MOSCOW

MOSCOW

Governing the Socialist Metropolis

TIMOTHY J. COLTON

THE BELKNAP PRESS OF
HARVARD UNIVERSITY PRESS
Cambridge, Massachusetts
London, England
1995

Frontispiece:
"Tall building" at ploshchad' Vosstaniya, under construction, 1952

Library of Congress Cataloging-in-Publication Data

Colton, Timothy J., 1947–
Moscow : governing the socialist metropolis / Timothy J. Colton.
p. cm. — (Russian Research Center studies ; 88)
Includes bibliographical references (p.   ) and index.
ISBN 0-674-58741-3 (cloth : alk. paper)
1. Moscow (Russia)—Politics and government. 2. Municipal
government—Russia (Federation)—Moscow. 3. Urban policy—Russia
(Federation)—Moscow. 4. Moscow (Russia)—History—20th century.
I. Title. II. Series
JS6082.C65 1995
947'.312084—dc20

95-14662

RUSSIAN RESEARCH CENTER STUDIES, 88

To
Patricia Anne Colton
and
Katharine Rose Colton

Contents

Figures

Maps

MOSCOW

Introduction

━━━━━━━━━━━━

I still confront its heaped-up beauty and tawdriness with a sense of fresh surprise. The fifteenth century and the twentieth are inextricably mixed and there is a foretaste of the twenty-first as well. Moscow is not merely a sight; it is a challenge to the intellect and to the senses. No matter how much you study it you cannot erase the margin of bafflement. Men may try to capture New York in a book, as [John] Dos Passos has done so well in *Manhattan Transfer* or as so many have done with Paris. But who will be foolhardy enough to try to compress this Moscow between the covers of a book?

—Eugene Lyons, 1935

WHAT sojourner to Moscow will ever forget that first eyeful of the convex expanse of Red Square and the ruddy battlements and golden spires of the Kremlin? Who would not be captivated, as Lyons was, by Moscow's mating of seemingly antithetical traits? It commingles not only the antique and the modern but the Occident and the Orient, the sacred and the profane, the picturesque and the squalid, the regimented and the chaotic.

Moscow does these things and more on a prodigious scale. Its nearly 9 million inhabitants make it mankind's fourth largest incorporated city (after Tokyo, Bombay, and Sao Paolo), second only to Tokyo in industrialized countries and to none in Europe. The 11 million in its metropolitan catchment area rank it ninth among conurbations (behind Tokyo-Yokohama, New York, Mexico City, Sao Paolo, Los Angeles, Chongqing, Bombay, and Shanghai), fourth among the industrial nations, and first in Europe.[1] Greater Moscow exceeds in numbers and economic mass dozens of member states of the United Nations and ten of the fifteen erstwhile republics of the Soviet Union.

For Russia watchers, local knowledge of Moscow commands attention because it evokes in fine grain country-level patterns. In medieval times Moscow was the mother city that lent its name to the very state—Muscovy. After Peter the Great moved the court to St. Petersburg, his window onto Europe, in the 1700s, the ancient capital was still thought of as Russia's social, cultural, and political bellwether and the barometer of its inner self. In a report in 1913, a group of progressive deputies in the city council remarked how aptly Moscow conditions "express the common causes defining the life of the entire country." Though not without idiosyncracies, its quotidian affairs were a microcosm of the nation's: "The general disorder of Russian life, with its characteristic features, is reflected all together in the life of Moscow—this great focus of the light and dark sides of the entire Russian system, of its bright and positive qualities and its great shortcomings, inextricably bound into a single whole."[2]

After the Russian Revolution all the more did Moscow, the seat of government again after a two-century hiatus, mirror the entire *Soviet* system. Its senior politicos, from Lev Kamenev and Nikolai Uglanov in the 1920s to Lazar Kaganovich and Nikita Khrushchev in the 1930s, Aleksandr Shcherbakov and Georgii Popov in the 1940s, Yekaterina Furtseva in the 1950s, Nikolai Yegorychev in the 1960s, Viktor Grishin in the 1970s, and Boris Yeltsin in the 1980s, headlined an all-USSR stage. Not a few political and programmatic trends gestated and were born in Moscow. With its size, capital status, and coverage in the media, Moscow displays these trends for the foreign scholar more clearly than most anywhere else in the country.

The venue in which Soviet leaders from Lenin to Gorbachev resided, worked, and played was the repository of their shared image of the good community. In the high Stalin era, when Kaganovich stood second in the central oligarchy, his Moscow barony was saluted as the USSR's "vanguard" city, the acme of its achievements. "Moscow," Joseph Stalin rhapsodized on the occasion of its 800th birthday in 1947, "is the standard bearer of the new, Soviet epoch." A generation later, Leonid Brezhnev hailed it as the "model Communist city," to be admired and emulated across the land. Moscow was in the 1980s the launching pad of *perestroika,* and Yeltsin was the first high-level victim of conflict over reform's itinerary. His eventual victory over Mikhail Gorbachev was a nail in the coffin of the Soviet Union.

Whatever else it has been, Moscow is in the final reckoning a city, a human settlement possessing the ingredients of Louis Wirth's foundational definition of urbanism: large size, high density, and social heterogeneity.[3] From this existential condition flow functional needs—for shelter, protection, and circulation, among others—that government must address and that lend themselves to comparison with similar aggregations elsewhere.

Early travelers' journals attest that, no matter how exceptional Moscow appeared from afar, closer contact revealed its kinship with other cities. "The sight of Moscow as one approaches the city is extraordinary," a Prussian visitor of the 1840s recounted, "and I know of no European city with which to compare it." "As one enters the gates," though, he continued, "the magnificent impression one had from outside vanishes. The city is then like any other."[4] This observation applied no less to the Soviet age, when Moscow's territory quadrupled, its population quintupled, and sections of it began to resemble foreign skylines.

Many if not all of the issues in the politics of Soviet Moscow have recurred in urban agglomerations on every continent, making Moscow a fitting case for comparative analysis of social policy and urban and regional governance. This is not to say that state responses to universal problems proved to be identical to, say, those in New York or Tokyo. The paradigm of urban design and management pioneered in Moscow was purposefully *socialist*.

The Marxist "integral socialism" at the core of the Soviet regime was a moral idea about human happiness and misery, yielding the prescription that a bountiful life in modern times depended on "the social appropriation of individual wealth" and consequently the control of all economic activity by the state.[5] The socialist urban paradigm as exemplified in Moscow contained distinctive political-economic elements: governmental ownership of the factors and means of production, including land; superintendence of administrative agents and clients via directive planning and administrative hierarchy; direct public provision of most goods and services at politically determined prices; and the lordship of investment and production goals over consumer welfare. Comprehensive planning, the proudest badge of socialist urbanism, was inculcated in such instruments as police curbs on in-migration, uniform formulas for allocation of housing and installation of infrastructure, and Moscow master plans, the two most important promulgated in 1935 and 1971.

Scholars have argued that great cities, in addition to their economic dimension, should be appreciated as "deliberate artistic creations intended not merely to give pleasure but to contain ideas, inculcate values, and serve as tangible expressions of thought and morality."[6] So it was in socialist Moscow, whose rulers exalted representations of the secular, the statist, and the collectivist over the religious, the commercial, and the individualist. They annihilated cathedrals, abbeys, fortifications, and ceremonial gates and towers and did their utmost to erect idols to themselves and their creed.

Pitchmen in the prime of Soviet power did not shrink from declaring that their capital, scientifically run according to socialist precepts, held a lesson for thinkers and practitioners around the globe. The new Moscow, went one canticle from the late Stalin years, was "a token of the emerging communist society, a plain example for the toilers of the entire world of the inexhaustible superiorities of the Soviet socialist system over the capitalist system." An equally perfervid statement from the 1960s read: "History shows that each epoch thrusts forward among the many capitals of states one that best personifies its characteristic traits, amasses the greatest cultural treasures, and carries the banner of the epoch. Such capitals in Europe were Athens and Rome in slave-holding society and Paris during the rise of the bourgeoisie. The socialist age has put forward Moscow."[7]

One time or another, many well-meaning non-Marxists bought at least partially into a version of this theory, shorn of its bombast and determinism. In 1936, for example, as the Great Depression still weighed down the Western countries, a quartet of liberal English urbanologists led by Sir E. D. Simon, a former lord mayor of Manchester, visited Stalin's Moscow for a month. About its planning potential they wrote:

> The [government of Moscow] has an opportunity unrivalled in the history of the world to reconstruct Moscow on the best town-planning lines. It has two overwhelming advantages compared with a capitalist democracy. The first advantage is socialism: the government owns the whole of the land and buildings; there are no interests of private owners to oppose or thwart its decisions. The second advantage is the one-party system, which makes the [city] notable for its ability to concentrate the whole energies

of the government in whatever direction it wishes, and its power to secure not only the acquiescence of the public to its plan, not only immunity from adverse criticism, but the active, and even enthusiastic, cooperation of the public . . . If there should be no great war . . . at the end of the ten-year plan [of 1935] Moscow will be well on the way to being, as regards health, convenience, and amenities of life for the whole body of citizens, the best planned great city the world has ever known.[8]

Although there were many things the Simon group got wrong, they were right that the substance of urban policy had to be investigated in concert with politics and the machinery for making and executing decisions. Except at the nativity of the system, the local politics that mattered revolved around the organs of the Communist Party of the Soviet Union (CPSU).[9] The Moscow first secretary normally belonged to the inner leadership of the partocracy. He and his underlings were entangled in the partywide struggle over patronage, precedence, and the general ideological line, walking a tightrope because of the glare of publicity and the general secretary's wariness of his Moscow lieutenant. Evidence from recently opened CPSU archives allows us to look anew at turning points in Moscow's political history, such as the tumbles off the tightrope of Georgii Popov in 1949 and Nikolai Yegorychev in 1967, about which probing analysis was previously impossible.

The constituted anchors of local government—the "soviets"— were never what they purported to be. As in any Soviet city, town, or village, the elections to them did not represent the people's choices of lawmakers but served as entries in what James C. Scott calls the "public transcript" of authoritarian regimes, "the symbolization of domination by demonstrations and enactments of power."[10] There was little spontaneous participation in local affairs, free association and assembly were out, and political discourse was abridged by censorship and official secrecy. The soviets existed primarily to repackage party decisions into legitimate legislative and administrative output, not to register societal input.

We can now see far better than Simon and his gullible colleagues did that this autocratic ethos, aside from traversing democratic values,[11] was anything but a guarantee of flow-chart efficiency or planning effectiveness. The preeminent CPSU apparatus fixed its sights on ensuring political conformity, industrial development, and the care and feeding of the Moscow-based political establishment, not on promoting local conveniences or welfare. Its muscle flexing on municipal issues was, accordingly, highly selective and inconsistent. Slack guidance by the nucleus of the local power structure let specific agencies pursue autarkic strategies, leaving gaping holes in regulation and service provision for which there was no market mechanism to compensate. Individual urbanites, subjects rather than citizens, had no power to demand redress.

The process of metropolitan governance may appropriately be characterized as one of *disjointed monism*. There was no political pluralism in the sense that it exists in a democracy, with independent power centers competing for popular favor, and next to no private property, which could have served as a base for a civil society. But monistic governance was not seamlessly monolithic: in the urban arena different points of view were tolerated, integration was haphazard, there was recurrent random behavior, and, diametrically opposite to Simon's assertion, slippage from approved objectives and norms was constant.[12]

Disjointed monism operated in the central-local plane as well. City authorities had to accept arbitrary intercession by national politicians who saw Moscow as the ideal receptacle for showboat programs and policy experiments. The works projects of Stalin's reign, often built with forced labor, were the vain stuff of dictators' dreams—the Moscow-Volga Canal, the marble-clad "underground palaces" of the first subway in the USSR, Parisian architectural ensembles on expansive boulevards and plazas, the never completed Palace of Soviets, intended to be the tallest building on earth and started on the ruins of what had been Russia's biggest church until Stalin had it blown to bits. The more prosaic suburban housing estates of the 1950s, the office towers and shops of prospekt Kalinina in the 1960s, the Olympic facilities in the 1970s, and the disputed World War II memorial in the 1980s were also icons of their time.

Besides accommodating interventions from glory seekers at the political mountaintop, Moscow's rulers reckoned with higher power in a different way, in a balkanization of authority among a myriad of centrally subordinated agencies. The Soviet hydra state relentlessly blunted local initiative and inhibited areal coordination, even when cooperation would seem to have been necessary to carry out objectives set above.

The hydra image pertains especially to the orchestration of urban development. Successive reorganizations never sufficed to give city hall the steering capacity to which it was supposedly entitled. On issue after issue city leaders were obliged to negotiate from a position of weakness with creatures of the center. Principal among the latter were economic planners, the production ministries, and their local affiliates. It was these business interests, after a fashion, that made most of the choices about capital investment, employment, and population growth. It was they who crashed through ceilings on migrant labor, slighted consumer-targeted endeavors, depopulated downtown Moscow in favor of hideous office complexes, despoiled historical landmarks, and used housing allocation for their particularistic purposes. Some of the entities most oblivious to local needs were associated with the military-industrial complex, the mollycoddled branch of the command economy and an imposing presence in and around Moscow.

Under the tsars, provincial and city governors appointed by the crown mitigated some of the disorganization of the central bureaucracy. After the destruction of this lever during the revolution, ad hoc commissions helped fill the void at first. Eventually, local Communist Party organs moved into the vacuum, carving out what Jerry Hough in his classic study of the party and industry identified as their role as "Soviet prefects." The Moscow experience helps illuminate why party prefectoralism arose, how it worked in the social sector, and its limitations.[13]

Moscow: Governing the Socialist Metropolis is an interpretive governmental, political, policy, and, in a limited way, social history of Moscow since 1917. I employ the bird's-eye technique of a "city biography" to map the course of events.[14] And I offer empirical generalizations to explain what may be observed on four cardinal dimensions: leadership and elites, including the involvement of Muscovites in the larger whirlpool of power politics; the evolution of metropolitan political institutions and their place in the overall state matrix; policy formation and performance vis-à-vis town planning and architecture, housing, and other key urban issues; and those societal, economic, and cultural variables needed to understand the big picture.

This is the first overview of the affairs of a Russian city throughout the twentieth century. The best studies of Soviet local politics to date have delved into one time segment and not traced themes longitudinally.[15] Earlier authors have also not had the evidentiary base I have been fortunate enough to assemble. Intellectual liberalization and Moscow's physical accessibility have allowed me to work in archives, sift through the full press record, interview officials, scholars, political activists, and ordinary urbanites, observe a polling station during the epochal election of 1990, and conduct laborious field inspections, wearing out the soles of more than one pair of sneakers. The book abounds with names and particulars—of persons, organizations, neighborhoods, streets, and buildings—in which local history and political studies in other countries revel, but which have been thin in the literature on the USSR.

Chapter 1 surveys pre-socialist Moscow, especially the geographic, sociocultural, economic, and architectural underpinnings, local self-government, and the Bolshevik movement (the prospective Communist Party).

In the next three chapters I turn to leadership, institutions, policy, and metropolitan development in consecutive periods of Soviet history. Chapter 2 covers the political revolutions of 1917 and "Red Moscow," the garrison city of the Civil War, when the foundations of single-party rule were laid and the first attempts at socialist solutions to city problems were made. Chapter 3 addresses the urban version of the moderate New Economic Policy of the 1920s, its repudiation in favor of transformation from above, and the febrile debate over how to create a "socialist city." Chapter 4 is an anatomy of Stalin's Moscow, an imperial capital run through the wringer of "socialist reconstruction" and violent purges. The apogee of Soviet urban monumentalism, enshrined in show projects and in Moscow's master plan of 1935, high Stalinism coincided with the low point for mass welfare and human rights.

The two chapters that follow are bracketed by the passing of Stalin in 1953 and Gorbachev's accession in 1985. In Chapter 5 I treat as a unit urban leadership and institutions during the Kremlin reigns of Khrushchev, who liberalized some controls and attempted to improve life through a vast increase in housing construction, and Brezhnev, who stuck closer to the preset course. In neither subperiod, I argue, did de-Stalinization go fast enough or far enough to alter basal realities of metropolitan governance. The chapter chronicles the interaction of local and national political bosses and the decay of the Moscow party machine, the turning points in policy, the relations between municipal and party structures and between urban and central government, the tentative openings in mass participation and public debate, and the difficulties in meshing city management with Moscow's districts and neighborhoods and with the green belt and urbanizing region surrounding it.

In Chapter 6 I focus on public policy and lay out its formation and attainment in four areas of basic need and urban amenity: town planning, notably demographic restrictions and the 1971 master plan; housing provision and location; transportation and consumer services; and conservation of the natural environment and the architectural patrimony of Moscow. In each sphere, particularly in housing, I consider the distributive implications of policies that made some Muscovites decidedly more equal than others. Along with the not negligible successes of urban programs after Stalin, the imbalances and failures that paved the way for the ensuing upheaval receive special attention.

In Chapters 7 and 8 I sail into uncharted waters, as I assess developments during and after Russia's anti-Communist revolution. Chapter 7 depicts the political awakening of Moscow up to the volcanic eruptions of the early 1990s. Episodes include Yeltsin's term as barnstorming Moscow party leader, the emergence of grassroots threats to the dictatorship, the 1990 election, the opposition's maiden ventures in government, and the final disintegration of Communist Party power. Chapter 8 discusses fledgling attempts to build stable democratic institutions in politics and a semblance of markets in economics. The book ends on a tentative note, since I leave the post-socialist metropolis a fragile newborn, with a more fulfilling future for its people a possibility but by no means a certainty. Moscow will remain "a challenge to the intellect and to the senses" as its odyssey continues.

Several technical points need brief explanation here:

Four appendixes at the end of the text furnish summary information on Moscow population, political and administrative machinery, leaders, and housing supply.

For events before February 8, 1918, when Russia adopted the Gregorian calendar, I employ the dates then in use, which were thirteen days behind the Western calendar.

For transliterating Russian words, I use the system of the U.S. Board on Geographic Names, with the modification that I transliterate the "short i" sound as "i" instead of "y." For well-known names such as Gorky, Trotsky, and Yeltsin, I retain the familiar English form. I have dropped terminal soft signs from place names and the first names of individuals.

In the interests of simplicity and authenticity, I retain transliterated Russian-language names for most addresses within the city, without translation into English. The main place designators are:

bul'var	boulevard
doroga	road
kol'tso	ring
most	bridge
naberezhnaya	embankment
pereulok	lane
ploshchad'	square
prospekt	prospect
proyezd	passage
ryad	row
shosse	highway
ulitsa	street
val	rampart
zastava	gate

1

Frontier Town
into Metropolis

THE MARXIST revolutionaries who took the reins of Moscow in October 1917, and welcomed their national administration there in March 1918, knew they were not dealing with any ordinary city. Since days immemorial, Moscow had been the focal point of Russia's being, and for three-quarters of the history of the Russian state Moscow was its capital. "A young and new Russia is raising its head," gloated *Izvestiya* (News), the tribune of the infant socialist government, in the very spot "where the old Russia in its time confirmed its greatness."[1]

While doffing their hats to "Red Moscow," the Bolsheviks could not put less endearing epithets out of mind: Holy Moscow, Third Rome, Gold-Domed Moscow, Calico Moscow, the Big Village of Russia. The ancestral home to Russia's Orthodox Christianity, nobility, and mercantile economy was, *Izvestiya* editorialized, "the embodiment of Russian thickheadedness, where Asiatic tradition uses the latest word in capitalist technology." It was a city they could not leave unreconstructed, even as they made it their own.

Rude Origins

The origin of the appellation Moskva, Moscow in English, has been lost in the mists of time. A seventeenth-century folktale had one

Mosokh, a descendant of the patriarch Noah, founding the city in Old Testament times, and Moskva as a crossbreed of his name and that of his wife, Kva. Historians agree on no more than derivation from the 473-kilometer-long Moskva River, on which Moscow stands.

Moscow, at 55°45′ north and 37°37′ east, squats near the middle of both the main East European Plain and the basin rimmed by the scimitar blade of the upper reaches of the Volga, the paramount river of European Russia (see Map 1). It also bestrides the seam between the deciduous woodlands of the temperate south and the bogs and conifers of Russia's north. The sepia Moskva meanders into the scene out of the west, looping like a carelessly tossed piece of yarn before sidling off to the southeast. The local geological dominant, the Teplyi stan Heights, reaches 235 meters above sea level, 115 meters above the riverbed. The wooded escarpment it demarcates to the southwest of the city, the Sparrow (Vorob'evy) Hills (the Lenin Hills from 1924 to 1991), affords the best panoramas. Moscow's terrain is more irregular than the legend that it "stands on seven hills" would imply. Swamps alternate with bluffs along the sinuous Moskva, and the ground is etched by brooks, lakelets, and arid gullies.

RUSSIA'S FORTRESS

The dank air, gusty westerly winds, and granular soil of Moscow and its environs, and the short growing season (141 days on average) and violent swings in temperature (from a mean of −10°C in January to +18° in July), hardly make a hospitable abode. Nonetheless, human habitation has been traced back five millennia by archaeologists. The hunters and fishermen who warmed themselves in the first clumps of huts had no written culture and left little but shards behind. By 500 B.C. their successors, the D'yakovs, livestock herders who wielded iron tools and conversed in an Ugro-Finnish dialect, had hacked walled encampments *(gorodishcha)* out of the wilderness, usually perched on embankment cliffs. These sites offered harbor from bandits, rain, and snow until the seventh or eighth century A.D.

Two farming tribes, the Vyatichs and Krivichs, colonized the region in the tenth and eleventh centuries. They were members of the Eastern Slav population family and trekked north and east into the Volga lands from their cradle of civilization in Kievan Rus, in the Dnieper River valley. Converted to Orthodox Christianity and speaking the precursor of the present-day Russian tongue, they came to stay.

MOSCOW AND EUROPEAN RUSSIA

The national boundaries and place names shown are those of 1995.

Moscow
Area of main map
RUSSIAN FEDERATION
SIBERIA

Murmansk
KOLA PENINSULA
Arctic Circle
White Sea
Arkhangel'sk
URAL MOUNTAINS
Ob R.
SIBERIA
FINLAND
Northern Dvina R.
L. Onezhkoye
Helsinki
Baltic Sea
Gulf of Finland
L. Ladoga
RUSSIAN FEDERATION
Perm
ESTONIA
St. Petersburg
Cherepovets
Yekaterinburg
Novgorod
Kostroma
Vyatka R.
Pskov
Tver
Yaroslavl
Volga R.
Nizhnii Novgorod
LATVIA
Ivanovo
Kazan
Suzdal
Vladimir
LITH.
Mozhaisk
Moscow
Moskva R.
Oka R.
Smolensk
Kolomna
Ul'yanovsk
Minsk
Kaluga
Ryazan
BELARUS
Bryansk
Voronezh
Saratov
Volga R.
Kiev
Dnieper R.
Khar'kov
Don R.
KAZAKHSTAN
UKRAINE
Volgograd
MOLDOVA
Dnepropetrovsk
Rostov on Don
Sea of Azov
UZBEKISTAN
CRIMEA
Stavropol
Caspian Sea
Sevastopol
Krasnodar
Black Sea
CAUCASUS MTS.
0 100 200 300 400 500 mi
0 100 200 300 400 500 km
GEORGIA
TURKMENISTAN

MAP 1

Seventy Vyatich burial mounds from the eleventh to thirteenth centuries have been excavated in modern Moscow.

As early as 1147 Moscow figured in written annals, which record Prince Yurii Dolgorukii of Vladimir-Suzdal, one of the loosely leagued Russian duchies, as inviting an ally to a banquet at a village of that name: "Come to me, brother, to Moscow."[2] He thought enough of Moscow to order his local vassal in 1156 to secure it with a dry moat and a wood palisade with blockhouses. Growth was swift around the fortified Kremlin *(kreml')* on Borovitskaya Hill, the high wishbone of land at the confluence of the Moskva and the tiny (7.5-kilometer) Neglinnaya River. Inside, the ruling family meted out justice and laws and rubbed shoulders with their aristocratic *(boyar)* retainers and the clergy. In the fashion of medieval Russian towns, a settlement for traders and artisans *(posad)* took shape eastward of the fortress gates, in the direction of the Moskva's main tributary, the Yauza. The oblong (later rectangle) between the posad and the Kremlin, skirted by vendors' stalls and religious grottoes but mostly kept free for parades, beheadings, and other rituals of state, was eventually named Krasnaya ploshchad' (Red Square).[3]

Warfare was integral to Moscow's development. The princes of Vladimir-Suzdal prized the city as a shield against Slavic warlords westward of the Volga basin, one of whom, Prince Gleb of Ryazan, put Moscow to the torch in 1176. The horse-mounted armies of the Mongol Tatars, from the far-off steppes of Inner Asia, posed a deadlier threat. Batyi Khan burned Moscow to the ground in 1237 and compelled the townfolk to pay tribute and accept his suzerainty.

The "Tatar yoke," by enfeebling Kiev and sundering the order of precedence among the Russian appanages, was politically a blessing in disguise for Moscow. Cushioned from the worst of the Tatars' depradations by other princedoms, it acquired a separate dynasty under Prince Daniel in the late thirteenth century. Daniel's son Yurii conquered neighboring Mozhaisk around 1305, gaining sway over the entire length of the Moskva River. Yurii and his younger brother, Ivan Kalita, tore free from Vladimir and Suzdal in the 1320s and 1330s. A few decades anon, Moscow had subjugated an orb of smaller towns—Zvenigorod, Volokolamsk, Kolomna, Serpukhov, and others—and arable land and forest. It was known as Podmoskov'e, literally "sub-Moscow."

Not content with equality, the Muscovite rulers employed cunning and duplicity with their peers and the Tatar khan, for whom Ivan Kalita (Ivan Moneybags) made himself chief tax collector, to grab top rank among Russian statesmen. Prince Dmitrii Donskoi's epic victory over the Tatar Golden Horde at Kulikovo Field on the Don River in 1380 betokened that primacy. Donskoi could not deter Tokhtamysh Khan, one of Tamerlane's generals, from sacking Moscow in 1382 after gaining admittance by a ruse—pretending he wanted to gaze upon its beauties. But Moscow resumed its expulsion of the Tatars and brought the Russian principalities to heel one by one.

Moscow's aggrandizement reached a crescendo toward the end of the fifteenth century in "the gathering of Russia," the welding together of an autocratic state with it as capital. Grand Prince Ivan III (the Great) subdued Novgorod and Tver, the holdouts among the free regions, and assumed the title of God-appointed *tsar'* (tsar, derived from Caesar) of all Russia. His son Vasilii III, king from 1505 to 1533, overran almost all the remaining appanages. So congruent were city and state that for another century the names Muscovy (or Moskovskoye) and Russia (Rossiya) were interchangeable.

In size if not amenities Moscow kept pace with its geopolitical clout (see Appendix A). Richard Chancellor, an Englishman who visited in 1553, when Moscow comprised about 100,000 inhabitants, thought it "greater than London with the suburbes." But, he added, it "is very rude and standeth without all order." After a mission in 1588–1589, his compatriot, Giles Fletcher, repeated the observation that the city was bigger than London.[4]

Ivan Kalita replaced the pine walls of the Kremlin castle, the embodiment of Muscovy's martial ethos, with stouter beams of oak in 1339–1340. In 1367 his grandson, Donskoi, built a new citadel, the mightiest in Russia, of albescent limestone. Ivan III, enlisting Milanese masters, undertook a total renovation in 1485. By 1495 the Kremlin had become the massive asymmetrical pentagon it remains today (Figure 1). The Faceted (Granovitaya) Palace, Ivan III's reception hall, was its first stone palace; the royal living quarters were scattered about until the tiered Terem Palace was put up in the 1630s. The Kremlin Wall, 2.2 kilometers of rubicund brick (painted white at first), averaged four meters in width and five to nineteen in height, depending on the relief. It was peaked with 1,045 twin-horned crenel-

Figure 1. Kremlin, c. 1880. (Museum of the History of the City of Moscow.)

lations and broken by five entry gates and eighteen individuated watchtowers that doubled as brigs; steep-pitched marquee or *shater* roofs were put over the towers in the seventeenth century. Sigismund von Herberstein, who headed Hapsburg legations to Moscow in 1517 and 1529, could barely believe how "very extensive and magnificently built" the Kremlin was: "from its size it might itself almost be taken for a city."[5]

For generations after the reconstruction of the Kremlin, just as the feudal walls of Western Christendom were coming down, Moscow only deployed more fortifications (see Map 2). Kitaigorod, the commercial quarter at the original posad, was surrounded, first by dirt breastworks, and then, between 1534 and 1538, by a brick wall, six meters thick for repelling siege artillery.[6] After the final punishing raid

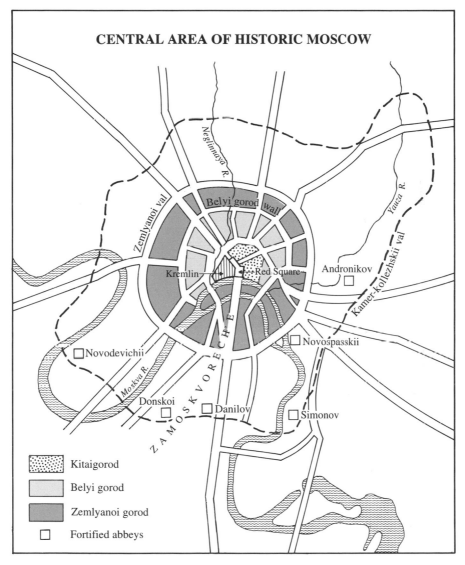

CENTRAL AREA OF HISTORIC MOSCOW

Neglinnaya R.

Zemlyanoi val

Belyi gorod wall

Yauza R.

Kamer-kollezhskii val

Kremlin

Red Square

Andronikov

Novodevichii

Moskva R.

Novospasskii

ZAMOSKVORECHE

Donskoi

Danilov

Simonov

Kitaigorod

Belyi gorod

Zemlyanoi gorod

Fortified abbeys

MAP 2

by Tatar cavalry in 1571, work gangs fabricated ten kilometers of whitewashed stone around the built-up area, setting apart Belyi gorod (the White City). In 1591–1592 followed a sixteen-kilometer soil rampart (Zemlyanoi val) and moat at a more forward line of defense, defining Zemlyanoi gorod (the Earthen City). The rampart, unlike the white wall, completed its arc south of the river, taking in Zamoskvorech'e, "the area across the Moskva River." As late as the 1740s, the government would throw up yet another earthen structure, the thirty-seven-kilometer Kamer-kollezhskii val (Customs House Rampart). It was used to keep out contraband until the abolition of internal customs in 1754, when its checkpoints were turned into police stations.

From Kitaigorod to Kamer-kollezhskii 109 high towers and gates studded the walls. Around many there coalesced farmers' and flea markets and votive shrines frequented by holy men, pilgrims, and beggars.

CULTURAL AND ECONOMIC CENTER

Moscow's ascent depended on more than the solidity of its walls and the guile of its princes. Religion was a potent asset. The Russian episcopate, impressed by its arms and prosperity, offered liege early on. Metropolitan Feognostii moved his residence in 1328 from Vladimir to what was already styled "Holy Moscow." "The presence of the metropolitan not only made Moscow the spiritual center of Russia, but . . . proved time and again to be helpful to the princedom in diverse material matters."[7] The holiest Russian abbey and seminary, the Trinity-St. Sergius Monastery, was founded shortly thereafter seventy kilometers north of Moscow.

Russia's bishops, dismayed by the fleeting union of the Greek and Roman rites, constituted a separate Russian Orthodox Church in 1443. When Constantinople fell to the Ottoman Turks ten years later, Moscow draped itself in the mystique of Byzantium. Ivan III married Zoe Paleologue, a niece of the last Byzantine emperor, and took the Byzantine two-headed eagle as his coat of arms. Vasilii III in the sixteenth century embraced the doctrine of Moscow as the "Third Rome," which—unlike Papal Rome and Constantinople—would stand for all time as the bastion of Christian piety.[8] The compact of the temporal and divine powers was cemented in the churches, chapels, and monasteries whose icons and frescoes were the glory of Russian art and whose bells, synchronized after 1625 with gonging chimes on the Spasskaya Tower of the Kremlin, rang in every hour of Moscow's day. Folklore put its churches at "forty times forty" *(sorok*

Figure 2. Chudov Monastery, c. 1880. (Museum of the History of the City of Moscow.)

sorokov)—a sum, perhaps understated, that toted up cupolas and spires, not buildings.[9]

Zlatoglavaya Moskva, "Gold-Domed Moscow," was no mere turn of expression. In the Kremlin, the Church of the Savior in the Wood (Spas na boru), built in planks in the 1200s and rebuilt in white stone by Ivan Kalita in 1330, was almost as old as Moscow. It chambered the Spasskii Monastery until Ivan III booted the friars out, after which it functioned as a parish church for servants of the court. Two abbeys remained in the Kremlin until the twentieth century: the Chudov (Miracles) Monastery (Figure 2), going back to 1357 and containing four churches, and the Voznesenskii (Ascension) Convent, founded in 1386 by Yevdokiya, Dmitrii Donskoi's widow, with three churches.

The spacious, cream stone Assumption (Uspenskii) Cathedral, erected on Sobornaya ploshchad' (Cathedral Square) in the Kremlin in 1326–1327 and done over for Ivan III by Aristotele Fioravanti of Bologna in the 1470s, was the nation's most sacred church (Figure 3).

Figure 3. Assumption Cathedral, c. 1880. (Museum of the History of the City of Moscow.)

It represented "a felicitous meeting of two cultures": the Russian, influenced by Byzantium, and the Western European, flowering in the Italian Renaisssance.[10] In it hung the most hallowed icon in Russia, the Virgin Mother of Vladimir; the tsars were crowned at the altar under its five gilt onion domes. Across the square, the Annunciation (Blagoveshchenskii) Cathedral boasted an iconostasis from the hand of the icon-painting genius Andrei Rublev. The scallop-roofed Archangel (Arkhangel'skii) Cathedral held the tombs of all grand princes and tsars from the fourteenth to the sixteenth centuries. Over Sobornaya ploshchad' reared the Ivan the Great Belfry, a slender octagon tipped with a gold-plated cupola and twenty-one bells.

Just outside the Spasskiye Gates, the Kremlin's main portal, Ivan the Terrible in the 1550s made St. Basil's Cathedral, properly the Cathedral of the Intercession on the Moat (Pokrovskii sobor chto na rvu), the voluptuous highlight of Red Square (Figure 4). Ever since, its ten turban domes and riot of arches, peaked gables, and roofs have been a logogram of all things Russian. The imbalance between St. Basil's extravagant outer surfaces and the plainness inside bespoke its political function: it was "conceived in terms of monumentality, of exterior effect, with little concern for decoration of the interior as a place of worship."[11]

At the opposite end of Red Square from St. Basil's stood the dainty Kazan Cathedral, built in the 1620s with pointed gables in the shape of tongues of fire pointing upward to a single cupola. It was a memorial to the expulsion of Polish oppressors from Moscow in 1612; twice-yearly processions paraded the icon that the Russian troops had carried into battle between the Kazan and Assumption Cathedrals and around the Kremlin and Kitaigorod Walls. Moscow experienced another wave of church building in the 1680s and 1690s. This time it was in the Moscow Baroque style best known for its sculpted architectural details and its borrowing from Western prototypes, a first for buildings designed by Russians.[12]

The six grand walled monasteries girding Moscow yielded in majesty to the Kremlin alone: Danilov (the oldest, founded by Prince Daniel in 1282) and Donskoi on the south; Andronikov on the east; Simonov (founded in 1370 and probably the premier monastery anywhere in Russia—see Figure 5) and Novospasskii (the continuation of the Kremlin Spasskii Monastery) on the southeast; and Novodevichii

Figure 4. St. Basil's Cathedral, c. 1880. (Museum of the History of the City of Moscow.)

Figure 5. Simonov Monastery, c. 1925. (From Alexys A. Sidorow, *Moskau,* Berlin: Albertus-Verlag, 1928, p. 163.)

(a convent for nuns established in 1520, whose cemetery would hold the graves of literati, generals, and revolutionaries) on the southwest. The monasteries held substantial amounts of land and peasant serfs until their confiscation by the state in the 1760s, Simonov owning 12,000 serfs in its heyday. They were places of refuge as well as prayer, especially on the city's south and east, the flanks most exposed to Tatar sabers.

Undergirding arms, politics, and godliness was the bedrock of geographic position. Moscow benefited immeasurably from being near the middle of a spacious shelf of land drained by a lacework of rivers and streams. The Moskva River empties at Kolomna into the Oka, which in turn joins the Volga, the water road to the Caspian and Persia, at Nizhnii Novgorod. Travelers could portage to the Klyaz'ma River and follow it to Vladimir or, alternatively, paddle down the Volkhov or Northern Dvina to the Baltic, the Dnieper or Don to Ukraine and the Black Sea, or the Kama into the Urals and West Siberia. The wagon roads that eclipsed the waterways also met in Moscow. By 1500 the nine highways splaying out from the Kremlin to Russian cities such as Tver, Kaluga, and Smolensk were its principal thoroughfares.

The collapse due to Tatar brigandage of the north-south trade pipeline through Kiev gave new import to the Volga and to lesser paths going east-west overland. The princes of Moscow were perfectly situated to police and tax this traffic. Its artisans and merchants, already well endowed with local building stone, fuel, minerals, and agricultural raw materials, enhanced their access to external markets and supplies.

The handicraftsmen who made clothing, boots, housewares, jewelry, armor, and weapons constituted the largest social group in Moscow by the fifteenth century. Fire hazard pushed them from Kitaigorod to "liberties" *(slobody)* near the edge of town, each with its own customs and obligations to the tsar. Some streets still bear the name of the artisans who plied their trade there. An enclave for foreigners, Nemetskaya sloboda (German Liberty), was set up on the west bank of the Yauza in the 1650s. The stalls of small traders and hucksters banked outside the Kremlin Wall and in swirling bazaars *(rynki)* that began to specialize by product in the sixteenth century. Moscow's big merchants *(kuptsy),* one-time petty traders who had amassed some capital, were the movers and shakers in long-distance trade, often enjoying state monopolies on foreign routes. If they struck gold, they could hope to win the tsar's ear or buy into the hereditary nobility whose woodsy estates *(usad'by)* dotted Podmoskov'e.

Our first reliable depictions of Moscow come from the early seventeenth century, by which time Russia was the largest state on the globe. A decade of tumult, the Time of Troubles, had bottomed out in the twenty-three-month Polish-Lithuanian military occupation of Moscow that was terminated in 1612 by the renowned warriors Kuz'ma Minin and Prince Dmitrii Pozharskii. It was Pozharskii who put up the Kazan Cathedral on Red Square in gratitude. The Romanov dynasty enthroned in 1613 brought Russia a measure of political calm and opened Moscow up to diplomats and traders from western Europe. They were struck less by its stability than by its indigence and uncouthness.

"Some of us, on approaching the city," a Dutch envoy who journeyed to Moscow in the 1630s remarked wryly, "said that it shines
like Jerusalem from without but is like Bethlehem inside." The traveler, Adam Olearius, drew a vivid portrait:

> The homes in the city (except for the stone residences of the boyars, some
> of the wealthiest merchants, and the Germans) are built of pine and
> spruce logs laid one on top of another and crosswise [at the ends] . . .
> The roofs are shingled and then covered with birch bark or sod. For this
> reason, they often have great fires. Not a month, nor even a week, goes
> by without some homes—or, if the wind is strong, whole streets—going
> up in smoke. Several nights while we were there we saw flames rising in
> three or four places at once. Shortly before our arrival, a third of the city
> burned down, and we were told that the same thing had happened four
> years earlier. When such disasters occur, the strel'tsy [troops of the tsar]
> and special guards are supposed to fight the fires. They never use water,
> but instead quickly tear down the houses nearest the fire, so that it will
> lose its force and go out. For that purpose every soldier and guard is
> obliged to carry an axe with him at night. So that the stone palaces and
> cellars may be spared from spreading flames, they have very small win-
> dows, and these may be sealed by sheet-metal shutters. Those whose
> houses are destroyed in a fire can quickly obtain new ones. Outside the
> white wall [around Belyi gorod] is a special market with many partly
> assembled houses. One can buy one of these and have it moved to his
> site and set up at little expense.
>
> The streets are broad, but in the fall and in rainy weather they are a
> sea of mud. For that reason, most of the streets are covered with round
> logs, laid parallel to one another, so that one can walk across as readily
> as a bridge.[13]

EARLY GOVERNANCE

Moscow as such had no government in the Middle Ages. The city was
a harlequin of feudal holdings weakly linked by the sovereign, who
shared management with lesser princes, often relatives or personal
favorites. From about 1400 until the middle of the sixteenth century,
he appointed several vice-regents (namestniki) to keep watch over
parts of it, although he gave them uncertain powers.

The crown's chief interests in the city were to preserve order,
maximize revenues, and carry out needed public works. Ivan the
Terrible created in the 1550s the first administrative body devoted to

Moscow. The Zemskii prikaz (Local Office) collected property imposts, supervised bridges and roads, patrolled and swept a few streets,
doused the worst blazes, and conducted summary trials of criminals
and drunkards. It elicited from time to time the advice and labor of
syndicates of elders from the several dozen territorial communities of
artisans and merchants. This did not alter the fact that the Zemskii
prikaz "carried out . . . mainly police functions" on behalf of its
Kremlin masters.[14]

Modern Moscow

Moscow passed a watershed at the turn of the eighteenth century
under Peter I (the Great), who took away its cachet as capital. A
century later a foreign emperor, Napoleon of France, caused it to go
up in flames for the last time. Moscow showed a remarkable ability
to rally from these setbacks and bound into a phase of headlong
development.

CALAMITIES AND RECOVERIES

The headstrong Peter was obsessed with molding the country into a
modern absolutist empire. Moscow he detested—like many Communists two centuries later—as a distillation of all that was archaic in
Russia. He fiddled early in his reign with Moscow works projects like
the ninety-meter Sukharev Tower (Figure 6), built over the years
1692–1695 at the Sretenskiye Gates, where in 1701 he opened the
College of Mathematics and Navigation Science, Russia's first non-
religious academy. After his sabbatical in western Europe in 1697–
1698, Peter enjoined inflammable wood construction in Moscow,
ordered architects to study with Dutch and Italian tutors, provided
for roads to be paved in cobblestone and regularly rinsed with water,
and installed streetlamps, a new sight in Russia.[15] But at every opportunity he fled to his country hunting lodges and drill grounds, as far
as he could get from the Kremlin. Taking the cue, noblemen began to
build their best houses in the foliaged swath of land angling northeast
from Kitaigorod to Peter's hideaways at Lefortovo and at Sokol'niki
and Preobrazhenskoye, across the Yauza.

Once squarely on the throne, Peter took a more sensational step.
In 1712 he quit Moscow entirely, conveying the court and bureauc-

Figure 6. Sukharev Tower, c. 1880. (Museum of the History of the City of Moscow.)

racy with him to St. Petersburg, under construction on the marshy approaches to the Gulf of Finland. He envisioned the Baltic capital as a Westernized town of secular monuments, steeples, orthogonally correct streets and squares, and columned palaces, its *regulyarnost'* a reproachful counterpoint to the bulbous domes, rabbit's warren of alleys, and homey timber residences of Moscow.

Plunged into depression, Muscovites saw their numbers sink by a fourth or more by 1725. To expedite the building of Petersburg, Peter issued a royal edict in 1714 proscribing stone and brick construction. The ban, poorly enforced, was revoked in 1728, but the city recovered slowly and was set back by a rash of fires in the 1730s and 1740s and, in the 1770s, an outbreak of bubonic plague, which inspired a "plague riot" in September 1771 put down by cannon fire. St. Petersburg eclipsed Moscow in numbers in the 1780s, and it took Moscow until 1800 to regain its earlier (1700) population of 200,000.

Where Moscow and Russia had once been synonymous, politically conscious Muscovites were now somewhat aloof from the national government. Popular culture accorded Moscow the aura of the steadfast parent or servant jilted by a parvenu—or, as the creator of the literary Russian language, Aleksandr S. Pushkin, portrayed it in a poem in the 1820s, the dowager queen in purple mourning clothes, curtsying before the new ruler. Muscovites consoled themselves that theirs was "a city of priests and merchants," a vessel of society's true values, whereas the cold and alien upstart to the north was "a city of bureaucrats and bankers." "Petersburg chatters," the adage went, but "Moscow gets things done." "Petersburg is a German city, Moscow is Russian. Petersburg lives on the money of the people and the peasantry, Moscow on its own, on earned money."[16]

The rupture was never total. Retaining the honorific epigraph "first-throned *(pervoprestol'naya)* capital," Moscow staged ceremonies such as the coronation of the monarch. Some state offices stayed there or left residues behind.[17] The army enlarged its barracks in Khamovniki, Lefortovo, and Khodynka. Many nobles and lesser gentry balked at moving to St. Petersburg; eventually, Peter III's revocation of obligatory state service for bluebloods in 1762 freed those who had gone to return without recrimination.

Moscow carried on. Under Peter I and his immediate heirs, a section of new palaces, parks, and hospitals graced Lefortovo. In 1755 the first institution of higher learning in Russia, Moscow University, was founded at the initiative of the encyclopedist and scholar Mikhail V. Lomonosov. It sparked a renaissance of ideas that confirmed Moscow as the cultural center of Russia and at least Petersburg's peer in science and letters. *Moskovskiye vedomosti* (Moscow News), Russia's first public newspaper, began publication at Moscow University in 1756, and the Office of Natural History of the university opened as its first museum in 1791.

In Podmoskov'e, construction of gentry estates multiplied after 1762. The manses and appurtenances of those with the most acres and serf laborers took on a novel scale and opulence. Kuskovo and Ostankino (domains of the princely Sheremetevs), Kuz'minki (once under the Simonov Monastery but given to the Golitsyns in 1757), Arkhangel'skoye (the property first of the Golitsyns and then of the Yusupovs), Petrovsko-Razumovskoye (the Razumovskiis'), Petrovsko-Alabino (the Demidovs'), Pokrovskoye-Streshnevo (the Streshnevs'), Cheremushki (the Men'shikovs'), Mikhalkovo (the Panins'), and Ostaf'evo (the Vyazemskiis') were but the stateliest of the manors.[18]

At the nadir of the city's fortunes, 1734–1739, the architect Ivan F. Michurin engraved its first semiaccurate geodetic map. The Cartesian precision of the streets on this brush with Enlightenment urbanism conveyed "pious hope rather than reality."[19] A 1748 rescript on fire protection marked off streets for straightening in the "red lines" *(krasnyye linii)* that were to be on all Moscow plans up to the twentieth century. A Commission for the Arrangement of the Capital Cities did a smaller-scale chart of the central area in 1775. It prompted some needed engineering work, although the bureau charged with implementation, the Kamennyi prikaz (Masonry Office), was disbanded after eight years. In 1782 Vasilii G. Ruban, the poet, journalist, and founder of Russia's discipline of local studies *(krayevedeniye)*, published the first guidebook to Moscow. The construction of major public buildings of a secular nature began under Michurin, the builder Dmitrii V. Ukhtomskii, and the Kamennyi prikaz. The rococo Red Gates (Krasnyye vorota), assembled on Zemlyanoi val to honor the coronation of Empress Elizabeth in 1724 (first in wood, then in stone by Ukhtomskii in 1753–1757), were a Moscow fixture until the 1920s (Figure 7).

The German-born Empress Catherine II (the Great), almost as

Figure 7. Red Gates, c. 1880. (Museum of the History of the City of Moscow.)

Moscophobic as Peter the Great, attempted to Europeanize the Kremlin on the principles of "order, perspective, and proportion." An Expedition for Building the Kremlin, appointed in 1768 with Vasilii I. Bazhenov as its chief architect, laid plans for knocking down many old structures and encasing the rest in an enormous four-story palace along the Moskva River, her answer to Versailles. The Kremlin cathedrals were to be enclosed in an oval piazza between the palace and two other grand edifices, and the riverbank in front of the palace was to be terraced. Several buildings, a span of the Kremlin Wall, and four towers were demolished; a bridge was built to cart in materials and a cornerstone laid in 1773. But finances, politics, and the settling of the buttresses put around the Annunciation and Archangel Cathedrals made Catherine abandon the scheme in April 1775 and have the wall and towers restored.[20]

Royal irresolution did not keep Bazhenov, his prize pupil Matvei F. Kazakov, and others from building landmark after landmark in the succeeding years. Catherine had the unlucky Bazhenov start a pseudo-Gothic royal palace at her estate in the village of Tsaritsyno, only to demolish most of it and turn it over to Kazakov, who also failed to complete the folly. The best products actually finished adopted the neoclassical idiom that characterized aristocratic taste in the West. Executed in the classical orders of Greek and Roman antiquity in pastels of amber, ochre, and rose, Moscow University on Mokhovaya ulitsa, the Senate building in the Kremlin, Petrovskii Palace, the Foundling Home (for abandoned infants), the Nobles' Club, and the great mansions along streets like Prechistenka, Tverskaya, Myasnitskaya, and Maroseika elegantly memorialized the age.[21]

In the economic sphere there was a trend away from artisan production and toward bigger industrial enterprises hiring wage labor. A mint, several weavers' mills, and a glassworks functioned in Moscow even before 1700. Thirty-two out of seventy-five Russian factories in 1725 were in the city; by 1770 it had 10,000 industrial workers, 90 percent of them in textiles. Concerned about the sanitary conditions blamed for the bubonic plague epidemic, Catherine tried in 1772 to expel large factories from Moscow and block new ones. No factories relocated, although proposals for factory construction were reviewed until the 1790s.[22]

Just when Moscow's comeback could be considered complete,

outside invasion wrought another calamity. Napoleon flung his Grand
Army at Moscow, having determined that it was Mother Russia's
beating "heart," indispensable as the "head" in St. Petersburg was
not. Inebriated French soldiers, Russian troops falling back from
Borodino, and vengeful Muscovites burned down two-thirds of Moscow's buildings during the occupation of September 2–October 11,
1812, its last ever by a foreign force. French sappers, hoping to
devastate Russian morale, tried and failed to dynamite the Ivan the
Great Belfry, the Kremlin Wall, and the Simonov Monastery. Nevertheless, when the embers cooled, Bonaparte posted a bill crowing that
"Moscow, one of the most beautiful and wealthy cities of the world,
exists no more."[23]

He could not have been more mistaken. Moscow's population
bounced back from 10,000 to 50,000 above its prefire level by 1830.
Triumphal Gates raised in enameled wood at Tverskaya zastava, on
the highway to St. Petersburg, to greet troops returning from European battlefields in 1814, signaled the recovery, even before architect
Osip I. Bove finished redoing them in stone and Greco-Roman statuary in 1834. In 1818 Ivan P. Martos, fired by love of country, completed his bronze and granite sculpture of Minin and Pozharskii,
Moscow's seventeenth-century liberators. Emplaced in Red Square by
order of Tsar Alexander I, it was the city's first monument to a specific
historical figure.

The Scotsman William Hastie compiled an inclusive rebuilding
program in 1813. The court rejected it as too costly, whereupon a
Commission for the Construction of Moscow, its mainstay Osip Bove,
devised a more operable Project Plan in 1817. The plan drew on both
Hastie's scheme and the 1775 chart of the committee for the two
capital cities. Put into action by Moscow's governor-general, Count
Fedor V. Rostopchin, it produced striking results before the commission was dismantled in 1843.[24]

The most spectacular sign of convalescence was the national commemorative monument to the war of 1812–1814: the Cathedral of
Christ the Redeemer (Figure 8). Architect Aleksandr L. Vitberg meant
it to reflect Russia's rank as "a mighty and expansive state"; it "had
to be great and colossal, surpassing in glory St. Peter's Cathedral in
Rome."[25] Told by the tsar not to put it in the Kremlin, he projected
an Italianate structure, taller and wider than St. Peter's, up on the

Figure 8. Cathedral of Christ the Redeemer, c. 1885. (Museum of the History of the City of Moscow.)

Sparrow Hills. But Vitberg was a feckless engineer and project manager, and Nicholas I transferred the commission in 1831 to Konstantin A. Ton. Nicholas agreed to build on the Moskva embankment, a half-kilometer upstream of the Kremlin, where the Alekseyevskii Convent had to be razed for the purpose. Ton's church was the biggest by far in Russia, the crucifix on the middle of its pentet of domes a dizzying 102 meters off the ground. Financed mostly by public subscription, it was under construction from 1838 to 1883.

If the Cathedral of Christ the Redeemer was a link to the past, most of the physical changes after 1812 looked forward. The mouth of the Neglinnaya River was confined to a subterranean pipe and Aleksandrovskii Garden was laid out as as a comely promenade along the Kremlin Wall. Between it and Moscow University, the Manezh, the 170-meter-long show stable for the imperial horse regiments, was a high point of the neoclassical *Ampir* (Empire school) that dominated in the reconstruction; it was later used for concerts and scientific exhibits. Submergence of the Neglinnaya enabled construction of Moscow's second great plaza, Teatral'naya ploshchad' (Theater Square). The square's jewel, the glittering Bol'shoi (Great) Theater opera house erected by Bove from 1821 to 1824 and altered after a fire in the 1850s (Figure 9), catered to Moscow's educated, middle-income denizens, as did other cultural temples and the first modern apartment houses.

CALICO MOSCOW

Recuperation laid the groundwork for a surge after 1860. The number of Muscovites rose an unexampled 65 percent between 1862 and the first proper city headcount in 1871. This rate never recurred, but it did not have to for Moscow to hit the 1 million mark in the 1890s and 1,618,000 in 1912, 6.5 times as large as before the Napoleonic blaze. A close second to St. Petersburg in Russia, it was the eighth or ninth biggest urban center under the heavens by World War I and one of the fastest growing.

The improvement in infant care and public hygiene stimulated some of this explosive growth: births (35.3 per 1,000) overtook deaths (32.8) in the local census of 1881. In-migration catalyzed by the emancipation of Russia's serfs in 1861 caused even more of it. Illiterate villagers looking for work coursed in, not only from Moscow

Figure 9. Bol'shoi Theater, c. 1880. (Museum of the History
of the City of Moscow.)

province, the source of one-third of late nineteenth-century migrants
to Moscow, but also from adjacent regions and further afield. Fifty
percent of Muscovites in 1882, and 61.5 percent in 1902, were first-
generation immigrants, nearly all of them peasants; they accounted
for over 90 percent of all factory hands in the city and four-fifths of
its population growth between 1890 and 1917.[26]

The rural floodtide reinforced the city's Russian ethnic character.
Ninety-five percent of the Muscovites counted in the first census in
1897 were Great Russians; the next largest national group, the Germans, came to merely 1.7 percent, followed by Poles at 0.9 percent,
Jews at 0.5 percent (they had triple that share until 1882, when
10,000 were expelled to the Jewish Pale of Settlement), and Tatars
and Ukrainians at 0.4 percent each. The Russian majority had edged

up to 95.2 percent by 1912, the fractions of the others remaining almost static.[27]

As rural poverty drove farmhands off the land, a vibrant urban economy attracted them to the city. Moscow was as much of a trade entrepôt as ever. Raucus open-air markets thrived on older sites such as Smolenskaya and Sukharevskaya Squares and Okhotnyi ryad (Hunters' Row), next to Red Square, and on new ones away from the Kremlin; hundreds of cart-pulling street hawkers peddled all things from meat and fruit to cigarettes and eyeglasses. The scions of the big merchant families shaved their beards, doffed caftans for business suits, and battened with the times. Establishment of the Moscow Commercial Exchange in 1839 was a testament to their self-confidence and supplied them with a lobbying voice. The banking and insurance businesses also expanded. The Moscow Merchant Bank, chartered in 1866, was the second largest commercial bank in Russia in 1900, and penny lenders and insurance firms proliferated.

For all the vigor of commerce and finance, industry was the driving force of Moscow's economy. Manufacturing leapt up in the 1840s, thanks to high tariffs and the importation of European machinery. Railroad construction took industry from strength to strength after the Nikolayevskaya railway, Russia's first, joined Moscow to St. Petersburg in 1851. No fewer than five new radial lines in the 1860s lengthened Moscow's reach to markets and to bountiful industrial supplies such as the coal reserves of the Donets basin, the oil of Baku on the Caspian Sea, the iron ore of the Urals, and the cotton plantations of Turkestan. Once four more lines were laid from 1899 to 1902, shiny steel rails converged from every point of the compass. The fifty-three-kilometer Moscow Circuit Railroad, hooking around the city and allowing shunting between radials, came into service in 1908.[28]

The Imperial Technical College, set up by the Yauza in 1830, supplied the engineers and mechanics for industry. The proprietors came from the old merchant lineages as well as the peasantry below and, less so, the nobility above. The factory owners of Moscow, in particular its textile tycoons, became the most perspicuous group of capitalists in Russia. Almost all ethnic Russians—unlike industrialists in most other parts of the empire—they did not rely on foreign capital or state orders and were oriented, like Moscow's bankers, toward domestic markets. They formed "the center of a powerful economic nationalism which carried strong political overtones" and frowned on state meddling in economic decisions.[29] Clannish and culturally right of center, many belonged to the Old Believers, the fundamentalist sect of the Orthodox Church, whose large congregations gathered around the Rogozhskoye and Preobrazhenskoye cemeteries.

The city's nickname at the time, Calico Moscow, provides a clue to its industrial forte. Manufacture of textiles, above all cotton cloth, was the mainspring of Moscow industry into the Soviet era. Giants like the Prokhorov Trekhgornaya Mill, founded in the Presnya area in 1799 and employing 6,000 workers by 1900, set the tone. Weaving and the needle trades were even more important in the sleepy towns of Podmoskov'e. Cloth was the principal product of what the government, mostly for the sake of factory inspection, defined as the Central Industrial Region, comprising Moscow and the provinces of Kaluga, Kostroma, Nizhnii Novgorod, Ryazan, Smolensk, Tver, Vladimir, and Yaroslavl.

All the same, Moscow's occupational profile was variegated and changing. Of 1,051,000 in the labor force in 1912, 418,000, about 40 percent, could be considered industrial workers, yet a majority of these toiled in artisanal shops rather than factories. Self-employed artisans still constituted 12 percent, administrative and clerical personnel 12 percent, and domestic servants 9 percent. In manufacturing, small- and medium-scale enterprises in a variety of industries predominated, which diversified the workforce far more than in St. Petersburg, where metals and machinery prevailed. Of 165,000 factory workers in 1912, 35 percent were in textiles (half the share of fifty years before), followed by metal working and machine building (16 percent), food processing (11 percent), printing (7 percent), and chemicals (3 percent).[30]

Some bureaucrats were as ambivalent as Catherine the Great had been about the manufacturing boom, fretting that it would corrode political order as much as medical health. The military governor of Moscow province, Arsenii A. Zakrevskii, informed Nicholas I in 1849 that "homeless and dissolute" workers would "easily join every movement, destroying social or private peace." On his recommendation, the government briefly barred Moscow to new cotton- and wool-spinning mills.[31]

Russia's system of mandatory identity documents, instituted by Peter the Great to facilitate surveillance, the draft, and taxation, and consolidated in 1857, might have lent itself to limitation of migration by coercive means. A reform in 1894, absolving most urban dwellers from it, did not cover Moscow and St. Petersburg, where passports issued by the police still had to be carried and migrants had to present their papers to the police for registration. But the government did not use personal identification as an instrument of social engineering until Soviet times. Rather, it sought to further internal security, especially by helping the constabulary and their informers—including building concierges, many of whom were non-Russians—to track political subversives.[32]

One big reason Zakrevskii's fears about anomie were not realized sooner than they were was that many clung to a stake in the villages they had walked away from. Surveys at the turn of the century showed 80 percent or more of the workers in some Moscow factories to be full or part owners of rural land. Many pitched in at sowing and harvesting, necessitating prolonged absences from the factory bench, and supported a wife and children in the countryside. Fraternization with *zemlyaki*, "landsmen" from one's village or district, was widespread in Russian cities but especially prevalent in centrally positioned Moscow, with its quick access to the interior. Tens of thousands of *otkhodniki*, seasonal workers, also flocked in each summer, working a few months in construction or industry before returning to the hearth for the winter. In politics, it was often said, the ties with the countryside gave many of Moscow's workers "village sympathies." In everyday life they lent a human face to what was otherwise a city of strangers.[33]

ANCIENT AND NEW INTERMINGLED

It sometimes seemed as if everyone in the first-throned capital was a *moskvofil*, a Moscow-firster. "Without taking into account this patriotic braggadocio," a citizen noted in 1912, "one would miss much in the psychology of the indigenous Muscovite."[34] Aleksandr Pushkin, who was born in Moscow in 1799 but spent most of his days outside it, wrote this tender hymn in his verse ballad *Yevgenii Onegin* (1831):

How many times in my sorrowful separation,
In my wandering fate,
Have I thought of you, O Moscow!
Moscow . . . how much there is in this sound
That flows together for the heart of the Russian!
How much echoes in it!

As expressed in this emotional appeal, in a way no other locale could Moscow represented the Orthodox roots, the traditions, and the very statehood of Russia. To millions, it stood as the symbol par excellence of their heritage. In the high culture, it was "the main stronghold of conservatism, mysticism, and resistance to rationalist, revolutionary, and liberal thought." In the parlors of the city originated the anti-Western Slavophile movement of the 1840s, a cause for which Moscow businessmen opened their wallets.[35]

Moscow's architecture reflected its citizens' regard for their past. "Everywhere," related a post-1812 observer, "we perceive variety, irregularity, and contrast, the marks of an ancient and modern city intermingled." To a later witness Moscow was "a natural product which has grown up slowly and been modified according to the constantly changing wants of the population," so unlike the "Baltic Venice," St. Petersburg, with its rectilinear plan and European mien.[36]

Prerevolutionary Moscow remained a religious treasure house, with 9 cathedrals, 15 monasteries for men, 10 convents, 292 Orthodox and 40 Old Believer congregations, 98 in-house chapels, and 20 other temples in 1913.[37] It never stopped putting up churches. The largest building under scaffolding when war broke out was the St. Alexander Nevskii Cathedral on Miusskaya ploshchad', drawn to be seventy meters high and to support twenty-one cupolas.

Churches and Moscow's nonecclesiastical architectural bounty were studied by local *krayevedy*, regionalists who poured out guides and almanacs and in 1909 came together in the Old Moscow Society, a committee of the more expert Moscow Archaeological Society. Tsar Nicholas I, wanting to feel at home in Moscow in the 1840s, put up a Great Kremlin Palace, designed by Konstantin Ton to be "replete with bastardized forms of ancient Russian and Byzantine styles."[38] Several of the older palaces and the Church of the Savior in the Wood were restored at the same time. Slavophile suggestions that Moscow

be reestablished as capital got a new lease on life after the assassination of Alexander II in St. Petersburg in 1881. Alexander III and
Nicholas II, unwilling to go quite that far, made it the center of court
ceremonial.[39] At the tercentary of the Romanovs in 1913, Nicholas
dedicated a plinth in Aleksandrovskii Garden engraved with the
names of twenty-nine outstanding Russians.

Late imperial Moscow presented as many markers of discontinuity
as of continuity, however. Indifferent to conservationist sentiment, a
plethora of churches and other historic structures were in decay.
And new, secular uses—business, leisure, and other—prevailed. Until
1880 or 1890, most retail goods were sold in the Asiatic bazaars or
in *lavki*, dim, unheated shops. By then, Moscow could also boast
specialty outlets, delicatessens, and paneled boutiques. Department
stores came a little later; the largest, designed by Roman I. Klein, was
opened by the British firm Muir and Merrilees on ulitsa Petrovka in
1908.[40]

Although most new building was bland, Moscow saw experimentation aplenty in architecture. The arts academy inaugurated in 1832
was renamed the Moscow College of Painting, Sculpture, and Architecture in 1865. In 1867 a professor at the school, Mikhail D. By-
kovskii, founded the Moscow Architectural Society; the first guild for
the profession in Russia, it contraposed itself to the poky Imperial
Architectural Society in St. Petersburg. Ideas and talent also came
from the Stroganov Arts and Crafts College, established in 1825 and
retitled the Stroganov College of Technical Design in 1869.

The Empire style dominant in construction after 1812 increasingly
came, from the 1830s to the 1860s, under the softening influence of
Eklektitsizm (Eclecticism), whose adaptation of idioms from art history was most fully expressed in the Great Kremlin Palace and the
Cathedral of Christ the Redeemer. Historicist borrowings in Moscow
were largely from medieval and seventeenth-century Russia. From the
1870s on Moscow was the center of a Neo-Russian Revival (or
Moscow Revival), which wove elements of church, village, and fortress structures into secular edifices of all descriptions, in a quest for
an authentic "national style."

Neo-Russianism culminated in the Historical Museum, by
Vladimir O. Shervud; in Aleksandr N. Pomerantsev's rebuilding of the
Upper Trading Rows, the future GUM department store, a three-

humped arcade for 1,200 different sales counters on Red Square; and in the Ryazan (later Kazan) Railway Station and the other work of Aleksei V. Shchusev. The Upper Trading Rows project, completed in 1893, was "a turning point in Russian architectural history, not only because it represented the apogee of the search for a national style but also because it demanded advanced functional technology applied on a scale unprecedented" in Russia. Its metal-ribbed sunlights, engineered by Vladimir N. Shukhov, weighed 2,500 tons and had 60,000 panes of glass.[41]

Moscow was home as well to *Modern* (Moderne or Art Nouveau), the primary modernist tendency in Russian architecture and the incubator of most of the design strains that contended after 1917. Moderne attempted to synthesize efficient and comfortable layout with an up-to-date decorative art stressing geometric and aquiline forms. Its prolific prophet, Fedor O. Shekhtel', a lecturer at the Stroganov College and the president of the Moscow Architectural Society from 1908 to 1922, built detached homes for the wealthy, apartment houses for professionals and the middle class, and commercial structures. His masterworks included the mansions of Stepan M. Ryabushinskii and Aleksandra Derozhinskaya, the Moscow Art Theater, and the Yaroslavl Railway Station.[42] In addition, a neoclassical revival had begun by 1910. Architects most boldly incorporated the style in banks, apartment houses, and the Alexander III Fine Arts Museum by Roman Klein, commissioned in 1912.

More and more, the shed roofs and smokestacks of industrial workplaces, rather than arresting architectural shapes, punctuated Moscow's skyline. This could be a letdown to anyone preferring a more picturesque silhouette. "The view . . . was not satisfactory," lamented a sightseer who peered out from a bell tower in the Simonov Monastery in 1859. "It began well with a perspective scene of the river coming down from the city [center]; but then appeared two powder-magazines, and ugly barracks, and after them were some horrid, black-smoking, factory chimneys only half a mile off and right in front of the fairylike Kremlin in the extreme distance, with its brilliant white towers and flashing points of gold." Even the historic center pulsed to new-fangled rhythms: "With [Moscow's] colossal houses, with its streetcars and automobiles, and with the reign of noise," one Muscovite fumed in 1909, "life is losing its former good nature, sociability, and sweet disorder and freedom. Life's tempo is being disciplined and shackled in the iron limits of the machine."[43]

Muscovites' ears soon picked up another of the metallic sounds of modernity: the drone of airplane propellers. Professor Nikolai Ye. Zhukovskii mounted one of the first wind tunnels in Europe at Moscow University in 1902; by the end of the decade he had opened an aerodynamics laboratory at the Imperial Technical College. In 1909 the Duks Works, founded by Yu. A. Meller in 1898 as a bicycle factory, built Russia's first domestically manufactured airship, the Farman-4 biplane. The test model took off from a gravel strip at the Nikolayevskiye Barracks on Khodynka Field, a neighbor of the factory. There, five kilometers northwest of the Kremlin, the Moscow Society of Aviators opened the Central Airfield in 1914.

Inevitably, Moscow gained in landmass as it did in townsfolk and economic activity. Engulfing the old artisans' settlements, nobles' lands, and farm villages, it distended from 1 square kilometer in the fourteenth century to 5.5 square kilometers in the sixteenth century and 19 in the seventeenth. The Kamer-kollezhskii val, encompassing 71 square kilometers, was decreed the official boundary in 1806. The city limits expanded in bits and pieces to 92 square kilometers until May 1917, when they jumped to the Circuit Railroad and in several locations beyond, taking in 233 square kilometers (see Map 3).

Moscow's layout showed strong points of affinity with the pre-industrial city. Successive works projects largely perpetuated the original array of transportation arteries. Bove's widening and straightening program left many streets and alleyways narrow and crooked. As before, main roads connected the Kremlin to the circumference of Moscow like so many spokes of a wheel. Concentric rings cut across, the inner two built mostly after 1812 on the site of razed medieval fortifications. The Bul'varnoye kol'tso, or Boulevard Ring, a mean of 1.5 kilometers out (except south of the Moskva River, where it was imperfectly closed only under the Soviets), supplanted the Belyi gorod wall. The Sadovoye kol'tso, Garden Ring, about as far out again, passed along the route of the anterior earthen rampart around Zemlyanoi gorod. Where the Bul'varnoye and Sadovoye rings intercepted radial avenues, major stone-paved squares were built. Both rings were lined with shaded esplanades and stately houses; many of the gates of the walls were left intact. Kamer-kollezhskii constituted a knobbly

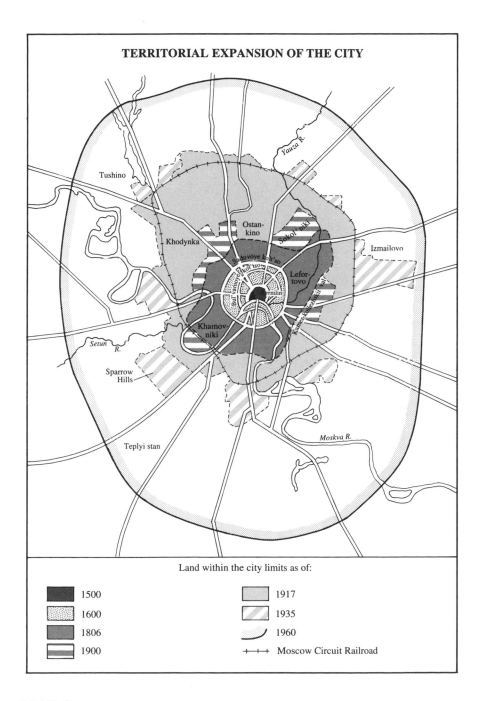

TERRITORIAL EXPANSION OF THE CITY

Tushino

Yauza R.

Ostan-
kino

Sokol'niki

Khodynka

Izmailovo

Sadovoye kol'tso

Bul'varnoye kol'tso

Lefor-
tovo

Kremlin

Kamer-kollezhskii val

Khamov-
niki

Setun R.

Sparrow
Hills

Teplyi stan

Moskva R.

Land within the city limits as of:

■ 1500	□ 1917
▨ 1600	▨ 1935
▨ 1806	⌐ 1960
▤ 1900	+‑+‑+ Moscow Circuit Railroad

MAP 3

third ring, giving way to a daisy chain of roads as it was demolished in the late nineteenth century.

SOCIAL GEOGRAPHY

A British correspondent who browsed inside the Sadovoye in the 1870s marveled at how "dilapidated buildings, which in West European cities would hide themselves in some narrow lane or back slum, here stand composedly in the face of day by the side of a palatial residence, without having the least consciousness of the incongruity of their position."[44] This architectural and social miscibility, common in Russian cities, was more pronounced in Moscow, and historians have used it to help explain Moscow workers' lower degree of class hostility.

No one would deny the existence of gradations. In the multistory apartment houses in ritzy areas, there was differentiation by floor: laborers, tradesmen, and domestics lived in cellars and garrets, the highest-status families on the first floor, and professionals and bureaucrats on the intermediate floors. Spatial integration of class groups "was possible precisely because the sharp legal and cultural segregation made neighborhood segregation superfluous."[45]

Despite this integration, income and occupational strata spread unevenly across the face of Moscow's seventeen police districts *(chasti)*, the forty-four police precincts *(uchastki)* within them, and the three detached precincts straddling the city limits (see Map 4).[46] Pockets of poverty festered in the seven inner districts bounded by the Sadovoye and the Moskva, notably the Khitrov Market, Moscow's den of thieves and prostitutes, in the southern precinct of Myasnitskaya, and the less sordid Zaryad'e trading area next door. But on the whole the central city was a residential space of relative comforts and privilege. The nobility continued to prefer the "gentry nests" of the Arbatskaya, Tverskaya, Prechistenskaya, and Myasnitskaya districts. Their low-lying stone and stucco-over-wattle villas *(osobnyaki)* were smaller and closer together than the wood mansions burned in 1812 and much simpler than the palaces of St. Petersburg. Tidy housing, trees, and grassy-banked bodies of water like Patriarshii (Patriarch's) Pond and Chistyi (Clear) Pond gave these neighborhoods a bucolic air. Steps away from milling thoroughfares, pedestrians felt they

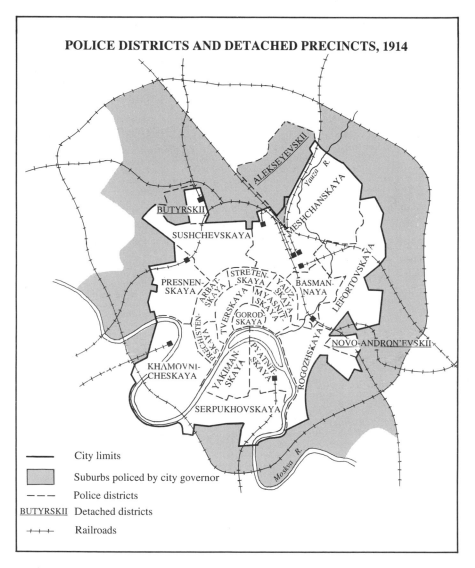

POLICE DISTRICTS AND DETACHED PRECINCTS, 1914

ALEKSEYEVSKII

Yauza R.

BUTYRSKII

MESHCHANSKAYA

SUSHCHEVSKAYA

PRESNEN-
SKAYA

STRETEN-
SKAYA

YAUZ-
SKAYA

BASMAN-
NAYA

LEFORTOVSKAYA

ARBAT-
SKAYA

MYASNIT-
SKAYA

TVERSKAYA

GOROD-
SKAYA

PRECHISTEN-
SKAYA

ROGOZHSKAYA

NOVO-ANDRON'EVSKII

KHAMOVNI-
CHESKAYA

YAKIMAN-
SKAYA

PYATNIT-
SKAYA

SERPUKHOVSKAYA

Moskva R.

—— City limits

▨ Suburbs policed by city governor

--- Police districts

BUTYRSKII Detached districts

+++ Railroads

MAP 4

walked among "the prettiest and most quiet and retired little country retreats one can imagine."[47]

With the redoubts of the wellborn intermingled merchants' and industrialists' homes, less immodest than in St. Petersburg but not lacking in luxuries and flanked by servants' wings and coach houses.

By 1910 the city had added several hundred European-type apartment houses, some of them five to ten stories high, with shops on their ground floors, mechanical elevators, and often the aforementioned upstairs-downstairs segregation. The best of them, put up in the Parisian Second Empire style by insurance companies, let fancy flats to well-heeled Russians and foreigners.

The prosperous sections also contained most of Moscow's banks and office buildings, many of them in Kitaigorod (especially on Il'inka ulitsa and Staraya ploshchad') or around Lubyanskaya ploshchad', the Upper Trading Rows, and carriage-trade shops at addresses such as Kuznetskii most, Petrovka, and Tverskaya ulitsa. Here, too, were the Praga, Slavyanskii bazar, and most of the good restaurants and cafés; the swank hostelries, led by the chicly Moderne Metropol' and Natsional'; the Yeliseyev Delicatessen and competing food emporiums; the sybaritic Sandunov Steam Baths; and all of the private academies and clubs, from the English Club and the Nobles' Club on down the social ladder.

The central section catered to intellectual and cultural establishments as well: Moscow University and its penumbra of salons and student flats and the bohemian quarter along Arbatskaya ulitsa, thick in bookshops and painters' lofts; the Bol'shoi, Malyi (Small) Theater, Moscow Art Theater, and other major stages; the Rumyantsev Museum (transferred from St. Petersburg in 1861), Historical Museum (opened in 1883), Polytechnical Museum (1877), and Alexander III Museum; the Moscow Conservatory (1866) and concert halls; all of the picture galleries except the Tret'yakov (in Zamoskvorech'e); and most of Moscow's movie houses (the first appeared in 1896 and the sixty-seventh by 1913). One time or another, many of the master spirits of Russian literature and art, philosophy, and science—Aleksandr I. Herzen, Nikolai V. Gogol, Aleksandr N. Ostrovskii, Timofei N. Granovskii, and Kliment A. Timiryazev, to fish out a few names at random—lived and worked in the downtown.

Although warehousing was plentiful in the core, industry, with its attendant clangor, soot, and odors, was scarce, except near the Yauza. Thousands of artisans, domestics, and clerical personnel lived in inner Moscow; the industrial working class by and large did not. The tenements, beer bars, consumer cooperatives, and other appurtenances of proletarian Moscow began to all intents and purposes at the Sadovoye kol'tso and the Moskva River.

South of the river, the three police districts of Zamoskvorech'e mixed merchants' and traders' homes (their occupants wickedly satirized in Ostrovskii's plays) with textile and machinery factories and workers' housing. Half of the Moscow plants with a thousand employees or more in 1917 were located in Zamoskvorech'e.

Beyond the Sadovoye in all directions, and farthest along the northern rim, sprawled the industrial belt, the "workers' outskirts" *(rabochiye okrainy)*. Here lived approximately three-quarters of the city's inhabitants and 90 percent of its industrial workers. Population density measured only a third to a half of that in the center, owing to tracts of industrial and waste land and the predominance of low-slung frame housing. Seventy-five percent of all buildings outside the Sadovoye in 1912 were wood, compared to about 60 percent between the two inner rings and under 10 percent within the Bul'varnoye kol'tso. It was the rustic, weathered log cabins and tenements, added to the leafy streets within the Sadovoye, that prompted Russians, with dashes of condescension and affection, to dub Moscow their "big village" *(bol'shaya derevnya)*. Semirural settlements, where factories overlooked meadows and pigsties, lay just across the city's frontier. A tourist could stand in a peripheral district and "conclude that he was in some distant village in the interior of the empire."[48]

The eastern perimeter of Moscow, taking in the Lefortovskaya, Basmannaya, and Rogozhskaya police districts, was handy to the Yauza and to the best rail transport. Hence it became the fastest growing and the most variegated area, holding dozens of textile and garment factories but also machinery enterprises and Moscow's one steel mill, the Goujon Works. Textile production nearly monopolized Presnya and Khamovniki (Presnenskaya and Khamovnicheskaya police districts) on the west and southwest, closer to the Kremlin, although many army installations and hospitals could be found in Khamovniki. The northern Sushchevskaya and Meshchanskaya precincts were the center of the food industry, but small foundries, metal plants, and artisans' shops of various kinds abounded here. The Sokol'niki area, in Meshchanskaya, hosted the city's three largest train stations on Kalanchevskaya ploshchad', its main freight yards, and the municipal tram park.

A mere 4.1 percent of the people in the Moscow melange lived in family-owned houses or apartments in 1912, much less than in comparable western European or New World cities. The proportions in institutional housing (dormitories, almshouses, prisons and barracks, and so forth), independent communal housing, and industrial or commercial buildings were also relatively low—6.6, 1.4, and 1.0 percent, respectively. The great majority of residents, 72.1 percent, were tenants or subtenants (more than half of tenants sublet to make ends meet), and 14.8 percent stayed in housing provided gratis by the employer. Maybe 1 percent were homeless.[49]

Huge disparities could be found within the broad housing types, especially among the tenants. The sorriest were the night lodging houses for transients *(nochlezhnyye doma),* notoriously in Khitrov's skid row (Figure 10). Five thousand souls slept here in 1912, in surroundings "undoubtedly threatening, both morally and biologically," to all Moscow.[50] A far greater number inhabited "cot-closet flats" *(koyechno-kamorochnyye kvartiry),* little more than semienclosed boxes in lice-ridden flophouses, where they got use of a cot, often on a shift basis, and a storage cubby. The 1912 census enumerated 319,000 Muscovites, 20.2 percent of the total population, in such flats, up from 17.4 percent in 1897; two-thirds of them lived in the proletarian wasteland outside the Sadovoye. Another 127,000 (8.4 percent) could get nothing better than rooms or corners under staircases, in attics, or in basements.

Of the 207,000 Muscovites in company housing in 1912, 59,000 were office workers and 32,000 were domestics and building superintendents; 117,000 were industrial workers, most though not all of them in the outer marches. While some still lodged with the master, normally they lived in barrack-style dormitories. Some employers also let small flats or family rooms, with or without kitchens. At the Trekhgornaya mill, 3,900 employees were housed by the factory, 2,800 of them in bunkhouses for unmarried workers, and all 6,000 could use the vocational school, hospital, maternity ward, library, and kindergarten. This paternalistic arrangement, aimed at socializing and disciplining the ex-villagers, did not please better-educated workers, who groused that they would rather be paid enough to afford their own housing and get amenities from local government. Although more resided in company housing in absolute terms in 1912 than in 1882, the percentage decreased from 21 to 15, and among factory workers from 90 to 30. For various reasons, the trend was to reverse under the Soviets.[51]

Figure 10. Flophouse in Khitrov Market, c. 1900. (Museum of the History of the City of Moscow.)

The Partial Modernization of Local Institutions

More than once did the tsars attempt to improve the administration of Moscow. In the nineteenth century the city was vested with the rudiments of urban self-government, but only that. Incompletely rationalized and democratized, local institutions could not meet many of the demands laid on them.

TOWARD SELF-GOVERNMENT

Peter the Great perpetrated the first fumbling efforts to retool local machinery. In 1699 he ushered in a citywide representative council, a Moscow Ratusha of a dozen notables chosen by state-monitored conclaves of merchants and artisans. He saddled it with most of the fiscal duties of the defunct Zemskii prikaz but granted no additional legislative powers. Incongruously, it was compelled to grub for revenues on behalf of the royal treasury from towns all over Russia, making it more "a financial organ of the whole state" than a local government.[52] Shedding this burden in 1710, the ratusha plugged away at the policing and housekeeping work of the Zemskii prikaz.

A longer-lived Petrine legacy, the *gubernii* (provinces), were territorial subdivisions of the empire entrusted to a personal agent of the monarch. The Moscow guberniya, one of the smallest of these territories but politically of stellar importance, was created in Podmoskov'e in 1709. Countylike areas for rural administration were later carved out within it, each called, from 1782 on, an *uyezd* and bearing the name of a main town. The guberniya originally held fifteen uyezds, reduced to thirteen by 1900.

Beginning in 1725, Moscow had not one but several overseers. They could quash any local decision, and their and their superiors' incessant yet fluctuating demands put city functionaries in an unenviable bind.

The military governor or governor-general *(general-gubernator)* of the guberniya, who resided in a Kazakov mansion on Tverskaya, bore responsibility for policing and security. A ranking soldier or bureaucrat, sometimes of royal blood, held this office. Grand Prince Sergei Aleksandrovich, governor-general from 1891 until he was blown up by terrorists in 1905, was an uncle of Tsar Nicholas II; the post remained vacant after his murder. The governor *(gubernator)* of the province, subordinate to the governor-general in law but autonomous in practice, busied himself with routine paperwork and headed the guberniya chancery. In addition, Moscow proper had a chief of police *(oberpolitseimeister)*, concerned with day-to-day law and order (including internal passports, censorship, and suppression of dissent) and with local services. After the urban unrest of 1905, the post was upgraded to city governor *(gradonachal'nik)*, coequal with the provincial governor.

The constitution and name of Peter's ratusha underwent several peremptory revisions. In 1785 Catherine the Great came up with a cumbersome tripartite structure: a mostly decorative Moscow City Assembly (Gradskoye obshchestvo), open to nobles and big merchants and convening every three years; a General Council (Obshchaya duma) of seventy-nine, picked by the city assembly; and an executive Six-Deputy Council (Shestiglasnaya duma), which included a city "headman" or mayor *(gorodskoi golova)*.[53] This system was disbanded in 1799, only to be resurrected suddenly in 1801.

Twice after 1800 committees set up by St. Petersburg to investigate local fiscal shortfalls "functioned for some time as the actual administration of the city."[54] Even in quiet times, the minute Moscow budget was haltered to the needs of the central state. As late as 1850 better than 50 percent went to policing, garrisoning troops, and maintaining government offices, and not a ruble could be spent without the say-so of the governor. Many of the skimpy services available, among them the aqueduct from the artesian wells at Mytishchi, completed in 1804, were in the hands of national agencies.

Here matters stood until the government, succumbing to fears that the city was being mismanaged, appointed a committee in 1859 to draft a special statute. The committee came up with a new charter in 1862 premised on public or voluntary administration *(obshchestvennoye upravleniye)* and more liberal in some respects than that passed for St. Petersburg in 1846. It did away with the toothless general assembly and recognized that Moscow officials had the right to take initiatives on issues of local interest. But it did not plainly bound their jurisdiction, and they remained at the governor's beck and call.

Political activity in the region quickened in 1864, when one of Alexander II's Great Reforms accoutered all guberniyas with a provincial council or *zemstvo*. The Moscow Guberniya Zemstvo, put under the thumb of landed squires by a franchise based on agricultural holdings, was one of the most active. While operating almost no programs in Moscow, it had taxation rights there and clashed repeatedly with the city. Each uyezd in the guberniya had its own zemstvo and was divided in turn into about a dozen *volosti* (volosts), cantons with limited judicial and administrative authority over peasants only.

In 1870 Alexander II undertook a comprehensive restructuring of urban government. When it took effect in 1873, Moscow had a semblance of Western municipal government.[55] The statute recited in some detail the decision powers of the Moscow City Duma *(gorodskaya duma),* as the council was now called, and its executive board *(uprava).* Both met at will and addressed matters of local taxation, streets, water and utility systems, public health and hygiene, fire fighting, and inspection of stores and markets; they also had partial responsibility for public schools, theaters, libraries, and museums. In many instances central ministries forfeited staff and facilities to the uprava.

The Moscow City Duma had 160 to 180 members, a lot by international standards. The mayor officiated at its meetings and those of the uprava, whose 7 members (9 after 1912) rarely belonged to the duma. The uprava set the duma agenda and disposed of most city business. It "looked on relations with the duma as a heavy burden of a formal character that hindered [its] actions and work," while the duma watched "with suspicion and preconceived mistrust" for executive abuses.[56]

Legislative-executive frictions were secondary to something more fundamental: on account of a blatantly discriminatory electoral system, both answered to a miniscule electorate. Citizenship in reform-era Moscow resembled a closed corporation more than an urban democracy. The dumas of 1862 to 1873 were chosen in a two-stage process predicated on assignment of voters to five estates fixed by inherited social position. A straightforward property-based franchise was imposed in 1873. This doubled the list yet left it piddlingly small; retrograde legislation in 1892 constricted it again. In 1889 24,000 persons were on the rolls (2.7 percent of the population), in 1892 a paltry 6,000 (0.5 percent), and in 1912 just over 9,000 (0.5 percent), of whom 3,400 cast their ballots (0.2 percent). The overwhelming majority of Muscovites, including essentially all manual workers and without exception all women and Jews, had no say in the choice of their local representatives.

FROM GENTRY TO BOURGEOIS DOMINANCE

The Moscow gentry had the upper hand politically until the 1860s, wielding it to guard special interests and occasionally to advance certain liberal causes, such as freedom of speech. Some merchants, their social inferiors but recognized as having a role in administration, participated deferentially.

Moscow's commercial blossoming and the advent of a property franchise and a form of government that put a premium on management skills quickly led to the displacement of the patrician elite. Businessman Sergei M. Tret'yakov, mayor from 1876 to 1882, was the first commoner to govern without bowing to it. Six of the ten mayors between 1870 and 1917, and four of the last five, were from the bourgeoisie. Entrepreneurs of one kind or another occupied 57.2 percent of all city duma seats in the late 1880s, 67.5 percent in the late 1890s, and 64.4 percent between 1906 and 1914.[57]

Moscow businessmen's push into politics drew on the same ethic of public service—grounded in altruism, religiosity, envy of the nobs, and the urge to leave monuments—that made them patronize a welter of cultural and charitable causes. The Tret'yakov family donated to the city in 1892 the gallery that bears its name, Russia's finest depository of native art, while the Shchukins, Morozovs, and Ryabushinskiis collected Paris impressionists, Picassos, and Art Nouveau fabrics. The railroad millionaire Savva I. Mamontov bankrolled the avant-garde Moscow Art Theater and the Abramtsevo arts and crafts colony north of the city. The Rukavishnikovs, Soldatenkovs, and Bakhrushins were benefactors of hospitals, orphanages, and homes for the aged. Philanthropy increased popular acquiescence in business's leadership in government. "This was a Moscow," an inside observer wrote later, "of merchant dominance, where the merchant was everywhere—in the warehouse and in the city duma and in the university—where nothing could be done without the merchant, where there was a sort of 'dictatorship of the sales counter.'"[58]

Moscow's burgher politicians lived mostly in the better neighborhoods within the Sadovoye. More than a quarter of the members of the city duma between 1897 and 1904 had relatives who also served,

the Guchkovs, Bakhrushins, and Vishnyakovs figuring most prominently. It was an amazingly cohesive community power structure. As
a councillor observed, "The duma leaders of the beginning of the
century . . . were tightly interknit and formed a a single integral
group."[59]

The cliques that existed in the city duma acted mostly on issues of
personality and patronage. The entry of political parties in 1905
altered little. The main rift between the two voting blocs in the duma,
the Right-Moderates and the Progressists, had to do with national
issues. The two groups compiled their slates of candidates desultor-
ily, had few differences on local matters, and were ill-disciplined in
council.

A MUNICIPAL BALANCE SHEET

The city duma and uprava made a contribution to urban well-being
that deserves to be acknowledged. For the last three decades of the
century, their members worked intently on innovating and stretching
their powers. Mayor Tret'yakov hired young physicians, teachers, and
engineers and convinced the duma to begin raising capital through
bonds, exhorting Muscovites to think of themselves as belonging to a
world city. The textile heir elected mayor in 1885, Nikolai A. Alekseyev, a prodigy "born to command and take charge,"[60] plumped for
public works and the taxes to underwrite them. His pride and joy was
a mansard-roofed city hall, the first in the country. Designed by
Dmitrii Chichagov, it opened in 1892 on Voskresenskaya ploshchad',
beside the Historical Museum and kittycorner from the Kremlin's
Nikol'skaya Tower.

When Alekseyev was shot by a deranged assassin in 1893, some
of the optimism of the political class died with him. Self-doubts welled
over the following generation, especially after the trauma of 1905.
Moscow government remained, nonetheless, a going concern. "Until
now," opined a writer at the respected journal on city issues,
Gorodskoye delo (Urban Affairs), in 1913, "Moscow has been the
only Russian city in which municipal government has attained a
European character and scale. It has been a model and example for
the rest."[61]

The duma had a solid presence in most of the conventional fields
of municipal activity. Only two services—gas lighting from 1868 to

1905 and horse-drawn trams from 1885 to 1901—were operated for any sustained time by private concessions. Moscow's budget counted for one-fourth of all spending by Russian cities in 1914, for less than one-tenth of all urbanites.

The city spent heavily on local roads and bridges, which it won possession of in 1875. By the early 1900s, it cobblestoned or asphalted most central streets, crossed the Moskva and Yauza with new bridges (nine of them in stone), and covered over many creeks and ditches. Mass transit, converted largely to electric-traction streetcars after the buyout of the two Belgian-owned tram firms, was disemploying thousands of Moscow's storied horse-and-buggy cabmen *(izvozchiki)*. To go with the arboretums at Sokol'niki and the Sparrow Hills, the uprava funded planting of neighborhood gardens. The waterworks, conveyed in 1870 and greatly enlarged under Alekseyev, were fed by a second aqueduct from the Mytishchi wells and a filtration station opened at Rublevo on the Moskva in 1913.

The duma also had credentials in social services. As of 1912, 5,700 transients slept nightly in its six lodging houses. It had an employment bureau, three almshouses where the penniless could work off their debts, a net of "district guardianships of the poor," ten shelters for juvenile delinquents and strays, eighteen hospitals, eleven birth clinics, and ten libraries and reading rooms. Desks in three-year elementary schools were available for all eligible children. A city college giving noncredit courses, Shanyavskii People's University, was opened in 1908. The uprava also operated nine "people's houses," whose lecture theaters, reading halls, and tearooms spread a gospel of cultural uplift and sobriety, not unlike American settlement houses.[62]

Against these achievements, however, have to be set grievous shortcomings. The duma has been faulted for its "underlying conservatism and political timidity" during the unrest of 1905, when it failed to provide a "civic alternative" to the polarities of left and right.[63] More disconcerting were the inadequacies of mundane city services, especially in areas like the outlying districts, or anywhere else populated by the lower classes.

In terms of the staple of urban life, housing, no solace could be taken from the consignment of so many Muscovites to cot-closet, flophouse, barrack, and basement accommodation. The duma was "very little and haphazardly concerned about the housing of the poorest of the people," one contemporary critic wrote; its efforts, said another, amounted to "a drop in the sea of the city's need."[64] The suggestion by deputy Emmanuil I. Al'brekht in 1913 that the city construct cheap housing for 35,000 people found little support. The Khitrov tenderloin outlived a generation of commissions of inquiry. Housing provision as a whole lagged between 1906 and 1915, as completions increased at half the rate of the population. Density per unit in 1912 was double or more that in western European capitals, and the gap was growing.[65]

Transport modernization, to take another program, gave short shrift to the dusty and corrugated roads outside the Sadovoye, and the extension of tram service proceeded there at a snail's pace. As Moscow's population surpassed a million, there was talk of a subway. In 1902 P. I. Balinskii, a municipal engineer, came up with a plan for an underground railway between Zamoskvorech'e and the Belorussia Railway Station (opened next to the Triumphal Gates in 1870), with an elevated trestle near Red Square. Experts put forward three alternative schemes in 1912, proposing to put shovels in the ground in 1914 and have the trains running by 1920. But the uprava dismissed these plans as beyond its means, and negotiations with private companies in 1902–1903 and 1913–1914 came to nought.

Comely parks and boulevards could not offset the ecological damage being wreaked by unchecked expansion of industry, rail yards, and population. Moscow had no planning department, no plan (the 1817 Project Plan, for the center only, was long since inoperative), and no zoning legislation. There were few checks on land use except for the height restrictions slapped on Kitaigorod in 1914 and the setback requirements ("red lines") along downtown streets, not applied to existing nonconforming structures.[66] Moscow's regulative vacuum was, of course, on a par with most industrial cities of the day. The harbinger of spatial planning in the United States, New York's zoning ordinance, dates from only 1916.

But Moscow fared worst by a cross-national yardstick with respect to basic sanitation. Although water supply was sufficient in the aggregate, about two-thirds of all houses in 1916, most of them cabins or tenements on the outskirts, were without a direct hookup. Hundreds of thousands of Muscovites had to buy supplies daily from water carts or tote them from the badly polluted rivers and from communal taps and wells. A city sewage system was not begun until 1893; wartime austerity halted the second leg of it, started in 1911. In 1916 just under three-quarters of all houses, and about every second resident, remained unconnected to the sewage mains. Unlicensed dumps and heaps of garbage and excrement littered the inner areas; cattle grazed, chickens pecked, and wild dogs wandered freely in the outer.

It is not surprising, therefore, that Moscow was the unhealthiest big city in Europe. Between 1883 and 1917, it endured eight epidemics of smallpox, ten of typhus, and four of cholera. In 1910 the death rate in Moscow, 26.9 per 10,000, was 10.2 per 10,000 higher than Paris's, 11.1 higher than Vienna's, and 12.2 higher than Berlin's; infant mortality exceeded western European levels by 50 to 75 percent.[67]

How can we explain such failings? The limitations of the burgher political elite undoubtedly figure in the answer. Nikolai I. Astrov, the longtime secretary of the duma and briefly mayor in 1917, wrote acidly in his memoirs that the duma benches were filled by men who were "sometimes very hard-working and well-intentioned but who had little culture and were accustomed to looking at public affairs, at the complex economy of Moscow, as they would look at their own . . . factories, bakeries, taverns, and inns."[68]

Granted, there is some truth here, but the point cannot be pushed too far. By no means all of the politicians were philistines, and it is unfair to tar the patrons of theaters and museums with being collectively uncultured. Their capitalist background and management experience, while blinkering them in some ways, yielded advantages on balance. As in national policy, Moscow's merchants and manufacturers had a commendable trust in the market. They were surely right to assume that a growing private sector would be more beneficial to overall housing and living conditions than government provision of a few thousand apartments a year. And their "dictatorship of the sales counter" was mild indeed compared to the iron-fisted socialist dictatorship that followed.

Of the many negligences in Moscow governance, some stemmed from exogenous circumstances. Russia was a backward country by European lights, and the most flawless municipal administration could not have equalized Muscovites' and Londoners' situations in 1900. The city was held back, moreover, by grossly inadequate financial resources. An impost on real property provided its only significant tax revenue, and the central government set a lid on that rate, jealously guarded other tax fields, and prohibited budget deficits. One council- man declared in 1913 that the squeeze between spending commit- ments and fiscal base made the duma's situation "so difficult that we are threatened by catastrophe."[69] It thus turned to fee-generating enterprises, such as the tram railways and the municipal gasworks, to bring in almost 60 percent of its monies in 1912. Programs that held out no prospect of turning a profit, such as drainage lines, a subway, or permanent shelter for the destitute, had commensurately less ap- peal.

The undemocratic nature of city government is as pertinent as the social origins of its members to understanding its uneven perfor- mance. Moscow politicians with good reason tailored their behavior to the interests of those who passed electoral judgment on them: a handful of citizens of above-average station who complained about expansion of public spending and taxation. Only universal suffrage and political competition would have forced them to be more respon- sive to the lower socioeconomic strata.

Another problem was the casual, not to say languorous, style of all Russian administration, a pattern from which Moscow was not exempt. The duma habitually deferred commonsense improvements until the last instant. It took decades to install lineaments of sound municipal decision making, such as a careful geodetic survey and real estate inventory. Mapping begun in 1845 still plodded along seventy years later; bureaucrats dallied, and the uprava considered the job "something easy, simple, and momentary."[70] Secrecy, endemic in Rus- sian government and business, obstructed legislative and public dis- cussion. Municipal pay was low and management practices high- handed, leaving thousands of employees tinder for revolutionaries. Duma politicians' preference for foreign consultants over city engi- neers offended nationalistic as much as professional sensibilities.

ST. PETERSBURG'S HEAVY HAND

The power of the national government further constrained the city. Many Moscow entrepreneurs felt a visceral antipathy toward the government, which stretched back to their Old Believer origins, battles over tariff protection for textile factories, and encounters with the likes of Governor-General Zakrevskii, who tried to halt industrial expansion in the 1840s.[71] Once at the municipal helm, though, they found it easier to swallow this hostility than to ford the gulf with the urban masses. Regardless of the last two tsars' mawkishness about Moscow, Astrov pointed out in 1913, few in St. Petersburg were more generous to the long-time rival than to Russia's other local authorities. The city duma, as Astrov said, was in a "tragic position." Its "lack of communication with the population of Moscow" left it with "vain hopes for support 'from above,' that is from a government that . . . does not distinguish Moscow, the cultural and industrial center of Russia, from any other city."[72]

Like any other Russian city, Moscow found that a raft of specialized agencies unceremoniously interfered in its decisions. The Ministry of Education's trustee for its schools, acting on a complaint by one of his inspectors, could overturn any duma decision. The Ministry of Internal Affairs (MVD) signed off on regulations for chimney sweeping and removing night soil. The Ministry of Finance circumscribed Moscow's taxation powers; during the prewar bargaining over the subway, it conducted parallel negotiations with concessionaires, admitting a city agent only at the last moment.[73]

No one at the center took on supportive oversight after the dissolution of the Commission for the Construction of Moscow in 1843. The MVD, responsible for local administration in general, was more interested in its other roles, of law enforcement and political control. It screened municipal employees for loyalty, billed city hall for police and army garrisons, and hounded two of Moscow's nineteenth-century mayors from office for political indiscretions. Several times it exercised its right of veto over the duma's choice as mayor—most gallingly following the 1912 election, when Moscow's first three nominees were turned down and the city was left mayorless for almost two years.

Abrasiveness varied with personalities and time periods. Count Zakrevskii, to one memoirist, "was of a type with the Asian khan or the Chinese lord." He threw tantrums over rulings that differed from his own, blurting out "I am the law" in Moscow.[74] Such willfulness seemed antediluvian by 1900, but ministers, governors, and police chiefs could still drive city officials to distraction with petty encumbrances. The "propriety and legality" of any municipal decision could be referred to a seven-member Special Board on City Affairs, chaired by the city governor (the guberniya governor before 1905) and seating three of his subalterns. "No matter what the question or how clear the rights of the city," one mayor related indignantly, "the government members always voted for the government's demands, and because they were in the majority the city could never achieve a just decision."[75] The board cashiered several dozen decisions a year, some retroactively.

Unavoidably, it fell to mayors to fulfill "the difficult role of smoothing over relations with the St. Petersburg departments." Their peregrinations to the capital were sardonically likened to the Moscow princes' abject carrying of petitions to the Golden Horde centuries before.[76]

REGIONAL STEPCHILDREN

Interrelations among groups and institutions within the extended region posed another knotty issue. The social mix of Podmoskov'e was in transition in the nineteenth century. Construction of country estates for the nobility slid in the 1830s and 1840s, and some fell into disrepair or were sold to mill and workshop owners. Railway building and congestion in Moscow after 1850 spurred the development of *dacha*—wood cottage—areas for middle-class Muscovites. Dachas came in all sizes and degrees of visual interest, the owners with the most to spend preferring Russian-looking tent tops and windowframe carvings. The best grounds had churches, summer theaters, tennis courts, electric lighting, and shops. Dachas were designed originally for vacations and weekends only, but from the largest aggregations— Kuskovo, Losinoostrovskii, Pererva, Perovo, Pushkino, Tsaritsyno— *dachniki* began to carry on small businesses or shuttle to work.

Industry followed into the circumferential curtain. By 1900 most of the 150 square kilometers out to the Moscow Circuit Railroad "was converted into a manufacturing district of the city and constituted a single entity with it, even though not included within its boundary."[77] Cottage and agrarian settlements along the radial railways transmogrified into grimy industrial villages, often around the branches of Moscow plants: Kuskovo, Lyublino, and Perovo on the east and southeast; Losinoostrovskii on the north; Spas-Setun and Tushino on the west and northwest; Biryulevo and Tsaritsyno on the south. Five to 10 kilometers out along Moscow's eastern horizon lay another crescent of factory villages: textile-based in Balashikha and Shchelkovo, heavy industrial in Lyubertsy and Mytishchi.

Moscow showed little curiosity about these lands, although reformers in the duma did favor gradual extension of services to the built-up fringe. The 85 square kilometers adjacent to Moscow, and the 150,000 people on it, were annexed in 1905 for policing purposes only, under the purview of the city governor (see Map 4).[78] These *prigorody*—"attachments to town," analogous to the English "suburbs"—remained for all other functions in Moscow uyezd, the donut-shaped county unit around the city. The 2,500-square-kilometer uyezd had none of the vehicles of village or township self-government rife in metropolitan areas in North America.

The territories Moscow did ingest were almost devoid of indigenous leadership, amenities, and corporate spirit. Like the rest of Moscow, they had no neighborhood or borough councils to stand up for them. Medieval self-help and elders' syndicates had fallen into desuetude before Peter the Great. The police districts and precincts, in existence since the 1780s, remained the one significant form of subdivision; their boundaries, often cutting across historic dividing lines, were periodically redrawn. The city duma conducted elections on a territorial basis after 1892, yet there were only six polling districts (three for the first few years), each returning thirty deputies. Boundaries, once again, were drawn out of administrative convenience. While injecting some local color into council debates, the voting districts had no intrinsic importance and were forgotten between elections.

Nor did regional cooperation arise to address emerging conundrums of metropolitan growth. The city's relations with the guberniya zemstvo instituted in 1864 were uneasy. Conservative, pro-industry, and pro-tariff merchants and manufacturers called the tune in the duma, and more liberal-minded, pro-agriculture, and anti-tariff gentry farmers did in the zemstvo. On local issues their only joint programs of any size were for insane asylums and sanitary inspection. The zemstvo alienated city politicians in the 1860s when it tried to exercise its right to levy a tax on Moscow real estate. During the debate leading up to the 1870 urban reform, Moscow representatives argued unsuccessfully that all big cities be off limits to the zemstvos.[79]

After a hiatus of two decades, Chairman Dmitrii N. Shipov revived the zemstvo's tax proposal. The guberniya got its way in 1895. Moscow officials concluded that the zemstvo "looked on the city of Moscow as its tributary"; guberniya leaders pilloried the Muscovites as unscrupulous skinflints. Bad memories of the tax fracas, Shipov wrote in his memoirs, "often prompted insufficiently tranquil discussion . . . of questions touching to one extent or another on the interests of the city of Moscow."[80]

In one of the nastier rows, the guberniya defeated Moscow's attempt to prohibit polluting industry near its new Rublevo pumping station. Skirmishes flared periodically between the city and Moscow uyezd. Not averse in principle to annexation of its urbanized sections, the uyezd struck a hard bargain during talks over this and cognate issues. In the 1890s its chairman, N. F. Rikhter, supported by St. Petersburg, extracted seven times the price offered for the land needed for the aeration fields of the city's new sewer system at Lyublino.

The tension bubbled over into the internal affairs of Moscow uyezd. Natives, supreme in its council due to franchise requirements, made up one-third of its population in 1914 but paid only one-fifth of local taxes. They were embroiled with factory owners and peasant migrants from other districts, always hungry for benefits and tax breaks, and with expatriate city dwellers. Many of these last commuted on the suburban railways, which doubled their ridership from 1905 to 1914.

The uyezd spared no effort to please affluent Muscovites. To encourage them to build plush homes on gentry farmsteads, and hence to pay high taxes, it let them plop them down almost wherever they pleased; some district roads had to zigzag around completed houses.[81] It was a different story for the typical exurbanites, white-collar workers of modest means. They gathered in dacha hamlets (dachnyye poselki) centered on a whistle-stop or natural landmark. Having no statutory recognition or tax rights, the hamlets had to rely on donations to fund fire, water, and other skeleton services.

Community representatives accused the uyezd of callousness and and of holding them hostage to border negotiations with Moscow. Five "hamlet congresses" after 1910 publicized their plight. The last, attended by thirty delegations in March 1914, "issued a reminder of the multifarious needs of our suburbs and hamlets and of the sad condition of these stepchildren of both city and zemstvo." The tatty settlements around Moscow were "living proofs of the extent to which the juridical, traditional city already fails to encompass the new, factual city." The real city, the congress declared, ought to be remade as "a Greater Moscow [Bol'shaya Moskva] for the satisfaction of the most elementary needs" of the populace.[82] This idea would be heard from again.

Some Muscovites saw salvation in another idea, the "garden city" propagated by the British social reformer, Ebenezer Howard. Howard's opus on verdant planned communities in which industry, housing, and greenery would happily coexist, was translated into Russian in 1904; a Russian Garden Cities Society was founded in 1913. Architect Vladimir N. Semenov, a Howard disciple who had worked for five years in London, blocked out Russia's first garden town in 1912 on 680 hectares at the Prozorovskaya station near Perovo, on the Moscow-Ryazan Railway. To his disappointment, the railroad provided no local employment when it built a village there in 1914. Prozorovskaya was "kept in bondage" to the company, which retained title to the land and cottages, renting mostly to its clerical employees and evicting tenants at pleasure.[83]

Nothing eventuated from a 1913 Moscow City Duma endorsement of twenty city-owned "garden settlements" to house 40,000 working-class families, the first to be at Khodynka Field. Just months before its abolition in 1917, the duma was holding a contest for a model settlement at Ostankino. The one garden scheme initiated from below also foundered. Rubber workers from the Bogatyr' (Hero) plant in Bogorodskoye, led by one S. I. Shesterkin, founded an association in 1914 for building a community named Druzhba (Friendship) north of the city limits. The 210-member group—no property owners or hirers of wage labor admitted—began collecting dues, but the provincial governor disallowed its charter and Shesterkin was conscripted into the army.[84]

The Revolutionary Alternative

The second city of the realm and the breeding ground of Slavophile ideology was also a hive of leftist opposition to the autocracy. The products of the revolutionary milieu amassed much experience in conspiracy and organization, but none in the art of local government and politics.

Moscow's pioneers in rebellion, the self-styled Populists (Narodniki) of the 1870s, directed their vague call for a village-based republic at the emancipated serfs in the countryside. Apathy among the peasants, and police retaliation for their turn from peaceful propaganda to terrorism, left them a spent force by 1880.

The torch passed to younger intellectuals and workers, excited by the newly translated socialist writings of Karl Marx and more attuned to urban Russia. The strike by the textile workers of Orekhovo-Zuyevo in 1885 gave them hope and affected the entire labor movement. By 1890 medical students Aleksandr N. Vinokurov and Sergei I. Mitskevich were running a socialist study group at Moscow University. Active in the circles were several members of the family of Vladimir I. Ul'yanov, known to posterity by the alias Lenin. Lenin's sisters Anna and Mariya and brother Dmitrii moved to Moscow from their birthplace, Simbirsk, around 1890. Lenin frequently visited and spent many weeks in the reading room of the Rumyantsev Museum.

In 1895 a handful of socialists tried to draw their local brethren into a single organization, the Moscow League for the Struggle for Emancipation of the Working Class. They sent a delegate to the founding congress of the first countrywide socialist party, the Russian Social Democratic Workers' Party (RSDRP), in Minsk in March 1898. Two days after the league affiliated itself with the party, the police threw its leaders in jail. An RSDRP committee finally began to function in the fall of 1898. One of its three members was Lenin's sister Anna Yelizarova; another was Mikhail F. Vladimirskii, a medical school dropout later to be important in the revolutionizing of Moscow.

Location guaranteed the committee's importance. Moscow "became the main junction for transporting literature in the central region of the country and for communication between *Iskra* [Spark, the party newspaper published abroad] and other Social Democratic organizations."[85] In 1902 the committee discovered a lucrative funding source in the proletarian writer Maxim Gorky and his mistress, actress Mariya Andreyeva. Businessmen, most of them Old Believers, provided other funds.

A schism developed within the RSDRP in 1902–1903 between

Lenin's "Bolshevik" faction, who conceptualized the party as a "vanguard" moving in advance of the masses, and the less zealous "Menshevik" group. Except for an unhappy marriage from 1906 to 1908, the two factions had separate Moscow committees as of March 1905 and carried on as separate parties.

The 1905 near-revolution was at once exhilarating and wrenching for socialists. Strikes and demonstrations, provoked by the government's bungling of the war with Japan and suppression of protest in St. Petersburg, erupted in January in Zamoskvorech'e and spread outside the Sadovoye. Labor unrest waned, exploded with renewed fury in the fall, and climaxed in a general strike in October 1905. When rail and other workers returned to work but conciliation failed, walkouts resumed in early December. This time radical workers and students formed militias and barricaded city roads. By December 17, after the Semenovskii Guards had shelled the strikers' holdouts in Presnya and pacified the protesters, as many as eight hundred lay dead.[86]

One by-product of 1905 was to reappear with a vengeance twelve years later: the "soviet" or revolutionary assembly. *Soviet,* a Russian word for council, connotes more extemporaneity than *duma.* The soviets had forerunners in the "workers' deputies," labor advocates elected in the spring and summer of 1905 within factories, shops, and offices. Some deputies formed committees and councils to assist them in fighting management. In August 1905, when the government announced restrictive electoral rules for the new national legislature, the State Duma, the Mensheviks proposed amalgamation of the factory deputies into working-class councils devoted to wider political issues. Striking printers set up the first such soviet in Moscow, on a trade basis, in September.

The Bolsheviks were initially cool to the soviets, saying the councils lacked socialist consciousness. They relented in mid-October, as the soviets gathered in popularity and white-collar personnel gained influence in them.[87] Soviets defined by territory formed in Moscow in early November, showing the advantage of being on a more intimate scale than any official body. Since late 1904 socialists had had committees at the level of the urban district, or *raion* as they called it, and it was here, starting with Lefortovo and Presnya, that the area-based soviets appeared.

A citywide Moscow Soviet of Workers' Deputies met November

22, 1905. The 170 delegates, some from raions and some from factories, claimed to represent 80,000 workers. The Mensheviks dominated proceedings, although the Moscow Bolshevik leader, Virgilii L. Shantser, was editor of the soviet's newspaper. The Moscow Soviet convened only five times, the last on December 15, and generally aped the St. Petersburg Soviet established five weeks before. It did, nevertheless, canonize revolutionary saints and herald mass political action by the urban working class.

Government repression following the uprising put the Bolsheviks and other socialists in a precarious position. In April 1907 there were about 6,200 Bolsheviks in Moscow (versus 1,600 Mensheviks) and another 3,000 of both in the guberniya; these were by far the highest totals recorded until 1917. One-fifth of the Bolshevik delegates to the Social Democrats' Fifth Congress in 1907 were Muscovites, as were three of five Bolsheviks on the combined Bolshevik-Menshevik Central Committee of 1907. Three years later Moscow's Bolsheviks had dwindled to 400. They were still only 600 in February 1917 (plus 200 in the guberniya), or less than 3 percent of the Bolshevik rank and file.

DEEP UNDERGROUND

Local circumstances, chief among them the proficiency of the Okhrana, the tsarist secret police, made the party's decline after 1907 worse in Moscow. Between June 1907 and November 1910, the Okhrana rounded up the city and guberniya Bolshevik committees on eleven occasions, often after an inside tip. The best-known Moscow Bolshevik from 1910 to 1914, Roman V. Malinovskii, the head of the party's caucus in the State Duma, was the most valuable of many double agents.[88]

The first Moscow Bolsheviks developed a well-ramified party machine. To organize the individual party cells, which existed surreptitiously within factories, they established areal party committees. The most important was the Moscow Committee, the organ of city scope, widely known by its initials MK (for Moskovskii komitet). General meetings of party members would confirm the five or so members of the early MKs, if not initiate their selection.[89] After it went underground in 1906, volunteer groups and committees performed much of the organizational work.

Starting in 1905, the MK designated one member as its prime organizer or secretary *(sekretar')*. The humble origin of this position belies its future towering stature. "In the Moscow Committee," one memoir states, "the secretaries . . . were not heads of the committee. They carried out the strictly administrative and technical functions that tied the committee together," among them collection of dues, record keeping, and publications.[90] Finances pulled them into unsavory dealings. Viktor K. Taratuta, the MK's secretary in 1906–1907, "was deeply involved in the shadier side of Bolshevik fund raising," handling cash from party "expropriations" (mostly bank heists) and using a sexual affair with the sister of a millionaire industrialist to embezzle a large inheritance.[91] Prominent members were passed over for the position. "In the interests of better conspiracy," the Bolsheviks tended to elect secretaries "who were relatively unknown by ordinary party members but possessed considerable experience of illegal work and connections abroad."[92] The brevity of service, necessitated by police raids and rotation to other assignments, further drained their authority. No fewer than eleven Moscow secretaries served between 1905 and 1910.

The quest for grassroots support led the Bolsheviks, as has been noted, to organize at the level of the city raion or district. Raion boundaries were fluid and had no governmental equal until 1917. The *raikom,* the raion party committee, aimed to link the factory cells to the city leadership. The raions proliferated to nine in 1905. Several subraion *(podraion)* committees, based as a rule in a single industrial plant, nested in the largest of them.[93]

To cultivate the manufacturing towns of the guberniya, the MK set up a special branch in the spring of 1905. In August this organ peeled off as a provincial committee *(okruzhkom),* reporting directly to the center. The Bolshevik leadership insisted on instituting yet another unit to check operations in what they termed Moscow *oblast'* (oblast, region), which encompassed the entire Russian heartland. The Moscow Oblast Bureau (Moskovskoye oblastnoye byuro), officially an arm of the Central Committee, oversaw Moscow guberniya and a dozen other provinces.[94]

Okhrana harassment after 1905 was most detrimental to the city and regional organs. In 1908 the Bolsheviks abandoned city conferences in favor of meetings of the closer-knit raions. The MK now consisted entirely of delegates from the raions, and a small executive commission *(ispolnitel'naya komissiya)* made most policy in its name.

A rash of arrests in mid-1910 knocked both the MK and the oblast bureau out of action. A shadowy "leading collective" from the five remaining raions briefly subrogated the MK in 1911. When all its members were jailed, the downtown Gorodskoi raikom claimed superiority, followed during the war by a string of ineffectual pretenders: the Bolsheviks on the city trade union bureau, two self-appointed "organizational commissions," two raikoms, and in 1916 a new oblast bureau, revived by an emissary of the Central Committee, Aleksandr G. Shlyapnikov. There were twenty-five attempts to reconstitute the MK—"Sysiphean work," said one participant.[95] Only in December 1916 was a small MK elected.

If the party fell far short of Lenin's ideal of flawless organization, the same was true of attitudes. The Moscow Bolsheviks were known for their "individuality and disunity."[96] Lenin had his confederates in the city—Taratuta, for example, the raffish MK secretary who became his financial consignee in 1909–1910—but they never got a firm hold on the organization.

Many local Bolsheviks were well to the right of Lenin. Their chief organizer in 1904–1905, Aleksei I. Rykov, was one of the least rigid of the Bolshevik leaders. Viktor P. Nogin, a prominent Moscow trade unionist several times on the central committee, assumed the role of "reconciliationist" and advocated entente with the Mensheviks. On the left, Moscow was the base of Bolshevism's syndicalist wing, which blended moderation on organizational questions with philosophical unorthodoxy (seeing Marxism as a secular religion and themselves as "god makers") and a radical social politics. The Muscovites Shantser, Stanislav Vol'skii, Martyn N. Lyadov, Anatolii V. Lunacharskii, and Mikhail N. Pokrovskii, Russia's leading Marxist historian, were fervent Bogdanovites, and Moscow was their best source of funds. The party cell at Moscow University hosted a less abstract and tactically more militant leftism. From 1908 to 1910 a splinter from it in Zamoskvorech'e, headed by Nikolai I. Bukharin, Valeryan V. Osinskii (Obolenskii), Vladimir M. Smirnov, and Varvara N. Yakovleva, pushed resolutions to this effect through party conferences, to Lenin's infinite annoyance.

Bolsheviks from differing coteries sometimes shared tasks amicably. Rykov and Bukharin, despite their divergent associations, had civilized relations and ultimately became allies in Soviet politics. Other times, relations were acrimonious. Several variables lay behind the heterogeneity of Moscow Bolshevism: the size and social diversity of the city; the party's layered structure; the constant influx of provincial revolutionaries, exiles returning from Siberia and abroad, and parolees from the political wards of the Lefortovo and Butyrki prisons; and the omnipresence of fifth columnists. The Okhrana factor bred paranoia. It got so bad, Bukharin said, that people "looked in the mirror and asked whether they themselves were provocateurs."[97]

The last thing such an exiguous and fragmented organization was competent to tend to was the workaday business of urban government. Bolsheviks ran for the State Duma, beginning in 1907, yet not in local elections, where the strict property franchise made them sure losers. Husbanding their energies for propaganda and shop-floor agitation, they, unlike socialists in the West, knew nothing of the ins and outs of social housing, sanitation, town planning, and transit. A connoisseur of underground printing presses or false-bottomed suitcases for smuggling pamphlets—the specialty of Osip A. Pyatnitskii, who would be Moscow party chieftain in 1920—was a politician in the fullest sense of the word but a stranger to the urban arena.[98]

From this sketch of Moscow under the old regime we can see the mismatch between the complexity and dynamism of its economic and social systems and the ineffectiveness of its political institutions. As workers, investors, and consumers, Muscovites built a city whose architecture, industry, and cultural adornments were not out of keeping with the "patriotic braggadocio" of its boosters. Though hardly without its horrors and injustices, the private Moscow responded gamely to intermittent crises and grew in its capacity to meet the needs of most of its inhabitants.

With the public city, it was a different story, as governance trailed behind social and economic change. For all the lattice of state controls, Moscow was, to use Frederick Starr's apt characterization of provincial Russia, an *undergoverned* place where "vital civic functions were not being fulfilled." Pro- and antigovernment rhetoric obscured this failing, as agitators on both sides adamantly asserted that the

Russian state was trimly organized. The reality of local decision making, as Starr put it, "was a pastiche of poorly assimilated procedures that were anything but rationalized."[99]

Moscow government, its good deeds notwithstanding, came up short in strategic purpose, administrative rigor, territorial scope, and ultimately in legitimacy. It was suspended between a fickle central state and an indifferent local population, hardly any of whom participated in its selection. Its leaders were not able to piece organizational tissue together into a whole that could reconcile the clashing expectations of the communities cohabiting the metropolis—locality and nation, city and region, consumer and producer, poor and rich. With time, there might have been evolution toward greater order and responsiveness, but the clock ran out in 1917.

When it did, the troubled agenda of the tsarist autocracy and its local creatures was bequeathed to a band of radical socialists who were utterly unprepared for it. Unexpectedly faced with the problems unsolved by the city duma, they and a new Moscow Soviet had a lifetime's homework to do overnight.

2

Red Moscow

────────────

WHEN 1917 dawned in Moscow, the twin-headed eagle still flapped over the Kremlin and over Mayor Alekseyev's city hall. When the sun set on that epic year, tsarism and the city duma were no more, the scarlet ensign of the socialist revolution flew atop the flagpoles, and the Bolsheviks in a reborn workers' soviet spewed decrees from the former governor-general's mansion at 13 Tverskaya ulitsa. The revolutionary tempest, far from petering out, would rage through three years of the Russian Civil War and its hubristic companion, "War Communism."

The Communists, as the Bolsheviks dubbed themselves in 1918, gladly threw the institutions, public policies, and social structures of the old order to the dogs. About the brave new world they would substitute, however, they had instincts only, nothing approximating an accepted design. "The revolution," an activist in Red Moscow recalled, "required us to organize brand new apparatuses, ones neither seen nor known before. We had to build something original, something of our own, something proletarian—all this was clear and incontestable. And yet, [we asked,] how to build? What to undertake? How to begin?"[1] On-the-job training, taking from the past, and conflict furnished the answers.

Neither the rabble-rousing soviets nor the Bolsheviks, who cribbed their program for the city duma election of June 1917 from another group, took naturally to urban issues. The municipal scepter passed to the soviets in 1918 just as the Communist Party, its leaders having made Moscow their national capital, began abridging freedoms of speech, assembly, and electoral choice and moving toward one-party dictatorship. The soviets as such, especially at the lowest levels, became essentially debating societies, leaving their executive boards—in collusion with city bureaucrats, the still inchoate and factionalized party apparatus, the police, and resurgent central agencies—to rule in peremptory and frequently erratic fashion. Some of the most promising policy innovations, a drawer full of city and regional plans included, could not be implemented because of disorganization; in other realms, such as housing and trade, changes spiraled out of control and produced division and privation so great that Red Moscow "deurbanized," plunging 50 percent in population and cannibalizing itself for fuel. Within government, the result was a self-defeating organizational gridlock that could be circumvented only by coming up with more and more arbitrary "extraordinary" instruments and methods.

1917

The ultimate cause of the Russian Revolution was the autocracy's unresponsiveness to urbanization and the sundry demands of modernization. The proximate cause was its blundering into World War I.

THE CRASH OF THE AUTOCRACY

Their nation's failure at total war stirred the upper and middle classes of Moscow into unprecedented activism. Duma leaders originated the All-Russian Union of Towns, a municipal alliance that tried to ease bottlenecks in rear services and that selected Mayor Mikhail V. Chelnokov as its chairman. The group joined in November 1915 in an All-Russian Union of Zemstvos and Towns, with Prince Georgii Ye. L'vov, a Moscow nobleman and landlord, as its president. Manufacturers and bankers fathered a Moscow War Industries Committee dedicated to gearing the local economy up to make munitions and war materiel. Its head, Pavel P. Ryabushinskii, a textile baron, philanthropist, and duma councilman, pressed the cabinet to step up the war effort.[2]

The court held the Moscow Duma in the usual scorn. The MVD

churlishly disallowed its successive choices for mayor following the 1912 election. After the election of December 1916, City Governor V. N. Shebeko barred the new council from meeting at all. He took umbrage at the 149-to-11 majority secured by the liberal Kadets (Constitutional Democrats), the first by a national party rather than a local list.

Muscovites' patriotic fervor did not take long to curdle. Draft call-ups unsettled family and work routines, as droves of unacculturated villagers and small-towners had to be imported as replacements. Nearly two hundred factories were evacuated to Moscow, some of them monsters like the Kauchuk (Rubber) Works in Khamovniki and the Provodnik (Wiring) Works in Tushino, both from Riga, Latvia. Military orders financed new plants, such as the AMO Auto Works built by a Ryabushinskii consortium at Simonovka, next to the Simonov Monastery, and expansions at the Goujon, Gustav List, Bromley, and other enterprises. Class-conscious metal and machinery workers almost doubled their share of Moscow factory workers to 28 percent and surpassed textile workers for the first time.

Moscow's population soared past 2 million by February 1917, 400,000 more than in 1912. An army garrison glutted to 100,000 men, thousands more sick and injured soldiers, and perhaps 150,000 refugees supplemented new workers and their dependents. With construction at a standstill, civilian arrivals herded into housing below the low Moscow norm, jacking up rents and consumer prices and deluging sanitation systems and schools. Snags in food distribution most frayed the public's patience. Mob disorders over shortages in Presnya in April and May 1915 frightened the Okhrana into preparing a contingency plan to use the Sadovoye kol'tso as a firebreak against a general insurrection. The ineptitude of the rationing and price controls introduced in 1916 only provided ammunition to the strike movement. The frigid winter of 1916–1917 piled power outages and plant shutdowns onto the city's cares.

The implosion of the autocracy was sudden and irreversible. As in 1905, Moscow took its lead from Petrograd (St. Petersburg's name from 1914 until its change to Leningrad in 1924). Bread riots and strikes there, gathering force February 23, achieved the abdication of Nicholas II and the formation of a Provisional Government of liberals and moderate socialists sworn to deliver the writing of a democratic constitution over to an elected Constituent Assembly. Moscow reached the flashpoint February 27–28, when work stoppages cataracted into a general strike, street skirmishes, and the defection of troops en masse. To the bewilderment of the insurgents, the police's blockade plan stayed on the shelf and only a handful of citizens died: "Everything happened of its own accord. There was no real opposition or rebuff. The authorities hid and kept quiet."[3] On March 1 the few functionaries who refused to accede to the new government were arrested.

INSTITUTIONAL GREENHOUSE

In national politics the February Revolution brought a last hurrah for the Moscow establishment. Georgii L'vov of the Union of Zemstvos and Towns, one of those denied the mayoralty in the period 1912–1914, became the hapless first prime minister of the Provisional Government. Lesser portfolios were held by more conservative Moscow plutocrats such as Aleksandr I. Konovalov (minister of trade and industry), Aleksandr I. Guchkov, the head of the Octobrist party and brother of two-time mayor Nikolai Guchkov (war minister), and Sergei N. Tret'yakov (chairman of the Economic Council). By September Muscovites made up half the cabinet in Petrograd.

Back in Moscow, the city duma's stock rose as the Provisional Government groped to keep radicalism at bay. Parleying March 1 with members of the guberniya zemstvo and other notables, the outgoing and incoming duma councillors passed a motion deploring "anarchy" and "every type of excess." The Provisional Government the next day made Mayor Chelnokov, a right-wing Kadet, its "commissar for the city of Moscow." He assumed broad powers over law enforcement, taxation, and food supply that had been exercised until days before by the city governor. All Russia's governors were sent packing March 5.

Preexisting organizations and graftings onto them could not contain revolutionary energies. As fast as they wilted, others budded and bloomed, some for only a few days or weeks. A first, evanescent claimant to authority over Moscow in this institutional greenhouse titled itself the Provisional Revolutionary Committee of Moscow. Formed February 27 by a cabal in the Moscow War Industries Committee, it was chaired by Aleksei M. Nikitin, a Menshevik politician.

After issuing several contradictory proclamations, it sank without a trace in forty-eight hours.

A sturdier player, the Committee of Public Organizations (KOO by its Cyrillic initials), took the grandstand March 1, instigated by the front benches of the Moscow Duma. Its members (339, and 222 nonvoting "candidates," by May) represented parties, trade unions, municipal workers, business groups, and cooperatives. Although based on nongovernmental organizations, the KOO craved, as its manifesto said, "to unite all power over the city of Moscow in [its] hands . . . to be the Provisional Government's representative and leader of all organizational and administrative work in Moscow."[4] Its chairman, physician Nikolai M. Kishkin, a liberal Kadet and an expositor of Moscow housing, replaced Chelnokov as city commissar on March 6. The KOO quickly acquired trappings of a legislative body: an executive board, a smaller presidium, and auxiliary committees, directorates, and "commissariats" to watch over central and local decisions.

March 1, 1917, was also the day of birth in the city duma chamber of a second Moscow Soviet of Workers' Deputies, a dozen years after the martyrdom of its predecessor. In its name, the Kremlin would before long be stormed.

Unlike the KOO and the duma, the soviet wooed only one social class, the industrial workers, equating protection of the interests of this class and other downtrodden groups (soldiers and peasants) with "democracy." Like the soviets germinating all over Russia, it exemplified a direct and folkish democracy, and its leaders disdained "bourgeois parliamentarism." Elections to it were public affairs, by show of hands at places of work; deputies who lost their voters' trust between polls could be recalled and replaced. The soviet's flowery debates were unencumbered by protocol and, rather like a meeting on the village green, all who wished to have their say did so. Deputies themselves, not a cabinet or a discrete executive branch, were supposed to be the main movers in the soviet and in carrying out its decisions.

The Moscow Soviet (the Mossovet in common usage) did not lack all structure, however. From the outset the 625 deputies designated an executive committee (*ispolnitel'nyi komitet*, or *ispolkom*, in the usual abbreviation), with 75, later 60, members chosen on a quota basis by the socialist parties. It in turn, as of April 11, delegated daily decisions to a presidium *(prezidium)* of 7 to 9 persons. The presidium set up a Municipal Department for relations with the city duma in May; it had eleven administrative divisions by October. Despite low party consciousness, the soviet was dominated, as in 1905, by moderate socialists partial to interclass collaboration. Its first chairman, the same Nikitin who headed the Provisional Revolutionary Committee, was succeeded March 5 by another Menshevik, Lev M. Khinchuk. The Bolsheviks' "fraction" or caucus *(fraktsiya)* came together March 19 with about 10 percent of the deputies.[5]

In Moscow, unlike Petrograd, an independent Soviet of Soldiers' Deputies represented discontented troops. Foursquare behind the pro-peasant Socialist Revolutionary (SR) party, this soviet stood close to the Mensheviks on policy. Soviets sprouted in Podmoskov'e as well. Here and there, especially in the industrial southeast, the Bolsheviks made rapid inroads; in the textile center of Orekhovo-Zuyevo they got control on March 19. When a Moscow Guberniya Soviet of Workers' Deputies was proclaimed May 27, the Bolsheviks caught the other parties napping and gained a majority in its executive, which they never lost.[6] Rural or village soviets also formed, representing peasants who were resorting to anarchic land seizures. These fed into a guberniya Soviet of Peasants' Deputies, where the SRs reigned supreme.

Politics effloresced at the subcity level, too. Eight raion (district) soviets were up and running by the end of March and twelve by autumn. Raions ranged in size from Simonovskii, with 45,000 people, to Gorodskoi (City) raion, covering all thirteen police precincts within the Sadovoye north of the Moskva, with 366,000 residents (see Map 5). The raion soviets patrolled streetcorners, distributed foodstuffs together with workers' cooperatives, and organized concerts and fairs. They mimicked the structures of the city soviet, except that most of them sat soldier delegates.

The raion soviets were a throwback to 1905, but territorial units within the official administration of the city were something else. Commissar Kishkin laid the groundwork in March 1917 by instituting in each precinct a *komissariat* to scrutinize police conduct. Around the commissariats city hall and the KOO then established "general citizens' committees," soon renamed "raion dumas." The raions here,

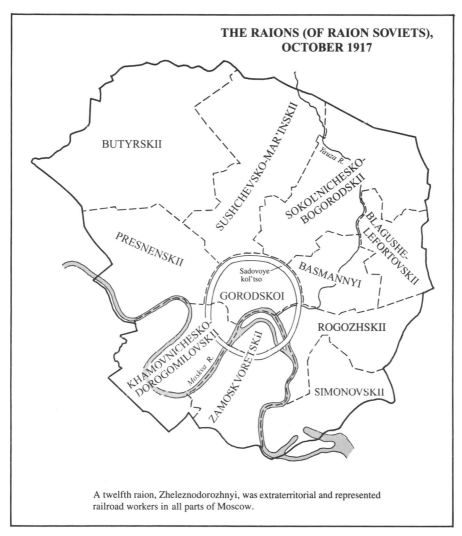

THE RAIONS (OF RAION SOVIETS),
OCTOBER 1917

BUTYRSKII

SUSHCHEVSKO-MAR'INSKII

Yauza R.

SOKOL'NICHESKO-
BOGORODSKII

BLAGUSHE-
LEFORTOVSKII

PRESNENSKII

Sadovoye
kol'tso

GORODSKOI

BASMANNYI

KHAMOVNICHESKO-
DOROGOMILOVSKII

Moskva R.

ZAMOSKVORETSKII

ROGOZHSKII

SIMONOVSKII

A twelfth raion, Zheleznodorozhnyi, was extraterritorial and represented
railroad workers in all parts of Moscow.

MAP 5

forty-four in total, were considerably smaller than the eponymous
raions of the soviets and generally coincided with a single precinct. A
number had their boundaries dilated when the Provisional Government on May 23, 1917, annexed a wide belt of suburban territory to
Moscow; even at that, their population averaged a mere 40,000.

The raion dumas initially comprised delegates from private associations and from semipublic agencies like the guardianships of the poor. Responsible first for food rationing, they redefined themselves as spokesmen at large for neighborhood interests. This volubility brought conflict with the raion soviets, their sponsor organizations, and newcomers like the "house committees" *(domovyye komitety),* which were elected within many apartment blocks, with the approval of the Provisional Government, in the summer and fall of 1917. "Endless misunderstandings" developed between the raion dumas and the precinct commissariats, which were run by unwieldy duumvirates (one commissar for crime prevention and one for maintenance of order) and were often staffed by conservative army officers. Squabbles had to be "moved toward compromise in interminable harangues and conferences."[7]

The patent dilemma was what to do with the Moscow City Duma. Mayor Chelnokov failed in early March 1917 to get KOO endorsement for legitimation, by cooptation of deputies from the lower classes, of the duma elected in December 1916. The duma met only twice in March, the second time anointing Nikolai Astrov as mayor.

The executive committee of the Moscow Soviet demanded that the duma be dissolved as a benighted vestige of autocracy. This call kindled torrid debate when it reached the floor of the soviet March 21. No one disputed the executive's position that the existing duma was "a defender of the interests of the landlords and merchants, concerned exclusively with the beautification of the city center and giving nary a thought . . . to the [workers'] outskirts."[8] But did this make it irredeemable? If so, who would take over its responsibilities?

Some deputies agreed with Yefim N. Ignatov that the soviet itself should accept responsibility for local government, as it offered "foxholes into which the workers ought to dig themselves" for protection against the propertied classes. Others sided with Il'ya S. Veger, who warned that if the Moscow Soviet enacted this proposal soviets all over Russia "will be changed over into city dumas and will worry about almshouses, sidewalks, and so on," which "would be the end of the revolution." Veger added that to take over from the Moscow Duma was in any event to assume an impossible burden: "The services we are being urged to take over have been in very poor condition for years. We will not get them in shape and will only harm ourselves."

The soviet's compromise resolution authorized liquidation of the current city duma and transfer of its administrative functions to the KOO, to be followed by free election, without property or gender qualifications, of a reformed duma. The KOO ordered the election for June 25 but declined to assume the duma's workload.

UP FROM THE CATACOMBS

The Bolshevik's mythology of the revolution would have them a tight phalanx tramping as one toward victory in 1917. Yet, as many events signified—beginning with the repartee between Ignatov and Veger, both of them members of the party—the column was a motley one.

After years in the wilderness, the Bolsheviks of Moscow felt out of sorts in open, legal politics. "Some comrades," in the words of one of them, Petr G. Smidovich, "could not get used to the idea that the underground was finally dead." Like groundhogs blinking in the noonday sun, they clung to cryptonyms, safe houses, and conspiratorial ways.[9]

The self-selected revolutionary vanguard waded into the scuffle for power with amusingly few weapons. The Bolshevik's MK, their resurrected city committee, had at its disposal only a wee "propaganda group," mostly students from the Moscow Commercial Institute. Its first appeals were broadcast courtesy of the SR party, and on various matters it cooperated with the Mensheviks. The Moscow Oblast Bureau began action—as Varvara Yakovleva, its secretary for most of 1917, testified—with "more or less random communication with random comrades, that is all."[10]

In March Secretary Rozaliya S. Zemlyachka leased offices for the MK in the Kaptsov boys' school on Leont'evskii pereulok. With the oblast bureau, which set up shop down the hall, she published the party's first Moscow newspaper, *Sotsial-demokrat* (Social Democrat), circulated leaflets, and proselytized. Now 6,000 strong, the Moscow Bolsheviks held their first legal conference at the city level April 3–4. The twenty-one-person MK elected there chose an executive commission of five. Raion organizations, their boundaries generally the same as the raion soviets', proliferated.

Guberniya and oblast organizing conferences gathered later in April. While the Moscow Oblast Bureau feigned oversight of Bolsheviks all over central Russia, six provinces were absent from its conference and, as Yakovleva confessed, "we were almost unconnected with the countryside and barely touched such [distant] guberniyas as Ryazan and Tambov." Her and Zemlyachka's best enrollees were the individuals who strayed into the Kaptsov school, for whom affiliation often "depended on whether they called on us . . . or on the Mensheviks" in the same building.[11] Membership reached 4,600 in Moscow guberniya by mid-April, and 18,000 in the provinces nominally under the oblast bureau.

The crop of popularly based political organizations presented a problem. Even in the Mossovet, where under a five-person presidium the party's fraction had a bridgehead, the Bolsheviks and the MK were at daggers drawn on big issues: "Some comrades even asked whether work in the soviet was really necessary, inasmuch as the question of the dictatorship of the proletariat was unresolved and there seemed no prospect of the soviets becoming state organs." Zemlyachka, who at the April conference supported a fraction in the Moscow Soviet, sniped at the soviets thereafter as "suspicious organizations." Vasilii M. Likhachev, who took her job in May, expressed more optimism, but as late as September 1, 1917, Innokentii N. Stukov of the oblast bureau was questioning Lenin's attachment to the soviets and proposing invention in their stead of "a new, fully empowered institution that would rely on the broad masses."[12]

Bolsheviks in the Mossovet received "no regular directives or steady, practical leadership," as the MK was "preoccupied with agitation at the factories and organizing the raions." Come the party's assumption of power, there were to be deputies who held that MK decisions were advisory only and that, as Ignatov said, "the fraction may choose not to subordinate itself" to them.[13]

LOCAL ISSUES AND BOLSHEVIK ASCENDANCY

Bolsheviks may have often looked askew at the soviets, but their attitude toward the dumas and the surrounding nuts and bolts politics manifested unvarnished contempt. Boris N. Volin, an organizer of the Moscow party conference in April, broke rank by coming out for an opening to municipal politics. To sugarcoat the pill, he observed that the city and raion dumas and the precinct commissariats could well influence the planned voting for the national Constituent Assembly. But his main contention was that alienation from local affairs was no longer sustainable on its merits: "Self-government plays an immense part in local life. Once the worker leaves the job, he gives himself over wholly to the power of the city. We must engage ourselves in city government."

Swayed by Volin and L. Ye. Gal'perin of Rogozhskii raion, the delegates endorsed a municipal presence in the interests of "widening the gains of the revolution," electing socialists to the Constituent Assembly, and achieving "those solutions to municipal problems most favorable from the point of view of democracy." They instructed party cells to get Bolsheviks into the raion dumas and called for establishment of a commission to write a program for the duma election.[14]

An MK Municipal Commission of Volin, Gal'perin, and Vadim N. Podbel'skii put pen to paper in mid-April. Volin provided a laconic description in 1922, skipping over Gal'perin, who absconded to the Mensheviks before the election:

> Neither Podbel'skii nor I had ever had any special interest in city issues. My entire acquaintance with questions of city services consisted in having read a couple of booklets, one in English and the other in German (their names I no longer remember), which treated urban questions from the point of view, it seemed, of the proletariat. These booklets, by the way, were very old and discussed the questions as they applied to England and Germany.
>
> We drew some others into this work. I remember Comrade Lizarev and, I think, Z. P. Solov'ev. We got a copy of the SR municipal program (they developed it, I believe, in 1905) and began to study it and put together our municipal program in a form much like it. We arranged a number of meetings with comrades from the raions somehow involved with the many and woolly-headed raion dumas.
>
> I cannot remember whether the MK examined the program we drew up or not. It was run off, but I never saw it after that. I do not know if a printed copy of it still exists. I do remember that when our program was written and printed, we received from St. Petersburg a program published by our CC [Central Committee], which in general and in detail corresponded to our own.[15]

It was this pirated program that Bolshevik candidates, approved as a slate by a city conference, took to voters in June. It tied local to national issues, saying Muscovites had to "organize city services for the sake of developing and consolidating the class struggle." The proletariat, it declared, would never live much better, "no matter how many representatives it has in the organs of city self-government," so long as the Provisional Government remained in office and Russia in the European war. Nonetheless, the Bolsheviks proposed to "tear the municipal economy from the hands of the bourgeoisie and its lackeys" in these ways:

1. Universal municipal suffrage at age eighteen.
2. "Full autonomy" from Petrograd for the cities.
3. Eventual nationalization of all urban land and transfer of it to the municipalities; immediate taxation of income, personal property, land transfers, and rents.
4. Municipalization of local transport and utilities; development of city nonprofit enterprises.
5. "Extensive municipal construction" of housing; aid to cooperative building; inspection of private premises.
6. Free elementary and vocational education, kindergartens, evening courses, and libraries; measures to counter juvenile crime.
7. Health care for all; improvements in hygiene and sanitation; meals for needy children.
8. Better amenities—blacktopped streets, lighting, sewers, water, and parks—especially on the city outskirts.
9. A city labor inspectorate and labor exchange; nurseries for working mothers; an eight-hour day and paid vacations for all city employees.
10. A popular militia, answerable to local government, in place of the regular police and army.
11. Permanent raion dumas with power over the most local services; city annexation of all near suburbs.
12. Municipal operation, in cooperation with the trade unions, of private factories idled by owners.
13. City works projects to employ demobilized soldiers.
14. Municipal control of veterans' services.[16]

The score on June 25 hinged on general as much as local issues. Open to virtually all residents aged twenty or older, and contested by seven parties, this election was the first in Moscow ever run by democratic rules. The 647,000 ballots cast multiplied almost 200 times the turnout in the last prewar election, in 1912.

As most everywhere in urban Russia, the SRs easily crossed the finish line first. Their 58.0 percent of the vote gave them a majority in the duma and the mayor's gavel to V. V. Rudnev, a transplanted country doctor and veteran of the 1905 soviet who had since moved to the right of the party. The Kadets, drawing best in genteel sections, were a distant second with 16.8 percent. The Bolsheviks ran fourth with 75,000 votes, or 11.7 percent of the total, a hair behind the Mensheviks' 11.8 percent. They scored worst in the city core, where their share was less than 5 percent, and best beyond the Sadovoye, especially to the south and east, where they came in second to the SRs. In the guberniya the Bolsheviks elected 28 percent of the deputies to the town dumas and a majority in Orekhovo-Zuyevo.

Democratization of the Moscow Duma let all agree on the redundancy of the Committee of Public Organizations. Its chairman, Kishkin, ordered it dismantled July 7. The city duma was now by default the Provisional Government's outpost in Moscow. Mayor Rudnev, a devotee of Prime Minister Aleksandr F. Kerenskii, mostly engaged it with national issues. The twenty-three Bolsheviks formed a duma fraction, as they had in the KOO and Moscow Soviet, with Ivan I. Skvortsov-Stepanov as chairman and Volin as secretary. Using the council to proclaim their revolutionary aims, they also pounded at local questions treated in the municipal program. In August 1917 they proposed that the duma hand over to the poor all Moscow properties of the royal family and Orthodox Church, ration apartments, and stick the gentry and the bourgeoisie with the entire burden of local taxes.

Four short months lay between the city duma election and the Bolsheviks' October Revolution. Their popularity grew not from their views on municipal issues but from their revulsion at the unending war, at economic decline, and at the monarchist putsch attempted in August by General Lavr G. Kornilov. Their ability in the last days of August to get the soviets of several Moscow raions to pass anti-Kornilov resolutions presaged their strength. At the beginning of September, the Zamoskvorech'e raion soviet was the first to elect a Bolshevik as its chairman.[17] Beyond the city limits, the Bolsheviks won majorities in zemstvo elections in two uyezds (at suburban Bogorodskoye and the more distant Podol'sk) and in the town soviets of Kolomna, Serpukhov, and Dmitrov.

The breakthrough occurred in the city soviet. Whereas about 10 percent of the deputies had been Bolsheviks in March and 30 percent when most mandates were renewed in June, by-elections and the conversion of sitting members propelled their share upward in late summer. On September 5 the Moscow Soviet voted to censure the Provisional Government, as the Petrograd Soviet had done August 31, and demanded the dismissal of Kishkin. Khinchuk resigned as chairman September 9, and on September 19, by 246 votes cast out of 466, the soviet chose an executive committee with a Bolshevik majority, 32 seats out of 60. Viktor Nogin, a thirty-nine-year-old, self-educated shop assistant's son whose autobiography boasted that he had sat in fifty different prisons, was elected chairman of the Mossovet. Five out of 9 on the new presidium were Bolsheviks: Nogin, Ignatov, Smidovich, Aleksei Rykov, and Varlam A. Avanesov. The Bolsheviks took as their rallying cry Lenin's "All Power to the Soviets!"

The September 24 balloting for the raion dumas, Moscow's second democratic city election in 1917, allowed another advance. Mikhail Vladimirskii masterminded the campaign against twenty-one rival parties, in seventeen redrawn raions (down from forty-four in the spring). He thundered out slogans about Moscow's housing shortage, "capitalist sabotage" of its economy, and bread lines, but the gravamen again concerned nationwide issues. "It is impossible," read the party's appeal, "to resolve food, financial, and other problems for Moscow without resolving them for all of Russia."[18]

The Bolsheviks, gleaning 51.5 percent of the votes and electing 50.2 percent of the 715 deputies, won a resounding victory. They earned 165 percent more votes than in June; all the other big parties lost votes as turnout declined almost 40 percent. Because SR and Menshevik votes fell off by more than 80 percent, the electorate polarized between the Bolsheviks and the most conservative of the large parties, the Kadets, who were down less than 10 percent. The Bolsheviks continued to be weakest in the central city, getting less than 20 percent of the votes in the silk-stocking Prechistensko-Arbatskii raion and about 30 percent in Myasnitsko-Yauzskii and Gorodskoi (the Kadets had a majority in the first and a plurality in the last two). They gained a plurality of votes in three raions and a clear majority in the remaining eleven, topping 60 percent in Petrovskii, Simonovskii, Pyatnitskii, Lefortovskii, and Butyrskii raions.[19]

The Bolsheviks went about staffing the raion dumas much as any party would. The MK Municipal Commission[20] scrutinized candidates for executives, and both a general meeting of Bolshevik deputies and the MK confirmed them. To be sure, muscle in the raions poorly transmuted into policy, for the MK was not in close touch with the raions, and the Moscow Duma, still an SR preserve, "tried in every way to impede" the raion dumas, refusing to formalize their legislative powers or give them funds. All the same, Bolshevik one-upmanship at raion level "loosened the [city] duma's foundation and facilitated the decline of [its] authority."[21]

These successes fired the hopes of radicals throughout the party. Lenin speculated that proletarian rebellion was imminent in the old capital and might spark a national revolution. As it happened, the Moscow Bolsheviks rested on their oars. They made no concerted move until their hand was forced by the October 25 coup in Petrograd, which overthrew Kerenskii and installed the new "Soviet" regime, run by Lenin's Council of People's Commissars (Sovnarkom).

The Moscow Soviet appointed the actual organizer of the local takeover, its Military Revolutionary Committee (VRK), only on October 25, with Petr Smidovich chairing in Nogin's absence. VRK commissars fanned out to transport and telegraph facilities, army units, and the offices of Commissar Kishkin and government bureaus. Raion VRKs and squadrons of the Bolsheviks' Red Guard from Moscow city and region provided reinforcements. Yet it took until November 2 for the Committee of Public Safety, the conservative prop rolled out by Mayor Rudnev, to surrender. Cadets at the Aleksandrovskoye Military School on Znamenka ulitsa rallied to Rudnev's colors and fought house to house in the Arbat area. Before terms were imposed, two truces were broken, the Kremlin changed hands twice, and Bolshevik ordnance attacked it from the Sparrow Hills and Zamoskvorech'e, doing shrapnel damage to the Spasskaya Tower's clock and bells, the Ivan the Great Belfry, and the Chudov Monastery. As many as 1,000 people perished in the gunplay; 238 soldiers and Red Guards were buried November 10, 1917, in a fraternal grave in Red Square.

Moscow's social diversity and the staying power of its establishment made the uprising more problematic here than in Petrograd. Moreover, the rebels had problems of their own. They split along territorial lines on the question of revolutionary strategy. The Bolshe-

viks' city committee contained some radicals (Vladimirskii and Zem-
lyachka, for example), yet the center of gravity rested with nail biters
like Secretary Likhachev, Nogin, Ignatov, Rykov, Smidovich, and Osip
Pyatnitskii, types who abounded in the contingent in the Mossovet.
The oblast bureau teemed with firebrands wanting prompt action.
Prominent were intellectuals long pacesetters on the party left—
Yakovleva, Nikolai Bukharin, Grigorii I. Lomov, Valeryan Osinskii,
Vladimir Smirnov, and Stukov (now accepting of the soviets), to
name the main ones. The guberniya committee shilly-shallied in the
middle.[22]

The city and regional leaderships went so far as to appoint competing "combat centers" to prepare the show of force. When they
finally formed a joint combat center on October 25, it had to wage a
"stubborn struggle" with the less venturesome Bolsheviks on the
Military Revolutionary Committee. The Bolsheviks in the Mossovet
voted to set up the committee only when persuaded it was a preserv-
ative device—"to assure order and tranquility in Moscow," Smidovich
stated—and none of their leaders was appointed to it or the combat
center.[23]

The air was thick with insults November 13 when the Moscow
Soviet met to elect a chairman, a touchstone of the city's new politics.
The Bolshevik fraction favored either Nogin or Rykov, soft-liners who
briefly served with Lenin in Sovnarkom and resigned to defend the
principle of coalition with other socialist parties. But the MK, where
the militants had strengthened their hand, spurned both. After an
attempt to nominate Grigorii Lomov, the MK and then the full soviet
went for the historian Mikhail Pokrovskii, only slightly less of a leftist.
Having dashed to power in the chariot of the soviet, the Bolsheviks
turned their backs on the makers of their victory in that very body.

Dilemmas of Power

Their intoxicating success set the Bolsheviks to searching their souls.
No question of the day failed to evoke a gush of speeches and resolutions in the soviets and party committees of Moscow. On the emotive issue of war and peace, Muscovites led the opposition to the
punitive Brest-Litovsk Treaty signed with Germany in February 1918.
The hard-line Zemlyachka was returned as MK secretary in December

1917, and the Left Communists had more support in the oblast bureau than anywhere in the republic. At the Seventh Party Congress, which ratified the peace in March, Lenin petulantly called them "our young Moscow friends." Chairman Pokrovskii, while not young, chaperoned an anti-Brest resolution through the Mossovet.

These events belong to the general biography of the regime. In Moscow itself the first task was to consolidate power in a setting replete with signs of its tenuousness.

FLYING SOLO

At one time or another that winter municipal employees, bank tellers, telegraph operators, physicians, civil servants in the state ministries, and school teachers, backed by parents' and pupils' groups, went on strike against the Moscow Bolsheviks. The "struggle for the governmental apparatus," said Pokrovskii, was as absorbing as the recent "struggle on the streets," and it left the soviet "no time for creative work." Dispersal of the pesky Constituent Assembly in Petrograd momentarily brought back street politics. At least 30 persons were shot or stamped to death when 200,000 paraded downtown on January 9, 1918.[24]

In this electrified atmosphere the Bolsheviks made the fateful decision to govern alone. To ask whether they did so of their own accord may be to miss the point. Nogin, Rykov, Likhachev, and other Muscovite moderates preferred coalition—but only with other socialists and only on Bolshevik terms. They did not quail at the suppression of the non-socialist press in late 1917, and they were less and less a factor as Russia careened toward one-party dictatorship.

The narrowing of partisan options in Moscow was most palpable in the Mossovet. The sixty-man executive committee chosen in November 1917 included twenty members from three brother socialist parties—ten Mensheviks, three Amalgamationists (advocates of a Bolshevik-Menshevik merger), and seven Left SRs—while three Left SRs and one Amalgamationist accompanied eleven Bolsheviks on the presidium. This ecumenism was spent in June 1918, when, by directive of the Central Committee, the Bolshevik (now Communist) majority expelled the first two groups from the ispolkom as "traitors to the working class." On July 23, after some Left SRs attempted a revolt against Lenin, they were shown the door; the two Left SRs on the smaller and more potent presidium were shut out the same day.[25]

A parallel if more gradual trend occurred in popular elections. In the polling for the Constituent Assembly in November 1917, pre-arranged by the Provisional Government, the Bolsheviks cornered 47.9 percent of the Moscow votes, a slightly lower ratio than for the raion dumas in September, although of a much larger whole; the Kadets drew 35.7 percent and the SRs 8.1 percent. When the Mossovet held its first post-October election in April 1918, the Bolsheviks used it to flaunt their support and isolate opponents. Yet they had already made a mockery of the precepts of uncoerced choice. Not only did they ban the Kadets and other non-socialist parties from the ten days of campaigning and voting, but also, as was to be the norm until the late 1930s, the ballot was cast in public and members of the old gentry, businessmen, clergy, former agents of the imperial police, and other pariah groups were disfranchised. The Bolsheviks swamped the opposition, getting nearly 70 percent of the seats to the less than 10 percent for the Mensheviks, several percent for the Left SRs, and the balance for smaller slates (see Table 1). Lenin was the first deputy declared elected.

Subsequent elections turned progressively more one-sided. Closure of Menshevik newspapers in May 1918 foretold the smothering of dissent with the outbreak of the Civil War that summer. Almost 80 percent of the deputies were Communists after the general poll of December 1918. When voters were next consulted in February 1920, opposition candidates were fiercely harassed and the ruling party's share exceeded 86 percent.[26] Some Mensheviks jumped ship with the 1917 chairman of the Mossovet, Khinchuk, and joined the ruling party; the remaining few, denied a national forum, treasured their soapbox in the Moscow Soviet.[27]

The reseating of the Soviet government in Moscow in March 1918—and with it its security police, the Cheka (All-Russian Extraordinary Commission for Combating Counterrevolution and Sabotage), under Feliks E. Dzerzhinskii—magnified the coercive component. The Cheka made Moscow's Black Guard anarchists an early target, arresting 600 and killing or wounding 20 in just one clash in April 1918. Raion-level Chekas joined with rank-and-file Communists in the Red Terror of the autumn of 1918, a paroxysm of arrests, shootings, and

Table 1. Elections to the Moscow Soviet, 1917–1927

Date	Deputies elected	Turnout (percent)	Deputies' party affiliation (percent)				
			Communist	Menshevik	SR	Other	No party
June 1917	700	—	32.9	31.6	18.9	9.0	7.7
April 1918	869	—	69.6[a]	9.9	3.6	7.5	9.4[b]
December 1918	662	—	79.5[c]	2.9	1.2	1.7	14.8[d]
February 1920	1,532	93.0	86.2[e]	2.6	0.0	0.4	10.8
April 1921	2,115	50.6	73.0	0.6	0.3	0.5	25.7[f]
January 1922	1,696	72.2	84.8	0.2	0.2	0.0	14.8
December 1922	1,902	70.6	90.7	0.0	0.0	0.0	9.3
November 1923	1,937	85.1	87.7	0.0	0.0	0.0	12.3
April 1925	2,203	63.8	69.9[g]	0.0	0.0	0.0	30.1
March 1927	2,283	66.7	70.0[h]	0.0	0.0	0.0	30.0

Sources: Number of deputies and party affiliation from *Moskovskii Sovet rabochikh, krest'yanskikh i krasnoarmeiskikh deputatov, 1917–1927* (Moscow: Izdaniye Moskovskogo Soveta, 1927), p. 132. Turnout from N. M. Aleshchenko, *Moskovskii Sovet v 1917–1941 gg.* (Moscow: Nauka, 1976), pp. 92, 251, 350.

a. Includes 13.1 percent declared sympathizers (*sochuvstvuyushchiye*) who had applied to join the Communist Party.

b. Includes 1.0 percent with unknown affiliation.

c. Includes 14.5 percent sympathizers of the Communists.

d. Includes 8.5 percent with unknown affiliation.

e. Includes 3.3 percent sympathizers of the Communists.

f. Includes 0.5 percent with unknown affiliation.

g. Includes 2.6 percent members of the Komsomol (Communist Youth League).

h. Includes 2.1 percent members of the Komsomol.

confiscations touched off by the August 30 assassination attempt on Lenin by an SR hothead, Fanya Kaplan, at the Mikhel'son factory in Zamoskvorech'e. There were mass slayings at Cheka headquarters, Petrovskii Park, Khodynka Field, Butyrki Prison, and Semenovskaya zastava. A wave of detentions followed the bombing of the Kaptsov school on September 25, 1919. Secretary Vladimir M. Zagorskii and eleven others attending an MK plenum died in the blast. Dzerzhinskii blamed upper-class reactionaries, learning belatedly that the anarchist band of Donat Cherepanov was responsible; hundreds of aristocrats, former Kadets, ex-gendarmes, and others were gunned down forthwith.[28]

The Moscow Cheka alone, from December 1918 to November 1, 1920, is said to have crushed fifty-nine "counterrevolutionary organizations," arrested more than 5,100 members, and executed 52 of them. Some of the 338 shot for "banditry" must have been political deviants, and these statistics take no account of killings by the All-Russian Cheka.[29]

Red Moscow had the dubious honor of being the testing ground for Soviet forced-labor camps. Appearing in late 1918 under the wartime term "concentration camps," they were populated by political and economic offenders detained for up to five years. The very first in Bolshevik Russia was in Novospasskii Monastery, whose seventeenth-century Spaso-Preobrazhenskii Cathedral held the burial vault of the Romanov family. By July 1920 the People's Commissariat of Internal Affairs (NKVD) and Cheka were operating three camps in closed-down monasteries (Novospasskii, Andronikov, and the Ivanovskii Convent), two other concentration camps, and two of the less strict "labor colonies." In October 1921, seven months after the conclusion of the Civil War, the seven camps in Moscow and three in the guberniya held a total of 4,217 inmates.[30]

THE MOSCOW SOVIET GOES MUNICIPAL

The Moscow Soviet, taking the bit in its teeth, brought the revolution a stride ahead of the party leadership. Besides legislating its own minimum wage, it was the most evangelical nationalizer in Russia, seizing thirty-seven factories before the uniform nationalization law of June 1918. It also levied punitive taxes on owners of real estate, authorizing collectors to cut off delinquents' electricity, take away their chattels, and send them to corvée labor.[31]

The soviet's radicalism burned hottest with respect to housing. In November 1917 it slashed all Moscow rents by 50 percent. It voted December 12 to "municipalize" the tenement housing owned by the biggest landlords; affected were 4,000 of 28,000 rental properties, with about 800,000 residents, 40 percent of the population. The raion dumas received rent, but collection and building management were turned over to the elected house committees. State control of urban housing did not become general Soviet policy until August 1918.[32]

The bravado of these proclamations was an index of the identity crisis that the Mossovet confronted once it completed the heroic task of mobilizing the proletariat for insurrection. Its leaders resolved the crisis by disposing of functional rivals and assimilating new missions they pooh-poohed—really those of a municipal council exercising delegated powers, albeit in a field of action widened by the regime's socialism. In so doing, they lessened the institutional anarchy in the metropolis.

A worry rampant after the October coup was that, as Vadim Podbel'skii voiced it, the soviet and its executive organs mistook high-flown phrases for action: "It becomes clearer every day that we have no real power . . . Our power in the person of the presidium [of the Mossovet] sits but does not govern . . . Our presidium has turned itself into a talking machine. Many of its resolutions are forgotten or lost." Moscow suffered, stated Mikhail Vladimirskii, from "divided sovereignty" (mnogovlastiye). The raion dumas, the revolutionary tribunals (political courts), the Red Guard, and the Moscow Food Committee, among others, were following their own lights and exercising "enormously more power" between them than the soviet. "If such a tangle was conceivable in the first days of the soviet," Vladimir-skii said, "now it is completely unacceptable. The [Moscow] Soviet . . . should be the single local center."[33]

One easy victory occurred on November 14, 1917, with the swallowing of the soldiers' soviet, now with a Bolshevik majority. A servicemen's section (of the Moscow Soviet of Workers' and Soldiers' Deputies), with the right to choose one-third of the executive, was retained until March 19, 1918. The VRK also succumbed resignedly to the Moscow Soviet, although it lurked in the background into

February. Other competitors had more tenacity. The soviet decided in November 1917 to leave intact the Moscow Food Committee, which—with the aid of the raion dumas—had been in charge of provisioning under Kerenskii. The committee took over private bakeries, sent off purchasing delegations, printed ration cards, and confiscated pantry stocks in excess of norms, all of them crucial acts in a famished city. Not until May 1918 did the Moscow Soviet reduce it to a subordinate Food Department.

The most glaring anomaly in 1917 was the Mossovet's estrangement from the core municipal activities carried out for fifty-five years by the Moscow Duma. Inevitably, the Bolsheviks felt enmity toward the duma as then constituted, with its SR allegiance. On November 3 the VRK appointed six commissars to oversee the duma. On November 5 it disbanded the city duma and uprava and ordered their powers transmitted to a four-member "council of commissars," which was superseded November 7 by seven "commissars for city services," and November 12 by a single "commissar of the city duma," the Bolshevik physician Nikolai A. Semashko. None of these assorted commissars achieved anything. They were matched in futility by Mayor Rudnev, who closeted himself with diehard members of his uprava and signed decrees, not stopping for a week or so after Lenin and the central government confirmed dissolution of the duma on November 16.[34]

The decree of November 5 unseated the councillors elected June 25; it did not extinguish the duma as such. The VRK intended, as earlier in 1917, for municipal work to resume in a duly reelected council. The committee in fact scheduled a duma election for November 26; it was soon postponed to December 6 and in the end never held. According to the only explanation we have, the Bolsheviks scrapped it reluctantly and only when all except one of the fringe parties boycotted.[35] Without its dismemberment ever being discussed, the Moscow City Duma was not to meet again.

City business lay for the next few hectic months with a product of inspired opportunism: the Soviet of Raion Dumas (Sovet Raionnykh Dum—SRD). The SRD's genesis was a meeting on October 27, 1917, of officers of the raion dumas, most of which had fallen to the Bolsheviks in the September elections. Lambasting the city duma for "taking the side of the counterrevolutionary bourgeoisie," they proposed an inter-raion organ to speed its defeat and help the Moscow

Soviet.[36] The VRK, taken with the idea, convened the first meeting of the SRD November 8. The SRD elected a bureau and named nine of its eighteen members heads of departments corresponding to salient local services—health, social security, schools, and so on. Besides Vladimirskii, its chairman, the bureau contained Boris Volin and Zinovii Solov'ev from the MK's original Municipal Commission, Semashko, lately commissar of the city duma, and, a bit later, Vasilii Likhachev, the ex-secretary of the MK. The Mossovet on November 27 recognized the SRD's authority on "all matters relating to city self-government."

A slapstick sign of the times was that the SRD's first stratagem for raising funds was to shanghai a railway car full of safes holding private bank deposits. When the VRK vetoed this stunt, Vladimirskii drove with gun-toting comrades to the Moscow headquarters of the State Bank, took 2 million rubles from the tills of the aghast clerks, and carried it back to his office in two battered suitcases. The loot was supplemented by subsidies from Petrograd, the accounts of the All-Russian Union of Towns, and new taxes—"a tax press," jubilated Vladimirskii, that "mercilessly squeezed the bourgeoisie."[37]

The SRD also had a great impact on personnel. Most of the white-collar staff of the Moscow Duma had stalked out in a dispute over pay and procedures the week before the October coup. The Bolsheviks, who had quarreled over the strike's merit,[38] took the management stance once in power. Many office workers returned in November 1917 but, according to Vladimirskii, "refused to carry out their work, whined, and abused us as usurpers." He retaliated in December by sacking them all and requiring them to reapply for their old jobs and sign a loyalty oath. Egged on, the Bolsheviks said, by former duma deputies, the union called a total strike.

Vladimirskii asserted with some cogency that the strike had its advantages:

> The strike of office employees was really a boon to us. If we had had to take into service all employees of the former uprava, whose staff was puffed way up under the free-spending SR duma, our revenues could never have supported this. Furthermore, we would not have looked so closely at the apparatus of city administration and mastered it wholly and in all its details, as we did with the assistance of 200 employees.

Among them were former uprava officials, without party affiliation, who came over to work with us in the very first days (M. I. Istomin, V. Rozanov, S. I. Chervyakov, and others).

We made out fine for a while without certain categories of "higher" employees (engineers). The city's enterprises, managed by the workers themselves, ran quite nicely . . . The majority of the uprava specialists had already under the SR duma found themselves in constant conflict with the workers, and thus their appearance on the job would only have been a distraction from work. It has to be noted that not only the workers but our responsible officials had an "antispecialist" attitude. We knew that many of "Rudnev's specialists" had earlier fought with the [opposition] White Guards against us.

After the strike committee, gutted by desertions, sued for peace in late February 1918, the strike collapsed of its own weight. The SRD "decided to take on a very small number of the most valuable former employees," forming by the beginning of March "a small but well chosen cadre of officials."[39]

The Moscow Soviet appropriated this winnowed bureaucracy and the books of the Moscow Duma (in their entirety) at the end of March 1918, although not without disputation. The Soviet of Raion Dumas and its bureau repeatedly expressed dissatisfaction with incursions—by the Mossovet, the house committees, the food committee, and other pretenders—into their area of responsibility. They more or less equated their bailiwick with the sphere of the old duma, whose city hall they worked out of and whose proprietary and policy interests they took to heart. A ringing protest was adopted at the bureau's meeting of January 15, 1918:

> The Bureau of the Soviet of Raion Dumas finds it necessary to inform the Presidium of the Moscow Soviet of Workers' and Soldiers' Deputies that there have been incidents of requisition of municipal buildings by the raion soviets, and even by the [Moscow Soviet's] requisition commission, without any preliminary communication with the organs of local self-government. In addition, these requisitions often take revolting forms and elicit fully justified dissatisfaction on the part of the poorest members of the city population. For example, representatives of the [city] soviet recently showed up at the Morozov shelter and the Presnya almshouse and demanded that they vacate their premises within several days. Besides this, schoolhouses . . . needed by the city are being occupied by the soviet

for its departments . . . to which the city administration [the Bureau of the SRD] could easily transfer private facilities freed up by military convalescent homes and other agencies connected with the war. The tying up of this space is impeding organization of school affairs and forcing excess expenditures upon the city.

The Bureau of the Soviet of Raion Dumas thus asks the Presidium of the [Moscow] Soviet (1) to order its requisition commission not to confiscate a single municipal building without prior approval by the Bureau of the Soviet of Raion Dumas, and (2) to take decisive measures so that the raion soviets not carry out requisitions without the permission of the [city] requisition commission.[40]

The Achilles' heel of the SRD was the ill-defined role of the raion dumas at its base, which duplicated the raion soviets. They were also hard to control, Bolshevik forces being spread wafer-thin between them and other tasks. The Mossovet dispersed the duma of Alekseyevskii raion, a Kadet redoubt, on January 24, and this prompted a vote January 29, at a joint session of the MK and the Bolshevik fraction in the soviet's executive, to fuse the SRD with the city soviet. On February 21 the Mossovet presidium followed suit. Most of the SRD's leaders, as Vladimirskii said, concurred in "the need . . . to pour our work into the general canal of soviet work and terminate our independent existence."[41]

The Soviet of Raion Dumas resolved March 18 to dissolve itself in favor of yet another council, a Soviet of City Services (Sovet gorodskogo khozyaistva), attached to the Moscow Soviet but with a fair measure of autonomy therefrom. The new municipal body was to be selected by the city soviet but to have its own board and chairman and be responsible for "direction and management" of all civic affairs. On March 29 Vladimirskii presented a tougher motion to an SRD meeting packed with representatives of the raion soviets. His plan, omitting the Soviet of City Services and placing all services unqualifiedly under the Moscow Soviet of Workers' and Soldiers' Deputies, passed by a narrow majority.[42]

There was as much resistance in the Mossovet to diving into municipal waters as there had been in 1917. When its ispolkom took up the issue March 31, Iosif A. Isuv, the head of the Menshevik caucus, piped up that the city and raion soviets could not man a municipal structure: "There are not enough people in the soviets, and there are even fewer specialists. To concentrate the work of city self-government in the soviets would only ruin the municipal activity of the city." The Bolshevik Romanov allowed that "many years of practice" would be needed before any realignment. Konstantin G. Maksimov rebutted for the Bolshevik majority. "The soviet must be not an advisory organ but a representative of the proletariat," he said, "and this rules out a separate city government," a recipe for organizational "bacchanalia." He carried the day, and the executive ordered the assimilation of the SRD and the raion dumas into the respective soviets.[43]

Thus was the character of the Mossovet shaped. Added to bureaus for local branches acquired or expanded since October, such as housing and trade, it henceforth had a Department of Soviet Enterprises (soon split into several) to administer customary municipal services and a Raions Department for liaison with the districts. The turnaround was complete by the end of April 1918. The soviet, now heir to the city duma, took on a daunting list of tasks. The meeting and office chambers it tamped into the palace on Tverskaya were, in effect, Red Moscow's city hall—the duma building on Voskresenskaya ploshchad' was signed over to other users—and the soviet's chairman was, in everyday language if not in legal title, the mayor.

SLAVOPHILES' DREAM

Without much forethought, the Soviet leaders early on made a decision about Moscow in the national scheme of things—to reinstate it as capital—which had momentous results for the city. The Provisional Government, citing military reasons but suspected by many of machinating to escape the aroused Petrograd proletariat, was the first to ponder a temporary removal there. In early October 1917 Kerenskii swore in Commissar Kishkin as "commander-in-chief for evacuation" and appointed a backup commission under Mayor Rudnev. A fortnight before being deposed, Kishkin did a numeration of Moscow buildings that might suit as offices and began to empty almshouses, schools, and orphanages.[44]

None of these preparations smoothed the evacuation actually done by the Bolsheviks, who had chided Kerenskii for considering it. Sovnarkom made the decision February 26, 1918, during the German drive on Petrograd aimed at knocking Russia out of the war. After

Figure 11. Rally welcoming Bolshevik government to Moscow, March 1918. (Museum of the History of the City of Moscow.)

toying with relocation to Nizhnii Novgorod, it settled on Moscow. Vladimir D. Bonch-Bruyevich, a guru of the quasi-religious syndicalists among the local Bolsheviks, conducted the operation in the utmost secrecy.[45] Train 4001 steamed into Nikolayevskii Railway Station March 11 with Lenin and a squadron of Latvian machine gunners on board. A workers' demonstration on Karetnyi ryad laid down the welcome mat the next day (Figure 11), and that evening Lenin addressed the Mossovet.

The Fourth All-Russian Congress of Soviets approved the move March 16, strictly as an interim measure. Grigorii Ye. Zinov'ev, the Bolshevik leader of Petrograd, harped on this point: "Bourgeois circles are gleeful about the fact that by a strange twist of fate we are realizing the Slavophiles' timeless dream of returning the capital to Moscow. I remind them on this score that he laughs best who laughs last. We are profoundly convinced that the change of capital will not last long and that the hard conditions dictating its necessity will pass."[46] Zinov'ev was dead wrong. Despite lingering references to "two capitals" and a delay in giving legal sanction, Moscow's position was never reexamined. It would be capital both of the Russian Soviet Federated Socialist Republic (RSFSR), whose constitution was adopted in July 1918, and of the multirepublic Union of Soviet Socialist Republics (USSR), founded in January 1924, of which the RSFSR was the largest integral unit by far.

To David K. Ryazanov, a party theoretician, the transplant purported a craven "capitulation to bourgeois traditions"; it would have been more high-minded to fight the Germans alongside the Petrograd workers, even if it meant going out with a bang like the Paris Commune of 1871. From the opposite perspective, another onlooker, while apologetic about Moscow's backwardness and "Asianness" (aziatchina), intoned that the change would confirm the popular character of the regime and its distance from the unfeeling tsarist bureaucracy. Moreover, swords could now be crossed with the nobles, priests, and capitalists indigenous to this "last sanctuary of the loose, lazy, bourgeois spirit" of Russia's past. If the revolution could tame Moscow, then there was no stopping it. "Raising its flag in Moscow, it graphically manifests the link between Russia's being and the fate of the whole world."[47]

This metaphysics left practicalities untouched. The gestatory problem of physical space metastasized as the government settled in. Many bureaucrats were hired locally, but they also came by the trainload from the old ministries in Petrograd, most of which were incorporated into the Soviet administration. Employment in the central bureaucracy mushroomed to 180,000 by 1920.[48]

Moscow did not contain the larger quarter for edifices of state of the typical European capital. Three sites were suggested for Sovnarkom headquarters: the eighteenth-century Foundling Home on the Moskva River, a shelter for patrician women near the Red Gates, and, naturally, the Kremlin. Although many Bolsheviks were reluctant to be identified with the acropolis of the tsars, the same security fixation that drove them to Moscow led them to favor the walled Kremlin.

Lenin, after a week in the Natsional' Hotel, picked out a small Kremlin apartment and office in the chambers of the crown procurator, on the third story of the Senate building. Yakov M. Sverdlov, the chairman of the quasi parliament (VTsIK, the All-Russian Central Executive Committee) and the main organizer of the party, moved in one floor down, and government agencies and guard units followed. Within days, the Bolshevik commandant, Pavel D. Mal'kov, barred the gates to civilian visitors and threw out all court servants and retainers and the cowled monks and nuns of the two abbeys, whom he charged with entertaining "dubious visitors" and selling Kremlin passes on the black market. The leaders and their families camped out in shared apartments—the Rykovs, Osinskiis, and Sverdlovs, for example, on the ground floor of the former Cavalry Guards Barracks. Even with this space and the making over of the Manezh, the show-horse stable, into Sovnarkom's parking garage, the Kremlin was sorely overtaxed.[49]

The Moscow Soviet responded to the space crisis March 7 by expropriating three hotels for government use. On March 11 it ordered all students, ex-soldiers, refugees, "parasites," and persons "without defined occupations" to leave town in three weeks, as of when they would be denied ration cards. Lenin's government formed its own "extraordinary evacuation commission" and proscribed agencies from snagging buildings, but it dissolved the commission April 3 and tossed the chestnut back in the city's lap. It unveiled a prolix new procedure for arbitrating conflicts in June and elaborations of it well into the autumn.[50]

As the scramble proceeded, makeshift offices and waiting rooms spilled higgledy-piggledy out of the Kremlin, into Kitaigorod, and on into abutting blocks. The Red Army grabbed the Middle Trading Rows on Red Square, pieces of Kitaigorod, and the Aleksandrovskoye Military School. The government-backed trade unions set up offices in the Foundling Home and meeting and reception rooms in the former Nobles' Club (now the House of Unions) on Bol'shaya Dmitrovka ulitsa. Some departments sardined staff into hotels: the People's Commissariat of Foreign Affairs in the Metropol', the NKVD in the Lyuks (which it shared from 1919 with the Comintern, the Communist International of revolutionaries), the party Central Committee in the down-at-the-heels Dresden. Others made do with gentry and merchant villas, graded according to "artistic value" by an expert committee.[51] When these could not be had, apartment houses, warehouses, and schools could.

The Cheka laid title to the Yakor' Insurance Company and Lloyd's Russian branch at 11 Bol'shaya Lubyanka, moving to the former Rossiya firm at 2 Bol'shaya Lubyanka in December 1920. The shorthand "Lubyanka" for the eight-story, mustard-yellow building has made Russians' flesh creep ever since. The Moscow Cheka got house 14 on the same street, the residence of Governor-General Rostopchin during the 1812 fire and later another insurance office. Asphalt-lined execution chambers, with faucets and gutters to cleanse the gore, were put beneath these buildings and a gentry villa on Varsonof'evskii pereulok.[52]

Subdivision of agencies was common. The VSNKh (Supreme Economic Council), which managed Soviet state industry, was said to be parceled out among 80 sites in August 1920, the People's Commissariat of Transport among 16, the military staff among 20, and the NKVD among 10. An article in January 1921 placed the first two agencies at 200 and 130 addresses, respectively.[53]

Pleas for nurseries, clubs, dispensaries, and storage followed requests for offices. If not satisfied at the Mossovet, officials carried their cases to Lenin and Sovnarkom. They displayed bucaneerish ingenuity in outwitting other claimants. The People's Commissariat of Posts and Telegraphs, for one, would sign over a building on Bol'shaya Dmitrovka to the MK in 1919 only if the party committee depopulated an apartment house for its use. To add insult to injury, MK staff found their new chambers shorn of office and kitchen gear, furniture, and light bulbs and the internal telephone cable ripped out of the walls.[54]

Muscovites remonstrated that national agencies "have occupied the best houses and villas and are now after new space." Some advised quarantining offices within the Bul'varnoye kol'tso or in Kitaigorod, others recommended "one place outside the city." Commentary echoed as late as 1920 on the "spontaneous seizure of mansions and apartment houses without any plan," and the departments' wont of "looking on Moscow as a kind of sponge" for soaking up endless demands.[55]

A pun of the day played on the nouns *glava* (a church cupola) and *glavk* (a chief directorate within a Soviet commissariat): Moscow's signature was now its "forty times forty" bureaucratic dens, not its fabled churches, most of whose bells had been stilled. Sixty percent of the city's home and institutional chapels, scores of its free-standing parish churches, and the majority of its abbeys were shut down and bound over to secular users by 1921. Many would never hold services again. Clerics stayed on at the monasteries and nunneries on suffrance of the government. At Novodevichii Convent, where the mother superior and about forty nuns and lay sisters still occupied the building formerly for the lay sisters only, the rest was taken up by workers' hostels and the dormitory of the Commissariat of Education. A nun interviewed by a foreign correspondent was "utterly uncomprehending of the great movement that had swept away her world."[56]

FACTIONAL REGIONALISM

A controversy in 1918 over regional governance embroidered resentment of central encroachment onto intraparty politics. The area in question was not Moscow guberniya, whose workers' soviet by the end of January 1918 annulled both the peasants' council and the gentry-led zemstvo, but an autonomous superregion.

The Moscow Oblast Bureau of the party, which originated in 1905 as a transmitter between the exiled leadership and Bolsheviks in central Russia, provoked the issue. The bureau's leftism on programmatic issues set it at odds with Lenin and central agencies. Selected at periodic conferences as of April 1917 and thus no longer a tailpiece of the Central Committee, it still affirmed a right to direct the party's work in Moscow (denied by the MK) and in the fourteen surrounding guberniyas.

Within the pyramid of soviets, something called a Moscow Oblast Bureau of Soviets, led by Mensheviks and SRs, existed from late March to early December of 1917. It professed writ over all soviets in thirteen guberniyas but had no way to back this up other than to convoke two "oblast congresses of soviets." The Bolsheviks summoned another congress December 10–16, 1917, and two weeks later its delegates and Moscow representatives decided to sire a convening board with the otiose title of Presidium of the Soviets of the City of Moscow and Moscow Oblast. The presidium, ten of its officers from the Mossovet and only five from the gigantic oblast, did little beyond rattle off a declaration or two, and the only member publicly active was Nogin, its commissar of labor.[57]

The party leaders of the city, guberniya, and oblast agreed in late January 1918 to a new governing body, this time to bear the nameplate of Lenin's cabinet: a "council of people's commissars," or sovnarkom. They resolved the next month that an oblast congress of soviets would be the right body to invest the Moscow Oblast Sovnarkom, and that the congress would supervise the sovnarkom through two additional entities—an oblast soviet, which would meet infrequently, and an oblast executive committee. The oblast congress duly sat March 10–11, 1918, and on March 19 a snap meeting of the oblast soviet elected the officers of the sovnarkom.

The Moscow Oblast Sovnarkom, once impanelled by this serpentine route, claimed the full plenitude of power over an area identified variously as thirteen, fourteen, or seventeen guberniyas. Its "people's commissars" (government ministers) spewed decrees for every function from city streetcars to family law and even foreign affairs. It intimated that it would recognize central authority only in the form of a voluntary federation—and not just of Russia with ethnically non-Russian areas, as many Bolsheviks wanted, but of aggregates within the Russian lands.

Pokrovskii gave up headship of the Mossovet to chair the sovnarkom. Aside from a few moderates like Maksimov (assistant chairman), Nogin (labor commissar), and Rykov (food commissar), its members were a "Who's Who" of the radicals from the oblast party bureau—Yakovleva (vice-chairman), Vladimir N. Maksimovskii (police and security chief), Arkadii P. Rozengol'ts (chancery head), Leonid P. Serebryakov (deputy and successor to Rozengol'ts), Smirnov (finances director), and Lomov (manager of economic matters). For most of them, the oblast was attractive "not for organizational or economic motives but for motives of a general political character."[58]

The oblast sovnarkom drew the wrath of central officials, most caustically Stalin, the commissar of nationalities in Sovnarkom and the party's authority on federalism. To them, Moscow oblast lacked economic and cultural unity and was ineligible for either self-government or partnership in a federal union. They threw cold water on Pokrovskii's attempt to find a precedent in the oblast bureau of the party, an optical illusion that had developed by "pure chance."[59]

The Moscow Soviet, which started out in favor, gave up on the oblast once it got a taste of having to please two feuding masters. It had to share local turf to boot, as the oblast sovnarkom paid no regard to its promise to clear with it all oblast decisions bearing on Moscow. Viktor A. Tikhomirnov of the city ispolkom described the snarl:

> Due to the parallel commissariats, people and [local] offices do not know where to turn and have to do business with the two levels simultaneously. They often get completely different answers to one and the same question. This occurs partly because the commissariats themselves are often not organized on the same principles . . . Things are still worse with the sorting out of conflicts. The two sides regularly appeal to both oblast and central commissariats, accepting as legal whichever decision is more beneficial. Thus the conflict spreads and, instead of a petty local spat, we have a standoff between commissariats. There have been cases where both center and oblast have sent people out to take care of some kind of local problem. Being in the dark about one another's work, these commissars usually do nothing but make a big mess out of local affairs.[60]

Lenin, who had chuckled with aides about the "Moscow tsardom," appointed a commission of himself, Sverdlov, and Stalin to investigate a mess that had become too big to overlook. The problem was forwarded to a second commission in May, by which time sentiment against the oblast was building. On June 9, 1918, a government rescript abolished the sovnarkom, to "economize on forces," and gave its assets to central and Moscow agencies.[61]

Much weaker multiprovince decision bodies survived for some months more. An oblast congress of soviets in late June 1918 appointed an oblast executive committee, containing such alumni of the oblast sovnarkom as Maksimovskii, Smirnov, and Serebryakov. But it was a lost cause from the start, and in December, at its only known meeting, it signed its own death warrant and passed its files and personnel to the NKVD.[62]

As for the oblast bureau of the party, the Central Committee decided in September 1918 to scrap it as well. Maksimovskii, Yakovleva's successor as secretary, tried the ploy of renaming it an oblast committee, but had to concede, as a final conference resolved in December, that the bureau was "an artificial amalgamation" and should be terminated. It was, in January 1919.[63] Laid to rest at the same time was still another regional agency, the Moscow Oblast

Economic Council (Sovnarkhoz), established in June 1918, which sought to govern most nationalized industry over fifteen guberniyas. A Moscow City Sovnarkhoz, chaired first by Vladimirskii and then by Likhachev, inherited its Moscow holdings.

The oblast's demise gave the Mossovet a primacy it had not had before. Its leaders were either repatriated to the city soviet (like Serebryakov, named its business manager, or Maksimov, head of the Food Department) or moved into RSFSR administration (like Pokrovskii and Nogin, deputy heads of the commissariats for education and labor, or Rykov, chairman of VSNKh). The withdrawal of the most fiery radicals—Bukharin, the main ideologist of the Left Communists, resigned from the city presidium in May 1918—the choice of a moderate soviet chairman, Petr Smidovich, and the annexation of the Soviet of Raion Dumas appeared to add up to a pragmatic turn in Moscow affairs. Smidovich, unable to keep the peace in the presidium between obstinate personalities (principally Vladimirskii and Yefim Ignatov), was in August 1918 succeeded as chairman by Lev B. Kamenev. Born Lev Rozenfel'd in 1883, Kamenev had been a Bolshevik since 1901 and a comrade of Lenin in the emigration. He was briefly ostracized in 1917 for disputing Lenin's strategy in Petrograd but as a socialist senior statesman had served as editor of *Pravda* (Truth) and as the Soviets' first head of state. Many took his arrival as a sign that Moscow was on the cusp of great things.

Urban Policy under War Communism

Red Moscow's leaders never devised a synoptic strategy for governing it. Least of all did they glance back at their municipal platform of 1917. The whorl of events overtook several of its planks, especially pertaining to soldiers, a militia, municipal autonomy, and shut-down factories. It is perhaps surprising, then, that they took action in eight of the fourteen areas they promised to reform—regarding the suffrage, land ownership, utilities, youth services, housing, health and hygiene, labor, and district administration. Extraneous factors and ineptitude vitiated some initiatives. In other fields—trade and housing stand out—the changes exceeded the most starry-eyed fantasies of 1917.

What unity policy had came from the ultrastatism and iconoclasm that made up the ethos of War Communism. The willingness to go for broke captured in the unofficial label Moskovskaya Kommuna, the Moscow Commune, had intriguing results. It also helped cut Moscow's population in half and degrade its habitat to a preindustrial state.

DEBUT AT SOCIALIST PLANNING

The 1917 municipal program was reticent about purposive town planning. But it is easy to see how vanguard socialists would espouse it once in power. Most on the left in the early twentieth century, Russians and others, considered planning—the exercise of rational foresight by the state—an elixir. In the national economy hitching the nationalized means of production to public goals would exalt the common and long-term good over the selfish and shortsighted. In the local community spatial and social planning would have the same beneficial effects.

In April 1918, the very month that it took over municipal administration from the Soviet of Raion Dumas, the Moscow Soviet established the first locally subordinated city design office in Moscow's history: an Architectural Studio affixed to its Buildings Department. Although the timing of the decision suggested a rush to get on with planning, caution toward its substance was betrayed by the appointment as studio head of Ivan V. Zholtovskii, a fifty-one-year-old member of the Imperial Academy of Arts and an afficionado of the Italian Renaissance and the classical orders. Zholtovskii gladly visited Lenin's office to hear the head of the Soviet government chat over tea about the downtown parks and other comforts he had admired in England and western Europe.[64]

Zholtovskii was swimming against the current in Russian architecture, as the ferment of the early 1900s had been keenly accelerated by World War I and the revolution. Such cultural avatars as the painters Wassily Kandinsky and Kazimir Malevich, the Cubist sculptor Boris Korolev, and the bard Vladimir Mayakovskii expressed the revolutionary trend toward linking the building process with the fine arts. Architectural education, reorganized in 1918, became a zone of combat between traditionalist and radical factions. Students in the First Free State Arts Studio (the former Stroganov College of Industrial Arts) and the Second Studio (the former Moscow College of Painting, Sculpture, and Architecture) rebelled against standpat teachers in 1919. In VKhUTEMAS, the renowned Higher Arts and Technical Studios resulting from their merger in 1920, a progressive curriculum reigned and students elected their professors.[65]

But the artistic and political avant-garde did not reign at the Architectural Studio of the Moscow Soviet's Buildings Department. The Zholtovskii team, which never exceeded ten architects and ten draftsmen, eschewed theory in favor of long-delayed works projects. Its first report to the city executive, in August 1918, recommended the likes of a cleanup of the Bul'varnoye and Sadovoye rings, bridges over the Moskva, a wide avenue to the Sparrow Hills, and public toilets. It stressed the thoroughfares and squares of the city center but did propose removal of smoky factories and preparation of "plans for new parts of the city, including . . . blocks of hygienic, beautiful housing for the needy."[66]

Another arm of the Mossovet, its Improvements Department, took a similar tack, although with more thought to the hardscrabble "workers' outskirts." Here it was possible, the department submitted in September 1918, to contemplate "socialist construction" on the basis of "a completely comprehensive plan of the future city." Beyond reference to sanitation and transport, it revealed little about how the new districts would be socialist.[67]

Zholtovskii in December 1918 presented a thicker planning sketch *(eskiz)* to the new national office for town planning, the City Planning Department of VSNKh's Chief Committee of State Buildings (Komgosoor). We know about it mainly from the comments of Grigorii D. Dubelir and V. A. Rozov, engineering consultants to the department. They paid tribute to Zholtovskii's counsel on traffic flow, overcrowding, and maintenance of the Kremlin but faulted him for a paucity of imagination and a narrow absorption in aesthetics. The City Planning Department's collegium resolved that Moscow's rewon capital status, chronic problems, and potential as exemplar of "a new socioeconomic way of living" elevated its development to "state and not only local significance." Moscow should have a subway, electrified suburban railways, a cincture of protected woodlands, and rows of snug one- and two-story workers' houses, kitchen gardens attached, out to the circuit railroad. This outcome would be feasible only if a "special organ" for planning carefully studied the area's economic, demographic, and other signs over a period of years.[68]

The city was so impatient to have a plan that it simply rerouted the Zholtovskii sketch (modified to mention a subway and a dusting of other ideas) to the City Planning Department's bureaucratic superior, Komgosoor, which mainly considered government construction projects. Komgosoor took it upon itself to consider the plan along with Moscow's 1919 construction estimates and approved it January 23, 1919. On February 8 the presidium of the Moscow Soviet proclaimed it to be in force.

Zholtovskii's plan remained a paper construct. The city did not publish the plan or pass zoning or other implementing ordinances; within months it was being treated as a worthy proposal, nothing more. The derangement of central and local government after 1917 helps explain this result. The plan was not fired by any larger vision, a distinct liability in a regime fighting to save its skin. Nor was it underwritten by the in-depth research needed to make it professionally respectable.[69]

Map fragments are all that remain of the plan. The studio, under a politically more astute architect, Aleksei Shchusev, worked on refinements into 1920. It completed drawings of eleven areas, projecting a uniform office and trade district for Kitaigorod, an industrial zone for Simonovka, low-density housing along the city fringe, and a two-kilometer-wide park apron joined to the downtown by shoots of lawn and forest.[70]

MONUMENTAL PROPAGANDA

Sparks of the excitement missing in the Zholtovskii plan flew in other sorts of planning projects. One of these contemplated individual structures that would make "monumental propaganda." The idea came from a Sovnarkom decree of April 12, 1918, "On the Removal of Monuments Raised in Honor of the Tsars and Their Servants and the Working out of Designs for Monuments to the Russian Socialist Revolution." It was evidently inspired by Tomasso Campanella's 1602 utopia, *City of the Sun,* which Maxim Gorky had brought to Lenin's notice.

In a destructive mode, the Mossovet and Bolshevik factory workers pried royalist regalia off buildings and pulled down old statues, including the figures of Alexander II in the Kremlin, of Alexander III before the Cathedral of Christ the Redeemer, and of Mikhail D.

Skobelev, the hero of the Russo-Turkish War of 1877, opposite the city soviet building. Imperial heraldry was ground off the Romanov memorial in Aleksandrovskii Garden. Lenin and members of his government helped tie ropes around the cross commemorating the assassinated Grand Prince Sergei Aleksandrovich in the Kremlin, crushing it on the pavement.[71]

The constructive side of the edict sought to turn Moscow (and Petrograd) into an outdoor museum and classroom, bedecked in art celebrating the revolution and its antecedents in Russian and world history. On July 30, 1918, the government approved an anthology prepared by a commission under architect Nikolai D. Vinogradov of the more than sixty Russian and European demigods to be honored, from Spartacus to Charles Darwin, Marx, and the Bolsheviks of 1917. Statues, busts, and bas-reliefs were commissioned for placement along holiday procession routes.

The first temporary monuments were unveiled in October 1918; they totaled twenty-five compositions by the time the scheme was dropped in 1922. Spats among the artists, Lenin's antipathy to the Cubo-Futurist designs put forward, and a shortage of materials kept most of them from realization. Some of those built were so unrecognizable that a supplementary written description had to be posted. Lenin helped christen an effigy of Marx and Engels in November 1918; both it and his favorite, a plaster Robespierre in Aleksandrovskii Garden, cracked to smithereens in the Russian frost. A mere half-dozen works have survived to the present day. Easiest to find are Nikolai A. Andreyev's renderings of Aleksandr Herzen and Nikolai Ogarev on the old Moscow University campus and the "Memorial to the Figures of the International Revolution" into which N. A. Vsevolozhskii turned the Romanov plinth. In keeping with the globalism of the moment, only five of the nineteen names engraved above the RSFSR's hammer and sickle were Russians; Marx, Engels, and Campanella led the list of the fourteen foreigners.

The flashiest piece of public art from this time was the Liberty Obelisk (Obelisk svobody), by architect Dmitrii P. Osipov and sculptor Andreyev, which Vinogradov persuaded Lenin to back as a symbol of emancipated Russia (Figure 12). Installed on the first anniversary of the revolution in place of the statue of General Skobelev, it was later embossed with a sculpture of the French revolutionary Goddess

Figure 12. Liberty Obelisk and Moscow Soviet building, c. 1925.
(Museum of the History of the City of Moscow.)

of Liberty and engraved with the text of the 1918 RSFSR constitution. Mayakovskii read his verses from its balcony. The obelisk appeared on Moscow's coat of arms until demolished in April 1941.[72]

There were intimations as well of projects more awesome than mere statuary. The most fetching, the Palace of the People (Dvorets naroda), represented a socialistic version of the pre-1917 "people's houses." The three large auditoriums of the proposed palace, at the former Shchukin estate on Karetnyi ryad, were supposed to expose the urban masses to high culture to a degree that the duma-controlled people's houses, the Bolsheviks said, had never done. At the ground breaking in November 1918, Kamenev enthused that it would be the second largest theater complex in Europe and "a palace not only for the Moscow but for the international proletariat."[73] The Palace of the People remained a gleam in Kamenev's eye—actual construction never began—but it would have many successors.

In a related change, forty or fifty of the capital's primeval street appellations fell victim to revolutionizing and rationalizing fervor. The Bureau of the Soviet of Raion Dumas, in one of its final acts, voted in April 1918 to begin renaming streets and plazas "whose names one way or the other bring up memories of the tsarist regime"; the first change, effective May Day, was of Voskresenskaya ploshchad' (Resurrection Square) into ploshchad' Revolyutsii (Revolution Square). Soon Staraya Basmannaya ulitsa (Old Basmannaya Street) had been made over into ulitsa Karla Marksa (Karl Marx Street), Skobelevskaya ploshchad' (Skobelev Square) across from the Mossovet into Sovetskaya ploshchad' (Soviet Square), and Yekaterinskaya ploshchad' (Catherine Square) into ploshchad' Kommuny (Commune Square). In 1919 came the first dedication to a living Communist leader—Lenin, whose acclaimed humility did not get in the way of the city retitling working-class Simonovka as Leninskaya sloboda (Lenin's Liberty) and putting Leninesque signs on five streets and two squares in Rogozhsko-Simonovskii raion. A Special Commission on Renaming Moscow's Streets appointed in 1920 redid hundreds of names, eliminating duplication but also removing verbal reminders of monarchs, saints, and religious holidays and substituting ideograms of the borning age. The best known to get new names were Vladimirskoye shosse (Vladimir Highway), which became shosse Entuziastov (Enthusiasts' Highway), Bol'shaya Nikitskaya ulitsa (Big Nikita Street), now ulitsa

Gertsena (Herzen Street), and Prechistenka ulitsa (Fresh Spring Street), now ulitsa Kropotkinskaya (Kropotkin Street).[74]

HISTORICAL CONSERVATION

A second type of innovation, pointing in quite a different direction, attempted to protect historical buildings, a goal that many Bolsheviks did not see as inconsistent with social progress. Decay due to neglect and air pollution, remarked on by sentimentalists before 1914, had been speeded by wartime deprivation and revolutionary vandalism. Many of the oldest and best landmarks no longer received care from their traditional keepers after the dissolution of the imperial court ministry (kept on as a Commissariat of Properties of the Republic until late 1918), the flight of the gentry and high bourgeoisie, and the nationalization of church property and of most private art collections.

The main exponent of conservation was Igor E. Grabar'. A painter, the doyen of Russian art critics and historians, and curator of the Tret'yakov Gallery, Grabar' was also head of the Central State Restoration Workshops created by Sovnarkom in 1918. His workshops provided a gathering place for scholars and enthusiasts like Petr D. Baranovskii, an architect and archaeologist from Smolensk guberniya who as a student had roamed the provinces with a camera, snapping pictures of disrepaired churches and manses. Grabar' found allies within the bureaucracy: Lenin's commissar of education, Anatolii Lunacharskii, a Moscow party activist in the early 1900s; the Department for Museum Affairs and Protection of Landmarks of Lunacharskii's commissariat; and the Mossovet's Commission on the Preservation of Landmarks, chaired by the same Nikolai Vinogradov who had shepherded the monumental propaganda program and organized eight "proletarian museums" to show expropriated private art to the Moscow masses. Lenin himself displayed a personal interest, ordering repairs to St. Basil's, several Kremlin structures, and the Sheremetev Hospital.

Grabar' was unfazed by the Civil War. His technicians and the mavens in the Old Moscow Society enumerated hundreds of buildings, publicized their treasures, and filled in shell holes. They commenced what loving therapeutic work they could find the materials for on the Kremlin, where the Spasskaya Tower chimes were working again by September 1918—pealing out the "Internationale," the

Marxist revolutionary hymn (and the Soviet national anthem until 1944). Novodevichii Convent, Simonov Monastery, the Sukharev Tower, and the Kitaigorod Wall also received care. One of the Old Moscow Society's more melancholy projects was a tabulation of frame buildings outside the Sadovoye about to be sacrificed for fuel; a photographic exhibit installed by the association in 1921 received the billing "Disappearing Wood Moscow."[75]

The conservationists recognized official ambivalence toward their work, a portent of far worse to come. The rectory of the Cathedral of Christ the Redeemer, converted into "a center of spiritual opposition" to Bolshevism after the first Russian Orthodox patriarch in two centuries was elected there in November 1917, was closed by the presidium of the Moscow Soviet in early 1918. Only an outcry by Patriarch Tikhon, collection efforts by the parish council, and letters by Lunacharskii to Lenin kept enough firewood in its boilers the next two winters to prevent its piping from freezing and splitting the delicate murals.[76]

Grabar', Roman Klein, and other arts figures proposed several times that the Kremlin be converted into a national museum and cultural center and that the Tret'yakov Gallery and Rumyantsev Museum be put into palaces vacated by the royal household. Lenin was not unreceptive, and there was discussion into 1919 of reopening the Kremlin, evacuating the barracks and apartments that infested it, and relocating museums. But all these plans were "deflected by VTsIK and the Kremlin Commandant's Office," a subunit of the Cheka. "The various offices and organizations servicing VTsIK and Sovnarkom swiftly, like a giant octopus, occupied and 'adapted' every vacant building in the Kremlin, distorting their interiors and external appearance."[77] In 1919 the government managed to pack an academy for Red Army officer cadets, the First Moscow Revolutionary Machine Gunners School, into the Kremlin.

GARDEN CITIES

The sweep of newborn ideas, if not achievements, was greatest in a third realm: planning for suburban and regional development. The most feverish activity occurred in 1918, and a central theme was Ebenezer Howard's garden city, which had been introduced in Russia before the war.

In August 1918 Mark T. Yelizarov, a Muscovite revolutionary and the government commissar in charge of fire protection (and coincidentally Lenin's brother-in-law), proposed the massive clearance of substandard housing in central Moscow, making way for offices for thousands of bureaucrats, combined with construction of a sash of garden cities "where the population that has to be resettled from Moscow can be placed." A subway would service the suburban communities and "moving sidewalks" the city core. Yelizarov was upbeat about cost: "A government made by the workers themselves cannot help but find the necessary resources."[78]

Yelizarov commissioned a plan for a model suburb, Privol'e (Free Place), to be built for 100,000 people on the Moskva River near Rublevo, west of Moscow. Drafted expeditiously by V. V. Voyeikov and V. D. Dubovskii, the plan made fine-drawn provision for utilities, municipal stores, a hospital, a crematorium, a communal refrigerator, a subway line to whisk residents to Moscow in fifteen minutes, and an "arts palace" to "stimulate, develop, and direct . . . spiritual interests." Residents would choose between blocks of sunlight-dappled apartments and family cottages set in cooperative truck gardens. With no allowance for industry or other urban employment in Privol'e, it resembled a sylvan dormitory town more than Howard's self-contained community.[79]

The final planning project came from a brilliant free spirit, Boris V. Sakulin. In his late thirties and certified as both an architect and a land surveyor, Sakulin was a professor at the Moscow Surveying Institute and a member of the collegium of the City Planning Department of Komgosoor. He believed that social and economic problems could be solved through creative application of mathematical methods. In October 1918 he handed Zholtovskii an ornate map he called an *inflyuentogramma* (influence chart) and an essay on a "city of the future" centered on Moscow (Figure 13).

Sakulin had traditional aesthetic concerns for Moscow proper: "artistic unity and integrity, with a perspective of enormous squares, gardens, and monumental buildings." What really enthralled him were the forces of technology and industrial production, which he saw as rupturing normal urban boundaries. Sakulin imagined nothing less than a vast, scientifically planned conurbation, over half the domain of the Moscow Oblast Sovnarkom of 1918.

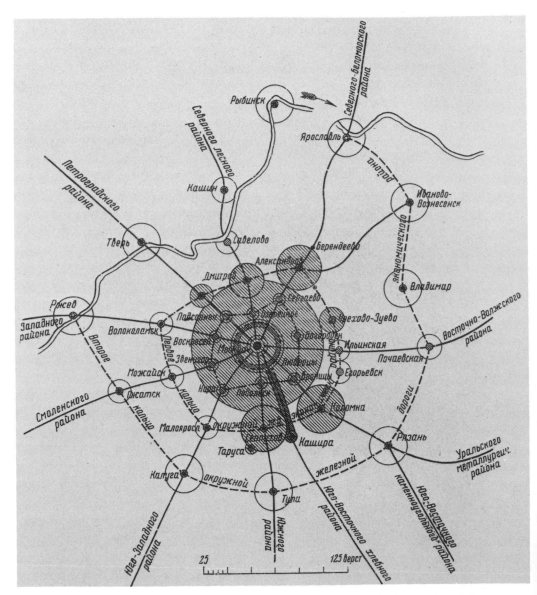

Figure 13. Boris Sakulin's regional plan, 1918. The large shaded circle is Moscow and its green belt. Smaller shaded circles enclose towns already under Moscow's economic influence. They and towns in blank circles were to be developed as satellites of Moscow. (From V. E. Khazanova, *Sovetskaya arkhitektura pervykh let Oktyabrya*, Moscow: Nauka, 1970, p. 79.)

Future growth was to be wheeled away from Sakulin's Moscow. The capital would be encased in a green belt *(zelenyi poyas)* reaching fifty kilometers out from the Kremlin, speckled with virgin and expanded industrial towns. Twenty kilometers out from the green belt, a ring railway would string together a necklace of satellite cities, each with its own economic base and zone of influence but interdependent with Moscow. Fifty to two hundred kilometers beyond that, a second circular railway, its arc closed between Rzhev and Yaroslavl by the Volga River, would link the centers of six adjoining provinces, all of them part of Moscow's "economic region" and wired into it by high-velocity radial railways. Sakulin left open the possibility of more expansion, paced by transportation advances, to "the limit of the natural development of the city."[80]

One beguiling work of fiction in 1920 gave freer rein to the imagination than any official report. Aleksandr V. Chayanov, an agricultural economist, devotee of peasant rights, and member of the Old Moscow Society, published *The Journey of My Brother Aleksei to the Land of the Peasant Utopia* under the pseudonym Ivan Kremnev. Chayanov spirits Aleksei Kremnev to Moscow in (of all years!) 1984. A peasant party has overthrown the Bolsheviks, eradicated big cities, and agrarianized the economy. Engineers—inspired, a guide says enigmatically, by Zholtovskii—have dynamited most landmarks and Soviet-built skyscrapers, leaving patches of Belyi gorod, gussied up like "a Russified Babylon." Down to 100,000 residents, but with hotels for 4 million, Moscow is heavily wooded and mainly a place for games and pageants.[81]

Chayanov intended his opus to amuse and provoke, and perhaps to apostrophize on revolutionary excess. As for the positive schemes of the architects and engineers, their ingenuity was not enough to save them. The Sakulin plan was not endorsed by Zholtovskii's studio, let alone by higher authority. Yelizarov's garden cities did get the avid backing of the city presidium, whose members hoped that the rehousing of workers would begin in the spring of 1919. But the NKVD replied for Sovnarkom that shortages of materials and rations for building crews would put off completion of a garden city (it referred to only one) until sometime between 1933 and 1948. Privol'e alone was kept barely alive for a few months in government committees.

Clearly, big planning initiatives would have to await postrevolutionary recovery.[82]

FROM TRADE TO DISTRIBUTION

If socialist dreams went begging in planning, this was not invariably so in Red Moscow. Radical experimentation effervesced in nearly every field of local policy, especially in trade and housing.

Price controls and rationing were widespread in Russia during the world war, levied on industrial materials, fuel, and many food items by 1916. The Communists of Moscow sharply tightened them, in essence because of their detestation of private property and capitalism. Many viewed the market, as one text put it, as "inconsistent with the communist way of life." And state supremacy in other parts of the economy rendered the trader's position practically untenable. "Private trade could not subsist under the conditions created—without credit, without the right of free circulation of capital, subject to constant requisitioning of goods, and . . . deprived of transport."[83]

The Provisional Government's monopolies on raw materials and fuels were transferred the winter of 1917–1918 to Sovnarkom agencies. Local powers controlled little beyond the provision of fuel to homes and light industry, which was assigned to departments of the city and raion soviets. Trade in consumer goods was different: here the Mossovet in July 1918 deputized a commission under A. I. Grozberg to "municipalize" all operations. This action well predated the decree of November 1918 making extirpation of private trade a national policy. Grozberg conveyed most large warehouses and wholesale facilities to the Russian government and retail outlets to the city. Typically, "a whole series of agencies took part" and "the work was not strictly coordinated."[84]

The picture was complicated by the blossoming of consumer cooperatives, which had been present in Russia since 1898, and by the yen of industrial and office employers for independent distribution outlets. City hall in the spring of 1919 welded all the cooperatives into a Moscow Consumer Association—the Moscow Consumer Commune by 1921—and gave it a monopoly on nonfood trade.

The remarkable commercial elite that had just months before reached into Moscow politics and philanthropy was no more: in the ultimate blow, it was driven out of commerce itself. Most merchants, shopkeepers, and petty traders and jobbers threw in the towel in 1918 or 1919. By 1920 private salesmen could be found in numbers only at the outdoor bazaars. Police intimidation was unremitting, although traders and customers were hard to keep down:

> You could almost always tell when a raid [at Sukharevskii Market] was about to take place. Warned by a mysterious system of wireless telegraphy, sellers and buyers alike began to grow restless, wares were gathered up in bundles, portable stands were dismounted, their owners scuttling down side streets and vanishing into open doorways. Then a panicky movement of the crowd began, the more timid simply taking to their heels and running. Those who were unlucky enough not to make a quick getaway soon found all exits blocked by militiamen, who examined all documents and looked into all packages. Those who were caught with illegal merchandise or who were unprovided with proper documents were herded en masse, surrounded by a cordon of militiamen, and marched off to the Cheka; the others were let out one by one. When everything was over, sellers and buyers began to reassemble, cautiously at first, then more boldly, and in half an hour everything was in full swing again.[85]

The Cheka shut down the butchers' market on Okhotnyi ryad in March 1920 and took the booths away; it closed Sukharevskii, the city's biggest and briskest market, in December 1920. The lower classes had a mixed reaction. "The workers are outraged at the Sukharevka," one orator told the MK plenum of July 1919; "nonetheless, they often demand [the return of] private trade and conveyance." The workers' backwardness was written off to "agitation" by profiteers.[86]

The abridgment of free exchange had as wrenching an effect on urban-rural relations. In Moscow guberniya, as across Russia, the peasants achieved spontaneous land reform in 1917–1918, taking over gentry fields and torching manor houses. They were suspicious of a new-fledged government whose policies on taxation, conscription, and culture seemed if anything less amicable to them than the old. When food deliveries shrank in the first half of 1918, Moscow led in the formation of "food detachments" *(prodotryady)*, armed posses that took at gunpoint whatever produce they could not buy. Moscow and the guberniya towns accounted for one-half of all Soviet detachments in 1918 and one-third in 1919 and 1920, even as Moscow's population dwindled.

In the city municipalization, inflation, and shortages caused an atrocious contraction of trade. Of over 20,000 stores, the soviet closed and sealed in wax the doors of all but 1,181 by February 1919 and 540 by June 1920. The number of shoe stores fell from 689 to 11 in 1920, millineries from 489 to 1, stationers from 429 to 9, jewelers from 900 to 1; there was not a single place to buy toys or furniture legally, and rarely an open food shop. Residents had to show certificates or coupons for almost every item, and most lined up for their main meal in a makeshift cafeteria *(stolovaya)*.

Empty stomachs and shortages chased many right out of Moscow; the remainder could not do without the black market. There were 1.1 million illegal ration cards in circulation in mid-1918 and 82,000 two years later. Street trade, it was admitted in 1920, had "only been converted to the illegal form," not stopped. "Things are being sold from baskets and bare hands rather than stalls and counters." Peasants and illicit "bagmen" bartered with contraband grain, "has-beens" *(byvshiye lyudi)* from the formerly privileged classes (and their footmen and butlers) with family heirlooms, and others with any knicknack or object they had. Trade flourished in passports, travel permits, ration cards, and foreign currency. "Other people, fantastic as it may seem, bought and sold real estate, on paper, of course, for future delivery when the right of private property would be re-established."[87]

Employers provided a crucial refuge. Many nationalized firms and state offices, their conscience and self-interest pricked, furnished their workers with nonmonetary wages through "closed distributors" *(zakrytyye raspredeliteli)* that they stocked and operated. City hall, its own larder empty, applauded them. In March 1919 Moscow had almost as many closed grocery stores (355) as publicly accessible ones (406). By March 1920 cafeterias had become the main providers of food; 196 were fastened to offices and 187 to factories, but only 125 municipal and 14 cooperative cafeterias existed. The closed canteens, while smaller, dished out 59 percent of the meals.[88]

Politicians of national rank knew about closed distribution firsthand. Many of them—including Lenin, Kamenev, and Bonch-Bruyevich—belonged in 1919 to a secret food cooperative, Kommunist. Fifteen hundred of its 9,000 members resided in the Kremlin. It had 1,000 employees: stock clerks, refrigeration specialists, agents who procured produce as far afield as Ukraine. Word leaked out, and Kommunist was liquidated when the MK received complaints that it was "grossly tactless" to operate such a thing during tough times. Not long thereafter, the Central Committee set up a dining hall and dispensary, colloquially the Kremlin Cafeteria, in the former mess of the Kremlin's guard regiment. It served 1,100 hot meals a day by the end of 1920 while distributing packaged foods to Kremlin dwellers and others on its list.[89]

After food and drink, heat was the most precious commodity in Moscow, and here a similar pattern appeared. Warfare isolated the city for months on end from the coal and petroleum of the Donets basin and Baku. Outhustling local agencies and the RSFSR's fuel regulator, Glavtop, industrial and administrative organizations availed themselves of coal and heating oil stocks and detailed thousands of workers to scavenge for brushwood and peat on the outskirts of Moscow. Fuel found its way into the home stoves of employees of the most rapacious procurers, mostly the central commissariats. The populace had recourse to only small municipal stores and the black market.[90]

THE HOUSING REPARTITION

Previously far-fetched solutions characterized housing policy, too. The Mossovet extended the 1917 municipalization of big apartment houses to all homes in August 1918. But the tenant-elected house committees were slow to pass on rent and often influenced by middle-class residents antipathetic to the regime. Accordingly, the city executive in July 1919 imposed much larger "block households" *(kvartal'nyye khozyaistva)* directly under its Housing Department, which previously had consisted of only a few dozen inspectors. By late 1920 about 450 block households embraced 90 percent of the population. Lesser house committees remained, reduced to distribution points for ration books.[91]

The real firecracker of a housing conflict concerned social justice and ideology, not administrative structure. The party spoke with some reason of a "housing repartition" *(zhilishchnyi peredel)* akin to the reallocation of land in the villages. This reallocation slashed previous disparities. In 1912 Muscovites in the most opulent quarters (with ten or more bedrooms) had, on average, 3.1 times the dwelling space of those in single rooms. By the end of the Civil War, that ratio was down to 1.6:1; between three and nine rooms, the range in which 80 percent lived, there were no gaps to speak of.[92]

The most brutal repartition was the coercive resettlement *(pereseleniye)* of workers and other have-nots into the homes of the nobility and bourgeoisie. The first intrusion, of more than 20,000 workers and family members into neighborhoods inside the Sadovoye, occurred in the final two months of 1917. There were fresh spasms in the spring and early autumn of 1918, then more gradual movement in 1919–1920, mostly in the summer months. One hundred thousand Muscovites relocated into higher-grade accommodation between October 1917 and the end of 1920.[93]

Of the several waves of resettlement, the most bellicose—pursued under the bloodcurdling slogan "Knock the Bourgeoisie Out of Their Nests!"—took place during the Red Terror after the assassination attempt on Lenin in 1918. A graphic description comes to us in the memoir of Yakov I. Bazanov, the secretary of the Basmannyi raikom (raion Communist Party committee) and chairman of the raion's "special housing commission." Basmannyi, near the Yauza, was where the Communists took resettlement the farthest:

> The moment we got word of the wounding of Comrade Lenin by the Whites [August 30, 1918], the commission declared Red Terror against the bourgeoisie and set about evicting them. We took over the big houses on Novaya and Staraya Basmannaya (formerly Nemetskaya) streets, ulitsa Bakunina (formerly Pokrovskaya), and others. We posted Red Guard sentries, some with machine guns, and gave the denizens three days to clear out. They were allowed to take with them necessary furniture, the rest remaining in the houses. We were successful in the eviction and freed several buildings in the designated period. Workers at first moved into the large homes slowly because of the fuel shortage. After our commission sent a detachment of Communists into 31 Bol'shaya Basmannaya, several thousand workers came over and occupied all the houses. The number of houses taken over by the workers reached 100. This is how we resolved the housing question.[94]

In 1917 official organizations had done little more than ratify reflexive workers' invasions; this time they led the way. The MK applauded the Basmannyi raikom's aggressive approach and appointed a commission on how to requisition home furnishings on a class basis.[95]

The expropriators were cheered on by leftist intellectuals and party members who wanted Moscow's best housing, denuded of its former owners and their worldly possessions, to become "workers' communes" *(rabochiye kommuny)*, foreposts of the solidary society they were all for forging. Nikolai Bukharin, the darling of the radicals, waxed lyrical on "the socialization of the household" in Moscow's "proletarian fortresses." Two thousand Muscovites, equally divided between blue- and white-collar households, banded into the first recognized commune in January 1919, in the big apartment house at 12 Tverskaya ulitsa, built in 1901–1902 as an investment property by the Bakhrushins. The commune had individual and family bedrooms but a common kitchen, dining hall, crèche, and laundry. In March 1919 the Eighth Congress of the Communist Party linked residential communes to the liberation of women, proposing transition from "the obsolete domestic economy" of feudalism and capitalism to "the house-commune, socialized eating facilities, centralized laundries, kindergartens, etc."[96]

A backlash against freewheeling transfers and collectivization was evident by late 1918. Proponents discovered that the bureaucracy, even the Cheka, contained "precious people . . . [who] are good at whining and weeping" about class enemies and squeamish about dumping them onto the street. Kamenev, the chairman of the Mossovet, countered by deploring "excesses," which had "sown panic among the bourgeoisie and among our local officials"and done "enormous harm" to the intended beneficiaries.[97]

The Communist MK, hoping to appease factory workers striking over bread lines, affirmed evictions of the bourgeoisie in July 1919 but solely on the basis of a close inquiry into residency patterns. In October the city soviet declared outright resettlement a proper remedy only for workers in "absolutely unsuitable quarters" and with the assent of a space commission, which began to think up and apply per capita norms. The preferred remedy, housing "compression" *(uplotneniye)*, divided rooms in large homes and allotted kitchen rights and a boudoir to the old inhabitants rather than shutting them out.[98]

Official zeal for eviction dampened over time as the original social target dispersed. Most of those displaced for communes in 1920 and 1921 were poorly paid clerical and service personnel, not the fat cats singled out in the early months. The distinction between classes was further blurred by the granting of exemptions from reapportionment initially reserved for the families of servicemen at the front to a series of professional groups—scientists, physicians, actors, musicians, painters, and others.

Leaders perceived that many proletarians, too, were balking at flat-out redistribution. "It has to be openly confessed," Ol'ga Stol'bunova, the head of the Housing Department of the Mossovet, wrote in June 1919, "that the mass of workers . . . will not, in spite of the deplorable condition of their own housing, go into bourgeois houses in the center of the city." The city soviet tried to collect rent in the expropriated flats, which it had not yet attempted in most of the outer areas. (Rents were to be abolished under War Communism, but only in its last month, February 1921.) An apartment in Arbat or Myasnitskaya, whatever its joys, dictated lengthy commutes to factories, which became hazardous as transit deteriorated, and placed workers at the mercy of failing central heating systems and utilities. Far better, Stol'bunova said, to put relocation out of mind and make the outskirts more livable.[99]

This was easier said than done. No private firms existed to do the job, and the city itself lacked the resources. The upshot, as with food and fuel, was that many people looked for housing help to a handy benefactor: their *employers*. The trade unions acceded in this development, as did most municipal leaders, Stol'bunova included. Since the Moscow Soviet indirectly influenced most factories through the city sovnarkhoz, jointly accountable to it and VSNKh, the jurisdictional issue did not seem pressing.[100]

The city first announced in March 1919 that, as fuel and transport were otherwise unavailable, all mass resettlements would be organized by enterprises. They would take rents and maintain the premises, incident to minimal check by the soviet. Factories were further instructed in July 1920 to rid buildings under their care of all nonemployees and, moreover, to add to their inventories any tenements in which more than half of the residents were their employees.

In 1919–1920 the phrase "house-commune" *(dom-kommuna)* supplanted "workers' commune," but more than the name tag changed. In June 1920 about 46,000 Muscovites, 33,000 of them factory workers and their relatives, lived in 300 house-communes. This population amounted to only about half the total number of persons resettled since October 1917, with fewer than 5,000 commune dwellers inside the Sadovoye. Clearly, most of the collectives produced by the early assaults on the bourgeoisie had come asunder. By April 1921, although resettlements had been rarities in the interval, the house-communes had grown to 471 in number; they slept 99,000, 65,000 of them industrial workers and dependents (constituting about 60 percent of Moscow's working-class population). The houses were standardly described as appurtenances of factories or, in inner Moscow, of offices.[101]

The insinuation of economic management into housing politics produced this result. The houses of interest to the factories were within walking distance and readily serviceable by them—structures outside the Sadovoye and in Zamoskvorech'e, not in the central area into which workers streamed before. Buildings came under factory tutelage in various ways: some were settled anew by workers of the enterprise; others were occupied for a time on a squatter basis; and still others (at Trekhgornaya, for instance) were nothing other than the barracks owned before nationalization by the private firm. The route mattered less than the destination. By 1921 "communal" living in Moscow almost coincided with existence in factory dormitories.

This random evolution had taken most of those caught up in it miles away from the original ideal of communitarian bliss:

> It might appear that nothing could be better than for people who think and work alike to live in common. The rub is that for the most part our housing collectives suffer from extreme disorganization. People live like Gypsies in them, and not even good furniture and solid buildings help with that. Everything is done in a hurry, any which way. The housing space is conducive to neither leisure nor work. And the main thing is that we have brought our petty bourgeois habits along with us into our communes. Everyone cooks in his own pot, hides in his own room, procures food and utensils for his own family, etc.[102]

The revolution had reconfigured property and power relations but not necessarily ways of living.

BOLSHEVIK GHOST TOWN

Writing from Paris exile toward the end of the Civil War, Rudnev, the last pre-Communist mayor, expressed sorrow but also a sense of exculpation in an essay on the "sick city" and "Bolshevik ghost town" Moscow had become. It survived, he said, like a medieval castle living off the society around it, and it would go on degenerating until the Soviet regime was overthrown.[103] The remarkable thing about Rudnev's article was that he minutely documented it from *Krasnaya Moskva* (Red Moscow), the Mossovet's own history of revolutionary Moscow.

Aside from administration, the only piece of the Moscow economy showing any sign of success was the war industry. In 1918 Nikolai Zhukovskii managed to establish a Central Aeronautics Institute in Moscow as a research center for Russian aviation. From one-half to three-quarters of the Soviet factories producing different kinds of military goods in 1920 were located in the capital. But such successes were few and far between. Overall manufacturing output collapsed by 1921 to one-tenth of the prewar level.

Demographic statistics provide the most unimpugnable chart of crisis. From a crest of 2,044,000 in May 1917, Moscow's population hemorrhaged to 1,716,000 in April 1918, 1,316,000 in September 1919, and 1,027,000 in August 1920—in spite of the continuing arrival of refugees and the expansion of the central bureaucracy. According to *Krasnaya Moskva*, the deurbanization *(dezurbanizatsiya)* of Moscow was "unprecedented in European history," with the exception of contemporary Petrograd's loss of 71 percent.[104]

The dip in birth rates, which made a slight recovery in 1919–1920, was a relatively minor cause of the demographic free-fall. The near-doubling of mortality, to about the level of the 1860s, had a far greater impact. Contagious diseases swept Moscow from the fall of 1918 on, the worst the rolling typhus epidemics that laid 18,000 low by mid-1920. Red Army enlistments also made inroads.[105]

Most dramatic was flight from the city, the cause of about two-thirds of the deurbanization. Many of the old gentry families and of the commercial and professional middle-class residents bailed out of Moscow and, indeed, Russia for good, porting whatever jewelry and valuables they could into diaspora. Tens of thousands of ex-peasants, mostly males, children, and nonworking women, melted into forest and steppe, often to native villages. Their defection cut the number of industrial workers by 50 percent and put "petty bourgeois" persons at many remaining workbenches.[106] The inflow of newcomers and the outflow of long-rooted residents, mostly Russians, affected Moscow's ethnic balance. Russians constituted 84.8 percent of the city's population at its 1920 low, more than 10 points less than their prewar proportion, and Jews, at 2.7 percent, had risen to the second most numerous group.

Hunger pangs prodded the exodus more than anything, although food was not as scarce as in Petrograd and few died of starvation. Fear of disease, of the Cheka, and of class warfare and loss of property also took a toll. The dire shortage of fuel contributed significantly to the chaos. It was mainly their empty coalbins that closed hundreds of factories. Cessation of electric power generation led to recurrent interruption of tram service and to the trams carrying only 8 percent of their 1917 passenger volume in 1920; most by this time hauled freight, trucks and horse carts having been taken off the road by shortages of gasoline and oats.

Some of the worst havoc was wreaked on the housing stock and its support systems. Many residents felt no obligation to do upkeep, uncertain "whether the apartments they occupy will remain theirs for long."[107] Shivering citizens bought Russian tile stoves or made their own, often in miniature versions styled *liliputki,* and fuelled them with sheds, fence pickets, trim, furniture, window jams, stair railings, and doors. Beginning in 1918 (well before the city sanctioned burning in July 1919), they crowbarred apart whole buildings and stuffed the wood into their stoves—twenty-five hundred frame houses and the Church of St. George in Khamovniki in the spree of the 1919–1920 winter alone. The fires were called *burzhuiki,* after *burzhui,* the bourgeoisie, even though they were licking through dwellings that now supposedly belonged to all classes.

Not even this could keep the frost from cleaving water meters and plumbing in the remaining houses that had them. Middle-class denizens, unaccustomed to lugging water and slop pails, felt more deprived than those in the small, unserviced houses away from the center. While the Rublevo filtration station and Mytishchi wells pumped as much water in 1921 as in 1917, much of it was coursing into the ground and one-quarter of the city had insufficient water

Figure 14. May Day subbotnik in Kremlin, 1920. (Museum of the History of the City of Moscow.)

pressure. The flooding, speeded by handmade chimney pipes butted through walls and roofs, brought on deterioration of plaster, floors, foundations, and even street pavement, where workmen had to string razor wire to keep pedestrians out of undermined zones.[108]

The first "Communist *subbotnik*," the Saturday cleanup day semivolunteered by the citizenry for chores such as sweeping sidewalks and courtyards, was held in Moscow on May 10, 1919. Neither subbotniks (see Figure 14) nor the ministrations of block households and the Mossovet could keep more and more of Moscow from becoming unlivable. By mid-1921 only 169,000 of the 231,000 housing units Moscow had in 1918 were still occupied; three-quarters of the rest were destroyed and the remainder uninhabitable.

Some had hoped that the dacha hamlets around Moscow, where the Moscow Uyezd Soviet declared full municipalization in August 1918, would be a refuge. Communist bigwigs helped themselves to the residences abandoned by patrician and mercantile "has-beens." Lenin vacationed at Gorki, the chateau nestled in a three-hundred-year-old copse of lindens on the Pakhra River south of the city and owned from 1909 to 1917 by Moscow's second-to-last city governor, A. A. Reinbot.

The Bolsheviks took special interest in the valley of the Moskva River westward of Moscow. Much of the land as far as Zvenigorod had originally been held by the boyar Golitsyn family; ownership diversified in the nineteenth century, but gentry manors and farms predominated and there was little manufacturing. The clean air, gentle hills, and stands of oak and birch forest had earned the district, with some overstatement, the name "Sub-Moscow Switzerland." In 1919 Joseph Stalin's family received Zubalovo-4, one of the country homes of the Baku petroleum magnate Zubalov, at Usovo. Other rising stars got houses at Zubalovo and nearby Barvikha, where a sawmill owner had planted a large fir forest. Arkhangel'skoye, some eight kilometers north, its country palace built up in neoclassical style by Prince Nikolai Yusupov after 1812, was famous for its drama theater, English garden, greenhouse, and picture and statue gallery. The Soviet government made part of Arkhangel'skoye into a museum but outfitted most of it as a Red Sanatorium, largely for military officers; one of those who summered there was Leon Trotsky, the head of the Red Army.[109]

Kremlin guards maintained these preserves, but for most of the outlying area a bodeful "desuburbanization," so to speak, compounded Moscow's deurbanization. Malakhovka, a dacha hamlet near the Moscow-Kazan railway with about three hundred cottages, two stores, and a summer theater where the great bass Fedor Shalyapin sang before 1914, went through a not untypical torment:

> The first years of the revolution were relatively quiet in Malakhovka, and some [Muscovites] came here to sit out the "Time of Troubles" . . . Then commissars started to frequent Malakhovka and to carry out regular searches and requisitions . . . Everything changed in the well-known way. [A resident who] spent the winter of 1920 in Malakhovka . . . reminisced that "everything was smashed and destroyed" here, "as if a sandstorm had whipped through the dacha settlement." Homeless dogs roved the streets; they were not mongrels but pedigree dogs left behind by the former owners of the dachas. The odd inhabitant hid out in a house. The

summer theater stood silent, boards nailed over its doors and windows. The old-fashioned park was plowed up for vegetable gardens, and students of the State Arts Studios were sent here to collect potatoes. One could not believe that not long ago engaged couples had strolled here and a brass band had played.[110]

All over Moscow uyezd, cabins by the hundred, forsaken even by the central and city agencies to which the uyezd soviet freely donated them after 1918, were given up to arsonists and the forces of nature. Others, broken up by peasant broadaxes, were hauled off in carts and sledges as kindling and clapboard for the villages of the guberniya.

Governing the Garrison

"War Communism"—how neat a hieroglyph of the regime's image of politics as an extension of warfare by other means. "The development of the Soviet state in all its respects," as Yefim Ignatov wrote some years on, "was adapted to the needs of the [civil] war, and there arose along with this an enormous degree of centralization."[111] So it was in Ignatov's city, Moscow: as power surged upward and authority came to be identified with the right to bark orders, ruling the city came to resemble the running of a besieged garrison.

This metaphor did not come true without resistance from middle officers and footsoldiers in the garrison. Nor did it come about under the influence of one acknowledged commander or quartermaster—the "single local center" Vladimirskii had hoped for. Centripetal forces played mainly in the vertical plane: between citizen and state, between local and national government, and from one floor of the local political house to the other. The organs of the Communist Party were still looking for a sure place in the new structure. And, when it came to the subtler kinds of coordination implicit in effecting complex programs of action at a reasonable social price, the metropolis was not better off than the mismanaged Moscow of old.

GOVERNMENT AND MASS

Red Moscow's rulers won acquiescence and active support from target groups and retained them under conditions of material hardship far more rueful than those that toppled the tsar. But this staying power does not obviate their illiberalism. Their bludgeoning of opposition parties and free recourse to police repression bespoke a bending of personal to collective and state needs. Their sundry rationing and identification papers, though sloppily applied, were no different in principle from Peter the Great's internal passports. The mandatory police permits for travel into and out of Moscow, and the fitful attempts to extrude "parasitic" groups from the city, outdid the imperial government in willfulness.[112]

In expressly local policy, the compulsory resettlement of housing best exemplified the new government's approach. The MK had the Cheka roust "bourgeois" tenants from next to its new lodgings on Bol'shaya Dmitrovka in June 1919 for no better reason than it deemed them "unacceptable neighbors" for a Communist Party office. Muscovites ended up regarded as transportable at the drop of a hat: "In the mind of many leaders of our administration, the idea of the ease with which the population can be shunted around has taken such deep root that they interpret any refusal to hand over real estate as a defense of the real or fancied bourgeoisie."[113]

If dissatisfied with an expropriator's or some other functionary's behavior, the average person's best alternative to standing stoically in line to file a complaint was to engage in petty bribery. The hunt for nutrition and safety left neither the time nor the social solidarity for normal political participation in the aggregate. An anarchist from the United States who lived in Moscow in 1920 watched adults and tykes fall from exhaustion without anyone lending a hand: "I spoke to friends about what looked to me like a strange lack of fellow-feeling. They explained it as a result partly of the general distrust and suspicion created by the [Cheka], and partly due to the absorbing task of getting the day's food."[114]

To the extent that Muscovites in the mass did take dissenting action, they did so chiefly at the workplace, and not through municipal avenues or interest groups. Consequently, the leaders' tolerance of strikes and autonomous labor organization was markedly less than their none-too-deep respect for opposition political parties.

The ubiquity of the begetter of "distrust and suspicion," the Cheka, raised questions about whether local civil authority was being trumped. Lev Kamenev, the MK, and the Gorodskoi raikom vocally supported the police reforms of early 1919, which dissolved the violent raion Chekas and removed some functions to courts of law. At an MK plenum that July, Aleksandr F. Myasnikov, the MK's military organizer, taxed the Cheka with "artificially sowing panic" in Moscow by overdrawing popular disaffection and thereby its own indispensability: "The Extraordinary Commission wants to gather all power into its own hands." Secretary Zagorskii accepted the barb, whereas Vasilii M. Mantsev of the Moscow Cheka considered it a "fairy tale" that diverted attention from the "fearful discontent against the Communists," which had to be countered come what may. As a bromide against abuses, Moscow party bodies in 1919–1920 reviewed security, bunkhouse conditions, and political education work at the local concentration camps.[115]

Anxiety about unconstrained police power was outweighed by the willingness to utilize that power to buttress political stability. When the MK the week following Myasnikov's outburst debated work stoppages in Sokol'niki and Lefortovo, the unanimously adopted resolution mandated locking workers inside strike-bound factories and deploying "Red Terror" against "agitators milking the food crisis for counterrevolutionary ends." In June 1920 strikes broke out among Moscow printers; the MK executive commission admonished the Moscow Cheka to make arrests as needed, clearing with it any names not consented to by either the printers' union or the raikoms of the party. To walkouts by tram drivers in August 1920 the commission responded by deputizing teams at every tram park for "filtration" of the workers into three categories; the Cheka was to put the strike organizers behind bars that evening "and, depending on the materials, to set up a trial" right away.[116]

Second only to police coercion as a check on heterodoxy was another sort of control: over the information needed to make independent political judgments. Moscow Communists haggled some over the severity of censorship but never over its necessity or morality. The seeds of what would grow into a boundless cult of secrecy were planted early and watered by the insecurity endemic to a minoritarian dictatorship. The urge to squelch information was greatest when disclosure would have revealed party use of violence, manipulation of other organizations, or intramural divisions.

Thus the press did not cover the exchange at the MK plenum of July 1919 over Cheka ambitions. The archival transcript shows one pro-Cheka secretary, Mgeladze of Gorodskoi raion, who had been rebuked for being loose-lipped about terror, chastising his confreres for "being ashamed of this side of our work." They should shout out the truth, he declared, even "if we have to Cheka-ize *(chekizirovat')* our entire party." Zagorskii went into a rage and moved a motion, passed by the plenum, that forbade local editors to print any story about a party decision on political controls or personnel without prior permission.[117]

THE REASSERTION OF CENTRAL AUTHORITY

War Communism whittled down local institutions in relation to central ones as surely as it reduced the individual before government as a whole. Kamenev traced the trend in a speech in June 1920. The first effect of the revolution, he said, had been to aggrandize Moscow's and all of Russia's local soviets. The soviets "took everything into their own hands, and the center was incapable of leading them, even though matters like military affairs, industry, food, and the railways demanded leadership." In the next phase, the center "began to control the activities of the local soviets." Lately, Kamenev explained, the screw had been tightened. Moscow had lost the right to budget for itself in 1919, its taxing and spending subsumed into the national budget. Ever more particularized conduits now exerted increasing control: "[Individual] central agencies consider that they themselves make decisions and local departments must obey."[118]

Few urban leaders, at least after the demise of the oblast sovnarkom, questioned that they had to comply with a central power that, in theory, spoke for all workers and peasants. Fewer yet caviled at national action in fields such as defense and rail transport. What most troubled them was the profusion of controls that impinged on due local responsibilities and did so in disjunct fashion.

To manage nationalized industry, for example, Moscow had a city economic council (sovnarkhoz); but, Konstantin Maksimov declared in 1919, the central sovnarkhoz, VSNKh, was preempting it: "VSNKh's centralization is producing a purely departmental policy," which was draining the ispolkoms of influence and "negates the main slogan of the October Revolution, 'All Power to the Soviets!'" In an unpublished address in November 1920, Kamenev reported that frictions between Moscow and higher-echelon officials were on the rise and had to be "liquidated once and for all." He mentioned as provocations a circular of the People's Commissariat of Food unfairly rebuking Moscow's rationing office, the demand by the State Publishing House (Gosizdat) that all Moscow books come out through it, and an order by the RSFSR commissar for posts and telegraphs to incarcerate his Moscow counterpart.[119]

Some Muscovites were moved to offer a general critique of over-centralization. At the Eighth Party Congress in 1919, Yefim Ignatov flayed the national commissariats for trying to appoint local adminis-trators, bribe them with subsidies, and hogtie them with regulations. The commissariats were, he said, "cutting the local departments off from the local executive committees and subjugating them." Timofei V. Sapronov, the chairman of the Moscow Guberniya Soviet, told the congress that the bureaucracy had grown "on a columnar principle," integrated from top to bottom but not laterally. National bodies "look at things from their own belfries . . . strive to improve the position of their own departments and to have nothing to do with other depart-ments" or with the localities.[120]

It was not that Moscow lacked assets in dealing with the center. It had prominence, for one thing, as the mastheads of the two pre-eminent newspapers indicated. The Mossovet was made copublisher of *Izvestiya,* the daily gazette of the Soviet government, June 22, 1918 (and remained so until July 1923). The MK was the party Central Committee's partner in *Pravda* starting March 14, 1918 (until Octo-ber 1952). Both papers devoted inordinate column space to Moscow stories.

The Soviet leaders could see Moscow's problems with the naked eye, without ever picking up *Pravda.* Because the Civil War so im-peded communication with the provinces, Moscow received even more attention. In the single month of February 1921, food and fuel shortages in Moscow made the agenda of Sovnarkom, the Politburo (the Communist Party's Political Bureau or inner cabinet), and other executive bodies ten times. Although Lenin said he felt more at ease with St. Petersburg–born officials than with "Moscow tea drinkers" and their "philistine" traditions, his family ties made him highly knowledgeable about the Moscow environment. As a sign of his affection for the Moscow proletariat, he accepted election to the Mossovet by preselected factory collectives. He gave 130 speeches in

Moscow and Podmoskov'e during the war and was photographed pushing a Russian twig broom in the Kremlin at a subbotnik in 1920. Local comrades "turned to him for help in writing, on the telephone, and in person"; he sent them memoranda on matters as petty as individual footwear and clothing needs.[121]

Muscovites enjoyed good representation above. Fifteen of fifty-four members of Sovnarkom to the end of 1922 were veterans of the Moscow organization. They included heavyweights like Rykov, the chairman of VSNKh, and Semashko, the commissar of health. Administrative positions of consequence in VTsIK and other state bodies went to ex-Moscow leaders such as Serebryakov (who while secretary of VTsIK remained on the presidium of the Moscow Soviet until the spring of 1920), Avanesov, and Sapronov. Muscovites' propinquity to central institutions, doubly important under wartime dislocation, factored into many promotions.[122]

In the Communist Party structure, Kamenev was a member of the Politburo from its founding in March 1919, and Bukharin, now the editor of *Pravda,* a candidate member. Serebryakov served as one of five original members of the party Orgburo (Organizational Bureau) in March 1919 and, more impressive, as one of the Central Committee's three secretaries from April 1920 to March 1921. His close Moscow colleagues, Maksimovskii and Nikolai V. Lisitsyn, were appointed successive heads of the party's personnel office (Uchraspred, the Registration and Assignments Department) from its inception in April 1919 to mid-1921.

There is no evidence that Muscovites acted as a disciplined pressure group. Interestingly, Kamenev, a voting member of the Politburo, found the need in commenting on misbehavior by the commissariats to implore the MK "to defend the Moscow ispolkom from such illegalities." Had he and others close to the vertex of power been capably defending local interests, there would have been no reason to invoke low-level protection.[123]

POWER CONCENTRATION

Locally, the soviets most clearly revealed the congealing of political control. As early as December 1918, Il'ya I. Tsivtsivadze told the MK that "fictive organs such as the plenums [of the Mossovet], which carry out no definite work," were becoming a laughingstock in Moscow. The MK returned to the question in November 1920, to hear again of a rubberstamp but now of public indifference to the institution. The plenum of deputies, said Kamenev, "only listens to communiqués and political speeches," resolving nothing on its own. According to one raikom secretary, Yakov V. Dorofeyev, most deputies had lost contact with their electors: "Members of the soviet never report on their work. It is as if the Mossovet did not exist."[124]

The near-disappearance of interparty competition in the soviet helped bring about this somniferous result. Another narcotic was the size of the Moscow Soviet, by 1920 about ten times that of the city duma. "We all know," Kamenev said in a public speech, "that businesslike discussion . . . is impossible at a meeting of 1,500." As Kamenev conceded in censored remarks, the point bore equally on the Communists' own fraction, which had more than 1,300 members after the February 1920 election.[125] Raw numbers and lung power, valuable in the street politics of 1917, disabled the soviet from collectively taking up issues of any intricacy. Its copious commissions were liquidated by early 1918. Seventy percent of the deputies signed into fourteen policy-specific members' sections *(sektsii)* in April 1920, but few attended the sections, which depended heavily on administrators.[126]

The executive committee of the Moscow Soviet, whose fifty or so members sat an average of once a week in 1920, twice as often as the full soviet, exercised somewhat more influence. A city decree of October 4, 1918, declared the ispolkom the "administrative and directive organ" of the Mossovet. All formal dispositions of the soviet and its officers were to be promulgated thereafter in its name, and all city departments were legally departments "of" the ispolkom.

But the ispolkom as such, too big to fit around one meeting table, rarely generated strategy. That task belonged to the more compact presidium of the Moscow Soviet, which met two or three times a week under the chairman of the full soviet. At one time disjunct in membership from the ispolkom, it from mid-1918 contained almost exclusively members of the ispolkom, usually about ten of them, most of whom were salaried municipal employees. The presidium was already said four months after the October coup to "decide every trifle," leaving the ispolkom "almost dead." It "takes care of all of the mundane business of managing the city," went the review in *Krasnaya Moskva*.[127]

Municipal centralization took place on a territorial as well as a legislative-executive plane. The soviets of Moscow's raions, in the thick of things in 1917, lost their footing as governance was bureaucratized.

The Mossovet's abolition of its division for liaison with the twelve raions in October 1918 was an ill omen. But two months later the MK held a torrid discussion about leaning the opposite way. Tsivtsivadze and several other members, citing city hall's isolation from public opinion, suggested that a "plenum of raion ispolkoms" supplant the Mossovet plenum and that future city soviets be assemblies of delegates from the raions. Opposing MK members parried with the point that raion leaders were "every bit as cut off from the masses as central ones," so that federalization would build on a rotten base.[128]

Although the raion soviets (to be practical, their ispolkoms and presidiums) remained vital in Moscow longer than most places, "soon the breadth and sweep of their work . . . was abruptly curtailed. They were reduced to simple executants of the orders of [the city], and then, as this also was shucked, were left with essentially nothing more than checking and observing the functions of other offices located on raion territory."[129] The greater frequency with which non-Communists were elected to the raion soviets, as compared to the Mossovet, caused some friction, but a convention (in effect until 1929) that Communist deputies sat on the soviets at both levels neutralized the tension.

The outbreak, in the spring of 1919, of an imbroglio over the raions' boundaries clearly signaled their slippage. Centralizers wanted fewer raions for economic and political reasons: it would save on money and manpower; raion autonomy was depleting "social discipline" and gumming up urban administration; and raions with too many intellectuals and office workers (Gorodskoi and Khamovnicheskii, mostly) would be more pliable if blended into "healthy proletarian raions."[130] Raion politicians, hardly any of whom concurred, managed to delay amalgamation for a year. In March 1920 the MK finally reduced the twelve raions to seven (see Map 6). The center-city Gorodskoi raion, whose abolition had been most sought on political grounds, postponed dissolution for two more years.[131]

The city radiated its authority into the enclosing province in addition to the districts of Moscow. In 1917–1918, after the obliteration of the antagonistic duma and zemstvo, Moscow city and guberniya had little to do with each other. Their one altercation came over the

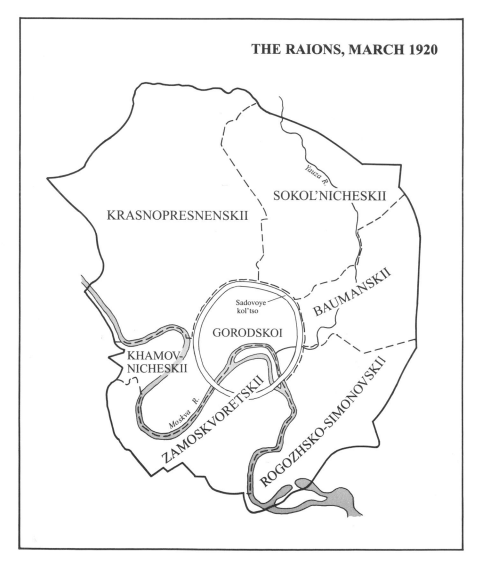

THE RAIONS, MARCH 1920

KRASNOPRESNENSKII

SOKOL'NICHESKII

Yauza R.

BAUMANSKII

Sadovoye kol'tso

GORODSKOI

KHAMOV-NICHESKII

ZAMOSKVORETSKII

Moskva R.

ROGOZHSKO-SIMONOVSKII

MAP 6

direction of nationalized industry, with the guberniya trying unsuccessfully to get its sovnarkhoz accepted in Moscow.

The presidium of the guberniya, the harder-pressed of the two
units, motivated by money problems and an accumulation of policy
irritants, approached the city in August 1919 with a plan for fusion

(sliyaniye) of their local governments. Sapronov predicted "enormous savings" and an end to "contradictory decrees" on issues such as food and fuel supply. City politicians were cool, and Zagorskii noted that Moscow had enough trouble handling its raions. Tsivtsivadze warned that the guberniya itself would suffer, as the city would "eat it up" and treat its citizens "as second-rate."[132]

A union of city and guberniya was forced in June 1920 as part of an RSFSR-wide consolidation of local administration. Its convoluted machinery assured urban supremacy. There was no directly elected provincial soviet, only a twice-yearly "guberniya congress of soviets." Plenums of the Mossovet formalized decisions for the entire region in between congresses, and a common ispolkom and presidium stood over both the Mossovet and the guberniya congress. A guberniya sovnarkhoz looked after local industry in city and guberniya. After a city-guberniya rhubarb refereed by the Central Committee, Moscow was given a lopsided majority of thirty-five of the fifty seats on the guberniya executive committee *(gubispolkom)* and seven of nine on the presidium.

COMPLICATIONS AND MUDDLES

Good as the executive corps of the Mossovet was at displacing back-bench deputies, the raions, the guberniya, and other nodes of local governmental power, it had a less than glowing record in delivering basic communal services. It lacked the ability to coordinate horizontally across policy and departmental lines.

Miscoordination to some extent followed from the segmentation of the central administration. At the Eighth Party Congress in 1919, the Moscow Bolshevik Valeryan Osinskii, now a delegate from the guberniya, made a startling appeal to a casualty of the revolution: the omnicompetent tsarist governorship, abolished in March 1917 and weakly continued in the office of the city commissar until October 1917. The Communists, Osinskii argued, should compel organizational "belfries" to toll in harmony by restoring the viceregal role and assigning it to the leadership of the local soviet: "Just as the old governor, being responsible to the central power, was at the same time boss of his own bureaucrats, so the ispolkom should be boss of all the bureaucrats acting on its territory."[133]

The regime, in no mood to tinker with the vehicle seeing it through a civil war, shunned Osinskii's demand. At the center, the NKVD was heir to many of the pre-1917 MVD's powers and responsible for municipal legislation. It had no interest in pushing for local autonomy or override powers.

The best the local soviets could get was codification of a principle that, strange as it may seem, was hailed as a small victory. Jurists articulated the concept of "dual subordination" *(dvoinoye podchineniye)* as early as 1918. It prescribed that a department of any soviet be doubly accountable to the executive of that soviet and to the analogous administrative division at the next highest plateau. In the Moscow Soviet's statute confirmed in April 1920, "The departments of the Moscow ispolkom are subordinate to it and are obliged to carry out all its orders and instructions, and also the instructions of the corresponding [central] commissariat." Heads of department appointed by the ispolkom could be removed for cause by the relevant commissariat; disputes were referred to the national government.

The bloating of the Mossovet's establishment also militated against effective horizontal coordination. It had 80,000 employees in May 1920, not counting the raion soviets, compared to 40,000 for the city duma in 1917, when the population was about double. The ceaseless reorganizations and hiring campaigns adulterated administrative standards even more woefully than in the central bureaucracy. The Housing and Land Department, for instance, kept "very, very approximate" statistics and slapdash records that often sanctioned dual and triple tenancies in the same building, "which produced disagreements and lawsuits."[134] The heading up of each of the soviet's departments by a collegium, usually of three persons, rather than one responsible officer, bred more confusion.

Equally debilitating was the tension between callow Communists and holdovers from the Moscow Duma. To a man, those at the apex of the municipal structure were tyros in government, thrust forward by their abilities as agitators and purgers. Tsivtsivadze characterized presidium members in 1918 as "good people in general" but "unfit for the work" undertaken. "All know something about everything, but in any given sphere none knows anything."[135]

Although a few of the party members placed at the head of agencies below were technically certified to be there, most were not (see Table C-1 in Appendix C on their backgrounds). Twenty-seven of fifty members of the 1920 gubispolkom had done time in tsarist prisons, seventeen had been in Siberian exile, and seven had lived abroad in political exile.[136] Below them operated both career city officials, usually without prior political involvements, and raw recruits and party loyalists who resented the "specialists" and found them convenient flogging boys.

The sad case of Vladimir V. Ol'denborger, a city duma employee since 1893 and the chief engineer of the waterworks since September 1917, brought the issue to national attention. Despondent over the breakdown of the water system and the vendetta against him led by the works' party secretary, T. I. Sedel'nikov, Ol'denborger counterattacked during the Civil War and committed suicide several months after it. The RSFSR's procurator general, Nikolai V. Krylenko, took charge of the trial of his tormentors; Sedel'nikov was sent to jail and the others repented.[137]

The Moscow Soviet might have risen above such difficulties with compelling leadership, but this it did not have. As noted above, its 1917 kingpins were at loggerheads over revolutionary strategy, and a number departed after October. The army and central civilian agencies claimed many of the soviet's best orators and organizers (see Figure 15). Some died as cannon fodder at the front, others of contagious disease at home. Chairman Kamenev, "surprisingly tactful and soft, even-handed with everyone,"[138] was a pacifier and a vacillator, not a forceful advocate. He abnegated most Moscow decisions to deputies of his like Mikhail I. Rogov and Mikhail S. Boguslavskii.

Disarray among the politicians encouraged municipal agencies to go their own way. "Each department," a member of the ispolkom groaned in 1919, "comes with its own needs to the presidium of the Moscow Soviet and gets some satisfaction, but . . . there is no overall plan." "Misunderstandings, complications, and muddles" beset urban services, from sanitation to kindergartens, with policies "not only not uncoordinated but contradictory."[139]

A PARTY IN QUEST OF A ROLE

If the Mossovet could not systematize local administration, what of the Russian Communist Party? It had 39,500 full and candidate members in Moscow in May 1920, many decision makers among them, and 6,800 in the guberniya. The best of its leaders lived out its

Figure 15. Members of Moscow Soviet leaving for Civil War front, 1919.
(Museum of the History of the City of Moscow.)

credal passions. Zagorskii, the MK secretary killed in 1919, had "ex-uded the healthy optimism" of someone "for whom the revolution sat not only in his head but in his blood"; Fedor A. Artem in 1920 seemed "as if fate had landed him in our century from the epoch of pure communism."[140]

Structurally, the party's foundation rested on its cells in workplaces and the fractions binding together the Communists in representative bodies. From there up, it matched the elected soviets, with committees for Moscow city (the MK or Moscow gorkom), the guberniya (the *gubkom*), and the raions (the raikoms); there were also eleven subraion party committees for parts of raions from 1919 until 1922. After the MK expressed some anxiousness that the very visible party fraction in the city soviet might "devour us all," the territorial organs slowly imposed their mastery. The statute that the Moscow party organization set down in July 1918, and the Eighth Party Congress made general policy in 1919, stipulated that any decision of the MK had to be "unconditionally implemented by all members of the Communist fractions of various establishments."[141]

City and province were stitched together in June 1920 into a city-ruled gubkom (still generally known by the initials MK). An executive commission of five or six persons had begun to make most time-urgent political decisions by one year after the October takeover, although MK plenums remained lively. The commission was restyled the MK bureau in August 1920, the same month that a second executive panel, a "secretariat of the bureau" for purely organizational matters (the secretariat of the MK from June 1922), began to convoke biweekly.[142]

As in the seven decades to come, the fulcrum of the party's power was its right to select elite personnel in the organizations it penetrated. Prime among these was local government. The procedure after October 1917 resembled the staffing of the raion dumas. In the Mossovet the party fraction would come up with names of preferred candidates for vacant posts, convey them to the MK for approval, and then use its voting strength to ram them through the plenum. This procedure covered only seats on the ispolkom and presidium. While the MK did have the final say, it and the Communist delegation in the soviet did bargain.

Accord over appointments disintegrated in 1919. A rumpus broke out in March when the bureau of the party's fraction in the Mossovet, with Ignatov as its spokesman, thwarted an MK demand to add two persons to the city presidium. Six weeks of wrangling yielded agreement on election of the ispolkom and presidium from scratch, a compromise that went out the window when the fraction held out for the return of five or six favorites whom Zagorskii and the MK could not abide. Through parliamentary maneuvers, the fraction bearded the MK executive commission, drawing accusations of refractoriness.[143]

The fraction argued that it was the last refuge of democracy in the soviet, what with the Communists' majority, the MK leaders' strutting about like "Soviet generals," and the death of interparty cooperation. They also maintained that the dignity of the city council required deference to the Communists working there. "It is impossible to treat it [the fraction] like some minor cell," Vasilii Likhachev, a former MK secretary and now head of a department of the soviet, lectured the MK in May, or to replace its seasoned nominees with yes-men "who humbly dance to your tune." Partisans of the MK granted the exceptional nature of the soviet, yet presented this as all the more reason for the fraction to knuckle under: "Since they decide matters of import for all Moscow, we may find ourselves answering for their actions. So it is understandable that we put forward our own candidates."[144]

It took a resolution of the party's central leadership in the final week of May 1919 to vindicate the MK, and incompletely at that. Four of the disputed MK nominees for the ispolkom were sustained, as compared to two of the fraction's, and the MK removed several errant members from the bureau of the fraction. Zagorskii gave up on an attempt to have the unsubmissive Ignatov purged from the soviet and sent to work for the Central Committee.

From its beachhead in the Mossovet, party influence over personnel extended outward in several ways. As concerns municipal positions, the roster confirmed by the MK lengthened, the biggest changes being the inclusion of delegates to the guberniya congress of soviets in 1920 and of municipal department heads and collegium members in January 1921.[145] By 1920 territorial party officials were taking the lead to nominate or designate (nametit') candidates up front, not waiting for proposals from the party fraction.

Cadres decisions were not confined to the soviets. Near the end of 1918 the MK and its executive began ruling on placements in law-and-order branches: revolutionary tribunals, the Cheka, and military commissariats (draft boards). In the summer of 1920 party confirmation rights were upheld in the local and regional committees of the state-sponsored trade unions and the Komsomol, the Communist Youth League.[146]

Local party committees engaged in cadres assignment on a wholesale basis as well. The mobilization (mobilizatsiya) of party members was a response to the fearful need for Civil War fighters. In the first resolution of its type, the MK in August 1918 enjoined party committees to provide lists of able-bodied Communists suitable for combat, for passing on to the Red Army. Thousands in the months to come would be conscripted through the lists.[147]

The pattern extended to civil pursuits in 1919, if never in the same quantity. MK directives sent slews of Communists, usually by raion quota, to priority enterprises and "fronts" like the Cheka, food distribution, and the railways. In the mop-up stages of the war one could see Communists being commandeered *(prikomandirovannyi)* as individuals to agencies that had requested party help, though not as yet to specific positions there.

The evidence speaks, therefore, to a decisive Communist Party voice on personnel matters, not least in the soviets. Equally important, however, the local party organs had not yet begun any all-encompassing orchestration. For one thing, even with respect to staffing the local party's prerogatives were not absolute. Documents throughout the Civil War refer to give-and-take negotiations *(peregovory)* over appointments. Ignatov, the thorn in the MK's side, remained on the presidium of the Moscow Soviet until the end of 1920 and even sat on the executive commission of the MK itself for the first half of 1920. Just weeks after the announcement at an MK plenum in November 1920 that the party fraction in the soviet had "ceased to work," it twitched to life. On December 16, 1920, Timofei Sapronov challenged Kamenev, though without success, for chairmanship of the fraction. Unable to come to closure about a recast presidium for the soviet, "on account of disagreements," the MK bureau accepted the whole slate proposed by the fraction; it also gave the soviet seventy-six acceptable candididates from which to pick the fifty-person ispolkom. In January 1921 the MK upheld the fraction when it overturned the MK bureau's nominees for the collegium of the city's schools department.[148]

When one casts about at broader policy, the immaturity of the dictatorship becomes apparent. In theory, Communists in every cell or fraction were obliged to carry out all decisions sent their way by the MK. In practice, when it came to local government, there were few such decisions on issues other than policing, personnel, organization, and plugging the war effort. The executive commission or bureau, it was flatly observed in late 1920, "has not been occupying itself with technical and soviet problems." An official history can claim no better than "unclearly defined relations" between the MK and the Mossovet, and the same would go for relations with almost every other actor of substance.[149]

Of the eventually major role of enforcer of the regime's cultural and intellectual fiat, there is but a murmur at this early point. Individual Communists and, to a point, party cells within host organizations carried out this job. Problems were almost never referred to the areal party committees.[150]

Nor was the party anything like the final arbiter on questions economic and social that it was to become. The MK and its bureau and secretariat seldom treated production and distribution and did not make economic appointments outside the branches of the city soviet. Save for irregular debate of housing resettlement and a plenum in April 1919 on workers' living conditions, the MK did not take up social services and welfare. Kamenev, reacting to complaints about the insolence of the fraction, reminded the MK in November 1920 that Communists in the soviet could always be hauled on the carpet as individuals: "There has been and still is MK control over the soviet in the sense that the MK can at any time summon any head of department and get an accounting from him." But this was in principle. Actual party records show virtually no instances of such a check being incurred for a breach of policy on an item on the municipal agenda.[151]

Why did the party's decision-making role emerge so slowly? Surely its blithe ignorance of territorial governance played a role. For urban management, its leaders had even poorer preparation than those of the local soviets (see Table C-1). Communists with an appetite for local issues gravitated to the soviets, where administrative work was of considerably higher status than in the party apparatus.

The party secretary, like his forebears in the underground, still toiled in the shadows. No fewer than nine MK secretaries served between October 1917 and the spring of 1921. Most were outranked by their municipal counterparts even in party terms. The Seventh Party Congress in March 1918 named Vladimirskii, the head of the Soviet of Raion Dumas, and not the MK secretary, Zemlyachka, to the Central Committee. "Mayor" Kamenev sat on the Politburo, his party counterparts not even making it onto the larger Central Committee.[152]

As happened with the Mossovet, group and individual mobilizations—which the MK often queried—siphoned talented activists off into central organizations. All five of the Moscow party secretaries who were neither assassinated (as happened to Zagorskii) nor demoted for miscues (Likhachev, Pyatnitskii, and Yakovleva, one month after the end of the Civil War) were reassigned to more crucial tasks—three in the army (Zemlyachka, Dominik I. Yefremov on two occasions, and Myasnikov), one in the trade unions (Fedor Artem), and one in the food bureaucracy (Isaak A. Zelenskii, who soon returned).

Beneath the apex, the party's administrative resources could not compare to the municipality's. Three days before the October Revolution, the Moscow Committee established eight small commissions; this embryo of an apparatus had dissipated by January or February of 1918. The MK's cupboard was so bare in March 1919 that its executive commission had to ask the Mossovet presidium for a one-day loan of two dray horses for transport. For most of 1919 Communists quipped that data on personnel and other party business were found "in Comrade Zagorskii's pocket." The first MK department *(otdel)* of salaried officials was created in early 1919, responsible for face-to-face party "agitation." Commissions also began to be re-appointed in 1919, and several of them were reconstituted as departments after Zagorskii's death.[153]

How much remained to be done MK Secretary Myasnikov laid out in *Pravda* in January 1920:

> Look first, if you will, at the [Communist Party] committees [in Moscow]. There is no uniformity in their organization and no system to their work. Not all of the raion committees even have their own executive organs . . . The youth league drags out a miserable existence, and it could be said that it is not really present in Moscow . . . Agitation and propaganda hobble along . . . Our clubs exist on paper only . . . Our party schools are barely alive and do not have stable and capable leaders. There are no party statistics and registration procedures, and neither is there an auditing commission. The Moscow Committee does not have properly functioning departments, which still have to be set up. Our office work is terrible. It would be hard for us to establish how many party members we have, and these forces are distributed unevenly.[154]

Not until July 1920 did the MK approve its first organization table, providing for eight administrative departments and roughly fifty professional staff members. An Organization and Instruction Department dealt with personnel questions and low-level party organization, but about two-thirds of the staff worked on political education and inspiration. The apparatus remained, as Zelenskii wrote, "in essence the party's agitation section" in Moscow. No unit specifically addressed either economic or municipal affairs.[155]

If inexperience and feeble organization characterized Communist Party chapters in most Soviet localities, the capital's had two peculiarities. The first, continuing a Moscow party tradition, was the strength of its districts. Under bylaws adopted in May 1917, the city party conference merely "confirmed" delegates from the raikoms as members of the MK, rather than choosing them directly. In consequence, the MK "did not consider itself . . . in the real sense of the word the leading organ" of the Moscow party.[156] Aleksandr Myasnikov, somewhat of a martinet and the first to oppose the raikoms, was rebuffed in 1920, but his efforts, the general centralizing current, and the decisions to redraw the raions and amalgamate city and guberniya abraded resistance. Only in October 1920 did a Moscow (now guberniya) conference negate the federative principle.

Party unity suffered as badly from a second shortcoming, ideological and personal infighting, as from the raions. Moscow was the first place to feel the sting of the Kremlin's most contentious policies. With its concentrations of students, artists, and trade unionists, it was a ready-made seedbed of nonconformity. The Moscow apparatus held "a special position," Kamenev observed, as "all the shades of party thought, which tend to arise at the center, can appeal to it directly." It had no senior statesman who could mediate among cliques through force of personality. Kamenev, a Moscow native yet poorly tutored in its party affairs, proved unwilling or unable to do so and stayed off the MK bureau until November 1920.[157]

Muscovites, Left Communists from 1918 supplemented by others, were integral to most of the bumptious groupings that protested one aspect or another of party policy until the Tenth Party Congress in March 1921 outlawed organized factions. Sapronov, irate at the bullying of the guberniya soviet, led the Democratic Centralists in their crusade against the dictatorial excesses of War Communism. At his side were Stepan I. Polidorov (Sapronov's successor in the guberniya), Osinskii, Smirnov, R. B. Rafail (the head of the Moscow Department of Public Education), and many activists in Gorodskoi raion. The Workers' Opposition of 1920–1921 had its stronghold in Moscow and in particular in Baumanskii (formerly Basmannyi) raion. Among its converts were Osinskii, Sapronov, Maksimovskii, Boguslavskii, Andrei S. Bubnov (an important economic administrator with a seat on the MK bureau), and Ignatov, who briefly had his own subfaction.

Moscow's main leaders could not stay out of the fray, and the party's central command was not yet able to inflict peace on its terms. Myasnikov, narrowly elected MK secretary in January 1920, was lost to the Polish front in June. When Secretary Pyatnitskii threw in with the Democratic Centralists that October, the Politburo tried to foist Myasnikov on the Moscow organization for a second stint. This attempt misfired, as Pyatnitskii would not resign or offer a list of candidates for MK membership for scrutiny by Central Committee workers "behind the back of the MK," something he said "has not been the practice in the Moscow organization."[158]

The Politburo did indeed recommend a list of MK members to the Moscow party conference in November, but the delegates picked and chose from it. Kamenev asked the new MK on the Politburo's behalf to make Zelenskii secretary. It opted instead for Artem, an outsider supported by some oppositionists. He lasted only five weeks and was replaced by Yakovleva, the former oblast secretary and Left Communist, who wavered on the factional question and then endorsed Trotsky's platform. Kamenev had difficulty without her getting a bare majority for pro-Lenin resolutions at Moscow conferences in early 1921; the MK was elected "as a result of negotiations among groups."[159]

The group free-for-all made party politics in Moscow looser than it was to be for decades, but it scandalized many Communists. It also deflected energy away from local problems. "In the Moscow organization," as Bukharin described it, "businesslike discussion of issues is often replaced by preposterous squawking, the kind of beating around the bush appropriate to market women but not to the proletariat."[160]

EMERGENCY MEASURES

The splintering of local authority led to exceptional means to overcome its particulars. Although the crisis style of decision making was a sorry substitute for institutional means, it did meet some dire needs.

Mobilizations for the front, food detachments, and subbotniks were emergency measures aimed at individuals. On two occasions— September 1919, when White regiments captured Orel and punched toward Moscow from the south, and May 1920, when war broke out with Poland—Moscow was put under martial law and a City Defense Committee, chaired by Kamenev but with party, Cheka, and military representation, was empowered to impose curfew, impress laborers to dig trenches, and the like.

More frequently, organizations and not persons had to be bridled.

The preferred expedient was the special-purpose commission, given a lofty title and the overriding powers thought necessary. Such entities were placed under the Russian government, the Moscow Soviet, or both, depending on the issue. The names fairly screamed urgency: Decongestion Commission, Extraordinary Fuel Troika, Special Collegium for Prisoners of War and Refugees, Special Commission for the Resettlement of Workers, Commission for Supply of the Two Capitals, Commission on Cutting Office Staffs, Extraordinary Commission on Electric Power Supply, Commission for the Improvement of the Workers' Living Conditions, and on and on.

Often one agency succeeded another in a game of revolutionary musical chairs. In October 1918 Sovnarkom appointed an "extraordinary commission" to clear the backlog of freight in Moscow's railyards and gave it "the rights of the Cheka" in doing so. When the commission relieved the congestion, with the help of requisitioned carts and soldiers, it was downgraded to a "collegium," with envoys of the city, railways, and industry. "It turned out," its chairman wrote, "that, without special rights vis-à-vis the agencies . . . involved with shipping, our collegium could not achieve the necessary results." The collegium had to beseech the government to redignify it as Moscow's "Unified Unloading Organ" for it to proceed.[161]

Time and again, special agencies failed to alchemize lavish titles and mandates into success. A case in point was urban construction, something all appreciated to be essential to mass welfare.

The Moscow Soviet's Buildings Department was frustrated by the lack of response to its requests for aid from government suppliers. Its prayers were seemingly answered in June 1919 when Sovnarkom gave it preferred access to construction materials, draft deferments and extra ration coupons for its workers, and the right to approve, through a Special Board on Construction Policy, the projects of all other organizations. In February 1920 an upstart Extraordinary Sanitary Commission invaded the department's terrain; chaired by a Mossovet official, it was entitled to undertake on its own whatever works were needed to improve hygiene. Three months down the road Sovnarkom merged the two bodies into a Special Temporary Construction and Sanitation Committee (Oskom), led by no less than the business manager of Sovnarkom, Bonch-Bruyevich, who briefed Lenin on it every second day.[162]

Oskom, established to do most building in Moscow and to coordinate the rest, declared a need for 110,000 workers. "Regardless . . . of repeated promises" from labor agencies, it acquired uncertain title to only 2,500. When it tried to collect fuel, cement, and timber, other departments "brushed off its demands," refusing even information on their hoards.[163]

In November 1920 Oskom was returned to full local control, renamed the Special Construction Directorate of the Moscow Soviet, and given the powers of a "construction monopoly" in the city and guberniya. January 1921 brought yet another name change, this time to Moskomgosoor, the Moscow Committee of State Buildings. The agency's floridly stated prerogatives never translated into apartments. The soviet instructed its 7,000 workers to concentrate on repair of houses and utilities. Little came of that, either, as the committee received only 3 percent of the supplies it put in for. The city executive, berating Moskomgosoor for having an "enormous bureaucratic apparatus" and no output to show for it, repealed its building monopoly in December 1921 and scuttled it altogether in March 1922.[164]

Taking the trophy for pretentiousness was the Commission for the Improvement of the Workers' Living Conditions, appointed at the tail end of War Communism, in March 1921, on request of the Mossovet. Formally under the soviet's presidium, it had a Sovnarkom charter and Dzerzhinskii, the fearsome head of the Cheka, as its chair. "Iron Feliks" singled out as his enemy those with line responsibilities for housing, food, and social services, relishing how he "did battle with all kinds of bureaucratism and red tape on the part of the organs of the [Moscow] Soviet." With a staff of fewer than twenty but "enormous assistance" from the secret police, the commission claimed in six months to have moved 11,000 workers into house-communes, given Moskomgosoor a mound of building materials, reopened laundries and pharmacies, rewritten the tram schedule, and impounded and redistributed tons of clothing.[165]

Health Commissar Semashko, who had been commissar of the city duma in November 1917 and was still attentive to Moscow politics, wrote tartly in the bureaucrats' defense that it was not their comfort but the development of local institutions that "shock tactics" impeded. Expedients like Dzerzhinskii's commission did not create resources; yanking the available ones around, they "impair and at times stop the work"of the organizations hereunto in place. "The good manager," Semashko counseled, "does not let today's evil blind him to tomorrow's needs."[166]

The "something of our own" that the Communists so dearly wanted to instill in revolutionary Moscow turned out to be shot through with borrowings from—and exaggerations of—the Russian legacy of autocratic administration and nonparticipatory, noncompetitive politics. Their collectivist and utopian ideology, the breaking of the restraints on government action posed by custom and private property, and the climate of violence and militarization all effected greater absolutism, not less. By any measure, the metropolis and its population were more *overcontrolled* than ever, as the Cheka and the presidium of the Moscow Soviet left so much less to chance than the Okhrana and the Moscow Uprava had in their day. The mushy "dictatorship of the sales counter" had been self-limiting and open-ended with respect to the future, acceptant as it was of "the differentiation of government and politics from other spheres of social life," which has been capitalism's gift to democratic development.[167] The flint-hard if untidy dictatorship of the state socialists took as axiomatic a denial of the autonomy or, for some purposes, the very existence of a private realm.

Statism without limit did not imply, however, either governmental efficacy or the successful prosecution of society-transforming experiments. One might say that Red Moscow, overpoliced and traumatized as it was, was a scarcely less *undergoverned* place than Calico Moscow. While the odd scrap of paper might point to a shining future, the bleak reality on the ground for most Muscovites was of dysfunctional bureaucracy, fear, and breakdown of civilized life.

Within the machinery of local governance, the new powers were at a loss to put their finger on Semashko's "good manager," the authoritative institution able to apply resources to Moscow's needs in an orderly and humane way. The quest for such an agent was to proceed long afterward and never really to succeed under Soviet rule. So, too, would the search for a better model of the urban condition in general. The writer Ilya Ehrenburg, wading through the Moscow snowdrifts in the final winter of the Civil War, was not alone in retaining the belief that "a new and extraordinary city would grow up in the place of the crooked little wooden houses familiar to me since childhood." But he was not the only one, either, to have had his faith shaken in the inevitability of the new and extraordinary being good and desirable. "I was often tormented," Ehrenburg reminisced, "by speculations about what the life of man in that city of the future would be like."[168]

3

From Reurbanization
to Hyperurbanization

M OSCOW was racked by the unrest that seized Soviet Russia as
the Civil War tailed off in 1920–1921. Displays of popular rage
exceeded the factional mayhem within the Communist Party. Short
rations sparked strikes at the AMO Auto Works, Kauchuk, and other
factories and rallies on the Kremlin's doorstep, capped by a 10,000-
strong march on February 23, 1921. Local officials were among those
calling for War Communism to be rethought.[1]

Out of this cauldron came the fascinating liberalizing interlude
known as the New Economic Policy (NEP). When promulgated in
March 1921, NEP highlighted freedoms for peasants that would coax
them to feed the towns. From there, it slid into a wider rapprochement
with the market in town and country: it legalized private trade, denationalized some small manufacturing, pared government spending and
subsidies, and solicited foreign investment. Left open to torrid debate
were the duration of the retreat and how to square it with "building
socialism." Every disputant invoked Lenin, who straddled the fence
until his death in 1924. The nay-sayers eventually won out, and NEP
was jettisoned in 1928–1929 for the titanic social engineering project
of the "revolution from above." Historians still argue about whether
this U-turn might have been avoided.[2]

For Moscow, the pragmatism of NEP did the trick of turning a
ghost town into a boomtown. And yet, its ideological baggage and

inner contradictions kept it from ever attaining full legitimacy. In local politics, the reform impetus was much slighter than in economics, and the drift was toward more systematic state controls. The imposition of the straitjacket of mobilized mass participation and of partocracy—the dominion of a now disciplined party apparatus, *nomenklatura* (appointment and patronage) procedures, and General Secretary Stalin—paved the way for the despotism that ensued. A fecund intellectual climate elicited scintillating designs for buildings and a reconditioned capital region, prompting no less a superstar than Le Corbusier to marvel at Moscow as "a factory of plans" and "the focus of architecture and city planning in the world."[3] But Russian poverty, uncertainty about how to treat Moscow's social and physical legacy, and a dearth of political will kept the plans from escaping the talking stage. By 1930, when the polemic over its future as a "socialist city" climaxed, pell-mell hyperurbanization was overrunning Moscow's beleaguered government and populace.

The Urban NEP

NEP in Moscow and the cities combined a global, guardedly pro-market orientation with specific local instruments for healing the wounds of war and revolution and refiring urban development.

REURBANIZATION

The incoming bureau chief of the *New York Times,* Walter Duranty, chanced in July 1921 upon an "incredibly broken" city. Skin-and-bone Muscovites wore garments "sewn together from blankets and curtains or even carpets." Many stores were shuttered, "but in most cases the boards had been torn away for fuel and you saw empty windows or no windows at all, just holes, like missing teeth." Back in town a few months later, Duranty was agog at the contrast:

> Everywhere dilapidated and half-ruined buildings were being refurbished and restored, and the fronts of the houses cleaned and painted. Shops, cafés and restaurants were being opened in all directions. Scores of shabby one-horse victorias like the old French fiacres had appeared, and traffic on the streets had increased tenfold. The city was full of peasants

selling fruit, vegetables and other produce, or transporting bricks, lumber and building materials in their clumsy, creaking carts. Suddenly goods began to appear from unexpected corners, hidden or hoarded . . . The people of Moscow, after a pause of bewilderment, seemed to realize NEP's possibilities simultaneously, and rushed at them like famished swine to a feeding trough.[4]

The commerce that put gruel in the trough and phased out rationing and wages in kind by 1924 was partly revived by city hall. It opened two jumbo five-and-dime stores downtown: GUM (the State Department Store) in the Upper Trading Rows on Red Square, and Mostorg (Moscow Trade) in the Muir and Merrilees premises on ulitsa Petrovka. It also superintended an armada of shops, kiosks, and service booths, together with outlets of the consumer cooperatives, dealing mainly in groceries and apparel.

More vital was reciprocity with the *Nepmen*, the small-time capitalists who came out of the woodwork in 1921. The city scurried to lease 4,000 buildings and rooms to businessmen by year's end and to license 7,400 street vendors. Sukharevskii and most of the open-air bazaars were soon in full swing (Figure 16). Private shops, their signboards overhanging the sidewalk, also proliferated. Nepmen rang up 77 percent of Moscow retail sales in fiscal year 1922/1923 (Soviet fiscal years in the 1920s began October 1). After several hundred businesses terminated operations in late 1923, their share dipped to 35 percent in fiscal 1923/1924, then held steady.

Even with the spate of closures, Moscow consumers could take their pick of 4,977 private shops and 606 cooperatives in May 1924 (versus 842 state stores) and of 5,600 market stalls (a 1927 figure), 24,000 self-employed buggy drivers (in mid-1928), and uncounted street hawkers. Walter Benjamin, a touring scholar from Germany, found the Smolenskii Market at Christmas of 1926 "so crowded with baskets of delicacies, tree decorations, and toys that you can barely make your way." Muscovites could sup and dance the foxtrot in privately owned restaurants and cabarets and patronize freelance physicians, tutors, opticians, photographers, seamstresses, and barbers.[5]

While divestment had scant direct effect on Moscow industry— private factories had only 4 percent of manufacturing employment in

Figure 16. Sukharevskii Market, 1925. (Museum of the History of the City of Moscow.)

1926 and cooperative firms 8 percent—the indirect payoff was great. With their workers fed and motivated, state factories recouped 1913 production levels in 1926. Textiles and other traditional specialties were joined in the recovery by branches of heavy industry that had grown since 1914.

Outside manufacturing, rail transport also resumed 1913 volumes by 1926. Moscow's first scheduled air passenger service lifted off from the Central Airfield for Nizhnii Novgorod in July 1923. Military research and development moved ahead around the main aviation laboratory of Russia, the Central Aeronautics Institute (TsAGI), led after Nikolai Zhukovskii's death in 1921 by Sergei A. Chaplygin. The aircraft industry's first design bureau, under Andrei N. Tupolev, was created in 1922 a stone's throw from TsAGI. In culture and the arts, literature, the theater, and film all staged sprightly comebacks. Mosfil'm, established in 1924, was the USSR's largest movie company; in 1927 it began a studio compound on the Lenin Hills, as the Sparrow Hills were renamed in 1924. Radio Moscow hit the airwaves from a Zamoskvorech'e studio in 1921.

Demographic changes provided the most heartening indexes of convalescence. From its 1920 low of 1 million, Moscow gained a half-million residents by 1923 and as many more by the census of December 1926, when it had eclipsed the war-gorged high of 2 million (see Appendix A). Deaths per 1,000, which had never been lower than 25 and tallied 45 in 1919, tumbled to 14.4 in 1923 and 13.6 in 1925. That, and a simultaneous baby boom, gave Moscow a natural increase of 16.6 per 1,000 in 1923 and 18.1 in 1925, 2.3 times the highest prewar rate. As under the monarchy, the preponderance of growth, 85 percent from 1921 to 1926, stemmed not from fertility but from in-migration, which was lubricated by the annulment of most administrative restrictions on mobility. Two-thirds of Muscovites in 1926 (not counting the 200,000 seasonal workers) had been born elsewhere, 5 percent more than in 1902; of the permanent entrants with continuous residence, 49 percent had landed after 1920.[6]

As earlier, the typical newcomer was an unskilled and unlettered peasant who left a dirt-poor village in central Russia to find economic opportunity. Ethnic Russians came to represent 87.8 percent of the population in 1926, although Jews, mostly from the former Pale of Settlement, gained as well, to a share of 6.5 percent. Two novel groups swelled the migrant pool: several tens of thousands of foreign political exiles and adventure seekers, and far more numerous economic refugees from the Russian provinces, on the run from the famine that ravaged the Volga and southern parts in 1921–1922. More than 75,000 of them descended on Moscow in 1922 alone. They contributed massively to the most heartrending spectacle of the time—the homeless children *(besprizorniki)* of the 1920s (Figure 17). Thirty thousand youngsters, orphaned or parted from their parents and frantic for food and shelter, joined the wave of famine refugees, and half stayed behind. Fifty thousand rag-clad waifs, migrants and natives, lived in Moscow in November 1923, keeping warm over smudgepots and burning truck tires. The fortunate ones earned their keep as messenger boys, bootblacks, and jugglers; the unfortunate

Figure 17. Homeless children, early 1920s. (From Alexys A. Sidorow, *Moskau,* Berlin: Albertus-Verlag, 1928, p. 123.)

took up prostitution and thievery. In 1926, after the problem had eased some, wraith-like seven- and eight-year-olds still sifted into Moscow to beg for crusts of bread. The bureau of the MK was displeased enough in 1927 to assign the deputy chief of the Soviet political police, Genrikh G. Yagoda, "to take all necessary measures to cleanse Moscow of homeless children and send them to other provinces."[7]

THE NEW MUNICIPAL POLICY

The so-called New Municipal or Communal *(Kommunal'naya)* Policy, a major yet overlooked corollary of NEP, was most strenuously pursued in Moscow. It addressed the ruination of housing and everyday functions by revolutionary convulsions. The wastage of the physical plant, Nikolai Semashko wrote in *Pravda,* grew out of local governance on "the principle of the loud voice and the clenched fist." The

Damocles' sword of confiscation, he warned, dangled over anyone who took care of his home and tempted Muscovites of average means to vandalize their own flats to avert "the watchful eye of 'the searchers.'" Unless the "orgy of annihilation" were halted, added another pundit, Moscow "in eight or nine years will not have one usable apartment."[8]

All appreciated that no turnabout could occur without a reanimation of local services. Here the leadership of the Mosssovet took the bull by the horns. Its omnibus "communal economy" directorate of the 1920s, MKKh (Moskovskoye Kommunal'noye Khozyaistvo), mended burst plumbing, patched potholes, and dug sidewalks and yards out from under stinking garbage and rubble. Streetcars restarted regular runs in May 1921. The fees levied on some services in August 1921 were a financial tonic, and in the spring of 1922 the city prepared its first budget since 1919; balanced books came in 1924, as the ruble stabilized.

When it came to salvaging the housing stock, the most exigent need, national statutes in 1921 provided a template for reform based on nongovernmental tenants' cooperatives. In September the city presidium led in execution by dissolving the official block households and offering to enter into six-year leases with "housing partnerships" (zhilishchnyye tovarishchestva) composed of the tenants of one or several dwellings. Houses of under five units could be "demunicipalized" outright to ex-owners or other persons. In the name of fairness, the RSFSR urban "sanitary norm" of 8.1 square meters of net dwelling space per person would be adopted as a ceiling and 10 percent of the partnerships' rooms would go to the city and raion soviets for the needy. The norm was varied for indulged groups such as officers in the Red Army and the Cheka (renamed the GPU in 1922 and the OGPU in 1923) and scientists.[9]

Quarrels over tenure got the housing partnerships off to a wobbly start. They were most clangorous inside the Sadovoye, where housing came up against shops and other profitable uses. Many members begrudged the rents instituted in May 1922, after a free ride of fifteen months. For all that, the partnerships did take shape and multiply to 10,000 by 1925. Relying on rents, volunteered labor, and market purchases of fuel and building supplies, most at least arrested the decay of their facilities.

The "house-communes" of Red Moscow remained a sticking

point. Conceived of as ventures in collective living, most had degenerated into seedy dormitories tethered to factories and government bureaus. "The hopes laid on the house-communes as breeding grounds of communist culture," one commentator put it, "have proven to be a mirage."[10] Their lack of success did not allay the question of control. The 1921 decrees foresaw temporary leasing by state organizations of some municipalized housing, an arrangement that constituted, officially speaking, a house-commune. Although legislation implied that the leases would be few, the 1,100 signed in the winter of 1921–1922 nearly tripled, to roughly 250,000, the Muscovites in the house-communes. About four-fifths of the homes were exclusively for employees of the leaseholder.

Regularization stiffened bureaucratic attitudes toward the exclusivity clause, which had been laxly enforced as the economic rebound spurred labor turnover. Sovnarkom in September 1922 authorized host enterprises to expel any house-commune tenants not on their payrolls. This decree was suspended when it raised the specter of mass evictions and ignited tit-for-tat eviction wars between commissariats. The difficulties tempted some employers to extricate themselves from the housing tar baby. A study of 255 factory-affiliated house-communes in Moscow in late 1922 ascertained that 42 percent of the workers living in them were unconnected with the factory and prophesied the "self-immolation" of these residences. In only 275 of the 1,000 communes nominally on the city's tally in April 1923 did residents feel they still lived in a dom-kommuna; in only 73 did management part with "miserly sums" for repairs.[11]

Events bore out neither the fright about evictions nor the forecast of an early burial of the Soviet form of company housing. An RSFSR circular in January 1924 cushioned manual workers from summary eviction upon change of job; the employer-landlord now had to work through a court and ensure alternate shelter. A Moscow ordinance in April further upheld gradualness in evictions by specifying that up to 50 percent occupancy by outsiders was permissible if the firm so wished. The house-comune of Civil War vintage died in the shakedown that ensued, whereas workplace-linked housing as such held its own.

The housing partnerships, their share of residents a whisker over 50 percent, dominated in July 1924, the last time arrangements were recorded in detail (see Table 2). Elective boards proverbial as "little

Table 2. Legal status of Moscow housing, July 1, 1924

Status	Dwellings		Residents	
	Number	Percent	Number	Percent
Housing partnership	8,358	30.8	908,740	51.8
Economic enterprise or administrative agency				
State lease from city	2,936	10.8	350,824	20.0
House-commune	120	0.4	58,846	3.4
Military	360	1.3	20,725	1.2
Nationalized	152	0.6	14,099	0.8
Private				
Leased from city[a]	2,865	10.5	108,376	6.2
Demunicipalized	7,536	27.7	96,793	5.5
Ownerless	4,780	17.6	193,156	11.0
Moscow Real Estate Directorate	78	0.3	3,199	0.2
Total	27,185	100.0	1,754,758	100.0

Source: "Rabota i dostizheniya MUNI za 1923–24 gg.," *Kommunal'noye khozyaistvo*, no. 24 (December 25, 1924), p. 79.
a. Includes 504 dwellings, with 5,825 residents, temporarily held until construction on site.

tyrants" governed the partnerships but not wholly without the tenants' say. The city kept almost no lodging as a public utility, save for a few dozen derelict buildings and five flophouses (four in Khitrov and other slums). Twenty-five percent of Muscovites lived in a private sector that comprehended a dwindling moiety of legally unassigned buildings. Private dwellings were small in size (26 residents on average, as against 109 in housing partnerships and 122 in state houses) and equipped with few conveniences.

This setup left a quarter of the population under the roof of a specialized state organization, usually in partial compensation for the labor of the breadwinner. The housing was of two subtypes: "nationalized," sequestered by a central agency in circumvention of the city soviet, or freely conveyed to the employer by city hall.

The most august group in the first and rare situation was the 500 or 600 officials left in the Kremlin, where the Politburo itself rendered the final verdict on tenancy. The flats were densest in the converted Cavalry Guards Barracks and along the White Corridor of the seventeenth-century Poteshnyi Palace. They had overstuffed furnishings, maids from the Romanov court, and access to a clinic, grocery store, and pharmacy, but no central heating or kitchens, tenants having to light their own ceramic stoves and carry out trays from the Kremlin Cafeteria in the former cavalry billet. Children bounced balls in courtyards and skied among the palaces and cathedrals after snowstorms.

The Kremlin had its own housing hierarchy. Lenin and his wife, Nadezhka K. Krupskaya, had four rooms. Aleksei Rykov, his successor as head of government, qualified for seven rooms for himself, his wife, and daughter, while a minor functionary might be thrilled with a bachelor flat in one of the two extinguished Kremlin abbeys. Every stick of furniture bore a government identification tag, and most residents still had to check in at the guardhouse at the Troitskiye Gates by the stroke of midnight. One party worker actually turned down a Kremlin apartment in 1922 because of the oppressive atmosphere: "Your every step was noted, and you could not even sneeze without the GPU knowing it."[12]

Several thousand members of the next political echelon crammed into Moscow's Houses of the Soviets, well-situated habitations cleaned out in 1917–1918. Thirteen of them existed in 1923 and about thirty in the early 1930s, when the term was abandoned. House No. 1 was the Natsional' Hotel, No. 2 the Metropol', No. 3 the former Orthodox seminary on Bozhedomnyi pereulok. House of the Soviets No. 5 was a red sandstone apartment block with Moderne touches and a courtyard garden at 3 ulitsa Granovskogo (formerly Sheremetevskaya ulitsa), two blocks from the Troitskiye Gates. Built in the 1890s and once owned by the aristocratic Sheremetevs, it rated next in prestige to the Kremlin.

Ordinary Muscovites in the state sector had originally been in the second subtype, the house-communes, in principle lodgings for manual workers only. These passed out of the picture in 1924. The device for closing them out was the "state lease" *(gosudarstvennaya arenda)*, whereby the city relinquished care of a tenement indefinitely, without charge, on the proviso that the lessee keep it in repair. Contracts, affecting white- as well as blue-collar staff, made news in the press. For many citizens, despite the extinction of the misnamed house-communes, a nexus between workplace and home had been retained. It had its demerits—*Pravda* caught a whiff of "the air of the old barracks"—but its merits, too. Most tangibly, government offices and enterprises had deep pockets. They performed 47 percent of Moscow housing repairs in 1924, for 26 percent of the residents; housing partnerships did only 30 percent, private actors 19.[13]

Historic buildings profited from a salutary side effect of urban revitalization. The Department for Museum Affairs and Protection of Landmarks, within the RSFSR People's Commissariat of Education, and the Moscow Soviet, its small restoration office directed by Nikolai Vinogradov, moved from first aid to all-round restoration. Religious edifices, 50 percent of the 474 officially protected landmarks when an inventory was done in 1925, often benefited, notwithstanding official atheism and the impoundment of 49 kilograms of gold and 57,000 of silver objects by the GPU in March and April 1922, ostensibly for famine aid. Vestigial communities of monastics lingered in Moscow's now state-owned convents and monasteries, eking out a living in tailoring and handicrafts.

Reclamation projects included St. Basil's and Kazan Cathedrals on Red Square, the Dulo Tower of the Simonov Monastery, the Malyi Theater, and the Sukharev Tower, made over into a Moscow Communal Museum directed by Petr V. Sytin between 1921 and 1925. An architectural museum specializing in rural church buildings opened at Kolomenskoye, a royal estate south of Moscow, in 1923. In 1924 its curator, Petr Baranovskii, and technicians from Igor Grabar's Central

Figure 18. Restoration of Golitsyn villa, 1925. (Museum of the History of the City of Moscow.)

State Restoration Workshops began rehabilitating the Moscow Baroque villa of the Golitsyn boyar clan on Okhotnyi ryad, completed in 1685 but hidden from view for generations (Figure 18). Vinogradov set up scaffolding in 1925 at the Kitaigorod Wall, which had grown a mane of shrubs and weeds, and in 1926 at the Red Gates, where thieves walked off with eighteen of the twenty carved figures during restoration.

NEP AND URBAN DEVELOPMENT

On top of effecting and stabilizing recovery, NEP sought to nourish dynamic growth, especially in the supply of housing, and to skew it toward the disadvantaged groups on whose shoulders the party had ridden to power.

Who was to be the agent of this laudable goal? The options were limited. The bankrupt city government still smarted from the debacle of its "extraordinary" construction departments under War Communism. The tenants' partnerships, the linchpin of the housing reform, had no legal basis for building and showed no wish to do so, so depressed were their revenues by rent controls that held them to 5 percent of members' incomes.

Several city officials suggested mimicking NEP in retail trade by uncorseting private capital in the housing market. A municipal statistician, Ippolit A. Verner, in 1921 urged the awarding of ninety-nine-year land leases to businessmen who would build apartments for a profit. Nikolai Semashko extolled "housing construction trusts" in which state and private firms owned shares. A transport engineer, Mikhail P. Sheremetevskii, and a member of the MKKh collegium, Isaak M. Benenson, pleaded for giving the green light to non-Russian firms. Sheremetevskii wanted all of Moscow earmarked a "territorial concession" of a single foreign company; it would supply housing and a marmalade of services in return for being allowed to collect government-approved fees.[14]

Moscow moved from words about housing construction to deeds only in 1923, after a nine-year caesura. Net completions climbed to about 500,000 square meters in 1929 (see Table D-1 in Appendix D).

The sponsorship question was resolved by opting primarily for municipal and cooperative control (see Table 3). While tolerating private building, which was decriminalized in August 1922, decision makers boxed it in by withholding credits, limiting it to dwellings of under six units, and imposing other prohibitions. Timber cottages slipped through the regulatory mesh, almost the only private houses to do so. As concerns foreign capital, in 1922–1923 Moscow entered into contracts with French and British companies on nine housing projects and bargained with a group of Swiss financiers. These endeavors got no further than sipping the champagne at the ground breaking for one building on Tverskaya in June 1923.

The presidium of the Moscow Soviet, shrugging off its earlier debacles, donned the hat of developer-in-chief. Drawing on tax revenues and proceeds from special housing lotteries, it acted through its own building trusts (the biggest, Mosstroi, fashioned from the wreck-

Table 3. Control of housing construction, 1923–1929

	Percent of expenditures on housing construction			
Fiscal year	Moscow government	Construction cooperatives	State bodies	Private
1923/1924	34.5	25.3	17.2	22.9
1924/1925	54.5	18.1	17.0	10.4
1925/1926	62.5	20.9	12.7	3.9
1926/1927	56.8	21.7	13.4	8.1
1927/1928	49.8	32.5	10.8	6.9
1928/1929	50.9	28.2	13.2	7.6

Sources: N. Popov (Sibiryak), "9 let na zhilishchnom fronte," *Stroitel'stvo Moskvy,* no. 11 (November 1926), p. 5; V. Zheits, "Rabocheye zhilishchnoye stroitel'stvo k XI oktyabryu," ibid., no. 19 (October 1928), p. 1; *Vsya Moskva* (Moscow: Izdaniye Moskovskogo Soveta, 1930), p. 28.

age of Moskomgosoor in 1922) and through contracts with private companies and *arteli,* peasant work gangs. By the end of the 1920s it was turning out estates of four- to six-story red brick buildings ranged around scrubby courtyards in the factory districts. Remnants can yet be found at Usachevka (built for the workers of Kauchuk, by the Novodevichii Convent—see Figure 19), Dubrovka (south of Taganskaya ploshchad'), Mytnaya and Shabolovka streets (in Zamoskvorech'e), and Dangauerovka (for what is now the Kompressor Works, in northeastern Moscow).

Construction cooperatives, the second preferred device, appeared in Moscow in 1923 (two years after the management-only partnerships, with which they should not be confused) and were regulated from 1924 by a national law on "housing-construction cooperative partnerships" *(zhilishchno-stroitel'nyye kooperativnyye tovarishchestva).* They fell into two categories, one for workers only and the second unrestricted; the first, to which about two-thirds of Moscow members belonged, was represented by city and guberniya federations. The co-ops assembled construction funds from dues and loans and operated the buildings once built. They were intertwined with the municipal administration, not a force apart. It gave them moral support, subventions, credits, and preferential treatment from Mosstroi and its other building trusts.

Figure 19. Workers' housing at Usachevka, 1930. (Museum of the History of the City of Moscow.)

The cooperative movement took quicker hold in Moscow than in any other Soviet city. In October 1925 42 percent of all building cooperatives in the RSFSR, and 31 percent of the members (28,600), were in Moscow; Moscow guberniya had an extra 10 percent of the co-ops and 28 percent of members. In January 1928 city and guberniya still had 29 percent of the cooperatives and 50 percent of the RSFSR membership (90,000), and in March 1930 their 100,000 members made up 29 percent of the USSR total.[15]

It was often claimed, without hard numbers, that white-collar Muscovites benefited disproportionately from the building co-ops. Some of the larger and longer-lived indeed served political personalities and professional groups, like Politkatorzhanin (for pre-1917 political prisoners), Medik (for medical specialists), and Vysshaya shkola (for professors). In 1926 the MK bureau deregistered six occupationally defined co-ops and endorsed organization on the territorial principle, saying this approach would aid working-class applicants. In 1928, reversing itself, it authorized cooperatives for the work forces of government agencies, such as the People's Commissariat of Foreign Affairs and the Commissariat of Trade; they were not mentioned in public.[16]

As for administrative and industrial employers, through happenstance the proprietor of hundreds of older homes, it was seldom suggested in the 1920s that they have much to do with providing new ones. State and party agencies whose staff could not get into the Houses of the Soviets commonly received allocations in projects completed by the Mossovet. What little housing the factories produced lodged mostly office personnel and engineers. This earned manufacturers opprobrium for spurning the needs of common workers; when they did build for workers, they were faulted for actuating an unsound "dependence on the leaders of the enterprise, [a relationship of] servant to master."[17]

A straw in the wind was the construction of the first large home exclusively for high officials, the "housing combine" of the USSR Council of People's Commissars on Vsekhsvyatskaya ulitsa (later ulitsa Serafimovicha), glancing obliquely at the Kremlin over the Moskva River (Figure 20). Started in 1928 and commissioned in 1931, it allowed the reconversion of the Natsional' and Metropol' to hotel use and a reduction in the colony within the Kremlin. Its architect, Boris M. Iofan, as an expatriate specialist and a member of the Italian Communist Party was detailed to accompany Aleksei Rykov during a trip to Rome for medical treatment in 1924. He became Rykov's bosom friend, returned to Russia, and won the commission after spreading out his drawings on the floor of the Rykovs' Kremlin apartment.

The eleven stories of the lumpish combine had 506 spacious, furnished flats, all with telephones and constant hot water, rarities in those days, and daily garbage pickup. It also had fifty passenger and cargo elevators, a department store, beauty salon, kindergarten, gymnasium, post office, and auto garage, branches of the Kremlin's cafeteria and clinic, and Udarnik, at the time the USSR's biggest cinema, where first-run films were preceded by light concert fare in the foyer. Apartments were issued to civilian and military VIPs, Old Bolsheviks, and their relatives, all arrayed by rank—those of highest standing with an unimpeded view of the Kremlin Wall. Generations of Muscovites

Figure 20. Government House residence on Moskva River. (Photograph by author.)

knew the home as Government House or simply "The House on the Embankment," the title of a best-selling novel in the 1970s by Yurii Trifonov (who lived in it as a boy). Moralists impugned it as an unholy extravagance. The residents' excitement at Government House's "almost fantastic" conveniences was dulled by the twenty-four-hour watch over them by OGPU sentries and by the cinder gray mastic in which it was finished. Iofan's plan called for cladding it in russet granite, but Rykov would not sign the chits for the expensive stone.[18]

All in all, to underline, the city soviet and cooperatives dominated Moscow housing construction, be it for party tetrarchs or factory hands. No one group within the municipal structure, it is true, called the shots, and building, as Mikhail V. Kryukov, the chief of Mosstroi, huffed in 1925, took place "day by day . . . without a plan."[19] A

Planning Commission advisory to the Mossovet presidium had been appointed in 1924, and the presidium began that year to ratify an annual "plan," in rubles, for outlays on house building. After Kryukov's blast, a Housing Construction Committee was attached to the presidium. The yearly plan bestowed little more than a summation of intent, and neither committee exerted any great influence.

Limp though the coordination was, municipal builders and the cooperatives constituted a localist coalition deciding on upward of 80 percent of housing construction in Moscow. Had NEP persevered, and had the alliance retained a say over the houses whose building it capitalized, chances are it would have lengthened its reach into housing management as well.

For nonhousing services, the Mossovet had the playing field to itself. It concentrated on inverting the social and spatial priorities of the old regime. "The first thing," Fedor Ya. Lavrov, the head of MKKh, said of his agency in 1924, "must be the extension of amenities to the outskirts of the city, so that the working class of Moscow can enjoy a civilized urban existence." His deputy, Il'ya Tsivtsivadze, added that party officials and workers themselves clamored for this Robin Hoodism every chance they got: "The comrades juxtapose the center to the outskirts: the center is bourgeois and the outskirts are working class; the center is theirs and the outskirts are ours."[20]

Old Moscow had grown more class-diverse than before, owing to the flight of gentlefolk and to proletarian forays into their neighborhoods. But former denizens crept back into the city center in the early 1920s, and workers and artisans trickled out as crowding worsened and factories on the outskirts were fired up. The outer zone, enlarged beyond the Kamer-kollezhskii val in 1917, retained its plebeian social face and physical decrepitude. Walter Benjamin marveled at its "village character," a feature of all Moscow, which "leaps out at you undisguisedly . . . in the streets of its suburbs." He had never seen another urban area "whose gigantic open spaces have such an amorphous, rural quality, as if their expanse were always being dissolved by bad weather, thawing snow, or rain."[21]

Chairman Lev Kamenev inaugurated the first tram line paid for by the Mossovet, northward to Petrovsko-Razumovskoye, in July 1922. Moscow had one-third more tram track by 1926 than it had had in 1914, carrying double the paying passengers, and was laying five to ten kilometers a year, much of it to working-class areas like Dangauerovka, Danilovka, and Leninskaya sloboda. Spokesmen exulted in the enlightenment that would be visited on the cloth-capped inhabitants of the outskirts. As motorized transport got them in range of theaters and lecture halls, they would feel "an uplift of cultural life" and perceive themselves as citizens.[22]

MKKh also began a large expansion of water and sanitation services in 1922, hiring the unemployed to dig drainage ditches and lay pipe. As of 1928, it was funneling three-quarters of its capital funds to the outskirts. Whereas less than half of the population was connected to sewage mains before the war, about 65 percent (of a larger total) was hooked up by 1927 and 68 percent by 1928. Municipal running water reached 65 percent in 1927, a like margin of improvement. Moscow in the late 1920s made 34 percent of all expenditures in the Soviet Union on urban water systems and 61 percent of those on sewage.[23] To this investment, and the parallel effort to improve hygiene and health through education and dispensaries, must go high marks and much of the credit for the decline in mortality.

DISCORDANT NOTES

The urban NEP was constantly buffeted by critics, and not even its upholders denied that it had flaws. What, then, was so irksome about government behavior that granted some relief from privation?

No explanation can omit the effect on public mores of veering from the puritanism of War Communism to the Moscow equivalent of the Roaring Twenties. The boulevards glowed with the red lights of brothels. Confidence men and traffickers in stolen goods popped up in Khitrov, Mar'ina roshcha, and other prewar haunts. Underground businessmen from all over the country cut deals under the potted palms at the Ampir and Ermitazh restaurants. Revellers at the casino in the Praga on Arbatskaya ploshchad' ogled the rouged chorus girls and wagered wads of dollars and francs—"a strange sight," Duranty mused, "in the center of the world's first Proletarian Republic." Journalists chronicled the bonanza in vice with a blend of revulsion and prurience, while Moscow's chief of police adjudged it "the reappearance of every malignant sore peculiar to capitalism."[24]

The official response vacillated between repression and grudging indulgence, with repression winning out in 1923–1924 and liberality getting a second wind after that. In legitimate trade and services, treatment of the Nepmen matched this course.[25] The boisterous Su-kharevskii Market was a barometer: closed in 1920 and reopened in April 1922, it was closed a second time at the end of 1924 and opened again in 1925, only to be shut for good in 1930 and its stalls burned.

We must not overlook the offensiveness of halfway marketization to socialist egalitarianism. Industrial workers sulked over the wage cuts and production speedups brought about by a "regime of economy" introduced in 1926. Unemployment reached about 200,000 in Moscow by 1927. Like the jobless, bemedalled Red Army veterans "discovered in their wanderings about Moscow that everything was beyond their reach, that the profiteers could snap fingers at them with impunity," and "began to wonder whether they had fought in vain." Guilt at the plight of Moscow's orphans and hoboes gnawed at appreciation of the bounty of markets and boutiques: "The streetcorners, particularly in those quarters where foreigners do business, are covered with bundles of rags—beds in the great open-air sickbay called Moscow."[26]

On housing and communal issues the chiliasm of 1917–1921 was never completely doused. As early as the summer of 1922, a year before salvos were heard against private trade, leftists preached "class struggle" in Moscow apartment houses and assailed excessive demunicipalization. Between September and December of 1922, an Extraordinary Housing Commission of the Moscow Soviet directed by Genrikh Yagoda of the GPU ferreted out violators of the square-meter quota, garnishing 12,000 rooms and sending many malefactors to trial.

Allegations flew in 1923 that Nepmen and rentiers had "swindled" their way into the housing partnerships. Evictions from Moscow accompanied inflammatory agitation. The OGPU heaved out 916 "socially dangerous" persons in but one lustration, in December 1923, and Yagoda won approval for an OGPU program (never carried out) to organize workers' housing projects in flats confiscated from deportees.[27] After emendation of the electoral rules, pro-government groups took over and "proletarianized" the boards of the housing partnerships in April 1924. Such jihads erased whatever chance there was that private capital would do much for housing construction.

Homogenizing policies kept differentials in housing supply low, although not nonexistent. Per capita housing supply in 1926 was 7.0 to 7.5 square meters in about 60 percent of the area inside the Sadovoye kol'tso, mostly in the western hemisphere (in the former Arbatskaya and Prechistenskaya police districts); at the other extreme, on the southeast periphery of Moscow and in the dilapidated Mar'ina roshcha neighborhood in the north, it was between 4.3 and 4.5 square meters. But all parts of Moscow, the better housed in particular, were socially much more mixed than before 1917. On average, workers and their families had 4.3 square meters per capita of housing in 1928 and all Muscovites 5.6 square meters; in 1930, the Moscow average was down to 5.5 square meters, that for workers up to 4.6.[28]

These trends attest that tensions with socialist values did persist but were not the main thing. Most unsettling was the inability to meet the irreducible material aspirations common to all classes.

Consider housing construction: annual completions never hit 50 percent of the 1913 level. Private enterprise measured a tiny fraction of its prewar attainment—perhaps 3 percent in the late 1920s—and state and cooperative builders did not take up the slack. Rehabilitation and building allowed Moscow to exceed its 1912 housing stock of 11,750,000 square meters only in 1928, when its population was 600,000 more. Per capita supply had nosedived to 5.6 square meters, already 24 percent less than in 1912, and fell far shy of the sanitary norm (hiked to 9 square meters in 1926), itself so stingy that citizens called it the "coffin norm" (grobovaya norma). (See Appendix D for time series on housing production and supply.)

The same officials who cried "housing crisis" in the early 1920s took pride then that thousands of proletarians had left cot-closet and basement flats and that most of Khitrov had been torn down. By mid-decade they were reciting housing horror stories: of individuals encamped on rooftops, under the arches of the Kitaigorod Wall, in railway stations, boxcars, parks, cemeteries, culverts, and even, for one set of urchins, in an ice-block igloo on Sofiiskaya naberezhnaya. Amorous but bedless Muscovites kept a small fleet of "bordellos on wheels" busy; these taxicabs for trysts were identifiable by their yellow stripes and opaque curtains. Rabochaya Moskva (Workers' Moscow) declared tongue-in-cheek that one day Moscow might "drop through the earth" and proposed making stretchable houses out of rubber to shelter the masses; this was in 1926, when conditions were gentle compared to later. An American who visited in 1927 remarked that, if there had been dreadful overcrowding in the slums before the war, "this evil has now been spread out, a little thinner, over the entire city." A British observer found the congestion "so terrible that it is almost impossible to describe."[29]

The pattern repeated itself for other facilities. The city returned to its discussion of a subway in 1922, and drawings were done for a tube under Myasnitskaya ulitsa in 1925. Again officials took no action, partly because they still hoped that foreign moneybags would come up with the funds. It had been general opinion in 1913 that the tram service, the workhorse of local transit, was scandalously overburdened; 816 streetcars carried an average of 705,000 riders a day that year, or 864 per car. In 1930 the city had 1,644 streetcars yet 2,603,000 riders; the daily load of 1,583 per car was 83 percent more than in 1913. During the rush-hour melee at Lubyanskaya ploshchad', "Every car that passed was stormed by would-be passengers" who stuck to ramps "like bunches of grapes." When one tried to get off, "the bunches fell off, many of the component parts taking a full-length sprawl in the snow."[30]

Casting the Institutional Die

NEP's verve in public policy washed over but feebly into the political process. Despite some betterment in administration and public access, the hallmarks of urban governance were the failure of the soviets to jell into strong agents of local control and the aggrandizement of the territorial apparatus of the Communist Party.

LOCAL GOVERNMENT COMES OF AGE

When Lev Kamenev was fleeced of the chairmanship of the Mossovet in 1926, the resolution spoke of the decision as evidence of institutional maturation. Kamenev, it averred, had been too tied up in Kremlin affairs "to take a real, direct part" in a government whose "enormous growth" and "complex and crucial" work made a full-time steward imperative. His replacement was Konstantin V. Ukhanov, a metalworker turned raion politician and then industrialist who had been chief of the State Electrotechnical Trust since 1922 and a candidate member of the Central Committee (CC) Orgburo since

January 1926. The press lionized Chairman Ukhanov as "the Red Director of workers' Moscow," a prototypical Russian public man, "boiling with sympathy and with a universal energy for all the 'fronts' opening up before him."[31]

The Communist-controlled municipal elite drew stature and confidence from several factors. The reintroduction of local budgeting made it downsize staffs (by 50 percent in some agencies), a premium to both efficiency and popularity. In June 1922 the substitution of heads of department for the ungainly collegiums further uncluttered the decision process. Also dispensed with were the special-purpose boards that abounded until 1921. The Yagoda commission of 1922 was the last major example of the type.

The concordance in the soviet as Moscow's main developer of housing betokened its political clout, as did its latitude to make representations abroad. City hall opened a Berlin trade office in 1922 and in 1922–1923 dickered with foreign companies over investment in a district heating grid and a canal to the Volga River. When it began planning for a subway, it wooed concessionaires; Siemens from Germany proffered a detailed sketch to Ukhanov in 1926, and conversations continued in 1928. Seabrook, an American firm, did 80 percent of Moscow's street paving in 1930. Municipal fact-finding delegations jaunted to Berlin, Paris, and the English garden towns.

Moreover, the easing of the spite between "Reds" and "specialists" boded well for cohesion within the city establishment. The leadership, as Tables C-1 and C-2 (in Appendix C) show for a pocket sample, still consisted of youthful, ill-educated jacks of all trades. Half had some steeping in local government, but the external milieu conferring the most prior experience was the Red Army. Most were also of humble social origin.[32] Other data offer a more multitoned picture for the year 1925. For 37 public servants more broadly selected than those in the tables—all heads and deputy heads of city departments, chairmen of raion soviets, and heads of raion departments of finance, education, and health—we find 100 percent Communist Party membership, but also rather more formal schooling (29.7 percent with higher education, though 64.9 percent with only elementary) and less lowborn origins (35.1 percent of worker or peasant parentage). Below this peak, the 1,241 "responsible workers" (managers) in local government sort into two piles. Of the 757 who held party cards, merely

14.9 percent had a postsecondary education, 60.4 percent had not gone beyond primary school, and 35.5 percent were from worker and peasant families. Of the 484 non-Communists, more than half (54.5 percent) had a higher education, only 29.0 percent had no better than a grade-school education, and a nugatory 4.5 percent were of proletarian or peasant background.[33]

This second subgroup is of special interest, for many in it, probably the majority, had been inherited from the Moscow Duma. While barred from peak positions, the veterans now had acceptance at intermediate grades, in technical branches especially, and Moscow government was the better for it. The chief of the city waterworks within MKKh until 1930, Nikolai I. Gushchin, had worked for the duma in 1912 (as shop boss at a tram depot); the heads of the works' equipment division and piping network in 1927 had filled the identical positions in 1912. The 1927 manager of the sewage division, Yakov Ya. Zvyaginskii, had also been a municipal employee in 1912, as had a number of his deputies. The tram service's chief engineer, Aleksandr V. Gerbko, was one of the first uprava experts, with Gushchin and Vladimir Ol'denborger, to desert to the Bolsheviks. "As far as the people presently heading up things in MKKh are concerned," went a 1928 testimonial, "the majority have practical experience in urban services of up to thirty years." Both political and press circles held technocrats like Gushchin and Gerbko in esteem.[34]

Besides being run in comparative amity, local institutions after 1921 were also, when rated against the Civil War and the Stalin era, relatively open to input gurgling up from below. An undergrowth of voluntary associations took part in some political decisions. Architectural groups and several conservationist organizations, led by the Old Moscow Society, participated most actively. The society, which had three hundred members in 1928, published a historical calendar, sponsored research on local history and folklore, registered ancient buildings and gravesites, and petitioned politicians to preserve the city's past.

The doors of local government were kept ajar to individual petitioners in the 1920s. City newspapers posted the reception hours and telephone numbers of officials, up to the soviet and party leaders of all Moscow. A Workers' and Peasants' Inspectorate (Rabkrin), in existence at all levels in the Soviet Union from 1921 until 1934, probed public complaints and exposed *byurokratizm*. The local press broached many subjects later penciled out by the censors. It raised no eyebrows when the 1923 city directory printed the entry "Concentration Camps," addresses and wardens and all, or when several reviewers nonchalantly corrected it on particulars of the camps. Handbooks also gave the exact names and locations of military offices and installations.

Mass participation centered on the sections of the city and raion soviets. Set up in April 1920 as commissions of deputies only, they began to add lay members in 1921. Their basic mission was checking up on the work of bureaucratic units and hearing gripes from below. They provided the preferred pool for rank-and-file promotees *(vydvizhentsy)* to leadership positions, who numbered 1,000 or more per year. The thirteen city and forty-four raion sections had 13,000 members in 1925, 8,700 of them nondeputies; by 1928 membership was 37,000, including 30,900 nondeputies.[35]

A ROAD NOT TAKEN

Although some of the rough edges of urban government had been smoothed, no comprehensive reform echoed NEP's other changes. Horizontal coordination was still choppy. The return of the municipal budget tempered dependency on higher authority, yet most of the other levers of vertical control went unaltered. The formation of the USSR in 1924, nominally a federal state with the Russian Republic (RSFSR) as one of its partners, merely substituted one superior for another on many decisions.

In 1929, for instance, Nikolai Gushchin sounded the bell about his helplessness to bring about the increase in clean water supply necessitated by population and economic growth. State industry had spurned pollution abatement in the Moskva River basin; the digging of gravel pits had dropped the water table near the Mytishchi artesian wells; railway officials foiled efforts to map out a canal to the Oka:

This short and incomplete sketch . . . prompts the conclusion of how much heterogeneous interests [*raznorodnyye interesy*], concurring and contradictory, come into collision in the resolution of every . . . issue. Planning, coordination of these interests, and the choice of the most rational settlement of the given problem . . . are beyond the means of the interested administrative organizations themselves, especially when their interests are opposed. This is why it is truly necessary to form an authoritative state organ to carry out planning in the field of water policy, concert different interests, and provide fundamental answers to the problem.[36]

Notice how Gushchin glided over his own master, the Mossovet. It did not figure in either his diagnosis or his prescription, which was to entrust the problem to yet another arm of the central (now USSR) government. Equally remarkable, his compendium of "heterogeneous interests" took in only bureaucratic actors, not individuals. How could this be?

For the subset of the population that had thrived under the old regime the problem lay in the vindictiveness still exhibited by the Soviet state. There was no restitution of the privileges and even, many times, the civil rights of Moscow's former nobility, big businessmen, and lesser bourgeoisie. The better part of those who had decamped from Moscow stayed away. Of the 134 deputies of the city duma as of mid-1912—a cross section of the pre-1917 upper crust—only 30 (22.4 percent) were listed as residents in any of the Moscow directories of 1923 to 1930. Nary a one reentered public life.[37]

Irrespective of lineage, anyone who availed himself of the chance he had under NEP to enter private commerce became a political outcast. Recipients of "unearned income" (from capital, property, or trade) made up most of the 7 or 8 percent of the adult Moscow population ineligible to vote. Clergymen also lived on the margins of the law and were frequently arrested.[38]

For most Muscovites the problem lay less in selective discrimination than in the devaluation of participation in general. Political life showed no cognate of NEP's stuttering appreciation of the value of the market in economics. Leaders did not become accountable to society. When all was said and done, community democracy was a road not taken.

Political communication went in one direction. Loudspeakers for piping in canned music, news, and propaganda appeared in squares, train stations, and courtyards in 1921–1922. In 1923 they began to be installed in the "workers' clubs," the latter-day "people's houses," and in 1924 in apartments. The synergy between local politicians and the organs of repression was undisturbed by NEP. The secret police had a seat on the MK as of 1920; the OGPU's vice-chief, Yagoda, filled it from January 1925 onward and joined the MK bureau in January 1927. The OGPU retained the Cheka buildings around ploshchad' Dzerzhinskogo (as the square in front of the Lubyanka became after Feliks Dzerzhinskii's death in 1926), and in 1928 began to construct two sleek office towers on Bol'shaya and Malaya Lubyanka streets. The local party organs exhorted Communists to oblige the police and made no bones about their readiness to use terror. "The OGPU," a speaker at a party gathering in 1923 stated point-blank, "looks into and fights against all those groups that are against our Communist Party and the working class. It knows how to clean things up from above, and we know how to clean things up from below."[39]

In electoral and interparty politics the Communists tightened restrictions, in counterpoint to the loosening of economic regulation. Local voting, especially, was harnessed to the construction of the regime's "transcript" of domination over the populace. For the city election of April 1921, one month into NEP, the Mensheviks' local leadership was jailed for the campaign, opposition speakers were drowned out by crowd noise, and a provision was put on the books (until 1924) permitting trade unions and army units, where the Communists' grip was close, to elect deputies separately. Voters returned the lowest proportion of anti-Communists up to that time (see Table 1), although turnout barely reached 50 percent and an unusual number of winners professed no party allegiance. One of the nonaligned deputies, a chemical worker named Mikhailov, formed a ginger group in the Mossovet and put himself forward for the presidium. *Pravda* sniffed that he "almost aspired to be chairman" of the soviet.[40]

Nine months later the Communists lifted turnout by 22 points and restored their vote ratio to about its 1920 level. Police and party roughnecks shut almost all election meetings to officers of the other parties.[41] Within the Moscow Soviet, nonpartisans were now expected to toe the line. GPU detention of two of the three Menshevik deputies in April 1922, for bringing out a "counterrevolutionary proclamation," opened a conformity drive. The SR Shteinberg was hooted down in June when he opposed a resolution endorsing the treason trial of a group of SR politicians.

The ballot of December 4–14, 1922, completed the transmutation of the local election from popular choice to spurious affirmation of the single-party state. The husks of the non-Communist parties did not field candidates. In many enterprises the precedent was set of voting by list presented by the party cell. At its session of November 9, the bureau of the Communist Party MK set the dates for the election and fixed on a commission (formally of the city soviet) to run it, chaired by the MK first secretary, Isaak Zelenskii. On November 18 a plenum of the MK accepted wording of a uniform mandate (*nakaz*) to be put before the electors by approved candidates. On November 23 the bureau instructed all departments of the MK and raikoms "to set aside all work not directly related to the reelection of the soviet." On December 12—two days *before* the balloting closed—it decided on the return of Chairman Kamenev and on who would sit on the Mossovet executive committee and the bureau of the Communist fraction. Kamenev hailed Moscow as the first Soviet city to place only Communists and "loyal non–party members" on its soviet.[42]

The party refined the process for the next city election, in November 1923. Army and union candidates were now cleared with the Communist Party raikoms. And candidates from the Komsomol, the party's youth auxiliary, all approved by the MK secretariat, were put through surreptitiously under the trade unions' allowance.[43]

What little had been left to chance was ironed out in the election of April 1925. Over and above the mandate, the MK bureau ordered the Mossovet to prepare a leaflet on its accomplishments, the Moscow Union of Consumer Cooperatives one on trade, and the Agitation and Propaganda Department of the MK colored posters and a film clip. It dunned several hundred Moscow and USSR leaders to give speeches. Most significant, the bureau transmitted to the city electoral commission and the raikoms quotas setting the political and demographic complexion of the deputy corps from stem to stern. Sixty percent of the members of the Moscow and raion soviets were to be Communists (of them 20 percent members admitted during the "Lenin enrollment" of 1924), 80 percent to be men, and 70 percent blue-collar workers; the bureau prepared separate synopses of factory directors, trade unionists, and political celebrities ("honorary members") to be elected.[44]

The worst anyone could think to say about the election at an MK plenum afterward was that a few assemblies in Krasnopresnenskii raion "were very noisy" and officials "had to apply pressure to get

[our] candidates through" there. First Secretary Nikolai A. Uglanov aptly reminded the committee that "the most basic thing is that the state machine is in the hands of the proletariat," that is to say, of the Communist Party. "Therefore," he continued, "there is not a candidate to be found who would come out in an election to the Mossovet against Kamenev. You could not find such a person." No one took Uglanov up on this point.[45]

The debasing of elections predictably had a stultifying effect on the proceedings of the Moscow Soviet. "Once the opposition was gone from the soviet," recalled Boris Dvinov, a Menshevik who sat in it until December 1922, "no one really spoke out on the reports, and it remained only to repeat the mechanics of raising hands, as just done in the [Communist] fraction . . . Politics was removed from the agenda, and all that was discussed were 'applied questions,' most of them uninteresting." The Mossovet, to Dvinov's mind, "died of boredom."[46]

The raising of hands was as metronomic in the sections of the soviet, where deputies, citizens, and administrators interacted at closer quarters. While the sections' quantitative embrace was great, the quality of participation was low.

Elected deputies, the Mossovet's secretary, Yakov Dorofeyev, declared in 1924, "look upon section work as an obligation," a penance to be discharged at minimal cost. Lay members came mostly from party-saturated groups such as the Komsomol and the unions. The bureau heading each section was chaired by none other than the director of the administrative office under scrutiny. As of 1922, the MK, through its Agitation Department, ratified membership in the bureaus. Each bureau was "guided by a prearranged plan coordinated with the department's work plan and approved by the presidium of the Moscow Soviet." For good measure, the bureau of the Communist fraction in the soviet got to review each section plan and the secretary of the soviet personally supervised "all current work" of the sections.[47]

Inflation of membership and intermittent upgrading campaigns in the late 1920s did not change the sections in character. Whenever problems were unearthed, one onlooker related, it was "not by the sections but by other organizations 'from the side.'" The sections "concentrate on vapid, applied questions, without tying these to general political issues." A story on the Tram Trust portrayed it as "ignoring its section 100 percent." One official is reported to have explicated, "We don't like having superfluous people at our meetings, since this only produces superfluous talk."[48]

Within the central, policy-setting machinery, the plenum of the Mossovet produced nothing but hot air. Kamenev admitted that its 1,500 members disqualified it for rational debate in 1920; by 1927 it was 50 percent bigger. The soviet's executive committee, with 187 members in 1927 (more than the whole duma before 1917) and 60 candidates, also performed a mostly ceremonial role. The soviet, which met every twelve days in the period 1917–1920, was doing so only once a month by the late 1920s; the ispolkom had gone from one session a week to one every forty to fifty days. The hot spot of decision making was again the presidium, comprising mostly senior municipal bureaucrats. It still sat twice a week and took up three times as many issues per sitting as in the years 1917–1920. At 27 members and 19 candidates in 1927, it also approached the bounds of manageability. From March 1921 to April 1925, and again from April 1927 onward, the soviet had a "small [*malyi*] presidium" consisting of 5 of the members of the presidium, to handle dross.[49]

TERRITORIAL VISTAS

On paper, local institutions in the 1920s diverged greatly in their areal dimension from Russian precedent and from the Western norm. Moscow's district soviets and its jurisdiction over all of its province offered vistas of a rich politics at the subcity and regional levels. Neither possibility panned out.

The embattled raion soviets were squashed further early in NEP. After partitioning the pugnacious Gorodskoi raion among its neighbors in June 1922 (see Map 7), the city dismounted all the raions' education, health, and property departments in August 1923 and pondered doing worse. One raion presidium pounced on the move as antiproletarian, since workers on the outskirts "meet people from their own milieu" in the district councils, and retorted that it was the Mossovet that should be curtailed. Mikhail Boguslavskii riposted for city hall that the raions should be grateful to be exerting "public control over the execution of decisions of the Moscow Soviet."[50] This opinion won out in February 1924, as the remaining raion de-

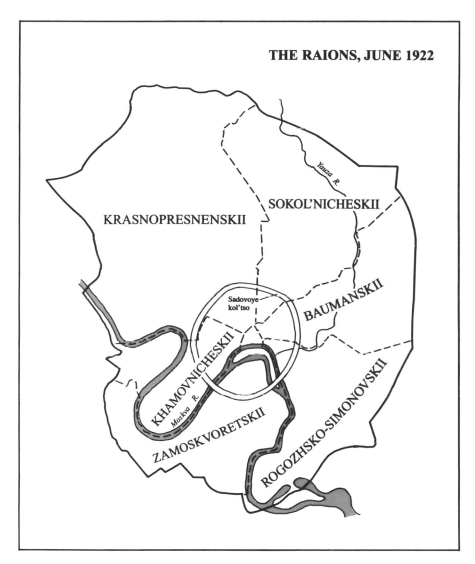

MAP 7

partments were replaced by emissaries *(upolnomochennyye)* of city
agencies.

The city backtracked in October 1925, reactivating most of the
raions' departments and vowing to respect their rights. But it repented
only halfheartedly, as city hall stipulated that it could countermand

any raion decision and that raion officials were in dual subordination to the kindred city department. "We cannot decentralize wholly or allot to the raions tasks of Moscow scale," Deputy Chairman Isidor Ye. Lyubimov of the Mossovet admonished. To prevent "raion parochialism," the city would "delegate to the raions [only] what is mostly local and district in character and not interlaced with city-wide interests."[51]

So the raions made do with a grab bag of jobs, such as outpatient clinics and kindergartens, and with tendering advice on the remainder. They had no budgetary capacity until 1929, merely filing spending estimates for the city's consideration. Further evidence of third string significance would come when, on account of population growth, the number of raions increased from six to ten in December 1930 (Map 8). The principles for boundary drawing were economic and administrative—"a more precise production specialization" of the raions and "a more equal distribution of the party and proletarian strata"—rather than responsive to popular needs or local tradition. The raions did not mount so much as a delaying action, and most of their names commemorated Soviet leaders (Lenin, Stalin, and Dzerzhinskii heading the roll) or doctrinal abstractions.[52]

The participants from below criticized less the overcentralization of decisions than the unjust distribution of their benefits. Representatives of the piebald exterior reaches of all six post-1922 raions expressed incredulity at statistics showing investment being directed away from the city interior and lost no opportunity to lodge the plaint, in the vernacular of class jealousy, that they were being short-changed.

At a plenum of the MK in June 1926, for example, a delegate working in the Cherkizovo area of Sokol'nicheskii raion charged Fedor Lavrov of MKKh with misleading the committee: "No, comrades, the periphery is still being badly developed." Scummy puddles were being used for bathing, drinking water, and laundering, and women were afraid to walk the pitch-black streets at night. An MK member from Blagusha, in Basmannyi raion, described the lack of sewage lines and pavement there, saying all it got from city hall, in the ninth year of Soviet power, was malapropos verbiage about "objective conditions" while repair of war damage and public works went full steam ahead inside the Sadovoye. According to another speaker,

THE RAIONS, DECEMBER 1930

OKTYABR'SKII
KRASNOPRESNENSKII
DZERZHINSKII
SOKOL'NICHESKII
Yauza R.
STALINSKII
Sadovoye kol'tso
BAUMANSKII
FRUNZENSKII
ZAMOSKVORETSKII
Moskva R.
LENINSKII
PROLETARSKII

MAP 8

workers at Danilovka, in south Zamoskvorech'e, were "saying that the center . . . is getting a better deal and are pointing to the absence of drainage and the presence of garbage dumps."[53]

More ill feeling festered outside the city limits. The 1920 merger of the city and guberniya soviets seemed to cast Moscow's influence outward and to allow for unified and equitable governance of the greater metropolitan area. Regional realities, though, jarred with the ideal of unity.

Moscow's hegemony over its hinterland, devised as a thrift measure in 1920, was real enough. The guberniya congress of soviets, held every six months until 1929, was no more a working assembly than the Mossovet. The joint executive boards of city and province, in which Muscovites predominated, took positions for the whole area, and the city's bureaucracy carried them out guberniya-wide.

Absent in these decisions—as gapingly as in the resolutions of the old guberniya zemstvo and city duma—was an ounce of regional consciousness. Line officials of MKKh, ostensibly the communal services directorate of the whole guberniya, "made it a rule to devote all their apparatus's energy, resources, and know-how to work in Moscow and to spare nothing for the uyezds." Outside Moscow, MKKh did not deliver water and other core services or defray local costs, and moreover charged a fee for technical advice. An ineffectual MKKh "out-of-town" *(inogorodnyi)* department was formed only in 1928.[54]

Accordingly, redistribution from the metropolis to smaller and poorer communities in the guberniya was minimal, and steep disparities persevered. In fiscal year 1926/1927 the guberniya authorities spent 84 percent of the monies collected in prosperous Moscow in Moscow itself, leaving only 16 percent for redistribution outside the city. Per capita expenditure in Moscow was still 2.9 times higher than in the uyezd towns and 3.8 times higher than in the rural areas. The insertion of organs for Moscow proper into the guberniya structure in April 1925 further thwarted regional consolidation. These organs encompassed a distinct presidium, subdepartments, and budget estimates. "Although Moscow was not an independent structural entity, special managerial units were extruded for . . . direction of city services."[55]

The paucity of regional thinking reinforced the wonted neglect of the urbanizing zone around Moscow. Ruination of its housing stock went on well after War Communism. In 1922 the soviet of Moscow uyezd proclaimed all of the 25,000 dachas there its property, this when personal houses in Moscow were being privatized. Most were leased to state offices or individuals (rarely the previous owners), under fuzzy terms that set afoot more desertion and plundering by peasants. Moscow took title to about 4,000 dachas in 1924, without speaking to the larger problem. The city's spiraling housing shortage spurred commuting from the dacha belt, which moved 120,000 individuals a day in 1923. Commencement of electrification of the suburban rail lines in 1925 invited the putting up of unserviced dacha and shanty housing near the platforms.

Even the nationalized country seats of Russia's vanished aristocracy deteriorated more quickly than in-town residences. Of 100 gentry estates in Podmoskov'e placed under state protection, only the 20 that were converted into public museums got any maintenance funds. Only 3—Arkhangel'skoye, Ostankino, and Pokrovskoye-Streshnevo—were guarded and kept up by staffs of more than ten persons. The rest were stripped of their valuables and either left bare and unheated or put to odd uses by a hodgepodge of unappreciative occupants. Without personnel, materials, and fuel, "everything inexorably went to pot."[56]

Havens of newly accrued privilege could be found in the guberniya. Party officials, mainly from the MK, built cottages at Serebryannyi bor, a nineteenth-century dacha hamlet west of Khodynka. The most construction was southeast of the city at Vyalki, Malakhovka, Bykovo, Udel'naya, Kratovo, and Il'inskii, along the Moscow-Kazan Railway or its spur line to Gzhel. The party requisitioned older dacha communities for Moscow functionaries and Old Bolsheviks and added several rest homes and children's camps. The Central Committee picked the prettiest, Kratovo—appreciated for its tall pines, sandy soil, and salubrious air—and Vyalki, a bit closer to Moscow. At Malakhovka the summer theater, closed during the Civil War, reopened for some years as a moviehouse.

The well-situated clump of summer houses upstream on the Moskva River between Kuntsevo and Zvenigorod had better growth prospects. At the end of the 1920s a group of academics, cultural figures, and politicians formed one of the first dacha-construction cooperatives in the USSR at Nikolina Gora, a village thirteen kilometers east of Zvenigorod that had attracted summer sojourners from the intelligentsia before 1917. Among the members were Nikolai Semashko, the novelist Aleksei Tolstoy, the former Moscow official and CC secretary Leonid Serebryakov, and Andrei Ya. Vyshinskii, the rector of Moscow State University and the future chief prosecutor in the Moscow show trials. Anastas I. Mikoyan, a member of the Politburo, got possession of a noble's masonry villa and mushroom and vegetable farm at the confluence of the river and Medvenka Creek. His property was known then—and is today—as the local *zamok*, castle.[57]

These clusters, elfin in size, served chiefly for part-time enjoyment. Most citizens roosting over the urban divide year-round were placed in as insufferable a position as ever by the asymmetry between city and province.

At the same 1926 plenum of the MK at which the nether marches of Moscow proper berated city hall's obliviousness, the refrain was taken up by guberniya residents for whom the disheveled periphery of the big city was something to be envied. Workers from Perovo, one *ukom* (uyezd party committee) official imparted, had to walk into Moscow to water their cattle and pay by the bucket at that. Rural roads subsidized before 1917 by crown parks and palaces, patrician estates, and factories were falling into rutted disrepair, and MKKh was demanding cash on the barrel to do a needs appraisal. The townsfolk of Kolomna, at the conflux of the Moskva and Oka Rivers, were quaffing "semiswamp water" and beholding Moscow's prosperity like children at a toy shop window: "At a time when services in Moscow are developing hand over fist and getting stronger, things are the exact opposite in the uyezds . . . Where we are, a properly constituted municipal economy simply does not exist."[58]

Places like Sokol'niki, paced out in the 1600s as the residency of the tsar's falconers, lived the dilemma in a special way. It straggled across Moscow's northeast edge, its older, inner blocks in Moscow's Sokol'nicheskii raion and its raw far parts in Moscow uyezd. Inner Sokol'niki got Moscow's utilities, streetcars, police patrols, and cooperative stores; the log huts on its unlit back streets, tended to by the uyezd soviet and the ukom, went without. Outer Sokol'niki, *Izvestiya* opined in 1928, "is not Moscow and not even an uyezd hamlet, it is a truly God-forsaken place."[59]

In September 1929 Moscow province amalgamated into an elephantine region comprising four former guberniyas (Moscow, Ryazan, Tula, and Tver) and 60 percent of a fifth (Kaluga). The new Moscow oblast, though smaller than its namesake of 1917–1918, ran over 156,000 square kilometers, almost equal to England and Wales, and contained 11 million people. It might have been more oceanic yet, said Konstantin Ukhanov, the head of its first presidium, were it not for the "truculent opposition" of regions further afield.[60]

The RSFSR-wide reform aimed to dilate areal boundaries on an "economic basis," enabling economies of scale and powering industrial growth. One-quarter of the USSR's factory labor and 30 percent of its manufacturing capacity were under the awning of Moscow oblast. The flax-growing east of the region would be a feeder for Moscow's textile manufacturies, pasture and truck farms would supply its food processing, and, of most appeal, the brown coal and iron ore of the Podmoskovnyi basin near Tula and Ryazan would load the blast furnaces of heavy industry. Moscow's was to be, in Ukhanov's words, "the foremost oblast" in the country "in resolving all problems in the building of socialism and in particular in fulfilling the five-year plan."[61]

The Soviet government also revamped the territorial layering beneath in 1929. It broke the uyezds down into rural districts about one-third the size (known as raions, the same label as the urban districts within Moscow), excised the diminutive volosts, and interposed an extra layer, the *okrug* or "circuit," between the oblast and the raions. There were 144 rural raions and 10 okrugs (a Moscow okrug encircling the capital and okrugs around Bezhetsk, Kaluga, Kimry, Kolomna, Orekhovo-Zuyevo, Ryazan, Serpukhov, Tula, and Tver) in Moscow oblast. The party structure, likewise, contained a Moscow *obkom* (oblast committee) at the top, raikoms at the bottom, and okrug committees *(okruzhkomy)* in the middle.

The oblast's institutions nearly copied the guberniya's. This arrangement, plus the enormity of the oblast and the attendant commotion—aggravated when the brand new okrugs were dispersed in July 1930—militated against any fast change in regional relations. It was variously estimated that the oblast government devoted 75 or 80 percent of its attention to Moscow. Nonetheless, some officials feared disruptive effects. The oblast had no more staff than the guberniya to deal with a quadrupled area, and snobbery and aversion to country living goaded those it did have to fight assignment to the raions. As for Moscow, some city-based politicians wondered if its problems might not be slighted as its growth snowballed. Qualms like these were to lead to the city's reacquisition of formal autonomy in 1931.[62]

THE RISE OF THE COMMUNIST PARTY MACHINE

The metamorphosis of the Communist Party, which trebled from 40,400 members and probationary members in Moscow in June 1921 to 135,900 in January 1930, was the biggest innovation in local politics. Moscow was a proving ground for the centralization and bureaucratization of the party. Minorities were subjected to majorities, rambling committees to compact bureaus, generalists to professional *apparatchiki* (party functionaries), nonparty to party agencies—and the whole conglomeration to a single person, Joseph Stalin.

The Tenth Party Congress's embargo on internal party factions drove them underground and, by sanctioning expulsion of the losers, made sectarianism deadlier. Moscow's chief tie to this demimonde was Kamenev, who, it was later alleged, regarded the city as an "independent principality" from which he could venture confidently into political battle.[63] Still the chief executive of Moscow, Kamenev was chosen deputy chairman of Sovnarkom and of the Labor and Defense Council, the governing board for industrial policy, in September 1922, after Lenin's first stroke. He both headed the council and chaired sessions of the party Politburo from Lenin's funeral in 1924 until early 1926.

In April 1921 Kamenev and the Politburo secured the recall of the last of the free-spoken MK secretaries, Varvara Yakovleva, and had Isaak Zelenskii, a savvy organizer and Kamenev's former deputy at city hall, voted in for a second term. Zelenskii's title, and his compeers' across the country, was dignified to "first secretary" in August 1922. He worked hand in glove with Kamenev—who gladly left party organizational questions to him—in the power struggle triggered by Lenin's illness.[64] In his finest hour Zelenskii aided the triumvirate of Kamenev, Zinov'ev of Leningrad, and Stalin in sidelining Leon Trotsky in 1923–1924. He delivered the ballots of almost 80 percent of Moscow's party cells and 92 percent of those cast for the MK in January 1924, declaring that the stability of the party in the aggregate "depends on the word of the Moscow organization."[65] Timofei Sapronov, R. B. Rafail, and other pre-1921 dissenters made a stand, but they gave Zelenskii a run only in Khamovnicheskii raion. The votes of indigent university students gave the one-time oblast secretary, Vladimir Maksimovskii, fleeting control as raikom secretary; Sapronov was deputy head of his organization department. Thirteen percent of Moscow's Communists were ousted in the party's purge of 1923–1924, the most in any large city.

Innokentii Stukov, a Moscow propagandist soon to be blacklisted as pro-Trotsky, made a prescient comment about changes in the party at a closed meeting in December 1923:

> Our party is being turned, and to a significant degree has been turned, from a politically functioning organism into an organ that in many respects resembles a state establishment or commissariat. If you look at the intraparty procedures we encounter in daily activity, you will notice how very developed the apparatus of the party has become. Party functionaries monopolize and perform all intraparty work. The remaining mass [of members] exist, all right, but they are passive and merely carry out the directives of our centers, centerlets, and subcenters. That is to say, we see here exactly the same relations you would find in any commissariat. I believe that I would not err to call Comrade Zelenskii not the secretary but the head of the Moscow organization.[66]

The Soviet political game was being rigged to the advantage of the full-time apparatchik, which Zelenskii impeccably typified. As the top Communist Party bureaucrat in Moscow edged out the chairman of the Mossovet as the predominant leader, MK chambers at 15A Bol'shaya Dmitrovka became the "centerlet" where decisions were handed down.

Zelenskii was prominent enough in his own right to be cross-appointed to the CC Secretariat in April 1923. The unique twofold tasking of the Moscow first secretary would be a convention for most of the next thirty years. The capital also had, as an unwritten right, a voting or a candidate's seat on the Orgburo. Between 1921 and 1925, Moscow officials went from 4 percent to nearly 10 percent of all members of the CC (see Table C-5).

This status bespoke Moscow's multiangled involvement in Communist Party operations. On a first, prosaic level, the Moscow party carried out liaison with the local bodies that sheltered, victualled, and doctored the Soviet leaders. Mosstroi built the infirmary of Lechsanupr, the Sanitation and Health Care Directorate of the Kremlin, at the corner of Vozdvizhenka and ulitsa Granovskogo (Figure 21). Designed by Boris Iofan as a thin insert in front of the Moscow Hunters' Club, the Kremlin Hospital, in casual parlance, was opened in 1926 as one of the first service centers expressly for the Soviet brass. The MK along with the OGPU managed the Gorki sanatorium in Moscow guberniya, where Lenin died, and the city health department supplied it with food. The MK also tended to the Comintern, the Moscow-based league of world revolutionaries, which had a large residence on Manezhnaya ploshchad'. A Comintern Radio Station opened on Voznesenskaya ulitsa (later ulitsa Radio) in 1922; it moved

Figure 21. Kremlin infirmary, ulitsa Vozdvizhenka. (Photograph by author.)

to the main Moscow station in Zamoskvorech'e in 1927 and transmitted to foreign countries from 1929.

Of greater import still was the Moscow organization's second, ideological function. If its management of city elections affected the "transcript" of control locally, its role in the sacralization of Lenin was transcript writing for the Communist system as a whole.[67]

The MK organized the first formal observance of Lenin's birthday, an evening of readings and discussion in April 1920. The Mikhel'son plant, where Lenin was wounded in 1918, became in September 1922 one of the earliest factories to acquire his name (the Vladimir Il'ich Electromechanical Works) and to have a statue of him erected before its gates. His speeches to the Mossovet were major rituals; he gave his last public address there on November 20, 1922. The MK founded the

Lenin Institute, the forerunner of the Institute of Marxism-Leninism, in 1923, handing it over to the CC in 1924. Kamenev served as the first director of the institute and of Lenin's archive as well as editor of his collected works. The Museum of the Revolution, another memorial to Lenin and 1917, opened its first exhibit in the House of Unions in 1923.

On January 27, 1924, Lenin was buried in Red Square, after a scrimmage with Petrograd/Leningrad over the honor. The embalmed corpse, in its glass-lidded, refrigerated sarcopohagus, was laid in a small wood crypt, topped by a statue of a waving Lenin, in front of the plot for fighters for the revolution at the Senatskaya Tower of the Kremlin. Carpenters threw it together in forty-eight hours from drawings by Aleksei Shchusev. A new frame structure, statueless but twice as big, had its festive opening August 1, 1924. Soviet rituals—of individual visits to the darkened crypt, solemn wreath layings on holidays, and the goose-stepping changing of the guard at the OGPU's "Post No. 1" at the tomb—began here. Stalin and two "god builders" from the Moscow revolutionary underground, Vladimir Bonch-Bruyevich and Anatolii Lunacharskii, made the mausoleum the tabernacle of Leniniana.[68]

The cult construction did not stop there. On February 7, 1924, city legislators passed a motion "To leave V. I. Lenin forever on the list of members of the Moscow Soviet" and to reserve deputy's ticket No. 1 for him. The Central Lenin Museum began as display cases in the MK's offices in 1924 and moved into the old building of the Moscow City Duma (since 1918 the home of the Moscow Union of Consumer Cooperatives) in 1936. The Rumyantsev Museum was renamed the Lenin Library in 1924 and made the USSR's state library in 1925.

Yakov Sverdlov had been buried between the Kremlin Wall and Lenin's future resting place in 1919. Starting in 1925 with Mikhail V. Frunze, the late head of the Red Army, and the next year with Dzerzhinskii, the party's greatest heroes were interred in a strip beside Sverdlov; urns holding the ashes of the less worthy were put in the wall. The permanent Lenin Mausoleum, also by Shchusev and built by Mosstroi—a ziggurat in polished, salmon-hued granite, trimmed in labradorite and porphyry—opened in October 1930 (Figure 22). In 1930–1931, to accommodate the altered semiotics of Red Square, its streetcar tracks were removed, cobblestones thick enough to take the

Figure 22. Lenin Mausoleum, lineup on anniversary of Lenin's death, 1931. (The Bettmann Archive.)

tracks of parading tanks and tractors were laid, concrete reviewing stands for 10,000 official guests were installed on either side of the tomb, and Martos's Minin/Pozharskii was moved toward St. Basil's.

The crucial overlap between Moscow and the center occurred in a third area, the positioning of personnel. As Communists reappeared from the army, the Moscow Committee in 1921 drew up a comprehensive register *(uchet)* of party members occupying responsible positions or qualified to do so. In 1922 and 1923 the emphasis shifted to cumulating for each party organ a list—a "nomenklatura"—of the jobs for which it was henceforth obligatory that the organ pass a minute of confirmation of any decision to hire or fire.[69]

Nomenklatura, as both the entire wickerwork of personnel controls and the people tangled up in it came to be abbreviated, regularized and amplified the jury-rigged mobilization and checking practices of the War Communism years. The nomenklatura of the Moscow Committee—in reality, of its bureau and secretariat—comprised 2,531 positions in the city and guberniya in March 1925. For each job candidate, party officials compiled an *ob"ektivka,* a confidential summary of family and educational background, career path, and political record. The 1925 nomenklatura was by eyeball estimate ten to fifteen times the set of posts being screened by the MK at the end of 1920—a figure that excludes the hundreds of seats on collegial bodies, mostly party, trade union, and Komsomol committees, passed "by the list" *(po spisku).*[70]

There was but a porous membrane between Moscow and central personnel systems at the incipient stages of nomenklatura, as the MK was empowered to clear many appointments in central bureaus. Only in mid-1922 did the CC assert itself. A parley in October 1923 laid down boundaries, yet as late as 1926 there was "inadequate delimitation of work." Adjustments took months more to thrash out and left a certain number of local positions requiring joint attestation by the MK and CC.[71]

Nomenklatura responsibility aside, Moscow positions often turned out to be stepping stones into major party or state offices, this at a time when dozens of Muscovites relocated earlier were still in place. In September 1921, for instance, the MK's second-ranking secretary, Isaak Min'kov, was rushed to Samara as guberniya first secretary, after dissension among Communists there; in October 1924 Secretary Nikolai K. Antipov became head of the CC's Organization and Assignments Department (personnel division); Vil'gelm G. Knorin, after a year as chief of the MK's Agitation and Propaganda Department, took over the analogous division of the Central Committee in March 1926. The MK and CC also dispatched Muscovites to the center and provinces in lots, far more than any other committee.[72]

Conversely (see Table C-2), numerous outsiders leavened Moscow's municipal and, more often, its party bureaucracy. As a rule, these were itinerants from the back country, but there were transfers from the center, too. Vasilii M. Mikhailov, a Central Committee secretary and a member of the Orgburo for the preceding year, was imported into the Moscow apparatus in March 1922, serving in various capacities until 1929. All five of the Moscow first secretaries from April 1921 to 1930—Zelenskii, Uglanov, Molotov, Bauman, and Kaganovich—had served in a senior position on the outside.[73] Underneath this superstratum, the CC Secretariat, establishing a counterflow to the intake of Muscovites, treated the MK as an employment service for provincial Communists, many of them penniless and homeless, who knocked on its door looking for work.

The personnel function gave the local party bureaus and, more explicitly, their secretaries the same hatchet Stalin wielded at the party's apex: power over the lesser office holders who stacked the very assemblies that put *them* in office. Not unlike the sachem of Tammany Hall, the Soviet party boss fixed his own election by distributing jobs in the public sector as spoils, liable to check only by the boss of bosses in the Kremlin. On the MK, party functionaries—administrative subordinates of the first secretary—formed a plurality from the beginning and a majority from 1925 to 1929. On the MK bureau, they were constantly in the majority (see Tables C-2 and C-3). The five-person MK secretariat had places for the head of the local trade unions and, from November 1928, for Ukhanov as chairman of the Mossovet, but again party secretaries were ascendant.

Patronage and top-down controls made a burlesque out of the party's democratic forms, much as the party had earlier subverted public elections. In 1921 a delegate to a Moscow conference already had "the impression that the MK does not quite exist" and that everything was up to its "powerful, intensely busy bureau." Beginning in 1922 election of the MK was reduced to checking off aye or nay for the nominees of the first secretary; the record does not indicate any being rejected, although smatterings of negative votes were lodged. Sapronov lamented that Lenin's vaunted "democratic centralism" had come down to "bureaucratic centralism," in which the triumphant apparatus "is beginning to stifle every hint of an idea and to throw objectionable people out."[74]

THE TSARDOM OF COMRADE STALIN

The quiet removal of Isaak Zelenskii in October 1924 was Stalin's opening gambit against Kamenev and his coalition partners. It brought to the fore the first party apparatchik to be undisputed chieftain of the Moscow organization. Nikolai Uglanov was in Stalin's good books for his orneriness and his dislike of the "discussion mentality" of the Moscow party. He won his party spurs in Petrograd, where he worked as provincial secretary from January 1921 to January 1922. After feuding with Zinov'ev, he was posted as party secretary in Nizhnii Novgorod. He was named Zelenskii's second secretary in August 1924; within two months, he had stolen both Zelenskii's Moscow position and his perch in the CC Secretariat, and in January 1926 he was promoted to candidate member of the Politburo.

Kamenev and Zinov'ev went along with the choice of Uglanov in the hope they could use him against Stalin. They soon rued it, for he turned on them, decimated their forces on the MK, and, after months of character assassination, pushed Kamenev out of the Moscow presidium in May 1926. When Kamenev and Zinov'ev formed an anti-Stalin troika with Trotsky, Uglanov savagely beat back their supporters. Kamenev, demoted to candidate member of the Politburo in January 1926, lost that rank in October 1926 and his seat on the Central Committee in November 1927.[75]

Uglanov nimbly hearkened to the legendary rivalry with Leningrad, the anti-machine forces' last redoubt. Leningraders in turn inveighed against "the tsardom of Comrade Uglanov" and Uglanov's "Moscow patriotism"and victimization of the ex-capital. Uglanov had gotten rid of "dozens and maybe hundreds" of officials, one Leningrader said, "so as to build a tsardom of indifference and calm in Moscow." Stalinists stuck up for Uglanov and his apparat, "a model of Leninist unity . . . the best in our party."[76]

The capsizing of Uglanov's career in 1928 clarified what Leninist unity connoted. Policy implications will be considered below, but the affair subsumed power as much as principle. While complimentary of Stalin, Uglanov comported himself as beholden to no one. He opposed any leader marking out "spheres of influence" or "turning our party's mightiest organization into a weapon of his personal politics"—the very thing Stalin had set out to do.[77]

Uglanov took concrete steps to buck up his position, ordering Muscovites to "stop bypassing the MK and petitioning the central organs" on disputed matters and enunciating a desire to groom cadres locally, "and for the time being to close the door to outsiders." "Let us not be accused of Moscow local patriotism, because we know our own people better, we can see what they are good for. I think we have to carry things to an extreme in this regard."[78] One text warrants that Uglanov meant "to concentrate in the MK the selection of cadres for all central economic, state, and party organs."[79] If at all true, Stalin's ire would have been assured.

Relations went from bad to worse in 1928. A meeting of Uglanov and Second Secretary Vasilii A. Kotov (a candidate member of the CC Orgburo) with Stalin in March did not clear the air. That summer surrogates of Uglanov and Stalin took potshots at one another in the press. Stalin's henchman in the CC Secretariat, Vyacheslav M. Molotov, courted accomplices in the local apparatus, notably Vladimir I. Polonskii, the head of the MK's Organization and Assignments Department. Others cut the legs out from under Uglanov in the raikoms, where Molotov and the Secretariat kept him from dismissing critics. On October 16, 1928, the CC and MK secretariats decreed the removal from the Moscow apparatus of Uglanov's most unquailingly anti-Stalin raikom secretary, Martem'yan N. Ryutin of Krasnopresnenskii district.[80]

The Politburo released a statement on "waverings" in the Moscow party on October 18, and events moved briskly to a finale. On October 19 Stalin vented his spleen at Uglanov at a special MK plenum packed with outsiders, stopping short of demanding his head. The committee censured Uglanov and drummed out his chief propagandist, Nikolai N. Mandel'shtam, and another loyal raikom secretary, Mikhail A. Pen'kov. On November 27 it accepted the resignations of Uglanov, Kotov, and the two raikom secretaries left on the bureau, Yevgenii F. Kulikov and Vladimir A. Yakovlev. Vasilii Mikhailov, the former MK and CC secretary, admitted to errors and was relieved five months later as head of the Moscow trade unions. Chairman Ukhanov of the Mossovet remained under a cloud from 1928 on, although not immediately purged.[81] Uglanov, downgraded to labor commissar in the USSR Sovnarkom, lost his positions on the party Politburo, Orgburo, and Secretariat April 29, 1929; he never again held a major job after July 1930.

The investiture of Molotov, a client rather than an ally of Stalin, as first secretary underlined that the city's party machine definitely belonged to the tsardom of Comrade Stalin. Uglanov's swan song to the MK implied as much, admitting that he had disagreed with Stalin on particulars but denying that the Moscow apparatus had or licitly could have a "special line." Ryutin of Krasnopresnenskii raion agreed that any exclusivity *(zamknutost')* or group stirrings *(gruppirovka)* in the capital city were harmful.[82]

THE LOCAL PARTOCRACY

Even as these theatrics went on at center stage, behind the scenes quotidian party activity gravitated toward a prefectoral or gubernatorial role keyed to areal coordination, not politicking. A number of the previous constraints on partocracy fast lost their applicability. The Communist fraction in the city soviet, a check on the party apparatus until 1921, lacked a meaningful voice as the party sidled, in Stukov's words, toward "the same relations you would find in any commissariat." Its meetings, held an hour or two before the soviet's, were costume rehearsals for the plenary spectacle. The raions of Moscow had been politically castrated, and ideological factions shriveled into little platoons of critics.

Also changed was the doctrinal claim, already a half-fiction, that sovereign power in the "Soviet" regime resided with the soviets and their executives, and that the party would act "through the soviets," high and low. The amended canon spelled out, in Zelenskii's words, that party committees and bureaus were "not to restrict the carrying out of their line to the transmission of directives to the soviets." No, they should put out grappling irons to anyone who could deliver results: individual officials, whole administrative divisions, mass organizations. Karl Ya. Bauman, head of the MK's Organization and Assignments Department, expostulated in 1925 that the party organs "are being turned more and more into supreme authorities [*vysshiye rukovodyashchiye organy*] which on basic matters . . . give instructions to all organizations, to 'officers of all branches of arms.'"[83]

The colonels and captains in this pliant troop got not only their marching orders but also their epaulettes from the party's field staff. As an MK resolution brusquely worded it, "The circle [of offices under local party control] is to encompass the basic command positions in all areas of organization. Initiative in selecting and appointing to them must be concentrated in the MK, the raikoms, and the ukoms."[84]

Fifty-eight of the "command positions" in the MK's primary nomenklatura in March 1925 were in the party's own administrative apparatus, with 75 more approved "by the list" and 27 posts (plus

75 by list) in the Komsomol apparatus. The 498 offices in the trade unions and 170 in the Moscow Union of Consumer Cooperatives (MSPO) brought the subtotal in mass organizations to 753 positions (29.8 percent of the total).[85]

In local government command points had previously been restricted to the Mossovet's presidium and ispolkom. After 1920 the bureau and secretariat of the MK took to monitoring Moscow department and subdepartment heads and scores of positions at the district level, by 1923 down to chief of department of a raion or uyezd ispolkom. "In the soviet line" were 913 (36.1 percent) of the slots in the MK's 1925 nomenklatura. The OGPU, nonpolitical police ("militia"), courts, and maybe higher education fell under this rubric, along with local executive panels and municipal bureaucrats subordinate to them.[86]

The balance of 865 nomenklatura entries (34.2 percent) consisted of economic jobs, which had hitherto been outside the party's ken. Of these, 670 were in manufacturing, transport, and building firms responsible to central offices or to local authority, chiefly the Moscow Guberniya Sovnarkhoz, and 195 were in banks and the guberniya insurance board. We know from archived protocols that the industrialists included not only trust and factory managers but in dozens of cases their deputies, too.[87]

The breadth of nomenklatura indicated a basal reality of Moscow politics by the halfway mark of the 1920s: the organs of the Communist Party were in the saddle. With the vanquishing of Kamenev, all could see the first secretary's precedence over the chairman of the soviet. The meeting of the MK bureau was the event of events in any week's political calendar, waited on by representatives of other organizations as the agenda required. In membership the bureau was as much a club of salaried party administrators as the presidium of the soviet was of municipal bureaucrats. On the MK, which seated a range of organizational leaders, city civil servants had been more than one-fifth of the members in 1920, the same ratio as the party apparatchiks; by 1927 their share was all of 2.3 percent (see Tables B-2 and B-3 in Appendix B).

The party also solidified its lock on sensitive information. As of February 1925, protocols of the MK bureau bore the stamp *Sekretno*, "Secret," and circulated in numbered copies to designated users only.

Tipping off this attitude, the MK in November 1926 renamed its General Department, the processor of intraparty information, as its Secret Department. Regulations governing document use multiplied. One of the most telling restrictions was on direct citation of any edict of a party organ in the corresponding governmental decision: "References in documents of the soviets to resolutions of the plenum, bureau, or secretariat of the MK are unconditionally prohibited."[88]

The party's bear hug on information, personnel, and, for that matter, local elections did not at first entail exertion of rights over every last policy decision. But before long party interference was rife.

Minutes of the bureau of the MK show it to be on the lookout from the start for issues bearing on support for the regime. Recurring examples included municipal rents and the price of rye bread, for which sharp increases were vetoed. On the housing problem, it several times either entreated central authorities (the Politburo, trade unions, Commissariat of Finance) on its own, going after funding for Moscow construction, or it enjoined the city presidium to do so with its blessing. The bureau ruled for the first time on local revenues in 1922, when it told city collectors to enumerate tax delinquents. Beginning in 1923 it signed off on the city's yearly budget, going over the presidium's draft motion before it was sent to the floor of the Mossovet. In 1924 it bade the presidium to submit an annual "plan of work" for the ispolkom and the bureaucracy. By the next year it was taking receipt of quarterly work plans from the sections of the city and raion soviets, twice yearly blurbs on budget fulfillment, and periodic bulletins from the presidium and municipal departments.

As of the mid-1920s, additionally, one sees the bureau dipping a toe in the minutiae of urban administration. So it was with its vote in January 1925 to "allow the [Communist] fraction of the Moscow Soviet" to go along with purchase of 100 European-made diesel buses for scarce foreign currency. After further cogitation, it told the soviet to order 100 more buses and 100 dump trucks from domestic suppliers.[89]

Whereas government officials would have thought this dictum unusual in 1925, at the finish of NEP it did not appear out of the ordinary. "We are now witnessing situations," Second Secretary Fedor G. Leonov of the obkom told a Kremlin conference in January 1930, "where the head of a [municipal] department does not consider a decision of the presidium of the Moscow Soviet to be binding until the [obkom] bureau has made a decision on the same question. This existed before, but not in so pronounced a form." He went on to report a decision overload not restricted to municipal issues: "We occupy ourselves with every possible thing and do not have the time to pose . . . fundamental questions about leadership and the direction of events."[90]

As noted above, the party organs were the ultimate guardians on local soil of the undemocratic setup at the nucleus of Soviet government. The MK's control perspective impelled it to scrutinize every proposal after 1921 to establish a new organization or publication in Moscow and region. It also put the local party at the forefront of consecutive ideological campaigns. In 1922–1923, for instance, the MK bureau went on the warpath against the brewing and sale of bootleg alcohol, tugging the mass media, magistrates, and police into the expedition. In 1925 it appointed a commission to filter admissions into Moscow postsecondary education, where it had been certifying appointments of deans since 1924, and to give preference to working youth and nominees of official organizations.[91]

Rozaliya Zemlyachka, the party leader in Zamoskvorech'e and a former secretary of the MK, called attention to a different line of advance in a prophetic speech in 1922. She maintained that the MK was ideally situated to act as a "regulating organ" in local production and distribution, and that it was already "calming down . . . conflicts" in the mixed NEP economy.[92] From this arbiter's role the MK embarked on a multifaceted economic prefectoralism that ripened under central planning.

Thus the conclusion of sectoral wage agreements, with limited increases for different industries, preoccupied the party in the 1920s. When cost cutting and regrouping of enterprises led to unemployment, the MK, wary of social tensions, told directors to keep on some redundant workers. Uglanov in 1925–1926 sponsored an inquiry into goldbricking and corruption in the State Aviation Trust; the director of Moscow's main aircraft plant, the Duks Works, was dismissed and the trust was prevailed upon to merge two engine workshops (Motor and Ikar) into an Aviation Motor Works in Baumanskii raion.

Examination of sore spots induced not only meddling but also some advocacy of local economic interests. In 1921–1922, for example, the MK bureau pestered VSNKh (the Supreme Economic Council) and the Politburo to get work on regional power stations at Shatura and Kashira finished, so that the electricity would speed recovery in Moscow. In 1923 it petitioned the Politburo to facilitate shipment of wool and cotton to the area's spinning mills, stating textile production had "as much political significance for Moscow and the guberniya as food provisioning did . . . in 1918–1920." In 1924 Zelenskii's bureau prayed the Central Committee, with no success, to add a Moscow representative to the board of VSNKh; in 1926 Uglanov's bureau repeated the demand for Gosplan (the State Planning Committee) of the RSFSR.[93]

It should be stressed that the prefectoral role remained incompletely scripted. The NEP-era party organs were after-the-fact fixers, without the sense of preemptive mission that would be ingrained later. For every story about their involvement, there are several about affairs proceeding without them.

The party was also malequipped for prefectoralism in terms of human clay and structure. Biographies collected for holders of high party posts in Moscow from 1921 to 1930 show them to have been younger than their municipal cousins, more inadequately schooled and more weakly prepared for making technical decisions, and more often than not with a history in the provincial or central bureaucracy, where they received no introduction to Moscow issues (see Tables C-1 and C-2).

Fuller data for the year 1925 back up these impressions, for the education variable, in any case. Not one of the 25 secretaries of the MK, raikoms, and ukoms in 1925 held a postsecondary diploma, and only 16 percent had graduated from secondary school; for 425 lower-ranking apparatchiks, the benchmarks were 7.1 and 41.6 percent. Both groups thus compared badly with ranking municipal officials who were Communists (14.9 percent of whom, as was noted, had a higher education in 1925) and miserably with municipal non-Communists (54.5 percent higher education). Seventy-six percent of the senior party officials were of worker or peasant descent, and 44.2 percent of the junior officials.[94]

Unlike their friends in the city soviet, the partocrats could not tap a substratum of specialists from the old regime. In fact, there were precious few administrative assets of any kind in their satchels. The "responsible workers" of all territorial committees in Moscow guberniya, from secretaries to instructors, amounted to 450 in November 1925. Rather than going up with the tempo of work, this number fell to 414 in 1926 and 339 in October 1927. Professional staff of the MK itself in autumn 1928, counting the 2 secretaries and 6 department heads, numbered 60 to 65; almost half toiled on cadres selection, most of the rest on propaganda and women's issues. The raions of Moscow had party staffs of 5 each.[95]

Zelenskii and Uglanov from 1924 to 1928 tried to stretch these sparse resources through ancillary forms, variously called commissions, councils, and colloquiums (soveshchaniya) of the MK. The interesting thing about these two dozen bodies was their targeting on very particular action areas, the inverse of the broadly functionalist departments thus far prevalent in the full-time apparatus. One forum addressed industry, a second cooperatives, a third the soviets, and so forth. They threw together MK functionaries (one of whom was chairman) and up to several hundred operators from the policy locale.

The commissions were harbingers of the branch departments that came into their own in the 1930s. In their day, though, they made little observable difference. All but three of them were attached to the MK Organization and Assignments Department and dealt exclusively with personnel matters, and that, evidently, in an advisory mode only. They had no existence aside from their occasional meetings and lacked implementing staff or budget.[96]

The Moscow Committee began to disband its ancillary commissions before Uglanov's fall, and all were gone by the end of 1928. The MK established a Department for Work in the Countryside in April 1928, a ground-breaking effort to implant the branch-specific approach within the apparatus itself. It did survive Uglanov, but it had negligible resources (five employees only) and acted essentially as a propaganda shop. At no time was there a comparable action unit for industry, municipal government, or any other specified realm. It would be a while yet before Moscow's party officials were organized so as to maximize their leverage over the minidramas of local administration.[97]

Feeling the Approach of Socialism

Moscow and the Soviet Union were changed forever by the transcending, state-promoted revolution that rang down the curtain on the New

Economic Policy. Arguably, this upheaval was of the same order of importance as 1917.

Once it met its first posited goal of recuperation, NEP got caught between two hostile bodies of opinion. One, to the right of center, stressed preservation of the market, while making concessions to the principle of greater regulation that underlay the First Five-Year Plan, adopted in December 1927. On the left, a second group chafed at NEP's lassitude and material shortcomings—loud in the litany of which were urban afflictions—and appealed to the visionary vanguardism in the Bolsheviks' original worldview. Stalin broke the standoff by abjuring moderation for unalloyed radicalism and gagging the last self-directing voices in the party.

Moscow, with its leadership revealed as the bulwark of the pro-NEP camp, experienced the most vicious political swordplay. The three full members of the Politburo around whom coalesced the Right Opposition, as Stalin soon dubbed it, all had Moscow pasts: Nikolai Bukharin, the erstwhile leftist, now the cheerleader for NEP; Aleksei Rykov, the chairman of the sovnarkoms of the USSR and RSFSR; and Mikhail P. Tomskii, the head of the Soviet trade unions. Uglanov, whom Stalin saw as "to the right of Bukharin," was the senior apparatchik lined up behind them, and the Moscow organization was the only big local branch of the party to side with Bukharin and the rest.[98] After caving in to Stalin's organizational power in 1928, Uglanov held fast to his convictions; Ryutin of Krasnopresnenskii raion defiantly circulated an anti-Stalin "platform" as late as 1932.[99]

The perceived iniquities of NEP did not go unnoticed in the capital, and were often set down to Uglanov personally. But rightism was unusually strong here, which made good sociological sense. The Moscow organization, by Uglanov's testimony, was "surrounded more than any other . . . by the negative manifestations of NEP."[100] NEP's overtures to entrepreneurs struck a chord in Russia's "Big Village" and trade entrepôt. Discord with the peasantry over procurement and prices, which set off Stalin's lunge to the left, was much less noticeable in the area than in the southern granary provinces. Light industry, particularly textiles, still bolstered economically the city and guberniya. Any acceleration geared exclusively to heavy industry, as Stalin was interpreting the five-year plan, threatened dislocation.

This is not to say that the Uglanov group disdained heavy industry. In 1927–1928 it persuaded VSNKh to expand chemical production in the Moscow region, picking as a first project a combine for superphosphates, chlorides, and artificial fibers at Bobriki. In August 1927 the MK bureau asked the Politburo to transfer the State Auto Trust (Avtotrest) whole hog to the Moscow Guberniya Sovnarkhoz and accepted municipal responsibility for enlargement of the AMO Auto Works. Two months later it proposed that a second auto plant be built in Moscow, to specialize in passenger cars and pickup trucks, and it subsequently requested hard currency to purchase equipment.[101]

The Uglanovites' antipathy was not to heavy industry but to exorbitant capitalization that would pauperize consumers and upset the social underpinnings of NEP. This was why Uglanov denounced party secretaries who witlessly sought metal-eating projects for their provinces. For the same reason, he tolerated private landholding and the relatively well-to-do farmer (kulak) and outspokenly criticized the "War Communism methods" of grain collection revived in 1928. For Moscow's cloth mills, whose output supported the standard of living and gave the towns something to swap for peasant produce, Uglanov lobbied so tirelessly that he gave Stalin a pretext to lampoon him as a perpetuator of Calico Moscow. "As secretary of the Moscow organization, in which the textile industry occupies the primary position," Uglanov told the climactic MK plenum of October 1928, "it is self-evident that I would very often have had . . . to argue, apply pressure, and make a fuss so that we would be given more money."[102]

SAYING IT BETTER THAN THE CENTRAL COMMITTEE

Against these heresies, the hard-boiled Molotov cracked the now customary Stalinist bullwhips: extraction of breast-beating apologies and the rousting of Uglanov's closest adherents. In unison with an all-party purge, 6.9 percent of the Communist ranks were expelled. Stalin felt confident enough to return Molotov to the Kremlin in April 1929; he replaced Rykov as head of the USSR government in December 1930. Molotov transferred the MK reins and Uglanov's former seats on the CC Secretariat and Orgburo to his second secretary and protégé, Karl Bauman, a Moscow Communist of Latvian origin. Bauman's 1913 papers from the Kiev Commercial Institute made him one of the best-educated Soviet leaders of the day, yet he was an unflagging leftist and a hater of the bourgeois values he imbibed in his youth.[103]

Bauman trained his guns on the lower decks of the bureaucracy, where purging commissions were ordered to pass on political credentials and biographies. Polonskii, one of Uglanov's accusers and now second secretary to Bauman, held that this purge, also national in scope, had to slash deepest in Moscow because "every sabotaging organization . . . open and concealed, has had its center" there. Of 83,000 soviet administrators screened in the oblast by mid-1930, 7.5 percent were furloughed as "alien, feckless, and harmful."[104]

The MK also choked off dissent in scientific circles, where Bukharin's pro-NEP thought had wide currency. No stone was left unturned in the Industrial Academy (the new incubator of economic executives), the Timiryazev Agricultural Academy, and the Communist Academy and the Institute of Red Professors, the two centers for social research. A 1929 enrollee at the Industrial Academy, Nikita S. Khrushchev, was one of the students who tangled with a rearguard among the faculty, bent, he alleged, on electing Uglanov and Rykov as delegates to the Baumanskii raion party conference. The thirty-five-year-old Khrushchev was rewarded with a ticket to the conference, his first foray into Moscow politics.[105]

How astounding, then, to see Bauman follow Uglanov into perdition in less than a year. No matter that he erred in the opposite direction—here was further testimony of the salience and volatility of Moscow politics. Bauman stumbled over his special interest, agrarian policy. Appointed chairman of a Politburo commission on the kulaks in the summer of 1929, he at first showed signs of moderation but soon succumbed to bullishness about "uprooting capitalism in the village"and substituting the collective farm (kolkhoz) for peasant smallholds. To the party's proposal in November 1929 to raise the "Twenty-five Thousanders," shock troops of collectivization, his machine responded with 6,600 of the 25,000 volunteers. The next month Moscow took shefstvo (wardship) over farms in the Volga, Central Asia, and other areas.[106]

Locally, Bauman spoke as early as August 1929 of a doomsday showdown with the kulaks and indeed of "dekulakization" and "liquidation of the kulaks as a class." The oblast's first party conference voted in September to collectivize 25 percent of 1.4 million farm households within five years; the obkom bureau in December aimed at 40 to 50 percent by the end of 1930; throwing caution to the winds, Bauman in January 1930 held out for full *(sploshnaya)* collectivization by spring. "With every step," one of his okrug secretaries, Anna S. Kalygina of Tver, exclaimed to the obkom in January, "we can feel the approach of socialism."[107]

Hundreds of thousands of peasants were bludgeoned and cajoled into hurriedly concocted collectives. Whereas only 0.5 percent of households in Moscow oblast had joined kolkhozes by August 1, 1929, and 3.2 percent had by October 1 (the oblast then ranked eighteenth in the USSR), 36.5 percent had by February 1, 1930, and 73 percent had (ranking the oblast sixth in the country) by March 1. Not all went meekly. The oblast party conference in September 1929 heard of "medieval forms" of protest, among them arson and the murder of abettors of the kolkhozes, one of them by crucifixion. Up to January 1930, Bauman said, there had been 603 "counterrevolutionary" crimes linked to collectivization; 19 officials had been killed, 82 wounded, and 112 beaten up, and 76 culprits had gone before firing squads. A party history counts more than 200 "anti-Soviet groups" in the oblast, and 301 "terrorist acts" between January and May 1930.[108]

One finds nothing here of the jackboot tactics of the collectivizers. A staff report to the obkom in January 1930 estimated "up to 75,000" kulak households in Moscow oblast. All were to be dekulakized, that is, removed from their farms to "uncultivated, undesirable land (hummocks, sand, etc.)," with "a minimum of tools" but no confiscation of clothing, crockery, and family wares ("as is taking place in certain cases"). Any who resisted were "subject at once to arrest, trial, and strict punishment" by exile or internment in a penal camp. Kulaks indulging in "sabotage," damage of farm property, or slaughter of livestock were "to be put down by all necessary means," including execution.[109]

Resistance to expropriation mounted so alarmingly across the country that the Soviet leadership pulled in its horns. The enthusiast Bauman, close at hand, was a tailor-made scapegoat. In *Pravda* on March 2, 1930, Stalin's article "Dizziness with Success" ascribed "excesses" to local reprobates who sounded mightily like the Moscow first secretary. At an obkom plenum in late March, Bauman, without owning up to basic error, revealed that Moscow's figures on collectivization "were in a number of cases unreal, as they counted kolkhozes that essentially did not exist."[110] Peasants streamed out of the sham collectives, only 7.3 percent of oblast households remaining in them by the end of April.

On April 22 Bauman was deposed and replaced by Lazar M. Kaganovich—a "200 percent Stalinist," in Molotov's words, so devoted "that when he was around you wouldn't dare say anything bad about Stalin." Stalin gave him the moniker "Iron Lazar."[111]

Born into a poor Ukrainian Jewish family in 1893, a bootmaker as a youth, and a party member since 1911, Kaganovich had been leagued with Stalin since participating in the Sovietization of Turkestan in 1920–1921, when Stalin was Lenin's commissar of nationalities. Once Stalin became general secretary in 1922, Kaganovich was made chief of the party's cadres section; in 1924 he chaired the caucus of CC department heads. He went on to be Central Committee secretary in 1924–1925, Ukrainian first secretary for three years, and, upon reentering the CC Secretariat in July 1928, the scourge of rightists in the party and trade unions. "If the Central Committee put an axe in his hands," his protégé, Khrushchev, wrote of him, "he would chop up a storm; unfortunately he often chopped down the healthy trees along with the rotten ones. But the chips really flew—you couldn't take that away from him." Ax in hand, Kaganovich was just the man to show Moscow into the era of high Stalinism.[112]

Addressing the next oblast party conference, Fedor Leonov—who had supplanted Ryutin in Krasnopresnenskii raion in 1928 and Polonskii as MK second secretary in 1929, and was soon to be downed himself—held that Bauman on the left had elucidated as well as Uglanov on the right that "any attempt to set the Moscow organization apart from the CC inevitably leads it . . . to a separate line." Paradoxically, "the Moscow organization, located on the same territory as the CC, has turned out to be less connected with it than a whole lot of other party committees a good distance from Moscow." "Any attempt" by Moscow, he went on, "to say 'more' than the CC or to say it 'better' can only end in the kind of error that has political connotations in principle and consequences in practice."[113]

METAL MOSCOW

The revolution from above reasserted the ethos of state allocation and class warfare over the mixed economy and interclass collaboration enshrined in NEP. "We must not forget," Bauman said in a distillation of the combat-centered mindset of the leadership, "that our Soviet apparatus is an organ of dictatorship, an organ of compulsion . . . surrounded by an ample quantity of enemies."[114]

In Moscow the first enemies to be bashed were the Nepmen. Harassment of shopkeepers and traders in 1926 and 1927 had been made light of, and it may be that Uglanov saw this attitude as either a passing phase or an innocuous compromise with the left. Instead, it presaged the evisceration of private commerce.

Restrictive bylaws, confiscatory taxation, and police raids closed down shops first, then cabmen and curbside peddlers, and finally Sukharevskii, Okhotnyi ryad, and most of the city's markets. Capitalists' fraction of retail trade pined from 36 percent in fiscal year 1925/1926 to 17 percent in 1927/1928 and 3 percent in 1930/1931, when only 900 private trading units in Moscow remained (versus 5,355 three years before). For "distorting the class line" on taxation by insufficiently mauling small entrepreneurs, the head and deputy head of the Moscow Finance Department were fired and purged from the party. At his last oblast party plenum, Bauman owned up to having "mechanically applied the methods of dekulakization" to the Nepmen; his policy, one member of the obkom bureau said, "to all intents and purposes put the city bourgeoisie outside the law."[115]

As farm deliveries fell and private marketing dried up, the rationing of bread was reintroduced in Moscow in February 1929, of sugar in March, and of meat and dairy products in September. In December 1929 bakeries began padding out bread dough with a potato admixture. The "closed distributors" of War Communism were reestablished in factories and offices in September 1930. City partocrats, who had rarely concerned themselves with food supply, now kept a close eye on rationing, clearing changes with the Politburo and commissioning reports on public morale from the OGPU. In March 1929 the MK bureau confirmed a classified "provisioning plan" for the city and guberniya; in October it passed an edict on potato supply, specifying to the last kilogram targets and time charts for procurement, storage, and sale.[116]

The hard line found vent in housing politics. The murder of an Old Bolshevik, Karavayev, by the son of his former landlord served as the pretext for advent of "class struggle on the housing front" days after Uglanov's ouster. Militants demanded the removal of ex-land-lords, profiteers, and other "nonlaboring elements" who were often, it was said, slyly concealing their identities. In January 1929 MKKh forbade private building of housing in all but two slivers of northern Moscow, Ostankino and Mikhalkovskaya ulitsa. Nikolai F. Popov, the chief of Moscow's Real Estate Directorate (the housing office), related to the MK bureau in May that expulsions from municipal housing were occurring apace and also that the city had adopted "a policy of deporting malicious, anti-Soviet types from Moscow . . . [using] the organs of the OGPU and the guberniya procurator." Raion-level commissions evicted something like 6,000 persons from 33,000 square meters of housing by year's end. There were calls in early 1930 for obtrusion of all 180,000 Moscow *lishentsy,* legally disfranchised individuals.[117]

State trade, ration books, and demonization of the bourgeoisie harked back to War Communism. Like collectivization, an act of dispossession vastly more draconian than grain requisitioning, other aspects of the Stalin revolution were new, in degree if not kind. State industry went into overdrive. To attain high rates of growth, categori-cal priority went to metal working, civilian and military machine building, and other branches of heavy industry underrepresented in and around Moscow. Calico Moscow, a post-Uglanov slogan bel-lowed, was being reborn as "Metal Moscow."

The city sported flagships for whole new branches of industry such as the First State Ballbearing Works, Frezer (metal-cutting machines), and Kalibr (measuring instruments). Extension and retooling made standard bearers out of older plants like AMO (trucks), Elektrozavod (the Moscow Electrical Works) and the Dinamo (Dynamo) Works (producers of motors, magnetos, and transformers), and Krasnyi proletarii (the Red Proletarian Works, formerly the Bromley factory, producing machine tools). The Bauman Higher Technical College on the Yauza, the USSR's top engineering school—the former Imperial Technical College named in 1930 after Nikolai Bauman, a revolution-ary who died in 1905, not after Karl Bauman—poured out engineers for Moscow and Soviet industry. Several of its faculties split off in

1930 as independent schools, such as the Moscow Aviation Institute and the Moscow Power Institute; soon after, they became national leaders in their areas.

In the defense sector Moscow benefited from the expansion in weapons-related science and from the military cooperation pact with Weimar Germany. At Podlipki, a village north of the city, several thousand German workers built a large plant for artillery pieces, Works No. 8, between 1929 and 1932.[118] Moscow industry specialized in aviation, which Stalin saw as essential to victory in a European war. Duks, Russia's original airframe factory, first concentrated on light reconnaissance craft but soon diversified into interceptors and bombers; test pilots took its prototypes up from the adjacent Central Airfield. Renamed Aviation Works No. 1 in 1928, it expanded during the five-year plan, as did two other big air plants: No. 22 in Fili, west of the city limits, built by Junkers under the agreement with the Germans; and No. 24, east of the Yauza, the engine maker created with Uglanov's help in 1926.

TsAGI (the Central Aeronautics Institute), on ulitsa Radio, near the Yauza and the Higher Technical College, was already the dominant institution for aviation research in the USSR. It spun off design bureaus, units that prepared preproject studies, drawings of aircraft systems and subsystems, and mockups. The earliest of these, the Tupolev bureau set up in 1922, was to be the most illustrious in Soviet aviation.

Other parts of a powerful aviation complex fell into place in and around Moscow. The Zhukovskii Air Force Engineering Academy, founded in 1922 in the Petrovskii Palace, across Leningradskii prospekt from Duks and the Central Airfield, yoked together users in the armed forces. In 1926 TsAGI opened a proving site at Ramenskoye Airfield, southeast of Moscow. Made the USSR Flight Test Institute in the 1930s, it conducted acceptance tests on all new Soviet aircraft. To back up the design bureaus, TsAGI between 1929 and 1932 spawned separate institutes for basic research on airframe materials (VIAM, the All-Union Institute for Aviation Materials), motors (TsIAM, the Central Institute for Aviation Motor Building), hydraulics (VIGM, the All-Union Institute for Hydraulic Machine Building), and jet turbines (TsVEI, the Central Turbopower Institute). All set up shop in Moscow and linked up with design bureaus, fabricating sheds, and test fields.

Some city officials had hopes that a local body would be at the helm of economic modernization. In addition to rebuilding AMO, Moscow was made liable in 1927 for constructing a regional power station, a cycle works, and several other factories. Local leaders dropped any notion of control in 1928 and 1929, as central trusts exerted dominion, but they were not deterred from plugging important projects. Their reasoning combined a desire for empire building (Bauman admitted that they looked like "imperialists" to other wooers of investment capital)[119] and uncritical acceptance of growth.

Neither of Bauman's pet schemes, a second Moscow steel mill and a tractor and combine plant, materialized. Yet in 1929 his MK sold planners on enlarging rather than, as some steel makers wanted, closing down the Serp i molot (Sickle and Hammer, formerly Gujon) Works and on a threefold expansion of the locomotive plant at Kolomna. Bauman grumpily told the MK plenum which elected him first secretary that the USSR Gosplan had picked Nizhnii Novgorod over Moscow for Russia's light auto plant, "despite our pertinacious resistance and every kind of support from Comrade Molotov." But he fought back from this reversal, too. In January 1930 the obkom bureau was admitted to a Politburo session and attained an agreement to speed up the AMO reconstruction. Later in 1930 work began on a second automotive plant, which had eluded Moscow in 1929. As a fig leaf, the Communist Youth International (KIM) Auto Works, the first Soviet factory to specialize in passenger vehicles, was formally a branch of the Nizhnii Novgorod (later Gorky) Auto Works until 1939.[120]

Few industrialists needed to be lured to Moscow. Dovetailing with its geographic centrality, labor reserves, and infrastructure was a new political desideratum. A history of the First State Ballbearing Works, erected at Sukino boloto (swamp) between 1929 and 1932, generalizes as follows about siting: "At a time of constant shortage of materials and unwieldiness of the administrative structure . . . not the last factor in selecting a building spot for a plant badly needed by the country was that Moscow was where the central party and economic offices were situated, with whose help production problems could swiftly be resolved."[121]

Moscow and Moscow oblast thus got a double dose of economic adrenalin from the First Five-Year Plan. They were showered with

Table 4. Social composition of city population, 1926–1933

Social group	December 1926	April 1931	July 1933
Employed			
Workers	293,200	673,000	823,400
Office employees	263,300	437,600	649,900
Service personnel	91,400	160,700	214,600
Handicraftsmen	91,100	94,300	76,200
Miscellaneous	65,400	64,800	59,000
Domestics	42,200	54,200	52,600
Those with unearned income[a]	35,000	3,600	1,300
Others			
Dependents	939,300	1,088,600	1,339,300
Unemployed	130,300	0	0
Pensioners	39,800	74,200	85,900
Students on stipend	34,900	98,100	89,100
Transitory individuals[b]	0	32,200	25,200
Total	2,025,900	2,781,300	3,416,500

Source: Moskva v tsifrakh (Moscow: Stroitel'stvo Moskvy, 1934), p. 16.
a. Mainly private traders and landlords.
b. Employable individuals in transition from one job to another.

construction projects: 100 of 518 Soviet factories coming on line in 1931, and a total of 300 enterprises rebuilt during the plan. And the plan also catered to the bureaucracy overseeing the effort nationwide, largely domiciled in the capital.

The demographic fallout was most evident for workers in Moscow industry, transport, and construction, whose ranks swelled 129.5 percent between the 1926 census and April 1931 (by which time unemployment was officially declared extinguished) and a further 22.3 percent by July 1933 (see Table 4). Most of the recruits were peasants keener than ever to pick up stakes when their villages, chiefly in the same central regions from which Moscow had always attracted immigrants, were turned upside down by collectivization. While Moscow's Russian-dominated ethnic makeup remained stable,[122] industrial growth redrew its social and economic profile. In large factories 70.4 percent of the workers added between January 1, 1929, and January 1, 1932, and 53.4 percent of all workers on the latter date (up from 35.0 percent in 1929), were in heavy industry. In offices (within production units as well as the central administration) the increments were also large, 66.2 percent from 1926 to 1931 and 48.5 percent from 1931 to 1933. Mercantile and handicraft pursuits wizened, although Moscow still had almost 53,000 registered domestics in 1933—46,000 fewer than in 1912 but 10,000 more than in 1926.[123]

The bottom line was what most alarmed Moscow's rulers. As Moscow raced past 2.5 million in population in 1930, housing construction continued at its tortoise's pace. Government officials commiserated with Bauman in 1929 when he proposed that they endow a "special fund" for developing Moscow's communal services. Yet, as he expressed it to the MK, "condolences are not the same as money."[124] Quandaries that had been around a decade or more now required resolution. How were monetary and other resources to be found to provide for human needs in such quantity? Equally vexing, what was to be done, qualitatively, at a moment of heady revamping of society, to make Moscow into a truly socialist city?

Factory of Plans

Thinking about how to reshape the urban environment was a robust cottage industry in 1920s Moscow. Futuristic ideas previously confined to the intelligentsia now found respectability and official protectors, sharing the platform with more conventional engineering, architectural, and administrative approaches. The multidisciplinary discourse, as much political as it was professional, was unstintingly cosmopolitan. VKhUTEMAS (the Higher Arts and Technical Studios), the stronghold of the modernist architects, had regular exchanges with the Dessau Bauhaus, and leading European architects such as Bruno Taut and Erich Mendelsohn frequently visited Moscow. Le Corbusier came three times between 1928 and 1930 and submitted two briefs for public works. Ernst May, the chief architect of Frankfurt, settled in Moscow in 1930, declaring his wish to take part in "the greatest national experiment of all times." The German-Swiss Hannes Meyer, Walter Gropius's successor as head of Bauhaus, traveled to the USSR with a Rotfront Brigade of seven Bauhaus students. Hundreds of foreign architects, many of them Communists or fellow travelers, made the same trek.[125]

Planning activity first centered on discrete building projects, on updating microscale prescriptions, such as garden communities and communal houses, and on a crude attempt to "unburden" Moscow from superfluous users. With time, the emphasis rotated to macrolevel schemes for the conurbation as a whole. Technical questions were interknit in the great planning debate with value questions, including attitudes toward Russian culture and the traditional family.

ARCHITECTURE AS TRANSFORMER

The government of Moscow was "the single greatest patron of avant-garde architecture during the 1920s," in Russia and perhaps the world.[126] Stirred by its design contests, experimentation with line, volume, texture, and color fizzed in classrooms and in the ateliers of state agencies and cooperatives. The venerable Moscow Architectural Society (MAO), revived in 1922 with Aleksei Shchusev as its president, umpired most building competitions. It was criticized for stodginess by a pair of organizational rivals based in the architectural faculty of VKhUTEMAS. The Association of New Architects (ASNOVA), founded in 1923 by Nikolai A. Ladovskii and inspired by Kandinsky and Malevich, fostered "Rationalists" who sought to achieve emotional uplift by mating architecture with the fine arts. The League of Contemporary Architects (OSA), organized in 1925 by Aleksandr A. Vesnin, Moisei Ya. Ginzburg, and other "Constructivists," took as their referents machines, technology, and industrial psychology. Rationalists and Constructivists, their disagreements aside, shared a common hope: "whether guided by form or function, the new architecture according to both groups would prove to be the transformer of life."[127]

They spread this demiurgic energy to objects as humdrum as department stores, bakeries, bathhouses, and parking garages. Vladimir Shukhov's 150-meter conical radio tower on ulitsa Shabolovka, made of hyperboloid turned steel for the Moscow and later the Comintern radio stations, was one of the visual totems of the interwar Soviet Union and "symbolized the revolutionary future" Russians saw themselves gliding into.[128] Not far away, ASNOVA architects, in an internal competition (with a multiplicity of prizes), sketched out the Shabolovka model housing estate. It called for twenty-four apartment houses, of five or six stories, for the 10,000 working-class tenants, a kindergarten, a day nursery, a social club,

Figure 23. Rusakov Club. (Photograph by William C. Brumfield.)

and a heating plant. The architecture was distinguished by the strong corner buildings, which rotated into view of the street through bays in the perimeter construction, the plentiful balconies, the flower gardens in the courtyards, and the finish in bright stucco.[129]

Konstantin S. Mel'nikov, a leader of the avant-garde, put his talents in 1924–1925 to replanning Sukharevskii Market and between 1927 and 1929 to turning out audacious workers' clubs, financed by the trade unions; five of his six clubs survive, the best known the Rusakov Club on ulitsa Stromynka (Figure 23). The Central Cultural and Recreational Park (later named after Gorky), a fairground for "building the new man," opened its gates in 1928 on the spot of the 1923 All-Russian Agricultural Exhibition along the Moskva, where the city's main dump had been before. Although never built, drawings propounded during the years 1922–1925 for a VSNKh office tower on Lubyanskaya ploshchad' and El Lisitzky's (Lazar M. Lisitskii's) pro-

posal for eight stilt-mounted "horizontal skyscrapers" along the
Bul'varnoye kol'tso had great influence on Soviet art and architecture.
Sergei Ye. Chernyshev's Lenin Institute and Grigorii B. Barkhin's
Izvestiya building (Figure 24), among the first office towers since
1917, were classics of spare modernism. Le Corbusier and the Russian
Nikolai Ya. Kolli won a commission for a headquarters for Tsen-
trosoyuz, the Central Union of Consumer Cooperatives, on Myasnitskaya ulitsa; it was finally completed, after seven years of travails, in
1935.

Outclassing all the others physically, two aborted proposals, driven
by state interests rather than advanced theory, foreshadowed the city-
sculpting monumentalism of the high Stalin period. The first, the
Palace of Labor (Dvorets truda), emanated in 1922 from Lev Kamenev, who likely saw in it an heir to the unbuilt Palace of the People
he espoused in 1918. He had in mind "one of the most grandiose
buildings in the world" on Okhotnyi ryad; with auditoriums and
other features largely for the Mossovet, it would have amounted to a
lavish town hall and club.[130]

At the congress that approved the formation of a federal USSR in
December 1922, Sergei M. Kirov, the head delegate from Baku and a
follower of Stalin, hijacked the idea—he is often wrongly credited
with originating it—and turned it into a national and international
facility. Noting that the Bol'shoi Theater, in which the congress convened, did not rise to that occasion, Kirov cast his thoughts ahead to
the day Moscow would be the capital of a world socialist commonwealth. His peroration gripped the hall:

> We are going to need a roomier space, one that can accommodate repre-
> sentatives of the toilers of the entire world. Therefore, we must take on
> the erection of a workers' palace on the best square of Moscow, the
> capital of the USSR, a palace that will be an emblem of proletarian might.
> We will show them [the bourgeoisie] that we, the "semi-Asiatics," are
> able to adorn the earth with the very finest monuments of art and
> proletarian inventiveness, with marvellous palaces. And then they will
> know that we have come to power seriously and forever![131]

Kirov's speech led to an open design contest arbitrated by an MAO
jury, chaired, in round one, by Kamenev. The drawings tendered were
tinged by a multitude of influences, among them European modernism, neoclassicism, and occultism. First prize was awarded in 1924 to

Figure 24. *Izvestiya* newspaper building. (Photograph by
William C. Brumfield.)

the Byzantine-looking entry of Noi A. Trotskii. When politicians disagreed over building details and financing, construction of the Palace of Labor stopped before it began, although architects continued to dream of a "Supreme Building" and sketches and budget estimates were done through the late 1920s.[132]

The entombment of Lenin in January 1924 led to a second flurry of blueprints, this time for a memorial to the patriarch. Leonid B. Krasin, the convenor of the funeral commission, foresaw a colossal Lenin Palace for athletics and theater on the Lenin Hills, tied to the Kremlin and the mausoleum by a broad highway. The complex's "significance for mankind," Krasin believed, would "exceed Mecca and Jerusalem."[133]

Aleksandr D. Metelev of the Kremlin commandant's office was one of many who were mortified: the project "would be like driving a massive tractor through old Moscow," splintering housing and landmarks. But destruction and reconstruction were precisely what captivated others. Literary critic Kornelii L. Zelinskii spoke exuberantly for a Lenin Tower, architecturally paired with the mausoleum and soldered to the Palace of Labor by a steel gangway. St. Basil's Cathedral would have to be disassembled and moved, but this prospect gave him no pause. A complex of this ilk, Zelinskii said, would be "the pith of a socialist Moscow," verily "the mental center of the world, the radio focus of the universe." A young member of ASNOVA, Viktor A. Balikhin, contended in a memorandum that a "grandiose monument" to Lenin, the Comintern, and the formation of the USSR should be put in place of the Cathedral of Christ the Redeemer. The church, being "of no value whatever," could be torn down without regret.[134]

Plans for a Supreme Building inspired not only ardor but also alarm, on the grounds that it might provoke a backlash among the hard-pressed population. *Pravda* refused to print a letter by Balikhin propounding his plan, fearing readers' reaction. In 1925 Valerii B. Zheits, a branch chief in the Real Estate Directorate of city hall, questioned the comparatively innocuous proposal for a ten-story office building for Gosbank (the State Bank) along the north side of Okhotnyi ryad. How could such an expense be justified, Zheits asked, when the city was unable to keep abreast of demand for ordinary housing? "The construction of so huge a building and the outlay of large resources . . . would most certainly produce great discontent in workers' circles . . . The project [is] politically impermissible." A smaller Gosbank tower designed by Ivan Zholtovskii went up on Neglinnaya ulitsa.[135]

Away from the grandiloquence of the megaprojects, Muscovites labored quietly to apply science and the Marxist social gospel to the props of daily life. They stressed two well-worn formulas: the garden city and the communal house.

Three Muscovites were instrumental in restarting the Russian Garden Cities Society in 1922: Nikolai Semashko, the RSFSR's commissar of health; his deputy, Zinovii Solov'ev, who had been an author of the MK's 1917 municipal program; and Vladimir Semenov, the London-trained architect who drew up the Prozorovskaya plan in 1912. Semenov still believed that garden cities, "neither town nor village," would have the strengths of each. Built by common sweat on public land, they would serve socialist goals; they would also let workers grow their own food in a pinch, which "anyone who survived the recent hungry years will appreciate."[136]

There was talk of a dozen or more garden towns around Moscow, and both of the major master plans of the 1920s incorporated swatches of them. The only one to get off the ground was Sokol, near Serebryanyi bor station, completed in 1930 after a five-year pause in construction. Its architect and organizer, polymath Nikolai V. Markovnikov, had been chief restorer of the Kremlin after 1917. Comprised of several hundred pert wooden houses filled mostly with artists and civil servants, Sokol was small, atypical in its social makeup, and plagued by cost overruns. In 1922 the Moscow rubber worker S. I. Shesterkin, who had been trying since 1914 for a proletarian garden settlement, Druzhba (Friendship), got it underway at Perlovka station, north of the city limits. His utopia fell by the wayside, and a standard factory hamlet was started at Perlovka in 1924.[137]

The garden city fell between stools. It did not suit the politically engaged intellectuals who befriended avant-garde policies. To their way of thinking, sodalities of prim, picket-fenced, single-family English cottages were either boring or morally dubious. Shesterkin's intention to build a communal dining hall notwithstanding, the neighbors thought the first houses at Druzhba so retrograde that they tried to tuck them away behind a high stone wall. The construction workers' union vilified the principle of the garden town as "contradictory to communist ideas . . . an expression of philistine, bourgeois ideology."[138]

To counter such purism planners promised garden cities chock-full
of collective services or, alternatively, stitched into a balanced regional
scheme like Mark Yelizarov and Boris Sakulin had offered in 1918.
Either way was devilishly expensive. Most policy makers were unwilling to provide more than lip service, preferring to spend on cheap
housing closer at hand.

Proponents of communal housing, a second recipe for better living,
initially had to overcome the memory of the ramshackle communes
of War Communism. But idealistic students, feminists, and workers
were flying the flag again by 1924, setting up residential collectives,
usually short-lived, in several buildings in Moscow. Citing Charles
Fourier's *phalanstere* and the communitarian strand in Marxist
thought, they believed that collectivism would be most authentic in
dwellings made to order for the purpose, not in the retrofitted older
houses tried before. Social reconstructionists in the movement, supported after 1925 by OSA, wanted abolition of the family and "socialization" of child rearing, food preparation, and leisure in the
housing complex, leaving private rooms only for rest and sexual
activity. City officials perceived the issue in generational terms, seeing
commune houses as a sop to hot-blooded youth while maintaining
that their elders could not be expected to go along. Nikolai Popov,
Moscow's housing chief, said in 1925 that, much as other Muscovites
wished pro-commune Komsomol members well, they clamored for
him "to let us die in our [private] kitchens."[139]

Aficionados could not agree whether collective living should be
introduced in a trice or through "transitional" homes with partial
pooling of facilities (leaving separate bathrooms and kitchens). A
transitional dwelling for staff of the People's Commissariat of Finance,
criticized by the radicals because only half of its tenants lived com-
munally, opened in 1930. Designed by Moisei Ginzburg and Ignatii F.
Milinis, it featured ribbon windows, roof gardens, and cement pilotis
at its base (since enclosed) that reminded some of an African lake
dwelling. It still stands at 25 Novinskii bul'var, near the American
embassy.[140]

Leftists were more dismissive of the Mossovet's model commune,
approved by Nikolai Popov in 1925 and finished in 1930 on
Khavskaya ulitsa in Zamoskvorech'e (Figure 25). The specifications
detailed an advanced abode for 750 toilers, complete with common
cafeteria, laundry, clubhouse, library, and daylong crèche and kinder-

Figure 25. Commune house on Khavskaya ulitsa, with Shukhov Tower in background, 1930. (Museum of the History of the City of Moscow.)

garten. As built to a design by Georgii Ya. Vol'fenzon of MAO, it doubled the projected size and skimped on shared services. The pledge signed by tenants—"to liquidate illiteracy in 1930 and struggle resolutely against alcoholism, unculturedness, and religion"—neither attracted nor made textbook socialists. Residents, mostly ex-peasants in conventional families, soon hung Christian saints' pictures on their walls and hand-washed longjohns out their bedroom windows to dry. The workers' commune built nearby at 8/9 ulitsa Ordzhonikidze, under the architect Ivan S. Nikolayev, and the several other commune houses done around the same time, had similar deficiencies.[141]

UNBURDENING MOSCOW

Three attempts at the beginning of NEP to acquire some steering power over the metropolis as a whole complemented patronage of individual architectural projects. In January 1921 the Russian government appointed a Commission for the Unburdening *(po razgruzke)* of Moscow attached to its NKVD (Commissariat of Internal Affairs). In April the city presidium, at Kamenev's prompting, set up a Special Learned Commission for "New Moscow" and asked it to come up with "a plan for the renaissance of Moscow" over twenty-five to thirty years. In addition, in October 1921 the MKKh launched an inquiry into Moscow's development in regional context, a Commission for the Creation of "Greater Moscow."

The first of these bodies had a purely inhibitive aim: to lessen the strain on Moscow's housing and infrastructure by evicting superfluous "offices, organizations, and enterprises" and vetting all transfers of the same into the city. Moscow immediately petitioned for the dispatch of 10,000 civil servants and 20,000 of their family members to Petrograd. The suggestion "ran into a mass of obstacles thrown up by the various agencies," a series of which were directly represented on the commission. When the city presidium called the commission biased, Sovnarkom took it under its aegis and withdrew the agencies' seats, leaving them the right of appeal. The commission now had one member each from Moscow, Rabkrin, and the NKVD, with the last acting as chairman. It also was empowered to jam bureaus into tighter working quarters if eviction proved impractical.[142]

The Commission for the Unburdening of Moscow cast a shadow out of all proportion to its staff of five or six persons. By April 1924 it had divvied up 838,000 square meters of Moscow office space in 735 buildings. More than half was grabbed from the central commissariats, which lost 56 percent of their office space and 82 percent of their buildings. About 447,000 square meters turned into housing space, enough for 70,000 persons at the 1924 norm. The remainder went mostly to clinics, schools, and other social programs, with roughly a quarter being recycled as offices.[143]

It never completed the reallocations because the commission acquired only 11 percent of its space through the preferred route of evacuation of agencies. It recommended the exodus to Leningrad of large establishments such as the People's Commissariat of Education; it had to settle for training institutes, archives, a ballet school, and the like. Worse yet, its performance deteriorated. It allotted almost 45 percent less floor area in 1924 and 1925 than in its best year, 1922, and almost 80 percent less in 1926, the last year for which data were made public.[144]

At first, the unburdening commission's niche in the top bureaucracy gave it an edge in bargaining. It surrendered this chip in 1925 when, without explication, it was appended to the government of the RSFSR rather than the USSR. Sensing their advantage, officials wore it ragged with appeals: "Each eviction calls forth a torrent of complaints, and some questions are reconsidered 500 times." It was widely agreed that "unburdening" had reached an impasse. Most easy reallocation was done by the mid-1920s. Bureaus spared the guillotine merrily recommenced their growth; "others often appeared in the place"of the handful evacuated; and the commission did nothing about the expansion of industry and the overall population. Better, one editorial declared, to drop this palliative for "a well-considered, integral system of long-range guidance" of development. Although the RSFSR government amended the commission's statute in April 1930, it lapsed into obscurity and, nearly forgotten, was scrubbed in 1937.[145]

Worth noting is that many Muscovites had badly wanted it to do better and to act with less liberality. They repeatedly called for it or some other board not only to curb in-migration but coercively to transport multitudes of people elsewhere. The pamphleteer Yurii Larin, for example, demanded in 1924 that limitations be set on the sale of inbound train tickets and that "whole categories of residents Moscow can do without" be resettled to ease congestion; he proposed a quota of 50,000 migrants a year and prompt deportation of 50,000 to Leningrad.[146] The passport and registry system of the mature Stalin regime took up this supposition that the city needed a regulative moat around it.

NEW MOSCOW

The chairman of the first of the two blue-ribbon planning panels established by city hall, the six-man New Moscow committee, was Vasilii G. Mikhailovskii, Moscow's chief statistician since 1911 and a learned critic of its unregulated development. The group's dynamo, Aleksei Shchusev, served as president of MAO from 1922 to 1930; fellow architects such as Sergei Chernyshev and Il'ya and Pantaleimon A. Golosov and gung-ho students at VKhUTEMAS carried out most of the work. In effect, New Moscow was an extension of Ivan Zholtovskii's city architectural studio, which Shchusev had directed before its dissolution in 1920.

More open than Zholtovskii to vogue, Shchusev had also been an

Figure 26. Aleksei Shchusev's New Moscow plan, 1925. Drawing shows the area north and west of the Kremlin. (From *Iz istorii sovetskoi arkhitektury, 1917–1925 gg.: Dokumenty i materialy*, Moscow: Izdatel'stvo Akademii Nauk, 1963, p. 47.)

academician and a proponent of the Neo-Russian Revival before
1917. Concerning Moscow he advocated making improvements while
protecting its priceless architecture and spider web of narrow roadways: "In the Moscow of the future, new streets should be interlaid
and squares should be rebuilt, but all these works should proceed in
full accord with the basic scheme of the old city, since its foundations
are marvellous and deserve the greatest regard and study."[147]

New Moscow (Figure 26) would have retained the city's landmarks but given it more of a European texture by weeding out minor
structures around them, inserting parks and gardens, widening avenues, ridding the Bulvar'noye and Sadovoye rings of houses, and
firming up squares and ensembles. Building more than five to seven
stories high in the central area was forbidden. The report quarried the
Zholtovskii plan and its elaborations for public works: a subway,
flood control for the Moskva and Yauza, a park belt with five green
wedges into the core. It also included such innovations as a third ring
road, a unified rail terminus, a river port, and theaters and stadiums.

New Moscow's most ambitious idea, for an agglutination of functions by district, was contrived to keep development damage to a
bearable minimum. It would have embayed administrative offices in
a "government center" near Khodynka Field, with the effect of de-
congesting downtown and permitting conversion of the Kremlin into
a museum. It called for most housing to be dropped in lightly settled
parcels of the north and northwest, industry in the south and southeast, and trade and banking in Kitaigorod and Zaryad'e. Higher
education and research laboratories were to be primarily in
Khamovniki and a Moscow sports center on the Lenin Hills. A wreath
of suburban garden towns would run twelve kilometers past the third
ring road.

The political decline of Kamenev, the plan's backer, weighed
against its acceptance, as did the architects' poor rapport with most
city bureaucrats (except for Mikhailovskii, who died in 1926). The
costs entailed—of central-city construction, rehousing those displaced
by it, and stringing utilities out to the housing areas—were staggering.
And New Moscow's demographics also created problems. Mikhailovskii's office in 1921 expected a population of 1,675,000 by
1935 or 1940; in 1923 it was still predicting only 2 million; Moscow
bumped these limits in 1924 and 1926, respectively. In 1925 Shchusev

upped his sights to 5 million but did not modify his prescriptions or state why a construct predicated on 2 million Muscovites was right for two and a half times as many. In a nutshell, New Moscow, as one analyst puts it, "was hopelessly out of date the moment it was born."[148]

The intended five-volume summary of New Moscow never saw the light of day, nor did the thirty-odd consultants' studies. Product dribbled out from 1923 to 1925 in lectures and articles, and much was not released at all. Neither Moscow nor the Soviet government formally turned thumbs up or down on the plan. Instead, it was left in limbo until the spring of 1925, when Shchusev deplored its suppression and implied that MKKh and Gosplan were at fault. His commission folded by December.[149]

NOT VENICE OR POMPEII

New Moscow, its name regardless, was based on a tenderness toward the old Moscow. It took a squall over the seemingly esoteric issue of care of historic buildings to shed added light on the plan's miscarriage and to clarify the symbolic stakes involved in replanning the socialist metropolis.

Urban conservation was never unopposed. Petr A. Krasikov, the chief of the Eighth (Church) Department of the RSFSR People's Commissariat of Justice, was one of many officials who thought different. An organizer of the impoundment of religious valuables in 1922, he unabashedly advocated closing churches and razing prominent keepsakes of tsarist Russia, claiming they gave "offense to revolutionary feelings." Krasikov was backed by the League of Militant Atheists, the official antireligious propaganda organization headed by Yemel'yan Yaroslavskii, a Moscow revolutionary and the first Bolshevik commissar of the Kremlin in 1917, and less deliriously by the Komsomol and some leftist intellectuals. Churches closed in a steady stream, with increasing frequency late in the decade; perhaps one-third of Moscow's Russian Orthodox churches were padlocked, leaving 224 still conducting services. The first three church demolitions occurred in 1924; the most notable, of the seventeenth-century Church of the Blessed Virgin on Bol'shaya Lubyanka ulitsa, made way for a political statue.[150]

For quite some time, the defenders of the traditional face of the city occupied the high ground. When they "came out against demolition boldly and consistently enough," a historian writes, "the initiators of destruction among the departments of the Moscow Soviet and the commissariats had to retreat."[151]

The Moscophiles were a supple and diverse lot. In 1925, for example, when two of the few secular relics of Petrine Moscow, the mansion of the Golitsyns (only just fixed up) and of the Troyekurovs, were marked for extinction for office construction, a coalition trussing together the Old Moscow Society, MAO, Glavnauka (the science division of the People's Commissariat of Education and overseer of the Department for Museum Affairs and Protection of Landmarks), and the Academy of Sciences contested the decision. S. F. Platonov of the academy, still based in Leningrad, wrote for the group that the demolition would be "utter barbarism." The campaign saved the Troyekurov home; the Golitsyns' was fenced off, to be demolished in 1932 when the headquarters of USSR Gosplan went up on Okhotnyi ryad. An old-time Moscow Communist from a gentry family, Mikhail S. Ol'minskii, reasoned from the affair that growth of the bureaucracy posed such a threat to Moscow's treasures that the seat of government should be moved to some town on the Oka River.[152]

By and by, the tables were turned against the keepers of the flame. Economic expansion increased the pressure on land, especially inside the Sadovoye kol'tso. Political radicalization made the urban heritage ideologically suspect. With respect to religious monuments, destruction became a financial boon with the passing of several decrees by the Soviet government as early as 1924–1925. These entitled municipalities to 40 percent of the proceeds from demolition of a church and sale of its materials and contents.[153]

The issue came to a head over one building, dragging Aleksei Shchusev into the melee and exposing the weakness of his New Moscow plan. The Church of Archdeacon Yevpl on Myasnitskaya had been built in the 1760s and was the only one in Moscow to hold services during the French occupation of 1812. In May 1925 Mosstroi announced it wanted to flatten the church to put up a Palace of Trusts for offices of several branches of VSNKh. The executives of the Soviet metallurgical, cement, and pulp and paper industries joined in Mosstroi's brief, and under pressure from them the presidium of VTsIK assented in the demolition. Suspended after a petition from the congregation, the decision was affirmed by the central government November 23, 1925. The building came down shortly thereafter, although construction of the palace never started for financial reasons.

The month before, Shchusev had penned a fiery personal letter to the government, insisting that Moscow had plenty of vacant lots and that the real choice was about "whether or not beauty is necessary to the city of the future." The "dreamers" who overthrew the tsar, he said, "thought that the generative spirit of the revolution would separate beauty from ugliness and would defend beauty."[154]

On November 22, on the eve of the final decision, *Izvestiya* carried a rebuttal of Shchusev's unpublished letter, and implicitly of his master plan, entitled "The New Moscow—Not a Museum of Antiquity." The author was the Moscow Real Estate Directorate's Nikolai Popov. His hymn to "multistory buildings of iron and reflecting glass" denounced Shchusev's whole approach. Moscow, he snarled, "is not a museum of antiquity, not a city of tourists, not Venice or Pompeii . . . not the graveyard of a past civilization but the cradle of a growing, new, proletarian culture, based on labor and knowledge."

Popov had scored a bull's eye. In a return missive, Shchusev lamely lauded preservation as much for showing off post-1917 architecture to advantage as for revering the past. Moreover, he granted that Moscow was encumbered with "building junk" and concurred with unnamed savants that "it is necessary to break Moscow up [*Moskvu nado perelomat'*]." Others who stood up for conservation over the next few years defensively warded off accusations, more barbed than Popov's, of "idealizing" the Moscow of nobles, caftaned merchants, and priests.[155]

The city presidium carried out the first removal of a major landmark, Ukhtomskii's eighteenth-century Red Gates on the Sadovoye northeast of the Kremlin, in June 1927. This gold-leafed pavilion, crowned by a copper archangel and possessing some of the sweetest-sounding bells in Moscow, had been eyed for razing as early as the 1850s but was avidly defended in the 1920s by the Old Moscow Society, educators, and the Academy of Sciences. The job "was done in a rush," the gates' decorations "simply being thrown onto the ground, where they broke up."[156]

Political radicalization put ever more landmarks at risk. Grabar' with some difficulty beat back a proposal in 1928 to take down the

Kitaigorod Wall. June 1928 brought the first dismantlement of a major Moscow church, the Church of St. Paraskeva on Okhotnyi ryad (originally completed in 1687). The city administration rejected the conservationists' despairing demand for time to study its unique tiled roofs and remove the altar and artwork. The deed was begun under cover of darkness, a tactic often followed over the next decade. In 1928, too, the twenty museums in the former gentry estates of the guberniya began to be closed to the public and turned over to state organizations.[157]

That same summer the very Kremlin was breached. In June 1928, on instruction of the VTsIK presidium, workers demolished the small Church of Konstantin and Yelena, built in 1470. Its restorer, Nikolai N. Pomerantsev, found no supporters despite making the point that it had been ordered repaired by Lenin ten years before. Museum officials were informed in September that most of the bells from the Kremlin churches would be melted down and the metal used in industry.[158]

Word came down in May 1929 of the impending removal of the two fourteenth-century Kremlin abbeys, the Chudov Monastery and the Voznesenskii Convent. Squeezed among the Spasskiye Gates, the Cavalry Guards Barracks, and the Sovnarkom (formerly Senate) building, they had been closed after the immurement of the Soviet government in 1918. Their shells were now to be leveled to further atheistic propaganda and construction of a new barracks for cavalry troops (the original having been made into a residence for Bolshevik politicos in 1918). Many of the tsars' children had been baptized in the male monastery, and the Slavonic-Greek-Latin Academy, Russia's earliest academic body, began here in 1687. The convent, its neighbor on Ivanovskaya ploshchad', contained the tomb of most of the pre-Petrine tsars' wives.

The Old Bolshevik Vladimir I. Nevskii, director of the Lenin Library, is the only one known to have protested the plan. In a letter to Stalin, he ridiculed the basing of a horse guard in the Kremlin ("a weak defense against contemporary means of attack," and sure to disturb officials and residents with noise and the smell of manure). It would make just as much sense to raze everything in the Kremlin "except the walls, so as to be freer to locate not only cavalry but also artillery barracks" there. And that, Nevskii said, would be a tragedy for Moscow and the country and would expose the regime to "propaganda against us Communists as destroyers of all that is Russian."[159]

Nevskii received his answer before sunup on December 17, 1929. The slumber of Kitaigorod and Zamoskvorech'e was broken by a roar: the Church of the Miracle of the Archangel Michael (1365) in the Chudov Monastery, known for its graceful lines and pale watercolor frescoes, had been sundered by dynamite. The rest of the two cloisters and the Small Nikolayevskii Palace next to them were ground to pieces in succeeding weeks. The army would build an officers' club and an enlarged Kremlin cadets' school on the site in the years 1932–1934, not the intended cavalry barracks; they were converted into the offices of the Secretariat of the Presidium of the USSR Supreme Soviet in 1939.[160]

The twenty-three monasteries and nunneries outside the Kremlin, most of them still housing some clergy, came under devastating assault at the same time. The seventeenth-century Strastnoi (Passion) Convent on Tverskaya was the first to be closed up, in March 1928, and then turned into an anticlerical museum. First to be physically expunged was the Sretenskii Monastery (founded 1397) near the Lubyanka, its refectory and belfry taken apart by MKKh in July 1928. Rozhdestvenskii, the oldest convent in Moscow (established 1386), became the Museum of the History of Chemistry in 1929; and the Danilov Monastery, the oldest of all Moscow's abbeys (founded 1282), became an orphans' detention center. By January 1930 the cloister churches had held their last services and the city's remaining friars and nuns had been sent to churches or farms in the oblast, all except for one or two stealthy holdouts—cassocked poltergeists amidst the wreckage of Holy Moscow.[161]

Thousands of church objects, from ten-ton bells to censers and candlabras, now went on scrap heaps and were disposed of by the kilo. Secret Moscow laboratories of the OGPU smelted gold and silver out of iconostases and, in November 1930, became responsible for extracting precious metals from church vestments and carpets from the length and breadth of the USSR. Even most of the cenotaphs and tombstones from the Simonov, Andronikov, Novodevichii, and Novospasskii cemeteries were given over to state building concerns. After the gangly bell tower of the Simonov Monastery was ripped down in July 1929, a party-sponsored workers' club, Proletarian Smithy, volunteered to do the same to its cathedral and fortress walls. They were sapped and blown up with 1,500 kilograms of ammonal and guncotton in early 1930, applying on a big structure the extirminative methods tested on Chudov.[162]

Moscow's and Russia's largest church, the Cathedral of Christ the Redeemer, had been denied maintenance since being exempted from Glavnauka's protection in 1923 but was spared public attacks because it was one of the several cathedrals that the government tried to deed over to the Renovated Church, a pro-Communist sect. At the end of the 1920s, the Renovators having dropped their claim, a press broadside against it began. One proposal recommended it be converted into a gymnasium; a more terrible fate was to be broached in a few months.

Nikolai Vinogradov, Petr Baranovskii, Nikolai Pomerantsev, Petr N. Miller, Petr Sytin, and the other guiding lights of the Old Moscow Society "feverishly sought out . . . compromise decisions" to accommodate street traffic and industry. But theirs was a successively more lonesome voice. In February 1930, beset by obloquy that it was not in step with the times, Old Moscow voted itself out of existence. Within months, its guardian angel in the central bureaucracy since 1917, the Department for Museum Affairs and Protection of Landmarks, was disbanded, and Igor Grabar' was replaced as head of the Central State Restoration Workshops.[163]

GREATER MOSCOW

By the time the furor over the city's heritage was astir in 1925, its leaders were seeking planning guidance from an oracle quite dissimilar to New Moscow. The Greater Moscow commission comprised mostly municipal engineers, not aesthetes. It was chaired by Sergei S. Shestakov, an erstwhile city duma man now teaching at the Higher Technical College and the Moscow Surveying Institute and author of a 1921 memorandum to MKKh on extension of the city's boundaries.[164]

Dacha dwellers and some city progressives had wanted a "Greater Moscow" before 1917 chiefly for the sake of equity. For Shestakov, the prime value was technical efficiency. The committee began with population projections—at first of 3 million Muscovites in 1955; then in its report, 4 million in 1945 and 6 million in 1960. With numbers like this, Shestakov said, Moscow would be "one of the world's greatest cities," provided massive spending went toward servicing rural land and raising the old town to standard—for which he was far more amenable than Shchusev to clearance methods. Scientific management of the process from first to last, he mooted, required that Moscow and environs be treated as a unit. Hence he arrived at a Greater Moscow of 1,800 square kilometers, eight times the 1925 city and triple the size of New Moscow, to be governed by a "joint directorate for Moscow and guberniya."[165]

Shestakov's most inventive proposal was for an inclusive rezoning of the metropolitan area into five concentric zones (Figure 27). He reserved a "central urban zone," nearly coterminous with the existing city, for housing, offices, and shopping. Thickets of factories were interspersed with parks in the second ring, and Howardian garden towns with parkland in the "garden zone," the third and broadest. Next came a "protective wooded zone" of solid greenery, feeding into the four park spokes. A slim fifth ring sheathed a circumferential railway for freight, which would free up the Moscow Circuit Railroad for passenger trains.

A final point responded to the fear of excessive in-migration. The life of Moscow, Shestakov said, "is too seductive for [other] people not to crave it." His plan's "seemingly reliable defense of the city against further expansion of its suburban appendages" would be overrun without bins for "surplus population." He thus assigned 3.5 million people to twenty-six garden cities, built from scratch and from historic Russian towns and arrayed in two tiers. The outer ring through Serpukhov and Volokolamsk, sixty to seventy kilometers out, reached as far as the first circle of satellites in Boris Sakulin's 1918 construct.[166]

Shestakov, unlike Shchusev, easily got his findings printed. In January 1925 a section of the Mossovet put its approval of the plan on record. The following month the presidium received it, agreed to widen Moscow's boundaries, and appointed a committee to "investigate possible conflicts."[167] Shestakov himself was put in charge of a new Land Planning Subdepartment in MKKh, a planning branch of which was to round out the sketch.

Local leaders often spoke, misleadingly, as if Greater Moscow were a done deal. Some admirers, foreshadowing the planning fracas of

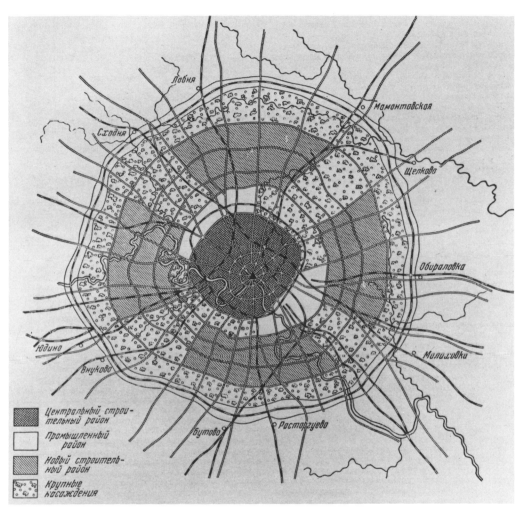

Figure 27. Greater Moscow plan, by Sergei Shestakov, 1925. The central urban zone appears in dark shading, new residential areas in intermediate shading, industrial districts blank, parks and forests in dotted sections. (From *Iz istorii sovetskoi arkhitektury, 1917–1925 gg.: Dokumenty i materialy,* Moscow: Izdatel'stvo Akademii Nauk, 1963, p. 49.)

1929–1930, put forth exotic variations. The mathematics-fixated Sakulin, who overlapped at the Moscow Surveying Institute with Shestakov for several years, wanted Greater Moscow to incorporate abstruse "harmonic planning networks." He proposed subways along four curlicue paths (his neologism for them was *kurazety*) to converge at the geometric center of Moscow, the Gorbatov Bridge in Presnya where workers fought the Semenovskii Guards in 1905; here would rise an Eiffel-like tower, a shopping plaza at its base and a weather station on its top floor.[168]

In the sequel, however, Greater Moscow made little more headway than New Moscow. No city or national assembly enacted it into law. Shestakov lasted only two years in his administrative position. When officials commented on the plan, they tended to keep their distance from its central concept, regional coordination, and to fasten on subsidiary recommendations for the old city, like widening radial streets by five to ten meters.

The reason for this insouciance was that Greater Moscow was as rich for the city's blood as New Moscow, maybe more. Its suburban and exurban housing would have been at low density and too remote for builders; the third ring's settlements would impinge on extant parks; and most of Moscow's 750 factories would have to be hauled into the two crescents of the second ring allotted to industry. The plan simply would have run into "sums which neither the proponents nor the opponents of 'Greater Moscow' have managed to calculate," one detractor stated. "The more our municipal officials have mulled over the idea, the more they have become aware of its illusoriness."[169]

CONSTRUCTION ANARCHY

The high-level political intervention that might have massaged Shchusev's or Shestakov's handiwork into a usable plan never came about. No party leader put his shoulder to the problem, and the MK bureau never once took it up. The Planning Commission and the Housing Construction Committee appended to the city presidium were both discontinued in 1929. The planning branch formed after release of the Shestakov plan was encoffined within the bureaucracy, three plateaus down in the structure of MKKh. Its measly nineteen staff members (in April 1929), none of them well known, did not have a monopoly over land allocation and had to go cap in hand for information to other departments. Solomon A. Gurevich, Moscow's main housing inspector, mourned that the capital "does not bear comparison so far as planning is concerned with the cities of the West or even with many cities in our country."[170]

With simple surveying in idle, a binding master plan looked as far off in 1930 as it had in 1914. There were no population guidelines for Moscow. Revised "red lines" for downtown streets lacked legal force. District plans had been fixed for but three small tracts in the north: Sokolinaya gora, Vsekhsvyatskoye, and Koptevo. Gosplan and other departments had garroted a city position paper on Kitaigorod.

Moscow was thus exceedingly vulnerable during the building frenzy of the First Five-Year Plan. "Due to the absence of [urban] planning," an inquiry by Moscow's Rabkrin found in early 1930, "we stand before the fact of absolute anarchy in the placement of construction on the city's territory." The whistle blowers could recite hair-raising snafus. An apartment house was going up on Pokrovka ulitsa fourteen meters in front of the setback. A printing plant and a university laboratory graced the path of a projected roadway. Dormitories were being put under the belching smokestacks of the Serp i molot steel mill. The railroads were shooting spur lines through to factories with nary a nod to the local councils. The State Electrical Trust had plunked a nitrogen plant smack in the middle of a quadrangle of Sokol'niki supposed to be for hospitals and clinics. A plot on Begovaya ulitsa readied at high cost for housing was being grassed over as a garden, while the Izmailovo deer park was overrun with shacks.[171]

The wildest disorder was in Proletarskii raion (Rogozhsko-Simonovskii raion until April 1929), the southeast quadrant now given over to heavy industry. The combination of new-laid factories, such as the ballbearing works, and reconstructions (of Serp i molot, AMO, and others) made it "the biggest construction site in the USSR" in 1930. Everything in this lunar landscape was "flowing out of a dozen departmental five-year plans," without concertation on social needs:

Let us begin with the housing problem. Its resolution is complicated by the fact that when plots were allocated for industrial building no plan was simultaneously worked out for the erection of housing, schools, hospitals, and eating places, one that would be haltered to industrial construction both spatially and in calendar terms. Then look at issues of a municipal nature, starting with urban transit. These, too, are to a significant degree suspended in thin air. It is unknown from where and to where workers are going to be transported . . . where the basic mass of the workers are going to live, who is going to put in . . . tram lines, water and sewage mains, roadways, playing fields, lawns, baths, laundries.[172]

Mikhail Kryukov, the chief of Mosstroi since 1922, sounded another alarm in November 1930 when he protested the sudden difficulty he was having spending his budget. Fifty-five percent of the funds given him in the just-completed fiscal year had to be returned. Moscow had been strapped for money in the 1920s, but what it had it could disburse, as the city still had wholesale and retail markets in physical goods and hordes of unemployed eager to sign on for a day's pay. Now allocation by administrative pronunciamento was devaluing the currency and setting, as Kryukov recognized, "an order of priorities [ocherednost'] in the supply of materials and labor."[173] In the emerging queue for resources, common people and the local authorities that gave them some succor would stand abyssmally low.

THE BATTLE OF THE DRAWING BOARDS

Young specialists, most of them Muscovites, had been busily visualizing new models of urbanism since the reform of Russian architectural education in 1918. Such was the thirst for emancipation from the past that the products often bore more resemblance to science fiction than to town planning. Some were literally castles in the sky: the diploma project of Georgii T. Krutikov, a student of Nikolai Ladovskii's at VKhUTEMAS, outlined a "flying city" in which atomic-powered aircraft transported urbanites from industrial work stations to beehive living colonies floating in space.[174]

The objective facts of the Moscow case—too many people, too little to meet their needs—would surely have quickened the long-simmering controversy over its trajectory. As it was, a subjective fact—the "cultural revolution" within Stalin's great break—took the urban debate to a full roil in 1929–1930. In no field was millenarianism more rampant than in city planning. At one another's throats over particulars, all involved shared a passion for reifying in local communities the state socialist values being pursued in the five-year plan for the national economy.[175]

The game began with denigration of preceding planning efforts as "bourgeois" and swipes at the timorousness and "uprava tempos" of the Mossovet. In the last months of 1929 Ladovskii, now the leader of a breakaway group from ASNOVA called ARU (the League of Urbanist Architects), offered the first proposal to fracture Moscow's basic layout. A polite panel discussion of the "socialist city" in the Communist Academy kicked off further argument, climaxing in May and June 1930 when the MKKh planners mailed a thirty-part questionnaire about Moscow to leading architects and thinkers.

Planners could have welcomed massive development with open arms, trying for more euphonious growth but not challenging any urban fundamentals. Most steered clear of such a solution. Sergei M. Gornyi, in charge of spatial planning in MKKh until May 1930, claimed this road to a Westernized "leviathan city" was cryptically favored by influential economic and political circles:

> Some among us make peculiar use of the slogan "Overtake and Surpass [Capitalism]," assaying not only to take the best from western European science and technology but also to compete with all the deformities . . . typical of the capitalist system. Due to this impetus, designs are being worked out to turn Moscow into a second New York with skyscrapers, subways, and a population of 10 million, to turn Tula [a provincial city south of Moscow] into a second Moscow, and so on. And suggestions like these are sometimes hotly defended by highly responsible establishments . . . We are likely here to replicate yesterday's Western mistakes, passing them off as "the latest Parisian fashion."[176]

Whatever was being imparted undercover, almost no one made a virtue of size in public. Boris Sakulin, who recycled his 1918 scroll about a gargantuan Moscow region, now a "federation of oblasts," was an exception. His idea was hardly novel, however, and it could as easily be construed as shunting growth away from the capital. The only unreservedly pro-growth epistle appeared in *Izvestiya* in March 1930. The anonymous writer believed that a hookup by shipping canals to the Volga and Oka, and thence to the Baltic and Caspian seas and the world ocean, was the algorithm for Moscow's greatness. Swelling to 7 to 10 million well-housed people, its economy buoyed by cheap water and electric current, Moscow was destined to be "not the third Rome but the first city of the world." Viktor N. Obraztsov, a transport engineer, agreed with the figure of 7 to 10 million in his response to MKKh, yet saw this as an unavoidable evil, not a good to be wished for.[177]

Boosterism and gigantism were minor sounds in the great debate

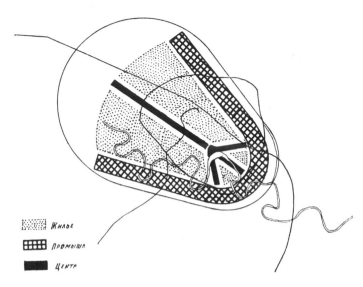

Figure 28. Nikolai Ladovskii's "dynamic city," 1930. The spotted area is for Moscow housing, checked area for industry, black strips for central functions. (From *Sovetskaya arkhitektura,* no. 1, January 1933, p. 22.)

of 1929–1930. The dominant harmonic was a reconstructionism derived from a diffuse animosity toward the industrial metropolis and a yearning for settlements convivial to a "new way of life" *(novyi byt)* marked by collectivism and harmony with the biosphere.

Thus Ladovskii opened with a declaration of liberation from "fetishism" toward the historic city. In place of the radial-concentric street plan, a residue of Moscow's "static" and feudal past now increasingly overtaxed by motorcars, he broached a "dynamic city" (Figure 28). The Kremlin area, frozen as a museum, was the only part not to be in motion. Ladovskii's center looked for all the world like a spaceship blasting off to the northwest, toward Leningrad (hence the caption "Rocket City" in some versions). It was expandable should the need arise, as was the parabolic zone for industry and the housing pods within it. Muscovites would travel to office or factory on foot and relax in gardens by their homes, not in a distant green belt.[178]

Ladovskii had much in common with the "deurbanist" perspective of the sociologist Mikhail A. Okhitovich, who embraced a planned builddown of the USSR's cities—not the forced flight of 1918–1920—

and pictured the country striated by bands of prefabricated and mobile residences wrapped around transportation lines. Also assonant with Okhitovich were the easel renderings for Moscow of the engineer German B. Krasin, who commended "workers' colonies" extending out in strips from the city (Figure 29), and of G. B. Puzis, an official in the RSFSR Gosplan aligned with OSA, whose solution called for extrusion of factories and insertion of wedges of parks and forests into the old town (Figure 30). OSA's Pantaleimon Golosov broached a "radial-tongue-shaped" mutant (Figure 31).[179]

Two epigones of the Constructivists, Moisei Ginzburg and the twenty-six-year-old Mikhail O. Barshch, in setting forth a linear scheme for Green City (Zelenyi gorod), a suburban resort north of Moscow espoused by the trade unions, wanted to shrink sharply the population of the mother city, stop construction there, and tear down functionless buildings for park space. As many ex-Muscovites as possible, now "agricultural proletarians" at one with nature, were to be distributed "along the main roads connecting Moscow with nearby centers." The pastoralism had a certain commonality with Chayanov's widely read *Journey of My Brother Aleksei to the Land of the Peasant Utopia*. Less drastically, Konstantin Mel'nikov proposed that construction beyond the circuit railroad be only along concentric transport loops. A wide tarmac around Moscow would form a "circular plaza for parades and popular celebrations," and all transit into and out of the city center would be on moving sidewalks.[180]

A group associated with Leonid M. Sabsovich, a functionary in the RSFSR Gosplan, weighed in with the most invasive proposals. Ye. Strogova announced in January 1930 that, rather than bloat into an "octopus city," Moscow should be decomposed into a "federation of towns" arrayed around big factories and designed by the workers themselves. Sabsovich, in a long response to the MKKh survey, advocated a ceiling of 1.5 million residents, to be lowered in due course (some pushed for a quota as low as 800,000). All investment, said Sabsovich, should be channeled to "new socialist towns" of 50,000 to 75,000 people thirty to fifty kilometers away. As first steps toward communization in the rump Moscow, everyone was to get meals from a single "food combine," while common laundries and nurseries were to liberate women from other domestic drudgery. A Sabsovich-

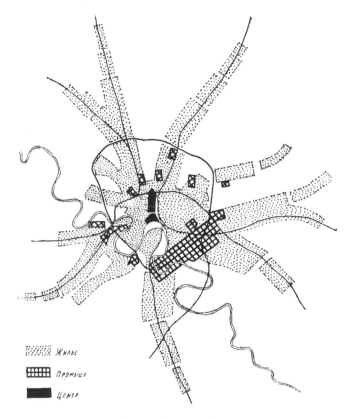

ЖИЛОЕ

ПРОМЫШ

ЦЕНТР

Figure 29. Moscow and "workers' colonies," by German Krasin, 1930. Housing areas appear in spots, industrial zones in checks, and space for central functions in black. (From *Sovetskaya arkhitektura*, no. 1, January 1933, p. 16.)

Figure 30. Sketch by G. B. Puzis, 1930. Wedges of cultivated parks (checked pattern) and woods (stripes) penetrate into city; factory zones appear in dark shading. (From S. M. Gornyi, *Sotsialisticheskaya rekonstruktsiya Moskvy*, Moscow: Tekhnika upravleniya, 1931, p. 113.)

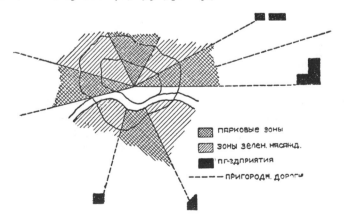

ПАРКОВЫЕ ЗОНЫ

ЗОНЫ ЗЕЛЕН. НАСАЖД.

ПРЕДПРИЯТИЯ

ПРИГОРОДН. ДОРОГИ

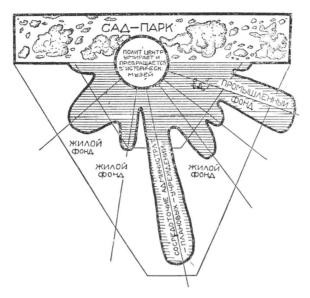

Figure 31. Pantaleimon Golosov's labile planning concept, 1930. A garden and park zone runs along the northern edge of Moscow. The circle contains the old downtown, converted into a museum. The lower protrusion is for administrative offices, others are reserved for industry. Residential areas are in white. (From Gornyi, *Sotsialisticheskaya rekonstruktsiya Moskvy*, p. 85.)

inspired sketch was forwarded by Stanislav G. Strumilin, USSR Gosplan's chief economist (Figure 32).[181]

Le Corbusier, winging a reply to the MKKh questionnaire from his Paris studio, recast Moscow into rectangles of housing, industry, and central uses (Figure 33). Housing would consist of hotel-like skyscrapers protuberating from grassy downs, 1,000 tenants per hectare. Le Corbusier's scheme depended on eradication of Moscow's established street pattern and the best part of its building stock, leaving only the Kremlin and a few other museum wards as mementos of Russian history. "It is impossible," he said, "to dream about combining the city of the past with the present or future. In the USSR more than anywhere, the question is one of two back-to-back epochs, with no factors in common."[182]

The exchange of views over the replanning of Moscow, short but sharp, subsided as the cultural revolution did. If its Prometheanism has a certain glamor in retrospect, one should not overlook the com-

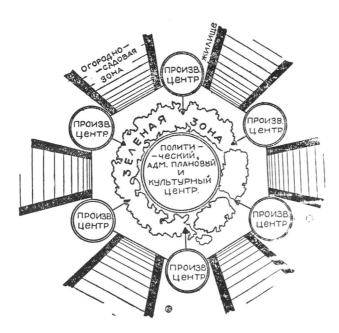

Figure 32. Stanislav Strumilin's proposal for a decentralized Moscow, 1930. The political, administrative, and cultural center is surrounded by a park zone, with six "production centers" on its fringe. The twelve dark strips, separated by agricultural and wooded areas, are for housing. (From Gornyi, *Sotsialisticheskaya rekonstruktsiya Moskvy,* p. 129.)

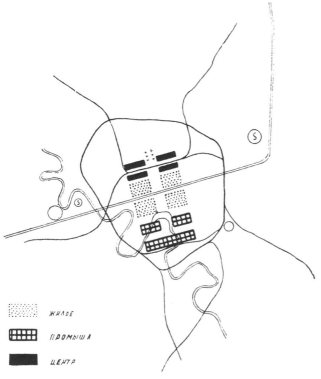

Figure 33. Le Corbusier's radical vision of Moscow, 1930. Housing is in spotted areas, industry in checks, and new city center in black. (From *Sovetskaya arkhitektura,* no. 1, January 1933, p. 12.)

batants' self-conceit and faddishness. Their scorn of the existing city had little empirical base and verged on sheer nihilism. Their ardor for reshaping time-honored institutions, from the family to the residential unit, had a totalitarian cast. Nikolai V. Dokuchayev of ASNOVA was one of the few to speak out against this trend in the MKKh poll, doubting the wisdom of dormitory housing and state child care that would emit budding socialists "in the spirit of incubators for chickens."[183]

On the matter of resources, the unaffordability of New or Greater Moscow applied doubly to these far more ostentatious ideas. A saving grace of Shestakov was that he let public policy bob with the spontaneous swell of urbanization. The new visionaries wanted to buck the current, talking of tamping down Moscow's population to 800,000—the level of the 1880s—when between 1930 and 1932 alone it increased by almost that many persons.

Although the official attitude remained loose until 1932 or 1933, it was blindingly clear in 1930 that remedial action of the most workmanlike kind could not be long postponed. In April the central government began to draft a rescript limiting industrial development in Moscow, the first concrete curb on its headlong growth. The decree, promulgated that October, forbade the construction of factories without municipal permission. The city presidium, for its part, dismissed from their posts Gornyi and the "reactionary engineers" said to have braked the work of MKKh's planners, and deputized a "shock brigade" within the planning branch to kick-start planning. As stopgaps, it decided to allot land to industry in only the southeast quadrant and to redo GUM and a series of downtown stores as offices.[184]

The handwriting was also on the wall for the more dewy conceptions of the planners. Most clairvoyant was the jargon-heavy resolution "On Work at the Reconstruction of the Way of Life" adopted by the Central Committee May 16, 1930—three weeks after Lazar Kaganovich replaced Bauman as Moscow first secretary. Singling out Sabsovich and Yurii Larin by name, the edict had harsh words for "semifantastic" and "utopian" theories about gaining socialism "at a single leap," by such means as the collectivization of cooking and child rearing or "the fundamental replanning of existing cities and the construction of new ones at the exclusive expense of the state." To the party leaders, such "leftist phrase mongering" ignored the Soviet

Union's "economic and cultural backwardness" and "the necessity at the present moment of concentrating the maximum of resources on the speediest possible industrialization of the country."[185]

The Central Committee document was released on May 29, as the first results of the MKKh questionnaire were coming out. By the time they were published in full a year later, they read like dusty diaries found in an attic. For Moscow, the gist of the resolution of May 1930 was unmistakable: speculation about an ideal socialist city was a luxury that Soviet society in its present fettle could not afford; schemes based on such quixotism were best left on the drawing boards. A police action several months later added a more ominous moral: fantasizing about the Soviet capital could be seditious as well. In September 1930 the economist Aleksandr Chayanov was arrested and charged with helping organize an anti-Communist Peasant Labor Party; he was shot in 1939. A main article in the OGPU's bill of indictment was that his ten-year-old fable about a ruralized Moscow, *Journey of My Brother Aleksei,* comforted kulaks and other reprobates. In so superheated an atmosphere, no-holds-barred contention about the morrow of the socialist metropolis was not possible.[186]

Walter Benjamin's diary for December 1926, noting Moscow's jam-packed sidewalks, electricity brownouts, and the martial arts needed to exit its streetcars, remarked that it had the air "of an improvised metropolis that has fallen into place overnight."[187] While not everything was of recent coinage, the most distinctive features of Moscow under NEP surely were formed on the run. Bounded liberalization brought with it reurbanization, the return of normal functions of big-city life, and, in the same breath, a desperate oversubscription of material assets and human beings. Its champions, as historians of NEP as a whole have demonstrated, failed to recognize it as anything more than a policy that perforce could be terminated "overnight" when the political wind changed. The "heterogeneous interests" detected in NEP politics by Nikolai Gushchin and others were almost entirely those of state institutions. They in the end were either co-opted or overpowered when political leaders stifled the ginger pluralism of the 1920s and embarked on the devil-may-care revolution from above.

Contrary to some stereotypes of Stalinism, this state-engineered revolution was itself improvised, and poorly so. Even as architects entertained visions of a bounteous tomorrow, Moscow's fabric was being tugged to the tearing point by the combination of unregulated population increase and willful neglect of social infrastructure and services. Demographic growth, preponderately from migration, billowed from 154,000 (6.7 percent) in 1929 to 256,000 (10.4 percent) in 1930. The worst was to ensue once farm collectivization deepened rural dolor: 411,000 new Muscovites (15.1 percent) in 1931 and a mortifying 528,000 (16.8 percent), or nearly 1,500 souls a day, in 1932. Between January 1, 1928, and January 1, 1933, Moscow would grow by almost 1.5 million people, or 70 percent. At the state norm, new housing was commissioned for maybe one incomer in six.

Socialist hyperurbanization invited comparison with two earlier experiences. First, as Solomon Gurevich wrote in 1929, the lack of horizontal coordination revisited the chaos of a dozen years before, the era of political coups and deurbanization. The term he used—"divided sovereignty" (mnogovlastiye)—was the very one Mikhail Vladimirskii had applied to Moscow government shortly after the October Revolution. Second, and more unflattering still, hyperurbanization was generating the bedlam socialists equated with capitalism—ironically, at just the moment that they were trying to extirpate the residuum of private capital and markets. As Gurevich observed glumly about the behavior of state industrialists, deaf to local agencies and residents, "We are getting . . . the random strewing of factories all over Moscow, the same state of affairs as before the revolution."[188]

Like the Bolsheviks of 1917, the Stalinist rulers of Moscow confronted an entropy that no one else but they had fathered.

4

Stalin's Moscow

THE LITURGY of Soviet politics from 1930 until 1953 consecrated the city "Stalinskaya Moskva," Stalin's Moscow. Read one psalm, from 1949:

> Comrade Stalin, in spite of all his multifaceted activity in leading the country, is concerned on a daily basis with the needs of Muscovites and pays special attention to the problems of rebuilding Moscow. There is no more or less significant aspect of the development of Moscow that Comrade Stalin has not addressed or on which he has not issued precise instructions. The Soviet people rightly call Moscow, the capital of the USSR, Stalin's Moscow. The great architect of socialism, Comrade Stalin, is the animator and organizer of Moscow's reconstruction . . . Stalin's genius has saved Moscow from the vegetative life [of the past], forever freed it from unemployment and poverty, liquidated its slums, and put it on the wide road of economic and cultural progress, the road of communism.[1]

Sycophants truckling to Stalin's ego tried to rename Moscow Velikii Stalingrad (Great Stalin City), Stalingrad-Moskva (Stalin City-Moscow), Stalinodar (Stalin's Bounty), or simply Stalin. The hawks on the issue were the "200 percent Stalinist," Lazar Kaganovich, and the nefarious police minister purged in 1938, Nikolai I. Yezhov. Stalin did not let them spit on a millenium of Russian history, perhaps because some sixth sense told him it would never be forgiven.[2]

No new signposting was needed for Moscow to be the lodestar of the Stalinist state. If not the "radio focus of the universe" mooned over in the 1920s, it was the communications hub of the USSR and, after post–World War II expansion, of the Communist bloc. Newsreels flashed Red Square and the Kremlin Wall onto unnumbered movie screens. Millions set their watches to *Moskovskoye vremya* (Moscow Time), the hour of calibration for all Soviet trains and telegrams under an edict of June 16, 1930, and to the staticky palaver of Radio Moscow, its broadcasts prefixed by the bells of the Kremlin's Spasskaya Tower and the sign-on "Govorit Moskva!" ("This is Moscow Speaking!").[3]

There would be no Moscow as we know it if the "Great Patriotic War," the offstage event halfway through the span of this chapter, had tilted against the Soviets. The Germans' Operation Typhoon uncoiled so swiftly in 1941 that the Politburo evacuated Lenin's mummy to Tyumen in Siberia and foreign embassies and many government bureaus to Kuibyshev. While Stalin fitted out a Douglas DC-3 for his disembarkment, bureaucrats burned office files, cowed Communists flushed their party cards down the toilet, and the Bol'shoi Theater and many public buildings were mined. Numerous Muscovites turned tail in the Great Panic of October 16–20, idling factories, stores, and transport. To muffle it, the police detained more than 120,000 persons and executed 372.[4] Nazi troops overran twenty-seven raions of Moscow oblast and mowed down regiments of undrilled home guards at the Vyaz'ma encirclement. Their panzers were revving in Khimki, twenty-nine kilometers northwest of St. Basil's, when General Georgii K. Zhukov on December 5, 1941, ignited the counteroffensive that heaved them from the oblast by February 1942.

Whereas two-fifths of its people were transported to the interior, fled, or enlisted in the army, and 10 percent perished in the forces or in the rear by May 1945, Moscow's physiognomy sustained mere pockmarks. Central and local party headquarters were burned out in a Luftwaffe raid in October 1941, but fewer than 350 buildings were damaged by bombs and shells in four years. Had its defenses buckled, Adolph Hitler's officers were under orders to outdo the conflagration of 1812 by submerging the cinders of Moscow in a sea of river water "that will conceal forever from the civilized world the capital of the Russian people."

The domestically induced terror of high Stalinism vied with the shooting war. The daily body count of the Great Purge of 1937–1938 matched that of the front in 1941, and the sour smell of death was never far away as party enforcers and the secret police did their ugly work before and after. Governance "in the Stalinist manner" was barely less militarized in style than it had been under War Communism, although its practitioners were by the late 1930s much better qualified for the technical side of administration. The Communist Party apparatus unquestionably dominated urban politics, and Moscow's partocrats, despite their vulnerability as individuals, had a unique vanguard status. The makers of urban policy conceptualized their task as giving Moscow a socialist visage, and they did so in decidedly martial terms—"one of the fronts of the great war we have been waging . . . for beautiful new things and a new man," as Kaganovich said of the construction of the subway.[5] Close scrutiny reveals this crusade to have been quite discriminating, and Stalin's capital to be really two cities: one, a temple and jamboree ground to the greater glory of the Soviet order and a hearth for the nomenklatura, built at great expense and under propitious political conditions; and the other, a shelter taking care of the barest needs of the majority of its people, pieced together with a minimum of care and investment and largely the province of the captains of industry and other employers, not of political generalists.

Socialist Reconstruction

Decisions reached in the first half of the 1930s had profound and lasting effects on Moscow. Their mutual aim was "socialist reconstruction" *(sotsialisticheskaya rekonstruktsiya)* for the sake of the values around which the Stalinist system had coagulated.

THINGS GET STARTED

The heads of the local and national partocracy took cognizance of the overwrought city around them just as its great planning debate wilted in late 1930. Not that they ignored its rural hinterland: the MK spearheaded the recollectivization that lassoed 80 percent of the oblast's farm families back into the kolkhozes by 1935. Rural worries did not keep Kaganovich from outdoing his predecessors in engrossment in the development of Moscow proper and resolve to enmesh the party in it. His apprentice, Nikita Khrushchev, would step into his shoes in 1935 and after 1953 be leader of the entire Soviet Union.

The MK on December 28, 1930, adopted its first incisive statement on Moscow's ills. It sounded a warning siren about a strategic vacuum: "the absence of well-conceived planning of urban service provision, poor integration with industrial construction, and inattention to the rising expectations of the masses."[6]

Aroused, the Politburo appointed its own commission of inquiry. It was at this time, its chairman Kaganovich later recalled, that Stalin boned up on Moscow and instigated action:

> Things got started when Comrade Stalin, having noticed certain hitches in the provision of fuel and water to the [Moscow] population, raised this matter in the Politburo together with housing difficulties and the poor shape of the pavement on Arbatskaya ploshchad'. As these questions were considered, Comrade Stalin kept enlarging the boundaries of the discussion until it got to the desirability of a general plan for rebuilding the city of Moscow.
>
> To probe Moscow's urban services, a special Central Committee commission was appointed, with Comrade Stalin as a member. Comrade Stalin faithfully attended the commission's many regular sessions. He suggested that it bring in specialists knowledgeable about the city. He spent hours hearing them out and discussing water supply, paving, the straightening of streets and squares, housing construction, and the like. From how to fix snags in fuel and water delivery, we moved on to matters such as a canal from the Volga to the Moskva, the installation of pumping stations and the augmentation of the Yauza's flow, the building of new bridges and of a subway, the demolition of the Kitaigorod Wall and of old and decrepit houses . . . and, to crown it all, a Stalinist master plan for reconstructing Moscow, whose execution has resulted in old Moscow becoming become Stalin's Moscow.[7]

The commission and the Politburo made a preliminary decision to reinstate Moscow's pre-1920 territorial autonomy. On February 20, 1931, the congress of soviets of Moscow oblast bisected itself into city and oblast soviets, each with executive, bureaucracy, and budget unto itself. Moscow was henceforth a "self-standing administrative and economic unit," answering directly to the Russian and Soviet governments. Konstantin Ukhanov, jinxed since the fall of Nikolai Uglanov, was left in the devalued oblast chairmanship and demoted in January 1932. The resurrected Moscow "mayoralty" went to Nikolai A. Bulganin, a product of the Cheka (organizer of the Red Terror in Nizhnii Novgorod in 1918) who had prospered in the electrical industry by taking on "conservative specialists."[8] An untidier partition occurred within the Communist Party. A Moscow city committee, or gorkom, was selected but subjugated to the oblast committee, the obkom (still widely referred to as the MK). To underline obkom control, Kaganovich was cross-appointed first secretary of the gorkom, as his successors would be until 1949.

On June 15, 1931, one month after the Politburo commission reported, a plenum of the Central Committee passed a resolution "On Moscow's Urban Services and the Development of Urban Services in the USSR." Never before or after did it have so much to say about Moscow or Soviet city affairs.[9]

Kaganovich's philippic to the CC took a sunny view of the regime's urban record, above all the reduction of social inequalities. Yet even his bathetic success stories had a down side. He adduced the case of a carpenter, Mikhail Bubentsov, who lived in an Arbat house that before 1917 lodged a tsarist general, the British consul, and "other bigshots and rentiers"; his family of four, Kaganovich noted in passing, was crammed into one of the mansion's fifteen-square-meter rooms. From homely detail, Kaganovich segued into his main message: overburdened and underserviced, the city was "a weak point in the socialist transformation of our country, from the point of view both of satisfying the material and cultural expectations of the working class and of the growth of industry."

The time had come, Kaganovich declared, to bring Moscow up "to the level of the technically advanced cities of Europe." He exempted institutional basics, since "with respect to society and politics we, of course, overtook and passed the leading capitalist lands long ago." He also pronounced a lapidary final anathema on those who had spilt so much ink over the ideal socialist city: "They forget that the cities of the USSR are already socialist cities" and had been so since 1917. "Idle chatter" about leapfrogging to communal kitchens or deurbanizing a Moscow or Leningrad "does not deserve a serious reply."

Consequently, in holding Moscow forth as Russia's "urban laboratory," Kaganovich stipulated tight limits for the experimentation. He focused on physical modernization through public works, instead of on the novel settlement forms around which controversy had lately eddied. Two giant undertakings to be commenced in 1932, an electric-traction subway and a canal from the Volga, topped a list that took in flats for 500,000 people in three years, extension of tram and sewage lines, new parks and bridges, and district plants to cogenerate electricity and heat.

It was unclear how the much-deplored lack of areal coordination was to be allayed. The CC bound unnamed "Moscow organizations" to prepare a "scientifically grounded plan" for it "as a socialist city," specifying only that there be no "extreme concentration" of growth. Otherwise, it dealt party, municipal, and other agencies problems one by one, without marking off turf or budget shares. Blandly recommitting itself to a long-range plan, the city council set up a new supervisory committee but gave it no guidelines.

Kaganovich, though acceptant of planning, portrayed it as a chore "of strictly practical significance, not abstract theoretical significance." In Moscow, "the big plan of works we have drawn up for housing . . . the subway, and other amenities has to be tied together" into a "unified plan" spliced to the five-year plan for industry. The technicians rendering it into work orders would take their straight-edges to historic Moscow: "build even and correctly combined roads, unkink curved and crooked streets and alleys," expurgate its "tumbledown hovels." To brake hyperurbanization, new factories were prohibited in Moscow (and Leningrad), effective 1932. On Moscow's population, Kaganovich volunteered only that it should neither sag nor be allowed to balloon out of "'tempting' thoughts of a Moscow of 10 million."[10]

UP WITH THE NEW

Gains in the Moscow salient of the "great war" for socialism were reckoned chiefly in the brick and mortar of blockbuster building projects. The party organs made a first incursion into the field with the appointment in March 1932 of an obkom-gorkom committee to supervise the preparation of a master plan. In September 1933 the gorkom and the Mossovet formed Arkhplan, a joint architectural commission chaired by Kaganovich. It took up not only whole-cloth planning, which did not come to fruition until 1935, but particulars of land use and construction as well.

The showpiece was the subway, a veritable icon of the modernity the regime sought. Kaganovich chortled that local bumpkins needed to learn the difference between a *metropoliten* (the word for subway taken from the French, often shortened to *metro*) and a *mitropolit* (a prelate of the Orthodox Church). Many planners played up the contrast with the bourgeois duma and the NEP-era Mossovet, which each dawdled for years over the issue.

Metrostroi, the new Subway Construction Trust, led by engineers and pit bosses out of the coal mining industry, broke ground on Rusakovskaya ulitsa in March 1932. Three months later it was declared a "shock" workplace, privileged in the receipt of materials and manpower. "The word 'metro' became a talisman . . . speeding up the turning of the supply gears. Into Moscow chugged innumerable trains loaded with wood, metal, and equipment."[11] Metrostroi's 70,000 workers, many of them unlettered hayseeds and nomads from Kazakhstan, Bashkiriya, and other non-Slavic areas, made it the USSR's largest civilian construction project at the end of 1934 (Figure 34).

The streams, gelatinous soil, and jumbled foundations in the bowels of Moscow confounded the workers' task. A switch in 1933 from shallow excavation to deep boring in cylindrical metal shields eased these hazards but brought on timber fires, cave-ins, and the torture of "the bends" from pressurized caissons. Dozens were killed and maimed: almost every one of the unpublished protocols of the city presidium authorizes severance payments to workers who had "lost their capacity for work" in Metrostroi. Deep tunneling also allowed the stations and the rail tubes between them to twin as air raid shelters, with sealing doors, vents, and provisions. This function was of some urgency with Hitler's takeover in Germany; at the end of the 1930s, the command post for Moscow's air defense system would be built into the Belorusskaya subway stop.[12]

A tunneler's nightmare, the metro was a propagandist's fondest wish come true. The *Metrostroyevtsy*, "metrobuilders," one flack re-

Figure 34. Underground workers building the first segment of the subway, 1934. (Museum of the History of the City of Moscow.)

cited, "not only carry out their role as individual cogs in an enormous mechanism" but teach other Soviets how to "grow in their work . . . be transformed into conscious builders of socialism."[13] On May 14, 1935, Stalin and Kaganovich, whose name the subway would carry until 1955, opened the first twelve kilometers of line, connecting Sokol'niki with the Gorky Park area by way of the railhead at Komsomol'skaya (formerly Kalanchevskaya) ploshchad' and Okhotnyi ryad. As the chiefs of the London and Paris undergrounds looked on, a half-million Muscovites filed by in approval.

The second colossus unveiled in June 1931, the Moscow-Volga Canal (Map 9), had been talked of since the 1670s and under earnest deliberation for a decade. The route chosen left the Volga near Kimry, passed through the oblast town of Dmitrov, and met the Moskva at Tushino. The canal, opened in July 1937, shocked with its sheer magnitude: 126 kilometers long, 70 of them up an incline, by an average 40 meters wide and 5 meters deep; 43 million cubic meters of earth displaced, more than the Suez Canal, and 3 million tons of cement poured; 17 weirs and dams, 13 pumping and power stations, 11 locks, 7 reservoirs, and 192 other capital installations. Raising the height of the Moskva by two meters and evening out its flow, it slaked the thirst of Moscow's residents and factories with fresh Volga water, abated spring flooding, and gave easy transit to and from main waterways for barges and liners up to 5,000 tons. With some license, it made Moscow the Port on Three Seas (the Baltic, White, and Caspian), and the Port on Five Seas when completion of the Volga-Don Canal in 1952 brought the Black and Azov seas into range.

Early documents had Moscow city hall in charge; by the time digging began, the project was in abler if unsavory hands. Certain state builders in Moscow, Metrostroi among them, had already employed some prison labor under police convoy. Moscow-Volga was made by this method alone, the second major commission of Gulag, the Chief Directorate of Corrective Labor Camps of the OGPU. Lazar I. Kogan, Semen G. Firin, and the other taskmasters of the White Sea–Baltic Canal, Gulag's first big project, traveled to Dmitrov in early 1933.[14]

There they inducted Mosvolgostroi, a labor army, eventually 200,000 strong, of political prisoners and a leavening of common

MOSCOW-VOLGA CANAL

MAP 9

criminals. It was the canal that gave Soviet convict workers their slang moniker, *zeki* or zeks, after *zaklyuchennyye kanal'stroya*, "prisoners of the canal-building directorate." Its chief engineer, Sergei Ya. Zhuk, served as the guiding voice in Soviet water resource planning until his death in 1957. Genrikh Yagoda, deputy OGPU chief and then head of the NKVD, the expanded police ministry, from July 1934 to September 1936, participated from the beginning; he knew the Moscow party well, having been a member of the gubkom/obkom since 1925 and of its bureau from 1927 to 1930. In late 1936, after two deadlines were missed, Matvei D. Berman, the chief of Gulag and a deputy of the new NKVD factotum, Yezhov, received a personal commission to finish off the canal.[15]

Moscow-Volga was the centerpiece of the Soviets' vile bid to represent forced labor as aerobic outdoor therapy. Firin rejoiced at the rehabilitation of the penal "enthusiasts," who "burned with creative fever" as they shoveled away. His charges dined well, made productivity suggestions, and relished the glee clubs, literary magazine, and "camp poets" nobly provided them. As Firin affirmed, their captors also did "not decline to use . . . coercive methods when persuasion fails."[16]

If truth be told, the "enthusiasts" north of Moscow were slaves, ill-fed and put up in sod huts and dugouts. They scraped the first two years without machinery, up to their knees in ground water. Pressure for completion worsened their pain. The channel flooded so quickly that wheelbarrows and setting forms remained and it had to be dredged before navigation could begin. The amnesty that freed 55,000 zcks in July 1937—mostly to languish in villages along the water's edge—came too late for those who had succumbed to undernourishment and exposure, exhaustion, and, after mechanization, explosions and unsafe machinery. Unmarked burial grounds for "tens of thousands" were put in the villages of Strogino and Korovino, in Tushino, and on Altuf'evskoye shosse, slightly eastward.[17]

On the eve of the June 1931 plenum, several secret panels had been discussing a third mastodonic endeavor: a Palace of Soviets (Dvorets Sovetov), a flamboyant revival of the Palace of Labor touted by Kamenev and Kirov. A "building council" for the palace, chaired first by Stalin's defense commissar, Kliment Ye. Voroshilov, and then by Vyacheslav Molotov, was established in February 1931. It proclaimed in July that the country could now afford the project and gazetted an open design competition for "a monumental structure, outstanding in its architectural formulation," to host meetings of up to 15,000 people.[18]

The codeword, "monumental," encapsulated the coming trend in Soviet architecture and planning, away from the avant-garde and toward overweening edifices in the genre of the Renaissance and neoclassicism. Moscow, the homeland of the picturesque and quirky in Russian architecture, gradually submitted to the rules of proportion, domineering size, and state-centeredness identified with St. Petersburg. The 160 entrants in the first design concourse (the field included 24 foreigners, headed by Walter Gropius and Le Corbusier) put forward a cornucopia of models. A fair number belied a Constructivist slant, while others—notably those taking a map of the USSR and a kolkhoz tractor as themes—exemplified politicized kitsch. The design of Ivan Zholtovskii, who already had a commission for the first sizable traditionalist building in Soviet Moscow, a Palladian apartment house on Mokhovaya ulitsa, was "a textbook of references to antique and classical architecture, with his main hall nothing less than a copy of the Colosseum."[19] Molotov's council awarded several prizes but declared no winner, binding future submissions to take account of "the best modes of classical architecture." In June 1933 Boris Iofan was judged the winner and appointed chief architect of the palace. On-site work began in January 1935.

Iofan's progeny was a terraced, colonnaded, and sculpture-frocked turret, knobbed by a 90-meter, 6,000-ton statue of a numinous Lenin holding his arm out to a grateful mankind (Figure 35). It was to be the tallest building on the planet—at 416 meters, 8 meters higher than the Empire State Building, opened in the capitalist Gomorrah, New York, in May 1931. Molotov thought it "absurd" that Lenin's head would be invisible from the entryway, but he signed when given an ultimatum by Stalin and Voroshilov.[20]

DOWN WITH THE OLD

Siting of this basilica of Soviet power displayed the ever more jaundiced view of the old Moscow. Specialists, Zholtovskii and Aleksei Shchusev in the group, advised erecting it on the empty Palace of Labor site at Okhotnyi ryad or in Kitaigorod. Stalin, after a walkabout June 1, 1931, with architects and Politburo members, insisted on the riverbank plot on Kropotkinskaya naberezhnaya, a half-kilometer southwest of the Kremlin, holding the cavernous Cathedral of Christ the Redeemer. Kaganovich said years later that he argued for the Lenin Hills, where Aleksandr Vitberg tried to put the cathedral in the 1820s, and warned that demolition of the church would be held by ethnic Russians against him, a Jew, and against the party and would "call forth a flood of anti-Semitism." Stalin was

Figure 35. Architects' rendering of the Palace of Soviets and surrounding area. (From *Arkhitektura SSSR,* nos. 10–11, October–November 1935, pp. 26–27.)

unmoved by this thought and by the knowledge that the high water table had hampered construction of the church on the embankment.[21]

The cathedral, likened by some to an oversized *samovar* (Russian kettle), may have had a questionable claim to pulchritude. It had been consecrated only thirty-four years before 1917 and lay on the bones of the fourteenth-century Alekseyevskii Convent, relocated to make way for it. It was, for all that, the largest house of worship in Russia and the Soviet Union. Paid for out of Muscovites' pocketbooks to honor the war of 1812–1814, it recalled to the popular mind patriotic and national customs. Thirty leading artists, led by Vasilii I. Surikov and Vasilii V. Vereshchagin, donated their time to create its high reliefs, iconostasis of albumen marble, twelve cast bronze doors (bought by Moscow's merchantry), 3,000 lamps, and the 177 wall plates commemorating Russian warriors in its nave. Thousands attended its Christmas and Easter services to listen to soloists from the Bol'shoi Theater and to hold tapers, which legend had it would bring good fortune if brought home lit.

Preparations for destroying the cathedral began in mid-July 1931, to the drumbeat from Yemel'yan Yaroslavskii and the League of Militant Atheists that it was "the ideological fortress of the accursed old world" (see Figures 36 and 37). Laborers under OGPU foremen pulled away marble and granite, crosses, ornaments, metal structurals, and the church's fourteen bells, saving them for smelting or reuse; they retrieved 422 kilograms of gold leaf from the five cupolas alone. Mikhail Kryukov, the chief of construction, intended to take down the entire church by hand and cable, but found the going slow. A team led by Aleksandr V. Kosarev, the head of the USSR Komsomol, called up youths to sling miners' picks and mallets. Kryukov's fears about safety were overruled in the interests of speed, and the building was expunged by high explosives at noon on December 5. When the first two charges left the dome and a pair of supporting columns standing, "believers in the crowd let out that the Lord had heard their prayers and would not let the church be destroyed."[22] A third and final explosion dashed their hopes.

Several clerics who protested the last-minute removal of relics December 5 were arrested and shot the same evening; two demolition experts had been sent to labor camps earlier for refusing to take part. Permission to save some artifacts was granted only halfway through

Figure 36. Cathedral of Christ the Redeemer during removal of cladding,
1931. (Museum of the History of the City of Moscow.)

Figure 37. Official rally at site of demolished cathedral, early 1932. Slogan on hoarding reads, "In Place of the Breeding Ground of the Narcotic [of Religion]—the Palace of Soviets." (Museum of the History of the City of Moscow.)

the stripdown. A few bells, murals, and reliefs made it whole to the Antireligious Arts Museum in the Donskoi Monastery and the Historical Museum, and some sculptures and stone fretwork to Kolomenskoye; facing materials were used in subway stations, the Lenin Library addition, and the Mineralogy Museum; the memorial plates ended up lining garden paths in Sokol'niki; the iconostatis was sold through intermediaries to Eleanor Roosevelt, who gave it to the Vatican.[23]

The city's other big memorial of 1812–1814, Osip Bove's Triumphal Gates on the road to Leningrad, suffered annihilation without protest in 1936. The last tsarist logos in Moscow, the Byzantine eagles on the main Kremlin towers, were dismounted in 1935 in favor of copper stars with the Soviet hammer and sickle. For the twentieth anniversary of the revolution in 1937, back-lit stars in ruby-red glass took their place.[24]

The biggest set-tos concerned a couplet of older landmarks: the sixteenth-century brick wall around Kitaigorod and the seventeenth-century Sukharev Tower, at the crossing of Sretenka and the Sadovoye. The 2.5 kilometers, fourteen towers, and six gates of the Kitaigorod Wall had been partially cleaned up in the 1920s. Nevertheless, the Kaganovich commission and public critics derided it as a traffic plug and "a relic of savage and medieval times"; ASNOVA, in a July 1931 letter to the MK and the city executive, retorted that its removal would be "vandalism." The conversation was truncated by the local party leaders' approval of excision of the ceremonial gates at Il'inka, Nikol'skaya, and Varvarka streets in June 1932. Workers did not complete the removal until autumn 1933 (partly because there were construction laborers living in the Varvarskiye Gates), and the idea circulated that Mosrazbor, the city's demolition trust, might stop there. In July 1934 the bureau of the gorkom ordered the wall's systematic destruction, except for two short sections, in the interests of street circulation (Figure 38).[25]

The Sukharev Tower, for generations the city's tallest structure, had since Peter the Great been variously a gatehouse, school and astronomical observatory, water tower, and, from 1925, the city museum. It was now mocked as "a symbol of hucksterism and fraud" due to associations with the Sukharevskii Market. In August 1933, after reading in the newspaper of its impending demise, Igor Grabar', Zholtovskii, and two other architects begged Stalin to help; a drawing enclosed with their letter showed how streetcar rails could be slotted through the pedestal. Kaganovich asked them to elaborate but also convoked a meeting of Communist architects to call them to arms in the "raving class struggle" surrounding the issue. Times were such, he sneered, that "we cannot deal with a single decrepit little church without a protest being delivered to us," and the bellyaching was turning many Muscovites against the regime.[26]

Stalin cabled confirmation of the decision from his vacation spa in September 1933, slamming the tower's defenders as short-sighted and retrograde. Action waited until April 1934, when Mosrazbor workers tore off the white stone balustrades. Grabar', Shchusev, and Zhol-

Figure 38. Tearing down Kitaigorod Wall, 1934. (Museum of the History of the City of Moscow.)

tovskii wrote Stalin again, claiming that the tower could be moved to a new foundation if traffic required. He spurned them coldly, and by June the tower was gone.

In a last dig at Sukharev's mercantile past, the intersection around its footings was rechristened Kolkhoznaya ploshchad' (Collective Farm Square) later in 1934. The new name betokened the blizzard of Sovietized street signs that blotted out such age-old names as Tverskaya and Pervaya Tverskaya-Yamskaya (now ulitsa Gor'kogo, Gorky Street), Il'inka (ulitsa Kuibysheva), Varvarka (ulitsa Razina), Myasnitskaya (ulitsa Kirova), and Ostozhenka (Metrostroyevskaya [Subway Builders] ulitsa). An engineer named A. I. Shumilin went so far as to moot that Red Square be renamed prospekt Mavzoleya Lenina—Prospect of the Lenin Mausoleum.[27]

By November of 1934 Lev M. Perchik, the chief of the Planning Department of Moscow, could taunt Moscophile antiquaries with having been outgunned and muzzled:

> We have completely snuffed out this kind of reactionary opinion and attitude. No one would dare speak up now in such a way, because millions know from experience that Moscow could not have lived another day in the stone swaddling clothes of its infancy. We still sometimes hear timid voices complaining about the undue severity of surgical methods. Such claims only amuse us. No one has identified a single demolished building which should have been saved; it is easy to find dozens more which must be demolished. We cannot reconstruct a city like Moscow without a surgeon's scalpel.[28]

"Reactionary" attitudes were not snuffed out by words alone. Petr Baranovskii, Moscow's restoration ace, received a reprimand in 1931 for his "apolitical" attitude. In October 1933 he was arrested and accused of plotting to assassinate Stalin. Six months into solitary confinement and interrogation, he signed a fictive confession and assumed a sentence to Siberia, there to remain until May 1936. The Central State Restoration Workshops were dissolved in 1934, and the NKVD bundled up many of his colleagues there. Vladimir Nevskii, who had tried to protect the Kremlin cloisters in 1929, was jailed in 1935 and shot two years later.[29]

The rota of state-protected Moscow buildings, already cropped from 474 to 216 in 1928, shrunk to 117 in 1932 and 74 in 1935.

The decertified buildings were often ecclesiastical, thanks to the surfeit of churches and a belligerently atheistic mood that saw the number of working Orthodox churches in Moscow dwindle from 224 in 1930 to about 100 in January 1933, 40 in 1937, and 16 in 1938. Once a church had been emptied, local councils and other agencies reaped financial rewards for bringing it down. A hidden clause in the 1933 economic plan assigned 252 tons of bronze bells from 20 closed churches to the city government.[30]

In the Kremlin, the Church of the Savior in the Wood, the most ancient in all Moscow, was wiped out in the spring of 1933. Aleksei Rykov believed this was because it darkened the windows of the flat that Kaganovich took over from him in 1932. The Church of the Annunciation, part of the Blagoveshchenskaya Tower, was demolished in 1932. In 1933 the Red Staircase (Krasnoye kryl'tso) of the Faceted Palace, from which medieval monarchs addressed the crowd on Sobornaya ploshchad', was pulled down for expansion of the Great Kremlin Palace; Stalin wanted the 1934 party congress held there rather than in the Bol'shoi Theater.[31]

The rape of the city's religious abbeys continued with brutal efficiency. Eleven of the twenty-five were wholly or partially demolished by 1937, when the last traces of the Strastnoi Convent, an atheistic museum since 1928, were swept away. The two Kremlin cloisters made way for office buildings, the Zlatoustovskii Monastery for an apartment house for the OGPU, and the Nikitskii Convent for a subway power transformer. The Zachat'evskii Monastery in 1932 became a garage for government limousines and a hostel for the drivers. Half of the Simonov Monastery, in its time the richest in Russia and Moscow's bastion against the Tatar heathen, was despoiled in 1931–1932 to extend ZIS, the Stalin Auto Works (formerly AMO) and allow for a "palace of culture" designed by the Vesnin brothers. The refectory went over to a fish cannery when a plan to open a cinema in it failed. *Nothing* of use covered over the rubble of five monasteries and nunneries: Georgiyevskii, Nikol'skii, Skorbya-shchenskii, Sretenskii, and Strastnoi.[32]

On Red Square, Kaganovich is said to have advocated deletion of St. Basil's Cathedral because "it interferes with the holiday columns of demonstrators" trotting into the square from the riverside. Closed to worshipers and assigned to the Historical Museum in 1929, it was

removed from the protected roster in the autumn of 1933 and Baranovskii was instructed by Dmitrii V. Usov, a deputy of Bulganin's, to
do a predemolition survey; his objections led to his arrest. Hearsay
has Kaganovich wanting the Kremlin itself obliterated—as staggering
a suggestion as could have been made in Moscow. Neither of these
ideas was acted upon, and St. Basil's was returned to the state list in
the mid-1930s. That either could be entertained is a mark of the
times.[33]

The approaches to the far terminus of Red Square had been
spanned since 1680 by the twin-marqueed Voskresenskiye (Resurrection) Gates; they enclosed the Shrine of the Iberian Virgin, where all
tsars since Peter I knelt in prayer before going into the Kremlin, and
a popular icon reputed to have healing powers. The shrine was closed
in 1929, but conservationists thought they had saved the gates when
they executed a plan, drawn up by Dmitrii P. Sukhov and supported
by ASNOVA, to widen their arches. The gates were effaced in one night
in June 1931.[34]

A few meters away, at the corner of Nikol'skaya ulitsa, stood the
flowerlike Kazan Cathedral, built to commemorate the defeat of Polish occupiers in 1612 and associated in pageantry with Russian generalship. Baranovskii had done restoration work there after 1925,
with the congregation's funds. He was halted in 1930 and the church
given to the city's cinema agency in 1933. When conversion into a
movie theater proved too expensive, it was demolished in July and
August 1936 to make way for an "artistic panorama" of Stalin's
Moscow. Funding went only as far as a summer café; after the war,
urinals and soda water dispensers were all that remained. Baranovskii,
commuting by rail from his place of administrative exile in Moscow
oblast, succeeded in photographing and measuring the half-destroyed
church.[35]

Lev Perchik's metaphor of the surgeon's scalpel was an injustice
to some of the techniques used. Seven tons of ammonal and 1,500
electric detonators were needed to fell the Cathedral of Christ the
Redeemer in 1931. It took five months of pile driving and blasting to
break apart the foundation and eighteen to cart off the 40 million
bricks. "In place of everything that had been there before, full of life,
there was now only black earth, over which there crawled back and
forth, like beetles over a grave, trucks of every type and make, ordered

to level everything, to take everything away." In November 1934 tens of thousands of Komsomols went at the remnants of the Kitaigorod Wall with cold chisels and spades. Watching them crumple, a witness was reminded of papier-mâché stage decorations coming down after a play. When Khrushchev blurted out at a meeting that old buildings had many partisans, Stalin replied, "Then you should blow them up at night."[36]

A PAPERWORK WALL

The same control reflex can be found in a crucial innovation in urban governance: a regulatory system of mandatory identity papers redefining some basic rights of the residents and would-be residents of Moscow. Like many features of the Soviet police state, this one borrowed from tsarist practice, only going much further in terms of socioeconomic content, universality, and severity of sanction.

The main decree, dated December 27, 1932, obliged all urbanites aged sixteen years and over to obtain renewable, pocket-sized passports from a new section of the OGPU. Residents had to register by April 15 in Moscow (and a 100-kilometer zone around it), Leningrad, and Khar'kov, with deadlines in other cities following in order of importance. Starting in May 1933 a page of the passport was reserved for stamping a residency permit—a *propiska*—giving title to work and habitation in the given city. Anyone without it was liable to imprisonment or summary banishment.[37]

To vindicate this callous step, the Kremlin pointed to the influx of villagers ("kulaks") into the towns, leaving unsaid that its own mailed fist lay behind the pandemonium impelling peasants, few of them genuine kulaks, off the land as fugitives. The exodus was becoming frantic, as the poor harvest of 1932 was about to visit mass starvation and disease on the countryside.[38] The legislation also spoke of shutting out "superfluous," "criminal," and "alien" people who were not from the peasantry. Besides softening pressure on the cities' infrastructure and provisions and tightening the noose of social controls, the government hoped to avert a further skid in food production by manacling peasants to the kolkhozes (they were normally issued documents only at the behest of an industrial employer, a provision not revoked until 1974).

For Moscow, the decree had been foretold in the plethora of

schemes to "unburden" it by obstructing in-migration and ejecting government offices and even individuals. The privations of the early 1930s must have firmed up support, albeit tempered by anxiety for friends and relatives. Kaganovich cagily pandered to it: "This is a big city, and people come here. There are no apartments for them, so they overload the city."[39]

The gorkom bureau in no time set up a formidable structure to carry out the decree. Each party raikom formed a "passportization assistance headquarters" under the head of its organization department, and each raion soviet a tribunal to hear appeals from police decisions; party secretaries chaired passport commissions within factories; the OGPU chipped in 1,000 staffers and the Moscow presidium 1,800 clerks and truck transport. In March 1933 a gorkom commission under Khrushchev began a reliability check of apartment superintendents and doormen, another committee (also led by Khrushchev) looked into the resurgence of street orphans, and Stanislav F. Redens, the chief of the Moscow OGPU, drafted a policy on doormen setting down that they "be selected and their work supervised by the organs of the militia," the regular constabulary. The militia were "in a planned way to inspect all houses, with the aim of flushing out persons who do not have the right to reside in Moscow."[40]

The teeth were quick to bite. Moscow between January 1933 and February 1936 experienced not a growth slump but a contraction of 91,000 in absolute numbers. A resolution at the beginning of 1933 set 3.3 million as the year-end target. Only promiscuous expulsions could have achieved such a thing, and this is what Moscow endured in the first half of the year, when, by official numeration, its population plummeted by 246,000 people. One politician drew guffaws at a meeting by likening the scarecrow peasants trudging out of Moscow to Napoleon's army in retreat.[41]

At least a portion of 1935's smaller decrease had political origins. The NKVD conducted thousands of arrests after the murder of Sergei Kirov, the Leningrad party leader, in December 1934, which Stalin exploited to magnify police terror. Khrushchev did not resist, thinking, he says in his tape-recorded memoirs, that Moscow was "constipated with many undesirable elements—nonworkers, parasites, and profiteers."[42]

Copious expulsions accompanied the interval of net growth in

Moscow's population (from mid-1933 to the end of 1934). An English resident saw police collar homeless juveniles and adults in November 1933. They were "to be taken forty or fifty miles outside Moscow and dumped on the road to die, like abandoned dogs or cats." The next spring, an OGPU man, Ivan N. Kuznetsov, was appointed head of cadres of Metrostroi and began a document review. "Former criminals, kulaks, and escapees from [political] exile," he said, hid out in shafts and tunnels. "Sometimes we literally had to drag them out into the light of day." Two thousand Metrostroi workers were kicked out of Moscow.[43]

Chairman Bulganin narrated a chilling companion tale to the city party plenum of March 1934. The 2,500 residents of 15 Smolenskii bul'var, he said, had been "taken prisoner by hooligans, orphans, homeless persons, beggars, and other riff-raff" who had barricaded themselves in the garret. The squatters offered protection from criminals in exchange for their presence being withheld from the police. When they were spurned, the illegals set the building ablaze, bringing fire trucks and the OGPU down upon their heads. The incursion, Bulganin said delicately, had been "liquidated," although some had infiltrated back into the attic.[44]

Moscow politicos did not ask where the ostracized were sent. "If you weren't told something," Khrushchev recalled, "that meant it didn't concern you; it was the state's business, and the less you knew about it the better."[45]

THE MASTER PLAN OF 1935

The socialist blueprint promulgated four years after the June 1931 plenum was a virtual bible for Moscow and for Soviet urbanization. To make it, organizational tools first had to be forged. Moscow's planning section was so bereft of data that the Kaganovich commission had to seek out information about communal services from Rabkrin and the OGPU. In September 1931 Vladimir L. Orleanskii became the third planning chief in two years to go under. His office was flayed as "a musty academic organ" infested with anti-Soviet specialists.[46]

A full-fledged municipal department for town planning, an Architectural Planning Directorate, finally coalesced in February 1932. Its chief was Mikhail Kryukov, a lathe worker's son talented enough to acquire an architect's papers before 1917 and after that become a construction organizer, first as head of Mosstroi and later in charge of building the Palace of Soviets. Co-opted to the city presidium, he retained 250 architects and engineers to draw up a master plan. Vladimir Semenov, the apostle of Ebenezer Howard who had been a consultant to Shchusev on New Moscow, directed this group.

"From June 1931 through 1932," Bulganin recapitulated in 1935, "we had no definite direction with respect to planning Moscow. We were seeking and striving for one."[47]

The soupiness of official thought allowed for disparate images of the future. Valeryan Osinskii, the USSR's chief statistician and a member of the old Bukharin group in the local party, conjectured Moscow as a "galaxy of socialist cities." German Krasin found fault with the subway and the ban on new factories, both already party policy, calling the former a waste of money and the latter a step toward "declassing" Moscow. Sergei Gornyi, Orleanskii's predecessor, was branded a "leftist" for propounding a blanket rezoning; and yet, Orleanskii took fire in his turn for having accepted Gornyi's population target of 3 million, "despite criticism of this stance in the press as right-opportunist and a brake on Moscow's maturation."[48]

A hundred flowers bloomed during an invitational contest for an outline plan, from October 1931 to October 1932. A brigade from VOPRA, the League of Proletarian Architects, pursed Moscow into five planning districts and imposed rectilinear streets beyond the city core. Nikolai Ladovskii and Krasin sallied forth with variations on their parabolic and deurbanist schemes of 1929–1930, Krasin clinging to the opinion that a Moscow strung out along railways should grow to 8 to 10 million people. V. B. Kratyuk projected a half-dozen Ladovskii-type planning "rockets" darting out from the the Kremlin and Kitaigorod, with the business and administrative center becoming a corridor pushed to the northeast and industry concentrated in the southeast (Figure 39). Kurt Mayer, the former chief architect of Cologne, presented a sparer, starfishlike rendition of Krasin. Ernst May adumbrated fifteen suburban "city collectives" of 100,000 persons each around a mostly intact core, and Hannes Meyer devised nine functionally specialized satellites, mostly to the east and south, making up a "system of cities" centering on an inner Moscow whose circular roads had been rebuilt as ellipses (Figures 40 and 41).[49]

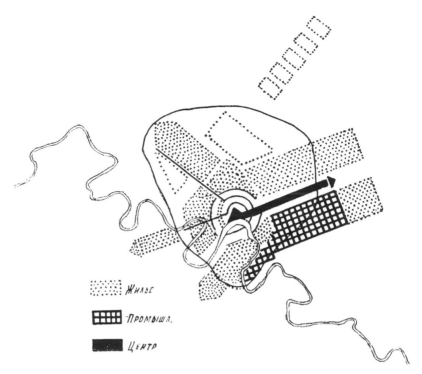

Figure 39. Planning sketch by V. B. Kratyuk, 1932. Housing areas are drawn in dots, factory zone in checks, and center in black. (From *Sovetskaya arkhitektura,* no. 1, January 1933, p. 20.)

If this cacophony recalled the 1920s, the barging in by politicians did not. In July 1932 Kaganovich chaired a meeting of 150 specialists and officials and gave general guidance incorporating "the direction for the future Moscow indicated by Comrade Stalin." The proviso was to "proceed first and foremost from the historically established forms of the present city, rebuilding it in accord with the dictates of our epoch."[50] All the entries in the concourse failed this litmus test and so were shortly found guilty of slighting the party's directives.

It fell to Vladimir Semenov to stencil in the 1935 plan. He shared the animus against utopian planning and seemed at home with the new monumentalism, praising majestic ensembles *(ansambli)*—the word evoked Napoleon III's Paris, Hapsburg Vienna, and St. Petersburg—over the utilitarian glass and cement of the 1920s. He tried to salvage something of the garden city by drawing in five "urban com-

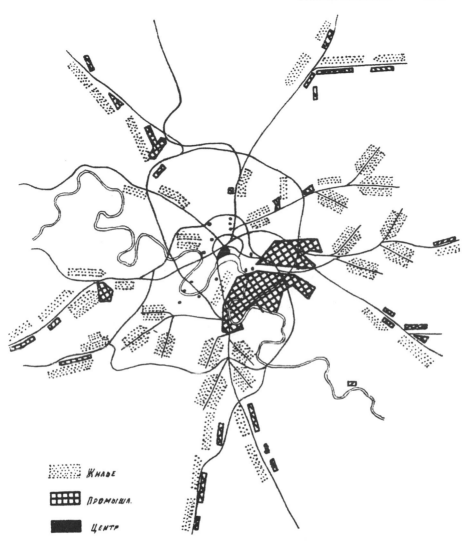

ЖИЛЬЕ

ПРОМЫШЛ.

ЦЕНТР

Figure 40. Ernst May's image of Moscow and outlying "city collectives," 1932. Housing areas are drawn in dots, industrial zones in checks, and center in black. (From *Sovetskaya arkhitektura,* no. 1, January 1933, p. 12.)

plexes," all to stir greenery in with industry and housing and to be set off from central Moscow by a girdle of parkland. By February 1933, when Semenov undraped the first gypsum maquette of the plan, the only Howardian remnant was the provision for downtown parks

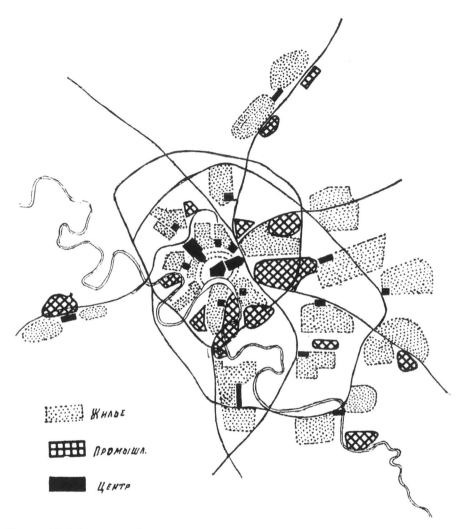

Figure 41. Moscow and environs as a "system of cities," by Hannes Meyer, 1932. Housing areas are drawn in dots, industrial zones in checks, and center in black. (From *Sovetskaya arkhitektura,* no. 1, January 1933, p. 14.)

and a suburban wooded zone. His plan stressed the ever more favored themes of street widenings and ensembles.[51]

Semenov was less than perfectly pliable, especially on conservation issues. With his stricture, repeated several times, that Moscow be "rebuilt, not wiped from the face of the earth," he reproached wanton demolition as much as social utopianism. He is reputed to have grabbed Stalin's elbow at a meeting when the leader picked up a model of St. Basil's to see how Red Square would look without it. This miscue would help account for his replacement in the spring of 1934 by Sergei Chernyshev, a functionary so cautious that he preferred to sign documents in pencil rather than ink. There were other hints of tension over the plan. In September 1933, during the fireworks over the Sukharev Tower, a Planning Department was detached from Kryukov's directorate. Lev Perchik, its first head, was the uneducated ideologist seasoned in the OGPU and the party apparatus of Ukraine under Kaganovich who advocated the scalpel treatment; he smeared planning ideas with which he disagreed as "Chayanovism," after the imprisoned author of *Journey of My Brother Aleksei*. For reasons unknown, he was supplanted in early 1935 by Kaganovich's former personal aide, Aleksandr I. Bulushev.[52]

The draft plan was far enough along to receive sanction on the highest plane on July 14, 1934, as Stalin and other Soviet panjandrums met with fifty of the planners in a Kremlin hall adorned with a large Moscow map. Stalin spoke in a soft voice. "The participants in the meeting rose from their chairs and, surrounding the leader in a tight circle, listened to him with rapt attention, hanging on every word."[53]

Stalin's soliloquy toasted the planners for winning "on two fronts," against "those who would deny the very principle of a city and leave Moscow as a big village" and against "proponents of hyperurbanization . . . who counsel building along the lines of a capitalist city, with skyscrapers and extraordinary overcrowding." On substance, he "paid special attention to the necessity of broadening streets and squares." But his crispest dictum fitted the plan into the overall political economy:

> Comrade Stalin [as paraphrased by Kaganovich] drew our attention at the meeting to the need to struggle resolutely with uncoordinated [*stikhiinoi*] construction . . . We long ago liquidated private property in land. However, we still observe certain builders taking a private-property approach to the plots allotted them. We must combat such antistate tendencies in the city's development. It is necessary to build . . . according

to a set plan. Anyone who tries to breach this plan should be brought to account. To rebuff antistate tendencies, we need a firm hand, a solid apparatus, and unshakable discipline. The plan precisely defining the line of street and square must be an inviolable law.

Moscow had been professed a socialist city in 1931—yet here was Stalin tarring its builders with comporting themselves like capitalists! It followed that a crucial function of the plan was to be an iron hand safeguarding collective and state interests.

The party-government resolution "On the Master Plan for the Reconstruction of the City of Moscow," cosigned by Stalin and Molotov, revealed the plan's contours on July 10, 1935. It assimilated the new planning orthodoxy and, without acknowledgment, snippets of prior endeavors. Its basal directives on population, territory, and physical plant, at the urging of Gosplan, projected only ten years into the future, not the twenty first envisaged.[54]

The document called for a Moscow of "approximately 5 million people, whose daily-life and cultural needs would all be fully met." Its area would jump from 285 to 600 square kilometers, close to what Shchusev urged in New Moscow, through staged annexation of "reserve territories." In a decision supposed to have come to Kaganovich during a clairvoyant sunrise drive around the outskirts,[55] half of the increment was to be to the southwest, past the Lenin Hills as far as Kuntsevo on the west and Lenino (formerly Tsaritsyno) to the south. Underpopulated and upwind of most industry, this high mesa, largely farmland but reserved by the city presidium in 1931 for a municipal airport, was severed from the body of Moscow by the hills and the snaking Moskva.

The plan embossed a gross functional zoning on the metropolitan area (Figure 42), another idea fashionable before 1935. Housing was destined mainly for the southwest (to hold 1.5 million people), northwest, and east. Sections were sequestered for industry, with most of the expansion in the southeast, and all unsanitary and fire-prone plants were to be evicted. A green belt (*lesoparkovyi zashchitnyi poyas,* "forest-park protective belt")—presaged by Zholtovskii, Sakulin, Shchusev, and Shestakov—circumscribed the city to a width of 10 kilometers, supplying recreation sites and oxygen. The housing built, 15 million square meters, would have reversed the downward

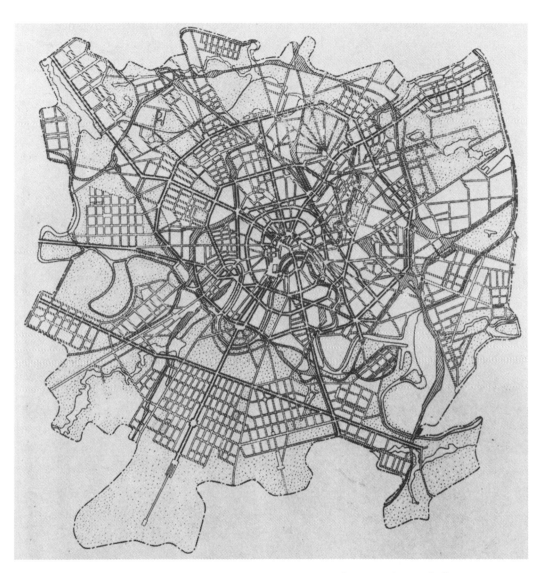

Figure 42. Moscow master plan of 1935. Drawing shows main roads (heavy double lines), residential blocks, and parkland (lightly dotted areas). (From M. I. Astaf'eva-Dlugach et al., *Moskva*, Moscow: Stroiizdat, 1979, p. 39.)

spiral of Moscow's supply per head. The plan also made allowance for 530 new schools, 11 bridges high enough to clear the vessels brought in by the Moscow-Volga Canal, and scores of other public facilities.

The planners saved their most acid words for the face of the pre-Soviet city, which "even in the best years of its growth . . . reflected . . . barbarous Russian capitalism." They retained and extended the radial-concentric street pattern but in their own way presaged the mutation of much that was familiar. Red Square was to be doubled in size and 23 other squares rebuilt. Kitaigorod, mostly cleared, would be a platform for "several monumental buildings of state-wide significance." Ulitsa Gor'kogo and other main thoroughfares were to be reamed out to no less than 30 to 40 meters "by demolishing buildings and immediately liquidating flower beds, lawns, and . . . trees . . . that impede traffic." There were to be 16 major highway projects: 5 radials, 5 links between squares, 3 ring roads, and 3 massive avenues traversing the city's midriff (from Izmailovo to the Lenin Hills, from Vsekhsvyatskoye to ZIS, and from Ostankino to Serpukhovskoye shosse).

Not for nothing did the press call it a brief for "an offensive on the old Moscow." Kaganovich in an off-the-record chat with officials used typically gladiatorial imagery. A scheme drawn up by armchair planners who did nothing but stare at documents would have been useless, he asserted. The master plan was a "plan of war," and like any strategy worth its salt it took account of the results of the first barrage: "Better one step in reality than ten steps in a design . . . Experience shows that a war plan worked out long before the war proves problematic. The present plan of war has been worked out after the opening battles with the adversary"—the adversary being, literally and figuratively, Moscow itself.[56]

All perspective was drowned in the hallelujahs about how the document would hoist Moscow above Athens, Rome, and Paris. Bukharin, his career nearing an ignominious end, lilted that "Stalin, the architect of the new world," had inspired a plan that was "almost a fairy tale, almost magical," which would make Moscow a latter-day City of the Sun, "a new Mecca to which fighters for the happiness of mankind will stream from all ends of the earth."[57] The bouquets to fabled worlds and humanity in the abstract must for some have masked disquiet about the here and now.

Power Play

Stalin's crabbed suspiciousness and the ambitions of his wards stoked a relentless and mostly furtive contest for power and standing. No account of Moscow government could fail to register how its elite fared in the game.

VANGUARD OF THE VANGUARD

It was right for the obkom and gorkom to be rehoused in 1933, after renovations by the OGPU, on Staraya ploshchad' (Old Square), three-quarters of a kilometer east of the Kremlin. Its new home, No. 6 Staraya ploshchad', stood yardarm to yardarm with No. 4, where the Central Committee Secretariat had been located since 1924; the two had been put up around 1910 as twinned luxury apartment houses.

Never was the tie between Moscow and national politics cozier than on Kaganovich's watch (see Figure 43). With his elevation to full Politburo member in 1930, and the move of his contender for Stalin's ear, Molotov, to government work, he became de facto second secretary of the party and high priest of Stalin's personality cult. He adhered unblinkingly to his idol's creed of government by combat and regimentation: "There are those who think that, since we have smashed the kulak and the opposition, we can work placidly and be liberal. This is false. Our enemies have not changed the struggle against us, only its form." During the Great Purge of the late 1930s, Kaganovich signed execution slips for 36,000 people.[58]

Within his bailiwick, Kaganovich treated the doctrinally suspect mercilessly as he rid himself of anyone who could be tarred with the faults of his predecessors. He had his pick of the footloose young Communists studying in Moscow or drifting in to find work, advancing them locally and in the provincial and central apparatuses. When political sections to enforce party policy were formed in Soviet state farms and tractor stations in 1933, Moscow provided one-third of the first 10,000 recruits.[59]

Kaganovich specialized in packing the Moscow establishment with a personal coterie. The rough-hewn and garrulous Khrushchev, for one, first made his acquaintance in 1917 and was a local secretary and deputy head of the Ukrainian party's personnel office under him before coming to the Moscow Industrial Academy as a trainee in 1929. There Khrushchev claims in his memoirs to have befriended

Figure 43. Revolution Day march, November 1934, beneath portraits *(left to right)* of Stalin, Lenin, and Kaganovich. (Museum of the History of the City of Moscow.)

Nadezhda Alliluyeva, Stalin's wife, a student in the textiles faculty, and to have been admitted into the Stalin household. Whether or not this was so (and one guesses that Kaganovich would have been wary), Kaganovich plucked him from the academy in January 1931, before graduation, to clean lingering rightists out of Baumanskii raikom. From there Khrushchev shimmied up the greasy promotions pole: first secretary of the largest raion (Krasnopresnenskii) in July 1931; second secretary of the Moscow gorkom in January 1932; overseer of the subway project (qualified by his youthful days as a coal miner) and in 1933 of passport issuance; gorkom first secretary and obkom second secretary, and thereby Kaganovich's right-hand man, in January 1934.[60]

Bulganin, the chairman of the Mossovet, had been with Kaganovich in Turkestan and in 1919 in his native Nizhnii Novgorod, where Kaganovich held his first big position. Coincidentally or not, Elektrozavod, the Moscow Electrical Works Bulganin directed until 1930, was in the same Baumanskii raion in which Khrushchev was making waves. The new head of the obkom's department for party personnel, Georgii M. Malenkov, had known Kaganovich since Turkestan and, in the CC apparatus, teamed with him in a 1925 purge of Moscow students and professors. Twenty-one other ranking Moscow functionaries between 1930 and 1937 (eleven who made it to obkom or gorkom secretary) can be identified as having earlier served in Kaganovich's presence, several twice: two at Nizhnii Novgorod, one at Voronezh (in 1919–1920), five in Turkestan, eight in the CC Secretariat, and eleven in Ukraine.[61]

In the wider amphitheater, Kaganovich was eulogized as Stalin's "best comrade-in-arms" and draped in offices and honors: head of the CC's agriculture and transport departments; superintendent of the party purge of 1933–1934, which ousted one Moscow Communist in nine; chairman of the Party Control Commission in 1934–1935. He gave the organizational report at the 1930 and 1934 party congresses and often served as Stalin's troubleshooter in the provinces. Aria upon aria extolled his political and administrative acumen. Kaganovich, an obkom official said at the Seventeenth Party Congress in 1934, "inculcated a Stalinist style of work from top to bottom and bottom to top" of the Moscow organization, turning it "into a forward column, a vanguard"—the vanguard of the Communist Party vanguard.[62]

Economics alone assured it a forward place. Moscow produced all of the USSR's ballbearings in 1934, two-thirds of its machine tools, 42 percent of its automobiles, and one-third of its instruments—not to mention aircraft and other military machinery, where the figures were classified. Firms such as ZIS, Aviation Works Nos. 1, 22, and 24, Frezer, Kalibr, the Moscow Radio Works, and the First State Ballbearing Works were *golovnyye predpriyatiya*, "head enterprises" whose technologies and management methods were evaluated and propagated to entire branches. In 1940, before wartime evacuation scalloped into its share, the city of Moscow put out 98 percent of the country's ballbearings, half of its machine tools and instruments, 49 percent of the autos, and more than 40 percent of the electrical equipment.

Stalinist economics dictated close cooperation with science, and science, being small by comparison with industry, could be more easily concentrated. The state commissariats first set up departmental research institutes in 1933, the first year of the Second Five-Year Plan. Moscow-based "academies" for broad sectors of learning proliferated, starting with the Lenin Academy of Agricultural Sciences, founded in 1929, and progressing through communal services (1931), architecture (1933), pedagogy (1943), medicine (1944), and art (1947). Most important, the USSR Academy of Sciences, after 210 years in St. Petersburg/Leningrad, moved to Moscow in 1934. Putting its presidium in the eighteenth-century Neskuchnyi Palace on Bol'shaya Kaluzhskaya ulitsa, southwest of the city center, the government posthaste began work in the district on lustrous facilities such as the Lebedev Physics Institute on Bol'shaya Kaluzhskaya and the Institute of Physical Problems on Vorob'evskoye shosse.

Beyond the production indexes and physics laboratories, an almost mystical aura rubbed off on Moscow. "As Moscow is rebuilt," the central press trilled after passage of the 1935 plan, "so shall all our Motherland's cities be rebuilt." The Kremlin parapets and the Lenin Mausoleum, the party and army leaders glued to it like mannequins, provided the backdrop to the armored parades marking May Day and November 7, organized by the Moscow party apparatus. Starting in 1931, they featured fascistic "physical culture promenades" of tens of thousands of gymnasts waving flags, portraits, and helium-filled dolls of Stalin. In 1933 the government denominated Aviation Day, to be held every August 18 to blare forth its technological achievements; the main air show, attended by Stalin and the Politburo, was held at either the Central Airfield or the newer terminal at Tushino. The Lenin Museum, the Museum of the Revolution, the Museum of the Soviet Army at ploshchad' Kommuny, and the All-Union Agricultural Exhibition, opened at Ostankino in 1939—these were but a few of the other Moscow sights the regime wanted its subjects to be instructed by. The Soviet Union's first television station took residence on ulitsa Shabolovka in 1938, broadcasting from the Shukhov Tower.

To the capital's benefit, the Stalinist hierarchy of individuals was superimposed, as one historian notes, "on a hierarchy of spaces, so that 'good' . . . people proved to be closer to the center of the world— Moscow, and even the center of Moscow—and 'the bad' occupied the periphery." Literature likewise cast Moscow as "a prefiguration of that which is to come . . . the place from which that Jacob's ladder rises, leading to 'higher' reality." In film, it appeared a shimmering court for the benevolent prince, whose subjects voyaged from near and far to tell his ministers their troubles.[63] In the plastic arts, Moscow was a showroom for likenesses of him in stone and metal. Sergei D. Merkurov's dyad of hulking granite statues of Stalin and Lenin—thirty-two meters (about twelve stories) high—flanked the Moscow-Volga Canal at Dmitrov. A Merkurov statue of Stalin almost as big was put up in the All-Union Agricultural Exhibition, and smaller ones materialized in front of the Tret'yakov Gallery and in the Kurskaya subway station. Said one Moscow guide book, "Tens and hundreds of artistic works—low and high reliefs, portrait busts, and figurative renderings . . . have been created by our sculptors on the Stalinist theme."[64]

On this sacral ground in 1935 the baton passed from Kaganovich to Khrushchev in the only honorable retirement of any but a short-term Moscow first secretary since 1917. Georgii Malenkov was made deputy head, to Yezhov (a rival of Kaganovich), of the Central Committee's Department of Leading Party Organs in 1934, and head when Yezhov took over the NKVD in 1936. Khrushchev, the first Moscow strongman since 1923 not to be made a CC secretary, concentrated on local issues. Although neither he nor any later boss equaled Kaganovich in sheltering cronies, he managed to give precedence to ex-Ukraine administrators whose careers had run in tandem to his.[65]

NECROPOLIS

Stalin's Great Purge cut a bloody swath through Moscow in 1937–1938. Denizens of its most desirable apartment houses trembled in their sheets at the rustlings of elevators or of oncoming automobiles they dreaded might be from the NKVD's argosy of *chernyye vorony* ("black crow") paddy wagons. Some were so sure the end was nigh that they kept a suitcase packed. Bukharin and Rykov, codefendants in the third of the Moscow show trials in March 1938, topped the scroll of pre-1930 oppositionists put in the dock in the Columned Hall of the House of Unions as fiendish "enemies of the people." For untold others, doom came as surreptitious seizure, conviction, and conveyance to a killing ground or penal colony. If forerunners had some rational connection to policy, this terror came without rhyme or reason, a witch-hunt driven by paranoia and malice.[66]

The dismal arithmetic of the fatalities for Moscow and the country remains uncertain. But one takes no risk in saying that the Muscovites massacred—in the Lubyanka, the NKVD "Inner Prison" completed on Fursakovskogo ulitsa in 1933, the execution cellar of the Military Collegium of the Supreme Court across ploshchad' Dzerzhinskogo, elsewhere in Moscow, and outside the city limits—have to be reckoned in *six figures*.[67]

The dead were interred covertly in grisly pits and mounds in the churchyards of the Donskoi and Novospasskii Monasteries; in the Kalitnikovskoye, Rogozhskoye, Vagan'kovskoye, Armyanskoye, Gol'yanovskoye, and other cemeteries; at Khodynka Field; at the Yauzskaya Hospital; at Kuz'minki, the former estate of the Golitsyns in southeast Moscow; and at the NKVD's compound at Butovo and its state farm at Kommunarka, to the south of Moscow. For the wolfish work of execution and burying, the police signed on village lads who had completed military service and handed them a Moscow propiska in recompense. Kalitnikovskoye—across Malaya Kalitnikov-skaya ulitsa from the Moscow Meat Combine—was a dump for nude corpses, tossed into pits with shovelfuls of lime by soldiers wearing rubber aprons and mitts; scavenging dogs loped through the grave-yard with body parts in their jaws. The municipal crematorium at Donskoi Monastery worked overtime incinerating bodies, and the ashes ended up in a great cavity in the ground, macadamized over.

Sobbing prisoners were brought alive to Vagan'kovskoye Cemetery in canopied trucks and forced to dig their own tombs, after which vodka-dulled guards put bullets in their skulls and tumbled them in. Novospasskii Monastery became a charnel house for German, British, and other foreign Communists, who were kept under lock and key and shot in a specially rigged shower stall; the cadavers were stacked like cordwood in furrows outside the abbey wall, regular graves and tombstones and drainage pipes placed over them to disguise the car-nage (see Figure 44). Isai D. Berg, a cutthroat section chief in the Moscow NKVD, ginned up a gas chamber (*dushegubka*) on wheels, an airtight lorry camouflaged as a bread van that suffocated internees with engine fumes on the drive out to Butovo. At Butovo, the central NKVD organized a phony shooting range to mask the gunshots; some-thing like 25,000 victims were buried in half-kilometer trenches in the

Figure 44. Secret burial ground for victims of the terror of the 1930s at Novospasskii Monastery. Bodies were interred in the shrubby area between the wall and the pond. (Photograph by author.)

three years 1937–1939. Perhaps 14,000 errant NKVD officers and others were eliminated and interred at Kommunarka, where Yagoda had a dacha before his arrest in 1937. At the end of 1938, when some 4,000 zeks at the Gulag camp at Dmitrov had wound up work on the Moscow-Volga Canal, "So as not to have to transport them or build new camps, almost all . . . were shot. There they rest now, along the banks and on the floor of the canal."[68]

The dragnet joined political nobodies to one-time worthies:

Investigations were "worked up" on the presumption of "the sharpening of the class struggle." The formula "Has-Beens Are Concealed Enemies" gave a free hand to overzealous [NKVD] servicemen . . . for whom the thing was to draw up lists: of former traders, former [pre-1917] constables, church elders, former kulaks, even people who had been dekulakized and lishentsy [persons without electoral rights]. The deputy chief of the NKVD's directorate for Moscow oblast, [G. M.] Yakubovich, signed arrest certificates daily and demanded that his subordinates work harder to expose hidden class enemies. And that is what they did, exposing whole lists at a time. People were sent to the troikas and special boards [execution tribunals] by the list, they were condemned by the list, and the [death] sentences were carried out by the list.[69]

The recreants merely arrested surely outnumbered those shot or gassed outright. A legion of misery, they filled Lubyanka, Butyrki, and Lefortovo, the three big political prisons, to the rafters; they were bound over for interrogation at Sukhanovka, the monastery due south of Moscow now the NKVD's worst dungeon; they coursed through Krasnaya Presnya transit jail on their way to the camp netherworld from which many would never return; their spouses, social lepers, lined up for letters at the Gulag postal wicket at 22 Kuznetskii most.

A pitiless settling of accounts claimed next to all of the old bulls of the Moscow party. Five of its nine living ex-heads—Pyatnitskii, Yakovleva, Zelenskii, Uglanov, and Bauman—were eliminated; only Molotov, Kaganovich, Khrushchev, and the long absent Zemlyachka came out alive, and Zemlyachka, Semashko, and Vladimirskii were the sole escapees among the main makers of the Bolshevik Revolution in Moscow. Of thirty-two others who had been city or regional party secretaries since 1917, only two threaded the needle. Slain, too, were both ex-chairmen of the Mossovet, Kamenev in August 1936 (after the first show trial) and Ukhanov in September 1937, along with, as best I can tell, every living deputy and ex-deputy chairman. The terror was serendipitous. Mikhail Kryukov, who had left Moscow government in 1933 to be the founding rector of the USSR Academy of Architecture, died in a Vorkuta camp after signing under torture a statement that he had been a saboteur since 1921 and passed data about numbered defense plants to foreign spies; Vladimir Orleanskii, disgraced when Kryukov replaced him as chief planner in 1931, still sat as deputy head of the planning office when the war broke out.[70]

The surrealistic turnover in territorial party committees gives an inkling of the impact on local institutions. Of the sixty-three persons selected to the Moscow gorkom in May 1937, only ten were returned in June 1938, and I have tracked eight to new jobs; the other forty-five (71.4 percent) were struck from the rolls, and the great majority, presumably, perished. Of sixty-four on the 1937 obkom, eight were reelected, ten are known to have gotten work elsewhere, and forty-six (71.9 percent) dropped from sight. In the Dzerzhinskii raikom of the city, three first secretaries in succession were detained within a few months in 1937.[71]

The city and regional party conferences in May and June 1937 were snakepits of mutual incrimination, as speakers tried to prove their "vigilance" by flagellating one another. To fan rivalry, delegates to the city conference had seventy-six names whence to choose the sixty-five members of the gorkom—the only deviation from full-dress slates from the early 1920s to 1990.

Khrushchev's oral reports raised a hue and cry about the "wreckers" swarming over the Moscow area: they had thrown machines at chemical and aviation plants off line, contaminated seed grain, arranged auto accidents, and sold military secrets to Western spies, all here because the sworn foe of socialism "wants to make his smudge in the most visible place" in the USSR. In the agencies of city hall, stated Bulganin, "a number of people . . . have turned out to be enemies of the people, Trotskyites, and scoundrels." A textiles executive, Sergeyeva, was one of the rare Stalinists to overplay the vigilance card; after she recounted chasing "400 assorted White Guards" out of her mill, she was accused of immodesty and voted ineligible for reelection to the gorkom. Furer, the head of a gorkom department, shot himself because of preconference stress, and Semen Z. Korytnyi, an obkom secretary (soon to be arrested), suffered a heart attack.[72]

Kaganovich, the erstwhile patron of many Muscovites and now a senior government minister, did not bestir himself to help those under siege. Khrushchev seems to have been no less craven, although he did tell school officials to give a teacher's job to Natal'ya Rykova, the twenty-one-year-old daughter of Aleksei Rykov; she was arrested in 1938, after his departure, and spent eighteen years in the Gulag. Dem'yan S. Korotchenko, briefly his second secretary in the obkom in 1937, and Stepan N. Tarasov, a gorkom counterpart, made it through the purge, but the other ten obkom and gorkom secretaries appointed while Khrushchev was Moscow boss did not, and several

34

423

of his personal assistants were arrested. If anything, Aleksandr I. Ugarov, the Leningrader who succeeded him in January 1938, was more aggressive, as he is averred to have "run down everything that had gone on before" in the organization.[73]

To opportunists, the purgers held out the carrot of eagle-winged promotion (see Table C-3 in Appendix C on external appointments). Hundreds of young Communists had been drawn upward or into posts in other regions, Ugarov raved in April 1938. "A year or a year-and-a-half ago . . . many of us would have doubted it would be possible for people to move so fast. This is what we call Bolshevik promotion!" So great was the outflow into other positions that the Moscow organs "sometimes end up in a kind of 'impoverished' state."[74] Bulganin's replacement as head of the Mossovet, Ivan I. Sidorov, reiterated the point.

Khrushchev (party viceroy in Kiev) and his office mate Bulganin (RSFSR premier in July 1937, then in many other posts) made prodigious strides, and both had Moscow wards in tow. Malenkov, designated a CC secretary in 1939, had less personalized a following, but, as Stalin's alter ego for cadres, dispensed more patronage. Khrushchev, Malenkov, and Bulganin, free of Kaganovich's apronstrings, entered the Politburo in 1939, 1946, and 1948, respectively.[75]

Two Moscow wheels besides Khrushchev were promoted to first secretary of a union republic—Aleksei A. Volkov, gorkom second secretary in 1937 (in Belorussia), and Dmitrii Z. Protopopov, a raikom first secretary (in Tajikistan). Arsenii G. Zverev, the first secretary of Molotovskii raikom and a favorite of Malenkov, earned an audience with Stalin by a rousing speech he gave to the party cell of the Commissariat of Heavy Industry, which was in his district. Stalin on the spot made him USSR deputy commissar of finance and, in four months, full commissar, a job he kept until 1960. The new boy in the raikom, Sergei G. Yemel'yanov, soon found himself deputy commissar of heavy industry.[76]

First Secretary Ugarov's comeuppance graphically demonstrated how the slightest miscue could make today's winner in the purge tomorrow's loser. Ugarov had barely settled in when Stalin chose to scapegoat him for gaps in the provision of food, clothing, and fuel that were occasioning citizen complaints. The Politburo discussed the Moscow supply situation in his presence September 13, 1938, whereupon Stalin invited Khrushchev back from Kiev to reconnoiter. Khrushchev never admitted to being in on Ugarov's demise, yet archive materials show him to have been massively complicit. He was the one on November 2 to read out a Politburo resolution on "the errors of the leadership of the Moscow organization," dated October 15, to a secret joint plenary of the obkom and gorkom. Ugarov, Khrushchev announced, "has been arrested and has confessed that he is an old enemy, recruited by Trotskyites and Rightists," and had "carried out hostile work" in Leningrad and Moscow for years.[77]

The motion removing Ugarov and his gorkom second secretary, Gleb A. Bratanovskii (also taken into custody in October), recorded that they had interrupted deliveries of green vegetables and meat to foment mass unrest and that "political blindness and carelessness" had let them do so. Ugarov was shot in captivity in February 1939. Sidorov, of the Mossovet, maintained his innocence at the plenum; he, too, was deracinated and vanished. The new chairman of the soviet was Aleksandr I. Yefremov, a factory manager who the previous May, as head of a local bridges commission, had reported to the NKVD about sabotage in the city service, and who at the plenum demanded the firing of Sidorov as "a person close to Ugarov and Bratanovskii."[78]

FORGE OF CADRES

The winding down of the terror left control of the Moscow organization to mutually mistrustful cliques. The all-important job of first secretary fell in November 1938 to Aleksandr S. Shcherbakov. Although Khrushchev officiated at his installation, the two men had no use for each other; Khrushchev had tried to demote him from his most recent position, head of the Stalino (Donetsk) obkom in Ukraine. Shcherbakov was a client of Andrei A. Zhdanov, Kaganovich's successor as second fiddle in the central Communist Party apparatus and Georgii Malenkov's archantagonist for Stalin's favor. He began his rise in the 1920s as a district secretary and propagandist in Zhdanov's Nizhnii Novgorod regional committee, worked with Zhdanov in the cultural field in the mid-1930s, and served as his deputy in the Leningrad obkom in 1936–1937. When Shcherbakov died of overwork in May 1945, at age forty-three, his assistant went to work for Zhdanov.[79]

Stalin did not let Zhdanov's coterie monopolize Moscow. When the gorkom second secretaryship came up in 1938, he admonished that it go to someone "who would watch [things] and, if there were any incident, report to the CC." The watcher was Georgii M. Popov, a Moscow-born aircraft engineer who that July had gone from graduation from the Industrial Academy to instructor in the Department of Leading Party Organs, headed by Malenkov. There he was responsible, his unpublished memoirs divulge, for a review of cadres in the NKVD and its organs in the army. Malenkov, happy with his performance, put him forward as second secretary and scout on Shcherbakov. Popov's relations with Shcherbakov thus began under a cloud.[80]

Popov made his mark as an economic manager. A former department chief at Aviation Works No. 1, he was well situated to take a lead in defense production, the priority sector of the Moscow economy. In September 1940 Stalin let fall to associates the cogency of his presentation at a Kremlin meeting on delivery of fighter engines to the air force. Soon afterward, Popov took charge of manufacture of the magnetos (at the Moscow Auto and Tractor Electrical Equipment Works) that Aviation Works No. 24 in Moscow needed to make more motors; he then fired the engine works' director, wrote a precise timetable for assembly, and briefed the Kremlin daily by special phone. At the Eighteenth Party Conference in February 1941, Stalin personally nominated Popov for membership in the Central Committee, lauding him as "a businesslike man."[81]

Moscow's place in the Soviet pecking order continued to be recognized after the Great Purge, albeit more formulaically and with more obsequiousness toward Stalin. "The Moscow organization," Shcherbakov effervesced at the Eighteenth Party Congress in 1939, "finds itself in a superior station in the sense that Muscovites work in the city where Comrade Stalin lives and works."[82] The same intonation would be pervasive in the artillery and firework fanfaronades to wartime victories and again during the gala 800th anniversary of Moscow's founding in September 1947, when Stalin issued a verbal salute to the city as "the standard bearer of the new, Soviet epoch."

Muscovites chalked up fewer top-level positions after 1938. Only the twin-appointed first secretaries joined Malenkov on the Secretariat: Shcherbakov, who was CC secretary for ideology from May 1941 onward; Popov, appointed March 1946, who had no specified field;

and Khrushchev in his second term in Moscow, who answered in the CC Secretariat for party organization (in part or whole) and kept a hand in agriculture. Stalin had a soft spot for Shcherbakov, who befriended his elder son, Yakov, and was at his side in the blackest days of 1941, and also, for a time, for Popov. Although dozens of Muscovites filled minor slots in the central apparatus, only one—Boris N. Chernousov, second secretary of the obkom from January 1939— headed a CC department, the crucial one for party personnel, for several months in 1948–1949. The seats apportioned to Moscow officials on the Central Committee, as high as 10 percent of the committee in the 1920s, hovered around 3 or 4 percent in the late Stalin years (see Table C-5).

Nevertheless, Moscow, commonly cited as the party's "forge of cadres" *(kuznitsa kadrov),* was still held to have special rights in staffing. Like all civilian units, it mobilized personnel for the war effort. The number of full and candidate members of the party in the city, having more than made up purge losses, dropped by 75 percent in 1941 as they sluiced into the military and the armaments industry. Shcherbakov added headship of the Chief Political Directorate of the Army and Navy and of the Soviet Information Bureau, the office in charge of all censorship and news management, to his duties in 1942. In wartime the gorkom alone placed about 5,000 Communists in external "leading work," not only in the army but in Ukraine, the security and foreign services, and other organizations.[83]

Alumni of the Moscow organization, city Second Secretary Ivan A. Parfenov wrote in 1947, were to be found in "numerous . . . state-wide positions . . . and in all oblasts, krais [territories], and republics." Popov disclosed in 1949 that since the war the obkom and gorkom had pitchforked more than 5,000 persons "into various sectors of socialist construction" outside the organization (out of the 40,000 given administrative appointments). They were "in leading work in the party CC, secretaries of obkoms and of central committees of the national [republic] communist parties, ministers and deputy ministers, and [in other] big state and party offices." Many showed up in newly annexed non-Russian territories.[84]

Moscow officials began to assume another role in power politics: riding herd on the Russian intelligentsia, the cream of which worked in the arts outlets, publishing houses, and institutes of the capital.

Mosfil'm filled out its roomy compound on the Lenin Hills, opening the USSR's first sound studio in 1931. The professional guilds made compulsory for artists after 1932 (Union of Writers, Union of Composers, and so forth) all worked out of Moscow. In science, the arrival of the Academy of Sciences, and its absorption of the Communist Academy and Institute of Red Professors, completed the centralization of intellectual life. As the regime used violence more sparingly after the Great Purge, it needed regularized and prophylactic instruments of control, and the Moscow apparatus fit the bill.

Shcherbakov was the first local boss to have experience here, having been conjointly head of the CC's Culture Department and secretary of the Union of Writers in the mid-1930s. When the party line on expression stiffened in 1944, after the laxness of the war years, the gorkom and central raikoms of Moscow spearheaded the crackdown and remained prominent when it was heightened in 1946–1948, as the cold war with the Western democracies unfolded. "A large place in the activity of the Moscow Committee," it was observed, "goes to the inculcation in intelligentsia personnel of . . . love and dedication toward the socialist Motherland."[85]

A MOSCOW AFFAIR

Shcherbakov's early death spared him entrapment in the turbid politics of late Stalinism. He surely would have sided with Andrei Zhdanov, who took a middle-of-the-road approach in relation to the alternatives. Elite conflict heated up after Zhdanov's own death in August 1948 and climaxed in the infamous Leningrad Affair of 1948–1950. In that incident, Malenkov and Lavrentii P. Beria, the overlord of the secret police after Yezhov, attacked loyalists in Zhdanov's Leningrad base and had a number of them put to death.

In December 1949 Stalin ordered Shcherbakov's Moscow heir, Georgii Popov, supplanted by Khrushchev, returned from Ukraine to be Moscow first secretary and a CC secretary. It was once believed that the affair was an epilogue to Malenkov's anti-Zhdanov purge, occasioned by loyalties running from Popov via Shcherbakov to Zhdanov.[86] We now know better, specifically, that Popov was no water bearer for Zhdanov or Shcherbakov. His demise better reflects his own recklessness and again the vulnerability inherent in the position of Moscow boss.

Popov was surprised in June 1945 that he and not Zhdanov got Shcherbakov's post. He briskly struck off on his own in the cadres realm, parting company with many Shcherbakov appointees, including seven of eight obkom and gorkom secretaries. His promotions favored officials from the gorkom (his sphere to 1945) over the obkom and also individuals with experience in aviation, the industry where he was trained and which Malenkov, his sponsor, supervised in wartime.[87]

Nothing implicates Popov in the Leningrad bloodletting. But other Muscovites in his and Malenkov's network were not so innocent. Circumstantial evidence ties in Boris Chernousov, the oblast second secretary who was appointed chief of the CC's personnel department in December 1948, when Malenkov was on the upswing, and accompanied Malenkov and a police team on an inquisitorial visit to Leningrad in February 1949. In March he was given the major position of chairman of the RSFSR Council of Ministers vacated by Mikhail I. Rodionov, a Zhdanovite from Gorky (Nizhnii Novgorod) about to be imprisoned and shot with Malenkov's connivance. Another Malenkov client to figure in events was Vasilii M. Andrianov, the person made first secretary of the Leningrad obkom in February 1949. He started his career in the Moscow gorkom in the 1930s and made a nimble ascent during the Great Purge.[88]

The paranoid climate that underlay the Leningrad Affair influenced Popov's demise. Subordinates of his had been grilled by Central Committee staff in 1945–1946 on the unfounded suspicion that they had embezzled party funds during the war. Popov remained aloof from that interrogation, but by early 1949, at the latest, he was the target of a whispering campaign by detractors who included Stalin's wastrel son, Vasilii—the commander of the air wing of the Moscow Military District and a member of the Moscow gorkom.[89] Popov succumbed to an intrigue that opened with receipt by Stalin of an anonymous letter against him in the early autumn of 1949. On October 4 Stalin fired Nikolai P. Firyubin, the gorkom secretary for military and civilian machine building (an aircraft engineer who was an obkom and gorkom secretary supervising airplane and ammunition production during the war), and set up a commission to look into Popov's leadership. Malenkov, washing his hands of his protégé, recommended a review by the Politburo while Stalin was on vacation, but Popov talked Stalin into delaying until the two of them could be present. Waving the inquiry report, Stalin told Khrushchev that Popov headed a band of "conspirators" in Moscow. Khrushchev, according to his memoirs, agreed that Popov had to go but tried to convince Stalin that he was not a traitor.[90]

The Politburo ruled in early December that Popov would be punished but disclaimed the graver charges against him. During December 13–16 a closed plenum of the gorkom and obkom confirmed the verdict and made Khrushchev head of the obkom after almost twelve years away. Lucky to have his head on his shoulders, Popov was routed to a minor government ministry at the end of the month. The charges against him were kept out of the press.

The plenum raised three main counts against Popov. First, he was accused of arrogance in demeanor: "Comrade Popov does not facilitate the development of criticism and self-criticism in the Moscow party organization."[91] He had secured the appointment of his brother Dmitrii as deputy editor of the newspaper *Vechernyaya Moskva* (Evening Moscow) and had served concurrently, unlike any Moscow party chief in the past, as municipal chief executive (a post he took while gorkom secretary in December 1944).

Second, Popov had been excessively occupied with economics, to the detriment of propaganda and political activity. "Comrade Stalin personally told me," he allowed at the December plenum, "that I exhibit a managerial deviation in my work."

The third substantial charge, an extension of the second, was that Popov had abused the ministries, as the central commissariats of the Soviet government were christened in 1946. Second Secretary Parfenov summarized it this way:

> [The MK] has been following an incorrect line in relation to the union [USSR] ministries and ministers, trying to put the squeeze on ministers and issue dicta to ministries, to supplant the ministers, the government, and the Central Committee . . . In the conceit that anything goes for him, Comrade Popov has been demanding from the ministries that they unconditionally submit to directives of the Moscow Committee, and that, as relates to all-union enterprises located in Moscow and Moscow oblast, they not address themselves to the government without the MK's consent. Comrade Popov has threatened ministers who disagree with these anti-state claims that the MK has, as it were, its own special residence to which he can invite ministers and give them a telling-off.

The indictment for an autocratic style had an empirical basis. Popov acknowledged that he was given to shouting orders, holding forth at inordinate length at party gatherings, and cutting in on speakers, and his joint tenure in the party and the city soviet was indeed unusual. Yet these peccadillos would hardly have brought him to earth in the absence of other offenses. Neither Khrushchev, his replacement, nor Kaganovich, the paradigmatic boss of the 1930s, was a model of etiquette. And Popov recalled having urged Stalin in 1945, without success, to find someone else for the municipal post.[92]

The second and third charges stuck more damningly. Popov's zeal on economic policy had more than once erupted into invective against senior officials. At the first postwar city party conference, in February 1949, he accosted Sergei N. Kruglov, the head of the MVD, the Ministry of Internal Affairs (as one-half of the prewar NKVD became in March 1946, the other half becoming the MGB, Ministry of State Security), and thus the minister in charge of Gulag labor. When the MVD began the Volga-Don Canal, Popov said, it had wrongly put work on Moscow's Kur'yanovskaya and Severnaya pumping stations "on the reserve track"—a mistake, he added with a wink, he learned from his "intelligence agents"; moreover, it assigned Severnaya to a Gulag official "who understands nothing about construction." At the December 1949 plenum, Popov revealed his sore relations with Dmitrii F. Ustinov, the Soviet minister of armaments. After one clash, Stalin warned him not to vent disputes at large meetings "when the matter concerns ministers."[93]

Not all of Popov's transgressions were in public. It was claimed in the Politburo motion of December 1949 that of 443 edicts of the gorkom and obkom since 1945 allocating production tasks to industrial enterprises, 255 were taken "in circumvention of the government." One such decision had stimulated the poison pen letter to Stalin in 1949. Taking the advice of research scientists and a gorkom department head, Secretary Firyubin instructed the USSR ministries for agriculture and farm machinery building that June to undertake development of a battery-powered harvesting combine at their Moscow plants. Neither he nor Popov asked permission of Gosplan or the USSR Council of Ministers (chaired by Stalin). It was this step that moved Stalin to sack Firyubin and start the fatal investigation of Popov.[94]

The wisdom of locking horns with an Ustinov or Kruglov aside, Popov's treatment of the economic bureaucracy was not as aberrant as it was made out to be. As he testified, the Moscow party had engaged in such practices "over a great many years."[95] The press was to print dozens of articles in 1950–1951 bearing witness to like activity in other parts of the USSR—activity that would persevere for decades afterward. Most likely, Popov, like Karl Bauman in 1929, was penalized as much for doing what he did under the noses of the Kremlin leadership as for his misdeeds.

True to Stalinist form, Khrushchev launched a Moscow purge. Popov's combination of municipal and party leadership was not to be repeated. Nor was the fusion of the obkom and gorkom headships, which had been the rule since the institution of the gorkom in 1931. The Politburo, Malenkov reported, had decided "to separate the post of first secretary of the obkom from the post of first secretary of the gorkom, keeping in mind, of course, that the gorkom will be entirely subordinated to the obkom."[96] Hence Khrushchev's selection to the obkom leadership only; a raikom first secretary, Ivan I. Rumyantsev, was promoted to first secretary of the gorkom, and Mikhail A. Yasnov, who was friendly with Khrushchev when in charge of building river embankments before 1938, became head of the city executive committee. Joint sessions of the bureaus and secretariats of the city and oblast party committees were discontinued.

Khrushchev, his gunsights on national politics, aimed the changes as much at allies of Malenkov as at residual clients of Shcherbakov and Zhdanov. The housecleaning thus pretested the Khrushchev-Malenkov struggle for Stalin's mantle. Of Popov's eight fellow secretaries in the obkom and gorkom, five were relieved in Khrushchev's first month, the other three by the spring of 1951. The gorkom propaganda secretary, Nikolai N. Danilov, a Leningrader and the only holdover from Shcherbakov, was the last to go. The sweep extended to lower party and soviet organs and to Muscovites in exterior agencies.[97]

The expurgation was unusual in that it was nonlethal, the antithesis of the sanguinary Leningrad Affair or the purge of 1937–1938. Few if any people were killed. Popov, after heading two ministries, was made director of an aviation plant in late 1951 and ambassador to Poland after Stalin's death; he was even reelected to the Central Committee at the 1952 party congress. In the same mood of clemency, for which Khrushchev takes credit in his memoirs, Firyubin was allowed to head a small unit in the Moscow executive committee in 1951 and promoted to deputy chairman in 1952; he began a long second career as a diplomat in 1953. Parfenov and Timofei A. Seli-vanov, Popov's first deputy in the Mossovet, obtained lesser municipal positions, and the obkom second secretary, Sergei A. Zholnin, found refuge in industry.[98]

Khrushchev's shakeup also demonstrated the new muscle he could flex, notably in the party committees in the state ministries, largely inactive since their formation in 1939. Malenkov had considerable support in the ministries, and here was one way to blunt it. Yekaterina A. Furtseva, Khrushchev's choice as gorkom second secretary, took a special interest in the subject and addressed a plenum on it in December 1951.

Jousting between Khrushchev and Malenkov would help explain the leniency of the Moscow purge. Neither had enough power to finish off the other's sympathizers, and so a certain balance prevailed, although the trend was in Khrushchev's favor. Repetition of key appointments points in the same direction. Both of Khrushchev's top deputies were shortly to be supervened as he gained strength: Rum-yantsev in the gorkom by a local candidate, Ivan V. Kapitonov; and the obkom second secretary, Viktor P. Alekseyev, by a camp follower of Khrushchev's from Kiev, Zakharii F. Oleinik. Khrushchev was unable to get unanimous votes for his slates of candidates for the city and oblast committees, a sure sign of intrigue. And as late as September 1952, he was speaking so mordantly of personnel abuses as to convey unease over his control.[99]

Governance in the Stalinist Manner

The governors of the socialist metropolis preened themselves on doing their job *po-stalinski,* "in the Stalinist manner." The algorithm would long outlive Stalin, in and out of Moscow.

WITHERED GRASSROOTS

Stalinism dessicated the grassroots of urban government close to the extinction point. In local elections the "Stalin Constitution" of 1936 substituted universal for class suffrage, areal for workplace precincts, and polling booths for voice votes. It did not ruffle Communist Party control. Turnout in the Moscow balloting, 84 percent in 1931 and 97 percent in 1934, rose to 99.8 percent in the numbered territorial electoral districts in 1939 (district 1 of the city soviet being a fictitious seat for the sainted Lenin), 99.98 percent in 1947, and 99.99 percent in 1950; 99.0 percent of the votes in 1939, and 99.4 percent after the war, were for the "bloc of Communists and non–party members." The asymptotic approach to mathematical perfection, and candidates' obligatory incurring of small debts to electors in what as of the 1934 election were plural, party-approved mandates *(nakazy),* were recited as exhibits of the regime's democratic character.

Egregious centralization of decision making accompanied these bogus elections. "The most conspicuous feature of the government of Moscow," E. D. Simon and his British experts concluded after their visit in 1936, "is the concentration of power and responsibility in the hands of the presidium," the camarilla of the Mossovet.[100] Forty or fifty guests sat in on its sessions, departing when the item requiring their attendance had been minuted. As in the 1920s, subcommittees within the presidium, their very existence not public knowledge, conducted lesser business.[101]

At the plenaries of the Mossovet, chopped from twelve to three or four a year, members gave unprecedented obeisance to Chairman Bulganin while aping his proclivity for debonair gray suits, starched collars, and neckties over proletarian tunics. The sections of the soviets, their Moscow membership peaking at about 60,000 in 1933, were marginalized by their formalism and by mounting distrust of them by officials. Bulganin found them wanting on both counts, stating that "in our sections the showy side prevails over real work" and that "class enemies . . . sometimes hide behind a sectioner's ticket."[102]

In the spring of 1937 journalists and a handful of political players called attention to "abuses of democracy" in Moscow. Their kowtowing to the constitution, a document mostly honored in the breach, inspires some incredulity, as does the coincidence with the opening of the Great Purge. For all that, the depositions were convincing about city hall's disdain for due political process. When expedient, they were able to show, local assemblies blithely co-opted dignitaries, waiving the formality of election for two members of the city presidium and scores of other officials. The subsidence of political participation could also be verified. Mincing no words, a member of the Moscow Soviet stated, "The presidium makes all the decisions, without drawing members of the soviet in . . . The questions the sections put to it usually go unminded." Deputy Chairman Yevgeniya S. Kogan broke ranks with the presidium to indict it as "divorced from deputies and voters." Other deputies submitted that it was it easier to get to see central than city office holders.[103]

Ersatz and impenetrable procedures, to take these witnesses at their word, diluted the meaning of what was left of local politics: "Not only rank-and-file workers and employees but many deputies of the Moscow and raion soviets are more and more losing interest in the work of their soviets." Bulganin's presidium, it was given out, had collegially considered fewer than one in seven of its 2,393 directives in 1936, arriving at most by telephone or written poll. Yurii Bovin of *Pravda* arraigned both the thronging soviet and the cloistered presidium: "Just as the plenum of the Moscow Soviet is too unwieldy to resolve practical problems, the presidium is too narrow and unrepresentative." To "broaden Soviet democracy" in Moscow, he envisaged a vigorous, mid-sized executive—the sixty-one members of the existing executive committee had sat only four times in two years.[104]

The revelations were a flash in the pan. Bulganin was promoted unimpeded, whereas Kogan, the highest-placed faultfinder (and once the wife of a member of Stalin's Politburo, Valeryan V. Kuibyshev), was caught in the maw of the purge.[105] The Mossovet voted the unelected members off the presidium and made nebulous calls for decorum in elections, staffing, and decrees. Instead of structural reform, the Kremlin in 1939 gave all local soviets a name switch (to "soviets of toilers' deputies") and other epidermal changes. Eliminating presidiums, it lodged all signatory power in executive committees, or ispolkoms.

The Moscow ispolkom that took office in January 1940, after elections in December 1939, resembled not at all the balanced, accessible cabinet Bovin had touted. It was a bloated version (twenty-one members, not thirteen) of the presidium, freed of so much as the fiction of an intermediate body scrutinizing it. "Current business," mainly financial and personnel, came under an "administrative colloquium" *(rasporyaditel'noye soveshchaniye),* an update of the former small presidium acting in total secrecy.[106] The municipality's chief executive was now chairman of the ispolkom alone, not of the full soviet, which was as meek and almost as overblown (at 1,400 deputies) as before. Perusing the 1940 budget, six months into the fiscal year, the soviet "suggested" to the ispolkom only staff bonuses worth 0.1 percent of the budget; discussions after the war had like results.

Four years of war, with soviet and ispolkom sessions irregular and cursory, fortified elitism. Vasilii P. Pronin, chairman until 1944, was well regarded by Stalin for his clipped style. New standing orders authorized him and his vice-chairmen "to decide urgent matters and give instructions in the name of the [entire] ispolkom." Pronin and two of his deputies, Mikhail Yasnov and Semen F. Frolov (an NKVD colonel in charge of civil defense), had the power to decide all "current questions" on their own.[107]

Then came Popov, under whom the ispolkom ceased to meet entirely in January 1945, resuming scheduled sessions only in April 1946. A new "bureau of the ispolkom" conducted all city business during this interlude and took precedence over the ispolkom after April 1946 and after the first postwar elections in 1947. Holding both party and municipal reins, Popov used his party office to exempt his municipal personage from questioning. "It is not coincidental," the plenum of December 1949 was informed, that since 1945 "nothing has been entered into decisions of the bureau and plenums [of the gorkom] that is critical of the Moscow Soviet or its agencies." Timofei Selivanov, who often substituted for Popov at soviet meetings, chaired sessions of the bureau of the ispolkom "with threats, aspersions on the worth of the officials present . . . and many cries and rejoinders."[108]

The full ispolkom sat twice as frequently, and had a tad more influence, after Popov's fall. But Yasnov, his replacement, exhibited a disarmingly similar decision style. Yasnov, the city party conference in 1951 heard, was never available for subordinates and ispolkom colleagues to see in his office. At executive meetings anyone who expressed disagreement with a draft bill handed down by the bureau was "asked if you want to keep working in the Mossovet system." "If you request help on this or that question, this is seen as an 'ultimatum to the ispolkom' . . . Try to get a revision of a part of a draft decision . . . and your intellectual qualities are thrown into doubt."[109] Yasnov gave a lazy apology and kept his job another five years.

The ispolkom, meanwhile, gave the fullest recognition yet, four-fifths of the seats in 1950, to municipal bureaucrats, of whom Yasnov was the first to become city chairman (see Table B-1 in Appendix B).

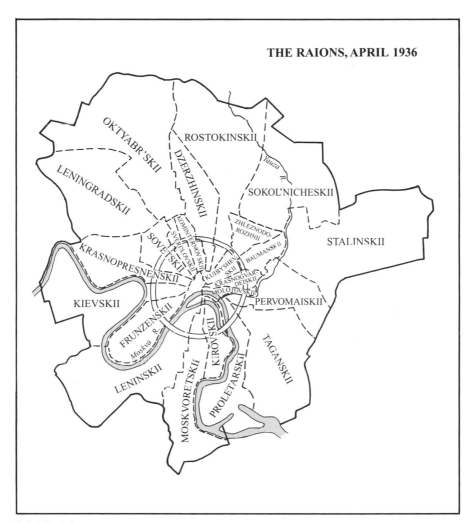

THE RAIONS, APRIL 1936

OKTYABR'SKII

ROSTOKINSKII

DZERZHINSKII

LENINGRADSKII

Yauza R.

SOKOL'NICHESKII

STALINSKII

ZHLEZNODO.
ROZHNII

KOMINTERNOVSKII

SVERDLOVSKII

SOVIETSKII

BAUMANSKII

KRASNOPRESNENSKII

KUIBYSHEV
SKII

KRASNOGVAR-
DEISKII

KIEVSKII

MOLOTOVSKII

PERVOMAISKII

FRUNZENSKII

Moskva R.

KIROVSKII

TAGANSKII

LENINSKII

MOSKVORETSKII

PROLETARSKII

MAP 10

And that group was much more competent, politically and technically, than before the Great Purge. All "Soviet men"—not a survivor of the duma service in the lot—nearly 60 percent of them had seen duty in the local party apparatus (Table C-2). Nearly half had a higher education (Table C-1), Aleksandr Yefremov in 1938–1939 being the first "mayor" thus qualified.[110]

Moscow's territorial raions, which increased from ten in 1930 to twenty-three in 1936 and twenty-five in 1941 (see Maps 10 and 11),

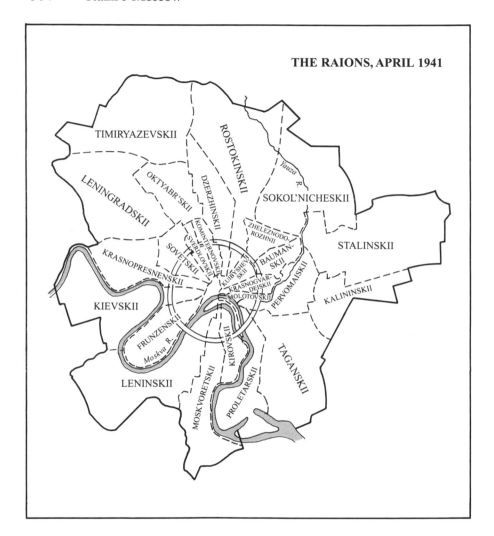

THE RAIONS, APRIL 1941

MAP 11

did little to bring the populace into the picture. The ease of reapportioning and renaming them spoke volumes about their mutability, which was seen as no less than that of the departments of city hall. "We Bolsheviks," Kaganovich explained in 1931 after the partition of a few months before, "never regard the form of organization . . . as an absolute," but rather "subordinate our work system . . . to the policy of the proletarian state."[111] Kaganovich believed that the raions, each being "a whole big city," should be supplemented by "subraion soviets," one for every "several streets." These would have been nonelected conclaves of deputies and section members, mobilizing residents for yard sweeping and other drudgery. The subraion soviets were never pursued, although citizens flickeringly had more contact with "deputies' groups" comprising the representatives of a given area in both layers of the local soviets.[112]

From the citizen's point of view, the ineffectuality of the raions detracted as much as their size. The commitment to bolstering raion powers, made in 1925, was retracted after 1930, and centralization was sanctified as a corollary of planning. In the last contrariety on the subject, in 1934, Stepan V. Kirillov, the soviet chairman of Frunzenskii (formerly Khamovnicheskii) raion, sniped at the attitude that the raion was "an appendage whose opinion can be disregarded." So lightly was his presidium regarded that it was learning about the city's master plan from the press and about the allocation of raion land from the startup of construction. Moscow's chief planner, Perchik, sternly rehashed the brief for central mastery: issues "must be decided on the scale of the entire city, not of the raion, subraion, block, or street," and be "carried out with all due strictness of state and party discipline." His remained the final word for decades.[113]

The standing commissions (postoyannyye komissii) of the soviets, as the sections were retitled in 1940, offered little relief. Whereas 60,000 laypersons participated in them in 1933, and 30,000 did in 1936, only 5,800 did in 1951 (2,500 in the city soviet and 3,300 in the raions). Most sections were chaired by an official, although no longer the head of the agency overseen. The Moscow gorispolkom's secretary, Pavel I. Leonov, fretted that commissions were often "ancillary organs," lapdogs of council executives—only to profess their job to be the ancillary one of "helping to carry out party and government directives and decisions of the local soviets" and to enjoin them from stepping on the toes of leaders and departments.[114]

THE POLITICS OF THE SUGGESTION BOX

So it was that Moscow's local soviets came to resemble utility companies more than units of self-government. To be sure, they were utilities with suggestion boxes nailed to their doors. On the most parochial issues, speeches by deputies, standing commissions, petitions to officials, letters to the editor, and the like might make a difference. An aroused individual might as well, though the results could be whimsical. During his hearing about St. Basil's with Dmitrii Usov of the Moscow administration in 1933, the lionhearted Petr Baranovskii threatened to commit suicide if the cathedral were demolished and then wired Stalin to that effect. The cathedral was spared; Baranovskii, incongruously, was sent to Gulag. Boris Sakulin asked several factual questions about the master plan at a Union of Architects conference in 1937; he was denounced as a "fascist" for his pains but not otherwise harmed, remaining active and dying a natural death in 1952.[115]

Even when Stalin and his minions had spoken, it was not impossible for an issue to be kept open. How else to comprehend the behavior on the conservation problem described by Perchik's replacement, Bulushev: "The Moscow Soviet has received many letters from 'old' Muscovites who love antiquity . . . expressing doubts about the need to rebuild central streets and squares and demanding retention of historical monuments of the ilk of the Kitaigorod Wall and the Shrine of the Iberian Virgin." This outpouring came in July 1937, in the midst of the Great Purge and after a decade of demolitions. Only three years later, Georgii Krutikov took the floor at an architects' conference and insisted that builders respect landmarks and "stop looking upon them as 'vanishing Moscow.'"[116]

Urban politics, in other words, was throttled but never given up for dead. The attenuation of debate and of the representative function of government was not quite enough to push it over the brink.

Stalinist local politics had two other trademarks, both mirroring changes throughout the Soviet system. First, it stubbed out the semiautonomous, nonstate organizations that had been in symbiosis with the municipal establishment before 1930. The housing partnerships, thrown into crisis by centralized planning, were forced in 1931 into *zhakty* (house-leasing cooperative partnerships) and, for buildings over 1,000 square meters, "housing trusts." The bureaucracy kept both on a short leash; and, as older Muscovites well remember, the police used them to keep tabs on tenants and monitor the passport rules. In 1937 raion "housing directorates" were imposed on all public housing, by then taking in the bulk of the dwellings held privately under NEP, except for a small reserve kept by city hall. Most building cooperatives and their Moscow federation were also eliminated and their property confiscated by the raion directorates.[117]

Among the more politically oriented associations, the Old Moscow Society and Garden Cities Society were closed down as early as 1930. ASNOVA, OSA, and the brawling architectural groups merged in 1932 into an official Union of Architects, which excluded heterodox figures one after the other. The only volunteers left in the municipal orbit were the few thousand green thumbs in the Moscow Society for Assistance to Tree Planting.[118]

Second, the Stalinist approach to urban affairs denied the dissemination of politically pertinent information. The quality of local newspapers, and of stories on Moscow in the national press, nose-dived in the mid-1930s, revived some after the purge, then sank again after 1941. Accounts of official meetings were exiguous and stylized, and advance notice of them and of leaders' schedules ceased. The voluminous staff papers done for the 1935 plan stayed in the planners' drawer. An Academy of Sciences commission on Moscow issues, formed in 1935, never publicly reported. The capital in the 1920s had two enlightening magazines devoted to local issues, *Kommunal'noye khozyaistvo* (Communal Economy) and *Stroitel'stvo Moskvy* (The Building of Moscow). The first was discontinued in 1931; the second reemerged after a wartime recess as the dishwater dull *Gorodskoye khozyaistvo Moskvy* (Moscow's Urban Economy), joined in 1952 by the equally sonorous *Arkhitektura i stroitel'stvo Moskvy* (The Architecture and Building of Moscow).

The famine extended to information seemingly innoffensive. Objective treatment of urban issues outside the USSR was impossible after about 1935, and foreign architects were gone by 1937. Moscow officials all but stopped junketing abroad and seeing foreigners. They made contacts after the war mostly with the capital cities of Soviet allies.[119]

The city directory *Vsya Moskva* (All Moscow), a gold mine of data since 1896, made its final, emaciated appearance in 1936. A slender statistical handbook, *Moskva v tsifrakh* (Moscow in Figures), came out only in 1934 and 1939. Next to no data about Moscow or any locality were released from the 1939 Soviet census. Under the spell of the spy mania and regulations on "state secrecy," the Chief Directorate of Surveying and Cartography, made a part of the NKVD in 1938, banned the printing of maps of Moscow and environs. Into the "special depositories" *(spetskhrany)* of libraries went extant Soviet maps, such as the oblast atlas published in 1934, and even tsarist-era charts going as far back as Catherine the Great.[120] The addresses and names of defense-related facilities no longer appeared. On issues of any complexity, Muscovites who wished to compose notes for the civic suggestion box had to do so handcuffed and nearly blindfolded.

NO POWER TO THE SOVIETS?

Stalin's Moscow reduced to dust whatever grit remained in the 1917 slogan "All Power to the Soviets!" so much so that it could be asked whether *any* power remained with local government. Its shallow and inert base left it unprepared to stand up to higher authority. The previous regard for municipal rights, on issues of mass welfare, in particular, gave way to a studied disrespect.

The focal issue of housing best illustrates the point. The crushing of the private and cooperative sectors made the majority of Muscovites tenants of the soviets' housing bureaus. Only 2.5 percent of the housing stock remained in private hands in the late 1940s; on the supposition that 1 or 2 percent was owned by building cooperatives (which made a slight comeback after the war) and about 40 percent by factories and central agencies, on the order of 55 percent of the population was municipally housed.[121] But the nominal nature of the rents paid (fixed at 1928 levels), and the phenomenal overcrowding, left municipal landlords with no slack resources and little discretion in expending their precious commodity.

Furthermore, company housing's 40 percent share considerably exceeded its 25 percent in the 1920s (and 15 percent in 1912), as it gained fast on the municipal total. In 1937 the largest factory in Moscow, ZIS, put up 27,000 of its 43,000 automakers, mostly in its encampment at Kolomenskoye, across the Moskva; it owned about 160,000 square meters of housing in 1950, enough to shelter perhaps 35,000 workers and relatives.[122] Over assets like these, city officials had no say. Their only recourse with a problem was to forward word of it to the centrally subordinated department with title to the facility, which might or might not have a subsection for Moscow real estate.

When it came to housing construction, local government suffered a devastating loss of leverage after 1930. Drafts of the First Five-Year

Plan showed no intent to lessen its role; Moscow was the only city to have a line in the national plan for its programs and to have a direct channel to USSR Gosplan. These were poor buffers, however, once the Stalin revolution engendered the bureaucratic rationing of resources and a suffusive bias toward defense and heavy industry. Favored builders sank their resources into production capacity and accommodation for their dependents, at first on a "nonplanned" basis (using materials scrounged inside the organization). In 1932, the concluding year of the First Five-Year Plan, Grigorii P. Konstantinopol'skii, the chief of Moszhilstroi (formerly Mosstroi), declared that diversion of supplies and workers into unplanned projects had been so great that "building organizations subordinated to the Mossovet took no great part in meeting the plan" for apartments and service facilities.[123]

The city government ended up with about one-quarter of housing completions in the first plan (see Table 5). More hardheaded quotas were set in 1933, assigning 17.4 percent of completions to the city, 18.7 percent to the cooperatives, 20.7 percent to the army and military industry, and 43.4 percent to other state bodies;[124] by year's end, municipal and co-op construction came to less than half of the low proportion given them. The city's share crept back to about 30 percent before 1940, then slithered almost to its 1933 low point. In

Table 5. Control of housing construction, 1928–1951

Year	Percent of net dwelling space completed			
	Moscow government	Construction cooperatives	State bodies	Private
1928–1932	24.7	16.9	55.6	2.9
1933	10.5	7.0	82.4	0.1
1937	24.3	—	—	—
1938	29.8	—	—	—
1948	11.3	—	—	—
1950	13.6	—	—	—
1951	17.8	—	—	—

Sources: For 1928 to 1933, *Moskva v tsifrakh* (Moscow: Stroitel'stvo Moskvy, 1934), p. 106. Total completions in other years, sources in Appendix D, Table D-1; completions by Moscow government in *Rabochaya Moskva,* March 28, 1938, p. 1; *Pravda,* February 3, 1939, p. 6; *Moskovskaya pravda,* April 22, 1951, p. 3; January 3, 1952, p. 2; September 28, 1952, p. 2.

absolute volume, city hall and the co-ops turned out 300,000 to 350,000 square meters of housing annually in the late 1920s, up to 250,000 on the city's account. Cooperative construction was negligible by the mid-1930s. Municipal output, done on a shoestring budget, reached only about 50,000 square meters in 1937. It was further damaged by the hand-over of brick kilns, sawmills, and other capital to industry during the war and did not again exceed 100,000 square meters until 1951.

By default, state organizations, looking out exclusively for their own, built or contracted for the lion's share of housing. And these organizations were increasingly differentiated. Segments of the central government, economic and noneconomic, multiplied like marigolds over the succeeding decade. The People's Commissariat of Heavy Industry, which owned all major factories from 1932 to 1936, splintered into commissariats (later ministries) for separate branches of civilian and military industry. Military industry was very well represented in Moscow. In 1932 Aviation Works No. 22, with 16,903 employees, had the third largest work force in the city, exceeded by only Elektrozavod and ZIS. Two other defense plants, Works No. 24 or the Frunze Works (13,634 workers) and Works No. 1 (11,714), counted among the top seven firms, while Works No. 39, also known as the Menzhinskii Works, and the Aviapribor (Aviation Instruments) Works ranked among the thirty-five biggest.[125]

Investment in defense R & D also leapt ahead, most noticeably in a belt of territory stretching northwest from downtown along Leningradskii prospekt. Sergei V. Il'yushin, a graduate of the Zhukovskii Air Force Engineering Academy, headed the major design bureau here from 1931 onward. By 1939 bureaus led by Artem I. Mikoyan, Pavel O. Sukhoi, and Aleksandr S. Yakovlev had become large concerns in the same area. Vladimir M. Myasishchev, formerly a deputy of Andrei Tupolev, was by the end of the 1940s running the prestigious Special Design Bureau No. 23 adjacent to Aviation Works No. 22. Sergei P. Korolev founded GIRD (the Group for Study of Jet Motion), the Russians' ground-breaking rocket institute, at 19 Sadovaya-Spasskaya in 1932.

And there was more. The Moscow Power Institute near the Yauza and the Radio Laboratory of the Communications Research Institute, opened at the Comintern Radio Station in Zamoskvorech'e in 1933, led the development of wireless communication and instrumentation that would help the Soviets coinvent radar. The Moscow Radio Works, a few blocks from the station, started making cockpit radios in the mid-1930s. The State Research Institute of Organic Chemistry and Technology was the Soviets' main laboratory for chemical weapons, and an attached factory produced blistering agents before and after the war, testing them on convicts. In the October panic of 1941, workers hurriedly buried tons of lewisite, mustard gas, and other toxic compounds on the grounds of the institute. The Red Army's chief test range for chemical-filled artillery shells, established in 1927 with German assistance, was at Kuz'minskii Pond, next to the Kuz'minki manor. Gas cannisters were buried all over the range.[126]

Local officials faced the bewildering task of attempting to gather intelligence on this fecundity. A 1938 list of nonmunicipal sponsors of housing construction comprised 24 central agencies—headed by the People's Commissariat of the Defense Industry, with 14.8 percent of the floor space underway—and an "other" category, with 12.6 percent, where the army and NKVD must have figured. Related sources list many others and show that large bodies often devolved control of housing to subunits. All told, 143 central agencies built apartments in Moscow in 1935 and about 100 did so in 1939; the number was put at 60 in June 1950 but at 130 that November and 100 in early 1953. Most saw housing as "an extra 'burden,'" a distraction from industrial construction to be discharged on the cheap.[127]

THE IMPERFECT PREFECTS

Communist ranks in Moscow, having tripled in the 1920s, tripled again to more than 400,000 members and candidates by January 1953.[128] The worst of times for the local soviets were the best of times for the apparatus that ruled within the ruling party. The first secretary and his retinue in some respects brought to mind the governor and the Special Board on City Affairs of the old regime, but the parallel does not begin to capture their reach and grasp. Party prefectoralism, once ad-libbed and erratic, now extended to almost every facet of metropolitan life.

Although Nikita Khrushchev after 1956 reported a degeneration of the party's central organs in the late Stalin period, the local partocracy suffered no such atrophy. Except at the height of the war, the bureaus of the Moscow gorkom and obkom met at a regular and at times frenetic pace. The gorkom bureau sat 117 times in 1940, 80 times in 1948, and 118 times in 1951. In 1948 the bureau of the obkom met separately on 65 occasions, and there were 17 joint sessions of the obkom and gorkom bureaus (these were stopped after Popov's ouster). The secretariats of the obkom and gorkom, though, were downgraded early in the 1930s, and were directly elected by party conferences last in 1931. They met 20 to 25 times a year in the 1930s but much less frequently after the war. In 1948 the gorkom secretariat met only 10 times, the obkom secretariat 8, and joint sittings 5. The secretariats' decision scope contracted accordingly, mostly to questions of internal party housekeeping and discipline.[129]

The party organs possessed in the high Stalin age three hitherto lacking prerequisites of full-fledged prefectoralism. Key was the belief in their irreplaceability, especially but not exclusively in the command economy. Their hand, Kaganovich commented in 1931, was indispensable to the most elemental operations: "For the annual and quarterly plans to be fulfilled, it is necessary for us to check regularly on plan fulfillment and immediately take the necessary measures in regard to lagging enterprises."[130] The case would be embellished later by appeals to the defense buildup, the war, and postwar healing.

The second departure concerned recruitment and training. Party functionaries rarely had an advanced education before 1937. Khrushchev, already second secretary of the gorkom, did not know what an escalator was when the subway was being planned and found an engineer's explanation "extremely complicated." This began to change during the Great Purge, which in other ways insulted technical rationality. One in four Moscow apparatchiks appointed in 1937–1938 had a higher education, and most had it from engineering institutes, the selfsame places Stalin was grooming his industrial elite (see Table C-1). It was policy in Moscow, said Fedor Ugarov, "to promote engineering and technical personnel into party leadership." He gave Chernousov, a raikom secretary at the time, as an example; Georgii Popov, who would become the first Moscow party leader to have a postsecondary education, would have been as convincing a case.[131]

The trend quickened after 1938. Just under half of Moscow's postpurge partocrats had graduated from a university or institute, the same ratio as municipal administrators. For almost 40 percent of the new breed, only 2 percent less than in the city service, the diploma was in engineering. Thirty-four percent had experience as economic managers, as many as the municipal officials and the highest ratio until the 1980s (Table C-2). Thus was the party acquiring some capacity for dealing with technically skilled elites on their own terrain.

Its territorial base also showed a turnaround. Postpurge apparatchiks in Moscow had rarely served beforehand in the provinces or central administration (Table C-2). Planting itself more firmly in local soil, the local party directorate was no more peripatetic than the municipal and far less than it had been.

The third novelty gave party organs the means to implement their prefectoral role. Partly this was a matter of size, for administrative staff grew by an order of magnitude in the 1930s and 1940s. Whereas the authorized strength (shtaty) of the MK in 1928 was about 60 responsible officials, the new Moscow gorkom alone received 94 positions (and 55 support staff) in 1931. Expansion slowed in the mid-1930s, but in 1948 the oblast and city committees had about eight times the cadres of the conjoint guberniya committee of two decades before: 277 professional and 126 auxiliary personnel in the obkom apparatus, 231 and 37 in the gorkom's. Another 400 to 500 responsible workers as well as support personnel were on staff in the raikoms of Moscow city, twelve or fifteen times the staff in the late 1920s.[132]

In addition to size, a restructuring, galvanized locally and nationally by Kaganovich, played a part. There had been attempts in the 1920s to supplement the prevalent "functional" scheme, pegged to broad roles like staffing and propaganda, with auxiliary commissions for discrete problems. Kaganovich entrusted the plenitude of control over a piece of the economic or administrative structure to a specialized division of the party apparatus, not a part-time offshoot. This "production branch" model allowed close supervision. Kaganovich himself headed the first branch Central Committee section, the Agriculture Department, in 1933.

Moscow trailblazed in 1930, fast upon Kaganovich's arrival in the MK and the liquidation of the ten okrugs within the enlarged oblast. The obkom created six "production-territorial sectors" within its Organization and Instruction Department, its primary administrative division at the time. Each sector (ten existed by mid-1931) was affixed to a set of raions bunched by economic profile: grain growing, light industrial, heavy industrial, and so forth. An article on the heavy industry group described a surge of activity:

> The sector has convened operational meetings with representatives of the appropriate organizations. This way a number of very important matters have been settled, such as: the mining and geological exploration needed to ensure supply of the Kosogorskii Works with iron ore; measures to implement the production and financial plan by cement plants; the construction of the Voskresensk Chemical Combine; preparation for spring planting in Bogoroditsk raion so as to retain personnel there; plan fulfillment, rebuilding, and reprofiling at the Kaluga Electromechanical Works; reconstruction of the Mytishchi Piping Works; and provision of raw materials to the Ryazan Footwear Factory.
>
> Most questions go through the MK secretariat or bureau. Certain decisions are made by summoning organizational representatives to the MK, and some through negotiations by telephone. Lately, the practice has been established of travel to the locality by officials of the sector and representatives of other MK departments and of industrial and trade union organizations . . . To solve problems of a more extended nature, liquidate breakdowns in production, or restructure the work being done, operational groups consisting of a party official, a manager, a union official, and engineering personnel are sent out. Such groups are now at work at the Mytishchi Wagonbuilding Works, the Podol'sk, Shurovskii, and Krasnyi stroitel' [Red Builder] works, and several cement plants.[133]

The territorial boundaries got in the way of business. Before the end of 1931, some sectors were operating outside the district, and branch sections without geographic referents were appearing (firstly for transport). In February 1932 the number of Moscow gorkom secretaries went from four to six, each designated in internal party documents as responsible for an itemized list of agencies and activities. Meanwhile, the Cadres Department, which handled personnel decisions outside the party apparatus itself, was given branch sectors, at first nine and then five.

In February 1934, after Kaganovich's report to the Seventeenth Congress, the party announced a full-scale switch to production branch organization. The Moscow obkom had, in addition to divisions for party personnel and for culture and propaganda, ones for industry and transport, agriculture, and the soviets and trade (by convention taking in law enforcement). The gorkom was given only a propaganda department but possessed "responsible instructors" assigned to organizations in thirteen branches, who operated much like staff in the obkom's specialized departments. Gorkom branch departments were introduced in January 1936.

Functionalism regained favor throughout the party in the spring of 1939, as staffing was concentrated in unitary personnel departments reporting to secretaries "for cadres." Yet Kaganovich's philosophy, espoused by his former understudy, Malenkov, was quickly reasserted for most nonpersonnel decisions. In December 1939 the Moscow obkom and gorkom again delineated branch departments, now reserved for economic tasks more exclusory than ever before; in September 1940 they began to appoint individual secretaries with jurisdiction over branches of industry. Branch departments and secretaries split off to the furthest extent during the war. By June 1943 the gorkom had no fewer than twenty-two departments, fifteen of them for branches of the economy, and thirteen secretaries, nine of them for production branches. The reclassification of most secretaries as deputy secretaries and heads of department in August 1943 did not alter the result.

In November 1948 the abolition of the cadres secretary and the single personnel department signified the aggressive reinstatement of the branch principle.[134] A Department of Party, Trade Union, and Komsomol Organs (under the second secretary) handled staffing in those three hierarchies and in the executive committees of the soviets, but everywhere else branch departments made personnel decisions. While the number of gorkom departments was slimmed to eleven, they were subdivided into thirty highly specific sectors that mostly replicated the earlier departments; and their number began to creep up again as soon as 1949.[135]

However activated, the apparatus's great formal asset was its power over other players' jobs and careers. The gorkom's nomenklatura in 1932 held 2,331 jobs, only 200 less than the MK's entire confirmation list in 1925, whereas the obkom confirmed a small residual of positions in Moscow, 122, and the raikoms confirmed 592. The nomenklatura of the gorkom contained approximately 8,000 posts in 1933, only to decline to 2,915 in April 1935 and 1,150 several years later. In 1939 it jumped to 7,340 and the raikoms' nomenklaturas to 31,000—fifty times more than in 1932. There had been no major change by 1950, when the Moscow gorkom's verification list was 6,367 positions long, the obkom's in Moscow 608, and the raikoms' 30,155, making a grand total of 37,130 positions.[136]

A fine-toothed listing for the gorkom in 1950 shows the largest group on its nomenklatura to be the 1,805 persons (28.3 percent of the list) supervised by the Department of Propaganda and Agitation. Nearly as many, 1,640 (25.8 percent), fell under the rubric of the several industrial departments of the gorkom and in transport, while 1,624 (25.5 percent) came under the Department of Party, Trade Union, and Komsomol Organs, whose writ embraced 174 positions of authority in the local soviets. The remaining positions spread across planning, financial, and trade agencies (496, or 7.8 percent), "administrative organs," defined at the time to take in the police, courts, health care, and civil defense (453 positions, or 7.1 percent), and municipal services and local construction (349 positions, or 5.5 percent).

Confirmation files in hand, the party organs could penalize and reward economic and other functionaries and replace them if necessary. Unofficial prerogatives were worth as much as codified rights. It was child's play for a raikom bureau, for example, to sack the head of a cinema or restaurant trust, a nonentity on its nomenklatura; if persuasive enough, it could topple the head of a large factory outside its nomenklatura and perhaps not on the gorkom's either. Serving a different policy goal, the Moscow party, at the end of Stalin's life, when official anti-Semitism was rampant, removed hundreds of Jews from the health and justice bureaucracies; Second Secretary Furtseva directed the purge.[137]

Hiring and firing was but one corner of the partocracy's empire. The mass media and the pyramid of committees and bureaus gave it a beeline to the population, deployable for so droll a task as selling lottery tickets, organizing a subbotnik, or partaking in "socialist competition" (contests for raising labor productivity) or so momentous an enterprise as press-ganging 500,000 Muscovites to dig trenches and fortifications in the face of the advancing Germans in 1941. In agriculture, the obkom and raikoms issued timetables—exact to the day— for sowing, tilling, and harvesting. When the regime tried to resuscitate peasant food sales in 1932, Kaganovich named members of the obkom bureau *oberkomendanty* for individual markets; when Moscow ran low on coal and firewood, he "distributed the basic kinds of fuel among us [on the bureau], so that each day we would look after our own sectors."[138]

In industry, the area's economic powerhouse, almost everything the party did rested on an informal foundation. Bureaus and secretariats dragooned members for major building or production sites. They gleaned information on individual factories on a weekly or even daily basis, archives reveal, and verified output and other targets. They reviewed planning estimates (*kontrol'nyye tsifry,* "control figures") and lists of construction projects (*titul'nyye spiski,* "title lists"). And they knocked heads together to get firms and industrial agencies to cooperate. Mikhail Z. Zelikson, the gorkom secretary for machine building, described this phenomenon during the war, when taut plans and evacuations brought it to its apogee: "We often have to take over as organizers of mutual assistance between plants . . . We transfer output or raw materials from factory to factory, so as to prevent down time, or help with qualified manpower or equipment. We resolve all these problems expeditiously, on the spot or on the phone, sometimes calling small meetings of the interested organizations."[139]

Grease was needed for the klunky wheels of a demarketized economy, but having the Communist Party apply it created a certain schizophrenia. Zelikson, with years of factory experience, observed that the party worker risked being so consumed by these machinations that he ended up a *tolkach,* the shady purchasing agent of Soviet lore; for their part, managers might "run to the gorkom for help whenever they had a supply complication." A later account accentuated the demeaning effects of officers of the ruling party "chasing around after bolts and screws."[140]

Interestingly, Zelikson was the department head in the gorkom in 1949 who came up with the idea for a party-forced product innovation (an electrocombine) that sparked the Popov affair. Moreover, Georgii Popov, in his testimony, laid his finger on the joint complicity of industrialists in the apparatus's exorbitant intercessions:

I have a whole sheaf of letters from ministries and agencies which have been turning to the Moscow Committee of the party, not for help in organizing socialist competition or concerning the state of party-political work. No, they have been appealing to us precisely to push through some [needed] machinery component or other such things . . . On the one hand, the Moscow Committee has climbed into industry; on the other hand, the ministries climb all over us so that they can grab hold of something for themselves.[141]

At its worst such attention to trivial detail degenerated into grandiloquence, with apparatchiks masquerading as satraps more than prefects. Here Kaganovich, the godfather of purposive party coordination, set the standard, revelling in an image of himself as a seer and an administrative miracle worker. "Whatever question Lazar Moiseyevich takes up," a hagiographer wrote, "he always penetrates to its heart," leaving experts "dumbfounded at his ability to find his way in the most minute and complicated subjects." To hear Yegor T. Abakumov, the chief of Metrostroi, tell it, Kaganovich, not content just to choose the location of the subway lines, plotted the tunnellers' every move: "He watched over how we put through the shafts, drifts . . . vaults, and walls . . . constantly visited us and gave us practical instructions on how to work." Policy making was a running seminar, with Kaganovich dispensing wisdom on a wondrous array of subjects: truck assembly; marble as a facing material; menus, prices, and hygiene in factory canteens; flax gathering and tractor repairs on the farms; and many more.[142]

The Moscow first secretary after Kaganovich, while more nervous about tripping off Stalin's jealousy, still walked the local stage with a swagger and was the *khozyain*—"boss" or "master"—to the subordinates he fusilladed with instructions and reprimands. He exploited his intimate ties to higher-ups and the superboss, Stalin. Popov, it was reported, "often cites in his utterances his conversations in the Central Committee and with Comrade Stalin," all of which, it went without saying, were totally secret.[143] Personalism and obeisance to power politics as much as economic criteria set the party boss apart from other local functionaries and from the classic, efficiency-seeking prefect of France or Italy.

THE PARTY-MUNICIPAL AXIS

The bread and butter issues under local institutions could not be treated the same as, say, ballbearing production. Structurally, the distinctive trait of party-municipal relations was the amount of cross-posting in leadership (Tables B-1, B-2, B-3). On the city presidium and ispolkom, party officials formed the biggest outside group. In the party organs, local government, after fading in the 1920s, was second only to the apparatchiks by the late Stalin period. Its seat share on the 1949 gorkom, 22.0 percent, was 1 percent higher than on the 1920 MK and eleven times as great as on the 1929 obkom; on the 1949 obkom, it was 15.4 percent; on the 1949 bureaus, it was the highest on record. And in the late 1940s, as has been seen, the local party organs and the city soviet had the same leader. "It has been difficult to distinguish," one of Popov's (municipal) deputies remarked in 1949, "whether instructions are coming from the chairman of the Moscow Soviet, the MK secretary, or a secretary of the Central Committee. In effect, the boundary between the Moscow Soviet and the Moscow Committee of the party has been effaced in our work."[144]

The interlocking of executives did not make the party and the soviets peers. Popov's bifold appointment, which made for perplexity until its discontinuation, in no way implied that his offices were on an equal footing: he was a party boss with the additional hat of municipal chief, not the other way around. Normally, the chairman of the soviet was, to quote Bulganin, "the practical worker in charge of urban services," happy to salute the party secretary because "as we go into battle . . . we should know our commander."[145]

Urban government, being wholly within the local party organs' span of supervision and the prize ring for periodic electoral tests of regime legitimacy, was subject to the party's urge to dictate more than most. The party used mainly the same levers here as it did in other spheres: nomenklatura to shape careers and administrative sections to affect decisions day to day.[146]

If there had once been some compunction about taking liberties with the elected soviets, there was no longer. The party fraction in the Mossovet, restyled the "party group" in 1934, ceased to meet regularly. When asked in 1938 if the group existed or not, Khrushchev answered that it did but that its sole function was to log in information from above; any voting would be improper, as Communists kept "no secrets" from loyal citizens and should raise their hands only in plenary session of the council.[147]

Joint decrees of party and municipal bodies, an exception under

NEP, were common after 1930. Also old hat were unilateral party decisions to obligate *(obyazat')* a city agency or assign *(poruchit')* it a job. Thus, to pick examples at random, we find the gorkom bureau and secretariat requiring the city presidium to spend 9 million extra rubles on housing for scientists; ruling "on improvements in the work of horses, fodder supply, and veterinary care" in the city's freight department; requiring introduction of diesel trolleybuses; directing that snow be flushed into sewers down special hatches; verifying quarterly the distribution of all new trucks and cars delivered to city hall; and adopting voluminous resolutions on trade in summer refreshments, setting precise dates for renovation of watermelon stands and lemonade carts. When the party wanted one of its buildings renovated, it simply instructed the municipal authorities to pay for or execute the work from their own resources.[148]

In the same vein, party decisions specified land use and project lists down to the last square meter, ruble, and tub of cement. Directives on public works laid down phasing and other arrangements in stupefying detail. Presidiums and other municipal bodies were portrayed as menials, as in this decree of the city party secretariat on a minor traffic question, dated July 29, 1935:

> *On removal of streetcars from ulitsa Kirova*
> [Resolved]:
> 1. To terminate streetcar traffic along ulitsa Kirova as of August 10.
> 2. To confirm new tram routes in the area, with gradual introduction from August 1 to August 10 [diagrams appended].
> 3. To obligate Mostramvaitrest [the city streetcar trust] and Gordorstroi [the city road building organization] to complete removal of the rails and paving of ulitsa Kirova in the following order:
>   (a) removal of the tram tracks from ulitsa Kirova between ploshchad' Dzerzhinskogo and the Kirovskiye Gates the night of August 10–11, and asphalting from August 11 to August 14;
>   (b) removal of the tracks from ulitsa Kirova between the Kirovskiye Gates and the Red Gates and from Myasnitskii proyezd the night of August 14–15, and paving of this segment from August 15 to August 19.
> 4. To assign the party group of the Moscow Soviet to formulate [*oformit'*] the present decision as a directive of the presidium of the Moscow Soviet.[149]

From nonlocal officials, the party's discipline could pry more compliance than the feeble writ of the soviets. Its executives could publicly summon economic administrators to meet their housing and related promises, and they repeatedly did so. Party pleas were more likely to identify powerful culprits, such as the military-industrial ministries.

The local partocracy also took direct action. Edicts of the apparatus wove back and forth across administrative lines, between dictate and entreaty, and between welfare and production goals. A March 1932 resolution of the obkom and gorkom bureaus on the First State Ballbearings Works had this to say:

Metallostroi [the builder] and Comrades Berze and Katushkin [its leaders] are obliged to complete construction of the second phase of the plant by no later than June 15, 1932, and all specialized work by June 1, 1932. They are to complete the oil tanks by May 1, the warehouses by May 15, the main shops by July 1, the courtyard by July 1, the railroad spur by June 1, the polyclinic [out-patient clinic] by August 1, the cinema by June 1, the day nursery by June 1 . . .

It is suggested that Comrade Katushkin complete ten apartment houses by April 1, fifteen by May 1, and twenty-one by July 1.

Comrade Konstantinopol'skii, the chief of Moszhilstroi [a city department], is obliged, in addition to the four houses already done, to turn over two houses by April 15, two more by May 15, and one by June 15 . . .

Considering that the plant is being built in a district thinly supplied with recreation, daily services, and stores, the People's Commissariat of Heavy Industry will be asked to allocate an additional 3 million rubles to such uses . . .

Comrade Bodrov [chief of construction of the plant] is obliged to build in 1932 a cinema, a clubhouse, a department store, a polyclinic, and a day nursery. MSPO [a retail cooperative subordinate to the city] is obliged to provide an advance for construction of the department store.

Since there are few roads around the site and poor communications between the plant and the city, the needed roads are to be put through by August 1.[150]

There was testimony during the flash of candor about local politics in 1937 that party commandism here could have some of the baleful effects it was having in industry. After the war Popov evinced a different version of the same problem at the city level. He did not so

Figure 45. Joseph Stalin with Politburo members marking a map of Moscow region, late 1940s. Leaders include Kaganovich (standing on far right), Malenkov (sitting to Kaganovich's right), Voroshilov (in military uniform on right), Beria (sitting to Stalin's left), Khrushchev (standing at door), Bulganin (in military uniform on left), and Molotov (sitting at table to Stalin's right). (From *Gorodskoye khozyaistvo Moskvy*, no. 12, December 1949, following p. 6.)

much fuzz the party-soviet boundary as exploit its ambiguity to suit himself. His disgrace did nothing to clarify the limits of party work. Moscow's municipal leaders held their tongues, reconciled to their handmaiden status.

ON THE INSTRUCTIONS OF COMRADE STALIN

We need not believe in the cliché of Stalin's big-hearted solicitude for Moscow to see that the dictator took a lively interest (see Figure 45). He was a homebody who seldom strayed far. The "city fathers," as he nicknamed Khrushchev and Bulganin, frequently dined with him in the 1930s and sometimes joined him in his theater box. "We always concentrated hard on what he was saying," Khrushchev said, "and then tried to do exactly as he had advised us." Stalin was beside himself when he did not hear from Georgii Popov about Moscow urban issues three months into his first secretaryship. He rang Popov up and demanded to know, "Why are you not phoning me? I cannot believe that Moscow is not in need of anything." Thinking fast, Popov put in a request for heating oil, steel tubing, and trucks; delivery began within minutes of Stalin's hanging up. "I figured out," Popov wrote, "that in my new role I was supposed to deal directly with Stalin."[151]

Stalin, after the suicide of his wife in 1932, rarely overnighted in his Kremlin flat overlooking the Ivan the Great Belfry, rigged with auditing and motion-detection systems that alerted bodyguards to every footstep or cough. His real home was the "Nearby Dacha" he built at Volynskoye, in suburban Kuntsevo just off the high road to Mozhaisk, in 1934. A one-story frame dwelling (a second floor was added in 1948), it had rustic furnishings, a sauna, and a hothouse for the lemons he offered his guests. The Politburo and its working groups often met there. The dacha was surrounded by fifty meters of asphalt, to aid detection of intruders, and then by a forest—land-mined, guarded around the clock by crack troops armed to the teeth, and hidden behind inner and outer stockades. At ground zero, Stalin slept on the sofa in his study, a pistol under his pillow.[152]

His daily commute took his armor-plated Packard convertible (a copycat ZIS-110 after 1948) from Kuntsevo, through the Arbat area, to the Kremlin's Borovitskiye Gates. Fanatical security accompanied him everywhere. A near-sighted housewife, who had the misfortune of trying to read a clock across Arbatskaya ulitsa out her apartment window just as his car wallowed by, was arrested when the sunlight glinted off her opera glasses. This happened in 1949; she did not see Moscow again until her release from a Siberian camp in 1955. As generalissimo during the war, Stalin saw another side of Moscow when he worked out of a cubicle in the bomb shelter of the General Staff—on the platform of the Kirovskaya subway station, only a plywood divider between it and the trains. The Politburo and State Defense Committee also held meetings in the station.[153]

Stalin remodeled the Volynskoye dacha every other year, as a balm to his nerves, according to memoirists. Renovating a whole city must also have satisfied a profound psychic need. Like his totalitarian confreres in Berlin and Rome, Stalin looked on his adopted hometown as a Brobdingnagian sandbox in which he could sift, heap, and bore at will. According to Albert Speer, Hitler's court architect, Hitler was "deeply irked" by the magnitude of the Palace of Soviets and Stalin's other projects; it can hardly be doubted that Stalin kept jealous watch on building plans for the Third Reich.[154]

Stalin's attention to Moscow planning issues can be traced to the remodeling of Red Square, the Kaganovich commission, the quarrels over landmarks, and the master plan. His more spasmodic entrenchments after 1935 usually reflected his interest in symbolism. In 1947 he ordered a sculpture of Yurii Dolgorukii mounted on Sovetskaya ploshchad', where the Liberty Obelisk had been until 1941; he admired the prince as an emblem of Moscow's and the USSR's links with Russian statehood. In 1950 he prescribed with a flick of the wrist from his limousine that the famous statue of Pushkin, by A. M. Opekushin, be portaged from the Bul'varnoye kol'tso, where it had stood since 1880, to a new Pushkinskaya ploshchad', at the site of the former Strastnoi Convent.[155]

Vastly more costly were several capital investments, made, as the saying went, "on the instructions of Comrade Stalin," notably: wartime continuation of subway construction, mostly by teenaged laborers who were kept on the job by withholding their passports; a natural gas pipeline from the city of Saratov, Moscow's first, begun in 1945 (and named after Stalin); eight office and housing towers, the Moscow "tall buildings" *(vysotnyye zdaniya)* enunciated in the jubilee year of 1947 and originating with a blue pencil drawing that Stalin handed to Popov; and a secret subway line from the Kremlin toward Stalin's sanctum at Volynskoye. Whereas some larger public purpose was served by the first two, and maybe the third, the hush-hush subway project revealed obscene incontinence. Stalin reportedly ordered it built near the end of the war, out of fear of assassination and of American atomic weapons. It was pushed out only as far as Kiev Railway Station, just across the Moskva River, and canceled after his death.[156]

It would be misleading to conceive of Stalin's role exclusively in terms of high policy and personal neuroses, for he excelled at the "petty tutelage" so deplored at the local level. Prowling the avenues of Moscow with his bodyguards, usually in the dead of night, he kept "a careful gaze on everything being built in the city," then "directed which public works were to be done first, and on what schedule." He telephoned city hall over watering a grove of parched lime trees and forbade use of double-decker trolleybuses, for fear they would tip over. He upped the cruising speed on the newly opened subway by 20 percent. He legislated on the granite to be used to face the river embankments—presenting engineers with a box of gray stones sent to him from the White Sea–Baltic Canal—on the underground duct to transport Volga water from a reservoir to the Yauza, and on ways to seat tram rails and to pave bridges and intersections.[157]

He conveyed the message to local apparatchiks that they could meddle just as relentlessly. Khrushchev recorded his reaction to Stalin's bull that he and Bulganin install more public toilets in Moscow: "This may seem like a trivial subject for Stalin to have brought to our attention, but I was impressed nonetheless"—enough to follow suit the rest of his career.[158]

The Two Cities

The salient feature of Moscow's development under Stalin was its dualism. Management of metropolitan growth in the 1920s had been society-oriented, populist, and periphery-focused: welfare goals rated passably high, and policy aimed to some degree to help have-nots living toward the edge of the city. The new formula was state-oriented, elitist, and centrist: it preferred ostentatious set pieces, it catered to the upper social strata, and its best efforts went to the center, not the workers' outskirts. Thus only a small circle of the population benefited from the larger-than-life building projects of idealized, monumental Moscow. For everyone else, Stalin's Moscow was a spartan place that frustrated and deferred gratification of basal needs. In both metropoles, but especially the second, resource scarcities and institutional immaturity conspired to keep attainment far short of aspiration.

The machinery for steering growth was far more elaborate than at earlier times. Even before 1935, provisions for continuous planning broke down along two planes. Microdesign *(proyektirovaniye)* at the

site level was the chief instrument of monumentalism; its poor relation, macroplanning *(planirovka)* of city and region, cared mostly for
minimal Moscow. These functions operated in separate city departments from 1933 to 1944 before combining in an Architectural Affairs Directorate, renamed the Architectural Planning Directorate in
June 1951. Headed by a chief architect of Moscow, the directorate
had 2,000 employees in 1950, one hundred times more than the
rudimentary planning office of 1929.

THE MONUMENTAL CITY

There is nothing aberrant about a great city being an alfresco gallery
for treasures that incarnate prevalent values. But Stalin took this
propensity to extremes. He pursued a monumentalism that cast into
shadow and at times annihilated artifacts of the pre-Soviet world
while surrounding the citizen with surrogates of the Soviet state's
might. It resonated with the brass-band nationalism of Stalin's Russia
and the "theme of victory" that took hold in all the arts after V-E Day.

Stalin fostered interorganizational competition. When the People's
Commissariat of Heavy Industry made an overture about a thirty-
three-story House of Heavy Industry in place of GUM and the Middle
Trading Rows in 1934, it expressed a tangible corporate interest, and
one that a soft budget constraint left it freer to chase than a bureau
or a private company in the West. Personality could reinforce organizational interest. The industrial commissariat, for instance, was
headed by a Georgian comrade of Stalin, Sergo Ordzhonikidze. His
death (at his own hand) in February 1937 was enough to put the Red
Square site out of reach; when planning resumed, the skyscraper was
assigned the riverbank traders' quarter, Zaryad'e, several blocks away.

Bigness and technical complexity, prized for going against the nap
of traditional Russian attitudes, received even more accolades if they
seemed to flout nature. Recollect that Bukharin characterized the
1935 plan as "almost magical." Khrushchev says that city administrators perceived the subway as "something almost supernatural." For
everyone except Molotov, a selling point of the Palace of Soviets was
that the raised arm of the Lenin atop it would stab the clouds eighty
days a year, as if emancipated from gravity. Speaking of the Moscow-
Volga Canal, an OGPU grandee cited the hydraulics for carrying water
and navigation uphill as proof of ideological elan: "The water does

not want to go into the Moskva River, so we have to force it to go. As we know, there are no fortresses Bolsheviks cannot storm."[159] Another act of forcing, starting in 1935, made the undulating Tverskaya into the arrow-straight ulitsa Gor'kogo. The only way to save the Mossovet's chambers, the one-time governor-general's palace at address 13, was to transport it. The building designed by Kazakov in the 1780s was shorn of its wings in 1939 and moved fourteen meters backward on rollers. By 1945 it had been jacked up a story, joined to a smaller house built in 1930, sandwiched between new ground and attic floors, and fitted with a high-arched portico. Workers also moved fifty houses on the old Tverskaya, many of which ended up in the courtyards of new buildings.

Finally, glamor projects made sense as a source of vicarious satisfaction for the population, a first installment on the good life to come. They would, as Kaganovich put it, refute the falsehood "that socialism is a barracks" peopled by look-alikes. He encouraged splurging on a subway with escalators, chandeliers, muscular proletarian statuary, stained-glass panels, fittings of brass and chrome, and walls of marble (twenty different kinds), porphyry, onyx, malachite, and other rare substances. "When our worker takes the subway, he should be cheerful and joyous," buoyed by the realization that "every screw [around him] is a screw of socialism," feeling as if in "a palace shining with . . . the light of advancing, all-victorious socialism."[160]

The magnification and gilding of ordinary pieces of urban tissue, the main ways the monumental principle was flaunted, could have winning results. The Mayakovsksaya metro station opened under ulitsa Gor'kogo in 1938, with its thirty-six oval ceiling cupolas, flecked marble, stainless steel trim, and mosaic panels, is as lovely a space as any the Communists built in Moscow. A model of it won a grand prize at the 1938 World's Fair in New York. Stalin evidently considered it his favorite station, and he made his most famous wartime speech here on November 6, 1941.

Often, the result was heavy and pompous. The twelve stations of the circular line completed beneath the Sadovoye between 1950 and 1954, jammed with odes to the conquest of the German dragon, look floridly overdone today. The vestibule of the Komsomol'skaya station was roofed by Aleksei Shchusev in a high cupola shaped like a Muscovite battle helmet, while Pavel D. Korin's mosaics within depicted

Aleksandr Nevskii, Dmitrii Donskoi, Mikhail Kutuzov—and Stalin, standing in the row of Russian men of mettle. New arterial roads in Stalin's Moscow spanning 100 or more meters across invited comparisons with the Unter den Linden in Berlin and the Vienna Ringstrasse, both a puny and unsocialist 50 meters. Whatever security reasons applied—the military thought it would be easier to sop up chemicals after aerial bombardment and may have intended to use the Sadovoye and other roads as landing strips—were second to "joyous" aesthetics.

Similar motivations determined building heights. The 1935 plan set a minimum of six floors for apartment houses; New Moscow in the 1920s had treated five to seven as an upper limit. Aligned along squares, avenues, and granite-coated river quays, houses and office buildings were to present the passer-by with walls of harmonious facade in proportion to the thoroughfare; 80 percent of all housing construction in Moscow was thus positioned in 1940. Bicentennials for Mikhail Kazakov in 1938 and Vasilii Bazhenov in 1939 were used to suggest kinship with Russian neoclassicism of the eighteenth century. But at the level of the individual building, the lusciously decorated look at best fell under pseudoclassical—resplendent in carved portals, cornices, friezes, pilasters, and vases—while at the level of street composition the inspiration seemed closer to the *grands boulevards* of Georges-Eugene Haussmann than to anything Russian or Marxist.

Architects saved their breath for unique and exceptional works, of which the subway, canal, and Palace of Soviets, the three behemoths hatched in 1931, were prototypes. In mid-Moscow, imposing new public buildings—the enlarged Lenin Library (started in 1928 but redrawn several times), the municipal Hotel Moskva on the Palace of Labor plot, Gosplan headquarters, and the Zholtovskii apartment house—skirted Okhotnyi ryad and adjacent squares by 1940. Two new auto bridges spanned the Moskva River to the right and left of the Kremlin (the Bol'shoi Kamennyi Bridge and the Bol'shoi Moskvoretskii Bridge, for which the Lower Trading Rows and seventy other buildings on Moskvoretskaya ulitsa were torn down in 1936), and Zaryad'e was being cleared for the heavy-industry staff.

Comparable ventures at various stages of fruition spangled the map: the star-shaped Red Army Theater on ploshchad' Kommuny, with a stage solid enough to bear the weight of ten-ton tanks; a Palace of the Arts on ploshchad' Vosstaniya; a Palace of Literature at Pushkinskaya ploshchad'; a Palace of Physical Culture at Kolkhoznaya ploshchad' and a 150,000-seat national soccer stadium in Izmailovo; a Komsomol Palace on Staraya ploshchad'; Palaces of Technology and Science near Gorky Park, for the Academy of Sciences and related bodies; an Administrative Palace for the police on ploshchad' Dzerzhinskogo; a House of Books for the publishing industry on Sadovaya-Spasskaya; a Radio House topped by a broadcasting mast at Miusskaya ploshchad' (on the foundation of the Aleksandr Nevskii Cathedral); a House of Aeroflot (the USSR airline) at Belorussia Railway Station. Most of these piles were never completed as contemplated and were quietly terminated after 1945. Even the Ministry of State Security had to make do with an enlargement of the Lubyanka designed by Shchusev.[161]

Once postwar construction tempos quickened, the "tall buildings" announced in February 1947 and blocked out under Chief Architect Dmitrii N. Chechulin, a student of Shchusev, took priority. Their completion rate was high; only the reworked Zaryad'e office block (slated for forty-six stories) went unfinished. They were conceived from the start as prestige projects. "We've won the war and are recognized the world over as the glorious victors," Khrushchev quotes Stalin as saying. "We must be ready for an influx of foreign visitors. What will happen if they walk around Moscow and find no skyscrapers? They will make unfavorable comparisons with capitalist cities?"[162] Vertically stepped, like the Palace of Soviets, and coiffed at Stalin's insistence by spires echoing the Kremlin towers, the tall buildings were often likened out of his hearing to thickly frosted wedding cakes. They pitched sixteen to thirty-six floors upward between 1947 and 1954. Two became brooding apartment houses (on ploshchad' Vosstaniya and Kotel'nicheskaya naberezhnaya); two served as hotels (the Ukraina and the Leningradskaya); and two held government offices (for the Ministry of Foreign Affairs on Smolenskaya ploshchad' and the Ministry of Transportation on Komsomol'skaya ploshchad'); the Ukraina and the Ministry of Transportation had residential wings (see Figures 46 and 47).

The largest product, a new campus for Moscow State University, provoked hidden swordplay. The campus was initially planned for the lanes behind the eighteenth-century university quadrangle on Mokho-

Figure 46. "Tall building" at ploshchad' Vosstaniya, under construction, 1952. This view is from the Moscow Zoo. (Museum of the History of the City of Moscow.)

Figure 47. "Tall building" on Kotel'nicheskaya naberezhnaya.
(Photograph by author.)

vaya ulitsa, but the realization that tens of thousands of downtowners
would have to be resettled convinced the government to redirect it to
the Lenin Hills. Architect Boris Iofan, supported by Andrei Zhdanov,
wanted to put a massive Lenin statue on its main tower and to site it
at the escarpment above the Moskva, whence a marble stairway
would descend to the riverbank. After Georgii Popov took it up with
Stalin, the design was simplified, the complex moved back from the
river, and Iofan replaced by Lev V. Rudnev, an architect specializing
in military and police buildings. Rudnev's skills would have come in
handy, for a closed atomic physics laboratory was constructed under
the campus and secret signals gear built into the roof and basement
of the campanile.[163]

All the foregoing projects were dollhouses by comparison with the
Palace of Soviets, the cynosure of the new Moscow designed to loom

over the Kremlin, the best of the old. The Lenin effigy acrest it grew under the ministrations of Iofan and the sculptor Sergei Merkurov from 50 meters high to 90 meters in the 1933 concourse drawings and then 100 in later plans, taking the structure in its entirety to more than 420 meters. Thirty-two meters across the shoulders, with 14-meter-long feet and 6-meter fingers, the statue was to be triple the size of the Statue of Liberty in New York harbor and visible from seventy kilometers on a clear day or under nocturnal floodlights. A hair taller than the Empire State Building, the broad beam of the palace would have made it a far more massive structure: its 350,000 tons of steel frame would outweigh the Empire State's six times, and its interior volume of 7 million cubic meters was supposed to exceed Manhattan's six largest skyscrapers put together.

As the political ganglion of the USSR, it was to put on all parliamentary and party congresses and big political festivals. Soldiers' and workers' cavalcades would march to it down a Prospect of the Palace of Soviets, 250 meters in breadth in some diagrams, running between the central squares and the Lenin Hills. The Pushkin (formerly Alexander III) Fine Arts Museum across ulitsa Volkhonka was to be rolled 100 meters out of the way and the Bul'varnoye kol'tso to be rerouted through the Arbat.

Publicists presented the Palace of Soviets as the apotheosis of opulence and mechanical refinement. In the final prewar drawings its Great Hall, huddling 21,000 people under a 100-meter dome, was ringed by a half-dozen lesser auditoriums (the Hall of the Building of Socialism, the Hall of Orders, the Hall of the Stalin Constitution, and so forth) and a warren of foyers and banquet and reception rooms. Six chanting verses of an oath to socialism that Stalin swore after Lenin's death provided the unifying artistic motif. Visitors would be air conditioned by a "weather factory," moved around by 281 elevators and escalators, and dazzled by 750 sculptures and busts, 20,000 square meters of frescoes and painted panels, 20,000 square meters in bas-relief, 6,500 in decorative glass, 5,000 in majolica, and 4,000 in mosaics. Exiting down a 115-meter processional staircase into the half-square-kilometer palace square—as befitting the largest building and the largest statue, nothing less than the world's largest plaza would do—they would proceed through statue gardens and banks of fountains toward the Kremlin, the embankment, or the subway. A

Museum of the World Revolution containing a monument to Karl Marx would purfle one side of the main square, while a new Institute of Marx-Engels-Lenin would stand on the square beside the Small Hall.

Some groused in private about the palace's luxuriousness and the demolitions it occasioned,[164] but in public all applauded. According to one disquisition, all historical antecedents, from the seven wonders of the ancient world to the Eiffel Tower, had been put up by exploiting classes. The Palace of Soviets would be the temple of the exploited, "a symbol in the people's eyes of all the achievements of socialism." The author went on to make the amazing declaration that, like the soul of the good Christian, it would have everlasting life. Long after a world Communist society had been formed, national boundaries erased, and the cosmos conquered, it would grace the shore of the Moskva: "The centuries will not leave their mark on it. We shall build it so that it stands without aging, eternally [vechno]."[165]

Alas, Stalin's palace—so unlike the Empire State Building, which rose up in nineteen months—never made it out of the womb. The first bulletin of the building directorate stated that it would be finished by the end of 1933, but excavation did not even begin until early 1935. Pouring of the foundation, to a depth of twenty meters below the riverbed, was completed in January 1938, by which time quarries and factories all over the country were preparing materials and components. The 1938 May Day parade in Red Square featured a huge float depicting the palace, with workmen putting the finishing touches on it. Cranes began that autumn to mount the ribwork of chromium-hardened steel girders, each with its "DS" (Dvorets Sovetov) monogram. In January 1939 notices went up of street closings to allow demolitions and transport of the Pushkin Museum, and Molotov put a motion to the party congress that March calling for completion of "basic work" by the end of 1942.

Water seepage into the base, not reported until September 1939, would have made the timetable unrealistic even without the war. To contend with the 117 springs discovered on the site, the engineers attempted to harden the muck by injecting bitumen. They then tried the ghoulish remedy of rafting hundreds of tombstones to the site from graveyards in Moscow and the region and thumping them into the gummy floor of the foundation pit. The treatment was stopped when war broke out, and most of the eleven stories of I-beams in the air in June 1941 were disassembled for tank traps and railroad trestles.[166]

Iofan, evacuated to the Urals, perfected his drawings and did a new gypsum model, which was displayed to deputies to the USSR Supreme Soviet in 1945. Maddeningly, the incursion of ground and river water was so bad by war's end that adolescents were skinny-dipping in the concrete foundation. Iofan hacked ninety-six meters off the palace's intended height, hoping this would give the project a push. The police general brought in to manage it, Aleksandr N. Komarovskii (a deputy of Sergei Zhuk's in Mosvolgostroi in the 1930s), stated later that it was already clear in mid-1948 that it would not go forward, but Stalin at a 1949 meeting of the Politburo told Popov that it would be built once engineers had perfected their technique on the tall buildings.[167] Without an official termination, the palace was put in abeyance. Its picture continued to be splattered on matchbooks and dustcovers, and the subway stop on Volkhonka remained the Palace of Soviets station, as if nothing had happened. Moscow grandmothers made the sign of the cross and clucked that the Communists had brought this upon themselves by defiling a hallowed place. Idlers and children stole through holes in the fencing to fish for carp that had somehow made their way into the lake in the foundation.

The mishap of the Palace of Soviets should not obfuscate the privileged station of monumental undertakings. The interest they elicited in the Kremlin placed them in a class apart. Another sign of favor was access to the labor reserves of the NKVD/MVD, numbering perhaps 100,000 in the Moscow region in 1939.[168]

The police were by no means confined to construction activity this grand. The three biggest camps in the area ringed the city, at Beskudnikovo, just north of Moscow, at Lyublino, to the southeast, and at Kryukovo, out the railway to Leningrad ("Kryuken'vald" in local argot, after the Nazis' Buchenwald). They supplied materials and mobile labor to dozens of compounds marked by Gulag's telltale watch towers. In Moscow oblast, the denizens of the Stalinogorsk (formerly Bobriki) women's camp mined coal and iron ore; at Dmitrov, zeks manned the Moscow-Volga Canal's locks and quays; and at Novyi Ierusalim and Zagorsk they dug clay and made bricks. Closer in, inmates at Izmailovo, Khovrino, the dacha zones of Serebryannyi bor and Pokrovskoye-Streshnevo, and Peschanaya ulitsa worked on ordinary blocks of flats and on closed factories and institutes. The future Nobel laureate Aleksandr I. Solzhenitsyn served at a prison laboratory (*sharaga* or *sharashka*) on the grounds of a former seminary at Marfino, in northern Moscow, from 1947 to 1950; as "Mavrino," the Marfino sharashka was the setting for his novel *The First Circle.*

Accountable for all interurban highways since 1936, the MVD was assigned standard road, water, and drainage projects inside Moscow after the war. Volume was enough to have its deputy minister for construction, Nikolai K. Bogdanov, selected to the bureau of the Moscow obkom. Solzhenitsyn spent a year at a minicamp at Kaluga Gates (later ploshchad' Gagarina) after the war, putting up a semicircular apartment block for MVD officers. It was, he wrote, "a tiny islet of the savage Archipelago, more closely tied to Noril'sk and the Kolyma [icy MVD colonies in the far north and east] than to Moscow."[169]

Nonetheless, the police specialized in showcase projects. Zeks put up the Kotel'nicheskaya naberezhnaya apartment tower, within sight of the Kremlin, and the Ministry of Foreign Affairs in the Arbat area. The Construction Directorate of the Palace of Soviets, an arm of Gulag from 1937, was left intact when the palace was suspended. Komarovskii used Soviet convicts and German and Japanese prisoners of war to craft the new university. "Every morning thousands of unhappy convicts in quilted jackets were marched from [a camp at the village of] Ramenki under convoy of short Bashkir guards, armed with machine guns, and under the eye of a multitude of sheep dogs . . . The column was several kilometers long, leading to the work yards . . . ringed by a barrier topped with barbed wire." Fifteen thousand prisoners worked on the classrooms and laboratories of the campus alone; an unknown number plunged to their deaths from scaffolding. Six thousand soldiers had to be deployed to dig sand from the riverbed and lug it up to the worksite. The checkpoints and lettered security zones stayed when the main building of the university opened in 1953; the barracks at Ramenki remained until torn down in the 1970s.[170]

Prestige projects not only received Politburo-level and police attention, they were also more likely to be shepherded by the most potent local agencies, those of the Communist Party. Arkhplan, the architectural commission of the gorkom and city soviet, had enough importance in the years 1933–1935 to be chaired by Kaganovich and then Khrushchev. Its agenda consisted mostly of demolitions, street widenings, and large buildings. It was revived as a municipal commission in January 1939, though with Shcherbakov at the helm.

Monumentalism's advantages did not make implementation steady or automatic. The party participated mostly to push individual buildings to completion. Integration on a wider basis was episodic; Arkhplan did not exist from 1935 to 1939, and in February 1944, under a new name (Architectural Council), it was downgraded to an ancillary of the city's chief architect. The city planning establishment considered the design studios formed in 1933, each headed by an eminent architect, responsible for imbuing building and street design with excellence. Four years later the studios were doing only 20 percent of blueprints in Moscow. In most instances, Shchusev sighed, "A commissariat decides to put up a building for itself, and its own studio does a design which ignores where it is to be constructed."[171] While municipal architects' share of the work rose to 45 percent by 1952, censure of agency exclusivism persisted.

It took lightning from the political Olympus to maintain discipline on the bedrock point of marshaling big buildings on main streets. Stalin gave word to this effect to Chairman Pronin in the spring of 1939. In 1949, discovering that 64 percent of all housing under way in his capital was in low-rise buildings, in contravention of the master plan and his 1939 edict, he had to reiterate it. This last broadside had shockingly little effect: only 22 percent of all housing space completed from 1951 to 1953 was on principal streets and embankments; 78 percent was "in peripheral districts and on secondary streets." The monumental city was not immune to the developmental entropy pervasive in the minimal city.[172]

Although most of Stalinist Moscow's true monuments were meant to be ogled and worked in, a good number of priority projects were residential. Invariably, they benefitted high- and middle-ranking officials and professionals. Elite housing construction picked up sharply after 1930, spurred by the precipitate expansion of the nomenklatura and the regime's desire to bestow material comforts on it. Government House (where Khrushchev stayed until 1938) was quickly overloaded, as were older buildings such as 3 ulitsa Granovskogo (where Shcherbakov, Malenkov, and Bulganin all lived, and Khrushchev after 1949). The Kremlin palaces substantially emptied out by 1940, with only Kaganovich, Molotov, and a few Stalin intimates remaining; a grass tennis court was laid out after 1945 on the wooded southwest corner where children had frolicked in the 1920s.

At first, building cooperatives got many of the permits for the new residences, typically for modest-sized houses on back streets in the old town. Hence the Kremlevskii Rabotnik (Kremlin Employee) co-op built at 16 ulitsa Malaya Nikitinskaya (later Kachalova), Nauchnyi Rabotnik (Scientist) at 18–20 Zubovskii bul'var, Sovetskii Pisatel' (Soviet Writer) at 19 Lavrushenskii pereulok and 43b ulitsa Gertsena, Sovetskii Kompozitor (Soviet Composer) at Miusskaya ploshchad' and 7 Bryusovskii pereulok, and Polyarnik (Polar Explorer) at 16–18 Sadovaya-Kudrinskaya. There were co-ops for aircraft designers and engineers on Pionerskii (formerly Patriarshii) Pond and at Pyataya Tverskaya-Yamskaya, for the People's Commissariat of Foreign Affairs and the Commissariat of Foreign Trade at 5–7 and 9–11 Kalyayevskaya ulitsa, and for the Union of Artists (in a compound containing studios and galleries) on Verkhnyaya Maslovka. The Central Committee directly funded a comfortable apartment house at 19 Starokonyushennyi pereulok in the Arbat (tearing down the Church of John the Baptist [1653]) and added two floors to 11–13 Arbatskaya ulitsa. The OGPU built at 1 Tverskoi bul'var, and the Red Army constructed a complex for its generals on Bol'shoi Ovchinnikovskii pereulok and a number of residences near its expanding offices and near the new Frunze and General Staff military academies, around the former Khamovniki Barracks.[173]

As of 1935 administrative organizations, not cooperatives, financed most of this accommodation, and much more of it took the form of larger and fancier buildings on thoroughfares, as the master plan demanded. Construction first concentrated on ulitsa Gor'kogo, the street taking the line of Red Square past Okhotnyi ryad to the northwest. By 1940, with Arkadii G. Mordvinov as the architect, it had been quadrupled in width at its base, to sixty meters, and a cliff of massive, honey-colored granite apartment houses put along its right side out to Sovetskaya ploshchad'. Dozens of eighteenth- and nineteenth-century homes were demolished or relocated. By 1950 a second

row in gray stone stretched up the left curb from city hall to ploshchad' Mayakovskogo. From here houses scattered along Leningradskii prospekt (the extension of ulitsa Gor'kogo) and clockwise and
counterclockwise along the Sadovoye, linking up with the high rises
at Kolkhoznaya and Vosstaniya Squares. Occupying them were Central Committee staffers, state functionaries, police and army generals,
industrialists, and approved intellectuals and performers.[174]

On quiet lanes not far away sat the homes of Beria (a former
merchants' house at 28/1 Malaya Nikitinskaya), Vasilii Stalin (a gentry villa at 7 Gogolevskii bul'var), and Malenkov (who had a mansion
built for himself at 28 ulitsa Alekseya Tol'stogo, but fell from favor
in the 1950s and never moved in). The large Kremlin clinic (Polyclinic
No. 1) was begun at 26–28 Sivtsev-Vrazhek pereulok in 1937 and
finished in 1950. At the several "Kremlin schools" in the vicinity,
politicians' offspring were dropped off by chauffeurs a block or so
away, to keep up egalitarian pretenses.[175]

By Stalin's death, activity bustled in two other areas. The smaller
was along Vorob'evskoye shosse, on the Lenin Hills not far from the
university and Mosfil'm. There a handful of two-story "villas"
(osobnyaki) for Politburo members were begun behind tall walls in
the late 1940s.

The second was, like ulitsa Gor'kogo, a fully visible street corridor—in this case along Kutuzovskaya ulitsa, Mozhaiskoye shosse, and
interconnected roads on the far side of the Moskva, heading toward
Poklonnaya Hill, Stalin's Kuntsevo dacha, and thence to points west.
Engineers began to cut the avenue through the proletarian slum of
Dorogomilovo in 1937–1938, putting the Ukraina Hotel as its anchor
there in the late 1940s. The plan had been to call it Stalinskii prospekt
upon completion, but Stalin's death interposed and it was named
Kutuzovskii prospekt, after Field Marshal Kutuzov, the commander
of Russia's armies against Napoleon. The first building, 22 Kutuzovskii prospekt, was settled in 1940. Two of the biggest, at 24 and
26 Kutuzovskii prospekt, were put over a Jewish cemetery and the
fraternal grave of 300 Russian troops who fell at the Battle of
Borodino in 1812; the soldiers' remains and a commemorative obelisk
were stealthily moved 1.5 kilometers away in 1953.[176]

Kutuzovskii (see Figure 48) had fewer facade embellishments than
ulitsa Gor'kogo, but it was much quieter. Flanked on the north by a
quay and footpath along the river, it had treed courtyards, several

Figure 48. Elite apartment house, Kutuzovskii prospekt, built in the early 1950s. (Photograph by author.)

small parks, service ateliers, and a movie theater built in. It housed, by rough guess, two or three times as many nomenklatura households as ulitsa Gor'kogo. Leonid I. Brezhnev, the future Soviet leader, moved into No. 26, a cream-tiled Central Committee property, in 1954. City schools 5 and 27, on the north side of Kutuzovskii, overtook the older buildings near ulitsa Gor'kogo as the preeminent Kremlin schools.[177]

THE MINIMAL CITY

Palaces and promenades were as distant as could be from the rounds of most inhabitants of Stalin's Moscow. Their world was defined by grinding shortages of, and differential access to, necessities and conveniences.

The most dehumanizing scarcities, of daily bread, occurred during the years of rationing, 1929 to 1935 and 1941 to 1947. As under War Communism, essentials were furnished by canteens and "workers' provisioning departments," as most of the closed distributors were titled in 1932, at work. In the lean winter of 1932–1933, enterprises fed 2.1 million Muscovites daily in their cafeterias, farmed 589,000 hectares of suburban land, and, under party pressure, bred tens of thousands of rabbits and carp on their grounds. The gorkom bureau confirmed monthly distribution plans for flour. All allotments correlated to status of user, with officials getting two or three times more than the common urban population.[178] In 1942, the year of the direst wartime shortages, "People in the Moscow streets looked haggard and pale, and scurvy was fairly common. Consumer goods were almost unobtainable, except at fantastic prices, or for coupons, if and when these were honoured," and "shop windows were mostly sand-bagged."[179]

Even when rationing was not in force, most blue- and white-collar staff counted on their employers for the main midday meal. ZIS, the Stalin Auto Works, paid 1,350 cooks and servers in 1940 to operate twelve cafeterias and fifty snack bars.[180] In addition, employees of the Central Committee and a few other agencies received passes to small shops selling consumer goods; they were known as *limitniki,* after the norming "limits" set for the goods.

In housing and physical comforts, the inelasticity of supply made rationing endemic. The new housing delivered in 1930, the last year of the NEP regimen, was equaled only once over the next two decades (in 1933). Builders consistently failed even to approximate production targets. Moscow received a niggardly 37.2 percent of the 4.5 million square meters set by the Second Five-Year Plan (1933–1937) and 24.8 percent of the 3 million given for 1936–1938 by the 1935 master plan. No housing goal was written into the Third Five-Year Plan (1938–1942), but fulfillment reached just half each annual quota before the war.[181] In the Fourth Five-Year Plan (1946–1950), the city fulfilled only 47.5 percent of the 3 million square meters assigned (see Table D-1 in Appendix D).

The only reason the housing shortage did not statistically worsen after the mid-1930s was the deceleration of population growth, for which restrictions on migration bore some responsibility. Although the mass expulsions of 1933–1935 were not, to my knowledge, repeated, passports and residence permits undoubtedly slowed down the influx, especially of peasants, demobbed servicemen, and ex-convicts from the camps and prisons. Building superintendents were expected to inform the police of unauthorized tenants, and many of these snoops were still chosen from minority groups—notably the Tatars, non-Slavs of Moslem religious background. Had hyperurbanization threatened to resume, the authorities could have forestalled it.

The impact of the controls should not be exaggerated. They did not bring Moscow down to the 3.3 million year-end figure posited by the gorkom in 1933 or prevent the addition of a half-million people in 1937–1938, despite the depradations of the Great Purge. Corrupt custodial personnel and police officers often took bribes to overlook violations of the passport law, and surveillance was never perfect, even in Stalin's Moscow. The 1941 document checks turned up thousands of residents without proper papers. The unplanned demographic effects of the war—low fertility, conscription, death at the front, and flight to the east—far exceeded those of the propiska system. Repopulation of Moscow after the German retreat seems to have been subject to few hindrances. And 280,000 persons managed to circumvent the propiska system in 1947 by commuting to work from outside the city.[182]

Neither did the government rigorously apply the policy to curb industrial growth by proscribing new manufacturing plants and relocating polluting ones. As Kaganovich told Arkhplan off the record in 1935, "No matter how much we talk about not building [factories], construction continues." Small-sized factories were "sprouting like mushrooms," he said, and the provision for modernization of enterprises through "reconstruction" provided a yawning loophole: "Under guise of reconstruction, immense new workshops are being added and new plants are being built." Several months after Kaganovich's remarks, Nikolai Yezhov, then still in the CC Secretariat, was appointed head of a "special commission" to investigate, but it stopped meeting in 1936 and did not report.[183]

Later accounts indicate no movement. "The least examination," Aleksandr Bulushev said in 1937, "shows that 'reconstruction' often amounts to the construction of large new factories. And, despite decrees by Sovnarkom and the CC, fire-hazardous and unsanitary enterprises are not being moved out of Moscow." Kaganovich had recommended that Gorplan, Moscow's economic planning board, cooperate with spatial planners in enforcing the rules. But it never did. Gorplan, it was reported, "sets down the data" on industrial investment presented by production agencies "but does not try itself to get at these problems."[184]

It cannot be overstressed that the stabilization of housing conditions occurred at a wretchedly low plateau. Projections for the First Five-Year Plan had per capita supply increasing by about 7 percent by the end of the plan; what actually happened was a decrease of 25 percent. The mean of just over four square meters sustained until the 1950s was under 60 percent of the claustrophobic figure for 1912 (see Table D-2).

What the median family in Stalin's Moscow called home was one monastically furnished room in a *kommunalka*—a "communal" flat, jointly occupied out of necessity, not Marxist conviction. The room had no running water; sheets or curtains marked off subareas where two or three generations slept and sat; food dangled out of winter windows in sacks. Shared sinks, toilets, washtubs, and cooking facilities (usually nothing more than Primus wood alcohol burners and cold water taps) lay either in a no-man's land between the dwelling rooms or down an unheated, laundry-festooned hallway—hence the epithet *koridorka.* A hot scrubbing was had at a public bath, once a week in winter, twice in summer. Muscovites who lived this way felt fortunate, for a great many did worse.[185]

During the First Five-Year Plan, tens of thousands of new construction and manufacturing hands were put up in open-bay wood bunkhouses, or *baraki* (see Figure 49). One hellhole at Cherkizovo, for Elektrozavod, held 550 men and women in 1932. At two square meters per tenant, the space was so tight that 50 slept on the floor and some used the straw-mattress beds in shifts.[186]

A local ordinance in 1934 forbade construction of any more barracks. It had nil effect. Building went on, now under the less pejorative name of *standartnyye doma,* "standardized houses." The prohibition notwithstanding, a Moscow official said in 1938, "we have contrived to find ways to build" barracks. Thirty-four percent of all the space completed from 1935 to 1937 was in standardized houses; the city held 5,000 barracks and expected 225 more to be built in 1938. Sixty

Figure 49. Workers' barracks, First State Ballbearing Works, 1933.
(Museum of the History of the City of Moscow.)

percent of the 7,500 production workers at Serp i molot lived in
hostels of one kind or another in 1937, 1,000 in ones "in very poor
condition." Fifty thousand people in Leningradskii raion resided in
barracks in 1940. E. D. Simon observed that 90 percent of Muscovite
families "would improve their housing conditions beyond recognition" if given "one of [the] houses which are being pulled down in
Manchester as unfit for human habitation."[187]

The barracks were not the worst the minimal city had to offer. It
was reported in 1933 that "conversion of coalsheds, warehouses,
cellars, and substairway spaces [into housing] has become a mass
phenomenon in Moscow." At about this time Stalin, during preparation of the general plan, branded as "demagoguery" a proposal to
eradicate all basement housing by 1945. One hundred Serp i molot
workers and their children in 1933 occupied windowless nooks on
the second floor of the Andronikov Monastery refectory. "There was
one washroom with two lavatory pans for the whole place . . . due

to which the garret was turned into a latrine." Three hundred and fifty dependents of the Soyuzformolit'e (All-Union Form Molding) Works in Dzerzhinskii raion lived in 1934 in a half-built boiler house, without water or toilets, while "several workers lived in mud huts next to the plant."[188]

Right after the war workers from the First State Ballbearing Works crammed up to 18 to a room. More than 4,000 charges of ZIS in 1946 were sheltered in wood houses and shacks leased outside the city. In 1948 barns, closets, dugouts, and rickety garages had been pressed into service. In 1950 the city had 3,318 officially recognized dormitories or hostels (obshchezhitiya), with 358,521 tenants. "Of these [dormitories], 2,680 were in barracks, 403 in basements, 69 in production facilities, and 22 in unfinished buildings. Only 144 of the dormitories were situated in permanent structures constructed specially for the purpose and equipped with all the necessary conveniences."[189]

This squalor reflected the neediness of society at large. The most resolute leadership could not easily have alleviated it. All too often, however, local institutions were far from resolute. Inasmuch as they did look out for welfare interests, they were hampered by the mincing of responsibility.

"The bulk of the projects," a city engineer mourned in 1939, referring to the four-fifths of all housing investment controlled by national agencies, "are carried out with really . . . *no control on the part of local organizations.*" A three-year-old municipal department for checking on the commissariats had only five clerks and "no control rights."[190] Both Metrostroi and operation of the Moscow subway itself were transferred to national commissariats in 1935, on Stalin's recommendation. After the war centrally subordinated organizations also built, by various accounts, about two-thirds of the capital's utility lines and half of its schools.

Fragmentation of responsibility gave rise to fragmentation and stratification of result. A city architect who designed apartment houses for Krasnopresnenskii raion in the early 1950s offered these examples in an interview:

> I worked on one building on the Sadovoye kol'tso which was for the staff of the Ministry of Ship Building [a defense production ministry]. Now

that was a rich patron. I received all kinds of goodies, like passes to rest houses, repairs to my family's apartment, and a nanny for my children. The ministry spared no expense. It had agents everywhere who searched out and procured high quality materials. It supplied the house with beautiful wood, of the grade used in captain's cabins. It traded a few automobiles with a quarry in Georgia for the top class of stone. We faced the exterior of the building in marble and the interior in Italian tufa . . .

I also drew up an apartment building for textile workers at Trekhgornaya. It was a great big structure, but done for a poor customer who couldn't afford anything. The home was simple and of conventional design.[191]

Inequity in outcome had a spatial dimension. As discussed above, residences for the senior nomenklatura overwhelmingly went up in the inner city. They contrasted sharply with the slovenly, factory-centered product toward the periphery. One readily sees it today around ZIL (ZIS) and the auto-related plants in the southeast, out shosse Entuziastov in the northeast, along prospekt Mira in the north, between Leningradskoye shosse and Volokolamskoye shosse in the northwest, and in Fili in the west. Somewhere between the two quality poles was the corridor of mostly joint-occupancy apartments built by Akademstroi, the construction arm of the Academy of Sciences, along Bol'shaya Kaluzhskaya ulitsa (later Leninskii prospekt), in southwest Moscow. A kind of white-collar factory town, this "residential cantonment of the Academy of Sciences," as it was denoted, had 5,000 residents in 1947.[192]

Installation of basic physical services lagged greatly after 1930, which mostly affected the outlying areas. The portion of the population served by municipal water crept up from 65 percent in 1928 to 72.5 percent in 1948; for city sewage, coverage seems actually to have *declined* from 1928's 68 percent.[193] Such amenities as existed outside the old town tended to be laid on by the factories for their labor forces, not by the areal governments. ZIS in 1940 possessed a "medical combine" (containing surgical and X-ray wards), two libraries, a palace of culture (with a gymnasium, banquet hall, and drama theater), kindergartens and nurseries for 2,000 youngsters, and a workers' resort and several Young Pioneers summer camps for children in Podmoskov'e. A big enterprise could also buy special treatment for its workers by subsidizing construction of a service facility.[194]

Outside the city limits the analogues to the stone houses on ulitsa Gor'kogo were the islands of state-owned cottages and resorts catering to the Soviet high and mighty. After 1930 urban construction and defense plants surrounded the dacha area along the Moscow-Kazan Railway. A newer zone took shape northwest of Moscow, between the Skhodnya and Ban'ka Rivers. Central Committee dacha settlements at Planernaya and Nagornoye, and a CC rest house in a noble's estate at Verkhneye Nagornoye, were enlarged by German prisoners of war after the war, and the police built their own compound at Novogorsk.

But the main country retreat for the nomenklatura spread along the axis to the west of Moscow defined by Stalin's Kuntsevo and Usovo dachas. The through road—nicknamed the *amerikanka,* "American way," for its satin-smooth blacktop—was barred to non-official traffic. The Arkhangel'skoye estate, confirmed as a sanatorium for the military, was thoroughly redone and expanded in the 1930s. For civilian officials, the main watering hole was the Sovnarkom (later Council of Ministers) sanatorium developed at Sosny, beside Nikolina Gora. Comintern officials (until that organization's dissolution in 1943), foreign Communists, and members of Lenin's family attended a compound at Zarech'e, just west of Kuntsevo. Dachas for functionaries sprawled along the highway from Rublevo to Uspenskoye and on the left bank of the river, usually behind green fences or barbed wire. The dacha of Procurator-General Andrei Vyshinskii, at Nikolina Gora, occupied a 15,000-square-meter lot and had a swimming pool. Molotov's colonnaded home at Gorki-2, looted by peasants in 1941, had three kilometers of riverbank. A villa near Barvikha, equipped with terraces, verandas, and a tennis court, "would have stood comparison with any of the rich houses which dot the neighborhood of Western capitals."[195]

The Russian intelligentsia also found its place in the summer sun of Podmoskov'e. As a sop for returning from abroad in 1931, Maxim Gorky was awarded a palatial dacha at Gorki-10 to go with a Shekhtel' mansion in Moscow. In 1934, by personal decision of Stalin, most of the village of Peredelkino, southwest of Moscow, was turned over to the Union of Writers for construction of dachas and rest houses for members. In decrees in the late 1940s Stalin ordered dachas built and given to academicians and contributors to the atomic weapons program. The scientists' cottages congregated in three areas: Zhukovka, two kilometers from Usovo; Mozzhenka, near Zvenigorod; and Abramtsevo, northeast of the city. The best two-storied houses at Zhukovka and Mozzhenka were on half-hectare lots and had garages and overnight huts for drivers. About one-third of Peredelkino was reserved for active-duty army officers; several thousand officers sent into the reserves after 1945 also received smaller plots west of Peredelkino, where they built cabins with their own hands and planted kitchen gardens.[196]

It made little difference to the sometime inhabitants of Barvikha, Nikolina Gora, or Peredelkino what local government did. Not so for the ordinary folk who peopled the urban fringe twelve months of the year.

Moscow oblast lasted only a few years in its amplitudinous 1929 boundaries. Together with other Russian regions, it began to be broken down into more manageable units in 1935, and by 1937 it had been reduced to more or less the pre-1929 guberniya.[197] Its government had only vestigial links with Moscow from 1931 onward. City and oblast constituted separate units of local administration, although, out of some garbled consideration or other, almost half of the deputies to the oblast soviet (143 of 305 in 1950) continued to be elected from the city of Moscow. There was next to no overlap between the executives of the two soviets (one deputy chairman of Moscow's ispolkom sat on the oblast's after the war) and next to no career switching from city to oblast.

In the party the subordination of the gorkom to the obkom made organizational connections closer. The two were also drawn together by shared responsibility for food supply. In addition to superintending farming, food processing, and distribution, the party organs required each raion of Moscow to carry out wardship *(shefstvo)* over a rural raion. Wardship, expressed chiefly in donated labor and surplus equipment, was an urban subsidy of collectivized agriculture.[198]

Much less cooperation existed in municipal services and metropolitan development. Party leaders took little interest, with one exception: the short-lived Fedor Ugarov in 1938. Ugarov was baffled by the "unhealthy disconnection" between city and oblast and by the lip service paid to "the leading role of Moscow." Highways leading into the city, he said by way of illustration, were often interrupted by graveled rights of way "for which neither Sidorov [chairman of the city soviet] nor Khokhlov [Ivan S. Khokhlov, chairman of the oblast soviet] answers" and which the party was doing nothing to help. Whatever Ugarov tried to do about the problem stirred up resentment. One of the charges made after his fall was that he "denigrated the role of the oblast [party] committee" and communicated with oblast party workers through gorkom departments.[199]

As the roads example demonstrated, some of the worst disconnects occurred in the territory abutting Moscow. The forested district of Izmailovo typified the problem; piecemeal annexation left the royal estate astride the city's Stalinskii raion and Reutovskii raion in the oblast. Housing construction, chiefly by factories, began in 1932. A press tableau from 1935 is worth quoting:

> The life of Izmailovites, who find themselves on the edge between town and country, abounds in every sort of incident. Thus the last in a row of standardized houses in the settlement does not have either a street address or a real master. The inhabitants of this house, workers from the Moskabel' [Moscow Cable] Works and others, live without residence permits. "And why are we not counted as living people?" residents write of themselves, not without humor, to *Rabochaya Moskva*. In the third quarter [of 1934] their children went without ration coupons; by the same token, no one asks them for rent . . .
>
> People say that that Izmailovo "is not being built for the ages," that pretty soon it will be torn down. But even provisionally it is unacceptable to build this way, without a general plan or account for the demands of daily life. When the residents of the addressless house write that they "sit without firewood, because there is no shed," that they "have to carry water 600 or 700 meters," and that they are "set apart from cultured life," their letters could well be signed by thousands of Izmailovites. They are hard-up for so much: drivable and walkable roads, bus service, water and drainage, stores, a school, a club . . .
>
> There is nobody to direct or organize a struggle for improvements. Each house directorate and zhakt "beautifies" its own building and yard. The result is tastelessness, anarchy . . . a crazy collage of houses, shacks, fences, and gates lacking any style or sense. What a dismal sight!

Life did get better in Izmailovo, but only slowly.[200]

An attempt to bring order was made in March 1933, when the city and oblast executives adopted a joint decree on land-use controls in fourteen raions adjoining Moscow. A forty-five-person board was to compose a plan for protecting forests and waterways and to approve all industrial construction, logging, and tilling of riverbanks within fifteen kilometers of the capital. The panel met several times in 1933, then evidently disbanded. The Moscow presidium voted in September 1933 to support a city-oblast "standing panel on satellite raions," but when a conference on the raions was held in July 1934, it came under the Institute of Economics of the Academy of Sciences. There was no follow-through on its idea of planning the suburbs in "special integrated districts."[201]

The 1933 decree was superseded by the 1935 master plan, with its 1,440-square-kilometer green belt (10 kilometers wide, not 15) external to the territory reserved for Moscow's growth. The belt, about half farmland, one-third wooded, and one-sixth urbanized, contained fifteen workers' hamlets, twenty-seven dacha settlements, and most of three towns (Kuntsevo, Lyublino, and Losinoostrovsk). Its 1935 population totaled 270,000.

But the master plan's provisions were not honored, a city-oblast resolution stated in April 1940; unauthorized (samovol'noye) construction abounded in the green belt, and industrial organizations dodging the 1931 rule against new factories in Moscow often got permission to build a few kilometers out. City and oblast planners in 1940 completed ambitious drafts that would have kept all new industry out of the green belt and placed a "suburban zone" of 1,800 square kilometers—laced with American-style parkways (parkvei)—under less stringent regulation.[202] They were never ratified.

The rush to put up defense-related factories and institutes further undermined regional planning. The terminus of the Moscow-Volga Canal, Tushino, was chosen for an airfield and in 1932 for a a major aircraft (later missile) plant, the Tushino Machine Building Works; aviation facilities were also built in neighboring Khimki. Bykovo, a military airfield laid out in 1933 southeast of Moscow, past Lyubertsy, drew aviation-related research and development to that subarea. Outside nearby Zhukovskii, New TsAGI, an offshoot of the Soviets' premier aviation research institute, had structural test bays and supersonic wind tunnels in operation by 1940, feeding prototypes to the Flight Test Institute at Ramenskoye Airfield. Mikhail L. Mil' and

Nikolai I. Kamov headed the two main design bureaus and experimental plants for Soviet helicopters, located near Bykovo and Ramenskoye fields, from the war on.

Military industry also thrived north and northeast of Moscow. Works No. 8, the artillery plant at Podlipki (renamed Kaliningrad in 1938), was important enough for its director to sit on the party obkom. Military science and terror fused for the outstanding aircraft engineer Andrei Tupolev in the bizarre experience of working for several years before 1940 as a political prisoner, in a convict design team locked up in a TsAGI sharashka at Bolshevo, the town next to Kaliningrad. Rocket designer Sergei Korolev, too, did research as an inmate in a northern suburb, in his case from 1938 to 1940 in a sharashka at Bolshino.[203]

Laboratory No. 2, the capital facility for Stalin's atomic weapons program, was put up in 1943 by zek labor under General Komarovskii at Pokrovskoye-Streshnevo, on forested land past the old Khodynka Field. At this laboratory, the future Kurchatov Atomic Energy Institute, the first Soviet atomic reactor was commissioned in December 1946. Radioactive wastes were dumped freely around its perimeter.

Beginning with a Stalin edict in May 1946, large plants for testing and building aerodynamic missiles were established, picking the brains of several thousand deported German scientists who had built Hitler's V-1 and V-2 rockets, at Khimki (Works No. 293, 301, and 456, where Petr D. Grushin, Semen A. Lavochkin, and Valentin P. Glushko served as chief designers) and Kaliningrad (Institute No. 88, the former Works No. 8, under Yurii A. Pobedonostsev and Korolev). The Kaliningraders made the Soviets' first reliable ballistic missile, the R-2, launched in October 1950. Each of these labs and plants had its own infrastructure and living quarters. Gulag began to build atomic research prison camps in 1946 at remoter points in the region like Podol'sk, Chernogolovka, Dubna, Pushchino, and Obninsk (in Kaluga oblast), where workers completed the first atomic power station in the world in 1954.[204]

In 1952, at the height of the cold war, Lavrentii Beria supervised the breakneck construction of a radarized air defense network around Moscow. "The grandiose work of building the underground fire points, bunkers, and launchers was done at fierce tempos by convicts and construction troops. Everything was held in the strictest secrecy.

Although many peasants in the surrounding villages could guess what was hidden behind the barbed wire, they wisely held their tongues." Even the paved roads linking the installations failed to appear on maps until the late 1980s.[205]

Neglect, ignorance, and secrecy kept regional planning off the public agenda. The only official response to the coordination problem was to expand the green belt. Four hundred and sixty square kilometers were transferred to it in 1948. In 1950 it was retitled Moscow's suburban zone *(prigorodnaya zona),* as recommended in prewar documents, and pushed out to 50 kilometers from the limit of the reserve territories. Its total area now encompassed 13,260 square kilometers, or not quite 30 percent of Moscow oblast, including 6,400 square kilometers of forest. Boundary changes were done without settling on new norms and procedures. As one analyst conceded in 1952, seventeen years after the master plan, "we have not fixed . . . the content of the concept 'suburban green belt' . . . or the principles on which to base the planning of the suburban zone."[206]

THE 1952 PLAN AND STIRRINGS OF CHANGE

All was not hidebound in Stalin's Moscow. Toward the end there were glimmerings of new departures in planning and policy.

For one thing, enthusiasm for destruction of the historic cityscape as an end in itself unmistakably declined, as part of the regime's "Great Retreat" away from the chiliasm of the early 1930s and toward selective reconciliation with the old culture.[207] Demolition of Moscow churches, already decelerating before the war, almost entirely ceased after it.[208] Petr Baranovskii was reissued a Moscow propiska in 1944 and allowed to work on the national restoration board through which Stalin had undertaken to rebuild some of the edifices and towns laid waste by the Germans. The League of Militant Atheists, moribund by the time of Yaroslavskii's death in 1943, was disbanded in 1946. In the 1944 reorganization of city planning, Moscow's Architectural Affairs Directorate was given a Department for Protection of Landmarks; a small sector for tabulating and photographing landmarks opened in the Culture Directorate in 1949. A USSR government decree of October 1948, "On Measures to Improve the Protection of Cultural Landmarks," became the first legislation in this area since the 1920s.

Although the city undertook no restoration comparable in magnitude to the rebuilding of the Romanov palaces outside Leningrad, Stalin did ask Igor Grabar' to recommend a project in connection with Moscow's birthday jubilee. He agreed to Grabar's suggestion of the Andronikov Monastery, founded on the Yauza in 1360 as a forepost against the Tatars and the place where the icon-making genius Andrei Rublev spent his last years. Specialists had been forced to stop work there in 1930, whereupon many of its walls and chapels were torn down as storerooms, two garages, and a hostel were inserted. A Council of Ministers decree in December 1947 authorized rehabilitation and ordered the casual users ejected. Baranovskii was put in charge of assembling a Rublev museum in the abbey. In 1952 he was permitted to do some preparatory work at the Krutitskoye Residence, the former palace of the senior metropolitan of the Orthodox Church near the Simonov Monastery. The structure, mostly dating from the seventeenth century, had been turned into an army barracks in the 1780s and was still occupied by the Ministry of Defense, warehouses, and worker tenants.[209]

Somewhat contradictorily, around this time Stalin considered three plans to put the heart of old Moscow under the knife. The only one realized laid out a "ceremonial alley" behind the Lenin Mausoleum in 1946, with busts by Sergei Merkurov erected between the fir trees to four beatified leaders buried below (Yakov Sverdlov, Mikhail Frunze, Feliks Dzerzhinskii, and Mikhail I. Kalinin); Andrei Zhdanov joined the row in 1948.

The second scheme called for building an overbearing monument to the defeat of the Nazis. The government's charge to the USSR Committee on Architectural Affairs specified only that the monument take the form of a sculpture on Red Square. Merkurov, addressing the committee in June 1947, enthused that he "could not imagine Victory without the figure of Comrade Stalin." His submission proposed that the Lenin Mausoleum be refashioned into a "Pergamon Altar," which would be the foreground for a massive Stalin statue mounted on the Senatskaya Tower of the Kremlin Wall, with tribunes radiating out from its corners. Dmitrii Chechulin, while not bold enough to oppose it, observed dryly that "nothing would remain of the Kremlin" if the plan were realized. Merkurov's fellow sculptor Vera I. Mukhina did speak against it, and Boris R. Rubanenko denounced changes to

Lenin's tomb, but Iofan and other participants recommended making room by razing GUM or the Historical Museum and standing the statue in the middle of the square. The idea was dropped, and Stalin seems not to have been personally engaged.[210]

The oddball third incident came about after conversations among Stalin, Georgii Popov, and Chechulin. On December 21, 1948, Popov sent Stalin a draft USSR government decree on "reconstruction of the walls and towers of the Moscow Kremlin." Their entire brick exterior, and part of the interior, were to be refinished in buffed red granite, a material already in use on ulitsa Gor'kogo and other central promenades and "capable of standing for centuries"; the crenellations were to be sheared off and rebuilt entirely in granite. The city was to do a test strip by August 1949, and the job was to be completed by ten implementing organizations, overseen by a state committee chaired by Popov, by the end of 1953. We know of no action being taken on Popov's memorandum and can do no more than scratch our heads about what convinced Stalin to ditch the project. The most plausible explanation is that it was overtaken by the process of working out a new general plan for Moscow.[211]

That mysterious story began February 1, 1949, when *Pravda* printed a party-government decree "On the Elaboration of a New Master Plan for the Reconstruction of Moscow." It stated that as the 1935 plan neared realization, "the powerful surge in the economy, science, and culture of the USSR" necessitated a new chart for Moscow's growth over a span of twenty to twenty-five years. One week later the gorkom and obkom bureaus assigned a commission chaired by Timofei Selivanov to prepare the framing documentation. Popov reported to the Politburo in June 1949 on reconstruction perspectives. It was then that Stalin spoke up for the Palace of Soviets and reiterated the height and location guidelines for housing. Little else of substance came up.[212]

The purge of Popov placed a different team in charge of the planning drill. There was no word of what they were doing until it was simply announced, in several communiqués in the summer of 1952, that the Council of Ministers had that past February enacted a Ten-Year Plan for the Construction of Moscow.

The document was not the ode to monumentalism that might have been expected. Covering only 1951 to 1960, not the twenty-five years first intended, it was not a master plan but essentially a recitation of production quotas, primarily for 10 million square meters of housing, and a brief description of where housing was to be located (two-thirds of it on avenues and embankments). It was devoid of population statistics, maps, gaudy projects, and the usual purplish lyrics about socialist splendiferousness. Architect Leonid M. Polyakov did a maquette of the city center, featuring the tall buildings and the Palace of Soviets, yet it, too, remained under wraps. "The most important part of the plan," Mikhail Yasnov asserted, "is housing construction."[213]

The 1952 plan, in short, was appreciably more realistic and more consumerist than any manifesto in decades. It no doubt reflected the influence of Nikita Khrushchev, who shortly after his return to Moscow got to appoint a new city chief architect. He selected Aleksandr V. Vlasov, the chief planner of Kiev during his tenure in Ukraine. When Chechulin was removed, shortly before Georgii Popov, he was charged in private with hauteur and misuse of state funds.[214] In public Khrushchev referred only to Chechulin's design overindulgences (izlishestva)—the very charge he was to hurl at the architectural profession as a whole after 1953. Chechulin remained head of the architectural atelier for the two tall buildings, the Zaryad'e office tower and the apartment house on Kotel'nicheskaya naberezhnaya, for which he was awarded a Stalin Prize in 1952.

Khrushchev campaigned from December 1949 until Stalin's death for a greater municipal role in housing construction and, following a personal yen, for fuller use of industrial techniques. He and Bulganin had sponsored an experiment in Zamoskvorech'e in the 1930s at making walls out of large masonry blocks. His new enthusiasm was for iron-reinforced slabs of concrete, which could be boomed into place and assembled factory-style. Anticipating resistance by Beria and the MVD, Khrushchev buttonholed Stalin and refuted the objection that ferroconcrete was "foreign." He got permission for pilot plants in Moscow and Lyubertsy; both came on line in 1952.[215] The 535,000 square meters of dwelling space completed in Moscow in 1950 was the most since 1933; the 735,000 in 1951 set a post-1917 record.

Stalin's Moscow may be read as an object lesson in the power of government to remake the world. Its rulers, survivors of a dog-eat-dog selection process, realized their shared values through methods that brooked no overt dissent and treated the physical and human matter of the city as almost infinitely malleable. Their exertions gave the socialist metropolis a distinctive morphology, texture, and rhythm. "On the instructions of Comrade Stalin," a normative image of the city, grounded in ideology and instinct, took shape over an entire generation. The effects were everywhere to behold: in the subway, the canal, the tall buildings, the handsome facades along ulitsa Gor'kogo and Kutuzovskii, and the manufacturers of the military gadgets that made the Soviet Union an international superpower.

But there were other patterns, too, at variance with the approved image, and they draw notice to the clay feet of state socialism. Even the ballyhooed monumental half of Stalin's Moscow had flaws, perhaps least among them the derivativeness and meretriciousness of its aesthetics of grandeur. More irksome was the difficulty its builders had—and in fact made for themselves—in executing the vision. Their greatest feats were not socialist constructions or reconstructions but, one might say, negative acts of "pre-socialist destruction." Although metro stations opened yearly beginning in 1950 and Gulag labor pushed the tall buildings skyward, a score of "palaces" and "houses" for this or that fine cause were discarded and the downtown was littered with sandy lots where an ancient building had been leveled while its replacement expired on the drawing boards. Most unrealized projects could decently be forgotten, but not the holy grail of monumentalism, the Palace of Soviets—a misshapen carcass within eyeshot of the Kremlin that mocked the ambitions of its conceivers and revealed the finiteness of the regime's resources and organizational capacity.

A supernal intervention, such as the 1947 edict on the tall buildings or the 1939 and 1949 directives on concentrating housing construction on main streets, could get a major project on or back on track. It is striking, however, how often the architectonic energy of Stalin and his men dissipated on trivia. Stalin himself saw fit to issue instructions on urinals, statues, and the speed of subway trains. His agents in the local party apparatus, dealing with matters of life and death at one sitting, would in the next be adopting resolutions on watermelon stands, tram tracks, and snow removal.

The disjointed monism of local governance, as I am calling it, showed most perspicuously in the jerry-built minimal city the vast majority of Muscovites inhabited but in whose politics they were no better than spectators. The municipal institutions that had the formal responsibility to minister to the populace's needs lacked the power to do so effectively. Nine times out of ten, the party organs that may have had the informal power to do the job lacked the motivation, distracted as they were by shadowy power contests, roles in elite and mass socialization, and conning the fulfillment of production plans. In spite of the verbal commitment to master planning, most aspects of urban development were shaped by a congeries of organizations only tangentially concerned with high policy and infected by what Stalin dubbed, for lack of a better term, a "private-property approach" to their mission. With respect to issues like population control, housing, urban infrastructure, many daily services, and the green belt, it was every department for itself. The losers were the ordinary Russians not blessed with an influential patron, sentenced by commission and omission to subsist under austere and sometimes bestial conditions.

Beneath the surface stirred some impetus toward change. Nikita Khrushchev's lobbying for construction reform, the surprisingly restrained city plan of 1952, and the spike in housing completions hinted that the tribulations of minimal Moscow were at last getting a hearing. The semisubmerged trend was to break into the open after Stalin's departure.

5

The Limits
of De-Stalinization

THE SAYING that the evil that men do lives on after them has seldom been more vividly exemplified than in Moscow on the heels of the death of Joseph Stalin. Having breathed his last at Kuntsevo on March 5, 1953, Stalin lay in state in the Columned Hall of the House of Unions, near the Bol'shoi Theater. Mourners and gawkers squeezed into a cordon wending from Trubnaya ploshchad' on the Bul'varnoye kol'tso, down Neglinnaya and Petrovka Streets to the garlanded bier. On the final day of the wake, March 8, milling, shoving, and the refusal of troops to let the file be broken incited hysteria; hundreds of Muscovites were asphyxiated or trampled to death in the ensuing melee. The transparent casket holding the body, pickled in preservatives and decked out in his generalissimo's uniform, was ensconced beside Lenin's in the mausoleum on Red Square the next day.

The ill-starred farewell eerily signaled the staying power of some of the most unappetizing sides of the system Stalin incarnated. Nikita Khrushchev bridled its gangsterish tendencies, yet "de-Stalinization" went only partway in reforming the country, and the day came for it to be attenuated by the more conservative Leonid Brezhnev. There would be no head-on challenge to Stalinism as a school of government until Mikhail Gorbachev—in 1953 a law student at Moscow University's old campus, blocks from the funeral maelstrom—was inaugurated in 1985. Russian theorists took under Gorbachev to describing their country's polity as an "administrative-command system" *(administrativno-komandnaya sistema)* that, once petrified under Stalin, could not be shaken off. The phrase has a ring of veracity to it. By chance, it was popularized by the Moscow economist Gavriil Kh. Popov, whom we shall see several years anon playing a large part in breaking up the partocracy in the city and in Russia.

Moscow affairs from Stalin to Gorbachev—during the Kremlin terms of Khrushchev, from 1953 to October 1964, and Brezhnev, who died in 1982 but whose influence in Moscow did not really lapse until Gorbachev ousted his lieutenant, Viktor V. Grishin, in 1985—are too complex to be covered in a single chapter. In Chapter 5 I dissect elites and institutions, providing overviews of power struggles and changes of political compass in its first two sections, of governing structures in the third section, and of relations with the polymorphous central state in the fourth. I leave in-depth investigation of the making and execution of selected urban policies, fleshing out points raised in the present chapter, to Chapter 6.

Khrushchev: Moscow for the Masses

Khrushchev knew Moscow inside out, having logged eleven years in district, city, and regional posts there in advance of his investiture as leader of the Soviet Union. His ascendancy, and in particular his extensive housing program, left an indelible stamp.

MOSCOW AND THE STALIN SUCCESSION

It said something about Moscow's past eminence that among the members of the CPSU Presidium (as the Politburo was known from 1952 to 1966) reconstituted after Stalin's death, six out of the ten had roots there.[1] Lazar Kaganovich had stayed on a good footing with Stalin to the very end. Khrushchev, his ex-client, gave up cross-posting as chief of the Moscow obkom March 7, 1953, to work wholly in the Central Committee Secretariat; he achieved appointment as its first secretary in September 1953. Two other key players, Georgii Malenkov and Nikolai Bulganin, had also won their spurs under Kaganovich in his Moscow heyday. Once Lavrentii Beria had been knocked out of the ring in mid-1953, Malenkov, as chairman of the USSR Council of Ministers, was Khrushchev's main adversary. When

Khrushchev gained the upper hand, Bulganin, then the Soviet defense minister, supplanted Malenkov as prime minister in February 1955. Both men had maintained decent contacts with Khrushchev since the 1930s, flareups notwithstanding, and Bulganin was the one to propose that Khrushchev be made first secretary.[2] Two more Presidium members had had glancing contact with Moscow: Foreign Minister Vyacheslav Molotov, briefly local first secretary in the 1920s; and the industrialist Mikhail G. Pervukhin, who was head engineer of Mosenergo, the Moscow electric power grid, before the war.

Moscow's party machine necessarily figured in the battle over Stalin's crown, though less centrally than in his rise. Moscow was home turf for Khrushchev, the prospective winner, albeit not unambiguously at first. His replacement in the obkom, Nikolai A. Mikhailov, knew both him and Malenkov from work in local factories and the Proletarskii raikom before the Great Purge but remained in Malenkov's ambit of control from 1938 to 1952 (as head of the USSR Komsomol). Squarely in Malenkov's camp in 1953, Mikhailov did hardly a thing to reshape Moscow elites or policies, maybe because he was ringed by Khrushchev loyalists like the gorkom first secretary, Ivan Kapitonov, and Grishin, the second secretary of the obkom. On March 31, 1954, he gave way to Kapitonov.[3]

In bout one of the succession hostilities, in 1953, Khrushchev and Malenkov sublimated their rivalry in a common front against the odious Georgian, Beria, Stalin's consort for police affairs. Confirmed as minister of a reunified MVD in March 1953, Beria tried to hopscotch around the Soviet power base, the secretarial apparatus of the party, and to come forth with a program that was, on paper, boldly reformist. Overplaying his hand badly, he was arrested June 26, 1953, condemned at a Central Committee plenum in July, kept in a cell by Moscow Air Defense District generals until December 1953, and then executed following a closed-doors trial at which Mikhailov sat as one of the judges.[4]

Civilian politicians had as early as mid-1952 sent emissaries into Beria's police fiefdom, capitalizing on Stalin's suspicions about him. Muscovites figured prominently in the action. "Excellent and honorable comrades," Mikhailov chirped at the plenum of July 1953, "were sent into the Chekist apparatus from the Moscow party organization."[5] Vladimir I. Stepakov, first secretary of the Pervomaiskii raikom, was a typical mole; he served as deputy chief of the Moscow directorate of the MGB from some time in 1952 into 1953.

Beria's power bid did not sit well with the Moscow partocrats, as Mikhailov explained:

> Beria wanted to put the MVD above the party and out of the party organizations' control . . . [He] made appointments in the MVD's directorate for Moscow oblast without finding it necessary to consult in any way with the Moscow [Oblast] Committee of the party.
>
> When the [USSR] ministries were reorganized, there were supposed to be party conferences and elections of party committees in all of them. The only exception thus far has been the Ministry of Internal Affairs. Despite our repeated posing of the need to convene a conference, Beria frustrated it. For almost three months, the secretary of the party committee [of the MVD] was unable to get in to see Beria to settle the question . . .
>
> We cannot find a case where issues in managing the MVD were investigated by the Moscow party organs without opposition on Beria's part. Let me cite some facts. Following directives of the Central Committee, the Moscow Committee of the party wanted to involve itself more closely in the work of the organs of the MVD. What came of this? The MK called a meeting that would take up deficiencies in the work of the Moscow directorate [of the MVD]. But right away there was a phone call from the ministry to the effect that it would be best to leave these matters alone and that there was no point mucking around in shortcomings.
>
> The Moscow City Committee of the party wished to look into defects in the work of the Moscow militia [everyday police]. There was renewed displeasure on this score, a demand to tone down criticism, etc. The Moscow obkom did a review of several raion directorates of the MVD in the oblast. But once again there was upset and a declaration that the Moscow party organization should not now be concerning itself with the MVD's work.[6]

With some relish, therefore, Moscow functionaries took part in the reassertion of the party's grip, and the assertion of Khrushchev's, over the police. The former first secretary of the Stalinskii raikom, Aleksei N. Nikiforov, appointed as secretary of the party committee in MVD headquarters in 1953, pressed upon Beria the demand for a party conference in the ministry. When a Committee for State Security—the KGB—split off from the MVD in April 1954, he became its first party secretary. The head of the Moscow obkom's Administrative

Department (for law enforcement), Konstantin F. Lunev, was made the MVD's first deputy minister in 1953, heading the Ninth Directorate, which handled the security of the Soviet leaders. He sat on the court that convicted Beria that December and was a deputy chief of the KGB from 1954 to 1959. Vladimir I. Ustinov, ex-first secretary of the Proletarskii raikom, moved into an undisclosed post in the MVD in July 1953, eventually taking over the Ninth Directorate from Lunev and remaining its chief when it was transferred to the KGB; from 1954 to 1957 he also served as a vice-chairman of the KGB. Yet another Muscovite, Nikolai P. Dudorov, as interior minister steered a bowdlerized MVD from February 1956, shortly before Khrushchev denounced Stalin's crimes in his "Secret Speech" at the Twentieth Party Congress, to 1960.[7]

Clipping the police's wings had a dramatic social impact in Moscow. Secret tribunals began to amnesty and "rehabilitate" victims of Stalin's lawlessness in 1955. A bedraggled host of ex-trusties melted into the population over two or three years, those from remote parts often having to do probation in Podmoskov'e. A Muscovite whose father was freed in 1956 after seven years in the wilds of the Komi region described the homecoming at the Yaroslavl Railway Station: "Out of the cars seethed a human mass in torn quilted jackets, in tattered earflapped caps, unnaturally high and stuffed with sand (to cushion the head in case of a whack from an axe, my father explained later), and in homemade rag footwear, wrapped in rope."[8]

National affairs now centered on the consolidation of Khrushchev's power. He made use of an armory of patronage and policy weapons not dissimilar to Stalin thirty years before, with the difference that no blood purge came as a finale. Moscow, by every indication, was as snug a harbor as he had. Its politics featured none of the histrionics or the Marxist sermonettes of years past. In recognition of their steadfastness, officeholders from the city and oblast hiked their share of the seats on the Central Committee from 3.2 percent in 1952 to 4.5 percent at the 1956 party congress, more than since the early 1930s.[9]

At the top of the local political heap in 1954, when Mikhailov was eased out of the obkom, stood Ivan Kapitonov. A diploma-holding construction engineer, a past head of two gorkom departments dealing with urban services (where he had criticized the ministries for shirking on housing and social supports), and an unflappable office worker, Kapitonov seemed custom-made for superintending the city's flat-out housing program (see below).[10]

But the coming force in Moscow turned out to be someone else: Yekaterina Furtseva, who in March 1954 took over from Kapitonov as first secretary of the gorkom. This one-time weaver, Komsomol worker, and party secretary in a scientific institute was the most noticeable of the many Soviet women whose party careers took off during and after the war. She focused on cultural issues more than Kapitonov had and acted as "a warrior against inertia, idle chatter, and violations of discipline, but especially against any ideological error or wavering." Furtseva also shared more of a personal bond with Khrushchev, who rescued her husband, Nikolai Firyubin, during the attack on Georgii Popov. A busybody with a mercurial temper, she was known as a *flyuger*, a weathervane swaying in every Kremlin breeze. Unsubstantiated gossip circulated that she for a time had been Khrushchev's mistress.[11]

Furtseva kept the state ministries, Malenkov's main constituency, under wary scrutiny, averring that the Moscow gorkom had a "special responsibility" for the character training of their personnel. As before March 1953, she pushed the party committees and secretaries in them to gather intelligence for Khrushchev, propagate his views, and call civil servants to account. She was a stalking horse for him in semi-closed party meetings, turning up the heat on Presidium members with whom he was having differences. She made the gorkom apparatus a transmission belt to the intelligentsia and to the minority of urban Communists who took the cultural "thaw" and the unfrocking of Stalin as license to question such bedrocks as one-party rule, uncontested elections, and the privileges of the nomenklatura. Furtseva's position before and after the Twentieth Congress, like Khrushchev's, was that unbounded liberalization was as pernicious as blind adherence to the past.[12]

On February 13, 1956, on the eve of the congress, Furtseva escaped Kapitonov's shadow when the Central Committee Secretariat uncoupled the Moscow gorkom administratively from the obkom. Now head of an independent organization, she was made a candidate member of the Presidium at the congress and cross-appointed to the CC Secretariat. Kapitonov was reelected to the Central Committee only.

In June 1957 Khrushchev, outgunned in a nonconfidence vote by a Presidium bloc he artfully labeled the Anti-Party Group, faced his acid test. He saved himself by appealing to the whole Central Committee. Furtseva threw herself body and soul into the fight. She called in political debts, telephoned party leaders in the interior, and arranged trips to the climactic CC plenum. In gratitude, Khrushchev made her a full member of the Presidium, the first female ever inducted into the inner sanctum—"Catherine III," quipped Muscovites who knew their Russian history. Khrushchev filed away for later use her report that her obkom counterpart, Kapitonov, had not extended himself when the chips were down.[13]

The ex-Muscovites in the leadership saw a grim outcome. The memory of common service did not keep Khrushchev from pitching them to the crocodiles once they united against him. Malenkov, Molotov, and Kaganovich, the threesome who knocked together the Anti-Party Group, were expelled from the Presidium in June 1957 and from the party in 1962. Pervukhin was demoted in 1957 and retired in 1961. Bulganin, a vacillator in 1957, was sacked from the chairmanship of the Council of Ministers in March 1958, allowing Khrushchev to add it to his party position, and from the Presidium in September 1958.

PANTHEONS

Moscow's physique, actual and planned, was instantly affected by the politics of recharting the country's course. One day after Stalin died, the Presidium resolved on a project that would have drawn a smile from his lips:

> In order to perpetuate the memory of the great leaders Vladimir Il'ich Lenin and Joseph Vissarionovich Stalin, and also of the outstanding figures of the Communist Party and the Soviet state buried in Red Square in front of the Kremlin Wall, a monumental building—a Pantheon—is to be built in Moscow, as a memorial to the eternal glory of the great ones of the Soviet land.
>
> Once the Pantheon is completed, the sarcophagi holding the bodies of V. I. Lenin and I. V. Stalin are to be transferred to it, along with the remains of the outstanding figures of the Communist Party and the Soviet state buried by the Kremlin Wall. There will be free access to the Pantheon for the wide toiling masses.[14]

The Presidium swiftly organized a design contest—closed and thus unbeknownst to the "toiling masses." Nikolai Kolli, a participant in Moscow planning since 1918 but out of favor after being forced out as chairman of the local chapter of the Union of Architects in 1951, submitted the sketch most seriously considered. A half-million square meters of floor space were to lie under his rotunda, amidst "monumental sculpture, bas-reliefs, memorial plaques, monumental paintings, and mosaics"; the exterior would be "tied in with the profile of the future Palace of Soviets." Kolli initially situated the Pantheon in the place of the GUM building on Red Square, but he eventually relocated it to Sofiiskaya naberezhnaya, across the Moskva from the Kremlin. Neither scheme, and none from any contestant, was approved.

The government announced a second concourse in July 1954, stipulating the Lenin Hills as the location.[15] Again nothing developed, in all likelihood because the Presidium could not agree on the Parthenon's occupants and presentation.

Even before the Secret Speech, Moscow's toponomy was showing the effects of Khrushchev's bid to put moral distance between himself and Stalin and the unregenerate Stalinists. Plans to make a museum out of the Kuntsevo dacha, still outside Moscow's western border, and to name the road to it after Stalin, were scratched in 1953; in 1957 the artery was dubbed Kutuzovskii prospekt. As a token of liberalization, Khrushchev had the Kremlin grounds and cathedrals opened to sightseers in July 1955, after thirty-seven years of barred gates and police passes. The remaining VIP flats were evacuated, partly because Khrushchev's wife, Nina, could not abide living in Stalin's digs. Molotov, Kaganovich, Anastas Mikoyan, and Kliment Voroshilov were among the last to leave, in 1957, by which time the tennis courts and other amenities had been closed. Most of the younger leaders followed Khrushchev to the stuccoed Central Committee villas begun on the Lenin Hills in the late 1940s.[16]

The Stalin Auto Works (ZIS), Moscow's biggest factory; the Stalin Filtration Station; and the Stalin Gas Pipeline all received new titles in 1956. Workers quietly dismantled the statues of Stalin at the All-Union Agricultural Exhibition, the Tret'yakov Gallery, and the Moscow-Volga Canal and blotted Stalin out of the murals in the Komsomol'skaya underground station. In the most operatic gesture, his body was carried out of the Lenin crypt on October 31, 1961, by vote of the Twenty-second Party Congress, and buried in the ground behind. Stalinskii raion in eastern Moscow became Pervomaiskii (First of May) raion the next month. The name of his henchman, Kaganovich, was taken down from the subway in 1955 and from the Okhotnyi ryad station in 1957; Molotovskii and Shcherbakovskii raions received new names in 1957–1958.

The debunking of Stalin left a spiritual void, and Moscow more than anywhere was the slate on which Khrushchev wrote a substitute doxology—adulating Lenin, the progenitor of the Soviet state. "Leninist commemorative places" were identified and spruced up by the dozen. Unlike the memorabilia-crammed Kremlin apartment where he had lived, opened to tours in 1955, Lenin had made but one speech or appearance at most of these. By 1980 the capital bore 130 Lenin shrines, 70 of them with inscriptions, and 30 statues and busts.

Countless facilities with which Lenin had no connection in life were bound to him in myth. The Moscow metro set the precedent when emblazoned with his name, not Kaganovich's, in 1955. The 103,000-spectator Central Athletic Stadium of the USSR took the same phrase, *imeni V. I. Lenina,* "Bearing the Name of V. I. Lenin," when the first soccer ball was kicked in 1956. Kaluzhskaya ulitsa, the traffic aorta into Moscow southwest, was reborn as Leninskii prospekt (Lenin Prospect) in 1957. The fetishization encompassed Lenin's wife, Krupskaya, to whom Moscow dedicated a whole museum, and the Ul'yanov family and his brother Dmitrii, after whom the city named streets. Tributes to him were slathered over the seventy-eight pavilions of the Exhibition of the Economic Achievements of the USSR (VDNKb), as the All-Union Agricultural Exhibition, reopened with a flourish in 1954, was restyled in 1958.[17] A topcoated bronze of Feliks Dzerzhinskii, Lenin's chief executioner, by Yevgenii V. Vuchetich, adorned the square in front of the Lubyanka in 1958. Karl Marx, Lenin's mentor, also received his due: an eight-meter statue by Lev Ye. Kerbel, unveiled at ploshchad' Sverdlova in 1961.

The quest for Leninist surrogates made for a slow and theatrical death for the Palace of Soviets, a white elephant since construction stopped in 1941. Boris Iofan manfully resumed drafting work in 1953, reducing the projected volume fourfold. But time worked against the waterlogged location on Kropotkinskaya naberezhnaya, for in 1955 excavation began at Luzhniki, the staging yard for the work there, for the Lenin Stadium, and the Palace of Soviets subway stop gained a new name (Kropotkinskaya). Puzzlingly, when the Council of Ministers proclaimed another design competition in August 1956, for "A Memorial to V. I. Lenin—the Palace of Soviets," it mandated the original site. The Great Hall was now to have only 4,600 places, versus the 21,000 specified in the 1930s.[18]

February 1957 brought yet another contrivance: a scaled-down Palace of Soviets (no measurements given) to be planted on the high and dry Lenin Hills, south and west of the new university compound. Land approximately three kilometers square, running across the Gulag barracks at Ramenki to the village of Amin'evo, was reserved. Architects were to shade in "space for the construction of a Pantheon" for some unspecified future date. The Pantheon, it was said in verbiage identical to the pronouncements of March 1953, was going to be "a memorial to the eternal glory" of Soviet immortals. A monument to Lenin would be erected separately northeast of the university, near the ridge of the hill. Drawings and maquettes went on exhibit in 1958, to be viewed by 200,000 people, but again no winner was declared.[19]

Khrushchev inspected plans for a Palace of Soviets and an attendant statue of Lenin, past the university, at the Moscow architects' club in November 1959. Last word of the project came in mid-1960, twenty-nine years after the ransacking and dynamiting of the Cathedral of Christ the Redeemer, although a Lenin memorial was discussed until Khrushchev's fall in 1964. For parliamentary sittings, party conventions, and other pageants, an antiseptic, glass-hulled Palace of Congresses, with 6,000 seats in its auditorium, was cupped inside the west wall of the Kremlin between 1959 and 1961, over the old Cavalry Guards Barracks. Workers sweated to finish it in time for the Twenty-second Party Congress. Muscovites unfondly nicknamed it Moscow's "punk amidst the nobles" *(stilyaga sredi boyar)*. The prime designer, Mikhail V. Posokhin, had other major commissions including the skyscraper at ploshchad' Vosstaniya and Khrushchev's vacation home at Pitsunda, on the Black Sea.

In a Kafkaesque postscript, the gaping foundation of the Palace of Soviets on the river embankment, ordered filled and grassed over in the pronouncement of February 1957, was reworked from 1958 to 1960 into an uncovered, heated swimming basin, the biggest in the Soviet Union and, so it was said, in the world (Figure 50). The

Figure 50. Moskva swimming pool in foundation of Palace of Soviets, 1988. (Photograph by author.)

designer, the resilient Dmitrii Chechulin, straightfacedly wrote of it as the latest word in aquatic exercise, making not a peep about its sorry prehistory. The Moskva pool emitted a vaporous miasma eating away at paintings and tapestries at the neighboring Pushkin Fine Arts Museum, the very one that was supposed to be moved away as if by a sorcerer's wand to accommodate the mightiest building on earth.

There would be no more cloud-parting palaces or pantheons in the socialist metropolis. Never again would its governors take up so ambitious or futile a project.

THE REINFORCED-CONCRETE FRONTIER

Khrushchev believed that the regime had to rely less on raw force and more on positive devices for building its authority. To this end, he appealed at the Twentieth Congress for reanimation of the moribund local soviets. A lengthy resolution of the Central Committee in January 1957, "On Improving the Activity of the Soviets of Toilers' Deputies and Strengthening Their Ties with the Masses," itemized their failings and promised to overcome them.[20] This overture would have a mildly leavening effect in Moscow.

The resurgent welfarism and consumerism in socioeconomic policy took priority over any burbling about political reform. As during NEP three decades earlier, Moscow symbolized the adjustment, which this time entailed state investments and not decontrol of nonstate enterprise.

On Red Square, GUM, a hetacomb of offices since the war, was cleaned up by Metrostroi and reopened as a municipal department store in December 1953; its 130 counters again had the largest trove of goods in the USSR. Moscow's biggest restaurant and night club, the Praga, was recommissioned in 1955, missing the baccarat tables it sported in the 1920s. In June 1957 Khrushchev and Bulganin snipped the ribbon at Detskii mir (Children's World), an emporium for toys and clothing fast by the KGB's lair on ploshchad' Dzerzhinskogo. Later that year the Manezh, the tsarist riding academy abased to a garage in 1918, was primped up as the USSR's Central Exhibition Hall, and Muscovites heard that dozens of shops, service salons, eateries, and entertainments would brocade Novyi Arbat (prospekt Konstitutsii in the 1935 plan, later prospekt Kalinina), a broad spoke avenue to be overlaid on the labyrinth of streets west of the Kremlin.

For Khrushchev, nothing was as germane to restoring popular trust as getting the smoldering housing problem in hand. He sought to make up for lost time on urban shelter with a major plank in his domestic platform, comparable in its repercussions to the program to revive agriculture and enrich the Soviet diet.

Moscow housing occasioned a high-level tiff, recorded in Khrushchev's memoirs:

> I remember once, not too long after the new leadership had begun to get its feet on the ground, that Molotov addressed a meeting of the [CPSU] Presidium about housing problems. There was panic in his voice as he said, "There's great dissatisfaction in Moscow over housing conditions!"
> You'd have thought he'd been born only yesterday. He acted as though he'd just learned that people were living in overcrowded, vermin-infested,

intolerable conditions, often two families to a room. At one of these Presidium meetings, I suggested we centralize our [Moscow] construction administration. Molotov literally exploded with rage: "How can you suggest such a thing? Here we are with an acute shortage of dwellings, and you want to liquidate all the building administrations in the city and put them under one authority? What makes you think that a single organization will do a better job than all these separate ones?"

Obviously, here was someone who didn't know the first thing about construction, nor did he understand the latest theories about division of labor and other progressive management techniques. It was a stormy meeting. The other comrades expressed their views. In the end, they supported me. When Molotov saw he was beaten, he withdrew his objections, and my proposal was approved unanimously.[21]

As the vignette reveals, the politics revolved around means, not the end of dignified accommodation. Molotov, chief minister to Stalin when the mishmash system for financing urban growth originated, stood by the status quo. Khrushchev's scheme, enacted by directive of the Presidium in April 1954, sutured a muscular developmental armature onto the city government, at the expense of central bureaus. Glavmosstroi, the Chief Directorate for Housing and Civil Construction of Moscow, was headed by a first deputy chairman of the ispolkom, Vladimir A. Kucherenko. As deputy minister of "medium machine building," Kucherenko had been in charge of building Soviet atomic weapons laboratories since the civilians took over that task from Beria in 1953, and he had worked in construction under Khrushchev's aegis in Ukraine. He and Khrushchev hoped that Glavmosstroi would show the flag to Leningrad and the other urban centers, where housing was no less deplorable.

The Moscow party committee saw to it that Glavmosstroi got seasoned and hard-driving leaders under and after Kucherenko. Vladimir F. Promyslov, his successor, went on to chair the Moscow municipal executive in the late Khrushchev and Brezhnev periods. Nikolai Ye. Pashchenko, deputy chief and chief from 1954 to 1968, did the most to mold Glavmosstroi; he was known for trusting middle managers and giving fat bonuses to productive workers.

Its employees (110,000 at first) Glavmosstroi drew from the dissolution of eighty-four building and installation trusts, culled from twenty-one central ministries and departments. Its mission was effectuation of construction plans for about 70 percent of Moscow's housing, local utilities, schools and nurseries, hospitals, shopping and recreation facilities, and office buildings—three or four times the municipal quotient in the late Stalin era. By concentrating resources and inculcating "industrial methods of building," it was to be Moscow's conveyor belt for manufacturing a livable urban environment.

The reshuffling left Gulag out. Zek construction battalions were in any event thinning out as the labor camps began to be emptied all over the Soviet Union. The police were divested of the Kurchatov Atomic Energy Institute and all nuclear arms–related installations the day Beria was jailed. Glavmosstroi assimilated Gulag's main Moscow building subsidiaries in 1954, leaving some of their cadres in city employ until going on pension.[22] Beskudnikovo, Kryukovo, Lyublino, Ramenki, and most of the barbed-wired enclosures in the environs were boarded up by the time of the Twentieth Congress.

Khrushchev repudiated more than rank political terror; as the party weaned itself from pharaonic works projects, forced labor lost its economic rationale. Khrushchev laid down the new, no-frills line in a jeremiad to Soviet builders and architects in December 1954. Jabbing a forefinger at the Muscovites in the hall, he said they had perpetrated the gravest sins of "overindulgence." The Stalinesque tall buildings, profligate with materials and labor, cost a fortune to heat, all for a pampered few. Aleksandr Vlasov, his designate as chief planner in 1950, was not doing enough to put away vainglorious "decorations" for catering to the populace. Houses from Grigorii A. Zakharov's atelier, Khrushchev spluttered, resembled museums or cathedrals: "He wants pretty silhouettes, but people want apartments. They are not in love with silhouettes. They need someplace to live."[23]

It was as stinging a blow to monumental Moscow as writing off the Palace of Soviets. Chechulin's forty-six-floor office minaret in Zaryad'e, the last of the Stalin high rises to get off the ground, was abandoned in early 1954 and its steel trunk put into the Lenin Athletic Stadium. The local authorities kicked off a campaign to pare prestige construction to the bone and load the surplus, plus a gobbet of fresh capital, into the housing and consumer sector.

The about-face convulsed an urban design profession set in its ways. The Moscow Architectural Planning Directorate underwent a nonviolent purge in 1954–1955. The demotees—Vlasov (brought in personally by Khrushchev in 1950 but now found lacking), Iofan, Chechulin, Chernyshev, Polyakov, and Zakharov at the head of the rogues' list—were kept on in lesser perches but browbeaten into recanting their "gigantomania," "blind imitation of old models," and "false monumentalism and embellishment." Leonid Polyakov, main author of the ten-year construction plan approved in 1952, had to give back the Stalin Prize and cash premium he won for the Leningradskaya Hotel, one of the tall buildings.

A new city architect, Iosif I. Loveiko, combed through 800 housing and other civil projects and subtracted 230 million rubles from price estimates. Several apartment houses already in production parted with their Corinthian columns, entablature, and decorative statues. Blueprints for Detskii mir and other public buildings were shorn of fancy touches. The paradeway of VIP housing on Kutuzovskii prospekt was completed at a slower pace, and the brakes were applied to plans for making more like it.

How then was a Moscow for the masses, without embellishments, to be crafted? A forcing device was the *tipovoi proyekt*, "type design," a three-dimensional, off-the-shelf template to which planners would fit the given builder. The "standardized houses" for factory workers in the 1930s had been primitive bunkhouses out of undressed wood, offering hardly any choices. The type designs marked out discrete living cells instead of unpartitioned barracks, in homes built of durable materials and to codes allowing repetitive, low-cost production.

A Special Architectural Design Bureau, emplaced in the Architectural Planning Directorate when Khrushchev was still obkom secretary, had been minting type designs for Moscow since 1951. The flats were ascetic, their doors opening out into vertical stairwells, not horizontal corridors. Staired sections, virtually identical, could be attached sideways to make multisegment buildings of as many spans as the land and budget would bear. The wonders of the cookie-cutter designs were propagated inside the city bureaucracy after 1953 by zealots like Vitalii P. Lagutenko, the chief engineer of the planning directorate, and Vasilii I. Svetlichnyi, Kucherenko's deputy. Apartment houses to their specifications spurted from 20 percent of those built in Moscow in 1954 to 85 percent in 1958 and 98 percent in 1962.

Homogenization carried over into building size. The preferred height was five stories, the maximum under Soviet law not to require an elevator or trash chute, a size that could be completed from cellar to roof in one building season. In March 1958 Khrushchev dictated that *every* new apartment house in Moscow would be exactly five floors. The Soviet General Staff had persuaded him that, along with being cheap, five-story buildings would be easy to evacuate in the case of nuclear war and, if repeated across the city, would deny American bombers navigational guides. The edict was rescinded in 1962, not before Nikolai I. Bobrovnikov was forced to resign as head of the Moscow government in September 1961 for appealing too strenuously for flexibility.[24]

Moscow systematized the housing drive around a monopoly technology, too. Khrushchev had been smitten for some time with a different methodology from the crude carpentry of the 1930s: mechanized, on-site assembly of precast parts in *zhelezobeton*, quick-setting concrete impregnated with steel rods or mesh. To this form Khrushchev switched the housing industry lock, stock, and barrel after 1953.

From the *krupnoblochnoye* ("big block") method, utilizing the reinforced concrete in kingsize bricks, Glavmosstroi graduated by the late 1950s to *krupnopanel'noye* ("big panel") construction, whereby prefabricated slabs for bearing walls, partitions, and floors, as well as structurals such as staircases, balconies, and doorjambs, were brought to the building yard on flatbeds, battened together, and lightly finished. It all comported well with the occupants' unexacting expectations and with the dearth of bricklayers, plasterers, and other skilled tradesmen.[25]

A fixity of Stalinist planning, not always honored, had been for permanent housing and other civil edifices to be knit into elegant ensembles lining major avenues, plazas, and river quays. Demolitions, rebuildings, and relocations were the price of the sensual and psychological benefits of "socialist reconstruction." Moscow officials at first intended to carry on this practice. They soon found that the abstemiousness of the party's urban policy and the technical dictates of mass production under Soviet conditions—presupposing large work gangs, supply stockpiles, and a flotilla of earth movers, lifters, and other heavy equipment—propelled them toward the low-density fringes of Moscow. It was a second coming of sorts for the 1920s theme of giving a wide berth to the "bourgeois center" and domesticating the "workers' outskirts" instead.

Almost 90 percent of the housing quota of the latter half of the 1950s was docketed for peripheral land requiring the fewest outlays on demolition and spadework. "The distribution of the bulk of housing construction on vacant city territories," a spokesman wrote, "will delay the reconstruction of certain main streets, embankments, and squares. In return it will give us the maximum feasible increase in the short haul of the dwelling space available to meet the pressing housing needs of Moscow's working people."[26] Belatedly fulfilling a stipulation of the 1935 plan, the lustiest growth occurred southwest of the old city, beyond the Lenin Hills and on either side of Leninskii prospekt, where the Academy of Sciences and other research organizations were putting up their institutes. Typical offspring of the age are the lackluster banks of walkups in Novyye Cheremushki in the southwest quadrant, Novyye Kuz'minki in the southeast, Khoroshevo-Mnevniki on the northwest, and Izmailovo to the northeast.

Reckoning on more sprawl, on August 18, 1960, the RFSFR government incorporated into Moscow the oblast towns of Babushkin (formerly Losinoostrovsk), Perovo, Lyublino, Kuntsevo, and Tushino and the cincture of virgin and semiurban land in which they fell. The rescript stopped at the Moscow Ring Highway (Moskovskaya kol'tsevaya avtomobil'naya doroga, or MKAD), 109 kilometers in girth, which soldiers had been laying over the bed of an old army road since 1956. Eighty thousand members of the Komsomol, living in tent towns, helped see it to completion in 1962. A secret circular highway in reinforced concrete, primarily for antiaircraft missile launchers and other military hardware, was finished 25 kilometers out into the oblast.

Moscow—fleetingly called, as from 1900 to 1930, Bol'shaya Moskva (Greater Moscow)—now extended 879 square kilometers, 17 kilometers on average from Kremlin to rim, with title to almost all the dacha hamlets and factory villages that encircled the tsarist city, and then some. The proletarian outskirts of the first decade after 1917 could have been nested many times over in the gigantic new colonization zone.

The more than 1 million people kenneled by the border distension helped push Moscow's population to 6.5 million by the midpoint of the 1960s. Ethnic Russians, because of their preponderance in the annexed areas and the quickening inflow of migrants, constituted more of the population than at any time since 1914. The Russian

Figure 51. The reinforced-concrete frontier: mechanized housing construction in Novyye Cheremushki, 1961. (Museum of the History of the City of Moscow.)

majority in Moscow went from 87.5 percent in the mid-1930s to 88.6 percent in the 1959 census and 89.2 percent in 1970.

To get a grip on development of the ever larger and more complicated metropolitan whole, the city set out to devise a new, multipurpose master plan. Drawn up by a collective under Mikhail Posokhin, appointed chief architect in place of Loveiko in 1960, it took until 1971 to enact.

If American city dwellers homesteaded after the war on a "crabgrass frontier" of single-family bungalows and landscaped lots,[27] many Muscovites felt blessed to be pioneers on the plebeian frontier marked by reinforced concrete and derrick cranes (see Figure 51). Housing completions sprinted upward in 1954, doubling by 1957 and

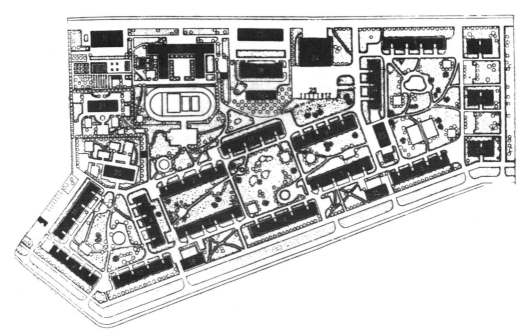

Figure 52. Ground plan of the Ninth Experimental Block of Novyye Cheremushki. Design provides for apartment houses (1–14), food shops (15 and
18), cafeteria (16), general store (17), telephone exchange (19a), day nursery
(20), kindergarten (21), school (22), consumer services building (23), cinema
(24), parking places for a few automobiles (25), and extensive landscaping.
(From *Devyatyi kvartal: Opytno-pokazatel'noye stroitel'stvo zhilogo kvartala
v Moskve [raion Novyye Cheremushki]*, Moscow: Gosstroiizdat, 1959, p. 17.)

just about quadrupling by 1961. The white-hot pace let builders, as
they had never done since planned construction began, overshoot
their annual targets. After thirty years of decrease and stagnation,
per capita supply swelled 50 percent between 1950 and 1961 (see
Appendix D).

The promise of the time was encapsulated in the Ninth Experimental Block of Novyye Cheremushki, three kilometers south of Moscow University. The twelve-hectare block (Figure 52), authored by
Natan A. Osterman and executed between June 1956 and November
1958, quartered 3,030 tenants in its sixteen mostly four-story houses.
It was billed as a harbinger of a brighter future for Moscow and the
urban USSR in part because it was the first large estate to aim to

accommodate ordinary families—not those in the first or second percentile of the population—in privacy, one household per two- or three-room flat. The project was oriented toward its own inhabitants and mutual spaces, not to the passersby along its perimeter. And it complemented bare apartment walls with a tempting basket of good things, both indoors (two-burner gas ranges, compact plumbing, modular furniture in some units) and out (school, kindergarten, day nursery, cafeteria, cinema, telephone exchange, playgrounds, duck pond, parking spots, and three small stores, all encased in the project).

A photocollage in a book publicizing the Ninth Experimental Block portrayed beaming residents picking roses and walking baby carriages amidst spanking new apartment low rises. Wan though it may appear against the suburban dream in the affluent West, it and the Khrushchevian building blitz did make the prospect of dignified living conditions no longer a phantasmagoric one.[28]

END OF THE VANGUARD

Khrushchev's rule provided an uneven boon to the Moscow establishment he had twice skippered. Much as it attenuated fear and spawned opportunities for advancement, as a scabrous pun about Furtseva went, *cherez Nikitskiye vorota* (through the eponymous Nikitskiye or "Nikita" Gates of old Moscow), it also sowed seeds of degeneration, most to be harvested later.

Moscow did remain a prime font of talent for Khrushchev and his coterie. It furnished almost as many heads of Central Committee departments from 1953 to 1964 as in all other periods combined (see Table C-3 in Appendix C); nine of the twelve were promoted after 1960. In 1958, after elbowing Bulganin out of the Council of Ministers, Khrushchev picked as head of its Business Office or chancery Petr N. Demichev, a Muscovite with a chemical engineering degree who had been his personal aide for four years and, as party secretary in a central raion of Moscow before then, had been coached in party liaison with the ministries. Demichev was to return as first secretary of the Moscow obkom in 1959 and, in 1960, of the gorkom. A Moscow coeval, Konstantin P. Chernyayev, got the same delicate assignment in Khrushchev's party office in 1962, and Grigorii T. Shuiskii, once a sidekick in the Moscow obkom (and in Ukraine), became one of his personal assistants in the CC.[29]

Muscovites were paramount in the economic sector where Moscow set the pace, construction, now a booming industry reliant on free labor. Nikolai Dudorov was the first head of the Central Committee's Construction Department in 1954–1956; two Moscow colleagues, Vasilii P. Abyzov and Anatolii Ye. Biryukov, held the position from 1961 to 1967. The State Construction Committee (Gosstroi) was upgraded in 1955 and its chief made a deputy premier in the USSR Council of Ministers; its chairman until 1961 was Vladimir Kucherenko, erstwhile director of Glavmosstroi, and his main deputy, Vasilii Svetlichnyi, also came from Glavmosstroi. Chief Architect Posokhin of Moscow served conjointly as chief of Gosstroi's civil construction arm (Gosgrazhdanstroi) from 1963 to 1967.

More sweepingly, the Soviet leaders still looked to the capital for pawns on the personnel checkerboard, especially when it came to the agencies, new and old, implementing Khrushchev's reforms. When the Presidium chartered a national manpower agency, the State Committee on Labor and Wages, Aleksandr P. Volkov from the Moscow oblast soviet, an obkom secretary and department head under Khrushchev, took its reins. When it hit upon revitalization of the Central Federation of Trade Unions, in came Muscovites. Chairmanship of the union board proved a suitable billet for Viktor Grishin, second secretary of the obkom, after Kapitonov requested his reassignment. The chief salesman for the Soviet school restructuring of the late 1950s was Russia's education minister, Yevgenii I. Afanasenko, an associate of Furtseva's since the 1940s and recently ideology secretary of the Moscow gorkom. Chairman Mikhail Yasnov of the city government was made premier of the Russian Republic in 1956, and Vladimir P. Mylarshchikov, former agriculture secretary of the obkom, became chief of the CC's Agriculture Department and Khrushchev's toughest emissary in the farming areas.[30]

Hands from the Moscow organization also directed the erratic organization overhauls that set the mood of the late Khrushchev period and hastened his downfall. The CC "bureaus" for Central Asia and the Transcaucasus that Khrushchev set up in 1962 were turned over to Vasilii G. Lomonosov, first secretary of the Kalininskii raikom, and Gurii M. Bochkarev, the gorkom secretary for industry. Moscow mates of theirs cropped up in the Party-State Control Committee, the superinspectorate that existed from 1962 to 1965, and in the pygmy sections issuing from the morseling of Central Committee departments by territory and branch.[31]

If all these interconnections substantiated the abiding import of the local machine, other signs pointed to a receding profile. Profuse as Khrushchev's Moscow ties were, his Ukrainian entourage was larger and less fractious. The ultimate winner in the palace intrigue against him, Brezhnev, a Russian from the south Ukrainian city of Dnepropetrovsk, had no Moscow vassals to speak of.

The drolleries of personality and small-group antagonism also told on the capital's position. The main promotee into the high command, Furtseva, relinquished her Moscow position in December 1957, working thereafter as Central Committee secretary for culture, science, and the media. Khrushchev soon wearied of her, and she grew jealous of Frol R. Kozlov, the Leningrader who materialized as his heir presumptive in 1960–1961. Furtseva and Kozlov were in-laws, which worsened matters when a family quarrel turned bitter. Kozlov prevailed on Khrushchev to demote her to Soviet minister of culture in May 1960 (replacing Nikolai Mikhailov) and to place him on the CPSU Presidium. Furtseva slit her wrists when dropped from the Presidium in October 1961 and had to be resuscitated by an ambulance attendant. Her fortunes did not revive when Kozlov's health failed in 1963. She served as minister until her death eleven years later, in dishonor because she used her position to build a dacha for her daughter near Peredelkino said to cost one million rubles.[32]

Furtseva still had the political wattage in December 1957 to impose a favorite, Vladimir Ustinov, as gorkom first secretary after her. He was one of the Muscovites moved into the MVD and KGB from 1953 to 1954 and, as another Moscow leader said later, during his four years at the Lubyanka he was unenthused about de-Stalinization and "not touched by the spirit of the Twentieth Congress."[33]

At the highpoint of his term Ustinov uncovered a corruption ring in Kuibyshevskii raion, in east Moscow. First Secretary Aleksandr K. Golushko of the raikom had been feathering his nest, extracting protection money for keeping the police away from black marketeers who operated out of a local boot factory. He also got several cohorts with criminal records reinstated in the party, found them housing, and drew the raion ispolkom into his web. Golushko was fired, expelled from the party, and bound over to prosecutors in October 1958, and the case was cited in the gorkom resolution as proof of "an atmosphere of indifference, lack of principles, and absence of Bolshevik criticism" in the local elite.[34] Deftly handled, the affair might have polished a reputation for Ustinov as a corruption fighter. The facts were hushed up, however, and he quickly acquired the image of an inferior administrator and something of a blowhard. In July 1960, two months after Furtseva left the Secretariat, Ustinov was dismissed without explanation, his party career over.

Petr Demichev, the former assistant of Khrushchev shunted from the obkom to relieve Ustinov, was an ideological moderate. He had a brighter but even shorter experience in the Moscow gorkom. Cross-appointed to the CC Secretariat in October 1961, he was co-opted full-time there in November 1962, in charge of Khrushchev's program to expand chemicals production. His second secretary and successor, a highflier named Nikolai G. Yegorychev, was to earn his spot in Soviet political history early in Brezhnev's reign. He showed himself to be the most liberal Moscow leader since Stalin's death when he attempted in 1963 to recruit Fedor M. Burlatskii, a Khrushchev adviser known for his anti-Stalinism, as his secretary for propaganda.[35]

Moscow's role in the party was complicated by the rejiggered relationship between its city and regional organs. The gorkom had remained a creature of the obkom in 1931, even as the city soviet and executive were amputated from the oblast. That affiliation changed in February 1956: the Moscow gorkom was henceforth the one city-level party committee in the Soviet Union to answer unmediatedly to the Central Committee.

The diseconomies of keeping together so large a local unit may have entered into the bifurcation decision. But the silence enveloping it and its awkward timing—after delegates to the Twentieth Congress had already been chosen by a pan-oblast party conference—point to a more political explanation.[36]

Khrushchev's desire to oblige Furtseva was undoubtedly a factor. And yet, her passage into the Presidium could just as easily have been lubricated by making her first secretary of the obkom and not tampering with institutions.

I would surmise that the Soviet leadership was juggling two discrepant objectives: to acknowledge the Moscow boss's natural authority and to avoid overconcentrating power in his or her hands. Recall that Stalin, in cashiering Georgii Popov in 1949, had already sundered the post of first secretary of the Moscow gorkom from obkom first secretary. The 1956 decision, curtailing the reach of the organization, carried the logic another step forward. The long-term effect was obscured by the short-term ascent of Furtseva: what had been an integrated structure since 1920 now stood as two smaller organizations with two leaders. City and oblast were uncoupled when it came to careers and decision making; Demichev's 1960 crossover posed a rare exception.[37]

To muddy the waters further, in 1959 the rump Moscow obkom suffered a quarrel bad enough to spark Kremlin retribution. It unsettled city as well as oblast officials, for the two pugilists had made their names in Moscow. Ivan Kapitonov, the obkom first secretary, had easily weathered a conflict of wills three years before with Second Secretary Grishin, very nearly pushing Grishin out of the power elite altogether before the assignment to the trade unions.[38] But this time he was not able to prevail over a lower-status politician, Nikolai F. Ignatov, the chairman of the ispolkom of the oblast soviet. In 1956 Khrushchev had been willing to condone Kapitonov's request; now, after Kapitonov's diffidence toward Khrushchev in his hour of need, in June 1957, help was not forthcoming.

The goldfish-bowl Moscow setting magnified the personality clash. Ignatov, who had a vocational school education only, was an intimate of Furtseva's and an easygoing man who rarely said no to a glass of vodka, not in the slightest like the punctilious Kapitonov. He became the obkom's secretary for industrial matters in March 1954 and replaced Grishin as second secretary in January 1956, only to be demoted to the oblast council that June. An accumulation of petty irritants led both men to the doors of Khrushchev and other Presidium members the winter of 1958–1959. "Kapitonov repeatedly proposed that Ignatov be removed as chairman of the Moscow oblispolkom. Ignatov considered that Kapitonov was unworthy of his position and should be fired. Their tense relations began to be felt in the apparatus, interfering with work and with fulfillment of the economic plan." In April 1959 both Kapitonov and Ignatov were sacked and publicly reprimanded for "incorrect and unpartylike relations."[39] They cooled their heels for some months, then were rusticated to Ivanovo and Orel provinces as obkom first secretaries.

A more subtle trend had to do with bureaucratic staffing. Whereas individual Muscovites did well in the promotion sweepstakes, mass recruitment came to a halt by 1955. Moscow was no longer spoken of as a "forge of cadres." It was also ceding some of its ideological aura. An augur of this change predated Khrushchev: the Central Committee daily, *Pravda,* ceased to be copublished by the Moscow obkom on October 14, 1952. While still afforded more media play than any other locality, Moscow was treated less reductively and worshipfully, and the "vanguard" terminology was dropped.

The stop-and-go cultural thaw gave rise to its own problems. It seesawed Moscow politicians between scholars and artists longing for more liberty and a Communist Party loath to give it unconditionally. Every first secretary, from Kapitonov to Yegorychev, found himself reassuring the intelligentsia one day and helping the next to stamp out a sign of independence at Peredelkino, a midtown picture studio, or an academic institute. Khrushchev's Falstaffian style added volatility. Yegorychev, on duty for only a few months, was obliged to second him in public when he bellowed invective at an infamous visit to a Manczh showing of abstract art in 1963. Yegorychev then compromised himself on all sides by trying to assuage the combatants behind the scenes.[40]

Brezhnev: Less of the Same

The Brezhnev era began amid optimism about stable, problem-solving government, without tantrums or trauma. The depositing of a marble bust over Stalin's grave in 1969, for the ninetieth anniversary of his birth, and the reversal of some (not all) of the Moscow place renamings of the 1950s, betokened the backsliding and desire to let sleeping dogs lie that soon set in.[41] Khrushchev lived out his days in a flat at 19 Starokonyushennyi pereulok and a state dacha at Petrovo-Dal'neye, both patrolled and bugged by the KGB's Ninth Directorate, and in the hospitals of the Fourth Chief Directorate of the USSR Ministry of Health, the contemporary name for the Kremlin Hospital complex. His body was consigned in 1971 to the graveyard at Novodevichii Convent, for public figures not meriting Red Square.

The Brezhnev Politburo did nothing to lay the long-term problems of the country or the city to rest. Its watch ended in disenchantment and the casting about for alternatives to the "epoch of stagnation" that unloosened the gyre of events from 1985 onward. In essence Brezhnev provided what urbanites had become used to by way of leadership and policy payoffs, but less of it.

YEGORYCHEV'S GAMBIT

Staraya ploshchad' was not big enough for both Leonid Brezhnev and the first secretary he inherited from Khrushchev. Like others before him, Nikolai Yegorychev did not outlast the solidification of the general secretary's authority.

The Moscow-born Yegorychev, a decorated war veteran and a graduate of the Bauman Higher Technical College, had twenty years' work in the Komsomol, the Moscow party, and the Central Committee under his belt. He was energetic, feisty, and *kar'ernyi,* undisguisedly ambitious. During the plotting against Khrushchev, he let it slip that he thought Brezhnev unworthy of the party chief's position. They got along at first "fairly well" in spite of this remark, Yegorychev reminisced. "I often met with him, giving him my recommendations, comments, and disagreement with this or that, and he heard me out and sometimes sought my advice. But after a while it became apparent that I was bothering him and even getting in his way." In early 1967 Yegorychev spurned a proposal by Brezhnev that he step down and take work in the Ministry of Foreign Affairs as a consolation prize.[42]

Yegorychev was eventually unlodged not by Moscow politics, narrowly speaking, but by the minefield of national issues into which he strayed. In September 1965, at the plenum of the Central Committee that approved Prime Minister Aleksei N. Kosygin's plan for administrative decentralization and worker incentives in Soviet industry, he warned that it would founder unless accompanied by investment in the consumer sector that would give workers something to buy with the rubles earned. Although not a direct assault on Brezhnev, the speech staked out the position that the Kosygin reform ought to be extended to a review of spending shares, including those of heavy and defense industry.[43]

In the spring of 1967 Brezhnev agreed to patch things up by cross-appointing Yegorychev to the Central Committee Secretariat, an honor that would have brought him into the party's inner circle. Brezhnev reneged on the commitment to deliver the promotion at the

Central Committee plenary of June 20–21, 1967. Yegorychev reacted by giving up on cooperation and regaling the plenum with the most uninhibited valediction it had heard since October 1964.

He addressed national security policy, by convention a preserve of the central leaders. Yegorychev flailed away at the performance of Soviet-supplied arms in the just concluded Six-Day War in the Middle East, at the USSR's diplomacy there, and at the condition of its own air and rocket forces. As the party's assignee to the city where Russia's most advanced weapons were developed, and to the Moscow Air Defense District, he was well placed to make these observations. By implication, he also questioned Brezhnev's passive mien and the party's loss of momentum on the domestic front. Yegorychev's speech was the final straw for Brezhnev and his claque, including Dmitrii Ustinov, the party's secretary for defense affairs—the selfsame Ustinov who, as minister of armaments in 1949, had bent Stalin's ear about Georgii Popov. They reacted by casting aspersions on Yegorychev's good judgment and loyalty.[44]

Brezhnev's enmity, incurred over personality and policy, was honed by the Moscow office's visibility, connections, and place in the party information grapevine. Yegorychev's admiration of the youngest member of the Politburo, Aleksandr N. Shelepin, who held Brezhnev in equally low esteem, did not help the situation. Yegorychev seemed of one mind with Shelepin on certain substantive questions. Coincidentally or not, he had been an official in the Komsomol when Shelepin was one of its leaders, and Shelepin had begun his own rise in the Moscow Komsomol during the war. Persons resembling them in background were to be downgraded farthest after 1967.[45]

The denouement bore out the durability of the party's culture of conformity. On tenterhooks for three days, Yegorychev stepped foward to abdicate—to Brezhnev, not the city leadership—on the supposition that he could not carry on without Kremlin backing. Brezhnev "was a bit afraid that the Moscow organization would not accept my resignation"; Yegorychev "assured him that everything would be all right and there would be no excesses."[46]

Yegorychev handwrote a note to the gorkom bureau admitting he had "forfeited the right to head the capital's party organization." On June 27 the gorkom met in plenary session to dispose of him, with the ideological vicar of the Secretariat and Politburo, Mikhail A.

Suslov, in attendance. Yegorychev's deposition before the Central Committee, Second Secretary Vladimir Ya. Pavlov explained, was "potentially harmful to our country." Pavlov added that Yegorychev had been flouting "the principle of collective leadership" within the gorkom and speaking in its name without consultation, slyly absolving himself and the bureau of responsibility. With no one else taking the podium, Yegorychev's resignation was accepted, and he moved on to a sinecure arranged by Brezhnev in the tractor-making ministry (becoming ambassador to Denmark in 1970).

GRISHIN AND THE DECLINE OF THE MOSCOW PARTY MACHINE

Suslov announced the chosen substitute: Viktor Grishin, a Moscow insider long absent from the local dais. Grishin hailed from Serpukhov, an industrial town in the south of the oblast, where he had been a party worker from 1940 until Khrushchev made him a department head in the obkom in 1950 and then second secretary in 1952. Since the altercation with Kapitonov in 1956, he had headed the Soviet trade unions, whose line on economic issues like price stability he defended, and since 1961 he had been a candidate member of the Politburo. Suslov reported that the gorkom bureau had "requested" his return to the city, a claim to be taken with a grain of salt. Grishin, Suslov said, could be spared for the greater good, especially as the impressment of someone with his experience "would signify the ever greater strengthening of ties between the Moscow party organization . . . and the Central Committee." The motion, true to form, was adopted unanimously.[47]

Grishin functioned as a quintessential member of the Brezhnevite oligarchy until it broke up in the 1980s. Promoted to full membership in the Politburo in 1971, he was one of only two persons on it at Brezhnev's death to have survived from Stalin's last Central Committee (the other was Dmitrii Ustinov).

Grishin could have given tutorials to all the party dukes in alliance crafting. While not a bosom friend, he was properly deferential to Brezhnev. At the Politburo table in 1976, he (among others) put the motion to confer the military rank of marshal on Brezhnev; in public he was quick to laud the ghost-written Brezhnev memoirs that came out in 1978. Overcoming an estrangement dating from his days in the trade unions, and notwithstanding his coolness toward economic reform, Grishin had a mutually appreciative relationship with Aleksei Kosygin and took family vacations with him. But he was also, he recollected, neighborly with Andrei P. Kirilenko, an economic neanderthal and Brezhnev's senior deputy in the party apparatus.[48] When Kirilenko lost ground in the late 1970s to Konstantin U. Chernenko, the majordomo of Brezhnev eventually elevated to the country's interim leader in 1984, Grishin lost no time paying court to Chernenko. For twenty years he played accordion at weddings of family of Politburo members and often subbed for Brezhnev as social host.

Grishin agreed viscerally with Brezhnev's policy priorities and never indicated doubts once retired, unlike some of his comrades. Sharing the belief in egalitarianism for society at large, he also superintended a methodical expansion of nomenklatura residences and leisure facilities in Moscow and its suburbs. To the man on the street, he appeared to be a kind of national toastmaster-general, genially officiating at testimonials and dedications from behind his breastplate of medals. "We all understand," Chernenko was to say at his seventieth birthday in 1984, "how great a responsibility lies on the shoulders of the party first secretary of our state's capital city. Moscow is always and for everyone on view, is it not?"[49] In Grishin, Brezhnev's Politburo had on view the qualities it admired and deserved.

It would be easy to make light of him. A half-dozen years Yegorychev's elder, the worst-educated first secretary since Khrushchev (his two diplomas were from vocational schools for surveyors and locomotive technicians), and a singsong orator, Grishin cut an unassuming figure. His speeches and writings give no inkling of more than a middling intellect.

For all that, less wily a political animal would not have made it through his never to be equaled eighteen and a half years as Moscow Communist leader. In that time he presented the party and municipal bureaucracies of each raion with fine new shared office buildings. Functionaries who enjoyed his trust found their telephone messages returned, their family anniversaries remembered, and their employ safe. Grishin was content to work with the human material at hand and not to insert toadies into the apparatus. Invoking Brezhnev's motto of "trust in cadres," he favored inchmeal rotation of personnel, not a hammer-and-tongs purge. He even treated protégés of Yegorychev gently. Second Secretary Pavlov stayed put for four years, and two gorkom secretaries whose tenure predated Grishin's, Leonid A. Borisov and Raisa F. Dement'eva, were still in the traces when he was ousted in 1985.[50]

With Vladimir Promyslov, Moscow's municipal chairman since 1963 and a member of the Central Committee, Grishin had testy relations. By account of a former aide, he tried to have Promyslov retired for mediocre work, but Brezhnev and several others on the Politburo stepped in. The two were to sling mud at one another as retirees.[51]

Grishin's one passion was his ideological conservatism. It was based not only on personal belief but on Moscow's towering presence in communications, high and mass culture, education, and science. In the capital resided the Soviet Union's national press and its television industry, broadcasting news and features out of the 539-meter Ostankino Television Tower, the tallest in Europe, which replaced the interwar Shukhov Tower in 1967. In 1970 Moscow hosted one-half of the USSR's cinematographers, one-third of its registered writers and composers, one-quarter of its painters and sculptors, one-sixth of its journalists, and almost 15 percent of its college-level students, and was the site of about one-third of all Soviet basic research and one-quarter of all applied research. In mass entertainment, as one analyst puts it, Moscow was Broadway, Tin Pan Alley, Motown, Nashville, and Hollywood rolled into one.[52] At a time when orthodoxy reigned among the national elite, no Moscow leader could have survived with a liberal position.

Grishin showed his colors when he supported the intellectual crackdown foreshadowing the 1968 Soviet invasion of Czechoslovakia. The city party conference that March, where he and Brezhnev gave stentorian speeches, proclaimed "the course toward 'turning the screws' on ideology and culture." At the Lenin jubilee the next month, Grishin took up the cudgels against "politically immature" intellectuals. An assault on heterodoxy in the performing arts, instigated by the first secretaries of the districts containing Russia's biggest live theaters (Krasnopresnenskii and Sverdlovskii raions), was an opening salvo in the campaign. Grishin's propaganda secretary, Alla P. Shaposhnikova, ordered a Moscow exhibit of modern painting closed down in July 1968.[53]

Grishin unaccountably took a shine in the early 1970s to the experimental Taganka Drama and Comedy Theater and its director, Yurii P. Lyubimov, and helped the vaudevillian and satirist, Arkadii I. Raikin, relocate from Leningrad to Moscow, angering the Leningrad leader Grigorii V. Romanov. But this latitudinarianism quickly yielded to intransigence.[54] Grishin outdid all previous first secretaries in patronizing politicized public art, unveiling the first and only Lenin statue in the Kremlin in 1967 (on the spot where the Bolsheviks took down the statue of Alexander II in 1918) and, in one of his final acts as leader, the largest Lenin figure in Moscow at Oktyabr'skaya ploshchad'. In between, he oversaw the installation of ponderous sculptures of Mikhail Kalinin, Yakov Sverdlov, Friedrich Engels, and dozens of minor Soviet heroes.

The Moscow KGB—whose section for "ideological counterintelligence" was as big as all others combined—obedient courts, and the party apparatus successfully suppressed overt political dissent in Moscow. Whereas more than half of all signers of dissident petitions in the USSR at the end of the 1960s were Muscovites, only about one-third were by the late 1970s.[55] The Moscow KGB chief, Viktor I. Alidin, entered the gorkom bureau as a candidate in 1974 and a full member in March 1975; no secret police agent had been so high in the local party since 1953. One of his assignments was to spy on the growing number of persons of Jewish nationality who wished to emigrate overseas. Although thousands were refused exit visas, the departures, combined with assimilation and low fertility, depressed Jews' share in the city's population from 3.6 percent in 1970 to 3.0 percent in 1979 and only 2.0 percent in 1989, leaving Ukrainians as the second largest ethnic group.

Grishin's propaganda secretary from 1971 to 1976 was Viktor N. Yagodkin, a know-nothing who had made his name hectoring faculty and students as party secretary of Moscow University. He drew notoriety in the world press in September 1974 by ordering the bulldozing of an unofficial outdoors art exhibit in southwest Moscow. In January 1976 he was kicked upstairs to USSR deputy minister of education for personnel; Grishin and Mikhail Suslov agreed on Viktor N. Makeyev, a less obstreperous raikom secretary who had been vice-rector of an economics institute, for the propaganda position.

So critical was ideology to the Moscow party in the late Brezhnev era that Makeyev did double duty as propaganda and second secretary. He spread dread about contamination by Western agents, corre-spondents, business professionals, and, during the 1980 Moscow Olympics, athletes. After the collapse of detente in 1980, Moscow headed up the jingoistic Soviet "counterpropaganda" policy. When researchers at the Academy of Sciences's main international relations institute questioned policy toward Eastern Europe in 1982, Grishin headed a Politburo inquiry that "tried to defame the work of the institute and its director," Nikolai N. Inozemtsev.[56]

The creedal conservatism of the Moscow apparatchiks would be a red flag to progressives after Brezhnev. But long before then indica-tions accumulated of a droop in Moscow's authority. There is no other way to interpret, for instance, the abrogation of the convention of cross-appointing the Moscow first secretary to the Central Com-mittee Secretariat. A routine laurel in the Stalin years, and conferred twice under Khrushchev (on Furtseva and Demichev), it was never bestowed on Grishin, for all his longevity.

Representation on the Central Committee itself demarcated influence. Moscow's contingent (Grishin, Dement'eva, and Promys-lov) constituted less than 1 percent of full members in 1981, in contrast to 1.7 percent in 1961 and much higher percents in bygone days (see Table C-5).

So it went with the lifeblood of the CPSU machine, patronage. Compare the Brezhnev column with Khrushchev's in Table C-3: over almost twice as long a time, far fewer Muscovites got coveted promo-tions. When appointments are annualized and grouped by rank (Table C-4), the dropoff is especially sharp in senior positions. Although members of the Grishin machine still stepped into Rank 2 posts at about half the rate of the pre–Great Purge Stalin regime or of the Khrushchev years, they were entering Rank 1 at a derisory one-tenth the rate of the Khrushchev period and still more slowly than almost every earlier time.

The careers of many of the Muscovites groomed by Khrushchev entered a blind alley under Brezhnev. Demichev, the junior party secretary for culture and propaganda, lost out to an apparatus reac-tionary in 1974 and was degraded, like Furtseva earlier, to culture minister. Retaining the candidate's seat on the Politburo he got after the 1964 coup, he stacked his ministry with Muscovites and was solicitous of nondissident intellectuals but had little wider impact.[57]

His Moscow contemporary, Vladimir Stepakov, head of the CC's Propaganda Department from 1965, was toppled in 1970. Besides Stepakov—no novice, as he had headed a department from 1961 to 1964—no Muscovite made it to the level of CC secretary or department head. Not one was posted as first secretary of a provincial party committee; the sole sitting secretary, Ivan T. Marchenko in Tomsk oblast, was demoted in 1965. A meager three Muscovites got onto the Council of Ministers, one of them Makeyev (deputy premier for cultural affairs from 1980 to 1983) and another a Grishin crony.[58]

One can readily understand promotion being blocked for cadres identified with Nikolai Yegorychev. But was some larger anti-Moscow phobia afoot? While that may be putting it too strongly, Brezhnev, a man of the hinterland, had no involvement with or empathy for the Moscow apparatus. And Grishin appears to have concluded that it would be safest for him to go along with reduced career mobility for Muscovites.

An intriguing personal note concerns Brezhnev's coadjutant for staffing the party—Ivan Kapitonov of Moscow. Brezhnev retrieved him from exile in Ivanovo in late 1964 to head the Central Committee's personnel division (Department of Organizational and Party Work), first for the RSFSR and then for the USSR. Kapitonov became CC secretary for party organization a year later. Five Muscovites, starting with his first deputy, Nikolai A. Petrovichev, can be spotted in the department under him.[59]

Kapitonov had begged off an invitation to return to Moscow under Yegorychev's wing in 1964, and by this juncture, Yegorychev said in an interview, "We did not consider him to be a Muscovite." Brezhnev had reason to be pleased by Kapitonov's knowledge of Moscow and also of the oblast, where the atoll of elite resorts and summer houses spread after 1964. At the same time, there was something comforting about the stain on Kapitonov's Moscow record and his indecorous ejection in 1959, a humiliation that may have biased him against Muscovites. And Kapitonov's set-to with Grishin surely appealed to Brezhnev as Machiavellian insurance against collusion between the two of them.

Nor can shifts in underlying variables be overlooked. Demographic and territorial changes steadily deflated Moscow in relation to the party's total mass. The obkom in 1930 held sway over 13.5

390 • The Limits of De-Stalinization

percent of all party members (and candidates), 8.1 percent of them in Moscow. By 1939, with Moscow's growth restricted and the oblast cropped back, the oblast accounted for 10.5 percent and Moscow within it for 7.7 percent. Moscow party ranks increased by 171 percent between January 1953 and Grishin's departure in 1985, but this jump was less than party-wide growth. The division of 1956 left the gorkom with 6.1 percent of all Communists (434,500) and the self-sufficient obkom with 2.9 percent. By Grishin's departure in 1985, these figures were down to 5.9 percent in the city (1,107,000 Communists) and 2.7 percent in the oblast. Size apart, the gorkom's severance from the obkom deprived its staffers of exposure to rural administration and hurt their entree to other regions.[60]

A last, unquantifiable point would recognize the maturation of Soviet institutions. Organizations that Moscow politicians once freely penetrated acquired a life of their own and resisted poaching on their staffing and other routines.[61] A not dissimilar calcification was taking place in the city bureaucracy.

MODEL COMMUNIST CITY

Where Khrushchevism in local affairs had placed stress on political inputs, Brezhnev's policy underscored outputs. This shift fit a general perspective that exalted regularity, order, and letting administrators with politically unthreatening knowledge ply their trade. "Scientific" and "businesslike" decisions, a pox on "dilettantism" and "subjectivism," integrated or "complex" programs—such were the new touchstones.

A Soviet fixation, this attitude struck a special chord in Moscow in part because of what had been occurring in the city's economy. Science and science services—science in the Russian meaning covering humanities and social sciences as well as the natural sciences and research and development with economic applications—vaulted from under 5 percent of employment in 1940 to 17 percent in 1965 and almost 20 percent in 1985 (see Table 6).

Grishin's obscurantism on intellectual freedom told the burgeoning specialist class to forget about democracy. The managerial philosophy, the flip side of the coin, said that within an autocratic polity there could be respect for systematically acquired knowledge. On local

Table 6. Distribution of employment, 1940–1985

Branch of economy	Percent employed in branch			
	1940	1965	1975	1985
Manufacturing	43.7	33.2	27.8	25.1
Construction	7.0	8.9	10.1	10.5
Transport and communications	10.0	9.9	9.5	9.5
Housing, trade, and consumer services	16.1	13.7	13.8	14.4
Health, education, and culture	7.4	10.6	11.6	13.0
Science and science services	4.8	17.0	19.0	19.6
Public administration and law enforcement[a]	7.9	4.2	5.5	5.9[b]
Other	3.1[c]	2.5[c]	2.7[c]	2.0[d]

Sources: *Moskva v tsifrakh, 1917–1977 gg.* (Moscow: Statistika, 1977), p. 64; *Moskva v tsifrakh, 1988* (Moscow: Finansy i statistika, 1988), p. 113.

a. Combines categories "apparatus of organs of administration" and "credit and state insurance." Evidently excludes military personnel.

b. Includes personnel in "information and computer services," previously subsumed under administration.

c. Unexplained residual.

d. Residual, but includes 1.8 percent "in other forms of activity in the sphere of material production."

issues there were no more shockwaves; by-the-book professionals now ran Moscow government.

Brezhnev himself pinned a unique badge of favor on Moscow in 1971, shortly before adoption of its latest master plan. Without asking Grishin's opinion, he gave word at the Twenty-fourth Party Congress that he wanted Moscow transmuted into the "model Communist city" *(obraztsovyi kommunisticheskii gorod)* of the Soviet Union. Brezhnev's anodyne phrase reinflated the regime's vision of Moscow and of its pedagogic function.[62]

Never did he spell out what a Communist paragon would consist of. Politicians kneaded it to their own purposes, often to back up budget claims. Grishin, though not its inventor, liked the concept and gave it ideological coloration: "We call on Muscovites to give a stellar example in the sphere of human relations as much as in solving problems of urban development. A model Communist city is a city where people with a high level of culture and consciousness live, a city of model public order. It is a city in which the atmosphere is of good will, mutual respect, and consideration."[63]

The concept glibly slid from the teleological to the empirical. Press columns under treacly headings like "Model Schools for a Model City!" and "Our Model City Deserves Clean Courtyards!" blurred aspiration and actuality. The spotlight swung to the latter, as if nirvana were an accomplished fact. "Moscow's experience," in the rapt words of one rendition, "is an inspiration for the entire country. The prospect of *also turning the remaining cities of our land into exemplary ones* rests to a great degree on how well it is studied and disseminated."[64]

Model standing had concrete implications for policy. Insofar as Moscow now shone as a lighthouse of communism, the dialectical perfection of socialism, notice was drawn to continuities with past benchmarks such as the 1935 master plan. There prevailed a receptiveness to projects lionizing Soviet exploits before domestic and foreign audiences. Although these did not regain the prominence or wastefulness they had before 1953, they were no longer demeaned as diversions of resources from more worthy ends.

Prospekt Kalinina, planned by Posokhin and made palatable to Khrushchev by its housing and stores, was christened to much ballyhoo for the fiftieth anniversary of the October Revolution in 1967 (Figure 53). The road, two kilometers long and eighty meters wide, was named after Mikhail Kalinin, who had been the figurehead Soviet head of state and a member of the Politburo from 1919 to 1946. It joined up at the Moskva River to Kutuzovskii prospekt. On the riverbank beside the bridge, a Chechulin-designed House of Soviets of the RSFSR (parliamentary and ministerial offices) was completed in white marble in 1980 (Figure 54); it would be in the world spotlight as the Russian White House from which Boris Yeltsin beat back the hardline coup of August 1991. Construction began in 1968 on the two and a half kilometers of Novokirovskii prospekt, a similar boulevard joining the train stations at Komsomol'skaya ploshchad' with the midtown squares (Figure 55).

In the residential areas Grishin made a hobbyhorse out of a "model, long-range housing district" on the eighty hectares of Severnoye Chertanovo, in Sevastopol'skii raion fifteen kilometers south of the Kremlin. "If Moscow in its development is called upon to be an

Figure 53. Prospekt Kalinina. (Photograph by William C. Brumfield.)

Figure 54. Russian White House. (Photograph by William C. Brumfield.)

Figure 55. Novokirovskii prospekt. (Photograph by author.)

example for the entire country," one encomiast descanted, "then Severnoye Chertanovo in turn should be an example for the whole capital."[65]

The biggest new public facility, the State Picture Gallery (New Tret'yakov Gallery) on Krymskaya naberezhnaya in Zamoskvorech'e, was occupied in stages in the 1980s. It took two decades to build and two decades to plan before that, going back to Ivan Zholtovskii. In 1983, after a quarter-century of planning,[66] construction began on the most colossal memorial since Stalin's death, an All-Union Victory Monument solemnizing the defeat of Hitler by Soviet arms. On a tractor-scalped polygon of 1.2 square kilometers on Poklonnaya Hill, a half-kilometer "parade alley" trimmed by fountains with 1,418 nozzles (one for every day of the war) was to terminate in a giant circular plaza holding the war monument to end all war monuments: a hemispheric gallery of sculptures; a white stone Central Museum of the Great Patriotic War; inside it, a crystal pylon encasing the Soviet flag raised over the Berlin Reichstag on April 30, 1945; before it, a ninety-meter ferroconcrete sculpture of workers and soldiers holding aloft a billowing banner, embossed with a Lenin head and surmounted by a ruby star. Grishin nursed the design along, involved himself in the choice of materials, and led a subscription campaign that collected 190 million rubles from the populace.

The largest of the undertakings taken to completion was the plant for the 1980 Summer Olympics. The pork barrel yielded Moscow a 40,000-seat roofed stadium, an Olympic Village, a 30 percent expansion of hotel space, and a second terminal for Sheremet'evo Airport. Municipal contractors did three-quarters of the work, which in 1979 came to 610 million rubles (a sum never made public), four times the funds plowed into Moscow trade, consumer services, roads and bridges, and parks put together. The government intended the sedulous choreographing of the games, to quote Grishin, to "show off the superiority of the Soviet way of life."[67]

To show Moscow at its best, 45,000 MVD and KGB officers were detailed to special guard duty, youngsters were kept over at summer camp, provincial shoppers were turned away at railway stations, Gypsies were rounded up and political dissidents tailed, laundry was whipped off of balconies along parade routes, buildings were spray painted (sometimes in such haste that window panes were coated), and a five-story apartment house breaking the line of Olimpiiskii prospekt in north central Moscow was torn down. Visitors saw gleaming new structures in "a city of dead streets, half-empty transport, and stores without crushes or lineups."[68]

Moscow in the Brezhnev era also presented model qualities through its own program for domestic and overseas aid. The time-honored practice of wardship over abutting rural districts grew into a patchwork of far-flung goodwill efforts. From the late 1960s to 1980, Glavmosstroi constructed 1 million square meters of housing space in Naberezhnyye Chelny, a new truck-manufacturing town almost a thousand kilometers away, and 600,000 square meters in Mongolia, in east Asia. City agencies had projects under way in twenty-two Soviet and foreign cities in 1985.

This dully ideological approach did not always mesh with the managerialism enshrined after October 1964. For a Moscow population that bulged from 6.5 million in the mid-1960s to more than 8.5 million twenty years later, the panegyrics to the dream metropolis jibed poorly with the banal realities experienced day by day. One poll in 1981 found Muscovites to be distinctly less satisfied with living conditions than residents of any other large Soviet city except Leningrad.[69] Among other causes of the ennui, local institutions failed in the main to keep the vows made with regard to housing, town planning, and a congeries of local issues.

The clouds appearing on the Soviet Camelot's horizon were many. Core provisions of the 1971 master plan were disregarded. Economic ministries resisted Moscow's effort to get them to dance in step. While per capita housing supply crept ahead, annual completions skidded by more than 40 percent. The reproaches about service provision at Novyye Cheremushki in the 1950s could have been read out almost verbatim about Yasenevo, Strogino, Bibirevo, or Brateyevo in the 1980s. Obligations incurred to curb water and air pollution and protect the treasures of historic Moscow were poorly met. On a mundane level, the unearthing of inefficiency and bribe taking by city produce retailers was to speed Grishin and Promyslov into retirement. Corruption, raised as a local issue in the Golushko affair in 1958 but not aggressively combatted, grew rank. Most basic, urban government remained at its core a bureaucratic structure, unattuned to opinion below.

For not a few, lukewarm performance and the ostrichlike response to it made the hype on the propaganda marquees a wellspring of incredulity and irritation instead of pride. How else can we explain the rise Yeltsin achieved after 1985, when he heaped scorn on Moscow's phony "modelness" *(obraztsovshchina)?* He was voicing out loud what many had been muttering under their breaths about the Brezhnev-Grishin mantra. "Window dressing [*paradnost'*], overemphasis on successes, and a hushing up of shortcomings have been instilled in its [the local establishment's] style of work," is how Yeltsin eventually rendered it, and this style had "given rise to conceit and inertia." The adulation was a hoax and a pity, he remarked, since Moscow *"used to be looked upon with great respect in the party."*[70] "Model Communist city," a last gasp of vanguardism, a claim for how high Moscow could fly, ended up a pointer to how low it had sunk.

Command Government Perpetuated

The house of urban governance did not fail to make some adjustments in late Soviet Moscow. When all is said and done, though, continuity eclipsed discontinuity in it, in its political climate, and in citizens' place therein.

THE ADMINISTRATIVE MUNICIPALITY

The leadership posited two enhancements for the soviets: in public responsiveness and in administrative capacity. Khrushchev-era policy bowed more to the first ideal and Brezhnev's more to the second, but both received steady play.

Results were more apparent on the second dimension, as Moscow evinced the increases in scale, complexity, and expertise that suffused the Soviet state. Growth in staff from 1.2 million in 1960 to 1.4 million in the mid-1970s and 1.7 million in 1988—roughly one in three working men and women—did not outstrip demographic growth, but it made an immense work force all the more so. About 30,000 of the 1.7 million in 1988 were managers. New York, with an almost equal population but a panoply of capitalistic firms to pull much of the load, had 300,000 city workers in the 1970s.

Hand in glove with governmental elephantiasis went an ever greater intricacy of structure. Between the early 1960s and the early

1980s, the Moscow ispolkom added three deputy chairmen and, mostly by cellular division of existing departments, eighteen agencies (see Table B-4 in Appendix B). Thanks to Parkinsonian grade inflation, eighteen of sixty bureaus in 1982, as compared to five of forty-two in 1961, were rated as "chief directorates," the loftiest category in Soviet organizational argot.

Professionalism did not accrete as painlessly as size and prolixity, although the technocratic style made deep inroads. Moscow's government opened itself up to contact with the external world in 1955. Exchanges of expert delegations, mostly with foreign capitals, involved fifty countries, socialist and capitalist, by the 1970s. While these had their frivolous side—Chairman Promyslov's jet travels and boozy banquets were legend—they did broaden horizons and perforate some ideological blinkers.

Of a piece, city hall began public opinion polling in the mid-1960s. In 1970 it instated automated information systems and a data center; thirty-three room-sized Soviet computers were whirring away by 1975 on everything from kindergarten enrollments to gasline repairs.[71] Glavmosstroi in 1972 took Khrushchev's building standardization to unheard-of heights by introducing a "Unified Catalog" of components. Troparevo, Orekhovo-Borisovo, and the mammoth housing developments of the 1970s and 1980s were pasted together almost exclusively with modular parts from the catalog.

Moscow also came to hire better-qualified personnel and enlarge its network of vocational and retraining courses. True, the payroll had not a few self-taught *praktiki,* and a classification grid less rigorous than in single-purpose central agencies inspired unease. But one-quarter of city employees in 1985 had specialists' papers, among them 30,000 engineers and technicians, 80,000 teachers and cultural workers, and 42,000 accountants and bookkeepers.[72]

At peak levels more than 60 percent of municipal workers from 1953 to 1964, and almost 75 percent after October 1964, had a higher education (see Tables C-1 and C-2). Engineers made up the largest subset by far, often with the construction profile shared by Yasnov, Bobrovnikov, Nikolai A. Dygai, and Promyslov, the chairmen of the city ispolkom between 1950 and 1986. Glaringly absent was a cadre of managers tutored in public administration, which never cohered as an academic discipline in the USSR. Instead, bureaucrats acquired generalist experience in the Communist Party. Rather more than half of Moscow municipal leaders under Khrushchev, and two-thirds under Brezhnev, had worked in the CPSU apparatus, the latter sum higher than even in the late Stalin years. Among Moscow's "deputy mayors," the deputy chairmen of the city ispolkom, party service exceeded 80 percent.[73]

Bureaucrats reporting to the soviet had always had more localistic career pathways than party officials; this correlation also obtained after 1953. One-fifth of municipal functionaries had some tempering in central administration, normally in a cognate bureau, while one ispolkom chairman, Dygai, was drafted from a construction ministry. Four out of five had Moscow-only biographics. Only several percent had worked in the provinces.

Another common qualification in the 1970s and 1980s was the venerability imparted by "trust in cadres." Promyslov spent twenty-three years in office. This span paled beside that of Iosif M. Goberman, who died in 1983 after running the city's cargo service since 1937, for twice as long.[74]

Why do these figures tell us so much about conditioning for bureaucratic service and so little about political aptitudes? The explanation is disarming: officials, up the chain of command to chairman of the executive board, were presumed not to be proficient in politics, in any case not in politics across the state-society divide. De-Stalinization actually reinforced the overpoweringly administrative ethos of city hall.

Moscow government under Stalin I compared to a utility company. A better analogue for post-1953 would be a building firm, given construction's place in the local economy. The skills demanded of executives had far more to do with internal control and mastery of arcane skills than with acquiring consent in, or responding to cues from, the environment.

A vice-chairman of the city executive was to put it lucidly when asked in 1990 why he had declined to run in Moscow's first contested local election in seventy years: "By way of thinking and living," he replied, "I am not a politician but a manager, a specialist in administration, and I have no intention of requalifying myself now." The speaker, Yurii M. Luzhkov, who actually did more requalifying than he predicted and threw his hat into the electoral ring the next year, in 1990 accurately summed up a deeply seated attitude.[75]

Nor did the machinery at the fingertips of Moscow's "specialists in administration" change materially. Local elections were, as ever, minuets in salute of the regime's cognitive control over the population. Party leaders touted turnouts of over 99 percent and overwhelming votes for the official slate as evidence of "socialist democracy" and the "monolithic unity" of party and people.

Every schoolchild could make out under the boilerplate what a Moscow party secretary was allowed to put into print only after 1985: "All personnel in the soviets, from the individual deputy to the chairman of the executive committee, were cleared within the halls of the party committee." Besides submitting candidates to a reliability test, Communist Party officials, sandpapering to perfection procedures devised in the 1920s, juggled the final lineup by age, occupation, gender, and other attributes, "down to tenths of a percentage point," as Yeltsin later admitted. It would not have been surprising if, as he also deposed, some deputies forgot who had signed their nomination papers.[76]

The dubious provenance, unmitigated amateurism, and sprawling size of the urban legislatures—the Mossovet hovered between 800 and 1,200 members—continued to disqualify them from a seat at the table of power. The four plenary meetings a year of the city soviet lasted five hours apiece, ending religiously at 3:00 P.M. with a buffet at city expense. Attendance was spotty, votes were unanimous shows of hands, and all procedures were scripted. Down to the choice of speakers and the themes of their speeches, the solons of the soviet had to clear everything with the ispolkom secretary before the gavel sounded. They could engage in special pleading, but to administrators or higher authority, not to their peers. Members of the public were admitted by invitation only.[77]

Any capacity for action inhered in the executive apparatus. As before, Moscow had outer and inner municipal cabinets. The ispolkom (executive committee), the larger of the two, convened less frequently, its twenty-five members sitting approximately once a month in the 1960s and 1970s.

The inner executive, about half the size, was called the ispolkom's bureau until March 1956 and its presidium thereafter. It comprised, without exception, city hall professionals already seated on the ispolkom: the ispolkom chairman (who also chaired the presidium), his deputy chairmen, each responsible for a subset of executive departments, and the ispolkom's secretary, in charge of relations with deputies and voters.[78] The presidium held three or four formal sessions for every one by the ispolkom, besides polling members by telephone. Meetings of both ispolkom and presidium were attended by official guests—as many as 75 or 100—who sat "along the wall" during those agenda items for which they were needed.[79]

The presidium was without doubt the more influential body. It alone considered certain questions of detail, such as land allocation and site plans, budgets, property transfers, and most personnel matters. It had a preliminary go at almost all issues headed for the full ispolkom. Not only was it more compact and more active, it was also more secretive—a sure sign of power in the USSR. The ispolkom published a bulletin on its activities twice a month; the presidium had none and was hardly ever mentioned in the press.[80]

The distinction between the two panels is somewhat theoretical, in that both took direction from the party organs. Furthermore, the city administrators on the presidium, together with two or three agency and district heads, made up 60 percent or more of the ispolkom (see Table B-1). Although not as high a percentage as in Stalin's lifetime, it allowed control of the proceedings should voting strength be required.

With Promyslov in the chair and not much of excitement on the order paper, executive meetings were, literally, drowsy affairs: "The sunny atmosphere of the hall," one journalist wrote later about the presidium, "would be broken by the sudden sound of someone snoring. Sedately and righteously the members would sit in state, knowing that something had happened but that no one was really bothered by it and no action was required." A raion chairman who belonged to the city ispolkom in the 1980s reported that orders awaiting the committee's validation were often printed and dated in advance. He found in his in-box ispolkom resolutions never discussed in his presence: "The structural subunits of the Moscow Soviet 'bake' them and then distribute them for compulsory discharge." Decisions taken at ispolkom meetings were nominally collegial; usually "there was no voting and in actual fact a wrapup decision was announced by the chairman."[81]

Innovations in legislative-executive relations after Stalin's reign bolstered the authority of the committees, the standing commissions, of the local soviets. Initial attempts at reform along these lines, by exhortation alone, met with ungratifying results. The ispolkoms and their presidiums "still decide all questions" in Moscow, a review in the city ispolkom's bulletin explained in 1961, with the exception of the few organizational items on which votes of the entire soviet were statutorily required. "During the course of the year," the author continued, the executive organs "make whatsoever amendments and supplements they wish" to plans and budgets; by December, these documents were but "loosely reminiscent" of the ones adopted by commissions and soviets.[82]

In May 1962, goaded by the antibureaucratism of the Twenty-second Party Congress, the Mossovet resolved to give its commissions the right to impose "binding decisions" on officials. But the prohibition of interloping in the city's economic plan, budget, and material allocations defanged the edict from the start. In reality, standing commissions were limited to tendering judicious advice and to publicly censuring reprobate administrators.[83]

The Brezhnev years brought a quantitative expansion of the committees. As against seventeen standing commissions with fifteen members each in 1965, the city soviet had twenty-one with a mean of forty-one members in 1982, and the proportion of deputies belonging rose from 23 percent to 98 percent. Unfortunately, the quality of their work did not keep up.

Native and foreign specialists had inklings of executive dominance in Soviet cities.[84] What was whispered before Gorbachev was said in full voice with the arrival of *glasnost'* (candor of expression). For Moscow, it is enough to quote Boris Yeltsin, who during his tempestuous tenure as city party leader from 1985 to 1987 several times addressed the issue.

In his most unsparing exegesis, before the city soviet in March 1987, Yeltsin disclosed that in the year just over, even after the disgrace of Promyslov and repeated summons to reform, not 10 percent of the questions ventilated in the ispolkom had been considered in a standing commission. In addition, some commissions had never met in full complement; half of their resolutions went unfulfilled; officials ignored innocent requests for information; and no commission had exploited the right to address a formal interpellation *(zapros)* to a dilatory leader.[85]

Conceding some blame to sloth and "a shortage of civic activism" among the deputies, Yeltsin insisted that the deeper cause was the operational code of the soviet. "The inertness of many deputies and their sense of a lack of rights and of the futility of their work have developed because of the arrogant, condescending attitude toward the commissions" long prevalent on the executive, among the agency chiefs, and across the Soviet system. Many officials "attend sittings [of the commissions] rarely, settle personnel questions without talking to the commissions, authorize their secretariats to keep mum, and ignore the commissions' appeals and suggestions." Years of impunity, Yeltsin said, oozing sarcasm, had bred "the fallacious habit of seeing the deputy as a tiresome supplicant or a runner of errands for 'his majesty the worker of the apparatus.'"

THE POLITICS OF THE RECEPTION ROOM

The mass participation to which the regime acceded after Stalin I would liken to behavior in a reception room. Urban government was now supposed to keep its door ajar, not merely post a suggestion box outside. Citizens were welcome, as long they waited their turn, kept their voices down, and, every now and then, rolled up their sleeves to lend a hand to the officials inside.

An incident recounted purringly in 1959 by a deputy in the soviet of Sverdlovskii raion, in central Moscow, conveys the effect sought:

> Emergency repairs had to be done to the flats on two floors of a house in my electoral precinct. So tenants of these apartments began to be evicted into "resettlement points." It suddenly transpired that several residents turned down the rooms made available to them, opposing even a temporary stay in them. The tenants came to me for help. I learned some details, that Shuvalova had just had a heart attack and Gurevich had lost 60 percent of her sight. I took a look at the resettlement point and discovered that the temporary housing was highly inconvenient and was at the top of a steep stairway.
>
> I went to the raion's housing directorate and tried to prove to them that the problem was not with any quirkiness on the tenants' part but with the new housing's unsuitability for them . . . Then I turned to the deputy chairman of the raion ispolkom. As a result of this, the ill women in a few days received better lodging in another resettlement point, one on the ground floor and one on the second.[86]

This Parable of the Good Deputy could be multiplied over and over again. It was taken as axiomatic that there would be legitimate grievances over the chaff of local policy and that conscience and common sense obligated government gatekeepers to act upon them.

At its most innocuous, constituency contact took the form of petition, a rock-bottom right not annulled even during the Stalinist terror. Some 19,220 residents came calling at the chambers of the Moscow ispolkom in 1981; 4,207 visited officials in city agencies, 116,855 the ispolkoms of the raions, and 75,075 raion departments. That same year, the city executive received 67,077 written requests, city agencies 137,120, and raion executives 147,363. In round numbers, 4,100 Muscovites saw municipal officials in the average work week, and another 6,800 had their letters opened.[87] Thousands of others—how many we do not know, but in all probability more—put stock in "covert participation" via human chains etched by kinship, contacts, and friendship and leading only in the end, if at all, to public officials.[88]

Devices to amplify what Donna Bahry characterizes as "compliant activism"—overt participation through the correct channels—gained currency in the early 1960s.[89] All had precedents in the 1920s and 1930s. One, the enlistment of up to 20,000 Moscow laypeople as unpaid, auxiliary *(vneshtatnyye)* members of local staffs, mostly got the amateurs and professionals stepping on one another's toes and writing fervid reports. It was so tarnished with Khrushchevism as to fall into desuetude after him.[90]

Official indifference, if not hostility, also hobbled another departure, the nurturing of state-initiated mass organizations at the neighborhood level. Most were coupled to the bureaucratic office managing the housing fund—known at this time as the *zhek* (short for housing-operation bureau) or, for buildings not under municipal control, the *domoupravleniye* (house directorate). House, division, and street committees embraced some 50,000 activists at their apogee in the late 1960s—about 0.8 percent of the population—with about a third that many in housing "repair detachments" and 30,000 in parents' committees at schools, library advisory boards, and similar bodies. This breakdown was out of a total *aktiv*, or corpus of activists, of 500,000 or thereabouts. Groups of this ilk survived, but in the 1980s, by

Yeltsin's testimony, many were wholly inactive or in "a lethargic state."[91]

Two other participatory forms found more fertile soil in the Brezhnev years. "Councils of deputies," subsuming the members of district and city soviets from one zhek or house directorate, arose in Moscow in 1961. In the mid-1970s 500 of the councils existed, usually with around fifteen members each. Their low-key sessions gave citizens a first avenue of appeal and bureaucrats a first moat of defense.

A final instrument was the familiar voters' mandate *(nakaz),* by which candidates for election swore to propound community projects —building playgrounds, caulking leaky roofs, adding bus routes, and the like—which had won approval from meetings of constituents. One nakaz was contracted for on average every three deputies elected. The Mossovet required all agencies and committees from 1969 onward to report annually on fulfillment.

Such procedures made city government less aloof, but again de-Stalinization had its limits. Other behaviors, foremost the authoritarian method of constituting the local legislatures, enfeebled links in the chain of feedback from below. The most that could have been anticipated of appointed, spare-time lawmakers was that they would act as fair-minded ombudsmen, not hale advocates of community interests.[92]

Especially corrosive of spontaneous participation was the joining of antidemocratic actions, such as rigged elections, to specious democratic rhetoric. The resultant cynicism seeped into activities that might otherwise have gotten respect. Many saw in all of local government a gestalt termed, after Brezhnev and Grishin, "democracy for the sake of the tick" *(demokratiya dlya galochki)*—ritual heeded so that boxes could be checked off on report sheets.

It did not escape Muscovites' attention that one and the same devices that afforded them portholes into governmental institutions lent themselves to reverse manipulation. That machination could be merely arithmetical, as in the distortion of summary data on mass participation by counting organizations established under Khrushchev to aid in the control of popular behavior. The most important of these, the *druzhiny* (red-armbanded street squads to combat crime and delinquency) and the "comrades' courts" (tribunals with a similar purpose), made up the majority of all participants in some statistical roundups.[93]

City authorities had more at stake than nice statistics. The residential committees afforded them a reserve of uncompensated labor; year-end reports spared no detail on how many apartments, lobbies, and fences activists had broomed and painted. The moth-eaten subbotnik tradition wound on. The spring cleanup on the Saturday in April nearest Lenin's birthday (the All-Union Leninist Communist Subbotnik as of 1970) dragooned 95 percent of the able-bodied population, by the government's reckoning; special-occasion subbotniks marked political anniversaries, drew on particular corps of volunteers, and dealt with urgent construction problems. Voters' mandates, to give another instance, served the purpose of officials as much as of electors. Yeltsin was to disparage nakazes "concocted . . . in the offices of the ispolkom," meaning mandates that shrewd administrators helped write to assure easy attainment or to give them trumps in bargaining for resources with superiors.[94]

Authentic voluntary associations would have lessened popular alienation, but there plainly was no freedom to build them. The Old Moscow Society, the Garden Cities Society, and the leagues of housing cooperatives, done in by Stalin, were not resurrected. Several dozen narrow-mandate organizations had some intercourse with the municipality but no effect on policy.[95]

Several organizations did point in the direction of a more spirited politics at the grass roots, although of a semiofficial nature. One, the Moscow City Society for Environmental Protection (the name as of 1966), descended from the Society for Assistance to Tree Planting of the Stalin years; it had 540,000 dues-paying members in 1963 and 1,900,000 in the late 1970s. The smaller Moscow Society of Nature Testers applied itself to environmental issues in scientific circles. Founded in 1805, it had only 3,500 members in 1978, but it and its president, Academician Aleksandr L. Yanshin, did much to interest the intelligentsia and sympathizers in government in ecology.

The All-Russian Society for the Preservation of Historical and Cultural Landmarks grew out of Rodina (Motherland), a youth club for aficionados of Russian art and buildings. Rodina was established in May 1964, on the suggestion of the indefatigable restorationist Petr Baranovskii, among students of the Mendeleyev Chemical Technology

Institute who had been working as volunteers at his Krutitskoye Residence restoration project. Mistrusted by officials because of its independence, Rodina expired in the early 1970s. But the All-Russian Society, generally known by the initials VOOPIK, thrived after its official founding by the RSFSR government in February 1966. Its Moscow branch had 650,000 members by 1978.[96]

Both the environmental and the landmarks societies worked under the gaze of party and municipal sentinels, and both had a generally inert rank and file. These constraints did not keep a resolute minority within and around them from figuring in an ecological politics that stirred in the late Brezhnev years and grew by leaps and bounds after 1985.

DISTRICTS WITHOUT COMMUNITY

As legislatures and mass organizations provided weak conduits to local government, the numbers and shapes of the raions gyrated. Two consolidations in Khrushchev's time took Moscow from twenty-five to twenty raions in September 1957 and to seventeen in August 1960. By contrast, under Brezhnev and Grishin the raions increased to thirty in November 1968 (counting the satellite town of Zelenograd),[97] to thirty-two in March 1977, and to thirty-three in October 1983, when Solntsevo, a town outside the Moscow Ring Highway, was annexed as Solntsevskii raion. Several more annexations between then and the end of 1985 extended five raions into the oblast without altering borders inside the MKAD. Maps 12 through 16 show the raions as of the redistrictings of 1957, 1960, 1968, 1977, and 1985.

Were the raions mere splotches on the page, or did they define politically relevant interests? Was there any objective basis for district identities and attachments?

By some criteria, late Soviet Moscow was remarkably homogeneous when held up against cities of its size in the West. This observation especially applies to ethnic origin, a potent generator of cleavage and conflict in many other places. A thumping 89.7 percent of Muscovites were Russians by nationality in the 1989 census. District-level data, available for the first time for that year (see Map 17), show a range of distribution of Russians across the thirty-three raions of only 8 percent, from a maximum of 93.3 percent in Zelenograd to a minimum of 85.6 in Sokol'nicheskii raion. Juxtaposition of the thirteen

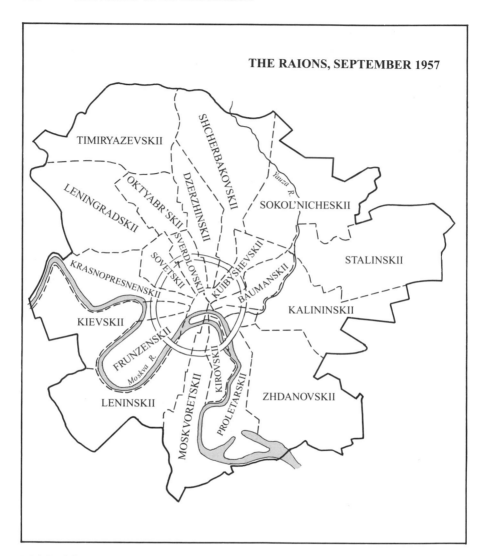

THE RAIONS, SEPTEMBER 1957

TIMIRYAZEVSKII

SHCHERBAKOVSKII

OKTYABR'SKII

DZERZHINSKII

LENINGRADSKII

Yauza R.

SOKOL'NICHESKII

SVERDLOVSKII

SOVETSKII

KRASNOPRESNENSKII

KUIBYSHEVSKII

STALINSKII

BAUMANSKII

KIEVSKII

KALININSKII

FRUNZENSKII

Moskva R.

KIROVSKII

LENINSKII

MOSKVORETSKII

PROLETARSKII

ZHDANOVSKII

MAP 12

raions jutting inside the Sadovoye kol'tso to the twenty outermost raions turns up but a slight difference—87.6 percent Russians in the inner raions, 90.2 percent in the outer.

The raions were far from being peas in a pod, however. They differed, most elementarily, in their blends of uses. The ratio of the number of persons gainfully employed in the raion to the number of

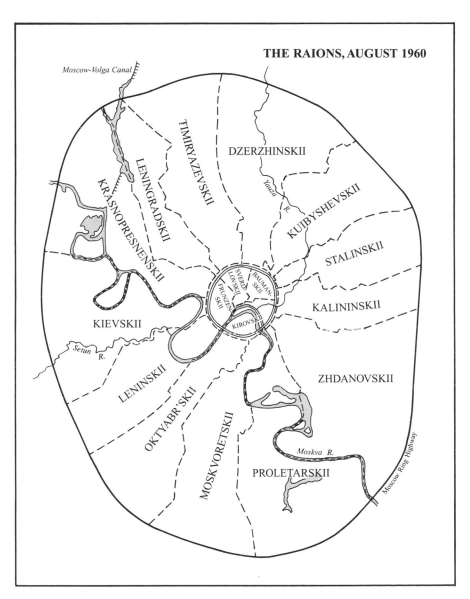

THE RAIONS, AUGUST 1960

Moscow-Volga Canal

TIMIRYAZEVSKII

DZERZHINSKII

Yauza R.

LENINGRADSKII

KRASNOPRESNENSKII

KUIBYSHEVSKII

STALINSKII

SVERD-LOVSKII

BAUMAN-SKII

FRUNZEN-SKII

KALININSKII

KIROVSKII

KIEVSKII

Setun R.

LENINSKII

ZHDANOVSKII

OKTYABR'SKII

MOSKVORETSKII

Moskva R.

Moscow Ring Highway

PROLETARSKII

MAP 13

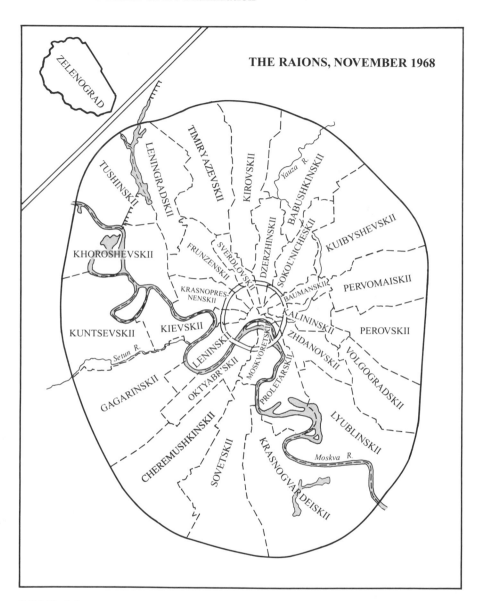

THE RAIONS, NOVEMBER 1968

ZELENOGRAD

TUSHINSKII

LENINGRADSKII

TIMIRYAZEVSKII

KIROVSKII

Yauza R.

BABUSHKINSKII

KUIBYSHEVSKII

KHOROSHEVSKII

FRUNZENSKII

SVERDLOVSKII

DZERZHINSKII

SOKOLNICHESKII

PERVOMAISKII

KRASNOPRES-
NENSKII

BAUMANSKII

KALININSKII

PEROVSKII

KUNTSEVSKII

KIEVSKII

Setun R.

LENINSKII

MOSKVORETSKII

ZHDANOVSKII

VOLGOGRADSKII

GAGARINSKII

OKTYABR'SKII

PROLETARSKII

LYUBLINSKII

CHEREMUSHKINSKII

SOVETSKII

KRASNOGVARDEISKII

Moskva R.

MAP 14

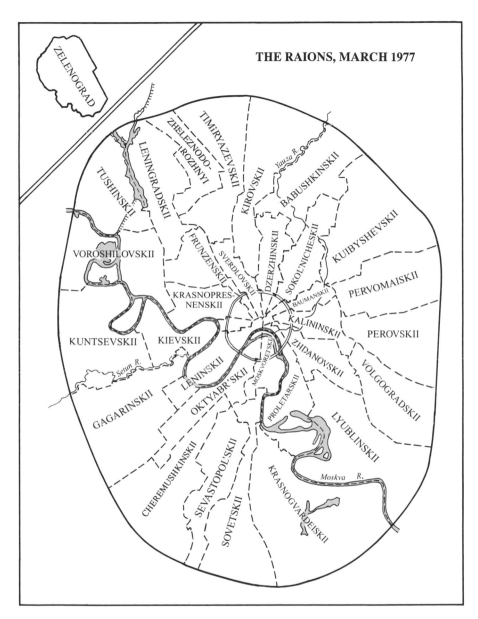

THE RAIONS, MARCH 1977

ZELENOGRAD

TIMIRYAZEVSKII
ZHELEZNODO-
ROZHNYI
LENINGRADSKII
TUSHINSKII
KIROVSKII
BABUSHKINSKII
Yauza R.
KUIBYSHEVSKII
FRUNZENSKII
SVERDLOVSKII
DZERZHINSKII
SOKOL'NICHESKII
VOROSHILOVSKII
PERVOMAISKII
KRASNOPRES-
NENSKII
BAUMANSKII
KALININSKII
PEROVSKII
KUNTSEVSKII
KIEVSKII
Setun R.
ZHDANOVSKII
LENINSKII
MOSKVORETSKII
VOLGOGRADSKII
OKTYABR'SKII
GAGARINSKII
PROLETARSKII
LYUBLINSKII
CHEREMUSHKINSKII
Moskva R.
SEVASTOPOL'SKII
SOVETSKII
KRASNOGVARDEISKII

MAP 15

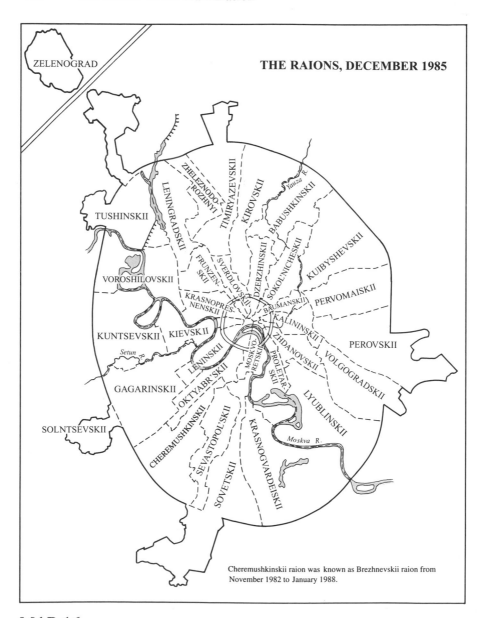

THE RAIONS, DECEMBER 1985

ZELENOGRAD

TUSHINSKII

LENINGRADSKII

ZHELEZNODO-ROZHNYI

TIMIRYAZEVSKII

KIROVSKII

BABUSHKINSKII

Yauza R.

KUIBYSHEVSKII

VOROSHILOVSKII

FRUNZEN-SKII

SVERDLOVSKII

DZERZHINSKII

SOKOL'NICHESKII

PERVOMAISKII

KRASNOPRES-NENSKII

BAUMANSKII

KALININSKII

KUNTSEVSKII

KIEVSKII

LENINSKII

MOSKVO-RETSKII

ZHDANOVSKII

VOLGOGRADSKII

PEROVSKII

Setun R.

GAGARINSKII

OKTYABR'SKII

PROLETAR-SKII

LYUBLINSKII

SOLNTSEVSKII

CHEREMUSHKINSKII

SEVASTOPOL'SKII

SOVETSKII

KRASNOGVARDEISKII

Moskva R.

Cheremushkinskii raion was known as Brezhnevskii raion from
November 1982 to January 1988.

MAP 16

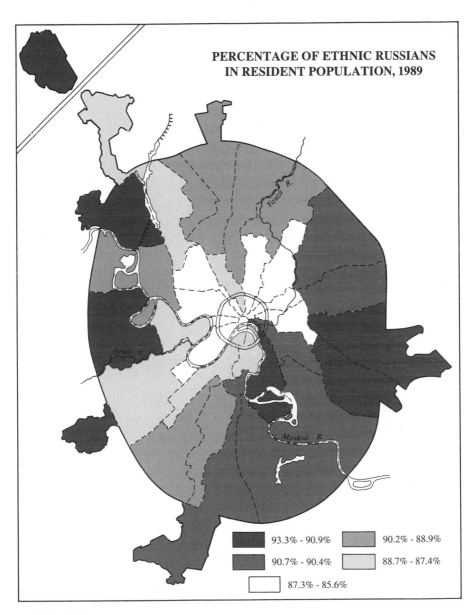

PERCENTAGE OF ETHNIC RUSSIANS
IN RESIDENT POPULATION, 1989

93.3% - 90.9%   90.2% - 88.9%

90.7% - 90.4%   88.7% - 87.4%

87.3% - 85.6%

MAP 17

persons housed there is a useful index of the balance of work and residential activities (see Map 18, again for 1989). The Moscow mean (weighted) was 0.54, or 54 workers per 100 residents, but there was great fluctuation. The ratio went as high as 2.08 for Baumanskii raion, where in-commuting meant that workers by day far outnumbered residents by night, and as low as 0.19 for Krasnogvardeiskii, a dormitory raion with very little employment.

The jobs-to-beds ratio roughly correlated with geographic centrality. The thirteen interior raions had, on average, 145,300 residents and 191,000 employees in 1989, 1.31 workers per resident, and contained 51.5 percent of all employment in the Moscow economy yet only 21.2 percent of the population. A typical exterior raion had 350,200 residents and 116,700 employees, thus only 0.33 workers for every resident. Within the inner and outer zones, sectoral differences were also apparent. Spurs of employment extended northeast, south-southeast, southwest, and northwest from the Kremlin, the wedges between being more residential in character.

Look next at Map 19, displaying the social class makeup of the raions, as measured (absent occupational and income data) by possession of a higher education. The Muscovite with a college-type diploma was likely to be in white-collar employment and to share some of the characteristics of the urban middle class in a Western society. The variance here, markedly less than on the previous indicator, registers much greater than on ethnicity. Leninskii raion had the top score, with 39.7 percent of inhabitants (aged ten or older) in the "middle class"; Lyublinskii had the lowest, 15.2 percent. The weighted average was 31.2 percent for the central raions and 23.3 percent for the peripheral raions.

Simultaneous plotting of the foregoing and other indicators would allow us to draw composite social portraits of the raions. But that would take us far afield.[98] Social and economic indexes predict political behavior on condition that (1) the interests they mark out are internalized by those concerned, and (2) some action mechanism links them to the world of power. By both these standards, the raions of Moscow fell far short.

In the first place, they far exceeded the intimate size that might have qualified them as minicommunities within an anonymous metropolis. They were nothing like neighborhoods, for their mean area

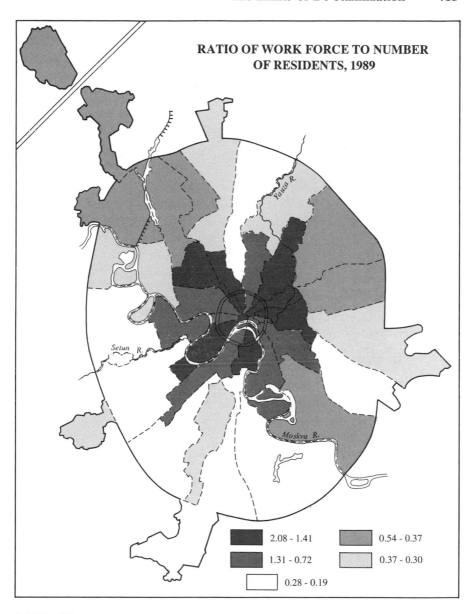

RATIO OF WORK FORCE TO NUMBER
OF RESIDENTS, 1989

2.08 - 1.41		0.54 - 0.37
1.31 - 0.72		0.37 - 0.30
0.28 - 0.19		

MAP 18

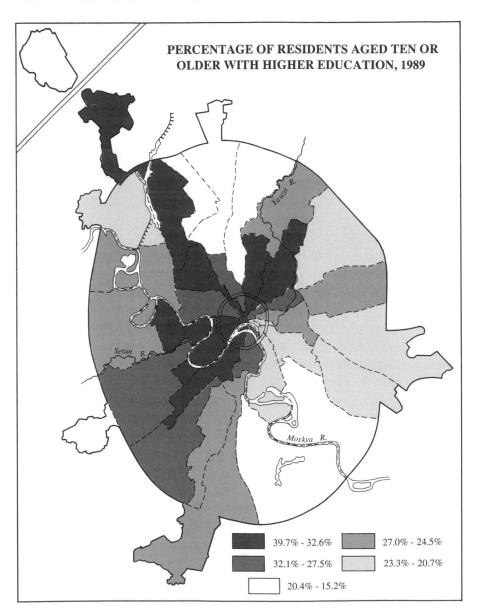

PERCENTAGE OF RESIDENTS AGED TEN OR OLDER WITH HIGHER EDUCATION, 1989

Yauza R.

Setun R.

Moskva R.

39.7% - 32.6%   27.0% - 24.5%

32.1% - 27.5%   23.3% - 20.7%

20.4% - 15.2%

MAP 19

in 1985 was thirty-two square kilometers and their mean population about 260,000 (from a high of 380,000 in the mid-1960s and a low of 190,000 in the late 1950s).

Nor did the periodic gerrymanderings give the raions any permanence. The primary criterion for boundaries remained "equal distribution of the party and proletarian strata," as it was termed in the 1920s. By this rule of thumb, numbers of working Communist Party members were symmetrized to standardize the supervisory load of the raion party committees and to ensure that no raion was the preserve of a single social stratum. Least of all were white-collar families and intellectuals in the central precincts to be set off from blue-collar workers. In a confidential speech in 1968 First Secretary Grishin gave the need for "correct socialization" as the best reason for shifting from four self-contained raions within the Sadovoye, in place since 1960, to the thirteen sloppily drawn wedges, each backing up into mainly working-class areas, that lasted through the 1980s.[99]

The effect of constituting raions out of organically unrelated subareas was to be commented on by an irate Moscophile, Irina Strelkova, in 1990:

> The capital has been skinned alive. Its integral, historically established parts have been chopped up and incompatible, alien patches forced together. Behind this has been a leveling idea—that Moscow should not have raions in which a majority are workers and raions where intelligentsia or office personnel predominate. If you were now to show a Muscovite from the olden days the narrow slices into which the city has been carved, he would hold his head in horror. How could you possibly unite in one Krasnopresnenskii raion the Nikitskiye Gates and Khoroshevskoye shosse? And put Teatral'naya ploshchad' into Sverdlovskii [raion] with out-of-town Petrovsko-Razumovskoye? And what do the Arbat and Fili have in common that would relate them to Kievskii raion, which has been named after a train station [the Kiev Station, named in turn after the Ukrainian city of Kiev]? Of course, the old Muscovite would suspect, and not inaccurately, that the lack of common interests among the residents of individual raions was deliberate—to rule out any [political] joining up. Cut into strips and de-Moscowized [*razmoskovlennaya*], Moscow is unable to offer resistance to the center.[100]

The very appellations of the raions were "de-Moscowized." Several were applied in succession to different quadrants of the city, as can be seen from the maps. Only eight of thirty-two raions in 1980 bore the historic designation of a locality, such as Presnya or Sokol'niki; the rest recognized political notables, events, or other cities of the USSR.[101]

Institutional factors as well contributed to the incapacity of the raions. Soviet Moscow was not the crazy quilt of municipalities that most American metropolitan areas have been. It was not even a federation of boroughs like Metropolitan Toronto or the Greater London Council. It was a unitary city with spatial subdivisions whose governments were sorely limited in authority and resources. Inter-raion differences were at root the product of state policies that rationed scarce goods like land and housing, and the policies that counted were made above, not by the raions.

The raions' subservience stood out at every turn. All their legislation was subject to review and emendation at city hall and, informally, by the party organs. They did not have their own land use plans. Their annual and five-year economic plans were articles in the city plan, and their budgets in the "consolidated" city budget, with raion tax rates affixed arbitrarily and variedly by the city finance department so as to balance its books. So tightly were purse strings held, one raion chairman groused in the 1980s, that he needed the city's permission to install a lavatory.[102]

City-raion relations tended to be bilateral and program-specific. Raion officials ran themselves ragged importuning city agencies— keyed to meeting Moscow-wide plan targets—into doing right by their districts. Neither time nor incentives encouraged inter-raion cooperation or attention to broader issues.

Within the raion subbureaucracies, departments remained in "dual subordination" to city-level departments. Promotion-bound officials used raion staff openings, posted citywide, as waystations. Functionaries in the ispolkom (or party committee) of one Moscow raion often resided in another.[103]

There was a riffle of interest among raion leaders in beefing up their powers in the late 1950s and early 1960s and some byplay on the issue in the press. These protestations went unanswered. Had an engaged citizenry wanted the raions to have more say, some degree of decentralization might have come off. But no such citizenry existed in socialist Moscow; even if it had, it most likely would not have made the raions its home. There was no such thing as a raion newspaper or electors' club. Raion institutions were as remote from the mass public as their city superiors.

INFORMATION SHORT CIRCUITS

Citizens cannot participate in politics effectively without substantial information about issues and processes, crossnational studies show. Here again de-Stalinization did not go far enough to sustain a robust urban politics.

This is not to deny that the slackening of censorship had an unclotting effect on the local media. The Moscow press gave signs of greater frankness, a nose for social questions, and an openness to outside commentators. In essays about air pollution in *Moskovskaya pravda* (Moscow Truth) in 1955, public health physicians wrote of industrial negligence in an acerbic tone not heard on such matters since the early 1930s. In a series on metropolitan transport in the monthly *Gorodskoye khozyaistvo Moskvy* in 1955–1956, authors disagreed on solutions. In 1958 residents could read judgmental stories on overcrowding and shoddy service on the Moscow subway, a sacred cow. An article on the raion soviets invited discussion of their plight and quoted the Russian proverb, "Truth is born in argumentation" *(Istina rozhdayetsya v sporakh).*[104]

In the scholarly realm publication of a textbook about Moscow by geographer Yulian G. Saushkin in 1955 signified the resumption of reputable research on the region. Historians and memoirists took up 1917, the Civil War, and World War II in Moscow. The 1959 national census gave Moscow its first hard population data in twenty years. Statistical handbooks, with economic and social policy as well as demographic indicators, made a comeback the year before.[105] Local political discourse also profited from the resumption of contacts with, and scholarship on, foreign cities.

If all these developments registered on the credit side of the ledger, a blowup in 1962 underscored the debit side. The March issue of the literary magazine *Moskva* ran a devastating critique of Moscow planning titled "How Now to Build Moscow?" written by Petr P. Revyakin, a professor at the Moscow Architectural Institute (the staid descendant of the avant-garde VKhUTEMAS), and three collaborators (a painter, an engineer, and a writer). *Moskva* wanted the article, a sequel to a roundtable with planners, to launch "a broad dialogue." It got the opposite. *Pravda,* the oracle of the Central Committee, released a full-page rebuttal, "Against Harmful Confusion on Problems of City Planning," signed by twenty-one members of the city's Chief Architectural Planning Directorate (GlavAPU), as the town planning office under Posokhin was now called. The dialogue ended before it began.[106]

Why the fuss? Revyakin and his coauthors recited a laundry list of planning errors fuller than any aired in the official media in a generation. Moscow, they said, was growing without guidance and was clogged with office blocks, smoke-vomiting factories, and traffic. They wrote with sorrow about the old center of Moscow, tying its fate to the 1935 master plan and to postulates of urban policy under and since Stalin. The Sukharev Tower, the Red Gates, the Cathedral of Christ the Redeemer, the shade trees on the Sadovoye—their annihilation had "imposed equal losses on the historical, national appearance of Moscow and on the live, daily interests and needs of Muscovites." The identical "fear of diversity," they charged, lay behind the "oppressive monotony" of the housing estates built up since 1953.

Nikita Khrushchev is said to have approved the *Pravda* riposte, and why not? Whatever his qualms about Stalinism, he was Kaganovich's deputy when the 1935 plan was drawn up and Moscow first secretary when implementation began. And he had given the order on five-story construction, which the *Moskva* treatise compared to the "dogmatic directives" on heights of 1935.

Revyakin and company queried in a more general vein the fashion in which city-shaping decisions had been and still were made. Planners and officials had dealt with Moscow's townscape as if they owned it. Intimations that they would clue in the public by regular reports had died on the vine:

> We have seen nothing of such accounts. And yet without them we cannot even approximate a science of urban planning, to say nothing of the Leninist norms about the answerability of the executive committees of the soviets and their departments and directorates to the population . . .
>
> Scientific planning demands more than anything wide publication of statistics in the press—ours and the foreign press—and the comparison of costs to the planning results achieved, in a word, analysis of the facts

and of practice. Without this there can be no guarantee that in future we will build on positive experience or that we will not repeat the mistakes of the past . . .

We are for renunciation of subjectivity and shallow empiricism in planning, of planning "by eye," of the settling of city planning questions by will of this or that leader . . . It is no longer tolerable that the Master Plan of Moscow, which decisively affects every Muscovite, is "kept secret" [*zasekrechen*] from the inhabitants of the capital. We must put an end to a situation where Muscovites see only "accomplished facts," where the magical tenet "This Has Already Been Decided" is king. This was used to suppress all opinions about "settled" questions, to eliminate any criticism that would transgress upon the "personal" decision of Stalin or of Moscow's "guardian," Kaganovich.

Pravda quarreled with the conclusions of the Revyakin group about historical preservation and other specifics. Of more moment, it impugned their motives to "scandalous irresponsibility, professional ignorance, and malice." With the approbation of the party apparatus, it put officials on record as having "categorically objected" to releasing the article in the first place and advised editors in the future to bear in mind their didactic function.

The broadside reduced dissenters from the mainstream of planning and development policy to "graveyard-like silence."[107] Nothing would rate with "How Now to Build Moscow?" until after 1985.

Political controls and inhibitions short-circuited information flows in post-Stalin Moscow. Writers could take issue with policy in bits and increments; they could not get away with holistic questioning of its thrust, of the subsoil of values beneath it, or of the integrity of political executives. Most of the time, without state censors having to step in, an "internal censor" showed journalists and editors the limits of the permissible.[108]

When they occasionally tested the boundaries, they tended to do so in publications not under the auspices of the Moscow partocrats. *Moskva* was an organ of the RSFSR Union of Writers. *Literaturnaya gazeta* (Literary Gazette), the weekly of the USSR Union of Writers, carried some of the most penetrating comments on Moscow community issues in the 1960s and 1970s. The Union of Architects' monthly *Arkhitektura SSSR* (Architecture of the USSR) was far more eloquent about Moscow than the analogous local journal. The same could be said of the Central Committee's *Sovetskaya kul'tura* (Soviet Culture), founded in 1974, which took a shine to urban conservation in Moscow, and of *Molodaya gvardiya* (Young Guard), a Komsomol magazine that weighed in on the same issue. *Arkhitektura* (Architecture), the Sunday supplement of *Stroitel'naya gazeta* (Construction Gazette), also did excellent features on Moscow, especially after 1975.

Moskovskaya pravda, the four-page morning newspaper of the gorkom and city soviet (1978 daily printing 450,000 copies), handled most local issues superficially. The evening *Vechernyaya Moskva* (press run 600,000) was of lower quality still, scanned mostly for television and theater notices.[109] A survey done for the gorkom in 1975, and never released, found that 56 percent of working Muscovites and 80 percent of college students were tuning in to Western radio stations. About Moscow radio and television, the researcher noted: "We all know that not infrequently they are boring in content and gray in form." Boris Yeltsin, again, spoke for many when he said the Moscow press "puts out few major analytical materials about the city's main problems or the activities of the party organizations or their leaders. Articles often do not reflect the real state of affairs."[110]

Perseverance of what Yeltsin branded "forbidden zones" crippled the Moscow media. With intraparty politics off limits, Muscovites had no information on the comings and goings and the likes and dislikes of their rulers. Principled conflict among them was rarely if ever disclosed.[111] Their privileges remained a closed book: the names of the Fourth Chief Directorate of the Ministry of Health, the Second Special Directorate of the Moscow Ispolkom, the purveyor of privileges to the local elite, or the Ninth Directorate of the KGB never graced a public document. Many of Soviet Moscow's founding fathers—Kamenev and the Right Oppositionists around Uglanov, most piquantly—were not exonerated during the Khrushchev thaw, and so, like Khrushchev himself after 1964, were stuck in an Orwellian memory hole.

The party kept other dirty linen under wraps. As discussed below, the secrecy blanket was almost as thick over the defense industry, the plum of Moscow's economy, and all aspects of metropolitan planning that could be related to national security. The Mossovet, though more communicative than bodies in these fields, revealed little about its executive organs and budgets. Much of the statistical information about social conditions used in this book was not released until the arrival of Gorbachev and Yeltsin. Yearbooks provided only selective data; the most common sophistry was the use of index numbers expressing an indicator as a multiple of a base year's value not itself given.

Moscow after Stalin was a city without disasters, as subway and construction mishaps, fires, and infectious disease went unrecorded and the mass media were barred from official inquiries made, depending on seriousness, by either municipal or party committees. When a five-story building collapsed in 1969 because of a karst produced by the working of underground water on soluble limestones, there was a news blackout and information was spoonfed to "an extremely limited circle of specialists"; when several more apartment houses fell down without word in the press in 1977, "disorientation and panic" spread in the area of the sinkholes.[112]

Moscow had no city directory or comprehensive telephone book, a subject a *Moskovskaya pravda* correspondent, Lev Kolodnyi, at last raised in 1987: "The blows at openness [under Stalin] were so strong that, regardless of the half-century that has passed, contemporary reference guides in no way approach in informativeness *Vsya Moskva*," the directory last published in 1936. "No one has yet lifted the taboo laid in 1937 on many of the best-known institutions," local and central, whose telephones and addresses remained unlisted. He cited the Ministry of Defense's office block on ulitsa Frunze in the Arbat, anonymous even though plaques on its walls commemorated generals and admirals who had worked there.[113]

Kolodnyi went on to discuss the most ignoble denial of all—of maps, which had an honored place in Moscow since Ivan Michurin's survey of the 1730s:

In 1937 . . . we stopped printing to-scale maps [of Moscow] . . . Why did this happen, who was bothered by [real maps]? . . . It was the same people who saw enemies of the people and saboteurs around every corner, who supposed that to stop publishing accurate maps of Moscow would mislead foreign intelligence services . . . Now, in place of maps to scale, "schematic plans" are put out . . . provisional charts full of omissions and distortions whose sense is impossible to comprehend. Not one of their big pages shows the network of Arbat alleys, which tourists need to know, or most of Moscow's other streets and lanes. Whom do they think they are kidding with such schemes? . . . Space-based reconnaissance is now capable not only of making out the exact web of streets and lanes but of detecting the vehicles driving along them. If anybody is being confused by these "schematic plans," it is the people and guests of Moscow.

The Chief Directorate of Surveying and Cartography of the USSR, swallowed by the NKVD in 1937, was transferred to civilian control after 1953, but it remained morbidly secretive and handcuffed to the police and the military. Planners and other municipal staff needed a security clearance *(dopusk)* to see the true maps stored in KGB-manned "second departments" within city agencies. Drivers in the Central Committee's car pool could not take accurate street maps on their rounds and thus had to scribble directions in the dispatcher's room. Diagrams of subway tunnels and all underground utilities were classified at one of the highest grades. If there was rational reason to safeguard bomb shelters and nuclear command posts, the proscription's global nature bore all the markings of Stalin's neurosis about espionage.[114]

Impenetrable security swaddled the below-ground facilities in the downtown area and the connected bunker system and shadow subway system for the safety of the leadership during wartime or civil unrest, known as Metro-2. Metro-2 took up where Stalin's half-built line to Kuntsevo left off. Democratic politicians with access to the data after the termination of Communist Party rule estimate it was as much as *one-third* the size of the public subway. They and other sources have described its main components as: a warren of bunkers and passageways beneath the Kremlin, Lubyanka, Central Committee, and other buildings out to the Bul'varnoye kol'tso; a deep line from there southwest, under the Moskva River (traversed above ground by a bridge for the regular subway) to the Lenin Hills; hilltop installations around the government villas; a much larger underground complex linked to the Lenin Hills, probably several kilometers square, in the area bounded by the Ramenki housing district and the prospekt Vernadskogo and Yugo-Zapadnaya subway stops; and a line from that shelter to Vnukovo Airport.[115]

For years there were rumors about Metro-2, which one or two

intrepid reporters tried to confirm. "Nothing came out. All sources of information were blockaded, and journalists who got anywhere close to this business were regularly threatened with trial for disclosure of a state secret."[116]

THE PARTY SOLDIERS ON

The last word in city politics, no different than in Stalin's time, lay with the territorial organs of the Communist Party. Aside from the 1956 severance of the gorkom from the obkom, they maintained a stable structure. Their backbone remained the apparatus of salaried party workers, who grew but modestly in number. The gorkom had 206 "responsible" officials (and 55 technical staff) in May 1956, right after the divorce from the obkom, 25 responsible workers fewer than in 1948, when the obkom still had some role in Moscow city. This total rose slowly to 222 responsible officials (and 60 support personnel) after the 1960 annexation, 254 and 72 in 1968, and 347 responsible officials in the mid-1980s. Raion party functionaries came to 973 responsible workers (and 452 technical) after the 1960 annexation, 1,068 and 509 in 1968, and about 1,250 responsible officials in the 1980s. The apparatchiks, never much over two thousand strong, constituted for most purposes "the party" in urban politics.[117]

The city party secretariat, comprising the gorkom secretaries only, was a relatively inconsequential body. It convened eight or nine times a year in the 1970s and, as it had since the 1930s, considered chiefly matters of internal party organization.

The authoritative cabinet of the local subsystem was still the bureau of the city party committee, dominated by party secretaries but seating a minority of officials working outside the party apparatus (see Table B-3). Members met in the bureau's fifth-floor conference room at 6 Staraya ploshchad' weekly in the 1970s, half as often as in the early 1950s but with about the same frequency as the presidium and ispolkom of the city soviet combined.[118] Congruent with party interests, the bureau had a far more catholic agenda than the municipal executive. Besides formal representation, it drew with regularity on the informal advice of outsiders. Thus, although the local KGB chief was not a member of the bureau until the mid-1970s, protocols in the party archive show him or his deputy sitting in on almost one-third of all bureau meetings in the late 1960s as an invited guest.

Organizational experimentation in the apparatus occurred mostly under Khrushchev, and to little lasting effect. His most controversial shakeup, the 1962 bifurcation of regional committees into industrial and farm wings, spared Moscow. Unpaid volunteers were briefly favored in party units, as in the soviets, only to be disavowed after 1964. Sixteen subraion party committees *(podraikomy)* were formed for localities within the newly annexed territories in 1961, to facilitate economic and residential development there. The party disbanded ten of these in 1963 and the rest in December 1968, when new raions were demarcated. In September 1963, during a campaign to step up involvement in the economy, the gorkom tacked five "production branch committees" (for communications, cargo transport, mass transit, trade, and construction) onto its existing departments. These, too, went by the boards in 1968.[119]

The party kept its ace in the hole, control over personnel. The reach of nomenklatura shortened after Stalin, as the positions confirmed by the Moscow party organs fell from about 37,000 in 1950 to 22,000 in 1956 and 17,000 in 1958. By 1960 the combined local nomenklaturas had crept back up to 22,526 (1,431 for the gorkom and 21,095 for the raikoms). The gorkom's total had grown to 2,005 in 1972, the last year for which a figure can be retrieved from the archive. Raikom nomenklaturas stabilized after 1960, coming to 22,991 offices in 1970 and 21,127 in 1980. The combined nomenklatura for the city and raion committees in 1980 would have been 23,000 to 24,000 positions—35 or 40 percent less than in the late Stalin era, but prodigious nonetheless.[120]

The 2,005 positions in the gorkom's 1972 nomenklatura are broken down in Table 7, following CPSU procedure, by department of the apparatus exercising supervision. The largest set, one-third of the total, performed "organizational and party work," an expansive category covering the ispolkoms of the local soviets as well as the trade unions, Komsomol, and People's Control inspectorates. Branches of manufacturing and transport comprised 26.9 percent of all positions confirmed, followed by 17.1 percent in socialization, cultural, and research pursuits, 9.0 percent in administrative organs (the KGB, regular police, and courts), 8.8 percent in construction (a small fraction in the municipal category in 1950), 3.3 percent in trade and services, and 1.7 percent in planning and finance.

Table 7. Positions in the nomenklatura of the Moscow gorkom, 1972, by department supervising the administrative area

Gorkom department	Positions confirmed	
	Number	Percent
Organizational and Party Work	662	33.0
Of which in apparatus of gorkom and raikoms	469	23.4
Of which in executive committees of city and raion soviets	103	5.1
Heavy Industry and Machine Building	163	8.1
Defense Industry	210	10.5
Light and Food Industry	75	3.7
Construction and Building Materials	177	8.8
Transport and Communications	92	4.5
Municipal Services	19	0.9
Trade and Consumer Services	48	2.4
Planning and Financial Organs	35	1.7
Science and Higher Education	222	11.1
Culture	56	2.8
Schools	8	0.4
Propaganda and Agitation	57	2.8
Administrative Organs	181	9.0
Of which in KGB	48	2.4
Total	2,005	100.0

Source: Tsentral'nyi gosudarstvennyi arkhiv obshchestvennykh dvizhenii Moskvy (Central State Archive of Social Movements of Moscow), f. 4, op. 175, d. 17, ll. 12, 34–71.

The party machine retained the branch architecture sanctified in 1948 (see Appendix B). Gorkom departments, after dwindling a bit under Khrushchev, were back up to nineteen by Brezhnev's death, almost as many as right after the war; twelve handled discrete economic sectors. The gorkom's six secretaries likewise had highly particular duties, economic and noneconomic.[121] Raikom structure, for the most part uniform, showed some variation by economic character of the district.[122]

The apparatchiks had more by way of formal schooling than ever before, Grishin's trade-school past to the contrary. The elite fraction with a higher education went from 63 percent in the period 1953–1964 to more than 80 percent in the years 1964–1985, almost 10 percent higher than municipal executives (see Table C-1). Fifty-three percent of the partocrats, 4 percent more than the municipal officials, had an engineering diploma. Fewer than 20 percent had any party leadership experience outside the Moscow apparatus, and less than 10 percent had served in the central government (see Table C-2).

Party leadership mixed the styles of the personalistic boss and the ambidextrous fixer, both found in Stalin's day, with the consultative technocrat celebrated in the Brezhnev period. In the first mode, a city first secretary could still make peremptory decisions in the way of the satrap of the 1930s. A movie house was designed into Novyye Cheremushki's Ninth Experimental Block because First Secretary Furtseva made up her mind during a tour of the area in 1957 that she liked it more than the parking garage already being built. The garage walls were torn down and blueprints for a cinema rushed through within a month.[123]

Grishin, to rid Moscow of pickpockets and thieves before the 1980 Olympics, instructed judges to slap minimum two-year sentences on all convicted of street crimes. He also directed Chairman Promyslov to purchase forty Mercedes limousines with hard currency to ferry VIPs around during the games; most of the vehicles were later presented to party and police officials, including Interior Minister Nikolai A. Shchelokov, as gifts. Anxious for the Severnoye Chertanovo model project to be finished by opening day, he excised several difficult objects from the site plan, including recreation places, a hotel, and what would have been the USSR's biggest poured-concrete building, thirty stories of apartments and service halls. Contradicting himself, he set back Chertanovo's progress by diverting manpower to the Olympic equestrian track in the same district.[124]

While cruising by in his limousine, so it was said after his retirement, Grishin resolved that the partially built headquarters of the TASS news agency at Nikitskiye Gates should be lowered by four stories from the approved design. When the architect remonstrated, Grishin dismissed him. While Grishin temporarily thought well of Taganka Theater, he granted its long-pending application to build a new hall. "Everyone who followed it knew that Grishin felt kindly toward [Director] Lyubimov. Excellent conditions were created for the authors of the design in their institute. First-class builders were sent to the project. All permits and sign-offs were issued without the tiniest delay." When Grishin soured on the theater in 1976, construction slowed to a crawl; Lyubimov went into exile in the West in 1984.[125]

Old-style bossism, especially at its apex, did not keep the apparatus from imbibing in "scientific" procedures after 1964. In 1966 the gorkom instituted a small sociology faculty within its school for propagandists (University of Marxism-Leninism); it did opinion polls and prepared reports on time budgets and transport problems. All the raikoms acquired survey research groups in the late 1970s. Advisory boards ancillary to *(pri)* the gorkom proliferated. The Arkhplan of the 1930s, which dealt with town planning issues on behalf of both the gorkom and the city soviet, was reborn as a Commission on City Planning, attached to the gorkom alone, under Yegorychev in 1964. Grishin dismantled it in 1967, only to set up a dozen other commissions, councils, and seminars, beginning in 1969 (see Table 8). They banded together party workers, nonparty officials, and academics to further a stated objective, which could be as narrow as introducing robotics into factories or as broad-gauged as "socioeconomic development" of Moscow.

The contribution of these panels is questionable. Grishin summoned the Commission on Socioeconomic Development, which he chaired, to act as a sounding board and also "an active instrument for practical attainment of the plans worked out."[126] It did not do much of either. It, its several sections, and its fellow commissions met infrequently, passed the odd desultory resolution, and left consummation entirely to the mainline apparatus. Most were dropped days after Grishin's retirement.

Apparatchiks still operated most of the time as economic prefects, keeping the command economy on keel. If Moscow was on the cutting edge in any field, it was technical progress, as an administrative substitute for market competition. Between 1967 and 1972, the gorkom hooked up with central planners and ministries to devise a "composite plan," bristling with deadlines and quotas, for modernizing the manufacture of machine tools, instruments, and other industrial goods in Moscow and the oblast in the 1970s. It worked out a similar scheme secretly with the military-related Ministry of the Radio Industry in 1968, for radar, radio, and television plants up to 1980, and for two other defense branches, shipbuilding and electronics, in

Table 8. Advisory committees of the gorkom, 1969–1985

Year established	Committee
1969	Standing Seminar of Directors of Industrial Enterprises
1973	Council of Rectors of Higher Educational Institutions
1974	Council of Directors of Vocational Schools
1976	Commission on the Socioeconomic Development of Moscow. Sections: Health and Child Care; Development of City Services; Problems of Population and Labor Resources; Industry and Transport; Education, Vocational Orientation, and Upbringing of Children and Youth
1976	Public Council on Problems of Efficiency and Quality of Industrial Production
1980	Coordinating Council for Working out an Integrated Program for Heightening Labor Efficiency and Economizing on Labor
1980	Scientific-Methodological Council on Problems of Creating and Installing Industrial Robots
1980	Commission on Transport
1981	Council on Coordination of the Social Sciences and their Relation to the Development of Moscow (with the Council of Rectors and the RSFSR Ministry of Higher Education)
1981	Commission on Development of the Production of Consumer Goods
1982	Commission on Fulfillment of the CPSU Food Program
1984	Commission on Carrying out the Economic Experiment in Moscow Industry[a]

a. The reference is to the experiment in streamlined management in several branches of industry adopted by the Soviet leadership in 1983.

1970. It completed plans for civilian machinery and consumer goods in 1980.[127]

At factory level, the Moscow apparatus attempted to answer technological lag by cultivating ties with research organizations. Six raikoms in the city center and southwest (later seven) originated departments of science and education and advisory councils on innovation in 1968. They and the gorkom induced institutes and factories to transact elaborate "contracts" to cooperate in the quest for new technology. There were 800 such nannying pacts in Moscow by 1976, and Brezhnev commended the program.

Very little of this activity could lay claim to novelty in objective or method. One sees, for instance, bureaus and officials publicizing production targets; punishing directors for not meeting quotas; fine tuning planning and building estimates; dispatching party members to urgent tasks; rationing industrial inputs; and participating in ministerial decisions on plant modernization. A breakdown or slowdown might be met with appointment of an "operational group" to clear things up on the spot. Every June, year in and year out, the gorkom bureau adopted a voluminous resolution on shipping and distributing the autumn harvest. For potatoes and the five staple vegetables (cabbages, carrots, beets, onions, and cucumbers), it fixed summary tonnage targets for all raions, setting down the source, mode of delivery, and time schedule (grafik) for each crop, the storage space to be built, the number of workers to be allocated to the loading, and the trucks and drivers to be borrowed from urban enterprises.[128]

None of this would have been out of place in the high Stalin era. Much of it involved compulsion or the threat of it, as did the nurturing of technical advance. "There was a strict hierarchy of subordination within the apparatus," said Yurii A. Prokof'ev, the last CPSU first secretary of Moscow, in looking back at Grishin's apparatus, in which he worked from 1968 to 1985. "We occupied ourselves with everything: from putting up vegetables and potatoes for storage to organizing recreational zones."[129]

The party prefects, in short, made do with the old tool kit. With the onset of stringency in the Soviet economy during the Tenth Five-Year Plan (1976–1980), they made clear their increasing reliance on the old way and its more unrefined devices, such as interference in supply procurement.

"Life itself," one raikom secretary said of his apparatus in 1979, "seems to be forcing it to assume administrative functions." Factory directors were "more rarely seeking out planning and managerial methods" of dealing with emergencies and were "dashing for help to the raikom." A secretary from another district commiserated: when enterprises flounder, their leaders "beseech the raikom to support their requests to superior organizations to reduce their plan." Party workers were intruding more into micromanagement: "pipes, reservoirs, cables . . . changes in blueprints and estimates, the laying of utilities, preparation of the front of work . . . working out mutually supportive relations [with other firms] . . . overcoming departmental barriers."[130]

BIG BROTHER AND THE WEAK SISTERS

The party organs did find time on this merry-go-round for social and municipal questions. Their appetite was likely greater than in the past, as many more of their officials, almost one-third of the Moscow party elite from 1964 to 1985, had career experience in local government (see Table C-2). The CPSU apparatus felt ceaseless pressure from above to intervene, since many urban agencies were large economic units with plans on whose fulfillment they had to report. All six gorkom secretaries and just under half of the gorkom's departments supervised the local soviets as producers.[131] The party organs also came under pressure from below. Almost 50 percent of the mail of some raikoms in the 1970s concerned peeves about housing repairs and queuing for flats—enough to spur hundreds of phone calls and letters from party workers on citizens' behalf.

Party and municipal executive bodies continued to interlock (with the gorkom first secretary and several party colleagues on the ispolkom and the chairman of the ispolkom on the gorkom bureau)[132] and to pass joint resolutions. The party bureau still cleared all agendas of the city ispolkom and spoke directly to the soviet through the party group within it, which assembled—an insulting thirty minutes before the plenary—to receive guidance. Gorkom and raikoms routinely organized field headquarters *(shtaby)* and appointed emissaries *(upolnomochennyye)* to expedite construction projects.

"The bureau of the gorkom," a member of it said in 1986, "has not ensured a precise demarcation of functions with the ispolkom of the Mossovet." Over half of the questions discussed in the bureau "are in the competence of the city soviet."[133] To construe it this way might overdraw the chances of boundaries being worked out under conditions of one-party rule. The soviet and the party committees and bureaus were related not so much by division of labor as by hierarchical subordination. The gorkom bureau still "assigned" municipal boards and officials to do its dirty work, as if electoral and accountability mechanisms were not worth a fig. Confidential minutes of the ispolkom and presidium leave no doubt that, while city hall might seek to soften decisions from Staraya ploshchad', in the final analysis it did as it was told.[134]

It does not follow that all incursions were unwelcome. Party workers could be of use to the weak sisters in the soviets. Often with a nudge from municipal bureaucrats, they jawboned central agencies and nationally controlled firms into expending labor or materials, usually of the "above plan" variety, on amelioration of a local sore spot—tarring of a dusty street, say, or completion of construction of a school, a grocery store, or a soccer field.

Grishin, in a postretirement interview, gave a superb example, on the unfading problem of food supply:

> Think about the food problem. Everyone, including me, was involved with that one. We had to help. There would not be enough meat in Moscow, and we in the gorkom could see that the Mossovet couldn't decide anything. So I would pick up the phone and ring up [Prime Minister] Kosygin and tell him, "Things are thus and thus, you must help us." And meat would be purchased abroad, mostly in Argentina. Or Gorky and Penza oblasts were supposed to supply Moscow with onions and failed to do so. With onions we always had to put up with big difficulties, to the point that some had to be imported from India. When this happened, I would make use of my position and authority. Most likely I would place a call to Central Asia or Kazakhstan and put it to them, "Comrades, this is the position we are in, come to our aid."[135]

On any one issue, party strong-arming might have been in the interest of the municipal officials nominally responsible. Over time, however, the umbilical cord made for debilitation and for a vicious circle in public opinion. Thinking local institutions to be ineffective, citizens looked elsewhere, and this made the institutions all the less credible.

Bluff acknowledgment came only with glasnost' in the 1980s. When an interviewer confronted a raikom first secretary with the popular impression that the elected councils were weak, the secretary conceded that "small change predominates" in council offices. "As soon as a thornier question arises, they come right to the raikom: 'Wake up, do something!'" Everyone had long since gotten used to the soviets being "whipping boys" for the party, another raikom boss said. "By and large the soviets are weak today, and the only real power is that of the party apparatus."[136]

Moscow and the Hydra State

What I have termed disjointed monism haunted central-local relations even when Stalin sat in the Kremlin. With the disappearance of the offsetting force of his monomaniacal personality, "the center" in many realms of policy, among them urban and regional development, lost focus further. Khrushchev, once his industrialization of housing production was under way, trespassed spasmodically in Moscow issues; Brezhnev was virtually absent. From the worm's eye view of Moscow government, the national state appeared as a many-headed hydra, not a one-headed leviathan. One head did not necessarily know what the other was doing, and knowledge about the best endowed segment of the beast—the military-industrial complex, which loomed large in the Moscow economy—was elaborately shielded from local decision makers and citizens. Reconciling the actions of the hydra state was a major and growing concern of the custodians of the socialist metropolis.

ARCHITECTS-IN-CHIEF

Of the two supreme Soviet leaders between Stalin and Gorbachev, it was Khrushchev who had by far the greater impact on the capital city. He achieved a takeoff in housing construction and an accompanying reorganization of the building industry, but his entanglement hardly ended there. "Although tremendously busy with affairs of party and state," Vladimir Promyslov avouched in a birthday accolade, "Nikita Sergeyevich Khrushchev keeps an attentive eye on the city's development, often visits its important construction sites, and scrutinizes plans for major buildings and for reconstructing individual districts." Each encounter with Nikita Sergeyevich, he said, has "incalculable purport for our further work."[137]

Stalin's circuits of Moscow were as a rule nocturnal and solitary, and climaxed in regal "instructions." Khrushchev plied city and region with a cortege of aides, scribes, and cameramen and spouted "advice and wishes" as well as dicta, often in a folksy, question-and-answer format (see Figure 56).

In 1958, in this traveling-circus spirit, Khrushchev suggested the

Figure 56. Nikita Khrushchev inspecting Moscow site plans at a sculptor's studio, May 1963. (From *Stroitel'stvo i arkhitektura Moskvy*, no. 6, June 1963, p. 3.)

construction of pedestrian walkways over or under Moscow thoroughfares. Taking the sun at the Klyaz'ma Reservoir in 1960, he proposed a chain of holiday hotels *(pansionaty)* for the lakes and canals of Podmoskov'e. In February 1963 he directed that the Stalin-commissioned monument to Yurii Dolgorukii be moved from Sovetskaya ploshchad' to the Novodevichii Convent and the Liberty Obelisk that stood there from 1918 to 1941 be rebuilt from photographs. In fine fettle in a three-day motorcade in May of 1963, Khrushchev counseled the building of more bachelors' flats; laid bare "his thoughts on how to organize vehicular and pedestrian traffic" on prospekt Kalinina; nagged youth to prune and pick Moscow's apple and pear trees; ordained substitution of reinforced concrete for granite cladding along roads and rivers; and got up to date on design work for monuments to Lenin and to Soviet space achievements.[138]

While most of Khrushchev's blandishments were adopted as policy, it would have taken more than that for him to be a genuinely integrating force. His openly reported Moscow interventions were casual and disconnected. His behind-the-scenes demarches could be downright cockeyed, disruptive of the cohesion of preexisting policy and the work of the local elite.

Khrushchev's druthers for five-story buildings have already been noted. He expressed a similarly doughty attitude toward precast ferroconcrete, as he made its use obligatory for fencing, plazas, and even complicated engineering works. The subway bridge across the Moskva River at the Lenin Hills, completed with reinforced-concrete girders in twenty hectic months in 1957–1958, deteriorated straightaway from vibration and rusting. The passenger station that Khrushchev insisted be placed on it had to be moved to land within a few years. The entire bridge was taken out of service in 1986, at tremendous inconvenience to commuters.[139]

Khrushchev's last years in power include egregious cases of interference. Out of the blue, he ruled in 1963 that all of Moscow's brickworks be closed and the switchover to concrete be made complete. The city treaded water by commissioning a feasibility study; by the time it was done, he had been overthrown. The same year Khrushchev resolved that a four-lane roadway on reinforced concrete pylons, arcing overhead from ploshchad' Dzerzhinskogo to the Bol'shoi Kamennyi Bridge beside the Kremlin, was the only answer to congestion in the medieval core of Moscow. The Manezh, Natsional' Hotel, and parts of the eighteenth-century university campus would have had to be bulldozed to make way for this eyesore. It was all Yegorychev and Promyslov could do to talk him out of it. In April 1964, to their horror, Khrushchev impulsively told Gosplan to slash Moscow's housing plan forthwith by 40 percent. Having heard from Yegorychev at the Lenin Day celebration that the city had already turned the key on 1 million square meters, the total for all of 1955, he got it in his head that Moscow was hoodwinking him and misspending the state's money. Only through an elaborate ruse, with Gosplan's connivance, did Yegorychev salvage Moscow's quota. In August 1964 Khrushchev thought it necessary to tell Yegorychev and Promyslov to switch all toilet seats in new Moscow housing from wooden to plastic make.[140]

The case for Khrushchev harmonizing policy from on high is unpersuasive; for Brezhnev it is nonexistent. Brezhnev, unlike Khrushchev, had no history of immersion in Moscow or urban affairs. Unlike Stalin, he had no inclination to take a crash course in either. His tack, as toward most social policy, was laissez-faire.

Brezhnev made the predictable insipid allusions to his "concern" for Moscow, but no backup ever materialized beyond his adage about Moscow as a model city. He never once paid a call on its construction sites or planners. The only known instances of him butting in on a local decision were trite ones. In 1974, after a visit to East Berlin, where he was shown a well-stocked supermarket, he advised Moscow planners to build larger food stores equipped with delivery bays for containerized goods. Following a tour of Kazakhstan, he asked that some construction techniques he witnessed there be copied; he backed down when Grishin questioned his cost figures. Brezhnev yawned over the nuts-and-bolts intelligence on Moscow that had mesmerized Stalin and Khrushchev. "His attitude," as Yegorychev put it, "was, 'You take care of it yourself.'"[141]

THE *VEDOMSTVA* DECIDE ALL

An aphorism of Stalin's—"Cadres Decide All"—condensed his view of a properly drilled staff as a crux of modernization. A Moscow witticism referred to the *vedomstva,* the multitudinous administrative arms of government. "The Vedomstva Decide All" conveyed exasperation at the inability of local institutions to get the limbs of the hydra state to pump in unison on issues focal to urban well-being.

The vedomstva under state socialism comprised more than the military and police, the post office, the tax collectors, and the other bureaucracies found in any modern country. They wore many additional hats: owners, occupiers, providers, customers, polluters, employers of almost everyone.

In dealing with them, Soviet municipalities continued to do without an institutional friend at court. No central unit acted as a patron and clearing house, like the Department of the Environment at Whitehall or the U.S. Department of Housing and Urban Development. At city hall employees jested that a miniscule Moscow subdepartment formed in 1971 within the State Planning Committee was "our embassy in Gosplan," while knowing full well that they sculled most of the shoals of intergovernmental diplomacy on their own.[142]

Moscow relied financially on the central government, collecting only those revenues reserved to it by the USSR Ministry of Finance and Gosplan, mainly a turnover or excise tax on consumer goods; deductions from the profits of local and other state enterprises, a larger item in its budget than in most localities; and a host of lesser imposts. Finance officers used impromptu and arcane "adjustment revenues" to keep the local budget out of the red.[143]

The hoary doctrine of "dual subordination" placed many city departments at the mercy of homologous bureaus in the government of the USSR or, commonly for social services, the RSFSR. These agencies frequently reversed momentary concessions. In 1975, for example, the USSR Ministry of Transportation, without discussion, reappropriated the subway, the pride and joy of the transit system returned in the 1950s after twenty years of ministerial control. The ministry managed it thereafter through an in-house directorate for all Soviet metros; its first head, Boris A. Shelkov, had been deputy chairman of Moscow's ispolkom for transport.

The ultrasecret Metro-2 was centrally managed from the beginning, and in a choking fog of secrecy. It was built by a special Tenth Directorate of Metrostroi and operated by the KGB's Fifteenth Directorate, headquartered in the bunker near the Yugo-Zapadnaya subway stop. Moscow's municipal impresario for a quarter-century, Promyslov, related that although he "heard" about its construction, he saw no documentation and was not permitted inside: "I was not of the rank or position to justify that. I was in the final analysis *only the chairman of the ispolkom of a city which in many ways was not governed by the ispolkom.*"[144]

Most parts of the hydra did not trouble themselves with local governance. But the city had to bother with them, by virtue of their economic presence and their provision of housing and other social goods to employees.

State-owned industry, although it slid in relative terms, remained the largest economic sector in Moscow, unusually so for a national capital. Its 1,100 factories in 1980 made about 19 percent of the trucks, 14 percent of the cars, 10 to 15 percent of the machine tools, 20 percent of the clocks, 10 percent of the televisions, and 13 percent of the wool cloth in the USSR. ZIL, the Likhachev (formerly Stalin) Auto Works in southeast Moscow, with about 80,000 on staff in the 1980s (and 40,000 outside Moscow), was one of the largest Soviet enterprises. Moscow had a second automotive giant, the Komsomol Small Car Works, producer of the Moskvich sedan, on Volgogradskii prospekt. Started at Karl Bauman's instigation as the Communist Youth International Works in 1930, it was updated with the help of the Renault firm in the 1970s.[145]

Three Moscow workers in five in 1980 toiled in metalworking and engineering plants, but old industries such as textiles, apparel, chemicals, and confectionaries still had sizable representation. Plants with more than 5,000 workers, only 5 percent of Moscow industry's total, had 40 percent of its personnel, 40 percent of production, and 42 percent of its fixed capital.

Diversification away from manufacturing compounded the burden of coordination for the local authorities. The growing sectors all had their own complicated anatomies. One hundred and twenty economic agencies had wholesale supply divisions in Moscow in 1979, and 80 percent of their warehousing was for out-of-town operations. Research and development, the most bustling sector, was highly diverse since almost 95 percent of its personnel worked in "branch science," tied to ministries or segments of industry rather than the Academy of Sciences. The USSR government alone had eighty-six ministries, state committees, and other divisions in 1980, twenty-five more than in 1966. Each had its chancery in Moscow, and most had a plethora of subdivisions and offshoots. Yeltsin was to shake his fist at the "bureaus, subsidiaries, and sections of various organizations" found in Moscow. "We cannot do a tally of them, as some do not have bank accounts or shingles on the wall."[146]

Governmental departments never literally "decided all" in Moscow. But time and again they dulled local initiatives and shunned contributions to the common cause. Even when giving ground, they refused to surrender. An illustrative issue was custody over the housing stock, which has a history in Moscow going back to 1917.

Soviet government policy since 1957 dictated that agency-owned housing should be deeded over to local councils. Moscow repeatedly endorsed transfer to the raion soviets, which acted as holding companies for municipal housing. In three decades of trying, it at best chipped away at this prosaic problem. Departments and enterprises owned 43.1 percent of its housing stock in 1961, more than before 1953, to 56.8 percent owned by the raions. The vedomstva's share perversely had increased to 44.9 percent in 1964. Still about 40 percent in 1974, it waned to about one-third in the early 1980s and, after a push for compliance, stood at 25.1 percent of the housing inhabited by permanent Muscovites in 1988; counting residents on temporary papers would likely have put it 3 or 4 points higher.[147]

The last figure was no cause for jubilation, what with the generation-old goal of total transfer. Over thirty years, the raions' share rose by less than 10 percent, to 64.9 percent, because apartments owned by housing cooperatives had gone from a negligible number to 9.6 percent of the total in 1988. In absolute volume, the departmentally owned fund had actually grown—from about 16 million square meters of net dwelling space in 1961 to perhaps 28 million in the 1970s and 26 million in 1988. The Ministry of Defense, for example, had dozens of apartment buildings scattered around Moscow, some near old barracks and bivouac areas.[148] More common was the "factory town" type familiar from the 1930s and 1940s, with housing arrayed around an industrial enterprise.

The economic ministries and other vedomstva impeded municipalization by foot dragging and obfuscation, not by openly contesting its validity. Compilation of memoranda, contracts, and fitness certificates "created a tangle of red tape which drags on for years on end."[149] In the course of backroom negotiations, departmental landlords skimped on building maintenance, diminishing the ardor of local officials for the transfer. At the rate hewed to, it would have been well after the year 2000 before the last departmental flat had been put on the soviets' books.

DEFENSE COMPLEXES

Governance of the pervasive defense-related business, the golden child of the Soviet economy, presented additional complexities. Moscow had always been the center of the Russian aviation industry, whereas army munitions were concentrated in the Urals, nuclear weapons making in the ten closed "atomic cities" in the east, and naval ship building in Leningrad and other seaports. Rocketry, resting on a proven foundation in airframes and propulsion systems, grew into a second strength for Moscow in the 1940s. A third specialization, drawing on the prewar radio industry, was in electronics, microelectronics, and computers; it came into its own in the Khrushchev period.[150]

In aviation, Moscow excelled at making prototypes and key components and subsystems (most important, engines and fuselages), not final assembly of the machines. Aviation work occupied scientific institutes, design bureaus and free-standing "special design bureaus" (KBs and OKBs, in Soviet jargon), related and colocated fabricating works, and a limited number of large airframe plants; some aggregations were integrated under Brezhnev into "science-production associations" (NPOs).

A declassified U.S. government study from 1971 shows the R&D function in Soviet aviation to have been overwhelmingly Moscow-centered. All basic data for aircraft and propulsion systems were provided by TsAGI and two other institutes separated from it during the First Five-Year Plan, TsIAM (for engine building) and VIAM (for aviation materials). The chief design bureau for jet engines, under Arkhip M. Lyul'ka, was in Moscow. Of the four Soviet design bureaus working on heavy bombers and transports, three (named after Tupolev, Il'yushin, and Myasishchev) were in Moscow, as were all three leaders in fighters and lighter fixed-wing planes (Mikoyan, Sukhoi, and Yakovlev). Two of the three design bureaus for helicopters and other support craft (Kamov and Mil') were in Moscow oblast, close by the city limits, as were all three related to aerodynamic missiles (the

Grushin, Lavochkin, and Vladimir N. Chelomei firms). The Flight Test Institute at Ramenskoye, still the principal aircraft test unit, possessed the longest paved runway and the most hangar space of any airfield in the country.[151]

As far as we are allowed to guess, the major manufacturing firms in aviation were either continuations of factories built up under Stalin or newer and usually smaller units associated with design bureaus. The purposive obscurity of terminology, and repeated reorganizations, make precision hard if not impossible. Most defense plants had standard industrial names until about 1930, when they were digitalized as a security precaution; in the 1950s, these were converted into (sometimes supplemented by) "post office box" numbers that were themselves classified; and in the 1960s and 1970s, some again got verbal names. Hence histories such as that of the Duks plant, Moscow's and Russia's first aircraft manufacturer: renamed Aviation Works No. 1 during the First Five-Year Plan and sometimes referred to as the Aviakhim Works; Works No. 30 from before the war; "Enterprise P.O. Box 2402" as of the early 1950s; and the Znamya truda (Banner of Labor) Machine Building Works during the Brezhnev period, when it was still one of the city's largest defense plants, making, among others, MIG fighters and Il'yushin passenger jetliners.

Aviation firms in Moscow clustered together (see Map 20). One area was anchored by Znamya truda, in Frunzenskii raion (using raion boundaries of 1977–1991), and the Central Airfield. A short ways to its east, in Sverdlovskii raion near the Dinamo Stadium, operated the Znamya revolyutsii (Banner of Revolution) Works (Works No. 39 in its day) and the Kommunar (Communard) Works, both makers of aircraft components. Behind checkpoints and in some cases under the ground, in a belt stretching northwest to the port and starboard of Leningradskii prospekt and Leningradskoye shosse, on through parts of Leningradskii, Voroshilovskii, and Tushinskii raions, sat a bevy of installations, often bearing founders' names from the hall of fame of Soviet aviation: the Zhukovskii Air Force Engineering Academy and the Ordzhonikidze Aviation Institute (the main college for aviation and rocketry engineers); the Il'yushin, Mikoyan, Sukhoi, and Yakovlev design bureaus and prototype plants; the Avangard (Avant-Garde) and Krasnyi Oktyabr' (Red October) works; and many others. The Voikov Iron Foundry on Leningradskii prospekt cast

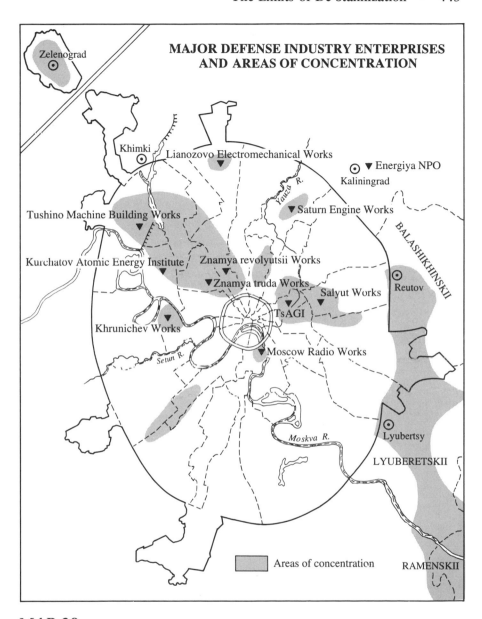

**MAJOR DEFENSE INDUSTRY ENTERPRISES
AND AREAS OF CONCENTRATION**

Zelenograd

Khimki

Lianozovo Electromechanical Works

Energiya NPO
Kaliningrad

Tushino Machine Building Works

Saturn Engine Works

BALASHIKHINSKII

Kurchatov Atomic Energy Institute

Znamya revolyutsii Works

Znamya truda Works

Salyut Works

Reutov

TsAGI

Khrunichev Works

Moscow Radio Works

Setun R.

Yauza R.

Moskva R.

Lyubertsy

LYUBERETSKII

Areas of concentration

RAMENSKII

MAP 20

444 • The Limits of De-Stalinization

high-tensile steel for airframes and missiles. Northward from this strip was the Saturn Engine Works in Babushkinskii raion, affiliated with the Lyul'ka design bureau.[152]

The second hive of aviation activity, located in the east end, fanned out from the Yauza-bank location of the original TsAGI and Tupolev design bureau, through the Lefortovo section and proximate to shosse Entuziastov. VIAM, in Baumanskii raion, and TsIAM, in Kalininskii raion, were both here, as were the Mil' Helicopter Works in Sokol'nicheskii raion, a national pace setter in that subfield, and the Salyut (Salute) Machine Building Works, the large jet engine maker on prospekt Budennogo in Pervomaiskii raion previously known as the Aviation Motor Works, Works No. 24, the Frunze Works, Works No. 45, and P.O. Box 299.

Ballistic rocket development was marshaled in Moscow from the time it captured Stalin's attention in 1945. Sergei Korolev, the chief designer of the Soviet ICBM (intercontinental ballistic missile) and space programs in the 1950s, chaired a "Big Six" council of heads of design bureaus. All six—Vladimir P. Barmin (for launch sites), Valentin Glushko (engines), Korolev (rocket frames), Nikolai D. Kuznetsov (gyroscopes and guidance), and Nikolai A. Pilyugin and Mikhail S. Ryazanskii (radio communications)—were Muscovites. "Practically all" designs for the Soviets' ICBMs and their launch facilities "were nurtured in quite modest Moscow buildings." One hundred and fifty Moscow organizations performed more than half the work on the Buran space shuttle, the top priority of the 1980s.[153]

R & D and production of missiles and manned and unmanned spacecraft abounded around Leningradskii prospekt, which over time became a dual aerospace corridor. Capital installations included the Mashinostroitel' (Machine Builder) NPO in Leningradskii raion (missiles) and the Tushino Machine Building Works and other divisions of the Molniya (Lightning) NPO, the prime contractor on Buran, in Tushinskii raion. A second cluster of rocket-related activity hinged on the extremely large Khrunichev Machine Building Works on Novozavodskaya ulitsa, in the Fili section of Kievskii raion. A bomber factory known as Works No. 22 under Stalin, this plant switched to missiles and satellites in the 1960s and made, among other things, equipment for the abortive lunar program of the 1960s, SS-19 ICBMs, the Proton rocket (the main Soviet space booster), and the Mir space station. It worked closely with the Salyut (formerly Myasishchev) design bureau abutting it and the All-Union Institute of Light and Special Alloys in the Bol'shaya Setun part of Kuntsevskii raion, founded in 1961 to innovate in airworthy materials.[154]

The interrelated radio (including radar and television), electronics, and computer industries were also strongly represented in Moscow. The one expansion plan approved by the gorkom and the Ministry of the Radio Industry in 1968 forecast 320 million rubles of investment by 1980, addition of 800,000 square meters of floor space in fourteen factories and twenty-nine institutes and design bureaus, and a trebling of output. Work in this sector spread out more than in aviation and rockets. Among the bigger assets were the Lianozovo Electromechanical Works in Timiryazevskii raion (making radars, televisions, and microcomputers), the Kuntsevo Mechanical Works in Kuntsevskii raion, the older Moscow Radio Works in Zamoskvorech'e, and the Almaz (Diamond) NPO, an electronics conglomerate whose design bureau and at least one plant were in Leningradskii raion. A good deal of R & D work for automated systems, computers, and space exploration went on in a cordon in southwest Moscow bisected by Leninskii prospekt, in Oktyabr'skii, Cheremushkinskii, and Gagarinskii raions.

The Ministry of Medium Machine Building, in charge of nuclear weapons production, also had a presence in Moscow. It ran big institutes in Zamoskvorech'e and on Kashirskoye shosse and an instrumentation works near the Central Army Park in Dzerzhinskii raion. Fundamental science was done at the seven research reactors of the Kurchatov Atomic Energy Institute in Voroshilovskii raion, which had 10,000 employees on its ninety-hectare site in the 1980s, and in three reactors at departmental and Academy of Sciences laboratories in southwest Moscow. A key installation was the ministry's Institute of Theoretical and Experimental Physics, on a former estate of the Menshikov family at 25 Bol'shaya Cheremushkinskaya ulitsa; founded in 1945 as Laboratory No. 3, it housed the USSR's first heavy water reactor.

Chemical and biological weaponry ranked low priorities in Moscow by comparison. Khrushchev closed the army's nerve gas test range at Kuz'minki in 1963, but the State Research Institute of Organic Chemistry and Technology remained a major R & D center for toxic agents. Academy of Sciences and departmental laboratories studied bacteriological substances.[155]

Military-oriented manufacturing and research was by no means confined to Moscow city. Seeking out open land and seclusion, defense industrialists located in Podmoskov'e as early as the 1920s. After 1945 the government gave impetus to proliferation of research facilities by creating a national system of *naukogrady*—closed, middle-sized "science towns" devoted to defense R & D. Of the approximately fifty, many (such as the "atomic cities") were in remote parts, but more than half were in Moscow oblast.[156]

Balashikhinskii, Lyuberetskii, and Ramenskii, the three oblast raions along the capital's eastern rim, had the thickest concentration of military production and R & D. New TsAGI in the science town of Zhukovskii, the Flight Test Center at Ramenskoye, Chelomei's Mashinostroyenie (Machine Building) NPO in Reutov (for cruise missiles, ICBMs, and spy satellites), and the Kamov Helicopter Works in Tomilino stood out as but the most important of the many facilities in this area.

Just northeast of Moscow lay Kaliningrad—containing, in the words of a Russian commentator, "the largest group of space-related design bureaus and institutes not only in the country but apparently in the world."[157] Institute No. 88, renamed the Central Institute of Machine Building in 1967, housed the Flight Management Center for all Soviet manned space flights and served as the research base for the booster rocket assembly works of the Energiya (Energy) NPO, at one time Korolev's shop. The cosmonauts' training town was at Shchelkovo, slightly to the east, military-related optics and electronics plants at Zagorsk, and the science town of Fryazino a hop and a skip to the northeast. Important atomic research emanated from Pushkino and also Dubna, with its cyclotron, started at the terminus of the Moscow-Volga Canal by General Komarovskii and Gulag in 1946.

To the northwest of Moscow lay Khimki, the site of the Glushko and Grushin OKBs (for propulsion systems), the main body of the Tupolev bureau, the Energomash (Energy Machinery) NPO (the main Soviet manufacturer of rocket engines), and related assets, some of them aided at birth by captive German scientists. Past Khimki, Khrushchev started Zelenograd from scratch in 1957 at the emptied Kryukovo labor camp, as a science city for electronics, optics, lasers, and precision instrumentation. Zelenograd has been called the Russian Silicon Valley; 90 percent of its economy depended on defense.[158]

What does this welter of activity add up to? Hard data were concealed until the late 1980s, when Yeltsin's successor as first secretary, Lev N. Zaikov, made some startling revelations. *"More than one-third"* of all manufacturing output in the city of Moscow, he said, and *more than one-half* of all research, experimental, and design work "of an applied character" took place in the plants and laboratories of the defense industry, and *one-quarter* of the entire Moscow labor force was "employed in the defense complex." Concerning Moscow oblast, another source said that one in five Communist Party members there worked in "enterprises connected with the defense industry."[159]

Easygoing definitions make these data awkward to interpret. Zaikov probably underplayed defense by excluding orders placed outside the military-industrial ministries (at ZIL, for example, which supplied amphibious vehicles, armored personnel carriers, and, by some estimates, half of its truck output to the army). In 1992, too early for post-Soviet structural change to occur, Yurii Luzhkov looked at the phenomenon from a different angle, asserting that Moscow city was the venue of "75 percent of all military-industrial science and 25 percent of defense production of the military-industrial complex of Russia." If we assume that about 70 percent of Soviet weapons work was done in Russia, the inference would be that at the end of the Communist era Moscow—with 3 percent of the USSR's population—was where 17 or 18 percent of its defense manufacturing and 50 percent of the related science went on.[160]

Whether or not estimates like this err on the high side, Zaikov was a master of understatement when he said, "The enterprises and organizations of the capital's defense complex play a vital role in its economy and in considerable measure influence its social makeup." We are dealing here not merely with economics or social structure but with culture and mindset.

It was a fact of political life that the cocoon around the defense industry muffled communication about the organizations furnishing the livelihood of hundreds of thousands of Muscovites. There was not and could not be any educated debate on how the military-industrial complex impinged on community issues.

Secrecy affected even Viktor Grishin, a member of the Politburo charged several times with supervising military programs. In the early 1970s he was unable, he testified, to get a reply from the munitions institute that occupied the Church of the Ascension at Nikitskiye Gates (beloved by many Russians because the poet Pushkin was married there in 1831) to a proposal to turn it into a theater; he had to press the matter on the minister of defense, a deputy prime minister, and the Central Committee secretary for armaments (Dmitrii Ustinov), and never received a straight answer. Valerii T. Saikin, the municipal chairman after Promyslov, later commented on how little his office knew about pollution thrown off by military plants: it was "very poorly informed about emissions from various kinds of closed enterprises and does not possess the necessary mechanism by which we could force these enterprises to present us with the information we require."[161]

Even less information reached the ordinary citizen of Moscow. No word went out about such public health hazards and nuisances emanating from secret enterprises as the deposits of radioactive wastes near the Kurchatov Institute and like facilities; the burial grounds for poison gases at Kuz'minki and the State Research Institute of Organic Chemistry and Technology; the epidemic of brucellosis in Krasnopresnenskii raion in 1976 caused by faulty venting from a germ warfare laboratory; and the leak of bacteriological agents from a veterinary institute in the early 1980s, a cloudlet of which nearly killed fifteen students in the Higher Party School in Frunzenskii raion.[162] Censorship resulted in suppression of the data contained in the foregoing paragraphs. The government closed Moscow's defense plants and institutes to journalists and made disclosure of their very existence an offense. It kept their telephone numbers off open lists. It denied most of them, and their superordinate agencies, geographic coordinates, as the withholding of street addresses and identifying signs was the whole point of the post office box system. It went so far as to classify the minutes of city conferences of the party as secret materials because of the references to defense enterprises.[163]

In Moscow oblast facilities like the Flight Test Center barred all foreigners and many Soviets and had perimeters patrolled by troops with machine guns and tracking dogs. The electronics specialization of Zelenograd and the rockets made in Kaliningrad were unmentionables. Kaliningrad, which had 100,000 residents by 1970, was omitted from most maps, and encyclopedia entries said only that it had woodworking and textile factories. The *betonka,* the secret ferroconcrete roadway parallel to the MKAD, was opened to civilian traffic around 1960 but not noted on openly circulated charts. As inside Moscow, cartographers went beyond omission to intentional distortion of locations of places they did not want prying eyes to see.[164]

THE COORDINATION MIRAGE

Overcoming fragmented centralism was for Moscow municipal and party leaders like the mirage of the oasis to the parched desert traveler, always beckoning but always over the next sand dune. If they failed to reach water, it was not for want of slogging. They worked principally with three organizing formulas after Stalin.

It is debatable whether the first, the "economic council" or sovnarkhoz of the late Khrushchev years, fits in this context at all. The sovnarkhoz of 1957–1965 was a means of streamlining the *command planning* function by resituating it from the central to the territorial level. Moscow had a sovnarkhoz before, from 1919 to 1932, to administer the portion of the local economy then under the city soviet's control. The sovnarkhoz instituted in May 1957, one of more than 100 in the USSR, was entirely a servant of central authority, with jurisdiction over 600 Moscow factories and almost 800,000 industrial personnel previously part of economic ministries; it did not govern defense R & D.

The program detoured away from serious economic reform. Any effect on local services or government was incidental. Certain kinds of information may have been easier to share, mostly through CPSU channels (the chairman of the sovnarkhoz was a member of the gorkom bureau), but neither relations with industry nor local leverage over it improved. The Moscow sovnarkhoz, with support of the gorkom, in fact offended the local councils after 1960 by taking over a series of municipal plants making furniture and housewares.[165] Few tears were shed when Brezhnev's Politburo discontinued the sovnarkhozes in 1965.

Compared to the first, the second strategy was more forthright and more benign. It operationalized coordination as *production* under local auspices, in monopoly or near-monopoly circumstances. The torchbearer was the seemingly esoteric Glavmosavtotrans, the Chief

Directorate for Automobile Transport of the Moscow ispolkom—the municipal cartage service. In 1951, when Khrushchev was Moscow viceroy, it was the first organization in the USSR assigned to do "centralized deliveries" by road of a prescribed set of products in a particular area, regardless of department of origin. This method represented advanced thinking at the time.

The schedule of cargoes over which Glavmosavtotrans had trucking rights, out to a radius of thirty kilometers from Moscow, extended from bricks to dozens of other commodities. Its chief, Iosif Goberman, allowed as he would not rest content until his empire was complete. Glavmosavtotrans by 1965 moved more than 70 percent of all local freight and boasted an electronic dispatch center, 40,000 vans, and 90,000 employees—how many American cities have this many workers on their whole roster? But it was never able to jostle other fleets off the highway and had to watch its share drop 10 percent by 1980. As Goberman remonstrated, the ministries lobbied ferociously to keep it in check.[166]

The local near-monopoly most pertinent to daily life was that dealt to Glavmosstroi in housing and civil construction in 1954. It demonstrates the attractions and the pitfalls of the production approach.

The problem transcended Glavmosstroi's failure to achieve complete control of housing production—its share climbed to 85 percent in 1970 and then sagged a few points. Irrespective of share, the local construction budget was never a simple item in the municipal accounts. The issue concerned more than taxation and money budgets, as currency in the command economy tended to follow in the stern of material allocations, not the other way around. Without markets for wholesale goods and capital, Glavmosstroi could use city rubles to purchase manpower but not much else. Legally, it was a contracting organization, meeting quotas by deadline on the basis of agreements. At no time did the indispensable "limits" *(limity)*, the chits entitling a builder to inputs of supplies and equipment, come entirely from the city.

To secure the limits, Moscow had to maintain a separate office, officially (as of a 1967 reorganization) its Chief Directorate of Capital Construction, generally going by the acronym GlavUKS. In 1967 GlavUKS was declared the exclusive broker—the "single client" *(yedinyi zakazchik)*—for the building of housing and service facilities in

Moscow. It was designed to link up resources from donors, in effect, to pool credits drawable on the central resource bank of Gosplan; the donors would be entitled to share the built proceeds, a mechanism denominated "proportional participation" *(dolevoye uchastiye)* in Soviet bureaucratese. Besides the city ispolkom and Gosplan, the shareholders were none other than the vedomstva, the very tribe of ministries and bureaus whose grip over urban development Glavmosstroi had been formed to break in the first place. As shall be seen in Chapter 6, this matrix approach to funding advantaged prosperous patrons and strained urban planning.

GlavUKS as such also proved to be a bottleneck in the development process. Long before 1967 its officials were disparaged as "cold-hearted paper pushers," ignorant of real building problems. A decade after the reform, GlavUKS was "not capable of . . . preparing the documentation on time," a barb regularly echoed. Although its charter remitted only 3 agencies from pooling (the Ministry of Defense, Ministry of Medium Machine Building, and Academy of Sciences), 174 disparate organizations commissioned their own housing and amenities at the turn of the 1980s, "leading to dispersal of material and labor resources among numerous construction sites and a growth in uncompleted construction."[167]

An extra complication was that Moscow chose to fragment the local construction industry itself. Three new builders with tongue-twisting names split off from Glavmosstroi: Glavmosinzhstroi (1968), for roads, water, and drainage; Glavmospromstroi (1972), for factories, offices, and public buildings; and Glavmosmontazhspetsstroi (1976), for industrial and "special" projects, some with a military flavor. The last two coexisted with the construction subunits of the ministries, which numbered a mind-bending 600 in Moscow in the mid-1980s, almost four times as many as two decades before.[168]

The chief of Glavmosstroi, who in Kucherenko's day had been a first deputy chairman of the city ispolkom, did not so much as sit on it after 1975. Glavmosstroi's progeny competed with it for resources and were more susceptible to bullying from above: Gosplan, rummaging for resources as the Soviet economy slumped, assigned two-thirds of Glavmospromstroi's capacity to the ministries in 1984 and brushed off city organizations as "transmission links and registrars of events." Glavmosstroi once gave Moscow a mighty building fist, several economists wrote, but "now this fist has become unclenched and on this account weak." Coordination construed as production had ended up being uncoordinated.[169]

The third and final recipe for interagency coordination relied on *regulation,* as separate from command planning or production. Physical town planning of the customary variety fell largely in this category. Its prescriptions as to architectural form and spatial allocation of functions, distilled in the metropolitan master plan, were mandatory for local agencies only, and that with much slippage; for other players, this guidance was loose and sometimes forgettable, experience would bear out.

It is of interest, then, that Moscow leaders ventured in the 1970s to supplement physical planning with regulation better meshed with production decisions. This modality was dubbed "social planning" or "socioeconomic planning." Unlike the sovnarkhoz of 1957–1965, it put social welfare first, at least on paper, and attempted to optimize social welfare by skewering it to economic development.

Industrial sociologists and party functionaries in Leningrad invented social planning in 1966. It reached Moscow only in 1971, as an experiment at the Automatic Line Works (formerly Crane Works), a machine tool plant in Zhdanovskii raion. The factory's social plan, jointly endorsed by management, party committee, and trade union local, tied targets for improvements in work safety and living conditions to increases in production. The raion adopted the first areal social plan in Moscow in August 1971, fixing commitments for better services and higher productivity districtwide up to 1975. In 1972 the gorkom bureau instructed all raions, with party committees out front, to follow Zhdanovskii's lead.[170]

The movement reached the city level in 1975, pushed by Second Secretary Leonid I. Grekov of the gorkom. Structural changes were made to Gorplan, the Economic Planning Commission of the Moscow Soviet; a new think tank, the abominably named Institute of the Economic Problems of the Integrated Development of the Economy of the City of Moscow, was put at its disposal. For the 1976–1980 accounting period, Moscow had an "integrated plan for socioeconomic development," no longer, in theory, a narrowly economic plan. In 1976 the gorkom's Commission on Socioeconomic Development gave the party apparatus a standing presence in the issue area.

As mentioned above, the gorkom commission was to be disestablished in 1986. Boris Yeltsin, who did so, was no less scathing about the social planning project, saying the documents produced were of low quality: "Many positions in them have not been checked out, are not thought out, are not balanced, and do not measure up to demands."[171]

Of the two species of local planning, physical planning was the more gainful and the one from which most can be learned. But neither caught up with the coordination mirage, as the rest of the story, taken up in Chapter 6, shows.

Moscow and Muscovites faded in national politics after 1953, especially after 1964. Personalities and petty squabbles helped make it so, but the irreducible fact was that a vanguard city, lighting the way forward to all and training pathfinders, had no place in a system not itself in motion. As the Soviet regime lost its sense of direction and settled into unlacquered conservatism, the Moscow leadership looked more like one blinkered elite among many, going nowhere in particular. Shouting "model Communist city" from the rooftops—putting a happy face on things as they were—only proved the point, and few were fooled into thinking otherwise.

Late Soviet Moscow displays an incongruity between social and political trends not dissimilar to that found in late imperial Moscow. Urban society was less dynamic than before 1917, but government was more incrusted: the gap between the two was of the same order of magnitude. Tectonic tension built up below the surface, imperceptibly.

The mature socialist metropolis had its able champions and administrators, but too often for its good they lost out to time servers and pedants. Ivan Kapitonov, the client of Khrushchev's who probably could have done the most for Moscow living standards, was passed over for Furtseva and the neo-Stalinist Ustinov; instead of Nikolai Yegorychev, Muscovites got the soporific Grishin. The denizens of 6 Staraya ploshchad' were judged in the final reckoning not by how well they listened to their subjects but by how they contained the political trouble that an energized Moscow could become, and did become after 1985. They bought stability, but, as Gorbachev said of

Brezhnev's Russia as a whole, it was "an artificial stability" that put in abeyance "the constant renewal . . . demanded by life."[172]

It was a stability, furthermore, that allowed for the stealthy sketching in the public mind of what James Scott calls the "hidden transcript" that reams out many authoritarian regimes—the imagining of a "counterfactual social order" in which subordinate groups reverse an established order of exploitation and status degradation, not infrequently invoking "the ritual symbols of [the] conservative hegemony" to do so.[173] Much as Soviet pseudofederalism by a strange irony sheltered the growth of ethnic consciousness in the republics of the USSR, and the deformed command economy raised expectations of a decent material life, pseudo-self-government in the socialist metropolis kept alive the intuition that there were such things as democracy and community control and that they might be worth fighting for, some day.

6

The Politics of Basic Needs
and of Urban Amenity

<hr>

To ASSESS how post-Stalin Moscow government took action in substantive areas of urban development, two macrocategories may be distilled from Abraham Maslow's "hierarchy of human needs" ranging from physiological requirements to higher psychological and emotional strivings.[1] How, first, did the city fare with regard to the *basic* material needs for which such miserly provision was made before 1953? A look at metropolitan planning and housing supply, the subjects of the first and second sections of this chapter, suggests the answer is, not well enough. And what was done to engender a state of urban *amenity* that, as the party promised, would afford Muscovites more than barebones subsistence? Nonhousing services and care of the natural and architectural environment, discussed in the third and fourth sections, reveal the true shortcomings of the system.

Planning for Metropolitan Development

The government used comprehensive normative guidance through master planning as the consummate means for shaping Soviet Moscow. The general plan, Viktor Grishin declared, was of "tremendous political, economic, and social import," and no dry engineering bulletin. "Incarnating the advantages of the socialist system, it defines our broad program for reconstructing, enlarging, and beautifying the city . . . for forming a communist way of life."[2] The upstart of the 1970s, social planning, was supposed to mobilize resources for realizing the conception of commonweal embodied in the master plan. It deserves some attention, but less than the dominant spatial mode, which retained the fusty title "architectural planning."

PLANS AND PLANNERS

The expiry of the 1935 Stalin plan and of the construction plan for 1951–1960 left Moscow without a development strategy, despite the ardent commitment to planning as such. This anomaly was finally erased July 9, 1971, when a joint session of the Mossovet and the gorkom with all due fanfare adopted the "Master Plan for the Development of the City of Moscow" given assent the month before by the Politburo and the USSR Council of Ministers (see Figure 57).

The document's lengthy incubation reflected how involuted an exercise town planning had come to be. The city soviet instructed its planning office, GlavAPU, to get down to it days after the suburban annexation of August 1960 and to have the precis of parameters, the TEO (Tekhniko-ekonomicheskiye osnovy, "technical and economic foundations") of the plan, ready by July 1961. When this deadline lapsed, Mikhail Posokhin, Moscow's well-connected chief architect, still predicted a wrap-up by 1965. As it turned out, the TEO were not ready until late 1963, and the USSR Council of Ministers gave the go-ahead to do a full-fledged plan only in September 1966. That ate up two years and was followed by three years more of horse trading with the government and "interested agencies" through a joint Gosplan–city hall commission.[3]

The TEO covered a span of twenty years, back-dated to 1961. The final version enacted in 1971 accordioned the duration out to "twenty-five to thirty years," establishing a cutoff some time between 1986 and 1991. Most spokesmen thereafter flippantly gave 1990 as the terminal year. The extension was due mostly to the fear that the plan could not be executed any quicker.

As in 1935 and in the half-baked plans of the 1920s, the plan's computations rested on an end-of-term population target. Following consecutive upward ratchetings (see below), the limit was fixed at 8 million, counting Zelenograd and several settlements in Podmoskov'e appended to Moscow. Annexations would cease; 100 square kilome-

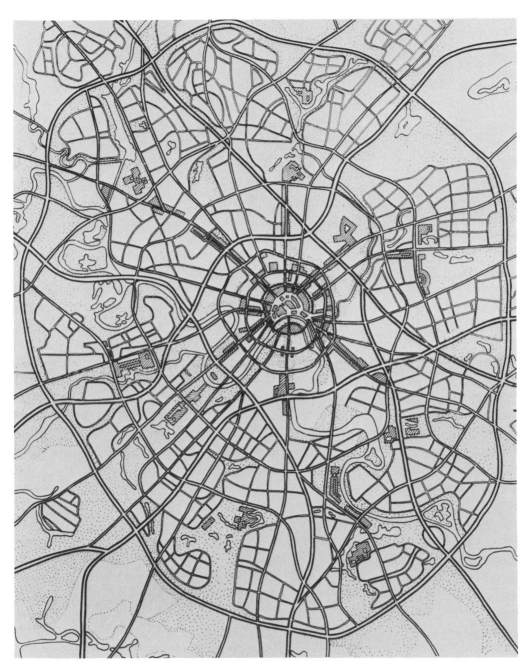

Figure 57. Moscow master plan of 1971. Design shows main roads, locations for public buildings (lined on map), and parkland (lightly dotted). (From M. I. Astaf'eva-Dlugach et al., *Moskva,* Moscow: Stroiizdat, 1979, p. 42.)

ters would be held for possible use after 1990. The population of an 1,800-square-kilometer green belt would increase by no more than 200,000.

Moscow's millions were to be furnished under the plan with the material wherewithal of a fuller urban existence. Housing provision was to swell by two-thirds, up to 13 to 13.5 square meters of net space per man, woman, and child,[4] and all apartments were to be decked with modern appurtenances. The plan set venturesome quotas for urban infrastructure. Subway track, for instance, was to be tripled over 1961, per capita seats in dining spots to be multiplied 3.2 times and public library capacity 5 times, and places in day nurseries, kindergartens, and hospitals to increase by more than one-half. Moscow was also to evict 356 noxious factories, preserve historical landmarks, build neighborhood and city parks, and adorn its streets with a "synthesis of the arts."

The master plan specified some of the capital facilities needed but paid less attention to them than the Stalinist plan of 1935. It put forth three main innovations in spatial control: parsing the city into eight "planning zones" around zonal subcenters; compacting manufacturing and warehousing into sixty-seven "production zones"; and implanting the "stepped" approach to service delivery that had gained acceptance in Russian planning theory.

The machinery for drawing up, modifying, and implementing the plan could not have existed in such proportions in a Western city. GlavAPU had 13,000 staff aboard by 1980, 2,500 of them architects and 700 in its Institute of the Master Plan, founded at Khrushchev's behest in 1951. Seven functional directorates dealt with matters like land allocation and old buildings, and 1,500 employees were in its surveying trust. Mosproyekt, the Moscow Design Institute established in 1951, divided in the 1960s and 1970s into five specialized Mosproyekts doing GlavAPU working drawings for (1) housing estates, (2) the city center, (3) the green belt, (4) health and recreation facilities, and (5) industrial construction. An Experimental Design Institute, successor to the Special Architectural Design Bureau of the 1950s, produced type designs in volume.[5]

For social planning organizational resources went to the composers of annual and five-year production plans for economic units (construction firms, shops, and so forth) on the local budget. Gorplan, the city's economic planning commission, headed by a deputy chairman of the ispolkom and with 400 personnel in the early 1980s, headed the effort. Rules enacted in 1975 granted it the right of "examination and consent" on the draft plans of all enterprises in Moscow, not just municipal ones. Its mandate was to see to Moscow's "integrated development in accord with the terms and indicators of the master plan . . . correspondence between the development of industry and of city services . . . harmonious evolution of the districts." Gorplan was endowed with branch departments in 1975, to which all producers now had to submit one- and five-year plans in precursory form for checking and comment before USSR Gosplan gave its approval for the central government. Its new Institute of the Economic Problems of Moscow provided backup; it by 1980 had a staff of 250, a computerized data bank, some capacity for econometric analysis, and a monograph series.[6]

REGULATING POPULATION GROWTH

The 1971 plan was typical of Soviet cities in singling out restraint of demographic growth as the precondition of progress. The digest of the TEO of 1966 expressed the point well:

> The axial problem for Moscow, like any great city, is control of the growth of its population. Only thus can housing and civil construction be fully used to improve the living conditions of its working people. The need to utilize Moscow's production and scientific potential to the full in the prewar and early postwar years caused its population to expand by way not only of natural increase but of mechanical growth, the inflow [of people] from the outside. Unfortunately, any further augmentation of the population would unavoidably worsen Muscovites' lives, sap the effectiveness of our efforts at city planning, and produce the kind of malady found in urban giants such as New York, London, and Tokyo. The conditions of the socialist system of management make it possible to resolve this problem.[7]

De-Stalinization had a moderating effect on some recent, draconian infringements on individual liberties but not on the principles of the passport system or the long-standing policy of using it to regulate migration-induced "mechanical growth."[8] Indeed, the central and city authorities turned a beady eye to evidence that curbs had not been

Table 9. Growth of the Moscow population, 1947–1989

Years	Average annual increase	Annual percentage increase (simple)
July 1947–April 1956	96,800	2.42
April 1956–1959	78,600	1.61
1960–1964 (including suburban annexation of August 1960)	257,400	5.00
1960–1964 (excluding suburban annexation of August 1960)	57,400	0.93
1965–1969	130,000	2.02
1970–1974	111,000	1.57
1975–1979	93,400	1.22
1980–1984	111,400	1.38
1985–1989	64,800	0.75

hewed to unswervingly enough since the war. Moscow's population grew an average of 2.4 percent a year between 1947 and 1956 (see Table 9), mostly because of migration. Nikita Khrushchev told the Twentieth Party Congress in 1956 that almost 300,000 people had relocated to Moscow from 1951 to 1955; that would have been approximately 60 percent of the increase in those years.[9]

In October 1956 the bureau of the Moscow gorkom ordered elimination of "serious violations" of the passport regulations. A follow-up edict in June 1958 conveyed indignation:

> The ispolkom of the Moscow Soviet (Comrades Bobrovnikov [chairman] and Rodionov [secretary]), the Directorate of Internal Affairs (Comrade Abramov), the raikoms of the CPSU [Communist Party], and the raion ispolkoms have not undertaken all possible measures to reduce the growth of the city's population due to migration and have not brought sufficient order to this work. The Moscow ispolkom and the ispolkoms of Sverdlovskii, Stalinskii, Baumanskii, Kuibyshevskii, and a number of raion soviets continue to enlist workers from other parts of the country and to give ungrounded permissions for propiska to certain citizens.
>
> The leaders of some construction organizations, enterprises, and offices are permitting individuals to live in their housing without registration, bringing in workers and putting them up in buildings unsuitable for habitation, and not seeing to it that employees whose temporary registration have expired leave Moscow.

The Directorate of Internal Affairs of the Mosgorispolkom is doing a poor job of checking on the work of militia bureaus in supporting the passport regime. In Moscow there reside a whole lot of people who have no propiska or passport, who have repeated criminal convictions, or who are not engaged in socially useful labor.

Several raion executive committees (Kalininskii, Leningradskii, Moskvoretskii, and Kuibyshevskii) are without sufficient validation issuing orders for occupancy of new housing space to persons who have never lived in Moscow and have housing in other regions.

The raikoms of the CPSU are only weakly involving themselves in strengthening the passport regime.[10]

The big-stick policy did have a stiffening effect. The annual percentage rise in Moscow's numbers declined by one-third, from 2.4 percent in the period 1947–1956 to 1.6 percent for the rest of the 1950s. The 1960 annexation hiked the population by 20 percent with a stroke of the pen, but it could be defended as a recognition of social realities and not a real enlargement. Factor it out, and Moscow's demographic growth for 1960–1964 dropped further, to 0.9 percent a year. Most encouraging to the government, about three-quarters resulted from procreation, not migration.[11]

Chief Architect Iosif Loveiko and the head of the drafting team for the new master plan, Nikolai N. Ullas, maintained in the spring of 1960 that Moscow should stand by the ceiling of 5 million inhabitants legislated in 1935, even though the population already exceeded that. In a speech to a national conference on town planning in June 1960, shortly before his replacement by Posokhin, Loveiko called on the city to resist the "great pressure" from branch agencies and agencies "seeking whatever way they can to expand their construction in Moscow."[12]

The boundary expansion of August 1960, which tipped Moscow over 6 million, did not dismay the restrictionists. In 1961 G. Ye. Mishchenko of GlavAPU chided past curbs as irresolute and mused that Moscow could accommodate no more than 5 to 5.2 million people in the 1980s, with perhaps another 0.8 million to 1 million in the green belt. Posokhin, less obdurate than Loveiko but still restriction-minded, asserted come 1962 that the plan would halt the upward march of population at the current 6.2 million.[13]

The TEO for the plan represented a partial yet hallucinatory win for the antigrowth camp. Affirmed in 1966, the year the population hit 6.5 million, it projected stabilization at 6.6 to 6.8 million. The problem that soon revealed itself was not in any wishy-washiness in the planners' preferences but in their being out of touch with demographic realities. The annual increase in population jumped in the second half of the 1960s to 2.0 percent, leaving Posokhin little alternative in a 1970 statement but to back off. His new target, 7 million, was 200,000 to 400,000 more than the TEO figure and, inexplicably, almost 100,000 less than the number clocked in the national census of January 1970.[14] The general plan finally adopted in 1971 marked the biggest retreat yet, to 8 million residents at the conclusion of the time allotment, or 3 million more than the goal flaunted in 1960.

Even that dike did not hold (see Table 9 and Appendix A). If growth moderated after 1970, it was from an unexpectedly high base and remained brisker than during the first half of the 1960s. Grishin in 1975 braced Moscow to expect 8.5 million denizens, not 8 million, in 1990. He, too, miscalculated. The city lumbered past 8 million in 1979, eleven years early, and past 8.5 million in 1983. It grazed 9 million in 1990–1991.[15]

Early planners had hoped for an urban steady state or a mild decrease. The TEO implied an annual increment of 7,000 to 20,000 between 1966 and 1981, and the approved version 53,000 a year until 1990. In fact, the average increment between 1971 and 1990 was 105,000, or twice the compromised estimate of 1971.

Whereas biological increase early in the 1960s, when the TEO were being cooked up, accounted for the bulk of population growth, and controls on in-migration acted fairly effectively, the tables dramatically turned in the mid-1960s. Lower fertility and higher mortality rates, the backwash mostly of wartime losses and the aging of the population, dampened natural increase. And at this very time in-migration ballooned. From 1965 to the late 1980s, roughly 85 percent of Moscow's demographic gain stemmed from mass influx from Russian towns and villages—movement of the kind debarred by the master plan.[16]

The administrative fetters in the possession of local authorities—personal passports and residential permits—might be thought more than adequate for retarding migration. Their implications for civil rights were not a question in Soviet Russia. It should have been possible for leaders to anticipate population trends and modulate them with some finesse, handing out or withholding residency as needed. Such was the intent of the tough talk of the 1950s, which for a time had the fancied result.

Without doubt, the passport-propiska regime had an extenuating effect in Moscow throughout the post-Stalin period. It shut hundreds of thousands of provincials out, helped keep growth consistently below the Soviet urban average,[17] and precluded hyperurbanization. It had the odd naysayer in the press and the specialist literature, but most Muscovites perceived it as beyond changing. More than that, many saw positive merit in it. Over and over, I heard it said that without coercive restrictions Moscow would be transmogrified, not into a New York or London, as the TEO preamble suggested, but into a Russian Calcutta or Mexico City, with brushfire growth, shanty-towns, and bruising competition between migrants and indigenes.

None of this alters the fact that Moscow grew twice as fast as the plan allowed, with acute repercussions on the standard of living. How could this be? To begin with, the propiska system had a humanitarian escape hatch to accommodate the 30 percent of all Moscow marriages that occurred with out-of-towners, and it was not uncommonly abused. In what was snidely called "matrimonial migration," nonresidents, usually males, contracted a fictitious marriage with a registered resident, dissolving it after acquiring a permanent propiska.

Nor was outright evasion of propiska unknown, as the directives of the 1950s trying to scare officials and residents into compliance recognized. Public policy and private desires constantly conflicted. Living "the bird's life" *(na ptich'ikh pravakh)*, as the phrase went, was easier in hypertrophied housing developments than in the closer and fearful setting of Stalin's Moscow, where most buildings had the intimate enclosed courtyards that characterized older Russian towns. The raion "passport desk" was staffed by the regular police, not the awesome OGPU, and not a few officers were prepared to live and let live. Especially under Brezhnev, corruption entered into the picture, as venal cops and concierges accepted bribes to look the other way while the "birds" fluttered into the black market and criminal under-world.

Another entryway, less underhand and more discriminating, was reserved for members of organizations—the party apparatus, ministries, defense plants and design bureaus, KGB, top science institutes, and a few others—that had the clout to get admission requirements waived. At maybe half of their sittings, Moscow's municipal executive organs reacted to the "fearsome flow of letters" (Vladimir Promyslov's words) from agencies on behalf of actual and prospective employees and their relatives. The city ispolkom considered 699 requests in 1971 and the presidium 3,620, covering between them about 15,000 individuals; about 80 percent of the applicants received propiskas. The practice was never mentioned in the press.[18]

It was, however, political tugging and hauling by corporate actors, involving the ordinary run of citizen, that underlay what I estimate to be two-thirds of the above-plan migration. The best way for outsiders to be logged into Moscow was by taking up a normal tender of employment and adhering to the city's procedures for gaining clearance. Some employers played fast and loose with the law—calling to mind the wooing of Mexican laborers in California—but that was the exception. Generally, the executive of the city soviet, advised by its small Labor Directorate (with a staff of 120 in the 1980s), granted labor "limits" (limity, the same term as for licenses to building materials) for Moscow. These annual certificates entitled factories, government offices, and other masters to add out-of-towners—limitchiki, in Russian newspeak—to their payrolls. Once the police inscribed their passports, usually for a probation of three to five years, the limitchiki and their families could receive temporary shelter and blend into waiting lists for regular housing and social benefits. It was a Faustian bargain; until given a permanent stamp, they were, as Boris Yeltsin was to say, twentieth-century "slaves," with "practically no rights at all."[19]

The authors of the 1971 plan intended to get at population growth principally by inhibiting migration and job creation. The published TEO foresaw a work force of 4 million, for little or no net increase in employment. Three hundred and fifty thousand jobs in manufacturing and construction, the "city-forming group," were to be redistributed to the "city-servicing group," primarily trade and retail services, and positions in state administration were to be slashed by 20 to 25 percent for the USSR and RSFSR bureaucracy and 30 to 35 percent for local offices. Additionally, daily commuters from Podmoskov'e were expected to decline from 500,000 to 200,000 out of the 4 million. The plan's final (1971) mandate on employment, which was not published then or since, must have looked to a total payroll in 1990 on the order of 4.5 million.

Bloated by the 700,000 limitchiki admitted between 1971 and 1986, 420,000 of them after 1980, Moscow job rosters in 1990 reached or exceeded 5 million—better than a half-million more than in the revised 1971 forecast and 1 million more than in the TEO. Commuters from the oblast totaled 650,000, a hike of 150,000 rather than a decrease of 300,000, and 20,000 "guest workers" from client states (mostly Vietnam) were toiling in factories on Soviet visas.[20]

What went awry here? Despite some contraction after 1980 and a depletion in relative terms, absolute employment in manufacturing went up slightly between 1960 and 1985 (see Table 10). Instead of 350,000 places being winkled out of manufacturing and construction, Moscow had perhaps 50,000 factory workers and 125,000 construction workers *more* in 1985 than at the start. In every other branch the work force surged by more than one-third. In health, education, and culture it was up by more than 100 percent. In science—much of it attached to industry and about half of it arms-related—it increased by 141 percent. Jobs rose most of all in public administration, by 150 percent. "On the initiative of particular ministries and vedomstva," in Grishin's words, "there continue the procreation of new enterprises and organizations and the expansion of existing ones, especially research institutes and administrative organs." In spite of the plan's flat prohibition, 30 manufacturing enterprises and more than 200 for science and science services were established between 1971 and 1990. In state administration only the army officers and family members admitted from provincial and foreign garrisons came to 5,000 persons per annum in the second half of the 1970s and about 9,000 per annum in the 1980s.[21]

From 1965 to 1980, at least, rises in the work force covaried with total population (compare Tables 10 and 9). For the first half of the 1980s, accelerated retirements imparted a new wrinkle. Although employment expanded by its pokiest rate since the war, population bounded forward, spurred by the signing up of batteries of limitchiki to fill vacancies in industry and services. Population growth did not decelerate appreciably until the onset of economic crisis in the late 1980s.

Local government sat on its hands as all this transpired. A GlavAPU

Table 10. Changes in employment by sector, 1960–1984

	Percent increase in employment					
Branch of economy	1960–1964	1965–1969	1970–1974	1975–1979	1980–1984	1960–1984
Manufacturing	3.8	1.5	0.1	0.6	−1.9	4.1
Construction[a]	−8.8	21.5	15.3	9.8	−1.8	34.4
Transport	7.6	6.6	6.9	10.5	0.6	36.3
Communications	24.4	2.9	16.9	9.4	−4.9	55.6
Housing and consumer services	−0.4	13.2	6.2	6.3	5.1	33.8
Trade[b]	28.6	10.1	4.6	13.0	3.0	58.2
Health	9.8	18.3	19.8	12.9	7.4	106.9
Education and culture[c]	22.9	17.9	9.4	18.0	7.3	100.5
Science and science services	55.6	15.4	14.9	15.0	1.2	140.5
Public administration and law enforcement[d]	31.2	42.3	16.5	12.8	1.9	150.2
Total	13.8	11.3	9.1	7.9	1.2	50.9

Sources: Taken and calculated from Moskva v tsifrakh, 1966–1970 gg. (Moscow: Statistika, 1972), p. 67; Moskva v tsifrakh, 1978 (Moscow: Statistika, 1978), p. 67; Moskva v tsifrakh, 1988 (Moscow: Finansy i statistika, 1988), p. 116.
   a. Production personnel only.
   b. Includes only personnel in retail trade until 1980.
   c. Averages separate figures for education and culture from 1980 on.
   d. Excludes small number of personnel in information and computer services from 1980 on.

specialist, Mikhail Dudik, warned as early as 1967 that the work force was not being closely monitored or reined in. "Through separate, unconnected decisions, individual vedomstva are year to year growing in significantly larger numbers than those foreseen by the TEO," he said. Sidestepping city hall, the agencies "go to the [central] government with requests for supplementary permission" to enlarge their plants, laboratories, and offices. GlavAPU, preoccupied with spatial and architectural issues, did not even figure in Dudik's account. At a plenum of the Moscow gorkom in December 1970, a deputy chairman of RSFSR Gosplan was the one to tell assembled officials that employer bids for staff increments in 1971 had totaled 203,000 places; 42,000 of these had been granted, and special pleading by the ministries had not subsided.[22]

The invigoration of Gorplan in 1975 and the interest in social planning made city officials better informed and more vigilant. Moscow rebuffed petitions for 77,000 limitchiki in 1978 and 104,000 in 1979. But the vedomstva still submitted requests for allocations of land, building capacity, and labor, "and they literally attack[ed] city organizations on these questions."[23]

In an interview in 1987, when glasnost' was loosening tongues, the director of the Institute of the Master Plan, Valentin I. Ivanov, described an ongoing guerrilla war between local and state business interests:

> Often the ministries and agencies adjust their plans without taking notice of the capabilities of the city, or its labor and territorial resources, and seek to expand output . . . by attracting extra staff, mainly from outside the city. Practically every ministry and agency has exceeded the [incremental] personnel limits laid down in 1980 by 20 to 80 percent . . . As a result, Moscow's population has expanded far above that provided for by the master plan . . . We bring the plan's provisions to the attention of the ministries and agencies, but this does not always suit them. They go around us, elicit sanctions from higher-ranking organizations, sometimes even get the Moscow ispolkom to agree . . . They make petitions to Gosplan, which then sanctions the further development of this or that branch in Moscow.[24]

Factories, military and civilian, exerted the strongest pull, causing the entry of 44 percent of migrant workers in the 1970s. Although manufacturing employment grew by only 2,000 during the decade, 250,000 limitchiki entered Moscow through the industrial revolving door. "After expiry of their work contracts on the limit [po limitu], and having acquired a Moscow propiska and housing, these people often move to jobs in more prestigious branches with more comfortable conditions of work."[25]

The city, a large employer itself, was not above reproach. Construction organizations, most of them municipally operated, accounted for 32 percent of all permits issued in the 1970s. Builders like Glavmosstroi became as addicted as heavy industry to an annual infusion of outsiders, and the filthy, dangerous, but passably high-paying work was often the best a migrant could fall into. Eighty-two percent of the new hands taken on by the building departments under the Mossovet in 1971 through 1977 were new or recent arrivals; more than 40 percent did not have a secondary education, and only 18 percent had the trade school diplomas recommended for blue-collar workers.[26] City agencies providing consumer and social services seldom had the funds to secure immigrants upon arrival, but many came their way—seeking easy and safe work, with moonlighting and graft opportunities—once they had paid their dues in manual labor.

Muscovites looked down on the migrants as uncouth and took offense at their resource claims. But few wanted the thankless jobs that the limitchiki took before clambering up the social ladder.

Nor were political and bureaucratic conditions auspicious for tightening up on population growth. GlavAPU and Gorplan, the planning bodies with a stake in the problem, were mutually suspicious and dismissive. In interviews architecturally trained GlavAPU officials slighted Gorplan's social planning as unmanly "stock taking," not real planning, while a Gorplan department head said bluntly of the 1971 master plan, "this is not our plan." A senior researcher in the Institute of the Economic Problems imparted that most of the time there was "absolutely no communication" between the two, and not much more with GlavUKS, the Chief Directorate of Capital Construction. No action was taken on Chief Architect Posokhin's proposal in 1978 for a tripartite coordinator of the coordinators, a "special planning and urban development committee or council for the city of Moscow" with representatives of the feuding parties.[27]

THE USE AND MISUSE OF LAND

Imperial Russia's cities were closely settled by Western standards, and Moscow was no exception. The chronic housing shortage and the ideological preference for apartments reproduced this pattern after the revolution and after Stalin's death. Moscow's gross population density of more than 8,000 persons per square kilometer in 1980, although 40 percent less than in the 1950s, paralleled that of 1914. Moscow as a whole approached the density of the core areas of London and New York.[28]

In 1975, four years into the master plan, First Secretary Grishin affirmed the commitment to keep Moscow within the MKAD highway, its circular outer limit since August 1960. Only three years later Posokhin suddenly stated to the gorkom that Moscow would run out

of land in 1981 and that planners were analyzing "variants for placement of construction, some of them utilizing the reserve territories."[29]

This expansion came to pass in October 1983, after Posokhin's
retirement but before Grishin's, when the town of Solntsevo west of
the MKAD was annexed as Moscow's thirty-third raion. In March
1984 and December 1985 Solntsevskii raion was padded out and
peninsulas affixed to five extant raions. The deepest, Novopodrez-
kovo-Kurkino on the northwest, stuck 10 kilometers into the oblast
at Khimki. Whereas the master plan provided for only the possibility
of garnisheeing 100 square kilometers, and not before 1990 at that,
the land grab of 1983–1985 took more than 200 square kilometers
and brought Moscow's surface area to 1,062 square kilometers, including Zelenograd and Tolstopal'tsevo, a small area 10 kilometers
past Solntsevo.

The oblast fought the change within the bureaucracy and insisted
on greenhouses and construction equipment as recompense for the
farmland lost. The fracas had to be adjudicated by the Politburo.[30]
Moscow officials, led by Posokhin's understudy and successor as chief
planner, Gleb V. Makarevich, opined vacuously that the breakout
would "strengthen the close mutual ties" between Moscow and the
green belt." Everyone else regarded it as proof of misgovernment.
That Moscow was still compact by global norms mattered less than
the betrayal of the no-annexation promise.

Moscow's inability to restrain its population growth and the resulting sprawl were compounded, as discussed below, by its failure to
match the human inflow with housing construction in surfeit of the
1971 targets. The city would have better dulled its ravenous land
hunger and compensated for population growth were it not for those
same features of its political economy that allowed development at
high densities in the first place.

One such trait was the substitution of administrative fiat for the
commercial determination of land values that obtains in capitalist
cities. In the West the interplay of supply and demand gives most
metropolitan areas a steep density gradient, sloping downward from
the high-priced and built-up business center to lightly populated outer
suburbs. Governments cannot assign most land, since it is private
property, but they wield influence through zoning and other devices
that affect the use, conveyance, and exchange value of pieces of land.

The density gradient in socialist Moscow was shallower, and it inverted the usual silhouette, resembling a low saucer with a bit of a convex center. Densities were highest in the core and along the radial roads feeding into it, built up by pre-1917 capitalism and by Stalinist monumentalism, and then toward the edge of the city, where technical advances enabled construction of successively taller generations of apartment high rises. Never after the abrogation of NEP did land's scarcity value or ruble price, at most a petty bookkeeping entry, enter into the picture.

Several Moscow economists and engineers, led by S. I. Kabakova and Aleksandr A. Segedinov, argued in the 1960s and 1970s for tenancy charges for land, which would have been tantamount to gradated rents, with a spread of up to twelve-to-one per hectare. They would have left it to planners to ascertain "rational use," via a prolix formula mixing capital cost, operating outlays, and the "economic and social effect" of any proposed investment. They were on the right track, though, in attacking "the misimpression that city land is 'cost-free'" and in urging that indirect as well as direct costs be brought into development decisions.[31]

Officialdom did not listen: it went on treating land as a free, administratively deployable good. The predictable effects ensued, beginning with the violation of the MKAD barrier. The most lamentable was the switch of almost 50 square kilometers of parkland—more than 30 percent of that designated by the 1971 plan—to housing tracts. This change occurred in the late 1970s and 1980s mainly in Strogino (in northwest Moscow), Krylatskoye (west), Orekhovo-Borisovo (south), and Nikulino, the Olympic Village, and Ramenki (southwest). Strogino, Krylatskoye, and Orekhovo-Borisovo largely caused the thinning out of the recreational land along the Moskva River by 12 percent.[32]

Planners and builders also spurned advice to relieve pressure by constructing garages and shopping malls underground, something the Russian climate alone recommended. While happily taking over parkland, which was mostly empty, level, and well drained, they shied away from putting housing and consumer facilities on the 200 square kilometers of underutilized territory within the MKAD—taken up by farms, warehouses, evictable factories, ravines, bogs, gravel pits, dumps, sewage aeration fields, rights of way for rail and high-voltage power lines, switching yards, and the like. They did not revamp off-the-shelf building designs to accommodate hilly relief and other nonroutine sites, wasting 15 to 20 percent of the land in many places. They caved in to industry, which by 1979 had spread over 32 more square kilometers in Moscow than the total allotted for 1990, and to the sponsors of office and public buildings, which encompassed 18 square kilometers more than budgeted.[33]

Obfuscation and legal indeterminacy clouded decisions surrounding land utilization. Not only were the master plan's summing-up tome and main maps (at a scale of 1:10,000) classified for official use only, but no codified Soviet law existed of either macroscopic land use planning or microscopic zoning. The general plan stipulated exact use of only small sections of Moscow. It set neither height nor density maximums. GlavAPU prepared 1:2,000 detail plans (*proyekty detal'noi planirovki,* or PDPs) for many plots on thoroughfares and intersections, and raion planners sometimes did the same for lesser parcels. Almost never, though, was the public alerted to this kind of assignment.

In the case of the parks Muscovites were apprised of the switch only retrospectively, and of its full dimensions only after 1985. To cite another example: the Komsomol lobbied into the 1971 plan a confidential clause agreeing to a Moscow Palace of Youth (exhibition hall and theater) on Arbatskaya ploshchad', minutes from the Kremlin. Giving no notice, the city bound the land over to the USSR Ministry of Defense, which was sequestered in tsarist- and Stalin-era buildings on the other side of ulitsa Frunze. The army at the end of the 1970s put up an office palace for the General Staff—eight stories high, a city block square, faced in marble, and connected to the subway—and the young people got theirs ten years later on Komsomol'skii prospekt in the Khamovniki area, well away from downtown.[34]

PLANNING ZONES AND PRODUCTION ZONES

Two of the master plan's more ambitious provisos aimed to rationalize land use. Both were signal failures. In the first of these, Moscow was carved into eight planning zones (Figure 58) with an average of 1 million inhabitants each, one in the middle of the city (out to the former Kamer-kollezhskii val) and seven between there and the

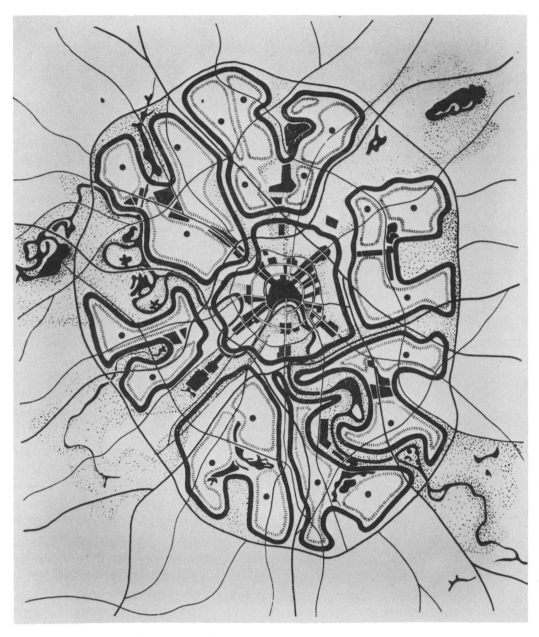

Figure 58. The eight planning zones of the 1971 master plan. (From M. I. Astaf'eva-Dlugach et al., *Moskva*, Moscow: Stroiizdat, 1979, p. 43.)

MKAD. Each was to have more or less parity between jobs and housing units and time-saving self-sufficiency in recreation and soft services. Individuals would "be able, if they find it convenient, to work at enterprises or offices located in their zones [of residence] and, without leaving the zone, pass their spare time or engage in sport."[35]

The boundaries of the macrozones, with populations from 650,000 to 1,340,000 (for the central zone), were set in 1977, as were plans for subcenters appropriate to their topography and social character and decorated with public art "displaying the heroic history of the Soviet people." The northern or Ostankino zone, for example, was to have a hotel, a restaurant featuring non-Russian cuisines, and a USSR House of Wholesale Trade by 1985; the northwest zone was to have a puppet theater and district library, the eastern zone a "marriage palace" and a fashion house at Izmailovo Park.[36]

Many Muscovites questioned the prudence of the planning zones after the fact, considering any attempt to replace Moscow's living core with a pleiad of artificial subcenters misguided: "You can relocate the selling of furniture from GUM to Medvedkovo [in the far north of Moscow], but the beauty and spirituality of the Kremlin and the memory of history cannot be picked up in the hand and moved out of place."[37]

Whatever their hypothetical value, the macrozones had a nugatory impact. The planning studios set up for them never asserted themselves over GlavAPU's other branches. Nor did their boundaries or work ever dovetail with the city's raions, which, on investment and works issues, could bring the influence of raion partocrats to bear.[38]

The planners found no hook whatsoever for getting commuters to work and reside within the same zone. Most planning and building activity was directed at the zones' physical nuclei, where the result was not much more inspiring. One or two zones lacked funds for any construction. In others, such as the southwestern (Lomonosov) zone, some clustering of recreation and shopping was discernible, yet not at the locations on the planners' charts. Elsewhere, a smidgeon of construction began at arbitrarily selected sites, commonly in semivacant areas where transport access was bad and there were no local conveniences for visitors.

The experience with the "production zones" *(proizvodstvennyye zony),* the second formula for rationalization of urban space, produced similar results. Partisans noted the irony that industry was distributed in socialist Moscow in much the same unorchestrated fashion as in tsarist times: "The building of industrial complexes . . . retains its traditional character. Industry as before is oriented toward the rivers and railway lines and constitutes a dispersed network located on the same general territory as housing."[39] In the name of efficient utilization of land and machinery, pollution abatement, and aesthetics, the 1971 plan set out to relocate some 800 of Moscow's factories and manufacturing shops. Three hundred and fifty-six were to be shooed out of Moscow entirely, and the balance rebased in production zones, many of them in the south, southwest, and west, where industry was scarce. Buffered from housing by sanitary cordons, the zones were to hold clean, up-to-date factory premises as well as shared utilities, transport, storage, other substructure, and services for workers.

Given the realities of the Soviet hydra state, the production zones never had a chance of success. One observer wrote in 1975 that the Institute of the Master Plan's sketches stayed on the easel because there was no political button for bringing behavior into conformity with plan: "No one bears responsibility for organizing the building or rebuilding of the production zone as a whole." Instead prevailed "the narrowly departmental approach . . . on the principle, 'The main thing is to look out for your own interest.'" In new zones most partners stuck to the plots allotted but maximized autarky in what they built; in the one zone in four being inserted into older areas, they fought to keep as many workshops, sheds, and boilers as they could.[40]

These were not teething pains only. The zones in the early 1980s were at only one-third of the approved density, and most lacked city input. Writing in 1987, three planners characterized the problem this way:

> The serious work of designing and building the production zones lies ahead. Scarce land is used in them ineffectively and often wastefully. The "estate" principle prevails. Every enterprise acquires its parcel of land and develops it at its individual discretion. As a rule, the only common things created are engineering communications. The formation of big "hotel" complexes for enterprises in the production zones, where each would have the necessary floor space for production but industrial infra-

structure and establishments for leisure and daily services [for employees] would be collectivized, is being hampered above all by the organizational principle whereby each director wants to have "his own" operation and to be autonomous.[41]

Only the local party organs could have begun to slice through bureaucratic bulkheads such as these. They never seized themselves of the problem. No Moscow leader made more than perfunctory mention of either the production or the planning zones until after Grishin's fall.

GREATER MOSCOW REVISITED

Moscow's rulers were not keen to take on the problems of the larger capital region. With Moscow oblast, its boundaries stable except for tiny changes in 1956 and 1957 (see Map 21), they had progressively fewer ties after 1953. The separation of the party gorkom from the obkom in 1956 did away with the main residuum of the fused city-province of the 1920s. Cross-seating between the city and oblast ispolkoms ended in 1955 and between the two soviets in 1957. Khrushchev's industrial reform in 1957 established separate sovnar-khozes for Moscow and the oblast, in spite of some sentiment for a joint one. In February 1958 *Moskovskaya pravda* was made a Mos-cow-only newspaper and a new mouthpiece, *Leninskoye znamya* (Leninist Banner), was founded for the obkom and oblast soviet.[42]

The city's sluggish geographic growth reflected diffidence toward Podmoskov'e. Authorized by the 1935 plan to go from 285 to 600 square kilometers, Moscow reached only 356 square kilometers by August 1960. Much of the oblast territory bit off in 1960 had been placed in its land bank twenty-five years before and could have been annexed any time.

The resultant neglect of border communities resembled the attitude of earlier years. An area like Izmailovo, a backwater in the 1930s, was well on its way to being a preferred district by the 1950s. But Staryye Cheremushki, a hamlet of a thousand in the oblast's Leninskii raion a half-kilometer past southwest Moscow, was as much a cast-away as Izmailovo a generation before, as a letter to *Moskovskaya pravda* related. In Moscow, where the adult residents were employed, most clinics, schools, and kindergartens turned them and their chil-

MAP 21

dren away. The soviets of the hamlet and of the oblast raion sullenly provided as few services as they could get away with. Washboarded roads were barely passable, the one social club had closed down, and water delivery and police protection were often interrupted:

> When something untoward happens in the settlement . . . the residents naturally turn to the housing office of the hamlet soviet. There the petitioners are sent "around the departments." "Ask in the raion center, Lenino," they are told.

It is a good twenty kilometers to Lenino. And if a desperate person has
the resolve to get there, he is met, shall we say, with no special enthusiasm: "You're from Staryye Cheremushki? What are you doing bothering
us? If you work in Moscow, we don't see you or know you. You really
belong to the city."

By the same token, the city authorities sweep aside all suggestions
about Staryye Cheremushki's belonging to Moscow. So we are neither
ours nor yours, I am afraid.[43]

In the territorial glacis external to the most quickly urbanizing
zone, lackadaisical staff work and the reserve between city and oblast
sank all efforts to devise a workable program. The long-awaited green
belt put forth by the 1935 master plan, dilated into a fifty-kilometer-
deep "suburban zone," was inoperative. City planners, after several
false leads, completed a secret plan for it in 1954. It went unconfirmed
by the participating governments and was excoriated for slipshod
research and for overlooking concepts such as the satellite city, ignored for two decades but briefly praised by Khrushchev at the Twentieth Party Congress. A reprise in 1956–1957 was "not seen by anyone except experts."[44]

The absence of binding objectives corresponded with the lack of
an institutional master, as the suburban zone lay in murky "dual
subordination" to the city and the oblast. Preponderant influence
wound up with the oblast, which was more affected, and with the
economic players who itched for locations close by Moscow. Policy
leaned toward "the industrial development of the green belt, with
insufficient account of its purport for the amenities available to the
capital."[45]

There were, to be sure, glints of a more visionary approach. Mikhail Barshch, who as a young blood coauthored a "deurbanist"
project for Moscow in 1929, offered a brief for the hinterland as the
centerpiece of metropolitan development. He pronounced the capital
starved of sunshine, oxygen, and "everything that is a normal need
for human beings." He proposed an aureole of sylvan satellite towns,
30,000 to 40,000 residents each and forty to fifty kilometers out along
high-velocity roads and railways. Intermixing cottages or small apartment houses with nonpolluting industry, gardens, and woods, they
would absorb surplus population, allow "animate communication

with nature," and let Moscow "breathe freely again." P. A. Pomozanov of the Institute of the Master Plan outdid Barshch, recommending that construction of garden cities be accompanied by demolition of the Moscow housing evacuated and its replacement, not by
new buildings, but by gardens and parks.[46]

Moscow took a step toward satellites in 1956, when the Institute
of the Master Plan fixed on six sites—at Chanovo, Golovkovo,
Kamenka, Krasnaya Pakhra, Ozeretskoye, and Voronovo—thirty-five
to fifty-five kilometers out of the capital. Officials put Kryukovo (later
Zelenograd) on the list in 1957—work began there in 1958—and
examined older provincial towns, such as Dmitrov and Zagorsk, for
refitting. By 1960 there were schemes for rehousing 1 million Muscovites in twenty satellite cities. Optimism welled among the advocates
of freezing or shrinking Moscow's population. Nikolai Ullas, for one,
coupled adherence to the 1935 plan's ceiling of 5 million to the
building of a double halo of outlying towns, those close to Moscow
with housing only and the outermost group offering employment as
well in plants and institutes evacuated from Moscow.[47]

Territorial explosion in 1960 touched off momentary gusto for
Greater Moscow. That phrase, in disuse for three decades, now connoted not only a much enlarged Moscow but a panregional perspective on planning choices.

The near tripling of Moscow's land surface did away with the
ours-yours dichotomy that had plagued the Staryye Cheremushkis
within and just outside the 1935 reserve lands. Services along the
periphery still lagged, but the annexation made it possible to lessen
the gap little by little.

The 1960 amalgamation decree reinstituted a compact green belt
(forest-park protective belt) exterior to the MKAD. Ten to 15 kilometers in radius—25 at a northern promontory around three reservoirs
of the Moscow-Volga Canal—and 1,800 square kilometers in area, it
measured one-quarter larger than the green belt of 1935–1950 but
only about one-eighth the size of the tumescent and mostly fictitious
suburban zone of 1950–1960. Novelly, the green belt, sectioned into
five new raions (Balashikhinskii, Krasnogorskii, Lyuberetskii, Mytishchenskii, and Ul'yanovskii), was placed in "administrative and economic subordination" to Moscow, the category an inch short of
annexation. Local deputies for each area stood down from the oblast

council and were co-opted into the Mossovet; raion party workers were likewise repositioned in the Moscow gorkom; the budgets of the green belt raions were incorporated into Moscow's. Municipal elections in March 1961 were jointly organized for Moscow and the green belt. Moscow officials held forth about city, forest belt, and satellite cities as a "unified organism," and they and suburbanites seemed to be going on the assumption that the capital itself would put in all needed transport, housing, and social infrastructure.[48]

The honeymoon ended quickly. The phrase Greater Moscow vanished from rhetoric in early 1961. The electronics workshop, Zelenograd, proved to be the only satellite city actually built; it had 132,000 people by 1980, twice the projected number, and was governed as a raion of Moscow. Both the 1966 TEO and the 1971 master plan left out mention of other satellites. Quietly, to minimize embarrassment, the government backpedaled on the green belt in November 1961. A decree removed the five raions and their 866,000 people from the city's pocket to Moscow oblast's and restored the pre–August 1960 status quo in the local soviets, party organs, and budgets,[49] Dual subordination was reinstated for physical planning of the green belt in September 1962.

The reasons for the flip-flop can be read between the lines. Oblast functionaries felt that slurs were being cast upon their past conduct. They were frosty toward the loss of prized territory in 1960 and toward satellite cities, which they insinuated would be haughty outposts with "a 'Moscow' regime separate from the oblast's."[50] But they could not have forced the retreat alone. Muscovites, too, had reservations, as they had in the past. After the first tingle of excitement over regional imperium, leaders and specialists fell back to earth when contemplating the resource implications.

Even boosters blanched at the price tag of carting labor and materials to Zelenograd, twenty kilometers from the MKAD. The same would have had to be done for future satellites several times remoter, in an economic setting that precluded contracting out. Abram M. Zaslavskii, Moscow's deputy chief architect and a senior planner since 1931, prophesied defilement of recreational land and warned that it would be "economically absurd" to shunt factories into Podmoskov'e to provide work for ex-urbanites. Better for the state to subsidize backward regions, and for Moscow to stick to improving the green belt "on a realistic basis . . . in proportion to the growth of economic capacity." This was the finding of experts from the Academy of Sciences and the construction bureaucracy asked to screen a preliminary version of the TEO. Predisposed to satellite development, they came around to a consensus that new towns be encouraged only in "exceptional circumstances."[51]

Strictly speaking, the costly satellites might have been discarded and unmediated physical control kept over the green belt. But the lesser commitment was still intimidating, and it suffered guilt by association with the satellite towns. Local and national decision makers kissed Greater Moscow goodbye and opted for a more tenuous and a more conventional relationship.

LIVING WITH THE AGGLOMERATION

Russian geographers and planners discovered in the 1970s their urban agglomerations *(aglomeratsii),* a phenomenon previously said to rear its head only in capitalist nations. They began to conceive of urbanization as taking place on a broader canvas and in response to a richer menu of stimuli than previously thought in the USSR. More accepting of the complexity of metropolitan regions, they were thus less enamored of trying to manage them through a single juridical entity, for one monopoly purpose, or by evoking a simple criterion such as optimal city size or proximity to the mother city.[52]

Definitions of the Moscow agglomeration varied widely. Some comprised those urban centers from which large numbers of workers commuted into the capital, others the population to a distance of 100 kilometers, and still others every resident of the oblast, 65 percent urbanized by 1980. All conceptions shared two aspects: the diversity of the interactions between Moscow and its hinterland; and the slight extent to which these interactions were influenced by city government.

Commuting across municipal lines has been the lot of tens of thousands of occupants of the Moscow region since the 1800s. Moscow could no more do without the 650,000 or so inbound day-workers in the 1980s, 13 percent of its work force, than without the limitchiki. Twenty-five to 30 percent of work-age residents of the green belt towns commuted into Moscow; this number declined to 2 percent 50 to 60 kilometers distant. Meanwhile 150,000 to 180,000 Muscovites (estimates vary) shuttled to work at factories, research institutes, and offices in the oblast (such as the polygon of the First Chief Directorate, the espionage branch of the KGB, opened just beyond the MKAD at Yasenevo in 1972, to which dozens of buses from Moscow streamed morning and evening).[53]

People also coursed across the divide for nonwork reasons, as typifies conurbations everywhere. The peculiarities of Soviet society tinctured these crosscurrents. The most careful study showed 610,000 oblast dwellers, from up to 110 kilometers away, visiting Moscow per day in the mid-1970s. Waxing about 4 percent a year, this movement accounted for 57 percent of all local rail traffic in summer and 45 percent in winter. Only one-sixth of the sojourners sought cultural enlightenment or spectator sports (see Table 11). Most wanted to satisfy basic household needs by doing what was achingly difficult to do in the Russian provinces—to consume, either foodstuffs or manufactured goods. Residents of the oblast scooped up 27 percent of all goods retailed in Moscow, a figure reported to be 35 or 40 percent by 1985.[54]

Recreational exploitation was where cooperation and city leadership were most noticeable. Forty percent of Muscovites in the 1980s debouched into Podmoskov'e for this purpose each week, 30 percent on summer Saturdays and Sundays (which became easier with the

Table 11. Motivation of nonwork visits by residents of Moscow oblast, 1974

Purpose	Percent of visitors reporting purpose
Purchase food	
At state store	38.1
At peasant market	1.7
Purchase consumer goods	37.7
Cultural pursuits	
Park	8.9
Theater or cinema	5.5
Exhibit or sporting event	2.1
Library	0.2
Public dining	5.8

Source: V. G. Glushkova and N. P. Shepelev, "Nekotoryye zakonomernosti kul'turno-bytovykh poyezdok iz Moskovskoi oblasti v Moskvu," *Vestnik Moskovskogo universiteta, Seriya V—geografiya,* no. 4 (July–August 1976), p. 99.

introduction of the five-day work week in 1968–1969); about 10 percent had access to dachas and produce gardens.[55] The forests of the green belt (see Map 22) supported about two-thirds of the individual activity. At Khrushchev's prompting, Moscow began in 1958 to organize "leisure zones" *(zony otdykha)* for raions undersupplied with parkland. There were twenty-one leisure zones by 1980, outfitted with picnic tables, play sets, and, in some zones, overnight campsites and hiking and ski trails; sixteen fell within the green belt, two on the Istra Reservoir west of the belt, and three inside the MKAD.

Even subsidized mass country recreation, one of socialist Moscow's successes, was less than perfect. The 1971 plan prescribed a 60 percent dilation of the green belt from 1,725 to 2,750 square kilometers, 1,480 square kilometers of it in forests, by 1990. This was not done. The green belt reached 1,775 square kilometers, then dropped to 1,720 after the 1983–1985 annexations; forest area fell to 720 square kilometers, a loss of 375 square kilometers.[56]

Static or ebbing area, penny pinching, and disorganization left the recreation system undercapitalized and oversubscribed. According to a 1982 account of defects (one of many that could be adduced),

> Out-of-town leisure, especially of short duration, still falls short of the organization of labor and daily life in the city. Most cutting are the following problems:
>
> 1. Lag of organization . . . behind real demand . . . especially when it comes to brief (Saturday and Sunday) outings and the recreation of families of diverse ages.
>
> 2. The insufficiency of professionally fitted-out and spacious areas . . . for utilization by large quantities of people. The concentrations of holidayers characteristic of many tracts of forests have not been counterbalanced by an effective system . . . for regulating their behavior, as a consequence of which there is occurring recreational degradation of woods and meadows.
>
> 3. Contradictions between the attractiveness of reservoirs for holidayers and the demands of the organs guarding water quality.
>
> 4. [Insufficient] maintenance of recreational resources because of: . . . the withdrawal of land for buildings, trans-shipping points, storage bases, warehouses; the fouling of water and atmosphere by factories, municipal facilities, transport, and agriculture; the worsening of the aesthetic qualities of territory due to ugly construction along roads, etc. . . . .

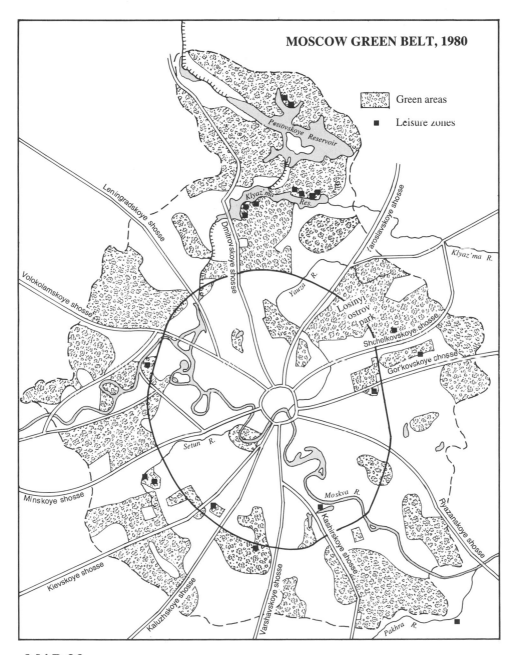

MAP 22

5. The underdevelopment of pieces of the recreational infrastructure like walking paths, automobile and bicycle roads, parking lots, trails, beaches, the marking of routes, and so on.[57]

Overuse was particularly hard on green areas closest in. Prime examples would be the beachfronts on the Moskva upstream from Moscow and the 110-square-kilometer Losinyi ostrov National Nature Park, brought under the aegis of the crown by Ivan the Terrible, which bridges Moscow's northeast boundary and the oblast. The drainage of bogs and swamps especially hurt Losinyi ostrov. Not even the nomenklatura dacha zone west of Moscow escaped. Local peasants damaged its forest through woodcutting and grazing of livestock, and construction officials through deleterious building practices, sometimes within sight of the Politburo châteaus.[58]

As for synoptic steering of the Moscow agglomeration, performance deviated sharply from promise. The TEO's population lid for the green belt, 1.2 million, stretched to the point that the 1971 plan called for stabilization at 1.5 to 1.7 million; since this subsumed 300,000 persons in areas to be amalgamated with the green belt, it would have meant growth of zero to 200,000 within the belt's 1971 borders. Aggregate demographic growth for Moscow, the green belt, and a 10,500-square-kilometer suburban zone hemming it, which would have slightly more leeway, was to be kept to 10 percent by 1990, or less than 0.5 percent a year. Expansion was to be pushed to the outer part of the oblast, which would gain population at double this clip—thirteen "basal centers" *(opornyye tsentry)* were identified as growth poles here—and even to other provinces in central Russia.

GlavAPU eventually prepared master plans for the towns in the green belt, but these and all normative documents had to be cleared with the oblast and Gosplan, and the belt was not considered a discrete planning object. Never restructured as intended, the belt took on new population about twice as quickly as planned, 85 percent of it from in-migration (mimicking Moscow).

According to the TEO, the green belt would function as "a limit preventing the merging of the capital with the nearby towns of the oblast." By 1980, though, the sizable green belt centers nearest to Moscow, all of them industrially based—Balashikha, Khimki, Lyubertsy, Mytishchi, and Reutov—had physically fused with the capital and had grown in combined population from 275,000 in 1959 to 606,000. This breach of the letter and spirit of the general plan raised the prospect of Moscow decomposing into an unmanageable blob a hundred kilometers across.[59]

Lyubertsy and Mytishchi, the eighth and sixth most populous cities in the oblast in 1959, had become the third and fifth in 1980; Podol'sk, the oblast's second city, abutted the green belt on the south; Kaliningrad, the nineteenth largest in 1959 and now the eighth, did so on the north. Kaliningrad, Khimki, Lyubertsy, and Reutov, in particular, were bastions of the unscrutinizable defense industry. Two of Moscow's airports—Vnukovo, to the west (opened in 1941), and Sheremet'evo, the international field, on the north (opened 1965)—sat right in the middle of green belt lands. The third and fourth airfields—Domodedovo, south of Moscow (1965), and Bykovo, the largest, southeast of the city (1933)—were located within several kilometers of the protected zone. All brought air and road traffic, noise, and fumes to woods and meadows.

On the policy of repelling economic and population growth, Table 12 traces a curve of good intentions gone astray. The green belt and suburban zone consistently outgrew the rest of the oblast, and in two subperiods out of three the green belt outgrew the suburban zone. The fringe of Podmoskov'e, its developmental magnets sickly, trailed behind—the diametric opposite of the objective. And neighboring oblasts were left in the dust by Moscow oblast as a whole. "The concept [of growth diversion] is not in practice being realized," one economist gasped in 1985. "There is too much inertia to the development of Moscow and the core of its agglomeration. The flywheel of their economy is devouring all the human resources set aside for the development of the periphery of Moscow oblast and the oblasts of the Central Economic Region."[60]

Housing

Citizens of the modern city have no more basic need than for the roof and walls that harbor their private lives. In most cultures homes are also powerful differentiators. Their size, beauty, furnishings, surroundings, and modes of acquisition and exchange set individuals, families, and social classes apart from one another. Housing politics

Table 12. Comparative population growth of Moscow and surrounding areas, 1959–1982

	Average annual increase (percent)		
Area	1959–1969	1970–1978	1979–1982
Moscow inside MKAD	1.4	1.4	1.2
Moscow oblast	1.8	1.2	0.7
Green belt[a]	2.9	1.2	1.1
Suburban zone[b]	2.1	1.5	0.8
External zone[c]	1.0	0.6	0.4
Other oblasts of Central Economic Region[d]	0.3	−0.2	−0.1
RSFSR	1.0	0.6	0.6
USSR	1.4	1.0	0.8

Source: V. Ya. Bekker, V. G. Glushkova, and B. S. Khorev, "Stolichnyi region: Problema ogranicheniya rosta yadra i sbalansirovannogo rasseleniya," in M. K. Bandman and O. A. Kibal'chin, eds., Ekonomiko-geograficheskiye problemy razvitiya stolichnykh regionov (Novosibirsk: AN SSSR—Sibirskoye otdeleniye, 1985), p. 32.

a. The seven raions encircling Moscow.
b. The eleven raions outside the green belt.
c. The remaining twenty-two raions of Moscow oblast.
d. Moscow oblast and eleven neighboring oblasts.

in socialist Moscow, as in most places, was one of the common denominators of urban existence and, potentially, one of the great segregators.

HOMES LIKE CARS

From its inception, the command economy attuned itself to quantity maximization, pursued through large, capital-intensive organizations geared to fulfill gross output quotas. The Khrushchevian reform of the housing sector, tested in Moscow, brought housing more in step with the economy as a whole. As billions of rubles in resources were ladeled in, investment and production were placed on an industrial scale instead of being done in driblets by isolated builders.

Glavmosstroi, the genotype of the new approach, explicitly aped the Soviet factory. A placard on its hoardings proclaimed, "Here We Assemble Homes Like Others Assemble Cars!" *(Zdes' sobirayem doma, kak sobirayut avtomobili!)* Three Glavmosstroi "house-building combines," integrating every stage of the process from cassette casting of concrete panels to wiring in kitchen appliances, were completing half of its volume by the mid-1970s. A step back in the cycle, another city conglomerate, Glavmospromstroimaterialov (the Chief Directorate for Building Materials), with 80,000 workers in 1980, supplied aggregates, modular components, glass, and finishing stuffs.

Small producers or proprietors had no role: a trifling 0.4 percent of Moscow's housing was privately owned in 1988,[61] and there were no private builders except for itinerant, gray-market repair and finishing crews (shabashniki). As a slight concession, local government made it easier for households wanting more congenial locations and room mixes to swap state-owned flats between themselves. City and raion exchange bureaus, which did no more than check on legalities before 1953, set up card files, an inspectorate, and a biweekly gazette for advertising offers, and the procuracy went easy on prosecutions of middlemen (called maklery) and tenants who made side payments to clinch deals. There were 100,000 official apartment trades in Moscow in 1981, as compared to 27,000 in 1961 and 3,500 in 1940.

A looser attitude toward the house-building cooperatives had greater consequences. Dormant since the 1930s, the co-ops received kindly words in the late 1950s and major USSR legislation in 1962, after which their production leapt to almost 20 percent of the Moscow total in 1970. Seven hundred thousand Muscovites lived in 2,000 cooperative buildings in 1980, and 9.7 percent of dwelling space in 1989 was in them. The cooperatives had little of the autonomy or political standing they had in the 1920s and mostly functioned as collection agencies for down payments, set at 40 percent of the principal by the 1962 law; state firms did all the construction.

Mechanized house making did bear out many of the hopes of its originators. Moscow completions, less than 500,000 square meters a year from 1933 to 1950, zoomed past 1 million square meters of net dwelling space (the 1913 level) in 1955, 2 million in 1958, and 3 million in 1960; they cleared that plateau until 1975. They at last propelled Moscow in 1963 or 1964—nearly a half-century after the Russian Revolution—over the 1912 index of per capita provision. (See Appendix D for completions and average supply.)

In-unit plumbing and conveniences also improved apace and approached saturation on most scores (Table 13). The trend was toward less cramped units as well, as they went from an average of 28 or 29

Table 13. Improvements to the housing stock, 1940–1984

Convenience	Percent of housing stock supplied				
	1940	1956	1966	1975	1984
Electricity	99.9	100.0	100.0	100.0	100.0
Running water	78.0	85.5	97.0	99.2	99.6
Sewage	73.0	83.1	96.0	99.1	99.5
Central heating	46.0	66.6	92.0	98.9	99.5
Natural gas	16.0	95.6	98.0	93.9	74.0
Electric range	0.0	0.0	0.0	5.4	25.6
Bath	22.0	39.0	71.0	93.9	97.3
Hot water	0.0	—	52.0	79.2	88.2

Sources: Moskva: Razvitiye khozyaistva i kul'tury goroda (Moscow: Moskovskii rabochii, 1958), p. 75; *Moskva v tsifrakh za gody Sovetskoi vlasti (1917–1967 gg.)* (Moscow: Statistika, 1967), p. 85; *Moskva v tsifrakh, 1985* (Moscow: Finansy i statistika, 1985), p. 144.

square meters (of gross area) in the first generation of standard designs to almost 60 square meters in the 1980s. Roomier apartments and responsiveness to consumer tastes made for better insulation of household functions (see Figure 59).

Quality did not advance anywhere as much as quantity. And how could it have? Builders were hostage to a single, jejune form: the cellular apartment on one floor of a matchbox tower stood on its end on barren ground (see Figures 60 and 61). Poured concrete was out of their reach technically, so no curvaceous or plastic forms relieved the monotony of cement slabs—this in the city of Fedor Shekhtel' and Vladimir Shukhov. Seventy-one percent of Moscow's housing in 1980 was in one of exactly three heights—five, nine, or twelve stories. Apartment interiors looked so shabby that most had to be redone before they could be occupied, with the tenant dipping into a thriving black market in wallpaper, paint, tiles, and hardware. There was no common-use space to speak of, ever since Khrushchev discarded finished lobbies as an "overindulgence." Hallways, staircases, elevator platforms, and breezeways were no-man's-lands—unsanitary, unaesthetic, and, due to pilfering of light bulbs, unlit. Without perpetual countermeasures, piping cavities and trash dumpsters pullulated with cockroaches and rodents.

This dreary state of affairs owed not a little to the decision to give

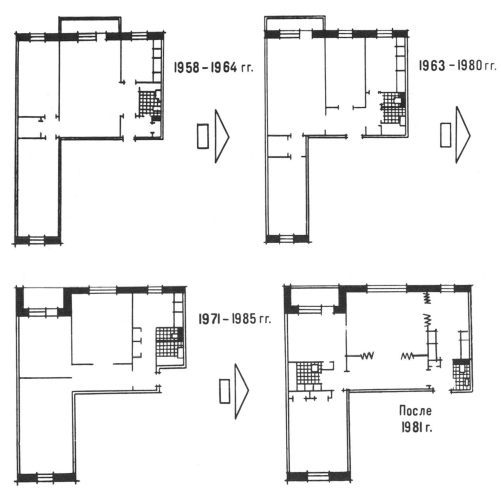

Figure 59. Changing dimensions of typical three-room Moscow apartment, 1950s to 1980s. (From Ya. Ye. Dikhter, *Mnogoetazhnoye zhilishche stolitsy,* Moscow: Moskovskii rabochii, 1979, p. 52.)

primacy to the amount of shelter provided, as the shortcut to amelioration of the housing crisis. Russians colloquially called the five-story houses of the 1950s and 1960s *khrushcheby,* "Khrushchev slums," a pun on *trushcheby,* "slums." Specialists have suggested to me that Khrushchev consciously lowered quality so as to defuse envy of the lucky citizens who got their mass-issue housing first.

Why, then, could the deficit not be made up in the Brezhnev

Figure 60. Bibirevo housing district, northern Moscow, built mostly in the 1970s. (Photograph by author.)

Figure 61. Krylatskoye housing district, western Moscow, built mostly in the 1980s. (Photograph by author.)

period, when quality was declaimed as a paramount goal? Official doctrine still treated housing as a commodity. It glorified installation of interchangeable, factory-tooled parts, preferably out of the Unified Catalog from which 70 percent of Moscow housing was constructed by 1980. Well executed or not, this approach chartered the sort of characterless environment spoofed in a Soviet movie of the 1970s. In the film a man got turned around on his way home and knocked on the door of an apartment identical to his own, in a matching building and housing block, only to be greeted by the wrong fiancée—with whom he spends the night, spoiling his wedding plans for the next day. Hyperstandardization made impersonality rampant within districts as well as between them. A study of one Moscow development found that 60 percent of the residents "still had no contacts at all with their neighbors" five years after moving in.[62]

Those responsible for the product were as immune as Soviet auto makers to an "invisible hand" of profit incentives or an "invisible foot" pushing the incompetent into insolvency. Practices such as "storming" *(shturmovshchina),* in which laborers madly completed plan assignments in the dying days of the month or year, invited poor workmanship. Output was doled out to long-deprived consumers with no alternate source of supply and, once received, was owned by the state—"held by everyone and by no one at the same time."[63] At foundation, housing in the socialist metropolis suffered from the prejudice against excellence suffusing the entire socialist economy. It condemned most Muscovites and other urbanites to life in one dinosaurian public housing project.

THE NEW HOUSING SCISSORS

Discontent with housing in Moscow incurred as many complaints to government as all other issues combined. Forty-six percent of the written petitions to the city ispolkom in 1981, 61 percent of the oral presentations, and 55 percent of letters to the raion authorities concerned housing.[64]

Although city hall and the Soviet government had long mouthed slogans about quality, few Muscovites would have taken exception to the verdict reached by a writer in *Moskva* magazine early in the Gorbachev administration:

For all its imposing quantitative accumulations, our construction colossus has not achieved the change in qualitative characteristics expected of it. Worse than that, it does not see the need for change. The big-panelled houses it puts up, although a lot higher than their predecessors, are every bit as drab and monotone. The bigger they get, the more distressing the impression they give off. Attempts by designers to introduce new series of homes or upgrade existing ones crack up against factory *val* [the gross output approach], where only one thing counts—not to change anything.[65]

There was angst about housing aesthetics and amenities—but also, despite the passage of time, about the quantitative response to the most basic wants. Freer speech after 1985 would bring forth such plaintive cries as this one:

The housing crisis . . . is Moscow's pain and shame . . . Our homelessness is never-ending . . . I would like to ask our city planners: in what other civilized capital would a woman take her husband for the night into a room where her mother is sleeping? No one finds that surprising here. Where else do people get married, settle down with children, age, and die in young people's dormitories? What other megapolis deserves more than Moscow to be known as the world's biggest collection of neurotics and impotents?[66]

The new housing scissors, to revisit a phrase of the 1920s, were defined by two diverging trend lines: an unforeseen increase in effective demand and a protracted slowdown in supply. Demand escalated when Moscow's population grew twice as fast as planned while Muscovites, given the regime's assurances, still felt entitled to "civilized" shelter. If any commitment of the master plan stuck in their heads, it was, in Chairman Promyslov's words, that there would be sufficient construction to "allow each family to enjoy a separate apartment and each family member to have a separate room" by the plan's end date.[67]

The sense of letdown might have been mitigated had the authorities taken resolute offsetting action on supply. They did not: they buried their heads in the sand as production subsided, more or less as the master plan anticipated it would, as if it had not been antiquated by the deluge of in-migration. From the high-water mark of nearly 3.5 million square meters of net dwelling space in 1973, output faltered 42 percent to a shade under 2 million square meters in 1985, the last year in power for Moscow's Brezhnevite leaders. This was the lowest absolute amount since 1957. The subtotal for construction cooperatives dropped by 66.7 percent between 1970 and 1981.[68]

Per capita housing as of 1985 (11.4 square meters of dwelling space) stood 2 square meters below the goal set by the master plan. Between 1971 and 1985, it stole forward by 23 percent, whereas it had soared by 52 percent from 1950 to 1961 and by 45 percent from 1961 to 1971.

The arithmetical mean does not convey the lumpy distribution of the disappointment. In mockery of the general plan, one resident in five in 1988, when new leaders published a thorough inventory, lived in joint occupancy (see Table 14). Most of them were shoehorned one family to a room into the mistitled "communal" flats, sharing kitchen, lavatory, door buzzer, and telephone. Although the last firetrap barracks of the Stalin years were removed in the 1970s, nearly 300,000 joint tenants, including 40,000 married couples, inhabited dormitories in 1988, only 66,000 less than in 1950; there were 40,000 in hostels

Table 14. The extent of the housing shortage, 1988

Category	Permanent residents affected		Of whom in joint occupancy	
	Number	Percent	Number	Percent
On queue of raion soviet	550,000	6.5	260,000	3.1
On queue of employer	330,000	3.9	174,000	2.6
In dilapidated building slated for demolition	250,000	2.9	150,000	1.8
In joint occupancy, not on queue	756,000	8.9	756,000	8.9
In dormitory	292,000	3.4	292,000	3.4
In 5 to 7 square meters of dwelling space, not on queue	750,000	8.8	0	0.0
In 7 to 9 square meters of dwelling space, not on queue	1,100,000	12.9	0	0.0
Total	4,028,000	47.4	1,632,000	19.2

Source: Moskovskaya pravda, March 25, 1988, p. 3.

at ZIL alone.[69] One Muscovite in ten stood in an administrative line for housing, which was lengthening by 20,000 to 30,000 a year. *Four million people* still had less than the state sanitary norm of nine square meters of dwelling space—the notorious "coffin norm" legislated in 1926—and so barely improved upon, and not infrequently did worse than, the 7.4 square meters the average Muscovite occupied in 1912.

RATIONING AND THE SOCIOLOGY OF PRIVILEGE

Exactly who came out ahead and who behind in the housing scramble, and why? Shelter remained a rationed good, meted out by government at a spurious price covering no more than 20 percent of maintenance costs, to say nothing of scarcity value. Action was sparked not by the sanitary norm but by the "triggering norm" *(norma postanovki)*, which in Moscow was three square meters of dwelling space per person from 1947 to 1969 and five after that. This coefficient's low value cut down on bureaucrats' case loads and let them minister to the most housing-deprived first. The housing codex brimmed with special allowances for holders of "personal pensions" from the state (on USSR, RSFSR, and local honor rolls), war veterans, invalids, academicians, artists with home studios, and others. For the mass of the population, the triggering norm was the index to watch.

Any lawful resident whose allotment fell below the norm had the right to be listed on the municipal registry *(uchet)* of "citizens needing an improvement in housing conditions." This chronologically ordered record functioned as a queue. The reward to *ocheredniki*, queuers, would after years of biding time be the keys to a much better apartment—about twelve square meters of net space per capita on average in the 1970s and 1980s. As entry to the queue depended on housing poverty, it could pay to impoverish oneself artificially. In one scam tried more than a few times, a Moscow family would carry out a legal exchange for a smaller flat, perhaps getting rubles under the table in the bargain, then file with the raion housing office for more space. Other ruses included sham divorces and adoptions and the legal but desperate act of early conception of a child.

Since rationing a supply-inelastic good on a first-come-first-serve basis inevitably discriminates against latecomers, the system especially hurt the young. In Moscow in 1984, 56.3 percent of "young families" (husband and wife aged thirty or younger) cohabited with parents or another relative, only about 13 percent of their own free will; the USSR mean was 42.6 percent. About 96,000 youthful Moscow families were on the city housing registry in 1988.[70]

Consumers, old or young, unwilling to cheat or to stand forever in the municipal queue had two options. The first, to join a building cooperative, was fraught with difficulty. The co-ops themselves had long waiting lists for admission, and eligibility turned on personal connections and on possession of the monetary nest egg (averaging 8,000 rubles, two or three years' wages) needed for the down payment. Blue-collar workers tended to balk at the cash requirement, leaving the field to the savings-oriented proto–middle class; writers, scientists and industrial designers, entertainers, and others with a shot at large pecuniary bonuses had a particular leg up. Many cooperatives emanated from an organizational patron such as a ministry, factory, or artistic union. When registration, loans, and even assistance in managing the building came courtesy of such a sponsor, unaffiliated persons had no chance to quality. Finally, cooperatives were less of a lively possibility with time because the Brezhnev-era leaders cut them back more than housing construction as a whole; from 18.8 percent of Moscow housing output in 1970, they fell to 8.6 percent in 1981.

Many Muscovites had a second option closer at hand. Numerous work units engaged in the funding of housing construction; they maintained "departmental registries" of dependents qualified for relief at their expense and made their own allotments from these lists. The 330,000 Muscovites on departmental queues in 1988 constituted three-fifths as many as the 550,000 on the city queue. (Table 14 does not double count; Muscovites often registered on both departmental and municipal queues but are accounted for here by the first waiting list joined.)

It seemed when Stalin died that company provision of housing would be curtailed as an atavism. Chairman Mikhail Yasnov of the city executive committee announced in 1954 that flats built by Glavmosstroi were to be dispensed exclusively by Moscow's housing bureaucracy, mainly the raion housing departments. Employers would hand out only the waning portion their own building crews erected, "with the consent" of city hall, which would peruse ledgers for accuracy and fit with policy.[71]

The edict had no effect, for it soon became obvious that employers wanted to keep their fingers in apartment allocation. Moscow enterprises and agencies in 1958 disbursed about half of the completed apartments in the customary way; the local housing authorities controlled only some of the other half. In 1960 the raions disposed of one-third of the total, or almost as little as before 1953.[72]

There were repercussions for fair play and public morale, as one or two Moscow officials were not bashful about saying. Valentin P. Semin, the head of the city's registration directorate, noted in 1960 that organizations with different resource bases took different attitudes toward allocation: "In some establishments a staff member who does not yet have a separate apartment is vouched needy, whereas in others a family would have to be at less than one-third of the sanitary norm per person." Such a "particularistic approach," he asserted, was considered unjust by "citizens who rightly think that housing ought to be distributed evenly to all those who need it, no matter where the person works." S. I. Matveyev, a specialist on city services in the gorkom of the party, added that agency headquarters, outmuscling even their Moscow branches, often assigned apartments to Muscovites in "significantly better" circumstances than those on municipal and other waiting lists.[73]

Semin and Matveyev objected mostly to the differential waits for housing, not disparities in the end result. Censorship would have precluded any searching discussion of the latter, but conditions were rendering it less problematic. Under Stalin the apartments that ministries and enterprises built from their own resources varied sharply in size and quality. The flat given a machinist in an aircraft plant might have one or two rooms more and be in better repair than that offered the worker in a textile mill or a bakery, and an NKVD captain would have fared better than a school principal. Glavmosstroi and the standardization of house building were forceful homogenizers. Inequalities in square meters allocated were further compressed by the establishment of GlavUKS, the "proportional participation" in financing introduced in the 1960s, and the municipalization of part of the departmental housing fund in the 1970s and 1980s.

Most Muscovites in 1970 or 1980 could expect to get *what* most everyone else in the same demographic category got *when* the rationing decision was made. Although data have not been released on per capita space allotment by employment and ownership category, there is some information on the not unrelated indicator of unit size. The average Moscow apartment in 1989 contained 33.0 square meters of net dwelling space. The mean was 32.9 square meters in houses in the general municipal fund, chiefly managed by the raion soviets; in houses kept by agencies and enterprises, it was a tad higher, 33.7 square meters; in housing cooperatives, where flats could be gotten more quickly by individuals qualifying for entry, it was somewhat lower, 30.5 square meters.

To say that a leveling of post-allocation housing attainment affected the vast majority does not imply that it affected each and every Muscovite. For a minority, it did not.

That charmed circle comprised the pith of the national establishment: the supreme leadership and senior apparatchiks of the party, executives in the military-industrial complex and other government branches, army and police generals, scientists in thriving disciplines, cultural luminaries. Their numbers were not astronomical. Yeltsin relates that the "Kremlin ration" of superior foods was delivered to 40,000 Muscovites in the mid-1980s.[74] If several times as many had lesser accoutrements of rank, the whole set would have approximated 150,000 to 200,000 people, counting dependents, or maybe 1.5 to 2.0 percent of Moscow's population.

Prime among the high nomenklatura's creature comforts was above-standard lodging paid for out of the state purse. In official-use documents, the euphemisms read "housing with improved layout" or "special houses"; not even these sanitized terms made their way into the mass media.

The best-endowed organizations played landlord, on their own or through an intermediary, to valued employees. The Ninth Directorate of the KGB guarded all elite housing and administered the residences on the Lenin Hills and other small parts of the special housing stock directly.

Central agencies themselves sometimes built special housing. The Repair and Construction Directorate of the Central Committee, which originated in the early 1940s but remained concealed from the public until 1991, occupied itself with housing and service outlets as well as office projects. With 1,200 workers in the 1980s (200 in a furniture plant and 1,000 in the field),[75] it has to have been smaller than the local construction arms of the army, KGB, and MVD. Staff complements for Akademstroi (the building unit of the Academy of Sciences) and the dozens of ministerial analogues are not known. What is known is that many of them built housing for internal consumption and, contractually, for leaders of other central departments. Moreover, Glavmosstroi's annual plans incorporated secret quotas for the party, Council of Ministers, and other clients.

At the upper end of the scale the edifices could be grand. The Lenin Hills villas had up to six bedrooms each, oak paneling, billiard tables, and reception salons—although they also had drafts and leaky plumbing.[76]

From 1954 on Leonid Brezhnev lived in a five- or six-room suite at 26 Kutuzovskii prospekt, the same building as Yurii V. Andropov, his KGB chief and later his successor as general secretary, moved into in 1951. Brezhnev directed Glavmosstroi in the 1970s to construct a residence in Kuntsevo (Kuntsevskii raion) for himself, Foreign Minister Andrei A. Gromyko, and several comrades. The site, on Zvenigorodskaya ulitsa, "was chosen without the participation of the Mossovet," Promyslov recounted in an interview in retirement. "The design was worked out on 'special order': downstairs, chambers for guards and servants; upstairs, everything on the principle 'two apartments per floor' . . . Neither first-class, imported building materials nor the latest in equipment was spared."[77] Brezhnev changed his mind, ceding the building to the Academy of Sciences, and resided mostly at the new, marble "palace" of a dacha built for him in Zarech'e, just west of Kuntsevo in the oblast. It had both heated and cold swimming pools and was set in a game park containing reindeer, peacocks, a dovecote, and a kennel for his dogs. When he went to his grave in 1982, he was preparing to set up in a sumptuous apartment with heightened ceilings covering half of the sixth floor of a new brick house at 10 ulitsa Shchuseva.[78]

It is not clear what space allotment the princely Kuntsevo house or the Zarech'e dacha afforded. On ulitsa Shchuseva, Brezhnev and his wife were to luxuriate in 441 square meters of gross space, or about 295 square meters of net dwelling space—thirteen times the Moscow mean each. In quarters for the not so highly placed, the assignment was, by ballpark estimate, 30 to 200 percent more than the Moscow mean.[79] Unit-area costs for some of the best appointed houses doubled or tripled the average. Promyslov maintained that the housing put up for the power elite "was as different from ordinary Moscow apartments as, let us say, a diamond is from ground glass."[80]

Whether or not Promyslov had no knowledge about Zvenigorod-skaya ulitsa, he was being disingenuous in his interview when he dissociated himself from VIP housing. Moscow government, in fact, had a crucial role in sheltering and victualing the Soviet top brass. Officials performing these functions, from the municipal ispolkom and the gorkom of the party, were commonly promoted into central managerial bodies such as the Central Committee's Business Office.[81]

For nomenklatura housing, city hall acted through an agent called, reconditely, its Directorate of Tall Houses and Hotels (UVDG). The directorate was founded within the USSR Council of Ministers in June 1952, as the first of Stalin's wedding-cake towers came into use, and most likely was kept in halter by the MVD and MGB. Its transfer to the Moscow ispolkom in June 1953, ten days before the detention of Beria, may have been a signal to the political class of the impending relief from police terror.[82]

The housing side of the UVDG, archive records show, held 213,000 square meters of dwelling space in 1960, 341,000 in 1965, and 402,000 in 1970. Besides two of the original tall buildings (at plo-shchad' Vosstaniya and Kotel'nicheskaya naberezhnaya), its 1970 inventory took in Iofan's Government House, five divisions of smaller houses, 1,500 housing staff, a furniture shop, and a repair trust. Accelerated construction, and the need for better management of the stock, prompted the Communist Party in the early 1970s to transfer its entire Moscow housing fund—Central Committee and gorkom—to the UVDG. Eight divisions within the directorate in 1990 are known to have operated for the Central Committee's Business Office; quite possibly the total was fifteen to twenty divisions. The eight CC divisions, open to ranking officials in other hierarchies as well as party workers, had seventy apartment buildings on their books. A realistic minimum estimate for UVDG net floor area in the middle to late 1980s would be 1,250,000 to 1,500,000 square meters; at 25 square meters per individual, these sums would have accommodated 50,000 to 60,000 occupants.[83]

The tenants of the Directorate of Tall Houses and Hotels and similar outfits were privileged not only in the "what," the quantity and quality of the housing received, but in the "when," the speed with which it was provided. According to Promyslov, most housewarmings in an immense project built for Central Committee staff in Kuntsevo were decided upon unilaterally by CC apparatchiks, "without any discussion in deputies' commissions or other 'formalities.'"[84] This process of licit queue jumping allowed the "covert participation" Sovietologists detected in Brezhnev's Russia—only by elites this time, not rank-and-file citizens. Local government got involved when space in normal city buildings was at issue or if a waiver of space norms or a local residency permit was needed. The city presidium and ispolkom discussed hundreds of cases each year, many of them raised by high-placed officials, including those on the Politburo.[85]

The foresaid may be considered a special application of a common feature of Soviet urban life: rationing of housing through the workplace. For 95 percent or more of Muscovites, the magnitude of the potential benefit, in terms of apartment size and quality, was more or less constant. But the timing of the benefit, its ease of procurement, varied dramatically. Although employers slowly turned ownership and maintenance of housing stock over to local government, they were much more possessive about entitlement decisions. Allocation by management remained *the most common means* of obtaining new housing. And work units, as Semin said in 1960, differed by orders of magnitude in their capacity to help.

The share of housing constructed directly by nonmunicipal organizations did tumble after Stalin, from approximately 80 percent to 15 or 20 percent of total volume. But the story was more complicated than these bald figures suggest.

First, the 15 to 20 percent retained was not to be scoffed at, especially as demands on local resources grew and overall building declined after 1973. Second, central organs held onto the prerogative to force city executives to earmark chunks of city-built housing to users they wished to favor, users who had no qualms about appealing to the center if an order was slighted.[86] Third, the systems of "single client" and "proportional participation" left the contributing agency with a decisive voice in the disposition of another slice of the housing pie. Moscow regulations obliged employers to consult on all housing decisions with the soviets' housing commissions and the trade unions, but these were the emptiest of words. When they paid the piper, the enterprises and ministries called the tune.

In 1968, as an example, Moscow's summary plan for assignment of new housing stipulated that "enterprises and organizations of ministries, agencies, and state committees" would receive, for doling out to their charges, 1,348,000 (36.6 percent) of the 3,680,000 square meters of living space available; 787,000 square meters of the subtotal were to be built by these organizations themselves, and the rest by Glavmosstroi. Another 451,600 square meters (12.3 percent) flowed on the same principle to departments in the city bureaucracy, the bulk of it for construction workers but some undisclosed portion for the UVDG. The housing cooperatives, with their largely white-collar clientele, got 550,000 square meters (14.9 percent). Miscellaneous uses, mostly resettlement of citizens displaced by urban renewal, ate up 432,800 square meters (11.8 percent). These disbursements left as a residual merely 897,200 square meters—24.4 percent of the gross—for distribution through the raions to queuers on the municipal registry.[87]

Later data reveal no improvement in the position of the municipal queue. In 1976, 12.7 percent of housing output was reserved for the cooperatives and 22.2 percent for employees and other priorities of the city soviet's; only 22.4 percent was apportioned to the general public by the raion ispolkoms, while 42.7 percent was given to centrally controlled workplaces. In 1979 the cooperatives and city agencies got 9.1 and 18.5 percent, the raions 29.6 percent, and central employers again 42.7 percent.[88]

All of these figures explain why time spent on the city queue would have been six to nine years in the mid-1980s, hinging on apartment type and size, whereas in enterprise or agency lineups it was "much less," perhaps three or four years.[89] Within the departmental category branch and status of the employer entailed drastic differences. Workers in consumer industry and the service sector, many of them paid by local government, experienced the longest delays. "Here live," said one polemic on the communal flats after 1985, "teachers, librarians, the physicians and nurses of the raion polyclinics, workers from small enterprises—in a word, everyone who has worked or works for Moscow and not for the center."[90]

At the opposite extreme, the CPSU apparatus, under UVDG cover, unsurprisingly benefited mightily. Heavy industry and construction also exerted strong claims, although high labor turnover in certain firms created a treadmill that kept lineups long.[91] In manufacturing and science, the defense complex was the best situated. Not only was a Khrunichev Machine Building Works or a special design bureau able, as a rule, to get recruits flats within one or two years, but many arms contractors possessed such bountiful housing supplies that they could guarantee workers perpetuation of their tenancy after termination of employment—an indulgence also found in the UVDG but rarely in any other industrial branch. Declassified files leave no doubt about preferential treatment of the military sector, or more broadly about the biases woven into the allocation mechanism.[92]

A GEOGRAPHY OF PRIVILEGE?

If housing condition varied according to social class, then one wonders about geography. Did "have" and "have-not" districts intermingle in the socialist metropolis? Did it possess the poor inner city and rich periphery that frequently characterize U.S. urban areas? Or, conversely, did it resemble Third World cities whose affluent centers are encircled by penurious suburbs?

Pre-Soviet Moscow exhibited the second archetypal pattern. The aristocratic and bourgeois core, though not a uniform area, outshone the "workers' outskirts." To counter this imbalance and to buttress their support, the Communists played to the periphery in 1917 and during the Civil War and NEP. The development focus switched to the city center after 1930, then back to the periphery in the 1950s, this time around in the form of mass housing expanding along a new frontier.

But aspects of the historical contrast between center and fringes remained after Stalin and were reinforced by events. A goodly portion of the choicest housing in late Soviet Moscow could be found in the center, be it defined as the territory out to the Sadovoye kol'tso or less restrictively as the thirteen raions (in the boundaries of 1977–1991) whose tips penetrated the Sadovoye. The old town and its near extensions out radial roads (like Kutuzovskii prospect) was still the most common location of nomenklatura housing, as can be seen in Map 23, displaying exact UVDG sites and subareas in which elite homes in general were concentrated.

The ulitsa Gor'kogo corridor was completed in the early 1950s, with a few side streets under construction until 1955–1956, and No. 30–32, the last Central Committee building on Kutuzovskii, was

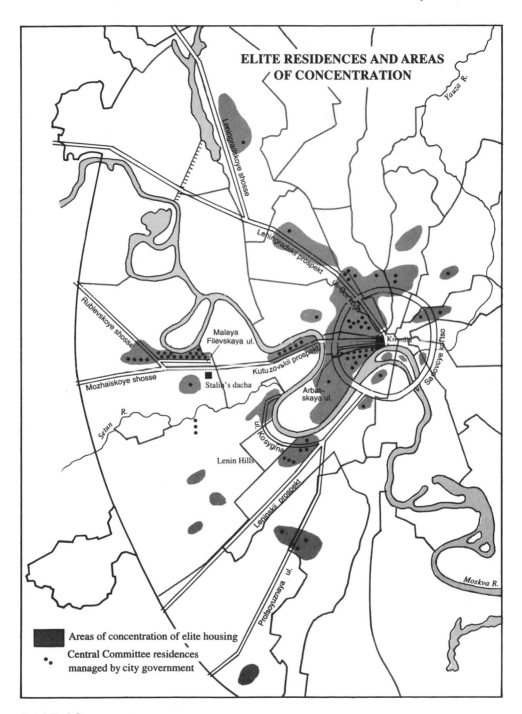

**ELITE RESIDENCES AND AREAS
OF CONCENTRATION**

Yauza R.

Leningradskoye shosse

Leningradskii prospekt

ul. Gorkogo

Rublevskoye shosse

Malaya
Filevskaya ul.

Kremlin

ul. Sadovoye koltso

Mozhaiskoye shosse

Kutuzovskii prospekt

Stalin's dacha

Setun R.

Arbat-
skaya ul.

ul. Kosygina

Lenin Hills

Leninskii prospekt

Moskva R.

Profsoyuznaya ul.

■ Areas of concentration of elite housing

•. Central Committee residences
managed by city government

MAP 23

finished in 1962 (most of Kutuzovskii was later signed over to the UVDG). The party opened its Oktyabr'skaya Hotel on Plotnikov pereulok, in the Arbat area, in 1962. In the late Khrushchev period only one major housing project reached completion: the seven-story building with a V-shaped floor plan at 15 ulitsa Stanislavskogo, two blocks west of city hall. Opened in 1962 or 1963, it boasted as inhabitants Dmitrii Ustinov, Andrei Gromyko, Vladimir Promyslov, and Khrushchev's son Sergei.

As nomenklatura housing construction flourished under Brezhnev, architect-drawn apartment blocks popped up all over old Moscow. Many if not most were in the UVDG fold by the mid-1970s. The curious could pick them out by their tawny or gray brick exteriors, inset balconies, parking lots behind wrought-iron fences, the blue-pointed fir trees in the yard, and, where the most puissant statesmen dwelt, the commemorative plaques by their entranceways. Unlike the ensembles on noisy avenues and plazas preferred by Stalin, they usually stood along back roads.

The densest new construction went up in the southern part of the Arbat area, on inconspicuous streets like Starokonyushennyi pereulok, pereulok Sivtsev-Vrazhek, ulitsa Ryleyeva, Bol'shoi Vlas'evskii pereulok, ulitsa Myaskovskogo, ulitsa Vesnina, and Plotnikov pereulok. Party pensioners from these buildings had dining rights at the Oktyabr'skaya Hotel. A second admired section, opened up under Stalin, was to the north of Arbatskaya ulitsa, bounded by the Bul'varnoye kol'tso, ulitsa Vorovskogo, Pionerskii Pond, and ulitsa Gor'kogo. The UVDG housed Mikhail Suslov and Brezhnev's amanuensis, Konstantin Chernenko, at 19 Bol'shaya Bronnaya, Yekaterina Furtseva at 12 ulitsa Alekseya Tol'stogo, and Grishin, Ivan Kapitonov, and Aleksandr Shelepin at 21 Alekseya Tol'stogo. The UVDG home prepared for the Brezhnevs on ulitsa Shchuseva was around the corner from Grishin and Kapitonov. There was a large Council of Ministers house on ulitsa Paliashvili.

The three most prestigious subdistricts—south and north Arbat and Kutuzovskii, which began one kilometer outside the Sadovoye—accounted for twenty-five out of seventy UVDG-managed Central Committee buildings, but were far from the only ones in the central city. Ulitsa Gor'kogo retained some allure, despite its thunderous traffic. In Calico Moscow's Khamovniki district, southwest of the

Sadovoye, elite apartment blocks (relatively few of them in the UVDG net) lined the Frunzenskaya and Smolenskaya quays (Lazar Kaganovich lived at 50 Frunzenskaya naberezhnaya until his death in 1991) and stretches of ulitsa Plyushchikha (for diplomatic personnel), Bol'shaya Pirogovskaya ulitsa, ulitsa L'va Tol'stogo, Komsomol'skii prospekt, and Obolenskii pereulok.

North of the downtown core, generals' homes clustered in the environs of the Sokol and Aeroport subway stations on Leningradskii prospekt. State and co-op buildings for writers and entertainers abounded near the Aeroport stop and Dinamo Stadium, in this general area, as well as by the artistic unions' clubs in the north Arbat.[93] A knot of UVDG and other buildings was put up in the 1980s on and around Olimpiskii prospekt and ploshchad' Kommuny, and there were two comparable nodules just east of ulitsa Gor'kogo, close to the Belorussia Railway Station and to ploshchad' Mayakovskogo. Smaller outcroppings perched on Bol'shoi Khariton'evskii pereulok and ulitsa Karla Marksa (northeast of Staraya ploshchad'), in Sokol'niki, near the VDNKh exhibition, in the Krasnopresnenskii district, and in western Zamoskvorech'e.[94]

Do composite statistics leave a more systematic trail concerning housing privilege? Yes and no. If one plots per capita housing by raion in 1978 and 1989, years for which good information is obtainable (see Maps 24 and 25), hints of an imbalance between inner and outer districts emerge. The general image suggests that attainment increased with proximity to the Kremlin.

But raion-level information must be interpreted judiciously, not least because Moscow's raions had populations of several hundred thousand and spanned zones built at very different times. Even taken at face value, the data do not bespeak a black-and-white contrast between center and periphery.

Although housing provision in the central raions was higher on average in 1978 and 1989, in both years the difference of the means (weighted) of the two macroareas was less than 1 square meter of dwelling space per capita: 0.8 square meters in 1978 (10.1 square meters in the thirteen inner raions, 9.3 in the outer raions); 0.9 square meters in 1989 (12.0 square meters in the midtown raions, 11.1 in the outer districts). No inegalitarian trend appears, and almost half of the augmentation of average supply in the belly of the city sprang

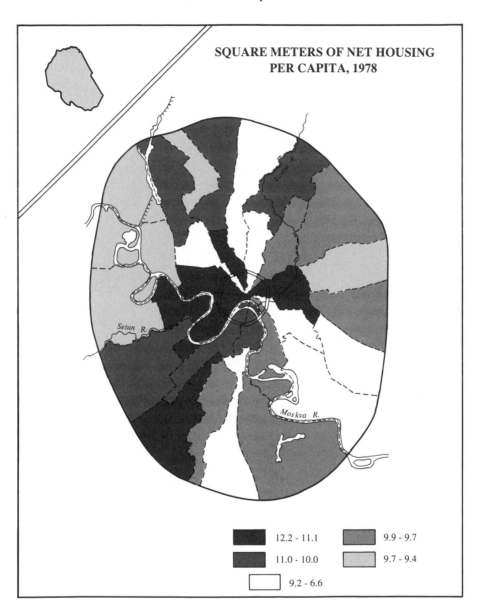

MAP 24

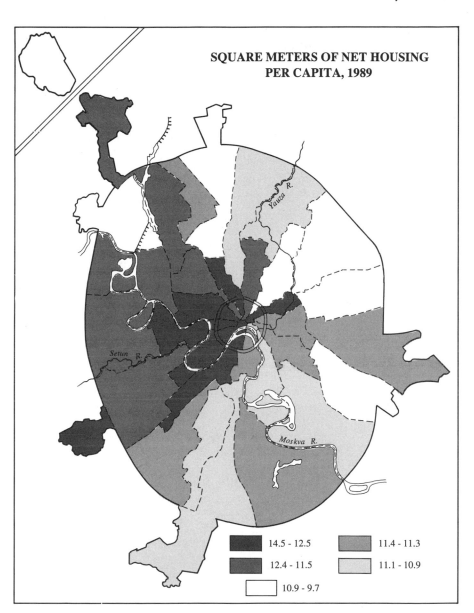

**SQUARE METERS OF NET HOUSING
PER CAPITA, 1989**

Yauza R.

Setun R.

Moskva R.

14.5 - 12.5	11.4 - 11.3
12.4 - 11.5	11.1 - 10.9
10.9 - 9.7	

MAP 25

from population decline rather than construction.[95] Moreover, there was much variation within each category. In 1978, for instance, the central zone had both the best-endowed raion (Leninskii, at 12.2 square meters) and the worst (Zhdanovskii, at 6.6); the outlying raions covered the waterfront from 11.6 square meters (Cheremushkinskii) to 6.6 (Lyublinskii).

One must also note the wide diversity of housing condition within most of the individual raions of central Moscow. Whereas many of the plushest residences in Moscow were located between the Kremlin and the Sadovoye, more than half of the population there inhabited joint accommodation in the 1980s, much of it in scraggly tsarist-era buildings confiscated after 1917. Queues for housing also tended to be longest in the central area (see Map 26), where some 19.5 percent of households remained on waiting lists in 1989, as opposed to 7.7 percent in the outer raions. In central raions like Frunzenskii and Kievskii, one could easily find aged widows on tiny pensions looking out of their communal flats onto deluxe homes, or a block of drab housing for factory workers a five-minute stroll from UVDG apartment houses.[96]

To further complicate the picture, Moscow's housing elect did not confine their attention to the city center (see Map 23 again). Of the UVDG/Central Committee buildings, for which we have an address book for the end of the 1980s, thirty of the seventy, or 43 percent, were in the outer twenty raions. Other nomenklatura groups, one suspects, dispersed out of the downtown more widely than that.

The Lenin Hills was slowly built up, despite curtailment of the construction of the grand postwar villas at about fifteen homes, perhaps half of which were refurbished as government guest houses. Prime Minister Aleksei Kosygin lived from 1968 to 1980 in a five-story UVDG residence at 8 Vorob'evskoye shosse (ulitsa Kosygina upon his death), and Mikhail Gorbachev, after first choosing ulitsa Shchuseva, was to have a new house built at 10 ulitsa Kosygina and to reside in it until his deposition in 1991. Just west of there, homes for middle-ranking officials came to hem Mosfil'movskaya ulitsa, and to the south there were three party buildings on Universitetskii prospekt.

Also well toward the periphery, clumps of top-drawer buildings were put up after Khrushchev in Gagarinskii, Cheremushkinskii, and

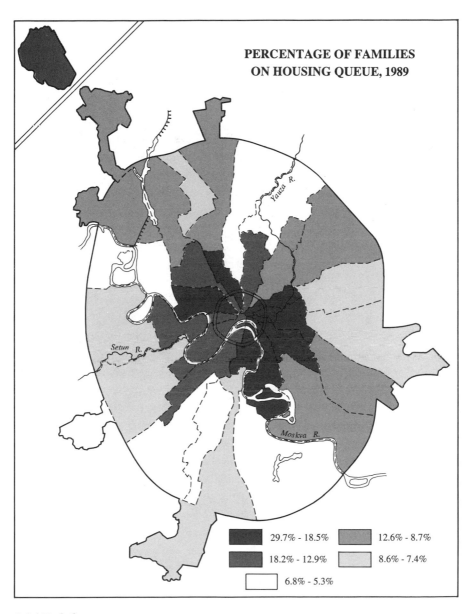

PERCENTAGE OF FAMILIES
ON HOUSING QUEUE, 1989

■ 29.7% - 18.5%		▨ 12.6% - 8.7%	
▨ 18.2% - 12.9%		▨ 8.6% - 7.4%	
□ 6.8% - 5.3%			

MAP 26

Figure 62. Elite housing project, Profsoyuznaya ulitsa, built in the 1980s. (Photograph by author.)

Sevastopol'skii raions, all in the south and southwest; others were begun near the scenic Khimki Reservoir in northwest Moscow, in Leningradskii raion. The biggest of these complexes—Tsarskoye selo, the Tsar's Village, to wisecrackers—was shared by the Council of Ministers and the Central Committee at street addresses 43–45 Profsoyuznaya ulitsa and 60–62 Novocheremushkinskaya ulitsa (in Figure 62). I would estimate it to have had no fewer than 10,000 residents.[97]

The most extensive effort at housing middle-level officials in the Brezhnev years occurred in Kuntsevo, the location of Stalin's Nearby Dacha and of a plethora of services for the nomenklatura. Endowed with leafy woods and frontage on the Moskva and Setun Rivers, it was kept largely free of polluting industry before and after its incorporation into Moscow in 1960. Perhaps one square kilometer of brick apartment towers took shape beginning in the late 1960s on the manicured streets between Malaya Filevskaya ulitsa and the Fili-Kuntsevo Forest Park, and then westward along Molodogvardeiskaya ulitsa and Rublevskoye shosse. The city's UVDG administered most of the Kuntsevo houses, although the Central Committee Business Office, as Promyslov said, did the assignments "without any formalities." Muscovites called the development Lyoningrad, after the Russian diminutive for Brezhnev's first name.

Kuntsevo had a unique place in Moscow's social geography because it adjoined the part of the oblast, in Krasnogorskii and (mainly) Odintsovskii raions, where summer houses and spas for the Soviet elite proliferated (see Map 27).

The Moscow Dacha Trust, a municipal agency, operated eighteen hundred cottages, largely in the older recreational area southeast of Moscow (centered on Vyalki and Kratovo) and in Serebryannyi bor. Its clients were mainly local government and party workers of junior and intermediate rank.[98] State dachas for lower- and middle-ranking officials were especially plentiful in the same two districts. For the high nomenklatura, four areas stood out: (1) the Skhodnya River, northwest of the capital, around the villages of Planernaya (for the newspaper *Pravda*), Mar'ino, Novogorsk (mostly for the KGB), and Nagornoye (Central Committee); (2) Pushkino and Mamontovka, due north of Moscow; (3) scattered sites to the south and southwest, in particular Peredelkino (for writers and generals) and Arkhangel'skoye-Yuzhnoye (for RSFSR officials); and (4) the "Sub-Moscow Switzerland" stretching the thirty-five kilometers up the Moskva River valley from Kuntsevo to Zvenigorod.

The last subset was by a long shot the most desirable. There army construction troops built the compounds, equipped with telephones and other conveniences rarely found elsewhere and guarded—lightly or heavily, depending on the occupant—by the Ninth Directorate of the KGB.[99]

A firm gradation of status underlay this premium dacha belt. Zarech'e, south of the axis out to Zvenigorod and containing the homes of Brezhnev and Gromyko, approximately forty dachas built for Comintern workers in the 1930s, and the thirty dachas assigned to the Ninth Directorate, ranked highest. It was followed in prestige

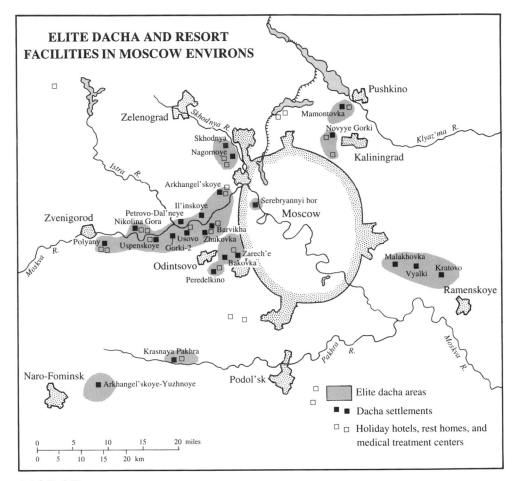

ELITE DACHA AND RESORT
FACILITIES IN MOSCOW ENVIRONS

Pushkino

Zelenograd

Skhodnya R.

Mamontovka

Novyye Gorki

Klyaz'ma R.

Skhodnya

Kaliningrad

Nagornoye

Istra R.

Arkhangel'skoye

Il'inskoye

Serebryannyi bor

Moscow

Zvenigorod

Petrovo-Dal'neye

Nikolina Gora

Barvikha

Usovo Zhukovka

Polyany

Uspenskoye Gorki-2

Zarech'e

Bakovka

Moskva R.

Odintsovo

Malakhovka

Vyalki Kratovo

Ramenskoye

Peredelkino

Moskva R.

Krasnaya Pakhra

Pakhra R.

Naro-Fominsk

Arkhangel'skoye-Yuzhnoye

Podol'sk

Elite dacha areas

Dacha settlements

Holiday hotels, rest homes, and
medical treatment centers

0   5   10   15   20 miles
0   5   10   15   20 km

MAP 27

by Barvikha, the next closest encampment to the city, holding a
government sanatorium (often used for foreign guests) and marble
dachas for Politburo members, and then by Zhukovka, where the
cottages built for scientists in the 1940s were supplemented after 1953
by three more settlements funded by the Council of Ministers.[100] After
that came, in rough order, Usovo, Uspenskoye, Nikolina Gora, and
Polyany, successively further to the west. Zvenigorodka, the Pioneer
camp for children of Central Committee workers, marked the end of
the chain.

Uspenskoye was the newest of the main dacha communities, while Nikolina Gora was one of the oldest and had cabins for the intelligentsia as well as politicians and bureaucrats. Khrushchev had dachas at Gorki-2 and Usovo and, after retirement, at Petrovo-Dal'neye, on the Istra. Il'inskoye, with cottages and a beach, was the retreat of the Moscow gorkom of the party. Arkhangel'skoye was after Stalin still mostly for the Central Military Sanatorium and military cottages, although the Soviet prime minister's mansard-roofed country place (Dacha No. 1 of the Council of Ministers) was also there. Aleksei Kosygin took an avuncular interest in the children of the local peasants and had an experimental school built for them.

Hard numbers for elite homes are sketchy. But we are told that the CC Business Office had dachas in Serebryannyi bor and Moscow oblast with a capacity of 1,800 families upon its dissolution in 1991. The Council of Ministers reserve in Nikolina Gora in 1990 had 219 winterized dachas, 373 summer-use dachas, and also 9 rest homes and holiday hotels. USSR civilian ministries owned 1,014 dachas in 1990, the Ministry of Defense 142; these were not all in the choice zone west of Moscow.[101] I would guess that, allowing for time sharing and the passing on of some into private hands over the years, the bowers out toward Zvenigorod accommodated 20,000 to 25,000 Muscovites on peak weekends.

So important were these homes in the Soviet scheme of things that the highway through them (Uspenskoye shosse) and the connecting city roads toward the Kremlin (Rublevskoye and Mozhaiskoye shosses and Marshala Grechko, Kutuzovskii, and Kalinina prospects) were dubbed the Government Route *(Pravitel'stvennaya trassa).* The pothole-free roadway—shouldered outside Moscow by mowed grass and glades of birch and pine, with its telephone polls removed and all wires put underground, and cleaned by mechanical street sweepers—was closed to all casual traffic until the late 1960s and oppressively policed afterward. Motorcades of bulletproof, upholstered ZIL limousines zipped down its reserved lanes.[102]

Not only the nomenklatura sought satisfaction outside the city's geometric center. The cooperative apartments prized by the Moscow middle class, loosely speaking, were located not in downtown Moscow but primarily toward the periphery (see Map 28), most thickly in the southwest quadrant. In the thirteen inner raions in 1989 they

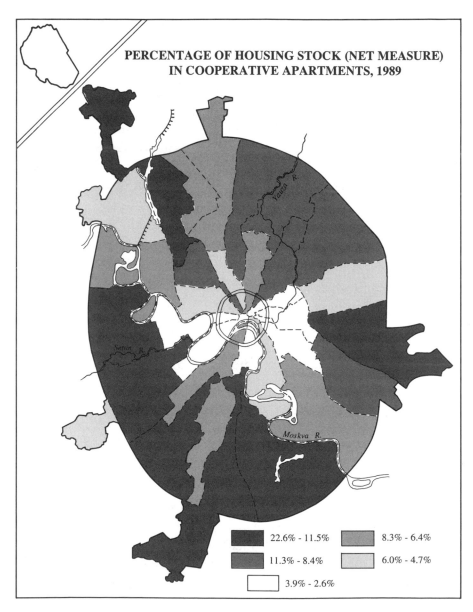

PERCENTAGE OF HOUSING STOCK (NET MEASURE)
IN COOPERATIVE APARTMENTS, 1989

22.6% - 11.5%   8.3% - 6.4%

11.3% - 8.4%   6.0% - 4.7%

3.9% - 2.6%

MAP 28

constituted 5.2 percent of the housing stock, in the outer raions 11.0 percent. When the residents of three housing estates near the MKAD were polled in the late 1970s on which sections of Moscow they considered the best and worst to live in, eleven of the twelve picks for "zones of a high level" were outside the Sadovoye (see Map 29). Residents chose only three in the eastern half of Moscow, although they agreed that the least appealing territory, stretching from Kitaigorod almost to the MKAD, was situated in the southeast. The southwest quadrant was the most popular, the northwest next.

Many factors, local and general, contributed to these perceptions. Kuntsevo's showing can be imputed to the residential choices of the Moscow-based national elite. The finger of well-appraised territory along Leninskii prospekt resulted primarily from the siting there of Moscow State University and most of the Academy of Science's institutes. These sources of livelihood gained strength in the 1950s and 1960s, the time of maximum housing production, which led to a clustering of professional employees in new apartments (many of them cooperatively owned) a short commute (by two subway lines) from, in Soviet terms, sought-after and clean work. The parkland on the Lenin Hills and the location there of three popular children's attractions (the Palace of Pioneers, Children's Musical Theater, and new Moscow Circus) were bonuses.[103]

In the case of the northwest corridor along Leningradskii prospekt and the island around Rechnoi vokzal, the decisive variables were the association with ulitsa Gor'kogo, Stalin's favorite paradeway, and the preponderance of aerospace factories, laboratories, and design bureaus in the district economy. High-paying and lightly polluting, these defense-related organizations also had the means to sustain expensive housing programs for their workers. In the northeast some combination of historical interest in Petrine palaces and villas (in the Baumanskii area), the park endowment of Sokol'niki and Izmailovo, employment mix, and newness of construction accounts for the spots of high appeal.

There can be little controversy about one thing: that the reviled quadrant was the southeast. Sweeping east and southeast of the conflux of the Yauza and Moskva was the city's worst rust and smokestack belt. It became the city's problem child in the First Five-Year Plan, when most of it was called Proletarskii raion, and remained

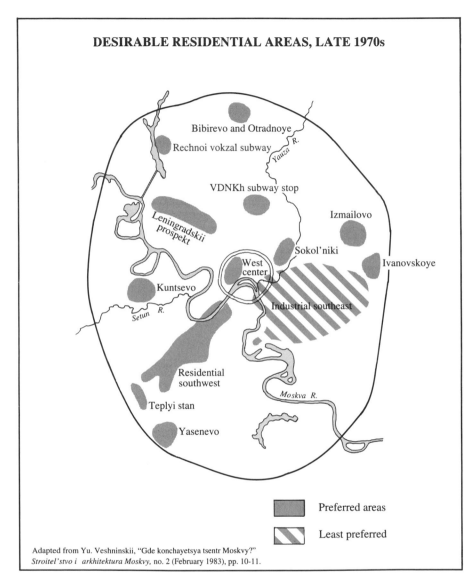

DESIRABLE RESIDENTIAL AREAS, LATE 1970s

Bibirevo and Otradnoye

Rechnoi vokzal subway

Yauza R.

VDNKh subway stop

Izmailovo

Leningradskii prospekt

Sokol'niki

West center

Ivanovskoye

Kuntsevo

Industrial southeast

Setun R.

Residential southwest

Moskva R.

Teplyi stan

Yasenevo

Preferred areas

Least preferred

Adapted from Yu. Veshninskii, "Gde konchayetsya tsentr Moskvy?"
Stroitel'stvo i arkhitektura Moskvy, no. 2 (February 1983), pp. 10-11.

MAP 29

thus under Khrushchev and Brezhnev. The area bore heavy, chiefly nondefense, manufacturing, including two auto plants, numerous manufacturers of industrial products, and an oil refinery (at Kapotnya, in Lyublinskii raion). Air pollution ran high, per capita housing and cooperative apartments were low, and few natural beauties compensated. Mass housing here, from older areas near Taganskaya ploshchad' and ZIL, through the Khrushchev-era projects at Novyye Kuz'minki, to new developments like Vykhino and Veshnyaki-Vladychino, was some of the most unappealing in Moscow.

Predominantly working-class areas in other parts of the city were less ghastly than the industrial southeast. Tushinskii raion, in the northwest, mostly inhabited by aerospace workers, benefited some from relatively generous employers and from the presence of the river and the canal. Zheleznodorozhnyi, Timiryazevskii, and Kirovskii raions, lying across the north of Moscow, had several attempts to vary Moscow's repetitive layout (at Lianozovo and Otradnoye) but bad air quality and public transit. Sovetskii and Krasnogvardeiskii raions, the mainly blue-collar raions along the southern rim, looked little different from the north, yet seemed to be slightly higher in prestige. Orekhovo-Borisovo in Krasnogvardeiskii raion, though, was one of the housing districts most censured for lack of consumer services, and misdeveloped Brateyevo adjacent to it was to be the locale of the most dramatic neighborhood uprising of the Gorbachev period.

If any one explanatory variable compels attention in all this description, it is the evergreen one of the link between welfare and employment. Having polled Muscovites on this bond in the 1980s, one social scientist condensed it in a statement about the city's "departmental [*vedomstvennaya*] geography":

> The bigger the enterprise and its profits, the more resources it can allocate to fortifying its "social home front," and vice-versa . . . So, sure, we have no poverty districts and no ghettos. But we do have a departmental geography, meaning that the quality of the urban environment depends greatly on bureaucratic patrons. The employees of rich enterprises, in whose development the state takes an interest (and, this means, enjoying a whole series of preferments and privileges), do more than take a proper pride in their collective and in their labor and achievements. They also feel superiority and exclusivity. In our survey, young workers at one such enterprise exhibited pure condescension toward the city's problems ("We have everything on our own!") and cared nothing for other work collectives ("They envy us and want to take everything from us!"). This produces the phenomenon of "corporate consciousness" and the danger of substitution of corporate goals for public, civil goals.[104]

Herein lies a primal distinction between urban and regional politics in Soviet Russia and in the United States. In a Westchester County, New York, a Grosse Point, Michigan, or a Beverley Hills, California, well-off townsfolk look principally to municipal government to secure their investments in "class" housing against "mass" encroachment. Town and county councils pass the restrictive zoning ordinances and building codes, the prohibitions on low-cost and multiple-family development, and the inducements to taxable commercial property.[105] In the socialist metropolis, spatial separation of socioeconomic groups was less prevalent, although not unknown. To the extent it was found, it took a different geographic form and sat on a different institutional foundation, one plugged into the life of the workplace rather than the local political arena.

A City for All Hours of the Day

It is a safe bet that no modern metropolis as big as Stalin's Moscow was ever as thoroughly defined by the two poles of workplace and bedroom. A principal goal of policy after 1953 was to enrich and diversify the urban tapestry. Put another way, Moscow's rulers sought to make it a city for all hours of the day, with widened amenities providing more opportunities for material satisfaction and repose off the job and outside the dwelling unit.

TRANSPORTATION

Transportation was the nonhousing service least politicized and most continuous with the past. There was no wrangling about the collectivist philosophy of urban transport, drawn from socialist values, to which Moscow had cleaved since 1917. Transportation was a public utility, to be provided along fixed routes by rail or bus monopolies, at heavily subsidized fares (five kopeks for a subway ride from 1935 until 1991). Private motor vehicles were frills.

With de-Stalinization, the wooing of the consumer, and the cutback on showcase projects, leaders attempted to make Moscow transit more user-friendly and efficient. New subway stations, no longer thought of as lush "underground palaces," were built to utilitarian designs with better accessibility to the street. At Khrushchev's beckon, workers dug several hundred underpasses beneath the broad streets and squares sanctified by the 1935 master plan, the rivers of concrete so expansive that pedestrians fording them were marooned between lanes of oncharging traffic.

Engineers and scholars disputed at length in the 1950s and early 1960s how best to calibrate metropolitan transport with demographic and economic growth. In keeping with the optimism of the times, they put forward exotic ideas for monorails, dirigibles, helipads, and the like. Politicians, official planners, and the generalist press paid little notice. The 1971 general plan held up as goals a "maximum of conveniences" to riders and a paring of the average trip to work to thirty or thirty-five minutes. To do so and to support shopping and recreation, it gave imprimatur to a prodigious works program, with the subway at the head of the list.

Modernization and extension of Moscow mass transit, a constant endeavor since the opening of the subway in 1935, continued in the latest planning period (see Table 15). Once reliant wholly on tram streetcars, the city now had massive and interlocking networks of subway trains, autobuses, electrified trolleybuses, and, in a few mostly proletarian areas, trams. The trunk of the system was the "metro" (Map 30). Moscow led the globe in subway traffic in 1980; the 6.3 million going through its turnstiles daily far outnumbered Tokyo's 5.0 million, Paris's 3.6 million, New York's 3.0 million, and London's 1.6 million. Another 1.6 million boarded electrified suburban trains *(elek-*

Table 15. Development of mass transit, 1935–1985

Indicator	1935	1947	1960	1970	1985
Total rides (billion)	2.038	2.640	3.659	4.562	6.003
Annual rides per resident	560	660	600	645	694
Rides by mode (percent)					
Tram	92	52	23	14	8
Autobus	5	7	27	33	36
Subway	2	30	28	36	42
Trolleybus	1	11	22	17	14

Sources: A. M. Zaslavskii, "Voprosy gorodskogo transporta Moskvy," *Gorodskoye khozyaistvo Moskvy,* no. 7 (July 1947), p. 2; *Moskva v tsifrakh za gody Sovetskoi vlasti (1917–1967 gg.)* (Moscow: Statistika, 1967), p. 77; *Moskva v tsifrakh, 1988* (Moscow: Finansy i statistika, 1988), p. 109.

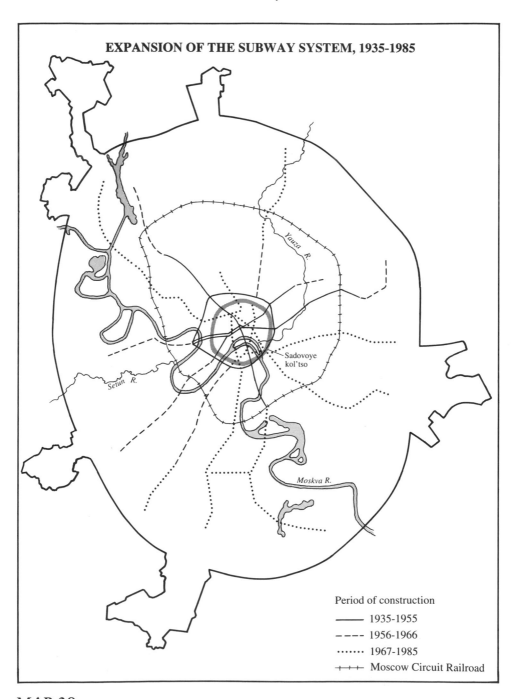

EXPANSION OF THE SUBWAY SYSTEM, 1935-1985

Yauza R.

Sadovoye
kol'tso

Setun R.

Moskva R.

Period of construction
——— 1935-1955
- - - 1956-1966
······· 1967-1985
+++ Moscow Circuit Railroad

MAP 30

trichki) into and out of the city. Moscow in this respect stood in flattering contrast to most metropolitan areas in the United States.

It could not be said that government met all policy objectives. Commuting times did not shorten. For Muscovites, they grew from an average of thirty-six minutes a day (each way) in 1945 to forty-one minutes for the much longer journeys of the mid-1970s and perhaps fifty minutes in the mid-1980s. For oblast residents employed in the city, they were about twice as lengthy.[106]

Moscow's transit system, like its housing stock, was swamped by demand springing from high population growth. To an even greater degree resources limited response. Subway expansion, after accelerating around 1960, fell spectacularly off schedule. In 1979, the year Moscow surpassed the 1990 population quota, it had 184 kilometers of tunnel, not the 320 envisaged by the master plan for that many people. (These figures exclude Metro-2, the secret reserve subway for the political leadership.) There were 208 kilometers in service in 1985, with the population still higher. The 55 kilometers completed between 1967 and 1985 exceeded by a mere 4 kilometers the subway track put into service between 1960 and 1967.

It was commonplace for new housing developments to be broken in ten or twelve years before the arrival of subway service. In the latter part of the 1980s, there were still four raions (Zelenograd, Solntsevskii, Zheleznodorozhnyi, and Timiryazevskii) with not one metro stop, one with one stop only, and three raions with three stops; these eight raions had a combined population of 2,344,000 in 1989. The dearth was greatest in the northern districts, in which Metrostroi had been digging the Timiryazevskii radius for twenty years but had opened only one station past the Sadovoye by 1990. Especially in the central area, where the radial lines connected and herds of passengers fought to transfer, platforms, escalators, and wagons were frighteningly crowded.

Overburdening was not limited to subways, as anyone who has squeezed onto a bus ramp at the most frantic rush-hour stops—at train stations or at subway terminuses toward the MKAD—can attest. Poor planning bred conflict over access to the grid. In 1979 one of Moscow's first local rebellions, of the kind that were to mushroom after 1985, broke out over such an issue.

Strogino, an uncut housing estate in Voroshilovskii raion already flush with 100,000 people (and the place of a burial ground for Gulag zeks), was cut off from the subway and main bus routes by the Moskva River, and residents could egress only by a tortuous bus path along the MKAD. Raion officials wheedled the gorkom bureau of the party into ordering a start on a bridge in 1978, but dallying led to a petition campaign and several street rallies urging a speedup. Only when Grishin and the party again interceded in 1979 was a temporary footbridge built allowing commuters to walk to the Shchukino station. This structure opened in December 1980 and a permanent bridge followed in 1983.[107]

The interdepartmental coordination that might have gotten the most out of transit resources was wanting in Moscow. The city, despite its socialist economics, never had a serious program for staggering work hours. A cavalcade of local and central edicts dating back to the 1930s, all lacking compliance mechanisms, took nothing out of peak traffic.

The paper trail of efforts to get cooperation from the Ministry of Transportation, the operator of the national rail system, also reached decades back. Before the war, it repeatedly clashed with Moscow over how to mesh the railroads with the new subway, pushing a plan for an unsightly elevated trestle over city protests. The elevated was not built, but neither did the central bureaucracy support planners on consolidation of Moscow's nine train stations, which stand today at the same places as in 1902. A tender spot was the Moscow Circuit Railroad, completed in 1908. City specialists repeatedly urged it be rebuilt as an above-ground metro track that would relieve occlusions on the Sadovoye kol'tso line. The ministry, adamant about keeping it for freight, stonewalled city requests and made things worse by refusing to electrify the line, making its diesels the dirtiest transport polluters in Moscow. Not even the ministry's assumption of administrative control over the subway in 1975 budged its attitude toward the circuit railroad.[108]

Another ministerial obstruction turned transport assets to private benefit. It would come to light during Boris Yeltsin's tenure as first secretary that 30,000 to 40,000 state-owned cars, most of them Volga and Chaika sedans, were functioning as limousines in Moscow. Several years later, and after budget cuts, the Transport Unit of the Central Committee Business Office alone had 1,400 drivers and mechanics and a fleet of 570 automobiles, 100 buses, and 140 trucks and ambulances. The injustice of the "family carriages," journalist Shod S. Muladzhanov noted, was that the city had to cancel bus runs when it came up 5,000 drivers short. The Moscow autobus park of the ministries and their local affiliates was 50 percent larger than the *entire* municipal fleet. Muscovites were inured to the sight of departmental buses, the sign "Reserved" clipped to their windshield visors, idling or being lightly used to ferry employees around, but were outraged to learn of its scope.[109]

In countries like the United States and Canada some of the most combustible transport politics has revolved around expressway construction. In Moscow the hegemony of mass transit and the low standing of private vehicles kept highway issues on the back burner. The number of individually owned autos did drift up over the years—from 27,000 in 1958 to 100,000 in 1967 and 500,000 in 1986—and with it the problems of giving cars short shrift. New roads were of low quality and consequently hard on vehicles and dangerous: the police called the racetrack MKAD, its four lanes unilluminated and with no center barrier, the "road of death." Moscow was so tardy to designate residential parking areas and okay garage-building cooperatives that automobiles had only 280,000 resting spaces in 1986. Except for weakly observed restrictions on trucks and no-stop strips on the biggest streets and near secured public buildings, it had no arrangements for orderly parking in commercial and work areas—no coin meters, no tickets, no tow zones. Hence the messy and unsafe strewing of vehicles along curbs and sidewalks.

The 1935 plan made provision for sixteen new highways, of which the only ones pursued with any vigor were in low-density outlying areas. Of the numerous proposals in the 1971 master plan, the most portentous called for four divided, high-speed *(skorostnyye)* highways, crisscrossing the city from northeast to southwest and southeast to northwest about five kilometers out from the Kremlin. Two circular roads were to be placed between the Sadovoye and the MKAD, an idea purloined from the earlier plan. Although Muscovites were reassured that tunneling and bridging would limit the disruption of residential districts, published estimates intimated to the contrary. The Third Transport Ring alone, to be strung together along the Kamer-kollezhskii val, would in one version have required the demolition of 566 apartment buildings and 72 factories and economic structures; displacing 50,000 people, it would have been a project to rival Robert Moses's South Bronx Expressway in New York City.[110]

No New York–style "highway coalition" took shape in socialist Moscow, as "the very low tempos and volume of highway and bridge construction" actually done after 1971, and the exponential increase in congestion, establish.[111] None of the large roads endorsed in 1971 was completed; there was substantial progress on the Third Ring only, and the diagonal superhighways were not so much as begun. Although trucking interests favored new roads, they were always politically junior to the railroads in the USSR. And, owing to the slender base of auto ownership, highway building never received the mass suburban support it has had in the United States. A weak highway program incurred only weak dissent against highways. Anti-expressway politics did not arrive in Moscow until after 1985.

CONSUMER SERVICES: THE WORKPLACE CONNECTION

Betterment of consumer trade and personal services came second only to housing among the announced goals of urban policy after Stalin. Broadcast figuratively in acts such as the reopening of GUM in 1953, it was reiterated time and again in verbal statements. Local channels, leaders agreed, had an indispensable part to play in getting the bounty of economic growth to the populace.

The services realm repeats a recurrent theme of our study, namely, the effect on urban welfare of producer—especially employer—interests. To this sector applied the same paternalistic practice of detouring consumer benefits through the workplace as a supplement or alternative to money wages.

The top echelon of the establishment again illustrates the syndrome. The Kremlin ration, the package of delicacies dispensed at the Central Committee commissary on ulitsa Granovskogo (readily identifiable by the parade of limousines outside its door), at Section No. 200 of GUM, and at other depots, was filled by, among others, a secret department of the Moscow Meat Combine that packed seven tons of cold cuts and roasts per day. The CC Business Office's "Daily Service Enterprise" had four closed retail goods "salons" and a shoe repair shop on Kutuzovskii. These enterprises represented the tip of an iceberg that extended to the "special workshops, special daily services, special polyclinics, special hospitals, special facilities" later bemoaned by Yeltsin.[112]

When members of the power elite had aches and pains, they could have them salved at the four unmarked polyclinics managed by the Fourth Chief Directorate of the USSR Ministry of Health and arrayed in strict order of status: the original infirmary at the corner of ulitsa Granovskogo and prospekt Kalinina; the Moscow Clinical Center opened at 6 Michurinskii prospekt, near Moscow University, in 1978; the 1940s building on Sivtsev-Vrazhek pereulok in the Arbat; and a clinic on ulitsa Zamorenogo in the Presnya area. The Fourth Chief Directorate also operated two in-patient hospitals: the Central Clinical Hospital off ulitsa Marshala Timoshenko in Kuntsevskii raion, formerly known as the Out-of-Town (Zagorodnaya) Hospital; and the surgical and therapeutic wings of the center on Michurinskii. The Central Committee Business Office gave out cradle-to-grave benefits, for, together with shops and sick bays, it ran two day nursery-kindergartens (at 45 Profsoyuznaya ulitsa and 1 ulitsa Davydkovskaya, next to Stalin's dacha), and, at the western end of Kuntsevo, an apparatchiks' burial ground (a corner of Troyekurovskoye Cemetery). It also had a rest home and burial area for Old Bolsheviks in Peredelkino.[113]

The carrying capacity of the Fourth Chief Directorate's wards and clinics roughly matched the class of beneficiaries of the Kremlin ration. In 1990, by which time it had been renamed and some economies made, the directorate had 23,649 patients on register in Moscow. Care was provided by 19,414 health personnel, with average annual expenditure of 1,400 rubles per patient—as compared to between 40 and 100 rubles per patient in standard municipal organizations. The Central Clinical Hospital had 140 candidates and 30 doctors of medical sciences—"in general . . . the best medical cadres in the country"—while the Moscow Clinical Center had more than 1,000 personnel for its 190 beds, diagnostic clinic, pool, and tennis courts.[114]

The ranking nomenklatura could also turn to the nearly thirty special rest homes, sanitoriums, and vacation hotels sprinkling Podmoskov'e to all sides of the capital. The most formidable was the Council of Ministers' sanatorium at Sosny, next to Nikolina Gora; several kilometers square, it was serviced at its peak, so it is said, by 2,000 employees. The Central Committee, besides its six rest houses, two sanatoriums, and three holiday hotels in the oblast, had five health and recreational camps for children there.[115]

A tread down the status ladder, the Fourth Chief Directorate of the RSFSR (not USSR) Ministry of Health operated three Moscow polyclinics for its charges, at 20 Kutuzovskii prospekt and on Grokhol'skii pereulok and ulitsa Plyushchikha, and two large hospitals, on ulitsa Davydkovskaya in Kuntsevo and Otkrytoye shosse in Kuibyshevskii raion. Next, the Moscow gorkom of the party and the several thousand top municipal staff had their own service network, administered by the gorkom's Business Office and the Second Special Directorate of the city government. On their books were two polyclinics (for senior and junior staff), the third wing of the Botkin Hospital, a rest house with 200 places in Serebryanyi bor, sanatoriums in Moscow oblast, Crimea, and Georgia, several summer Pioneer camps for youngsters, a children's health camp in Litvinovo (west of Moscow), and a gorkom/obkom "food combine" operating canteens and direct-order desks.[116]

Moscow's largest industrial enterprises, too, had amassed enormous capital in soft services. For instance, the Frezer Works, a maker of metal-cutting tools in Volgogradskii raion, maintained in 1980 a day nursery, three kindergartens, a primary and a vocational school, one Pioneer camp, a sports stadium, and a "house of culture." The First State Ballbearing Works a few years earlier had kindergarten and nursery spots for 2,600 children, 200 medical personnel, a Pioneer camp on the Black Sea, and reserved places in six sanatoriums in Moscow oblast and southern climes. The Komsomol Small Car Works had more than thirty kindergartens and day nurseries, a "palace of culture," gymnasiums, a hockey rink, a trade school, and several polyclinics. ZIL, Moscow's biggest factory, possessed in 1966 thirty-five kindergartens, 614 physicians and nurses, a 500-bed hospital and nineteen shop clinics, resorts in Yalta, the North Caucasus, and Podmoskov'e, a 10,000-seat soccer stadium and a covered swimming pool, a library of 533,000 volumes, and a culture palace with a planetarium, concert hall, and rooms for dozens of hobby clubs; in the 1980s it opened a "hospital complex" with 1,000 medical personnel.[117]

Administrative cubbyholing brought forth in consumer services the same kinds of diseconomies and disproportions long deplored in the housing sphere. The stylish outlets for the national elite reflected a pervasive style of behavior in Moscow and the USSR, not a singular abuse.

So, of the 5.7 million Muscovites who availed themselves of public dining daily in 1983, those seeking nourishment in residential districts stood in long queues, whereas "the greatest concentration of places is found in the canteens of leading branches of industry." Eighty-four percent of the Pioneer camps, rest houses, and other out-of-town recreation facilities for Muscovites were built and run by employers for their own staff and families. Many structures were "crumbsize" and prodigal of green belt and resort land, and the absence of common standards bred "fundamental disparities" in access between wealthy and poor sponsors. "The departmental factor has given birth to and reproduced to this day a situation of 'recreational inequality' . . . and irrational use of the precious territory of Moscow's environs."[118]

Similarly, departmental hospitals or wards inaccessible to the general public held 20.7 percent of Moscow's sickbeds in 1982, up slightly from 19.4 percent in 1965.[119] The Fourth Chief Directorates of the USSR and RSFSR health ministries owned only the best of these. The Ministry of Defense had health complexes in Lefortovo and Sokol'niki, the KGB a polyclinic on Varsonof'evskii pereulok and a hospital in Pokrovskoye-Streshnevo, and the Academy of Sciences its own hospital on ulitsa Fotiyevoi in southwest Moscow, while the Ministry of Transportation had well-regarded hospitals in Sokol'niki and Tushino.

Out-patient polyclinics on departmental budgets burgeoned in the Brezhnev years. In 1987 forty or so exempted about 500,000 Muscovites from the lines in city clinics:

They are constituted upon petition of a ministry or agency, a genesis that right away gives them advantages over the raion polyclinics. The Ministry of Health, again on application of the ministries and agencies, agrees to staffing quite a bit more generous than within the city health service. And not only staff sizes are better. The physician or nurse has a lower case load and a higher salary, 15 to 20 percent more than normal. This produces a "shoving off" every year of specialists from the raion polyclinics into the departmental ones, which is why the departmental polyclinics have so many more specialists. The polyclinic of the Ministry of Foreign Trade has three times as many neurologists and oculists and five times as many otolaryngologists as the average . . . the polyclinic of the Ministry of Finance . . . [has] twice the surgeons and four times the neuropathologists, and so on . . . And almost all the departmental polyclinics are in good buildings and outfitted with the latest equipment.[120]

Had employer "company stores" been generalized to all social and consumer programs, local institutions would have been made quite irrelevant. But things were not taken to this extreme for the bulk of the population of post-Stalin Moscow.

Service provision by the employer chiefly involved simple needs bearing proximately on the occupational function—not confounded by lengthening commuting times—in which auxiliary organizations, mainly the trade unions and party apparatus, took a strong interest. Day care was often furnished because without it mothers of young children could not work. Organized out-of-town recreation, the most fragmented of all the services, fortified staff morale and identification with the enterprise. Midday meals and medical clinics drew on Russian traditions of industrial hygiene and on managers' preference for well-fed and healthy workers.

Most Muscovites did not regularly obtain any but these basic services through the workplace. Four in-patient beds in five, after all, were in public hospitals, and the clientele of municipal clinics outnumbered the departmental polyclinics' sixteen to one. Of preschoolers in group care, 64.9 percent in 1980 attended local nurseries or kindergartens. Three-quarters of the places in eateries were open to all comers without restriction. Of the books and magazines shelved in nonacademic libraries in 1982, 55.6 percent were municipally held, 5 percent more than in 1965. The city owned sixty-four of the capital's ninety-two athletic stadiums. The workers' clubs, quartered in palaces of culture at the job site and bearers of a heritage going back to the avant-garde of the 1920s, received regular visits from only 15 percent of the population in the early 1980s; over 60 percent routinely patronized cinemas and theaters, all of which were on the city's ledger.[121]

Although the bond between workplace and welfare was nowhere near disappearing, it was giving indications of fraying. Remaining firmest in several areas of bedrock need, it had less to offer when it came to the amenities a more sophisticated citizenry had come to expect. In a private-enterprise economy, urbanites would have bought amenities on the market. In the socialist metropolis, the only place to turn was to local government.

ATTEMPTS TO RATIONALIZE SERVICE DELIVERY

City agencies and firms participated in all phases of satisfying consumer demand. They manufactured some household wares and foodstuffs, although most were made by central bodies. They built almost every shop and service counter. And arms of the municipal bureaucracy, jointly supervised by higher (mostly RSFSR) ministries, operated the bulk of the retail economy, from GUM on Red Square, with its 8,000 employees, to the tiniest newspaper stand. I will bear down here on the developmental mission. It is not one of the prouder chapters in the history of Soviet Moscow.

Central and local authorities committed to two objectives: lifting the aggregate level of provision and spreading the largesse around through a set of coordinating mechanisms. Just how short of attainment of the first goal they came up is evident from a juxtaposition of expansion quotas for the consumer sector posed in the 1971 general plan with results as of 1986 (see Table 16). The master plan still had four years to run in 1986, but its defects were plain; selecting any other year in the 1980s would make no great difference.

Fulfillment fell shortest of the targets for cafeterias and restaurants, places of entertainment, and libraries, where Moscow in 1986 had between one-third (cinemas) and two-thirds (eateries) of the per capita assets charted by the master plan. Hospitals, schools, and preschools fared much better, with shortfalls of under 10 percent. As with housing, the investment effort slackened. When construction rates by five-year planning period are compared for five of the seven types of facility given in Table 16, as well as for retail stores, in no category was as much capacity brought on stream in 1981–1985 as twenty years before (see Table 17). In three categories less was done than in 1956–1960, when Moscow's population was under 5 million.

Equally at odds with hortatory policy was the unsatisfactory distribution of the capacity made available. Soviet planning theory aimed at ensuring the even placement of consumer resources through a

Table 16. Actual and planned levels of provision of selected consumer facilities, 1961–1986

Type of facility	Provision per 1,000 residents		
	Actual 1961	Target in 1971 plan	Actual 1986
Hospital beds	11	16–17.5	14.7
Places in day nurseries and kindergartens	39	60	55.4
Places in elementary and secondary schools	85	120	102.2
Seats in cafeterias and restaurants	48	150	98.3
Seats in live theaters, concert halls, and circuses	6	15	6.4
Seats in cinemas	8.1	35–40	11.7
Volumes in mass libraries	2,000	10,000	5,900

Sources: For first and second columns, "Osnovnyye napravleniya razvitiya goroda," Stroitel'stvo i arkhitektura Moskvy, no. 11 (November 1966), p. 20 and interleaf. Third column calculated from figures in Moskva v tsifrakh, 1987 (Moscow: Finansy i statistika, 1987), supplemented by information from other handbooks for seats in live theaters, concert halls, and circuses.

Table 17. Construction of selected consumer facilities, 1956–1985

Type of facility	Construction completed (thousands)					
	1956–1960	1961–1965	1966–1970	1971–1975	1976–1980	1981–1985
Hospital beds	10.3	14.4	10.1	24.5	8.7	12.8
Places in day nurseries and kindergartens	71.0	120.4	99.3	55.7	76.7	68.0
Places in elementary and secondary schools	133.4	187.6	163.4	132.0	99.7	127.1
Seats in cafeterias and restaurants	59.5	137.9	162.9	159.3	159.7	134.5
Seats in cinemas	17.3	23.6	30.7	12.5	5.2	8.8
Square meters of floor area in retail stores	—	286.1	263.6	332.0	156.1	242.8

Source: Moskva v tsifrakh, 1988 (Moscow: Finansy i statistika, 1988), pp. 173–176.

"stepped" *(stupenchataya)* system. This was to allocate the proceeds of development fairly and "bring the expenditure of time on all kinds of service to a minimum," freeing up hours for socially meritorious tasks and leisure.[122]

In the 1960s some in Moscow considered making the dwelling unit itself the basic step in the service ladder, slackly on the model of the post-1917 "house-communes." In 1965 city hall approved a design drafted by a group of planners under Natan Osterman for a House for the New Way of Life (Dom novogo byta, or DNB), to hold 2,200 young adults in the Tenth Block of Novyye Cheremushki (at 19 ulitsa Shvernika) and serve as a prototype for the urban USSR. The DNB's twin sixteen-story towers were to be joined by a service pod containing an auditorium, dance hall, swimming pool, and calisthenics rooms; meals were to be taken in messes rather than in the bantam apartments; there would be extended care for toddlers and after-hours programs for schoolchildren. While disclaiming any mimicry of the early communes, Osterman highlighted the advantages of "scientific fantasy" for "the formation of communist consciousness."[123]

Debate raged over the project, mainly on the pages of *Literaturnaya gazeta,* even as cranes levered wall panels into place (see Figure 63). Osterman was disparaged for wanting to sterilize daily life in a "common kettle," for misestimating upkeep costs, and for evincing a snobbish love for "villas" with perquisites out of reach of the unwashed masses. He and his allies replied that tenancy would be voluntary, that their costing was realistic, and that superior collective services should accompany all new housing. Although the local authorities never publicly disavowed the DNB, their support had chilled by the time it was completed in 1969, shortly after Osterman died. Unwilling to make it a municipal responsibility, and unable to talk ZIL or other possible patrons into stepping in, they signed it over to Moscow State University, on the flimsy excuse that the university could best do the sociological research needed to evaluate the experiment. Vetoing the swimming basin and other extras, the deans made the DNB a dormitory for graduate students, many of them from Africa and Asia. The research and discussion soon lapsed.[124]

Russian social scientists argued, on the basis of surveys in Moscow and other cities, that urbanites did not want the communal dining and child rearing at the core of the DNB.[125] It was thus a mark of some

Figure 63. Natan Osterman's House for the New Way of Life. (Photograph by William C. Brumfield.)

reasonableness on the part of policy makers that they chose to service the populace after Stalin by emplacing the needed resources not in the individual apartment house, and not in rivalry to family activities, but in concentric rings around the home.

Architects had presaged the decisive ring, the *mikroraion* (microraion or microdistrict), in their work on "enlarged blocks" before the war and on "service blocks" in the mid-1950s. The microraion was first used systematically in the Khimki-Khovrino area of northern Moscow in 1959–1960. It typically held 8,000 to 10,000 inhabitants, who were to have within walking distance food stores, child care, a school, and the most essential daily services, all installed according to per capita norms as the housing itself was built. More specialized purchases, health and episodic consumer services, and leisure opportunities were to be procured in the bounds of a larger *zhiloi raion* (housing district), for which special norms were worked out. These districts appeared in the 1960s as aggregations of 30,000 to 40,000 persons (the 1971 plan set a ceiling of 70,000). By the 1970s and 1980s they had reached 250,000 residents in places such as Ore-khovo-Borisovo and Yasenevo (in southern Moscow), Lianozovo (in the north), and Krylatskoye (in the west). And beyond the housing district there lay the city's eight planning macrozones and their service subcenters, discussed above.

Making the case for rationalization in 1957, one planner gave the counterexample of Butyrskii khutor, a development for 70,000 people under way in Dzerzhinskii raion. As tenants moved furniture into its apartments, they found themselves among little besides houses and dirt lots. The area had no baths or laundries, only two barbershops, a dire shortage of classrooms, and no club, library, movie house, playground, or clinic. "Each builder," the author said, "tends to his own departmental concerns, making no connection between them and common ones."[126]

Stepped planning made some improvements on this state of affairs. Nonetheless, the criticisms of later years sounded a great deal like what was said about Butyrskii khutor. Most microraions and housing districts in 1975 provided their occupants with only a portion of their planned features and with a distribution that "takes a random char-acter and does not correspond to any sort of system of rational organization of service." Imbalances were worsening, one planning official stated a few years later: "The disproportion between the ever growing housing fund and the service network is not lessening but growing," and the gap had become "like a vested tradition."[127]

Numerous vignettes suggest that the last spokesman was not cry-ing wolf. A study of 108 microraions completed in the 1960s discov-ered that, when 100 percent of the housing had been done, completion rates were 86 percent for preschool and school facilities, 74 percent for trade and consumer services, 69 percent for health, and 63 percent for recreation and culture. In 1982, when the key had been turned on 93 percent of the Teplyi stan district's housing, and completion of day care and schools stood at 90 and 80 percent, ratios for food stores were 70 percent and for other stores, dining places, and polyclinics a scant 27 percent. In Yasenevo the same year, 94 percent of the housing space had been deployed but merely 70 percent of capacity for nurs-eries and kindergartens, 58 percent for classrooms, 31 percent for food stores, 27 percent for polyclinics, and 5 percent for dining.[128]

Evidence of the systemic nature of the problem comes from trial projects aimed at perfecting coordination techniques. The most instructive is Severnoye Chertanovo, the model development born with every political advantage at a joint session of the gorkom bureau and the ispolkom of the Mossovet in May 1971. Viktor Grishin doted on it as the gem in the crown of the model Communist city, and it was designed by a bevy of 300 planners headed by Chief Architect Posokhin. Outside their spacious apartments, Severnoye Chertanovo's 20,000 people were to enjoy a subway connection on the new Serpukhovskaya line, a below-ground parking garage, a spherical, 10,000-square-meter commercial center, and a banquet of recreation and service depots.[129]

It would take more than the backing of a member of the Politburo to see this kind of venture to fruition. Severnoye Chertanovo was first scheduled to be fully functioning in the late 1970s, a date soon pushed back to the summer of 1980, in time for the Olympics. That date came and went without comment. Seven years later, Grishin was on pension and 18,000 tenants had set up house in what was *still* a work in progress:

> The trade center's . . . carcass towers stand naked, saplings vegetating in its brick walls and its metal beams and long forgotten derrick cranes rusting away . . . "The experiment has not worked out and will not work out," is how the first secretary of the Sevastopol'skii raikom, Aleksei Mikheyevich Bryachikhin, without slandering it, appraises the situation. "The design was cut off from real life. The work is stuck in the mud. We promised the residents the city of the future, but so far there is a dearth of even the simplest daily conveniences . . . The people of the microraion have nowhere to buy so much as a needle and thread, nowhere to get their hair cut, nowhere to get together after work" . . . The polyclinic, trade center, service combine, and cultural center bring up the rear of the construction. There is no club, no public library, no place for work with children, no café or canteen, no sports fields, no store for manufactured goods, no telegraph office . . . The microraion's planning isolation makes the inhabitants feel the absence of the most important services all the more.[130]

As a visitor in 1984, I was taken by the bright ceramics and airy lobbies of the apartment houses. But the only working services at Severnoye Chertanovo were one of two projected schools and one of

Figure 64. Severnoye Chertanovo in 1988: apartment buildings, uncompleted parking garage and stores, construction debris. (Photograph by author.)

two day nurseries, a small general store *(universam),* a postal and telegraph branch, bread and vodka shops, a pair of vegetable stalls, a newspaper kiosk, and a reception point for laundry. When I returned in 1988 (see Figure 64), there had been added the subway stop, the second school, a polyclinic, a kindergarten (as yet unopened), three refreshment stands, and a car wash and gasoline pump, and final touches were being put on a swimming pool and gymnasium. The trade emporium was far from finished, the general store had burned down and been replaced by a metal tent, and residents still hauled mesh bags of groceries and other necessities off public transit. The area was littered with workers' shacks and detritus and ripped by bulldozer treads. Although the underground auto park was open, a leaky roof, high monthly fees, and vandalism had persuaded many owners to angle their vehicles on ramps and walkways.

Why was the product so mottled, after almost twenty years of effort, in even the cream of Moscow's housing estates? Clearly, the same order of priorities that made Soviet urban development on the whole so threadbare affected this development. Housing trumped all. Fulfillment of the annual quota of square meters built was a do-or-die imperative for economic and political executives; every other aspect of public welfare could wait.

The balkanization of the bureaucracy worsened the effect of resource stringency. An unwritten rule held that 5 percent of the capital assigned to any housing project was to be set aside for cognate services. This left a minimum of half of the costs of schools, stores, and the rest to be covered in dribs and drabs from other sources. The matrix system for funding social overhead made bargaining over these matters an almost completely vertical process, involving specialized local bodies and the higher-ranking bureaus (such as the USSR and RSFSR school and trade ministries) superintending the programs: "Each of the participants strives to finish only his own object and feels no responsibility for the entire district."[131] Resources were not miscible between program areas, so horizontal transfers to right imbalances were rarely tried, and then only with the aid of the local party organs. Even in Severnoye Chertanovo, eleven agencies shared leadership of the project.

The development formula worked to the advantage of older districts and against newer ones. As neighborhoods aged, the deviation from the norm generally narrowed. But the time lag could be reckoned in decades rather than years, and maturation did not have uniform effects on all services.

The age factor was correlated with a second, spatial bias. Since Moscow's growth went from the inside out, its best-equipped areas were as a rule those closest to its center. At the same time, marked irregularities of provision on all variables occurred within the inner and outer raions alike. These points are best illustrated for 1989, a year for which I have unusually full raion-level data and for which most indicators are the result of investment decisions taken before 1985.

For each of five measures of service provision (see Maps 31 through 35), mean provision in 1988–1989 is much higher in the thirteen innermost raions taken together than in the twenty outlying

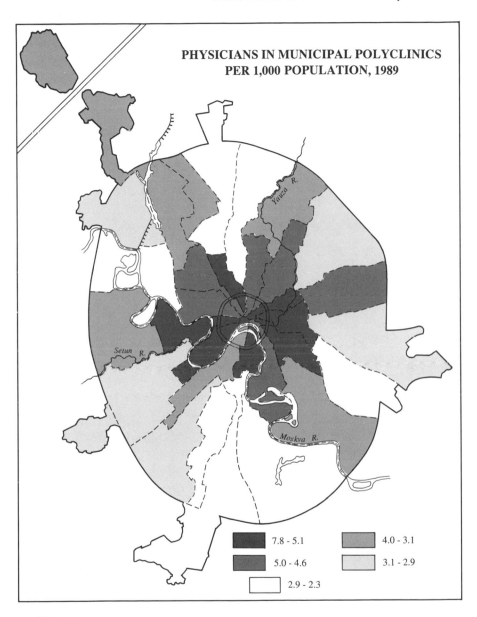

**PHYSICIANS IN MUNICIPAL POLYCLINICS
PER 1,000 POPULATION, 1989**

7.8 - 5.1	4.0 - 3.1
5.0 - 4.6	3.1 - 2.9
2.9 - 2.3	

MAP 31

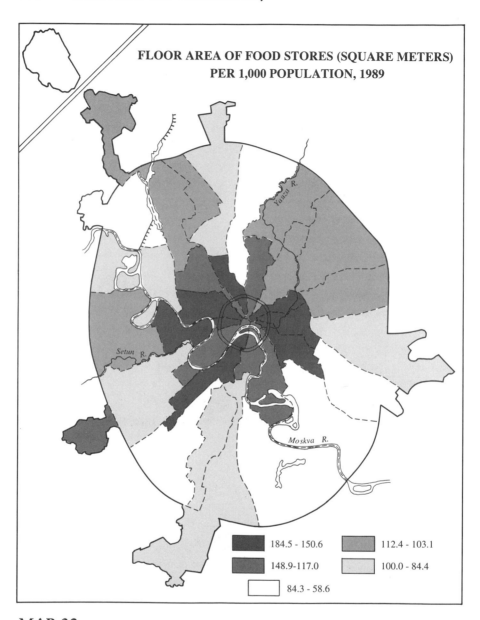

FLOOR AREA OF FOOD STORES (SQUARE METERS)
PER 1,000 POPULATION, 1989

Yauza R.

Setun R.

Moskva R.

184.5 - 150.6	112.4 - 103.1
148.9-117.0	100.0 - 84.4
84.3 - 58.6	

MAP 32

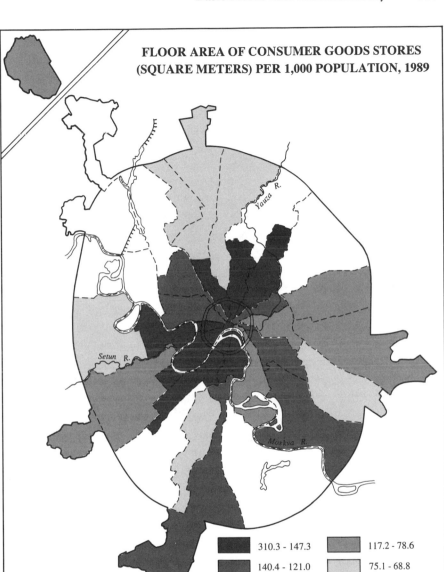

FLOOR AREA OF CONSUMER GOODS STORES
(SQUARE METERS) PER 1,000 POPULATION, 1989

310.3 - 147.3	117.2 - 78.6
140.4 - 121.0	75.1 - 68.8
67.2 - 55.9	

MAP 33

PLACES IN PUBLIC DINING ESTABLISHMENTS
PER 1,000 POPULATION, 1989

220.9 - 62.8	30.4 - 16.9
46.8 - 31.5	15.7 - 11.8
11.3 - 4.7	

MAP 34

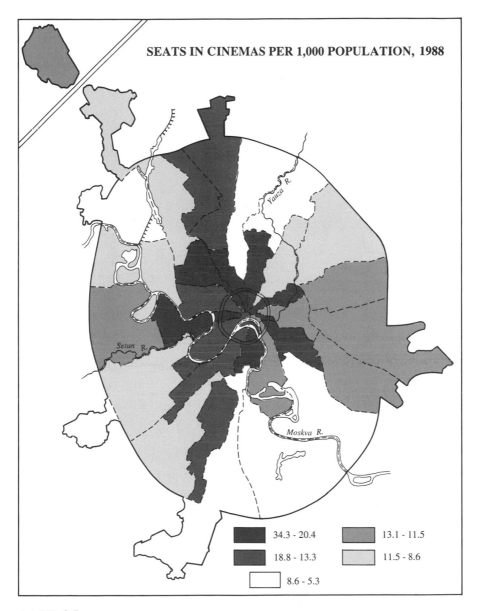

SEATS IN CINEMAS PER 1,000 POPULATION, 1988

Yauza R.

Setun R.

Moskva R.

34.3 - 20.4   13.1 - 11.5

18.8 - 13.3   11.5 - 8.6

8.6 - 5.3

MAP 35

raions and differs appreciably within each group of raions. Thus the inner raions had an average of 1.88 times the per capita density of physicians in polyclinics (Map 31). But among the inner raions the ratio of the best-supplied raion (Kievskii) to the worst (Oktyabr'skii) was 1.96:1, and among the outer raions the ratio of best (Pervomaiskii) to worst (Krasnogvardeiskii) was 2.06:1. For food stores (Map 32), the inner/outer ratio was 1.62:1, while in the inner group the ratio of best (Kievskii) to worst (Sokol'nicheskii) was 1.64:1 and in the outer group it was 2.09:1. For nonfood stores (Map 33), inner raions exceeded outer raions by 2.42:1, and best/worst ratios were 3.20:1 for the inner raions (where Sokol'nicheskii, the worst-supplied with food stores, was best-supplied with nonfood stores) and 2.27:1 for the outer raions.

Besides the age and location of the residential district, the nature of the service induced significant fluctuation. Table 18 (pp. 544–545) pulls together data on inter-raion differences in endowment with social and consumer facilities in 1978 and 1988–1989. The summary device is a standardized measure of statistical variation, the coefficient of variability (the ratio of the standard deviation of the distribution to its mean). For Soviet policy makers, the ideal would have been a standard deviation and thus a coefficient of variability of zero for each service, meaning equality of provision from one raion to another. Failing that, they would have preferred low coefficients and ones that fell over time.

The values for per capita housing space came closest to the ideal. The coefficient of variability was only 0.082 in 1989, a low score, and that was almost 50 percent less than for the 1978 baseline. Housing, in short, was being provided quite equally across raions, and more equally in 1989 than eleven years before. The 1989 coefficient of variability came to less than 0.3 for two other services, school classrooms and food stores, and to less than 0.4 for (among others) physicians in polyclinics, drugstores, and laundry facilities. Housing, elementary education, bread stores, health clinics, pharmacies, laundries—all met *basic needs,* and their flat distribution within Moscow reflected a governmental belief in relatively egalitarian allocation of these fundamental benefits in a socialist society. Of the most essential services, the only one with a coefficient of more than 0.5 in 1989 was subway transportation (0.990); indexes for other transit modes would in all likelihood show a more even allotment.

When we look, however, at programs that bear on *urban amenity,* a comfortable and satisfying life above and beyond the rudiments, the range of availability is much greater. At the extreme, the 1989 score for seats in live theaters, music halls, and circuses was 1.964, twenty-four times the score for housing, and the coefficient of variability for seats in publicly accessible cafeterias and restaurants was 1.106, thirteen times the housing score. Stores retailing manufactured items showed a much wider spread than food stores.

The enriched-curriculum "special schools" specializing in music and in English and other foreign languages, which appealed to parents in the would-be middle class, were far more maldistributed than ordinary grade and secondary schools. Four outer raions (Krasnogvardeiskii, Solntsevskii, Sovetskii, and Zelenograd) were without a foreign language school in 1989, while Krasnopresnenskii raion, in old Moscow, had eight, and Otktyabr'skii, in the southwest, had seven. Only 6 percent of the first-grade pupils in the special schools in 1987 were from workers' families, and in the final grades their representation "often fell to zero." "The location of these 'palaces of knowledge,'" an investigative journalist wrote, "often importunately coincides with the addresses of those blocks where the greater part of the population consists of the families of officials in the ministries and departments and of doers of intellectual labor."[132]

The different scores for 1978 and 1989, given the lead times necessitated by five-year plans, capture the outcome of investment choices made no later than 1975 and 1985. Of the twelve rows for which we have coefficients of variability for both 1978 and 1989, eight show a decline. But in five of the eight the drop in variability was less than 10 percent of the 1978 score. And in four cases, three of them, surprisingly, having to do with basic needs—subways, hospital beds, and care of preschoolers—variation was greater in 1989 than in 1978. State policy made at best irregular progress toward the equality it espoused.

Environmental Concerns

The ground for the militant environmentalism of post-1985 was prepared by a generation of inadequate policy and of growth in apprehensiveness about pollution and about the imperilment of the architectural patrimony.

Table 18. Cross-raion variability in selected social and consumer facilities, 1978 and 1989

Indicator	Coefficient of variability[a]	
	1978	1989
Housing (actual dwelling) space per capita	0.160	0.082
Proportion of households on housing queue	—	0.548
Subway stops per capita[b]	0.952	0.990
Hospital beds		
Per capita	0.690	0.756[c]
Per person of pension age	—	0.702[c]
Physicians in municipal polyclinics per capita	—	0.385
Pharmacies per capita	0.359	0.352
Places in day nurseries and kindergartens		
Per capita	0.126	0.445[d]
Per preschool child	—	0.480[d]
Places in daytime elementary and secondary schools		
Per capita	0.144	0.117
Per school-age child	—	0.191
Day music schools		
Per capita	—	0.570
Per school-age child	—	0.624
Foreign language schools		
Per capita	—	0.967
Per school-age child	—	0.974
Seats in cafeterias and restaurants per capita		
All	0.551	0.605
With unrestricted clientele	—	1.106[e]
Floor area in retail stores per capita		
Food	0.308	0.289
Manufactured goods	0.644	0.611
Seats in live theaters, concert halls, and circuses per capita	—	1.964
Seats in cinemas per capita	0.510	0.476[f]
Volumes in mass libraries per capita	0.783	0.750
Personal service outlets per capita		
Laundry	—	0.362[g]
Dry cleaning	—	0.363[g]
Shoe repair	—	0.425[g]
Hair cutting	0.565	0.478[g]
Locksmith	—	0.693[g]
Photo developing	—	0.697[g]

NURTURING NATURE

Official solicitude for natural ecology had a lengthy pedigree in Moscow. As long ago as 1935, the master plan dictated removal of all factories fouling the city's air or water. The USSR Sovnarkom promulgated special regulations on smoke emissions in Moscow in February 1937, and the Council of Ministers issued new ones in 1948. National and local resolutions on defense of streams and ponds in the area came out in 1947, 1949, and 1955.

By and large, these early prohibitions slipped into the bureaucratic bog. There were few extrusions of noxious enterprises (isolated cases began to be recited only after 1960), and technology created new hazards. Through the 1950s, the Kurchatov Institute and other atomic research laboratories buried isotopic wastes in their yards and casually trucked them to unlicensed dumps near radial highways. Not until 1961 did Radon, a disposal unit of the Ministry of Medium Machine Building, open an underground disposal plant near Zagorsk, north of Moscow. Radon did little about the pollutants generated before it. Only under Gorbachev did Muscovites learn that there was radioactive soil underneath the cellars of large housing developments such as Novyye Kuz'minki, Novyye Cheremushki, Khoroshevo-Mnevniki, and Khimki-Khovrino. The very existence of Radon and of the radiation-monitoring First Chief Directorate of the Ministry of Geology could not be publicly discussed.[133]

The sketchy data passed by the censors admitted a steady deterioration of the Moskva River, until clogging of the current by upstream

Table 18 (footnotes)

a. A standardized measure of variation, expressed as the standard deviation of the distribution divided by its mean. The higher its value, the greater the variation of the indicator, in this case across raions.

b. Subway stations on boundaries between raions are counted in each raion.

c. Hospital beds used in calculating these coefficients are for 1988. The coefficients for beds in public hospitals only in 1989 were 0.754 (per capita) and 0.712 (per person of pension age).

d. Day care places for these coefficients are for 1988.

e. For eateries with restricted clientele, the coefficient is 0.495 for 1989. It could not be computed for 1978.

f. Cinema seats for this coefficient are for 1988.

g. Excluding Zelenograd, for which no information was available.

hydroelectric dams left it not able to oxygenate itself by the turn of the 1960s. The Yauza was a reeking porridge of raw wastes from eighty-two manufacturing plants; an oil-soaked creek tributary to it burst into flame in 1971. "It is no secret," a journalist said later, "that [the Yauza] is called a river only by force of habit. When you get down to it, there is no river here at all. It is really the biggest gutter for waste in Moscow."[134]

Air quality gained from the major exception to governmental inaction. Upon completion of the natural gas pipeline from Saratov in 1946, Moscow organizations began to convert their boilers from coal and peat to gas firing. The biggest investment was made by Mosenergo, the regional division of the USSR Ministry of Power, in gigantic district stations for cogeneration of heat and electricity—the acronym is TETS, for "thermopower central." There were to be fourteen TETS stations in Moscow by 1985, supplying 80 percent of its radiator steam, hot tap water, and electric current (see Figure 65).

Retooling reduced throwoff of soot and sulphur compounds by more than two-thirds as of the mid-1960s. The changeover was incomplete, however, and gaseous discharges from transport and industrial furnaces worsened during this same period. Contaminated air, the city's chief sanitary physician, Mikhail S. Sokolovskii, said in 1961, "is harming people's health" in Moscow. Without elaborating on human effects, he stated that atmospheric pollution had wiped out 87 percent of the pine trees and 98 percent of the spruces in Izmailovo Park since 1930.[135]

Sokolovskii could afford some candor because of a vagary of Kremlin politics. In May 1958 the Central Committee had resolved on a precipitous expansion of Soviet output of fertilizers and industrial chemicals. One of the firms to respond was the Dorogomilovo Chemical Works, a maker of paints, dyes, and special materials for the armed forces founded in 1916 across the Moskva from Novodevichii Convent. By chance, a choking cloud from its chimneys wafted one day in the autumn of 1960 over the government villas on the Lenin Hills, about a kilometer away, where Khrushchev was squiring a foreign delegation. Dyspeptic, he ordered instant conversion of the plant to plastics production and the evacuation by 1963 of eighty-seven of Moscow's filthiest metal foundries and chemical workshops. In a crash campaign the Dorogomilovo works was reprofiled

Figure 65. Smokestack and cooling towers of a district thermopower station, visible behind apartment buildings, western Moscow. (Photograph by author.)

and some of the transgressing plants were ousted. But complaints persisted.[136]

Leaders after Khrushchev put a more balanced program in place. In August 1968 the executives of the gorkom and city council undertook to rescue the Moskva River, vowing to end the emptying of untreated municipal sewage into it by 1971 and demanding that industry do so by 1976. The Moscow-Volga Canal began to ration water to Moscow industry that same year. Viktor Grishin early in his reign helped defeat a proposal to build an atomic power station on the outskirts of Moscow, disputing the claim of President Anatolii P. Aleksandrov of the Academy of Sciences that Soviet nuclear power was so safe that a reactor could be built on Red Square.[137]

Moscow in the 1970s, capitalizing on the Brezhnev Politburo's receptivity to pollution abatement, pumped local and ministerial budgets for water and air purification up to 100 million rubles for 1971–1975 and 500 million for 1976–1980. The 1971 master plan bound Moscow to several environmental initiatives—production zones, accelerated shutdown of unsanitary factories, high-temperature incineration of solid waste, a bigger and cleaner green belt, and muffling of urban noise. The budgets and staffs of the Moskva-Oka Basin Inspectorate, the main enforcer of the water code, and the city's fifty "sanitary-epidemiological stations," the guardians of air quality since the 1890s, were enlarged. Lay members of the Moscow Society for Environmental Protection were encouraged to take part in mop-ups, and the press gave more regular coverage of ecology.

This investment reaped dividends. The unsung policy of water rationing forced industry's draw on fresh water down from 39 percent in 1968 to 26 percent in 1986 and induced almost half of the water system's manufacturing clients to engage in recycling. Cleansing of the Moskva also showed results. Effluent evidently did diminish some, and dredging barges suctioned and strained millions of cubic meters of river muck over ten years. Classified data recorded a recovery of oxygen content by the mid-1970s.[138] A few intrepid anglers defied "No Fishing" signs to toss in a line for pike and perch here and there along jetties in downtown Moscow.

I do not mean to suggest that successes merited the accolades heaped. Privately distrusted by many Muscovites at the time, the propaganda about Moscow the Immaculate would be held up to ridicule after 1985. "Of the manifold myths of the epoch of stagnation," two naturalists were to write, "one of the most popular and oft repeated was the myth that Moscow is one of the cleanest capitals in the world and, of course, the cleanest city in our country. Smugness on this account was rudely broken off by glasnost'."[139]

The production zones, as detailed above, were a travesty. Of the 44 polluting enterprises marked for evacuation from Moscow in the first five years of the 1971 master plan, no more than 5 were actually removed in that time; of the 356 targeted in total, 139 were gone by 1987. Eleven percent of solid waste was being burned in 1990. The green belt was reduced in area, not expanded, and demographic and industrial growth there far exceeded the quota. "The special status of the green belt is ignored by the local powers," a researcher at Russia's leading environmental institute said in 1989. "Right next to Moscow large forests are being cut down and swamps drained—in a word, things are going on that can be classified as ecological crimes." Noise pollution had worsened; from 6 to 41 percent of Muscovites, depending on the raion, lived in "zones of acoustic discomfort."[140]

Although open sources provided no summary index of the condition of the Moskva River, they conceded that "in places" it and the Yauza overshot state norms for impurities by twenty to fifty times and that a main reason was "the release of untreated sewage within the city limits," amounting to 2.2 billion cubic meters a year. More than half of factory waste water in Moscow was being discharged uncut into municipal drains, and only 8 percent of the cleaning was being done with efficient equipment.[141]

In exurban raions in Podmoskov'e, especially to Moscow's east, free use of urban sewage as fertilizer produced abnormal readings for zinc, chromium, nickel, iron, and cobalt; 40 percent of the vegetables shipped to Moscow from these districts exceeded state limits for metal content. By dint of industrial emissions and farm runoff, "the majority of the bodies of surface water in the Moscow region" were "not fit for recreational or household use." The worst readings were at Lytkarino, Zhukovskii, Ramenskoye, Voskresensk, and Kolomna, all factory towns on or near the Moskva downstream of the capital, and, for human fecal counts, in the Istra basin, upstream of Moscow.[142]

The fix for water pollution that environmentalists have learned to distrust most is dilution with fresh flow, which was what the Moscow-Volga Canal of the 1930s accomplished. Engineers in Gidroproyekt, the USSR's main hydraulic institute, actively pursued this remedy again from 1974 onward. They planned to dam the Volga River above the town of Rzhev in Kalinin oblast, about two hundred kilometers northwest of Moscow, and to increase throughput in the canal by running water from the reservoir through a chain of ditches, underground tubes, and streams. Work began in the early 1980s. Until defeated in the Gorbachev period, the project threatened to damage the ecology of the upper Volga basin and to take the heat off purification and conservation efforts in Moscow.

Performance on air pollution was no less unsettling. A *samizdat* (underground) manuscript by Boris Komarov reported in the late

1970s that carbon monoxide fumes in Moscow's air measured ten to thirteen times the "maximum permissible content" set by the government, while hydrogen sulphide levels surpassed the norm six months out of the year. Attacking misleading Soviet comparisons to Western urban centers in which car ownership was ten or fifteen times higher, Komarov concluded that Moscow's air was more breathable than that of Los Angeles and some American cities but less clean than in western European capitals, despite much larger auto fleets there.[143]

Official data declassified after 1985 proved supportive of Komarov. Exhaust from cars and trucks, which numbered fewer than 1 million in Moscow on any given day (800,000 based in the capital, about 200,000 in transit), accounted for 73 percent of the 1.3 million tons of atmospheric emissions in 1988. It was unimpeded by no-lead gasoline, catalytic converters for motor vehicles, or local exhaust checks. Of the 27 percent of air pollution from point sources, the largest share came from Mosenergo's TETS stations and from the 50 smaller power plants and 2,500 individual boilers that had survived rationalization. Only 18 percent of the smoke spewing from the TETS units was being filtered, and that only to snag large particles. The five built after 1960 went up close to the MKAD, where they intruded on the green belt and were engulfed by new housing districts.

Other scofflaws besides Mosenergo included the heavy industrial plants of the Ministry of Ferrous Metallurgy (Serp i molot and the Voikov Iron Foundry, for example), the Ministry of Petrochemicals (the Kapotnya Oil Refinery, specializing in diesel fuel), the Ministry of the Chemical Industry (the Dorogomilovo works and Mosbytkhim, a producer of household chemicals), and the Ministry of the Automobile Industry (ZIL, the Komsomol Small Car Works, the First State Ballbearing Works, and others). Late Soviet-era sources spoke not only of oceans of smog, nitrous oxide, sulphur anhydride, and carbon monoxide in Moscow's air, but of unspecified doses of lead, mercury, phenol, cobalt, cadmium, molybdenum, zinc, and other more toxic substances in air and ground.[144]

Pollution levels differed enormously from district to district. For fixed sources only in 1987, the first year for which any raion-level environmental statistics were given (see Map 36), they ranged from 40 tons settling on each square kilometer in Oktyabr'skii raion to 1,153 tons in Lyublinskii and 1,345 in Timiryazevskii raion. Factoring

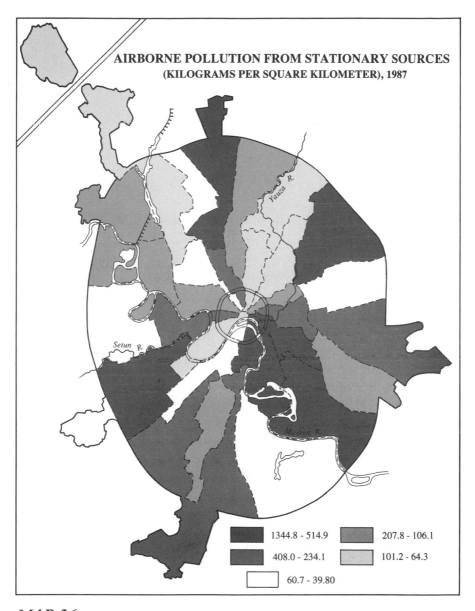

AIRBORNE POLLUTION FROM STATIONARY SOURCES
(KILOGRAMS PER SQUARE KILOMETER), 1987

1344.8 - 514.9   207.8 - 106.1

408.0 - 234.1   101.2 - 64.3

60.7 - 39.80

MAP 36

in autos, for which information is spotty, the grimiest air overall was in Proletarskii, Sverdlovskii, Zhdanovskii, Timiryazevskii, Moskvoretskii, and Lyublinskii raions. Four of the worst six were thus in southeast Moscow.[145]

Moscow scholars after Brezhnev's death correlated air quality with personal health. Researchers from the Institute of Genetics of the Academy of Sciences and several medical laboratories examined records at twenty-four children's polyclinics. They found a linear relationship between pollution and respiratory diseases: in badly soiled raions the incidence of bronchitis, acute pharyngitis and tonsilitis, and chronic otitis ran 40 to 60 percent above the average, and asthma rates, which grew sevenfold in Moscow between 1949 and 1981, were 200 percent higher there. For the 9 percent of children in "zones of extreme ecological discomfort," reports of respiratory illness were 100 to 150 percent above the city mean and "deviations from normal physical development" 30 to 50 percent above. The scientists also noted a link with genetic damage, as had been rumored for years: "Study of the frequency of congenital defects revealed that in the 'dirty' raions developmental anomalies are encountered more often than in the control group of less polluted raions."[146]

Why could socialist urbanism not achieve decent pollution standards? One reason was the same skimping on resources we have seen in housing and consumer amenities. Planners boasted of laying aside 500 million rubles for state capital investments in nature conservation for 1976–1980. It transpired that only 280 million rubles' worth of construction and installation work was done in Moscow, and 297 million more from 1981 to 1985. Funds allocated to the main category, water purification, were tied up in uncompleted projects, in vintage Soviet fashion, and so bought progressively less capacity; 63 percent less filtering power was added in Moscow in the years 1981–1985 than in 1976–1980. Air quality received the pittance of 12 million rubles of investment over ten years. It was hurt even more by diminishing returns; a mere 23 percent as much scrubbing capacity was added in 1981–1985 as in 1976–1980.

The second disabling factor was the perennial difficulty of coordinating vertically oriented state organizations. One of many anguished commentaries on delays faced in relocating polluting factories put the standoff this way: The enterprises "are in no hurry, all the more so because they firmly expect support from their ministries . . . With truths and untruths, the ministries secure from USSR Gosplan a 'temporary waiver' of measures sanctioned by Gosplan itself. The enterprises that are supposed to be taken out of the capital continue 'temporarily' and 'by way of exception' to poison its air and water."[147]

Where a local unit had an enforcement device with bite—like the Moscow-Volga Canal's spigot for rationing water—agency interests could be overridden. But they seldom were. The Moskva-Oka Basin Inspectorate was "a semi-amateur organization" manned mostly by retired army officers.[148] The Mossovet had an advisory committee with a psychedelic title—Interdepartmental Scientific-Technological Council on Problems of Strengthening Conservation of the Environment and Rational Utilization of Natural Resources in the Capital and the Green Belt—and a filing cabinet full of verbose "integrated plans" for nurturing nature, but it had few firm regulatory powers. The prefects of the Communist Party confined themselves to fluffy exhortation and supervision of what works projects existed.

ARCHITECTURAL CONSERVATION AND THE FATE OF THE CENTRAL CITY

Environmentalism applied more to Moscow's man-built heritage than to its biological setting. The issue was not new. Nor was it played in the same apocalyptic key as under Stalin, who ruthlessly stamped out pre-socialist talismans. But urban conservation, and the kindred question of social policy in the inner city, refused to quit the agenda and put leaders more and more on the defensive.

Khrushchev's one direct encounter with historical conservation came over a Civil War–era structure, the Osipov-Andreyev Liberty Obelisk on Sovetskaya ploshchad'. His ear bent by liberal intellectuals, he ruled that this tribute to the emancipating spirit of the Russian Revolution, dismantled by Stalin's writ in 1941, be resurrected and take its place on the square back from the statist Dolgorukii statue. The planners got advice from the aged Nikolai Vinogradov, who had been Lenin's expert on monumental art, and the widow of Dmitrii Osipov.[149] They proceeded in vain, as work on the plinth ceased once Khrushchev was retired.

Khrushchev showed no similar obligingness toward bits of the city forged before 1917, any more than he had as local party boss in the

1930s. His atheistic drive closed ten or twelve of Moscow's fifty functioning Russian Orthodox churches and had six of them torn down.[150] He twitted fixers of old buildings with squandering "the people's money," had spending on restoration trimmed, and encouraged vituperative counterattack to Petr Revyakin's pro-conservation essay in *Moskva* magazine. His Moscow legates voted in secret to locate the Palace of Congresses in the Kremlin. They resumed street relabelings: the 156 in 1964 surpassed the total of any year since 1922. Among the prominent names to go were Bol'shaya Kaluzhskaya, Bol'shaya Yakimanka, and Meshchanskaya streets (which became Leninskii prospekt, ulitsa Dimitrova, and prospekt Mira in 1957) and Okhotnyi ryad and Mokhovaya ulitsa (prospekt Marksa in 1961).[151]

All this abuse did not keep some Muscovites, mostly intellectuals, from doing their small part to protect old Moscow. Petr Baranovskii worked quietly at rehabilitating the Andronikov Monastery and the Krutitskoye Residence. The aircraft designer Andrei Tupolev accompanied him to a meeting in 1959 with the prime minister of the RSFSR, Dmitrii S. Polyanskii, to try to forestall demolition of a sixteenth-century mansion north of the Lubyanka. In early 1964 Baranovskii and Revyakin met with Yekaterina Furtseva, now Soviet minister of culture, and pleaded futilely for her help; she told them she was not sure what a "communist city" would look like, but "it would be without churches." In 1962 arose the first known street protest against a demolition in decades. Tipped off that the city would raze the eighteenth-century Church of the Savior of the Transfiguration to facilitate subway expansion, residents of Preobrazhenskoye in the east end organized a round-the-clock guard. The sentries were driven away one night in police vans and the church was sapped and dynamited before dawn; their later treatment is unknown.[152]

If the reinforced-concrete suburbs took precedence over the central city under Khrushchev, what downtown renewal he allowed bore no small resemblance to the steamshovel 1930s, minus the venom toward unique antiquities and the mock-classical taste in new edifices. When road builders began to knock through the route for prospekt Kalinina, *Pravda* cooed that it was "hard for even long-time residents to recognize" that portion of the Arbat. "It looks like someone's gigantic hand has removed everything decrepit and outdated."[153] The "outdated" was, as ever, a matter of opinion; here it took in Sobach'ya plo-shchadka and some of the finest houses put up in Moscow's aristo-cratic enclave after the fire of 1812, one of them the mansion of Aleksei S. Khomyakov, a founder of the Slavophile school. Artists' drawings showed Kalinina's twin rows of 25- to 30-story towers as free-floating, vacant of contextual references to the Arbat or Moscow.

It was in the same surgical spirit that a competition for a detail plan (PDP) for inner Moscow was conducted in 1966–1967. One entry proposed the demolition of all existing structures in Zamoskvorech'e; several would have converted 40 to 50 percent of the area inside the Sadovoye into parkland; others provided for skyscrapers of 50 stories or more. A collective in the Institute of the Master Plan headed by Simon M. Matveyev won first prize. It made these recommendations: a green strip 300 to 700 meters wide along the outer edge of the Sadovoye, to be studded with ministerial office towers; a new zone in the southwest for the highest organs of party and state; a park belt along the Moskva, dominated by monuments to Lenin and wartime victory; elimination of housing inside the Bul'varnoye kol'tso and "active reconstruction" out to the Sadovoye kol'tso in clusters of apartment high rises "amidst open, green spaces"; and the laying out of "splendid, broad radial prospects" converging on the Kremlin.[154]

By this time, however, respect for the urban heritage had begun to rise. Although some historical sites were razed during Leonid Brezh-nev's long administration, only three churches were and demolitions declined overall.[155]

When the Politburo decided in 1965 to spare the dowry box of tiny Orthodox churches along the southern margin of ulitsa Razina (see Figure 66), it portended a new phase of accommodation. The Church of the Conception of St. Anne, St. Barbara's Church, Zna-menskii Monastery, and nine lesser cousins had been endangered by their proximity to the cumbrous, 3,000-room Rossiya Hotel, the largest in Europe, designed by Dmitrii Chechulin to replace the office tower left unfinished in the devastated Zaryad'e district in 1954. Instead of the churches being pulled down, the hotel's ramps were redrawn and the shrines and the final long fragment of the Kitaigorod Wall were given state protection.

Other conciliatory decisions followed. The central government cooperated in the formation of republic-level conservation associa-

Figure 66. Church of the Conception of St. Anne and Rossiya Hotel. (Museum of the History of the City of Moscow.)

Figure 67. Rebuilt Triumphal Gates. (Photograph by author.)

tions, in Russia the All-Russian Society for the Preservation of Historical and Cultural Landmarks (VOOPIK); in 1976 it was to adopt a
new USSR landmarks bill. City hall between 1966 and 1968 built a
facsimile of Osip Bove's Triumphal Gates, the memorial of the 1812–
1814 war razed in 1936, on Kutuzovskii prospekt (Figure 67). In
1967, after discussion in the Politburo, it accepted a jog in prospekt
Kalinina so as to salvage the 300-year-old Church of Simeon Stolpnik.
It agreed in 1968 not to remove the classical villa on Bol'shaya
Gruzinskaya ulitsa that once belonged to the greatest Russian lexicog-
rapher and enthnographer, Vladimir I. Dahl. Street renamings fell
from 134 in 1965 to 33 in 1968, and then to a mere 2 in 1969, the
fewest since 1917; they averaged 5 a year in the 1970s. Restoration
budgets climbed from about 2 million rubles a year in 1965 to 4

million in 1972, 15 million in 1976, and 25 million in 1984. Mikhail Posokhin, the circumspect chief architect, came out in 1978 for rebuilding the Sukharev Tower, demolished by Stalin in 1934. In 1979 the city ispolkom voted for auto-free malls on Arbatskaya ulitsa, Kuznetskii most, and Stoleshnikov pereulok, scenic old Moscow alleys.

The 1971 master scheme was confirmed without a final decision on a PDP for the central area, but in June 1972 the gorkom and Mossovet delineated nine "reserve zones" within the Sadovoye kol'tso where clearance would be strictly limited. The following December the gorkom bureau subjected a pro-demolition PDP draft to "sharp criticism," and in April 1974 a downtown plan was approved which, compared to earlier projects, lowered permissible building heights and cut back on housing and office construction.[156]

Following the precedent of the "lengthy, exhausting struggle by cultural workers, historians, and architects" over ulitsa Razina, the Moscow intelligentsia participated throughout these decisions on the downtown area. Intellectuals had been writing protest letters about the Rossiya Hotel and the threat to the street's surviving churches since 1961. It was a petition from them that got the matter on the Politburo's agenda of December 31, 1965. Brezhnev and Suslov made speeches "to demonstrate that they were not indifferent to the hopes of our cultural figures," and it was all Vladimir Promyslov, invited to the meeting, could do to get approval for the revised site plan.[157]

Pressure was mostly applied behind the scenes, but drum beating was again permissible in the press, by advocates such as the painter Il'ya S. Glazunov, the mosaic artist Pavel Korin, who chanced censure in the 1930s to speak up for the Sukharev Tower, the nature novelist Leonid M. Leonov, and Oleg V. Volkov, a once-persecuted writer who helped spark the countrywide crusade on behalf of Lake Baikal in Siberia. They worked free-lance and through VOOPIK, whose Moscow chapter operated out of the former abbot's chambers in Znamenskii Monastery. Architect L. I. Antropov took the rare step of a nonwritten protest in 1967; he lay down in the bucket of an earthmover at the Church of Simeon Stolpnik until assured that it would not be demolished.[158]

The indomitable Petr Baranovskii lived long enough to lobby for Simeon Stolpnik and the Dahl house and to establish a school for restoration technicians at the Krutitskoye Residence in 1969. In November 1971, at Krutitskoye, he led VOOPIK's first festive Sunday outing *(voskresnik)* of amateur restorers. He died in 1984 at the ripe old age of ninety-two.

VOOPIK members and other lay citizens sat on the "representative commission" to advise GlavAPU on demolition permits appointed in 1976. The presidium of the organization in May 1980 sent letters to the RSFSR government and *Literaturnaya gazeta* recommending a second coming for the Sukharev Tower. Viktor Grishin later indicated something approaching fear of VOOPIK:

> It was practically impossible to do anything in Moscow with [an old] structure that presented any sort of interest without incurring the active interference of the Society for the Preservation of Landmarks. I remember how on one street, Sadovaya-Karetnaya, a stone pedestal stood in the middle of the sidewalk. We thought that we had better tear it down—it was right in the center of the sidewalk, you see, and it was getting in the way. But no way, the Society for the Preservation of Landmarks got its dander up and claimed this was a valuable antiquity. And what do you think happened? We had to retreat.[159]

With public policy thus enlightened, why did the issue not fade away? How can we explain the pent-up resentment that was to find vent after 1985? As in one sphere after the other, expectations were aroused here that could not be met. "Before our very eyes," two planning scholars wrote in 1980, "public opinion has radically changed and professional attitudes toward protection of our city's precious legacy have changed." "Much has been done," they went on, "but all the same we have more problems than accomplishments."[160]

Yet again, accomplishment was constrained by the resources deployed. Rehabilitation budgets were a drop in the bucket of true needs and were under 0.5 percent of capital investment in the city. Moscow, never given its own restoration trust, had to solicit the Soviet and Russian cultural bureaucracies for manpower. It asked for control of the RSFSR Ministry of Culture's new Moscow trust, Mosrestavratsiya, in the late 1970s, only to see the ministry dissolve it rather than hand it over. Rejuvenation projects puttered along from one planning period to the next. "The plan might be fulfilled in rubles, but completion of restoration of the landmark would be put off" as contractors took on new assignments rather than finish off old ones.[161] There were stories of small churches taking twelve or fifteen years to restore. The Arbat mall was not given over to pedestrians until 1985; those on Stoleshnikov and Kuznetskii most were never begun.

Hundreds of designated landmarks ended up with no help at all. And caring for some did not keep the average state of old Moscow from worsening by reason of past mistreatment, the careless property management that goes with public ownership, and technical blunders. Inattention to subterranean water flows in laying the foundation of the Rossiya Hotel and the new wing of TsUM (the Central Department Store) in the 1960s and 1970s undermined the ulitsa Razina churches, the Malyi Theater, and the colonnade of the Bol'shoi. Digging for the Palace of Congresses knocked the walls of the Great Kremlin Palace off vertical, caused the Assumption Cathedral to settle, cracking some of its frescoes, and disturbed the medieval piles beneath the Ivan the Great Belfry. Thoughtless replacement of the cobblestones on Sobornaya ploshchad' with macadam and concrete forced moisture to build up in the soil and infiltrate the basements of several of the Kremlin churches, notably the tsars' crypt beneath Archangel Cathedral.[162]

Even relatively young buildings of Soviet provenance made the list of architectural cripples. The Lenin Library was mangled by overuse and by foundation cracking, sagging of walls (so severe it pushed some windows out of frames), and flooding of its depository in 1984, brought on by ill-conceived tunneling for subway lines and Kremlin parking in the area. Engineers feared that the eighteenth-century Pashkov House, by Bazhenov, part of the library complex, was about to fall down. Estimates for overhaul of the Lenin Library alone were five to ten times the annual restoration outlays for all Moscow.

The paladins of heritage buildings had to master byzantine procedures for classifying them and conferring protected status. The three main brands of officially impanelled landmarks (architectural, cultural, and historical) overlapped, and the seal of approval could be bestowed by any of three levels of government (USSR, Russia, and Moscow). The exact size of any subcategory or the city total was anyone's guess. Moscow was said in the mid-1980s to have about 1,200 architectural landmarks, the largest group, but at fewer than 600 street addresses; perhaps two-thirds were located inside the Sadovoye. A covey of special-purpose agencies kept inventories, classified as state secrets, as were the central-area PDP (which Posokhin repeatedly spoke of as a recommendation only) and the bylaws about the reserve zones.

Regardless of the receipt of 1,100 applications, no buildings were appended to the rolls after 1974. "As a result of endless delays, a lot of landmarks of old Moscow were destroyed," among them traders' rows near Tagankskaya ploshchad' and mansions in Lefortovo. One tally puts the number of "historic buildings" removed between 1971 and 1988 at more than 2,200. Many buildings inside the reserve zones remained unprotected by the regulations, and the "red lines" authorizing street widening written into the 1935 master plan were mostly left in effect. New construction was frequently "allowed by way of exception and special exception." "The whole system of reserve zones," a member of VOOPIK's volunteer inspectorate said in 1987, "has not yet been thought through."[163]

The closer one looks, the more fragile the consensus about the conservation issue appears. The Sukharev proposal drew a hail of bad notices (by Dmitrii Chechulin, among others) and was stopped in its tracks in 1980. But by then the friends and foes of preservation were trading imprecations that echoed the Shchusev-Popov exchange of the 1920s and bore a family resemblance to the controversy between Slavophiles and Westernizers in the nineteenth century. According to one modernizer, Moscow should be glad to part with "the shameful symbolism of the dark past." He accused its upholders of maligning socialists and seeking to embalm even slums like Mar'ina roshcha and the remnants of Khitrov. This was planning "recidivism," shot back a VOOPIK activist, assailing those "who mouth words about a 'scientific approach' but in deeds are all for a sweeping demolition of historic Moscow." As "patriots, feeling moral responsibility before the people," builders ought to care for what their forebears had made.[164]

Although most of the liberal intelligentsia concurred in the goals of retention and restitution, the cause had its deepest appeal for the growing number of Muscovites whose loyalties lay with tradition, nation, and religion. This aspect of urban conservation came through in varying combinations and degrees of frankness in the published dialogue. On the uncensored pages of samizdat, it could take pathological forms that misrepresented the larger movement but wormed into the politics of the issue.

One unsigned pamphlet from the early 1970s arraigned Moscow's politicians and planners, from the first demolitions of the 1920s through the destruction on prospekt Kalinina, for cleaving to "an ideology of militant anti-Russian chauvinism." It dropped the innuendo that the non-Russian, usually Jewish, ethnic origins of certain officials, past and present, influenced this policy.[165] A tract that made the rounds a couple of years later made the grotesque claim that Kaganovich, a secularized Jew, iniquitously tried to twist Moscow in the 1935 master plan into the form of a Hebrew Star of David.[166]

It was no coincidence that architectural conservation became an anthem of Pamyat' (Memory), the xenophobic group that gained notoriety after Brezhnev. The loosely structured Pamyat' came into being during the buildup to the 600th anniversary of the Battle of Kulikovo Field in 1980, receiving logistical support from well-wishers in the Ministry of the Aviation Industry. Moscow photographer Dmitrii D. Vasil'ev, its acknowledged leader, railed at union halls and clubs against corrupt Communist officials and the "Zionists" and "Masons" he said were in cahoots with them. His standard address screened slides of the Cathedral of Christ the Redeemer and other vanished local sights.[167]

Concerning famous landmarks, the nub of the post-1964 reforms, conservationists of all stripes had some reason to rejoice. When it came to the overall physical and social character of the old town, the result was more mixed. Socialist Moscow experienced no commercial thrust for downtown redevelopment. Yet its historic core was beset by different pressures, symptomatic of Soviet conditions. The outcome disappointed a large and diverse constituency.

The most profound changes were demographic and social. At the turn of the 1960s, when the master plan was under revision and wholesale clearance was still palatable, the nineteen square kilometers inside the Sadovoye had about 900,000 residents; planners projected a decline to between 200,000 and 350,000 people, all to live in updated housing. The actual numbers were 500,000 in 1969 and 240,000 in 1988, toward the bottom of the targeted range. The housing stock in 1988 was 47 percent smaller than in 1960. The streets on which millions of Muscovites were reared, the backdrop to some of Russia's most enchanting novels and poetry, "today do not inspire the most undemanding romantics," Lev Kolodnyi wrote glumly. Whole sections of inner Moscow "have been partially or fully depopulated." At dusk, when the sacrament of switching on the lights occurs, they "stand mute and in darkness, deserted by the former inhabitants of the Arbat, Sretenka, Strastnoi bul'var, and the like. If here and there a lamp twinkles, it is only until the end of the work-day."[168]

The great majority of the downtown population was relocated in the date-stamped tract housing of the outlying districts—a psychological loss often not defrayed by the gain in floor space. Suburbanization was involuntary: once older houses had been emptied, they were either wrecked or remodeled for different users; there was no program for rehousing the displaced in the same neighborhood or raion. In an echo of the worst of postwar urban renewal in the United States, tenants took up relocation offers one by one, leaving older houses partially vacated and allowed to decay and be vandalized for up to ten or fifteen years.

Who was left behind? Increasingly the center had a two-class population—not unlike American inner-city areas undergoing "gentrification." Sixty percent of the 240,000 living in central Moscow, mostly natives of the city and oftentimes elderly, still occupied communal flats in 1988, "frequently without simple conveniences."[169] Many of the other 40 percent belonged to political and professional elites who, as discussed above, received high-class accommodations.

It would have been one thing if the core area were acquiring cultural and other attractions that would grace the metropolis as a whole. This was decidedly not what was happening. The inner raions retained their edge in terms of retailing and services, but these sectors were not the focus of redevelopment. Unlike prospekt Kalinina, which for all its faults had thirteen stores, ten service establishments, and restaurants and cafés with a seating capacity of 5,600, Novokirovskii prospekt in north central Moscow, the applauded road project of the 1970s and 1980s, had almost nothing for the consumer. Compared to western European capitals, central Moscow remained devoid of the small walking and sitting pleasures. Almost one-quarter of all retail sales were still rung up at the dowdy points of what was smirkingly called the shopper's "Bermuda Triangle": GUM, founded as the Upper Trading Rows in 1893; TsUM, which began as Muir and Merrilees in 1908; and Detskii mir, the only one to open under Soviet rule, in 1957. All three of these museum pieces aimed to please non-Muscovites.

If resident and consumer interests lost out, who came out on top in downtown politics? The answer, as so many times in this book, is the producers and the functionaries.

Employment in central Moscow grew by 25 percent between 1977 and 1987 alone, while office space increased by 40 percent. The Ministry of Defense and the KGB, which flanked the Lubyanka with two forbidding office blocks, one for its directorate for Moscow and oblast,[170] led the parade of central agencies building in every cranny of the central area. By directive of Aleksei Kosygin in the mid-1960s, the four double-winged apartment houses on the south side of prospekt Kalinina were transfigured into ministerial offices before their residents could move in; the five much smaller towers on the north held only 900 flats, perhaps one-quarter of those planned. The windswept Novokirovskii prospekt was lined from the beginning with cold administrative haunts, their portals glistening with brass name plaques. The bureaucracy also took over hundreds of older apartment houses that landlords, usually the raion ispolkoms, could not afford to maintain or rehabilitate and were willing to lease without charge. "Unappealable decisions in a command voice about 'transferring,' 'resettling,' 'providing,'" rained down on the city and district authorities.[171]

The opinion that central Moscow was in a bad way rested less on crisp calculation of cost and benefit than on emotions and a feeling that something comfortable and cherished was being denatured without any offsetting good coming of it. If Moscow had always been Russia's heart, as the saying went, then this came down to saying that Moscow's own heartbeat was at risk.

The socialist urban paradigm, as modified under Stalin's heirs, was not without its accomplishments. Reckoned among them in Moscow would be devising the 1971 master plan, expanding the city's boundaries, doubling per capita housing provision, laying out exurban leisure zones and the green belt, putting together the world's most extensive transit system, investing in infrastructure and service networks, achieving advances against water and air pollution, and making efforts to conserve architectural landmarks.

Goals low in the hierarchy of human needs, beginning with crude shelter, were the ones served best and most uniformly by public policy. By comparison, urban amenity, strivings transcending mere subsistence, fared poorly and betrayed greater spatial and socioeconomic variability in outcome.

Moscow's experience would seem to bear out, therefore, Charles Lindblom's axiom about communist regimes possessing the "strong thumbs" suitable for simple and direct tasks, but "no fingers," none of the dexterity requisite in an intricate, truly modern society.[172] But it points also to the wisdom of reshading Lindblom's metaphor somewhat. On complex issues urban governance lacked not so much fingers as the capacity to get fingers and limbs—the segments of the hydra state, using slightly different imagery—to work in tandem. Disjointed monism, as I have formulated it, was more accurately "all fingers" than "no fingers." Examples abound in post-1953 Moscow: planners posited demographic and territorial limits to growth, yet the unintegrated actions of business and administrative units shredded them; producers winked at planning and industrial zones as they followed the principle "look out for your own interest"; the green belt and suburban zone outgrew outer Podmoskov'e, contrary to the letter and spirit of the law; housing projects, even paragons like Severnoye Chertanovo, lacked the accouterments of a rounded existence; ministerial bus fleets were half again as large as the city's; polluting factories sidestepped evacuation orders, and the occupants of historical buildings tore them down or defaced them.

The Moscow case demonstrates another tendency at some variance with Lindblom: a discernible slackening over time of the thumbs of the state and of the political will and acumen behind them, and thus of the ability to satisfy basic needs, not just the preference for amenity. The 40 percent decline in housing production, at a time of demographic growth far in excess of the anticipated amount, provides the best illustration by far of this syndrome.

A single-minded executive power—local or central, democratically or autocratically constituted—might conceivably have imposed order. But no such actor was to be found in the socialist metropolis. Unelected municipal and party officials derived no authority from below; from above, they got a limited urban-development mission and, in addition, a host of other orders that frequently overrode it, especially for the much more potent party apparatus.

The record of the Directorate of Tall Houses and Hotels suggests that, given resources and a mandate to act, the system could in theory support a decent urban life. Unfortunately, only a picayune minority was invited to feast at the table. Information control kept the majority as ignorant as possible of the housing and the other well-bounded privileges of the nomenklatura, yet this secrecy fed popular suspicion and envy. On less neuralgic policy issues (stepped service delivery, for instance), or where the good produced was less readily divisible (air pollution and building aesthetics, say), or where bad conscience or the urge to please a target group made for less smothering censorship (architectural conservation under Brezhnev would be an example), querulous notes sounded in local discourse well before 1985. Here the bosses' own promises did as much as anything to convince Muscovites that they deserved better. Leaders did enough to make such causes legitimate yet nowhere near enough to realize the headway that the people saw as theirs by right.

7

The Mold Shattered

ORDINARY socialist governance, in the metropolis and the country, was shattered by the extraordinary events issuing from Mikhail Gorbachev's accession as Soviet leader in 1985. Personnel and policy changes grew in short order into a ginger liberalization, a partial opening of the regime under Communist Party tutelage. For a plethora of reasons—pent-up demand for change, economic downturn, demoralization of the party high command and scruples there about the use of force, and the demonstration effect of revolts in Eastern Europe, among them—the process spun out of control. With the acceptance of legal opposition and competitive elections, liberalization cascaded into democratization and reform into revolution.[1]

"All the variety and contradictoriness" of the transmutation were reflected in Moscow "as if in a drop of water," a local party worker declared in 1988.[2] Seismic events had already occurred: the ouster of Viktor Grishin, the rock-ribbed local chieftain and Kremlin rival to Gorbachev; the hyperkinetic reform efforts of Grishin's replacement as first secretary, Boris Yeltsin; and, most rivetingly, the break between Yeltsin and Gorbachev. In wider circles Muscovites graduated before most of their compatriots from passive disaffection with conditions to uncensored discourse about them and active protest in autonomous organizations.

A mutinous election in March 1990 would pass the tiller of Moscow government to a conspicuous band of radicals, allied to a resurgent Yeltsin in the RSFSR legislature. "The model Communist city," the chairman of the redrawn Mossovet, Gavriil Popov, remarked as the political temperature rose, "is becoming the symbol of the whole crisis of perestroika."[3] It took until only the dog days of the following summer for the crisis to spark a bungled reactionary coup that saw the capital overrun with tanks. That drama "may in time be recognized to have been the most important single political happening of the second half of the twentieth century," writes one historian.[4] As public theater, Moscow in August 1991 ranks after only the breaching of the Berlin Wall in the imagery of the self-immolation of Soviet-bloc communism.

Chapter 7 addresses the revivification and realignment of Moscow politics from the last days of Leonid Brezhnev to the crumpling of the partocracy in 1990–1991. In Chapter 8 I deal with the institutional and policy choices post-Communist leaders have barely begun to resolve.

The Change to Change

The overdue Brezhnev succession, and the deepening awareness of the exigency of Soviet problems, lowered elite resistance to innovation. When the change to change came, Moscow was where its early watchwords—*uskoreniye* (accelerated development), *perestroika* (rebuilding), and *glasnost'* (candor or publicity about failings)—were put to the test.

INTERREGNUM

Foreshocks of the earthquake to come rumbled in Brezhnev's final months and in the abbreviated terms of his two sickly successors, Yurii Andropov and Konstantin Chernenko, who were interred beside him in Red Square within twenty-eight months. Until Brezhnev passed away in his country house at Zarech'e on November 10, 1982, the tremors were mostly palace intrigues and rustlings about corruption in his household. Andropov, the former chief of the KGB, anticipated in his moment in power his then understudy, Gorbachev, by broaching the unspoken topic of Soviet malaise. He issued a bugle call for "discipline and order," effectuated as an assault on malingering and corruption. Brezhnev's legatee, Chernenko, continued the program not without backsliding.

The stolidly Brezhnevite leadership of Moscow had to feel the quaverings. Grishin's dealings with Andropov were strained, reportedly owing to an altercation over a fire that killed twenty guests at the Rossiya Hotel in 1980.[5] But Grishin and his confreres fell in like lambs behind the punitive measures against the urban rank and file instated by the Politburo. A cannonade of gorkom motions in January 1983 instructed Moscow police and employers to clamp down hard on drunkards, unregistered residents, and job truants.

Not so easily absorbed was Andropov's clean government crusade, which trained its sights on functionaries more than on the populace. Grishin allegedly wanted some of the state dachas in Podmoskov'e donated to local councils.[6] The gift was not made, and the threat could not be defused by tokenism. Moscow was fair game for whistle blowers and enforcers; the timing if not the content of the charges manifested succession contingencies.

The announcement April 14, 1983, of the arrest of Yurii K. Sokolov, the manager of the famous Delicatessen No. 1 on ulitsa Gor'kogo (the Yeliseyev Delicatessen before 1917), made the loudest slap thus far at graft and influence peddling in the USSR. A procurator's inquiry into the diversion of state foodstuffs in Moscow was said to have begun in November 1982. Later accounts put the start in April of 1982 and pinpointed the detention of Sokolov at October 30, 1982, while Brezhnev was still alive. They also confirmed the identity of one of Sokolov's backroom customers: Brezhnev's daughter, Galina Churbanova, whose lover, the circus clown Boris Buryatiya, had been unloading her haul on the black market.

The trail led into the innards of the city bureaucracy. Vladimir A. Ural'tsev, the head of the Chief Directorate for Fruits and Vegetables, Sokolov's wholesaler, was sacked and expelled from the CPSU in April or May 1983. Later that year the KGB, now master of the hunt, called on Sokolov's supervisors in the Moscow Chief Trade Directorate. Nikolai P. Tregubov, the head of the agency since 1967, was jailed in July 1984. A court sentenced him in 1986 to fifteen years in prison; dozens of accomplices got lesser terms; Sokolov, having profited to the tune of 3 million rubles, was executed.[7]

It should not go unmentioned that neither Grishin nor Chairman Vladimir Promyslov of the Moscow ispolkom was ever indicted for a crime. Writing after Grishin's death, a former aide, Yurii P. Izyumov, exonerated him by arguing that while "everyone knew" about the

Sokolov ring, no one could do anything because of warnings from the Soviet minister of internal affairs, Nikolai Shchelokov, a hunting companion of Brezhnev (who was fired in December 1982 and committed suicide in 1984). Izyumov adds that Moscow's police chief, Vasilii P. Trushin, wanted Sokolov detained, and that Grishin himself gave the final order. Trushin, a Grishin promotee out of the local party and a member of the bureau of the gorkom since 1976, must have played his cards well, as he moved up in December 1984 to the position of first deputy interior minister vacated by Brezhnev's son-in-law, Yurii M. Churbanov, and held top offices for six or seven years.[8]

Tregubov, Grishin insisted in 1991, was framed, as part of a plot by "very influential forces" to bring shame upon Grishin: "This was whacked together as a political rather than a criminal affair, aimed at also touching Grishin . . . I doubted then . . . and I doubt now that Tregubov took bribes." Izyumov does not doubt Tregubov's venality and qualifies Grishin's faith in Tregubov by revealing that Grishin "more than once had him checked out by the KGB." But he agrees that the flap was contrived, with the aim "one more time to incriminate Moscow and the head of its party organization." Grishin, he says, signed off on the Tregubov arrest warrant "to avoid suspicion of a coverup."[9]

The point is not that some were guilty but that the investigation was a political football and was so perceived on all sides. The Moscow leaders were bespattered by their proximity. Tregubov had been praised in a confidential evaluation by the city party secretariat as a "principled worker" who took "an active part in public life." It did not go unnoticed that he had sat on the gorkom since 1974, as had Ural'tsev as a candidate member since 1981, or that they were feted as salutary urban managers. An article by Yurii Sokolov in 1982 drew Delicatessen No. 1 as a picture perfect enterprise, and Ural'tsev bragged in the same magazine of his directorate's prowess.[10]

The aroma of dishonor did not keep Grishin from vying in 1984–1985 for what remained the brightest trophy in Soviet politics, the general secretaryship of the Communist Party. Grishin tried to deny later that he ever coveted it;[11] his behavior at the time spoke otherwise.

The death or decampment of old-timers like Mikhail Suslov and Dmitrii Ustinov made the party's Moscow wheelhorse, the longest sitting member of the Politburo, the most credible counter to the youngish, reform-minded Gorbachev. Grishin's position had with-stood the commerce scandal and his personal dullness, ill health (he had suffered two heart attacks), and exclusion from the Central Committee Secretariat. His very limitations were his strength: he would give the oligarchs a few years more of peace and quiet.

Deceleration of Moscow cadres' career mobility under Brezhnev left Grishin's clientele stunted by the standards of his forebears. And he had no purchase on the personnel weapon. The one Muscovite who did in 1982, Kapitonov, was not much of an asset, as he and Grishin had fallen out in the 1950s. In April 1983 Andropov and Gorbachev obviated any danger by replacing Kapitonov as head of the party's Organizational and Party Work Department by Yegor K. Ligachev, a straitlaced Siberian apparatchik who abhorred Grishin and his machine. Ligachev joined the group of CC secretaries in December 1983; Kapitonov left it in 1986.[12]

Grishin chose the unsubtle tactic of riding Chernenko's coattails—playing Chernenko to Chernenko, as it were—and mouthing Soviet pieties. When an Order of Lenin was pinned to his chest for his seventieth birthday in October 1984, a tribute by Chernenko recalled the apothegm of Moscow as "a good example for the whole country." Grishin reciprocated by hanging on Chernenko's elbow and acting as his proxy at most protocol events. In February 1985 he read out the speech of a hospital-bound Chernenko to electors in his RSFSR parliamentary district and hosted a crass pantomime in which Chernenko, panting from terminal emphysema, received his deputy's card. Television broadcasts were arranged, to Ligachev's disgust, "to implant in public opinion the idea that Grishin was the second person in the party, and thus that the right of continuity in supreme power belonged to him and him alone."[13]

The bubble burst upon Chernenko's death. Grishin may or may not have drawn up a standpat platform and a list of candidates for leading posts: Yeltsin maintains that he did, Ligachev that he did not. In any case, there was so much latent support for the avatar of change, Gorbachev, that Grishin, a caricature of the geriatric status quo, had no chance. The Politburo and Central Committee unanimously approved Gorbachev as general secretary on March 11, 1985, and Grishin, as Yeltsin recalled the scene, "dared not make a move."[14]

The also-ran was a marked man. The People's Control Committee of the USSR set off a gasp of bad publicity by looking into the inflation of housing construction statistics in Moscow; it eventually concluded that 500,000 square meters of unfinished flats were improperly commissioned in 1985. The city and central press brimmed with mordant letters about the Moscow consumer economy, singling out housing and the paucity of potatoes and greens. Grishin vowed to "activate reserves" and waxed obsequious about Gorbachev. As protégés outside his Moscow base retired, he made what looked like preemptive cadres changes inside it.[15]

Grishin's contortions lasted only nine months. Told by Gorbachev to quit for the health of the party, he asked to go out in style by delivering the keynote at the upcoming Moscow party conference. Gorbachev refused and invited Boris Yeltsin in, explaining that Moscow needed "to be rescued."[16]

The gorkom met in special session on December 24, 1985. Gorbachev, his attendance showing the gravity of the occasion, thanked Grishin for his "big contribution" and wished him well in the honorific post of counsellor to the Presidium of the USSR Supreme Soviet. Grishin said stoically that "new energy" was needed in Moscow and there were "no small number of defects and derelictions" to be ironed out. He would be relieved of his sinecure in 1987 and drop dead in May 1992 in a lineup at a pension wicket.[17]

Gorbachev, in introducing his "exacting" designee, Yeltsin, expressed a sentiment, vented many times before, that helped set up the clash that ensued. He was, Gorbachev said, "counting on the [Moscow] party organization to go in the van of our party and people, to give an example and be a true political guide, as it has been at every stage of the struggle for socialism." Yeltsin took up the gauntlet, confident that "any profound, well-conceived initiative by Muscovites will quickly find resonance in the whole party and country." The motions on Grishin and Yeltsin were adopted without a peep. The next meeting of the Central Committee dropped Grishin from the Politburo and made Yeltsin a candidate member.

WHITE KNIGHT

Yeltsin was one of the brace of provincials from eastern Russia—including Yegor Ligachev and Nikolai I. Ryzhkov, the new chairman of the Council of Ministers—who were catapulted into high office as the reforms gathered steam. Born on a prosperous peasant homestead in the Urals in 1931, he had experienced Stalinist repression as a child—his father spent three years in a labor camp as a kulak—yet had always minded Soviet political rules. He was a civil engineer by trade and climbed the ranks in Sverdlovsk oblast, the fourth most populous region in the RSFSR and a powerhouse of heavy and defense industry. His aptitude for organization convinced superiors to put up with what he concedes is "a difficult, obstinate character."[18]

Yeltsin was co-opted into party work in 1968. In November 1976, after reconnoitering by Kapitonov and Brezhnev, he was appointed first secretary of the Sverdlovsk obkom; this position automatically slotted him into the Central Committee in 1981. In Sverdlovsk, he stated in his autobiography, he was infallible "god, tsar, and lord" and was thoroughly "steeped in the administrative-command methods" of his milieu. He had been friendly with Gorbachev, a fellow regional leader until 1978, although they had a spat over farm policy in Sverdlovsk oblast around 1980, when Gorbachev was CC secretary for agriculture.[19]

Gorbachev, on the advice of Ligachev, who soon regretted it, named Yeltsin head of the Construction Department of the Central Committee in April 1985, with the additional title of CC secretary bestowed July 1. Yeltsin and his wife were issued an apartment in a UVDG house on Vtoraya Tverskaya-Yamskaya ulitsa. He reluctantly took the Moscow viceroy's job, he says, relenting when convinced Grishin "lacked any sense of moral decency" and had let Muscovites' lot get "worse than several decades before."[20]

Yeltsin, the first incoming leader since Aleksandr Shcherbakov in 1938 not to have worked in Moscow administration, barreled into the job, casting himself as the white knight taking on the indecency and misrule of the local old guard. Working "flat out" was the only way, he related, "to reach the turning point" in reforms; he was at it eighteen hours a day, with four hours off for sleep and two for calisthenics and "self-improvement."[21]

He flourished the populist style that became a Yeltsin trademark. In safaris to factories and offices, he buttonholed employees, jotted down complaints, and chewed out errant managers. He rode public transit with commuters and dropped in without warning on microraions and stores. He took issue in party committees with the Gorbachev policy most unloved by blue-collar workers—the drive against alcohol consumption, an enthusiasm of Ligachev's—and turned back a proposal to close Moscow's main brewery.[22]

From the rostrum, the clenched-jaw intensity of Yeltsin's rhetoric—the "Bolshevik truth," he phrased it—jolted listeners, especially after the pabulum spouted by Grishin. He expounded at the city party conference in January 1986 that Moscow had been brought low by years of misgovernment and lacquering over the truth: "There may be some to whom these judgments sound overly harsh, but sooner or later they had to come out." He regaled the Twenty-seventh Congress with a vinegary premonition of political instability in the USSR that earned him headlines at home and abroad. Metropolitan Moscow's ills he ascribed to "fallacious methods of leadership . . . window dressing, idle talk, the yen . . . for a quiet life."[23]

Life was anything but quiet for officialdom, as Yeltsin meant "to start with personnel" to rattle the city out of its torpor. He did so by orchestrating the biggest cold purge there since Khrushchev's in 1949–1950. He believed his approach to be "agreed upon" with Gorbachev, who had been carrying out his own housecleaning in the central and regional party apparatus and the ministries: "He knew my character and was certain I would be able to clear away the accumulated debris, to fight the [party] mafia, and, having character and courage, that I would carry out a wholesale cleanup of personnel."[24]

At city hall, Yeltsin waited but one day to get Vladimir Promyslov's resignation. He settled as municipal chairman on an extramural candidate, Valerii Saikin, the director of ZIL and twenty-nine years younger than Promyslov. In two years less a month, Yeltsin chucked out eight of Promyslov's ten deputies and seventeen of nineteen heads of chief directorates of the ispolkom. Eight hundred employees in the Moscow retail network were arrested for kickbacks in his first four months.

In the party apparatus, Second Secretary Raisa Dement'eva (a secretary of the gorkom since 1960) headed the procession of supernumeraries. Of the other gorkom secretaries, four were put out to pasture by the spring of 1986 and the fifth in 1987. Out went the heads of fifteen of the nineteen departments of the gorkom and the first secretaries of twenty-three of the thirty-three raions. The Moscow sections of national organizations like the KGB and the trade unions underwent collateral changes.[25]

Yeltsin's appointments showed an emphasis on youth and education. For those post-1985 Moscow officials for whom the data are available (see Table C-1 in Appendix C),[26] the average year of birth was 1940 for holders of municipal and party positions, making them twenty and fourteen years younger than the comparable groups for 1964–1985. Ninety-four percent of the municipal officials, and 100 percent in the party, had a postsecondary diploma, with more than 80 percent in each set trained as an engineer.

Yeltsin further stirred up the bureaucracy by cross-fertilizing with external talent. Not much more than half of the new municipal executives, less than since the late Stalin era, came out of local administration (Table C-2); 65 percent had seen some local party duty, unchanged since 1964–1985, while over 40 percent had been, like Saikin, economic managers outside city government. For CPSU counterparts, prior tempering in the Moscow apparat was still the norm (65 percent), but at its lowest percentage since the 1920s; 58 percent had worked as economic managers, by far the most ever, and 42 percent in Moscow government, also a high; the number with Komsomol experience had plummeted. Recruitment of nonlocals was way up. Of all new party officials, 27 percent, more than at any time in the past, had served in a central party office; this figure included both of Yeltsin's second secretaries, Vasilii G. Zakharov, a Leningrader, and Yurii A. Belyakov, who had been his assistant in the CC Secretariat. Several arrivistes came from Sverdlovsk.[27]

If some departures occurred with dignity, a vituperative mood more often characterized them. So it was for the managers of a butcher shop, sacked on the spot amidst "noise and hubbub" after Yeltsin, waiting in line, discerned that they were going to resell a load of veal out the back door. The first ranking party officer to be deposed, Second Secretary I. V. Danilov of Oktyabr'skii raikom, was let go because, Yeltsin jabbed, he "built himself a palace of a home . . . with a personal fireplace and a personal chimney pipe" in an apartment house. Five of the raikom first secretaries he weeded out were cited for similar infractions, most scathingly Anatolii P. Averchenkov of Perovskii raion and Boris A. Gryaznov of Frunzenskii, the only raion official on the gorkom bureau. As much as they deserved this retribution, the arraigned were deprived of all chance of rebuttal, and anyone who expressed reservations about their guilt was considered to be supping with the devil.[28]

Besides transfusing new blood and deterring vice, Yeltsin used the cadres weapon to personalize responsibility and compel better performance. He regularly ran down checklists of office holders' "assignments," saying heads would roll if they did not shape up. In July 1986 he revived the somnolent Communist Party fraction in the Mossovet. With him in the chair, the group gave Tregubov's replacement in the Chief Trade Directorate, Nikolai F. Zav'yalov, fourteen days to bring about an "essential improvement" in the supply of summer vegetables; when he failed to achieve the impossible, he was summarily dismissed.

Yeltsin wedded the purgation of staff to the broad theme with which he most identified himself: "social justice." In comments to Moscow propagandists in April 1986, he drew a link between criminality, like Danilov's, and a more nebulous "misuse of authority" and contravention of socialist egalitarianism, as when executives had their limousines take them or their spouses on errands. A few months later he lambasted Moscow's foreign language and other "special" schools and described how the sons and daughters of officials were being driven to class by chauffeurs. Party secretaries in the hall smiled knowingly, he stated with mock conviviality to the propagandists, because, now that he had set things aright in the motor pool, they had all come to the meeting in one car. The techniques deployed on this issue were the ones he preferred to use on elite privilege: "a quiet talk with the offender, drawing the necessary conclusions."[29]

Yeltsin's strictures stirred up a hornet's nest in the Kremlin, where most moderates surmised that he was going too far: "The situation was especially inflamed by several serious clashes in the Politburo with Ligachev about perquisites and privileges."[30]

The Moscow functionaries involved found the retirements, demotions, and homilies devastating. Ill will rubbed off even on some of the ostensible beneficiaries, which helps explain their eagerness to join in once it was Yeltsin's turn to be pounded. One district secretary grimaced in November 1987 that the blitzkrieg had "demoralized" them and "induced bewilderment and diffidence." Others testified to being promoted, only to be downgraded or furloughed in the blink of an eye.[31]

In the policy realm Yeltsin, to his credit, trained his energy on social questions. He took a pugilistically pro-consumer approach. One by one, he lit into Moscow's sacred cows, grinning as he punctured "the legend of the reliability" of its subway or bellowed that its prefab houses were "ugly boxes." He cashiered Chief Architect Gleb V. Makarevich, the long-time deputy of Mikhail Posokhin, in March 1987 and lashed out at the planners' "fear of making decisions and even making bold suggestions." Parrying suggestions to hem in the Moscow agglomeration by freezing its economy, he also echoed the critics' disquiet at unmanageable sprawl. Accordingly, he took umbrage at central agencies' labor-intensive expansionism and twisted their administrators' arms to expend resources on urban utilities and soft services.[32]

During the winter of 1985–1986 the gorkom bureau dispatched letters to forty-two ministries demanding 50 to 100 percent increases in their output of consumer goods in Moscow, evacuation of noxious factories, consignment of half of their local building capacity to city needs, and manpower-saving automation; thirty ministries replied affirmatively by the end of March. Yeltsin's office also inveigled central planners into authorizing a doubling of the rate of subway construction in the 1986–1990 five-year plan. A few months later it mediated a pact with Gosplan canceling a bushel of industrial investment projects and "funneling the funds released to building social and cultural facilities and improving communal services." Yeltsin devised a characteristically blunt solution to the chronic infringement of population ceilings by migrant workers: inform employers in March 1986 that further requests for annual supplements to strength would be turned down. In September an indefinite ban on limitchiki, starting in 1987, was laced at his request into a Politburo decree on Moscow planning. Thirteen months after that came a Council of Ministers edict on centrally funded reconstruction of the downtown infrastructure.[33]

Yeltsin could not have cared less about economic theory. He had little to say about the 1986 bill authorizing individual and family firms or about the Central Committee's commitment at its plenary of June 1987—in words that mostly remained on paper—to a transition to decentralized management. Following his spell in political purgatory and rebirth as an elected politician, he was to discover the market. For the present, however, he reflexively left the theorizing to others and pressed familiar switches.

In 1986, for instance, he proclaimed an inspection of research facilities, with the aim of lessening duplication: "Closing down the first ten or fifteen institutes, and airing this in the media, will have quite an effect in activating the rest." Nervous about food shortages, the gorkom stopped a ministry from shipping oranges and treats earmarked for its Moscow workers to Siberia. Yeltsin prevailed upon the Central Committee Secretariat and the Council of Ministers in July to allocate 5,000 tons of extra meat and stocks of fish, juices, and berries to local stores. That autumn produce from state farms, trucked and flown in by arrangement with provincial party committees and the military, was put out at seasonal food fairs; Yeltsin rationalized them as a way "to put the squeeze on the market traders." On no less than twenty-six microissues, from vocational training to macaroni making, party and soviet panels enacted "special purpose integrated programs."[34]

The gaily painted stalls, amusement areas, and low prices of the fairs were widely appreciated. The slingshot special programs, by contrast, were jeered at after Yeltsin's ouster as "unbalanced, poorly worked out, and only for advertising." The pruning of deadwood research units got nowhere. As Yeltsin remonstrated a year after he took out the shears, 7 institutes had been terminated but the total number had bloated from 1,041 to 1,087.[35]

BLACK SHEEP

Yeltsin's whirlwind tour of duty in Moscow rates a mixed assessment. With some justification Gorbachev charged, after their estrangement, that he reveled in "hit-and-run attacks, pressure, shouting, and management by mere injunction," musketry from "the old arsenal" of autocratic rule.[36] Yeltsin was indeed confrontational and given to purging, and many of his prefectoral interventions, such as the "integrated programs" splicing new missions onto an unreconstructed bureaucracy, would not have been amiss for Grishin.

Nevertheless, Gorbachev had to admit that Yeltsin's exertions on behalf of intensified change—which he derided as "pseudorevolutionary" and "phony leftist"—outran his own, not to mention those of more cautious figures like Ligachev, Yeltsin's implacable foe by 1987. While both Gorbachev and Yeltsin were changing with the times, Yeltsin was doing so more rapidly and more profoundly, particularly as gauged by repugnance at the status quo and readiness to incur conflict. Although Yeltsin made ample use of command methods, he sensed, as he wrote later, that they were "running up against a brick wall" and that "new steps" had to be taken and new tools of governance fashioned: "But Gorbachev did not want to take those steps. Most of all he was afraid of laying hands on the party-bureaucratic machine, that holy of holies of our system . . . Our relations began to worsen."[37]

Yeltsin's disappointment with gradualism impelled him to flirt with unconventional political ideas. He became "two Yeltsins," as an associate recalled in a memoir. One was the party boss, the neo-Bolshevik "used to power and homage," the other the protodemocrat, "beginning to reject the rules of the game woven into the system." These two Yeltsins "fought it out" between 1985 and 1987 and for long after that.[38]

In one of his first accommodating gestures, Yeltsin in August 1986 had the half-completed All-Union Victory Monument at the end of Kutuzovskii prospekt, begun three years earlier by Grishin, mothballed (see Figure 68). He was prevailed upon to do so by intellectuals who felt it a pompous monstrosity and were offended by the flattening of Poklonnaya Hill, where Marshal Mikhail Kutuzov held his council of war during the Napoleonic invasion of 1812. The day after the Politburo commissioned a new design concourse for the memorial, Saikin and the city ispolkom, citing "the wishes of the population," restored the historic appellations of two old streets renamed under Stalin, Ostozhenka ulitsa (Metrostroyevskaya since 1935) and Khamovnicheskii val (formerly Frunzenskii val), and named a subway station after the Red Gates, torn down in 1927.

More telling, from Yeltsin's lips (see Chapter 5) came the most penetrating critique of the top-down nature of Moscow government and the hammerlock of "his majesty the worker of the apparatus." In October 1986, three months before Gorbachev's maiden speech on democratization, Yeltsin implored the regime to *break out of the narrow circle of the nomenklatura and put an end to its self-reproduction.* One of the first swipes at one-party rule, this recommendation came from someone who had unswervingly used the nomenklatura to suit his purposes.[39]

In early 1987 Yeltsin commended the "informal organizations,"

Figure 68. Unfinished All-Union Victory Monument in 1993.
(Photograph by author.)

the voluntary associations springing to life in Moscow (see below).
When the new Arbatskaya ulitsa pedestrian mall started attracting
unlicensed peddlers, some of whom sold homemade posters and dolls
caricaturing Soviet leaders, he defended them from the police. He
sponsored the opening of an unregulated weekend mart for artists and
craftspeople at Bittsa Park (it moved to Izmailovo in May 1987).

Yeltsin took an interest in electoral mechanisms in 1987. From
March through the late summer, he experimented with selection of
the secretaries of raion party committees from among two or three
candidates vetted by the gorkom, a degree of unpredictability not
countenanced since Lenin's day. Although the regular election to the
Mossovet in 1987 went unreformed, press discussion was lively and
one of the 800 nominees (the cafeteria manager at Moscow State
University) actually lost.

On May 6, 1987, Yeltsin broke new ground by meeting on a public square with leaders of the first unauthorized street rally in Moscow since the 1920s. The rally, as it happened, was staged by the rabidly nationalist Pamyat', hardly a hotbed of democracy, but by receiving their petition he acknowledged the notion of spontaneous assembly. In August 1987 a much larger demonstration, by ethnic Tatars deported from their Crimean homeland by Stalin, tied up Red Square for several weeks. On August 20–23 Yeltsin provided a meeting hall in southwest Moscow for the first Soviet symposium of unofficial political groups. Partly organized by former dissidents but with raikom aides present, it passed forceful resolutions about democracy.[40]

The chronology of Yeltsin's fall from grace is well known.[41] He first crossed swords with Gorbachev over his personnel shakeup, which he was reprimanded for overdoing in the Politburo in January 1987. In front of the Central Committee in June, he castigated Ligachev and the Secretariat for uncooperativeness in his Moscow reforms and for mismanaging the party overall. On September 12, 1987, after a tense Politburo meeting at which he and Ligachev clashed again on perks for officials, he asked the vacationing Gorbachev in a letter to be relieved of all his posts. Gorbachev deferred decision, only to have Yeltsin put it before the assembled Central Committee on October 21 at a plenum on appraisals of Soviet history.[42] Committee members took turns attacking Yeltsin, and Gorbachev referred the case to the Politburo.

On November 11 Gorbachev, saying Yeltsin was insubordinate, had the Moscow gorkom supplant him with CC Secretary Lev Zaikov, a Politburo member eight years older and with a go-slow attitude toward change. Yeltsin, pasty-faced and under a physician's care, had to listen to his ex-subordinates rake him over the coals and to submit an abject apology.[43] *Pravda* carried a tendentiously edited transcript of the plenum on November 13. Given a secondary government post by Gorbachev after his recuperation (first deputy chairman of Gosstroi, the State Construction Committee), Yeltsin was voted off the Politburo February 18, 1988, two years to the day after his promotion.

Although systemic issues were at stake, the clash was a "logical climax," as Yeltsin said, of the frustrations of trying to govern Moscow: "In order to deal with Moscow's sorest problems, I needed the help of the whole Politburo. The capital city is such a complicated conglomerate, where everything crisscrosses and intertwines, that without joint efforts things would never be moved off the mark. But I had noticed lately an active unwillingness to help the city solve its acute problems. In those circumstances, how could I carry on?"[44]

Butting heads with Ligachev and Gorbachev also followed the dance of oneupsmanship iterated time and again in the past by Moscow CPSU leaders. Like more than one of them, Yeltsin met resistance to his staffing moves from central apparatchiks who worked cheek by jowl with Moscow organizations, posed a convenient court of appeal for the local losers, and instinctively looked for the national fallout.[45]

Yeltsin's visibility further irked the Kremlin leadership. A livid Gorbachev in October 1987 asked testily whether he sought "the separation of the Moscow organization." "You are not content," he blustered, "to have Moscow alone revolve around your person. Now do you want the Central Committee, too, to devote itself to you?" Nikolai Ryzhkov scowled at Yeltsin's incessant press interviews: "He is starting to be cited everywhere . . . He obviously enjoys being in a detached position." Yeltsin thought his subway and neighborhood tours the greatest irritant to his Politburo peers: "In Sverdlovsk this had been completely normal . . . In Moscow it was an event arousing an immense amount of gossip."[46]

This was not the first time a Moscow leader, trying to make the USSR's first city a beacon to all, had become more Catholic than the pope—a maximalist and evangelist who then had to be reined in. Like Karl Bauman during collectivization, Yeltsin was fired up by none other than the general secretary—had not Gorbachev himself asked him "to give an example and be a true political guide" in making social change? Both times, the Muscovite overlearned the lessons of the preceding fracas with the party right wing and became a liability on the left. Both times, local malcontents were encouraged to pummel him and didactic use was made of the episode.

If Bauman furnished a mere hiccup in the cementing of Stalin's dictatorship, Yeltsin provided a milestone on the highway to a new kind of politics altogether. The episode etched Gorbachev's core conundrum, of being at one and the same time architect-in-chief of reform and steward of the house under reconstruction. And Yeltsin, his self-incrimination soon repudiated and the glitches in his Moscow record overlooked, was from this day forward the radicals' charismatic David. Not only would he live to stand up to Goliath another day, but changes in the structure of political opportunities would make the terrain unrecognizable.

SEARCHING FOR EQUILIBRIUM

As with Bauman in 1930, the substitute for the outcast was a loyalist, senior in standing, with a mission to restore stability. Kaganovich did so with a rod of iron, solidifying the Stalinist mold. Lev Zaikov reigned but one month longer than Yeltsin and rates only a historical footnote. As Yeltsin underwent a miraculous resurrection and sparred with Gorbachev for national leadership, Zaikov's star sank.

Zaikov, like Yeltsin, was a latecomer from the provinces. He made his name in the armaments industry in Leningrad, ending as director of a major research and manufacturing firm. Appointed municipal chairman there in 1976, he received his first party post, the high one of first secretary of the Leningrad obkom, only in 1983. He journeyed to Moscow as Central Committee secretary for the military sector in July 1985 and vaulted into voting membership on the Politburo in March 1986. He retained his CC secretaryship after November 1987, the only Moscow kingpin after Petr Demichev to be cross-appointed to the Secretariat. This was not a formality, as he supervised all Soviet defense production and chaired a Politburo commission on military policy, overseeing arms control and the withdrawal from Afghanistan. He remained, too, on the USSR Defense Council, the arbiter of military and military-industrial policy in the state apparatus.

That Zaikov had few options but to delegate many local decisions to underlings does not account for the slightness of his impact on Moscow events. Kaganovich's workload had not prevented him from pursuing a vision of a remade city and region; Zaikov sought what proved to be an elusive equilibrium. On macropolicy his views were close to those of Ligachev, with whom he made two showy Moscow tours in 1988 and who browbeat him on administrative questions. At his Moscow desk, he attempted to brake change and to nudge it down an incremental path.[47]

Zaikov held out an olive branch to officials, spurning Yeltsin's "cadres carousel" and promising "comradely support." Personnel change slowed to a saunter. Saikin and most of the promotees at city hall went undisturbed. In the party apparatus three of the five gorkom secretaries added by Yeltsin lost their jobs, yet they were not publicly rebuked and got good work elsewhere. Only seven raikom first secretaries were replaced, five of them to receive promotions. Not one of the ten raikom leaders appointed before Grishin's departure was touched.

Zaikov renounced the importation of Sverdlovskers and other "political limitchiki" and selected associates from within. His pick as second secretary, Yurii Prokof'ev, had been Grishin's last deputy for cadres (head of the gorkom's Organizational and Party Work Department) and a full member of the bureau in 1985, and was shuffled by Yeltsin to secretary of the municipal executive.

On substantive issues, Zaikov remarked as he vacated office, it would have been futile to try to "overcome all our accumulated problems at a single stroke"; better to trowel in "a sound foundation for steady, sequential movement forward."[48] Hence he supported mild adjustments in economic policy and rationalizations of the municipal and party bureaucracy.

Zaikov avidly backed Chairman Saikin's "General Scheme for Management of the Economy of Moscow," a streamlining plan approved in April 1988. It rejigged the Mossovet's fifty-two production branches into twenty-five bigger units, integrated by seven committees headed by deputy chairmen of the ispolkom. It produced Mosstroikomitet, the Moscow Construction Committee, which swallowed Glavmosstroi and the city's fragmented building departments, some of its design studios, and the Chief Directorate of Capital Construction.

In December 1988 Zaikov made a stab at reorganizing the city CPSU apparatus, slashing cadres and putting "political work" ahead of economic supervision. The Moscow party conference of January 1989 selected an unprecedented number of rank and file Communists to the gorkom—30 percent of the membership, the same as the party apparatchiks—and made big increases in the shares allotted to economic managers, academics, and cultural personnel (see Tables B-2 and B-3 in Appendix B).

Zaikov carried some of Yeltsin's policy initiatives forward and unveiled one or two of his own. He stood behind the curbs on closed service facilities for the nomenklatura enacted in 1988 and 1989. He was noticeably warmer than Saikin toward cooperative firms, which

Soviet legislation now gave legal status. He and Saikin negotiated a fresh Council of Ministers decree on eviction of polluting factories and a reduction of 2.4 billion rubles in the industrial investment planned for the first half of the 1990s. The Mossovet voted in 1988 to take possession of all ministerial housing by the year 1993. Glavmosarkhitektura (as GlavAPU was renamed in 1988) released a draft of a new Moscow master plan in April 1989; it extended to the year 2010 and put a premium on social services, regional integration, and ecology. In July 1989 the city loosened the allocation rules for city and departmental housing, making several hundred thousand Muscovites eligible for the housing queue.

Zaikov's pride and joy was "Progress-95," an "integrated territorial and branch program" for guiding the economic and social development of Moscow until 1995. The program, approved by the Politburo in April 1989, aimed "to smash interbranch barriers and concentrate all the city's forces on priority directions," set forth in a dozen categories.[49] In that it looked at all sectors at once, it perhaps had advantages over Yeltsin's twenty-six special-purpose programs. In every other respect, though, Progress-95 was a placebo, a conventional study in command planning replete in dubious quantitative indicators (for machine tools hooked up, kilometers of power cable laid, and so forth) and phlegmatic about consumer welfare.

Zaikov's early exit from Moscow government resulted not from any one flaw in his reorganizations and multisector plans but from the dissonance between the leaden, administrative style he personified and the newly kaleidoscopic context of metropolitan politics. The new politics was induced by the Gorbachev leadership's momentous commitment to *demokratizatsiya* and the societal response to the opening.

The Democratic Impulse

A democratic impulse, released by the changes rippling through Russia and the USSR, reworked the Moscow political game in four pivotal realms: communication, grassroots organization, voting, and institutional setup. This section of the chapter deals with the first and second areas and the dress rehearsal in free voting that proved lethal to Zaikov. The electoral extravaganza of 1990 merits a separate major section. I treat governing structures later in the chapter and, along with public policy, in Chapter 8.

CONVERSING ABOUT EVERYTHING

Full-throated glasnost', uncorked by the repeal of most of the Stalinist restrictions on expression, came to Moscow in 1986 and 1987. Seized as a lantern for bringing festering problems to light and mustering indignation against recalcitrant bureaucrats, it was soon accepted by most reformers as a value in its own right.

Yeltsin, what with his abhorrence of "forbidden zones," instantly warmed to the cause. About the print media, his appointee as editor of *Moskovskaya pravda,* Mikhail N. Poltoranin, exclaimed: "The city's journalists cannot be led around on a short leash. The time has come for broad independence, deep-going and fruitful inquiry . . . a frank and honorable conversation about everything."[50] And converse the Moscow press did, with ever more of an affinity for disallowed themes and formulations. *Moskovskiye novosti* (Moscow News), a weekly notorious for its connections with the KGB and boilerplate stories for tourists, led the way to journalistic freedom, as did the previously run-of-the-mill *Moskovskii komsomolets* (Moscow Komsomol Member). Yeltsin also recognized the suasive power of television. New managers of Moscow's state TV station moved the gray current affairs program *Dobryi vecher, Moskva!* ("Good Evening, Moscow!") to the frontier of glasnost'.

Attacks on Yeltsin's media allies in October 1987 seemed to foretell a clampdown. On January 8, 1988, *Moskovskaya pravda* carried a stinging essay about Brezhnev and his government's policies in Moscow by correspondent Lev Kolodnyi. Gorbachev excoriated Poltoranin and Kolodnyi at a conclave the next day, and the newspaper then printed a sheaf of disapproving letters from readers. Within a month, Valerii P. Lysenko, a more timid editor advanced by Ligachev, had superseded Poltoranin.

But no media counterreform followed. While muckraking softened, the quantity and quality of the information circulating about local affairs continued to increase apace under Zaikov. Progressives' victories in most of the battles over freedom of expression in the USSR at large countered the dampening effect locally of the dismissal of Yeltsin. The Nineteenth Communist Party Conference in June and July

1988—at which the defrocked Yeltsin (a delegate) was allowed to address the meeting (and an enthralled national television audience) and to spar with Ligachev—marked a point of no return for glasnost'.

Moscow's official outlets printed less about elite privilege after November 1987, but as if to compensate disclosed more social and economic data than during the six decades before and widened and systematized their coverage of welfare problems. *Moskovskaya pravda* in March 1988 issued a compendious inventory of housing conditions. The following year it and *Gorodskoye khozyaistvo Moskvy* began their exposés of environmental degradation. Moscow's 1989 handbook provided novel statistics on atmospheric emissions, tabulating these and other sensitive figures by raion. By newspaper, television, and radio, Muscovites were notified of street crime, transit accidents, and all the misfortunes they had always heard of by word of mouth only.

Information previously stifled on national security grounds began to surface. Kolodnyi's *Moskovskaya pravda* article on overclassification of maps and telephone directories (see Chapter 5) appeared in December 1987. Zaikov made a point of publicly visiting defense contractors, named some in speeches, stated that "post office boxes" had been accorded street addresses, and called on military plants to wake up to Moscow's social needs. Detailed and to-scale maps of the city and oblast went on sale in August 1989. *Vsya Moskva,* the city directory last seen in 1936, was reborn in 1990 as an "information and advertising annual" from a Russian-German joint venture.

In another sign of life district soviets and party committees began to publish Moscow's first-ever raion newspapers. The first, *Izmailovskii vestnik* (Izmailovo Herald) in Pervomaiskii raion, hit the streets in March 1989. Perturbed at the Central Committee Propaganda Department's slowness, Zaikov and the gorkom gave approval to them on their own. Twenty-six *raionki,* with diverse political positions, were coming out once or twice a month by year's end.

A dig at Brezhnev may have been the excuse for getting rid of Poltoranin, but historical revisionism escalated across the board after his departure. After taking up smaller fry in 1987, the party in February 1988 rehabilitated Bukharin, Rykov, and the rest of the Moscow-rooted Right Opposition to Stalin. The floodgates unstopped, revelations, reassessments, and recriminations about the city's and the nation's burdened past poured out. The Workers' Opposition, Kamenev, Zelenskii, Uglanov, Ryutin, even Georgii Popov, Khrushchev, and Yegorychev—their names and scores of others enshrouded in silence were restored to the language. Damning new tidbits, though rarely a modulated assessment, were divulged on unsympathetic figures like Molotov, Kaganovich, Shcherbakov, and Grishin. Kolodnyi wrote several of the most trenchant pieces.

Even the dicey theme of the impact of terror on the population at large, untouched during the Khrushchev thaw, came up in 1988. From the autumn of 1988 until 1991 Aleksandr A. Mil'chakov, a Moscow writer and the son of a former Komsomol leader imprisoned in the 1930s, waged a bulldog campaign to find, study, and mark the mass graves of prisoners who were murdered or died of neglect under Stalin. Using aging witnesses, geological instrumentation, extrasensory diviners, and some tips from KGB files, he located the abattoirs and burial grounds at Kalitnikovskoye Cemetery, Strogino, Novospasskii Monastery, and Butovo. Moscow television and *Vechernyaya Moskva* publicized his findings and invited Muscovites to participate in digs and soil sifting.

History was brought to bear on questions of urban planning and management. Local journals presented new and hushed-up information on the city's pre-1917 philanthropists, the Old Moscow Society, the cooperative housing and garden city movements, and specialists like Igor Grabar', Konstantin Mel'nikov, Mikhail Kryukov, and Petr Baranovskii. As a prick to the imagination, *Arkhitektura i stroitel'stvo Moskvy* in 1988 serialized Aleksandr Chayanov's 1920 fantasy *Journey of My Brother Aleksei to the Land of the Peasant Utopia*, set in a Moscow of 1984; Chayanov, arrested and shot in the 1930s, had been retroactively pardoned by a judge in 1987.

By 1988, too, the venerated master plan of 1935 was at last open to criticism. Asserting that it had reduced Moscow to an altar for the "pathological enshrinement" of Stalin and the omniscient state, an art historian, Nina Moleva, called for "emancipation from its methodological principles" and "endlessly recycled . . . stereotypes." A Moscow painter, Yevgenii Kuman'kov, pushed further, asserting that "the fate of the city demands a somber, courageous realization of the senselessness of its losses" since 1917, not merely 1935. Only making a clean breast of what was done in the people's name would show whether Moscow had merely to correct "isolated shortcomings" or, as he thought likely, "to save what is almost irreparable."[51]

THE INFORMALS AND MOSCOW'S HYDE PARK

The second flaring of the democratic impulse related to organization and political techniques. Starting right after it eased censorship, Gorbachev's government suspended or disabled prohibitions on association and assembly as old as Soviet power itself. As new regulations on "amateur organizations" promulgated by the RSFSR Ministry of Culture in July 1986 foretold, despite intermittent attempts to restrict protest in the center of Moscow, the secular drift was toward liberalization.

The nova of independent secondary associations went by the generic name "informal organizations" or simply "informals" *(neformaly)*. Unlike the trade unions, Komsomol, and other registered "public organizations," the informals were voluntary and loosely structured and did not enjoy monopolies granted by the Communist Party. Although lonely examples existed before Gorbachev—Pamyat' was one—only now did the genus proliferate.

Moscow was reported to have 500 informal associations in October 1987, when they began to be noticed, and about 1,500 in September 1988. These are approximations, given the informals' fluidity. Many, in the recollection of one activist, Valerii V. Fadeyev, "existed in words only, fictitiously, in that their frisky informal thinking far outdistanced their meager practice."[52] For all that, they had a far from meager impact on events.

Former dissidents or amnestied political prisoners participated in some of the alternative associations. But the leaders were, for the most part, young, white-collar men and women previously inactive in both the CPSU and the human rights movement. The motive to join, the head of the gorkom's Propaganda and Agitation Department, Yurii A. Vinogradov, had the grace to say, was "displeasure with the formalism, overbearingness, and idleness of official organizations." Mere mention of them in the media gave participants "a certain metaphysical satisfaction," says Fadeyev, as they began to think, "They write about me, therefore I exist."[53]

The great majority of the informals formed around cultural and recreational issues, with interests as apolitical as break dancing, body-building, and philately. About a hundred of the 1988 tally were "politicized" *(politizirovannyye)* groups oriented toward public issues. Fadeyev estimates that no political group in mid-1988 had more than fifty members and most had ten to fifteen. Despite their small size, these aggregations sent a shiver up officialdom's spine: "The city's party, soviet, Komsomol, and other structures were unprepared," to quote Vinogradov, "for the stormy increase in their number and level of activity."[54]

Organizations with catholic political interests took the field during the Yeltsin interlude. The two most seminal, the Club of Social Initiatives, founded in late 1986, and the Perestroika Club, organized at the Central Mathematical Economics Institute in the spring of 1987, began as low-key discussion circles of young Muscovites. Influenced by the cultural ferment and by members of socialist underground groups closed by the KGB in the early 1980s, the two clubs turned into proponents of "democratic socialism," referring fuzzily to Scandinavian models. The lack of clear goals and internal structure inclined them to winding debates in which success "was directly proportional to the number of speeches made at sessions, never mind in what connection."[55]

Older liberals led by Academician Andrei D. Sakharov, the great Russian dissident freed from internal exile by Gorbachev, created in August 1987 the society Memorial, committed to fixing the scale of the Stalin terror and honoring those who suffered. It collected 50,000 signatures on a petition to the CPSU conference in 1988 asking for construction of a memorial in Moscow to the casualties of Stalinism. A Moscow Association of Victims of Illegal Repressions followed shortly; it had 2,200 members by 1990, about the same as Moscow Memorial. In October 1988 Sakharov, Tat'yana I. Zaslavskaya, and 100 members of the intellectual establishment inaugurated Moscow Tribune, a club advocating radical economic reform, release of the last political prisoners, representative democracy, and "spiritual and moral renewal."

Most memorable in 1988, younger and more uninhibited participants made incursions into politics. They were energized by the feel-good atmosphere of that year, the growth in public disobedience in the non-Russian republics, and the party conference, at which Gorbachev articulated his conception of democratization and delegates argued over how far it should go.

Beginning with the anniversary of Stalin's death on March 5, they began staging small street demonstrations, broken up by the militia, with anti-Stalinist and even anti-Communist themes. Members of the two wings into which the Perestroika Club split in January 1988, Perestroika-88 and Democratic Perestroika, were among the founders in May of Democratic Union, the first self-styled opposition party in the USSR. In early June the police began to tolerate extended political conversations at Pushkinskaya ploshchad' (Pushkin Square), a spot in central Moscow where nonconformists met and were arrested in the Brezhnev years.

On June 25, 1988, three days before the Nineteenth Conference, a few dozen youths put up signs in front of Pushkin's statue and held a peaceful public rally. And so, "One of the solidest Soviet traditions, affirmed by the bitter experience of several generations of dissidents, was buried."[56] A crowd gathered and signed petitions directed to the conference delegates. The meeting lasted ten hours without disruption. For months thereafter, the area was known as Moscow's Hyde Park. Organized demonstrations occurred daily and received coverage by Soviet and Western television. Thousands of other townsfolk converged to read posters on a Democracy Wall on the *Moskovskiye novosti* building and buy unofficial newspapers and magazines.

An important coalition, the Moscow Popular Front (Moskovskii Narodnyi Front), was founded on a nearby alley in July 1988. A grouping of associations of radical bent, it emulated the "popular front in support of perestroika" formed in Estonia the previous month. Its first leader was Yevgenii Dergunov, later an extreme conservative. Dedicated in theory to defending reform, in reality it was miles out in front, laying preparations for the elections promised by Gorbachev and voicing solidarity with Yeltsin. It "sought to unite all the popular fronts of the USSR under its aegis, but failed, given the long-standing provincial distrust of movements run from Moscow." The thirty-four groups constituting it had about 1,000 members at the end of 1988; only "50 to 80" of them, by its leaders' estimate, were activists.[57] Prime among them were alumni of the now-dissolved Club of Social Initiatives and Perestroika Club and of newer groups like Socialist Initiative, an association of liberal Communist Party members.

On the ideological right "national-patriotic associations," often sponsored by the xenophobic RSFSR Union of Writers, held organizational meetings in Moscow starting in the fall of 1988. Pamyat' had stooped to outright fascism, and VOOPIK, the landmarks association, was encumbered by its official sponsors and its bloated membership. New groups like Yedinstvo (Unity, subtitled the Association of Lovers of Russian Literature and Art), the League for Spiritual Rebirth of the Fatherland, and the Foundation for Restoration of the Cathedral of Christ the Redeemer mixed cultural Russophilia with the causes of keeping the USSR intact and promoting Russia's interests within it.

THE GREENS

The bulk of the politicized informals dwelt on local issues, and chiefly on problems of urban amenity rather than basic need. They shared an environmentalism defined in terms of both the man-made city and the nature around it. They espoused an eclectic ideology. Their style mingled the culture- and aesthetics-driven historical conservation of an earlier time, the "Not in My Back Yard" syndrome familiar in the United States, and the Green movements of Western Europe. The last label—*zelenyye,* "greens"—stuck.

Moscow environmentalists were appalled by the Chernobyl nuclear disaster of April 1986 and inspired by the Politburo's overturning in August 1986 of plans to divert Siberian rivers to Central Asia. In 1988 complaints about nuclear safety convinced the Kremlin to close down the 1940s heavy water reactor at the Institute of Theoretical and Experimental Physics. That same year the 183-year-old Moscow Society of Nature Testers joined several intelligentsia groups in defeating the plan to build a conveyance system for Volga water from Rzhev to the Moscow-Volga Canal. Aleksandr Yanshin, its president and a vice-president of the Academy of Sciences, chaired the government commission whose advice Gorbachev took. The anti-Rzhev forces benefited greatly from opposition among army veterans to the flooding of World War II graveyards by the reservoir that would have been formed.

The greens had no mean success in halting or modifying Moscow works projects they considered odious. As many as two hundred construction sites were idle in March 1988 owing to petition campaigns, pickets, and other forms of protest.[58] All this helped break the population's psychological inertia and politically educate many who were to seek local electoral office in 1990. Several imbroglios are emblematic.

A first swirled around Lefortovo, a quarter of east central Moscow, mostly in Baumanskii raion, called after a Swiss-born admiral of Peter the Great's. Originally on the left bank of the Yauza, after 1812 its boundaries looped around the right-bank zone of Nemetskaya sloboda. Blended in here with apartment housing and small factories are Moscow's second-ranking prison and landmark buildings from the 1700s and 1800s, including the well-known Lefortovskii and Yekaterinskii Palaces and the Budrenko Main Military Hospital.

The threat to Lefortovo's tranquillity came from the northeast arc of the Third Transport Ring. An eight-lane roadway was designed to approach from the west, dip in an underpass under Bakuninskaya ulitsa, and discharge its roaring traffic onto a bridge across the Yauza and thence into old Lefortovo. Massive clearance and excavation were projected. Execution of the plan, drawn up in concealment by GlavAPU and the RSFSR cabinet, the funder of most of the work, began in 1984.

A solitary building initially aroused excitement: the Shchcrbakov Mansion on Bakuninskaya, the finest specimen of classical home architecture in this quadrant of Moscow (Figure 69). The two-story house was erected as a store and home by a merchant family in the 1790s and turned into a tavern and hostel after 1917; VOOPIK had been trying to get it on the register of landmarks since 1978. The mansion would have been ripped down to make way for the tunnel were it not for the "dozens of volunteers [who] began a struggle to save [it], utilizing all measures, including the extreme ones of picketing, collecting signatures, sending telegrams to the very highest offices, interfering in the press." Teenagers and college students kept watch by night and several times brazened out police officers and wrecking crews. Their pouring of sand and sugar into the fuel tanks of the demolition equipment prompted a scuffle and the arrest of Kirill Parfenov, a student at the Bauman Higher Technical College. The arrest brought Yeltsin into the fray. He agreed to protection of the house in January 1987, and the city ispolkom passed a bylaw shortly thereafter.[59]

Moscow VOOPIK and two community groups, Sloboda and In Defense of Lefortovo, then opened hostilities against the whole northeast crescent of the Third Ring. Alleging it would be a "stationary gas

Figure 69. Shcherbakov Mansion, 1988. (Photograph by author.)

chamber" for residents and foliage and render the Budrenko Hospital unusable, they lobbied Yeltsin, Saikin, and even Gorbachev and pelted the press with letters. Wisely, they dunned central organs such as *Literaturnaya gazeta, Sovetskaya kul'tura,* and the Ministry of Defense's *Krasnaya zvezda* (Red Star) as well as local newspapers. After literary lions, army officers, the Ministry of Culture, and Chief Architect Leonid V. Vavakin came to the protestors' assistance, city hall directed in May 1987 that the highway be rerouted.

The proxy path sketched by the engineers provoked a further hubbub in 1988 when it was learned that the spot in Nemetskaya sloboda where the national bard, Aleksandr Pushkin, was born in 1799 (where a school now stood) would be asphalted over. In March 1989 the RSFSR revoked the 1984 decree authorizing construction and instructed the road planners to bypass Lefortovo.

The battle royal over the Moscow Zoo provides a second case in environmental politics. The city's zoo, dating to 1864, had been crammed onto a postage stamp of downtown land (17 hectares) in Krasnopresnenskii raion. A modern zoo, with better viewing for the public and humane conditions for the wildlife, was proposed as far back as 1925. The Moscow and USSR governments decided in 1975 to emplace "the best zoo in the world" on 200 hectares of Bittsa Forest Park, a semirural section of Moscow's southern periphery. By the time implementation began more than a decade later, Bittsa was at the doorstep of hundreds of thousands of apartment dwellers in three of the fastest growing raions (Cheremushkinskii, Sevastopol'skii, and Sovetskii). An information meeting at a local club in February 1988 showed that political conditions had also changed:

> At the front of the small stage the architects had put an attractive exhibit centered on a plan of the new complex. Beside the exposition was the presidium [of the meeting], seating experts and representatives of the MGK [Moscow gorkom] of the CPSU, the party raikom [of Sevastopol'skii raion], the raiispolkom, the Academy of Sciences, and the zoo staff. They seemed almost to outnumber the ordinary folk in the chairs of the viewing hall.
>
> Discussion of the draft began with complaints about the organizers of the meeting. The residents said indignantly that hardly anyone knew about the gathering, that the notice was sent around at the last minute, that it was not posted at all apartment house entrances, and in general that the whole thing was contrived . . .
>
> As soon as the director of the zoo, V. Spitsin, had reported, tempers flared. Old and young people, saying they spoke for the residents of the raions, categorically declared that they didn't need the zoo and that they wanted to live in peace, to breath fresh air, to enjoy the natural landscape that stretched right beneath the windows of their flats. "We are not going to let you cut down 'our' woods," said one orator, "just as it was not allowed to turn the northern [Siberian] rivers around or ruin Lake Baikal."
>
> In vain did the experts try to get through other lines of argument. Nor did the thorough speech of I. Vinogradovskii, the head of the design collective, bring the nature lovers around. New arrivals at the meeting kept cutting in, and the argument dragged on. When it came time to sum up, the audience squawked. They declared the meeting null and void and warned that they would go to higher authority and force a nationwide

discussion of the plan, because it was concocted during the [Brezhnev] period of stagnation and now there was a different situation in the country.[60]

At neither this nor any subsequent gathering would the Bittsa Initiative Group heed the return plaint: that the zoo would serve all Moscow and occupy the scruffiest 10 percent of the park's land. GlavAPU rashly shifted the site to a patch of the park where Cheremushkinskii residents, shoveling and raking on weekends with the encouragement of the raikom, had built a dirt ski hill. This served only to anger sports enthusiasts and fitness buffs across Moscow.

Letters and articles about the zoo problem abounded in the newspapers (local and national) in the spring of 1988. The pro-Bittsa forces branded their antagonists "group egoists"—an aphorism picked up from Valerii Saikin at city hall—and got schoolchildren to sign in crayons a petition branding them cruel to animals. The Bittsa Initiative Group retorted by building support among other neighborhood-based groups, such as Sloboda and Tushino, an association fighting interloping on the Tushino Birch and Oak Woods in Tushinskii raion. In June 1988 scrimmaging spilled onto the streets, as several hundred opponents of the zoo project rallied in front of the Bol'shoi Theater, brushing aside an invitation from a deputy of Saikin's to meet with him at Bittsa.

In September 1988 First Secretary Zaikov, who earlier agreed with the epithet of "group egoism," caved in. The fight over the zoo, he said, stemmed from "our neglect of the city's ecology" and "a lack of culture on matters of democracy." "It obviously is necessary," he concluded, "to take account of the opinion" of the residents, implying that the Bittsa plan should be scrapped.[61] His prediction that the authorities could settle on a site and "inform Muscovites" of it within two weeks proved wildly optimistic. The following month city hall formed a committee of planners, scientists, party workers, and, novelly, delegates of the Bittsa group. Most specialists preferred Nikulino, four kilometers northwest of Bittsa, but the panel was deadlocked when last reported in session at the end of 1989.

No less clamorous was the third case, the dispute over Brateyevo, a microraion set amidst an unusual stew of planned and unplanned uses in Krasnogvardeiskii raion. Brateyevo consisted of unswerving rows of standard high rises constructed in the late 1970s and 1980s on a city dump in marshes along the Moskva River. Flush across the river sat the six-smokestacked TETS No. 22, a thermopower-central station built a decade before on green belt land and fueled by coal; just upstream from the TETS rose the cracking towers of the Kapotnya Oil Refinery, the Kur'yanovskaya Aeration Station for sanitary sewage, and the Lyublino Mechanical Foundry. On its side of the river, Brateyevo abutted a landfill site and municipal trash incinerator, the MKAD, and the heavily populated Orekhovo-Borisovo district.

Many of the inhabitants (12,000 in 1987 but about 50,000 by 1990) resented the combination of visual and atmospheric pollution and the barren microraion design. Brateyevo had no cinema or club, and only one tiny department store sold consumer goods. The straw that broke the camel's back was the enunciation of a previously classified plan to lay out an adjacent "production zone" for a typographic combine, an auto repair works, several garages, and a building materials plant. One of Brateyevo's two filaments of greenery was to disappear with consignment of Gorodnya Creek to an underground pipe, leaving only the weeds under power transmission pylons for children to play on.

On July 28, 1988, just after construction began, demonstrators from a Brateyevo Initiative Group blocked truck access to the production zone. Within two weeks the city had agreed to suspend work on the zone, stop the enclosure of the Gorodnya, and consult the denizens of Brateyevo and Orekhovo-Borisovo about future construction. The plan eventually adopted elided all but two small plants in the zone. In October 1988 the initiative group secured the raion's consent to its conversion into a "committee for social self-government" *(komitet obshchestvennogo samoupravleniya)*. Without having any formal legislative powers, the committee, the chairman of the raion ispolkom said, would "take under control all questions affecting the life of the microraion."[62] It was described as the first such committee in the Soviet Union.

The buffeting of the Northern TETS (also known as TETS No. 27) offers a final example of the inroads made by the informals. Sited in the oblast town of Mytishchi, in the green belt within walking distance of the MKAD at Babushkinskii raion, the Northern TETS was to have an end capacity of 900 megawatts, the most of any power generator in Europe. Its smokestacks were to shoot 250 meters into the air, and twenty-nine enterprises (including a trash incinerator, asphalt yard, and cattle feed plant) were to be in a production zone in their shadow. Like most Soviet capital projects, it took several five-year plans to win the requisite clearances. Design work began in 1974, the Moscow ispolkom gave approval in 1976, the RSFSR government allocated the land in 1983, and steamshovels bit into the ground in 1986. About 40 million rubles' worth of work had been completed when opposition crystallized in 1989.

Once forced to do so openly, Mosenergo, the parent USSR Ministry of Power, and municipal executives defended the Northern TETS. It would be, they said, the last district generator built in or near Moscow, as later ones were to be twenty to thirty kilometers into the oblast; its output would aid population growth and subway extension in north Moscow and buy time for rehabilitation of older, high-polluting stations; and foreign-made scrubbers and utilization of gas fuel would keep emissions within acceptable limits. General Director Nikolai I. Serebryanikov of Mosenergo wrapped the argument up in the ribbon of local pride and self-reliance. "Only through our own efforts" can Muscovites secure the energy to underwrite a better life, he asserted. "We cannot count on help from the outside."[63]

The counterargument was made by individuals, neighborhood groups, and, in 1989, by Severo-vostok (Northeast, a "regional association of ecological societies"). They threw doubt upon the power industry's claims about energy demand, citing classified data to the effect that Moscow's existing plants made it a net exporter of electric power. Mosenergo, they said, lied in depicting the plant as nonpolluting: the scrubbing technology was unproven, and the natural gas to be burned was to be diverted from other Moscow stations, which would have to substitute heavy oil.

The anti-TETS forces placed greatest stress on the harm they maintained the facility would do to the regional environment. They supplied a long cadastre of injuries: nonobservance of the green belt's protected status for a second time (TETS No. 22 already blighted it in Lyublinskii raion); annihilation of the picturesque villages of Chelobit'evo and Volkovo; encroachment on microraions in Mytishchi and Babushkinskii raion, 1.2 kilometers away; damage to Losinyi ostrov National Park from fumes and transport; fouling of the Yauza headwaters and five drinking-water reservoirs; strewing of contaminants over a thirty-mile radius; and loss of arable land. The more they pressed the indictment, the shriller their language became: the station would be a "death sentence" for the area; its chimneys were "artillery barrels" aiming a "poisonous cloud" at Moscow; its construction would equal economic vandalism, criminality, and even "genocide."[64]

Protest groups in early 1989 picketed Chelobit'evo and gathered 300,000 signatures from Moscow and Mytishchi on a petition. At the opening of the Soviet deputies' congress that summer, Vladislav A. Gorokhov, the director of Losinyi ostrov and the member from Mytishchi, handed the petition, cosigned by 74 deputies, to the congress's presidium, lodged a formal complaint with Prime Minister Ryzhkov, and made a fiery peroration linking the TETS to "the hostages of the ministries" in other parts of the country.[65]

Ryzhkov, visiting the site with Gorokhov, Zaikov, and Saikin, made concessions in July 1989. He announced that polluting objects would be removed from Losinyi ostrov, that the city of Kaliningrad would be prevented from expanding toward the park, that a planned aircraft test complex would not be built here, and finally that the Kremlin would "take under review the appropriateness of building the Northern TETS and a number of other facilities."[66] Three months later, the production zone was canceled, although the station itself remained under study and, slowly, under construction.

INCLUDING THE MILLIONS

Glasnost' and nonstate organizations harrowed the Communist Party. The contested elections to which Mikhail Gorbachev won agreement in principle at the 1988 party conference dealt it a sledgehammer blow.[67]

The elections, as Zaikov paraphrased it, would "include millions of people" in the perestroika dialectic through "rebirth of the power of the soviets in the Leninist sense." To titillate the public and give ammunition to deputies, whose relations with executives had been "stood head over heels" by Stalin, lawmakers were henceforth to be chosen in truly secret elections with a multiplicity of candidates. The CPSU apparatus would retain its tutelary function: "as a rule," deputies after the election would choose the corresponding party first secretary for the revived position of chairman of the soviet. This "combination of posts," Zaikov averred, would "boost the role and authority of the organs of the popular will" and make the party solicitous of them.[68]

Muscovites first nibbled the forbidden fruit on October 23, 1988, in the homely skin of by-elections for several local councils. For 2 of 6 seats up for grabs on the Mossovet, the standard single candidate ran; in three districts there were 2 candidates and in one district 3. Turnout (in the range of 85 to 90 percent) and the winners' vote shares (55 to 75 percent) fell short of the unanimity of yore.

The ante rose mountainously higher in the election of the new USSR Congress of People's Deputies, which in turn parented a new Supreme Soviet, a standing parliament. Citizens chose two-thirds of the 2,250 deputies in several rounds of direct voting March 26 to May 18, 1989; the party, Academy of Sciences, and other approved public organizations designated the remaining third. The electrifying races were the popular ones, where in Moscow 81 candidates jostled in twenty-six territorial districts and 2 more battled in a city-wide "national-territorial" district.

Lev Zaikov was absent from the hustings, opting, like Gorbachev, for delegation to the congress by the Central Committee and assigning Second Secretary Prokof'ev to a local district. The election authorities tried in many districts to keep vocal critics off the ballot by channeling nominations through workplaces and manipulating the "assemblies of electors" charged with screening them. Several well-known progressives were forced to find districts in other cities. In the postnomination phase, voters were urged to turn out for "responsible," pro-Gorbachev candidates.

Far from heeding the call, Muscovites delivered a stinging rebuff. They elected only 4 or 5 candidates of plainly centrist views and 1 obscurantist; all others sent to the congress from areal districts were self-described radicals. The largest group of winners came from the arts, sciences, and communications (15 deputies elected out of 24 nominees), all progressives. Five deputies (of the 12 nominated) were engineering and technical personnel. Neither factory workers nor public administrators were well received: 1 of 9 workers nominated won a seat, 5 of 25 directors of enterprises, and none of the 6 military officers.[69]

All 5 stalwarts of the city political machine to try their luck were humbled. The municipal chairman, Saikin, fared best, getting 42.5 percent of the valid votes in his district and placing second. Prokof'ev was trounced by 2 other candidates, getting 13.5 percent. Only Petr S. Surov, the chairman of Mosstroikomitet, made it to a runoff vote (required when no one earned a majority in the first round), there to be buried with 25.8 percent of the votes. Two raikom first secretaries, Aleksei M. Bryachikhin of Sevastopol'skii raion and Vladimir M. Syrtsov of Timiryazevskii, got 20.2 and 10.1 percent in their districts. Chief Architect Vavakin was elected to the congress, but from the USSR Union of Architects.

Most unwelcome to the nomenklatura, Boris Yeltsin profited from a trampoline effect. Having kept his name in the news by giving speeches and interviews, he decided to run in the all-Moscow district, where he would be a favorite son and media attention would be greatest. "He wanted to obtain a vote of confidence from 6 million Muscovites," one of his campaign aides wrote later.[70]

Yeltsin, opposed by Yevgenii A. Brakov, the director of ZIL, called for a speedup of reforms and the rescinding of unjust privileges. Media attacks and a probe of his conduct by a party tribunal boomeranged and gave him the aura of a martyr. He won a landslide victory with 89.4 percent of the votes. His advisers joked that Zaikov must have secretly been one of his ten electoral agents.

Autonomous organizations played an auspicious role in the election. Memorial, the Moscow Popular Front, and Democratic Perestroika circulated pro-Yeltsin petitions, pasted up posters, and organized impromptu rallies. Collaborating with them were ad hoc "voters' clubs" formed within most electoral districts by boosters of progressive candidates. Muscovites elected with their help became household names: Sergei B. Stankevich, a specialist on American history, an organizer of the Popular Front, and the drafter of an open telegram from candidates in defense of Yeltsin; physicist Arkadii N. Murashev and economist Oleg T. Bogomolov; Il'ya I. Zaslavskii, a textile researcher and seeker of rights for the handicapped; and others. Twelve of the 16 candidates supported by the Moscow Popular Front were elected.

Public organizations also elected 168 Muscovites, many of them liberals. All told, the Moscow deputation—containing Yeltsin, Sakharov, about 30 members of Moscow Tribune, and a stable of young stars—was "the most active and militant" of any region's. The inauguration of the deputies' congress in May 1989 featured "confrontation and verbal skirmishing between Moscow and non-Moscow."[71]

It was the economist Gavriil Popov, a Muscovite representing an organization (the Union of Scientific and Engineering Societies), who proposed formation of the Interregional Deputies' Group, the opposition caucus in the USSR parliament, that June. Twenty of the 27 directly elected Moscow deputies, and 22 other Muscovites, were founding members. Four of its 5 cochairmen (Sakharov, Yeltsin, Popov, and Yurii N. Afanas'ev) came from Moscow, and Arkadii Murashev served as the group's secretary. An opinion poll in late 1989 found 32 of the 100 "most popular deputies," and 6 of the top 10, to be residents of Moscow.[72]

The election stimulated the nascent opposition within Moscow to redouble its organizing efforts. The Popular Front, the lead taken by Sergei Stankevich, chose a thirteen-person "coordinating council" in May 1989, but yielded the stage over the next six months to the more innovative voters' clubs. They mostly reconstituted themselves as raion-level clubs and by autumn were working with "support groups" for the radical USSR deputies and with voters' clubs in more than a hundred workplaces. In October 1989 they formed an umbrella body, the Moscow Association of Voters (Moskovskoye Ob"edineniye Izbiratelei). The association, which young politicos again dominated, put out an unregistered tabloid newspaper, *Golos izbiratelei* (Voice of the Voters).

In the city headquarters of the Communist Party, by contrast, gloom and disbelief spread. At an election postmortem in June, Zaikov deplored the fling with candidates "who based their election platforms on criticism of the soviet and party organs." Yet much of the fault, he conceded, was the party's. It still recruited leaders on the dog-eared "technocratic" criterion, "not a Communist's ability to cooperate with people or convince them . . . so much as knowledge of the ins and outs of production, economic and technical literacy." The election had changed little: "We confine ourselves as in the old days to giving directives. We are not teaching people how to act in new ways and we ourselves have not learned how to work under conditions of democratization."[73]

Zaikov believed he would learn new tricks in time for the local elections scheduled for 1990. Expecting to chair the next Mossovet, he commissioned renovation of a city hall office, with private lift. But the bungling of the antecedent campaign was not forgotten.

On November 21, 1989, Gorbachev stood before his third organizational plenum of the gorkom. Hiding behind the fig leaf of Zaikov's indispensability in the Politburo and Secretariat (from which he and Ligachev retired eight months later), Gorbachev asked the committee to accept his resignation as first secretary. A struggle over Zaikov's successor was concealed from the press. In meetings with the bureau, Gorbachev tried to inflict Vladimir I. Resin, the head of industrial construction within Mosstroikomitet—a baffling choice, since Resin was as much a captive of the party's technocratic culture as Zaikov. The bureau held out for Second Secretary Prokof'ev, and the gorkom approved him, though not without 18 candidates being discussed and 20 of 144 votes cast going to a raikom first secretary, Aleksandr V. Rudakov. Sixteen years Zaikov's junior, a Moscow insider, more personable, and not chained to the military-industrial complex, Prokof'ev was a sounder bet to be a vote getter. He pledged to move election management onto the party's front burner and improve on "the mistakes and miscalculations" of the previous spring.[74]

It is hard to say which of three breakthroughs was the more noteworthy. First, no general secretary had ever failed to dictate the choice of Moscow leader. Prokof'ev was not close to Gorbachev and would not become so even after being added to the Politburo the next summer, but Gorbachev "considered it impossible" to ignore the opinion of the Moscow Communists.[75] Second, not since the Civil War had the selection of the leader not been by acclamation. And, third, never before had a rotation of the party guard come from worry about an election or control of representative institutions. Bigger shocks lay in store.

A Stunning Election

Democratization, Samuel Huntington observes, commonly rolls forward with a "stunning election" in which authoritarian rulers try to renew their legitimacy at the ballot box, misjudge the public mood, and go down to defeat.[76] In the Soviet Union the setbacks in the 1989 ballot were a surprise, but centrists and conservatives outnumbered radicals in the federal congress, and Gorbachev sailed through as its chairman. The truly stunning elections came the next year, in the union republics and localities.

The last time Muscovites had any choice in a city election was in January 1922, and they last saw non-socialist candidates in the voting for the raion dumas in September 1917. Although opposition parties as such did not figure in the 1990 ballot, near-parties did, and, as Yurii Prokof'ev said afterward, it was "in essence carried out on a multi-party basis."[77] This quasi-party election, three-quarters free, ushered into city government an arm of Democratic Russia (Demokra-ticheskaya Rossiya, or DR), a league of Westernizing democrats who simultaneously gained narrow leverage over the RSFSR parliament and cabinet. The 1990 election marked the beginning of the end of the Communist partocracy.

RULES

The vote was conducted under an amended electoral statute passed by the outgoing Russian Supreme Soviet October 27, 1989, extending the safeguards already written into the USSR election code out of both a sense of fairness and the fear that chicanery would abet radicals. The law reserved no seats for official organizations and provided for no winnowing electors' assemblies. Also, to make the local soviets more effective once elected, it reduced them somewhat in size (from 800 to 498 deputies in Moscow) and made senior bureaucrats (heads of directorates and departments) ineligible to sit in them.

The franchise was universal. Virtually all Muscovites aged eighteen or over—6,713,548 in all—were eligible to cast a vote in one of 3,048 polling precincts within reapportioned electoral districts (numbered 2 through 499 because district 1 was still a notional seat for Lenin). City hall's Department for Work of the Soviets, a capable organizer, spent 10.2 million rubles on election logistics, five or six times the amount of the last stage-managed election in 1987. Electoral commissions in precincts, districts, and Moscow city, with 5 to 21 part-time members, acted as returning officers and umpires of complaints.

Candidates, who could be nonresidents employed in Moscow as well as qualified Moscow voters, began to be nominated in early December. The electoral law authorized "labor collectives," approved public organizations, and convocations in residential areas to bring names forward. The first two were fixtures of the past, with workplaces, under the collar of CPSU committees, always having made the main body of nominations. Work units had more leeway than in 1989: subunits of 30 workers in large enterprises could nominate an unlimited number of candidates. Residential groups were also less encumbered, as only 150 persons had to attend the nominating meeting, not the 500 in the USSR election.

Filed by the deadline of January 2, 1990, were 3,793 nominations for the Moscow Soviet, about 5 percent of them put by more than one source. Only 1.8 percent of the nominees had ever before served as a deputy; 73.8 percent came out of workplaces, 23.3 percent from public organizations, and 7.0 percent from neighborhood caucuses. Almost 14,000 persons were nominated for the raion councils and the five hamlet and village soviets in the Moscow orbit; 78.2 percent of these originated in workplaces.[78]

The district electoral commissions were to rule by January 23 on acts of registration that would put nominees' names on the ballot, but there was slippage from that timetable and no cap on appeals. Hefty inserts in *Moskovskaya pravda* of February 2, 6, and 8 printed the names and vital statistics of 3,329 city-level candidates, expunging the 464 who had been denied registration or dropped out. This was not the final repertory, as several dozen were reinstated on appeal, 1 candidate was deregistered, and others withdrew. Come election day, March 4, 3,262 certified candidates remained.

The attrition pales before the survival of 6.6 candidates per electoral district—6.6 times as many as there would have been in years gone by. No district went begging for candidates. In only 3 of 498 was there a single candidate unopposed, and in only 18 were there two-way races. In 70 districts 10 or more contestants stood (14.1 percent of the districts, but 27.0 percent of the candidates), and 23 ran in the most contested case.

Central districts were thickest in candidates, averaging 10.6 each, compared to 5.5 in the raions not traversing the Sadovoye kol'tso. Nonresidents of the raion, generally commuters to jobs in the district, constituted 43.4 percent of all candidates, but 61.2 percent in the downtown raions and only 34.2 percent closer to the city limits. In-raion candidates were close to equal in the two zones: 4.1 per electoral district in the inner 13 raions, 3.6 per district in the outer 20.[79]

Aside from residing within the raion, the typical candidate was male (85.4 percent) and middle-aged (average age forty-five). Three-quarters were affiliated with the Communist Party: 72.8 percent as members, 1.1 percent as probationary members, and 1.4 percent in the Komsomol. And they were overwhelmingly from the Russian approximation of the urban middle class, which has been found in virtually every country to be the strongest constituency for democratization. A piffling 6.7 percent were blue-collar workers. Almost one-quarter were professors and researchers, followed by those in basic administrative pursuits, managers in industry, transport, and construction, and engineers and technical specialists. Those four groups, plus a smaller set of media and arts figures, accounted for 72.9 percent of all candidates. Managers and professionals in human services, personnel in semiofficial and unofficial organizations, and miscellaneous categories raised the nonclerical white-collar ratio up over 90 percent.

The contenders could not campaign without restriction. The law required local authorities to cover all expenses (200 rubles for each candidate for the Mossovet). No oral forums other than district all-candidates' meetings were approved. The only acceptable posters were officially prepared composites, presenting for every candidate in the district a mugshot, biographical cameo, and statement of "program." These appeared on display only during the penultimate week of the campaign.

Nomination, registration, and campaigning all had their share of rancor. About seventy appeals against registration decisions of the district electoral commissions percolated to the city commission by mid-February. They usually concerned the credentials of the nominating entity in cases where the Department for Work of the Soviets maintained that the radical voters' clubs, in that they were founded purely to nominate candidates, were not licit public organizations. When the clubs and legal experts took issue, the city commission decided to rule case by case, invoking as criteria the club's longevity (it had to predate October 27, 1989) and area of operations (raion or larger) and finding in favor of the appellant on about sixty of the seventy petitions. Most of the thirty cases adjudicated later involved the wording of official posters or dirty tricks—defacement of posters, heckling, telephone harrassment—which pinned commissioners in a crossfire.[80]

Procedurally, the election was incomparably fairer than any in

Moscow since the Bolshevik Revolution. The sheer multitude of contestants crossed one of democracy's Rubicons. Far less was done to stifle entry of unorthodox candidates than in 1989. Oppositionists remonstrated only mildly about abuses.

True, political parties other than the Communist Party continued to be excluded from nominations and campaigning. It would not be so again, for the Gorbachev leadership had just come to the historic decision to rescind Article 6 of the Soviet constitution, the legal underpinning of the CPSU's monopoly on party activity. The change took effect too late, March 14, 1990, to alter the Russian and Moscow balloting. But enough had already transpired to make this a transitional election with abundant real competition.

As salient as the revised nomination procedures were those governing confidentiality, a rampart of due process flouted in the past. Article 47 of the RSFSR law specified physical layout, dictating that "booths or rooms sufficient in quantity for secret voting" be placed in each voting place and that ballot boxes be "installed in such a way that as voters approach them they will necessarily pass through" the booths.

To judge from precinct 51/218 in Kievskii raion, where I spent the morning of March 4, the spirit if not the letter of the law prevailed. The polling station, an auditorium in a printing shop decorated in cut flowers and a bust of Lenin, with a subsidized snack bar downstairs, was open from 7:00 A.M. to 8:00 P.M. Voters flashed passports and took color-coded ballot slips from precinct electoral commissioners, who ticked off their names on lists. Two-thirds of those voting, give or take, entered four curtained cubicles to bend over their ballots in privacy. But four was not enough to handle demand, so the rest wrote on their knees or on open tables in the main hall, bantering with neighbors and accompanying youngsters. They sidled around the booths and joined the file exiting them, popping their slips like the rest into two plywood ballot urns.

This nonchalance flagrantly trespassed Article 47. But the fact remains that the intimidation and fear of surveillance that sullied past elections were gone. Voters interviewed gave every appearance of having made a free choice. Heretofore, ever since nominally secret balloting was introduced in the 1930s, they had but one option: ratify the official nominee by inserting an untouched ballot into the box, or cross off that name, for which they had to duck into the polling booth and draw attention to themselves. In 1990 the profusion of candidates forced all voters to address their ballots. Eavesdroppers could find no signal as to how voters had chosen, whether or not they used the polling cubicle.

Three other electoral technicalities, oddities in Anglo-American terms and since revised, warrant mention. First, a turnout component dictated that no one could be elected at any phase unless 50 percent of qualified voters had cast valid ballots. Second, in a carryover from the past, voting was done negatively, by scratching out the names of candidates disfavored. This system applied even when only a single name appeared on the ballot, precluding acclamation. All-negative ballots were possible; though not tallied in any positive vote ledger, they counted for turnout purposes. Third, there was a baroque formula for runoff and repeat elections in the eventuality that no candidate won a majority in the opening round. In Moscow, 35 candidates were elected in the first round (3 of whom ran unopposed) and 428 in the second, held March 18 after two weeks of desultory runoff campaigning; only a plurality was needed for victory in the runoff. Supplementary elections began in April and limped on into late 1990; I will not scrutinize them here.[81]

THE PARTY THAT COULDN'T

Near-parties, if not full-fledged parties, were given their opening by the electoral ineptitude of the CPSU, the only accredited party, as much as by the liberalized electoral rules. The Communists, Prokof'ev said afterward, "did not manage to become aware in time" of the altered situation, in spite of the cold shower the preceding March.[82] Prokof'ev did gallantly contest a territorial district (No. 388 of the Moscow Soviet, in the Butovo section of Sovetskii raion, past the MKAD). And the gorkom did adopt on December 20, 1989, a month after his installation as first secretary, "Political Theses" looking ahead to the campaign and pledging "political stability" and "constructive dialogue" with other groups.

If these steps betokened progress, blistering testimony could be offered to the contrary. Here is one raikom first secretary:

> The gorkom of the party has been less and less successful at shaping public opinion, directing it down a constructive channel, and harmoniz-

ing the activity of the raion party organizations . . . The absence of coordination by the gorkom was especially noticeable during the preelection campaign. We entered it disarmed, with no strategy or tactics for action, without objective appraisal of the situation or experience of a political struggle for power. The political leaders, theoreticians, and ideologists of the city party organization came across as downright helpless. Their whole approach was disconnected and unprofessional. There was no single platform to unite everyone. A significant portion of the party aktiv was passive. All this is what brought us to those reverses whose fruits we are now reaping.[83]

The apparatchiks were "helpless" largely because nothing in their careers had groomed them for the slings and arrows of campaigning. Anchored in work units, the party had busied itself primarily with economic plan fulfillment. Apart from chapters in some apartment blocks, mostly for retirees, it still had a spectral presence in the domestic realm where voting and other acts of citizenship take place.

In terms of campaign message and delivery, the local Communist Party did not comport itself like a win-oriented political party. Neither Prokof'ev, preoccupied with his Butovo district, nor anyone else took charge of its campaign. Its Political Theses, unmodified after December 20 despite popular restlessness, were mostly a marmalade of good wishes, with scant allusion to Moscow, and of warmed-over promises about local amenities. They waffled on some divisive issues (property ownership, for one) while annoying non-Communists by belaboring schismatics within the party's own walls. Some made allegations that unnamed oppositionists, "taking cover under the slogans of perestroika," were conniving to "restore capitalist relations" in the USSR and bind Moscow over to profiteers and money changers.[84]

As Prokof'ev confided, what concrete agitation the party did mount in the districts "was oriented as before to the personality factor."[85] This had been the sales pitch in the age of the one-name ballot, but now a slew of *Communist* candidates appeared—almost five per electoral district—lacking any device to keep them from tripping over one another. Three-quarters of the Communists in the race ran without the benediction of any of the several slates that devised more exact programs. The smartest fended for themselves, knowing that the pro-Communist vote would be split. Even the sympathetic voter had to decide "by intuition or . . . guesswork," in Prokof'ev's words.[86]

To take blandness an extra notch, the gorkom's theses, hewing to the mobilizational lexicon of earlier times, counseled Muscovites to embrace worthy "Communists and non–party members," therein diluting the very admonition to vote Communist. As they realized that the radical slate was hitting home with an audience, party publicists peddled the bromide of "consolidation of healthy forces." Most press coverage took the form of roundtables, with the tone of a quest for dispassionate custodians of a unitary public interest.

We will never know how the Communist Party would have fared had it nominated single candidates by district and pulled out all the stops to get them elected, brandishing the pork barrel as well as more philosophical positions. Some pessimists claimed that this strategy would not have helped: "The backing of party committees would have guaranteed some candidates' complete downfall."[87] And yet, as this same onlooker points out, some Moscow apparatchiks did go unscathed. Quantitative analysis (see below) brings out no tilt against CPSU officials or against ordinary members of the party. Bad election generalship must take partial responsibility for the result.

THE NEAR-PARTIES THAT COULD

Urban democrats stepped into the breach left by the Communists. A corps of several thousand radicals, initiated in discussion circles, green movements, the Moscow Popular Front, and the USSR election, had been waiting for Russian and local elections for some months. The spark for formation of the Moscow Assocation of Voters in October 1989 was the belief that Gorbachev could be outflanked in the voting but that more of an organizational springboard would be needed.

Boris Yeltsin considered making a run for the Mossovet, and then getting himself elected chairman and hitting back at the partocrats who turned on him in 1987. He opted instead to stand for the Russian parliament in Sverdlovsk.[88]

Since Yeltsin's priorities lay elsewhere, several academics who had been elected USSR deputies in 1989 and had national reputations mounted the effort in Moscow. The Interregional Deputies' Group first chose the anti-Stalinist historical scholar Yurii Afanas'ev for Moscow coordinator, but decided by the end of the year that he was better cut out for the USSR parliament. The caucus then lit upon Popov—an ethnic Greek, a former dean of economics at Moscow University, a government adviser on management reform since 1965, and the editor of the journal *Voprosy ekonomiki* (Problems of Economics). Except for a few months of work in the Moscow sovnarkhoz (territorial economic council) in the 1960s, Popov, at the age of fifty-three, had never had any great acquaintance with local issues. But he soon realized that city government would be an invaluable beachhead in the larger political war:

> The more familiar I became with the situation in Moscow, the more clearly I saw that in principle it was possible not only to elect Moscow democrats to the Russian parliament, but also for us to attempt to take control of the Moscow City Soviet. From the point of view of the present and future development of the country's democratic movement, the significance of this event is impossible to overestimate. If the reactionary forces were to attempt a comeback, the outcome would in many respects be decided here in Moscow. If we had to take the offensive, then once again the Moscow rallies and mass demonstrations would prove deciding factors. According to Russian custom, the country would most likely accept whatever was decided in Moscow. It is one thing when at the Congress a thousand obedient deputies vote yes and two hundred Interregionals vote no, but it is something else altogether when two hundred deputies are backed by hundreds of thousands of people in Moscow's streets and public squares. Yes, for Moscow it was worth making changes in our plans.[89]

Popov's fellow member of the Interregional Group, Sergei Stankevich, had been more involved all along in local agitation, and he took responsibility for the radicals' organizational decisions. A researcher at the Institute of World History of the Academy of Sciences, Stankevich was only thirty-five years old. Three other instigators stand out: Vladimir O. Bokser, aged thirty-six, a pediatrician and a leader of the Society for the Defense of Animals, an animal rights group; Mikhail Ya. Shneider, forty-two, a scientist at the Institute of Geomagnetism and the Ionosphere and a member of a splinter discussion group, Lingva; and Aleksandr I. Muzykantskii, forty-nine, a civil engineer who was Yeltsin's very first electoral agent in 1989 and his main link to the Moscow activists. Popov (in his student days the secretary of the Komsomol committee at Moscow State University),

Stankevich, and Bokser were members of the CPSU; Muzykantskii and Shneider were not.[90]

During the Moscow and RSFSR nominations, Stankevich and Shneider put out a Popular Front primer on how a "democratic bloc" could break through. They noted that voters exhibited "a certain fatigue with political globalism" and would look for "much more concretization and program" than in the USSR election. For candidates to the city council, they submitted this war cry:

> Here what should prevail, obviously, is the theme of a Megapolis in which the problems of the whole land are incredibly densely layered. A winning moment in the program of a candidate to the local soviet should be [the need for] a Law on the Capital which will give special powers to the city authorities to curb agency dictate and in which removal of the seat of government from Moscow is not to be excluded. [We should speak about] granting Moscow special administrative status, about making Moscow comfortable for Muscovites, about declaring a three-to-five-year moratorium on industrial construction and simultaneously reorienting all building capacities to housing, of converting raion road departments into contract units to rid the streets of rubbish, of making municipal property out of all enterprises dealing with the recycling of scrap materials, the sanitary cleaning of the streets, and the manufacture of the goods that Muscovites need. Protection of green zones, and conferring on them the status of city and raion parks, is another very important idea. An indispensable theme will be anything connected with the development of self-government.[91]

From policy the pamphleteers went on to tactics, dispensing cool counsel on agitation, positive and negative symbols, picketing and visual aids, and coping with "apparatus candidates." They told nominees to use participatory process to turn omissions in the action program into an asset:

> When you are in contact with the voters, underline that your task as a deputy will not be to settle every problem in the district on your own—to say that would be deliberately misleading—but to open up as many opportunities as possible for citizens themselves to come together in associations for the defense of consumer rights, in ecological groups, in neighborhood patrols to guard playgrounds and transport stops, and so on. Every time a voter heaps doubt upon the practicality of resolving

these or other problems—and there will be dozens of times—suggest to him right off that he join the aktiv of the future deputy, that he become your plenipotentiary for dealing with the issue that is sorest and most urgent to him . . . It is especially important that the candidate react flexibly to the situation, carry out polemics in "enveloping style," following up an attack with agreement and confession of the gravity of the problem, and then with a summons to reflection: "Yes, you are right, you have a basis for believing that way, but let us THINK TOGETHER about these other things that you have not yet brought out."[92]

The Moscow Association of Voters held ice-breaking discussions in October and November about forming an "Alternative-90" slate solely for the soviets of Moscow. Efforts to expand its horizon culminated January 20–21, 1990, in the founding conference in Moscow's Youth Palace of Democratic Russia, an "electoral bloc" of candidates for republic and local deputy throughout the RSFSR. The 175 delegates were from Moscow, Leningrad, and twenty smaller centers, representing voters' clubs and associations and a variety of other groups, such as Memorial and Moscow Tribune. Hailing the testament of Andrei Sakharov, who had died the previous month, their manifesto vowed to take Russia, "following the majority of the European countries," down "the difficult but peaceful and democratic path of parliamentary transformations, which in the final analysis will give bread and freedom to all." Otherwise, it said apocalyptically, the country faced "bloody shocks" and breakdown.[93]

On politics, the Democratic Russia declaration was unquailingly liberalizing and Westernizing. It touted multiparty democracy, Russian "sovereignty" in a voluntary Soviet federation, abolition of censorship, parliamentary control over the KGB, and constitutional enshrinement of civil and religious liberties. It repeated the demand to "eradicate all privileges of nomenklatura officials" that Yeltsin had been voicing since 1986.

On the economy, by contrast, the democrats were circumspect. They were noncommittal about socialism: "The argument now heating up about economic policy . . . often acquires ideological coloration: socialism or capitalism? Moving the conversation onto this plane will not tell us what kind of economy we need. It is time to draw practical conclusions from what the experience of the entire world has proven." The "basic regulator of the economy" was to be the market, but the Democratic Russia manifesto stopped short of embracing private ownership, calling instead for "legal equality of the various forms of property" and conversion of "a significant portion" of state assets "into other forms." It also espoused "mighty mechanisms for ecological security and social defense"—like a guaranteed minimum income, retail price controls, subsidized food prices, and indexed pensions—that would be hard to square with rapid marketization.

The coalitional nature of the opposition's economic program eventually caused it grief. On local issues the problem ran deeper: it did not make any comprehensive statement on urban or municipal policy at all. The only reference by Democratic Russia on January 21 was to "public control" of the allocation of state-owned apartments. Individual candidates either fell back on earlier positions taken by the Moscow Popular Front and Association of Voters or filled in the blanks themselves.

Inexact as it was, Democratic Russia had a platform with the thrust and allure needed to fight and win the Moscow election as a near-party. It turned the municipal vote into a referendum on Communist rule more searching than that of 1989.

Unlike a normal party, Moscow DR had no stylized decision-making structure, relying instead on bargaining and on self-appointed leaders like Popov and Stankevich. Nor did it enjoy legal shelter. It did not exist until three weeks after nominations ceased; not being an authorized organization, it could not have nominated candidates in any event. Election posters and ballot slips ignored it and all the blocs, and it was shut out of the official local media, getting its first mention in *Moskovskaya pravda* March 2.

How, then, did the insurgents position themselves for victory? Although Stankevich and others tempted some candidates into the ring in vacant districts,[94] the locomotive power in the early stages came from individual nominees and from troops of boosters, all with minimal orchestration.

The DR party exerted itself more after January 21. It tendered invitations to sign on to nominees—though not always, as a few names got onto DR lists without consent. The four-page newspaper of the DR candidates, *Pozitsiya* (Position), managed to publish in late February but was amateurish.[95] With lax coordination, DR tended to misplace its efforts. Only 264 of the 619 members of the slate (42.6 percent) stood as the exclusive DR candidate in the electoral district; 128 districts had 2 DR candidates each, 30 had 3 or more, and 78 had none. Fratricide was rare, as the other players were too disorganized to capitalize, but the empty districts cost DR 40 or 50 seats.

One might predict the radical roster's relative youthfulness (see Table 19) but not necessarily its subaverage proportion of women. Slightly more than half were members or affiliates of the Communist Party—the enemy within. The slate fell between the rightwing and center slates but far above the city mean in terms of closeness of district to residence.

Most striking about the democratic list was its occupational profile. With 64.3 percent of its candidates coming out of higher education, science, the media and arts, or engineering pursuits, it was above all representative of Moscow's humanistic and technical intelligentsia. A not negligible 10.3 percent were members of the inner administrative elite. Twenty-two army officers, 2 from the KGB, and 7 from the local police bore the Democratic Russia ensign, as did 8 Komsomol leaders, 2 trade unionists, 8 USSR and RSFSR civil servants, and 7 municipal officials. Senior among the last was Nikolai N. Gonchar, the chairman of the executive committee of Baumanskii raion, who had won respect among the informals during the fight over Lefortovo and Nemetskaya sloboda. DR even had 10 fellow travelers within the Communist Party apparatus: one was the forty-two-year-old Aleksandr F. Kapustin, the first secretary of the Krasnogvardeiskii raikom.

Circumstances obliged the radicals to be inventive about transmitting their appeal. They received a blaze of publicity at two thronging street demonstrations, on February 4 and February 25. Banished from the main city newspapers, they eked out space in the callow raion press and in liberal national publications, notably the weekly newsmagazines *Ogonek* (Spark) and *Argumenty i fakty* (Arguments and Facts). DR's listing in *Pozitsiya,* an unregistered newspaper priced at fifty kopeks, was reproduced in thousands of mimeographed and photocopied handbills doled out free and in posters slapped up during the stretch drive of the campaign at shops, subway stations, house stairwells, and the like. The authorities did nothing about these bald contraventions of the election law.

Table 19. Some characteristics of the 1990 candidates by slate (percent)

Characteristic	Dem. Russia (N = 619)	Right (N = 146)	Center (N = 265)	None (N = 2,232)	All candidates (N = 3,262)
Age under 40[b]	35.2	15.8	24.5	26.1	27.3
Women	15.2	17.8	18.5	13.7	14.6
Member or affiliate of Communist Party	50.7	54.8	97.0	80.9	75.3
Residence in same raion as electoral district	73.3	85.6	57.0	50.0	56.6
Occupational group					
Faculty member or researcher	37.0	29.5	9.8	19.1	22.2
Media/arts figure	6.1	13.0	0.4	3.2	4.0
Manager in production sector	2.9	4.8	21.1	16.1	13.5
Core public administrator[c]	10.3	8.2	37.0	22.4	20.6
Engineer or technical specialist	21.2	19.2	5.7	10.6	12.6
Manager or professional in service sector	7.4	6.2	14.0	13.5	12.0
Employee of semi-official or unofficial organization[d]	5.3	5.5	3.0	4.0	4.2
Other white-collar	1.1	1.4	0.8	0.9	1.0
Blue-collar worker	4.4	5.5	5.7	7.4	6.6
Miscellaneous	4.2	6.8	2.6	2.8	3.2
Running as exclusive candidate of slate in district	42.6	82.2	39.2	NA	NA

Note: NA = not applicable.

a. Twenty candidates were endorsed by two slates. Nineteen times, the second listing was by the center bloc, which did not reveal itself until the eve of the first round of the election. As a simplifying assumption, cross-endorsed candidates are reckoned to belong to the slate that endorsed them first. Thus thirteen candidates endorsed by both Democratic Russia and the center bloc are counted as DR candidates, and six backed by the center as well as the right are considered right candidates. In one case, a DR candidate was subsequently endorsed by the right bloc; he is counted as DR.

b. Average year of birth 1945 for all candidates, 1943 for right, 1944 for unendorsed, 1945 for center, and 1946 for Democratic Russia.

c. Includes officials in USSR and RSFSR government, local soviets, CPSU apparatus, People's Control, trade unions, Komsomol, military, KGB, MVD, and local police.

d. Includes artistic unions, established mass associations, youth units, cooperatives, and informal political associations.

Leaders of the Communist Party paid homage later to the opposition's tactics. One bears quoting at length:

> Mastery of agitation deserves special study, because here the Democratic Russia bloc in every respect outstripped the party [CPSU] committees. Those "all-encompassing" official election posters, with their boring portraits of each candidate, faceless biographical texts, and indistinguishable programs, naturally could not captivate the voters.
>
> Everyone remembers the veritable "war of the pamphlets" that erupted on the eve of the election. It is difficult to say who came out on top in this . . . but Democratic Russia, while taking part in the pamphleteering, placed its bet on forms of agitation significantly more incisive and popular, and consequently more effective: preelection rallies; people with megaphones in underground passageways and on the streets; posters that slammed the target right on, showing not only the merits of the candidates supported by the bloc but criticizing their rivals, and sometimes discrediting them; support groups acting in the microraions, in sections of apartment houses, at traditional places of congregation of city dwellers; and sound trucks. Let us be frank about it: all this made an impression.
>
> Meanwhile, the official structures—not only party committees but also the trade unions and all the other public organizations—neglected to carry out this kind of operative and purposive work.[96]

On the sidewalks of their districts candidates were free to extemporize on Democratic Russia's program. Many did so with alacrity, highlighting their life experiences or directing appeals, not infrequently emotion-laden, to defined groups of voters.

Thus Lazar Z. Shugol', a DR nominee in electoral district 451 (Tushinskii raion), described in his poster his internment by the KGB in the 1950s for writing an article finding fault with Leninist ideology, and Boris Yu. Kagarlitskii in district 460 (Frunzenskii raion) told of being arrested as a theater student in 1982. In district 334 (Proletarskii raion), Valerii Fadeyev detailed his work for Memorial and Yeltsin's 1989 campaign and said he would seek "the moral rebirth of our society." Father Aleksandr I. Borisov in district 269 (Moskvoretskii raion) said little more than that he had been a parish priest since 1973 and was "for a significant increase in the number of working churches" in Moscow.[97]

Vladimir K. Abushayev, the DR standard bearer in district 3 (Leninskii raion), proposed a municipal payment to central Moscow's copious old-age pensioners and demanded an end to "the seizure by the Central Committee, Council of Ministers, and other agencies of land [in the raion] for their mansions" and to issuance of residency permits to "bankrupt" dignitaries. Yulii S. Gusman in district 185 (Krasnopresnenskii raion) called for a state health insurance scheme, financed in part by profits from "big sport," and for dedicated flats in rebuilt downtown housing for native Muscovites dislocated by urban renewal. In district 337 (Proletarskii raion), Irina V. Bogantseva posited eviction from Moscow of all of ZIL's foundries, diversion of factory investment budgets to housing, and a public park instead of industrial wasteland for the Nagatino Floodlands.

Viktor M. Matveyev in district 189 (Krasnopresnenskii raion) construed DR's platform as "municipal socialism," such as, he said, had been "successfully implemented by left forces in the countries of Western Europe"; his poster asserted that grassroots groups should have the right to space in local newspapers and time on TV and radio. One of the few incumbents in the race, Nellya N. Rogacheva in district 86 (Gagarinskii raion), campaigned on her record of helping to scuttle a nomenklatura apartment project. Aleksandr P. Braginskii in district 117 (Kievskii raion) declaimed in favor of a "radical improvement" of sanitation, more auto service stations, and orders to defense plants to make spare parts for cars and buses. The DR candidates in the Brateyevo housing project (districts 182, 183, and 184, Krasnogvardeiskii raion) relied on their opposition to overdevelopment there, and Gaik B. Zulumyan in district 182 also stressed his role in the Brateyevo self-government committee. Lyudmila T. Shekhova in district 149 (Kirovskii raion) highlighted her leadership against the Northern TETS and repeated the indictment of it as "ecological genocide."[98]

Democratic Russia was not the only quasi party in the race. Two smaller groups, from different bands on the political dial, also ran candidates.

An arch-conservative slate, the Bloc of Public and Patriotic Movements of Russia, was the more diminutive but also the more viscerally motivated of the two. Making up for the time lost in 1989, it, like DR, conducted concurrent RSFSR and Moscow campaigns. Its declaration, "In Favor of a Policy of Social Harmony and Russian Rebirth," was published in December 1989 in *Literaturnaya Rossiya,* the organ of the RSFSR Union of Writers. A dozen extant societies and clubs signed the broadside, among them VOOPIK, Yedinstvo, the League for Spiritual Rebirth of the Fatherland, the Foundation for Restoration of the Cathedral of Christ the Redeemer, the Rossiya (Russia) Deputies' and Voters' Club, the United Toilers' Front of Russia, the Russian Branch of the International Foundation for Slavic Literatures and Cultures, and the Voluntary Society of Book Lovers of the RSFSR. All these organizations were Russian rather than Muscovite in scope.[99]

The Russophiles' platform was not without its subtleties. Its championing of republic prerogatives commanded wide public sympathy and appeared in some guise in every faction's program. It supported environmental causes, such as cleaning up the Volga and halting atomic power plants. It shrewdly phrased its reverence toward Russian Orthodoxy and its critique of past mistreatment of the church to cast the issue, in part, as a civil libertarian one.

These, however, were secondary notes in the chorus on the right. The primary chord raged at perestroika and defended an imperial nationality policy. It condemned proposals to cut the defense budget and espoused institution of a "Leninist" Russian Communist Party as the epicenter of a redisciplined Soviet party. Russian liberals it lumped together with anti-Russian nationalists in a "bloc of separatists and 'left radicals,'" itching "to dismember the USSR and sell out our national wealth" to foreign and indigenous "swindlers." On local issues the bloc reiterated the stock oath to protect and restore architectural landmarks. To ease development pressure, it proposed building a new "administrative center for the USSR" somewhere outside Moscow. It kept silent on housing and other welfare questions.

The Russophiles were slow to solidify organizationally. The list of approved candidates for the Mossovet in the mid-February edition of the Rossiya Club's newspaper, *Rossiya,* named only 34 candidates. The preelection *Literaturnaya Rossiya* had 150 names, of which 146 actually appeared on the ballot March 4; these counts do not include Yevgenii B. Balashov in district 171 (Krasnogvardeiskii raion), who was somehow endorsed by both DR and the anti-DR right.

Here and there, backers put together outdoor pep talks the weekend of the election but otherwise mustered little presence on the streets. Extremists who may or may not have been in the bloc hung out placards alluding to perfidious ties between Democratic Russia and the three planetary bogeys of "international Zionism," the big banks, and the U.S. Central Intelligence Agency. "If we do not stop them," one poster warned, "Russia may share the sad destiny of Poland, Panama, and Palestine. Keep in mind that every vote given to the yellow bloc falsely calling itself 'Democratic Russia' is a shot in Russia's back, a blow at the future of our children."[100]

The right bloc disputed only 133 electoral districts but avoided intrabloc rivalry (120 districts had lone candidates and 13 had pairs) and managed to fly the flag in 30 raions. Its nominees, deservedly for conservatives, were the oldest of any slate's (see Table 19). They were also more apt than the democrats to be women, to run in their raions of residence, and to belong to the Communist Party. Hardly any fewer (61.7 percent of the slate) were in higher education, research, the media and arts, and engineering occupations, with about twice as many of them in the media/arts category as DR had. Core public administrators were scared off by the right's vitriol. In all Moscow, only 3 military commanders and 9 other bureaucrats sported its colors.

The third and last slate, a centrist group, barely qualifies as such. It was cobbled together at the eleventh hour by gorkom and raikom party workers, acting with the approval of First Secretary Prokof'ev. According to interviews, a prime mover was Aleksei Bryachikhin, the construction engineer and municipal manager Yeltsin installed as first secretary of Sevastopol'skii raion in 1987. The only borough official on the gorkom bureau, a rival to Prokof'ev for the second secretary-ship in 1988, and one of two raikom leaders to run in 1989, Bryachi-khin had been urging Moscow Communists to take elections more seriously and was one of the few to court the politicized clubs and associations. He chose to stand in district 355, half of which was the nomenklatura housing project on Profsoyuznaya and Novochere-mushkinskaya streets.

The March 3 *Moskovskaya pravda* and *Vechernyaya Moskva* splashed the following announcement, autographed by 284 candidates for the Mossovet and several dozen for RSFSR deputy, over a half-page:

Esteemed voters!

We candidates for deputy in your districts are waging an honorable struggle for the votes and trust of the electors. We have diverse programs. Judge for yourselves which is better. But we have a common concern: the fate of perestroika is in jeopardy!

We see the egress from the crisis in political stability and civil accord, in assertion of democratic order and legality, in a just allocation of national property. We are convinced that this alone will make it possible to build the life that you and your families deserve, provide a better future for your children, and resolve the people's problems with housing, work, food, and consumer goods.

We call upon you to make your choice March 4, 1990.

Thirteen of the signatories had previously been endorsed by the democrats and 6 by the Russophiles. Saying nothing tangible about urban problems, they adopted the soothing intonation of the round-tables in the official press. Setting aside the 19 who were cross-endorsed, 97 percent of the centrists were associated with the Communist Party (Table 19). The slate had more women and many more out-of-raion candidates than the other two blocs, and was about average in age. Senior administrative personnel made up almost three-quarters of it. It was especially well stacked with officials in central or local government (29) and the party organs (36). No less than 8 other raikom first secretaries joined Bryachikhin.

The centrists' last-minute debut gave voters only a few hours to digest their epistle. Their chances were further reduced by capricious territorial organization. The bloc's 265 candidates spread over just 178 electoral districts. Fifty-five percent were huddled in the 9 raions where raikom first secretaries were on the slate, and another 20.8 percent in Krasnogvardeiskii raion. In 14 raions it had no candidates whatsoever, as compared to 3 empty raions for the tiny right bloc and none for DR.

THE VOTERS SPEAK

Once the returns had been laboriously tallied and published, as they were without incident,[101] it became clear that not right, center, or independents had spoiled Democratic Russia's parade. For a movement but a few weeks old, the achievement was dazzling. It returned the most legislators in the initial round and in the runoff rounded out its popular vote by 300,000 and stockpiled the most deputies' mandates by far (see Table 20). Two hundred and eighty-two of the seats filled by March 18, or 60.9 percent, were Democratic Russia's, dwarfing the right (12 deputies) and center (19) and, less one-sidedly, the 150 unendorsed entrants.

DR had drawing power in all sections of Moscow (see Maps 37 and 38). Its vote allotment March 4 fell to no less than the 14.7 percent it received in Perovskii raion and rose to 49.9 percent in Zelenograd; it was between 25 and 35 percent in twenty of thirty-three raions. In the runoff it ranged from 17.0 percent (Baumanskii raion) to 75.7 percent (Zelenograd).

The gaping holes in the other slates produced a jagged geographic array of votes. The right bloc got zero first-round votes in the three raions where it had no candidates and an anemic 0.8 to 8.1 percent in the others; in the runoff it was ignored in sixteen raions and polled between 2.3 and 12.0 percent in the rest. The center sat out fourteen raions in the first round and sixteen in the runoff; where it was suited up, its vote bounced between 0.5 and 24.3 percent March 4 and between 2.0 and 20.9 percent March 18. Unaligned candidates, meanwhile, harvested from 19.7 to 62.4 percent in the first race and from 12.0 to 60.2 percent in the second.

It is hard to say how much the radicals' breakthrough owed to the local Moscow campaign and how much it resulted from autonomous swings in public opinion, spurred by exogenous events such as Soviet economic woes and the 1989 upheavals in Eastern Europe. A poll at the end of January detected a radicalization of mass attitudes and found that a majority of Muscovites "intend to support those candidates in the elections who come out for immediate and decisive changes in our life."[102] The tide was running the democrats' way.

And yet, the attitudinal shift did not foreordain the result. The democrats still needed to get enough credible names on the ballot to have a shot at a majority and to persuade Muscovites that they and no one else would best transact "immediate and decisive" reforms.

Intercandidate variability in votes attained suggests how loosely articulated popular preferences were and that at a minimum those citizens with subliminal democratic leanings had to have them activated by good signaling. By district, DR candidates' joint share in the first round was as lofty as 86.1 percent and as dismal as 8.8 percent.

Table 20. The 1990 election results

	Slate				Straight negatives[a]	All votes
	Dem. Russia	Right	Center	None		
First round						
Districts contested	422	133	178	2,232	NA	NA
Candidates	619	146	265	487	NA	NA
Votes received	1,313,374	138,414	284,658	1,833,131	748,250	4,317,827
Percent of total votes	30.4	3.2	6.6	42.5	17.3	100.0
Percent of votes in districts contested	35.7	12.0	17.9	43.3	17.3	NA
Deputies elected	22	0	3	10	NA	NA
Candidates advanced to runoff	418[b]	32	65	383[c]	NA	NA
Runoff						
Districts contested	365	32	64	382	NA	NA
Candidates	416	32	65	320	NA	NA
Votes received	1,615,790	104,340	193,428	1,223,496	404,793	3,541,847
Percent of total votes	45.6	2.9	5.5	34.5	11.4	99.9
Percent of votes in districts contested	56.0	41.9	37.2	48.9	11.4	NA
Deputies elected	260	12	16	140	NA	NA
Total deputies elected	282	12	19	150	NA	NA

Note: NA = not applicable.
a. Valid ballots where voter rejected all candidates.
b. Includes two second-place finishers who withdrew before runoff.
c. Includes one first-place finisher who withdrew before runoff.

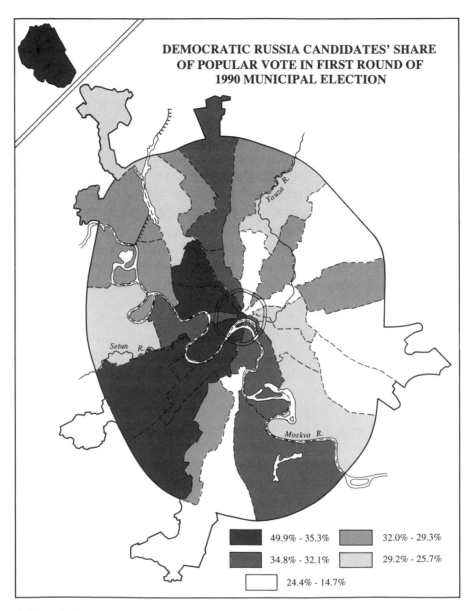

DEMOCRATIC RUSSIA CANDIDATES' SHARE
OF POPULAR VOTE IN FIRST ROUND OF
1990 MUNICIPAL ELECTION

49.9% - 35.3%   32.0% - 29.3%

34.8% - 32.1%   29.2% - 25.7%

24.4% - 14.7%

MAP 37

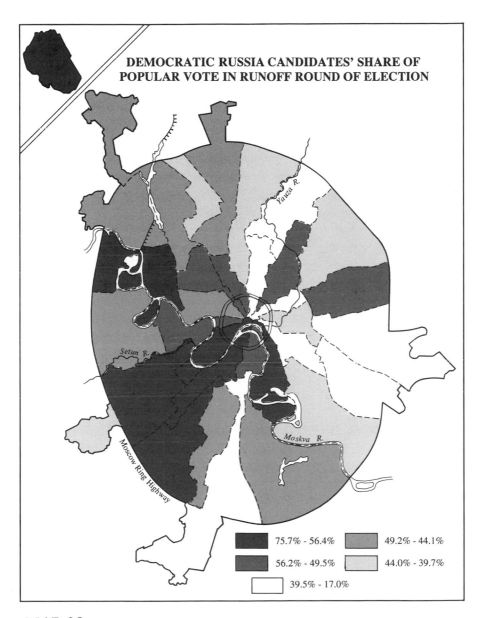

DEMOCRATIC RUSSIA CANDIDATES' SHARE OF
POPULAR VOTE IN RUNOFF ROUND OF ELECTION

75.7% - 56.4%   49.2% - 44.1%

56.2% - 49.5%   44.0% - 39.7%

39.5% - 17.0%

MAP 38

For rightists, first-race shares by district ranged from 0.9 to 38.2 percent, for centrists from 0.44 to 59.4 percent, and for independents from 0.2 to 69.2 percent.

Neighborhood- and street-level issues were a factor in some races. Where there was a recent history of environmental agitation, radicals, especially if experienced in green politics, ran unusually well. Democratic Russia won handily, for example, in Brateyevo and in Babushinskii and Kirovskii raions abutting the Northern TETS.

Citywide, Democratic Russia was victorious, but it was no steamroller. In the first round, when options were least constrained, its 30.4 percent of the votes (35.7 percent in the 422 districts it contested) came up well short of a majority. Unlabeled candidates outdrew it by a half-million votes, and almost one in every five electors chose to pencil out all of the names on the ballot. DR's share would have been less had its opponents not been so disorganized: the right and center slates secured 12.0 and 17.9 percent of the votes where they fielded candidates, almost as many combined as DR.[103]

In the runoff DR got 45.6 percent of the ballots, but with 46.5 percent of the candidates and a 6 percent drop in turnout signifying a sag in voter interest. Independents rather than the decimated right and center again yielded the principal competition, reeling in 34.5 percent of the votes and 32.7 percent of the seats. Straight-negative votes declined almost 6 percent, as first-round naysayers unwilling to jump on the democrats' bandwagon became abstainers.

The published returns tell us how well the radicals did overall in Moscow's stunning election. They do not tell us *under what conditions* they fared more or less well. To understand this question and its implications for democratizing politics, quantitative analysis is helpful. Table 21 sets forth the results of an ordinary least squares regression in which a variety of causal variables are tested for their power to predict democrats' electoral success. That success, the dependent variable, I measure here as the amalgamated vote share of Democratic Russia candidates by electoral district on March 4. As the first pair of coefficients show, and as common sense would suggest, DR votes tended to go up with the number of DR candidates, and, less sharply, down with the number of other candidates.[104]

Some interesting associations reveal themselves for characteristics of the district and its population. Statistically significant coefficients

Table 21. Regression coefficients for Democratic Russia's percentage of valid first-round votes, 1990 election[a]

Variable	Coefficient[b]
Intercept	26.32 (4.01)
Characteristics of district contest	
Number of DR candidates	8.32 (0.74)
Number of other candidates	−2.07 (0.23)
Characteristics of district	
Percent of population 10 and older with higher education	0.29 (0.11)
Books in public libraries (millions, per capita)	0.99 (0.22)
Foreign language schools (per 1,000 school-age children)	−0.15 (0.07)
Characteristics of DR candidates	
Age	−0.16 (0.06)
Woman	−5.56 (1.47)
Resident of raion	8.11 (1.37)
Occupation	
Health professional	8.78 (3.69)
Military or police officer	6.98 (2.83)
Media/arts figure	5.70 (2.58)
Leader of cooperative	−6.62 (3.43)
Manager in production sector	−6.74 (3.00)
Characteristics of other candidates	
Occupation	
Komsomol official	30.58 (8.31)
Researcher in Academy of Sciences	15.50 (7.01)
Trade union official	14.27 (5.92)
Blue-collar worker	−7.16 (4.28)
Military or police officer	−10.40 (3.78)

Note: Standard error of the regression is 9.87. R^2 is 0.47.

a. N = 420 (excludes 76 districts in which there was no DR candidate and 2 in which there was no other candidate).

b. Numbers in parentheses are standard errors of the coefficients.

were obtained for three independent variables, having to do with educational level, public libraries, and schools functioning in foreign languages. They converge on a single interpretation—the strong attraction of the democratic opposition for Moscow's proto–middle class.[105]

All other things being equal, Democratic Russia pulled in 2.9 percent more votes for every 10-point increase in the population possessing a higher education. Well-educated, white-collar voters, it may be inferred, sided more often than other Muscovites with DR, while lower-status voters went for other, largely more conservative candidates.[106] There was also a positive correlation with book holdings in public libraries, which tended to be largest in older raions (Baumanskii, Krasnopresnenskii, Frunzenskii, and Leninskii, in particular) with high concentrations of intellectuals and professionals. Foreign language primary and secondary schools showed a negative correlation. A reasonable explanation is that the influentials whose children went to such schools were hostile to Democratic Russia, and especially to the populist parts of its program. Selective data for districts with concentrations of elite housing support this interpretation. It was not likely a coincidence that First Secretary Bryachikhin of the Sevastopol'skii raikom, one of the organizers of the centrist slate, achieved his unusual first-round victory in a district containing a large UVDG housing estate.[107]

Note that all other district characteristics except these three are useless in explaining the democrats' vote share. It mattered not whether the electoral district was downtown or suburban or whether Russians, women, the elderly, or criminals were overrepresented there, or if it was a have or a have-not in social services, housing supply, and most amenities. Note also that district characteristics were far from the only correlates of Democratic Russia's strength. Voters weighed the quasi-party programs they were presented with against their concerns, but the connections drawn were exceedingly crude and left ample room for other information. In another marker of the transitional nature of the election, the largest number of valid coefficients in the regression were generated for characteristics of the candidates.

Among radical candidates, the electorate preferred youth, men, and, very strongly, residents of the same raion. While job status of the candidate did not matter, DR nominees in three occupational subgroups were favored (health care professionals, military and police officers, and media and arts figures) and in two were disfavored (managers of state enterprises and leaders of economic cooperatives). These findings, though not conclusive, indicate ambivalence and perhaps disorientation among the Moscow electorate just as it was making its presence felt. Voters registered comfort with some democratic politicians who were also authority figures from the old regime (army and police officers), but not invariably so (they were uncharitable toward industrial managers). Dismissive of the Soviet economic establishment, they were equally unhappy with personnel from the quasi-private cooperatives—despite the radical slate's pledge to accelerate market reform. And there was a strong "friends and neighbors" effect among pro-DR voters, suggesting, like the support for military and police personnel, that some Muscovites were trying to balance their leap into the unknown with affirmation of the known (in this case an identical raion of residence).

Surprisingly, the electors showed no sensitivity toward the livelihoods of the core public administrators on the radical list or to most of the subgroups among them. Nomenklatura reformists, like Chairman Gonchar of Baumanskii raion (a winner in the first round) and First Secretary Kapustin of Krasnogvardeiskii raion (who got a handsome majority in the runoff), could do very well. Nor, for that matter, did membership in the Communist Party, little more than a year before the party's demise, turn pro-democratic voters off. A radical candidate who belonged to the party or Komsomol stood to get no more and no less of the votes than if he or she were unconnected. As a result, 134 of the 280 Communists and Komsomols elected were nominees of Democratic Russia.

As for the characteristics of non–Democratic Russia candidates, whom I have merged into a single group, the picture is murkier. It is not self-evident why age, gender, and residency would not matter for these contenders when they did for DR candidates, or why Academy of Sciences researchers would be one of the leper groups. It is easier to understand why voters would be prejudiced against trade union and Komsomol functionaries—although, again, there is no effect one way or the other for Communist Party apparatchiks or government administrators. Yurii Prokof'ev and Valerii Saikin, both runoff victors in their districts, were but the most senior of sixty bureaucratic leaders, thirteen CPSU secretaries in their ranks, elected.[108] Blue-collar workers, who had not been beneficial to Democratic Russia when flying its banner, were a boon when they ran for other slates or as independents, presumably because more conservative (and lower-class) voters saw merit in candidates of plebeian social background. Again, military, regular police, and KGB officers were magnets for votes for the non-DR forces, exactly as they had been when they ran for the radicals. Some voters seemed to be looking past ideology and formal program to individual traits and institutional auras.

Exit the Partocracy

Winners and losers readily agreed on one familiar chestnut: that in a season of high political drama all eyes would be glued to Moscow. He now could see, Sergei Stankevich held after two months of perusing its books, that the capital's "superconcentration" of problems "exceeds all our preconceptions." With sound governance, though, Moscow could be "an appropriate testing and demonstration ground" for the transition to a normal life. On the other side of the fence, Yurii Prokof'ev admonished the Communist Party congress in July 1990 to scrutinize what was germinating in Russia's "seedplot of political movements." "Social processes always develop more quickly at the center," and sooner or later the swell of change would reach out to the farthest provinces. The party, he said, "must forestall this wave" by redeeming socialist values through "healthy pragmatism."[109]

Neither side had any idea how quickly the overriding issue of legitimacy would come to a head. The democrats' brain trust foresaw "years of tough and exhausting struggle" with the Communist Party griffin. The struggle turned out to be reckoned in months. Its termination was so "swift and unexpected," Aleksandr Muzykantskii would observe, that it "caught us democrats unprepared" and looking—like the Bolsheviks in 1917, he might have added—"as if we do not know what to do with victory."[110]

FROM OPPOSITION INTO POSITION

The popularly based Moscow Soviet convoked April 16, 1990. Gavriil Popov, nominated by the DR caucus, was duly chosen for the resuscitated office of chairman April 20, getting 280 of the 420 ballots cast and handily defeating four other deputies. Stankevich was voted his vice-chairman and Nikolai Gonchar a second deputy chairman.

Cross-examined about his biography, the headmasterly Popov recounted a loss of faith in Soviet verities. "I was not born an opponent of administrative socialism . . . I believed in the system I lived in" and did "everything I could to help [it] adapt." Only around 1980 had he reasoned "that repairs won't do and principled changes to the entire system are needed." On Moscow priorities Popov was coquettish, pleading he was "not a specialist" on street crime or landmarks. He dodged a query about the possible transfer of shops to private hands. He even had a kind word for the CPSU, saying it "still has a chance of leading the country's development along the correct path."[111]

The public seemed fascinated by the proceedings. Moscow television stations broadcast uncut film of them each evening. On opening day alone, seventy-three deputies dashed off five-minute speeches, nineteen speaking more than once. The *mikrofonomaniya* did not seem out of place.

By the end of the debut session on June 30, it was clear that the lawmakers would not be enacting "principled changes" just by virtue of being freely elected. The session passed only eight motions on the substance of local policy, most reactive to rather than formative of events. The main decision on consumer welfare was to impose a residency requirement for purchase of durable goods, as many Soviet towns and regions had already done. In the social sphere, the council appointed several investigatory panels and amended the budget to provide parents of preschoolers with a small portable allowance for day care. On ecology, the deputies came out against completion of the Northern TETS, a decision that had to be framed as a request to the USSR Council of Ministers. On land use and the housing fund, they adopted hazy pro-market declarations without means of implementation.

Why was it so hard for the now empowered opposition to accomplish real change? In part, the enormity of city problems that had rankled for generations and were nested in organizations, spending priorities, and mentalities would have frustrated quick redress by the most angelic reformers. For another thing, it was patent early on that Moscow's council, like all late Soviet and post-Soviet legislatures, had congenital defects going back to its parentage and that these were being magnified by personalities and by emergent ideological rifts among the radicals.

The overt machinery of local government could no longer be covertly propped up by the Communist Party. The Mossovet on May 28, 1990, receded recent decrees transferring to the party legal title to forty-three buildings and parts of buildings constructed jointly from party and municipal funds, mostly under Grishin. The day after, it declared its stake in Moscow's daily newspapers, *Moskovskaya pravda* and *Vechernyaya Moskva*. When the gorkom would not negotiate, the soviet established two new papers—*Kuranty* (Chimes), appearing in September 1990, and *Nezavisimaya gazeta* (Independent Gazette), in January 1991—and in August 1990 a radio station, *Ekho Moskvy* (Echo of Moscow).[112] Media diversification was one index of the crumbling influence of the CPSU. Another was Popov's and Stankevich's decision in July 1990, three months after Popov expounded on the salvageability of the party, to follow Yeltsin in renouncing membership in it.

Popov responded to the multifold crisis of authority by leaning on and strengthening the executive wing of government. To that end, he favored collaboration with enlightened servants of the old order, from either the state or the party hierarchy. He had fought "an apparatus that usurped power and made decisions that were rightfully the people's," he said, but "once the people have power, the apparatus is necessary" to act. He lobbied unsuccessfully to retain as chief bureaucrat—chairman of the city ispolkom, now unhooked from chairmanship of the city soviet—Valerii Saikin, who had been appointed by Yeltsin in 1986 but had since antagonized radicals with his ponderous manner, gibes at "group egoism," and obligingness toward the CPSU. Popov's second choice was Yurii Luzhkov, Saikin's deputy for food supply and interim successor. The new soviet confirmed Luzhkov as ispolkom chairman April 26; most in the DR caucus wanted an outsider.[113]

The test of wills continued between Popov and members of the Mossovet, including a growing subset of the Democratic Russia majority, over the balance between executive and legislative powers and, as a corollary issue, between city hall and the raions. The revisions of legislative-executive relations initiated by Gorbachev proved unworkable. The restored office of chairman of the soviet had few intrinsic powers and was supposed to gain luster from being filled by the local CPSU boss, a nonstarter in Moscow. And the reborn presidium of the soviet—a deputies' tool consisting of the chairman, deputy chairmen, and committee heads—was hamstrung by changes in the political context. The blossoming of political groups in the Mossovet, as Popov stated, "opened up a gulf" between the presidium and "the real leaders of the Moscow Soviet, those who head the fractions."[114]

It took until January of 1991 for a new ispolkom, three of its fifteen members non-Communists—another first—to gain ratification by the Mossovet. By then an exasperated Popov had sketched a plan for overhauling local government (see Chapter 8). The centerpiece was a separately elected office of mayor *(mer)*. It would be analogous to the state presidency being considered by the RSFSR and, in Popov's reading, would be both stronger and more democratic than the unelected USSR presidency that the federal deputies' congress had awarded to Gorbachev in March 1990.

Although many points remained unresolved, Popov did get direct election of a mayor put to the electorate as an extra question at the USSR referendum on Soviet federalism March 17, 1991. Eighty-one percent favored his proposal. An enabling decree by the presidium of the Russian parliament April 27 allowed Moscow to hold the first democratic election of a local chief executive in its history on June 12, 1991. Following a three-week campaign, Popov won in a cakewalk; Luzhkov was elected vice-mayor on the same ticket. Nikolai Gonchar succeeded Popov as chairman of the soviet when Stankevich declined what would have been certain election.

A larger context shaped Moscow's postelection politics and mini-constitutional debate: the breakdown of the organizational and psychic underpinnings of state socialism and of Gorbachev's pattern of guided change. It called into question no less than the principles by which Russia and the other nations of the Soviet Union were to define themselves as human societies. The all-consuming crisis, as one of the candidates for Mossovet chairman said in 1990, was erupting in "elemental, unregulated, and uncontrolled processes" that washed over and through the actions of leaders and governments.[115]

Signs of systemic instability abounded in Moscow. Rallies drawing scores of thousands of marchers to the Kremlin gates were only the most ostentatious. The economy began to contract in 1990; shortages, hoarding, and inflation resulted in wending lineups and fist fights in front of stores. Crime rates soared while the birth rate dropped. Perhaps 10,000 evacuees from southern republics torn by communal violence flocked to the capital in 1990. Refugees begged for rubles and food in railroad and subway stations, soon joined by panhandlers. A tent city on the lawn of the Rossiya Hotel was "a gathering place for deprived, offended, and disgruntled people from across the land" from July to December.[116] Until police closed it, the several hundred campers heckled USSR and RSFSR deputies walking to the Kremlin.

Polar positions gained in this disordered environment. A traditionalist from the Krasnodar region, Ivan K. Polozkov, was chosen first secretary of the RSFSR chapter of the Communist Party founded in June 1990. In the beleaguered union government, Gorbachev, having blown hot and cold on economic reform, rejected the "500 Days" plan for crash marketization and banked to the right the winter of 1990–1991, promoting hardliners and emitting stern decrees. The Moscow KGB set up an office to combat trade "sabotage"; army troops started joint foot patrols with militiamen on February 1.

Russia's radicals, outside their urban bastions in Moscow and Leningrad, exhibited strength in the legislative chambers of the RSFSR. By the skinniest of margins, the Congress of People's Deputies on May 29, 1990, picked as head of the Russian Supreme Soviet the maverick ex-Muscovite, Boris Yeltsin. The parliamentary position, combined with his charisma and his flashy exit from the CPSU in July 1990, at the Twenty-eighth Congress, made Yeltsin the unquestioned leader of the democrats. On June 12, 1991, the same day as the Moscow mayoral contest, the republic's citizens elected him president of Russia with 57 percent of all the votes (72 percent in Moscow). His publicity materials were coproduced with Popov's, prominently displaying a snapshot of them in conversation.

Moscow government unavoidably became a battle zone in the confrontation between standpatters and radicals, Communists and anti-Communists, USSR and RSFSR, Gorbachev and Yeltsin. The game reached its meanest in a jurisdictional dispute over the militia (regular police) force. Along with crime prevention and traffic control, Moscow's Chief Directorate of Internal Affairs maintained public order, a ticklish job as street actions intensified.

Democratic Russia deputies stirred the pot when they served notice that they would not accept organization of the 1990 May Day ceremonies by the Communist Party apparatus. On April 21 President Gorbachev directed that the USSR cabinet alone would grant permits for assemblies inside the Sadovoye kol'tso. The Moscow Association of Voters nonetheless marched its own columns into Red Square on May 1. When noisy revelers brandished antigovernment and anti-Gorbachev signs—effrontery never seen at such an event—the Soviet leaders stalked off the reviewing stand.

Popov adopted a middling position on the May Day controversy, but disputatious Moscow deputies took out their anger on Petr S. Bogdanov, the chief of police since 1986 (and concurrently a USSR deputy interior minister since 1988). In November 1990 they held hearings into his handling of security at the Revolution Day parade. On January 23, 1991, the full soviet voted to replace him with one Vyacheslav S. Komissarov, a provincial policeman recently on an anticorruption assignment in the USSR MVD. It did so against the wishes of Popov and Luzhkov and without getting the consent of superior line officials obligatory under "dual subordination."

In the past the RSFSR and USSR interior ministers, particularly the latter, would have been consulted. Any difference would have been resolved by the CPSU organs; until the mid-1980s the position had been invariably filled by ex-party officials in any case.[117] This time, an almost slapstick sequence of events ensued in March and April 1991: (1) Gorbachev, acting as USSR president, put out a decree stopping Komissarov's appointment; (2) sixteen pro-Komissarov city deputies went on a three-week hunger strike; (3) Yeltsin's government announced Komissarov appointed by its writ; (4) Komissarov began to sign orders even though federal agents kept him physically out of his headquarters; (5) Gorbachev instituted a Chief Directorate of Internal Affairs for Moscow and Moscow Oblast inside the USSR ministry and named General Ivan F. Shilov, lately chief of the oblast police, to head it; (6) Gorbachev's interior minister, Boris K. Pugo, appointed yet another officer, Nikolai S. Myrikov, a specialist in crowd control, commander of the Moscow militia beneath Shilov; and (7) Popov stated that Moscow could not do without a "municipal militia" under his control.

Leaving aside the KGB—whose local directorate was as large as ever and was tapping the telephones of Yeltsin and Popov—Moscow in the space of a few months had four police chiefs. Two of them, Komissarov and Myrikov, nursed claims, and Shilov and a hypothetical municipal force also contended. In unadorned fact, no one at all commanded this vital urban function, and all involved, as Myrikov said, were "playing with fire."[118]

Intractable problems, institutional immaturity, social unrest, economic recession, a sectarian and uncivil politics, the "war of laws"—the deck was stacked against policy innovation. And, by and large, Moscow did not get effective innovation in the year after the stunning election. On economic reform Popov and his allies "began to think that we should not try to start something or rack our brains in Moscow, that we should wait until a general program had been adopted for the USSR and Russia." When no program evolved, they "were left with measures of an administrative character," such as rationing of cigarettes and some foodstuffs, "and did not get around to any really large-scale transformations."[119]

The people of Moscow tolerated this wheel spinning with remarkable forgiveness, as they showed beyond a doubt at the polls June 12, 1991. Turnout in the mayoral election was 2.2 percent higher than in the first-round voting for the Mossovet. Whereas Democratic Russia's candidates won 30.4 percent of the votes in 1990, Popov (and Luzhkov) got 65.3 percent against four opposing teams. The second-place ticket, topped by Valerii Saikin, trying to make a comeback, received only 16.3 percent. To put it another way, 298,024 more Muscovites went to the polls in June 1991 than in March 1990, but Popov attracted 1,700,874 (129.5 percent) more supporters than Democratic Russia had the previous year and 2,259,858 more than his nearest opponent.

With social and economic change stalled, democrats harped on the symbolic politics for which the city had always been a peerless stage. In April 1990 the Mossovet disclaimed the customary motion awarding Lenin a Moscow deputy's papers. It refused to participate in the yearly Leninist Communist Subbotnik, pronouncing its weekend meeting "a democratic subbotnik." In May DR militants carted off the plaster bust of Lenin at the head of the council auditorium (Figure 70). Orthodox Communists stormed out at this "blasphemy," but the majority had the statue permanently removed in July. In November 1990 a city commission denied Ivan Polozkov of the RSFSR Communist Party a Moscow residency permit, saying he did not have valid work because the party had not been registered. The ispolkom in the spring of 1991 signed a document renting part of the Lenin Museum to a business association.

Addressing the historical record, the ispolkom resolved in June 1990 to rebuild from municipal coffers Kazan Cathedral, the seven-

Figure 70. Newly elected leadership directs a meeting of the Moscow Soviet under bust of Lenin, May 1990. Sergei Stankevich is speaking into the microphone, and Gavriil Popov is seated at the far right end of the table. (Photograph by author.)

teenth-century church on Red Square razed in 1936; the cornerstone was laid November 4, 1990.[120] Two months later the city closed down the Moscow House of Scientific Atheism, the center for antireligious propaganda. In front of the Lubyanka on October 30, 1990, the Mossovet cosponsored with Memorial the unveiling of a stone commemorating "the millions of victims of the totalitarian regime." Hundreds of Gulag survivors attended the ceremony and, in another departure from Soviet precedent, Russian Orthodox clergymen offered prayers. A featured speaker was Oleg Volkov, a ninety-year-old former political prisoner and an advocate of architectural preservation.[121]

Nor was any time lost desacralizing public spaces stamped in socialist iconography. Yeltsin and Saikin had made several rechristenings in 1986, and in 1988 Brezhnevskii raion was renamed Cheremushkinskii. Memorial had circulated petitions in 1988 and 1989 demanding new designations for three Moscow raions named after members of the Stalin Politburo—Zhdanovskii, Voroshilovskii, and Kalininskii—and had succeeded in the first and second cases. A few other changes had been made, none terribly offensive to the party apparatus. In November 1990 the city presidium upped the ante in two respects: quantitatively, by retitling twenty-seven streets and squares at once and giving notice that many more would follow; and qualitatively, by picking on appellations holy to the Soviet regime.

Among the demigods chiseled from the map were Karl Marx, Maxim Gorky, Feliks Dzerzhinskii, Mikhail Frunze, Sergei Kirov, Valeryan Kuibyshev, Yakov Sverdlov, and Mikhail Kalinin. Prospekt Marksa reverted to the medieval Okhotnyi ryad and Mokhovaya ulitsa, ulitsa Gor'kogo to Tverskaya, and ploshchad' Dzerzhinskogo to Lubyanskaya ploshchad'; ulitsa Frunze returned to Znamenka ulitsa, ulitsa Kirova to Myasnitskaya, and ulitsa Kuibysheva, between the Kremlin and Staraya ploshchad', to Il'inka; the Bol'shoi and Malyi theaters were back on Teatral'naya ploshchad', not ploshchad' Sverdlova, and prospekt Kalinina had reverted to Vozdvizhenka and Novyi Arbat. Nikol'skaya ulitsa in Kitaigorod won out over ulitsa Dvadtsat'-pyatogo Oktyabrya (Twenty-fifth of October Street), Manezhnaya ploshchad' over ploshchad' Pyatidesyati-letiya Oktyabrya (Square of the Fiftieth Anniversary of the October Revolution), and Sukharevskaya ploshchad', once home to the Sukharev Tower, over Kolkhoznaya ploshchad' (Collective Farm Square).

Communist Party officials accused Democratic Russia of "a well calculated political action," aimed at "revving up public opinion" on the eve of the Revolution Day festivities. They wanted a plebiscite before money was spent on street signs and maps. Why, someone wanted to know, were noble Bolsheviks like Dzerzhinskii being besmirched by "petty populism," and why were "the one-sided positions of 'retro' ideology" gaining the upper hand? What about rededicating prospekt Kalinina to Aleksei Rykov, the Muscovite prime minister who fought against Stalin to save NEP, and Nikita Khrushchev, the de-Stalinizer who pushed this modern boulevard through the decrepit Arbat?[122]

A short while before, it would have been daring to exalt Rykov or Khrushchev over Stalin or Kalinin. Such talk was now dated, as Moscow and Russia hurtled beyond de-Stalinization to de-Communization.

THE AGONY OF THE COMMUNIST PARTY

"If Communists want hereafter to carry out the mission of a political vanguard," Lev Zaikov orated after the USSR elections, "the party has to rebuild itself faster than society as a whole does." The balloting had brought out "a crisis in the forms and methods of work of our party committees." How much tougher it would be, he said, to find a place in a democratizing society than "simply to hold onto power" in an inert dictatorship.[123] Zaikov's plaint could as well have come from Yeltsin before him or Prokof'ev after him. Had more been done about it, Yeltsin might not have given up on the party's reformability and Prokof'ev might have been spared the ignominy of being its last Moscow chieftain.

Intraparty reform from 1985 to late 1988 addressed only three areas. It trimmed a bit of organizational fat, mainly commissions ancillary to the gorkom.[124] Yeltsin and Zaikov radiated a modicum of glasnost' into the CPSU's inner works through press interviews, communiqués about the weekly gorkom bureau, and printed transcripts of speeches at plenums and biographies of new party officials. And they delegated some electoral choice to raion party committees, allowing them to choose among several acceptable candidates for first secretary.

The Nineteenth Party Conference in 1988 committed the party to bigger changes, though without forsaking Lenin's "democratic centralism." The Twenty-eighth Congress in July 1990 approved further reforms.

In Moscow two gorkom plenums in autumn 1988 began to retool machinery with the objective of more open-minded leadership. Extraordinary city party conferences were summoned in January 1989 and November 1990, the second preceded by a no-holds-barred discussion of organization and policy. As of December 1988 all elections of secretaries of the gorkom were competitive and by secret ballot. Prokof'ev, chosen leader this way in 1989, at the 1990 conference fended off a challenge for his job—another first for a sitting Moscow leader—by Valerii P. Shantsev, the old-line first secretary of the Perovskii raikom since October 1988 ("the Moscow Polozkov"). Unlike Aleksandr Rudakov in 1989, Shantsev got to make his pitch in public, berating Prokof'ev as a political chameleon and Gorbachev, present at the session, for inaction. He drew almost 30 percent of the delegates' votes, twice as many as Rudakov had, and was then elected second secretary of the gorkom.[125]

The party also took on reorganization of its administrative fist, its full-time apparatus, in 1988. It shifted the theoretical basis of the apparat, in Prokof'ev's words, "from the branch principle, the principle of running everything, to the principles of making recommendations, of studying and advising on the methodology of party work" at the grassroots.[126] This abdication of the traditional prefectoral definition of the party's role had consequences for structure.

First, the gorkom more than halved its staff, from 437 responsible workers in July 1988 to 217 in 1989, not counting several dozen in its Business Office, and 201, including 27 in the Business Office, in February 1991. Gorkom departments dropped in number from eighteen to eight in 1988, edging up to nine in 1991, and secretaries were cut from six to five. The raikoms underwent comparable reductions.

Second, the production branch principle was jettisoned for a throwback to the functionalism prevalent until the 1930s. Of the eight gorkom departments instituted in December 1988, an omnibus Socioeconomic Department dealt with economic policy generally, and only one section, the Defense Industry Department, was specific to an economic branch. The second was dissolved at the beginning of 1991, and departments were formed for relations with the soviets and "public and political organizations."

Third, the secretariat of the gorkom stopped operating as a collegial organ in 1988, and the bureau chopped back its sessions in 1990 to two per month.

Fourth, the nomenklatura system, the mainstay of party personnel control, was well-nigh done away with over three years. Local party confirmation of appointments of most economic managers ceased in 1988, of most municipal executives in 1989, and of most raion-level officials in 1990. By 1991 the gorkom's nomenklatura had dwindled to about 200 positions, roughly 10 percent of its size in the mid-1980s and less than 3 percent of its size in 1939. Everyone on the list was a Communist Party staffer, not a state civil servant.[127]

Fifth, there was a concerted attempt to co-opt nonapparatchiks onto the gorkom (see Table B-2). Zaikov extended Khrushchev's and Brezhnev's policy of recruiting blue-collar members, also increasing the representation of economic managers. Prokof'ev stressed managers and intellectuals, not the faceless rank and file.

And, sixth, to give nonleaders a say in party policy, commissions of members of the gorkom, several dozen members each and chaired by gorkom secretaries, were organized. From three in January 1989, the commissions grew to five in 1991: for party organization, ideology, socioeconomic problems, relations with the soviets, and mass organizations.

This restructuring, then, was the therapy laid on. Why did it not save the patient? The fundamental causes of death resided outside the local arena. The party's underlying and broad-based pathology had taken an eon to evolve. Diagnosing a low-grade fever, what he termed "crisis symptoms," Mikhail Gorbachev pursued a treatment schedule that, as Yeltsin recognized before almost anyone, was raising the sick man's temperature and bringing on morbidity.

The Gorbachev leadership's miscalculations were beyond counting. It timidly attempted to reform the economy and ineptly managed economic developments at the very time that it encouraged mass political mobilization outside the partocracy's hierarchical framework. The stepping up of change in the localities and republics in 1990 detonated intergovernmental conflicts and ethnic separatism and cut the feet out from under Gorbachevian moderates the USSR over. Thus political liberalization coincided with economic distress and a mushrooming constitutional and ideological crisis.

The reformation within the party that made old-fashioned suppression of these multiple strains impossible came too late and aimed too low for them to be peacefully internalized. The unchecked pluralization of politics rendered nonsense of the "vanguard" mission, leading liberal Communists to defect and conservatives to fume. Frantic to shore up his authority, Gorbachev wagered on state institutions and on his opportunistic entente with rightists in the armed forces, police, and production bureaucracy. It was they who moved against him in August 1991 and catalyzed the final disintegration of pere-stroika and, in tumbling sequence, of the CPSU and the imperial Soviet center.

The Moscow Communist Party lived through every aspect of the pan-Soviet crisis except interethnic strife. In 1990, the year of maxi-mum ferment within the party, the spokesman for the largest liberal group, Democratic Platform, was Vyacheslav N. Shostakovskii, the rector of the Moscow Higher Party School and a member of the gorkom. Dismissed after the Twenty-eighth Congress voted down his program, he left the CPSU and helped organize the Republican Party, one of Russia's first non-Communist parties.

The structural reforms produced some results. They offset the party's authoritarian ethos, by and large. Smaller staffs, the disem-bowelment of nomenklatura, and the end of branch departments demonstrably lessened the apparatus's ability to interfere in nonparty business. Although a few dissident Moscow Communists were ex-pelled, "democratic centralism" was pretty well a scholastic phrase by 1990–1991.

Intraparty reform failed in that it did not and maybe could not match destruction of the old with construction of robust new proce-dures. Some well-intentioned changes might have served the Moscow party in the long term had they been given the time to work. Others were so badly conceived or implemented that they either had no impact or hastened the party's comedown.

In field after field, the local party, having been on a treadmill of inconsequential reforms since 1985, suddenly found itself with new units that had yet to find their legs and long-standing ones that needed reprogramming. Prokof'ev conceded in November 1990 that the com-missions of the gorkom had "become neither generators of ideas nor directors of the work of the corresponding departments" of the ap-paratus. Members paid them no mind, and their chairmen "depend greatly, as before, on the apparatus, which is always at hand." As for the once fearsome bureau, "The sharp contraction in questions about economics and cadres," most of its docket until recently, "has posed the hard question of how to redefine the position of this elected organ." It was supposed to be bearing down on "analysis of the situation," working out of "positions," and "coordination" of the party's efforts, but who knew what these rubbery terms meant?[128]

If they meant anything, it should have been masterminding a vigorous presence in urban government. But here again the party let others define its agenda.

The predicament would have been less dire had Gorbachev's 1988 reform formula been realized. The city party boss would have been chosen head of the Mossovet and held both posts, as Georgii Popov had under different conditions in the 1940s. But this was not to be in Moscow, although obkom first secretaries were selected chairmen of soviets in about two-thirds of Russia's regions.

Democratic Russia's majority stood between Prokof'ev and the chairmanship. Gavriil Popov did not feel bound by Communist Party discipline and left the party in July 1990. Moreover, the new soviet would out of principle not seat any CPSU functionary on its presidium or ispolkom. Nor did anyone from those bodies seek or accept a place in the gorkom bureau, snipping a cord stretching back to Lev Kamenev. Municipal officials constituted only 4.3 percent of the 1990 gorkom, less than at any time since the 1920s, and they were mostly minor administrators and raikom secretaries recently moved over to chair raion soviets. The interlocking of the monopoly party with city government, a constant of the Soviet era, had effectively been undone.[129]

Refusing to let his name stand for chairman and go down to defeat, Prokof'ev did try to salvage something in the Mossovet. At an off-the-record organizational meeting, he asked all deputies belonging to the Communist Party to stay behind to take counsel. It was a moment of epiphany: 200 of the almost 300 Communists in the room exited. When Democratic Russia deputies, half of them nominally CPSU members, delivered on their intention of forming a voting bloc in the council, Prokof'ev authorized formation of a countergroup, Moskva, with 94 members.

Prokof'ev would have nothing to do with leading Moskva, leaving a pair of deputies to become cochairmen. The first, Aleksei Bryachikhin, was its agreed nominee for presidency of the whole soviet. But a group of Moskva deputies backed another bloc member, Igor N. Preobrazhenskii, who nearly doubled Bryachikhin's vote. Insulted, Bryachikhin put his time into the Sevastopol'skii raion soviet, which he was chosen to head, and the RSFSR Communist Party.[130] Chairmanship of Moskva devolved upon an unsung bureaucrat, Yurii Vinogradov. Secretary of the Moscow ispolkom since 1988 (he had replaced Prokof'ev there), he was purged from that position by Popov and took a stipend as a graduate student in a Central Committee institute.

Charges and countercharges about these embarrassments flew at the 1990 city party conference. It passed a motion pinioning the gorkom: "The gorkom has proven unprepared for parliamentary activity. It exercises *practically no influence* on the work of the Moscow Soviet and its executive organs." One delegate, elaborating on points in Valerii Shantsev's election speech, flung questions and implicitly the charge of cowardice at Prokof'ev:

> Why did none of the secretaries of the gorkom get into the struggle for deputies' mandates in the [repeat] election for deputies to the Mossovet on November 25? . . . Yurii Anatol'evich [Prokof'ev] would not put up a fight for chairman of the Mossovet even though this would have given him the possibility of again putting out the position of the city party organization. The group Moskva is run by a graduate student . . . while the first secretary is again in the shadows. One has to ask, why? What kind of position is this? Either the city organization has a leader or it does not.[131]

Adjustments were finally made after the conference. Shantsev, Prokof'ev's accuser and now his second secretary, was made both head of a new gorkom commission for the soviets and chairman of the Moskva fraction, and a party department was established for liaison with soviets. These changes raised morale in the Moskva group, but Prokof'ev was still on the sidelines and the delay had been costly: the Mossovet was making almost no law, locked as it was in its conflict with Popov.

In June 1991 the Moscow party organization flunked its third straight electoral test, the race for mayor. A Popov victory may have been inevitable, given his connection to Yeltsin, but the party worsened the odds by reliving some of the mistakes of 1989 and 1990. Prokof'ev begged off without explanation, saying in private that he could not win—true enough, as a poll in mid-May showed only 1 percent of Muscovites wanting him to be mayor—and could do more for Moscow by concentrating on his gorkom job and seat in the Politburo.[132] Shantsev showed no interest. The gorkom did not convene a plenum to nominate and send off any candidate. Rather, the bureau nine days before the election endorsed *three nominees*—the inexhaustible Bryachikhin and Saikin, and factory director Vladimir V. Klyuyev. Saikin would have received half as many votes again had those for Bryachikhin and Klyuyev gone his way, and the party would have looked less forlorn.[133]

One final time Prokof'ev had to apologize to the gorkom for an electoral fiasco: "The Communist Party was unable to put forward any kind of serious rival to the main candidates for president of Russia and mayor of Moscow. This is no coincidence. The party's ranks are divided and perplexed."[134]

Perplexity turned to panic, owing not only to the election but to two menacing actions by opponents and the intensification of one negative tendency. The first threat was Gavriil Popov's decision, outlined in mayoral directives July 5 and 10, 1991, to rejig the territorial basis of Moscow government (details in Chapter 8). The executive and bureaucratic machinery of the raions—though not, right away, their soviets—were to be phased out for ten large "administrative okrugs" (districts) and more than a hundred "municipal okrugs" and "territorial directorates" within them (see Map 39). The unelected "prefects" and "subprefects" in charge—the very terminology harked back to the glory days of the party apparatus—would report directly to the mayor.

The liquidation of the raions, and with them their names, many straight out of Communist scripture, took one more swipe at the party's symbols. It had practical consequences, for the raions had always been CPSU transmission belts and had about 80 percent of the party's Moscow staff and large holdings of real estate. Redistricting them had always been a party call. Popov threw that tradition out the window. In an unpublished side decree, he instructed city agencies to begin August 1 to evict raikoms from the raion office buildings claimed as city property by the Mossovet in May 1990, and after that to sell them by auction.

Prokof'ev got no response to a protest to Gorbachev. At the gorkom plenum of July 17, 1991—the last, as it turned out—he said the party would stick with the raions. But in a letter August 1 to Vladimir A. Ivashko, the CPSU's deputy general secretary, he asked for urgent action "to preserve the structures of the Moscow city and oblast party organizations." He requested authorization to incorpo-

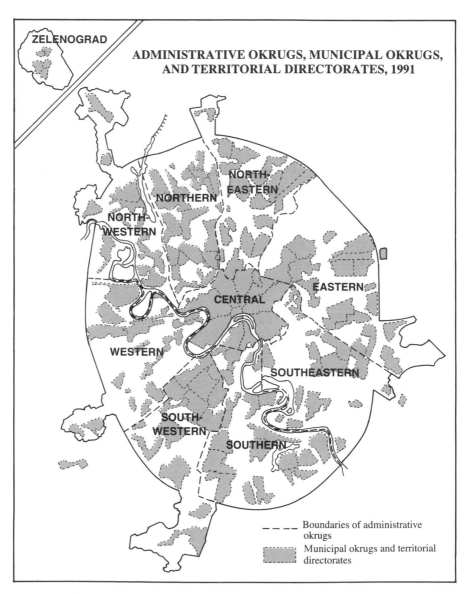

ZELENOGRAD

ADMINISTRATIVE OKRUGS, MUNICIPAL OKRUGS,
AND TERRITORIAL DIRECTORATES, 1991

NORTH-
EASTERN

NORTHERN

NORTH-
WESTERN

CENTRAL

EASTERN

WESTERN

SOUTHEASTERN

SOUTH-
WESTERN

SOUTHERN

- - - - Boundaries of administrative
okrugs

Municipal okrugs and territorial
directorates

MAP 39

rate a "commercial joint stock company" to which the gorkom and obkom would transfer "the balance of the basic resources of the party organs [of Moscow], with a value of 116.6 million rubles"—including, it seems, buildings, equipment, and bank accounts. The CC Secretariat agreed August 9. Prokof'ev would have gone ahead had he been given the chance.[135]

Russia's President Yeltsin tightened the vise in a decree dated July 23. He ruled that political parties—to all intents and purposes, the Communist Party—were forthwith to disband their organizations at places of work and could no longer carry on any activity during business hours. The *departizatsiya* edict pulped the broad base where the party had been recruiting, socializing, taxing, and disciplining members since the early 1900s.

The final cause for despair was a trend, not a unique event: the uncoordinated, headlong exodus of members from the party. Its ranks in the city of Moscow actually grew slowly until the beginning of 1990, to an apogee of about 1,160,000. A mere 1,000 Muscovites turned in their party cards in 1988; 3,000 did so in 1989. In the first five months of 1990 their numbers reached 14,000, and for 1990 as a whole 155,000; in the second half of 1990, departures were about 2 percent of the entire membership per month. For the last recorded interval, January through April 1991, 67,000 are reported to have withdrawn. By May 1, 1991, the 865,000 Communist Party members and candidates in Moscow were 295,000, or 25 percent, fewer than on January 1, 1990. Across the USSR the party lost approximately 20 percent during that same period.

A great many other Muscovites had withdrawn in all ways short of formal resignation. According to Shantsev, 128,000 Moscow Communists, roughly one in eight, were delinquent in their dues in January 1991, and "a lot of them have in fact lost all connection with the CPSU"; in some raions one-fourth to one-third of the membership neglected to pay up. Wastage was especially high among working-class Communists, whose membership share dropped 4 percent between January 1990 and May 1991. Party rolls declined by almost one-half in the Salyut jet engine plant and almost one-third in Krasnyi proletarii and the Komsomol Small Car Works.[136]

Figures like these led some in Moscow to speculate that the presidential rescript on cells in workplaces might have been superfluous.

"Let us look the truth in the eye," a columnist wrote about Yeltsin's disposition. "The CPSU is in agony . . . Maybe a decree is not needed, maybe everything will be decided of its own accord."[137] All "maybes" would vanish in a few weeks time.

COUP DE GRACE

In August 1991 a bid to turn back the political clock of the Soviet Union at gunpoint melted within sixty hours into a celebration on the sidewalks of Moscow of the values the plotters despised. A couple of days more and a coup d'état had resolved itself into a coup de grace for the Communist system.

Rumors had flown for months of a national crackdown, with or without Gorbachev. On June 17, 1991, "an acquaintance with access to the highest echelons" whispered to Mayor Popov that neo-Stalinists were about to declare martial law and turn all Soviet local administration over to the armed forces. Knowing he was tailed by the KGB, Popov thought it unwise to go straight to Gorbachev. He pondered calling a preemptive rally but concluded that "battles around the Kremlin would provide the excuse for introducing a state of emergency." He passed the tip to Yeltsin, who was on a state visit to Washington, via U.S. Ambassador Jack F. Matlock, Jr., and both Matlock and President George Bush notified Gorbachev. Gorbachev reined in his prime minister, Valentin S. Pavlov, and the danger momentarily passed.[138]

The shoe finally dropped during Gorbachev's summer vacation in the Crimea. When it did, the eight-man State Committee for Emergency Rule in the USSR that tried to usurp him introduced troops into the national capital, as most Praetorians have. At sunup Monday, August 19, armored vehicles of the Tamanskaya Motorized Rifle Division and Kantemirovskaya Tank Division of the Soviet Army rolled in from bases in Moscow oblast, as did the Twenty-seventh Brigade of the KGB's Special Forces from its barracks at Teplyi stan, in southwest Moscow. Their treads gouged asphalt softened by the summer heat. By noon T-80 tanks were idling at railroad stations, bridges, and government offices, pointing their turrets at the traffic, and KGB armored personnel carriers were in the Kremlin by early afternoon. The army soldiers, at least, bore light arms and instructions that they would be rounding up draft dodgers and stifling "provocations." They were joined over the next twenty-four hours by troops from the MVD's Dzerzhinskaya Motorized Rifle Division, paratroops from Tula and Ryazan, and units of the Vitebskaya Division of the KGB.[139]

The first decree of the emergency committee (GKChP, in its Russian initials) forbade protests and strikes anywhere in the USSR. Muscovites, nonetheless, had gathered by lunch hour at the "White House," the headquarters of the RSFSR on Krasnopresnenskaya naberezhnaya, and watched Yeltsin, in a bullet-proof vest, fulminate at the GKChP from atop a tank—the tableau that will be forever associated with him in the history books. Other citizens congregated on Tverskaya ulitsa between the Moscow Soviet and the Natsional' Hotel, blocking tanks with two pirated trolleybuses, and on Manezhnaya ploshchad', where protestors beat back an attempt to clear the square with water cannon. At 3:30 P.M. demonstrators began to build barricades out of paving stones, benches, trash bins, and building materials on the plaza in front of the White House. Soviet Vice-President Gennadii I. Yanayev then issued a special order for the GKChP to designate Nikolai V. Kalinin, the commander of the Moscow Military District, as military commandant of the city, citing "attempts to organize rallies, street marches, and demonstrations and to incite disorder."[140] General Kalinin imposed an 11:00 P.M. curfew Tuesday, August 20.

The show of firepower was not overwhelming. It has been estimated that at its height the GKChP deployed no more than 3 armored battalions in open positions and 500 KGB commandos, most of them in its Alpha Group, on high alert. At 4:00 P.M., August 20, 54 tanks and 74 other heavy vehicles shuttled among seventeen chokepoints in central Moscow. Up to 30,000 KGB troops and an untold number of infantrymen and airborne troops were kept in staging areas toward and beyond the MKAD, secluded from the population. Still, there is no question that the forces were adequate and that the GKChP could have called upon plenty more. Yeltsin himself says that the Russian White House, where he, his vice-president (and future enemy), Aleksandr V. Rutskoi, parliamentarians, and irregulars were holed up with 400 tommy guns, "could have been stormed by a single company."[141]

Exactly why the command to do so was not given may never be known. The disorganization that prevented the putschists from arresting Yeltsin at his dacha in Arkhangel'skoye-Yuzhnoye at the beginning of the adventure again reared its head. Guilty consciences kicked in, especially as the crowds grew and began to fraternize with the troops and "morally disarm" them. Situation reports to the White House resistors flowed from friendly army and KGB commanders.

A labyrinthine Moscow subplot went with the wider game. The KGB intended to arrest 7,000 Muscovites and preprinted 300,000 warrant forms. Vitalii M. Prilukov, the chief of the city and oblast directorate of the KGB, cut short senior staff's weekend leave Sunday afternoon and set up an "operational headquarters" to "oppose the diversionary and subversive activity of the adversary" Monday morning. He commanded officers to prepare for the mass arrests and to mingle with the crowds. Later that day plainclothes agents were sent into the group milling around the White House.[142]

Toward the city's elected government the GKChP took a double-tipped approach. It first tried naked repression. Seven of the seventy arrest warrants personally signed by KGB Chief Vladimir N. Kryuchkov the morning of August 19 were for Moscow political personages: Gavriil Popov, who would be back from a trip to Central Asia only that evening; Sergei Stankevich, the first deputy chairman of the soviet; Il'ya Zaslavskii, the chairman of the Oktyabr'skii raion soviet; Democratic Russia organizers Mikhail Shneider, Vladimir Bokser, and Arkadii Murashev; and Aleksandr Muzykantskii, now the prefect for the Central Administrative Okrug. Popov, Stankevich, Zaslavskii, and Murashev were also deputies in the USSR congress. None of the seven was among the handful the GKChP managed to detain.[143]

But the committee waved a carrot as well as the stick, in the hand of Yurii Prokof'ev of the CPSU gorkom. In the preceding months, pressed from the right within the Moscow party and exasperated with Gorbachev, Prokof'ev had been sounding the tocsin with conservatives, initiating two manifestos cosigned by the party committees of Great Patriotic War "hero cities." Though not in the hard core of the conspiracy—no serving party apparatchik was—he was well briefed on the planning and reportedly was one of the two members to proselytize for it at the Politburo's meeting of August 19. At the last meeting of the coup makers, on August 21, he would be, according to Yeltsin, in "hysterics" and would ask for a pistol so he could kill himself (which he did not do).[144]

Prokof'ev invited three Moscow statesmen that first day to throw in with the GKChP: Vice-Mayor Luzhkov, the acting mayor in Popov's absence; Boris V. Nikol'skii, a deputy of Luzhkov's; and Leonid A. Belov, a deputy chairman of the Mossovet and the alternate for the vacationing chairman Nikolai Gonchar.

Luzhkov was the first to be wooed. Prokof'ev suggested to him in a telephone conversation at 8:00 A.M., he recounted, "that I come to him for instructions." Luzhkov "answered that I was preparing to go to see Yeltsin. He [Prokof'ev] said that I would be sorry about this later."[145] Luzhkov's name was affixed to Kryuchkov's arrest list after this exchange.

Nikol'skii, a secretary of the Moscow gorkom under Viktor Grishin in the early 1980s, may have seemed a likelier bet to cave in. The only description we have of the sales pitch is from Popov: "Prokof'ev summoned Nikol'skii and suggested that he head up a [local] junta that had to be formed in Moscow. Nikol'skii replied that he had made his life's choice and categorically refused to participate in the affair."[146]

Belov should have been the softest target, being a military officer and a member of the Moskva fraction in the soviet and of the gorkom of the party. In Popov's telling, Prokof'ev sent for Belov "and demanded that [he] lead a presidium session about liquidating the mayoralty, liquidating the mayor's office, and so on. This the presidium of the Moscow Soviet completely ignored."

The intrigue around the Moscow leaders did not end with the attempts to suborn Luzhkov, Nikol'skii, and Belov. Gavriil Popov was convinced that he was about to be imprisoned on August 20. He told the Mossovet August 22 that only "thanks to efforts of the leadership of the Directorate of the KGB for Moscow and Moscow Oblast was the arrest of Yurii Mikhailovich [Luzhkov] and myself staved off" that day. We hear from other sources that the commanders of the directorate decided the evening of August 20 not to participate further in the putsch. The attempt to arrest Popov presumably preceded that decision, but we cannot say for certain. Nor can we be definite about the meaning of Popov's public thanks to General Prilukov for passing him "exceptionally valuable information" about goings-on, or about his failure to allude to Prilukov's pro-coup actions of August 18–19, which were surely known to him. Most likely, Popov was buying time until a decision about Prilukov could be made at higher levels. And soon it was: a week later Prilukov was relieved of his command on suspicion of collusion with the GKChP.[147]

In the regular Moscow police, Nikolai Myrikov, the latest commissioner, was made General Kalinin's martial law deputy August 20. He collaborated with the state of emergency. According to a published story, he dismissed the guard detail at the Moscow Soviet in the predawn of August 21, when an assault on the White House seemed imminent, so as to make its capture easier. Deputy Chairman Belov, setting aside doubts, agreed then and there to flee and form an "underground presidium" if the troops arrived, which they never did. Myrikov is also said to have acted with Prilukov to prevent cadets in police academies from coming to the White House siege scene. He, too, was fired when the dust settled, despite defending himself by saying he would have been arrested had he not complied. Even Vyacheslav Komissarov, the policeman the deputies had preferred to Myrikov as Moscow chief constable, is reported to have behaved questionably. By one account, he advised Popov not to fight arrest and gave him pointers on how to make himself comfortable in a jail cell.[148]

The GKChP also made overtures to Moscow oblast, where the 1990 elections had installed a government loyal to the obkom of the Communist Party. The chairman of the oblast soviet, Ivan M. Cherepanov, and other regional officials were promised "high posts in the new leadership of the country if . . . they would 'hand over' Moscow oblast." Cherepanov abstained on an anti-putsch vote in the soviet's presidium August 19; for this dereliction he was booted from office after the failure of the coup. About a third of the raion soviets in the oblast, more of the CPSU raikoms, and most district newspapers "directly or indirectly backed the GKChP."[149]

The deal making, back stabbing, and temporizing should not soil the valor of August 1991. Muscovites earned their places in the heroes' gallery. Members of the Mossovet, congregating at city hall August 19, walked in the first anti-coup demonstrations at midday, stuffing flowers in tank gun barrels in Manezhnaya ploshchad' and spray-painting graffiti on hoardings. Deputies Valerii Fadeyev of the city soviet and Ivan Novitskii and Dmitrii Chegodayev of the Oktyabr'skii raion soviet organized a teeming rally on Manezhnaya several hours later. Some deputies put up barricades at the RSFSR parliament and abutting streets. Father Aleksandr Borisov, the city representative from district 269, distributed hundreds of Bibles to the tank crews at the White House and its defenders. Acting Mayor Luzhkov released a curt condemnation of the GKChP for the administration that afternoon, asking Muscovites not to do its bidding.

With censorship of radio and television and the ban on most newspapers, it fell to the Moscow government to keep some lateral information channels open. Luzhkov was "a kind of anchor man on the telephone bank dealing with civilian Moscow,"[150] linking the Yeltsin team with local agencies and central ministries. By refusing to shut down Echo of Moscow, he gave the democratic forces their only radio outlet in central Russia during the tensest hours. Municipal workers were ordered to print and copy Boris Yeltsin's defiant decrees, and they and deputies were distributing them by 7:00 P.M. August 19, out the windows of the Moscow Soviet on Tverskaya. *Kuranty* put out a special issue Monday night, its 1,000 copies run off on a city Xerox machine. It did four more issues that week, one of them disguised as originating in the suburban town of Mytishchi, and printed several political pamphlets. Five locally controlled newspapers and magazines were among the eleven to join in the anti-coup paper *Obshchaya gazeta* (Common Gazette).

Mayor Popov gave a rousing speech outside city hall August 20 and joined the White House defense brigade that night. He cautioned the coup makers not to misgauge the Moscow populace. They had hoped, he speculated, to copy Poland in Eastern Europe, where martial law, imposed in 1981, prolonged the life of the regime. A more likely scenario was Romania in December 1989; there "the tanks went over to the people and a bloody massacre inflicted by the apparatus on the people was turned into the bombardment of the apparatus" and the execution by firing squad of President Nicolae Ceausescu. The only way for a gruesome outcome to be avoided, he said, was for the diehards to give up.[151]

Yeltsin in a public appearance August 20 thanked the capital for its support and expressed confidence "that in Democratic Moscow aggression [of troops against the democrats] will not happen." A snap phone poll that day found a mere 10 percent of Muscovites willing to say they fully or partly supported the GKChP, while 79 percent gave negative answers. If 72 percent agreed with the restoration of "basic order" in the USSR, 64 percent believed this could only be done by constitutional means and 59 percent felt the coup would sow "disorders and chaos."[152]

Although the great bulk of Muscovites did not externalize their discontent, enough of them took part with enough passion to make the bloodshed of which Popov spoke believable. The multitude before the White House wavered between 50,000 and 100,000; more than 100,000 may have heard Popov and other orators on Tverskaya on August 20. The throngs were almost always good-humored and self-policing. The only fatalities occurred when three young men—Dmitrii Komar, Il'ya Krichevskii, and Vladimir Usov—died in a firefight on the Sadovoye kol'tso in the wee hours of August 21.

The standoff at the White House stayed the coup committee's hand long enough for its resolve and hold on its agents to be shaken. The Tamanskaya Division was already wheeling out of the city when the trio were killed. A withdrawal of troops not based in Moscow began at 5:00 A.M. August 21. General Kalinin canceled the curfew and announced a speedup of the pullout that afternoon.[153] The barricades began to come down and the instigators to surrender, all except for Interior Minister Boris Pugo, who shot himself. President Gorbachev was back in Moscow by nightfall.

The three martyrs were buried Saturday, August 24. Popov and Gorbachev, hours away from stepping down as general secretary of the CPSU, eulogized them at a funeral meeting in Manezhnaya ploshchad'. Popov used the occasion to burnish Democratic Moscow's reputation. Muscovites' birthright, he said, was the opportunity "to be the first to take up the business of their people" in good times and bad. This last week, "Moscow has been preserved as the great city of Russia because in the decisive days it knew how to stand to the end."[154] He could be forgiven for puffing out his chest some.

THE IDOLS FALLEN

Despite Prokof'ev's machinations, the Moscow CPSU leadership stayed publicly silent during the putschists' two days in control. The gorkom's daily newspaper, *Moskovskaya pravda,* one of the nine in Moscow allowed to publish normally, accepted the coup but complained about certain aspects of it.[155] Several members of the gorkom urged Prokof'ev to call a plenum to adopt a position on the crisis. He declined, afraid the committee would cleave down the middle.

The afternoon of August 21, as the troops took to their billets, a meeting of bureau members and secretaries of the raikoms released the last ever public declaration of the Moscow CPSU. Stating that the GKChP's goals "cannot but evoke sympathy," it conceded that its methods had occasioned "concern and misunderstanding among the majority of the population." Party committees had been trying "to explain the real state of affairs" and "to preserve in this extreme situation the normal life rhythm of the city." The communiqué even-handedly condemned all "acts of confrontation" without recommend-ing the immediate retraction of martial law. Mostly it refuted "groundless accusations" of complicity in the putsch and asked mem-bers of the party "to carry out their civic duty at their places of work and not to participate in mass political actions."[156]

But mass political actions, abetted by politicians, erupted again and again over the next three days and exposed with laser clarity the party's loss of legitimacy. A carnival spirit seized Moscow on August 22, fed by news of the arrests of the coup leaders and the televising of proceedings of the RSFSR Supreme Soviet, at which Yeltsin jauntily initialed a presidential decree "suspending" the Communist Party on Russian soil until the coup could be investigated. The Mossovet also convened an extraordinary session. Mayor Popov briefed the deputies and was one of the first Russian leaders to call for what ensued—"na-tionalization of the property of the CPSU apparatus" and a settling up with the structures "that made the putsch possible."[157]

At 4:30 P.M., as the debate droned on, Popov took the law into his hands and signed a directive suspending the city and raion com-mittees of the party. The order, whose general clauses were redundant in light of Yeltsin's action that morning, declared that the gorkom's and raikoms' assets were forthwith to go over to the mayoralty for safekeeping until blame for the putsch could be affixed. Popov was aware that a crowd of several tens of thousands had made their way from the White House through Red Square to Staraya ploshchad', where they blocked the entrance to the Central Committee and tossed rocks through the gorkom's windows. Vasilii S. Shakhnovskii, the business manager of the Moscow executive branch, pulled up about 6:00 P.M. with Moscow and RSFSR deputies and a squad of city police and announced that the premises had been sealed and he was beginning an inventory of contents.[158]

Friday afternoon, August 23, Popov took the rasher step of asserting jurisdiction over the physical plant of the Central Committee. An executive order, read out by Prefect Muzykantskii, laid claim to the entire complex on Staraya ploshchad' and ordered it evacuated and sealed. Yurii Prokof'ev and his secretary for ideology, Lyudmila S. Vartazarova, were surrounded by demonstrators chanting his name as they exited the gorkom building, to which they had been readmitted that morning. Patrolmen and deputies rescued them from possible bodily harm and helped them into a taxicab. At 4:00 P.M. August 24, Popov ordered KGB sentries at the Central Committee replaced by a municipal commandant and constables. He was acting, he said, to prevent party workers from shredding archives and other records.[159]

Popov's demarche at Staraya ploshchad' came to naught. He was rebuffed, not by the CPSU but by Russia's president, who coveted the Central Committee quarters for himself. Popov and Muzykantskii took the position that the offices rightfully belonged to the city, since Moscow construction trusts had built them. Yeltsin showed what he thought of that view on August 30, after negotiations failed: armed RSFSR troops evicted the city commandant from the CC building. Within days Russian ministries moved desks and filing cabinets into the suites.[160]

The August days were to provide yet more galvanic testimony to a transfer of power. On Thursday, August 22, the crowd that had besieged Staraya ploshchad', swelling to some 50,000, surged the four blocks to the Lubyanka and daubed swastikas and slogans on the main KGB building. The staff inside had armed themselves and plugged entranceways and corridors. This defensive posture and the urgings of city officials, dispatched by Popov, staved off a run at the offices. Anger fixated on the fifteen-ton bronze statue of Dzerzhinskii, the father of the Soviet police state, on the traffic island in the square (see Figure 71). Demonstrators put a cardboard dunce's cap on its head and tried to rock it off its feet with wire hawsers until Muzykantskii and Sergei Stankevich persuaded them that the falling metal might cause fatalities or crush the ceiling of the subway station below. Under blazing television lights, several of city hall's mobile building cranes waded in, but even they could not handle the statue's mass. At about

Figure 71. Dismounting of Dzerzhinskii statue in front of Lubyanka, August 1991. (Reuters/Bettmann.)

11:00 P.M., to hurrahs from the audience, three imported Krupp cranes lifted "Iron Feliks" onto a flatbed. As Muscovites, drunk and sober, chipped flakes from the granite base for souvenirs, fireworks went off over the old town.

Toppled that same week were three more major monuments: to Mikhail Kalinin, at the foot of the former prospekt Kalinina; to Yakov Sverdlov, facing the Bol'shoi Theater; and to Pavlik Morozov, the teenager who entered the Soviet pantheon by tattling on his parents during collectivization, at the Krasnopresnenskii Children's Park. They, and most of a dozen or so minor mementos, were also taken down by municipal work gangs in hardhats, tightly supervised by high-placed officials. The city carted them to a Garden of Sculptures of the Epoch of Totalitarianism opened on the grounds of the New Tret'yakov Gallery August 31.

Institutional symbols also fell. Mayor Popov, called "the most eminent ideologist among the new administrators" in Russia by the historian Leonid M. Batkin,[161] laid claim three weeks after the August days to the tallest skyscraper in Moscow, the thirty-one-story home of the defunct Council for Mutual Economic Assistance (CMEA, the agency for Soviet–East European trade) next to the White House. From there, he fired off reform directives and appeared in his signature baggy suit and sweater in almost nightly interviews on Russian television. Popov had the satisfaction in September 1991 of seeing two of his associates from the democratic movement put at the head of the capital's political and regular police forces. Yevgenii A. Sevast'yanov, the head of his mayoral staff, was on his recommendation appointed chief of the Moscow KGB; a second Moscow DR leader, Arkadii Murashev, took over the Moscow militia, returned from USSR to RSFSR and local subordination. And Popov's deputy, Luzhkov, was from August to November one of the four members of the Committee for Operational Management of the Economy, the panel that directed the central government as Gorbachev tried in vain to patch the Soviet Union together.

The entity at the intersection of all vectors in Moscow politics for seventy years—the local apparatus of the Communist Party—was put on the organizational scrap heap with no more decorum than the statues. The party as a whole was living on borrowed time, as was the Soviet Union that it had baled together. President Yeltsin exterminated it outright by decree on November 6, 1991. Mikhail Gorbachev resigned as USSR president and the Soviet federation went out of business on December 25, 1991. The Russian red, white, and blue tricolor flew over the Kremlin as of 7:35 P.M. that day. Yeltsin took over Gorbachev's Kremlin office the next morning.

The Moscow party organs' expiry was rich in bathos. Yurii Prokof'ev, his deputy's immunity to prosecution waived by the Mossovet August 22, was interrogated by the police. Although he avoided indictment, his reputation was left in tatters. The gorkom lost its press mouthpiece August 27, as *Moskovskaya pravda*'s board registered it as an independent newspaper and replaced Valerii Lysenko with Shod Muladzhanov as editor-in-chief.[162] Prokof'ev at first hand-sorted office files at Staraya ploshchad', without electricity or telephone service, which had been disconnected by city hall. In early September he was relegated to several rooms, with two telephones, at 4 ulitsa Ar-khipova. His skeleton staff shrunk to thirty by month's end, all occu-pied with finding employment for themselves and other apparatchiks.

The gorkom secretaries tried without success to convoke a plenum at the close of the coup week. On ulitsa Arkhipova, they managed an improvised meeting in the courtyard; it took no decisions. The rump apparatus would have run out of money for salaries by November 10 had not the decree by Yeltsin put it out of its misery. An order by Yurii Luzhkov on November 22 confiscated all bank accounts, build-ings, commercial subsidiaries, and other possessions of the now "for-mer" gorkom and raikoms.[163]

The democratizing revolution that reached a crescendo in Moscow and Russia in the August days shattered in a half-decade a mold the Communist Party had taken seven decades to make and fortify. Ironi-cally, the opposition alliance that waylaid the partocracy had one foot planted inside the party itself.

Real and estimable as the turnabout was, it was also incomplete. There were moments when it might have gone much further than it did, and conceivably have taken an ugly turn. Popov wrote later of having had to contend in August 1991 with Muscovites and out-of-towners "spoiling for action to prove how ready they were to fight for democracy." Political liberals were joined on the street, he said, by thrill seekers, looters, and former KGB stool pigeons who wanted to invade the Lubyanka to seize records of their past treacheries. Without Boris Yeltsin's support, Popov stated, "I as mayor could never have blunted the 'revolutionary' ire of the masses." He was proud that he and the president "rejected the idea of turning the victory over the GKChP into a global purge of the previous system, into a revolution of the Leninist type," replete in "pogroms and anarchy."[164] Herein lies another irony: at their very minute of triumph, the main pacifiers of the situation were the self-professed democratic governments themselves. Semiotic acts such as the sealing of CPSU buildings and the dismounting of statues halted mass spontaneity as much as they swiped at the past.

The democratic initiation drew to an end the *disjointed monism* exhibited by city government throughout the Soviet era. It did not, however, introduce the *democratic pluralism* that would be its negation. Monism yielded, not to a well-buffered pluralism, with crosscutting cleavages among socially grounded interests and mutual restraint, but to a postauthoritarian free-for-all in which many interests went unrepresented. And disjointed coordination among bureaucratic agencies was replaced, not by majority rule exercised through legitimate institutions but by a ferile struggle for power and control in which responsiveness to public wishes was of secondary concern. The hard work of building a post-socialist metropolis was just beginning.

8

Toward a Post-Socialist
Metropolis

FROM the onset of competitive politics to the consolidation of
democratic governance there runs, as Adam Przeworski says, a
mined path.[1] The booby traps on it have been as plethoric in proto-
democratic Moscow as anywhere in Russia or Eastern Europe.

Dzerzhinskii's statue and the insignia of Communist Party domination have been easier to dismantle than procrustean organizations
and mentalities, and the fit between legacies and new facts lacks
resolution. Successor institutions take root but haltingly, amidst acrid
debate over their anatomy. Elites play inconclusive roles, as old hands
from the nomenklatura dig themselves in and leaders cast up on the
democratizing wave sometimes prove themselves unworthy. The
philosophical rupture with the state socialist paradigm has not kept
fundamental reform of practice from coming in squirts and spasms,
the modalities from being bruisingly contested, or the standard of
living of the population from deteriorating. Almost everything in
transitional politics is up for grabs.

Chapter 8 deals in its opening part with the coalition making and
confrontations that have accompanied Moscow's jerky steps toward
post-socialist stability. Next I discuss the dynamics of reconstituting
metropolitan institutions. In a third section I treat public policy
choices and the vortex of "capitalist reconstruction" in the city that
once flew the pennant of "socialist reconstruction." After a fourth

section about the challenge of civility and civic community, I offer brief concluding reflections on Moscow and Russia's future.

The Minefield of Democratic Consolidation

Democratic Russia and the *anti*-Communist coalition arrayed around it, like inclusive opposition fronts in many other democratizing countries, could not recast itself as a cohesive *post*-Communist coalition in Russia and Moscow, and for that reason did not long outlast its victim. It fissured every which way and was riven by crises that came to a head in the tragic clash of September–October 1993, one more drama in the country's politics to be acted out in downtown Moscow. That trauma eventuated in a coerced restructuring of local representative bodies and an air-clearing municipal election that carried city politics into the mid-1990s on more or less the trajectory it had been on since the flameout of perestroika.

THE ANTI-COMMUNIST COALITION UNRAVELS

The alliance that bested the CPSU broke its teeth on three issues. The first, a matter of style and temperament, pitted instinctive "agitators" (in Harold Lasswell's typology), mired in the mode of moral outrage and direct action, against the democrats' "administrators," who comfortably worked the levers of the state.

Gavriil Popov at his peak in 1991 struck many as the very model of the latter. Leonid Batkin went so far as to ruminate that "the Command System which in its day G. Kh. Popov delineated so well [in his writings] . . . may be regenerating" in Moscow—in, he said drily, "a Completely New Democratic Form." But Batkin did not know how out of his element the academic-turned-politico felt. As Popov said sheepishly later, he had prepared himself only "to be mayor in a society commanded by the CPSU," where he would be "standing up for Muscovites' interests in a regime that did not need me to function." After the implosion of the Communist Party, "I became mayor in a whole other sense: boss of everything and everyone. I was not ready for such a role."[2] Most of the deputies elected in 1990 were agitators, and Popov was perhaps a hybrid sort; Popov's vice-mayor and successor, Yurii Luzhkov, and Boris Yeltsin in the

Kremlin were congenital administrators. Tension between the psychological types bedeviled the democratic camp.

Conflict broke out, second, over policy content. Democratic politicians differed from the 1990 elections forward over how best to reorder socialistic governmental, economic, and social systems. The very heterogeneity and cloudiness of program that gave the democrats advantages at the polls converted into laming disadvantages once they took office. The demise of the CPSU eliminated their common foil and opened up fresh areas of disagreement. Popov, for example, felt entitled as capital-city mayor to ply Yeltsin with advice after August 1991—urging him to summon a constitutional convention, delay economic "shock therapy," hold new provincial and local elections, and keep Russia in a Soviet confederation. When the president and his acting prime minister, Yegor T. Gaidar, snubbed this counsel, Popov threatened to resign and then did so on June 6, 1992, one year into his term.[3]

In the local arena contradictions over global issues were compounded by divisions over municipal policy, in particular the Popov-Luzhkov government's economic stabilization program and plans for rapid privatization of city housing and commercial assets. The group structure of the Moscow Soviet best illustrates the centrifugal tendencies among the democrats of 1990–1991.

More than 90 percent of the Mossovet deputies sorted themselves at the maiden session of the soviet in April 1990 into four groupings: the majority Democratic Russia Bloc, the Moskva Group of Communist Party loyalists, and the smaller Independents and Otechestvo (Fatherland) factions (see Table 22). The fractions allowed within the DR bloc grew in number and independence as its strength dwindled to 202 members by December 1990.[4] Otechestvo had dissipated by that time, and the blocs and groups in the soviet had increased to fourteen. But one of these caucuses (the Initiative Fraction) operated within the DR Bloc; six others—Democratic Platform (soon to redeploy as the Republican Party), Democratic Party of Russia, Sodruzhestvo (Concord), Voters' Clubs, Liberals, and Greens—stayed close in outlook to Democratic Russia, and many of their deputies held dual memberships. Only 12.7 percent of the deputies were outside the group structure.

The Mossovet lineup, substantially the same in April 1991,

Table 22. Membership of deputies' groups in the Moscow Soviet, 1990–1992

Group	Full Moscow Soviet				Small Soviet
	April 1990 (N = 472)	December 1990 (N = 472)	April 1991 (N = 472)	February 1992 (N = c. 460)[a]	February 1992 (N = 99)
Democratic Russia Bloc (Fraction)[b]	292	202	204	63	22
Moskva Group	94	81	82	44	9
Independents Group	35	49	49	23	5
Otechestvo (Fatherland) Group	10	NA	NA	NA	NA
Republican Party of Russia	NA	NA	37	24	6
Democratic Platform Group	NA	26	26	NA	NA
Sodruzhestvo (Concord) Group	NA	25	24	NA	NA
Voters' Clubs Group	NA	23	23	NA	NA
Initiative Fraction of Democratic Russia Bloc	NA	21	21	NA	NA
Liberal Fraction	NA	13	13	10	3
Greens Group (Fraction)[c]	NA	13	13	8	3
Democratic Party of Russia	NA	12	12	7	1
Moscow Lefts Fraction	NA	6	6	6	1
Fraction of Christian Democratic Union of Russia	NA	4	4	2	1
Christian Democratic Fraction	NA	3	3	4	3

Konsolidatsiya (Consolidation) Fraction	NA	2	2	NA	NA
Vozrozhdeniye (Rebirth) Fraction	NA	NA	NA	7	2
Constitutional Democratic Party	NA	NA	NA	5	3
Fraction of Labor	NA	NA	NA	14	5
Social Democratic Party of Russia	NA	NA	NA	4	0
People's Party of Free Russia	NA	NA	NA	12	6
Union of Communists Fraction	NA	NA	NA	5	2
Not in any group	c. 40	60	Unknown	252	39

Sources: For the first column, press reports of group totals. For the remaining columns, listings of individual members supplied by the Moscow Soviet.

Note: NA = not applicable.

a. Exact size unclear, because some deputies had become inactive without formally resigning their mandates.

b. Renamed Democratic Russia Fraction in 1991.

c. Renamed Greens Fraction in 1991.

changed dramatically by February 1992, six months after the putsch and one month into the Yeltsin-Gaidar economic reform. DR (now a fraction, not a bloc) had lost two-thirds of its members and made up a mere 13.7 percent of the council. Five of the 1991 fractions had gone belly up, eight of the ten survivors had shriveled, and six midget fractions had arisen. About 55 percent of the active deputies did not belong to any group—evidence of political dealignment, not mere realignment. Dealignment was most pronounced among the deputies elected on the Democratic Russia ticket (see Table 23). Already in

Table 23. Percent of Moscow Soviet deputies affiliated with deputies' groups, 1990–1992, by slate on which elected in 1990[a]

	Slate on which deputy elected in 1990			
Affiliation	Dem. Russia (N = 282)	Right (N = 12)	Center (N = 19)	None (N = 150)
December 1990				
Number of groups				
1	62.4	100.0	84.2	80.0
2	24.8	0.0	0.0	4.0
None	12.8	0.0	15.8	16.0
Specific groups				
Democratic Russia	60.6	0.0	0.0	18.0
Moskva	2.1	8.3	73.7	40.0
Independents	2.5	91.7	10.5	19.3
Other	46.8	0.0	0.0	10.7
February 1992				
Number of groups				
1	36.2	41.6	52.6	40.7
2	7.8	33.3	0.0	2.0
None	56.0	25.0	47.4	57.3
Specific groups				
Democratic Russia	21.3	0.0	5.3	0.7
Moskva	2.3	0.0	42.1	20.0
Independents	1.4	50.0	5.3	8.0
Other	27.0	58.3	0.0	14.0

a. Includes the 463 deputies elected in the first round and runoff elections in March 1990. Nine other deputies were selected later.

December 1990, 12.8 percent of them did not belong to a deputies' group. By February 1992, more than half, 56.0 percent, were unaffiliated (just 1 percent more than deputies elected without anyone's endorsement in 1990), and only 21.3 percent participated in the Democratic Russia Fraction.

If the first two sources of conflict had a scattering effect, the third—institutional interest—polarized the democrats. It drove a wedge between the legislative and executive branches of local government.

No sooner had the Westernizing democrats risen to power in the folkish soviets than, like the Bolsheviks in their day, they set about subverting them. Gavriil Popov, still Mossovet chairman, proposed in a searching essay in a national magazine in December 1990 that the soviets be recognized as "no less incompetent than the economic system of socialism" and that Russian government be "de-sovietized." Their dysfunctionality could no longer be masked now that the party was coming undone: "Under the CPSU, the real administrative power of the party stood behind the facade, and the decorations moved and did something. Under the democrats, there is no firm administrative hierarchy behind the decorative soviets, and the motions of the decorations accomplish nothing." Not accomplishing anything did not, in Popov's reading, mean that the elected soviets were idle. Far from it, they engaged in "daily nursemaiding, verging on daily terrorizing" of all other actors.[5]

Popov's critique, though self-serving, made a broader point. The Mossovet, manumitted from the party apparatus, still had almost 500 members sitting in a dozen or more factions, with no governing majority. Two-thirds of them utilized the option of taking leave from permanent jobs and drawing pay from the city. Partly for this reason and partly as a corrective to the perfunctoriness of the past, their deliberations were marathons; the soviet met for twenty weeks in its first year.

The time and energy on deputies' hands outpaced their information and their lawmaking prerogatives. That mismatch, and the giddy atmosphere of the times, elicited posturing for the TV cameras and incendiary oratory about extraneous issues. As early as June 1990 Sergei Stankevich lamented that members' immaturity was "leading to waste of time, a refusal to hear one's opponent out, a tendency to hop ahead in thought and verbalize it as quickly as possible." So far, the soviet resembled "not an institution of power but an unruly get-together in which there is lots of struggle but far less real work."[6] While Stankevich criticized this "style of the street rally," a better analogy might be to the intelligentsia political clubs of the late 1980s, where points accrued for the number of speeches made. Conduct off the council floor could be obnoxious, as the 1991 hunger strike over appointment of a chief of police showed. The organizer of that caper, Yurii P. Sedykh-Bondarenko, was chosen a deputy chairman by the soviet in June 1991. Allies in the raions—like the head of the Krasnopresnenskii soviet, Aleksandr V. Krasnov, or Sergei P. Pykhtin of the Cheremushkinskii council, who was also a Democratic Russia deputy in the Mossovet—resorted to civil disobedience to try to nullify city actions.

Popov hoped institution of a separately elected mayor would answer to the incapacity of the city soviet. But the deed was done hurriedly in May and June 1991 and without consensus on mayoral powers. Popov warned of rough water ahead:

> Arguments between the Mossovet and the mayor are inescapable, and they are all to the good if they protect both sides from mistakes. But unfortunately the position presently taken by deputies in the soviet is not about the kinds of arguments natural to a democracy. The problem now is that there are various views as to the role of the mayor. If the situation does not change, if agreement is not reached, then there will be no escaping a prolonged conflict between the Mossovet and the mayor . . . I do not want, in case I am elected, to be the mayor who wages war with the Mossovet and its deputies.[7]

"War" is not too strong a word for the interbranch acrimony that ensued. The Mossovet and, after January 1992, the Small Soviet, the standing subcouncil selected by it, adopted dozens of resolutions challenging Popov's reorganizations and took their brief to the public, the government of Russia, and in several instances the procuracy and the courts. Mayor and council adopted discrepant edicts on economic reform. "How much more," one pundit asked in late 1991, "do Muscovites have to put up with these decisions, decrees, and programs, spraying like a fountain from an abundance of sources, supposedly mandatory but in reality contradictory?"[8] They did not let up even after Popov's resignation in June 1992. By 139 votes to 84, the Mossovet voted nonconfidence in Yurii Luzhkov and appealed for a new mayoral election by the end of the year. When Luzhkov demurred, there was talk of retracting the mayoralty, the prefects, and all of the organizational innovations of 1991.

BLACK OCTOBER

Events in national politics blasted Moscow government out of this morass. A brouhaha drawing on the same essential causes developed there between President Yeltsin and the legislative arm, marshaled by Chairman Ruslan I. Khasbulatov and by Yeltsin's renegade vice-president, Aleksandr Rutskoi. Slower to build than its Moscow microcosm, this conflict acquired explosive force in 1992–1993.

On September 21, 1993—the date delayed two days to avoid associations with August 19, 1991—Boris Yeltsin carried out a presidential coup by proroguing the Russian Congress of People's Deputies and Supreme Soviet and ordering elections held for a substitute Federal Assembly. A quorum of the parliament refused to comply, passed a resolution impeaching him and making Rutskoi president, and barricaded themselves in the Moscow White House. After a day of murderous pandemonium there, on the Sadovoye kol'tso, and at the Ostankino Television Tower, Yeltsin on Sunday, October 3, imposed a state of emergency in Moscow and ordered in armor and troops, including most of the army and MVD regiments deployed in the putsch of 1991. The next morning tanks and SWAT teams quelled the parliamentarians and their heavily armed guard; 300 of them were convoyed from the smoke-licked White House to Lefortovo Prison. The official toll in Moscow's "Black October" was 145 dead and 733 wounded. It was by far the city's worst public carnage since October of 1917.

Jousting among Russia's political titans as usual took place in Moscow. Few Muscovites accepted Yegor Gaidar's televised invitation Sunday evening to "defend democracy" with their bodies, but violence would probably have billowed had the tanks not intervened. The first target of the anti-Yeltsin mob October 3 was the Moscow mayoralty, housed in the former CMEA tower next to the White House. About fifty ruffians smashed its glass doors with truck bumpers and rushed up the stairs, where they roughed up employees, killing two of them, and set two floors ablaze. Deputy Premier Aleksandr Braginskii was held hostage in handcuffs for eight hours as the battle raged.[9]

The city administration served as a lightning rod because it had always been unqualifiedly aligned with Yeltsin. Mayor Luzhkov sat in on Yeltsin's councils of war, concurred in all of his edicts and ultimatums, cut off the encircled White House's electricity and water, was one of three government agents at last-minute talks brokered by Patriarch Aleksii II at the Danilov Monastery, demanded strict punishment after the deputies' capitulation, and used local constables and vigilante groups to close offending newspapers. Ten Moscow policemen perished in the fighting.

Many city lawmakers lined up on the other side. Chairman Nikolai Gonchar of the Mossovet tried to mediate with Rutskoi; after that flopped, he stayed out of sight. Extremist deputies took action as individuals and small groups, since Gonchar would not convoke the soviet and its building was under guard. Deputy Chairman Sedykh-Bondarenko led several stone-throwing disturbances, and Viktor I. Anpilov, elected in 1990 on the Bloc of Public and Patriotic Movements slate, commanded a thuggish paramilitary group at the White House. According to fragmentary reports, deputies from the Sverdlovskii and Krasnopresnenskii raion soviets distributed firearms to protestors. At 6:00 P.M., October 3, following the occupation of the mayor's chambers, Aleksandr Rutskoi, in his most wild-eyed pronouncement—summoning the crowd to take the Kremlin by storm—gave notice that he had "appointed" the Krasnopresnenskii chairman, Aleksandr Krasnov, as mayor of Moscow in Luzhkov's place. Several hours later about fifteen Mossovet deputies were arrested; police beat one of them, Boris Kagarlitskii, elected as a DR candidate in 1990 but now leader of the Moscow Socialist Workers' Party.[10]

Although violent ultras were a minority in the Moscow-area soviets, mutual suspicion and fear of their potential for rallying resistance made them targets of swift suppression. Yeltsin on October 4 ordained Luzhkov's government the sole martial-law authority in Moscow and "suspended" until further notice the activities of the city and raion soviets. The mayor, whose frustrations with the Mossovet went back to 1990, upped the ante October 6: without any legal crutch whatever, he declared the soviets of Moscow permanently disbanded. He was, he said, "doing away with a loathsome creature" that would forever have held the metropolis back. He further directed that a new council with an old name—Moscow City Duma—be elected December 12, the day of the Russia-wide balloting. Yeltsin seconded him in one decree October 7 and another October 24, which also compelled election of a Moscow Oblast Duma; that same week, Yeltsin prescribed reformation of all Russian local governments over the next eight months.[11]

The failure to find middle ground and the opportunistic quashing of duly elected councils did not bode well for community democracy in Moscow. Nor can comfort be taken from the incidental use of raw police power against citizens whose misdeeds had no relation to the political warfare. The city's military commandant remarked that the presence of extra troops and heavy weaponry provided a chance "to liquidate as many breeding grounds as possible of criminal 'infection'" in the capital. In addition to detaining 37,000 for violation of curfew before the emergency was canceled October 18, the police and army deported almost 10,000 persons from public places and apartment houses for not having valid residence papers.[12]

FROM BULLETS TO BALLOTS

The parliamentary election of December 12, 1993, two months after the shootout, brought a bone-weary truce to Russian politics. Although conservatives and ultranationalists fared much better than expected, Yegor Gaidar's Russia's Choice Movement, the remnants of Democratic Russia at its core, returned the biggest delegation to the Federal Assembly, and the population concurrently ratified an executive-centered draft constitution. In one of its first acts the lower house (the State Duma) granted amnesty to the perpetrators of the rebellions of both August 1991 and October 1993.

Moscow's sideshow municipal election settled local accounts for the moment. Like the countrywide campaign, it exemplified "democracy by design": conducted under duress, hurriedly, and by rules written to serve the government's purposes of electing friendly deputies and fostering party formation.[13] To make the duma a more businesslike body than the soviet, it was to be limited to thirty-five full-time deputies, chosen in districts within the administrative okrugs. Nominations were permitted from residential groups and registered "electoral formations" (parties or coalitions of parties) but not from workplaces. Parties could have no more than one candidate per district, precluding the duplication common in 1990, and it was a further boon to them that nominees had to submit four thousand signatures of voters from their districts in order to qualify. Winners were to be determined on a simple plurality basis, with no runoff and with the turnout requirement dropped to 25 percent.[14]

Adherents of the quasi-parties had been but 31.6 percent of the field of aspirants in March 1990, vastly outnumbered by independents. In 1993 this ratio was more than reversed, as 73.9 percent of the nominees formally represented a political party.

Five of the thirteen parties in the 1993 national race laid slates before the Moscow electorate. The fulsomely pro-Yeltsin Russia's Choice ran in all but three districts, while a trio of moderately reformist groups had smaller rosters: PRES (the Party of Russian Unity and Accord), a new party emphasizing regional issues; RDDR (the Russian Movement for Democratic Reforms), the descendant of an association founded by Gavriil Popov in 1991; and Citizens for Popular Sovereignty, supporters of the Yabloko (Yavlinskii-Boldyrev-Boldin) list Russia-wide. The only right-leaning ticket was from the Moscow chapter of Civic Union, a group consisting largely of industrialists which had been losing influence for a year. The two most muscular reactionary parties—the Communist Party of the Russian Federation (KPRF), the Russian successor to the CPSU started up in 1993, and the misnamed Liberal-Democratic Party of Russia (LDPR), led by the chauvinist Vladimir V. Zhirinovskii—chose to sit out the Moscow ballot.

Compared to the stunning election less than four years before, this municipal contest was low-key. The 161 candidates, less than 5 percent of the 1990 total, averaged 4.6 per district, one-third fewer than in 1990. With a mean age of forty-two, they were three years younger than in 1990, and born six years later; about 6 percent more were female, although women remained woefully underrepresented (see Table 24). Two-thirds resided in the electoral district in which they were running, 10 percent more than the candidates in 1990 who dwelt in the same city raion. One in five had been members of the last Mossovet.

In class terms, blue-collar workers (1.9 percent of the contestants) were even rarer birds than in 1990. Twenty percent of the candidates were again core public administrators, but there were also significant departures. The intelligentsia and engineers who accounted for 34.8 percent of the 1990 candidates were down to 15 percent in 1993, and production managers in state or quasi-privatized enterprises were down to 4 percent from 13.5 percent. The slack was taken up by four other white-collar groups whose joint share trebled to 49.4 percent: managers and professionals in services, leaders of voluntary associations, private entrepreneurs, and elective politicians (mainly full-time deputies from the local soviets). The third and fourth of these categories had not existed in 1990, and the second was barely present.[15]

The national campaign was waged chiefly on the airwaves. City duma candidates had to depend on word of mouth and on posters and handbills, which I observed to be in incredibly short supply compared to March 1990. The fire-and-brimstone rhetoric of the foregoing election was also scarce, as contenders gave primacy to socioeconomic issues, crime, and local governmental structure.[16] Russia's Choice emphasized cooperation between the duma and the mayor and the charms of privatization. RDDR had a murky message on "social partnership." Civic Union's selling cards were corruption fighting and income maintenance. Citizens for Popular Sovereignty gave the most play to ecological problems, while PRES advocated mayoral responsiveness, free medical care, and crime control.

The radical democrats in Russia's Choice, who also did exceptionally well in the national balloting in Moscow,[17] prevailed, capturing nineteen of the thirty-five seats in the city duma and outpolling all other parties (see Table 25). Civic Union bagged only three seats, while the moderate reformist groups got five among them and independents eight. The draw of Russia's Choice by district—from 10.2 percent in district 8 to 31.7 percent in district 28—shows some correspondence with Democratic Russia's strength in 1990, although with numerous anomalies (see Map 40). Three of its top five districts were in Moscow southwest, where DR excelled, and another (district 14) was around Izmailovo, in the northeast, where democrats had done well since 1989. Personalities and neighborhood issues clearly played a role. Russia's Choice's worst performance was in district 8, near the Northern TETS, where residents were enraged at the resumption of construction of the station; the party fielded no candidate in district 9, abutting the TETS, and in adjacent district 12 it did miser-

Table 24. Some characteristics of the 1993 candidates by slate (percent)

Characteristic	Russia's Choice (N = 32)	Moscow Civic Union (N = 31)	PRES (N = 18)	RDDR (N = 17)	Citizens for Popular Sovereignty (N = 21)	None (N = 42)[a]	All candidates (N = 161)[a]
			Slate				
Age under 40[b]	40.6	58.1	33.3	28.3	23.8	26.8	36.9
Women	21.9	6.5	11.1	11.8	23.8	19.0	20.5
Residence in same electoral district[c]	62.5	64.5	55.6	70.6	66.7	75.6	66.9
On 1990 Moscow Soviet	28.1	19.4	38.9	11.8	14.3	11.9	19.9
Occupational group							
Faculty member or researcher	21.9	9.7	11.1	11.8	0.0	4.9	10.0
Media/arts figure	3.1	3.2	0.0	11.8	23.8	2.4	6.2
Manager in production sector	9.4	0.0	5.6	11.8	0.0	2.4	4.4
Core public administrator	21.9	3.2	33.3	11.8	14.3	29.3	19.4
Elective politician	15.6	19.4	33.3	0.0	4.8	7.3	13.1
Engineer or technical specialist	3.1	12.9	0.0	0.0	4.8	4.9	5.0

Manager or professional in service sector	9.4	9.7	16.7	17.6	19.0	24.4	16.3
Employee of voluntary association	9.4	32.3	0.0	23.5	9.5	19.5	16.9
Private entrepreneur	0.0	0.0	0.0	11.8	4.8	4.9	3.1
Other white-collar	0.0	0.0	0.0	0.0	0.0	0.0	0.0
Blue-collar worker	3.1	3.2	0.0	0.0	4.8	0.0	1.9
Miscellaneous	3.1	6.5	0.0	0.0	14.3	0.0	3.8

a. No information except gender and incumbency is available on one incumbent candidate.

b. Average year of birth 1951 for all candidates, 1948 for PRES, 1949 for Citizens for Popular Sovereignty, 1950 for Russia's Choice and independent candidates, and 1955 for Moscow Civic Union.

c. Uses home addresses obtained from Moscow Electoral Commission.

Table 25. The 1993 election results

Slate	Candidates	Deputies elected	Percent of total votes received	Percent of votes in districts contested
Russia's Choice	32	19	19.6	21.5
Moscow Civic Union	31	3	11.5	13.2
PRES	18	2	7.3	14.4
RDDR	17	2	5.6	11.6
Citizens for Popular Sovereignty	21	1	7.0	11.8
Independent candidates	42	8	18.5	25.3
Voted against all candidates	NA	NA	30.5	30.5

Note: NA = not applicable.

ably, too. Russia's Choice also stayed out of district 22, containing the unhappy Brateyevo area, while in the adjoining district 23 it drew its second lowest vote total.[18]

Information for microanalysis of the municipal election is not available, but preelection survey data gathered for the national campaign provide a snapshot of the general state of mind of post-Soviet Moscow. Table 26 tallies voters in a random citywide sample who had already decided to support Russia's Choice, one of the three moderate reformist parties that participated locally (PRES, RDDR, and Yabloko), or one of the two authoritarian populist alternatives, the Communists or Liberal-Democrats.[19]

Socioeconomic status, at least for Russia's Choice and Zhirinovskii's LDPR, is predictive of Muscovites' political orientation: the more educated the voter and the more prestigious his or her work, the more likely the vote for the radical democrats.[20] A second association links policy attitudes. Voters who strongly approved of Yeltsin and favored a rapid transition to the market went for Russia's Choice. The moderate parties found the greatest resonance among those with in-between positions on Yeltsin and the market; among deep-dyed conservatives, the two authoritarian parties together outpoll the moderates by about 50 percent and Russia's Choice by several times over. Personal and family welfare also show a correlation. Almost 60 percent of Muscovites whose economic situation was much improved over a year before were partial to Russia's Choice, and almost 20

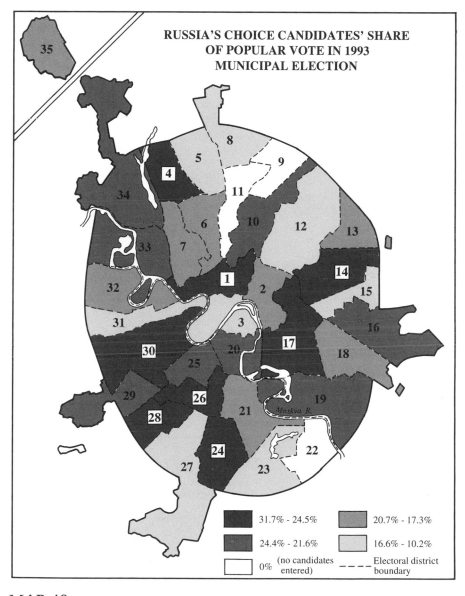

RUSSIA'S CHOICE CANDIDATES' SHARE
OF POPULAR VOTE IN 1993
MUNICIPAL ELECTION

31.7% - 24.5%   20.7% - 17.3%

24.4% - 21.6%   16.6% - 10.2%

0%   (no candidates   Electoral district
       entered)   boundary

MAP 40

Table 26. Some factors associated with support for national parties among Moscow voters, November–December 1993

Factor	Percent intending to vote for party[a]			
	Russia's Choice	Moderate reformers[b]	LDPR	KPRF
Education				
Higher	46.3	25.3	5.3	5.8
Elementary or secondary	35.6	25.9	13.4	5.9
Occupational ranking				
Upper management	45.8	28.0	2.8	11.1
Middle management, technical, professional	44.2	24.9	5.8	2.6
Clerical or manual	35.0	25.9	16.1	6.3
Attitude toward President Yeltsin				
Approve strongly	68.3	19.5	6.1	2.4
Approve on the whole	50.0	30.4	4.6	0.5
Disapprove	9.1	22.7	16.7	16.7
Attitude toward market economy				
Favor rapid transition	69.5	17.6	3.8	1.5
Favor gradual transition	32.0	31.0	8.9	6.4
Opposed to transition	4.9	24.2	22.0	17.1
Economic situation of voter's family over past year				
Much better	59.3	18.5	3.7	3.7
Same or slight change	45.4	27.1	6.7	3.5
Much worse	22.4	24.1	19.0	12.1

Source: Russian Election Project, funded by the Carnegie Corporation, MacArthur Foundation, and National Science Foundation and organized by the author, Jerry F. Hough, and Susan G. Lehmann.

  a. Voters who had decided on vote for party list for State Duma, who constituted 429 out of the 990 voters interviewed.

  b. The three most reform-oriented centrist parties (PRES, RDDR, and Yabloko).

percent of these Muscovites supported the moderate reformers; among those who felt themselves much worse off, Russia's Choice barely cleared 20 percent, trailing the moderates by a few percentage points and the combined LDPR-KPRF vote by almost 10 percent.

    In Moscow politics, there was a dark lining to the radical democrats' silver cloud of victory. First-past-the-post rules let Russia's Choice Movement achieve its slight majority of seats in the city duma with under 20 percent of the vote—no more than this, despite the abstention of its most dangerous opposition. The movement's take of the vote was 10.8 percent less than Democratic Russia's in the first round of the 1990 Mossovet election and 45.7 percent less than Popov's in the 1991 mayoral election. The 51.0 percent turnout was also much lower—14.3 percent less than in 1990 and 16.5 percent less than in 1991—and 5.7 percent of those who showed up spoiled their ballots. The starkest warning sign was the abundance of straight-negative votes, against *all* the pretenders; they came to 30.5 percent of the valid votes cast and were the leading option in thirty-one of thirty-five electoral districts. "A pox on all your houses" was the modal response of the citizenry in this first post-CPSU election.

A POST-COMMUNIST COALITION

Gavriil Popov wrote on the anniversary of the putsch of August 1991 that the democrats' heroic behavior then "did not carry [them] to power" in Russia. It could not have done so, he said percipiently, because, disunified and inexperienced, they "were not ready for power." They could stay in the match only by joining in *"a coalition of democrats and reformist apparatchiks"* such as Popov believed he had tried to organize in Moscow.[21]

Such an alliance of convenience functions, barely, in post-Soviet Moscow. The city has a "ruling elite," as one local sociologist observes, but it "has gone through only the first stage of its evolution." "No longer totalitarian, it is not yet democratic. It interweaves three orientations: reformist, populist, and bureaucratic. It is characterized by features such as social mobility, openness, pluralism of political ideology, and constant turnover."[22]

In the nascent post-Communist coalition, it is not elected democrats who have the upper hand but apparatchiks, broadly construed. Popov has used the analogy of a taxi in which the cabbie has been discourteous and has run fares up needlessly. The passengers revolt and take turns driving, only to discover that they navigate and steer poorly. Lately the professional driver, chastened, has returned to the wheel, while the passengers "give him advice and check him" without thinking they can cruise the streets on their own.

Popov personally was relieved to be out of the Moscow driver's seat by June 1992. The gruff Yurii Luzhkov, the archetypal "reformist apparatchik," succeeded him. Born in 1936 (the same year as Popov), and for most of his career an engineer and factory director in the Moscow chemical industry, Luzhkov was brought into city government by Yeltsin in 1987, supported Democratic Russia from the beginning, and yet, in his own words from 1990 (see Chapter 5), is "not a politician but a manager."

The heterogeneity of the post-Communist coalition is illustrated by background information on four subgroups of Moscow leaders: city hall "ministers" and subprefects in the executive branch, deputies in the defunct Small Soviet and the Moscow City Duma in the legislative branch (see Table 27). They share certain denominators with the Soviet-era establishment out of which they emerged. They are overwhelmingly male, although women make up 20 percent of the new city duma. They are somewhat younger than the municipal and CPSU functionaries appointed after Grishin's fall, less so for the ministers and Small Soviet members than for the city duma and subprefects. They prolong the trend of many years toward formal education and technical competence. They are slightly better schooled on average than the arrivistes of the late 1980s, the difference being that the elected deputies and to a lesser extent the subprefects were more likely to have trained in the social sciences or humanities rather than in an engineering institute. A fair number have postgraduate diplomas.

Almost 60 percent of the cabinet ministers, 40 percent of the duma members, more than one-quarter of the subprefects, and two-thirds of the deputies in the Small Soviet had work experience in science and higher education. For most legislators before and after December 1993, this was their only professional experience before entering politics.

Several administrators in the Popov-Luzhkov cabinet, which includes the ten okrug prefects, had proven themselves in democratizing politics the same way many deputies in both the soviet and the duma had. Aleksandr Muzykantskii of the Central Administrative Okrug, a former electoral agent for Yeltsin, is an example, as are the two of the five first deputy premiers (Ernest A. Bakirov and Konstantin E. Buravlev) who were Democratic Russia activists and prominent figures in Popov's electoral races.

The government ministers, though, have collectively had considerably more diverse, more high-powered, and more bureaucratic careers

Table 27. Background of senior executive and legislative officials of post-Soviet Moscow

Characteristics	Executive officials			Legislative officials	
	Government ministers, January 1992 (N = 22)[a]	Subprefects, January 1992 (N = 106)[b]		Members of Small Soviet, November 1991 (N = 87)[c]	Members of city duma, December 1993 (N = 35)
Percent male	100.0	98.1		96.6	80.0
Average year of birth	1942	1949		1945	1952
Education (percent)					
Higher	100.0	94.3		97.7	97.1
Higher engineering	81.8	72.6		58.6	42.9
Postgraduate degree	31.8	18.7		12.6	22.9
Percent with professional experience in science and higher education	59.1	27.4		67.8	40.0
Prior administrative experience (percent)					
CPSU apparatus	22.7	24.5		6.9	0.0
Moscow local government	45.5	15.1		4.6	14.3
Other government	27.3	6.6		3.4	8.6
Political police	0.0	0.9		1.1	2.9
Trade unions	0.0	0.9		0.0	2.9
Economic management	31.8	28.3		8.0	5.7
Komsomol	22.7	10.4		0.0	0.0
Military	4.5	9.4		12.6	5.7
Science and higher education	45.5	3.8		10.3	2.9
Miscellaneous	4.5	15.1		14.9	5.7

Source: Moscow city government.
a. Data for 22 of 23 ministers.
b. Data for 106 of 135 subprefects.
c. Data for 87 of 99 members.

than the legislators. While science and higher education was again the most common background, almost half of the ministers had been administrative leaders in this area, unlike the homely lab researchers and instructors in the legislative branch. An equal proportion had worked as municipal bureaucrats before the election of 1990, merely 7 percentage points less than the comparison group of 1986–1991. One-third of the ministers had been economic managers outside the city service and more than one-quarter had miscellaneous experience in government administration.

Most indicative of continuity, 23 percent of the ministers had at one time been in the apparatus of the Communist Party and 23 percent had been Komsomol officials. The ex-partocrats included First Deputy Premier Boris Nikol'skii, the former gorkom secretary who spurned Yurii Prokof'ev in August 1991; Aleksei Bryachikhin, the erstwhile raikom secretary and aspirant to be chairman of the city soviet and mayor, presently prefect of the Western Administrative Okrug; and Yevgenii A. Panteleyev, prefect of the Eastern Okrug (later a deputy premier), who headed the Kuibyshevskii raikom from 1986 to 1991. In January and March 1994 they were joined by the most conspicuous crossovers yet from the CPSU machine, when Luzhkov recruited Anatolii V. Ivanov, a former Central Committee worker, as a deputy prime minister, and Valerii Shantsev—the second secretary of the Moscow gorkom and the anti-DR head of the Moskva Group in the city soviet in 1990–1991—as his prefect in the Southern Ok-rug.[23] The subprefects were in most cases strangers to local government and to the intelligentsia but had abundant bureaucratic experience elsewhere. Twenty-five percent had served in the CPSU apparatus, 28 percent in economic management, and about 10 percent each in the Komsomol and the army officer corps.

In sum, there has been no cleanly revolutionary displacement of governmental personnel in post-Soviet Moscow. Elected democrats—anything but monolithic themselves—are one partner only in a ruling coalition, and a junior one at that. The other players are not carbon copies of their predecessors at city hall and Staraya ploshchad', and some helped batter down the CPSU, but the largest group consists of "reformist apparatchiks" out of the old establishment. This coalition will no doubt carry on for some time to come.[24]

Reinventing Metropolitan Institutions

Social forces plug into the urban political process through local institutions. Mikhail Gorbachev's recipe for them had been for improvement through competitive elections and some legislative reform. Moscow was the first major jurisdiction where deeper structural change was proposed and effected.

ALL POWER TO THE MAYOR?

The overhaul of governmental machinery carried out in Moscow, and widely imitated elsewhere, was first outlined in an open letter by Gavriil Popov in January 1991.[25] He proposed a sheer break with the increasingly rambunctious amateurism of the soviets. For local decision making, all Russia, in his view, should have town and district councils of no more than several dozen members, to be elected every two or three years. In Moscow, until this could be achieved, he recommended the Mossovet be downgraded to a featherweight congress that would convene once a year, chiefly to select 10 percent of its members to a standing Municipal Soviet (Munitsipal'nyi Sovet) and to approve the city budget. The Municipal Soviet was to meet for one week per quarter, and the raion soviets were to be dissolved in favor of advisory boards attached to the raion ispolkoms.

Urban governance as Popov saw it was to revolve around a popularly chosen mayor who would "lead the building of state organs and the economic, social, and cultural development of Moscow" and dispose of all land and city property. This local president could veto all decisions of the Municipal Soviet, and a two-thirds vote would be needed to override. He was to structure and staff all city agencies, supervise the ispolkom, appoint the raion authorities, and set all raion boundaries. Two consultative bodies—one on law-and-order issues and the other a citizens' "roundtable"—would buck up his authority.

Although a chorus of derision from city deputies and raion leaders greeted Popov's plan, few disputed the need for a more concerted executive power or for democratic election of its head. The CPSU caucus in the Mossovet had proposed a public ballot for the soviet chairman in April 1990, an idea acceptable to Popov at the time but not to Democratic Russia. The soviet, while lodging reservations, did not impede the mayoral election that Popov handily won in June 1991. Public opinion obviously favored the change.[26]

Buoyed by his thumping victory at the polls, and given a nearly free hand to reorganize by the RSFSR government, Mayor Popov on June 21, 1991, put into effect five crowning elements of a new executive structure:[27]

1. A Mayor's Department (Departament mera), to be the mayoral brain trust and political staff. Through six committees and groups, it was to draft proposals on "problems of the strategic development of the city."

2. A Government (Pravitel'stvo) of Moscow, headed by a premier (prem'er) appointed by the mayor, to manage the municipal bureaucracy, replacing the ispolkom. It contained two dozen ministers, the most important ranking as "deputy prime ministers" and superintending six administrative "complexes" (for city infrastructure, economics and city property, social policy, building and investment, foreign economic relations and science, and consumer affairs). Vice-Mayor Luzhkov was named premier.

3. A Moscow Capital Collegium (Moskovskaya stolichnaya kollegiya), for intergovernmental relations, "coordination of the city executive branch with union [USSR] and republican [RSFSR] organs." It was also to study "long-term issues" and "work out a policy for the city executive branch on principal questions in the life of the city." The collegium was chaired by the mayor and, as of October 1991, had twenty-nine members.[28]

4. A City Assembly (Gorodskoye sobraniye), to be the mayor's liaison with the city's "basic public and political movements." Its two hundred members would be from Democratic Russia, the CPSU gorkom, trade unions, womens' and environmental organizations, and similar institutions. Although the mayor was identified as chairman in June, when the assembly met in August it was headed by Aleksandr N. Yakovlev, a former liberal member of Gorbachev's Politburo; Luzhkov took the chair in September.

5. A single Business Office (Upravleniye delami) for the executive branch, separate from that of the Mossovet, to provide logistical support. The business manager heading it, Vasilii Shakhnovskii, was the most powerful municipal mandarin.

Appearance of this formidable edifice prompted a minireform in the Mossovet, which tacitly accepted some of the criticism of its excesses. It took advantage of a new RSFSR law to deputize a Small Soviet of 20 percent of its members, ninety-nine deputies, to act as its proxy in between plenary sessions.[29] The Small Soviet's weekly sittings, open to journalists but not televised, provided fewer opportunities for grandstanding and eased information sharing and intergroup bargaining. But its factional complexion mirrored that of the Mossovet, whose convocations, while less frequent, remained volatile. The Mossovet presidium was left in place, and rivalry soon emerged with the Small Soviet.

Nor did jealousy between the soviet and the aggrandized executive wing dissipate. The interim rules adopted by the Mossovet in April 1991 defined the pivotal mayor's office in only the haziest of terms. The mayoral veto turned out shakier than Popov pushed for, as it could be negated by 50 percent of the deputies present for a vote, and other key clauses were ambiguous.[30]

Unable to mold the city soviet, Popov and Luzhkov ignored it, leaving it to snipe and obstruct while they issued virtually all the rules and regulations defining economic reform as unilateral rescripts. Although the mayor could not shush critics, he made policy in the new political universe as the CPSU first secretary had in the old.

The Mayor's Department and Business Office gave him a chancery for initiating policy, solidifying press relations, and dispensing patronage and favors. The consultative apparatus performed mostly cosmetic tasks.[31] The Government of Moscow for most purposes operated as a continuation of the pre-1991 ispolkom, more correctly—in that the government consisted of city civil servants and met weekly—of the inner municipal cabinet that went by the name of presidium of the ispolkom from 1956 to 1990. The pompously titled office of "premier," another artifact of 1991, became an oxymoron when Luzhkov, promoted from vice-mayor to mayor, kept the premier's title. A city that had had an elected mayor and an elected vice-mayor who doubled as premier now had a combined mayor/premier. References to the premiership faded in 1993.[32]

The bureaucracy beneath came through no less bulky and opaque than before. The deputy premiers under Luzhkov when the rewiring was done totaled only one less than the eleven deputy chairmen of

Vladimir Promyslov's ispolkom a decade before. Nameplates were changed, as groupings of agencies became "complexes"[33] and sundry bureaus became "associations," "committees," and "concerns." The seventy-one municipal agencies reporting to the premier and deputy premiers in 1992 *exceeded by eleven* the number for 1982. And this tally did not count the *twenty* subunits internal to the Mayor's Department and the Business Office, most of them descendants of offices subordinate to the ispolkom.[34]

The arrangements foisted on the capital in 1993 formalize the executive power that Popov and Luzhkov had heretofore asserted mostly by fiat. In the same way as the Yeltsin constitution for Russia is "hyperpresidential,"[35] these local structures are "hypermayoral." Despite discussion going back to the 1980s of American-style separation of powers and checks and balances, they are premised on fusion of governmental powers. The mayor, under a "provisional statute" promulgated by Yeltsin, can legislate by executive directive *(rasporyazheniye)* on any question pertaining to the city's services or "socioeconomic problems." The Moscow City Duma can "suggest" changes to directives but can remonstrate against them only in the courts; pending judicial disposition, implementation is obligatory. The mayor can veto duma bills—and line items within them—and the proportion for override is now two-thirds of all the deputies, the ratio Popov sought in 1991. He also has absolute control over all executive appointments.[36]

Moscow's hypermayoral charter, like the new Russian constitution, is "retrospectively crafted" to rectify problems of the preceding several years, in particular, the legislative-executive impasse. It remains to be seen whether, as some predict of Russia, its corollary is "fig-leaf parliamentarism," in which fractious lawmakers argue fruitlessly over side issues while Caesarist executives run the show.[37]

Inasmuch as effective representative institutions are likely to develop only in step with an effective party system, Moscow, where the big radical party has a majority in the city duma, will be an interesting test case. Pledging "partnership and equality," Luzhkov handled the duma with kid gloves in its early months. He met individually with members before inauguration and, although not obliged to do so, consulted them on appointments and compromised on several policy decisions. Luzhkov promises a "depoliticized" administration and made a point of staying out of the 1993 national election, unlike the many chief executives of Russian regions who won seats in the upper house, the Council of Federation. For Muscovites, Luzhkov said, what matters is not "how pretty I look on the television screen" but what "real results in terms of improving life in the city" he can effect.[38]

The thirty-five councillors in the Moscow City Duma have far lower expectations than the "agitator" class of 1990 of being at the center of the local political game. They have picked as their speaker *(spiker),* not chairman, Viktor A. Maksimov, the Russia's Choice delegate from district 19, in the working-class Lyublino area. Maksimov is a professional police officer and sat on the final Mossovet in the Democratic Russia Fraction. His campaign poster favored "resolution of the problems of the city with account of the opinion of the population, a search for compromises, and achievement of security and stability"—a far cry from the militancy of 1990.

An ironhanded mayor can probably exclude the duma from real influence over policy in the near future, but only at a price. Even in presidential systems, parliaments "can help bind various constituencies to the polity," be a training and recruiting ground for leaders, and "keep the government usefully aware of simmering social problems, not to mention of the errant behavior of its own agents."[39] Strong executives are needed to drive economic and social change forward in post-socialist Moscow, but if they seek omnipotence they jeopardize the popular base of reform and the legitimacy of democratic principles.

REPLANTING THE GRASSROOTS

Some of the same juices feeding the row between executive and legislature nourished another structural tension, with Moscow's subcity governments. The soviets of the thirty-three raions were competitively reelected in the general balloting of March 1990. Their flabby size (an average of 130 members) and verbosity earned them Popov's enmity as quickly as the Mossovet did and goaded him toward drastic remedies.

Partisan and factional rivalries fanned the embers, as the raion leaders for the most part ranked more conservative than the city's. Eight raion soviets were chaired by first secretaries of CPSU raikoms, who ranged from centrists (such as Aleksei Bryachikhin in Sevastopol'skii raion and Yevgenii Panteleyev in Kuibyshevskii raion) to hardliners (such as Valerii Shantsev in Perovskii raion and Igor S. Lukin in Proletarskii raion).[40]

Radicals elected in the Democratic Russia insurgency controlled a handful of raions, which antagonized the city administration the most. In Krasnopresnenskii raion Chairman Aleksandr Krasnov—whom Rutskoi would try to anoint mayor of Moscow in October 1993— announced his district's "sovereignty," much as republics of the Soviet Union were doing, and asserted ownership of all land, mineral resources, and air rights within its boundaries. In Oktyabr'skii raion Il'ya Zaslavskii, a USSR people's deputy, was accused of awarding appointments and contracts to friends and business associates. The presidium of the Cheremushkinskii council, headed by Sergei Pykhtin, voted in October 1990 to eliminate the raion ispolkom and then to fire its officials and bolt their doors for noncompliance. Luzhkov and Popov had Moscow police reopen the ispolkom offices and froze the raion's budget until Pykhtin gave in.

Popov's epistle on governmental reform in January 1991 advocated replacement of the raion soviets with advisory committees made up of city deputies. The raions and their ispolkoms were to persevere. Popov went on to endorse as the "base level of government" what he called "self-government councils of the microraions." These were to be elected by the residents once rules for them had been approved by the mayor, and until then were to be manned by out-of-work deputies from the raion soviets.

Popov's blast at the raions did not fit previous criticism of overcentralization, but his nod to the microraions continued a line of thought pursued by reformers and conservatives alike since the birth of the Brateyevo "committee for social self-government" in 1988. Thirty-two neighborhood committees and soviets had sprung up in Moscow by mid-1989 and over 150 were active by November 1990. In July 1989 the Saikin-led Moscow ispolkom adopted a model charter that let the self-government committees incorporate themselves, open bank accounts, engage in commerce, and advise on city and raion appointments. It did so with the support of Lev Zaikov and the CPSU apparatus, who thought they would head off the "initiative groups" and other informal associations in the neighborhoods.[41] The committees were to multiply to 275 in 1993, 142 of them members of a Moscow Association of Organs of Territorial Self-Government headed by Gaik Zulumyan of Brateyevo.

The city in early 1991 approved "experimental municipal okrugs" in two hotbeds of home rule, Brateyevo and Krylatskoye. Unlike the citizen committees, their councils (after a bridging period, to be elected by the residents) were to be mini–town halls dispensing budgeted services in addition to acting as self-help groups and community advocates. To this end, they would receive an unspecified portion of the municipal apartment houses, schools, clinics, and other property on their territories.[42]

The raions received a harsher blow than first intimated once Popov was elected mayor. He wasted no time repartitioning the city in directives between July and September 1991 and finishing the raions as going concerns. He terminated their ispolkoms and administrative departments October 26. Since the mayor was not judged to have the right to dissolve their soviets, they continued to function after a fashion—holding meetings, passing motions, and in Dzerzhinskii raion briefly forming a militia and blockading their building to keep the prefect's hirelings out. The sight of deputies furiously adopting resolutions they had no means of carrying out was comical but also sad, for they had run in good faith in 1990 and were not all the fools Popov made them out to be.[43]

Raion territory and assets were redistributed in 1991 to kingsize administrative circuits or okrugs *(administrativnyye okruga),* nine in the trunk of the city and a tenth for Zelenograd (see Map 39 in Chapter 7). Fifteen raions were incorporated whole into one of the okrugs, eighteen apportioned among two or more. The okrugs in Moscow proper were supposed to be roughly equal in population; the ratio between the most populous okrug (the Southern) and the least (Northwestern) turns out to be more than two-to-one (see Table 28). The Central Administrative Okrug, essentially the pre-1917 city and some of the older Soviet-era sections out to the Moscow Circuit Railroad, is the smallest macrodistrict and the only one where the daily work force exceeds the overnight inhabitants. The eight sectoral okrugs all have more residents than workers.

The administrative okrugs function purely to output policy and do not take input from representative organs of their own. Each is headed by a *prefekt* appointed by the mayor; he sits on the city cabinet with

Table 28. Vital statistics of the administrative okrugs (September 1991)

Okrug	Area (square kilometers)	Residential population	Jobs
Central	64.2	789,900	1,477,600
Eastern	152.3	1,219,400	518,600
Northeastern	100.6	1,070,200	318,400
Northern	104.6	947,800	565,900
Northwestern	92.6	612,300	204,400
Southeastern	118.0	813,400	425,000
Southern	130.5	1,365,400	451,100
Southwestern	110.5	961,100	315,300
Western	142.5	980,900	359,100
Zelenograd	36.0	165,300	83,000

the rank of minister, the prefect of the central okrug also being a deputy premier of Moscow. All of the first appointees were seasoned bureaucrats, and several, notably Bryachikhin and Panteleyev, were veterans of the Communist Party apparat. Of the seventeen functions ascribed in the statute to the prefect and *prefektura* (prefecture, support staff), the first was to "see to the execution of the decrees, orders, and directives of the mayor and government of Moscow on the territory of the okrug."[44] The marching orders were as centralist and commandist as anything the CPSU organs ever uttered.

The second innovation in subcity governance in 1991 was the subdivision of the residential sections of the ten administrative okrugs into neighborhood units coinciding by and large with the hitherto powerless microraions. In most of Moscow they were dubbed "municipal okrugs" *(munitsipal'nyye okruga),* the same title as the pilot units at Brateyevo and Krylatskoye; only the Central Administrative Okrug called them "territorial directorates" *(territorial'nyye upravleniya).* The 129 municipal okrugs and territorial directorates, raised to 135 by 1992, had an average population of 65,000 to 70,000. The ten in the central city were all named after historic sections; elsewhere, old village and hamlet names replaced Sovietisms in most instances.[45]

The subprefect *(suprefekt)* of the minidistrict was another appointed functionary, selected in this instance by the prefect over him. He was to be advised by a council in the municipal okrug, comprising for the time being only those deputies elected from the area in 1990 to the city and raion soviets (some of whom refused to serve without pay). The subprefect, to quote Popov's order, was to "direct and coordinate the work of all [local] agencies" on his assigned territory and "achieve the practical execution of the policy of the mayor and the government of Moscow." He also had a laundry list of specific duties, including enforcement of environmental codes and assistance to the police. But, in contrast to test tube projects like those at Brateyevo and Krylatskoye, to which property could be deeded from the raions at no cost to city hall, the municipal okrugs were endowed with no physical assets apart from their tiny offices and reception rooms and were far punier in legal and budgetary terms than the maligned raions. Several subprefects used for the municipal okrug the simile of a prematurely born baby, "with feeble legs and arms and poor blood circulation."[46]

The territorial reform was done abruptly and with a wanton disregard for public opinion. The spacious, artificially bounded, and socially heterogeneous raions had over the years not formed communities of interest, but they were familiar administrative vessels, and erasing them at so tumultuous a time caused no minor inconvenience. Given inadequate publicity, most Muscovites lacked the barest knowledge of the new units. One survey in February 1993 showed only 11 percent preferring the new system to the old, 32 percent thinking it was worse, and 34 percent seeing no difference. Another poll, at the end of the year, showed slightly more (16 percent) liking the new but more (43 percent) also expressing a preference for the old. The February investigation "demonstrated that the majority of Muscovites are confused about the terms 'prefecture,' 'municipality,' 'okrug,' and 'raion' and cannot define their functions and interrelations." Fifty-three percent of the respondents could not say which administrative okrug they resided in, and 81 percent could not identify their municipal okrug. Only 9 percent could give the last name of their prefect, and only 3 percent could name their subprefect.[47]

The municipal shakeup of 1993 belatedly allowed some rationalization of the situation. The absurdly functionless (and raionless) raion soviets were laid to rest during the October crisis. A presidential decree in December, drafted by Luzhkov, confirmed the status quo on the administrative okrugs: they would remain bureaucratic servants of the mayor. But a modicum of popular control was introduced for the municipal okrugs, now in the usual Russian fashion to get new labels—"municipal districts" *(munitsipal'nyye raiony)*. Each district, including those in the Central Administrative Okrug, was to have an elected "municipal assembly" of five to seven lay "advisers," who were to consider neighborhood problems and approve budgetary estimates for the minidistrict. The subprefect, retitled the "chief of municipality" *(glava munitsipaliteta)*, was still to be appointed by the mayor, but with the consent of the municipal assembly.[48]

Moscow's governmental sandwich—an elected duma and strong mayor on top, unelected prefects in the middle, and elected minicouncils and accountable administrators at the bottom—has a fighting chance of evolving into a valued system. At the grassroots, the new participatory structures will mainly be neighborhood pressure groups and will likely supersede or co-opt the spontaneous self-government committees, which were falling into disuse before December 1993.[49] The municipal districts, of more human proportions than the large raions of the Soviet era, jibe better with felt social needs and with real cycles in urban development. They have the potential to be building blocks of a decently governed metropolis.

TOWN AND COUNTRY

Moscow's relationship to its hinterland was yet another institutional question sharpened by political change. The issue personally concerned Yeltsin and Zaikov, the third- and second-last leaders of the Moscow CPSU, who as obkom first secretaries in Sverdlovsk and Leningrad had been accustomed to the Soviet norm of the rulers of a region controlling its main city. Unhappy over the Moscow anomaly of putting town and country in sealed compartments, they encouraged discussion of overarching problems. Zaikov asked Gorbachev to form a unified party obkom for city and oblast, but oblast partocrats objected and Gorbachev did not override them.[50] The draft master plan presented in 1989 (see below) was the first Moscow plan to be couched in a regional framework. Its prime mover, Chief Architect Leonid Vavakin, had previously held that position in Moscow oblast.

Of the broader stimulants of regional consciousness, the most trenchant was the ecological issue. Although many "green" associations were fiercely parochial, the inherent ambience of pollution led some of them to widen their spatial terms of reference. When the Rzhev aqueduct project faced opposition in 1988, conservationists from around the Russian heartland could take credit for blocking it. Moscow environmentalists aided protests in the oblast towns of Zhukovskii (against construction on green belt land), Podol'sk (against industrial overdevelopment), and Zagorsk (against a proposed receptacle for radioactive sludge). The salvos against the Northern TETS were fired from the northern raions of Moscow and from Mytishchi and Kaliningrad, in the oblast.

The day before the 1990 election, eight candidates from Reutov, on Moscow's eastern border, published an unusual essay from the outside looking in about the segregation of Moscow from Podmoskov'e. Although, they said, intense economic and social intercourse went on between the two, in governmental terms they had no connection. How could Reutov be outside the city while Zelenograd and Solntsevo had long since been ingested? "More than 18,000 Reutovites [about one-third of the work force] are employed in Moscow and practically every resident makes purchases in Moscow stores. So why does the Mossovet not answer for social and living conditions in Reutov, where, by the way, the population density index is one of the highest in Europe, infant mortality is extremely bad, housing is falling down, and the roads are undrivable?" The signatories called for a "Soviet of the Moscow Region," an umbrella authority for development problems. Bills would be approved by concurrent majorities in chambers deputized by the city and oblast soviets.[51]

Neither this nor any other sweeping regional reform has yet been enacted. Oblast politicians have steadfastly opposed it. Rural and small-town areas, politically to the right of the big city, prefer to steer their own course. Their leaders worry about loss of discretion and job security and have bridled at what Anatolii S. Tyazhlov, the chief administrator of the oblast, has called "populist declarations" about unification that would have the oblast "get down on its knees."[52]

Meliorists from Moscow rather than the oblast pushed for city-oblast amalgamation after March 1990. Many liberals found the juxtaposition of Moscow to the underserviced areas reprehensible and dissented from the passport and propiska regulations that kept oblast dwellers out. Others were galvanized by the stories about environmental degradation in Podmoskov'e that underlined both Moscow's complicity in its problems and exposure to them should they go unremedied. Gavriil Popov, again the inciter of action, responded to the economic consideration that the city limits impeded the flow of goods, services, and capital. Amalgamation was further recommended by politics: a combined region of 15.5 million people would likely come under the sway of Moscow's radicals and would be a formidable force nationally.

Popov won Boris Yeltsin over to amalgamation, and on September 1 Yeltsin stated his support. At their request, Gorbachev appointed a nine-person presidential commission to investigate "governance of the city of Moscow, the capital of the USSR and the RSFSR." He chose as its head Nikolai D. Pivovarov, the chairman of the USSR Supreme Soviet's commission on local government. Popov's confidential memorandum recommended immediate action on a "Unified Capital Region of Moscow." It would in due course be administered by a popularly elected legislature and mayor, but for now would have a board with representation proportional to population, and thereby slanted toward the capital, and a mayor chosen by the Mossovet.[53]

The Pivovarov commission met several times, never coming to a vote on a pro-unification draft report.[54] Hostilities between the Soviet and Russian governments ruled out common action.

When Popov resuscitated the issue, he skated around Gorbachev and the fading USSR and wagered on public opinion and Russia. In April 1991 the Presidium of the RSFSR Supreme Soviet, on a motion by a committee chairman representing a Podmoskov'e district (Sergei M. Shakhrai), instructed the city and oblast soviets to poll residents on June 12, at the presidential and mayoral elections, on their views of "incorporation of the city and oblast into a unified capital region with a single propiska, supply system, and trade and services network."[55]

The Moscow electorate welcomed the proposition; 61.1 percent cast votes in its favor. The oblast soviet, though, kept it off the ballot. The unification question, it said, was juridically incorrect and worded so as to "seduce" oblast dwellers "with capital-city standards of living and quotas for consumer goods and food." Deputies from raions along the Moscow border voted about two-to-one for the main motion, while among deputies from outer raions support reached almost four-to-one.[56]

All was not lost. Days before the one-legged referendum, the city and oblast administrations, anticipating the result, signed a "general treaty" committing them to "gradual, planned socioeconomic integration," with emphasis on food processing, construction, and communal services. Talks on functional integration continued, and in January 1992 the two agreed to consolidate their propiska procedures and eventually remove all barriers to cross-border migration. In January 1993 they formed a Joint Collegium of the Organs of Government of Moscow and Moscow Oblast, a discussion forum for mutual aid cochaired by Luzhkov and Tyazhlov.

The sorest point between city and oblast has been not pollution or consumer supply but the resource endowment of the region. The oblast soviet's resolution rejecting participation in the June 1991 poll said so bluntly: "The most complicated problem in relations between Moscow and Moscow oblast is the use of the oblast's land and natural resources. A 'unified capital region' . . . would deprive the population of Moscow oblast of their constitutional right to independence in the utilization of land and natural resources on the territory they inhabit."[57]

The oblast authorities, remember, resented Moscow's land annexations outside the MKAD between 1983 and 1985 as a way of making them pay for the city's mismanagement. In the late 1980s conflict flared over the dedication of rural land to dachas and kitchen gardens (single-family and communal) for part-time cultivation by Muscovites, a policy pushed by Gorbachev and successive Moscow party secretaries. Village and oblast officials were wary about ceding land under any terms, about the competition from weekend farmers for scarce farm inputs such as seed and fertilizer, and about the overload of local shops and the rural infrastructure.

The oblast in 1990 pulled in its horns on dacha and garden plots. The annual allotment increased tenfold, although Moscow says many parcels are remote from commuter rail platforms. Roughly 1.8 million Muscovites (estimates vary) now have some access to cabins and gardens, double the figure of 1980.[58]

Decrees by President Yeltsin in September 1991 and January 1992 threw yet another stick on the fire: accommodation of permanent, low-density housing. The first promised to fund the building of detached houses in the Moscow area (and other provinces) for Soviet

Army officers repatriated from Eastern Europe. The second set aside 400 square kilometers of the oblast for sprinkling with frame housing, three-quarters of it for Muscovites, over a ten-year period. Most was to be within 50 kilometers of Moscow. The Ministry of Defense was to fork over 200 square kilometers more from military reservations.

The oblast government, exploiting the sloppy draftsmanship of the Yeltsin decrees, has taken a go-slow approach, withholding two-thirds of the acreage due for transfer in 1992 and 1993. District-level officials "see the future settlers as uninvited guests who will occupy their lands, and are obstructing things as much as they can." The military has been more recalcitrant, transferring no land at all yet. The territory surveyed for the housing is remote from the MKAD, "far from roads and utilities . . . in out-of-the-way places, ravines, pits, and bogs."[59]

Progress has been made at the level of attitudes and two-way communication. Luzhkov and other Moscow leaders now eschew amalgamation, arguing they are in no position to take on more burdens. Planners speak openly of the "one-sided colonization" of times past. The city's new Department for Development of the Moscow Region has accepted an oblast estimate of the investments needed to underwrite the present volume of garden and dacha activity. The document mentions 900 kilometers of roads and railway track, 3,000 hospital beds, dozens of stores, and 1,200 fire engines, ambulances, and garbage trucks: "Moscow should either finance the development of the social, engineering, and transport infrastructure of Podmoskov'e or take on this work itself."[60] Either way, regional cooperation would be advanced.

OUTGROWING DEPENDENCY

In the perennial problem area of relations with higher authority, Moscow at least suffers no longer from the abnormal tension bred by the frenetic competition among its superiors in the final months of the Soviet Union. Not only did USSR and RSFSR ministers appoint rival Moscow police chiefs, but Gorbachev and Yeltsin advanced separate draft laws on Moscow governance to give them leverage there.

There had been discussion of special USSR or RSFSR legislation covering Moscow since the mid-1980s. Gavriil Popov took up the cause in 1990, stressing Moscow's right to mandated relief for the costs of serving as capital city. A bill reported out of a USSR Supreme Soviet committee in April 1991 contained, besides a vague promise to pay rent for real estate occupied, clauses giving the Soviet Union and Russia cognate jurisdiction in Moscow, making federal property inviolate, and entitling the Soviet government to adopt "state programs for development of the [capital] district." A resolution taken by the Presidium of the RSFSR Supreme Soviet gave nearly exclusive primacy to Russia.[61]

The sparring is over. The Commonwealth of Independent States formed by Russia (now, officially, the Russian Federation) and ten former republics in December 1991 is an assemblage of sovereign countries, not the USSR reincarnated. Post-Soviet Moscow answers to but one center: the government of Russia, seated in its timeless Kremlin. Parliament's passage of a statute "On the Status of the Capital of the Russian Federation" in April 1993 was, therefore, anticlimactic. It bound Russia to offset capital city-related costs borne directly—a narrow reading of its liability—and was otherwise unnoteworthy.

Competition for resources continues. Popov and Yeltsin, it will be recalled, did not see eye to eye over the disposition of Communist Party headquarters at Staraya ploshchad' in August 1991. Almost all went to the Russian administration, the Moscow oblast soviet getting the former quarters of the gorkom and obkom. Popov received only a row of dachas at Kuntsevo-2 and the nearby Zarech'e country house of Brezhnev.

Yurii V. Petrov, the head of Yeltsin's Presidential Chancery, rebuffed Luzhkov's proposal that party-owned and party-reserved property either be put up for sale and the profits divided or, for medical facilities, be "given over to Moscow's jurisdiction and used for social objectives and not for the elite." Eyes-only instructions by Petrov and Yeltsin—only a half-decade before, the bane of nomenklatura privilege—commandeered almost all fixed assets of the Central Committee and the USSR Council of Ministers. In the main document, on March 21, 1992, Yeltsin assigned thirty-three properties to his office. Nine (three kindergartens, two hotels, the Serebryannyi bor dacha settlement, and a polyclinic, pharmacy, and laundry) were in Moscow and twenty-three (mostly rest homes, dacha colonies, and children's facilities) in the oblast. Other decrees carved up the former Fourth Chief Directorate of the Soviet Ministry of Health between a Russian Governmental Medical Center and a Chief Social-Production Directorate of the Presidential Chancery. Of its clinics and hospitals, only the Moscow Clinical Center on Michurinskii prospekt is available to Muscovites, and only because of a decision taken by Gorbachev in 1990. In October 1993 Yeltsin took over even the former CMEA building beside the White House that Popov sequestered in 1991; it housed the State Duma until returned to the city with equal suddenness in April 1994.[62]

In the workaday world, one may ask whether Moscow as capital of Russia has more leeway or less than it did under Soviet rule to make decisions about the local community. There is no simple answer to that question.

All factions in the Russian leadership favored local autonomy before the 1991 coup, and only six weeks prior to it passed a liberal enabling law on local self-government, which embodied many past criticisms. Since then, attitudes have diversified and policy has wavered.

The decentralist line has been continued de jure in some pieces of legislation, including a 1992 law on regional councils, and de facto in acceptance of quite a bit of local ingenuity in the economic and social spheres. Yet the executive branch has imposed vertical checks that brazenly resemble the prefectoralism of the Communist Party apparatus—or, it might be added, the tsarist governor. Key was a Yeltsin order gazetted August 24, 1991, taking some local functionaries' support of the GKChP as his cue, to designate "presidential representatives" in provinces and the cities of Moscow and St. Petersburg (as Leningrad had just been renamed). The envoys (appointed temporarily, ostensibly) were to report on violations of Russian laws and presidential decrees.

Moscow was better positioned than other localities, as Yeltsin named Popov himself his representative for the city and oblast the week after the putsch. The president brought the capital into line in January 1992, after he and Popov fell out over policy, when he designated Vyacheslav F. Komchatov, a Russian parliamentarian, as his plenipotentiary. Komchatov, who referred to himself as "the eyes of the president," had little impact, yet the mere fact of his appointment signaled that Moscow would not be immune to scrutiny.

When all is said and done, post-Soviet Moscow remains painfully reliant on the guidance, munificence, and bureaucracy of the center. While released from blatant subserviency, it is far from in charge of its own destiny. The boldest gambits in Moscow government since March 1990 were made possible only by politically motivated backing from the Russian level. Without it, the impasse between Popov and the Mossovet might have been utterly paralyzing. Dicta of either the presidium of the RSFSR parliament or Yeltsin authorized the 1991 mayoral election and let Popov gut the raions and take the lead in privatizing city property. Luzhkov could not have gotten away with his annihilation of the Moscow and raion soviets in 1993 without Yeltsin's aid.

Dependency has been no less noticeable in public finance. Although Russia's approach to local taxation has been more permissive than the USSR's, Moscow still taps mainly its traditional pools of revenue. These have been stretched to the limit by: declines in the profits of state enterprises, Moscow's most voluminous revenue source since the 1960s; reductions in the budgets of central (now Russian) departments, especially in funds available for investment; and the galloping inflation brought about by decontrol of prices and macroeconomic imbalance.

Moscow budgets, consequently, have been written in red ink since 1991, with yawning deficits having to be made up in good part from the Russian Federation treasury. City leaders alternate between resignation and anger. "Our good president," Luzhkov said wistfully in 1992, "will not leave the capital in poverty." In a moment of fury in 1994, after complaining that the federation still owed the city 250 billion rubles (about $150 million) from 1993, he said the Russian government "reminds me of a Gypsy who has stopped feeding his horse but continues to ride it until it drops."[63]

Moscow will outgrow its fiscal peonage only so far as it expands its local revenue base. That will not happen overnight. Success will hinge less on the charity of Russian authorities than on economic reform and recovery, especially in the nonstate sector.

Nor will there be instant relief of the city's vulnerability to functionally specialized national agencies. Hardly any of the heads on the Soviet hydra state have been lopped off as it has been Russianized. Moscow has scored certain successes, most gratifying the recapture of the subway from the Ministry of Transportation in 1992 and, in an area where it was denied even information on national-security grounds, the reassignment of some of the KGB-administered bomb shelters, which it is now trying to lease as storage or office space.[64] But the larger problem remains.

Concessions have sometimes been offset by prolongation of controls in a different costume. The subway is a case in point. Metrostroi, the organization that builds subway lines, was not consigned to Moscow in 1992; Russia has bargained hard over funds for it, telling Moscow it has to raise much of the capital on its own credit. The axiom of dual subordination stays locked in, submitting city departments to central bureaucrats in many operational aspects. The Federal Security Service, the thrice-renamed internal security branch of the former KGB, keeps watch on city offices. A maze of Russian ministries and departments occupy prime Moscow land without compensation, from the Ministry of Defense, the Federal Security Service, and the Foreign Intelligence Service (the other heir of the KGB) to economic production and regulatory bodies by the dozen. The April 1993 Russian law on Moscow promises recompense for direct costs, but it is being interpreted as stingily as possible. "As mayor," Popov reminisces, "I regularly received directives and assignments [from the Russian government] with respect to buildings, apartments, dachas, and so forth. The country's territory, population, and industry had been cut almost in half, but the state apparatus could not fit itself into the buildings that the USSR, Russia, and the CPSU Central Committee put together used to occupy."[65]

As employers, governmental bureaus and firms located in Moscow still commit and constrain urban government in dimension after dimension. They and their bureaucratic superiors engage local actors in multicornered games that are almost as difficult for local interests to prevail in as ever. Assuming that marketization of the economy lurches onward, we can predict this influence will dwindle in the long term. In the short term, however, it persists and city hall cannot yet do without it.

Urban Development after Socialism

In another age, the Bolsheviks grudgingly backed into the New Economic Policy. The post-Communist coalition plows ahead affirmatively into what its leaders envision as a humane and efficient version of Russia's capitalist and mixed-economy past. While the underlying tectonics that produced the breakout may be irresistible, the uncharted stretches and contradictions along the way forward are legion.

CAPITALIST RECONSTRUCTION

Radical reform of the command economy requires correlated progress along two axes: (1) the dominant mode of exchange among economic units, from central planning toward mutual adjustment through the market mechanism, and (2) control of productive assets, from uniform public ownership to forms of nonstate property. Transition on the marketization axis is the natural province of central governments. Local governments can best get traction on the second dimension, privatization, in that they possess a trove of capital they can convey to enterprising owners, provided central authorities do not sabotage the move.

Gorbachev occasioned less action than talk about economic reform, and far less than Lenin's NEP in the 1920s. He did lift restrictions on some small private businesses: individual and family firms (as of 1987) and, to greater effect, cooperatives of unrelated individuals sharing risks and proceeds (under a law adopted in May 1988). Although Moscow did not set the pace, it got its fair share when the cooperative movement took off in 1988–1989. Most co-ops had the hired labor permitted under the 1988 law. Economic cooperatives active in the city mushroomed to 3,537 on January 1, 1989, and 12,327 on January 1, 1990. On the latter date 489,000 Muscovites were working in them, mostly part-time (although precise data on hours are unavailable)—222,000 as members and the rest as wage workers. The largest share of the Moscow co-ops in 1990 (23.8 percent, much above the Soviet average) specialized in construction, followed by handicrafts (11.2 percent) and consumer services (4.1 percent); a growing subset did not have a fixed profile, catching opportunities as catch can.[66]

The cooperatives met with a mixed reception. The populace saw them as doing some good yet also as taking liberties with the law and providing frills rather than necessities. Chairman Saikin and the Moscow ispolkom briefly suspended licensing in late 1989. Democratic

Russia candidates identified as members of cooperatives did poorly in the election the next spring.

The democrats entered office buzzing with ideas about gearing up economic transformation. They gave moral backing and office leases to such novel capitalistic ventures as the Russian Commodities and Raw Materials Exchange (established in October 1990) and the several hundred commercial banks fighting for a foothold in the city. On most policy questions, however, they were handcuffed by their weak statutory powers and by the "war of laws" between the USSR and Russia.

Wanting to protect consumers from spiraling shortages, and armed with estimates that 40 percent of all retail wares in Moscow were being bought by goods-hungry outsiders, Popov and his executive took regressive administrative measures of the customary Soviet type. They first limited purchases of food and manufactured essentials to certified residents of Moscow and Moscow oblast. In February and March 1991 they added cigarettes and vodka to the several staples (sugar and salt) rationed by monthly scrip and forbade export from Moscow of refrigerators, televisions, and many consumer durables. Frightened that conservative farm areas would embargo food shipments, they considered reinstating the comprehensive rationing not seen since 1947.

The upheaval of August 1991 cleared some of the detritus blocking forward-looking policies. Yeltsin chose a national cabinet led by Yegor Gaidar and other youthful marketeers and allowed them in January 1992 to take the intrepid steps of deregulating most retail prices and giving a green light to private commerce. Nine months later Russia began to distribute shares in state companies.

Moscow city government has contributed principally to asset privatization, since marketization per se lies mostly with the center. Ideological convictions have been foremost in the privatizers' thinking, above all the sense that a propertied middle class, not the salaried and insecure proto–middle class of Soviet times, forms the backbone of a productive economy and a stable society. "We have the task," Yurii Luzhkov declared in 1992, "of creating a middle stratum in Moscow."[67] Financial calculations have also figured, as reformers have posited that devolution of state property will benefit the city treasury either sooner (through buyout charges) or later (through taxes and assorted fees).

Plumbings of Moscow public opinion in 1990–1991 showed citizens well disposed toward privatization. The aforementioned random survey of voters during the 1993 election confirmed this assessment, revealing that in each of five sectors residents of Moscow were more bullish about privatization than voters across the country (see Table 29). Twice as many approved acceleration or continuation of privatization as a general policy as favored a slower pace or policy reversal; a plurality was strongly or reservedly for the state relinquishing big factories, and majorities supported privatization of housing, retail

Table 29. Moscow and Russian attitudes toward economic reform, November–December 1993 (percent)

Question	Moscow voters (N = 990)	All Russian voters (N = 3,900)
Privatization of state property		
Favor acceleration	27.1	16.7
Favor present rate	21.8	17.9
Favor slowdown, cessation, or		
reversal	23.5	30.9
Privatization of big factories		
Favor strongly	21.6	17.3
Favor on the whole	25.3	20.2
Oppose	30.6	35.6
Privatization of retail trade		
Favor strongly	35.3	21.3
Favor on the whole	26.5	20.7
Oppose	24.8	40.2
Privatization of housing		
Favor strongly	42.6	40.0
Favor on the whole	27.0	22.3
Oppose	14.7	21.7
Private purchase and sale of land		
Favor strongly	19.0	14.5
Favor with restrictions	46.6	35.6
Oppose	33.4	39.6
Foreign investment		
Favor strongly	24.5	12.1
Favor with state controls	42.7	42.1
Oppose	21.7	29.6

Source: Russian Election Project (see Table 26).

trade, and land. Foreign investment, at least with some state regulation, also had majority approval.[68]

Actual privatization commenced in the very housing sector where Red Moscow in 1917–1918 showed the rest of Russia how to bolt in the opposite direction by municipalizing bourgeois and gentry property for the benefit of the proletariat.[69] Popov and Luzhkov in September 1991 promulgated the decree "Conversion of the State and Municipal Housing Fund of Moscow into the Property of Citizens." For a nominal fee, almost any permanent resident—all save those in dormitories, buildings condemned for demolition, landmarks, and the houses of army garrisons—could apply for title to his or her place of residence. The privatization office owed a reply within two months. The tenant for whom no impediment was found had only to file a notarized consent form for the deeding to be considered final.

Given over gratis would be eighteen square meters of gross living space per family member (about twelve square meters of net dwelling space, close to the city average), plus an additional twelve square meters gross per family. A pittance would be paid for validly allocated space in excess of the quota. An individual or household could exercise the privatization option one time only, forfeiting the right to reenter the housing waitlist. The housing unit could henceforth be bought and sold for the market price and passed on in a will.[70]

Sure enough, the procedure proved more cumbrous than billed, with lineups, shortages of forms, and some imprecision in wording beclouding the program launch. Many Muscovites have been nervous about future confiscation, possible denial of municipal maintenance and utilities, and onerous property taxation.

But anxiety did not keep Muscovites from taking to the program. They snapped up more than 250,000 apartments, 170,000 of them in municipal buildings, in the first year. By January 1993 the total was 310,000, roughly 10 percent of the housing stock, and by March 1994 it reached about 1.3 million apartments, or roughly 40 percent. Brokerage firms have sprung up to handle resales, and condominium-like "housing partnerships"—the same term as used in the 1920s in demunicipalized housing—have been organized to pool maintenance and improvement costs.

Privatization has made two other inroads in Moscow housing. First, the city supplements the sale of older apartments by offering a portion of housing output to private buyers at scarcity prices. In 1992, the first year of the program, one-sixth of the new flats becoming available went on the auction block to the highest bidder.

Second, the city now allows private and quasi-private enterprises to build houses, which had been forbidden since the 1920s. Most indigenous players to date have been public bureaus reborn as a joint stock company or cooperative, usually without a change in leadership. Mospromstroi (the former Glavmospromstroi) and Mosinzhstroi (formerly Glavmosinzhstroi), two big municipal building agencies set up in the Brezhnev period, went through such a laundering process in 1991 and began to seek out profitable housing and office building projects.[71]

Typically, the local firms have operated in joint ventures with foreign partners. The pioneering projects have been small, expensive, and targeted at international customers able to buy or lease them in hard currency. In 1992, for instance, the joint venture Perestroika began 25 townhouses on the bank of the Setun River for rental at $5,000 to $20,000 per month; a principal in Perestroika was Mosinzhstroi, whose chairman, Andrei Stroyev, became president of the joint venture. A Russian-Danish outfit made a start on 30 bungalows at Kuskovo Park, in southeastern Moscow, while Rosinka, a Russian-U.S. concern, broke ground for 500 cottages in Krasnogorskii raion, northwest of Moscow.[72] Granted that this activity is in its infancy, we can expect continued growth if it finds ways to expand into catering to upper-income local folk.

After housing, privatization spread to consumer trade and services, where again the city had a prior hold on most existing facilities. Mayor Popov's privatization formula, announced in November 1991, covered all stores and kiosks, consumer convenience outlets (dry cleaners, repair depots, beauty parlors, and so forth), and dining places on the municipal books. Preference normally went to the current employees, who were to set themselves up as an "entrepreneurial collective." Shops under 150 square meters were to be sold to the collective (with their inventories and accounts receivable) for 1,000 rubles per square meter, a fraction of their market value. Most larger premises were leased to workers for one year, with the option of purchase at a negotiated price after that. GUM, TsUM, and the very biggest trade concerns, as well as wholesale distributors, were to be rechartered as joint stock companies. The municipality would hold no less than 25 percent of the equity and the workers no more than 25 percent, with the balance tendered to investors.[73]

The advantage given to staff members caused the most controversy. Larisa I. Piyasheva, Popov's chief aide for retail privatization, maintained that giveaways to employees were the fastest and most equitable solution in this and every part of the economy. She traded barbs with Yeltsin's deputy premier for privatization, Anatolii B. Chubais, who argued that an alternative to "nomenklatura privatization," namely, citizen purchase of stock through government-issued vouchers, would be more lucrative and would win fans for privatization. Piyasheva resigned in September 1992, three months after Popov, to protest adoption of Chubais's program Russia-wide.

The tiff with Chubais and the tendency for the fine print in the rules to change from day to day notwithstanding, divestiture of Moscow trade and services soared, and along the lines mapped by Popov and Piyasheva. Six thousand trade and service enterprises had gone private by May 1992, more than half of all the firms denationalized in Russia up to that time. By the spring of 1993 more than 90 percent of Moscow's retail shops and about 70 percent of its restaurants, cafés, and service outlets had been turned over to private operators and the city was being praised as "an example of fast and daring privatization." In 95 percent of the cases the state-owned property had been bought out by work collectives. The privatized firms range in size from GUM on Red Square (incorporated as the GUM Trading House Joint Stock Company) to newspaper kiosks and cobblers' stands.[74]

Foreign capital has also made its presence felt in Moscow trade and services. The startup in January 1990 of the world's largest McDonald's restaurant, a joint venture with the city at Pushkinskaya ploshchad', introduced Russian palates to American fast food. McDonald's plans to have twenty eateries in Moscow by the end of the 1990s, and there are outlets in the central city for Pizza Hut, Dannon Yogurt, and Baskin Robbins. Boutiques featuring global brand names in luxury and specialty paraphernalia—Nina Ricci, Estée Lauder, Christian Dior, United Colors of Benetton, Yves Rocher, and Nike, to mention a few—dot Tverskaya and other central avenues. Showrooms for Porsche, Maserati, Mercedes Benz, Alfa Romeo, and

Rolls-Royce appeared in 1992–1993, although heavy duties on imported cars levied in 1994 have cut into their business. The Radisson Slavyanskaya Hotel at the Kiev Railway Station initiated a fleet of three-star hotels. McDonald's constructed a needle tower off of lower Tverskaya, the first contemporary office building put up with Western money (Figure 72). A slew of other hotel and office developments are in the works, almost all with foreign credits and building contracts for foreign firms.

At the bottom end of the market there has been an upsurge in boisterous public commerce, with a bloodline going back to the bazaars of old Moscow and the Nepmen. For several months after the Yeltsin administration revoked decades-old proscriptions in January 1992, the *tolkuchka,* a sea of tens of thousands of peddlers, lapped unimpeded over downtown sidewalks, plazas, and train and subway stations, leaving them littered with wrappers and crates at nightfall. One Western correspondent thought Moscow "a phantasmagoria, a post-Communist world as painted by Hieronymus Bosch." Muscovites, the young especially, "rush headlong into some weird, pleasurable, vulgar world of primitive capitalism."[75] By summer, city hall was confining the ambulatory sellers to designated areas and cracking down on the ubiquitous unlicensed stalls in plywood, canvas, and tin. At present the city lists about 15,000 reasonably sturdy registered stalls (Figure 73).

Privatization of the factories and industry-related research institutes that were the princesses of socialist Moscow's economy proceeds along a more leisurely timetable. The capital's hunk of the defense industry has barely been nicked, as it, along with most Russian enterprises in communication, energy, raw materials, and brewing and distilling, until 1995 at the earliest will be fully owned by the state, administered through branch departments corresponding to the old Soviet ministries. Denationalization of civilian factories caught fire only after the Russian Supreme Soviet accepted a framework privatization program in June 1992. In July 1992 President Yeltsin mandated that all large state enterprises not exempted from privatization be reorganized as joint stock companies with corporate boards and publicly traded shares; distribution of the shares was to vary with the circumstances. In August he announced a "people's privatization" feature under which each citizen would receive a privatization voucher

Figure 72. McDonald's office building, Gazetnyi pereulok. (Photograph by author.)

Figure 73. Shoppers and private trading stalls near Kiev Station, 1993. (Photograph by author.)

with a face value of 10,000 rubles, which could be used to purchase equity in firms undergoing privatization. The emergence of stock exchanges would allow the sale of shares in a secondary market and their valuation by supply and demand.[76]

Thus ZIL, the biggest factory in Moscow, was reorganized in 1992 into the Likhachev Works Joint Stock Moscow Company—the first three letters of the Russian short form, AMO, being identical to the forerunner auto factory built by the Ryabushinskiis during World War I. Twenty-five percent of the AMO-ZIL shares were to be donated free to all employees, 25 percent discounted or auctioned to them, 35 percent sold to the public, 10 percent kept for marketing to foreigners in hard currency, and 5 percent reserved for Moscow and the municipalities where ZIL has plants. Another demonstration project, the

Bol'shevik Confectionary Factory on Leningradskii prospekt, in December 1992 became the first Russian state company to be bought in its entirety with privatization vouchers.

Corporatization and stock distribution was completed for three-quarters of Russia's and Moscow's factories by June 1994. The near-term winners have been industrial managers, who typically have used purchase options, favors to workers, and other schemes to gain formal control over assets over which they have had effective informal control since the evisceration of most of the economic ministries. As macroeconomic stringency forces managers to look at restructuring options, the privatization process is becoming more openly political, and some of the politics is local.

In Moscow the most closely watched case has been ZIL, where Mayor Luzhkov, alarmed at the enterprise's decline, bargained the city's share of equity up to 25 percent in exchange for agreeing to take over ZIL's entire stock of housing and social facilities. He then persuaded the ZIL directors to make Aleksandr P. Vladislavlev, the deputy head of the League of Industrialists and Entrepreneurs of Russia, chairman of their board and to bring back Valerii Saikin (lured from ZIL to city hall by Yeltsin in 1986) as director. Vladislavlev and Saikin, with Luzhkov in their corner, try to negotiate loans from foreign and Russian banks and to make the wrenching decisions about which divisions of the plant to salvage and which to abandon as unprofitable.[77]

"Capitalist reconstruction" has had one pronounced outcome much desired by liberal reformers: a greater individuation of incomes and hence of incentives to economic efficiency. Assessments on this point cannot be precise: Russians rarely disclose their earnings, the baseline is unclear, and existing information does not allow us to disentangle the effects of government policy and other factors. Still, some estimates are suggestive. Muscovites surveyed during the 1993 election reported a mean individual income before taxes of 85,000 rubles for that October (about $70 at the official exchange) and a mean family income of 168,000 rubles ($140). A family at the 25th percentile of the distribution earned 67,000 rubles, or 40 percent of the mean, while one at the 75th percentile earned 200,000 rubles, 119 percent of the mean and 3.0 times the absolute income of the 25th-percentile household; the 90th percentile marked 300,000 rubles, 179 percent of the mean and 4.5 times the 25th percentile. Among individuals, the 75th percentile took home 3.0 times as many rubles as the 25th percentile and the 90th percentile 5.2 times as many.[78]

SOCIAL PROTECTION

Under the best of circumstances, structural transformation of a statist economy produces a temporary economic deterioration, hurts large social groups, and sows political opposition. Russia and Moscow have not avoided this syndrome, which appears to be nowhere near over.

The Moscow economy staggered into recession in 1991, with an absolute drop of 2 percent in industrial production and a spike of 180 percent in retail prices. That degenerated in 1992 into outright depression, near-hyperinflation, and deindustrialization: manufacturing production was down 27 percent, food processing down 28 percent (and sales of some foods 40 or 50 percent), and consumer prices up by 2,500 percent. In 1993 inflation slowed to 700 percent, but industrial output was off another 15 percent.

Even the once sacrosanct military-industrial complex has been hammered, the cutbacks in state procurements compounded by the rethinking of priorities now that the cold war is history. In the first half of 1993 Moscow's total defense production was 27 percent less than one year before. "Conversion" of arms contractors, begun under Gorbachev, has made slow headway. "In theory, everyone is for conversion," one analyst concludes. "In practice, things are more complicated, and for one reason or another the 'demobilization' of defense industry is bumpy." Some plants, laboratories, and design bureaus have gone months without orders, their production lines hard to civilianize on anything but a make-work basis. The renowned Tushino Machine Building Works, its Buran space shuttle canceled in 1991, turns out light training craft and, oddly, hypodermic needles. Former "post office boxes," "instead of occupying themselves with Buran or Energiya [the rocket engine works in Kaliningrad], are forced to chase targets for fly swatters, vegetable peelers, and mattresses." The Kompozit NPO, an engineer of alloys for missiles, gets kudos for fabricating pushcarts for hot dog vendors, while the Khrunichev Works and other giants try out ozonizers, aerosol fire extinguishers, and air filters for industrial tools. Although defense plants have been enjoined to look to the mass market, their output of consumer goods waned by 9 percent in the first half of 1993.[79]

The one ache of the transition that Moscow has been spared in the early innings is unemployment. Fewer than 20,000 Muscovites, mostly middle-aged women and furloughed research personnel, were officially out of work and receiving a government allowance in January 1994. Incomparably more are underemployed—on short work weeks or assigned long vacations at reduced pay—than are unemployed. Managers have preferred to trim real wages, leaving many fringe benefits intact, than to lay off workers; the federal government, apprehensive of social unrest, has emitted cheap, inflationary credits to help them stay afloat.

Featherbedding is but one outcropping of the larger phenomenon of "social protection" *(sotsial'naya zashchita)*, a term analogous to social insurance or social security in the West. Post-Soviet politics must determine how much of this security there will be, for whom, and at what price to marketizing reform.

The government of Moscow has cushioned some redistributive effects of economic shock therapy through pecuniary and in-kind subsidies. Senior citizens have had passes for mass transit since June 1991, and fares for the general population (although several thousand times what they were before the inflation) come to less than 20 percent of the cost of running public transportation. City soup kitchens ladle out 60,000 dinners a day, and all pupils through fourth grade receive two meals each schoolday. City hall makes small cash contributions to a host of needy groups—old-age pensioners, families with handicapped children or very low incomes, some college students, and single mothers on assistance from the Russian government—and since 1991 has paid a monthly allowance to military officers living in municipal flats. New and old transfer payments to individuals soak up 3 or 4 percent of the Moscow budget and affect 3.6 million Muscovites, not counting hidden subsidies such as those built into transit tickets.

The city's safety net has reached economic units as well as individuals. Military-industrial enterprises have been prime supplicants.

A municipal conversion-assistance plan tabled by a mayoral advisory panel in August 1991 still saw defense industry as a source of largesse for Moscow. By 1992 Luzhkov in speeches and backstairs lobbying came to the relief of the industry. He reminded the government that Russia cannot be a world power without a mighty, well-equipped army and overseas munitions sales. He twisted bank managers' arms to float loans to local defense plants and bureaus, pledged Moscow property as security, and allocated 5 billion rubles to contracts with defense enterprises. In 1993 the city provided 10 billion rubles' worth of credits and got arms contractors to sign 350 agreements governing use of their technology for civilian purposes. A knot of aviation, missile, and other firms have surrendered their apartment buildings to the okrug prefectorates and solicited mayoral subsidies to keep clinics and kindergartens open.[80]

In city government's bedrock areas of activity, housing policy presents the most problems for those promoting social protection. In the palmy days of glasnost' privilege emerged as a key issue. It was unconscionable, Boris Yeltsin and others then held, for a minority to live in airy apartments in "special houses" when millions were stuck in prefabricated boxes or squalid communal flats. Similar sentiments applied to the state dachas in Moscow oblast. Potshots at nomenklatura housing crackled in the Democratic Russia campaign in 1990 and in the press after the 1991 coup.

The democrats' populist indignation was short-lived. Concerning medical facilities and other services, they at least made the effort, blunted by Yurii Petrov, to gain either control or financial compensation. In housing, they attempted no redistribution at all. Aside from the resolve to avoid an anarchic "revolution of the Leninist type," there has been an element of studied self-interest in their stance. The 180-degree political turn has given some of the new elite the chance to acquire for themselves housing plums once reserved for the old, which would be degraded if social leveling were enforced.

There has thus been no purge of such preserves as the Directorate of Tall Houses and Hotels, since 1991 a section of the city government's Association for Operation of Housing and Administrative Buildings. Disruption has been minimized, and the residents have with few exceptions gone undisturbed. Meanwhile, the housing needs of the new rulers have not gone begging. Elective officials and bureaucratic promotees have filtered unobtrusively into nomenklatura buildings. Ruslan Khasbulatov, the speaker of the Russian parliament until October 1993, occupied the high-ceilinged suite at 10 ulitsa Shchuseva built for Leonid Brezhnev. Yeltsin, unhappy with Gorbachev's concrete house on ulitsa Kosygina, moved his in-town residence to a new UVDG building at 4 Osennaya ulitsa in Kuntsevo; Luzhkov and Prime Minister Viktor S. Chernomyrdin are housemates. Lower-ranking officials find places in lesser but still very desirable homes, occasionally with token concessions to ordinary citizens.[81]

In the lagoons of cottages, rest houses, and holiday hotels outside the city, the turnover has been more rapid. Barvikha (where Yeltsin's presidential dacha is), Usovo, Uspenskoye, and most of the exurban preserves are now sanctuaries for the post-Soviet establishment. Wrote one Moscow oblast deputy about the Russian Council of Ministers' seizure of a CPSU dacha and resort compound on the Klyaz'ma Reservoir: "This is the replacement of one elite proprietor by another. For many years the masters of Klyaz'ma were party functionaries. Now look at this new wave, this marvellous corps of bureaucrats, making themselves at home." Construction booms in the preferred dacha zone west of Kuntsevo. "Luxurious villas are going up . . . next to moss-covered villages without running water or sewage."[82]

Making themselves at home has been immeasurably eased for both incoming and carryover elites by the privatization legislation. It permits those assigned VIP accommodation by a present or past patron to perpetuate that benefit by taking out lawful ownership at exceedingly low cost. They pay exactly the same sum for each square meter in an elite building as residents of reinforced-concrete prefabs pay, although "prestige apartments," as they are being advertised, command 10 to 20 percent per meter more on the open market. Nomenklatura houses in inner Moscow were among those whose denizens acquired deeds as soon as they were available. Government House across the river from the Kremlin, the Central Committee alley on Kutuzovskii prospekt, and 12 and 21 ulitsa Alekseya Tol'stogo (where Yekaterina Furtseva and Viktor Grishin lived) are among several cases mentioned in interviews. Some state dachas in the oblast have also been acquired at fire-sale prices, although there is no privatization program for them and success hinges on personal connections.[83]

This fortification of privilege has a kernel of rationality, as long as it imbues owners with pride of possession, rewards upkeep and improvement of the asset, and creates collateral that encourages saving and investment. But what of everyone else? The wider the circle of winners, the greater the economic payoff should be. Obversely, the fewer the winners and the leakier the protective shield, the greater the flack the reformers will encounter. For stability to be maintained, covert elite privilege must ultimately give way to a normal stratification of rewards, overtly related to effort and moderated by the state, such as characterizes a modern capitalistic economy.

In the housing realm post-Soviet Moscow is not striking the necessary balance. Much of the population does not get tangible payoffs from the reformed system. Conditioned to expect a flat distribution of supply by socialist ideology and the democrats' rhetoric, they confront steep gradients in reality.

In privatized housing, growing inequalities in incomes and purchasing power, absent constraint by government, will cause sharp inequalities in attainment. Much new state-built shelter will be allocated, as under Soviet rule, by position on administrative queues. The municipal and departmental registries that list qualified applicants have lengthened dramatically in Moscow, from 880,000 in 1988 to more than 1,200,000 in the early 1990s. The rank-and-file city queuers slated for new apartments in 1994 were those who signed up before July 1, 1982![84]

Runaway demand results, in part, from democratization, which has spurred once bashful citizens to place claims with the housing bureaucracy. A more potent factor has been the decision in 1989 to hike the "triggering norm" delineating eligibility for rationed housing to six or seven square meters per capita, from five square meters.[85] Besides those on waiting lists, 150,000 Muscovites live in dilapidated buildings slated for demolition (100,000 less than in 1988), and 1 million reside in joint-occupancy flats, without the right to enter the queue (about 250,000 more than in 1988).

Aggregate housing supply has lagged behind demand owing to the downward curve construction has taken since the 1970s. Production has sufficed to keep per capita provision at the plateau achieved but not to heighten it or satisfy the cohorts of new claimants. Policy decisions under Gorbachev not only failed to check the decline in capacity but also let it escalate.

The Mossovet in 1988, implementing the decision of the Twenty-seventh Party Congress to give every Soviet family a separate apartment by the turn of the century, set an objective of 50 million square meters gross (about 33 million net) of housing space added in Moscow by the year 2000. Yearly increments of 2.7 million square meters of net dwelling space, the annual pace realized in 1978, would have been required. In 1991 the soviet set a subgoal of 20 million square meters gross (13 million net) for the four years 1992–1995, or 3.25 million square meters net per year. Most of the work was to be done by Glavmosstroi, whose privatization was postponed indefinitely. Builders and planners questioned all these targets, considering them out of touch with capacity. Meanwhile, housing industry specialists, reasoning from sunk costs, believe that they must continue to stress high-rise buildings and that it will take years to begin on the low rises and cottages on exurban plots promised in Yeltsin's presidential decrees.[86]

As it was, 1990 and 1991 were the worst years for the Moscow housing industry since the early post-Stalin years (see Table D-1 in Appendix D). The barely 1 million square meters (net) completed in 1991, the skimpiest total since 1954, just exceeded 30 percent of completions in 1973, the peak year. Production bounced back in 1992 and 1993, as multiyear projects were finished off, but was still only about 55 percent of 1973's, when Moscow had 1.6 million fewer people than in 1992. Municipal construction accounted for 69 percent of the 1993 total, as compared to 85 percent in 1973, and in absolute volume totaled only 45 percent of what was completed under the reviled Grishin and Promyslov in 1973. If production sticks at this level, the Moscow housing industry will have made by the end of the 1990s around 60 percent of the housing projected in 1988, or as much on annual average as was built in 1957.[87]

Sluggish supply has stagnated per capita provision at the level of the mid-1980s.[88] Its effect on those deprived of housing, already serious, is exacerbated by a decision to put a lid on the share devoted to households on the needy list. Whereas 45 to 50 percent of all output was funded by the city government and set aside for municipal purposes in the 1970s and 1980s, the quotient is now one-third, and that subsumes allocations for urban renewal and sundry city uses as well as for families on the queue. Housing have-nots are thus in a double bind, as the city allots them *a lower proportion of a lower volume* of housing completions. Besides the one-third distributed through municipal channels in 1993, about 10 percent went to housing cooperatives, 27 percent was auctioned off to all comers at stratospheric prices, and 30 percent was acquired by "enterprises and organizations" for their employees. Although state employers, who are divesting themselves of management of company town housing, are apt to exert a smaller claim on new construction in future, in 1993 their share was still of the same magnitude as the unrestricted municipal share.[89]

Moscow leaders make a virtue today out of exercising less influence than before over fragmented decisions affecting housing and living conditions. "That which enterprises and organizations build on their own money is their property," Mayor Luzhkov avers. "The city government has no business climbing into it." About the socioeconomic groups who will benefit, he candidly says, "The prose of market life is such that much of [the housing] is now being acquired not by those who get by from one payday to the next but by people of substance."[90]

Tension also surrounds the city's rent and utility fees, which in the Soviet canon were combined in a single "apartment payment" *(kvartirnaya plata)* owed to the municipal or departmental landlord. These charges were unrelated to the unit's scarcity value and did not meet the maintenance costs of housing, to say nothing of amortized construction or cognate state investments. The inflation of the early 1990s further depressed them in real terms, as local housing authorities, petrified about public reaction, raised them more slowly than other prices. By some calculations, apartment payments by 1992 covered less than 15 percent of real costs.

In reaction to this discrepancy, the city resolved on an important change in May 1994. It for the first time aims to recoup operating and capital costs, both for the dwelling (for publicly owned units) and for electricity, sanitation, and other utilities (for privatized flats as well). The ratio to average family income is to rise gradually from 5 percent in 1993 to 10 percent in 1994 and 20 percent in 1998. Muscovites whose fees exceed that figure will be eligible for a sliding municipal subsidy; those who do not pay their bills can be summarily evicted within six months. At the insistence of the city duma, Luzhkov accepted three amendments that soften the blow for poorer families: (1) households with a monthly income of under 52,000 rubles (to be adjusted for inflation) will pay nothing; (2) the charge will vary with the quality of the building; and (3) there will be triple fees for all square metrage exceeding "social norms" (96 square meters of gross space for a family of three). Clearly, socialist egalitarianism still influences city administrators, and it can be expected to linger on combustible social issues for the indefinite future.

PLANNING PERSPECTIVES

Had Moscow not been dilatory in cranking up the machinery, it would, like Leningrad, have spawned another town plan before perestroika came knocking.[91] Instead, its last socialist planning exercise was eclipsed by change, leaving great uncertainty about what comes next.

Moscow leaders in January 1982, eight years before the expiry of the obsolescent city plan of 1971, ordered the drawing up of parameters (the TEO, "technical and economic foundations") for a new one. There was no outward sign of alarm. "The basic goal of the TEO," purred Chief Architect Makarevich, "is . . . to foretell a further molding of Moscow that will smoothly continue the urban planning ideas incorporated in the general plan of 1971." Working forecasts were to be done out to the year 2010 with general prognoses to 2050.[92]

Draft TEO, cooked up under a lid of secrecy, were approved by the city bureau of the CPSU in October 1984 and filed with the Soviet government for study. They set a notch for Moscow's population of 9.5 million in 2010, only 400,000 more residents than expected in 1990. Somehow the city was to be confined to annual increments of 20,000 people, less than one-fifth of those realized under the 1971 plan. It was to annex 110 square kilometers more of oblast land. A "system of satellite cities" was to catch overspill, while the green belt was to be "significantly expanded." Recalling Sergei Shestakov's schema of the 1920s and the abortive attempt to mate capital and green belt in 1960–1961, city officials called it a prospectus for Greater Moscow.[93]

The slender published summaries made no mention of targets for housing construction. They did adumbrate public works (subway lines, two filtration stations, the Rzhev water system, the Northern TETS, and the like) and improvements to trade and conveniences that would supposedly clip the hours spent on shopping and housework by 40 to 50 percent. Greater Moscow was to be sectioned into four "planning sectors" and then into sixteen "planning zones," eight inside the MKAD (the same as in the 1971 plan) and eight in the expansive green belt. The sixteen zones were to have "advanced centers for services" interlaced by high-speed transit. All polluting factories were to be extruded.

One can read unease about this doodle in wishful thinking into the airtight security surrounding it and the absence of the debate found in the early 1960s. Printed materials gave no clue how Moscow would avoid the mistakes of the preceding plan. Analytical gaps were papered over with clichés about the marvels of socialism.

Gorbachev's political thaw and Boris Yeltsin's ascent ultimately did in the draft TEO. In his first big local speech Yeltsin portrayed metropolitan planning as a signal failure. Moscow, he charged, was turning into "an ungovernable formation," and prescriptions for it were built on sand: "The question of how and where the city is to develop has still not been resolved in principle. It is apparent that we need one edict more that will nullify most previous ones and take a position on the integrated socioeconomic development of Moscow." The gorkom in March 1986 adopted a policy of cutting off residency permits for migrant laborers, and Yeltsin got the USSR Council of Ministers to submit the TEO to a review committee chaired by the economist Stanislav S. Shatalin, the future begetter of the 500 Days reform plan. The industrial interests that perennially stymied attempts to bring population growth and living standards into balance stuck to their guns—putting in for labor allotments "with a steadfastness that would be best put to use elsewhere," Yeltsin explained to the gorkom in July 1986. "There are leaders who voted for the decision" of March 1986, he said, "who then returned to their offices and put their signatures to applications to the Mossovet for the allocation of limits—'by way of exception,' it goes without saying."[94]

Yeltsin and the Shatalin committee agreed that the combination of unrepentant behavior by economic elites and the pie-in-the-sky TEO spelled disaster. Shatalin's vice-chairman, Leonid Vavakin, and several expert witnesses pushed a mandate for negative population growth, to 8 million or perhaps 7 million by 2010, together with urbanization of selected tracts of the Moscow region. Yeltsin drew the line at population reductions, which catered to "narrow localism," but expressed interest in the other findings.[95]

Shatalin and Vavakin came up with a compromise resolution that

Yeltsin accepted and the Politburo adopted, along with an indefinite ban on limitchiki, in September 1986. The "Conception of the Integrated Socioeconomic Development of Moscow to the Year 2000" tore up the draft TEO and stipulated that new guidelines should "take full account of current problems," shoot for "organic unity" with the oblast, and undergo "broad discussion." It posed a population quota of 9.5 million for 2000 and of 10 million for 2010; even those figures would require a two-thirds slackening of population growth. Work was to be completed first on realizable social and economic programs for the 1990s and, after that, on new TEO and a draft general plan out to 2010.[96]

Vavakin, Gleb Makarevich's replacement as chief architect in early 1987, superintended the most transparent planning process ever seen in Moscow. A Public Council on City Planning, about half of its 400 members from the intelligentsia, met monthly to consider the revised TEO (now "technical and economic indicators," TEP) and their applications. It was chaired by Valerii Saikin, the municipal chief executive, but dominated by Yeltsin until his ouster and after that by Vavakin, who also headed a Consultative Council of Experts. Discussion irrupted into the press; green groups and other voluntary associations joined the fray in 1988–1989.

Participants most fervidly stated the point of view that the economic and demographic mass of Moscow was inundating its infrastructure and amenities. Saikin wondered if the blunderbuss of the interwar Commission for the Unburdening of Moscow might not be revived "to unload from Moscow offices which could as well be located in other cities." Sociologist Igor V. Bestuzhev-Lada claimed that within a decade or two Podmoskov'e was going to be paved over from one end to the other and Moscow would surpass 25 million. A satirist forecast that the capital would gulp down the Soviet Union in its entirety: "there will be orange groves in the southern outskirts . . . and the denizens of the northern outskirts will draw bonus pay for living in Arctic conditions."[97]

Against this backdrop, Vavakin at last released a digest of the "Master Plan of Development of Moscow and Moscow Oblast to the Year 2010" in April 1989.[98] The Moscow population goal for 2000 was kept at 9.5 million and that for 2010 pared to 9.8 million, with 6.9 million more in the oblast. After—but only after—2010, the proposal endorsed a drawing down (not quantified) in the population of both city and region. Moscow's municipal boundaries were to be stabilized, although 60 percent of new housing was to be on the protuberations outside the MKAD. Density would be stepped up by infilling empty and underused lands, among them the Lyublino aeration fields, refuse heaps, and gullies. Four "research and production" satellites of 100,000 persons each were to be implanted in neighboring oblasts, while in Moscow oblast the development bulldozers were to be forced out to transportation corridors external to the green belt.

The plan's social improvements were touted without the drumrolls of 1935 and 1971. The paragraphs on shelter show fewer completions than the Mossovet had projected in its 1988 housing program and a self-effacing target for per capita supply in 2010—12.0 square meters of net dwelling space, a tad more than the current 11.4 square meters and *less* than the 13.0–13.5 promised in the 1971 plan. The slummy five-story walkups of the 1950s were to be revamped and, where necessary, taken down for modern buildings. The newer housing estates on the perimeter were to be rendered "psychologically comfortable" by adding greenery, enclosing small spaces, and finishing off service facilities. One hundred and fifty kilometers of subway track were to be laid and the four controversial cordon highways of the 1971 plan would be dropped for a pair of apostrophe-shaped roads several kilometers beyond the Sadovoye, allowing vehicular bypass of the central area. Also abandoned were the fictional planning macrozones of the 1971 legislation. Rather, twenty-one "specialized centers" and four "regional multifunctional centers" were to be nodes of leisure and commercial activity (see Figure 74).

The 1989 draft, which probably deserved a kinder fate than it got, did not reach far enough in curbing growth to quiet the restrictionists. Composing a brief for the slimming down that Vavakin originally favored, two geographers noted that multiple exemptions to the ban on limitchiki had been granted since 1986. They proposed slicing the work force by 1 percent a year until a population of 7 million was attained, forbidding new factory dormitories and any high-rise housing past the MKAD, and capping subway construction at five kilometers a year, since several thousand migrant laborers and their kin needed to be admitted for every kilometer. Conversely, the architectural critic Valerii Rabinovich rebuked the draft as too restrictive—a

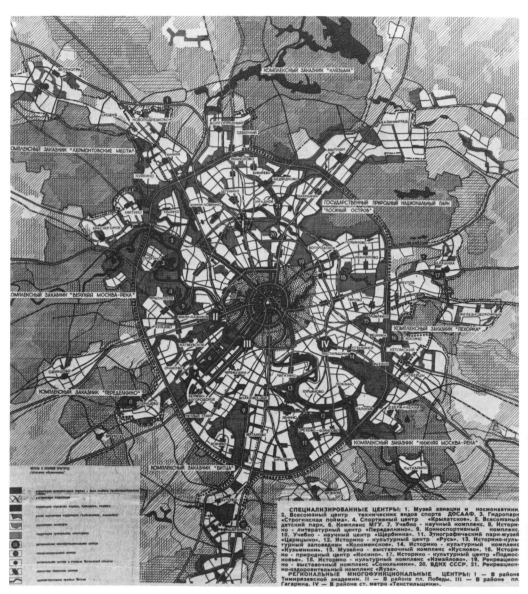

Figure 74. Unratified draft master plan, 1989. City parks appear in dark shading, green belt forests in small checks. Twenty-one mostly recreational "specialized centers" are indicated in Arabic numbers; and four "regional multifunctional centers" are shown in Roman numerals. (From *Moskovskaya pravda*, April 13, 1989, p. 3.)

last gasp of "the antiquated and antiscientific administrative-command principles" of state control. Not only would population maximums be shattered sooner or later, but the police-state devices buttressing them were "residues of territorial serfdom."[99]

The planners could not have picked a worse moment to come forward. They strove to reanimate the levers of socialist urban management at the very instant when the forced consensus about state socialism was coming asunder. They wrote in the metier of the central bureaucracy, only to see the center lose power and to be slapped with the reproach that in a democratizing society local governments ought to chart their own futures. The democrats elected in 1990 felt no stake in Vavakin's sketch and did not appoint him to the ispolkom in 1991 or as a government minister in 1992. And specific contours of the plan had been outdated by revised expectations about public policy, leaving it susceptible to assault by single-issue opponents.

The fatal shot was fired by Goskompriroda, the fledgling USSR State Committee on Environmental Protection, one of several regulatory bodies to which Vavakin's report was referred in 1989. In September 1990 the Goskompriroda collegium conducted the equivalent of an American environmental impact hearing. It heard evidence that the plan was "extensive in character" and did "not take into account the quickly changing ecological situation," especially population dynamics, water and air pollution, and the mottled green belt. After "stormy discussion," the collegium voted against the package, inviting Vavakin to come back some day with a revision. Without friends at court, the draft plan went into indefinite abeyance.[100]

The consummate irony is that unplanned extraneous trends had begun to bring about the very demographic outcome the planners had so doggedly sought, and then some (see Appendix A). Mean annual increases in Moscow's population from 1985 through 1988 were 77,800, or 0.90 percent of the 1985 base, already the most tepid rate of the postwar period. In 1989 and 1990 the increments were tiny, 13,000 and 23,000, or two-tenths of a percentage point per year. In 1991 and 1992 the unthinkable happened: permanent residents *declined* by 46,000 and 76,000, 1.4 percent in the two years—the first time the population decreased in peacetime since the evictions by the NKVD in the mid-1930s. Current forecasts predict a further drop to 8.5 million within two or three years.[101]

We can attribute this revolution to reinforcing declines in both biological and migration indexes, themselves a reflection of economic disarray, poorer nutrition, and mental stress. Lower birth rates and higher death rates produced a natural decrease in the population in place. That effect was mitigated by resettlement into Moscow, but net migration for its part declined and in 1992 turned negative. In 1992 more Muscovites died than were born, and more people moved out of the city than moved in.

The population outflow is the most arresting indicator. It has set tongues wagging about a replay of the "deurbanization" of the War Communism years. Price inflation has been higher in the capital than anywhere else in European Russia, and wage increases slower. This pincer movement put Moscow residents' standard of living 8 percent lower than the national average in April 1993. Although "mass flight" into the provinces was not under way, the head of the Russian Ministry of Labor stated, "we do not know where we will end up if things keep going the way they are."[102] The very fact that a cabinet member would mention such fears was telling.

Urban planning in Moscow undoubtedly must adapt to altered conditions. Faith is hard to come by in Russia nowadays in the perspicacious shaping of society by the state. Economic reform sunders the instrumentation through which Soviet plans were implemented, from Gosplan to compliant, government-owned factories and construction trusts.

If doctrinaire comprehensive planning has seen its day, there are reasons to believe that urban planning in a less grandiose form will persevere. Moscow's planning machinery has proven remarkably resilient. GlavAPU, the core agency, changed labels twice in three years—it is now Moskomarkhitektura, the Committee for Architecture and City Planning—but it has the same chief (Vavakin) and 10,000 of the 13,000 employees it had at its prime. Although land allocation was taken over in 1991 by a new bureau, Moskomzem (the Committee for Land Reform and Land Resources), and some design institutes and studios are being spun off as private ateliers, Moskomarkhitektura intends to retain a large professional cadre and faces little resistance from politicians.[103] Architects at its Institute of the Master Plan continue to rework the 1989 draft, confident that a revision will be legislated. Articles calling Moscow's lack of a plan a disgrace have appeared in the local and central press.

In another subfield, Gorplan, the City Planning Commission of Soviet times, continues in wizened form as a Committee on Long-Range Planning within the Mayor's Department. The former Gorplan think tank is now the Institute of the Long-Range Development of Moscow. GlavUKS, the Chief Directorate of Capital Construction, hums along as Moskapstroi, the Moscow Capital Construction Department.

The stagnation and now diminution of Moscow's population will not put all or most of the planners out of work, for in many societies urban planning has been most prized precisely when cities are in decline. Only time will tell if the dip of the early 1990s signals temporary stress or a secular change. The marketizing New Economic Policy of the 1920s, it may be remembered, was accompanied by robust demographic growth in Moscow. Should the decline persevere, a governmental response will be expected for that, too. Planning is essentially a hedge against uncertainty, and the one certainty in Moscow life is that uncertainty will be a staple of it.

Policy makers give no sign of terminating the passport and residential permit system that underbraced Soviet town planning. Its morality and efficiency came into question under Gorbachev, and it seemed on its way out until the dissolution of the USSR intervened. The Russian identity cards replacing Soviet internal passports perform most of the same functions, although general Russian policy recommends doing away with the propiska stamp.[104] Moscow's government has fought the abolition of propiska every step of the way and has stated repeatedly that it intends to retain the system as a condition of permanent residency. Despite its Stalinist origins, propiska has almost universal public support in Moscow. Asked about it in October 1993, 26 percent of a sample of Muscovites said they wanted it left unchanged and 54 percent wanted it tightened up; only 4 percent favored relaxation and 4 percent abolition.[105]

Moscow officials justify continuation of residential controls, first, as a law-and-order measure, since 35 to 40 percent of all crimes in the city are committed by nonresidents and propiska is a handy weapon for the overburdened police force. The eviction of 10,000 unregistered individuals during Black October played to a widespread fear of victimization by outsiders, especially ethnic non-Russians. Second, officials hold that the advent of market pricing of housing and high income differentials make restrictions necessary for purposes of social policy. According to this argument, high-income migrants, not lower-class criminals, "will gush into Moscow" and will "buy housing at free prices . . . and wash away the most marvellous of plans."[106] Third, they raise an economic consideration and treat Moscow papers as a good that can be sold to would-be immigrants to raise municipal revenue. A limited commercialization of propiska went into effect June 1, 1994; it may yet be overruled by the Russian government and will in any event be open to corruption.[107]

Urban planning would survive even if mobility were unrestricted, because local government will retain a legitimate role in urban development. Pent-up demand and the grinding down of infrastructure over the last generation leave many Muscovites wanting more public services, not less. They cannot get all they expect in an era of wasting budgets, yet they have needs that cannot sanely be neglected. Privatization of housing and retail trade will put some of the bigger problems in nonstate hands—such as refurbishing the vast stock of five-story "khrushcheby" and building stores and dry cleaning outlets in outlying housing projects—but classic public-goods dilemmas will make government investment crucial in certain areas. The subway department, for example, estimates that 233 kilometers more of track and 133 stations, on six lines, will be necessary to meet commuter demand by 2010. If funding cannot be found, locational decisions will have to be varied. To achieve this kind of interissue and interagency coordination, problem-solving planning must be undertaken.[108]

The regional dimension of Moscow's development, a key point of the unratified 1989 plan, demands strategic vision. Specialists from the Institute of the Master Plan, showing unusual political savvy, argue that only by thinking on a regionwide scale can Moscow achieve the "democratization of suburbanization" prevalent in the urban agglomerations of the industrial West. Staged insertion of low-density housing into Podmoskov'e would be a great improvement over the present chaos, where the green belt is being chewed away and even middle-income housing mandated by presidential decree is being put at unlivable sites, while only the "new bourgeoisie," by hook or crook, gets well-located plots to put up second homes. The optimal outcome for twenty-five or thirty years hence, the experts say, would be a Moscow reduced to 7 million residents (the Shatalin-Vavakin target in 1986), surrounded by 5 million suburbanites living in communities governed confederally with the city.[109]

Lest this scheme appear to be another pipe dream, one hastens to add that planners' skills will be in demand for a job that needs to be done for private as much as public purposes: installation of the rudiments of a modern system of land use control. Private ownership of rural and urban land became an option in Russia only after several presidential decrees on the subject in late 1993. In 1991, however, the RSFSR did permit local governments to levy "payments for land," essentially surrogate rents related to economic value. Moskomzem in March 1992 subdivided Moscow into sixty-nine "territorial-economic assessment zones" and set annual charges on a sliding scale from 135,000 rubles per hectare (in parts of Zelenograd) to 826,000 rubles (in south-central Moscow); it granted exemptions to scientific and cultural organizations, law enforcement bodies, and agencies catering to war veterans, invalids, or orphans. A year later, Moscow began to auction off forty-nine-year leases, charging for new users whatever the market would bear rather than the arbitrary and relatively flat fee structure approved earlier.[110]

These changes are bound to modify the behavior of builders and government regulators. As differentiated prices and rents give rise to differentiated uses, architects and planners will have to do more than crank out location-blind designs and site plans. Clients will demand, and the market should dictate, particularized structures whose height, layout, and configuration will be tailor-made. Working out those individual designs, the customized network of utilities and services, and safeguards for nearby communities will be a generation's labor for the surviving part of the overblown planning bureaucracy.

CONSERVATION CONUNDRUMS

No cause vaulted up the Moscow political agenda as quickly during the liberalization of the 1980s as the parallel questions of defense of the natural and the man-made environments. Their salience has since declined, although it would be an error to think that either has been extinguished.

To some extent both species of environmentalism, especially the first, bloomed as surrogates for the questioning of ideological fundamentals. "You were still not allowed to yell, 'Down with the CPSU!'" one participant recalled, "but you could say, 'Give Us a Clean Environment!'"[111] Mobilization around ecological issues occurred first in the protest arena and then in electoral politics. Many winners in the

1990 election came out of neighborhood controversies like those over the Moscow Zoo and Brateyevo. One of the Mossovet's first acts was to demand a stop to construction of the Northern TETS, the power generating giant in the far north of Moscow. It acceded in the veto of the draft master plan for defects in the ecological sphere.

Mindsets have changed since 1990. Political figures who rode the so-called green stallion to office often saw things otherwise when their roles changed and the end of Soviet power obviated environmentalism's shock value. Among the population, environmental angst has lost out to concern over the most rock-bottom individual and family needs. As early as December 1991, a poll found that only 15 percent of Muscovites identified pollution and ecology as an urgent problem in city life. Twenty-seven percent mentioned housing, 33 percent urban transport, and 87 percent food supply.[112]

The Moscow administration thus took no great risk in January 1992 when it decided to collaborate with the Russian government to complete the Northern TETS. Attacked months before as a bomb for "ecological genocide," the plant had been reengineered and its industrial zone canceled. More pointedly, its projected electricity and heat took on a different glow under conditions of economic crisis than when pickets went up in 1989. Deputies in the Mossovet resisted but did not reverse the decision. The first boiler was fired up in November 1992 and began delivering power to the Bibirevo and Medvedkovo housing districts and to Mytishchi in the oblast. The station, the largest of its class in Europe, is to be fully operational by 2000.

Governments cognizant of the tradeoffs between economic and environmental variables salvaged the Northern TETS. So it would be if, as officials suggest, the Rzhev conveyance project, torpedoed by Gorbachev, were to be revived to augment Moscow's water supply.

Absent-minded environmental disruption looks quite different from conscious choice of this kind. The former abounds in and around Moscow and is being compounded by the lag in revising environmental laws and implementing mechanisms, the budget deficit, and the overall decline in state authority.

Plantings in Moscow parks and gardens, for example, have fallen off markedly. The financially strapped city puts in about one-half of the trees, 40 percent of the shrubs, and one-third of the flowers it did in 1985. Muscovites now own 1 million automobiles, and annual increases in the fleet have tripled since 1990. Municipal inspectors cannot keep up with the parking garages being thrown together in corrugated metal and brick in microraions and nature reserves: "Rarely is the law observed. The basic patterns are willful seizure, willful construction, and [occupation of] illicitly allocated or grabbed green space, which influences the ecological condition of the whole city."[113] Garage "shanghais," in the vernacular, have encroached since 1990 on the Setun and Skhodnya Rivers, Golovinskii Pond, the patrician estates at Mikhalkovo and Tsaritsyno, and Bittsa Park. Sanitation has visibly worsened all over Moscow, as trash and snow removal lag owing to aging equipment and to many municipal workers' absorption in side activities. Largely because of worsening hygiene and cutbacks in vaccination programs, epidemic diseases absent for decades have returned. In 1993, 2,544 Muscovites fell ill with diphtheria (unknown in Moscow from 1975 to 1988), and 99 died; cholera, not sighted since 1973, also cropped up in 1993.

The circumferential green belt and contiguous districts, flush with truck gardens, summer and weekend dachas, and year-round cottages, have lately been similarly squeezed. Biologists warn that ecosystems to all sides of Moscow are being overtaxed by haphazard drainage of wetlands, woodcutting, beating of trails, and cabin building on the banks of creeks, lakes, and reservoirs. No environmental assessment preceded Yeltsin's decrees on cottage construction in the oblast; planners try to do it post facto. The twenty-one Moscow leisure zones are falling into wrack and ruin: "Endless reorganizations, relocations, proprietary changes, and plain disorder have left our leisure zones masterless. A wave of vandalism has struck beaches and boat houses. Buildings and equipment have been burglarized, wrecked, and burned. Riverside areas are all cluttered up and water channels are not being checked and dredged."[114]

Elite and mass consciousness about environmental issues has not come full circle. Muscovites have stayed alert to hazards they see as posing an acute health or genetic danger, such as dumps for nuclear or toxic waste. Natural scientists and city planners discuss ecological problems freely and have no shortage of ideas about remedy. Militant neighborhood groups block construction projects in Lefortovo, Brateyevo, and Mitino.

Paradoxically, the draft master plan of 1989 that was axed on ecological grounds had incalculably more to offer on such questions than its forerunners. Its suggestions were sound if expensive: liquidation of 13 industrial zones; closing of 77 factories in Moscow and 104 in the oblast, reprofiling of 148 factories, and rebasing of 195 in industrial zones; construction of 19 trash incinerators, treatment plants, and processors for poisonous substances; 62 kilometers of sound deflection barriers on heavily traveled streets; and large anti-erosion and reclamation works. Moscow could do worse than to return to these investments when finances permit.

The messy springtime of the transition away from a planned economy and a passive society has exacerbated ecological problems and made solutions seem more unattainable than ever. In subsequent phases radical economic reform ought to have salutary effects. The more private ownership there is of housing and businesses, the more incentive individuals and small groups will have to care about the condition and appearance of their physical world. Successful privatization would duplicate the material basis for the common-law doctrine of nuisance that has been the basis for land use zoning and its accompanying defenses in the West.[115] With diversification of ownership and stabilization of the currency, monetary levers can be devised to deter abuses, a process that proved so hard to establish in the command economy. Market or near-market pricing of natural resources—urban and exurban land and fuels at the head of the line—will dampen demand for them and reduce waste.

The politics of the architectural environment has had much in common with ecological politics. Protest over incursion on Moscow's older sections helped foal the green movements, and the two groups have used similar tactics of protest. But differences have been observable, too. The architectural conservationists are more aroused than the ecologists by history and symbols. They link the sins of the Soviet past to questions of Russian national identity (sometimes but not always chauvinistically) and spirituality.

Under fire from VOOPIK, city planners held a contest in 1986–1987 for a design to rebuild the Sukharev Tower on the stone sill left over from its excision in 1934; the USSR Merchant Marine Ministry agreed to foot the bill and put a naval museum in the tower. The city's standing request for its own restoration agency was granted in 1987. The integrity of historic districts generated the most emotive discussion during deliberations on the draft master plan, at the very time that glasnost' triggered revisionism about the demolition binge of the 1920s and 1930s, the 1935 and 1971 plans, and the ramming of prospekt Kalinina through the Arbat. A Foundation for Restoration of the Cathedral of Christ the Redeemer, trained on the most sensational of the Stalin-era razings, formed in 1988 and held an arabesque inauguration in September 1989, on the 150th anniversary of the laying of the cornerstone of the church by Tsar Nicholas I. In February 1990 the Old Moscow Society, 60 years after its dissolution, was revived as a discussion circle. In June 1990 Popov's government resolved to resurrect the Kazan Cathedral, the small seventeenth-century church on Red Square ground to dust in 1936.

The fruit of these efforts is impressive. Although the Sukharev reconstruction was scrapped for lack of funds, several acts of symbolic restitution have been speedily effected. City building trusts rebuilt the Kazan Cathedral in two years flat, from drawings and photographs done in the 1930s by Petr Baranovskii; Patriarch Aleksii consecrated it November 4, 1993, in the presence of Yeltsin, Luzhkov, and the Russian press (Figure 75). In the Kremlin, the Red Staircase of the Faceted Palace, pulled down in 1933, was resurrected on Yeltsin's order and opened for viewing in May 1994; work has commenced on reversing Stalin's changes to the Great Kremlin Palace and the Senate building. Ground was broken in 1994 on a re-creation of the Voskresenskiye Gates of the Kitaigorod Wall, which Stalin demolished in 1931; the gates, and a new Shrine of the Iberian Virgin within them, are to be ready by 1997.

The Russian Orthodox Church, from which the Soviet government seized many of the desecrated and expunged landmarks, has taken a back seat to secular Moscophiles and Russophiles in restoration politics. It has had two other priorities: construction of a new national basilica, for which it received permission to build at Tsaritsyno in 1988, and ownership of all extant religious buildings. The first task is beyond its means for the moment, while the second has been so successful that the episcopate finds itself saddled with scores of crumbling parish churches and even a handful of Moscow's ancient abbeys. So far the Moscow patriarchate has been given the keys to the Danilov Monastery (handed back as a church headquarters by Gorbachev in 1988, the millennium of Russian Christianity), the Donskoi, No-

Figure 75. Rebuilt Kazan Cathedral. (Photograph by author.)

vospasskii, and Simonov Monasteries, and the Rozhdestvenskii Convent; small groups of monks and nuns have returned and once again peal the bells.[116] The church has also been allowed to observe holy days in some venerable temples that remain state property (St. Basil's and the Kremlin Assumption Cathedral, conspicuously).

The most celebrated reconstruction cause has, of course, been the Cathedral of Christ the Redeemer. After several years in which that issue was left mostly to jingoists, Luzhkov and the Moscow government in December 1993 decided to cooperate. They closed the Moskva swimming pool in the circular foundation of the Palace of Soviets that never was and deeded the site to the cathedral foundation, which raises subscription funds for the project. Municipal contractors began foundation work in the autumn of 1994 and had a forest of building cranes in the air by year's end. On Orthodox Christmas, January 7, 1995, the patriarch and the mayor, in a nationally televised ceremony, laid the cornerstone of the church. The city government plans to complete construction of the shell—in ferroconcrete, faced in brick—by the 850th anniversary of Moscow in September 1997, with decorative work to go on for some years after that.[117]

Rebuilding the dynamited cathedral may make sense politically but not economically and culturally. The faithful would be far better served if the funds were spent on fixing up neighborhood churches and erecting new ones on the Moscow outskirts, where only old village and estate churches survive—and where, as in all of Russia, not a single house of worship was built under Soviet rule. The mammoth neocathedral smacks of post-Soviet monumentalism, conceived in exactly the same spirit as the nineteenth-century original (which architect Aleksandr Vitberg saw as an ode in stone to the "mighty and expansive" Russian state) and as the socialist pagoda that Joseph Stalin tried in vain to put up here.

A companion dilemma during this rediscovery of old Russia's legacy has been what to do with evocative structures built in the Soviet period. In March 1987 the city put forty-eight buildings from the 1920s and 1930s, many of avant-garde design, on its landmark registry. Few decisions have been this easy. An attempt in the late 1980s to get backing for reassembly of a vanished talisman, the Liberty Obelisk of 1918–1941 (as Nikita Khrushchev had favored), found no takers. The Victory Monument on Poklonnaya Hill, a new project, was suspended in 1986 because of its gracelessness and its transgression on a site sacred to Russian nationalists. After an unavailing search for a different concept and venue, construction resumed in 1992. The semifinished pavilion admitted its first visitors in May 1993 and had its grand opening by Yeltsin on the fiftieth anniversary of victory over Germany on May 9, 1995. The plans call for construction of an Orthodox church, a synagogue, and a mosque in a half-moon to the west of the main gallery; the public sculpture has yet to be decided upon.

The 1991 coup honed the dilemma of what to do with socialist icons, as Communist Party buildings and public art became the targets of avenging crowds. After municipal workers took down the showpiece statues of Dzerzhinskii and the others, some wanted all visual memorials of the party pulverized. But the view prevailed in the city's commission on the subject that indiscriminate destruction would be mimicry of "the true Leninists whose extremism and Bolshevik intolerance we are rejecting."[118] It was decided to leave seven of the sixty-eight large statues and busts of Lenin on their pedestals, including Lev Kerbel's bronze behemoth at Oktyabr'skaya ploshchad' but excluding the pensive sitting figure in the Kremlin. The Marx on Teatral'naya ploshchad' will be undisturbed, except for the worshipful inscription, as will nineteen of the forty-eight major sculptures of Soviet personages. Remaining works of political art are to be stowed over several years in museums or warehouses. President Yeltsin removed Post No. 1, the fixed-bayonet guard at the Lenin Mausoleum, in October 1993; the tomb seems likely to stay, although debate continues on whether Lenin's body and the other remains in Red Square should be buried in a more suitable place. Mayor Popov closed the Lenin Museum, the pre-1917 city hall, which demonstrators very nearly invaded on August 22, 1991. The new Moscow City Duma has declined the offer of use of the building; it will reopen after renovation as a wing of the Historical Museum.[119]

Moscow's carousel of place names rolled on unabated through 1993, so that by now the Lenin Hills are once again the Sparrow Hills, the Lenin Library has become the Russian State Library, and the big athletic stadium's title no longer includes "Bearing the Name of V. I. Lenin" (although the subway's, for some reason, does). Oktyabr'skaya ploshchad' and Novokirovskii prospekt (solemnizing the October Revolution and Sergei Kirov) are Kaluzhskaya ploshchad' (Kaluga Square) and prospekt Akademika A. D. Sakharova (Academician Sakharov Prospect). Renamings have now been decelerated because they cost too much and confuse many who grew up with the Soviet-era appellations.[120]

Grassroots fury in the 1980s targeted the despoilment of picturesque old Moscow by demolitions and construction of faceless buildings dwarfing their surroundings. The protestors, who had access to the national media and sympathy from liberals and conservatives alike, won a great and probably irrevocable victory. The planner or investor who proposes in the 1990s to take apart an object on one of the city's protected ledgers does so at his or her peril. No one would dream today of shoving a Rossiya Hotel or a prospekt Kalinina into a heritage area. The "red lines" of the Stalinist master plan, used to justify street widenings since 1935, have been rescinded.

This hard-won solicitude might be negated if commercialization of land use were to breed high-density redevelopment of the old town. But planners would most likely resist that temptation for political reasons.

Domestic and international financiers are currently negotiating several blockbuster mixed-use projects. Most will be in or just out of the Central Administrative Okrug; not one will be inside the Sadovoye kol'tso. The grandest, a Moscow International Business Center organized by a SITI (as in City of London) joint stock company, has been approved for a square kilometer of industrial land on Krasnopresnenskaya naberezhnaya, three kilometers west of the Sadovoye. SITI signed a lease with the city in November 1992 and is seeking up to $8 billion from foreign lenders. Its "Crystal Palace" stock exchange, seventy-story tower for banks and insurance companies, hotels, and other niceties should be finished by 1999 if all goes well. Other sites being haggled over include the Badayev Brewery across the river from SITI (for offices and shops); the ploshchad' Gagarina area along Leninskii prospekt (for shops, hotels, and housing); Leningradskii prospekt at the Central Airfield (for an Aviation Center with offices and transport terminals); the Sparrow Hills (for a "scientific business park" linked to Moscow University); and the Exhibition of the Economic Achievements of the USSR at Ostankino (for mixed uses).

Conflict has erupted over several of these proposals, yet retention of scenic townscape has seldom been the issue. Residents perturbed about overcrowding and overpricing of local services have signed "Not in My Back Yard" petitions and staged sit-ins at ploshchad' Gagarina. The SITI consortium had to reckon until October 1993 with Aleksandr Krasnov, the chairman of the Krasnopresnenskii raion soviet, who campaigned for construction of apartments for raion residents on the unused portion of the site.

In the inner city, too, residents have rallied against menaces to the peace. They object vociferously to the dragging out of the infrastructural improvements begun in 1987, which tie up roadways year in year out as tsarist-era sewage collectors and water mains are excavated. The uncouth market culture of the streets has brought with it litter and commotion. At its worst, as in the several pedestrian malls—

overrun with hustlers and prostitutes, bargain-seeking provincials and foreign tourists, and food sellers with smoke-spewing grills—petty commerce has been a torment for surrounding apartment dwellers.

But the most wrenching issues inside the Sadovoye are more social than sanitary or aesthetic. The government of Moscow seeks to end demographic depletion, halt the involuntary relocation of native Muscovites to distant microraions, and maintain a balance among income groups. Not least of the pathologies before it is the profusion of derelict apartments and houses between the Kremlin and the Sadovoye kol'tso. In the second half of the 1980s, with the slowdown in construction on the outskirts and the authorities chary about coercing tenants into resettlement, aging tenement houses tagged for rehabilitation or demolition were frequently evacuated piecemeal and then, after maintenance had dwindled, abandoned to the wind and rain. More than 2 million square meters of gross living space went unoccupied in central Moscow in 1992—enough if in good trim to shelter about 120,000 Muscovites at the per capita norm, or half of the present population out to the Sadovoye.[121]

The city has made its priority in the old center the capital reconstruction of vacant, semivacant, and substandard housing, much of it of pre-1917 construction inhabited for decades on a communal basis. Seemingly feasible targets for the mid-1990s set 200,000 square meters (gross) of existing floor area to be reconditioned annually, plus another 200,000 square meters of newly constructed space in architect-designed apartment houses.

The city will have a harder time achieving the proclaimed social objective of class diversity than the physical targets. Under the policy worked out in 1992–1993, any organization or enterprise that undertakes to rehabilitate decrepit buildings in the Moscow center is entitled to receive and dispose of half of the housing itself. Most will either be assigned to organizational leaders or sold at the going price. Privatization also discriminates: offers to buy joint-occupancy flats or rooms in them, usually for a combination of cash and a factory-issue flat near the MKAD, are posted all over downtown Moscow. Bought-out kommunalki are being refitted as roomy single-family apartments for clients with the wherewithal to pay for them.

The city administration accepts a responsibility to rehouse free of charge displaced residents of the central area, but that position, too, has a sticking point. A recent summary says:

> Who is going to live in this . . . first-class housing in the very center of Moscow? Won't the tens of thousands of Moscow families so favored be exclusively from the new rich, from those with high incomes? How different will it be from past years, when it was bureaucratic folk, retainers of the [Communist Party] throne, who made themselves at home in these "gentry nests"?
>
> The answer is simple: we are not talking here about an elite, bureaucratic or commercial, but about all residents without exception . . . There will be sufficient new housing for all inhabitants of the old quarters . . . *But* it is another question whether every family can subsequently afford to live in new, high-quality apartments once the impending reform of apartment charges [rent and utilities fees] is taken into account. In time, what one pays for housing will depend on the location of the accommodation and on its level of comfort. This will be the choice of each family. The task ahead is to give people new housing. They will do with it as they see fit.[122]

The city has committed itself, then, to one-time allotment of a flat at the per capita minimum in size. That done, residents will be thrust without further ado into a market in which the dimensions, quality, and location of their shelter will depend on their economic resources. The result can only be intensification of the exodus of blue-collar and lower-status households from the central city and its steady conversion into far more of an oasis of well-being than it ever was under the Communist Party.

Already the center and the periphery show a discernible contrast in housing affordability (see Map 41). The priciest zone is inside the Sadovoye, with an extension to the southwest. Two small areas outside the Sadovoye and the quadrant past the university come next in value. Most of the outlying raions fall into a third category. The fourth and least desirable zone is in plebeian Moscow southeast.

Some of the polemics about downtown development interlard class and spatial imagery much as socialist ideologues did in 1917 and afterward. "Traders in real estate and the city authorities," states one tract, value the windswept housing estates of the outer districts only

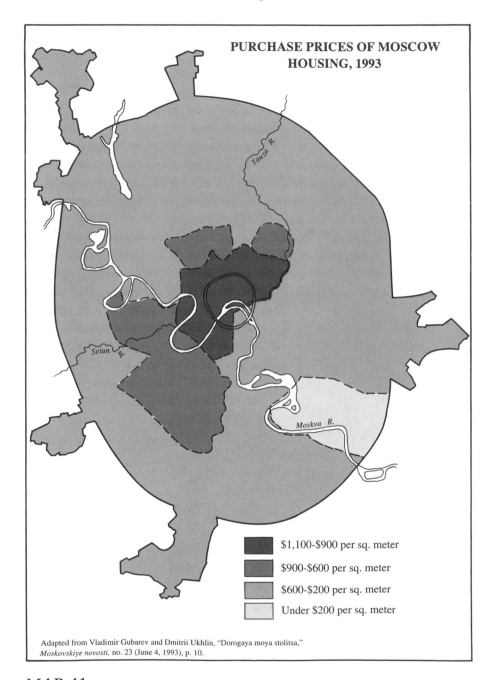

PURCHASE PRICES OF MOSCOW
HOUSING, 1993

$1,100-$900 per sq. meter

$900-$600 per sq. meter

$600-$200 per sq. meter

Under $200 per sq. meter

Adapted from Vladimir Gubarev and Dmitrii Ukhlin, "Dorogaya moya stolitsa,"
Moskovskiye novosti, no. 23 (June 4, 1993), p. 10.

MAP 41

as somewhere to put Muscovites dislodged by their plans to gentrify the inner city: "It is precisely to here, into dormitory 'reservations,' that the tiresome 'aborigines' will be expelled once businessmen and foreigners have finally managed to turn the center of Moscow into their own forbidden city."[123] Herein lies the grist of a politics of territorial division and envy that Moscow has seen before and that it behooves reformers to nip in the bud.

Making a Civic Community

Moscow has in a blink of history's eye traveled no small way from dictatorship toward democratic self-government. World experience teaches, though, that going the distance to a well-ordered regime will take much longer than the voyage thus far.

How long might that be? Where the imprinting of robust democratic values and institutions is concerned, says Robert Putnam, time is metered in decades if not in generations. A narrower "two-turnover test" has been recommended by Samuel Huntington, who considers democracy consolidated "if the party or group that takes power in the initial election at the time of transition loses a subsequent election and turns over power to those election winners, and if those election winners then peacefully turn over power to the winners of a later election." Even by this criterion, Moscow and Russia have miles to journey, since the group that rose upon the CPSU's collapse came asunder, rather than surrendering power to another group, and since the showdown that solidified one subgroup's control in 1993 was not peaceful. We could not speak under the Huntington rule of a local democratic order being consolidated in Moscow until two municipal elections hence, in the late 1990s at the earliest.[124]

A crucial indicator of political development, as Putnam's study of regional reform in Italy reminds us, is "civic community," or patterns of "civil involvement and social solidarity." Civic community, in Putnam's understanding, is innate in democratic politics, an endogenous sign that the people are ruling themselves. It also interweaves a mesh of causal connections with exogenous variables. Profoundly shaped by state behavior, civic community shapes the state in turn. It evolves with glacial slowness, and its retardation may trap polities in "vicious uncivic circles," yet it is not impervious to intervention.

This last point is particularly germane in Moscow in that its past, under the tsars and under the CPSU partocracy, cannot by any stretch of the imagination predispose it toward a democratic future. Civic community in pre-socialist and socialist Moscow was conspicuous by its absence. Mobilized participation, "compliant activism," and "covert participation" could not substitute, and their aftereffects may be impeding post-socialist development. Putnam, abstracting to Russia and the other former Communist countries from his findings about southern Italy, bets against them surmounting their histories: "Without norms of reciprocity and networks of civic engagement, the Hobbesian outcome of the Mezzogiorno—amoral familism, clientelism, lawlessness, ineffective government, and economic stagnation—seems likelier than successful democratization and economic development." "Palermo," he writes figuratively, "may represent the future of Moscow." And so it may be—but not necessarily.

As Putnam himself shows, institutional change in the form of the reconstitution of regional governments made a difference to the public life of the Mezzogiorno in the 1970s and 1980s. Regional politics became more competitive, more pragmatic, and less derivative of the ministries in Rome. "These trends transpired in the South no less than the North . . . Compared to the North, the southern regions are no better off today than they were in 1970. Compared to where the South would be today without the regional reform, however, the South is much better off."[125] Organizational and procedural reform and experimentation, in other words, may inculcate some if not all of the features of civic community, even when societal chromosomes seem biased against them.

What can we speculate about Moscow's chances of making progress toward civic community similar in order of magnitude, say, to what was done in the southern provinces of Italy? I limit myself to two sides of the question: policy performance and engagement of the citizenry in political activities and discourse.

GOVERNMENT THAT DELIVERS

Sophisticated students of political change know that a complex and multifaceted relation exists between material well-being and the inauguration and consolidation of democratic rule. Contextual problems such as extremes of poverty, inequality, and inflation are not a deterministic death sentence for new democracies, and, as Huntington reasons, a certain disillusionment with government policy may actually promote stability if it deflates popular expectations. Also, as Putnam argues, civic community and democracy may just as well be causes of economic prosperity as the other way around. This having been said, transnational and case studies speak with one voice that levels of socioeconomic development covary with democratization. "Empirically speaking," in Putnam's words, "few generalizations are more firmly established than that effective democracy is correlated with socioeconomic modernization."[126]

Although we cannot say fatalistically that policy failure would foreclose the consolidation of civic community and democratic norms in Moscow, we can say that policy success will shorten the odds of the best outcome eventuating. The imperfectly democratized government of the post-socialist city will answer for its deeds in the dock of public opinion, just as the Communist Party did once it untightened its grip on society. The better it does at redressing chronic problems of basic need and urban amenity, the greater its authority will be. The more socioeconomic development it engenders, the tougher it would be for neoauthoritarians to control the local economy, the more resources will be available for intergroup accommodation, the larger and more secure the pro-democratic urban middle class will be, and the more achievement-oriented and tolerant the population as a whole.

Democratization in Russia and Eastern Europe, in a distinctive twist, coincides with the attempt to marketize the command economy, a project that at the outset depresses output and manufactures privation. Popular reactions to economic and related social ills have, predictably, been pained. In Moscow a sample of adults surveyed in early 1993 did not give local government a positive report card on a single dimension of economic reform or urban services. Forty-four percent considered privatization work good or satisfactory, the best grade assigned; 31 percent rated social protection of the needy good or satisfactory, while only 18 percent said so of housing policy, 16 percent of the maintenance of overall living standards, 2 percent of the physical appearance of the city, and 1 percent of law and order.[127]

It is reassuring in light of these statistics that so few Moscow voters followed the authoritarian pied pipers in the 1993 parliamentary election and that, helped along by generous rules, Russia's Choice was able to gain its majority in the city duma. Most Muscovites are not yet ready to surrender their newly won political, civil, and economic liberties, despite their understandable discontent with policy performance in general.[128]

But the last word has hardly been spoken, for Muscovites are just now encountering the critical costs of structural adjustment—bankruptcies and unemployment. Democratic Russia's manifesto in 1990 promised that the democratic path "in the final analysis will give bread and freedom to all." In the final analysis bread as well as freedom will have to be delivered, or else freedom will be tarnished in the eyes of many. The literature on political transitions gives us no basis for forecasting how long the democrats will have to make good on their promises. What it does suggest is that deliver they must.

As if crafting economic and social structures were not a tall enough order, Moscow government must cope with the effects of the decay of public mores, a process that began as the old regime decomposed but has continued under the new. The slippage of state and social controls and wider access to weapons have markedly worsened common criminality in Russia. Muscovites now triple-bolt their doors, cast nervous glances over their shoulders as they go about after dark, and consume an ocean of crime reportage in the mass media. They tend to associate the 25 percent annual increases in many serious crimes with cultural permissiveness and political liberalization: hence much of the support for the propiska system and the acceptability, indeed, popularity of the sweeps of the streets during the state of emergency of October 1993.

A pair of interrelated phenomena that Russians also associate with democratization has a more direct political impact: organized crime and corruption. The country's *mafiya* has not yet been seriously investigated by social scientists. We do know that it functions as a loosely woven assemblage of criminal and violent gangs, that its structure is clan-based, that a disproportionate number of its leaders are of non-Russian nationality (often from Chechnya, Azerbaijan, and elsewhere in the Caucasus region), and that it feeds parasitically on private and quasi-private firms in the transitional economy. Protection rackets, an especially odious manifestation, first came to notice in the heyday of the cooperatives around 1990. Some estimate that 80 percent of all Moscow and Russian entrepreneurs today are forced to remit monthly fees to remain safely in business.[129]

Criminal syndicates shade at the edges into a still more insidious behavior: corruption. As the later years of Leonid Brezhnev go to show, corruption is a sulphur that eats at public credence in authoritarian governments. No less so can it affect the democrats, especially since to a member they made hatred of venality and favoritism one of their rallying cries. The good many who have tolerated or dabbled in vice once in office, uninhibited by meaningful Russian law on conflict of interest, invite the charge of duplicity as well as illegality.

Higher expectations of kickbacks and "presents" *(prinosheniya)* have been widely reported since 1990 among all branches of the Moscow police (most notoriously, traffic patrol officers), clerks in the housing bureaus, registrars of new businesses, school principals, and taxation officers. The respected columnist Yurii Shchekochikhin claims that the most solvent businesses are pseudoprivatized firms with one foot in the bureaucracy, whose good will must be bought by "bribes in the form of participation in profits in kind . . . or of valuable gifts or trips overseas as the guest of a private firm."[130]

Some tales of scandal have featured the names of present or former ranking officials. Petr Bogdanov, the former Moscow chief of police, presides over a Russian-Kuwaiti joint transport venture reputed to have worked out sweetheart deals with regulators; he was on its payroll while still in uniform. Vladimir N. Smyshnikov, the subprefect of the Krylatskoye municipal okrug, was jailed in 1992 for pocketing a 500,000 ruble payoff. Shchekochikhin describes Yevgenii I. Bystrov, a former KGB colonel, deputy head of the Moscow ispolkom, and business manager of Gorbachev's presidential office, and now an adviser to Luzhkov, as "one of the biggest holders of property in Moscow." Andrei Stroyev of Mosinzhstroi and the Perestroika company took flight in 1993, apparently to evade prosecution after being denounced in the press for fraudulent dealings. Gavriil Popov in an interview before his retirement glibly likened bribes to tips for a café waiter and recommended that civil servants publish "tariffs" setting down their price, "let us say 10 to 20 percent of the value of the transaction."[131]

Even Mayor Yurii Luzhkov is alleged to have allied himself improperly with influential local firms and to have signed sweetheart deals with them in exchange for political support. He is good friends with Vladimir A. Gusinskii, the president of the Most financial group, and, according to persistent reports in the Russian media, has given Most preference in the opening of city bank accounts and has sold it municipal real estate at bargain prices. In return, journalists said in late 1994, Most was helping finance a campaign to elect Luzhkov president of Russia in 1996.[132]

We have no mathematical barometer of corruption in post-Soviet Moscow. It may well be that popular perceptions outrun the reality. In a survey taken in December 1993, for example, 60 percent of Muscovites agreed that graft was widespread in city government, and 19 percent said it was probably so. But many fewer, 22 percent, reported having personally encountered bribe taking among municipal officials.[133] Nonetheless, it is the larger number that speaks loudest politically. The indifference of the ruling coalition to corruption's effects is impolitic as well as immoral. No government of Moscow that does not bestir itself on this disease can make the requisite headway on the path of democratic consolidation or will deserve to do so.

ENGAGEMENT AND DISCOURSE

Psychological and organizational involvement in politics distinguishes the rounded civic community. Civil engagement seemed to take a quantum leap in democratizing Moscow, as public debate opened up on all manner of issues, ferment broke out in the Communist Party and its subordinate organizations, protest activity jumped, political associations sprang to life, and high rates of electoral participation were achieved. On one score after the other, regrettably, there has been a pronounced dissipation of energy since the watershed of 1990–1991. Three specific areas raise warning flags about prospects for civic comunity and democratic consolidation: urban mass communications, the organizational framework for participation, and attitudes toward civic life.

In a full-throated democracy the local communications media, principally the press, put out much of the information needed for lively community politics and give citizens vicarious participation in public affairs. The media in the Soviet dispensation did neither of these things, conveying the party's chosen message and dampening discussion of issues. During the thaw of the 1980s the CPSU first loosened and then relinquished its horse collar on editors and writers; they were allowed to broach taboo subjects and dissent from deep-seated truths, and they presented their audiences with reams of fresh information. Unfortunately for civic community, they could not sustain this progress. Although there is little likelihood of an old-time information monopoly being revived, the monologue typical of the former regime has not been replaced by the interactive, multichannel, data-rich media that would complement democratic politics. The post-Soviet local press has reached a state of impoverishment; far freer to criticize and enlighten than before, it lacks the resources to pursue the opportunity to the fullest.

The depletion is to a large extent monetary. As everywhere in Russia and the Commonwealth of Independent States, state subsidies of newspapers and periodicals have been cut and advertising revenues have not compensated; consequently, prices have been hiked and circulation has dropped. Consumer tastes have also changed, away from "serious news" and toward lighter, apolitical fare. The most popular daily newspaper in Moscow (and Russia) is *Moskovskii komsomolets,* the former local organ of the now defunct Komsomol; 42 percent of Muscovites said in a survey in 1993 that they read it loyally. Sixteen percent read *Vechernyaya Moskva* and 9 percent *Moskovskaya pravda*—these two mainstays of Soviet Moscow now have print runs of about one-third of the late Brezhnev years—and 7 percent read *Kuranty.* The most oft-read national papers were *Trud* (Labor), the trade union daily, and *Izvestiya,* with 11 percent and 6 percent of readers. *Nezavisimaya gazeta* and *Segodnya* (Today), another liberal daily established in 1993 (and owned by the Most group), got only several percent each; the raion newspapers that appeared out of nowhere in 1989 disappeared in 1991 for lack of paying customers.[134]

The economics of publishing has precipitated personnel cuts and a general coarsening of editorial content, which fits with the drift of popular interest away from things political. Consequently, although local newspapers reach more readers than national newspapers, there is a dearth of local political news and commentary in Moscow today.

What is available is often poorly researched and unabashedly partisan. *Moskovskii komsomolets,* the first Russian paper to print advertisements in the 1980s, has kept its readership up by turning itself into a tabloid featuring scandalous, bite-size stories; it rarely covers city government in depth. The most instructive information source since September 1992 is a four-page insert in each Thursday's *Moskovskaya pravda* called *Tverskaya, 13;* paid for and controlled by the mayor's office, it unfailingly takes his side in disputes. Public affairs takes a back seat to television listings and horoscopes in *Vechernyaya Moskva,* and *Kuranty,* founded by the Mossovet, has backed off from local issues.[135]

It should come as no surprise, therefore, that 53 percent of Muscovites questioned in 1993 said they were poorly informed or completely uninformed about local issues. Eighty-three percent "know practically nothing about the basic programs of the mayor's office," and one-third protest the "unobjectivity" of the information they do receive.[136]

Other printed media do even worse in terms of literate discourse on local politics. The political broadsheets and pamphlets that were given out and sold by the hundreds of thousands in 1990 rarely appear now, their distributors' places taken on streetcorners by a swarm of hawkers of pornography, holy pictures, occult books, and *biznes* (business) and real estate manuals. City hall's (admittedly dull) monthly journal on urban management has been transformed into *Moya Moskva* (My Moscow), an illustrated magazine carrying some short essays on government but mostly pieces on crime, shopping, and entertainment. The Moscow monthly on urban development became *Moskovskii zhurnal* (Moscow Magazine), which focuses on architectural history to the exclusion of all other subjects and has a penchant for churches and icons.[137] The statistical yearbook *Moskva v tsifrakh* (Moscow in Figures), revived in 1958 after a two-decade hiatus and upgraded in the late 1980s, preceded the raion newspapers into oblivion in 1990. Quantitative data on population and social policy is back to a rivulet. As for television, its coverage of metropolitan politics crested in 1990–1991. The half-hour newsmagazine *Moskovskii teletaip* (Moscow Teletype), though of decent quality, mixes all-Russian with Moscow stories. Sessions of local councils are no longer broadcast.[138]

Civil engagement in post-Soviet Moscow has been lacking in the organizational sphere as well. Again, the story began optimistically; again, the sunny glow has given way to gloom. The groups that took to the field at the end of the 1980s, unlike the top-down "public organizations" reporting to the CPSU, were genuinely voluntary associations that seemed to typify what Robert Putnam terms "the social ability to collaborate for shared interests."[139] Most of them turned out to be transient.

Like Democratic Russia and its contingent in the Mossovet, many of the general-purpose and heavily ideological organizations in the new flock quarreled internally and splintered. The discussion clubs and circles that battened in the Hyde Park euphoria of the late 1980s have almost without exception disbanded. Without formally dissolving, the Moscow Popular Front went down the drain in 1990, followed by the Moscow Association of Voters in the autumn of 1991. Moscow Memorial, created for the noble purpose of commemorating Stalin's victims, has been divided between rancorous cliques since 1992.

Of Moscow's more issue-specific groups and movements, some have been victims of their own success, as accommodating city policies on questions like the Third Ring roadway and the zoo defused the original controversy. In some cases their initiators have taken government jobs, and their successors have "proved themselves weaker and less far-sighted."[140] In other instances, such as the Northern TETS, changing opinions of economic development took a toll. Moscow's green groups and most of its neighborhood-based organizations were, as the label said, "informal organizations" that gloried in their shapelessness; once enthusiasm ebbed, their leaders had no structure to fall back on.

Many newer associations are exceptionally flimsy. The Moscow League of Housing and Housing Construction Cooperatives has more potential than most but for now is little more than a letterhead. The reborn Old Moscow Society, headed by a writer, Vladimir B. Murav'ev, has no membership list; it meets once a month at the Historical Library and passes a hat around to pay for notices of the upcoming meeting. A new breed of pressure groups—business lobbies—is only now making a debut. The Moscow League of Industrialists and Entrepreneurs, on paper the most puissant, looks out for state manufacturers and their employees. It has been absorbed thus far in national affairs, where it functions as the Moscow chapter of the League of Industrialists and Entrepreneurs of Russia. Nikolai Gonchar, then head of the Mossovet, served as a cochairman of its organizing committee in 1992; he survived the debacle of October 1993 and was one of two Moscow politicians elected to the Federation Council in December.[141]

Over and above the shortcomings of the press and of Moscow's associational tissue, attitudinal factors impede the growth of civic community. Civic traditions are fragile. History predisposes Russians toward mutual mistrust rather than trust and toward stoic acceptance of what the government does rather than self-confident influence over it. The passions of the opening stages of the democratic transition are spent, the high hopes disappointed. Times are hard. The regnant mood is one of withdrawal from politics and concentration on economic survival and social stability.

Although the majority of Moscow residents do not relish an authoritarian restoration, most at this juncture rate civil engagement low on their personal scale of priorities. Asked in July 1992 to indicate the two "most important things for you at present," a mere 3 percent circled political participation and 22 percent free speech, whereas 67 percent indicated economic betterment and 69 percent public order. A poll in May 1993 elicited similar responses: 6 percent for political participation, 15 percent for free speech, 64 percent for a higher standard of living, and 63 percent for public order.[142]

One study estimates that Muscovites contact local political institutions only *one-fourth to one-sixth as often* as in the early 1980s, before perestroika. Of citizens surveyed in 1993, fewer than 5 percent had in the foregoing twelve months called upon a prefecture, about the same number had been to their municipal okrug or to a raion deputy, 1.6 percent had contacted a city agency, and 1.9 percent had approached a Mossovet deputy; 11 percent had turned to a police station; 25 percent sought out the management of their workplace. Asked whom they could count on to deal with their personal and family problems, they mentioned self-reliance first—the answer that ranked last in the early 1980s—and then, in order, their relatives, their friends, their employer, the police, the courts, and, "bringing up the rear of the long list, their hopes for the prefecture and mayor's office (5 percent) and their elected deputies (4 percent)."[143]

No panacea exists for this triad of communicational, organizational, and attitudinal problems. Engagement cannot be decreed by marketizing democrats any more than a "model Communist city" could be by socialist autocrats. Patience and forbearance have their virtues in the present situation. A public-spirited press, one could argue, will be there to read when Muscovites vote with their pocketbooks for it. Secondary associations will gather members and credibility when individuals find it congenial to sign up. Political participation will rate higher when citizens learn how to do it right and the burdens and distractions of daily life are lightened some. Political interests will emerge as economic transformation spawns property rights and a civil society, in which members have pecuniary and psychic stakes in what the government does.

To say that gradualism makes sense as a global strategy is not to make a case for benign neglect. Institutional design, by structuring opportunities, *can* influence participation: Soviet authoritarianism depressed it; Russian protodemocracy can elicit it. Governments with self-control and orderly procedures will be worth influencing; today's jerry-built and corruptible structures often are not. Instead they encourage private and frequently secretive interpersonal networks that "serve profoundly particularistic needs and possess an inward-looking ethos" and "are not well-positioned to operate effectively in the public sphere."[144]

An open electoral system must be maintained for civil engagement to be fostered, inasmuch as free and clean elections most unambiguously mark popular sovereignty. Electoral competition is also necessary to stimulate the evolution of political parties. Ideally, political executives and not just legislators should take a hand in electoral and party politics—a point lost thus far on both Boris Yeltsin and Yurii Luzhkov, but not apt to be ignored so blithely by their successors a few years hence. As for community participation, a successful democratization of Moscow's new "municipal districts," and transfer of some budgeting and custodial responsibilities to them, would stimulate civic culture, without the threat to metropolis-wide governance that larger units might pose or be seen to pose. Even selective revival of aspects of mobilized participation may have its uses. Beginning April 1992, city hall has sponsored a Spring Beautification Day—a replacement for the Leninist Communist Subbotnik carried away with the CPSU—and Luzhkov has authorized *druzhiny*, citizen street patrols, in high-crime areas. The abuse of such mechanisms by the Communists should not rule out their adoption in reformed version by a city woefully short of cooperative endeavors.

A Rip Van Winkle who nodded off in Moscow before World War I and woke up in the middle 1990s might feel crushed by the scale of a metropolis six times the land surface and five times the population of the one he knew before he fell asleep. Many of the structures and contraptions around him, from the subway to the ferroconcrete housing estates and the hulking thermopower stations, would be strange. He would wonder where the Kitaigorod Wall, the Sukharev Tower, and the Cathedral of Christ the Redeemer had gone to, and maybe he would ask about that statueless pediment on Lubyanskaya ploshchad' or about the vanished "Moscow Soviet" whose inscription still adorns the entranceway of the former governor-general's palace on Tverskaya. But his senses would also tune in much that was recognizable. One glimpse of St. Basil's and the Kremlin would tell him he was in Moscow.

Nor would it be any mystery to this Rip Van Winkle what country he was in. He would be happy to hear that a now extinct party of Bolsheviks had hauled Russia's seat of government back from St. Petersburg in 1918. If he chanced to board a train out of any of the city's nine railway stations (all familiar, as the youngest was twelve years old in 1914), what he witnessed outside the MKAD would bring back to his mind how much the physical and human face of Moscow, warts and all, is the face of Russia.

It would not take our time traveler long to realize that he had landed in a fundamentally troubled metropolis and society. The signs would be omnipresent. Were he to thumb through back volumes of Russia's journal on urban affairs, he could pick out the passage written on the eve of World War I and quoted in the Introduction of this book: "The general disorder of Russian life, with its characteristic features, is reflected all together in the life of Moscow—this great focus of the light and dark sides of the entire Russian system." How prophetic the words are of the 1990s: "general disorder" in Russia, mirrored in its primate city.

For post-Soviet Moscow, order will not be brought forth out of disorder, nor civic community out of uncivility, unless they are also brought forth for Russia. That is as elementary yet as powerful a conclusion as emerges from the present study. Under the CPSU, no amount of repainting of street signs, wrecking of medieval walls, or erection of socialist statuary was able to blot out Moscow's Russian-ness. Under the post-Communist coalition, no amount of sagacious policies, incorruptible administrators, data-laden newspapers, ebullient associations, or conscientious citizens will save Moscow for democracy if political gridlock keeps Russia from tackling its economic problems, if fratricide breaks out between it and its erstwhile colonies, or if the country itself descends into civil war and anarchy, as it so nearly did in 1993.

Moscow will not be without clout in the new Russia. Indeed, head-counting considerations alone should give it more say in the politics of postimperial Russia than it had in the USSR. Moscow accounted for about 3 percent of the Soviet population in 1991; the city totals roughly 6 percent of the Russian Federation's population, and with the oblast adds up to 10 percent. Economically, there is no a priori reason to think that radical reform will lessen the role of Moscow. Although demilitarization will hurt the defense industry complex, many counterbalancing factors will compensate, including: Moscow's geographic centrality, its transport links to the former Soviet republics and the outside world, its exposure to foreign capital and international organizations, and its overweening presence in advanced technology, postsecondary education, mass communications, and highbrow and lowbrow culture. Moscow ought to weigh as heavily in Russian public and private affairs as New York City and Washington, D.C., combined in the United States, or London in Britain, and quite likely more than that.

Relatively few Muscovites are found in Boris Yeltsin's inner circle at the moment, but they will come and go, and their role may bound forward if, as is widely expected, Mayor Luzhkov makes his run at the presidency after Yeltsin's death or retirement.[145] In public policy practitioners, journalists, and oppositionists will continue to watch every step taken in or by Moscow. Successful revitalization of a ZIL or a Khrunichev Works would have resonance far "beyond the beltway," as would the bankruptcy of such an industrial landmark or a major strike at one. A riot that might go unnoticed in Novosibirsk will make the evening news if it is in Red Square.

When Gavriil Popov was pondering resignation, an editorialist

described him as subconsciously emulating some of his Soviet forebears:

> Moscow is a part of Russia, of this gigantic country that lost its name,
> a special part but a part nonetheless. And any attempt to bring order to
> it through homeopathic means—[microdoses] by statewide standards—is
> doomed to fail. The drama of G. Kh. Popov, I think, lies above all in his
> wish "to be an example for the country." It is surprising but true: each
> Moscow ruler wants to make our long-suffering capital a model. They
> conduct tests on us and then they isolate us, which gives rise to an
> understandable reaction in the provinces.[146]

In good times and bad, governments have used the theory of
Moscow as a model to reconcile the tension between city and nation.
A model metropolis, be it socialist or capitalist, is a part of the whole
but not just any part: it sets a standard and a tone for the others.

It would be unfortunate if democratically elected leaders were not
wise enough to resist this siren song. They would be well advised to
let their agenda flow from the innate properties of urbanism, as Louis
Wirth detected them earlier this century—large size, high density, and
social heterogeneity—and from Moscow's wealth of experience of the
contradictions of the state socialist paradigm of urbanization. They
should be husbanding their energies for their own city, which will be
best served if on issues of local scope it looks to its needs and interests
and lets others draw conclusions for themselves. Russia, too, will be
best served this way, assuming it pursues formulas that work and not
just ones that look pretty.

It has been observed that Russia's national government, to achieve
only its most urgent objectives, "probably needs to be the most effective and well-disciplined state in the history of the world."[147] Russia's
capital, to do all it is being asked, might have to be the best-governed
city in human history. The likelihood of this happening is not high,
and the memory of preachy Soviet claims in this regard ought to be
enough to dissuade post-Soviet perfectionists. Achievements at the
urban level may have to be undramatic, measured in the currency of
everyday life rather than of world-conquering ideas. Looking back at
the pages of this book, I see several macroissues with which Moscow
government must grapple, along with several questions that might

reasonably be asked about governmental performance over the next, say, ten to fifteen years:

Service and responsiveness: For seven decades (and for most of its pre-socialist history, too), Moscow government did what its leaders believed the city needed, not what the population told the leaders they wanted. Competitive elections have begun to reverse this guiding assumption, but only begun. Can progress be continued, even as city leaders retain their commitment to facilitating social change? Can city bureaucrats be motivated to put provision of services ahead of their private welfare? Can the presumption that citizens are entitled to know what their government is doing be enshrined?

Scale: Socialist urban government is too big and smothering. It must become smaller and suppler. Can it be downsized without paralyzing conflict? Can this be done without savaging those functions for which government provision and regulation are necessary?

Accessibility: Socialist or not, a city of almost 10 million people governed from a single point would be inaccessible to most urbanites. The weak subcity governments inherited from the Soviet regime, the raions, have been eliminated, but a superior arrangement has not yet been put in place. Will the municipal districts do the trick? Must other channels be found to link communities to city hall?

Coherence and accountability: Imbedded in the Soviet command system, Moscow government prior to the 1980s could be held together by informal mechanisms, especially the supremacy of the CPSU organs, and accountability to the population did not count for anything. Now that local government has been formalized, strife abounds over jurisdiction and mandate. Can some local charter be worked out that will recognize both the obvious imperative of strong executive power and the equally obvious needs for some constructive role for elected representatives and for procedures for executive accountability to the public?

Regional cooperation: Thoughtful Muscovites since the discussion of Greater Moscow before 1917 have appreciated that their city cannot be properly managed in isolation from the urbanizing region surrounding it. What instruments, short of the amalgamation that is today politically and, most likely, technically unfeasible, can be found to get Moscow and Podmoskov'e to pull together on matters of common concern?

Local-central diplomacy: The disjointed monism of the Soviet period resulted from the malintegration of the central bureaucracy, the tendency for top leaders to intervene in Moscow affairs without regard for the costs and consequences, and the denial to the city of basic tools of self-management. Moscow remains the national capital and will never have the autonomy of a small town in the Russian interior, but ways must be found for it to limit its exposure to Kremlin "ad hocery," to integrate the decisions of various pieces of the central state, and to raise the revenues to pay its own way.

Strategic planning: Comprehensive socialist planning, the effectiveness of which was problematic at the best of times, is as dead as the CPSU. How can planners learn to think strategically instead of synoptically about the city's development, doing less but doing it better?

An expanded policy repertoire: Socialist urbanism relied on a small set of monopoly policy formulas that, when they were enforced, produced monotony and, when they were not, left a void of purposive action. Can Moscow diversify this repertoire? Housing supply is a good test: can Muscovites get the opportunity to purchase or rent some of the plenitude of dwelling forms (detached single-family houses and townhouses, to mention two) that have been denied them for political reasons? Another touchstone might be historic conservation: can Moscow learn that there is something in between razing or dishonoring an old structure and turning it into a museum exhibit?

This by no means exhaustive brief sets forth work enough for a generation of Moscow leaders, planners, builders, and entrepreneurs.

Muscovites had enough during the Soviet period of radiant blueprints, drawn for the edification of the entire country or all humanity, of a glorious future in whose name all kinds of self-denial and self-delusion could be justified. They threw out the Communists partly because that future never arrived. They deserve better now.

There are signs that better will be coming their way, slowly and painfully. Muscovites have made some of the needed choices about forging democratic institutions, a civic community, and a normal, market-coordinated economy. If given the room to labor and the leadership to help them organize themselves, they in all likelihood will construct a post-socialist metropolis, although, to paraphrase Karl Marx's concept of human agency in history, it will not be exactly the one they want.

APPENDIX A

The Population of Moscow

Year[a]	Population[b]
1400	30,000–40,000
1550	c. 100,000
1650	c. 200,000
1700	c. 200,000
1725	140,000–150,000
1790	c. 175,000
1812 (before September fire)	251,000
1812 (after fire)	c. 10,000
1830	306,000
1852	337,000
1862	364,000
1871	602,000
1882	753,000
1897	1,039,000
1907	1,346,000
1912	1,618,000
1915 (November)	1,984,000
1917 (February)	2,017,000
1917 (September)	1,854,000
1918 (April)	1,716,000
1919	1,550,000
1920 (August)	1,027,000
1921	1,148,000
1922	1,278,000
1923	1,521,000
1924	1,628,000
1925	1,744,000
1926 (December)	2,026,000
1928	2,167,000
1929	2,314,000
1930	2,468,000
1931	2,724,000

Year[a]	Population[b]
1932	3,135,000
1933 (January)	3,663,000
1933 (July)	3,417,000
1934	3,614,000
1935	3,641,000
1936 (February)	3,572,000
1937 (May)	3,604,000
1939	4,137,000
1941 (December)	c. 2,500,000
1947 (July)	c. 4,000,000
1956 (April)	4,847,000
1959	5,046,000
1959 (in August 1960 boundaries)	6,040,000
1960	5,140,000
1961	6,242,000
1965	6,427,000
1970	7,077,000
1975	7,632,000
1980	8,099,000
1985	8,656,000
1989	8,967,000
1990	8,980,000
1991	9,003,000
1992	8,957,000
1993	8,881,000

Sources: For 1400, 1550, and 1941, *Istoriya Moskvy: Kratkii ocherk,* 3d ed. (Moscow: Nauka, 1978), pp. 24, 39, 355; for 1650, 1700, 1725, and 1790, *Istoriya Moskvy* (Moscow: Izdatel'stvo Akademii Nauk SSSR, 1952–1959), I, 447, and II, 60, 63, 306; for 1812 through 1918, 1920, 1939, and 1959–1965, M. Ya. Vydro, *Naseleniye Moskvy* (Moscow: Statistika, 1976), pp. 11–14; for 1919 and 1921–1934, *Moskva v tsifrakh* (Moscow: Stroitel'stvo Moskvy, 1934), pp. 13, 16; for 1935, N. M. Aleshchenko, *Moskovskii Sovet v 1917–1941 gg.* (Moscow: Nauka, 1976), p. 490; for 1936, *Pravda,* February 20, 1936, p. 6; for 1937, Tsentral'nyi gosudarstvennyi arkhiv obschestvennykh dvizhenii Moskvy (Central State Archive of Social Movements of Moscow), f. 4, op. 8, d. 1, l. 35; for 1947, A. M. Zaslavskii, "Voprosy gorodskogo transporta Moskvy," *Gorodskoye khozyaistvo Moskvy,* no. 7 (July 1947), p. 1; for 1956, *Moskva: Razvitiye khozyaistva i kul'tury goroda* (Moscow: Moskovskii rabochii, 1958), p. 6; for 1970–1989, various editions of yearbook *Moskva v tsifrakh;* for 1990 and 1991, *Raiony g. Moskvy v 1990 godu: Statisticheskii spravochnik* (Moscow: Mosgorstat, 1991), p. 6; for 1992, Mosgorkomstat, *Statisticheskii press-byulleten',* no. 6 (1992), p. 43; for 1993, *Moskovskaya pravda,* January 11, 1994, p. 2.

a. January, unless otherwise specified.

b. For Moscow within the administrative boundaries of the day.

Composition and Administrative Structure of the Municipal and Communist Party Organs of Soviet Moscow

Moscow municipal government, beginning with the Russian Revolution, centered on a noncompetitively elected local council known as as the Moscow Soviet, often abbreviated colloquially to Mossovet. In official parlance it was variously the soviet of "workers', peasants', and soldiers' deputies" (to 1940), of "toilers' deputies" (1940–1977), and of "people's deputies" (after 1977). The last title endured until the extinction of the Mossovet in October 1993.

The Mossovet had a complex two-tiered leadership structure. Soon after 1917 the larger of the two presiding bodies, the executive committee *(ispolkom)*, grew unwieldy in size and became essentially decorative. The much smaller presidium *(prezidium)* made most decisions. Until changes initiated by Stalin took effect in 1940, the individual leader of the local government simultaneously chaired the entire soviet as well as the ispolkom and the presidium. From 1940 to 1990 the ispolkom was held to a more moderate size than before and had a greater role in policy, although the inner executive—formally "the presidium of the ispolkom" most of this time—prevailed on a good part of the city's more detailed business. The chief executive during this period was referred to as chairman of the ispolkom only, not of the entire soviet.

Reforms initiated by Mikhail Gorbachev came into effect after the competitive city election of 1990. I discuss these and subsequent reorganizations in Chapters 7 and 8.

As for who sat on municipal executive panels, lists of members were printed in even the most secretive years of Communist Party rule. Their identities can generally be ascertained from published sources.

The changing membership of the main leadership body of the Mossovet, the presidium (to 1940) and the executive committee (after 1940), is indicated in Table B-1. I have used representative panels from historical periods for illustration. The post-1940 presidium is not included in the table, but if it were the message would be simple: no one but municipal administrators sat on the presidium all that time.

The territorial organs of the Communist Party—committees and their executives, known as bureaus as of 1920—were more powerful than the municipal structures but also more secretive. The citizen or researcher needed to do careful detective work to ascertain their composition. I was able to rectify gaps and errors in my knowledge with archival research when that was finally allowed in the 1990s.

Information on the composition of Moscow's controlling party committees is provided in Table B-2. The timing of selection decisions necessitates somewhat different dates from the civic executive. Table B-3 shows the occupations of full and candidate members of the bureaus.

Administrative machinery was reconfigured as missions evolved. In the case of Moscow's municipal government, it would be tedious and unnecessary to recite the many changes. Table B-4 summarizes the results. The trend toward greater complexity of organization is obvious.

For the Communist Party, mapping the administrative apparatus is more complicated yet also more essential, given its wide-ranging prefectoral role.

Locally, as at the center, the party's key leaders and administrative officers were called secretaries. Except for August–November 1918, there was only one secretary of the Moscow party committee until August 1920, when another was added; the two were designated first and second secretaries in 1922.

As party influence deepened under Stalin, the secretarial team became larger and its division of labor more elaborate. Beginning in 1923, the Moscow gubkom (the party committee of Moscow guberniya) had a trio of secretaries, with the second secretary generally answering for personnel and internal party organization and the third for economic matters. The Moscow obkom (oblast committee) had three secretaries upon its creation in 1929 and also from April 1934 to April 1939, with the third-ranking secretary usually concentrating on agriculture. In 1932–1933 there was an unusual number of secretaries, six (including secretaries tending to industry, transport, food distribution, and agriculture). This structure signaled a trend toward "production branch" organization, as opposed to the less differentiated "functional" model prevalent in the 1920s. The subordinate Moscow gorkom (city committee), established in February 1931, had four secretaries at first (including specialists in industry, transport and city services, and propaganda), then six in 1932–1933, and three from March 1935 to early 1939; the third secretary was primarily occupied with propaganda until June

1936, and with industry and other things economic after that. The number of obkom and gorkom secretaries increased to five after the Eighteenth Party Congress in the spring of 1939.

Following a change in policy at the congress, the Moscow obkom and gorkom returned to general functionalism as their organizing principle. A secretary "for cadres" *(po kadram)* was accountable for all personnel decisions, and the only "branch" secretary was the obkom's overseer of agriculture. Soon, however, the party was overlaying branch upon functional organization. The gorkom created seven production branch departments in December 1939 (for defense industry, machine building, and other industries), and others followed as prewar and wartime mobilization drew the party more and more into running the economy and society in all its aspects. In late 1940 secretaries of both the gorkom and the obkom were designated "for" the aviation industry; beginning the next spring, the two committees installed a dozen branch-specific secretaries (eight or nine at a time) to cope with the war effort. Their mandates were very narrow: transport, machine building, construction, light industry, food industry and trade, local industry, and, in several combinations, fuels and electric power. The obkom also had secretaries for defense industry and livestock rearing, while the gorkom had one for the electrical industry and several "for industry," one species or another of munitions production. The downgrading of most of these functionaries to deputy secretaries and heads of department in August 1943 did not greatly change their behavior, as best one can tell.

After the war's end, the obkom had five secretaries: first, second (usually responsible for industry), and those for agriculture, personnel, and propaganda; in 1947–1948 the second secretary took charge of agriculture. The gorkom also had five secretaries: first, second (he had broad duties because the top man, Georgii Popov, also headed the obkom and the municipality), and those for personnel, propaganda, and industry. Branch organization was fully reasserted in November 1948; the personnel secretary was discontinued as party cadres returned to the purview of the second secretary. A new secretary handled mostly industry in the obkom and construction and (in an odd blend) municipal affairs, police matters, and military and civilian machine building in the gorkom. Briefly, beginning September 1952, there were only three secretaries in both obkom and gorkom, but the set of five was reinstituted in March 1954 and remained after the gorkom's severance from the obkom in 1956.

After the addition of a sixth secretary in December 1960 until the 1980s, the secretarial lineup in Moscow stabilized. The gorkom first secretary provided overall leadership and the second secretary normally dealt with party personnel matters and "administrative organs" (the police and the judiciary). The four other secretaries tended to ideology, propaganda, and culture; construction and municipal administration (this secretary invariably sat, along with the first secretary, on the ispolkom of the city soviet); the industrial economy; and trade and services. From July 1976 to October 1980, the second secretary directed ideology and another official handled personnel and administrative organs. When Raisa Dement'eva became second secretary in 1980, she reassumed jurisdiction over personnel and policing, and the man most recently responsible for those areas was reassigned to trade and services. In February 1985 a seventh secretary, for managing the gorkom's foreign ties, was appointed, but this position was dissolved by Boris Yeltsin in March 1986, and another secretarial position was removed shortly thereafter.

Beneath the secretaries operated the administrative departments of the local party bureaucracy. Like the secretaries, they were arrayed mainly by broad function until the early 1930s, then by branch of operations, by a mix of the two in the 1940s, and by branch from 1948 until Gorbachev reinstated functionalism in the late 1980s. Table B-5 displays the departmental structure at selective points in its evolution.

Table B-1. Occupations of members of municipal executive (percent)[a]

Occupational position	Presidium					Executive committee		
	1919 (N = 10)	1920 (N = 11)	1924 (N = 17)	1935 (N = 13)	1940 (N = 21)	1950 (N = 25)	1961 (N = 25)	1982 (N = 25)
Local party organs	0.0	18.2	5.9	30.8	14.3[b]	12.0	12.0	8.0
Guberniya or oblast	0.0	18.2	5.9	15.4	4.8	4.0	0.0	0.0
Moscow city	0.0	NA	NA	15.4	9.5	8.0	8.0	8.0
Moscow raion	0.0	0.0	0.0	0.0	0.0	0.0	4.0	0.0
Non-Moscow district	0.0	0.0	0.0	0.0	0.0	0.0	0.0	0.0
Workplace	0.0	0.0	0.0	0.0	0.0	0.0	0.0	0.0
Central party organs	0.0	0.0	0.0	0.0	0.0	0.0	0.0	0.0
Municipal organs	70.0	63.6	76.5	69.2	57.1	80.0	60.0	64.0
Guberniya or oblast	0.0	63.6	58.8	7.7	0.0	0.0	0.0	0.0
Moscow city	70.0	NA	NA	61.5	52.4	72.0	52.0	60.0
Moscow raion	0.0	0.0	17.6	0.0	4.8	8.0	8.0	4.0
Central government	0.0	0.0	0.0	0.0	0.0	0.0	0.0	0.0
Political police	0.0	0.0	0.0	0.0	4.8	4.0	0.0	0.0
Trade unions	0.0	9.1	17.6	0.0	0.0	0.0	4.0	4.0
Economic management	10.0	9.1	0.0	0.0	0.0	0.0	4.0	4.0
Komsomol	0.0	0.0	0.0	0.0	0.0	0.0	0.0	0.0
Science, education, culture	0.0	0.0	0.0	0.0	0.0	0.0	0.0	0.0
Military	10.0	0.0	0.0	0.0	4.8	4.0	0.0	0.0
Newspaper editor	0.0	0.0	0.0	0.0	0.0	0.0	0.0	0.0
Procuracy and courts	10.0	0.0	0.0	0.0	0.0	0.0	0.0	0.0
Rank and file	0.0	0.0	0.0	0.0	19.0	0.0	16.0	16.0
Other	0.0	0.0	0.0	0.0	0.0	0.0	0.0	4.0[c]
Unknown	0.0	0.0	0.0	0.0	0.0	0.0	4.0	0.0

Note: NA = not applicable.

a. Except for 1919 and 1920, the table covers the new executives selected after the most recent Mossovet election. The 1919 figures are for May, when the executive was reshuffled without an election being held. The 1920 figures are for June, following the amalgamation of Moscow and its province and four months after the local election.

b. The obkom first secretary (A. S. Shcherbakov), who served simultaneously as gorkom first secretary, is counted here as an obkom official.

c. Chairman of Moscow "people's control" committee.

Table B-2. Occupations of full members of Communist Party committees (percent)[a]

Occupational position	MK 1920 (N = 38)	Gubkom 1927 (N = 131)	Gubkom 1929 (N = 201)	Obkom 1932 (N = 118)	Obkom 1938 (N = 65)	Obkom 1949 (N = 91)	Subordinate gorkom 1932 (N = 112)	Subordinate gorkom 1938 (N = 65)	Subordinate gorkom 1949 (N = 91)	Subordinate gorkom 1961 (N = 123)	Independent gorkom 1976 (N = 171)	Independent gorkom 1989 (N = 176)	Independent gorkom 1990 (N = 255)
Local party organs	21.1	51.9	33.8	39.8[b]	53.8[b]	42.9[b]	40.2[c]	61.5[c]	47.3[c]	44.7	39.2	30.1	35.3
Guberniya or oblast	0.0	7.6	8.5	9.3	9.2	15.4	4.5	6.2	6.6	0.8	0.6	0.0	0.0
Moscow city	10.5	NA	NA	5.1	4.6	5.5	8.0	7.7	12.1	16.3	13.5	8.5	4.3
Moscow raion	10.5	9.9	8.5	5.1	15.4	2.2	14.3	35.4	23.1	17.9	18.7	18.2	13.7
Non-Moscow district[c]	0.0	18.3	15.7	18.6	13.8	19.8	0.0	0.0	0.0	0.0	0.0	0.0	0.0
Workplace	0.0	16.0	1.0	1.7	10.8	0.0	13.4	12.3	5.5	9.8	6.4	3.4	17.3
Central party organs	2.6	0.8	1.0	3.4	4.6	3.3	4.5	1.5	3.3	0.0	0.0	0.0	0.0
Municipal organs	21.1	2.3	2.0	3.4	13.8	15.4	11.6	10.8	22.0	12.2	14.0	9.1	4.3
Guberniya or oblast	0.0	2.3	1.5	1.7	4.6	9.9	0.9	1.5	1.1	0.0	0.0	0.0	0.0
Moscow city	7.9	NA	NA	1.7	3.1	3.3[d]	4.5	7.7	14.3[d]	9.8	12.9	8.5	2.0
Moscow raion	13.2	0.0	0.5	0.0	0.0	1.1	6.3	1.5	6.6	2.4	1.2	0.6	2.4
Non-Moscow district[c]	0.0	0.0	0.0	0.0	6.2	1.1	0.0	0.0	0.0	0.0	0.0	0.0	0.0
Central govt.	0.0	2.3	2.5	5.9	1.5	4.4	3.6	3.1	3.3	0.8	0.6	0.0	0.0
Political police	2.6	0.8	1.0	2.5	1.5	4.4	3.6	6.2	3.3	0.8	0.6	0.6	1.6
Trade unions	10.5	9.9	6.0	3.4	0.0	3.3	4.5	0.0	3.3	1.6	0.6	0.6	0.8
Economic management	5.3	8.4	19.9	23.7	7.7	11.0	14.3	1.5	8.8	11.4	7.6	14.8	16.1
Komsomol	0.0	2.3	2.5	1.7	3.1	1.1	1.8	1.5	2.2	0.8	0.6	0.6	1.2

Science, education, culture	0.0	0.8	2.0	1.7	0.0	1.1	1.8	0.0	1.1	7.3	5.3	11.4	19.2
Military	5.3	5.3	4.0	4.2	3.1	7.7	2.7	7.7	2.2	2.4	2.3	1.1	2.4
Newspaper editor	0.0	2.3	2.0	2.5	1.5	2.2	0.0	0.0	1.1	1.6	1.2	0.6	2.4
Procuracy and courts	2.6	0.8	0.0	0.0	1.5	0.0	0.0	0.0	0.0	0.8	0.6	0.0	0.4
Rank and file	0.0	10.7	23.4	7.6	7.7	3.3	11.6	6.2	2.2	15.4	26.9	30.1	13.3
Other	0.0	1.5[e]	0.0	0.0	0.0	0.0	0.0	0.0	0.0	0.0	0.6[f]	1.1[g]	0.8[g]
Unknown	28.9	0.0	0.0	0.0	0.0	0.0	0.0	0.0	0.0	0.0	0.0	0.0	0.0

Note: NA = not applicable.

a. The table covers the new committees selected at the party conference held in the given year. The 1920 figures are for the MK selected that March, the last to be from the city of Moscow only. Several gubkoms were selected at conferences later in the year.

b. The obkom first secretary (L. M. Kaganovich, A. I. Ugarov, G. M. Popov), who served simultaneously as gorkom first secretary, is counted here as an obkom official.

c. Uyezds in 1920 and 1927; okrugs and raions in 1929; raions and small cities in 1932, 1939, and 1949.

d. In 1949 the head of the Moscow municipality (Popov) was simultaneously first secretary of the obkom and gorkom; he is counted as an obkom official.

e. Two leaders of cooperative organizations.

f. Chairman of people's control committee.

g. Chairman of people's control and leader of official veterans' organization.

Table B-3. Occupations of full and candidate members of Communist Party bureaus (full members recorded by number, candidate members by number with "C")[a]

Occupational position	Gubkom			Obkom			Subordinate gorkom			Independent gorkom			
	1920	1927	1929	1932	1938	1949	1932	1938	1949	1961	1976	1989	1990
Local party organs	4	11,3C	20,4C	13,5C[b]	4,2C[b]	6,2C[b]	12,3C[c]	6,2C[c]	7,3C[c]	8,3C	8,2C	7,2C	8
Guberniya or oblast	4	4,1C	7,1C	7,1C	3,2C	5,1C	1	1	2	0	0	0	0
Moscow city	NA	NA	NA	4,1C	1	1	5,3C	2	4	6	8,1C	6,1C	5
Moscow raion	0	6	6	0	0	0	6	3,2C	1,3C	2,3C	1C	1	1
Non-Moscow district[c]	0	1,2C	7,3C	2,3C	0	1C	0	0	0	0	0	0	0
Workplace	0	0	0	0	0	0	0	0	0	0	0	1C	2
Central party organs	0	0	0	1C[d]	0	0	0	0	0	0	0	0	0
Municipal organs	1	2	1	2,1C	2	2,1C	1,1C	1	2,2C	1	1	1	0
Guberniya or oblast	NA	2	1	1,1C	1	2,1C	0	0	0	0	0	0	0
Moscow city	NA	NA	NA	1	1	0[e]	1,1C	1	2,2C[e]	1	1	1	0
Moscow raion	0	0	0	0	0	0	0	0	0	0	0	0	0
Non-Moscow district[c]	0	0	0	0	0	0	0	0	0	0	0	0	0
Central government	0	0	0	0	0	0	0	0	0	0	0	0	0
Political police	0	1	1	1	1	1	0	0	1	0	1	1	0
Trade unions	1	1,1C	3	1	0	1	0	0	1	1	1	1	0
Economic management	1	1,2C	1,1C	1C	0	0	1	0	0	0	0	1	2
Komsomol	0	1C	1C	1C	0	1C	1C	0	0	1C	0	1C	0

Science, education, culture	0	0	0	0	0	1C	0	0	0	0	0	0
Military	0	1	1	1	0	1	0	0	1	0	0	1
Newspaper editor	0	0	0	0	1C	0	0	0	0	0	0	1
Procuracy and courts	0	0	0	0	0	0	0	0	0	0	0	0
Rank and file	0	0	0	0	0	0	0	0	0	1[f]	2	0
Other	0	0	0	0	0	0	0	0	0	1[f]	1C[f]	1C[f]
Unknown	0	0	0	0	0	0	0	0	0	0	0	0
Total	7	17,7C	27,6C	18,9C	7,2C	11,5C	14,6C	7,2C	11,5C	10,4C	13,2C	13,4C	13

Note: NA = not applicable.

a. The table covers the new bureaus selected at the first meeting of the party committee chosen at the conference held in the given year. The 1920 bureau shown is that of the gubkom, selected in May of that year. I was unable to ascertain the membership of the bureau of the city-only MK selected in March and used in the previous table.

b. The obkom first secretary (Kaganovich, Ugarov, Popov), who served simultaneously as gorkom first secretary, is counted here as an obkom official.

c. Uyezds in 1920 and 1927; okrugs and raions in 1929; raions and small cities in 1932, 1939, and 1949.

d. This individual was an official in the Central Control Commission of the party.

e. The head of the Moscow municipality in 1949 (Popov) was simultaneously first secretary of the obkom and gorkom; he is counted as an obkom official.

f. Chairman of people's control committee.

Table B-4. Administrative structure of municipal government[a]

Feature	1919	1925	1935	1950	1961	1982
Number of deputy chairmen of executive (including secretary)	1	3	3	11	8	11
Number of administrative agencies						
Overhead (mainly finances, housekeeping, relations with citizens)	4	3	2	7	8	11
Physical services (mainly utilities)	3[b]	1[b]	3	4	2	2
Transportation (including freight as well as passenger transport)	1[b]	0[b]	3	6	4	5
Social services (mainly housing, schools, health, social security, job placement)	4	5	4	5	6	10
Consumer and cultural services (mainly retail trade, public dining, daily services, parks, recreation)	2	3	4	8	7	14
City planning (architectural and physical)	0	0	3	1	1	1
Economic planning	0	0	1	1	1	1
Local industry	1	1	2	2	7	6
Agriculture	1[c]	1[c]	0	0	0	0
Construction and building materials	1	0	1	4	4	7
State administration (mainly police and courts, conscription, civil defense, vital statistics)	4	7	1	0	2	3
Total agencies	21	21	24	38	42	60

a. The table describes the structure ratified at the post-election session of the Mossovet in the given year.

b. Streetcars were administered in 1919 by a composite department of "soviet enterprises" and in 1925 by one for "municipal services." Both of these large agencies provided mostly physical services.

c. These agricultural agencies dealt mostly with emergency food growing in 1919 and with farming in the surrounding province, which was then under Moscow jurisdiction, in 1925.

Table B-5. Administrative structure of the party organs[a]

	Gubkom		Obkom	Gorkom							
Feature	1920	1928	1936	1936	1939	1945	1948	1960	1981	1988	1991
Number of secretaries	2	2	3	3	5	5	5	5	6	5	5
Number of departments	8	6	11	10	6	24	11	16	18	8	9
List of departments											
For general functions											
Confidential communication[b]	*	*	*	*	*	*	*	*	*	*	*
Business office	*	*	*	*	*	*	*	*	*	*	*
Propaganda and agitation[c]	*	*	*	*	*	*	*	*	*	*	*
Personnel and organization[d]	*	*	*	*	**	**	*	*	*	*	*
Work among women	*	*									
Subbotniks	*										
Rural work	*	*									
Military (mass defense work)					*	*					
Socioeconomic problems										*	*
Work with soviets								*			
Work with public and political organizations										*	*
Analytical center										*	*
For economic branches and sectors											
Agriculture			*					*			
Industry			*								
Industry and transport											
Industry, transport, and city services				*							
Heavy industry							*		*		
Transport							*				
Transport and communications								*	*		
Power stations						*					
Medium and heavy machine building (munitions)						*					
Machine tools						*					

Feature	Gubkom		Obkom	Gorkom						
	1920	1928	1936	1936	1939	1945	1948	1960	1981	1988	1991
Machine building							*		*		
Chemicals and metallurgy								*			
Local industry								*			
Aviation industry						*					
Electrical industry						*					
Food industry						*					
Construction and building materials						*	*	*	*		
City services						*	*	*	*		
Trade						*					
Trade and consumer services									*		
Public dining						*					
Ancillary food growing						*					
Defense industry						*	*	*	*	*	
Textile industry						*					
Light industry									*		
For other specific matters											
Press			*	*	*	*					
Schools			*	*	*	*		*	*		
Soviets and trade			*	*	*	*		*	*		
Culture			*	*	*			*	*		
Science			*	*							
Planning and finance						*					
Trade, finance, planning							*	*	*		
Science and higher education							*	*	*		
Administrative organs (police and judiciary)[e]							*	*	*	*	
External ties								*	*	*	*

Note: * = one department; ** = two departments.

a. Times chosen to illustrate major periods of development: July 1920 (after confirmation of the first organization chart); June 1928; January 1936 (during first period of branch organization); May 1939 (after return to functional model); January 1945; November 1948 (after confirmation of branch organization); August 1960; March 1981; and December 1988 and January 1991 (time of Gorbachev-era reforms). In some cases, the structure described was approved by a local party conference, in other cases not.

b. Called variously the General Department (to 1926), Secret Department (1926–1934), Secret Unit (1934–1939), Special Sector (1939–1966), and again the General Department (from September 1966 on).

c. Also called the Department of Agitation and Propaganda (1920–1931, 1935–1939), Department of Culture and Propaganda of Leninism (1931–1935), and Ideological Department (1962–1964, 1988–1991). There was a separate Agitation and Mass Work Department from 1931 to 1935.

d. A bewildering series of organizational formulas was employed for these central functions of the partocracy. An Organization and Instruction Department was responsible at the outset for the party's at the time modest personnel decisions as well as for lower-level party organization. These two tasks were split in 1923, then reunited in 1924 in an Organization and Assignments Department. Organization and Instruction was reinstated in 1930, with responsibility for appointments within the party apparatus only and also for general party organization; a separate Personnel Department controlled patronage in the government bureaucracy and mass organizations. Between 1935 and 1939, party personnel and related organizational matters were under a Department of Leading Party Organs, with appointments outside the party apparatus supervised by branch-specific departments. The Personnel Department set up in 1939 was supposed to answer for all cadres policy, but it was in fact hemmed in by a new wave of branch-specific departments and dealt in large part with party staffing; a new Organization and Instruction Department also existed at this time, dealing mainly with minor party housekeeping. The unified Personnel Department was abolished in November 1948, never to return. In-party appointments and general organization were handled thereafter by a Department of Party, Trade Union, and Komsomol Organs (1948–1956), Department of Party Organs (1956–1965), Department of Organizational and Party Work (March 1965–December 1988), Department of Party Organization and Personnel (December 1988–February 1991), and Organizational Department (February–August 1991). Appointments in most state organizations were delegated to branch departments.

e. Known as the Administrative Department from 1948 until 1956 (except for fourteen months in 1953–1954, when it was fused with the Department of Trade and Financial Organs), and as the State-Legal Department in 1988–1991. Its jurisdiction included health care and social security agencies until November 1967, when they were transferred to the Department of Science and Higher Education.

Careers of Municipal and Communist Party Officials in Soviet Moscow

Information about career pathways provides clues to how any political elite develops and functions. The tables below present data on hundreds of Moscow officials, culled from official biographies and, if these were unavailable or incomplete, from sightings in the press and other sources. They deal with holders of offices in local government and the Communist Party organs between October 1917 and the regrouping following the election of March 1990, which effectively terminated Soviet-era arrangements in the city.

General and professional backgrounds of senior decision makers are summarized by period in Tables C-1 and C-2. They rely necessarily on the full biographies.

Table C-3 tracks promotions into external positions. Here the net is cast more widely, in terms both of rank (the officials did not necessarily attain the positions specified in the preceding tables) and of the fullness of the record (for quite a few there is fragmentary information only, which is sufficient for my purpose). Table C-4 groups these same positions into two rank ranges and gives annual averages for appointments by time period. Tables C-3 and C-4 present only the frequency of appointment of Muscovites, not their durability in office or their mobility systematically compared to non-Muscovites, but the information is, nonetheless, useful.

Table C-5 summarizes the representation of Moscow officials on the Communist Party Central Committee.

Tables C-6 and C-7 provide biographical details on the topmost municipal and Communist Party leaders of Soviet Moscow, to many of whom frequent reference is made in the text.

Table C-1. Background of senior municipal and Communist Party officials[a]

Officials	Percent male	Average year of birth	Percent members of CPSU	Average year of CPSU admission	Percent with higher education	Percent with higher engineering education
Municipal						
1917–1920 (N = 21)	95.2	1882 (N = 20)	95.2	1906 (N = 20)	23.8	0.0
1921–1930 (N = 14)	92.9	1885 (N = 10)	92.9	1909 (N = 12)	7.1	0.0
1931–1938 (N = 32)	87.5	1896 (N = 29)	100.0	1919 (N = 31)	15.6	3.1
Of whom appointed 1937–1938 (N = 9)	88.9	1902 (N = 7)	100.0	1926 (N = 9)	33.3	11.1
1939–March 1953 (N = 41)	87.8	1904 (N = 41)	100.0	1929 (N = 33)	48.8	41.5
March 1953–October 1964 (N = 36)	97.2	1910 (N = 35)	100.0	1936 (N = 29)	61.1	50.0
October 1964–1985 (N = 41)	97.6	1920 (N = 44)	100.0	1945 (N = 33)	73.2	48.8
1986–April 1990 (N = 17)	94.1	1940 (N = 17)	100.0	1967 (N = 15)	94.1	82.4
Communist Party						
1917–1920 (N = 20)	85.0	1884 (N = 18)	100.0	1906 (N = 18)	10.0	0.0
1921–1930 (N = 25)	100.0	1889 (N = 23)	100.0	1910 (N = 23)	4.2	0.0

1931–1938 (N = 80)	92.5	1898 (N = 64)	100.0	1919 (N = 79)	11.3	8.8
Of whom appointed 1937–1938 (N = 28)	92.9	1901 (N = 20)	100.0	1923 (N = 28)	25.0	21.4
1939–March 1953 (N = 94)	89.4	1906 (N = 89)	100.0	1929 (N = 84)	48.9	39.4
March 1953–October 1964 (N = 60)	88.3	1915 (N = 60)	100.0	1940 (N = 54)	63.3	48.3
October 1964–1985 (N = 51)	90.2	1926 (N = 50)	100.0	1951 (N = 44)	82.4	52.9
1986–April 1990 (N = 26)	92.3	1940 (N = 26)	100.0	1966 (N = 18)	100.0	80.8

Sources: The Moscow daily press, especially obituaries and, in certain periods, election portraits and notices of appointment; the major USSR and RSFSR newspapers; biographical entries in encyclopedias and encyclopedia yearbooks; handbooks of Supreme Soviet deputies; Moscow Communist Party archive; and the occasional election poster viewed on Moscow streets.

a. The municipal positions in which service is recorded here are: chairman or deputy chairman of the executive of the city soviet; head of a city agency; and chairman of a raion executive committee. The Communist Party positions are: secretary of the city party committee (1917–1920, 1931–1990); secretary of the guberniya (1920–1929) or oblast (1929–1956) party committee; head of a department of any of these committees; and secretary of a raion party committee.

Individuals whose careers spanned several periods are counted in those periods when they held office for at least two years. Anyone who served in several periods but did not put in a full two years in any is counted once, in the period of the longest service. Officials who held both municipal and party positions are counted in both categories. Of the 414 officials represented in the table, 300 have a single entry, 87 have two entries, 21 have three entries, 5 have four entries, and 1 (V. F. Promyslov) has five entries.

Table C-2. Prior administrative experience (percent)[a]

	Party			Government			Political police	Trade unions	Economic management	Komsomol	Military	Miscellaneous
Officials	Local Moscow	Provincial	Central	Local Moscow	Provincial	Central						
Municipal												
1917–1920	0.0	0.0	0.0	19.0	0.0	4.8	0.0	0.0	4.8	0.0	0.0	0.0
1921–1930	14.3	28.6	0.0	50.0	21.4	7.1	7.1	14.3	21.4	0.0	35.7	0.0
1931–1938	31.3	18.8	6.3	34.4	9.4	6.3	9.4	6.3	21.9	6.3	15.6	9.4
Of whom 1937–1938	44.4	0.0	0.0	44.4	0.0	0.0	0.0	22.2	22.2	11.1	0.0	11.1
1939–March 1953	58.5	4.9	4.9	51.2	9.8	7.3	0.0	4.9	34.1	19.5	4.9	17.1
March 1953– October 1964	55.6	0.0	5.6	58.3	8.3	16.7	2.8	2.8	41.7	19.4	2.8	8.3
October 1964–1985	63.4	2.4	4.9	80.5	4.9	22.0	2.4	2.4	36.6	17.1	0.0	14.6
1986–April 1990	64.7	0.0	5.9	52.9	5.9	11.8	0.0	0.0	41.2	5.9	0.0	17.6

Party												
1917–1920	10.0	5.0	0.0	15.0	20.0	0.0	0.0	5.0	0.0	0.0	20.0	10.0
1921–1930	56.0	64.0	24.0	12.0	16.0	12.0	16.0	20.0	0.0	0.0	28.0	4.0
1931–1938	72.5	51.3	20.0	13.8	17.5	2.5	8.8	11.3	8.8	17.5	28.8	6.3
Of whom 1937–1938	82.1	25.0	7.1	10.7	3.6	0.0	3.6	10.7	7.1	21.4	21.4	3.6
1939–March 1953	81.9	9.6	8.5	11.7	4.3	6.4	0.0	4.3	34.0	30.9	5.3	20.2
March 1953–October 1964	88.3	6.7	11.7	25.0	5.0	6.7	5.0	1.7	30.0	40.0	6.7	26.7
October 1964–1985	94.1	5.9	13.7	31.4	0.0	9.8	0.0	5.9	27.5	37.3	2.0	33.3
1986–April 1990	65.4	11.5	26.9	42.3	7.7	3.8	0.0	0.0	57.7	23.1	0.0	30.7

Sources: Same as Table C-1.

a. Positions the same as those in Table C-1. If an official served in more than one position in the municipal or CPSU hierarchy in the same period, he is counted in the highest position occupied.

Table C-3. Number of Moscow officials appointed to external positions[a]

Position to which appointed[b]	Period when appointed							
	1917–1920	1921–1930	1931–1938	Of whom 1937–1938	1939– March 1953	March 1953– October 1964	October 1964–1985	1986– 1990
Central Committee secretary	1	8c	0	0	4	2	0	1d
Central Committee department head	3	6	4	0	1	12e	1	0
Other central party position	1	18	13	4	22	30	13	2
Provincial party first secretary	3	8	18	12	11	5	0	0
Other provincial position	6	14	14	8	19	4	3	0
Member, USSR Council of Ministers[f]	10	10	4	4	4	7	3	2
Member, RSFSR Council of Ministers[f]	0g	0g	6	2	11	6	3	1
Other government position	18	20	15	7	29	31	52	4
Political police	2	0	0	0	2	3	0	0
Trade unions	2	10	4	1	2	5	6	0
Military[h]	12	0	1	1	10	0	0	0
Miscellaneous[i]	2	9	4	2	5	6	6	1

Sources: Same generally as Tables C-1 and C-2. For postings to other union republics, a search was conducted of obituaries in five republic dailies from 1955 to 1990: *Kazakhstanskaya pravda* (Kazakhstan), *Pravda Ukrainy* (Ukraine), *Pravda Vostoka* (Uzbekistan), *Sovetskaya Latviya* (Latvia), and *Zarya Vostoka* (Georgia). For persons appointed to relatively minor party and government positions, the directories of Soviet officials put out by the Directorate of Intelligence, U.S. Central Intelligence Agency, were invaluable.

a. The 397 individuals referred to here held municipal and party positions at various ranks. Only 218 are included in Tables C-1 and C-2. More or less complete biographies were located for 310. Most served primarily in party positions. For the first decade, a handful are counted who did not hold administrative office in Moscow's party or municipal hierarchy but were active in the city's politics and sat on the Moscow party bureau. Included also are a few career party officials who at the moment of transfer from the Moscow organization were still employed by the Komsomol.

b. Entries refer only to positions to which the official was appointed within the given period and by no later than the fifth year after his transfer out of the Moscow administration. Individuals named in the same period to more than one position in a category are counted only once in that category.

c. Includes two leaders (V. M. Molotov and L. M. Kaganovich) who were already Central Committee secretaries at the time of appointment as Moscow first secretary and who remained so.

d. The official here is L. N. Zaikov, who was already a Central Committee secretary when appointed Moscow first secretary and who remained so throughout his two-year term.

e. Includes two appointments to head "bureaus of the Central Committee," whose status was roughly that of a department.

f. Council of People's Commissars to 1946.

g. RSFSR commissariats for the most part functioned as countrywide agencies from the formation of the USSR in 1922 until about 1930. Appointments to them at this time are counted as USSR-level appointments.

h. Most in this category were political officers.

i. Includes director of a factory or institute; newspaper editor or deputy editor; secretary of an artistic union; and official of the Comintern (before 1943), the Komsomol (one case), and the trade cooperatives.

Table C-4. Annual rate of appointment to external positions

Period	Rank 1 posts[a]	Rank 2 posts[b]	All posts[c]
1917–1920	5.4	13.6	18.9
1921–1930	3.2	7.1	10.3
1931–1938	3.3	7.1	10.4
Of which 1937–1938	8.0	12.5	20.5
1939–March 1953	1.4	7.1	8.5
March 1953–October 1964	2.2	7.3	9.5
October 1964–1985	0.2	3.9	4.1
1986–1990	0.6	1.6	2.2
Average (weighted)	2.0	6.5	8.4

a. Central Committee secretary or department head, first secretary of a provincial party committee, member of the USSR Council of Ministers.

b. All other positions in Table C-3.

c. Because of rounding, numbers in this column do not always equal the sum of the numbers in the previous two columns.

Table C-5. Representation of Moscow officials on the CPSU Central Committee

Years of congress[a]	Full members		Candidate members	
	Number	Percent	Number	Percent
1918	1 of 15	6.7	0 of 7	0.0
1919	1 of 19	5.3	0 of 8	0.0
1920	1 of 20	5.0	1 of 12	8.3
1921	1 of 25	4.0	0 of 15	0.0
1922	2 of 27	7.4	0 of 19	0.0
1923	3 of 40	7.5	0 of 17	0.0
1924	4 of 51	7.8	1 of 35	2.9
1925	6 of 63	9.5	0 of 43	0.0
1927	7 of 71	9.9	3 of 50	6.0
1930	6 of 71	8.5	5 of 63	7.9
1934	3 of 71	4.2	7 of 68	10.3
1939[b]	1 of 71	1.4	4 of 68	5.9
1952	4 of 125	3.2	1 of 112	0.9
1956[c]	6 of 133	4.5	1 of 122	0.8
1961	3 of 175	1.7	1 of 155	0.6
1966	3 of 195	1.5	2 of 165	1.2
1971	3 of 241	1.2	2 of 155	1.3
1976	4 of 287	1.4	0 of 139	0.0
1981	3 of 319	0.9	1 of 151	0.7
1986	3 of 307	1.0	2 of 170	1.2

a. Excludes the party's last congress, in 1990, which elected numerous nonofficials to the Central Committee.

b. At the Eighteenth Party Conference in 1941, two of the Moscow candidate members, G. M. Popov and V. P. Pronin, were promoted to full members, making Moscow's share 4.2 percent of the full members and 2.9 percent of the candidate members.

c. Delegates to the Twentieth Congress were elected from the unified city and oblast organization, which was divided several days later. Of the 6 officials on the Central Committee, 3 worked in city posts and 2 in oblast posts. In addition, V. V. Grishin, who had been relieved as second secretary of the obkom several weeks before, was reelected to the Central Committee. He was not given a new assignment (as head of the trade unions) until some time after the congress.

Table C-6. Careers of municipal chief executives[a]

Chief executive	Term of office	National party office	Prior career	Subsequent career
Viktor P. Nogin[b] (1878–1924)	September–November 1917	Already CC[c]	Revolutionary	Demoted for factional reasons (too moderate in revolution), worked in Moscow Oblast Council of People's Commissars, in trade unions, as deputy head of RSFSR labor commissariat, as head of textile industry
Mikhail N. Pokrovskii (1868–1932)	November 1917–March 1918	None	Revolutionary and teacher	Chairman of Moscow Oblast Council of People's Commissars March–May 1918, then deputy head of RSFSR education commissariat and leading historian
Petr G. Smidovich (1874–1935)	March–August 1918	None	Revolutionary	In Red Army, head of Moscow guberniya economic council and of Moscow schools department, honorific positions only after 1920
Lev B. Kamenev (1883–1936)	August 1918–May 1926	Already CC; P in March 1919; PC in December 1925[d]	Revolutionary, first chairman of All-Russian Central Executive Committee (VTsIK), envoy to Finland	Briefly government trade commissar, then minor positions, executed after show trial
Konstantin V. Ukhanov (1891–1937)	May 1926–February 1931	Already CC and OC (OC to December 1927 only)	Revolutionary, chairman of raion soviet in Moscow 1918–1921, director of Dinamo Works, head of Soviet electrotechnical industry 1922–1926	Remained as chairman of oblast soviet to January 1932, demoted to deputy head of a national agency, head of two RSFSR commissariats, purged

Name	Term	CC/CCC membership	Career before	Career after
Nikolai A. Bulganin (1895–1975)	February 1931–July 1937	CCC in February 1934	In Cheka 1918–1922, industrial oficial, director of Moscow Electrical Works 1927–1930, deputy chairman of oblast soviet in late 1930	Chairman of RSFSR Council of People's Commissars, then many senior government and military posts, ending as chairman of USSR Council of Ministers 1955–1958
Ivan I. Sidorov (1897–?)	August 1937–November 1938	None	Financial and farm administration in Moscow oblast, head of city land department 1934–1937	None (purged)[e]
Aleksandr I. Yefremov (1904–1951)	November 1938–February 1939	None	Engineer and factory director, first deputy chairman of Mossovet and chairman of oblast soviet 1937–1939	Head of Soviet machine tool industry, eventually deputy chairman of Council of Ministers
Vasilii P. Pronin (1905–1993)	April 1939–December 1944	CC in February 1941	Local Komsomol and party work in Moscow, head of personnel section and third secretary of gorkom 1938–1939	First deputy chairman of RSFSR Council of People's Commissars 1944–1946, USSR minister of state reserves from 1946, demoted to a deputy minister spring 1953

Table C-6 (continued)

Chief executive	Term of office	National party office	Prior career	Subsequent career
Georgii M. Popov (1906–1968) (See entry in Table C-7)	December 1944–January 1950			
Mikhail A. Yasnov (1906–)	January 1950–January 1956	CC in October 1952	Construction engineer, deputy chairman of Moscow ispolkom 1938–1949, briefly deputy minister of urban construction	Chairman of RSFSR Council of Ministers to December 1957, first deputy chairman to December 1966, then ceremonial head of state of RSFSR to retirement in 1985
Nikolai I. Bobrovnikov (1909–1991)	January 1956–September 1961	CC in February 1956	Municipal engineer in Moscow, deputy and first deputy chairman of ispolkom, 1950–1956	Deputy chairman of a scientific committee, then deputy chairman of Gosplan (for construction and urban management) from 1963 to retirement in 1986
Nikolai A. Dygai (1908–1963)	September 1961–March 1963	Already CCC; CC in October 1961	Mostly construction administration, rising to chairman of government commission on capital investment	None (died in office)

| Vladimir F. Promyslov (1908–1994) | March 1963–January 1986 | CC in April 1966 | Mostly construction administration, including deputy and first deputy chairman of Moscow ispolkom for construction and secretary of gorkom for construction, deputy chairman of RSFSR Council of Ministers in 1963 | None (retired in disgrace) |
| Valerii T. Saikin (1937–) | January 1986–April 1990 | CC in March 1986 | Engineer and manager at ZIL auto works in Moscow, director 1982–1986 | Appointed deputy chairman of RSFSR Council of Ministers, later held positions in USSR government and returned as ZIL director 1994 |

a. Chairman of the Moscow Soviet until 1940, chairman of the executive committee (ispolkom) of the soviet from 1940 to 1990.

b. For a few days, Nogin was simultaneously commissar of trade and industry in Lenin's national government, but he resigned in a dispute over whether to form a coalition with other socialist parties.

c. CC = Central Committee

   CCC = candidate member of Central Committee

   P = full member of Politburo (or Presidium, in 1952–1966)

   PC = candidate member of Politburo (or Presidium)

   OC = candidate member of Orgburo (1919–1952 only)

d. From September 1922 to early 1926, Kamenev held two important offices in the national government along with his Moscow post: deputy chairman of the Council of People's Commissars and deputy chairman (chairman from February 1924) of the Council of Labor and Defense, which was then the main body for making economic policy.

e. After being purged from the Moscow position, Sidorov was arrested in another post in the Siberian city of Tomsk. His exact time of death is still unknown, but it was probably in 1939.

Table C-7. Careers of Communist Party first secretaries[a]

First secretary	Term of office	National party office[b]	Prior career	Subsequent career
MK (Moscow Committee, city only), October 1917–May 1920				
Vasilii M. Likhachev (1882–1924)	October–November 1917[c]	None	Revolutionary with long periods in foreign exile	Demoted in factional dispute (too moderate in revolution) to district-level position, then economic management in Moscow, head of MK propaganda department
Rozaliya S. Zemlyachka (1876–1947)	December 1917–May 1918	None	Revolutionary, MK secretary March–May 1917, then raion secretary	Transferred to army, then local party work (including raikom in Moscow), later in government inspectorate
Dominik I. Yefremov (1881–1925)	May–September 1918	None	Revolutionary, active in Sokol'nicheskii raion 1917–1918	Political work in army
Vladimir M. Zagorskii (1883–1919)	September 1918–September 1919	None	Revolutionary, secretary of Soviet embassy in Berlin	None (assassinated)
Dominik I. Yefremov (*see above*)	September 1919–January 1920	None	(*See above*)	Returned to army, then local party work, head of government insurance board
Aleksandr F. Myasnikov (1886–1925)	January–June 1920	None	Revolutionary, elected commander of Western Front, head of Belorussian party committee	Transferred to head of Armenian government, chairman of Transcaucasus federation, secretary of Transcaucasus party committee

Gubkom (guberniya committee), May 1920–September 1929

Isaak A. Zelenskii (1890–1938)	June–August 1920	None	Revolutionary, chairman of raion soviet 1917–1918, then head of food department of Mossovet	Transferred to Siberian branch of national food commissariat, then back to Mossovet
Osip A. Pyatnitskii (1882–1938)	August–November 1920	Already CCC	Revolutionary, member of combat center of Mossovet, then in trade unions	Demoted for factional reasons (support of Democratic Centralists) to position in Comintern, later in CC apparatus, then purged
Fedor A. Artem (1883–1921)	November–December 1920	Already CC	Revolutionary, seven years in Australia, military and party leader in Ukraine	Transferred to head of miners' union, died in air crash
Varvara N. Yakovleva (1884–1944)	December 1920–April 1921	None[d]	Revolutionary, secretary of regional bureau of party 1917, Left Communist 1918, head of Petrograd Cheka, in food organs and Siberian party apparatus during Civil War	Demoted for factional reasons (support of Trotsky platform) to party position in Siberia, then in RSFSR education commissariat, head of RSFSR finance commissariat, purged

Table C-7 (continued)

First secretary	Term of office	National party office[b]	Prior career	Subsequent career
Isaak A. Zelenskii (see above)	April 1921–October 1924	Already CCC; CC and OC in April 1922; S in April 1923; O in June 1924	(See above)	Demoted for factional reasons (support of Kamenev) to secretary of CC's Central Asian bureau, then head of Soviet consumer cooperatives, purged
Nikolai A. Uglanov (1886–1937)	October 1924–November 1928	Already CC, S, and O; PC in January 1926	Revolutionary, trade unionist, party secretary of Petrograd and Nizhnii Novgorod	Demoted for factional reasons (support of Right Opposition) to people's commissar of labor, then minor positions, purged
Vyacheslav M. Molotov (1890–1986)	November 1928–April 1929	Already CC, P, S, and O	Revolutionary, provincial party work, CC secretary since 1921	Returned to full-time work as CC secretary, head of Soviet government 1930–1941, many high posts until forced out by Khrushchev in 1957
Karl Ya. Bauman (1892–1937)	April–September 1929	Already CC and OC; PC, S, and O in April 1929	Revolutionary, party secretary in Kursk, deputy head of CC personnel section 1923–1924, head of personnel of MK 1924–1928, head of CC's rural department 1928	First secretary of new Moscow obkom

Obkom (oblast committee), September 1929–February 1956

Karl Ya. Bauman (*see above*)	September 1929–April 1930	(*See above*)	(*See above*)	Demoted for mismanagement of farm collectivization, remained briefly as CC secretary, then secretary of CC's Central Asian bureau, head of CC science department, purged
Lazar M. Kaganovich (1893–1991)	April 1930–May 1935 (also first secretary of gorkom February 1931–January 1934)	Already CC, PC, S, and O; P in July 1930	Revolutionary, Civil War commissar, head of CC personnel section 1922–1924, CC secretary 1924–1925 and again in 1928, head of Ukrainian party 1925–1928	Transferred to high government positions, but remained CC secretary until 1939, retired 1957
Nikita S. Khrushchev (1894–1971)	March 1935–January 1938 (first secretary of gorkom from January 1934)	CC in February 1934	Junior commissar in army, party work in Ukraine in 1920s, head of raion soviet and raikom secretary in Moscow 1931–1932, gorkom second secretary 1932–1934	Promoted to first secretary of Ukrainian party
Aleksandr I. Ugarov (1900–1939)	February–October 1938 (also first secretary of gorkom)	Already CCC	Political work in army and Moscow, party official in Leningrad 1926–1938, ending as second secretary of gorkom	None (purged)

Table C-7 (continued)

First secretary	Term of office	National party office[b]	Prior career	Subsequent career
Aleksandr S. Shcherbakov (1901–1945)	November 1938–May 1945 (also first secretary of gorkom)	CC and O in March 1939; PC in February 1941; S in May 1941	Provincial party work in Nizhnii Novgorod, Leningrad, Siberia, and Ukraine, in CC apparatus 1932–1936 (instructor and head of culture department)	None (died in office)
Georgii M. Popov (1906–1968)	May 1945–December 1949 (also first secretary of gorkom)	Already CC; S and O in March 1946	Komsomol work, aviation engineer, in CC apparatus, second secretary of Moscow gorkom from November 1938, simultaneously municipal chief from December 1944	Demoted to head minor government ministries, ambassador to Poland, economic manager
Nikita S. Khrushchev (*see above*)	December 1949–March 1953	Already CC and P; S in December 1949	(*See above*)	Selected first secretary of CC 1953, also chairman of Council of Ministers from 1958, deposed October 1964
Nikolai A. Mikhailov (1906–1982)	March 1953–March 1954	Already CC and S (until March 14, 1953)	Journalism and party work in Moscow, head of Komsomol 1938–1952, CC secretary November 1952	Demoted to ambassador to Poland, later minister of culture, head of government press committee

Ivan V. Kapitonov (1915–)	March 1954–April 1959	Already CC	Construction engineer, local party and soviet work in Moscow from 1941, second secretary of obkom 1951–1952, first secretary of gorkom 1952–1954	Demoted to first secretary of Ivanovo obkom, promoted to head of CC department in 1964, CC secretary in 1965, demoted to chairman of party auditing commission in 1986, retired 1988
(Gorkom (city committee), subordinate to obkom, February 1931–February 1956[e]				
Ivan I. Rumyantsev (1913–)	January 1950–September 1952	None	Party secretary in a Moscow defense plant, first secretary of a raikom	Demoted to economic management work, eventually director of Znamya revolyutsii aviation plant in Moscow
Ivan V. Kapitonov (*see above*)	September 1952–March 1954	CC in October 1952	(*See above*)	Promoted to first secretary of Moscow obkom (*see above*)
Yekaterina A. Furtseva (1910–1974)	March 1954–February 1956	Already CCC	Komsomol work, local party work in Moscow from 1942, second secretary of gorkom 1950–1954	(*See below*)
Independent gorkom, after February 1956				
Yekaterina A. Furtseva (*see above*)	February 1956–December 1957	CC, PC, and S in February 1956; P in June 1957	(*See above*)	Promoted to full-time work as CC secretary, demoted to minister of culture 1960

Table C-7 (continued)

First secretary	Term of office	National party office[b]	Prior career	Subsequent career
Vladimir I. Ustinov (1907–1971)	December 1957–July 1960	None	Engineer, local party work in Moscow 1946–1953, then official in KGB (deputy chief 1954–1957)	Demoted to ambassador to Hungary, head of department of CMEA secretariat
Petr N. Demichev (1918–)	July 1960–November 1962	CC and S in October 1961	Party work in Moscow from 1945, several years in CC apparatus, secretary of Moscow obkom 1956–1958, business manager of Council of Ministers 1958–1959, first secretary of Moscow obkom 1959–1960	Promoted to full-time work as CC secretary, demoted to minister of culture in 1974, first deputy head of state 1986–1988
Nikolai G. Yegorychev (1920–)	November 1962–June 1967	Already CC	Komsomol work, local party work in Moscow from 1954 (except in CC apparatus 1960–1961), second secretary of gorkom 1961–1962	Demoted to deputy head of industrial ministry, ambassador to Denmark, deputy minister again, then ambassador to Afghanistan 1988
Viktor V. Grishin (1914–1992)	June 1967–December 1985	Already CC and PC; P in March 1971	Local party work in Moscow oblast from 1941, head of obkom department 1950–1952, second secretary of obkom 1952–1956, head of trade unions from 1956	Advisory position (retired in disgrace)

	December 1985–November 1987	Already CC; S (until February 1985); PC in February 1986	Construction administration and party work in Sverdlovsk, first secretary of Sverdlovsk obkom 1976–1985, head of CC construction department from April 1985, CC secretary from July 1985	Demoted to first deputy chairman of state construction committee, resigned May 1989 to sit as Moscow representative in new Soviet parliament, elected chairman of RSFSR parliament May 1990, elected president of Russia June 12, 1991
Boris N. Yeltsin (1931–)				
Lev N. Zaikov (1923–)	November 1987–November 1989	Already CC, P, and S	Manager in defense industry, municipal chief of Leningrad 1976–1983, first secretary of Leningrad obkom 1983–1985, CC secretary from July 1985	Returned to full-time work in party Secretariat and USSR Defense Council, served in lesser positions in Defense Council after July 1990, retired 1991
Yurii A. Prokof'ev (1939–)	November 1989–August 1991	CC and P in July 1990	Local Komsomol and party work in Moscow, secretary of Moscow ispolkom 1986–1988, second secretary of gorkom 1988–1989	Left politics in disgrace, now a businessman

a. The top-ranking party official was designated the "first secretary" in August 1922.

b. Symbols same as in Table C-4, with the additions S = Central Committee secretary and O = member of Orgburo.

c. Likhachev had been secretary since May 1917.

d. Yakovleva had been a candidate CC member in 1917–1918.

e. From 1931 to 1949, the prevailing practice was for the obkom leader to serve simultaneously as first secretary of the Moscow gorkom. The two offices were split in December 1949.

Housing Construction and Supply in Soviet Moscow

In that housing provision was considered a key index of governmental performance in socialist Moscow, a detailed record of it is of value.

Soviet statisticians used at various times two different definitions of housing completions and supply: (1) "overall housing space" *(obshchaya zhilishchnaya ploshchad')*, a gross measure of total floor area, and (2) "dwelling space" *(zhilaya ploshchad')*, a more restrictive measure excluding hall, kitchen, bathroom, and storage space. Unless otherwise indicated in the text, this book employs the second, net definition throughout, to maximize comparability. For new construction (Table D 1), I have located "dwelling space" figures for all years up to 1963; after that, they usually have to be computed from a coefficient inferred from other data. The coefficient ranges from 0.62 for the mid-1960s to 0.65 for 1973 and following years. For the housing stock as a whole (Table D-2), dwelling space per capita is available up to 1971. Thereafter I have employed a coefficient of 0.67, following standard Soviet practice.

Table D-1. Annual housing construction

Year	Square meters of dwelling space completed
[1913	1,089,000]
1923	30,000
1924	58,000
1925	114,000
1926	223,000
1927	404,000
1928	432,000
1929	497,000
1930	516,000
1931	455,000
1932	512,000
1933	624,000
1934	384,000
1935	247,000
1936	210,000
1937	211,000
1938	324,000
1939	430,000
1940	370,000
1941	140,000
1942	8,000
1943	29,000
1944	53,000
1945	253,000
1946	86,000
1947	129,000
1948	270,000
1949	405,000
1950	535,000
1951	735,000
1952	782,000
1953	812,000
1954	910,000
1955	1,065,000
1956	1,374,000
1957	1,810,000
1958	2,352,000
1959	2,925,000
1960	3,033,000
1961	3,433,000
1962	3,430,000
1963	3,420,000

Table D-1 (continued)

Year	Square meters of dwelling space completed
1964	3,369,000
1965	3,113,000
1966	3,286,000
1967	3,150,000
1968	3,276,000
1969	3,276,000
1970	3,392,000
1971	3,392,000
1972	3,328,000
1973	3,445,000
1974	3,315,000
1975	3,185,000
1976	2,925,000
1977	2,860,000
1978	2,795,000
1979	2,600,000
1980	2,545,000
1981	2,522,000
1982	2,369,000
1983	2,176,000
1984	2,142,000
1985	1,999,000
1986	1,986,000
1987	2,141,000
1988	2,046,000
1989	2,055,000
1990	1,466,000
1991	1,070,000

Sources: For 1913, *Rabochaya Moskva,* March 9, 1924, p. 5; for 1923–1933, *Moskva v tsifrakh* (Moscow: Stroitel'stvo Moskvy, 1934), p. 5; for 1934–1935, N. M. Aleshchenko, *Moskovskii Sovet v 1917–1941 gg.* (Moscow: Nauka, 1976), pp. 498–499; for 1936, *Rabochaya Moskva,* March 26, 1937, p. 1; for 1937–1940, annual and summary figures in *Moskovskii bol'shevik,* June 15, 1939, p. 2, January 8, 1940, p. 1, and March 21, 1941, p. 1; for 1941–1944, N. M. Aleshchenko, *Moskovskii Sovet v 1941–1945 gg.* (Moscow: Nauka, 1980), pp. 198–199; for 1945–1950, N. M. Aleshchenko, *Moskovskii Sovet v 1945–1961 gg.* (Moscow: Nauka, 1988), pp. 39, 109; for 1951–1958, V. Ye. Poletayev, *Rabochiye Moskvy na zavershayushchem etape stroitel'stva sotsializma, 1945–1958 gg.* (Moscow: Nauka, 1967), pp. 257–258; for 1959–1963, Yu. G. Saushkin, *Moskva: Geograficheskaya kharakteristika,* 4th ed. (Moscow: Mysl', 1964), p. 162; for 1964–1988, various editions of yearbook *Moskva v tsifrakh;* for 1989, indirect reference in *Moskovskaya pravda,* January 15, 1991, p. 1; for 1990, *Vedomosti Mossoveta,* no. 4 (1991), p. 47; for 1991, *Moskovskaya pravda,* January 21, 1992, p. 3.

Table D-2. Housing supply per capita

Year	Square meters of dwelling space per capita
[1912	7.4]
1920	9.5
1922	7.4
1923	6.8
1924	6.2
1925	5.9
1926	5.8
1927	5.7
1928	5.6
1930	5.5
1931	5.2
1934	4.2
1940	4.1
1950	4.2
1961	6.4
1966	8.2
1971	9.3
1976	10.3
1980	11.0
1985	11.4

Sources: For 1912–1926, Moskovskii Sovet rabochikh, krest'yanskikh i krasno-armeiskikh deputatov, 1917–1927 (Moscow: Izdaniye Moskovskogo Soveta, 1927), p. 363; for 1927–1928, V. Zheits, "Rabocheye zhilishchnoye stroitel'stvo Moskvy k XI oktyabryu," Stroitel'stvo Moskvy, no. 19 (October 1928), p. 1; for 1930–1931, Vechernyaya Moskva, May 22, 1930, p. 2, and April 13, 1931, p. 1; for 1934, calculated from housing stock figures in Moskva v tsifrakh (Moscow: Stroitel'stvo Moskvy, 1934), pp. 13, 182; for 1940, calculated from housing stock figure in N. M. Aleshchenko, Moskovskii Sovet v 1917–1941 gg. (Moscow: Nauka, 1976), p. 500; for 1950, estimated on assumption that 1 million square meters was added to housing stock in 1940s and that population was 4,300,000; for 1961–1985, housing and population data in various editions of yearbook Moskva v tsifrakh.

Notes

The following two Russian abbreviations are used for archival references:

TsGAODM: Tsentral'nyi gosudarstvennyi arkhiv obshchestvennykh dvizhenii Moskvy (Central State Archive of Social Movements of Moscow), the Moscow Communist Party Archive until 1991;

TsGIAGM: Tsentral'nyi gosudarstvennyi istoricheskii arkhiv goroda Moskvy (Central State Historical Archive of the City of Moscow).

I follow the standard form for citations from these archives: f. (fund), op. (register), d. (file), then l. or ll. (folio page or pages).

Introduction

The epigraph is from Eugene Lyons, *Moscow Carrousel* (New York: Knopf, 1935), p. 1.

1. According to National Geographic Society (NGS) data, the populations of Tokyo, Sao Paolo, and Bombay in 1990 were approximately 11.9 million, 9.9 million, and 9.5 million, respectively. Metropolitan area figures are harder to come by because of differing national definitions, but the NGS puts Tokyo-Yokohama at 30.4 million, New York, the Consolidated Metropolitan Statistical Area (CMSA), at 18.1 million, Mexico City and Sao Paolo at 15.0 million, Los Angeles (CMSA) and Chongqing at 14.5 million, Bombay at 12.6 million, and Shanghai at 12.5 million. The 11.0 million for Moscow is an estimate for the city of Moscow, its green belt, and the commuter population outside the green belt. In Europe, Paris is the second biggest metropolitan area (9.0 million), but has a city population of only 2.2 million; London comes next, with a metropolitan (Greater London) total of 6.8 million and a city (Inner London) figure of 2.5 million.

2. M. Novikov, "Moskva: Progressivnaya duma i gorodskoye khozyaistvo," *Gorodskoye delo,* no. 23 (December 1, 1913), p. 1589.

3. Louis Wirth, "Urbanism as a Way of Life," *American Journal of Sociology,* vol. 44 (July 1938), pp. 1–25.

4. August von Haxthausen, *Studies on the Interior of Russia,* ed. S. Frederick Starr (Chicago: University of Chicago Press, 1972), p. 17.

5. Martin Malia, *The Soviet Tragedy: A History of Socialism in Russia, 1917–*

1991 (New York: Free Press, 1994), pp. 33–34. As Malia points out, socialism has many meanings, but "integral socialism" is the appropriate concept for understanding the Soviet experience.

6. Donald J. Olsen, *The City as a Work of Art: London, Paris, Vienna* (New Haven: Yale University Press, 1986), p. 4.

7. T. A. Selivanov, "Velikii Stalin—vdokhnovitel' i organizator rekonstruktsii Moskvy," *Gorodskoye khozyaistvo Moskvy*, no. 12 (December 1949), p. 14; Yu. G. Saushkin, *Moskva: Geograficheskaya kharakteristika*, 4th ed.(Moscow: Mysl', 1964), p. 14. The second author, I should note, was not a party hack but a distinguished geographer.

8. E. D. Simon et al., *Moscow in the Making* (London: Longmans, Green, 1937), pp. 211, 234.

9. This was the party's official name from October 1952 until its abolition in 1991. It was known from December 1925 to 1952 as the All-Union Communist Party (Bolshevik), from March 1918 to 1925 as the Russian Communist Party (Bolshevik), and prior to that as the Bolshevik wing of the Russian Social Democratic Workers' Party.

10. James C. Scott, *Domination and the Arts of Resistance: Hidden Transcripts* (New Haven: Yale University Press, 1990), p. 45.

11. Simon and his coauthors were under few illusions on this point. They wrote, for example, that there was "an extraordinary atmosphere of suspicion" in the city, that "the government flatly refuses to tolerate opposition or criticism," and that "any overt protest means immediate arrest." Simon et al., *Moscow in the Making*, pp. 224–225.

12. Gordon Skilling wrote about the Soviet system as "a kind of imperfect monism," but he drew attention to interest-group behavior more than I do here. Thomas Remington's concept of "fragmented centralism" comes closer to my meaning; his notion, somewhat narrower than mine, applies mostly to the early years of the regime. H. Gordon Skilling, "Interest Groups and Communist Politics: An Introduction," in Skilling and Franklyn Griffiths, eds., *Interest Groups in Soviet Politics* (Princeton: Princeton University Press, 1971), p. 17; Thomas F. Remington, *Building Socialism in Bolshevik Russia: Ideology and Industrial Organization, 1917–1921* (Pittsburgh: University of Pittsburgh Press, 1984), esp. chap. 3.

13. Jerry F. Hough, *The Soviet Prefects: The Local Party Organs in Industrial Decision-Making* (Cambridge, Mass.: Harvard University Press, 1969). Hough discusses mainly the 1950s and 1960s. Some of his themes are updated in Peter Rutland, *The Politics of Economic Stagnation in the Soviet Union: The Role of Local Party Organs in Economic Management* (Cambridge: Cambridge University Press, 1993). Both authors give only brief consideration to the party and urban and consumer services.

14. Two excellent examples of city biography are Jonathan Kandell, *La Capital: The Biography of Mexico City* (New York: Henry Holt, 1988), and Robert Hughes, *Barcelona* (New York: Knopf, 1992).

15. Besides Hough's *Soviet Prefects*, the most influential work on Soviet local

affairs has been Merle Fainsod's *Smolensk under Soviet Rule* (Cambridge, Mass.: Harvard University Press, 1958), which is about a province in western Russia between the wars. For a thoughtful city study concentrating on the Brezhnev period, see Blair A. Ruble, *Leningrad: Shaping a Soviet City* (Berkeley: University of California Press, 1990). On the same city in the 1950s and 1960s, see David T. Cattell, *Leningrad: A Case Study of Soviet Urban Government* (New York: Praeger, 1968). Two useful monographs with thematic organization and a post-Stalin focus are Theodore J. Friedgut, *Political Participation in the USSR* (Princeton: Princeton University Press, 1979), and Jeffrey W. Hahn, *Soviet Grassroots: Citizen Participation in Local Soviet Government* (Princeton: Princeton University Press, 1988). The brief but meaty volume by William Taubman, *Governing Soviet Cities* (New York: Praeger, 1973), opened up some of the questions explored in the present work. I have learned a good deal from three recent monographs dealing with subperiods of Soviet Moscow politics: Richard Sakwa, *Soviet Communists in Power: A Study of Moscow during the Civil War, 1918–21* (London: Macmillan, 1988); Catherine Merridale, *Moscow Politics and the Rise of Stalin: The Communist Party in the Capital, 1925–32* (London: Macmillan, 1990); and Nobuo Shimotomai, *Moscow under Stalinist Rule, 1931–34* (London: Macmillan, 1991).

1. Frontier Town into Metropolis

1. *Izvestiya,* March 14, 1918, p. 1.

2. There is no general scholarly work in English on Moscow's formative history. Much can still be learned from Arthur Voyce, *Moscow and the Roots of Russian Culture* (Norman: University of Oklahoma Press, 1964). The fullest Soviet-era Russian source is the six-volume *Istoriya Moskvy* (Moscow: Izdatel'stvo Akademii Nauk SSSR, 1952–1959). P. V. Sytin, *Istoriya planirovki i zastroiki Moskvy* (Moscow: Moskovskii rabochii, 1950–1954), ably reviews physical development. Some studies by Russian geographers are useful, especially, among the panoramic works, Yu. G. Saushkin, *Moskva: Geograficheskaya kharakteristika,* 4th ed.(Moscow: Mysl', 1964), and Yu. G. Saushkin and V. G. Glushkova, *Moskva sredi gorodov mira* (Moscow: Mysl', 1983), p. 101. Valuable accounts of building trends are Kathleen Berton, *Moscow: An Architectural History* (London: Studio Vista, 1977); William C. Brumfield, *Gold in Azure: One Thousand Years of Russian Architecture* (Boston: David R. Godine, 1983), esp. chap. 4; and Albert J. Schmidt, *The Architecture and Planning of Classical Moscow: A Cultural History* (Philadelphia: American Philosophical Society, 1989). On the development of Russian architecture in general, the authoritative source is William C. Brumfield, *A History of Russian Architecture* (Cambridge: Cambridge University Press, 1993).

3. The name did not stick until after 1650. *Krasnaya,* "red," could also be translated "beautiful."

4. Quotations in Anthony Cross, ed., *Russia under Western Eyes, 1517–1825* (London: Elek Books, 1971), p. 61, and Lloyd E. Berry and Robert O. Crummey,

eds., *Rude and Barbarous Kingdom: Russia in the Accounts of Sixteenth-Century English Voyagers* (Madison: University of Wisconsin Press, 1968), p. 124.

5. Quoted in Cross, *Russia under Western Eyes,* p. 58.

6. Kitaigorod has sometimes been misrendered as "Chinatown," as *Kitai* means China in Russian. In fact, the name stems from *kita,* an antiquarian term for a pole fence such as originally surrounded the area.

7. Nicholas V. Riasanovsky, *A History of Russia,* 5th ed. (New York: Oxford University Press, 1993), p. 98.

8. Despite controversy over the Third Rome theory, scholars agree that it was first articulated in 1510 in a letter to Tsar Vasilii by Filofei, an abbot from the town of Pskov.

9. A visitor estimated that every fifth house in the 1630s contained a private chapel and put the total of churches at over 2,000. Historians do not dispute these figures. Samuel H. Baron, ed., *The Travels of Olearius in Seventeenth-Century Russia* (Stanford: Stanford University Press, 1967), p. 116.

10. Brumfield, *Gold in Azure,* p. 146.

11. Ibid., p. 172. Brumfield makes this observation of two other large local churches, the Ascension at Kolomenskoye and John the Baptist at D'yakovo, as well as of St. Basil's.

12. The disputed question of how much Moscow Baroque owed to Western models is fully considered in James Cracraft, *The Petrine Revolution in Russian Architecture* (Chicago: University of Chicago Press, 1988), chap. 4.

13. Baron, *Travels of Olearius,* pp. 112–113.

14. *Istoriya Moskvy,* I, 243. For the first fifty years of its existence, this agency was called the Zemskii dvor, Local Household.

15. See Cracraft, *Petrine Revolution,* pp. 141–145.

16. Quoted in G. Vasilich, "Ulitsy i lyudi sovremennoi Moskvy," in *Moskva v yeye proshlom i nastoyashchem* (Moscow: Tovarishchestvo Obrazovaniye, 1909–1912), XII, 13. See also Sidney Monas, "Petersburg and Moscow as Cultural Symbols," in Theophanis G. Stavrou, ed., *Art and Architecture in Nineteenth-Century Russia* (Bloomington: Indiana University Press, 1983), pp. 26–39.

17. Large offices of most agencies were maintained, and the work done in Moscow before 1800 "was no less" than that done by the collegiums in St. Petersburg. Monarchs spent twenty of the seventy-five years following Peter's death in Moscow. *Istoriya Moskvy,* II, 127.

18. N. Ya. Tikhomirov, *Arkhitektura podmoskovnykh usadeb* (Moscow: Gosudarstvennoye izdatel'stvo literatury po stroitel'stvu i arkhitekture, 1955), pp. 63–94.

19. Schmidt, *Architecture and Planning,* p. 22.

20. A. I. Mikhailov, *Bazhenov* (Moscow: Gosudarstvennoye izdatel'stvo literatury po stroitel'stvu i arkhitekture, 1951), pp. 49–110, and *Istoriya russkogo iskusstva* (Moscow: Izdatel'stvo Akademii Nauk SSSR, 1953–1964), VI, 96–102. The latter points out that realization of the project might have made Moscow grander than St. Petersburg and forced Catherine to shift her residence back there. An English traveler,

Edwarde Clarke, believed that the palace "would have surpassed the Temple of Solomon, the Propylaeum of Amasis, the Villa of Adrian, or the Forum of Trajan." Quoted in Schmidt, *Architecture and Planning,* p. 40.

21. See especially the beautifully illustrated discussion in Schmidt, *Architecture and Planning,* chaps. 3–7.

22. John T. Alexander, "Catherine II, Bubonic Plague, and the Problem of Industry in Moscow," *American Historical Review,* vol. 79 (June 1974), pp. 637–671.

23. Quoted in Berton, *Moscow,* p. 152.

24. Albert J. Schmidt, "The Restoration of Moscow after 1812," *Slavic Review,* vol. 40 (Spring 1981), pp. 37–48.

25. Ye. I. Kirichenko, G. A. Ivanova, and Ye. G. Klodt, *Khram Khrista Spasitelya v Moskve* (Moscow: Planeta, 1992), p. 29. This is the irreplaceable study of the cathedral.

26. *Istoriya Moskvy,* V, 16.

27. All statistics in this book on Moscow's ethnic composition until the 1970s are taken from M. Ya. Vydro, *Naseleniye Moskvy* (Moscow: Statistika, 1976), pp. 30–32.

28. The number of central stations has remained constant at nine, one less than the radial railroads, because the freight lines to Kursk and Nizhnii Novgorod have always shared the Kursk Station.

29. Alfred J. Rieber, *Merchants and Entrepreneurs in Imperial Russia* (Chapel Hill: University of North Carolina Press, 1982), p. 135.

30. Statistics taken or derived from Vydro, *Naseleniye Moskvy,* p. 38, and Diane Koenker, *Moscow Workers and the 1917 Revolution* (Princeton: Princeton University Press, 1981), pp. 21–25.

31. Walter M. Pintner, *Russian Economic Policy under Nicholas I* (Ithaca: Cornell University Press, 1967), pp. 235–236.

32. See especially Mervyn Matthews, *The Passport Society: Controlling Movement in Russia and the USSR* (Boulder, Colo.: Westview Press, 1993), chap. 1.

33. The best discussion is Robert Eugene Johnson, *Peasant and Proletarian: The Working Class of Moscow in the Late Nineteenth Century* (New Brunswick, N.J.: Rutgers University Press, 1979), chaps. 2–4. Johnson shows that, although rural contacts exerted a calming effect, they also exposed Moscow workers to potentially destabilizing influences. See also Joseph Bradley, *Muzhik and Muscovite: Urbanization in Late Imperial Russia* (Berkeley: University of California Press, 1985), chap. 4, and Victoria E. Bonnell, *Roots of Rebellion: Workers' Organizations and Politics in St. Petersburg and Moscow, 1900–1914* (Berkeley: University of California Press, 1983), pp. 52–57.

34. Vasilich, "Ulitsy i lyudi," p. 13.

35. Andrzej Walicki, *The Slavophile Controversy,* trans. Hilda Andrews-Rusiecka (Oxford: Oxford University Press, 1975), p. 70. Walicki points out that Moscow in the eighteenth century was the chief center of the Rosicrucians, the mystical wing of Freemasonry.

36. Robert Lyall, *The Character of the Russians and a Detailed History of*

Moscow (London: T. Cadell, 1823), p. 36; Sir Donald Mackenzie Wallace, *Russia on the Eve of War and Revolution*, ed. Cyril E. Black (New York: Random House, 1961), p. 203 (originally published 1877).

37. I. P. Mashkov, *Putevoditel' po Moskve* (Moscow: Moskovskoye Arkhitekturnoye Obshchestvo, 1913), p. 147.

38. Berton, *Moscow*, p. 170.

39. Richard Wortman, "Moscow and Petersburg: The Problem of Political Center in Tsarist Russia, 1881–1914," in Sean Wilentz, ed., *Rites of Power: Symbolism, Ritual, and Politics since the Middle Ages* (Philadelphia: University of Pennsylvania Press, 1985), pp. 244–274.

40. Robert Gohstand, "The Shaping of Moscow by Nineteenth-Century Trade," in Michael F. Hamm, ed., *The City in Russian History* (Lexington: University Press of Kentucky, 1976), pp. 160–181.

41. William C. Brumfield, *The Origins of Modernism in Russian Architecture* (Berkeley: University of California Press, 1991), p. 20.

42. See especially ibid., chap. 4; Ye. I. Kirichenko, *Fedor Shekhtel'* (Moscow: Stroiizdat, 1973); Catherine Cooke, "Fedor Shekhtel: An Architect and his Clients in Turn-of-Century Moscow," *Architectural Association Files*, nos. 5–6 (Summer–Autumn 1984), pp. 5–31.

43. C. Piazzi Smith, *Three Cities in Russia* (London: Lovell, Reeve, 1862), II, 47–48; Vasilich, "Ulitsy i lyudi," p. 6.

44. Wallace, *Russia on the Eve*, p. 204.

45. Bradley, *Muzhik and Muscovite*, p. 236. James H. Bater found a roughly similar picture of "admixture of classes" in the capital: see *St. Petersburg: Industrialization and Change* (London: Edward Arnold, 1976), pp. 402–407.

46. In addition to Russian sources on social geography, I am indebted to Koenker, *Moscow Workers*, chap. 1; Bradley, *Muzhik and Muscovite*, pp. 229–238; and Laura Engelstein, *Moscow, 1905: Working-Class Organization and Political Conflict* (Stanford: Stanford University Press, 1982), chap. 3.

47. G. T. Lowth, *Around the Kremlin* (London: Hurst and Blackett, 1868), p. 14.

48. Lyall, *Character of the Russians*, p. 381.

49. For the broad types of living unit I rely on Bradley, *Muzhik and Muscovite* (pp. 200–201), counting boarding houses as rental accommodation. Bradley's book gives the best description of Moscow housing before 1917. Other housing statistics cited are from *Entsiklopedicheskii slovar' t-va Br. A. i I. Granat i Ko.*, 7th ed., vol. 29 (Moscow: 1914), 366–367, and *Istoriya Moskvy*, V, 696.

50. S. K. Aleverdyan, *Zhilishchnyi vopros v Moskve* (Yerevan: Izdatel'stvo AN Armyanskoi SSR, 1961), p. 49 (originally published 1915).

51. The Trekhgornaya case is described in ibid., p. 61, and P. A. Buryshkin, *Moskva kupecheskaya* (New York: Izdatel'stvo imeni Chekhova, 1954), p. 146. Bradley, *Muzhik and Muscovite*, p. 204, points out that statistical imprecisions may exaggerate the drop in employer-supplied housing, but the trend does not seem to be in doubt.

52. *Istoriya Moskvy*, II, 120.

53. A Moscow mayor was first appointed in 1766, but his relationship to other officials was not specified until 1785.

54. Walter Hanchett, "Tsarist Statutory Regulation of Municipal Government in the Nineteenth Century," in Michael F. Hamm, ed., *The City in Russian History* (Lexington: University Press of Kentucky, 1976), p. 91.

55. On the 1862 and 1873 charters, see Walter S. Hanchett, "Moscow in the Late Nineteenth Century: A Study in Municipal Self-Government," Ph.D. diss., University of Chicago, 1964, chap. 2.

56. D. N. Shipov, *Vospominaniya i dumy o perezhitom* (Moscow: Tovari-shchestvo Pechatnya S. P. Yakovleva, 1918), p. 560.

57. Thomas W. Owen, *Capitalism and Politics in Russia: A Social History of the Moscow Merchants, 1855–1905* (Cambridge: Cambridge University Press, 1981), p. 161; Robert W. Thurston, "Urban Problems and Local Government in Late Imperial Russia: Moscow, 1906–1914," Ph.D. diss., University of Michigan, 1980, pp. 115–116. The six business mayors were I. A. Lyamin (1871–1873), Tret'yakov, N. A. Alekseyev (1885–1893), K. V. Rukavishnikov (1893–1896), N. I. Guchkov (1905–1912), and M. V. Chelnokov (1914–1917).

58. Buryshkin, *Moskva kupecheskaya*, p. 230. Philanthropy is thoroughly treated in Jo Ann Ruckman, *The Moscow Business Elite: A Social and Cultural Portrait of Two Generations, 1840–1905* (DeKalb: Northern Illinois University Press, 1984), and Beverly Whitney Kean, *All the Empty Palaces: The Merchant Patrons of Modern Art in Pre-Revolutionary Russia* (London: Barrie and Jenkins, 1983).

59. Buryshkin, *Moskva kupecheskaya*, p. 275. On residential and family connections, see Engelstein, *Moscow, 1905*, pp. 51–52. Engelstein found that almost two-fifths of the 113 councilmen elected in 1900 for whom street addresses could be located lived in Prechistenskaya, Arbatskaya, and Tverskaya districts, and almost half lived on the same nineteen streets.

60. B. N. Chicherin, *Vospominaniya: Zemstvo i Moskovskaya Duma* (Moscow: Kooperativnoye izdatel'stvo Sever, 1934), p. 182.

61. "Moskovskii gorodskoi golova," *Gorodskoye delo*, no. 9 (May 1, 1913), p. 564.

62. My account draws on Thurston, "Urban Problems and Local Government," chaps. 5–7, and *Istoriya Moskvy*, IV, 516–545, and V, 690–717.

63. Engelstein, *Moscow, 1905*, p. 146.

64. N. M. Kishkin, "Zhilishchnyi vopros v Moskve i blizhaishiye zadachi v razreshenii yego gorodskoi dumoi," *Gorodskoye delo*, no. 5 (March 1, 1913), p. 292; G. Yaroslavskii, "Gorodskoye samoupravleniye Moskvy," in *Moskva v yeye proshlom i nastoyashchem*, (Moscow: Tovarishchestvo Obrazovaniye, 1909–1912), XII, 40.

65. Ye. I. Kirichenko, *Moskva na rubezhe stoletii* (Moscow: Stroiizdat, 1977), p. 110, and Aleverdyan, *Zhilishchnyi vopros*, p. 34, citing contemporary statistics that show 8.7 persons per apartment in Moscow, 4.5 in London, 4.3 in Paris, 4.2 in Vienna, and 3.9 in Berlin.

66. Soviet historians, who for decades flatly condemned late imperial Moscow's

lack of planning, eventually allowed that some good surveying and inspection work was done, much of it a continuation of rudimentary plans such as those of 1775 and 1817. One went so far as to say that Moscow "developed relatively harmoniously and healthily in comparison with the big cities of western Europe." Kirichenko, *Moskva na rubezhe stoletii,* p. 30.

67. Information in these two paragraphs comes from *Istoriya Moskvy,* V, 709, 718, and Thurston, "Urban Problems and Local Government," pp. 29–30. Although Bater writes in his superb study (*St. Petersburg,* pp. 351–352) that St. Petersburg was the least healthy city, the statistics cited by Thurston do not bear him out. In the early 1880s total deaths were 33.3 per 10,000 in Moscow and 32.8 in St. Petersburg; in 1910 Moscow still led in deaths, with 26.9 (as compared to St. Petersburg's 24.1) per 10,000. In 1909 infant mortality in Moscow was 3,160 per 10,000, as compared to 2,420 per 10,000 in St. Petersburg, 2,100 in Madrid, 1,920 in Munich, and 1,730 in Vienna and Cologne.

68. N. I. Astrov, *Vospominaniya* (Paris: Y.M.C.A. Press, 1941), p. 261.

69. "Krizis gorodskikh finansov," *Gorodskoye delo,* no. 2 (January 15, 1913), p. 90.

70. "Sobraniye gorodskikh zemlemerov," ibid., nos. 15–16 (August 1–15, 1913), p. 163.

71. James L. West, "The Moscow Progressists: Russian Industrialists in Liberal Politics, 1905–1914," Ph.D. diss., Princeton University, 1974.

72. "Krizis gorodskikh finansov," p. 90.

73. Thurston, "Urban Problems and Local Government," pp. 98, 216–217, 291.

74. N. A. Naidenov, *Vospominaniya o vedennom, slyshannom i ispytannom* (Moscow: Tovarishchestvo I. N. Kushnerev, 1903–1905), I, 90.

75. Chicherin, *Vospominaniya,* p. 206, writing about his term as mayor in the early 1880s. Tsarist governors generally had worse relations with the urban dumas than with the zemstvos, because of the governors' aristocratic origins and their unfamiliarity with city government. Richard G. Robbins, Jr., *The Tsar's Viceroys: Russian Provincial Governors in the Last Years of the Empire* (Ithaca, N.Y.: Cornell University Press, 1987), pp. 166–172.

76. Astrov, *Vospominaniya,* p. 277.

77. A. A. Trifonov, "Formirovaniye seti gorodskikh poselenii na territorii Moskovskoi oblasti (seredina XIX v.–1976 g.)," in *Russkii gorod* (Moscow: Izdatel'stvo Moskovskogo universiteta, 1982), p. 21.

78. Three police precincts (Butyrskii, Alekseyevskii, and Novo-Andron'evskii) were split between Moscow and the suburban area, but only their inner parts were subordinated to the city for municipal purposes.

79. Lester T. Hutton, "The Reform of City Government in Russia, 1860–1870," Ph.D. diss., University of Illinois, 1972, pp. 80–82.

80. Quotations from Astrov, *Vospominaniya,* p. 273, and Shipov, *Vospominaniya i dumy o perezhitom,* p. 40.

81. I. Verner, "Predstoyashchaya planirovka Moskvy," *Kommunal'noye khozyaistvo,* nos. 2–3 (February 1, 1925), p. 61.

82. "Poselkovyi s"ezd," *Gorodskoye delo,* no. 9 (May 1, 1914), pp. 577–578.

83. V. N. Belousov and O. V. Smirnova, *V. N. Semenov* (Moscow: Stroiizdat, 1980), p. 32.

84. "Pervyi v Rossii sad-gorod 'Druzhba 1 marta 1917 g.,'" *Kommunal'noye khozyaistvo,* no. 13 (November 1922), pp. 16–17.

85. *Lenin i moskovskiye bol'sheviki* (Moscow: Moskovskii rabochii, 1969), p. 56.

86. This is the figure cited in Engelstein, *Moscow, 1905,* the best account of the upheaval.

87. M. Vasil'ev-Yuzhin, "Moskovskii Sovet rabochikh deputatov v 1905 godu i podgotovka im vooruzhennogo vosstaniya," *Proletarskaya revolyutsiya,* no. 4 (April 1925), p. 94. See also Robert M. Slusser, "The Moscow Soviet of Workers' Deputies of 1905: Origin, Structures, and Policies," Ph.D. diss., Columbia University, 1963.

88. Ralph Carter Elwood, *Roman Malinovsky: A Life without A Cause* (Newtonville, Mass.: Oriental Research Partners, 1977).

89. Party histories speak of the early MK being freely elected, but a founding father's memoir indicates the 1905 MK "was built from above." "The core of the committee was selected by the central committee and expanded and supplemented itself through cooptation. There were no elections at all, which were quite impossible in underground conditions." S. I. Mitskevich, *Revolyutsionnaya Moskva* (Moscow: Goslitizdat, 1940), p. 351.

90. "Vospominaniya V. P. Nogina o moskovskoi organizatsii," *Proletarskaya revolyutsiya,* no. 2 (February 1925), p. 207.

91. Robert C. Williams, *The Other Bolsheviks: Lenin and His Critics, 1904–1914* (Bloomington: Indiana University Press, 1986), p. 117.

92. *Ocherki istorii Moskovskoi organizatsii KPSS (1883–noyabr' 1917)* (Moscow: Moskovskii rabochii, 1979), p. 213.

93. Eight raikoms were for the Gorodskoi, Second Gorodskoi, Zamoskvoretskii, Presnya-Khamovnicheskii, Butyrskii, Rogozhskii, Lefortovskii, and Sokol'nicheskii districts. The ninth, the Zheleznodorozhnyi raikom, took in all railroad employees, regardless of location.

94. In addition to the nine guberniyas of the Central Industrial Region, the Moscow Oblast Bureau in the early days encompassed Orel, Smolensk, Tambov, and Voronezh guberniyas.

95. P. G. Smidovich, "Vykhod iz podpol'ya v Moskve," *Proletarskaya revolyutsiya,* no. 1 (January 1923), p. 171.

96. Williams, *Other Bolsheviks,* p. 68, makes this comment of the MK lecture group, but it applies to the whole organization.

97. "Vystupleniye N. I. Bukharina posvyashchennoye pamyati I. I. Skvortsova-Stepanova," *Voprosy istorii,* no. 5 (May 1988), p. 78. Alliances shifted with circumstances. For example, G. I. Lomov, a leftist allied with Bukharin, worked closely with Rykov in 1913 in Lefortovskii district, but then turned against him in 1917. Lomov, like Rykov, was born in the Volga city of Saratov, and the two may have been friends from an early age.

98. Pyatnitskii's specialty is discussed in Ralph Carter Elwood, *Russian Social Democracy in the Underground* (Assen: Van Norcum, 1974), p. 139.

99. S. Frederick Starr, *Decentralization and Self-Government in Russia, 1830–1870* (Princeton: Princeton University Press, 1972), pp. 46–47.

2. Red Moscow

1. A. Shlikhter, "Oktyabr'skiye dni," *Proletarskaya revolyutsiya,* no. 5 (May 1922), p. 238. The best studies of the revolution in Moscow are Diane Koenker, *Moscow Workers and the 1917 Revolution* (Princeton: Princeton University Press, 1981), and A. Ya. Grunt, *Moskva 1917-i: Revolyutsiya i kontrrevolyutsiya* (Moscow: Nauka, 1976). Especially useful on party politics and ideology are B'Ann Bowman, "The Moscow Bolsheviks February–November 1917," Ph.D. diss., Indiana University, 1973, and Richard Sakwa, *Soviet Communists in Power: A Study of Moscow during the Civil War, 1918–21* (London: Macmillan, 1988). Summary works on War Communism are Silvana Malle, *The Economic Organisation of War Communism* (Cambridge: Cambridge University Press, 1985), and Thomas F. Remington, *Building Socialism in Bolshevik Russia: Ideology and Industrial Organization, 1917–1921* (Pittsburgh: University of Pittsburgh Press, 1984).

2. Lewis H. Siegelbaum, *The Politics of Industrial Mobilization in Russia, 1914–17* (London: Macmillan, 1983), chap. 3.

3. P. G. Smidovich, "Vykhod iz podpol'ya v Moskve," *Proletarskaya revolyutsiya,* no. 1 (January 1923), p. 173.

4. E. N. Burdzhalov, *Vtoraya russkaya revolyutsiya: Moskva, front, periferiya* (Moscow: Nauka, 1971), p. 45.

5. A. V. Lukashev, "Bor'ba bol'shevikov za revolyutsionnuyu politiku Moskovskogo Soveta rabochikh deputatov v period dvoyevlastiya," *Voprosy istorii KPSS,* no. 8 (August 1967), p. 61. Early organization of the soviet is best described in Ye. Ignatov, *Moskovskii Sovet rabochikh deputatov v 1917 godu* (Moscow: Izdatel'stvo Kommunisticheskoi akademii, 1925).

6. Yu. P. Aksenov, "Trudyashchiyesya Moskovskoi gubernii v boyakh za pobedu Oktyabrya," in D. A. Chugayev, ed., *Ustanovleniye Sovetskoi vlasti na mestakh v 1917–1918 godakh* (Moscow: Gospolitizdat, 1959), pp. 15–110.

7. A. N. Voznesenskii, *Moskva v 1917 godu* (Moscow and Leningrad: Gosizdat, 1928), p. 26.

8. Quotations from Ignatov, *Moskovskii Sovet,* p. 161, and I. Veger, "K istorii Moskovskogo Soveta rabochikh deputatov," *Proletarskaya revolyutsiya,* no. 1 (January 1926), pp. 225–226.

9. Smidovich, "Vykhod iz podpol'ya," p. 177.

10. V. A. Obukh, "Iz vospominanii o Fevrale i dnyakh Oktyabrya," in P. N. Pospelov, ed., *Moskovskiye bol'sheviki v ogne revolyutsionnykh boyev (Vospominaniya)* (Moscow: Mysl', 1976), p. 73; V. Yakovleva, "Partiinaya rabota v Moskovskoi oblasti v period fevral'–oktyabr' 1917 g.," *Proletarskaya revolyutsiya,* no. 3 (March 1923), p. 197.

11. Yakovleva, "Partiinaya rabota v Moskovskoi oblasti," pp. 202, 198.

12. Obukh, "Iz vospominanii," p. 77; TsGAODM, f. 3, op. 1, d. 46, ll. 48, 95–96, 237.

13. Obukh, "Iz vospominanii," p. 77; TsGAODM, f. 3, op. 1, d. 46, l. 283.

14. TsGAODM, f. 3, op. 1, d. 46, ll. 56–59. Volin (a revolutionary alias) is referred to here and in most other party documents from 1917 and 1918 by his given name, Yefim Fradkin.

15. B. Volin, "Vokrug Moskovskoi Dumy," *Proletarskaya revolyutsiya,* no. 6 (June 1922), p. 98. At an MK session on April 23, Volin spoke for the commission and said that a draft program had already been prepared by Gal'perin. Archival documents from May to June 1917 refer to an MK Municipal Group, which may have had a somewhat different composition than the Municipal Commission and which was assigned 1 percent of Moscow membership dues in late May.

16. Program reproduced in Ignatov, *Moskovskii Sovet,* pp. 440–445.

17. The Gorodskoi and Lefortovskii raion soviets were briefly under Bolshevik leadership as early as April.

18. Grunt, *Moskva 1917-i,* p. 229.

19. See especially Koenker, *Moscow Workers,* pp. 212–215.

20. This body was referred to during the election campaign for the raion dumas as the Municipal Bureau but was renamed the Municipal Commission by the MK on October 22. That resolution also named Podbel'skii chairman and Volin (Fradkin) and Vladimirskii members. The commission was charged with organizing the party for elections to the Constituent Assembly as well as in the municipal arena. TsGAODM, f. 3, op. 1, d. 46, l. 271.

21. M. Vladimirskii, "Moskovskiye raionnyye dumy i sovet raionnykh dum v 1917–1918 gg.," *Proletarskaya revolyutsiya,* no. 8 (August 1923), p. 80; Voznesenskii, *Moskva v 1917 godu,* p. 105.

22. See especially V. Yakovleva, "Podgotovka oktyabr'skogo vosstaniya v Moskovskoi oblasti," *Proletarskaya revolyutsiya,* no. 10 (October 1922), p. 304, and O. Pyatnitskii, "Iz istorii Oktyabr'skogo vosstaniya v Moskve," *Istorik-marksist,* no. 4 (44) (1935), p. 9.

23. *Triumfal'noye shestviye Sovetskoi vlasti* (Moscow: Izdatel'stvo Akademii Nauk SSSR, 1963), I, 313, 255.

24. TsGAODM, f. 3, op. 1, d. 46, l. 296; *Pravda,* January 22, 1918, p. 3, and January 24, 1918, p. 3; Jan M. Yarkovsky, *It Happened in Moscow* (New York: Vantage Press, 1961), pp. 267–275.

25. Beginning in June 1920 and continuing for some years, the Moscow ispolkom contained several nonaligned members but never included members of other parties. The presidium remained 100 percent Communist.

26. Because of the frequent by-elections, 91 percent of the deputies had been Communists or sympathizers when the election was called. The 1920 vote, in other words, slightly reduced the party's numerical dominance.

27. See Boris Dvinov, *Moskovskii Sovet Rabochikh Deputatov, 1917–1922: Vospominaniya* (New York: Inter-University Project on the History of the Menshevik

Movement, 1961), p. 98: "The Moscow Soviet of Workers' Deputies was the single place, the single tribune, from which we could appeal to the masses. Naturally, we valued it." Khinchuk went on to hold major offices, including Soviet trade envoy to Britain and Germany and people's commissar of trade of the Russian Republic; he was purged in 1938 and died in 1944.

28. *Pravda*, April 21, 1918, p. 3; TsGAODM, f. 3, op. 1, d. 56, l. 72, which reveals that shootings were still being carried out "absolutely mercilessly" in December 1918; Sergei P. Melgounov, *The Red Terror in Russia* (London and Toronto: J. M. Dent, 1925), pp. 4–8; George Leggett, *The Cheka: Lenin's Political Police* (Oxford: Clarendon Press, 1981), p. 199.

29. *Krasnaya Moskva, 1917–1920 gg.* (Moscow: Izdaniye Moskovskogo Soveta, 1920), p. 633.

30. Statistics in *Izvestiya*, July 1, 1920, p. 2, and *Kommunisticheskii trud*, October 27, 1921, p. 3. Forty-three percent of the inmates in July 1920 had been sent by the Cheka and 7 percent by revolutionary tribunals; the rest were sentenced by the ordinary courts for the economic crimes of profiteering, bribery, and graft. There are photographs of a workshop and kitchen of the Pokrovskii camp in *Krasnaya Moskva*, opp. p. 631, and a description of the Andronikov camp in Marguerite E. Harrison, *Marooned in Moscow* (New York: George H. Doran, 1921), pp. 110–111. Several concentration camps had been opened for German and Austrian war prisoners in Moscow in the spring of 1918. Some of the premises evidently were used to incarcerate Russians later. Aside from the monasteries, the camp most often mentioned in accounts was at Kozhukhovo, just south of the city. For general background, see Michael Jakobson, *Origins of the Gulag: The Soviet Prison Camp System, 1917–1934* (Lexington: University Press of Kentucky, 1993), chap. 3.

31. G. S. Ignat'ev, *Moskva v pervyi god proletarskoi diktatury* (Moscow: Nauka, 1975), p. 148; *Pravda*, March 1, 1918, p. 3.

32. *Krasnaya Moskva*, p. 335. The Moscow decrees, drafted by D. V. Kuzovkov of the Finance Department of the Moscow Soviet, served as the model for the national directive eventually adopted August 20, 1918. V. V. Zhuravlev, "Nachal'nyi etap resheniya zhilishchnoi problemy v SSSR," *Voprosy istorii*, no. 5 (May 1978), pp. 36, 40, 42.

33. TsGAODM, f. 3, op. 1, d. 53, l. 10, and d. 54, ll. 31–32.

34. *Triumfal'noye shestviye*, I, 301; V. A. Kondrat'ev, ed., *Moskovskii voyenno-revolyutsionnyi komitet (oktyabr'–noyabr' 1917 goda)* (Moscow: Moskovskii rabochii, 1968), pp. 277–278; P. A. Buryshkin, *Moskva kupecheskaya* (New York: Izdatel'stvo imeni Chekhova, 1954), p. 347.

35. See Volin, "Vokrug Moskovskoi Dumy," p. 166, and *Moskovskii Sovet rabochikh, krest'yanskikh i krasnoarmeiskikh deputatov, 1917–1927* (Moscow: Izdaniye Moskovskogo Soveta, 1927), p. 77. The Soviet of Raion Dumas (discussed below in text) set the December 6 date at its meeting of November 21 (TsGIAGM, f. 1363, op. 1, d. 8, l. 2), but archival records do not indicate that it or its bureau ever returned to the question. The Bolsheviks' city conference on November 25 and an MK meeting at "the end of November" were still addressing the party's slate for

the election (TsGAODM, f. 3, op. 1, d. 46, ll. 291, 302). The only party that refrained from the election boycott was a fringe group, the Lithuanian Social Democrats.

36. The resolution is reprinted in *Triumfal'noye shestviye*, I, 276–277. Accounts of the chaotic meeting are in A. Shlikhter, "Pamyatnyye dni v Moskve," *Proletarskaya revolyutsiya*, no. 10 (October 1922), pp. 192–197, and Vladimirskii, "Moskovskiye raionnyye dumy," pp. 81–82.

37. Vladimirskii, "Moskovskiye raionnyye dumy," pp. 84–86.

38. At the MK's debate October 20, Bukharin voiced support for the workers' demands, while Rykov feared the strike would demoralize the population and cause "pogroms and lynchings." The issue was referred to the presidium of the city soviet. TsGAODM, f. 3, op. 1, d. 46, ll. 263–265.

39. Quotations from Vladimirskii, "Moskovskiye raionnyye dumy," pp. 87, 89–90, 91.

40. TsGIAGM, f. 1364, op. 1, d. 14, l. 16. The SRD had voted November 17 to reserve all requisitions to the raion dumas, but this action was unenforceable.

41. Vladimirskii, "Moskovskiye raionnyye dumy," pp. 92–94.

42. TsGIAGM, f. 1364, op. 1, d. 8, ll. 34, 43–44, 50–51.

43. N. M. Aleshchenko, *Moskovskii Sovet v 1917–1941 gg.* (Moscow: Nauka, 1976), pp. 79–80; *Pravda*, April 3, 1918, p. 3.

44. *Izvestiya*, October 12, 1917, p. 2.

45. Yu. P. Malinovskii, "K pereyezdu TsK RKP(b) i Sovetskogo pravitel'stva iz Petrograda v Moskvu (mart 1918 g.)," *Voprosy istorii*, no. 11 (November 1968), pp. 99–103.

46. *Izvestiya*, March 17, 1918, p. 2.

47. Ibid., March 17, 1918, p. 2, and March 14, 1918, p. 1.

48. M. P. Iroshnikov, "K voprosu o slome burzhuaznoi gosudarstvennoi mashiny v Rossii," in *Problemy gosudarstvennogo stroitel'stva v pervyye gody Sovetskoi vlasti* (Leningrad: Nauka, 1974), pp. 46–66; *Krasnaya Moskva*, p. 55.

49. P. D. Mal'kov, *Zapiski komendanta Kremlya*, 3d ed. (Moscow: Molodaya gvardiya, 1968), pp. 116–120; author's interview with Natal'ya A. Rykova (daughter of Aleksei Rykov), July 1992.

50. *Leninskiye dekrety o Moskve* (Moscow: Moskovskii rabochii, 1978), pp. 39, 58, 113–115.

51. *Izvestiya*, March 23, 1918, p. 4.

52. Melgounov, *Red Terror in Russia*, pp. 206–207; *Moskovskaya pravda*, January 22, 1992, p. 7; Leggett, *Cheka*, pp. 217–218.

53. *Krasnaya Moskva*, p. 347; *Izvestiya*, January 25, 1921, p. 4.

54. TsGAODM, f. 3, op. 1, d. 71, ll. 169, 187–188.

55. *Izvestiya*, December 1, 1918, p. 2, and August 23, 1918, p. 2; *Kommunisticheskii trud*, August 11, 1920, p. 3, and August 24, 1920, p. 3.

56. Harrison, *Marooned in Moscow*, p. 135. Rozhdestvenskii Convent held a police station, Strastnoi Convent military offices, and the Simonov Monastery and the Vsekhsvyatskii Convent workers' quarters.

57. Aleshchenko, *Moskovskii Sovet v 1917–1941 gg.*, pp. 33–34, and Maksimovskii in *Izvestiya*, June 28, 1918, p. 4.

58. *Izvestiya*, April 30, 1918, p. 1. The election was so hastily arranged that some appointees "either could not be reached or had still not found substitutes for the offices in which they had worked earlier" (*Pravda*, March 20, 1918, p. 3).

59. Stalin and M. I. Latsis of the NKVD in *Izvestiya*, April 3, 1918, p. 3, and March 28, 1918, p. 1.

60. Ibid., April 30, 1918, p. 1.

61. *Leninskiye dekrety*, pp. 62–63; Aleshchenko, *Moskovskii Sovet v 1917–1941 gg.*, pp. 86–88; Ignat'ev, *Moskva v pervyi god*, pp. 85–87; A. M. Anikst, *Vospominaniya o Vladimire Il'iche* (Moscow: Partiinoye izdatel'stvo, 1933), p. 8. Moscow guberniya quietly had its own sovnarkom from April to July 1918.

62. *Izvestiya*, June 29, 1918, p. 3, and December 10, 1918, p. 4. A government decree on December 23, 1918, dissolved Moscow oblast, while continuing three others. The RSFSR constitution of July 1918 had allowed (without requiring) oblast executive committees, but this reference was eliminated in January 1920.

63. *Pravda*, December 13, 1918, p. 4; M. A. Kitayev, "Iz istorii partiinogo stroitel'stva v Moskovskoi oblastnoi organizatsii (noyabr' 1917 g.–yanvar' 1919 g.)," *Voprosy istorii KPSS*, no. 6 (June 1971), p. 93.

64. I. V. Zholtovskii, "V 1918-m," in *Vospominaniya o Vladimire Il'iche Lenine* (Moscow: Gospolitizdat, 1957), II, 319–321.

65. See especially Selim O. Khan-Magomedov, *Pioneers of Soviet Architecture*, trans. Alexander Lieven (New York: Rizzoli, 1983), chaps. 2–3.

66. *Iz istorii sovetskoi arkhitektury, 1917–1925 gg.: Dokumenty i materialy* (Moscow: Izdatel'stvo Akademii Nauk, 1963), p. 32.

67. Ibid., pp. 32–33.

68. Ibid., pp. 37–38.

69. In fact, the city ordered a detailed inventory of real estate only the week after adoption of the plan, and a basic land survey only in June 1919. *Vecherniye izvestiya Moskovskogo Soveta Rabochikh i Krasnoarmeiskikh Deputatov*, February 15, 1919, p. 3, and July 1, 1919, p. 4.

70. V. E. Khazanova, *Sovetskaya arkhitektura pervykh let Oktyabrya* (Moscow: Nauka, 1970), p. 80.

71. Sergei Romanyuk, *Moskva: Utraty* (Moscow: PTO "Tsentr," 1992), pp. 40–42.

72. See generally Richard Stites, *Revolutionary Dreams: Utopian Vision and Experimental Life in the Russian Revolution* (New York: Oxford University Press, 1989), pp. 88–90; A. Strigalev, "K istorii vozniknoveniya leninskogo plana monumental'noi propagandy (mart–aprel' 1918 goda)," in I. M. Shmidt, ed., *Voprosy sovetskogo izobrazitel'nogo iskusstva i arkhitektury* (Moscow: Sovetskii khudozhnik, 1976), pp. 213–251; John E. Bowlt, "Russian Sculpture and Lenin's Plan of Monumental Propaganda," in Henry A. Millon and Linda Nochlin, eds., *Art and Architecture in the Service of Politics* (Cambridge, Mass.: MIT Press, 1978), pp. 182–194. V. D. Bonch-Bruyevich, *Vospominaniya o Lenine* (Moscow: Nauka, 1965), pp. 376–

377, 380–381, describes Lenin's antimodernist views, his use of soldiers to tear down offending art work, and his inability to get a statue of the novelist Leo Tolstoy put up in the Kremlin.

73. *Pravda,* November 12, 1918, p. 4.

74. TsGIAGM, f. 1364, op. 1, d. 8, l. 68; A. M. Pegov et al., *Imena moskovskikh ulits,* rev. ed. (Moscow: Moskovskii rabochii, 1979). Renamings averaged 1.1 a year in 1900–1917, but 14 a year in 1918–1921 and 202 in 1922, the peak year for the commission. In addition to Lenin's adopted surname, streets and squares evoked his Russian patronymic (Il'ich), his family name (Ul'yanov), and one of his revolutionary aliases (Tulin).

75. Yelena Ovsyannikova, "Staraya Moskva i 'Staraya Moskva,'" *Arkhitektura i stroitel'stvo Moskvy,* no. 9 (September 1988), p. 25. The beginning of the inventory of architectural treasures is reported in *Vecherniye izvestiya,* February 15, 1919, p. 3.

76. Vladimir Kozlov, "Gibel' Khrama," *Moskovskii zhurnal,* no. 9 (September 1991), pp. 9–13.

77. Vladimir Kozlov, "U istokov," *Arkhitektura i stroitel'stvo Moskvy,* no. 7 (July 1990), p. 13. See also *Izvestiya,* December 22, 1918, p. 4, and December 28, 1918, p. 3.

78. *Izvestiya,* August 23, 1918, p. 2. Yelizarov (1863–1919) had belonged to the MK in the early 1900s and was married to Lenin's older sister, Anna.

79. The Privol'e plan is excerpted in *Iz istorii sovetskoi arkhitektury, 1917–1925 gg.,* pp. 33–36, and analyzed in Khazanova, *Sovetskaya arkhitektura pervykh let Oktyabrya,* pp. 51–53.

80. M. Astaf'eva[-Dlugach], "Pervyi sovetskii plan Bol'shoi Moskvy," *Nauka i zhizn',* no. 5 (May 1967), pp. 26–27.

81. Ivan Kremnev, *Puteshestviye moyego brata Alekseya v stranu krest'yanskoi utopii,* pt. 1 (and only) (Moscow: Gosudarstvennoye izdatel'stvo, 1920).

82. *Iz istorii sovetskoi arkhitektury, 1917–1925 gg.,* pp. 36, 40; *Izvestiya,* November 14, 1918, p. 4; M. Astaf'eva-Dlugach, "Proyektnyye razrabotki zony vliyaniya Moskvy v pervyye poslerevolyutsionnyye gody," in V. L. Glazychev, A. M. Zhuravlev, and Yu. S. Aralov, eds., *Problemy teorii i istorii arkhitektury: Puti formirovaniya i perspektivy razvitiya arkhitektury Sovetskoi Rossii (Podmoskov'ya)* (Moscow: TsNII po grazhdanskomu stroitel'stvu i arkhitekture, 1978), p. 65. Under Shchusev, the Zholtovskii studio did do a rough drawing of a system of garden towns around Moscow in 1919, but no debt to Sakulin was acknowledged. After declaring Privol'e an urgent project some time in 1920, the government took no further action. Komgosoor faulted the draft for being unconnected to any plan for resolving Moscow's housing crisis.

83. *Krasnaya Moskva,* pp. 287–288.

84. Ibid., pp. 291–292.

85. Harrison, *Marooned in Moscow,* p. 154.

86. TsGAODM, f. 3, op. 1, d. 71, l. 42.

87. *Krasnaya Moskva,* pp. 53–54, 302, and Harrison, *Marooned in Moscow,* p. 93. Harrison also reported (p. 156) that peasants who earned large profits

from trade in Moscow, unable to find needed farm implements, rope, and clothing, bought "useless luxuries" such as bedroom sets, fine china, silk gowns, and gramophones.

88. *Krasnaya Moskva*, p. 299. For more on natural wages, see William J. Chase, *Workers, Society, and the Soviet State: Labor and Life in Moscow, 1918–1929* (Urbana: University of Illinois Press, 1987), pp. 37–38.

89. TsGAODM, f. 3, op. 1, d. 71, ll. 10–13, 24, 29, 31; "Otchet upravleniya delami TsK RKP," *Izvestiya TsK RKP(b)*, no. 27 (January 27, 1921), p. 12; Lidiya Shatunovskaya, *Zhizn' v Kremle* (New York: Chalidze Publications, 1982), p. 40. The MK of the party set up its own cafeteria in December 1919.

90. "Toplivosnabzheniye Moskvy v 1916–1921 godakh," *Kommunal'noye khozyaistvo*, nos. 1–2 (May 1921), pp. 4–8.

91. *Krasnaya Moskva*, pp. 334–342. The first block households were formed in July 1918, but they acquired control over the house committees only the following year. Complaints about the influence of former proprietors were still being heard at an MK plenum in September 1920 (TsGAODM, f. 3, op. 1-a, d. 6, ll. 34–35).

92. *Moskovskii Sovet . . . 1917–1927*, p. 357.

93. Aleshchenko, *Moskovskii Sovet v 1917–1941 gg.*, pp. 68, 193–195, accounts specifically for 96,000 resettlements, but his figure for 1918 seems incomplete, and other Soviet historians give a total of 100,000.

94. Baumanskii raionnyi komitet VKP(b), *Ocherki po istorii revolyutsionnogo dvizheniya i bol'shevistskoi organizatsii v Baumanskom raione* (Moscow: Moskovskii rabochii, 1928), pp. 118–119.

95. TsGAODM, f. 3, op. 1, d. 54, l. 133. One week before, the MK did oppose a plan by the Cheka to open a police store selling confiscated possessions (ibid., l. 131).

96. *Pravda*, August 27, 1918, p. 1, and August 12, 1919, p. 2. Congress resolution quoted in Hugh D. Hudson, Jr., *Blueprints and Blood: The Stalinization of Soviet Architecture, 1917–1937* (Princeton: Princeton University Press, 1994), p. 57.

97. *Pravda*, October 23, 1918, p. 1; *Izvestiya*, September 13, 1918, p. 3, and December 1, 1918, p. 3; *Vecherniye izvestiya*, October 2, 1918, p. 3.

98. TsGAODM, f. 3, op. 1, d. 71, l. 42; *Vecherniye izvestiya*, September 3, 1919, p. 3.

99. *Pravda*, June 26, 1919, p. 2.

100. See Stol'bunova in ibid., February 4, 1919, pp. 1–2. In October 1919 ownership of all factory housing was transferred to the soviet, but the issue remained one of practical responsibility rather than legal rights.

101. Statistics in *Krasnaya Moskva*, p. 360, and T. V. Kuznetsova, "Revolyutsionnyi zhilishchnyi peredel v Moskve, 1918–1921," *Istoriya SSSR*, no. 5 (September–October 1963), p. 146. One nonfactory with its own housing was the Central Committee of the Communist Party, which in 1921 acquired three buildings as dormitories near its Mokhovaya ulitsa headquarters ("Otchet upravleniya delami TsK RKP," p. 12). There are several references in archive documents to a house-commune of the Moscow Committee, but I could not trace its location.

102. *Kommunisticheskii trud,* April 17, 1920, p. 4.

103. V. Rudnev, "Bol'noi gorod," *Sovremennyye zapiski,* no. 11 (July 18, 1922), pp. 311–337.

104. *Krasnaya Moskva,* p. 54. On in-migration, the 1926 census found 161,000 Muscovites who reported migrating to Moscow in the years 1917 through 1920. It did not specify how many 1917 arrivals came before October, but the number was probably not large.

105. Some 314,000 Muscovites served in the army; many were posted locally, and others soon returned from the front.

106. Aleshchenko, *Moskovskii Sovet v 1917–1941 gg.,* p. 222; Diane P. Koenker, "Urbanization and Deurbanization in the Russian Revolution and Civil War," in Koenker, William G. Rosenberg, and Ronald Grigor Suny, eds., *Party, State, and Society in the Russian Civil War* (Bloomington: Indiana University Press, 1989), pp. 90–95.

107. *Ekonomicheskaya zhizn',* June 17, 1921, p. 2.

108. See C. E. Bechhofer, *Through Starving Russia* (London: Methuen, 1921), pp. 134–135, and Walter Duranty, *I Write As I Please* (New York: Simon and Schuster, 1935), p. 112.

109. Arkhangel'skoye, one of the oldest of the nobles' estates in Podmoskov'e, belonged to the Sheremetevs in the 1600s, to the Golitsyns from 1703 to 1810, and to the Yusupovs from 1810 onward. Nikol'skoye-Uryupino, just north of Arkhangel'skoye, Petrovskoye Dal'neye, to the west, and Vyazemy, near Zvenigorod, remained with the Golitsyns until 1917. Ubory, an estate near Usovo, was owned by the Sheremetevs. On Arkhangel'skoye and Zubalovo after 1917, see Svetlana Alliluyeva, *Twenty Letters to a Friend,* trans. Priscilla Johnson McMillan (New York: Harper and Row, 1967), pp. 26–27, and Vladimir Kozlov, "Voina dvortsam," *Moskovskii zhurnal,* no. 8 (August 1991), p. 38.

110. V. Bessonov in *Moskovskaya pravda,* February 21, 1992, p. 3.

111. Ye. Ignatov, *Gorodskiye raionnyye sovety kak forma uchastiya rabochikh v upravlenii gosudarstvom* (Moscow: Izdatel'stvo Kommunisticheskoi Akademii, 1929), p. 38.

112. Apart from local rationing and travel, the most important document was the "labor book" instituted in September 1918 for the bourgeoisie and extended to the entire working population that December. "There are many indications," a specialist writes, "that the new regime was not able to enforce these stringent new practices." Mervyn Matthews, *The Passport Society: Controlling Movement in Russia and the USSR* (Boulder, Colo.: Westview Press, 1993), p. 18.

113. *Kommunisticheskii trud,* August 11, 1920, p. 3. The MK eviction incident is in TsGAODM, f. 3, op. 1, d. 71, l. 78.

114. Emma Goldman, *My Disillusionment in Russia* (Garden City, N.Y.: Doubleday, Page, 1923), pp. 33–34. A typical locus for small-scale corruption was the municipalized house in which former owners had to share space with newcomers: "Those [former proprietors] who know how to get on the good side of the [district] commissar, by bribery or otherwise, are frequently allowed to keep their old quarters,

and if they give up any of their rooms, to choose their own tenants." Harrison, *Marooned in Moscow*, p. 95.

115. TsGAODM, f. 3, op. 1, d. 70, ll. 27–32; op. 1, d. 158, ll. 22, 48; op. 1-a, d. 7, ll. 13 (concerning a hunger strike in several camps), 31, 39.

116. Ibid., op. 1, d. 70, ll. 40–43; op. 1-a, d. 7, ll. 10, 27.

117. Ibid., op. 1-a, d. 7, ll. 20–21.

118. *Kommunisticheskii trud*, December 21, 1920, p. 1.

119. *Izvestiya*, January 14, 1919, p. 5; TsGAODM, f. 3, op. 1-a, d. 7, l. 91.

120. *VIII s"ezd Rossiiskoi kommunisticheskoi partii (bol'shevikov): Steno-graficheskii otchet* (Moscow and Petrograd: Knigoizdatel'stvo Kommunist, 1919), pp. 170, 174–175.

121. Quotations from *Sto sorok besed s Molotovym: Iz dnevnika Feliksa Chuyeva* (Moscow: Terra, 1991), p. 221, and A. F. Myasnikov, "Moi vstrechi s tovarishchem Leninym," *Voprosy istorii*, no. 3 (March 1957), pp. 27, 30.

122. An illustration of the propinquity effect is the appointment of Semashko as health commissar in July 1918. "Since Ye. P. Pervukhin [Semashko's rival] was lo-cated in Petrograd, where he [worked] in the Petrograd Soviet, and Semashko was here [as head of the Mossovet's Health Department], Pervukhin was left where he was . . . and Semashko was named to head the new commissariat" (Bonch-Bruyevich, *Vospominaniya o Lenine*, p. 261). Avanesov was the sole secretary of VTsIK from October 1917 to the spring of 1919, then served with Serebryakov until transferred to the Cheka at the end of 1919. Sapronov, although active in intraparty opposition, was appointed head of the Small (Malyi) Sovnarkom, which dealt with government business of a routine nature, in late 1920.

123. TsGAODM, f. 3, op. 1-a, d. 7, l. 92. A personal connection of particular importance existed between MK Secretary Zagorskii and Sverdlov, the powerful party and state leader who predeceased him in 1919. The two were boyhood best friends in Nizhnii Novgorod, and Sverdlov was behind Zagorskii's appointment in 1918. N. G. Dumova, *Sekretar' MK* (Moscow: Politizdat, 1966), pp. 5–12, 91.

124. TsGAODM, f. 3, op. 1, d. 56, l. 105; op. 1-a, d. 7, l. 93.

125. *Kommunisticheskii trud*, December 19, 1920, p. 1, and TsGAODM, f. 3, op. 1-a, d. 7, l. 93.

126. Kamenev said in November 1920 that attendance at the sections was aver-aging 15 percent. "Everything depends here on the [department] head. If he does not know how to interest the members of the section, then nothing comes of it." TsGAODM, f. 3, op. 1-a, d. 7, l. 93.

127. Nogin in ibid., op. 1, d. 53, l. 12; *Krasnaya Moskva*, p. 32. Only one of the fifteen members of the presidium of November 1917 was also on the ispolkom, but nine of eleven in July 1918 sat on both. Until the end of the Civil War, all but one presidium member overlapped, and after that all members did. Beginning in the early 1920s, the presidium was sometimes referred to as "the presidium of the ispolkom," but there was evidently no statutory basis for this designation.

128. TsGAODM, f. 3, op. 1, d. 56, ll. 94–110.

129. Ignatov, *Gorodskiye raionnyye sovety*, p. 57.

130. These were the arguments made at the MK plenums of February 15 and March 31, 1919, the second of which appointed a commission to study the question. TsGAODM, f. 3, op. 1, d. 69, ll. 19, 79–80.

131. The only group that actively sought amalgamation was the leadership of the soviet of Lefortovskii raion, which believed that workers there would benefit from access to the superior housing of neighboring Basmannyi raion. This belief was not shared by the Lefortovskii party committee, which fought amalgamation tooth and nail. Raion politicians often gave clever rebuttals to the demand for amalgamation. Gorodskoi raion, for example, conceded that it contained a large nonproletarian population but warned that dissolution of the raion would only spread social contamination to other raions.

132. TsGAODM, f. 3, op. 1, d. 70, ll. 93–94.

133. *VIII s"ezd*, p. 267.

134. A. Kudryavtsev, "Zhilishchnoye delo v Moskve," *Kommunal'noye khozyaistvo*, no. 3 (March–April 1922), p. 2.

135. TsGAODM, f. 3, op. 1, d. 53, l. 12.

136. *Kratkii obzor deyatel'nosti Moskovskogo Soveta* (Moscow: Gosudarstvennoye izdatel'stvo, 1920), p. 41.

137. The trial can be followed in *Izvestiya*, March 9 to 15, 1922.

138. Ibid., February 27, 1923, p. 5.

139. *Vecherniye izvestiya*, December 19, 1919, p. 3.

140. *Pravda*, September 29, 1919, p. 1, and August 14, 1921, p. 2.

141. TsGAODM, f. 3, op. 1, d. 54, l. 10 (Zemlyachka to the MK in January 1918); *Pravda*, July 14, 1918, p. 5.

142. The first meeting of the executive commission to produce numbered protocols was August 19, 1918. From April 1919 onward, almost every MK plenum opened with a report from the commission. A three-man MK "secretariat" (Vladimirskii, Tsivtsivadze, and Pyatnitskii) was appointed October 22, 1917, but the party archive contains no minutes of meetings or decisions. A similar organ was named in July 1918 (consisting of D. I. Yefremov, Zagorskii, and B. A. Breslav) and existed for several months, but again there is no record of activity and Yefremov was referred to throughout as "the secretary of the MK."

143. The three members of the ispolkom who most offended the MK were S. S. Belorussov, A. V. Radzivillov, and Korzilov (initials unknown). All had been among the city soviet's leaders since 1917 and were friends of Ignatov.

144. TsGAODM, f. 3, op. 1, d. 69, ll. 151, 153–154, 183.

145. On January 3, 1921, the MK for the first time passed on a complete list of all members of the collegiums (ibid., op. 2, d. 17-a, l. 1). Its bureau had previously discussed only candidates for work in especially sensitive municipal agencies. The first case (dated September 10, 1918) involved the collegium of the Food Department of the Mossovet.

146. The first recorded intervention on law-and-order positions occurred July 26, 1918, when the MK assigned its executive to submit to it lists of suitable candidates for judges in the revolutionary tribunals (ibid., op. 1, d. 54, l. 97). Protocols

show confirmation of the collegium of the Moscow Cheka and of local military commissars beginning in November 1918, of the board of the guberniya trade union council in June 1920, and of the Moscow leadership of the Komsomol in September 1920.

147. The decree of August 3, 1918 (in ibid., ll. 99–100), called for mobilization of one-fifth of all Moscow Communists, which would have come to about 4,000 persons. This was evidently not achieved, but fragmentary figures for later mobilizations are suggestive: more than 1,000 sent to the Southern Front from October to November 1918; 650 to the Southern Front from July to August 1919; 3,000 to the Western Front against Poland in the summer of 1920.

148. Ibid., op. 1-a, d. 7, ll. 93, 107–110; d. 6, ll. 79, 88; op. 2, d. 17-a, l. 2.

149. Quotations from *Krasnaya Moskva*, p. 658, and TsGAODM, f. 3, op. 1-a, d. 6, l. 43 (speaker N. V. Lisitsyn). Sakwa, *Soviet Communists in Power,* p. 185, notes the former reference but gives the party more credit for direction of the soviets than I would.

150. A rare exception is the MK's decision December 1, 1920, on two controversies in the performing arts. It fired the head of the Arts Subdepartment of the Moscow Soviet for staging an "unsatisfactory" concert in honor of Friedrich Engels at the Zimin Theater and canceled the play *Rubbish* at the Theater of Revolutionary Satire because it "cast the idea of communism in a negative light." The Zimin Theater affair was raised by the Central Committee. TsGAODM, f. 3, op. 1-a, d. 7, l. 98.

151. Kamenev's statement is in ibid., l. 93. In April 1919 Petr Smidovich complained about MK annulment of decisions of the city ispolkom, but his example was the esoteric one of an ispolkom attempt to turn over adult education in Moscow to the League for Proletarian Culture (ibid., op. 1, d. 69, l. 116). Outside municipal services, the only economic appointment passed on by the MK was in the city sovnarkhoz; Vasilii Likhachev was approved as chairman by the MK bureau on August 3, 1920.

152. Fedor Artem was already a Central Committee member when named Moscow party secretary in November 1920. Both Pyatnitskii (appointed in August 1920) and Isaak Zelenskii (when he started a second term in April 1921) were already Central Committee candidate members. Zelenskii in April 1922 became the first serving Moscow party secretary to gain full Central Committee membership.

153. Quotation about Zagorskii in Dumova, *Sekretar' MK,* p. 93, and request for the horses in TsGAODM, f. 3, op. 1, d. 71, l. 30. The eight commissions appointed October 22, 1917, were for party finances, preparation of political reports, municipal and soviet affairs, the military and the Red Guard, and work in the trade unions and cooperatives. Several were formally dissolved by the MK, but most simply lapsed. In 1919 a commission to organize subbotniks was the first one created, in May. It was converted into a department in November, and a department for work with ethnic minorities was set up the same month.

154. *Pravda*, January 11, 1920, p. 2.

155. Zelenskii's statement in *Rabochaya Moskva,* November 7, 1922, p. 5. Although ten departments were approved in May 1920, those for youth and ethnic

minorities were abolished before staffing levels were settled in July. The full authorized strength of the departments was 242 persons, but 112 were in the three housekeeping units grouped into the MK's Business Office later in 1920, and 21 were in the General Department, which was responsible for secret correspondence. To judge from the archive entry, 40 or 45 percent of the remainder were what would several years later be termed "responsible workers," with some decision power. The Department of Agitation and Propaganda had the most staff, 43 in all, and the other sections for political education had 40. There were 29 persons in the Organization and Instruction Department. TsGAODM, f. 3, op. 1-a, d. 6, l. 9.

156. *Krasnaya Moskva,* p. 658.

157. Quotation from *Kommunisticheskii trud,* January 21, 1921, p. 2. Kamenev, born to the family of a Moscow railway machinist in 1883, had studied for several years at Moscow University and was active in Moscow in 1904 and 1907, but mostly served the party in western Europe and Petrograd. Remember that no MK existed at all between 1910 and late 1916. Of the ten secretaries from 1905 to 1910, only six (V. K. Taratuta, L. Ya. Karpov, F. I. Goloshchekin, N. A. Skrypnik, Yu. P. Figatner, and M. P. Tomskii) were active in government after the revolution and only two (Taratuta and Tomskii) kept any connection with Moscow. Taratuta held a minor industrial position (head of the Moscow cloth trust); Tomskii, after helping with raion duma elections in 1917 and heading the Moscow trade union council, moved in 1918 to union administration on the national level.

158. TsGAODM, f. 3, op. 1-a, d. 6, l. 41. Pyatnitskii had awful relations with Myasnikov, who had worked in Moscow as a military organizer and raikom secretary in 1919. Myasnikov was unpopular with almost all his colleagues, perhaps because of his criticisms of the raions and the Cheka. In December 1919, shortly before his election as secretary (by a split vote), the MK executive had requested the Central Committee to remove him from Moscow. Ibid., op. 1, d. 71, l. 248; op. 1-a, d. 6, ll. 43–44, 59, 64.

159. *Kommunisticheskii trud,* February 22, 1921, p. 3. Kamenev's initiative and the elections of Artem and Yakovleva appear in the minutes in TsGAODM, f. 3, op. 1-a, d. 6, ll. 41–45, 66–68, 88.

160. *Pravda,* November 16, 1920, p. 1.

161. Ye. P. Shterenberg, "Na prodovol'stvennom fronte," in *Pervoye desyatiletiye: Vospominaniya veteranov partii—moskvichei* (Moscow: Moskovskii rabochii, 1982), p. 55.

162. *Izvestiya,* May 11, 1919, p. 1, and June 5, 1919, p. 4; Bonch-Bruyevich, *Vospominaniya o Lenine,* p. 377.

163. "Stroitel'noye delo v Moskve 1920 g.," *Kommunal'noye khozyaistvo,* nos. 1–2 (May 1921), pp. 13–14.

164. See the criticisms in *Kommunisticheskii trud,* February 18, 1921, p. 2, and December 3, 1921, p. 3.

165. *Pravda,* April 5, 1921, p. 3, and September 15, 1921, p. 1.

166. *Kommunisticheskii trud,* July 26, 1921, p. 1.

167. Dietrich Rueschemeyr, Evelyne Huber Stephens, and John D. Stephens,

Capitalist Development and Democracy (Chicago: University of Chicago Press, 1992), p. 41.

168. Ilya Ehrenburg, *People and Life, 1981–1921,* trans. Anna Bostock and Yvonne Kapp (New York: Knopf, 1962), pp. 386–387.

3. From Reurbanization to Hyperurbanization

1. On the demonstrations, see Richard Sakwa, *Soviet Communists in Power: A Study of Moscow during the Civil War, 1918–21* (London: Macmillan, 1988), pp. 240–247. Lev Kamenev and several of his deputies had for some months favored a relaxation of War Communism.

2. Different scholarly perspectives are offered in Stephen F. Cohen, *Bukharin and the Bolshevik Revolution: A Political Biography, 1888–1938* (New York: Knopf, 1973), and *Rethinking the Soviet Experience* (New York: Oxford University Press, 1985), pp. 71–92; Alexander Erlich, *The Soviet Industrialization Debate, 1924–1928* (Cambridge, Mass.: Harvard University Press, 1960); Sheila Fitzpatrick, Alexander Rabinowitch, and Richard Stites, eds., *Russia in the Era of NEP: Explorations in Soviet Society and Culture* (Bloomington: Indiana University Press, 1991); Moshe Lewin, *The Making of the Soviet System: Essays in the Social History of Interwar Russia* (New York: Pantheon, 1985); and Richard Pipes, *Russia under the Bolshevik Regime* (New York: Knopf, 1994), chaps. 8–9.

3. Quoted in V. E. Khazanova, *Sovetskaya arkhitektura pervoi pyatiletki* (Moscow: Nauka, 1980), p. 260, and Jean-Louis Cohen, *Le Corbusier and the Mystique of the USSR,* trans. Kenneth Hylton (Princeton: Princeton University Press, 1992), p. 90.

4. Walter Duranty, *I Write as I Please* (New York: Simon and Schuster, 1935), pp. 109, 111, 138–139.

5. Quotation from Walter Benjamin, *Moscow Diary,* ed. Gary Smith (Cambridge, Mass.: Harvard University Press, 1986), p. 37. Trade statistics from *Pravda,* November 2, 1921, p. 4, May 16, 1924, p. 5, and July 24, 1928, p. 5; N. M. Aleshchenko, *Moskovskii Sovet v 1917–1941 gg.* (Moscow: Nauka, 1976), pp. 287, 411; *Moskovskii Sovet rabochikh, krest'yanskikh i krasnoarmeiskikh deputatov, 1917–1927* (Moscow: Izdaniye Moskovskogo Soveta, 1927), p. 350.

6. Many of these issues are ably discussed in William J. Chase, *Workers, Society, and the Soviet State: Labor and Life in Moscow, 1918–1929* (Urbana: University of Illinois Press, 1987), chap. 2. The labor books and other registration documents were done away with in June 1923, although several decrees later in the decade subjected some urban dwellers to registration.

7. *Rabochaya Moskva,* January 27, 1926, p. 6; TsGAODM, f. 3, op. 8, d. 34, l. 74. Statistics in *Izvestiya,* March 24, 1923, p. 3, and *Pravda,* November 24, 1923, p. 5. On Moscow's attraction to the homeless children, see Alan Ball, "The Roots of *Besprizornost'* in Soviet Russia's First Decade," *Slavic Review,* vol. 51 (Summer 1992), p. 261.

8. *Pravda,* May 20, 1921, p. 1, and October 11, 1921, p. 1.

9. An early summary of exceptions is N. I. Bronshtein, *Uplotneniye i pereseleniye* (Moscow: Zhilishchnoye tovarishchestvo, 1924). See in general John N. Hazard, *Soviet Housing Law* (New Haven: Yale University Press, 1939), and Gregory D. Andrusz, *Housing and Urban Development in the USSR* (London: Macmillan, 1984), chaps. 1–5.

10. S. Gurevich, "O domakh-kommunakh," *Kommunal'noye khozyaistvo*, no. 1 (January 1922), p. 10.

11. See I. Gel'man, "Zigzagi zhilishchnoi politiki," ibid., no. 11 (October 1, 1922), pp. 4–5; "Doma-kommuny," ibid., no. 3 (February 1, 1923), p. 9; "Khronika," ibid., no. 8 (May 1, 1923), p. 38.

12. Boris Bazhanov, *Vospominaniya byvshego sekretarya Stalina* (Paris: Tret'ya Volna, 1980), p. 54. The Kremlin residences are described in S. Dmitriyevskii, *Sovetskiye portrety* (Berlin: Strela, 1932), pp. 15–18; Lidiya Shatunovskaya, *Zhizn' v Kremle* (New York: Chalidze Publications, 1982), pp. 20–31; and Larisa Vasil'eva, *Kremlevskiye zheny* (Moscow: Novosti, 1992), pp. 118–120. I learned a great deal about them in an interview with N. A. Rykova, Rykov's daughter, in July 1992.

13. *Pravda*, February 10, 1925, p. 5; "Remont stroyenii i zhilishchnoye stroitel'stvo goroda Moskvy i Moskovskoi gubernii v 1924 g.," *Stroitel'stvo Moskvy*, no. 2 (August 1924), p. 7.

14. I. Verner, "Uluchsheniye zhilishchnykh uslovii v krupnykh gorodakh," *Kommunal'noye khozyaistvo*, no. 8 (December 1921), pp. 5–7; *Pravda*, August 22, 1922, p. 1, and September 13, 1922, p. 1; M. Sheremetevskii, "O vosstanovlenii MKKh kontsessionnym sposobom," *Kommunal'noye khozyaistvo*, no. 6 (July 1922), pp. 4–7.

15. "Pervyi god shirokoi raboty zhilishchno-stroitel'noi kooperatsii," *Kommunal'noye delo*, no. 5 (March 1926), p. 35; *Pravda*, February 1, 1928, p. 2; *Vechernyaya Moskva*, March 19, 1930, p. 2.

16. The cooperatives banned in December 1926 were for sanitation specialists, teachers, tanners, meat packers, tram workers, and municipal office employees. In January 1928 the MK secretariat secretly approved the merger of building cooperatives of the trade and foreign affairs commissariats, as well as a new cooperative for diplomats. TsGAODM, f. 3, op. 7, d. 13, l. 213, and op. 9, d. 35, l. 1.

17. *Pravda*, July 9, 1926, p. 5.

18. Details from Shatunovskaya, *Zhizn' v Kremle*, pp. 66–70, and, especially on Iofan's role, from my interview with Rykova.

19. TsGAODM, f. 3, op. 6, d. 25, l. 194.

20. F. Lavrov, "Kakiye raboty po blagoustroistvu Moskvy byli proizvedeny MKKh v 1924 godu," *Stroitel'stvo Moskvy*, no. 2 (October 1924), p. 10; I. Tsivtsivadze, "K voprosu o blagoustroistve okrain g. Moskvy," *Kommunal'noye khozyaistvo*, nos. 19–20 (October 25, 1924), p. 8.

21. Benjamin, *Moscow Diary*, p. 112.

22. S. Gurevich, "O tramvainoi politike Moskovskogo Soveta," *Kommunal'noye khozyaistvo*, no. 23 (December 1, 1923), p. 3.

23. F. Lavrov, "Pochemu Moskve nuzhny novyye vodoprovod i kanalizatsiya," *Stroitel'stvo Moskvy*, no. 3 (March 1927), p. 6; *Izvestiya*, April 14, 1927, p. 4, and

April 5, 1928, p. 5; N. Avinov, "Dolya Moskvy v kommunal'nom khozyaistve Sovetskogo Soyuza," *Kommunal'noye khozyaistvo*, nos. 11–12 (June 25, 1928), p. 5.

24. Duranty, *I Write as I Please*, p. 145; *Pravda*, October 26, 1921, p. 2.

25. The definitive national study is Alan M. Ball, *Russia's Last Capitalists: The Nepmen, 1921–1929* (Berkeley: University of California Press, 1987). Ball observes (p. 101) that 6,310 of 16,500 licensed private traders in Moscow went out of business in 1924.

26. Alexander Barmine, *One Who Survived* (New York: Putnam's Sons, 1945), p. 125; Benjamin, *Moscow Diary*, p. 22.

27. *Rabochaya Moskva*, December 30, 1923, p. 1; TsGAODM, f. 3, op. 5, d. 11, l. 137.

28. S. M. Gornyi, *Sotsialisticheskaya rekonstruktsiya Moskvy* (Moscow: Tekhnika upravleniya, 1931), map on p. 44; TsGAODM, f. 3, op. 9, d. 19, l. 196; *Vechernyaya Moskva*, May 22, 1930, p. 2. The 1928 figures show quite a range among workers, from 3.1 square meters in the food industry to 4.5 among metal workers and 4.9 among printers.

29. *Rabochaya Moskva*, February 7, 1926, p. 3; Dorothy Thompson, *The New Russia* (New York: Henry Holt, 1928), p. 17; H. J. Greenwall, *Mirrors of Moscow* (London: George G. Harrap, 1929), p. 40. The igloo story is in *Rabochaya Moskva*, January 26, 1926, p. 7, and the taxi-bordellos are mentioned in Shatunovskaya, *Zhizn' v Kremle*, p. 10.

30. Jane Seymour, *In the Moscow Manner* (London: Denis Archer, 1935), p. 86. Tram occupancy figures derived from city statistics.

31. *Pravda*, May 8, 1926, p. 3.

32. Table C-1 does not tabulate social origins, since this information is not reliably available for all categories. For the 1921–1930 municipal leaders, however, we know that ten of fourteen came from working-class or peasant families; three were of middle-class background, and one's origins are unknown.

33. *Moskovskaya organizatsiya R.K.P.(b) v tsifrakh*, 2d ed. (Moscow: Moskovskii komitet RKP[b], 1925), pp. 41–42, 46–47. The 1,241 officials worked for Moscow city and guberniya, the raions of Moscow, and uyezds in the guberniya. Social origins, party saturation, and education varied from one specialty to the other. For example, 46.7 percent of those in general government were of worker or peasant origin, 82.8 percent were Communists, and 10.1 percent had a higher education; for health officials, the figures were 0.0 percent, 35.7 percent, and 26.6 percent.

34. Quotation from A. Sayeshnikov, "Neskol'ko slov po povodu stat'i inzh. Ivanova 'Zemel'noye delo v Moskve,'" *Kommunal'noye khozyaistvo*, no. 6 (March 25, 1928), p. 17. Information on personnel continuity was taken from the 1912 and 1928 editions of *Vsya Moskva*, the city directory. Of the thirty-four waterworks officials listed in 1928 (for 1927), five had held administrative positions within the works in 1912 and eight others were listed in the 1912 directory (four of them identified as engineers). Five of thirty-nine sewage officials in 1927 had been identified in administrative positions there in 1912; three others had been municipal employees (one of them in the sewage department), while six more had been listed in the

directory (two as engineers). The only holdover from the duma to be an agency head was V. G. Mikhailovskii, chief of the Statistics Department since 1911 and a member of it since 1897. See his obituary in *Pravda*, October 13, 1926, p. 4.

35. Aleshchenko, *Moskovskii Sovet v 1917–1941 gg.*, pp. 237, 336–337.

36. N. Gushchin, "Soglasovaniye interesov v razlichnykh oblastyakh vodnogo khozyaistva na primere vodosnabzheniya g. Moskvy," *Kommunal'noye khozyaistvo*, nos. 1–2 (January 25, 1929), p. 77.

37. *Vsya Moskva* for the respective years. Nikolai Guchkov, the mayor in 1912, is the only pre-Soviet mayor to appear in the directories; he is listed in 1925 only, as living in his old neighborhood and working for a peat-gathering organization. For twelve members of the 1912 duma, later yearbooks reveal close relatives living at their 1912 addresses.

38. Vladimir Kozlov, "Delo ob ograblenii tserkvi," *Moskovskii zhurnal*, no. 7 (July 1991), p. 19, states that twenty-seven Moscow priests were taken into GPU custody on March 31, 1922, alone, during the raids on church possessions.

39. TsGAODM, f. 3, op. 4, d. 36, ll. 34–35.

40. *Pravda*, August 26, 1921, p. 2.

41. Reprisals against the Mensheviks during the 1921 and 1922 campaigns are described in Boris Dvinov, *Moskovskii Sovet Rabochikh Deputatov, 1917–1922: Vospominaniya* (New York: Inter-University Project on the History of the Menshevik Movement, 1961), pp. 100–103, 118.

42. *Pravda*, December 15, 1922, p. 3. Protocols of the decisions on the election are in TsGAODM, f. 3, op. 3, d. 6, ll. 60, 61, 63, 64, 69.

43. TsGAODM, f. 3, op. 4, d. 7, ll. 151, 159.

44. Ibid., op. 5, d. 11, l. 219.

45. Ibid., op. 6, d. 6, ll. 90, 97.

46. Dvinov, *Moskovskii Sovet*, pp. 106, 107.

47. Quotations from TsGAODM, f. 3, op. 11, d. 154, l. 41 (Dorofeyev), and *Otchet o rabote sektsii Moskovskogo i Raionnykh Sovetov Rabochikh, Krest'yanskikh i Krasnoarmeiskikh Deputatov s aprelya 1925 g. po yanvar' 1926 g.* (Moscow: Izdaniye Moskovskogo Soveta, 1926), pp. 4–5.

48. *Rabochaya Moskva*, January 9, 1930, p. 1; "Plenum sektsii Mossoveta po GZhD 15/IV 1931 g.," *Kommunal'noye khozyaistvo*, no. 10 (May 1931), p. 40.

49. The 1927 small presidium was charged with "resolving a series of minor problems" (TsGAODM, f. 3, op. 8, d. 33, l. 78) but also seems to have influenced major decisions. Its head was the second-ranking deputy to Chairman Ukhanov; in 1921–1925, it was Kamenev's first deputy, Rogov. In addition, the chairman of the Mossovet and his top two or three deputies each answered for the monitoring *(nablyudeniye)* of a segment of the city bureaucracy on his own. Information on meetings taken from *Moskovskii Sovet . . . 1917–1927*, pp. 130–131, which points out that the presidium's workload "measurably increased" in comparison with 1917–1921. Municipal officials were not nearly as overrepresented on the ispolkom as on the presidium. Of 125 members in 1924, 14.4 percent were from the city bureaucracy and 15.2 percent from the raion soviets.

50. *Izvestiya,* June 19, 1923, p. 5; *Rabochaya Moskva,* September 16, 1923, p. 1.

51. *Izvestiya,* October 27, 1925, p. 3.

52. Quotation from the MK bureau resolution of November 24, 1930, in TsGAODM, f. 3, op. 12, d. 58, l. 80. One raion was named in 1920 after the revolutionary Nikolai Bauman, and in 1929 Rogozhsko-Simonovskii was renamed Proletarskii (Proletarian) raion. Of the ten raions formed in 1930, one was again named after the proletariat, one after the October Revolution, and five after leaders (Lenin, Stalin, Bauman, Dzerzhinskii, and Frunze). Many places in Podmoskov'e (and the USSR as a whole) were also renamed for political reasons around this time. For example, Sergiyev posad, the location of the Trinity–St. Sergius Monastery, was renamed Zagorsk (after Vladimir Zagorskii) in 1930 and Bogorodsk was renamed Noginsk (after Viktor Nogin).

53. Ibid., op. 7, d. 7, ll. 31–32, 38, 60.

54. M. Sovetnikov, "K usileniyu svyazi s mestami," *Kommunal'noye khozyaistvo,* no. 13 (November 1922), p. 1; S. Koshkin, "K organizatsii Inogorodnogo otdela pri MKKh," ibid., nos. 1–2 (January 25, 1929), pp. 122–126.

55. Aleshchenko, *Moskovskii Sovet v 1917–1941 gg.,* p. 229.

56. Vladimir Kozlov, "Voina dvortsam," *Moskovskii zhurnal,* no. 8 (August 1991), pp. 37–38.

57. I have learned the most about elite dacha sites from interviews. Nikolina Gora is described in Arkady Vaksberg, *Stalin's Prosecutor: The Life of Andrei Vyshinsky,* trans. Jan Butler (New York: Grove Weidenfeld, 1991), pp. 86–87.

58. TsGAODM, f. 3, op. 7, d. 7, ll. 27–28, 29, 63.

59. *Izvestiya,* March 20, 1928, p. 4.

60. As first proposed in 1928, the oblast was to encompass nine guberniyas (Ivanovo, Kaluga, Kostroma, Moscow, Nizhnii Novgorod, Ryazan, Tula, Vladimir, and Yaroslavl), 420,000 square kilometers, and 19 million people. This plan was resisted by the guberniyas and by leaders of what became the five super-oblasts ringing Moscow oblast—Leningrad in the north, Ivanovo Industrial oblast to the east, the Middle Volga and Central Black Earth oblasts in the south, and Western oblast to the west. Moscow, Ukhanov said, avoided "battles" by renouncing several territorial claims. TsGAODM, f. 3, op. 10, d. 65, ll. 111–112.

61. Ibid., d. 73, l. 9.

62. The main institutional difference was that Moscow did not have the separate presidium it had since 1925, but rather had twenty-five of the fifty-one seats on a joint city-oblast presidium.

63. *XIV s"ezd Vsesoyuznoi Kommunisticheskoi partii(b): Stenograficheskii otchet* (Moscow: Gosizdat, 1926), p. 394.

64. Unlike Zinov'ev, Kamenev did not try to install persons loyal to him in the party machine of his city. "Zinov'ev in Leningrad organized his own clan, planted it in position, and kept a close hand on the second capital. These techniques were foreign to Kamenev. He did not have any clan and sat in Moscow by inertia." Bazhanov, *Vospominaniya byvshego sekretarya Stalina,* p. 177.

65. *Pravda,* January 11, 1924, p. 4.

66. TsGAODM, f. 3, op. 11, d. 85, l. 102.

67. "Nothing conveys the public transcript more as the dominant would like it than the formal ceremonies they organize to celebrate and dramatize their rule. Parades, inaugurations, processions, coronations, funerals provide ruling groups with the occasion to make a spectacle of themselves in a manner largely of their own choosing." James C. Scott, *Domination and the Arts of Resistance: Hidden Transcripts* (New Haven: Yale University Press, 1990), p. 58.

68. Consult in general Nina Tumarkin, *Lenin Lives! The Lenin Cult in Soviet Russia* (Cambridge, Mass.: Harvard University Press, 1983), chap. 6.

69. The MK bureau adopted its resolution on "a register of responsible workers of the Moscow organization" on March 23, 1921. It covered all cardholders considered capable of working at positions no lower than secretary of a party cell or chairman of an uyezd executive committee. A meeting in December 1923 seems to have been the first to establish an itemized list of positions constituting the MK's nomenklatura. TSGAODM, f. 3, op. 2, d. 17-a, l. 53, and op. 11, d. 85, l. 35.

70. Resolution of the MK secretariat of March 14, 1925, in ibid., op. 6, d. 45, ll. 37–38. The 2,531 positions were divided into three "groups," apparently those cleared by the MK itself (584), its bureau (920), and its secretariat (1,027). Such divisions fluctuated constantly and were never crucial, as the same secretaries predominated in both the bureau and the secretariat, and the full MK showed no independence on personnel questions. Contemporary sources were often inconsistent on nomenklatura size, mainly because they sometimes included positions that the party organ registered but did not confirm (often described as its "second nomenklatura"). An example would be the reference to 5,000 positions in the MK nomenklatura in 1924 and 4,470 in late 1926. V. Markovich, "K uporyadocheniyu nomenklaturnoi sistemy raspredeleniya rabotnikov," *Izvestiya TsK RKP(b),* nos. 45–46 (November 22, 1926), p. 6. The MK secretariat voted in August 1928 to cut the MK's nomenklatura in half, but no figures for before or after were given; TsGAODM, f. 3, op. 9, d. 35, l. 210.

71. Quotation from N. Kozlov, "O raspredelitel'noi rabote partii," *Izvestiya TsK RKP(b),* no. 1 (January 18, 1926), p. 2. The CC's nomenklatura had 5,500 positions at the start of 1926, but at year's end an unspecified number of jobs in central agencies were moved to MK control. This seems to have been a passing phase. I have not found figures on dual confirmations, but numerous individual instances, mostly for economic positions, are visible in archival materials.

72. See, for example, the statement about MK supply of 730 activists for work in the provinces in *Pravda,* December 5, 1925, p. 5.

73. Other examples would be the appointment of N. N. Popov, a deputy head of the CC's Agitation and Propaganda Department, as head of the same department of the Moscow Committee in 1928, and of G. N. Kaminskii, head of the CC's Department of Agitation and Mass Campaigns, as third secretary of the MK in 1930. Mikhailov had been a member of the Mossovet and MK in 1917 and a Cheka and army officer during the Civil War. It is unclear why he skyrocketed to prominence in 1921. Molotov, the Stalinist who served with him in the CC Secretariat, said he had

at most the abilities of a regional administrator. *Sto sorok besed s Molotovym: Iz dnevnika Feliksa Chuyeva* (Moscow: Terra, 1991), p. 229.

74. Quotations from *Kommunisticheskii trud,* November 5, 1921, p. 3, and *Pravda,* December 14, 1923, p. 4. The Moscow party archive's file on the guberniya party conference of June 1922 (f. 3, op. 3, d. 4, ll. 245–246) contains a handwritten original of a "draft of a list of members of the MK" prepared "at a meeting of active officials of the MK" and signed by Zelenskii. The list contains twenty-four names as well as quotas to be filled by the raikoms and the Komsomol.

75. The rout of Kamenev is well described in Catherine Merridale, *Moscow Politics and the Rise of Stalin: The Communist Party in the Capital, 1925–32* (London: Macmillan, 1990), chap. 1. On Uglanov's career and appointment, see esp. *XIV s"ezd,* pp. 192, 193, 509–512, 954–955, and "N. A. Uglanov: K politicheskomu portretu," *Izvestiya TsK KPSS,* no. 2 (February 1990), pp. 116–126.

76. *XIV s"ezd,* pp. 184, 394.

77. Ibid., p. 193.

78. *Rabochaya Moskva,* October 18, 1924, p. 3, and *Shestoi ob"edinennyi plenum MK i MKK VKP(b) (18–19 oktyabrya 1928)* (Moscow: MK VKP(b), 1928), p. 10. The second remark, made in September 1928, was one of those Stalin demanded retracted when the disagreement went public. Within a month, Uglanov was so pressed that it was hard for him "to replace the lowliest technician" (ibid., p. 119).

79. *Ocherki istorii Moskovskoi organizatsii KPSS (1883–1965 gg.)* (Moscow: Moskovskii rabochii, 1966), p. 445.

80. See *Shestoi ob"edinennyi plenum,* pp. 25, 29, 33, 50–52, 58, 62, 70–71, 73–81, 95–97; "M. N. Ryutin: K politicheskomy portretu," *Izvestiya TsK KPSS,* no. 3 (March 1990), pp. 155–156; Merridale, *Moscow Politics and the Rise of Stalin,* chap. 2.

81. It was alleged during the Great Purge in 1937 that Ukhanov and other "right deviation elements" in the Mossovet presidium continued to resist the party line in 1929–1930. TsGAODM, f. 4, op. 8, d. 3, ll. 169–170.

82. *Shestoi ob"edinennyi plenum,* pp. 19, 114.

83. *Rabochaya Moskva,* June 4, 1924, p. 5, and *Pravda,* December 3, 1925, p. 5.

84. Plenum resolution of February 1926 in TsGAODM, f. 3, op. 7, d. 2, l. 16.

85. References are to the listing in ibid., op. 6, d. 45, ll. 37–38.

86. Of the 913 positions, 253 were specifically identified as being in the Moscow Education Department, 21 in the Executive Committee of the Mossovet, 61 in its Finance Department, and 90 in municipal trade organizations. Minutes show the MK confirming senior posts at Moscow University and other postsecondary institutions beginning in 1924; it is possible that these were included in the education figure, although, strictly speaking, most postsecondary training was not under this department. No details were given on 488 positions, but it is clear from other references that they embraced law enforcement and various municipal positions, many of them at the raion and uyezd level.

87. The first personnel decision noted of the MK bureau or secretariat to involve an economic administrator (the director of a printing trust) was taken by the bureau in February 1922.

88. Decision of the MK secretariat of January 1927, in TsGAODM, f. 3, op. 8, d. 52, l. 5. The Secret Department was to be retitled the Secret Unit in 1934, the Special Sector in 1939, and the General Department again in 1966.

89. Ibid., op. 6, d. 31, ll. 1, 3.

90. *Pravda,* January 19, 1930, p. 3.

91. The directive on "the struggle with homebrewers" is in TsGAODM, f. 3, op. 3, d. 6, l. 48. The commission on admissions dealt with Moscow University, diploma-granting institutes, workers' preparatory faculties, and technical schools. It reserved 8,000 of 18,000 places in higher schools for graduates of the workers' faculties and 10,000 for organizational candidates, including 1,500 each for the party, Komsomol, and trade unions. In June 1927 the MK secretariat dissolved it and named representatives to the admissions committees of Moscow's seventeen higher schools. See ibid., op. 11, d. 154, ll. 75–98, and op. 8, d. 52, ll. 137–138.

92. Ibid., op. 3, d. 4, l. 171.

93. Examples of economic activity all taken from archival records. The 1923 statement on the textile industry is in ibid., op. 4, d. 7, l. 47.

94. *Moskovskaya organizatsiya R.K.P.(b) v tsifrakh,* 2d ed., p. 24.

95. One published source put the MK's authorized strength in 1928 at 56 responsible workers and 91 support staff ("technical workers") (note in *Izvestiya TsK RKP[b]*, no. 27 [September 10, 1928], p. 8), but the departments listed did not include the Secret Department, which, according to the archive, had 13 professional and support staff upon its creation in 1926. The totals for responsible workers are given in *Moskovskaya organizatsiya R.K.P.(b) v tsifrakh,* 2d ed., p. 24; *Moskovskaya organizatsiya VKP(b) v tsifrakh,* 3d ed. (Moscow: Moskovskii komitet, 1927), p. 18; *Moskovskaya organizatsiya VKP(b) v tsifrakh,* 4th ed. (Moscow: MK VKP[b], 1927), p. 22.

96. The Higher Education Colloquium, an adjunct of the Agitation and Propaganda Department, was a partial exception; it discussed matters as diverse as Marxism classes, science policy, and the student press. The Rural Colloquium may also have aspired to a wider role. My source on the commissions is various files in the Communist Party archive. The first for which a record appears is the MK's Cooperatives Council, in April 1924. Next came the Industrial Commission; it met every second week in 1925, making seven or eight personnel decisions per meeting. Aside from the bodies for higher education and rural work, the only one of the twenty-four I found that was not identified as an add-on to the Organization and Assignments Department was the Colloquium for the Communal Economy. Created in April 1928, it was also the largest, with 429 members. In several cases (e.g., for officials in finance and trade), a pair of commissions were appointed in 1926–1927, one to discuss appointments and the other to consider recruitment and evaluation of officials.

97. The Cooperatives Council, the oldest of the auxiliaries, was the first to be dissolved, in May 1928. Within the Organization and Assignments Department, a "sector" for cooperatives and soviets, established in December 1928, was a forerunner of the more specialized approach of the 1930s. It is unclear why this area was singled out for special treatment.

98. Quotation from a memoir by Bukharin's widow: A. M. Larina, "Nezaby-

vayemoye," *Znamya,* no. 10 (October 1988), p. 142. In an interview with me in March 1993, Larina reported that Stalin was especially anxious about Uglanov because, like Tomskii but unlike Bukharin and Rykov, Uglanov was of proletarian origin and might have found support among industrial workers.

99. Persecuted together with his family from 1930 on, Ryutin was shot in January 1937 and posthumously exhonerated only in 1988. Uglanov, after being fired as people's commissar of labor in July 1930, was made head of a fishery station in Astrakhan. He was expelled from the party in 1932, reinstated in 1934, and allowed to work mainly in the fish-processing industry in Siberia. He was arrested in August 1936 and shot May 31, 1937. Uglanov was absolved of all charges by the USSR Supreme Court only in July 1989.

100. *Rabochaya Moskva,* October 18, 1924, p. 3.

101. TsGAODM, f. 3, op. 8, d. 33, l. 108; d. 34, ll. 34, 67–69; op. 9, d. 19, l. 133.

102. *Shestoi ob"edinennyi plenum,* p. 17.

103. As commissar of the banks of Kiev in 1917, Bauman had seized their gold stocks and sent them to Moscow. In 1923–1924, after several years in Kursk, he was deputy chief of the party's personnel section, which was headed by Kaganovich but supervised by Molotov. He became the MK's head of personnel in August 1924, and for most of his term the central secretary overseeing this function was Molotov. In April 1928, after Molotov shifted to supervision of agriculture, Bauman became a candidate member of the Orgburo and head of the Secretariat's new Department for Work in the Countryside, thus Molotov's closest aide. He followed Molotov to the MK that November as second secretary.

104. *Chetvertyi plenum MK VKP(b) sovmestno s plenumom MKK (5–7 avgusta 1929, 14–15 avgusta 1929)* (Moscow: MK VKP[b], 1929), p. 79; *Vechernyaya Moskva,* June 2, 1930, p. 2.

105. *Khrushchev Remembers,* trans. Strobe Talbott (Boston: Little, Brown, 1970), pp. 39–42.

106. A. M. Gak and I. I. Sanina, "Karl Yanovich Bauman," *Voprosy istorii KPSS,* no. 12 (December 1967), pp. 103–104; L. Kozlova, *Moskovskiye kommunisty v bor'be za pobedu kolkhoznogo stroya (1927–1933 gg.)* (Moscow: Moskovskii rabochii, 1960), pp. 20–21.

107. *Vechernyaya Moskva,* January 8, 1930, p. 1.

108. Ibid., September 18, 1929, p. 1; *Rabochaya Moskva,* January 17, 1930, p. 2; *Ocherki istorii Moskovskoi organizatsii KPSS (1883–1965 gg.),* p. 467.

109. TsGAODM, f. 3, op. 12, d. 62, l. 121.

110. *Rabochaya Moskva,* March 29, 1930, p. 3. On Bauman's and the Moscow organization's role in the conflict, see Lynne Viola, *The Best Sons of the Fatherland: Workers in the Vanguard of Soviet Collectivization* (New York: Oxford University Press, 1987), pp. 75, 93–94, 130–131.

111. *Sto sorok besed s Molotovym,* p. 319. There have been reports that Kaganovich's daughter Maya was Stalin's mistress, but Kaganovich before his death in 1991 emphatically denied them, and they seem to have no base in fact.

112. *Khrushchev Remembers,* p. 34. Kaganovich had a prior interest in Moscow.

While working in the Secretariat, he was appointed to the 1924, 1925, and 1929 Moscow Committees. One of his former Ukrainian subordinates, I. L. Bulat, was made head of the MK's personnel section in April 1929 and third secretary in January 1930. Bazhanov, *Vospominaniya byvshego sekretarya Stalina,* p. 197, says Kaganovich was Stalin's first choice for Moscow leader at the time of Zelenskii's departure in 1924.

113. *Pravda,* June 20, 1930, p. 5. Bauman lost his candidate's seat on the Politburo at the congress but was not officially removed from the Orgburo or Secretariat until October 2, 1932. According to a former party official (Abdurakhman Avtorkhanov, *Tekhnologiya vlasti* [Frankfurt: Posev, 1976], p. 325), he stayed in Stalin's secret "cabinet" and in charge of the daily operations of the Secretariat until late in 1930. The only explanation would be protection by Molotov. Leonov, who most likely was close to Molotov, too, was removed as second secretary in July 1930 and sent to head a regional party committee in Siberia.

114. *Pravda,* August 20, 1929, p. 4.

115. G. Merkov, "Rekonstruktsiya torgovoi sistemy i planirovka Moskvy," *Kommunal'noye khozyaistvo,* no. 8 (April 1931), p. 6; TsGAODM, f. 3, op. 12, d. 59, l. 83; d. 42, ll. 4, 82.

116. TsGAODM, f. 3, op. 10, d. 75, ll. 35–36; d. 76, l. 27.

117. I estimate 6,000 persons evicted from the 33,000 square meters of living space cited in "Plenum tsentral'noi zhilishchnoi sektsii 31 yanvarya," *Kommunal'noye khozyaistvo,* no. 3 (March 1930), p. 120; this is also the source for the call for eviction of all 180,000. The Popov quote is from TsGAODM, f. 3, op. 10, d. 75, l. 75.

118. Details of the early days of Podlipki, the future rocket-producing city of Kaliningrad, are only now emerging. See Anatolii Zak in *Nezavisimaya gazeta,* April 13, 1993, p. 6.

119. TsGAODM, f. 3, op. 10, d. 74, ll. 52–53.

120. *Pravda,* September 18, 1929, p. 3; *Ocherki istorii Moskovskoi organizatsii KPSS, Kn. II, Noyabr' 1917–1945* (Moscow: Moskovskii rabochii, 1983), p. 361; TsGAODM, f. 3, op. 10, d. 65, ll. 43–44; *Istoriya Moskovskogo avtozavoda imeni I. A. Likhacheva* (Moscow: Mysl', 1966), pp. 141–142.

121. *Pervyi podshipnikovyi: Istoriya pervogo gosudarstvennogo podshipnikovogo zavoda, 1932–1972* (Moscow: Mysl', 1973), p. 12.

122. Russians' share of the Moscow population declined marginally, from 87.8 percent in 1926 to 87.5 percent in 1933, and Jews rose marginally, from 6.5 to 6.6 percent, an all-time high. Ukrainians posed the largest proportional gain, from 0.8 percent of the populace in 1926 to 1.5 percent in 1933. A likely reason was the severity of the hunger and dislocation produced by collectivization in Ukraine.

123. Aside from the figures given in Table 4, the data on big factories are found in the same handbook, p. 91. Continuity in the sources of migration during this period is proved in David L. Hoffmann, "Moving to Moscow: Patterns of Peasant In-Migration during the First Five-Year Plan," *Slavic Review,* vol. 50 (Winter 1991), pp. 847–857.

124. TsGAODM, f. 3, op. 10, d. 74, l. 93.

125. Quotation in Anatole Kopp, "Foreign Architects in the Soviet Union during the First Two Five-Year Plans," in William C. Brumfield, ed., *Reshaping Russian Architecture: Western Technology, Utopian Dreams* (Cambridge: Cambridge University Press, 1990), p. 179. The first German architect moved to Russia in 1924. According to Kopp (p. 177), there were 800 to 1,000 foreign-born architects in the USSR in 1936, about half of them Germans.

126. S. Frederick Starr, *Melnikov: Solo Architect in a Mass Society* (Princeton: Princeton University Press, 1978), p. 41.

127. Hugh D. Hudson, Jr., *Blueprints and Blood: The Stalinization of Soviet Architecture, 1917–1937* (Princeton: Princeton University Press, 1994), p. 24. Further information on the groups is in *Iz istorii sovetskoi arkhitektury, 1926–1932 gg.: Dokumenty i materialy* (Moscow: Nauka, 1970), pp. 7–25, 39–105, and Selim O. Khan-Magomedov, *Pioneers of Soviet Architecture*, trans. Alexander Lieven (New York: Rizzoli, 1983), chaps. 2–5.

128. Blair A. Ruble, "Moscow's Revolutionary Architecture and Its Aftermath: A Critical Guide," in Brumfield, *Reshaping Russian Architecture*, p. 126. This is an excellent primer on the city's public buildings of the period.

129. Selim Khan-Magomedov, "ASNOVA i kompleks na Shabolovke," *Arkhitektura i stroitel'stvo Moskvy*, no. 9 (September 1988), pp. 21–23.

130. "Khronika," *Kommunal'noye khozyaistvo*, no. 11 (October 1, 1922), p. 24.

131. *Izvestiya*, December 31, 1922, p. 1.

132. The MK bureau was told in September 1927 that foundation work would begin by the Revolution Day holiday (November 7) that year, but it did not. TsGAODM, f. 3, op. 8, d. 34, l. 55.

133. *Izvestiya*, February 7, 1924, p. 2.

134. Ibid., February 12, 1924, p. 4, and February 24, 1924, p. 2; Selim Khan-Magomedov, "K istorii vybora mesta dlya Dvortsa Sovetov," *Arkhitektura i stroitel'stvo Moskvy*, no. 1 (January 1988), pp. 21–23. The design contest for a permanent mausoleum in 1925–1926 also brought forth grand schemes. One of the 117 entries, entitled "Dawn of a New Life," would have filled Red Square and illuminated central Moscow with floodlights; another called for a Lenin statue fifteen to twenty floors high containing meeting halls for government and party organizations. Tumarkin, *Lenin Lives!* p. 203.

135. Vladimir Kozlov and Valerii Sedel'nikov, "Konets Okhotnogo ryada," *Arkhitektura i stroitel'stvo Moskvy*, no. 4 (April 1990), p. 26.

136. V. Semenov, "O gorode-sade," *Kommunal'noye khozyaistvo*, nos. 8–9 (September 1, 1922), pp. 7, 10.

137. On Sokol and its inhabitants, see N. Markovnikov, "Poselok 'Sokol,'" *Stroitel'naya promyshlennost'*, no. 12 (December 1929), pp. 1069–1076, and *Vechernyaya Moskva*, August 13, 1928, p. 2. It was named after the Sokol'niki district, in which it was originally supposed to be situated.

138. "Khronika," *Kommunal'noye khozyaistvo*, no. 12 (June 15, 1923), p. 29.

139. TsGAODM, f. 3, op. 6, d. 25, l. 207. A fine general treatment of communal housing is Milka Bliznakov, "Soviet Housing during the Experimental Years, 1918–

1933," in William C. Brumfield and Blair A. Ruble, eds., *Russian Housing in the Modern Age* (Cambridge: Cambridge University Press, 1993), pp. 101–118. On communes set up in preexisting buildings, consult Richard Stites, *Revolutionary Dreams: Utopian Vision and Experimental Life in the Russian Revolution* (New York: Oxford University Press, 1989), pp. 215–217.

140. The building is ingeniously designed and pioneered some of the prefabricated materials that came into wide use in the USSR in the 1950s. Most of its flats were split-level "Type F" units of about thirty square meters with small kitchens, washrooms, and sleeping alcoves. Two similar houses were built on Gogolevskii bul'var and at Rostokino, northeast of the city center.

141. Information on the Khavskaya house taken from M. Ancharova, "Dom-kommuna," *Revolyutsiya i kul'tura*, no. 1 (January 15, 1930), pp. 77–80, and *Rabochaya Moskva*, February 9, 1930, p. 4. The contest announcement is in *Iz istorii sovetskoi arkhitektury, 1917–1925 gg.: Dokumenty i materialy* (Moscow: Izdatel'stvo Akademii Nauk, 1963), pp. 63–64. The surviving part of the building, at the modern address 18 ulitsa Lestcva, is used as office space. The Nikolayev commune on ulitsa Ordzhonikidze still exists as a student dormitory, as does another house by him at 21 Kotel'nicheskaya naberezhnaya.

142. *Pravda*, January 21, 1921, p. 4; *Leninskiye dekrety o Moskve* (Moscow: Moskovskii rabochii, 1978), pp. 420–421, 453–454, 461–462.

143. "Zasedaniye sektsii MUNI Mossoveta," *Kommunal'noye khozyaistvo*, no. 8 (April 20, 1924), pp. 15–16.

144. From ibid., p. 16; *Rabochaya Moskva*, January 29, 1926, p. 6; *Izvestiya*, February 2, 1927, p. 5.

145. Quotations from *Rabochaya Moskva*, January 29, 1926, p. 6, and *Izvestiya*, June 19, 1926, p. 1. The new statute (*Izvestiya*, April 8, 1930, p. 4) iterated appeal procedures and placed on the commission a member of the collegium of the NKVD (as chairman), two representatives of the Mossovet, one of Rabkrin, and one of the trade unions. The 1936 city handbook had an entry for the commission, identifying D. Z. Lebed', a deputy premier of the RSFSR, as chairman. The last reference I have found is in July 1937.

146. *Pravda*, August 15, 1924, p. 1.

147. A. Shchusev, "Problemy 'Novoi Moskvy,'" *Stroitel'naya promyshlennost'*, no. 3 (March 1925), pp. 194, 196. The best summaries are this article, pp. 193–200, and *Iz istorii sovetskoi arkhitektury, 1917–1925 gg.*, pp. 42–47.

148. Yurii Zhukov, "Moskva: Genplany 1918–1935 godov i sud'by pamyatnikov arkhitektury," *Gorizont*, no. 4 (April 1988), p. 34. Population estimates in I. Verner, "Plan razvitiya g. Moskvy," *Kommunal'noye khozyaistvo*, no. 7 (November 7, 1921), p. 13; *Rabochaya Moskva*, August 26, 1923, p. 2; Shchusev, "Problemy 'Novoi Moskvy,'" p. 199, referring to 4 million in a central area and 1 million in a suburban area.

149. See Shchusev in *Izvestiya*, April 16, 1925, p. 5.

150. Precise numbers on churches and their closings are elusive. The 1930 figure—as with most subsequent totals cited in this book—comes from a personal

communication to the author from Professor Nathaniel Davis of Harvey Mudd College, who has compiled a database on Orthodox churches in Russia and Ukraine. The starting point for the early 1920s is not so clear. The 1923 *Vsya Moskva* lists 9 Orthodox cathedrals and 279 churches, but monastery and convent churches are not included and a number of the churches given seem to have been closed at the time.

151. Vladimir Kozlov, "Pervyye snosy," *Arkhitektura i stroitel'stvo Moskvy*, no. 8 (August 1990), p. 29.

152. Platonov and Ol'minskii in *Izvestiya*, October 23, 1925, p. 6, and November 12, 1925, p. 5.

153. See Kozlov, "Delo ob ograblenii tserkvi," p. 21.

154. Shchusev's letter is reprinted in Vladimir Kozlov, "Na perelome: Moskovskaya starina v 1925–1926 godakh," *Arkhitektura i stroitel'stvo Moskvy*, no. 9 (September 1990), p. 26. This article is also the source of the information about the Palace of Trusts affair.

155. The Popov and Shchusev letters are reprinted in *Iz istorii sovetskoi arkhitektury, 1917–1925 gg.*, pp. 49–50.

156. V. Murav'ev, "Krasnyye vorota," *Arkhitektura i stroitel'stvo Moskvy*, no. 6 (June 1987), p. 33.

157. I. E. Grabar', "Pamyatniki staroi arkhitektury i novoye gorodskoye stroitel'stvo," *Stroitel'naya promyshlennost'*, no. 5 (September–October 1928), p. 378; Kozlov and Sedel'nikov, "Konets Okhotnogo ryada," p. 28; Kozlov, "Voina dvortsam," pp. 40–41.

158. Kozlov, "Pervyye snosy," pp. 26–27. Between 1925 and 1938, 385,000 church bells were smelted down in Russia, Ukraine, and Belorussia, and only several percent were spared. Oleg Platonov, "Puteshestviye v Kitezh-grad," *Moskva*, no. 4 (April 1990), p. 158.

159. Vladimir Kozlov, "Tragediya monastyrei: God 1929-i," *Moskovskii zhurnal*, no. 1 (January 1991), p. 40; *Moskovskaya pravda*, January 28, 1990, p. 3.

160. The military school, eventually named the RSFSR Supreme Soviet Higher All-Forces Command School, was moved out of the Kremlin in 1935, presumably in connection with the tightening of police control over Kremlin installations.

161. "Several clergy, regardless of [state policy], remained beside their abbeys and in some cases even within their walls." The mother superior of the Alekseyevskii Convent survived there until the 1980s. Kozlov, "Tragediya monastyrei," p. 37. See also Vladimir Kozlov, "Chernyye gody moskovskikh obitelei," *Moskovskii zhurnal*, no. 11 (November 1991), p. 10.

162. Information mostly from Kozlov, "Tragediya monastyrei," pp. 32–41, and Kozlov, "Delo ob ograblenii tserkvi," pp. 23–24. The blasting at Simonov is related in *Rabochaya Moskva*, January 24, 1930, p. 6, and *Vechernyaya Moskva*, July 26, 1930, p. 2.

163. Yelena Ovsyannikova, "Staraya Moskva i 'Staraya Moskva,'" *Arkhitektura i stroitel'stvo Moskvy*, no. 9 (September 1988), pp. 26–27; D. A. Ravikovich, "Okhrana pamyatnikov istorii i kul'tury v RSFSR," *Istoriya SSSR*, no. 11 (November 1967), p. 196.

164. Besides Shestakov, the commission had five members (four of them known to be city employees) and one representative of the New Moscow commission. Shestakov is identified in the 1912 Moscow directory as an engineer in the streets and drainage branch of the city uprava.

165. S. S. Shestakov, *Bol'shaya Moskva* (Moscow: Izdaniye MKKh, 1925); early population projection in *Izvestiya,* March 1, 1924, p. 5.

166. Shestakov, *Bol'shaya Moskva,* p. 30, 33.

167. *Pravda,* February 15, 1925, p. 3.

168. Boris Sakulin, "Garmonicheskaya grafika v primenenii k planirovke i zastroike gorodskikh raionov," *Kommunal'noye khozyaistvo,* nos. 19–20 (October 25, 1926), pp. 12–18.

169. Yu. Korob'in, "Vozmozhnosti razmeshcheniya naseleniya g. Moskvy na yeye sushchestvuyushchei territorii," ibid., nos. 3–4 (February 25, 1929), p. 19.

170. S. Gurevich, "Yeshche raz o planirovke Moskvy," ibid., nos. 7–8 (April 20, 1929), p. 26. Khar'kov, the Ukrainian capital in the 1920s and a much smaller city, had thirty-six planners; Leningrad had forty-five. The planning office and MKKh authorized construction on vacant land, the city's real estate directorate on occupied lots.

171. Quotation and some examples from "MORKI o sostoyanii raboty v Zemel'no-planirovochnom otdele MOKKh," ibid., no. 3 (March 1930), p. 118. Other examples taken from *Pravda,* April 3, 1930, p. 5; Ya. Yakshchin, "K voprosu o planirovke Moskvy," *Stroitel'stvo Moskvy,* no. 5 (May 1929), pp. 27–28; *Vechernyaya Moskva,* February 26, 1929, p. 2.

172. P. Arutyunyants, "O rekonstruktsii Proletarskogo raiona," *Kommunal'noye khozyaistvo,* no. 7 (July 1930), pp. 4–5.

173. M. V. Kryukov, "God bor'by na stroitel'nom fronte," *Stroitel'stvo Moskvy,* no. 11 (November 1930), p. 10.

174. Khan-Magomedov, *Pioneers of Soviet Architecture,* pp. 282–283.

175. See S. Frederick Starr, "Visionary Town Planning during the Cultural Revolution," in Sheila Fitzpatrick, ed., *Cultural Revolution in Russia, 1928–1931* (Bloomington: Indiana University Press, 1978), pp. 207–240.

176. Gornyi, *Sotsialisticheskaya rekonstruktsiya,* p. 61. Another time, Gornyi identified the economic planning commission of the Mossovet (which at the time concerned itself with all of Moscow oblast) as a source of such thinking. S. Gornyi, "Planirovka Moskvy," *Kommunal'noye khozyaistvo,* no. 6 (June 1930), p. 17.

177. B. Sakulin, "K probleme rekonstruktsii g. Moskvy," *Kommunal'noye khozyaistvo,* no. 10 (October 1930), pp. 22–27; *Izvestiya,* March 1, 1930, p. 5; Gornyi, *Sotsialisticheskaya rekonstruktsiya,* p. 109. Sakulin was a founding member of ARU, but as usual his ideas were highly individual.

178. See ARU, "K voprosu o novoi planirovke Moskvy," *Stroitel'naya promyshlennost',* no. 9 (September 1929), pp. 798–800, and N. Ladovskii, "Moskva 'istoricheskaya' i 'sotsialisticheskaya,'" *Stroitel'stvo Moskvy,* no. 1 (January 1930), pp. 17–20.

179. For Krasin's comments, see his "Osnovnyye problemy planirovki Moskvy,"

Stroitel'stvo Moskvy, no. 1 (January 1930), pp. 21–33. For Puzis and Golosov, see Gornyi, *Sotsialisticheskaya rekonstruktsiya*, pp. 110–113, 85–86.

180. M. Barshch and M. Ginzburg, "Zelenyi gorod: Sotsialisticheskaya rekonstruktsiya Moskvy," *Sovremennaya arkhitektura*, nos. 1–2 (January–April 1930), pp. 17–37; Gornyi, *Sotsialisticheskaya rekonstruktsiya*, pp. 107–108.

181. Strogova's article is in *Pravda*, January 2, 1930, p. 4. Sabsovich and Strumilin are in Gornyi, *Sotsialisticheskaya rekonstruktsiya*, pp. 116–125, 128–130.

182. Gornyi, *Sotsialisticheskaya rekonstruktsiya*, p. 191. See the sympathetic discussion in Cohen, *Le Corbusier and the Mystique of the USSR*, chap. 6.

183. Gornyi, *Sotsialisticheskaya rekonstruktsiya*, p. 90.

184. M. Nefedov, "Opyt ischisleniya budushchego rosta naseleniya Moskvy," *Kommunal'noye khozyaistvo*, no. 6 (June 1930), p. 8; *Izvestiya*, March 15, 1930, p. 4; Gornyi, "Planirovka Moskvy," pp. 16–17; *Izvestiya*, October 10, 1930, p. 4. The decree prohibiting new industrial construction was issued by the government of the RSFSR. Most of GUM was closed in 1930, but it reopened as a retailing facility in 1933; it was converted to offices during the war.

185. *Pravda*, May 29, 1930, p. 5.

186. Pavel Penezhko, "Kak udarili po 'Chayanovshchine,'" *Ogonek*, no. 10 (March 1988), pp. 6–8, and Yaroslavskii in *Pravda*, October 18, 1930, p. 2. Chayanov was politically rehabilitated by the Gorbachev administration in July 1987. Puzis, a major voice in the debate of 1929–1930, and one who survived Stalinism, recalled many years later that the Central Committee resolution "put an end to free research" on urban planning and the future of Moscow. Sabsovich, he says, "was very hurt by this affair" and, after losing a leg in a streetcar accident, "completely abandoned the battle" and died, forgotten, in 1943 or 1944. Okhitovich was to be arrested in 1936 and died in a camp in 1937. See Anatole Kopp, *L'architecture de la période stalinienne* (Grenoble: Presses universitaires de Grenoble, 1978), p. 389, and Hudson, *Blueprints and Blood*, pp. 159–160.

187. Benjamin, *Moscow Diary*, p. 31.

188. Gurevich, "Yeshche raz o planirovke Moskvy," p. 27.

4. Stalin's Moscow

1. T. A. Selivanov, "Velikii Stalin—vdokhnovitel' i organizator rekonstruktsii Moskvy," *Gorodskoye khozyaistvo Moskvy*, no. 12 (December 1949), pp. 9, 14.

2. "Kak Moskva chut' ne stala Stalinodarom," *Izvestiya TsK KPSS*, no. 12 (December 1990), pp. 126–127; *Sto sorok besed s Molotovym: Iz dnevnika Feliksa Chuyeva* (Moscow: Terra, 1991), p. 264.

3. The bells, tolling the "Internationale" until 1935 and a traditional peal after their restoration in 1937, rang at only 6:00 A.M. and midnight. The hourly musical signal on radio was changed to "Song of the Motherland," by Isaak Dunayevskii, in 1939. In 1956 a ditty with a local motif—Vasilii Solov'ev-Sedoi's "Evenings around Moscow," popularized in the West as "Midnight in Moscow"—was substituted.

4. Of 121,955 individuals detained between October 20 and December 13, 1941,

47,575 were accused of military offenses, 2,610 of "counterrevolutionary crimes," and 71,825 of other violations. Besides the executed, 11,419 were sent to prison or labor camp and 2,959 expelled from Moscow. "Moskva na osadnom polozhenii," *Izvestiya TsK KPSS,* no. 4 (April 1991), p. 210.

5. *Pravda,* May 20, 1935, p. 3.

6. Ibid., January 10, 1931, p. 2.

7. Ibid., December 21, 1939, p. 5 (comments for Stalin's sixtieth birthday). The second secretary of the obkom, K. V. Ryndin, stated in 1931 that street lighting was the issue that attracted Kremlin attention, and credited Kaganovich with having "raised [the question] to a principled, political, all-party level." TsGAODM, f. 3, op. 24, d. 1, ll. 5, 11.

8. *Vechernyaya Moskva,* December 11, 1937, p. 2.

9. The resolution is in *Pravda,* June 17, 1931, pp. 2–3. Local implementing measures are in ibid., June 21–25, 1931, and Kaganovich's speech in ibid., July 4, 1931, pp. 3–4.

10. Ibid., July 4, 1931, p. 4.

11. A. I. Levchenko, "V Moskvu potyanulis' sostavy," in *Istoriya metro Moskvy* (Moscow: Izdatel'stvo "Istoriya fabrik i zavodov," 1935), I, 416.

12. See *Vechernyaya Moskva,* January 7, 1933, p. 2, and *Khrushchev Remembers,* trans. Strobe Talbott (Boston: Little, Brown, 1970), pp. 68–69. Construction of the air defense post is described, without identification of the station (which I know from interviews), in *Moskovskaya pravda,* July 30, 1992, p. 3.

13. *Pravda,* December 19, 1933, p. 4.

14. The city presidium made Kogan chief of construction in May 1932, replacing P. Ya. Bovin (whom it appointed in September 1931), but continued to treat the canal as its own until December 28, 1932, when it transferred all equipment, contracts, and workers (except for diggers, who presumably were replaced by prisoners) to a Gulag subunit then called Moskanalstroi. Moscow found itself short of the materials and machinery needed, appealing to the USSR government in September 1932 to help out. TsGIAGM, f. 150, op. 1, ll. 257, 539, 756–757.

15. There were 196,000 prisoners working on the canal at the start of 1935. O. Khlebnyuk, "Prinuditel'nyi trud v ekonomike SSSR, 1929–1941 gody," *Svobodnaya mysl',* no. 13 (September 1992), p. 78. Speaking in 1937, after Yagoda's arrest, Khrushchev claimed that Yagoda opposed construction and that the MK had to threaten him with an appeal to Stalin. TsGAODM, f. 4, op. 8, d. 1, l. 28.

16. *Rabochaya Moskva,* November 28, 1934, p. 2.

17. Quotation from "Voskhozhdeniye 'Memoriala,'" *Gorodskoye khozyaistvo Moskvy,* no. 11 (November 1989), p. 31. A. V. Krokhin, "Ya byl kanalarmeitsem," ibid., no. 8 (August 1990), p. 33, describes the dredging and states that political prisoners among the zeks, himself included, were sent off to other camps east of Moscow. Notice of the amnesty is in *Pravda,* July 22, 1937, p. 4. Journalist Aleksandr Mil'chakov has asserted that the toll from the canal was 500,000 (David Remnick, *Lenin's Tomb: The Last Days of the Soviet Empire* [New York: Random House, 1993], p. 139), but it is hard to see how this number could be accurate without a

much larger labor force than reported. Dental analysis of prisoners' bodies showed, according to Mil'chakov, that many ate bark, roots, and grass to supplement their thin rations.

18. The decree and design parameters are in *Izvestiya*, July 18, 1931, p. 2, and background in Isaak Eigel', "K istorii postroyeniya i snosa khrama Khrista Spasitelya," *Arkhitektura i stroitel'stvo Moskvy*, no. 7 (July 1988), pp. 30–33.

19. Alexei Tarkhanov and Sergei Kavtaradze, *Architecture of the Stalin Era* (New York: Rizzoli, 1992), p. 27. See also Catherine Cooke and Igor Kazus, *Soviet Architectural Competitions, 1920s-1930s* (London: Phaidon Press, 1992), pp. 58–83, and Peter Lizon, "The Palace of the Soviets—Change in Direction of Soviet Architecture," Ph.D. diss., University of Pennsylvania, 1971.

20. *Sto sorok besed s Molotovym*, p. 265.

21. See F. I. Chuyev, *Tak govoril Kaganovich: Ispoved' stalinskogo apostola* (Moscow: Otechestvo, 1992), p. 47; *Moskovskii bol'shevik*, December 22, 1939, p. 3; Selim Khan-Magomedov, "K istorii vybora mesta dlya Dvortsa Sovetov," *Arkhitektura i stroitel'stvo Moskvy*, no. 1 (January 1988), pp. 21–23; Ye. I. Kirichenko, G. A. Ivanova, and Ye. G. Klodt, *Khram Khrista Spasitelya v Moskve* (Moscow: Planeta, 1992), pp. 232–236, 244–246.

22. "Etot pamyatnik na veka," *Literaturnaya Rossiya*, no. 38 (September 22, 1989), p. 11.

23. Among contemporary sources, the newspaper *Vechernyaya Moskva* covered this and other demolitions most fully. For other details, see retrospective reports in Oleg Platonov, "Puteshestviye v Kitezh-grad," *Moskva*, no. 4 (April 1990), p. 161; *Vechernyaya Moskva*, June 9, 1990, p. 3; D. Popov, "Osvobozhdeniye iz t'my," *Arkhitektura*, no. 21 (November 3, 1990), p. 4; Vladimir Kozlov, "Gibel' Khrama," *Moskovskii zhurnal*, no. 9 (September 1991), pp. 16–18. There are remarkable photographs in *Razrusheniye Khrama Khrista Spasitelya (Samizdat)* (London: Overseas Publications Interchange, 1988), and in Kirichenko, Ivanova, and Klodt, *Khram Khrista Spasitelya*, pp. 242–267.

24. Stars were put up in 1935 on the Borovitskaya, Nikol'skaya, Spasskaya, and Troitskaya towers. The Vodovzvodnaya Tower was included in the 1937 scheme. M. A. Topolin, *Kremlevskiye zvezdy* (Moscow: Znaniye, 1975).

25. The main decisions are given in R. G. Grigor'ev, *Iz istorii rekonstruktsii Moskvy (sotsial'no-politicheskii aspekt)* (Moscow: Znaniye, 1991), pp. 34–41. The decision of June 1932 is in TsGAODM, f. 4, op. 2, d. 8, l. 146. Public comments are in V. A. Makovskii, "Kitaigorodskuyu stenu nado snesti," *Stroitel'stvo Moskvy*, no. 4 (April 1931), p. 31, and P. Gel'bras, "Uroki Gorzemplana," ibid., no. 11 (November 1931), p. 2.

26. "K istorii snosa Sukharevoi bashni," *Izvestiya TsK KPSS*, no. 9 (September 1989), pp. 109–116. Kaganovich claimed in retirement that he initially opposed demolition and wanted a traffic tunnel beneath the tower but concluded it would be too expensive. Chuyev, *Tak govoril Kaganovich*, p. 48.

27. On Red Square, see A. Yastrebov, "Pokusheniye na Krasnuyu ploshchad'," *Nedelya*, no. 47 (November 21, 1988), p. 12. After the late 1920s, it was not the pace of the renamings that changed but the importance of the streets. Name changes

averaged twelve a year in 1929–1935, but only five in 1936–1952. Among the most prominent to be retitled in the late Stalin era were Pokrovka (which became ulitsa Chernyshevskogo in 1940) and Maroseika (ulitsa Bogdana Khmel'nitskogo, 1953).

28. L. Perchik, "Moskva na stroike," *Stroitel'stvo Moskvy,* no. 11 (November 1934), p. 9.

29. Yu. A. Bychkov, *Zhitiye Petra Baranovskogo* (Moscow: Sovetskaya Rossiya, 1991), pp. 63–82; Platonov, "Puteshestviye v Kitezh-grad," p. 160.

30. Yurii Zhukov, "Moskva: Genplany 1918–1935 godov i sud'by pamyatnikov arkhitektury," *Gorizont,* no. 4 (April 1988), pp. 39–44; Vladimir Kozlov, "Delo ob ograblenii tserkvi," *Moskovskii zhurnal,* no. 7 (July 1991), p. 23.

31. Author's interview with N. A. Rykova, July 1992; *Moskovskaya pravda,* June 24, 1990, p. 3; Ye. B. Ovsyannikova, "'Rabota byla ves'ma interesnaya,'" in L. V. Ivanova and S. O. Shmidt, eds., *Krayevedy Moskvy* (Moscow: Moskovskii rabochii, 1991), pp. 210–211. In the palace the builders joined the Aleksandrovskii and Andreyevskii halls into one and expanded kitchens over the site of the Red Staircase.

32. Sergei Romanyuk, *Moskva: Utraty* (Moscow: PTO "Tsentr," 1992), entries under individual structures; Vladimir Kozlov, "Chernyye gody moskovskikh obitelei," *Moskovskii zhurnal,* no. 11 (November 1991), pp. 8–15; Valentin Sukhodolov, "Kinoteatr v trapeznoi Simonova monastyrya," *Arkhitektura i stroitel'stvo Moskvy,* no. 5 (May 1990), pp. 28–30.

33. Bychkov, *Zhitiye Petra Baranovskogo,* pp. 63, 75–78; O. B. Nebogin and M. S. Slanskaya in *Moskovskaya pravda,* January 7, 1989, p. 4. Kaganovich hotly denied in retirement that he had his eyes on St. Basil's (Chuyev, *Tak govoril Kaganovich,* p. 51). The church was locked up in the spring of 1939, perhaps because the question of demolition was reopened at that time. Some architects were told that the government feared it had become unstable and might fall down during a military parade.

34. See Vladimir Kozlov, "Tragediya Kitai-goroda," *Moskovskii zhurnal,* no. 2 (February 1992), p. 20, and the firsthand account in Allan Monkhouse, *Moscow, 1911–1933* (Boston: Little, Brown, 1934), pp. 221–222.

35. The proposals to make the church into a cinema, and then to replace it with a panorama, were never made public. They are in TsGIAGM, f. 150, op. 1, d. 159, ll. 7 and 437, and TsGAODM, f. 3, op. 49, d. 44, l. 32. The cathedral's bell tower was torn down during restoration work in 1928. Romanyuk, *Moskva: Utraty,* p. 52, says the church was given over to Metrostroi in 1933 for a warehouse and cafeteria, but the documentary record contains no trace of this development.

36. M. L. Pasternak, excerpted in *Razrusheniye Khrama Khrista Spasitelya,* p. 36; Lev Nikulin, quoted in Vladimir Papernyi, *Kul'tura "Dva"* (Ann Arbor: Ardis, 1985), p. 21; Aleksei Adzhubei, *Te desyat' let* (Moscow: Sovetskaya Rossiya, 1989), p. 131. Landmarks were destroyed in some other Russian towns to further Moscow's reconstruction. The stone kremlin and some of the churches of Serpukhov, in the south of Moscow oblast, were torn down in 1932 to make fill for the bed of the subway.

37. The decree was published in *Pravda* December 28. An edict of April 28, 1933, designated twenty-five cities, beginning with Moscow, which had "regime districts" around them, subjected to unusually strict conditions. The passports showed the bearer's full name, date and place of birth, nationality, social position, and place of employment, along with the place of permanent residence. Photographs were added in 1937, making the system more airtight, and there were further minor changes in 1940. Mervyn Matthews, *The Passport Society: Controlling Movement in Russia and the USSR* (Boulder, Colo.: Westview Press, 1993), pp. 27–31.

38. The area was hit relatively lightly in the famine. Mortality in Moscow oblast increased from 16.1 per 1,000 in 1932 to 20.0 in 1933; the USSR average in 1933 was 37.7 deaths per 1,000, and the RSFSR average 31.4. S. G. Wheatcroft, "More Light on the Scale of Repression and Excess Mortality in the Soviet Union in the 1930s," *Soviet Studies*, vol. 42 (April 1990), pp. 361–362.

39. *Pravda*, January 20, 1933, p. 2.

40. TsGAODM, f. 4, op. 2, d. 10, ll. 200–202; op. 3, d. 7, l. 128; d. 31, ll. 171–172.

41. A. S. Yenukidze in *Izvestiya*, February 2, 1933, p. 4; he claimed that literal equation of the two events would be "anti-Soviet fantasy." The January 1933 resolution is in *Sbornik vazhneishikh postanovlenii MK i MGK VKP(b): Materialy k 4 oblastnoi i 3 gorodskoi konferentsii VKP(b)* (Moscow: VKP[b], 1934), p. 13.

42. *Khrushchev Remembers*, pp. 78–79. In June 1935 the city party secretariat asked municipal officials to suggest uses for apartments "freed up in connection with decisions by judicial and administrative organs on expulsion from Moscow" (TsGAODM, f. 4, op. 5, d. 33, l. 8).

43. Freda Utley, *Lost Illusion* (London: George Allen and Unwin, 1947), p. 40; I. N. Kuznetsov, "Universitet glubokogo zalozheniya," in *Istoriya metro Moskvy* (Moscow: Izdatel'stvo "Istoriya fabrik i zavodov," 1935), I, 431.

44. TsGAODM, f. 4, op. 4, d. 2, ll. 193–194.

45. *Khrushchev Remembers*, p. 79.

46. TsGAODM, f. 3, op. 24, d. 1, l. 28, and Gel'bras, "Uroki Gorzemplana," p. 2. N. P. Udalov, acting head of the department until its dissolution in early 1932, was also removed from Moscow planning work.

47. *Vechernyaya Moskva*, July 11, 1935, p. 1.

48. *Izvestiya*, August 7, 1931, p. 3; essays by Krasin and Gornyi, interspersed with editorial comments, in *Sovetskaya arkhitektura*, no. 4 (July–August 1931), pp. 13–23; Gel'bras, "Uroki Gorzemplana," p. 3.

49. Descriptions of the seven designs are in P. and B. Gol'denberg, "Zadachi sotsialisticheskoi rekonstruktsii Moskvy," *Sovetskaya arkhitektura*, no. 1 (January 1933), pp. 6–25, and V. Semenov, "Arkhitekturnaya rekonstruktsiya Moskvy," in *Voprosy arkhitektury* (Moscow: OGIZ, 1935), pp. 119–158.

50. Bulganin in *Vechernyaya Moskva*, July 11, 1935, p. 1.

51. S. Boldyrev, P. Gol'denberg, and V. Dolganov, "Moskva: Voprosy pereplanirovki," *Sovetskaya arkhitektura*, no. 4 (July–August 1931), pp. 32–37; *Izvestiya*, February 26, 1933, p. 4. Semenov identified himself, S. A. Boldyrev, A. M. Levitin,

K. V. Orlova, and P. V. Pomozanov as authors of the kernel of the document of July 1935.

52. I heard the story about Stalin and Semenov in interviews. A good biography of Perchik is in *Rabochaya Moskva*, March 14, 1935, p. 1, and a sketchier one of Bulushev in *Izvestiya*, June 12, 1956, p. 4. Archive materials show Bulushev as Kaganovich's assistant from early 1931 to 1935; he was also head of the gorkom's Secret Department from February 1932 to September 1933, and then secretary of Arkhplan, the party/soviet commission on architecture and planning. Perchik was a raion party secretary in Moscow until he was purged in 1937. Chernyshev was chief architect of Moscow's planning division until 1941 and died a natural death in 1963.

53. Quotations here from Kaganovich in *Pravda*, July 30, 1934, p. 3, and Selivanov, "Velikii Stalin," p. 7.

54. Officials told visiting British experts about Gosplan's intervention. E. D. Simon et al., *Moscow in the Making* (London: Longmans, Green, 1937), p. 45. In July 1934, when he first gave details of the plan, Kaganovich spoke of a time frame of fifteen to twenty years. All citations from the plan are from *O general'nom plane rekonstruktsii gor. Moskvy* (Moscow: [n.p.], 1935).

55. Kaganovich's inspiration reported by Khrushchev in 1935, who said the drive let Kaganovich focus "the ebullience of his Bolshevik energy" on the problem. Kaganovich came out for expansion to the southwest at the Arkhplan meeting of February 21, 1935, but defined its extent rather more broadly than in the final version. TsGAODM, f. 4, op. 5, d. 71, l. 12; f. 3, op. 49, d. 79, l. 3.

56. Kaganovich to Arkhplan July 20, 1935, ibid., f. 3, op. 49, d. 79, l. 15.

57. *Izvestiya*, July 14, 1935, p. 2.

58. L. Kaganovich, "O vnutripartiinoi rabote i otdelakh rukovodyashchikh partiinykh organov," *Partiinoye stroitel'stvo*, no. 22 (November 1934), p. 12; O. B. Nebogin and M. D. Slanskaya, "'Nel'zya ostavit' v ryadakh partii,'" *Voprosy istorii KPSS*, no. 5 (May 1989), p. 100.

59. V. Markovich, "Derevnya poluchila moguchii otryad bol'shevikov," *Partiinoye stroitel'stvo*, nos. 13–14 (July 1933), p. 63.

60. Kaganovich later said without qualification that he "promoted" Khrushchev (Chuyev, *Tak govoril Kaganovich*, p. 31). Khrushchev recollected (*Khrushchev Remembers*, p. 34), "I was widely regarded as someone who had been very close to Kaganovich, and it's true, I had been." Of Alliluyeva, who committed suicide in 1932, Khrushchev calls her (p. 44) his "lucky lottery ticket" and says that she "helped determine Stalin's attitude toward me."

61. These are the twenty-one, with N in brackets standing for service with Kaganovich in Nizhnii Novgorod, V for Voronezh, T for Turkestan, CC for Central Committee apparatus, and U for Ukraine: N. V. Andreas'yan (CC), A. I. Bulushev (CC), N. Ye. Donenko (CC, U), N. A. Filatov (CC), G. N. Kaminskii (CC), V. M. Klement'ev (T, U), Ye. S. Kogan (T), D. S. Korotchenko (U), S. Z. Korytnyi (U), N. V. Margolin (U), B. V. Margulis (U), I. P. Nosov (N, V), L. M. Perchik (U, CC), Ya. Kh. Peters (T), K. V. Ryndin (CC), K. F. Starostin (N, U), S. N. Tarasov (U), Ya. Ya. Tsirul' (CC), A. A. Volkov (T, U), S. B. Zadionchenko (U), and

I. G. Zhuravlev (T). Donenko, obkom secretary for transport in 1932–1933, had arguably held the most strategic posts, having been Kaganovich's assistant for party cadres in the Secretariat in 1923–1924 and head of personnel of the Ukrainian party in 1928–1929 (see *Rabochaya Moskva,* June 8, 1933, p. 2).

62. *XVII s"ezd Vsesoyuznoi kommunisticheskoi partii (b): Stenograficheskii otchet* (Moscow: Partizdat, 1934), p. 102.

63. Papernyi, *Kul'tura "Dva",* p. 88; Katerina Clark, *The Soviet Novel: History as Ritual* (Chicago: University of Chicago Press, 1981), p. 46; Richard Stites, *Russian Popular Culture: Entertainment and Society since 1900* (Cambridge: Cambridge University Press, 1992), pp. 91–92.

64. N. Sobolevskii, *Skul'pturnyye pamyatniki i monumenty v Moskve* (Moscow: Moskovskii rabochii, 1947), p. 19.

65. For instance, D. S. Korotchenko (his name Russified to Korotchenkov at the time) had been a department head in the Baumanskii raikom and chairman of the raion soviet in 1931, when Khrushchev was raikom secretary; he made it to second secretary of the obkom in 1936–1937. S. B. Zadionchenko, another Baumanskii official (head of organization of the raikom, then deputy chairman of the soviet), received major promotions in 1937 and later. S. Z. Korytnyi, who had worked in close proximity to Khrushchev in Kiev and was head of the personnel section of the Krasnopresnenskii raikom when Khrushchev was secretary, became obkom secretary for ideological questions in 1936.

66. There is by now a massive scholarly and memoir literature on the terror. The best starting points are Robert Conquest, *The Great Terror: Stalin's Purge of the Thirties* (London: Macmillan, 1968), and J. Arch Getty and Roberta T. Manning, eds., *Stalinist Terror: New Perspectives* (Cambridge: Cambridge University Press, 1993).

67. Several Russian sources (cited in Alec Nove, "Victims of Stalinism: How Many?" in Getty and Manning, *Stalinist Terror,* p. 270) give the number of Soviets executed in 1937–1938 after trials for political offenses as 681,692; this excludes persons who were shot without a hearing or who died under interrogation or in confinement. On the assumption that the numbers killed in any area would have been in proportion to the area's share of total Communist Party membership, approximately 90,000 in Moscow city and oblast would have been shot in the two years. Other revelations suggest such an estimate would be low. A journalist given access to some NKVD files reports that at some point in 1937 executions in Moscow began to exceed 300 a day, which would have produced roughly 200,000 deaths over two years. Another investigator, citing KGB sources, claims they averaged 900 a day in 1937–1938, yielding a not credible total of 600,000, about one-sixth of Moscow's total population. Yet another analyst found that the daily lists of persons arrested and shot ranged from about 100 to 400 names. Finally, the head of the special NKVD troika for Moscow oblast for the first half of 1938, Mikhail Semenov, testified when arrested in 1939 that his group dealt with "up to 500 cases" per day, "sentencing several people each minute to the death penalty and various terms of imprisonment." See *Komsomol'skaya pravda,* October 28, 1990, p. 2; *Vechernyaya Moskva,* April

14, 1990, p. 3; *Moskovskaya pravda,* November 19, 1991, p. 2; Irina Osipova, "Five Cases," in *Resistance in the Gulag: Memoirs, Letters, Documents* (Moscow: Vozvrashchenie, 1992), p. 64.

68. Quote about the Dmitrov massacre from *Moskovskaya pravda,* November 19, 1991, p. 2, and story about Berg from *Komsomol'skaya pravda,* October 28, 1990, p. 2. The estimates about Butovo and Kommunarka are from police data summarized in *Moskovskaya pravda,* July 8, 1993, p. 1. Most other details are from interviews with A. A. Mil'chakov in *Vechernyaya Moskva,* April 14, 1990, pp. 1, 3; May 12, 1990, p. 3; July 12, 1990, p. 3; October 20, 1990, p. 4. Mil'chakov, the son of a prominent victim of the terror, first brought the mass grave sites to public attention in a television interview in late 1988.

69. KGB spokesman A. Oligov in *Moskovskaya pravda,* October 26, 1989, p. 2. Referring to detentions by the list, Khrushchev reported to Stalin July 10, 1937, early on in the purge, that 41,305 "criminal and kulak elements" had been arrested in Moscow oblast, including Moscow city. He relegated 14,369 of them to the "first category" of enemies, deserving the death penalty; it is unclear how many were actually executed. A Yezhov directive of June 30, 1937, ordered that 35,000 more residents of Moscow oblast be arrested and 5,000 shot; family members of the executed were to be exiled from the oblast. A memorandum by Stalin to Yezhov and others dated January 31, 1938, enlarged the first category by 4,000 persons in Moscow oblast. Nataliya Gevorkyan, "Vstrechnyye plany po unichtozheniyu sobstvennogo naroda," *Moskovskiye novosti,* no. 25 (June 21, 1992), pp. 18–19; Yevgeniya Al'bats, *Mina zamedlennogo deistviya (Politicheskii portret KGB SSSR)* (Moscow: Russlit, 1992), document after p. 314.

70. On Kryukov, see T. Shul'gina, "Pervyi rektor Vsesoyuznoi akademii arkhitektury," *Arkhitektura SSSR,* no. 3 (May–June 1990), pp. 105–107.

71. On the Dzerzhinskii raikom, see the account in *Moskovskaya pravda,* October 15, 1989, p. 3. For rare cases of raikom secretaries arrested but reinstated in other positions, see the skeletal obituaries of M. P. Sigal and N. V. Andreas'yan in ibid., April 8, 1959, p. 4, and November 14, 1973, p. 4.

72. Khrushchev's most vitriolic remarks are in TsGAODM, f. 4, op. 8, d. 1, ll. 4–21, 59–76; the quotation about the "smudge" is at p. 61. Bulganin's statement is in d. 2, l. 83, and Sergeyeva's in d. 3, ll. 144–150. Korytnyi's fate was probably sealed by the fact that he was married to the sister of Iona Yakir, one of the Red Army leaders shot by Stalin in June 1937.

73. Quote from N. M. Dedikov, second secretary of the obkom, in November 1938 (TsGAODM, f. 3, op. 24, d. 150, l. 19). One Khrushchev aide, I. P. Aleksakhin, spent seventeen years in the camps (see *Moskovskaya pravda,* December 4, 1990, p. 4). N. Ya. Osipov, who worked in Ukraine in the 1920s and was Khrushchev's assistant from 1932 to 1936, disappeared in 1937, as did V. Ya. Simochkin, who worked in his office a shorter time. I learned of Rykova's experience from my interview with her.

74. A. Ugarov, "Vybory partorganov v Moskovskoi organizatsii," *Partiinoye stroitel'stvo,* no. 9 (May 1, 1938), pp. 15–19.

75. Some ex-Muscovites were to prosper with Khrushchev in Ukraine, most, like him, originally brought from there to Moscow by Kaganovich. As early as March 1937, the Moscow second secretary (Margolin) took over the Dnepropetrovsk obkom. His Moscow successor (Korotchenko) was briefly obkom boss in Smolensk, but Korotchenko replaced Margolin in Dnepropetrovsk by the end of 1937 and became Ukrainian premier once Khrushchev arrived. A vice-chairman of the Mossovet (K. S. Karavayev) became chairman of the Dnepropetrovsk oblast soviet in 1938 (he was later a deputy premier of Ukraine), by which time Zadionchenko of Moscow was first secretary there. Within several weeks of Bulganin's appointment as head of the RSFSR government, one Muscovite (Zadionchenko) had become deputy premier and another (I. N. Kuznetsov, from the OGPU and Metrostroi) head of his chancery. A promotee who seemed especially reliant on Malenkov was F. F. Kuznetsov, the first secretary of the Proletarskii raikom who rose in 1938 to head the cadres section of the army's political directorate. P. I. Seleznev, Malenkov's subordinate in the Moscow obkom and CC department, was designated first secretary of the Krasnodar regional committee in 1939. All told, thirteen Moscow officials were named provincial first secretaries in 1937–1938.

76. Yemel'yanov's biography, which does not identify the raikom, is in *Moskovskaya pravda*, December 5, 1962, p. 4. Zverev's big break is described in his memoir, "O nekotorykh storonakh istorii sovetskoi finansovoi sistemy," *Voprosy istorii*, no. 2 (February 1969), pp. 139–140. In February 1948, when Malenkov was engaged in a factional struggle with other leaders, Zverev was demoted to deputy minister, but he was reinstated in December 1948, after Malenkov's recovery. As for the two first secretaries, Protopopov's earlier service in the secret police may have facilitated his promotion, and Volkov in the late 1920s worked in Nizhnii Novgorod under Zhdanov, by 1937 a CC secretary and Malenkov's main rival. Volkov was purged in 1938, but Protopopov lasted in Tajikistan until 1946. Volkov followed a long line of Muscovites in Belorussia. The first secretary from 1932 to 1937, N. F. Gikalo, had been a Moscow obkom and gorkom secretary before 1932. Two Moscow veterans, V. G. Knorin and A. I. Krinitskii, headed the organization in the 1920s. The leader in 1930–1932, K. V. Gei, served as a Moscow secretary for the next two years.

77. Transcript in TsGAODM, f. 3, op. 24, d. 150; quotation from Khrushchev at l. 13.

78. Yefremov statement in ibid., ll. 48–50. He was confirmed as chairman of the Mossovet on November 3. Sidorov was transferred to a position in the Siberian city of Tomsk before being arrested.

79. A. N. Krapivin's obituary (*Pravda*, January 10, 1947, p. 4) stated that he had worked since Shcherbakov's death as "assistant to a secretary of the CC." Zhdanov, who signed the obituary first, must have been the secretary. Shcherbakov's feud with Khrushchev is described by his son Aleksei in ibid., March 12, 1991, p. 4. Aleksei also refutes the charge made in Khrushchev's memoirs that his father was an alcoholic.

80. In the tape recordings on which his memoirs were based, Khrushchev states

flatly that Malenkov "promoted" Popov. Popov's own account says that as party screener of the NKVD he reported directly to Malenkov, and that the decision to send him to the gorkom was made by Malenkov. G. M. Popov, "Vospominaniya" (unpub. ms., TsGAODM, n.d. but apparently 1966), pp. 30–31. Popov denigrates both Zhdanov and Shcherbakov in his memoir, stating at one point (p. 70) that Shcherbakov was a coward during the Moscow panic of October 1941.

81. Popov, "Vospominaniya," pp. 36, 43–46.

82. *XVIII s"ezd Vsesoyuznoi Kommunisticheskii partii (b): Stenograficheskii otchet* (Moscow: Gospolitizdat, 1939), p. 70.

83. *Boevoi otryad srazhayushcheisya partii: Moskovskaya partiinaya organizatsiya v gody Velikoi Otechestvennoi voiny* (Moscow: Moskovskii rabochii, 1985), p. 393.

84. I. Parfenov, "Bol'sheviki stolitsy v bor'be za sotsialisticheskuyu rekonstruktsiyu Moskvy," *Partiinaya zhizn'*, no. 16 (August 1947), p. 29, and *Moskovskii bol'shevik*, February 2, 1949, p. 6. I have found biographies of twelve Muscovites transferred to a wide range of positions outside the RSFSR between June 1941 and March 1953. Most important were the obkom secretaries, A. N. Isachenko and A. S. Yakovlev, who were made secretaries of the Lithuanian and Kazakhstan central committees.

85. *Moskovskii bol'shevik*, February 3, 1949, p. 2.

86. Robert Conquest, in *Power and Policy in the U.S.S.R.: The Struggle for Stalin's Succession, 1945–1960* (London: Macmillan, 1961), p. 100, described the affair as an assault on "some rather less close associates of Zhdanov's, through his ally Shcherbakov . . . in the Moscow party machine." The interpretation is similar in Werner G. Hahn, *Postwar Soviet Politics: The Fall of Zhdanov and the Defeat of Moderation, 1946–53* (Ithaca, N.Y.: Cornell University Press, 1982), p. 40.

87. A. Ya. Sekachev, who had been in the aircraft industry and was first secretary of Leningradskii raion, one rich in aviation facilities, was made obkom secretary for cadres in June 1948 (and for machine building, administrative organs, and transport that autumn). The gorkom secretary for machine building and municipal matters from June 1945 onward, N. P. Firyubin, had a similar background. The obkom second secretary after Chernousov was S. A. Zholnin, former director of a defense plant and the gorkom's personnel secretary. O. V. Kozlova, a Moscow raikom secretary, was made obkom propaganda secretary in July 1946, replacing a protégé of Shcherbakov who took over one of his lesser posts, head of the Soviet Information Bureau. Some removed by Popov experienced precipitate demotion. M. I. Malakhov, responsible for cadres decisions in the obkom, was made Gosplan representative in Moscow oblast in 1948. V. K. Pavlyukov, the gorkom secretary for food supply in wartime and briefly second secretary under Popov, vanished after being appointed USSR deputy minister of trade. A death notice in 1956 (*Moskovskaya pravda*, November 14, p. 4) said his last post was the humble one of repair chief of Moscow's bakeries.

88. Chernousov had a personal rapport with Stalin, having caught his attention before his elevation to the obkom in 1939 (author's interview in 1991 with

K. F. Kalashnikov, former secretary of the gorkom and obkom). At least one Muscovite, G. N. Kotel'nikov, first secretary of the Baumanskii raikom, followed Chernousov into the CC department as head of a sector (*Moskovskaya pravda*, July 30, 1950, p. 4). Andrianov worked for the Moscow gorkom from 1932 to 1934 and was a student at Moscow University from 1934 to 1937. The minutes of the city party secretariat show him being confirmed as an instructor for the transport sector in March 1932. He rose rapidly during the purge and in 1938 was appointed first secretary of the Sverdlovsk obkom. Malenkov's son describes him as close to Beria by the late 1940s. Andrei Malenkov, *O moyem ottse Georgii Malenkove* (Moscow: Tekhnoekos, 1992), p. 58.

89. Vasilii said ten years later that he found Popov's behavior at the Moscow party conference in February 1949 "disgraceful" and that after it he "told Comrade Stalin about many sides of Popov." *Iosif Stalin v ob"yatiyakh sem'i: Iz lichnogo arkhiva* (Moscow: Rodina, 1993), p. 132.

90. L. A. Openkin, *Ottepel': Kak eto bylo* (Moscow: Znaniye, 1991), pp. 17–26; *Khrushchev Remembers*, pp. 262–265. According to Vasilii Stalin, Malenkov was reluctant to push for Popov's dismissal but was reproached by Stalin, who said, "How can it be that you are right next to him, in the same city, and yet cannot see what is going on?" *Iosif Stalin v ob"yatiyakh sem'i*, p. 132.

91. Quotations from the transcripts of the plenum of December 13–16 and of the closed meeting of Moscow party activists on December 28–29, 1949, in TsGAODM, f. 3, op. 117, d. 6, l. 12; f. 4, op. 60, d. 174, ll. 2, 5–6. The extreme charges, which the plenum resolution branded "unfounded and slanderous," were that Popov was "politically unreliable," that he chased "proven cadres" out of Moscow positions, and that he implanted "his own people" (ibid., f. 4, op. 60, d. 174, l. 7).

92. Popov, "Vospominaniya," p. 118.

93. TsGAODM, f. 3, op. 117, d. 156, ll. 111–112; d. 6, ll. 21–22.

94. Ibid., f. 4, op. 60, d. 174, ll. 12, 107–113.

95. Ibid., f. 3, op. 117, d. 6, l. 6.

96. Ibid., l. 167.

97. Chernousov, Malenkov's man in the RSFSR Council of Ministers, was removed in August 1953, presumably at Khrushchev's behest, and thereafter held only inferior jobs (his obituary is in *Moskovskaya pravda*, January 3, 1978, p. 3). The wartime chairman of the Moscow ispolkom, V. P. Pronin (who, as head of the gorkom's personnel department in 1938, worked hand in glove with Malenkov), was dropped from the position of minister of labor reserves in the spring of 1953. His obituary in 1993 mentions him holding only one other, minor position—deputy head of a construction ministry—before retirement.

98. Popov ("Vospominaniya," pp. 141–143) said he was sent to the plant, in Kuibyshev, after "political intrigues" by Beria and Malenkov. Khrushchev's version (*Khrushchev Remembers*, p. 249) is that he and Malenkov got Popov out of harm's way. Selivanov was reinstated as deputy chairman of the city executive in 1954 and served on the gorkom from 1958 until his retirement in 1970. I know of the fates of seven of the eight secretaries besides Popov. Sekachev of the obkom, like Zholnin,

became a factory director. Firyubin's fellow gorkom secretary, I. M. Kolotyrkin, became a deputy head of the city ispolkom. Kozlova, the obkom propaganda secretary, became an academic, and Danilov, her counterpart in the gorkom, was made deputy head of state radio and later deputy minister of culture. This leaves unaccounted for only N. F. Solov'ev, the obkom third secretary, whose main task was rural electrification; he had already been fired by the time of the December 1949 plenum.

99. At the city party conference in April 1951, the 874 delegates approved the usual slate of 85 candidates for 85 seats on the gorkom. But 37 of the candidates had at least 1 negative vote cast against them. One delegate voted against Khrushchev. The largest numbers of negatives (11 and 39) were against Furtseva and Yasnov, two officials conspicuously promoted by Khrushchev. The press, needless to say, did not mention these votes. TsGAODM, f. 4, op. 71, d. 2, ll. 408–409. If Khrushchev's interest in replacing Alekseyev by Oleinik, a farming specialist from Kiev oblast, is clear, the transfer of Rumyantsev to economic management in September 1952 is less so. He was almost identical in background (aviation industry, first secretary in Leningradskii raion) to Popov's deputy for cadres and then machine building, Sekachev, whom Khrushchev sacked in January 1950. But Khrushchev's son-in-law states that his fall "was unrelated to Khrushchev's attitude toward him" and "was decided somewhere higher up." Adzhubei, *Te desyat' let,* p. 29.

100. Simon et al., *Moscow in the Making,* p. 13.

101. The presidium in August 1932 denominated a five-person "small presidium" under Bulganin's senior deputy; the last meeting recorded in the city archive was in January 1933. An "implementation commission" *(komissiya ispolneniya)* of the presidium also did some work in its name, subject to subsequent confirmation, from July 1931 to March 1934.

102. TsGAODM, f. 4, op. 3, d. 4, l. 50. Two former employees of the soviet told me of Bulganin's dress code, which was ahead of official fashion by only a few years.

103. *Rabochaya Moskva,* March 27, 1937, p. 1; *Izvestiya,* March 28, 1937, p. 4; *Vechernyaya Moskva,* March 27, 1937, p. 2.

104. Quotations from *Izvestiya,* March 8, 1937, p. 2, and *Pravda,* March 8, 1937, p. 2.

105. Kogan, a career party propagandist and a survivor of the ideological wars of the 1920s, divorced Kuibyshev in 1930 or 1931. She was demoted from gorkom secretary for propaganda to deputy chairman of the soviet in 1936, one year after his death. She was sent to a camp in Central Asia in mid-1937 and died there shortly thereafter.

106. The conference's members consisted of the chairman of the ispolkom and his deputies. Some unofficial documents refer to it as the "narrow" *(suzhennyi)* ispolkom.

107. N. M. Aleshchenko, *Moskovskii Sovet v 1941–1945 gg.* (Moscow: Nauka, 1980), p. 23. The full ispolkom met nineteen times in 1942 and only about a dozen times in 1943 and 1944 combined.

108. TsGAODM, f. 3, op. 117, d. 6, l. 169. Protocols in the city archive (TsGIAGM, f. 150, op. 1) show the ispolkom meeting seven times in 1946 and ten

times in 1947, whereas its bureau met thirty times in 1946 and thirty-two times in 1947.

109. G. S. Gorin, chief of the city waterworks, in TsGAODM, f. 4, op. 71, d. 2, l. 167. Ispolkom and bureau sessions occurred with equal frequency in the early 1950s: the ispolkom met twenty-three times in 1950 and the bureau twenty-two times.

110. Yasnov did not have a college-level education, although he studied part-time in construction institutes. He had worked for the city since 1930 (as a deputy chairman of the executive committee, 1938–1949) and was best known for directing the digging of fortifications around Moscow in 1941. The purged Sidorov had been head of a city department (for land allocation) but was ill-educated and was in rural administration until 1934. Popov, who had a higher education, and Pronin, who did not, came to the chairman's office from party work.

111. *Rabochaya Moskva,* February 25, 1931, p. 1. Of twenty-five raions in 1950, only three (Krasnopresnenskii, Moskvoretskii, and Sokol'nicheskii) had localized names. Twelve commemorated individual leaders and revolutionaries, one a Russian scientist, six political organizations or events, one the railroads, and two other Soviet cities.

112. *Pravda,* July 30, 1934, p. 3. Deputies' groups were first formed in Moscow in 1926.

113. *Rabochaya Moskva,* July 14, 1934, p. 2, and July 28, 1934, p. 2.

114. *Izvestiya,* July 21, 1951, p. 2. The twelve chairmen of city commissions included four party officials, four heads of raion ispolkoms, a school principal, and directors of the Moscow subway, an aviation plant, and a medical institute.

115. See Bychkov, *Zhitiye Petra Baranovskogo,* p. 76, and *Izvestiya,* June 9, 1937, p. 4. Molotov reported that Stalin personally "saved" St. Basil's from unnamed supporters of demolition (*Sto sorok besed s Molotovym,* p. 267).

116. *Pravda,* July 22, 1937, p. 4; *Arkhitekturnyye voprosy rekonstruktsii Moskvy (Materialy VIII plenuma pravleniya Soyuza sovetskikh arkhitektorov SSSR, 8–12 iyulya 1940 goda)* (Moscow: Akademiya arkhitektury SSSR, 1940), p. 47.

117. There were 112 building cooperatives in Moscow before the change. Membership is unknown, but 70,000 members were waiting for housing. The co-ops sponsored 19 of the 478 houses under construction and still managed 1.8 million square meters of built housing, about 11 percent of the city total. *Rabochaya Moskva,* April 1, 1937, p. 3, and May 12, 1937, p. 2; "Moskva na stroike," *Stroitel'stvo Moskvy,* no. 10 (May 1937), p. 32; *Pravda,* October 23, 1937, p. 6.

118. This group, founded in 1933 on the initiative of the former chairman of the Mossovet, P. G. Smidovich, with the approval of the gorkom bureau, was known as the Moscow Society of Friends of Greenery until 1945. It had 30,000 members after the war and was often criticized for inactivity.

119. A large delegation led by Bulganin visited western European capitals in autumn 1936. I have found no record of another tour until one to Stockholm in 1947.

120. A 1774 map of Moscow guberniya was still in the special map depository of the Lenin Library in 1989. Yurii Golubchikov, "Vremya otkryvat' prostranstvo," *Ogonek,* no. 26 (June 1989), pp. 25–26.

121. Selivanov, "Velikii Stalin," p. 9, puts 86.6 percent of all dwellings and 97.5 percent of floor space in Moscow housing in the "socialist sector." Forty percent was given as central agencies' share in numerous postwar sources. According to *Moskovskaya pravda*, November 23, 1952, p. 2, there were "quite a few" cooperatives in Moscow, most of them putting up small buildings; the examples given were for professional artists and athletes.

122. ZIS figures from TsGAODM, f. 4, op. 8, d. 1, l. 114, and estimated from incomplete data in *Istoriya Moskovskogo avtozavoda imeni I. A. Likhacheva* (Moscow: Mysl', 1966), pp. 434–435.

123. TsGAODM, f. 4, op. 2, d. 2, l. 97. On Moscow and Gosplan, see "Oral Memoirs of Nikita S. Khrushchev" (Oral History Collection, Columbia University), pt. 2, pp. 152–153.

124. TsGAODM, f. 4, op. 3, d. 7, l. 107.

125. Ibid., op. 2, d. 10, l. 141.

126. The story of the chemical warfare institute was broken by Lev Fedorov and Vil Mirzayanov in *Nezavisimaya gazeta*, October 30, 1992, p. 1. The Kuz'minki test range is described in Vladimir Voronov, "Kuz'minki . . . zarinki . . . zomanki," *Stolitsa*, no. 8 (February 1993), pp. 1–3. Research on biological weapons was also done, but details are still secret.

127. Ya. D. Zager, "O 'perekhodyashchem' stroitel'stve," *Stroitel'stvo Moskvy*, no. 8 (April 1938), p. 10; *Pravda*, December 17, 1935, p. 2; *Moskovskii bol'shevik*, June 15, 1939, p. 2 (source of quotation); *Moskovskaya pravda*, June 9, 1950, p. 3, and November 4, 1950, p. 2; A. Zaslavskii, "Plan gigantskikh rabot," *Arkhitektura i stroitel'stvo Moskvy*, no. 5 (May 1953), p. 4. In Moscow oblast outside the city, central agencies were carrying out 98 percent of housing construction in 1948. The secret police had a distinctive method of augmenting its housing fund. According to Al'bats, *Mina zamedlennogo deistviya*, p. 92, an agreement in 1950 specified that it received the flats of all Muscovites arrested on political charges.

128. Total members and candidates in Moscow were 242,000 in January 1933, 158,000 in 1937, 229,000 in 1941, 61,000 in 1942, 227,000 in 1946, and 408,000 in 1953.

129. Source: minutes in party archive.

130. *Pravda*, February 28, 1931, p. 2.

131. *Khrushchev Remembers*, p. 69; TsGAODM, f. 4, op. 9, d. 1, l. 31.

132. Information for (March) 1931 and (November) 1948 taken from TsGAODM, f. 4, op. 1, d. 37, ll. 26–30; f. 3, op. 38, d. 14, l. 284; d. 23, ll. 41–50. Other archive protocols show obkom and gorkom positions to have been cut in November 1933 from 403 to 287, leaving 106 responsible and 86 support positions for the obkom, 78 and 17 for the gorkom. Responsible jobs in the gorkom apparatus numbered 93 in January 1939 and 148 that May. The gorkom bureau in April 1934 approved 249 responsible and 120 support positions for the 10 raions.

133. "Opyt differentsirovannogo rukovodstva raionami," *Partiinoye stroitel'stvo*, nos. 15–16 (August 1931), p. 48.

134. The personnel officers' role was diluted before then. Popov observed that in Moscow they "limit their activity in a number of cases to the selection of party

cadres" (*Pravda*, March 28, 1948, p. 2). The explanation may lie in a respect for specialized competence resulting from the industrial backgrounds of many cadres officials. Of the eight personnel secretaries of the Moscow obkom and gorkom between 1939 and 1948, five had engineers' diplomas; six had extensive experience in industry (three of them in defense plants) and one in rail transport.

135. Two new economic departments were created in June 1949, one of them an Aviation Industry Department. The Department of Propaganda and Agitation was broken down in 1952 into four departments.

136. Source: memorandum prepared for the author from archive minutes by A. S. Novikov of the Central State Archive of Social Movements of Moscow (for 1932 and 1950); a partial listing in TsGAODM, f. 4, op. 3, d. 33, l. 94 (for 1933, omitting posts within the party and Komsomol organs, which probably ran to more than 1,000); Z. Sibiryachka, "Pod znakom ukrepleniya organizatsionno-partiinoi raboty," *Partiinoye stroitel'stvo*, no. 10 (May 1935), p. 21 (for 1935); *Moskovskii bol'shevik*, March 18, 1940, p. 2 (for 1939). Of the 30,155 positions confirmed by the raikoms in 1950, 2,024 were subject to repeat confirmation by the gorkom.

137. In 1952 and the first quarter of 1953, 158 Jews were fired in the city's pharmacies directorate, 67 in the city and raion procuracies, and 13 in senior medical positions. Ye. V. Taranov, "Pervaya dama Moskvy," pt. 1, *Kentavr*, nos. 11–12 (November–December 1992), p. 71. For cases of directors of important factories (Kauchuk, the Borets [Fighter] Works, and the Trailer Works) being removed by raikoms, see "Samokritika i vnutripartiinaya demokratiya," *Partiinoye stroitel'stvo*, nos. 11–12 (June 1930), p. 27, and *Moskovskii bol'shevik*, March 30, 1941, p. 2, and May 15, 1941, p. 3.

138. *IV Moskovskaya oblastnaya i III gorodskaya konferentsii VKP(b), 16–24 yanvarya 1934 g: Stenograficheskii otchet* (Moscow: Moskovskii rabochii, 1934), pp. 48, 416; hereafter *Konferentsii*. Like incidents are described in Nobuo Shimotomai, *Moscow under Stalinist Rule, 1931–34* (London: Macmillan, 1991), which also contains much general information about Moscow government at the time.

139. M. Zelikson, "Rabota sekretarya gorkoma po promyshlennosti," *Partiinoye stroitel'stvo*, no. 8 (April 1942), pp. 23–24.

140. M. Zelikson, "Iz opyta raboty promyshlennogo otdela," ibid., no. 7 (April 1941), p. 23; *Moskovskaya pravda*, August 26, 1950, p. 2.

141. TsGAODM, f. 3, op. 117, d. 6, ll. 7–8. Zelikson was dismissed before the December 1949 plenum, his career ruined. He worked afterward in a Moscow factory and an economic exhibition. Zelikson was of Jewish background, and it is possible that the anti-Semitism of the late Stalin years affected his fate. His obituary is in *Moskovskaya pravda*, December 24, 1977, p. 4.

142. Ye. T. Abakumov, "Kto stroil metro," in *Istoriya metro Moskvy* (Moscow: Izzdatel'stvo "Istoriya fabrik i zavodov," 1935), II, 5; *Rabochaya Moskva*, March 5, 1935, p. 2.

143. TsGAODM, f. 3, op. 117, d. 6, l. 163. There were several references to Popov as khozyain at the plenum. Popov, remember, was also a national leader, like most of his predecessors since Zelenskii. As one speaker observed (p. 203), Popov

"has not been an ordinary secretary, he has also been a secretary of the Central Committee and has great authority."

144. Ibid., f. 4, op. 60, d. 174, ll. 62–63. Bulganin, the chairman of the Mossovet, was a member of the last city party secretariat to be publicly elected (in February 1931). After that time, the secretariat consisted of party secretaries only.

145. *Konferentsii,* p. 561.

146. I could find no summary figures on municipal officials covered by nomenklatura. One of the five branch departments formed in the Moscow obkom in 1934 was the "soviet-trade" section, while five of the thirteen groups of instructors in the gorkom dealt to some degree with municipal issues (those for construction and building materials, communal services and housing, the food industry and public dining, state and cooperative trade, and the soviet apparatus). A Department of Construction and City Services was established under the gorkom in December 1939, and it persisted through various renamings and reorganizations. See Table B-5 for a summary of changes over the years.

147. TsGAODM, f. 3, op. 24, d. 150, l. 107.

148. For example, the gorkom secretariat instructed the party fraction in the presidium of the soviet to have 500,000 rubles transferred to the OGPU for renovation of its new quarters at Staraya ploshchad' in 1933. The funds were to be "found in the city's own budget in the process of implementation," that is, without adopting a formal budget line. In November 1939 the secretariat decided to wall over the gap between two of its buildings, adopting a motion "to assign the party group of the Moscow Soviet . . . to organize the construction and conclude it no later than May 1, 1940." TsGAODM, f. 4, op. 3, d. 33, l. 83; op. 11, d. 137, l. 3. Examples of small interventions taken from *Sbornik vazhneishikh postanovlenii,* pp. 14, 307; *Rabochaya Moskva,* May 10, 1933, p. 3; *Pravda,* December 8, 1937, p. 6; TsGAODM, f. 4, op. 3, d. 34, l. 66; op. 11, d. 6a, ll. 7–8.

149. TsGAODM, f. 4, op. 5, d. 33, l. 218.

150. *Sbornik vazhneishikh postanovlenii,* pp. 60–61.

151. *Khrushchev Remembers,* p. 62; Popov, "Vospominaniya," p. 137.

152. Volynskoye, settled by a Muscovite prince in the fourteenth century, had a string of aristocratic owners until it was bought in the late 1800s by the Knopps, a merchant family. The dacha, southwest of the present intersection of prospekt Marshala Grechko and Minskaya ulitsa, survives but is hidden from view. Members of the Stalin family continued to use the Zubalovo dacha ("Far Dacha") at Usovo, about twice as far out the same radius from the Kremlin. Stalin had two other dachas in the Moscow area, Lipki and Semenovskoye, but visited them rarely.

153. I heard the story of the arrested woman from her nephew, a Moscow playwright. Wartime use of the subway station is described in S. M. Shtemenko, *General'nyi shtab v gody voiny* (Moscow: Voyenizdat, 1968), pp. 34–35. Stalin moved his military office in 1943 to the former villa of the Soldatenkovs at 37 ulitsa Kirova, which later held the reception hall of the Ministry of Defense.

154. Albert Speer, *Inside the Third Reich,* trans. Richard and Clara Winston (New York: Avon Books, 1971), p. 215. Speer's plan for a "New Berlin" was adopted

in 1937, two years after the Moscow master plan and the year the Germans celebrated Berlin's 700th anniversary. Reminiscent of Moscow, old buildings were torn down in large numbers, "destroying Berlin's historical substance at the very moment when one pretended to celebrate it." Gerhard Weiss, quoted by Gordon A. Craig in *New York Review of Books,* vol. 38 (November 7, 1991), p. 34.

155. The Dolgorukii piece was not completed until 1954. Popov ("Vospominaniya," pp. 217–218) claims responsibility for moving the Pushkin statue, but I have heard the story about Stalin doing it from knowledgeable architects.

156. Stalin's role in the first three projects has been openly written of, and Popov (ibid., pp. 111, 213–215) gives some details. I learned about the fourth almost entirely from interviews. The Arbatsko-Pokrovskaya line of the regular subway linked the Kremlin area to Kiev Station by 1937, crossing the river on a bridge built for that purpose. The secret project involved a parallel and wholly underground line. Stations for public use were evidently built into at least the first part of the duplicate line, because the section to Kiev Station was opened—without explanation—one month after Stalin's death, at which time the original spur to Kiev Station was mysteriously mothballed. The Khrushchev leadership eventually completed the "Fili line" to Kuntsevo, but mostly in a cheap, cut-and-fill and surface form. The 1937 line to Kiev Station was reopened in the late 1950s. An amateur subway buff, Vladimir Gonik, has reported ("V kruge vtorom," *Moskovskiye novosti,* no. 31 [August 2, 1992], p. 24) that he once spoke with an old man who claimed to have helped design an underground tunnel to Kuntsevo for regular, two-way automobile traffic. Gonik concluded that there was insufficient evidence to validate this or any version of the story.

157. Quotations and most examples from *Moskovskii bol'shevik,* December 22, 1939, p. 3; *Pravda,* November 25, 1936, p. 3, and December 19, 1939, p. 4; Selivanov, "Velikii Stalin," p. 13.

158. *Khrushchev Remembers,* p. 63.

159. Ibid., p. 63; *Konferentsii,* p. 158.

160. *Pravda,* May 20, 1935, p. 3.

161. The Red Army Theater was finished to specifications in 1940. The Palace of Science was begun in 1939 but dropped in the early 1950s; the State Picture Gallery now occupies the site. The unfinished Aleksandr Nevskii Cathedral, a warehouse and children's clubhouse since the Civil War, was demolished in 1940–1941, but Radio House, according to press accounts, was still being built in 1950; construction stopped several years later. Izmailovo got a smaller stadium, and the central stadium for the USSR was built at Luzhniki in the 1950s.

162. *Khrushchev Remembers: The Last Testament,* trans. Strobe Talbott (Boston: Little, Brown, 1974), p. 98. See also Tarkhanov and Kavtaradze, *Architecture of the Stalin Era,* pp. 141–142.

163. Disagreements over the university project are described by Dmitrii Semenov in *Moskovskaya pravda,* May 18, October 12, and October 26, 1991, and in Popov, "Vospominaniya," p. 214.

164. A Soviet diplomat resident in Moscow in the late 1930s heard some covert

grumbling about the palace but observed that anyone who tried to raise the issue overtly "would have been regarded as a fool, or, worse still, a counterrevolutionary." Alexander Barmine, *One Who Survived* (New York: Putnam's Sons, 1945), p. 216. Mariya A. Svanidze, a member of Stalin's extended family, wrote in her diary in 1936 that the tearing down of housing near the construction site was "embittering a whole mass of the people" against the government. She also condemned the uprooting of trees in downtown Moscow and the construction of "villas and mansions" for the nomenklatura. *Iosif Stalin v ob"yatiyakh sem'i,* p. 188.

165. N. S. Atarov, *Dvorets Sovetov* (Moscow: Moskovskii rabochii, 1940), p. 15. This book is the source for many of the technical details in the preceding paragraph.

166. Chronology pieced together from scattered press references and interviews. Some interesting details are in the letter by I. Yu. Eigel' in *Arkhitektura i stroitel'stvo Moskvy,* no. 1 (January 1989), p. 27, and in Eigel's book, *Boris Iofan* (Moscow: Stroiizdat, 1978), pp. 108–117. See also Nikolai Malinin, "Moskva iz-pod stola," *Stolitsa,* no. 2 (January 1991), p. 45, and Lidiya Pol'skaya, "Dvorets vo imya . . . ," *Literaturnaya gazeta,* no. 35 (August 29, 1990), p. 13. V. M. Mikhailov, the chief of construction, reported in *Pravda,* March 28, 1936, p. 6, that soil studies conducted by Academician B. Ye. Vedeneyev had "confirmed that the site selected is entirely favorable," but he also outlined the plan for bitumen injections.

167. A. N. Komarovskii, *Zapiski stroitelya* (Moscow: Voyenizdat, 1972), p. 166; Popov, "Vospominaniya," p. 211.

168. The census of February 1939 put "prisoners of camps, prisons, and colonies" under NKVD central at 16,551 and under the NKVD directorate for Moscow oblast at 91,080, out of a USSR total of 3,742,914. "Research Materials: 1939 Census Documents," *Journal of Soviet Nationalities,* vol. 1 (Winter 1990–1991), pp. 165–167.

169. Aleksandr I. Solzhenitsyn, *The Gulag Archipelago, 1918–1956,* trans. Thomas P. Whitney and Harry Willetts (New York: Harper and Row, 1973–1978), II, 287. Bogdanov was on the obkom bureau from February 1949 to September 1952. On MVD responsibility for roads, water, and sewage, see *Moskovskii bol'shevik,* April 3, 1949, pp. 2–3.

170. Quotation from Lev Kolodnyi in *Moskovskaya pravda,* December 3, 1989, p. 4. The police took charge of the palace in October 1937, when A. N. Prokof'ev, an NKVD boss, replaced the executed V. M. Mikhailov as chief of the directorate. Prokof'ev, who combined this with several other posts, was not punished when the palace foundered. He was named deputy head of a construction ministry in 1949 and died a few months later (*Pravda,* October 21, 1949, p. 4). Komarovskii's directorate was assigned 326,000 square meters of housing construction in the 1951–1955 economic plan and was also in charge of the Zaryad'e high rise.

171. *Rabochaya Moskva,* May 9, 1937, p. 3.

172. *Arkhitekturnyye voprosy rekonstruktsii Moskvy,* p. 7; M. A. Yasnov, "O razvitii gorodskogo khozyaistva v 1950 godu," *Gorodskoye khozyaistvo Moskvy,* no. 6 (June 1950), pp. 2–3; P. B. Abramov, "Voprosy razmeshcheniya stroitel'stva i inzhenernoi podgotovki zastraivayemykh territorii," ibid., no. 7 (July 1954), p. 7.

173. Examples taken from protocols in the archives of the city party committee and soviet.

174. The elite houses on ulitsa Gor'kogo (since renamed Tverskaya ulitsa) have addresses 4, 6, 8, 9, 15, 17, 19, 25, and 27. There was some specialization of clientele. Politicians were overrepresented in house 6, where Georgii Popov lived. House 25 was mainly for dancers and directors from the Bol'shoi Theater, and No. 27 mainly for writers and police officials. 1 Sadovaya-Sukharevskaya, 5 Sadovaya-Samotech-naya, 3 Bol'shaya Sadovaya, and 14–16 and 28–30 Sadovaya-Kudrinskaya were built, I have been told, expressly for the police establishment. A large house was opened in 1938 on Glinishchevskii pereulok (later ulitsa Nemirovicha-Danchenko), just off of ulitsa Gor'kogo, for the actors of the Moscow Art Theater, and several homes for composers were finished on ulitsa Nezhdanovoi in the mid-1950s.

175. On the Malenkov residence (now the Cuban embassy) and rumors that a dungeon was found in the basement of Beria's house (now the Tunisian embassy), see Mikhail Voslenskii, *Nomenklatura: Gospodstvuyushchii klass Sovetskogo Soyuza,* 2d ed. (London: Overseas Publications Interchange, 1990), pp. 356–357. On Vasilii Stalin's house, which had a billiard room, film-viewing room, and pantry full of luxury foods, see the reminiscences of his former driver, A. Brot, in *Argumenty i fakty,* no. 14 (April 1991), pp. 6–7. The "Kremlin schools" were No. 110, on Merzlya-kovskii pereulok, No. 20, at 6 Vspol'nyi pereulok, and Model School No. 25, near city hall. The principal of No. 25, which Vasilii and Svetlana Stalin attended in the 1930s, was elected to the USSR Supreme Soviet in 1937.

176. The story of the Borodino grave is recounted in *Izvestiya,* September 24, 1991, p. 9. I learned about the Jewish cemetery from interviews.

177. The schools, which offered foreign languages, have since been renumbered 711 and 1232. School 56, behind house 22, was an ordinary city school.

178. In the third quarter of 1931, 47.8 percent of all consumer durables were reserved for the closed distributors (TsGAODM, f. 4, op. 1, d. 5, l. 16). Flour quotas for September 1934 are in ibid., op. 4, d. 6, ll. 157–160: 44,544 tons for individal consumption, including 528 in two "special" categories (mostly for nine closed distributors and NKVD and military units); 9,007 tons for public dining, with 392 tons here to special users, 20.4 to the "Dining Hall of the Central Aktiv," presumably in the Kremlin; and 1,063 tons for consumer co-ops, miscellaneous uses, and reserves. General analysis of rationing privileges is in Ye. A. Osokina, *Iyerarkhiya potrebleniya: O zhizni lyudei v usloviyakh stalinskogo snabzheniya, 1928–1935 gg.* (Moscow: Izdatel'stvo MGU, 1993), chap. 3.

179. Alexander Werth, *Russia at War, 1941–1945* (London: Dutton, 1964), p. 350.

180. *Istoriya Moskovskogo avtozavoda,* p. 273.

181. I have been able to calculate completion rates for 1938 (51.3 percent) and 1940 (52.9 percent) but not for 1939.

182. Last point from A. M. Zaslavskii, "Voprosy gorodskogo transporta Moskvy," *Gorodskoye khozyaistvo Moskvy,* no. 7 (July 1947), p. 7. For general discussion of loopholes in the passport system, see Sheila Fitzpatrick, *Stalin's Peas-*

ants: Resistance and Survival in the Russian Village after Collectivization (New York: Oxford University Press, 1994), chap. 3.

183. TsGAODM, f. 3, op. 49, d. 79, ll. 17–18; op. 50, d. 42, l. 118.

184. *Pravda,* June 9, 1937, p. 4; TsGAODM, f. 3, op. 50, d. 42, l. 94. Until such statistics became classified in the late 1930s, factories pointed to increases in their work force with pride. The rebuilding of ZIS between 1934 and 1937 employed 11,000 construction workers and more than doubled its payroll.

185. Andrei Sakharov was "delighted" when, as a promising young physicist in 1948, he was assigned a single room in Kitaigorod with his wife and daughter. It was so tiny they had to eat off the windowsill. Andrei Sakharov, *Memoirs,* trans. Richard Lourie (New York: Knopf, 1990), p. 95.

186. Andrew Smith, *I Was a Soviet Worker* (New York: Dutton, 1936), pp. 47–48.

187. TsGAODM, f. 3, op. 50, d. 42, l. 95; *Rabochaya Moskva,* May 28, 1937, p. 2; G. V. Bezrukov, "Nasushchnyye zadachi rekonstruktsii raiona," *Stroitel'stvo Moskvy,* no. 10 (May 1940), p. 2; Simon et al., *Moscow in the Making,* p. 155.

188. "Moskva na mesyats," *Stroitel'stvo Moskvy,* nos. 2–3 (February–March 1933), p. 37; Arnosht Kol'man, *My ne dolzhny byli tak zhit'* (New York: Chalidze Publications, 1982), pp. 164–165; Kozlov, "Chernyye gody moskovskikh obitelei," p. 11; TsGAODM, f. 4, op. 4, d. 6, l. 18.

189. *Pervyi podshipnikovyi: Istoriya pervogo gosudarstvennogo podshipnikovogo zavoda, 1932–1972* (Moscow: Mysl', 1973), p. 180; *Istoriya Moskovskogo avtozavoda,* p. 435; *Moskovskii bol'shevik,* July 16, 1948, p. 2; V. Ye. Poletaycv, *Rabochiye Moskvy na zavershayushchem etape stroitel'stva sotsializma, 1945–1958 gg.* (Moscow: Nauka, 1967), p. 256. In remarks to a closed conference in February 1949, First Secretary Popov said that 300,000 Muscovites lived in baraki (TsGAODM, f. 3, op. 117, d. 156, l. 367). A fictional portrayal of postwar Moscow describes the destitute students "who practically lived on the streets," sleeping with friends and in railroad stations. Yuri Trifonov, *Another Life and The House on the Embankment,* trans. Michael Glenny (New York: Simon and Schuster, 1986), p. 248.

190. *Moskovskii bol'shevik,* June 15, 1939, p. 2; emphasis added.

191. Defense plants tended to build better housing than others, but when they were growing the fastest they sometimes had to begin with barracks. The standardized houses being put up at Works No. 22 in Fili in 1938 gave residents 2.5 square meters of space each. TsGAODM, f. 4, op. 9, d. 3, l. 75

192. There was also maldistribution between the sexes. Despite the drafting of women into heavy industry during the war, they were still overrepresented in the light, food, and chemical industries, which had the least to expend on amenities. The unmarried were most affected, as married women could queue for housing through their husbands' employers.

193. Statistics for 1948 from N. M. Aleshchenko, *Moskovskii Sovet v 1945–1961 gg.* (Moscow: Nauka, 1988), p. 41, which states that 45 percent of the housing stock was plugged in to both running water and sewage. Standard handbooks put the sewage figure at 73.3 percent in 1940. The discrepancy may reflect a deterioration

of connections to sewage mains during the war. The chief of Moscow's water and sewage directorate stated in 1951 that "almost nothing" had been done to expand the network since the late 1930s. TsGAODM, f. 4, op. 71, d. 2, l. 165.

194. ZIS data from *Istoriya Moskovskogo avtozavoda*, pp. 272–273. In 1934 the city presidium authorized renovation of the surgical wing of the Blagusha Hospital by Works No. 24, Moscow's main aircraft engine plant. The building was to be "earmarked for the workers of Works No. 24," and the city health department was obliged to supply it with equipment and personnel. TsGIAGM, f. 150, op. 1, d. 366, l. 5.

195. Quotation from Barmine, *One Who Survived*, p. 269.

196. Interviews and personal observations.

197. From its 1933 maximum of 146 raions, Moscow oblast lost 26 raions to a new oblast centered in Kalinin (formerly Tver) in 1935, and 38 and 39 raions to the newly founded Ryazan and Tula oblasts in 1937. Other adjustments followed: 8 raions gained from Tula and Ryazan oblasts in 1942, and 11 ceded to Kaluga, Vladimir, and Ryazan oblasts in decrees in 1944 and 1946.

198. This assistance was not negligible. In 1947 Moscow's Kirovskii raion donated 21,300 man-days of labor to electrify villages in Kommunisticheskii raion of the oblast, while Krasnopresnenskii raion sent machine tools, building materials, and library books to Zaraiskii raion. *Moskovskii bol'shevik*, May 7, 1948, p. 2, and May 28, 1948, p. 2.

199. TsGAODM, f. 4, op. 9, d. 2, ll. 22–23; f. 3, op. 24, d. 150, l. 35.

200. Excerpt from *Rabochaya Moskva*, May 20, 1935, p. 2. Compare to later references in ibid., August 14, 1938, p. 4, and *Moskovskaya pravda*, June 30, 1950, p. 3.

201. *Rabochaya Moskva*, March 29, 1933, p. 2; *Vechernyaya Moskva*, July 9, 1934, p. 1; TsGIAGM, f. 150, op. 1, d. 159, l. 624.

202. *Moskovskii bol'shevik*, May 8, 1940, p. 4; A. I. Kuznetsov, "Arkhitekturnyye problemy planirovki prigorodnoi zony," *Stroitel'stvo Moskvy*, nos. 21–22 (November 1940), pp. 3–7.

203. A memoir of the Bolshevo institute is G. A. Ozerov, *Tupolevskaya sharaga* (Frankfurt: Posev, 1973).

204. On suburban defense works and laboratories, see esp. *A Summary of Soviet Guided Missile Intelligence*, US/UK GM 4–52, July 20, 1953, Secret, Declassified February 28, 1975; and Central Intelligence Agency, Office of Scientific Intelligence, *Scientific Research Institute and Experimental Factory 88 for Guided Missile Development, Moskva/Kaliningrad*, OSI-C-RA/60–2, March 4, 1960, Declassified April 30, 1979. According to *Rossiiskiye vesti*, February 20, 1993, p. 6, Works No. 456, the future Energomash concern, was founded in 1929.

205. *Moskovskaya pravda*, August 13, 1992, p. 3.

206. V. I. Vasil'ev and G. I. Makeyenko, "Prigorodnaya zelenaya zona Moskvy," *Gorodskoye khozyaistvo Moskvy*, no. 5 (May 1952), p. 20, which gives a summary figure for forests only.

207. The argument about this change was first made in Nicholas S. Timasheff, *The Great Retreat* (New York: Dutton, 1946).

208. Romanyuk, *Moskva: Utraty,* provides a valuable if incomplete inventory of Moscow churches demolished between 1917 and 1991. Of the 116 churches lost, 84 were torn down between 1930 and 1936. Only 14 churches were demolished before 1930, 7 of them in 1928. Seven were razed between 1936 and the war and only 2 between the war and Stalin's death. No monastery demolitions were undertaken after 1937.

209. Bychkov, *Zhitiye Petra Baranovskogo,* pp. 100–102, 149.

210. Yastrebov, "Pokusheniye na Krasnuyu ploshchad'," p. 12.

211. I have in my possession a handwritten copy of Popov's memorandum, given to me in 1992 by a Russian scholar with access to materials of the Central Committee Secretariat. No one I have questioned knows any more about the affair. It was not mentioned in Popov's memoirs. I have been told that the red granite was taken by the Soviet Army from a train confidently sent by Hitler to the Moscow front in 1941, containing materials for a gigantic memorial to German victory to be built at Moscow. Perhaps with the aim of acclimatizing the public to changes in the Kremlin, a biography of Catherine the Great's court architect depicted his unrealized plan for a Versailles-like palace in the Kremlin as expressing "a grandiose image of a new, enlightened Russia, in which social justice would prevail." A. I. Mikhailov, *Bazhenov* (Moscow: Gosudarstvennoye izdatel'stvo literatury po stroitel'stvu i arkhitekture, 1951), p. 108.

212. TsGAODM, f. 3, op. 117, d. 11, ll. 3–4; Popov, "Vospominaniya," p. 213.

213. *Pravda,* October 12, 1952, p. 4.

214. TsGAODM, f. 3, op. 117, d. 6, l. 36.

215. "Oral Memoirs of Khrushchev," pt. 2, pp. 167–169.

5. The Limits of De-Stalinization

1. Three other members of the "expanded Presidium" selected at the Nineteenth Party Congress in October 1952 (V. M. Andrianov, D. S. Korotchenko, and N. A. Mikhailov) had Moscow connections in their past, as did one candidate member (N. G. Zverev). All were dropped when a much smaller Presidium was appointed March 6, 1953. Korotchenko's clientelist ties were with Khrushchev, and the others' just as clearly with Malenkov.

2. Khrushchev and Bulganin occupied adjacent suites on the fifth floor of 3 ulitsa Granovskogo after 1949. "Even during the silent times, when mutual suspicion was everywhere, they dropped in on one another and, unseen by outsiders, drank a glass of tea or a tumbler of Georgian cognac." Sergei Khrushchev, *Pensioner soyuznogo znacheniya* (Moscow: Novosti, 1991), p. 16. As concerns Malenkov, who lived on the fourth floor, Khrushchev himself stated: "I had been friends with Malenkov since the days when I worked in the Moscow organization before the war. We often spent our days off together. We had dachas near each other in the country. Therefore, even though Malenkov showed a certain amount of condescension toward me during the war, especially when Stalin displayed his dissatisfaction with me, Malenkov and I never had a falling out." *Khrushchev Remembers,* trans. Strobe Talbott (Boston: Little, Brown, 1970), pp. 313–314.

3. Malenkov's son remembers Mikhailov as a supporter of his father (Andrei Malenkov, *O moyem ottse Georgii Malenkove* [Moscow: Tekhnoekos, 1992], p. 58). Mikhailov, a Moscow native, had been a Central Committee secretary since October 1952, and would have been stronger if he had retained this post along with the Moscow job to which he was appointed March 7, 1953. On March 14, however, he lost the position. The best study of the succession (Robert Conquest, *Power and Policy in the U.S.S.R.: The Struggle for Stalin's Succession, 1945–1960* [London: Macmillan, 1961], p. 202) exaggerates when it says Khrushchev "lost Moscow" then.

4. See Amy Knight, *Beria: Stalin's First Lieutenant* (Princeton: Princeton University Press, 1993), chaps. 9–10.

5. "Delo Beria: Plenum TsK KPSS, Iyul' 1953 goda," *Izvestiya TsK KPSS,* no. 2 (February 1991), pp. 159–160.

6. Ibid., p. 160.

7. It is not clear when Lunev took over the directorate, but a recently declassified document (in *Moskovskaya pravda,* July 17, 1992, p. 2) has him signing as chief on July 23, 1953. After police service, Stepakov and Nikiforov both returned to local party work, Nikiforov as first secretary in Dzerzhinskii raion, where the KGB was headquartered. Nikiforov was a deputy chairman of the city ispolkom from 1959 to 1963. Another ex-first secretary of the Stalinskii raikom, A. G. Yakovlev, was in "leading work" in the MVD in 1957–1960 (ibid., June 1, 1968, p. 4). Dudorov made his way back to Moscow government in 1960, serving for some years as chief of Glavmospromstroimaterialov, its agency for making building materials.

8. Erik Kotlyar in ibid., September 11, 1991, p. 7.

9. See the explanatory note in Table C-5, Appendix C. Besides incumbent Moscow officials and persons (like Bulganin or Korotchenko) with that experience some time before, several had post-1950 Moscow experience but current positions elsewhere: four on the full Central Committee, or 3.0 percent of its membership (Dudorov, Grishin, Vladimir Kucherenko, and Mikhailov); and three, or 2.5 percent, of the candidate members (Nikolai Firyubin, Lunev, and Vladimir Mylarshchikov).

10. Kapitonov graduated from the Moscow Institute of Communal Construction Engineers in 1938 and joined Moscow administration in 1941. He was municipal chairman of Krasnopresnenskii raion in 1947–1948, head of the Planning, Finances, and Trade Department of the gorkom in 1948–1949, and head of its Department of City Services from October 1949 to January 1951.

11. Quotation from Ye. V. Taranov, "Pervaya dama Moskvy," pt. 1, *Kentavr,* nos. 11–12 (November–December 1992), p. 67. Furtseva finished the Lomonosov Institute of Precise Chemical Technology in 1942, after a stint as party secretary there. She was appointed a secretary of the Frunzenskii raikom in 1942 (she was much feared in Moscow State University and the many research institutes in the raion) and gorkom second secretary in January 1950. She married Firyubin in 1952 or 1953, in a second union for both. Firyubin, after two years of municipal work, transferred to the diplomatic service in 1953 and served as a USSR deputy foreign minister from 1957 to 1983; he was selected a candidate member of the Central Committee in 1956.

12. In early 1954, for example, Furtseva read the riot act to members of the Union

of Artists who refused to accept the gorkom's candidates for leadership of the Moscow local (ibid., pp. 73–74). N. G. Yegorychev, then a raikom secretary and later Moscow first secretary, agreed in 1990 with the statement that the questions raised then by the most liberal Moscow Communists were "almost the same" as under Gorbachev, including "the issues of a multiparty system, of how to elect deputies, of privileges, etc." After the Twentieth Congress, it was further observed, these questions came up in meetings of party cells in Moscow but "did not make their way into the press." "Beseda s Yegorychevym N. G.," in *Neizvestnaya Rossiya, XX vek* (Moscow: Istoricheskoye naslediye, 1992), pp. 297–298.

13. Some details are in Ye. V. Taranov, "Pervaya dama Moskvy," pt. 2, *Kentavr*, no. 1 (January–February 1993), p. 106.

14. Vladimir Bessonov, "Sovetskii sotsialisticheskii Panteon," *Moskovskii zhurnal*, no. 2 (February 1991), p. 13.

15. *Pravda*, July 4, 1954, p. 2.

16. Sergei Khrushchev, *Pensioner soyuznogo znacheniya*, p. 49, inaccurately says that Malenkov commissioned the villas after March 1953. Excavation of the bunkers beneath them was a factor in the decision to locate the Moscow State University campus well behind the brow of the Lenin Hills in 1947 or 1948. In February 1952 the bureau of the Moscow obkom, chaired by Khrushchev, instructed a commission to suggest where to locate an unspecified number of villas by 1955 (TsGAODM, f. 3, op. 146, d. 36, l. 141). On Mrs. Khrushchev and the decision about the Kremlin, see Larisa Vasil'eva, *Kremlevskiye zheny* (Moscow: Novosti, 1992), p. 421.

17. There is an irony here, because as architecture the exhibition was "the last argument of the Stalinist style, prolonging its triumph beyond its chronological limits." Alexei Tarkhanov and Sergei Kavtaradze, *Architecture of the Stalin Era* (New York: Rizzoli, 1992), p. 160.

18. I. Yu. Eigel', *Boris Iofan* (Moscow: Stroiizdat, 1978), pp. 117–119; *Pravda*, August 25, 1956, p. 1.

19. *Pravda*, February 7, 1957, p. 1; V. Bykov and Yu. Khripunov, "K itogam obshchestvennogo obsuzhdeniya konkursnykh proyektov Dvortsa Sovetov," *Arkhitektura SSSR*, no. 8 (August 1958), pp. 9–13.

20. On the institutional framework, consult David T. Cattell, *Leningrad: A Case Study of Soviet Urban Government* (New York: Praeger, 1968); Ronald J. Hill, "The Development of Soviet Local Government since Stalin's Death," in Everett M. Jacobs, ed., *Soviet Local Politics and Government* (London: George Allen and Unwin, 1983), pp. 18–33; Jeffrey W. Hahn, *Soviet Grassroots: Citizen Participation in Local Soviet Government* (Princeton: Princeton University Press, 1988), chap. 3; Blair A. Ruble, *Leningrad: Shaping a Soviet City* (Berkeley: University of California Press, 1990), esp. appendix A; and Jerry F. Hough and Merle Fainsod, *How the Soviet Union Is Governed* (Cambridge, Mass.: Harvard University Press, 1979), chap. 13, which discusses government and party bodies together.

21. *Khrushchev Remembers: The Last Testament*, trans. Strobe Talbott (Boston: Little, Brown, 1974), p. 100–101.

22. Solzhenitsyn relates the case of one Mamulov, the warden of the Khovrino

camp, in *The Gulag Archipelago, 1918–1956,* trans. Thomas P. Whitney and Harry Willetts, (New York: Harper and Row, 1973–1978), II, 549–550. Four identifiable Gulag subunits are listed in "O perestroike stroitel'nykh organizatsii v Moskve," *Gorodskoye khozyaistvo Moskvy,* no. 6 (June 1954), p. 2, as having gone over to Glavmosstroi: the Construction Directorate of Moscow State University (originally of the Palace of Soviets), the Chief Directorate for Construction of Tall Buildings, and Osobstroi (builder of the Ministry of Foreign Affairs tower) and Stroitel', both trusts specializing in industrial construction.

23. *Pravda,* December 28, 1954, p. 3.

24. Interview with Promyslov in *Vechernyaya Moskva,* July 16, 1992, p. 5, and author's interviews.

25. The advantage of reinforced concrete was not so much cost as the speed with which its production and use could be expanded, since this did not depend on skilled laborers. Most brickworks in the area dated from before 1917 and required setting of the clay and straw by hand. Several used the cruel traditional technique for moving bricks over the baking fire—rotation by a blinded horse.

26. N. Ya. Kovalev, "Plan razmeshcheniya zhilishchnogo stroitel'stva v Moskve v shestom pyatiletii," *Gorodskoye khozyaistvo Moskvy,* no. 7 (July 1957), pp. 2–3.

27. Kenneth T. Jackson, *Crabgrass Frontier: The Suburbanization of the United States* (New York: Oxford University Press, 1985).

28. The photos follow p. 42 of *Devyatyi kvartal: Opytno-pokazatel'noye stroitel'stvo zhilogo kvartala v Moskve (raion Novyye Cheremushki)* (Moscow: Gosstroiizdat, 1959). The project, a short walk from the Akademicheskaya subway stop, has by now visually merged with its surroundings.

29. Demichev, secretary of Sovetskii raikom from 1947 to 1950 and then an official of the gorkom, was made Khrushchev's assistant in the obkom in 1952, moving with him into the Central Committee apparatus in 1953. From 1956 to 1958 he was ideology secretary of the Moscow obkom. Chernyayev was a gorkom secretary in 1950–1952; his whereabouts until 1962 are unknown. Shuiskii's official biography placed him in the CC apparatus as of 1950, but the local press identified him as Khrushchev's aide in the Moscow obkom.

30. This is by no means an exhaustive list of the Muscovites who landed in these agencies. In the State Committee on Labor, for example, I. V. Goroshkin, a former secretary of the Moscow gorkom, was first deputy chairman from 1955 to 1959 and then deputy chairman until he retired in 1977. S. S. Novozhilov, a colleague of Volkov from Moscow oblast, supplanted him as first deputy in 1959. Another former gorkom secretary, V. I. Prokhorov, was named to the second-ranking position in the union bureaucracy in 1955, and remained there for thirty years.

31. For example, when four "ideological departments" sprouted in 1963 (for the agricultural and industrial sectors in the RSFSR and the other republics), both RSFSR units were entrusted to Moscow men: that for agriculture to Stepakov, head of an antecedent CC department since 1961; and that for industry to M. I. Khaldeyev, first secretary of the Timiryazevskii raikom. Two ex-raikom first secretaries, Ye. M. Chekharin and V. A. D'yakov, led CC/RSFSR departments for science and administrative

organs in 1962–1963. D. A. Polikarpov, a former gorkom secretary, had been head of the CC's Culture Department since 1955; his title but not his function varied in 1963–1964.

32. Some details in Taranov, "Pervaya dama Moskvy," pt. 2, pp. 107–109. I owe others to interviews with Moscow cultural figures. Furtseva's daughter Svetlana was married to Kozlov's son, and when they separated there was a fight for custody of their daughter.

33. Author's interview with N. G. Yegorychev, January 1990.

34. TsGAODM, f. 4, op. 107, d. 12, l. 12, and d. 31, ll. 89–90.

35. Author's interview with Burlatskii, December 1992.

36. The decision was unannounced. I ascertained its exact date and wording ("To subordinate the Moscow City Committee of the CPSU directly to the Central Committee") from the archive in 1991.

37. The gorkom and obkom continued to have their offices and a joint chancery at 6 Staraya ploshchad'. But the only obkom or gorkom secretary besides Demichev to move to the other committee after 1956 was Anatolii Biryukov, who in 1959 left the gorkom (where he was head of the Construction Department) to be obkom secretary for construction. Returning to the gorkom in 1960 as construction secretary, he spent 1964 to 1971 in the CC apparatus and RSFSR government, then finished his career as a deputy chairman of the Moscow municipal executive.

38. Kapitonov pushed through the removal of Grishin in January 1956 before the Presidium settled on a new job for him. The first offer was of a lowly posting as a counsellor in the diplomatic corps. Grishin won the union appointment only in March 1956, after a tearful appeal to Khrushchev. He was reelected to the Central Committee in February, a sign it had been decided to retain him in a high post.

39. Quotations from the obkom plenum of April 2, 1959, taken from TsGAODM, f. 3, op. 184, d. 14, l. 1. The sketchy official condemnation is in *Partinaya zhizn'*, no. 8 (April 1959), pp. 10–11.

40. Yegorychev was adamant in his interview with me that, besides criticizing the artists, he "transmitted pressure from below and helped pacify the situation."

41. No district or street was ever renamed in honor of Stalin. In 1966, however, a subway stop in north Moscow was named after Aleksandr Shcherbakov (Khrushchev had excised his name from it in 1962), and in 1970 Khoroshevskii raion was renamed Voroshilovskii raion, for K. Ye. Voroshilov, a member of the Stalin Politburo.

42. "Napravlen poslom," *Ogonek*, no. 6 (February 1989), p. 28.

43. "Beseda s Yegorychevym N. G.," p. 302.

44. "Napravlen poslom," p. 29. Khrushchev's son-in-law wrote that Brezhnev obtained an advance text of the speech and thus had ample time to rehearse a response. Aleksei Adzhubei, *Te desyat' let* (Moscow: Sovetskaya Rossiya, 1989), p. 297.

45. Yegorychev was Komsomol secretary in the Bauman College in 1947–1949, when Shelepin was second secretary of the USSR Komsomol. N. A. Kuznetsov, a Komsomol veteran who was Yegorychev's second secretary, was appointed RSFSR

minister of culture in 1965; he was retired at the age of only fifty-two in 1974, a year before Shelepin's exit from the Politburo. The new second secretary, V. Ya. Pavlov, had been second secretary of the Moscow Komsomol in 1952–1956; he remained in the Moscow gorkom until reduced to ambassador to Hungary in 1971. The extent of Yegorychev's agreement with Shelepin remains unclear. The standard Western version has been that he advocated domestic neo-Stalinism and a more forward policy abroad. I read him as having more nuanced views. In the interview with me, he stated that he had not been close to Shelepin and would have preferred Kosygin as general secretary should Brezhnev have been forced out. Fedor Burlatskii among other insiders has described Yegorychev as considerably more reformist than he has been depicted.

46. "Napravlen poslom," p. 29.

47. Quotations from TsGAODM, f. 4, op. 144, d. 8, ll. 5–13.

48. See on these points Krasnaya zvezda, September 9, 1992, p. 4, and the interview with Grishin in Nezavisimaya gazeta, February 19, 1991, p. 5. On early dealings with Kosygin, Yu. P. Izyumov, a former assistant of Grishin, reports that as head of the unions he "came out so sharply against the government's suggestion to raise [consumer] prices that for several years his relations with Kosygin were cut off. Then they were again harmonized, on the basis of mutual respect." Moskovskaya pravda, October 10, 1992, p. 3.

49. Pravda, October 5, 1984, p. 1.

50. There are many other examples of this phenomenon. L. V. Petrov, head of gorkom personnel when Yegorychev fell, was made chairman of the city's trade unions and stayed until 1986. P. A. Voronina, Yegorychev's deputy in the Baumanskii raikom and earlier a Komsomol worker, survived equally long in party and municipal work. Muscovites with Komsomol connections found berths in agencies such as Novosti news, the State Committee on Vocational and Technical Education, the State Committee for Television and Radio, the USSR Union of Writers, and Mosfil'm (where N. T. Sizov was director into the 1980s). There were exceptions to Grishin's tendency not to hire cronies. L. D. Novozhilov, his personal assistant, had been the same in the Moscow obkom and then in the unions. A. I. Yashin, who worked early in his career in Serpukhov and later with Grishin in the obkom, returned to Moscow as first deputy mayor for construction in 1973.

51. See Izyumov in Moskovskaya pravda, October 10, 1992, p. 3. Grishin "sharply criticized" Promyslov, he writes, and "more than once" recommended his replacement. "But Brezhnev, [Foreign Minister] Gromyko, and other influential members of the Politburo stood up for him. Promyslov was extremely useful to them: he swiftly and accurately resolved all questions (about apartments, garages, dachas, and so on) for their numerous relatives and protégés."

52. Statistics from encyclopedia and press sources. Observation on entertainment by Richard Stites, Russian Popular Culture: Entertainment and Society since 1900 (Cambridge: Cambridge University Press, 1992), p. 163.

53. Georgii Arbatov, "Iz nedavnego proshlogo," pt. 1, Znamya, no. 9 (September 1990), p. 214 (March conference); V. V. Grishin, Izbrannyye rechi i stat'i (Moscow: Politizdat, 1979), pp. 119–137 (Lenin jubilee); Sovetskaya Rossiya, scattered articles from February to October 1968 (theater campaign); Politicheskii dnevnik, 1964–1970

(Amsterdam: Alexander Herzen Foundation, 1972), p. 391 (art exhibit). The theater crackdown broadened from criticism of the director Anatolii Efros's rendering of Chekhov's *Three Sisters*. Both principals were rewarded. S. S. Gruzinov, first secretary of Krasnopresnenskii raikom, was appointed ambassador to Algeria, and B. V. Pokarzhevskii, of Sverdlovskii raion, was made chief of the city cultural bureaucracy in 1968 and secretary of the ispolkom in 1975. The two raikoms created sections for keeping up with cultural affairs in November 1968.

54. Mikhail Shcherbachenko, "Stroitel'nyye dramy i komedii na Taganke," *Arkhitektura i stroitel'stvo Moskvy*, no. 10 (October 1989), p. 7; Izyumov in *Moskovskaya pravda*, October 10, 1992, p. 3.

55. Yevgeniya Al'bats, *Mina zamedlennogo deistviya (Politicheskii portret KGB SSSR)* (Moscow: Russlit, 1992), p. 278; Ludmilla Alexeyeva, *Soviet Dissent: Contemporary Movements for National, Religious, and Human Rights* (Middletown, Conn.: Wesleyan University Press, 1985), p. 345.

56. Georgii Arbatov, "Iz nedavnego proshlogo," pt. 2, *Znamya*, no. 10 (October 1990), p. 201.

57. Demichev knew many arts figures through his wife and daughter, both opera singers. Three of his four vice-ministers as of 1980 (Ye. M. Chekharin, G. A. Ivanov, and T. V. Golubtsova) were ideological specialists out of the Moscow organization.

58. The crony, Yashin, was appointed minister of building materials in 1979. The third individual was A. K. Mel'nichenko, a deputy chairman of the Moscow ispolkom who became minister of the medical industry in 1975. Two other Muscovite ministers are excluded from Tables C-3 and C-4—Demichev and Lomonosov, who was made chairman of the State Committee on Labor in 1975—because they had been out of Moscow positions for more than five years.

59. Four of the five joined the department before Kapitonov: Petrovichev, deputy heads B. N. Moralev and A. G. Skvortsov, and sector chief V. M. Serushkin. A. T. Kosarev, first secretary of the Kirovskii raikom of Moscow, came in as head of a sector (responsible for Moscow and the surrounding oblasts) in 1966.

60. By way of comparison, from 1960 to 1985 five officials out of the Moscow obkom were made first secretary of another region, for which some competence in agriculture was expected—Yu. N. Balandin (Kostroma), N. F. Ignatov (Orel), A. A. Kandrenkov (Kaluga), P. A. Leonov (Sakhalin and Kalinin), and Ye. I. Sizenko (Bryansk)—but not one from the gorkom. Four Muscovites became second secretaries of non-Russian republics, for which general political skills were more pertinent— L. I. Grekov and V. G. Lomonosov (Uzbekistan), B. V. Nikol'skii (Georgia), and V. N. Rykov (Turkmenistan).

61. A good illustration is the Council of Ministers of the RSFSR. From 1937 to 1957, five Muscovites chaired it: Bulganin (1937–1938), Khokhlov (1940–1941), K. D. Pamfilov (acting, 1942–1943), Chernousov (1949–1952), and Yasnov (1956– 1957). None served after Yasnov. Three were first deputy chairman—Pronin (1944– 1946), A. M. Safronov (1949–1957), and Yasnov (1957–1966)—but, again, none after Yasnov. Eight Moscow officials served as deputy chairman between 1937 and 1960, only three after that.

62. A Grishin aide said later (*Moskovskaya pravda*, October 10, 1992, p. 3) that

one of Brezhnev's assistants inserted the passage at the last moment, and that "it is possible that not even he [Brezhnev] was warned about it."

63. Ibid., March 22, 1975, p. 2.

64. Ibid., May 21, 1981, p. 2; emphasis added.

65. Ya. Ye. Dikhter, "Severnoye Chertanovo—raion kommunisticheskogo byta," *Gorodskoye khozyaistvo Moskvy,* no. 2 (February 1973), p. 10.

66. The first design contest for the monument was organized in 1957. Poklonnaya Hill was selected as the site, and a ninety-eight-hectare Victory Park laid out on it, in 1961.

67. *Moskovskaya pravda,* May 8, 1979, p. 2; outlays given in TsGAODM, f. 4, op. 188, d. 4, ll. 36–39.

68. Georgii Yelin, "Olimpiiskii god," *Ogonek,* no. 52 (December 1990), p. 30, and Anatolii Prokopenko in *Vechernyaya Moskva,* February 23, 1994, p. 2.

69. O. B. Bozhkov and V. B. Golofast, "Otsenka naseleniyem uslovii zhizni v krupnykh gorodakh," *Sotsiologicheskiye issledovaniya,* no. 3 (July–September 1985), pp. 95–101. There is corroborating evidence from emigrants: Brian D. Silver, "Political Beliefs of the Soviet Citizen: Sources of Support for Regime Norms," in James R. Millar, ed., *Politics, Work, and Daily Life in the USSR* (Cambridge: Cambridge University Press, 1987), pp. 130–133.

70. *Moskovskaya pravda,* January 25, 1986, p. 1; emphasis added.

71. *Byulleten' Ispolkoma Moskovskogo gorodskogo Soveta,* no. 3 (February 1975), pp. 32–38. On the growth of a "management" philosophy in Soviet cities, see Carol W. Lewis and Stephen Sternheimer, *Soviet Urban Management* (New York: Praeger, 1979).

72. *Byulleten' Ispolkoma,* no. 3 (February 1986), p. 1.

73. Twenty-eight of thirty-four deputy mayors in 1960–1985, or 82.4 percent, can be identified in prior positions in the party apparatus. Seven had been secretary or department head in the gorkom, fifteen were raikom first secretaries, three had both gorkom and raikom experience, and three had other party roles. In some cases, party and municipal experience were closely related functionally. N. I. Ulezlo, the deputy head of city government for transport from 1982 to 1987, was trained at the Moscow Institute of Railroad Transport Engineers, worked sixteen years in a transport design institute, and was raikom first secretary in Sokol'nicheskii raion, location of the city's main railroad yards (obituary in *Moskovskaya pravda,* December 13, 1990, p. 4).

74. Goberman's biography is in ibid., June 28, 1983, p. 4.

75. Ibid., April 5, 1990, p. 3. Luzhkov made his career to 1987 in industrial administration, but his approach varied little from the municipal norm.

76. A. M. Bryachikhin, "Prioritetnyye napravleniya," *Gorodskoye khozyaistvo Moskvy,* no. 6 (June 1989), p. 7; *Moskovskaya pravda,* February 23, 1987, p. 1.

77. Statements here based on press reports, interviews, and attendance at one soviet session in June 1988. Compare with the depictions of meetings of raion soviets in Henry W. Morton, "The Leningrad District of Moscow—An Inside Look," *Soviet Studies,* vol. 20 (October 1968), pp. 206–218; Theodore H. Friedgut, "A Local Soviet

at Work: The 1970 Budget and Budget Discussions of the Oktyabr Borough Soviet of Moscow," in Everett M. Jacobs, ed., *Soviet Local Politics and Government* (London: George Allen and Unwin, 1983), pp. 18–33; Hahn, *Soviet Grassroots,* pp. 199–205, 234–241.

78. Management responsibilities were given in the ispolkom bulletin. In 1982, for example, Chairman Promyslov provided "general leadership" and oversight of finances and external relations. Two first deputy chairmen and eight deputy chairmen handled the following portfolios: (1) personnel, housing admistration, and roads, (2) construction and town planning, (3) personal services, (4) economic planning, (5) utilities, office buildings, and the ispolkom's housing reserve, (6) health, schools, and social security, (7) trade and public dining, (8) police and courts, (9) housing allocation, cooperatives, and local industry, and (10) transportation and environmental protection. The ispolkom's secretary answered for administrative housekeeping, citizen relations, culture, and recreation.

79. In 1950, after the purge of Georgii Popov, the bureau of the ispolkom had one fewer meeting than the full ispolkom (twenty-two meetings versus twenty-three), but from 1953 onward the smaller body always met more often. The bureau met forty times in 1954 and the ispolkom twenty-two times. In 1960 presidium meetings outnumbered ispolkom meetings fifty-four to sixteen; in 1971, it was thirty-nine to eleven.

80. Observations here rest largely on the minutes of the presidium and ispolkom for 1970 and 1971, the last two years the city archive let me examine. Western studies of Soviet local government based on public records almost ignored the presidiums.

81. Mikhail Polyatykin in *Moskovskaya pravda,* July 26, 1990, p. 2; A. A. Zheltov and Yu. M. Luzhkov in ibid., June 1, 1988, p. 2, and January 18, 1991, p. 1.

82. *Byulleten' Ispolkoma,* no. 22 (November 1961), p. 15.

83. See ibid., no. 9 (May 1962), pp. 15–21. As late as 1988, several chairmen of raion standing commissions told me that they could see no circumstances under which they could issue a binding decision.

84. Soviet discussions are summarized in Ronald J. Hill, *Soviet Politics, Political Science, and Reform* (Oxford: Martin Robertson, 1980), chap. 4. I heard the same themes in conversations in the early 1980s. There is sound analysis of council procedures, with illustration from Moscow, in Theodore H. Friedgut, *Political Participation in the USSR* (Princeton: Princeton University Press, 1979), pp. 188–200, and Hahn, *Soviet Grassroots,* chap. 6. Both note the continued dominance of executives as well as the existence of some opportunities for deputies to contribute.

85. *Moskovskaya pravda,* March 15, 1987, p. 3.

86. *Byulleten' Ispolkoma,* no. 3 (February 1959), p. 33.

87. Ibid., no. 6 (March 1982), pp. 24–25. The information provided makes no allowance for double counting.

88. See Wayne DiFranceisco and Zvi Gitelman, "Soviet Political Culture and 'Covert Participation' in Policy Implementation," *American Political Science Review,* vol. 78 (September 1984), pp. 603–621.

89. Donna Bahry, "Politics, Generations, and Change in the USSR," in James

R. Millar, ed., *Politics, Work, and Daily Life in the USSR* (Cambridge: Cambridge University Press, 1987), pp. 76–84. See also Friedgut, *Political Participation,* pp. 216–219, and Robert J. Osborne, "Public Participation in Soviet City Government: The Vision of the Future Community in the Light of Current Problems of Urban Organization," Ph.D. diss., Columbia University, 1963.

90. The figure of 20,000 is from M. F. Konovalov, "Sovety stolitsy—massovyye obshchestvennyye organizatsii," *Gorodskoye khozyaistvo Moskvy,* no. 1, (January 1963), p. 11.

91. *Byulleten' Ispolkoma,* no. 6 (March 1966), p. 11, and *Moskovskaya pravda,* February 23, 1987, p. 2. Thirty thousand Muscovites were reported in "voluntary assistance commissions" attached to housing units as early as 1957. Moscow organized about 500 zheks between 1959 and 1961, replacing the roughly 2,000 domoupravleniyes. In the 1980s it replaced many zheks by larger boards going by the initials DEZ.

92. Hahn uses the ombudsman analogy in *Soviet Grassroots,* pp. 194–199.

93. Of the 500,000 activists reported for 1966, 240,000 were *druzhinniki* and 52,000 were members of the comrades' courts. *Byulleten' Ispolkoma,* no. 6 (March 1966), p. 11.

94. *Moskovskaya pravda,* February 23, 1987, p. 1.

95. Typical organizations mentioned in documents were the Moscow branch of the Red Cross, the Moscow Society of Dog Fanciers, and the Moscow Society of Hunters and Anglers. Cooperative housing construction was revived in the late 1950s, but the city cooperative federation dissolved in 1937 was not.

96. Rodina's doors were padlocked at the request of the architect of Proletarskii raion in April 1968 but reopened when members wrote to the Central Committee. It died quietly several years later. VOOPIK served most of the purposes of its founders. Yu. A. Bychkov, *Zhitiye Petra Baranovskogo* (Moscow: Sovetskaya Rossiya, 1991), pp. 166–168.

97. Zelenograd was classified as a town in the oblast when established in 1958. In 1960, while remaining such, it was subordinated to Leningradskii raion of the capital. It began to report to the Moscow ispolkom in February 1965. As of 1968 it was treated for most purposes as a raion of Moscow.

98. For an imaginative effort at mapping residential differentiation, see Ellen Hamilton, "Social Areas under State Socialism: The Case of Moscow," in Susan Gross Solomon, ed., *Beyond Sovietology: Essays in Politics and History* (Armonk, N.Y.: M. E. Sharpe, 1993), pp. 192–225.

99. Grishin also referred to an unwritten rule about rough equalization of CPSU memberships. Gorkom plenum of November 1968, in TsGAODM, f. 4, op. 152, d. 30, ll. 12, 15.

100. *Sovetskaya Rossiya,* May 16, 1990, p. 4.

101. Those with a historically significant name were Cheremushkinskii (renamed after Brezhnev from 1982 to 1988), Krasnopresnenskii (in the Presnya quarter), Kuntsevskii (Kuntsevo), Lyublinskii (Lyublino), Moskvoretskii (Zamoskvorech'e), Perovskii (Perovo), Sokol'nicheskii (Sokol'niki), and Tushinskii (Tushino). Thirteen

raions commemorated persons (eleven revolutionary and political heroes, one astronaut, and one scientist); five, aspects of the Russian Revolution; and four, other cities. Zheleznodorozhnyi stood for the Moscow railroad junction, and Zelenograd means "green city."

102. *Moskovskaya pravda,* June 1, 1988, p. 2.

103. Of ninety-nine raion-level municipal officials who ran for election to the Mossovet in the competitive election of March 1990, during which place of residence was disclosed, 34.5 percent—and 44.4 percent of raion ispolkom chairmen—lived in other raions. The ratio was 44.4 percent among raion party officials and 60 percent of raikom first secretaries.

104. *Moskovskaya pravda,* March 7, 1958, p. 3.

105. The first to come out were small volumes in 1958 and 1964. Annual tomes of several hundred pages began to appear in 1966, all produced by the USSR Central Statistics Directorate.

106. A. Korobov, P. Revyakin, V. Tydman, and N. Chetunova, "Kak dal'she stroit' Moskvu?" *Moskva,* no. 3 (March 1962), pp. 147–160, and *Pravda,* May 11, 1962, p. 4. The signatories in *Pravda* included three former chief architects (Chechulin, Vlasov, and Loveiko) and Boris Iofan. Chief Architect Posokhin did not sign but affirmed current policy in an essay in the May issue of *Moskva.* Revyakin, a member of the city soviet's commission on landmarks, anticipated some of his 1962 arguments in "Litso stolitsy," *Literatura i zhizn',* no. 76 (June 26, 1960), p. 2.

107. Oleg Platonov, "Puteshestviye v Kitezh-grad," *Moskva,* no. 4 (April 1990), p. 164.

108. Journalist Lyudmila Nechiporuk described this phenomenon after the collapse of CPSU rule: "Working in a single-party newspaper, I, to be honest, cannot even say quite when my internal censor took up residence within me. With 'him' I had to clear all materials, 'he' advised me to avoid 'incorrect' conclusions and evaluations. Because you do not want to write for the wastebasket, you willy-nilly become a conformist, you kid yourself, you adapt. Conformism evolves quietly, unnoticeably. The most frightening thing is that you begin to believe sincerely that what you have written is the truest of truths." *Moskovskaya pravda,* August 28, 1991, p. 2.

109. *Moskovskaya pravda*'s lineage went back under various titles to 1918. *Vechernyaya Moskva* was established in 1923 and was much more informative up to the late 1950s. *Moskovskii komsomolets,* the Moscow Komsomol newspaper (established in 1919), stressed youth issues but occasionally commented seriously on local affairs. For information on the gorkom's supervision of *Moskovskaya pravda,* see Lilita Dzirkals, Thane Gustafson, and A. Ross Johnson, *The Media and Intra-Elite Communication in the USSR,* R-2869 (Santa Monica: Rand Corporation, September 1982), pp. 54–59.

110. M. N. Rutkevich to the March 1975 plenum of the gorkom, in TsGAODM, f. 4, op. 183, d. 1, l. 51, and Yeltsin in *Moskovskaya pravda,* March 30, 1986, p. 2. Moscow assuredly complied with the finding of one Western study concerning the pervasive distrust of the Soviet local media, an estrangement stemming "not . . . from

lack of interest in things local, but rather from dissatisfaction with the failure of the local media to provide truly local coverage." Ellen Propper Mickiewicz, *Media and the Russian Public* (New York: Praeger Special Studies, 1981), p. 48.

111. As James C. Scott argues (*Domination and the Arts of Resistance: Hidden Transcripts* [New Haven: Yale University Press, 1990], p. 56), denial of internal conflict characterizes authoritarian regimes: "If the dominant are at odds with one another in any substantial way, they are, to that degree, weakened, and subordinates may be able to exploit the divisions and renegotiate the terms of subordination."

112. A. Gordon, "Etot opasnyi karst," *Arkhitektura i stroitel'stvo Moskvy*, no. 4 (April 1990), p. 7.

113. *Moskovskaya pravda*, December 20, 1987, p. 3. Kolodnyi did not actually name the military as occupant, probably because censor's rules still prohibited it.

114. Seventy-five of the Soviets' 2,000 underground sanctuaries against nuclear attack were in Moscow (Daniel Ford, "The Button—II," *New Yorker*, vol. 61 [April 8, 1985], p. 59). A former Central Committee chauffeur described the withholding of maps to me in an interview in 1993.

115. Some of these details are in or may be inferred from an interview with the engineer Vladimir Gonik: "V kruge vtorom," *Moskovskiye novosti*, no. 31 (August 2, 1992), p. 24. I learned others on my own. Ventilation ducts and entrances can be spotted near the Yugo-Zapadnaya station and at the south edge of the Fifty Years of October Park. The four office towers on the west side of prospekt Vernadskogo, still unfinished, are said to have been started by the KGB to service the subterranean complex. There is a large underground garage joined by mechanical elevator to the Kremlin arsenal courtyard, and also passageways of various sorts connecting it to Staraya ploshchad'. The estimate that Metro-2 grew to one-third the size of the regular subway was made by Gavriil Popov, the chairman of the Mossovet and then mayor of Moscow in the early 1990s, in an interview with the author in October 1994.

116. "V kruge vtorom," p. 24.

117. The statistics, again referring to authorized strength, are from TsGAODM, f. 4, op. 102, d. 19, ll. 92–94 (for 1956); op. 17, d. 25, ll. 11, 31 (1960); op. 152, d. 44, l. 61 (1968); *Moskovskaya pravda*, July 9, 1988, p. 2, and July 26, 1990, p. 1 (1980s). There were also full-time party staffers ("released" secretaries) in places of work; in 1988 they totaled about 3,200. The gorkom's eight office buildings were on Staraya ploshchad' and on nearby Kuibysheva, Arkhipova, Bol'shoi Cherkasskii, and Malyi Spasoglinishchevskii streets.

118. The archive shows the bureau sitting 118 times in 1951, 60 times in 1961, 71 in 1968, 51 in 1975, and 48 in 1978.

119. The subraion committees had only 35 responsible workers and 18 support staff in January 1968. The production branch committees, for activities occupying about 15 percent of Moscow's party members, had 123 responsible officials and 63 technical workers. TsGAODM, f. 4, op. 152, d. 37, ll. 88–89.

120. Figures for 1956 and 1958 were found in V. K. Gorev, "Deyatel'nost' Moskovskoi partiinoi organizatsii po uluchsheniyu rukovodstva promyshlennost'yu

(1956–1959 gg.),'' in K. I. Suvorov, ed., *Nekotoryye voprosy organizatsionno-parti-inoi raboty v sovremennykh usloviyakh* (Moscow: VPSh i AON pri TsK KPSS, 1961), pp. 298–299. Others are from a tabulation prepared in 1992 by A. S. Novikov of the Central State Archive of Social Movements of Moscow. Some of the raikom-confirmed positions were subject to repeat confirmation by the gorkom, but I do not know the exact number.

121. The gorkom created a unitary Industry and Transport Department in May 1953; by July 1954 it had been reorganized into five separate departments, one of them for defense industry. An Industrial Department was established in 1960, but it did not cover defense production, local industry, or building materials, and in 1963 two new industrial departments were christened. There was no serious attempt to cut down on departments in the Brezhnev years.

122. After the last reorganization of the raions in 1968, instructors in raikom propaganda departments ranged from three to eleven in the five raions with the greatest concentration of cultural facilities. Instructors for industry varied from three to six, and for party organization (responsible at that time for trade and services as well as party work in the narrow sense) from three to fourteen. Departments for science and higher education were set up in six raions only.

123. Source: former construction engineer interviewed in Israel in 1982.

124. Interviews with a former official in the Moscow procuracy, a Russian parliamentarian with access to official information about Shchelokov, and Moscow planners.

125. Letter by E. Dorfman in *Arkhitektura i stroitel'stvo Moskvy*, no. 3 (March 1988), p. 32; Promyslov interview in *Vechernyaya Moskva*, July 16, 1992, p. 5; Shcherbachenko, "Stroitel'nyye dramy i komedii," p. 7.

126. *Moskovskaya pravda*, April 14, 1977, p. 1.

127. The plans for civilian industry were discussed in the press. The radio industry scheme is in TsGAODM, f. 4, op. 152, d. 43, ll. 126–127, 141–173, and there is brief reference to those for shipbuilding and electronics in ibid., op. 169, d. 3, l. 116.

128. In 1968 the directive of the gorkom bureau on the harvest ordered the mobilization of 24,000 loaders and more than 36,000 trucks and drivers (TsGAODM, f. 4, op. 152, d. 41, ll. 25–59). Such figures were never published.

129. Interview in *Izvestiya TsK KPSS*, no. 8 (August 1990), p. 36.

130. *Moskovskaya pravda*, April 17, 1979, p. 2, and July 7, 1979, p. 2.

131. Two gorkom secretaries, for construction and municipal administration and for trade and services, were almost wholly occupied with local government. In addition, the first secretary gave general leadership and the others supervised the local police (second secretary), industry (industry secretary), and health, education, and culture programs (ideology secretary). Eight of eighteen gorkom departments in 1981 dealt with this range of issues. Several raikoms in inner Moscow had departments for trade and services by the 1980s, but most continued to deal with municipal issues through their organizational and industrial departments.

132. Although the municipal chairman regularly attended the city party bureau, the gorkom first secretary rarely went to meetings of the ispolkom, leaving this to the

secretary for construction and local services or, sometimes, to the second secretary, who was not a member of the ispolkom. Minutes show First Secretary Grishin to have missed every meeting of the city ispolkom in 1970 and 1971.

133. *Moskovskaya pravda,* January 25, 1986, p. 3.

134. In December 1971, for example, Promyslov made this comment about the 1972 plan for housing distribution: "The gorkom bureau has studied this question and given basic approval to a line [of policy]. Of course, there may be oversights here and it may be possible for us to make some changes, but essentially we must adopt this plan." TsGIAGM, f. 150, op. 1, d. 3830, l. 405.

135. *Nezavisimaya gazeta,* February 19, 1991, p. 5.

136. *Moskovskaya pravda,* June 1, 1988, p. 2, and November 5, 1988, p. 2.

137. V. Promyslov, "Po leninskomu puti," *Stroitel'stvo i arkhitektura Moskvy,* no. 4 (April 1964), p. 4.

138. *Pravda,* August 7, 1958, p. 1, and February 10, 1963, p. 1; V. I. Fedorov, "Nekotoryye voprosy razvitiya lesoparkovogo poyasa i organizatsii otdykha naseleniya," *Gorodskoye khozyaistvo Moskvy,* no. 2 (February 1961), p. 10; communiqués in *Stroitel'stvo i arkhitektura Moskvy,* no. 6 (June 1963), pp. 1–3.

139. Superficial repairs in 1965 did not stop the decay and were complicated by the placement of the footings on a highway bridge below. Some experts wanted the bridge demolished, but this would have halted rail and possibly river traffic for years. When a temporary bypass was opened in 1986 and capital renovation began, it was planned for six years (four times as long as it took to build the bridge). Even that timetable was inoperative, and reopening is now slated for 1996 at the earliest.

140. I owe this information to my interview with Yegorychev. Moscow's 1964 housing plan was 3,400,000 square meters (net), and Gosplan was ordered to cut it to 2,000,000. Yegorychev arranged for 500,000 square meters to be assigned for bookkeeping purposes to the construction cooperatives and 700,000 to central agencies, and for the final 200,000 to be reported as plan overfulfillment. Again, Khrushchev was on pension before the matter could be reviewed.

141. Interview with a former engineer in the Chief Architectural Planning Directorate; Grishin in *Nezavisimaya gazeta,* February 16, 1991, p. 5; Yegorychev interview.

142. The Gosplan subdepartment for Moscow and Leningrad was in the territorial planning department, one of Gosplan's least influential. There were four Moscow specialists in it in 1982 (author's interviews). The RSFSR had a Ministry of Housing and Municipal Services, in which Muscovites held leading posts, but it had no general custody over cities and no great interest in Moscow.

143. Carol W. Lewis, *The Budgetary Process in Soviet Cities* (New York: Center for Government Studies, Graduate School of Business, Columbia University, March 1976).

144. *Vechernyaya Moskva,* July 16, 1992, p. 5; emphasis added.

145. Most statistics in this section from Yu. G. Saushkin and V. G. Glushkova, *Moskva sredi gorodov mira* (Moscow: Mysl', 1983), chap. 4.

146. *Moskovskaya pravda,* February 23, 1987, p. 1.

147. Statistics from articles in *Gorodskoye khozyaistvo Moskvy,* no. 10 (October

1964), p. 4, and no. 2 (February 1973), p. 22, and *Moskovskaya pravda,* March 25, 1988, p. 3. Such data must be used with care because of the various ways of reckoning housing space and classifying owners. The departmental total properly included housing under agencies of the city itself, and not available to the general public. Naturally, subtotals for major firms were large. The First State Ballbearing Works owned 359,000 square meters of housing (with 27,000 tenants) in 1973, Serp i molot 250,000 square meters in 1979, and the Komsomol Car Works 800,000 square meters in 1991. *Pervyi podshipnikovyi: Istoriya pervogo gosudarstvennogo podshipniko-vogo zavoda, 1932–1972* (Moscow: Mysl', 1973), p. 276; *Moskovskaya pravda,* April 29, 1979, p. 1, and November 6, 1991, p. 7. Net dwelling space under departmental control in 1989 ranged from 5.6 percent in Zelenograd to 39.6 percent in Lyublinskii raion.

148. Clusters of military housing can be identified at Sadovaya-Kudrinskaya, ploshchad' Kommuny, and Smolenskaya naberezhnaya in central Moscow; somewhat further out, on Komsomol'skii, Kutuzovskii, and Leningradskii prospects, Mozhai-skoye shosse, and in the Khoroshevo and Lefortovo subareas; and in Babushkin and Medvedkovo, in the far north of the city, where the army once had artillery ranges. These buildings are either "generals' houses" or low-quality housing for personnel on temporary duty in Moscow. Most officers permanently stationed in the capital lived in the common housing stock. In the March 1990 election, 57.7 percent of the military candidates for the city soviet were from seven raions (Babushkinskii, Cheremushkinskii, Krasnogvardeiskii, Kuntsevskii, Perovskii, Sovetskii, and Timirya-zevskii), and there were no military nominees in seven raions.

149. *Moskovskaya pravda,* November 11, 1983, p. 2.

150. The information that follows draws on my own observations, interviews, scattered items in the press and local archives, and several declassified U.S. government documents.

151. Defense Intelligence Agency, *Estimated Expenditures for Research and Development by the Soviet Ministry of Aviation Industry,* DIA-450-2-6-71-INT, July 1971.

152. The nomenclature can be bewildering. The design and production operations associated with Mikoyan and Sukhoi were known in the 1980s as "machine building works" named after them, while the complexes associated with Il'yushin and Yakovlev were called Strela (Arrow) and Skorost' (Speed). The Mikoyan works, Strela, Skorost', and the Aviapribor (Aviation Instruments) NPO were in Frunzenskii raion, the Sukhoi and Avangard works in Leningradskii raion, and Krasnyi Oktyabr' in Tushinskii raion. Another large producer in this area was the Del'ta NPO in Timiryazevskii raion; it was in the Ministry of the Defense Industry, but I am not aware of its specialty.

153. *Moskovskaya pravda,* October 24, 1989, p. 1, and July 13, 1991, p. 2; *Izvestiya,* March 11, 1992, p. 3.

154. See among other sources *Rossiiskiye vesti,* November 21, 1992, p. 4; *Neza-visimaya gazeta,* October 27, 1992, p. 6; and the obituary of the founder of the alloys institute, A. F. Belov, in *Moskovskaya pravda,* December 26, 1991, p. 4.

155. See for some details *Nezavisimaya gazeta,* October 30, 1992, p. 2; Vladimir

Voronov, "Kuz'minki . . . zarinki . . . zomanki," *Stolitsa*, no. 8 (February 1993), pp. 1–3; and *Izvestiya*, June 26, 1993, p. 15.

156. Estimate in *Argumenty i fakty*, no. 25 (June 1993), p. 8.

157. Sergei Leskov in *Izvestiya*, January 4, 1992, p. 2.

158. Readily identifiable in Zelenograd are three production plants for electronics (Elion, Ion, and Mikron) and six research institutes (Electronic Technology, Materials, Microinstruments, Molecular Electronics, Precision Technology, and Zenit). The 90 percent estimate is from *Kuranty*, March 4, 1993, p. 4. Energomash, joined from its birth in 1929 with the Glushko design bureau, made the engines for the rocket launchers for all of the Soviet Union's manned and unmanned space vehicles, beginning with Sputnik in 1957.

159. *Moskovskaya pravda*, October 24, 1989, p. 1 (emphasis added); *Leninskoye znamya*, December 5, 1989, p. 2.

160. *Nezavisimaya gazeta*, July 11, 1992, p. 6. One Western scholar estimates from unexplained residuals in unpublished Soviet data that 24.4 percent of all industrial employees in Moscow in 1985 were in the military-industrial ministries, and 20.8 percent in Moscow oblast. Brenda Horrigan, "How Many People Worked in the Soviet Defense Industry," *RFE/RL Research Report*, vol. 1 (August 21, 1992), pp. 36–37. Horrigan's figures are lower than public Soviet/Russian estimates such as Zaikov's and Luzhkov's, and they exclude R & D and military production in civilian ministries, both of which were unusually high in Moscow. Even at that, they put Moscow military-industrial employment in 1985 at 300,000 in absolute figures, and the city-oblast total at 525,000, by far the highest in the USSR.

161. *Nezavisimaya gazeta*, February 16, 1991, p. 5; *Moskovskaya pravda*, July 5, 1989, p. 2.

162. The brucellosis incident is reported in Vladimir Golyakhovsky, *Russian Doctor*, trans. Michael Sylwester and Eugene Ostrovsky (New York: St. Martin's, 1984), pp. 206–210. The case at the Higher Party School is taken from *Izvestiya*, June 26, 1993, p. 15.

163. The Defense Industry Department of the CPSU gorkom could not be mentioned in the press, although the name of its head from 1954 to 1986, N. T. Pimenov, was occasionally printed, without his position. Only his obituary, in the Gorbachev era (*Moskovskaya pravda*, August 23, 1990, p. 4), disclosed that he had carried out this important job.

164. For distortion of maps of the oblast, see Yurii Golubchikov, "Vremya otkryvat' prostranstvo," *Ogonek*, no. 26 (June 1989), pp. 25–26.

165. Yegorychev in *Moskovskaya pravda*, December 8, 1962, p. 1, and, in general, David T. Cattell, "Local Government and the Sovnarkhoz in the USSR, 1957–62," *Soviet Studies*, vol. 15 (April 1964), pp. 430–442.

166. Early statements by Goberman on this point are in *Pravda*, March 13, 1957, p. 2, and September 28, 1962, p. 3. Glavmosavtotrans carried 71 percent of all loads (measured in ton-kilometers) in 1965, 67 percent in 1970, 61 percent in 1980, and 59 percent in 1985.

167. *Moskovskaya pravda*, September 15, 1960, p. 3; February 23, 1977, p. 2; June 16, 1981, p. 2.

168. This number is cited in several sources. There were 173 such organizations in 1963 (*Byulleten' Ispolkoma*, no. 17 [September 1963], p. 1).

169. *Moskovskaya pravda*, January 18, 1984, p. 2, and January 8, 1986, p. 2.

170. Ruble, *Leningrad*, chap. 6; *Moskovskaya pravda*, August 28, 1971, p. 2; October 22, 1972, p. 1; December 10, 1972, p. 1.

171. *Moskovskaya pravda*, January 25, 1986, p. 2.

172. *Pravda*, January 28, 1987, pp. 3–4.

173. Scott, *Domination and the Arts of Resistance*, pp. 81, 101.

6. The Politics of Basic Needs and of Urban Amenity

1. Abraham H. Maslow, *Motivation and Personality* (New York: Harper, 1954), and *Toward a Psychology of Being* (Princeton: Van Nostrand, 1968).

2. V. V. Grishin, *Izbrannyye rechi i stat'i* (Moscow: Politizdat, 1979), p. 221.

3. The best sources on TEO and plan are the special issues of *Stroitel'stvo i arkhitektura Moskvy* of November 1966 and July–August 1971. The Siberian-born Posokhin had once worked for Shchusev and designed the skyscraper on ploshchad' Vosstaniya. Criticized for extravagance in 1955, he repented and won the trust of Khrushchev and local leaders. In 1961, shortly after becoming chief architect, he was hastily admitted into the CPSU. From 1963 to 1967 he was head of the civil construction arm of Gosstroi, the State Construction Committee, as well as Moscow planner.

4. This was the target given in the final draft in 1971. The 1966 TEO expressed it as 12 to 15 square meters.

5. My sources here are interviews in GlavAPU.

6. The changes in Gorplan are laid out in *Byulleten' Ispolkoma Moskovskogo gorodskogo Soveta*, no. 22 (November 1975), pp. 2–6. The most important new departments were for heavy industry and machine building, the second with a subdepartment for "specialized" machinery, a euphemism for defense industry.

7. "O Tekhniko-ekonomicheskikh osnovakh General'nogo plana razvitiya Moskvy," *Stroitel'stvo i arkhitektura Moskvy*, no. 11 (November 1966), p. 9.

8. The main liberalization was the return in 1956 of the workers' right to change jobs at will, which had been revoked in 1940. The passport system was amended in minor ways, in general and for Moscow, by mostly unpublished decrees in 1953, 1958, 1964, and 1972. See Mervyn Matthews, *The Passport Society: Controlling Movement in Russia and the USSR* (Boulder, Colo.: Westview Press, 1993), pp. 30–37.

9. *XX s"ezd Kommunisticheskoi partii Sovetskogo Soyuza: Stenograficheskii otchet* (Moscow: Gospolitizdat, 1956), I, 79.

10. Resolution of the gorkom secretariat, in TsGAODM, f. 4, op. 107, d. 121, l. 129.

11. Vladimir Promyslov in 1968 gave somewhat different figures from the ones relied on in Table 9, but pointing to a similar conclusion. He said Moscow's population had increased by 1,400,000 from 1946 to 1955 but by only 540,000 from

1956 to 1965, "thanks to measures such as the limitation of entry into Moscow." Ibid., op. 152, d. 3, l. 125.

12. N. Ullas, "Nekotoryye voprosy perspektivnogo razvitiya Moskvy," *Stroitel'stvo i arkhitektura Moskvy,* no. 3 (March 1960), pp. 7–8; I. Loveiko, "Gradostroitel'nyye problemy Moskvy na novom etape," ibid., no. 5 (May 1960), p. 4; *Vsesoyuznoye soveshchaniye po gradostroitel'stvu (7–10 iyunya 1960 g.): Sokrashchennyi stenograficheskii otchet* (Moscow: Gosstroiizdat, 1960), p. 297.

13. G. Ye. Mishchenko, "Regulirovaniye rosta naseleniya Moskvy i yego rasseleniye," *Gorodskoye khozyaistvo Moskvy,* no. 3 (March 1961), pp. 7–9; *Pravda,* July 8, 1962, p. 6.

14. M. Posokhin, "Cherty Leninskoi Moskvy," *Stroitel'stvo i arkhitektura Moskvy,* no. 4 (April 1970), p. 21.

15. Compare to Leningrad, where the optimal population ceiling also "bore little relationship to reality." The limit of 3.5 million was exceeded in 1966, the year the plan was ratified. Blair A. Ruble, *Leningrad: Shaping a Soviet City* (Berkeley: University of California Press, 1990), p. 81.

16. Natural increase in Moscow, which was 11.7 per 1,000 in 1940 and 7.4 per 1,000 in 1950, was 7 per 1,000 in 1960 (14.6 births per 1,000, 7.6 deaths), or about 42,000 persons. It was down to 2.3 per 1,000 in 1965 (10.8 births, 8.5 deaths), or about 15,000 persons, and bottomed out at 1.5 per 1,000, or about 10,000 persons, in 1968. Natural increase was roughly 17,000 persons in 1970, 16,000 in 1980, and 15,000 in 1985. Calculated from data in *Moskva v tsifrakh,* various editions.

17. See on this point Cecil J. Houston, "Administrative Control of Migration to Moscow, 1959–75," *Canadian Geographer,* vol. 23 (January–March 1979), pp. 32–44.

18. I originally heard about this procedure in not-for-attribution interviews. I compiled the totals for 1971 from ispolkom and presidium minutes in the city archive. Promyslov's statement is in TsGIAGM, f. 150, op. 1, d. 3830, l. 147.

19. Boris Yeltsin, *Ispoved' na zadannuyu temu* (Moscow: PIK, 1990), p. 94.

20. The exact size of the work force at the end of the 1980s is unclear. *Byulleten' Ispolkoma,* no. 4 (February 1988), p. 4, gives Moscow's total employment "limits" as 4,890,000. But *Itogi sotsial'no-ekonomicheskogo razvitiya raionov g. Moskvy v 1985 g.* (Moscow: Statisticheskoye upravleniye goroda Moskvy, 1986), p. 107, breaking down employment by raion, gives a grand total of 5,128,500. *Moskva v tsifrakh, 1989* (Moscow: Finansy i statistika, 1989), p. 24, the first of the annual handbooks to provide employment totals, said there were 5,271,100 employed in 1985, including 337,300 in organizations outside the city limits subordinated to Moscow organizations; these figures were said to be 5,097,000 and 309,800 in 1988. The estimates of migrants for 1971–1986 are from *Moskovskaya pravda,* July 20, 1986, p. 2, and October 12, 1986, p. 2.

21. *Moskovskaya pravda,* March 22, 1975, p. 1 (Grishin); B. Khorev and V. Glushkova, "Skol'ko stoit chistyi vozdukh," *Gorodskoye khozyaistvo Moskvy,* no. 10 (October 1990), p. 25; *Argumenty i fakty,* no. 21 (May 1991), p. 5. An example of a brand new factory would be the Second State Ballbearing Works in

southeast Moscow, opened in 1979. Modelers found in the 1970s that increases in industrial production exerted twice the indirect pressure on population that other forms of activity did. M. G. Zavel'skii et al., "Prognozirovaniye razvitiya narodnogo khozyaistva Moskvy s ispol'zovaniyem imitatsionnoi modeli," in *Problemy sovershenstvovaniya sistemy planirovaniya i upravleniya narodnym khozyaistvom g. Moskvy* (Moscow: Institut ekonomicheskikh problem kompleksnogo razvitiya narodnogo khozyaistva g. Moskvy, 1981), pp. 52–53.

22. M. Dudik, "Na pervom plane—interesy goroda," *Stroitel'stvo i arkhitektura Moskvy*, no. 1 (January 1967), pp. 8–9; TsGAODM, f. 4, op. 169, d. 3, l. 39.

23. *Moskovskaya pravda*, June 5, 1980, p. 2.

24. "Vremya bol'shikh peremen," *Arkhitektura i stroitel'stvo Moskvy*, no. 1 (January 1987), p. 4.

25. V. Ya. Bekker, V. G. Glushkova, and B. S. Khorev, "Stolichnyi region: Problema ogranicheniya rosta yadra i sbalansirovannogo rasseleniya," in M. K. Bandman and O. A. Kibal'chin, eds., *Ekonomiko-geograficheskiye problemy razvitiya stolichnykh regionov* (Novosibirsk: AN SSSR—Sibirskoye otdeleniye, 1985), p. 35.

26. Ibid.; TsGAODM, f. 4, op. 188, d. 3, l. 96.

27. TsGAODM, f. 4, op. 188, d. 3, l. 38.

28. Population per square kilometer was 7,600 in 1907, 9,100 in 1912, 12,900 in 1941, and 14,200 in 1959. The annexation of 1960 depressed it to 6,900, after which it crept back up to 8,100 in 1980. Density in the Census Bureau Consolidated Area of New York in 1980 was 3,058 per square mile, or about 1,200 per square kilometer; in the core (the four main boroughs of New York City, Hudson County, and Newark), it was 9,600 per square kilometer. See for general discussion R. A. French, "The Individuality of the Soviet City," in R. A. French and F. E. Ian Hamilton, eds., *The Socialist City: Spatial Structure and Urban Policy* (New York: John Wiley and Sons, 1979), pp. 79–90, and Yu. G. Saushkin and V. G. Glushkova, *Moskva sredi gorodov mira* (Moscow: Mysl', 1983), pp. 248–250.

29. TsGAODM, f. 4, op. 183, d. 1, l. 10; op. 188, d. 3, l. 40.

30. Author's interviews. About two-thirds of the land transferred was planted in vegetables, berries, and feed crops.

31. Quotation from S. Lyashchenko, "Dorogiye gektary," *Stroitel'stvo i arkhitektura Moskvy*, no. 4 (April 1978), p. 5. Kabakova was an economist at a construction research institute. Segedinov, a city employee, was chief engineer of the team that drew up the TEO of the 1971 master plan and addressed the pricing issue as early as 1961.

32. N. O. Peshkova and A. I. Chuvelev, "Tupiki ekstensivnogo puti," *Gorodskoye khozyaistvo Moskvy*, no. 7 (July 1988), p. 6.

33. See among other sources S. Matveyev, "Novyye rubezhi zhilishchnogo stroitel'stva," *Stroitel'stvo i arkhitektura Moskvy*, no. 12 (December 1978), pp. 3–5, and A. Kudryavtsev, "Vazhnyye i aktual'nyye voprosy gradostroitel'stva," ibid., no. 3 (March 1979), p. 29.

34. Even though it violated the master plan, the city's chief architect and the main

author of the plan—Mikhail Posokhin—accepted the General Staff building as his last personal architectural commission.

35. "Arkhitekturno-planirovochnaya organizatsiya goroda," *Stroitel'stvo i arkhitektura Moskvy,* nos. 7–8 (July–August 1971), p. 23. The eight planning zones were not part of the TEO, although these did project "integrated city districts" with populations of 350,000 to 500,000, which would feature "all the necessary conditions for labor, daily life, and leisure."

36. "Tsentry planivorochnykh zon," ibid., nos. 10–11 (October–November 1977), p. 65.

37. *Moskovskaya pravda,* January 9, 1986, p. 3.

38. Author's interviews.

39. T. Kh. Slavkina, "Ot otdel'nykh predpriyatii do promyshlennykh zon," *Gorodskoye khozyaistvo Moskvy,* no. 6 (June 1976), p. 21.

40. *Moskovskaya pravda,* February 12, 1975, p. 2.

41. Ibid., August 20, 1987, p. 2.

42. A factory director named Konovalov proposed to the obkom that a unified sovnarkhoz be created. "Participants in the plenum applauded . . . when he said, 'Moscow and Moscow oblast have always been in their historic and economic development a single region'" (*Sovetskaya Rossiya,* April 13, 1957, p. 2). The central offices of the oblast soviet did remain in city hall, at 13 ulitsa Gor'kogo; administrative branches were scattered in other buildings in central Moscow. In all other big Russian cities the Communist Party apparatus was under oblast control, and this predisposed them to more regional coordination than was achieved in Moscow. See Ruble, *Leningrad,* pp. 102–103.

43. *Moskovskaya pravda,* June 14, 1957, p. 2.

44. N. F. Yevstratov, "Lesoparkovyi poyas stolitsy," *Gorodskoye khozyaistvo Moskvy,* no. 9 (September 1960), p. 4; V. V. Shilo, "Raionnaya planirovka Moskvy i Moskovskoi oblasti," ibid., no. 3 (March 1961), p. 42; *Moskovskaya pravda,* July 9, 1957, p. 2.

45. Yevstratov, "Lesoparkovyi poyas," p. 4.

46. M. Barshch et al., "Novyye zhilyye raiony vokrug Moskvy," *Arkhitektura i stroitel'stvo Moskvy,* no. 5 (May 1956), pp. 21–26; P. Pomozanov, "K voprosu o proyektirovanii gorodov-sputnikov," ibid., no. 11 (November 1957), p. 26.

47. K. F. Knyazev, "Goroda-sputniki i razvitiye krupnykh gorodov," *Izvestiya Akademii stroitel'stva i arkhitektury,* no. 2 (April–June 1960), pp. 50–51; Ullas, "Nekotoryye voprosy," p. 8.

48. See First Secretary Demichev and M. K. Solov'ev, chairman of the executive committee of Krasnogorskii raion, in *Moskovskaya pravda,* December 10, 1960, pp. 2–3. Plans for subway construction in *Leninskoye znamya,* October 14, 1961, p. 3, showed lines being extended north and southeast into the oblast. In the party apparatus, the five first secretaries from the green belt were put on the gorkom in December 1960, other officials were transferred to its books, and the head of the Mytishchenskii raikom was made a candidate member of the gorkom bureau.

49. The decree by the Presidium of the Supreme Soviet of the RSFSR was pub-

lished in *Vedomosti Verkhovnogo Soveta RSFSR,* no. 43 (November 16, 1961), p. 646, but not mentioned in the local press. It reunited the five raions created in 1960 with the pieces severed from them. The next plenum of the oblast soviet added two of their chief executives to its ispolkom, again without explanation. Perhaps 100,000 persons in the green belt remained administratively subject to Moscow through seven hamlet councils (in areas containing pumping stations and other city enterprises) and the Zelenograd soviet.

50. A. I. Kononenko, "Blagoustroistvo gorodov Podmoskov'ya," *Gorodskoye khozyaistvo Moskvy,* no. 11 (November 1962), p. 22.

51. *Moskovskaya pravda,* December 29, 1960, p. 2; A. Zaslavskii, "Sozdadim nauchno obosnovannyi general'nyi plan!" *Stroitel'stvo i arkhitektura Moskvy,* no. 3 (March 1961), pp. 1–2; Kononenko, "Blagoustroistvo gorodov," p. 23.

52. See James Bater, *The Soviet City: Ideal and Reality* (London: Edward Arnold, 1980), pp. 81–83.

53. Figures in Yu. D. Fedorov, "Ob osobennostyakh rasseleniya v prigorodnoi zone Moskvy," *Voprosy geografii,* vol. 87 (1961), p. 86; V. G. Glushkova and N. P. Shepelev, "Opredeleniye granitsy zony aktivnogo vliyaniya Moskvy," *Vestnik Moskovskogo universiteta, Seriya V—geografiya,* no. 5 (September–October 1974), pp. 93–96; T. Badalov and Yu. Bocharov, "V zone vliyaniya stolitsy," *Stroitel'stvo i arkhitektura Moskvy,* no. 4 (April 1978), pp. 18–19; Saushkin and Glushkova, *Moskva sredi gorodov mira,* pp. 235–236.

54. V. G. Glushkova and N. P. Shepelev, "Nekotoryye zakonomernosti kul'turno-bytovykh poyezdok iz Moskovskoi oblasti v Moskvu," *Vestnik Moskovskogo universiteta, Seriya V—geografiya,* no. 4 (July–August 1976), pp. 95–99.

55. Fifteen percent regularly exited the city on off-work days in 1939, but 18 percent in 1959, 23 percent in 1970, and 28 percent in 1975. V. G. Glushkova and N. P. Shepelev, "Problemy territorial'noi organizatsii zagorodnogo otdykha naseleniya krupnykh gorodov v vykhodnyye dni (na primere Moskvy)," *Vestnik Moskovskogo universiteta, Seriya V—geografiya,* no. 1 (January–February 1976), p. 31.

56. Compare "Lesoparkovyi zashchitnyi poyas i sistema otdykha naseleniya," *Stroitel'stvo i arkhitektura Moskvy,* nos. 7–8 (July–August 1971), p. 57, with B. L. Samoilov and G. V. Morozova in *Moskovskaya pravda,* August 11, 1989, p. 3.

57. V. S. Preobrazhenskii et al., "Problemy territorial'noi organizatsii rekreatsionnoi deyatel'nosti v Moskovskoi oblasti," *Izvestiya Akademii Nauk SSSR, Seriya geograficheskaya,* no. 6 (November–December 1982), pp. 93–95; numbers added for clarity.

58. A case in point is Katina Hill, a once verdant mound at the conflux of the Istra and Moskva Rivers, close by the elite dachas at Petrovo-Dal'neye and Gorki-2 (and a favorite walking site for Stalin). The hill was deforested by local inhabitants seeking firewood during World War II. Much of it was then carted off as by army construction battalions, after which the local state farm turned the pit into a garbage dump. Pine seedlings planted in the 1950s were eaten by peasants' goats. In the 1970s farm families, without authorization, sowed parts of the hill in potatoes.

59. "The city, spreading like an oil spill, may swallow up the surrounding land

the same way it did the recreational territory inside the MKAD." Leonid Volkov, "Vybor general'nykh napravlenii," *Arkhitektura i stroitel'stvo Moskvy,* no. 3 (March 1988), p. 3.

60. A. Yu. Bekker, "Opyt planirovaniya gradostroitel'nogo razvitiya Moskvy," in M. K. Bandman and O. A. Kibal'chin, *Ekonomiko-geograficheskiye problemy razvitiya stolichnykh regionov* (Novosibirsk: AN SSSR—Sibirskoye otdeleniye, 1985), p. 25.

61. *Moskovskaya pravda,* March 25, 1988, p. 3. Most of the private housing consisted of rundown cabins on the outskirts, but there were a few palatial homes given to scientists and weapons designers, among them Vladimir Chelomei, Petr Kapitsa, Sergei Korolev, and Pavel Kurchatov.

62. Z. A. Yankova and I. Yu. Rodzinskaya, *Problemy bol'shogo goroda* (Moscow: Nauka, 1982), pp. 63–64. I owe the term "hyperstandardization" to Blair Ruble. See his essay "From *Khrushcheby* to *Korobki,*" in William C. Brumfield and Blair A. Ruble, eds., *Russian Housing in the Modern Age* (Cambridge: Cambridge University Press, 1993), p. 254.

63. Ruble, "From *Khrushcheby* to *Korobki,*" p. 244.

64. *Byulleten' Ispolkoma,* no. 6 (March 1982), p. 25.

65. Sergei Suyetin, "Gorod dlya cheloveka," *Moskva,* no. 4 (April 1987), p. 168.

66. S. Smolkin, "Veto bezdomnykh," *Arkhitektura,* no. 7 (April 14, 1990), p. 1.

67. *Byulleten' Ispolkoma,* no. 22 (November 1966), p. 6.

68. Until 1980 the problem lay in unambitious plans, not in failure to fulfill them. In the period 1981–1985 Moscow for the first time since the 1940s fell significantly short of a five-year housing plan, not completing 4.2 percent of the 11,700,000 square meters assigned. City leaders did express private regret at performance. As early as August 1971, at a meeting of the ispolkom, Promyslov apologized that the Politburo and the Soviet government "cannot give us what we request" for housing investment because they preferred to spend on agriculture. He did not mention military industry, the other big claimant on resources. TsGIAGM, f. 150, op. 1, d. 3830, l. 196.

69. ZIL figure given in *Moskovskaya pravda,* June 11, 1988, p. 2. The Mossovet in 1969 voted to empty all barracks by 1976, and evidently did so. In 1971 there were still 16,000 Muscovites living in 340 barracks, 200 owned by the city and 140 by enterprises. TsGIAGM, f. 150, op. 1, d. 3830, l. 75.

70. *Moskovskaya pravda,* May 17, 1988, p. 3.

71. Ibid., June 22, 1954, p. 2.

72. Ibid., April 29, 1958, p. 2, and December 15, 1960, p. 3.

73. Ibid., December 15, 1960, p. 3; S. I. Matveyev, "Ustranit' nedostatki v obespechenii moskvichei zhiloi ploshchad'yu," *Gorodskoye khozyaistvo Moskvy,* no. 8 (August 1961), p. 17.

74. Yeltsin, *Ispoved',* p. 116.

75. *Izvestiya,* August 27, 1991, p. 1; *Komsomol'skaya pravda,* August 31, 1991, p. 3.

76. I saw the amenities during an evening in one of these buildings in May 1991. Problems with the houses are described in Larisa Vasil'eva, *Kremlevskiye zheny*

(Moscow: Novosti, 1992), pp. 421–422. They are on both sides of ulitsa Kosygina between Michurinskii prospekt and Mosfil'movskaya ulitsa.

77. *Vechernyaya Moskva,* July 16, 1992, p. 5, omitting the name of the street.

78. Details mostly from Yevgenii Chazov, *Zdorov'e i vlast'* (Moscow: Novosti, 1992), pp. 86–87, and *Nezavisimaya gazeta,* April 17, 1992, p. 1. There were rumors that Brezhnev designed the house on ulitsa Shchuseva, but family members have denied this and said he and his wife found it too luxurious. Yurii Churbanov, *Ya rasskazhu vse, kak bylo* (Moscow: Nezavisimaya gazeta, 1992), pp. 17–19, 69, and Vasil'eva, *Kremlevskiye zheny,* p. 457.

79. On size, only anecdotal data are available. Four members of the Soviet political elite (the son of a former Politburo member, two parliamentarians, and an ex-ambassador to India) were given apartments in the new elite building at 26 ulitsa Dimitrova in the late 1980s measuring 17.8, 25.6, 23.7, and 25.8 square meters of dwelling space per capita (*Argumenty i fakty,* no. 37 [September 1990], p. 5). But these did not approach the upper limit. The two apartments sharing the sixth floor of the ulitsa Shchuseva house with the Brezhnevs had 116 and 115 square meters of net dwelling space, which would give a family of four almost 30 square meters each.

80. *Vechernyaya Moskva,* July 16, 1992, p. 5. The house at 26 ulitsa Dimitrova cost 871 rubles per square meter of dwelling space to build; the Moscow average at the time was 271 rubles.

81. For example, Yu. P. Valov, head of the gorkom's Department of City Services, and before that the deputy chairman of the city ispolkom in charge of the directorate for nomenklatura housing, was named first deputy head of the CC's Business Office in 1983. An ex-gorkom official, K. P. Chernyayev, headed the office in the late Khrushchev period.

82. The changes in the directorate's status are recounted in TsGIAGM, f. R-496, op. 1. Municipally owned hotels were put under its wing only in September 1954 and removed in the late 1980s.

83. Details for 1960, 1965, and 1970 taken from ibid., d. 424, 587, 728. UVDG buildings for the Central Committee only are listed on pp. 86–89 of the classified *Spisok telefonov rabotnikov apparata TsK KPSS,* the CC telephone directory for March 1990, a copy of which was shared with me by a former official several years later. The divisions given are numbered 1, 3, 5, 6, 7, 9, 10, and 11. This means that at least three other UVDG divisions existed, but the number is in all likelihood quite a bit higher. I know from interviews that there was at least one division for Soviet cosmonauts and one for persons involved in foreign intelligence (including defectors from other countries). If the pre-1970 numbering scheme had been retained, Government House and the two tall buildings at ploshchad' Vosstaniya and Kotel'nicheskaya naberezhnaya would also have had separate divisions—and this cannot have been the end of the list. A specialist in a municipal institute told me confidentially in 1988 that the UVDG had "about 2 million square meters" of total space (which would be approximately 1.3 million square meters of net dwelling space), with plans to increase it to 3 million.

84. *Vechernyaya Moskva,* July 16, 1992, p. 5.

85. In January 1971, for instance, the city presidium agreed to a request by two members of the Politburo, N. V. Podgornyi and K. T. Mazurov, that the widow of a radar scientist keep a large apartment upon her husband's death. That July it accepted a petition by a vice-president of the Academy of Sciences, M. D. Millionshchikov, and the minister of medium machine building, Ye. P. Slavskii, to allocate a four-room flat to the director of the Institute of Biophysics, G. M. Frank. The allotment was 18 square meters per person, and as partial recompense the Franks agreed to donate 7,000 rubles to local kindergarten construction. TsGIAGM, f. 150, op. 1, d. 3831, l. 10; d. 3832, l. 4. The secretary of the ispolkom, A. M. Pegov, stated that the city allocated 200,000 square meters of dwelling space in 1970 to individuals previously lacking a Moscow propiska, a figure he thought unduly high. But it included rooms in dormitories and ordinary apartments as well as prime accommodation. Ibid., d. 3830, l. 75.

86. In July 1971 the Central Design Bureau of Experimental Machine Building of the Ministry of General Machine Building—the ministry that built missiles and space vehicles—reminded the city presidium that a Politburo resolution of November 19, 1968, had obliged it to allocate 2,500 square meters of dwelling space to specialists from the institute and that less than half of the space had been provided. The presidium agreed to comply forthwith. Ibid., d. 3832, l. 118.

87. TsGAODM, f. 4, op. 152, d. 37, ll. 76–77.

88. *Byulleten' Ispolkoma*, no. 14 (July 1976), pp. 14–15, and no. 11 (June 1979), p. 19.

89. Ibid., no. 14 (July 1987), p. 35. The three-year estimate is mine, based on interviews.

90. *Sovetskaya Rossiya*, May 16, 1990, p. 4.

91. This is why ZIL, Moscow's largest factory, had a seven-year wait (*Moskovskaya pravda*, May 7, 1987, p. 2).

92. The fullest list I have found of housing projects actually built by nonmunicipal bodies is for 1958 (TsGAODM, f. 4, op. 107, d. 28, ll. 1–2, 9–73, 153–154). Of 640,000 square meters of dwelling space scheduled for construction, the largest lump (147,100 square meters, or 23.0 percent) went to defense contractors, mostly in aviation. Next came allocations to civilian heavy industry and construction (18.7 percent each), the Ministry of Defense (16.6 percent), the Council of Ministers and assorted central agencies (7.8 percent), and the MVD and KGB (7.6 percent). Light and food industries got a mere 2.8 percent. The Academy of Sciences received 2.6 percent, but research personnel would have been included in several other categories. Culture and health got least of all, 0.5 percent. The army's portion in 1958 was probably abnormally high, and I suspect that defense industry got less than usual. In addition to these quotas, 424,000 square meters of Glavmosstroi's output were designated to specific branches, of which 33.3 percent went to the reserves of the city and raion ispolkoms, 25.9 to Glavmosstroi workers, 21.0 percent to miscellaneous municipal employees (mostly in housing and transport), 18.9 percent to the military, and 0.9 percent to the Ministry of Foreign Affairs. We know from another source that from 1969 to 1985 the Ministry of Defense received 65,000 square meters a year from the city under a government directive and an average of 64,000 more under

annual allocations, excluding apartments built by the military itself. *Argumenty i fakty,* no. 21 (June 1991), p. 5.

93. A group of cooperative buildings for writers and the polyclinic of the USSR Writers' Union were sited on Krasnoarmeiskaya and Chernyakhovskogo streets, right at the Aeroport metro station, causing some of the neighbors to refer to the area as "The Gentry's Nest" (after the title of a short story about the tsarist nobility by Ivan Turgenev). An UVDG house for party officials was located at 4 ulitsa Lizy Chaikinoi.

94. There were nomenklatura houses near Olimpiiskii prospekt on ulitsa Durova, Troitskaya ulitsa, Delegatskaya ulitsa, ulitsa Dostoyevskogo (formerly Bozhedomnyi pereulok), and Vtoroi Samotechnyi pereulok. Addresses near the Belorussia Station were on Vtoraya and Tret'ya Tverskaya-Yamskaya ulitsa, ulitsa Aleksandra Nevskogo, Pervaya and Vtoraya Miusskaya ulitsa, and Lesnaya ulitsa; several KGB houses were on Malaya Gruzinskaya ulitsa. The housing project close to ploshchad' Mayakovskogo was at the corner of ulitsa Medvedeva and Vorotnikovskii pereulok, and there was also a KGB building at the corner of Medvedeva and ulitsa Chekhova. For the small outcroppings, the main addresses were 5–7 Bol'shoi Khariton'evskii, 26 ulitsa Karla Marksa, 4 Vtoroi Polevoi pereulok (Sokol'niki), several buildings for astronauts and space engineers on Zvezdnyi bul'var and ulitsa Akademika Koroleva (VDNKh), 22 pereulok Pavlika Morozova (Krasnopresnenskii), and 26 ulitsa Dimitrova and 5 Donskaya ulitsa (Zamoskvorech'e).

95. In the thirteen inner raions, net housing stock increased by 9.3 percent, but population decreased by 7.8 percent. In the outer raions, housing stock increased by 38.2 percent and population by 16 percent.

96. An excellent example of juxtaposition of social types was in the vicinity of Kutuzovskii prospekt. The residents of the next two streets south of Kutuzovskii, Studencheskaya and Kievskaya, were almost all blue-collar, and Kievskaya bordered on both the noisy open-cut subway to Kuntsevo and the rail lines feeding into the Kiev Station. The housing here included cramped hostels built for college students before the war and rows of houses put up by the Ministry of Transportation for railway workers in the 1940s and 1950s, containing mostly communal apartments. Pupils from this subarea did not attend the select elementary schools north of Kutuzovskii.

97. These buildings are on the east side of Profsoyuznaya at the Novyye Cheremushki subway station. Those still under construction for the Central Committee in 1990 had 510 apartments ("Kak vybirali predsedatelya Mossoveta," *Gorodskoye khozyaistvo Moskvy,* no. 7 [July 1990], p. 15). In 1990 the municipal electoral district (No. 355) of which the project made up about two-thirds had 10,424 voters, for a total population of about 15,000. Other projects in the south and southwest of which I am aware were the Ministry of Foreign Affairs complex in Nikulino (Gagarinskii raion); KGB buildings on Michurinskii prospekt (Gagarinskii); the adjacent homes for the Moscow party committee and Moscow Soviet on ulitsa Udal'tsova (Gagarinskii); the party-government developments on ulitsa Akademika Pilyugina and at the corner of Vlasova and Garibaldi streets (Cheremushkinskii raion); and the several houses for KGB foreign intelligence personnel in Yasenevo (Cheremushkinskii). The buildings in Leningradskii raion, on Vyborgskaya, Festival'naya, Flotskaya,

and Lavochkina streets, were started only in the mid-1980s and were for party, government, and KGB workers.

98. *Kuranty,* September 11, 1991, p. 1.

99. I learned about elite dachas mostly from interviews and personal observation. The inventory here is suggestive, not comprehensive, but there is no mistaking the clustering in the Kuntsevo-Zvenigorod strip. The government's Zavidovo hunting preserve was at a remote location northwest of the city, in Moscow and Kalinin oblasts.

100. Stalin's daughter, who had a dacha at Zhukovka for years, describes the different food supply arrangements for the officials, scientists, and local peasants there and recounts how these groups "led entirely different and separate lives." Svetlana Alliluyeva, *Only One Year,* trans. Paul Chavchavadze (New York: Harper and Row, 1967), pp. 251–252. In a drive with a friend in 1992, I was shown subareas in the Council of Ministers territory designated for KGB officers, MVD officials, and other specialized groups, as well as the dacha occupied for many years by Brezhnev's brother Yakov.

101. *Izvestiya,* August 27, 1991, p. 1; *Kuranty,* June 7, 1991, p. 1; *Moskovskaya pravda,* July 2, 1991, p. 3; *Argumenty i fakty,* no. 35 (September 1991), p. 6.

102. Leninskii prospekt, the road from the city center to Vnukovo-2 Airport, the landing field for official flights, was also known as a government route.

103. Oktyabr'skii, Cheremushkinskii, and Gagarinskii, the three raions flanking Leninskii prospekt, had 11.6 percent of Moscow's 1989 population but were the originating raions for 22.7 percent of the candidates for the 1990 municipal election engaged in higher education and general science. The largest proportion of the candidates from institutes under specialized ministries, 6.9 percent, were from Voroshilovskii raion in the northwest. Of the candidates who were writers, artists, and entertainers, by contrast, 34.5 percent were from Frunzenskii, Kievskii, Krasnopresnenskii, and Leninskii raions, which had only 6.6 percent of Moscow's population; 23.0 percent of the journalist candidates came from the same four raions.

104. *Moskovskaya pravda,* July 7, 1988, p. 3.

105. See, for example, Michael N. Danielson and Jameson W. Doig, *New York: The Politics of Urban Regional Development* (Berkeley: University of California Press, 1982), chap. 3.

106. Detailed data to 1975 are in G. A. Gol'ts, *Transport i rasseleniye* (Moscow: Nauka, 1981), p. 139. A later planning document stated that Muscovites expended "about an hour" in transit to work (*Moskovskaya pravda,* April 13, 1989, p. 5). One-way commuting times in 1900 were thirty-three minutes for Moscow residents and ninety minutes for residents of the guberniya working in Moscow.

107. The main decisions on Strogino, but not the protest, were chronicled in *Moskovskaya pravda.*

108. O. K. Kudryavtsev, "Bol'shoye kol'tso metropolitena—na baze Okruzhnoi zheleznoi dorogi," *Gorodskoye khozyaistvo Moskvy,* no. 4 (April 1958), pp. 19–21; *Moskovskaya pravda,* July 15, 1969, p. 2, and June 15, 1988, p. 2.

109. *Moskovskaya pravda,* March 31, 1987, p. 3, and February 11, 1986, p. 2, and for the CC fleet *Kuranty,* September 12, 1991, p. 1.

110. L. Z. Kaplan and G. Ye. Mishchenko, "Za nauchnyi podkhod k organizatsii dvizheniya," *Gorodskoye khozyaistvo Moskvy,* no. 6 (June 1966), p. 18.

111. Quotation from summary of draft of new master plan, in *Moskovskaya pravda,* April 13, 1989, p. 5.

112. Author's interviews and Yeltsin, *Ispoved',* p. 117. One source (*Argumenty i fakty,* no. 39 [October 1991], p. 8) has 6,000 to 7,000 persons a month being serviced at ulitsa Granovskogo prior to closing in 1988.

113. List put together from many (mostly oral) sources.

114. *Moskovskaya pravda,* July 23, 1991, p. 3, and December 4, 1991, pp. 1–2; *Izvestiya,* December 29, 1993, p. 5.

115. Aside from interviews, I draw on a list of assets seized in an unpublished decree by Boris Yeltsin, as president of Russia, in March 1992, and on the 1990 Central Committee phone guide. Andrei Mal'gin, "Petrov zhil, Petrov zhiv, Petrov budet zhit'," *Novoye Russkoye slovo* (New York), May 18, 1992, p. 5, and *Spisok telefonov rabotnikov,* p. 83. Jurisdiction over assets cannot be established in every case. In the USSR as a whole, the Central Committee's nineteen sanatoriums and various rest houses had a combined capacity of 7,100 persons and employed 400 physicians and 1,500 nurses (*Izvestiya,* August 27, 1991, p. 1).

116. Information mostly from interviews. A few details emerge in *Kuranty,* September 10, 1991, p. 1, and October 16, 1991, p. 2.

117. *Nash "Frezer"* (Moscow: Moskovskii rabochii, 1981), pp. 252–254; *Pervyi podshipnikovyi: Istoriya pervogo gosudarstvennogo podshipnikovogo zavoda, 1932–1972* (Moscow: Mysl', 1973), pp. 276–277; *Moskovskaya pravda,* November 6, 1991, p. 7; *Istoriya Moskovskogo avtozavoda imeni I. A. Likhacheva* (Moscow: Mysl', 1966), pp. 556–567; A. Gadasina, "Forposty meditsiny v zavodskom raione," *Gorodskoye khozyaistvo Moskvy,* no. 11 (November 1988), p. 22.

118. "Obespechivaya kompleksnyi podkhod," *Gorodskoye khozyaistvo Moskvy,* no. 2 (February 1983), p. 4; L. Karlik and Ye. Yampol'skii, "Vazhnyi sotsial'nyi zakaz," *Stroitel'stvo i arkhitektura Moskvy,* no. 7 (July 1985), p. 27; N. Shklyayev and V. Lapshin, "Vedomstvennyi faktor i zagorodnyi otdykh moskvichei," *Arkhitektura i stroitel'stvo Moskvy,* no. 7 (July 1987), p. 10.

119. Unless otherwise indicated, statistics in this section are taken from various issues of *Moskva v tsifrakh.*

120. *Moskovskaya pravda,* March 14, 1987, p. 4.

121. *Moskva v tsifrakh,* various issues, and I. Bobkov and V. Patsiorkovskii, "Obshchestvennyi tsentr zhilogo raiona," *Stroitel'stvo i arkhitektura Moskvy,* no. 3 (March 1983), p. 11.

122. "Osnovnyye napravleniya razvitiya goroda," *Stroitel'stvo i arkhitektura Moskvy,* no. 11 (November 1966), p. 18.

123. N. Osterman and A. Petrushkova, "Zhiloi dom-kompleks s obshchestvennym obsluzhivaniyem," *Arkhitektura SSSR,* no. 7 (July 1965), pp. 13–37.

124. See esp. Ya. Zhuchok and Ye. Zuikova, "Arkhitektura i sotsiologiya byta," *Stroitel'stvo i arkhitektura Moskvy,* no. 4 (April 1967), pp. 22–23; Yurii Polukhin, "Ne fantaziya, a real'nost'," *Literaturnaya gazeta,* no. 45 (November 6, 1968), p. 11.

See in various issues of the same journal N. Osterman, "Razvedka budushchego," no. 10 (March 5, 1968), p. 11; Leonid Zhukhovitskii, "Byt' li DNB?" no. 2 (January 14, 1970), p. 12; and the letters in no. 9 (March 4, 1970), p. 11.

125. See, for example, Yankova and Rodzinskaya, *Problemy bol'shogo goroda*, pp. 29–47.

126. *Moskovskaya pravda*, May 9, 1957, p. 2.

127. V. Nesterov, "Novyi zhiloi raion," *Stroitel'stvo i arkhitektura Moskvy*, no. 1 (January 1975), p. 11; A. Shcherbachenko, "Delo pervostepennogo znacheniya," ibid., no. 6 (June 1979), p. 9.

128. S. A. Kravtsova, "Obosnovaniye prodolzhitel'nosti zastroiki mikroraionov," *Gorodskoye khozyaistvo Moskvy*, no. 10 (October 1968), p. 15; A. Voronin, "Kompleksno planirovat', proyektirovat', stroit'," *Stroitel'stvo i arkhitektura Moskvy*, no. 3 (March 1982), p. 20; S. Misharin, "Proyektirovat' i stroit' kompleksno," same journal, no. 11 (November 1982), p. 2.

129. A good preliminary description of the project is L. Dyubek, "Moskva, Severnoye Chertanovo," *Stroitel'stvo i arkhitektura Moskvy*, no. 9 (September 1972), pp. 2–8. I have relied heavily on interviews for my account.

130. *Moskovskaya pravda*, September 15, 1987, p. 3.

131. Voronin, "Kompleksno planirovat'," p. 20.

132. *Moskovskaya pravda*, February 18, 1987, p. 2.

133. See the article and map in ibid., May 16, 1991, p. 3; the map in *Rabochaya tribuna*, January 30, 1991, p. 1; and the article on Radon in *Nezavisimaya gazeta*, December 26, 1992, p. 6. A similar case would be the blistering agents buried in 1941 in the yard of the State Institute for Organic Chemistry and Technology; this matter was not brought to light until 1992.

134. *Kuranty*, July 21, 1992, p. 3.

135. *Moskovskaya pravda*, February 9, 1961, p. 3.

136. Decision summarized in ibid., December 18, 1960, p. 3. I learned of the background politics from interviews. It is impossible to be precise about the number of evictions. Stories in ibid., September 4, 1964, p. 2, and October 9, 1966, p. 2, said that 50 plants and 100 workshops were moved out of Moscow between 1948 and 1966, 18 and 61 of them between 1959 and 1964.

137. Yu. P. Izyumov in ibid., October 10, 1992, p. 3.

138. See *Moskovskaya pravda*, September 12, 1987, p. 2, and Thane Gustafson, *Reform in Soviet Politics: Lessons of Recent Policies on Land and Water* (Cambridge: Cambridge University Press, 1981), pp. 195–196.

139. *Moskovskaya pravda*, August 29, 1990, p. 2.

140. TsGAODM, f. 4, op. 183, d. 1, l. 43; *Moskovskaya pravda*, August 11, 1989, p. 3, and August 7, 1990, p. 3.

141. *Moskovskaya pravda*, July 5, 1989, p. 2.

142. Ibid., April 13, 1989, p. 6; *Sovetsksaya Rossiya*, January 26, 1990, p. 3; *Leninskoye znamya*, January 16, 1990, p. 2.

143. Boris Komarov (Ze'ev Wolfson), *Unichtozheniye prirody: Obostreniye ekologicheskogo krizisa v SSSR* (Frankfurt: Posev, 1978), pp. 44–45.

144. Figures from *Moskovskaya pravda,* July 5, 1989, p. 2, and August 29, 1990, p. 2; the city handbook for 1989; I. Tsarev and A. Trushin, "Otkuda sleduyushchii udar?" *Gorodskoye khozyaistvo Moskvy,* no. 4 (April 1990), pp. 28–29; and "Za-gryazneniye atmosfernogo vozdukha Moskvy," *Energiya, ekonomika, tekhnika, ekologiya,* no. 11 (November 1989), p. 18. In 1988 the Kapotnya Oil Refinery was the source of 91 percent of the hydrogen sulphide emitted in Moscow, Mosbytkhim of 93 percent of the fluorine compounds, and the Foton Works of practically all of the mercury.

145. *Moskovskaya pravda,* August 29, 1990, p. 2.

146. Ibid., August 29, 1990, p. 2. See also D. Sokolov, "Chelovek v megapolise Moskva," *Nauka i zhizn',* no. 10 (October 1990), pp. 2–6.

147. *Moskovskaya pravda,* March 22, 1987, p. 2.

148. Gustafson, *Reform in Soviet Politics,* p. 113.

149. T. Shul'gina and N. Shchepetil'nikov, "Vydayushchiisya pamyatnik revolyutsii," *Stroitel'stvo i arkhitektura Moskvy,* no. 4 (April 1963), pp. 22–24.

150. Communication to the author by Professor Nathaniel Davis, Harvey Mudd College, Claremont, Calif.; Sergei Romanyuk, *Moskva: Utraty* (Moscow: PTO "Tsentr," 1992).

151. Name changes averaged twenty-eight a year from 1953 to 1964, more than five times the average of 1935–1952. Not all were politically motivated. Some were done for technical reasons, and in some cases it was Soviet-era names that were changed. A proposal in the 1950s to change all streets called after pre-1917 property owners or with religious intonations was watered down after resistance by writers and the Moscow Geographic Society. Yurii Yefremov, "Poema moskovskikh imen," in *S lyubov'yu i trevogoi* (Moscow: Sovetskii pisatel', 1990), pp. 155–156.

152. Yu. A. Bychkov, *Zhitiye Petra Baranovskogo* (Moscow: Sovetskaya Rossiya, 1991), pp. 5–7, 140–141; Georgii Kokun'ko, "Khronika odnogo unichtozheniya," *Arkhitektura i stroitel'stvo Moskvy,* no. 5 (May 1988), pp. 9–10.

153. *Pravda,* October 18, 1957, p. 6.

154. Summaries in *Stroitel'stvo i arkhitektura Moskvy,* no. 3 (March 1967), pp. 2–39.

155. Among the demolitions were those of the "Famus House" on ulitsa Gor'kogo once occupied by the Rimskii-Korsakov family (1967), the seventeenth-century Church of Sts. Joachim and Anna (1970), the eighteenth-century nobles' villa at the intersection of Kropotkinskaya and Metrostroyevskaya streets (1972), and the library of the novelist Ivan Turgenev (1972). These cases are described in Romanyuk, *Moskva: Utraty,* pp. 174–176, 214–215, 232, 264–265, who says the nobles' villa was torn down because it was in a dilapidated state and the Politburo did not want U.S. President Richard Nixon to see it on his visit to Moscow in 1972.

156. See M. Posokhin, "Povysit' kachestvennyi uroven' gradostroitel'stva," *Stroitel'stvo i arkhitektura Moskvy,* no. 3 (March 1975), p. 4, and A. Ganeshin, "Novyi etap rekonstruktsii tsentra," *Arkhitektura i stroitel'stvo Moskvy,* no. 2 (February 1987), pp. 14–16.

157. "Sud'ba Russkoi stolitsy," in *Arkhiv samizdata,* vol. 21 (Munich: Radio

Liberty, 1972), p. 91; Romanyuk, *Moskva: Utraty,* pp. 70–71; Promyslov in *Vechern-yaya Moskva,* July 16, 1992, p. 5.

158. "Sud'ba Russkoi stolitsy," p. 95; Oleg Platonov, "Puteshestviye v Kitezh-grad," *Moskva,* no. 4 (April 1990), p. 161.

159. *Nezavisimaya gazeta,* February 19, 1991, p. 5.

160. V. Glazychev and G. Zabel'shanskii, "Zapovednaya zona: Zapovednik ili zapoved?" *Stroitel'stvo i arkhitektura Moskvy,* no. 10 (October 1980), p. 31.

161. Vladimir Rezvin, "Istoriya odnogo pamyatnika so prologom, no bez epi-loga," *Arkhitektura i stroitel'stvo Moskvy,* no. 8 (August 1989), p. 17.

162. *Moskovskaya pravda,* June 11, 1987, p. 3, and January 13, 1994, p. 4; L. Bobylev, "Bol'shomy teatru—bol'shoye plavaniye?" *Arkhitektura,* nos. 5–6 (July 1991), p. 13; *Nezavisimaya gazeta,* October 17, 1991, p. 6.

163. V. Apenin, "Paradoksy zapovednykh zon," *Arkhitektura i stroitel'stvo Moskvy,* no. 11 (November 1987), p. 7; letter by V. Makhnach and S. Filatov in ibid., no. 7 (July 1988), p. 12; Peshkova and Chuvelev, "Tupiki ekstensivnogo puti," p. 6.

164. *Moskovskaya pravda,* July 20, 1980, p. 2; Ye. Sorin, "Garmoniya starogo i novogo," *Stroitel'stvo i arkhitektura Moskvy,* no. 19 (October 1978), p. 10; N. Apol-lonskii, "Snova o garmonii starogo i novogo," same journal no. 6 (June 1979), p. 32.

165. "Sud'ba Russkoi stolitsy," passim.

166. I heard about this document in interviews but never saw a copy. Another target of chauvinistic criticism was Yemel'yan Yaroslavskii, the chairman of the League of Militant Atheists under Stalin. Yaroslavskii, whose given name was Gubel'man, was, like Kaganovich, Jewish in origin.

167. Author's interviews. There is general information in "Pamyat," special issue of *Nationalities Papers,* vol. 19 (Fall 1991).

168. *Moskovskaya pravda,* November 20, 1987, p. 3.

169. Ibid., October 22, 1988, p. 3.

170. Despite the new office space, the KGB felt pressed. The seven-story building at 7 ulitsa Dzerzhinskogo, into which the Moscow directorate moved in 1980, was supposed to be almost twice as high but was cut back by planners. A spokesman told a journalist later that his colleagues were working "in conditions inappropriate for officers" (*Moskovskaya pravda,* December 11, 1991, p. 5). The KGB's largest facility was the Moscow Training Center it built on Michurinskii prospekt in the 1970s; it also had major buildings near Rublevskoye shosse, in Kuntsevskii raion, and, as has been mentioned, its foreign espionage branch outside the MKAD at Yasenevo.

171. *Moskovskaya pravda,* October 27, 1987, p. 3.

172. Charles E. Lindblom, *Politics and Markets: The World's Political-Economic Systems* (New York: Basic Books, 1977), chap. 5.

7. The Mold Shattered

1. On the distinction between liberalization and democratization, I follow Samuel P. Huntington, *The Third Wave: Democratization in the Late Twentieth Century* (Norman: University of Oklahoma Press, 1991), p. 9.

2. V. K. Belyaninov in *XIX Vsesoyuznaya konferentsiya Kommunisticheskoi partii Sovetskogo Soyuza: Stenograficheskii otchet* (Moscow: Politizdat, 1988), I, 110.

3. *Vedomosti Mossoveta*, no. 1 (1991), p. 18.

4. James H. Billington, *Russia Transformed: Breakthrough to Hope* (New York: Free Press, 1992), p. 3.

5. According to one account, Grishin blamed the fire on sabotage, while Andropov and the KGB cited poor construction and violation of codes. Zhores A. Medvedev, *Gorbachev* (New York: Norton, 1986), p. 173.

6. Mark Frankland, *The Sixth Continent: Russia and the Making of Mikhail Gorbachov* (New York: Harper and Row, 1987), pp. 95–96.

7. The fullest account of the affair is the series of articles in *Moskovskaya pravda*, September 10–16, 1986.

8. See ibid., October 10, 1992, p. 3. Trushin, a former head of the Moscow Komsomol, worked from July 1976 to October 1979 as secretary of the gorkom supervising party organization and law enforcement, then as chief of police, keeping his seat on the gorkom bureau. In January 1984 he was reappointed gorkom secretary, responsible this time for trade and services as well as administrative organs. He succeeded to Churbanov's job December 10, 1984, and in 1989 was appointed the first head of the resurrected RSFSR interior ministry. He lost this position in 1990, but in August 1991, after the failed anti-Gorbachev coup, served one day as USSR minister of internal affairs.

9. *Nezavisimaya gazeta*, February 19, 1991, p. 5; *Moskovskaya pravda*, October 10, 1992, p. 3.

10. TsGAODM, f. 4, op. 152, d. 122, l. 59 (1967 assessment of Tregubov, signed by Secretary R. F. Dement'eva); Yu. K. Sokolov, "Berech' vremya pokupatelya," *Gorodskoye khozyaistvo Moskvy*, no. 4 (April 1982), pp. 19–20; V. A. Ural'tsev, "Na uroven' sovremennykh trebovanii," same journal, no. 8 (August 1982), pp. 8–10.

11. See his interview in *Nezavisimaya gazeta*, February 16, 1991, p. 5.

12. Ye. K. Ligachev, in his memoir *Zagadka Gorbacheva* (Novosibirsk: Interbuk, 1992), p. 13, says that Kapitonov was an "honorable" official but would have been replaced by any new leader. In an interview with me in November 1991, he stated that Kapitonov was eased out for "objective" reasons but also that there was some concern that he might use his position to assist Grishin. Kapitonov supervised light industry in the Secretariat until March 1986.

13. Ligachev, *Zagadka Gorbacheva*, p. 56.

14. Boris Yeltsin, *Ispoved' na zadannuyu temu* (Moscow: PIK, 1990), pp. 102–103. The only person on Grishin's list whom Yeltsin identifies is V. I. Dolgikh, who he says was to have become prime minister.

15. V. N. Makeyev, the gorkom second secretary elevated to deputy premier of the USSR, had been demoted to the trade unions in January 1983. The other Grishin clients on the Council of Ministers, A. I. Yashin and A. K. Mel'nichenko, retired in July and December 1985. The provincial first secretary with the closest past links to him, P. A. Leonov of Kalinin oblast (a Moscow raikom and obkom official from 1945 to 1955), retired in August 1985. In Moscow three of nineteen heads of gorkom

departments, and seven of thirty-three raikom first secretaries, were replaced between March and December 1985. All three of the new department heads, and four of the seven raikom secretaries, were to be retired or demoted by Yeltsin.

16. Yeltsin, *Ispoved'*, p. 83; *Nezavisimaya gazeta*, February 16, 1991, p. 5. Grishin blamed Ligachev more than Gorbachev for his removal, saying Ligachev "wanted to be the second person in the state" and saw him as an obstacle.

17. References to the plenum are from the transcript in TsGAODM, f. 4, op. 207, d. 8, ll. 1–12. *Pravda* on December 25 said only that Grishin had been removed "in connection with his going on pension." Some Western journalists have written highly fanciful accounts of the plenum. Dusko Doder and Louise Branson claim in *Gorbachev: Heretic in Power* (New York: Viking, 1990), p. 102, that the gorkom actually reelected Grishin to the post and retracted only when Gorbachev demanded they do so.

18. Yeltsin, *Ispoved'*, p. 7. I survey Yeltsin's career and style in "Boris Yeltsin, Russia's All-Thumbs Democrat," in Timothy J. Colton and Robert C. Tucker, eds., *Patterns in Post-Soviet Leadership* (Boulder, Colo.: Westview Press, forthcoming 1995). The best narrative biography is John Morrison, *Boris Yeltsin: From Bolshevik to Democrat* (New York: Dutton, 1991). His father's persecution is first described in Boris Yeltsin, *Zapiski prezidenta* (Moscow: Ogonek, 1994), pp. 121–125.

19. Yeltsin, *Ispoved'*, pp. 55, 56. Ya. P. Ryabov, the Sverdlovsk first secretary until 1976 and later CC secretary for the defense industry, recommended Yeltsin for his early promotions. Also from Sverdlovsk was Ryzhkov, who supervised Yeltsin's work in the Secretariat from April 1985 until he became prime minister that October. He graduated from the same polytechnic as Yeltsin and was director of the city's largest factory until 1979.

20. Ibid., p. 83. One then colleague in the Soviet leadership wrote later that Ligachev "calculated that Yeltsin would be 'his man' in Moscow," as the two were from adjacent provinces and were not dissimilar in personal style. Vadim Medvedev, *V komande Gorbacheva* (Moscow: Bylina, 1994), p. 67.

21. "Vypiska iz vystupleniya t. Yeltsina B. N. 11 aprelya s. g. pered propagandistami g. Moskvy," Radio Free Europe/Radio Liberty, *Materialy samizdata*, no. 23/86 (July 18, 1986), p. 9.

22. We have only Yeltsin's word for his stand on the anti-drinking campaign (*Ispoved'*, p. 96).

23. *Moskovskaya pravda*, January 26, 1986, p. 1; *XXVII s"ezd Kommunisticheskoi partii Sovetskogo Soyuza: Stenograficheskii otchet* (Moscow: Politizdat, 1986), I, 141. Yeltsin's congress speech attracted the most public attention, but some insiders were more struck by his preceding address to the Moscow conference. One compared it in his diary to Khrushchev's anti-Stalin speech to the Twentieth Congress in 1956. A. S. Chernyayev, *Shest' let s Gorbachevym* (Moscow: Kul'tura, 1993), p. 63.

24. *Moskovskaya pravda*, January 26, 1986, pp. 1, 3; Yeltsin, *Ispoved'*, p. 83.

25. Among those discharged were the chief of the Moscow KGB, V. I. Alidin, and that of the Moscow union council, L. V. Petrov, both members of the gorkom bureau.

Eight of the raikom first secretaries were given higher-ranking jobs, although three had lost them by the time of Yeltsin's removal.

26. Tables C-1 and C-2 put post-Grishin personnel into a single temporal category, extending to April 1990. Within this period, however, ten of the fifteen municipal officials, and twenty-one of the twenty-four Communist Party officials, began their service under Yeltsin.

27. One Sverdlovsk man was A. N. Tsaregorodtsev, named head of the gorkom's General Department in October 1986 and removed after Yeltsin's fall. Two of Yeltsin's three personal assistants also hailed from Sverdlovsk. I do know of outsiders given high municipal posts, but incomplete biographies keep them from figuring in Table C-2. As an example, V. A. Karnaukhov, appointed head of the Chief Trade Directorate in 1986, had served in the party organs of Tomsk oblast under Ligachev.

28. Quotations from Yeltsin, *Ispoved'*, p. 88, and "Vypiska iz vystupleniya t. Yeltsina," p. 7. The other raikom bosses dismissed in disgrace were Yu. A. Grafov (Timiryazevskii raion), I. F. Komzolov (Kuibyshevskii raion), and I. V. Shakhmanov (Leningradskii raion). All five were expelled from the gorkom in February and March 1987.

29. "Vypiska iz vystupleniya t. Yeltsina," p. 8; *Moskovskaya pravda*, September 21, 1986, p. 2.

30. Yeltsin, *Ispoved'*, p. 96.

31. *Pravda*, November 13, 1987, pp. 2–3. The harshest charge regarding Yeltsin's cadres policy was that it caused a former raikom first secretary (who can be identified as A. V. Korovitsyn of Kievskii raion) to commit suicide in 1987. Yeltsin denied this, saying that the death had nothing to do with the official's removal from the raikom some months before. See *XIX Vsesoyuznaya konferentsiya*, II, 104, and Yeltsin, *Ispoved'*, pp. 119–120. A former assistant to Yeltsin, who is not uncritical of him, told me that Korovitsyn's dismissal was prompted by remarks made by President François Mitterrand of France in 1986 about the decrepitude of food stores in central Moscow, and that Yeltsin actually tried to keep Korovitsyn from being expelled from the party.

32. Quotations from *Moskovskaya pravda*, July 20, 1986, p. 2; November 23, 1986, p. 1; April 14, 1987, p. 1.

33. Ibid., March 30, 1986, p. 2; July 20, 1986, p. 2; October 5, 1986, p. 2; October 24, 1987, p. 1; Yeltsin, *Ispoved'*, pp. 93–94.

34. *Moskovskaya pravda*, March 30, 1986, p. 2; "Vypiska iz vystupleniya t. Yeltsina," pp. 2, 4; "Kak reshalsya v Moskve prodovol'stvennyi vopros," *Izvestiya TsK KPSS*, no. 12 (December 1990), p. 125.

35. *Pravda*, November 13, 1987, p. 2; *Moskovskaya pravda*, August 9, 1987, p. 2.

36. *Pravda*, November 13, 1987, p. 1.

37. Ibid.; Yeltsin, *Ispoved'*, pp. 95–96.

38. Lev Sukhanov, *Tri goda s Yeltsinym: Zapiski pervogo pomoshchnika* (Riga: Vaga, 1992), pp. 40–41.

39. *Moskovskaya pravda*, October 5, 1986, p. 2; emphasis added. Yeltsin was

perhaps thinking more broadly about party structure, as he recommended to Gorbachev around this time that first secretaries of territorial committees be kept out of the Politburo because membership would make it impossible to criticize them. See "Plenum TsK KPSS—oktyabr' 1987 goda: Stenograficheskii otchet," *Izvestiya TsK KPSS*, no. 2 (February 1989), pp. 279–280.

40. Doder and Branson, *Gorbachev*, pp. 263–265; Vera Tolz, *The USSR's Emerging Multiparty System*, Washington Papers/148 (New York: Praeger, 1990), pp. 26–29; *Nyeformaly: Civil Society in the USSR* (New York: Helsinki Watch, 1990), pp. 58–59.

41. Main sources are the transcript of the CC plenum of October 1987, the report on the Moscow gorkom plenum of November 11, 1987, speeches at the Nineteenth Party Conference in June and July 1988, and Yeltsin's autobiography.

42. Yeltsin made no mention of the Stalin question or the other historical issues on the agenda, which were of no more interest to him than economic theory. To the extent that he had views, they were seen at the time as less liberal than Gorbachev's. See Chernyayev, *Shest' let s Gorbachevym*, p. 177.

43. In an interview five years later (*Trud*, December 26, 1992, p. 2), Gorbachev stated that he found the plenum distasteful and that it got out of hand when Moscow officials "said not only what he [Yeltsin] deserved but more than that."

44. Yeltsin, *Ispoved'*, p. 129.

45. The facts on personnel politics are hard to pull out. Yeltsin is said to have asserted at the June 1987 CC plenum that Ligachev was sending agents into Moscow to gather "negative materials" on cadres ("Plenum TsK KPSS—oktyabr' 1987 goda," p. 240). Another source has him saying he could not purge officials with patrons above (Kevin Devlin, "El'tsin's Supporter on Struggle against Party 'Mafia,'" Radio Liberty/Radio Free Europe Research, *Background Report [USSR]*, no. 85 [May 20, 1988], p. 4). At the plenum that removed Yeltsin, V. V. Skitev, the head of the gorkom's cadres department, said he had contact with the Secretariat, but only "surreptitiously" and because Yeltsin lost interest in staffing. A. M. Larionov, a former raikom secretary, said Yeltsin's Moscow colleagues failed to take their misgivings about his personnel decisions to the top: "Surely these comrades could have gone to the CC, which is not far from here." *Pravda*, November 13, 1987, p. 3.

46. "Plenum TsK KPSS—oktyabr' 1987 goda," pp. 241, 280, 256; Yeltsin, *Ispoved'*, p. 93. Gorbachev's first remark was prompted by anger at Yeltsin's suggestion that his resignation from the Moscow leadership, as distinct from the Politburo, be dealt with by the gorkom alone.

47. Although the public impression was that Zaikov and Ligachev were friendly, their relations were, in fact, poor. Gorbachev's principal aide recalls a scene when Zaikov was "practically in tears" as he told his boss about Ligachev's interference in his work. Valery Boldin, *Ten Years That Shook the World*, trans. Evelyn Rossiter (New York: Basic Books, 1994), p. 184. Boldin characterizes Zaikov as a weakling for whom even Gorbachev had little respect.

48. *Moskovskaya pravda*, December 6, 1987, p. 1, and November 22, 1989, p. 1.

49. Ibid., May 6, 1989, pp. 3–6.

50. Ibid., February 23, 1987, p. 4.

51. Nina Moleva, "Vremya istoricheskoi pravdy," *Arkhitektura i stroitel'stvo Moskvy,* no. 3 (March 1988), p. 11; Yevgenii Kuman'kov, "Mysli khudozhnika," ibid.

52. Valerii Fadeyev, *Pokhozhdeniya neformala (ocherk 88 goda)* (Moscow: Russkoye slovo, 1992), I, 15. Numerical estimates in *Moskovskaya pravda,* October 14, 1987, p. 3, and September 20, 1988, p. 2.

53. *Moskovskaya pravda,* September 20, 1988, pp. 2, 4; Fadeyev, *Pokhozhdeniya neformala,* I, 30.

54. Fadeyev, *Pokhozhdeniya neformala,* I, 16; *Moskovskaya pravda,* September 20, 1988, p. 4.

55. Fadeyev, *Pokhozhdeniya neformala,* I, 10.

56. Ibid., p. 37. It so happens that I was present at the square for several hours of the rally. I did not appreciate its significance at the time.

57. *Nyeformaly,* p. 68; *Samodeyatel'nyye obshchestvennyye organizatsii SSSR (spravochnik)* (Moscow: Moskovskii Narodnyi Front, 1988), pp. 17–18. According to Fadeyev, Dergunov became leader because he lived near Pushkinskaya ploshchad' and was thus able to attend all the meetings there.

58. *Moskovskaya pravda,* March 2, 1988, p. 2. On particular conflicts, I derived much of the important information from interviews.

59. A. Musatov, "Palaty Shcherbakova," *Stroitel'stvo i arkhitektura Moskvy,* no. 11 (November 1986), p. 14; Vladimir Gurbolikov, "Kak my spasali palaty Shcherbakova," *Gorodskoye khozyaistvo Moskvy,* no. 11 (November 1990), p. 18; Doder and Branson, *Gorbachev,* pp. 185–186.

60. *Moskovskaya pravda,* March 3, 1988, p. 3.

61. Ibid., September 25, 1988, p. 2.

62. Ibid., November 11, 1988, p. 3.

63. Ibid., June 21, 1989, p. 2.

64. Details taken from numerous articles in the Moscow and oblast press and from materials distributed by anti-TETs lobbyists at meetings of the Mossovet in May 1990.

65. *Pervyi S"ezd narodnykh deputatov SSSR: Stenograficheskii otchet* (Moscow: Izdaniye Verkhovnogo Soveta SSSR, 1989), IV, 318–323.

66. *Moskovskaya pravda,* July 30, 1989, p. 1.

67. For informed general discussion, see Michael Urban, *More Power to the Soviets: The Democratic Revolution in the USSR* (Aldershot: Edward Elgar, 1990), and Brendan Kiernan, *The End of Soviet Politics* (Boulder, Colo.: Westview Press, 1993).

68. *Moskovskaya pravda,* September 25, 1988, p. 2.

69. V. A. Kolosov, N. V. Petrov, and L. V. Smirnyagin, *Vesna 89: Geografiya i anatomiya parlamentskikh vyborov* (Moscow: Progress, 1990), pp. 223, 231–232 (amended to count P. S. Surov as a political leader).

70. Sukhanov, *Tri goda s Yeltsinym,* p. 78. According to Boldin (*Ten Years,*

pp. 214–215), one of the reasons Gorbachev did not contest a territorial district in Moscow was his fear that Yeltsin would oppose and defeat him.

71. Kolosov, Petrov, and Smirnyagin, *Vesna 89,* p. 238; R. Z. Sagdeyev in *Pervyi S"ezd,* I, 151.

72. Kolosov, Petrov, and Smirnyagin, *Vesna 89,* p. 239.

73. *Moskovskaya pravda,* June 22, 1989, p. 2.

74. Ibid., November 23, 1989, p. 1. I learned of the attempt to impose Resin, born in 1936, from participants in the negotiations. According to a then member of the Politburo, Zaikov asked Gorbachev to relieve him of the Moscow post. Medvedev, *V komande Gorbacheva,* p. 121.

75. Medvedev, *V komande Gorbacheva,* p. 121.

76. Huntington, *Third Wave,* pp. 174–192.

77. *Moskovskaya pravda,* November 30, 1990, p. 1.

78. Source: Moscow City Electoral Commission.

79. Nomination close to residence was also more common among women and persons of pension age. Among employment-age candidates, Communists were less likely than most to stand in their home raions, evidently because of their engrossment in some political issues in their job units through party cells there. Among candidates born after 1930, 52 percent of CPSU members ran in their raions of residence as against 67 percent of the other candidates.

80. Author's interview with Vladimir S. Afanas'ev, secretary of the commission.

81. Fourteen districts went straight to a repeat election, in which the original candidates were ineligible, 1 because of low turnout and 13 because neither of 2 candidates had gotten a majority. In the runoff vote of March 18, 898 candidates were eligible, but 3 of them withdrew; low turnout prevented a decision in 21 districts. First-lap frontrunners prevailed in 79.9 percent of the districts decided. The total number of deputies elected was 472. In addition to the 463 elected March 4 and 18, 2 candidates were declared elected in early April after the city electoral commission revised turnout figures from the runoff vote, and 7 in the repeat election and runoff April 24 and May 15. The city postponed further voting until November 25, when a repeat election in the 26 remaining districts, in which turnout was abysmally low, failed to settle anything. Yet another round of elections should have occurred in 1991, but it was never held.

82. *Moskovskaya pravda,* November 30, 1990, p. 1.

83. V. S. Afanas'ev of Pervomaiskii raion in ibid., December 1, 1990, p. 2.

84. Ibid., December 21, 1989, p. 1. Among the promises rehashed were those to provide every family with a separate flat by 2000, equip every microraion with shops and consumer services, and restore architectural landmarks.

85. Ibid., November 30, 1990, p. 1.

86. Ibid., February 15, 1990, p. 3.

87. V. Shutkin in ibid., November 3, 1990, p. 2.

88. Sukhanov, *Tri goda s Yeltsinym,* pp. 240–241.

89. Gavriil Popov, "Strasti po Moskve: Nestoyavshiisya mer," unpub. ms., p. 61. This manuscript is Popov's forthcoming memoir.

90. Popov says in ibid., pp. 20–21, that he once considered careers in both the party apparatus and the KGB. Stankevich joined the CPSU only in 1987, and was active in Socialist Initiative, a Marxist-oriented reform group. Fadeyev, *Pokhozhdeniya neformala*, I, 41, describes him as defending the single-party system in 1988. Lev A. Ponomarev, a Moscow physicist who began in politics in the Memorial society, was another important organizer, but his involvement was mainly at the RSFSR level, not Moscow.

91. S. Stankevich and M. Shneider, *Rekomendatsii po taktike kandidatov demokraticheskogo bloka i ikh komand v izbiratel'noi kampanii, 1989–90 gg.* (Moscow: Informtsentr Moskovskogo Narodnogo Fronta, n.d. [1989]), pp. 5, 7.

92. Ibid., p. 12.

93. "Sozdan izbiratel'nyi blok 'Demokraticheskaya Rossiya,'" *Ogonek*, no. 6 (February 1990), pp. 17–18.

94. In an interview with the author in May 1990, Stankevich could not say how many eventual DR candidates had been talked into running but stressed that it was a minority.

95. *Pozitsiya*, identified as a publication of the Concord Foundation (Obshchestvennyi fond "Sodruzhestvo"), published a complete list of DR candidates for the Mossovet in its issue no. 3 (February 1990), pp. 2–3. Five of those mentioned had withdrawn from contention by mid-February, 7 had never been duly registered, 2 were running in different districts, and one's name was misspelled.

96. *Moskovskaya pravda*, November 3, 1990, p. 2.

97. The candidates' positions are taken from posters I saw at the time in Moscow. Shugol' and Fadeyev were the only DR candidates in their districts, while Kagarlitskii and Borisov were 1 of 2 in theirs. Father Borisov won his seat in the first round; the other 3 were victorious in the runoff.

98. Abushayev, Bogantseva, Braginskii, and Shekhova, the sole DR candidates in their districts, won their seats in the runoff. Rogacheva, 1 of 3 DR candidates in her district, finished second to another DR candidate March 4 but won the runoff. Gusman, 1 of 6 DR nominees, and Matveyev, 1 of 2 DR nominees in his district, both finished third March 4 and were eliminated. In Brateyevo, Democratic Russia candidates all won first-round victories: Zulumyan against another DR candidate; V. E. Gefenider in district 183, unopposed; and S. Ye. Nikiforov against 2 non-DR candidates in district 184.

99. There were two exceptions to this pattern: the Rossiya Club, founded in October 1989, which originated in the USSR parliament as a counterweight to the Interregional Group; and the United Toilers, founded in June 1989 in Leningrad with the intent of pulling ordinary workers into the battle. References to the declaration are to "Za politiku narodnogo soglasiya i Rossiiskogo vozrozhdeniya," *Literaturnaya Rossiya*, no. 52 (December 29, 1989), pp. 2–3.

100. Quotation from a poster seen March 3 in the Medvedkovo area of Babushkinskii raion. The same day, I saw Stars of David scrawled over several DR posters in central Moscow, a vulgar attempt to link the radical slate with Jews.

101. Official results were printed in the local press but with numerous omissions,

apart from the remediable lack of reference to candidates' slates. I could not have done my analysis without the supplementary data I received from the Department for Work of the Soviets.

102. *Moskovskaya pravda*, February 3, 1990, p. 2.

103. In one raion, Sevastopol'skii, where the center was well organized (but the right was not particularly so), center and right together marginally outpolled DR in the first round.

104. The statistical information concerning districts and their populations is all aggregated by city raion and thus subject to considerable measurement error. Noninterval candidate characteristics—gender, raion of residence, and CPSU affiliation—were coded as dummy variables, scored 1 for quality-present and 0 for quality-absent. Occupations were ranked on an 11-point prestige scale, in the same order as the major groups in Table 19. For additional testing, each of the groups, the discrete occupations, and batches of them were recoded as dummies. The multiplicity of nominees, not found in an election contested by mature parties, was dealt with by averaging individual-level values.

105. Altogether, I ran twenty district (raion) characteristics as independent variables. One was a dummy variable for geographic centrality. Five were sociodemographic indexes, giving the proportion of the population ethnic Russian, female, of pension age, having a higher education, and convicted of a crime the preceding year. Fourteen were yardsticks of public policy or its results, roughly capturing provision of health care, schooling, housing, retail and consumer services, recreation, and environmental protection. All were for 1989 except for day care, cinemas, and air emissions, which were for 1988. Most indicators were taken from *Moskva v tsifrakh, 1989* (Moscow: Finansy i statistika, 1989). Several were from the data set *Sistema kompleksnoi otsenki sostoyaniya sotsial'no-ekonomicheskogo razvitiya Moskvy i yeye administrativnykh raionov*, prepared by the Central Mathematical Economics Institute and kindly shared with me by Professor Vladimir Treml of Duke University.

106. A positive coefficient was also obtained when a measure of the cooperative housing stock—another index of what I am calling the middle-class population—replaced the educational variable in the regression. The regression coefficient for the percent of the raion's dwelling space cooperatively owned was 0.22; it fell slightly short of statistical significance at the .05 level.

107. Yet Democratic Russia won runoff victories in districts 4 and 5 in Leninskii raion (near Komsomol'skii prospekt and Frunzenskaya naberezhnaya); 114 and 115 in Kievskii raion (Kutuzovskii prospekt); 185 in Krasnopresnenskii raion (ulitsa Alekseya Tol'stogo); and 216 in Kuntsevskii raion (Malaya Filevskaya ulitsa). Either some well-connected voters betrayed their class and went with the radicals, or they voted against DR and were outvoted by their neighbors.

108. Prokof'ev drew 43.3 percent in the first round against two other candidates in district 388, defeating a DR candidate in the runoff with 69.6 percent of the final vote. In district 150 (Krasnogvardeiskii raion), Saikin finished first of three candidates in the first round with 43.7 percent. When the runner-up (a DR nominee) withdrew from the runoff, Saikin ran unopposed and won with 62.2 percent of the vote. The

apparatchiks elected included two of four gorkom secretaries in this group, five of twenty-four raikom first secretaries, and six at lower grades. Twenty-nine of the sixty were army, regular police, or KGB officers.

109. *Moskovskaya pravda*, June 17, 1990, p. 7, and July 5, 1990, p. 2.

110. Ibid., October 15, 1991, p. 2.

111. "Kak vybirali predsedatelya Mossoveta," *Gorodskoye khozyaistvo Moskvy*, no. 7 (July 1990), pp. 9–11. Popov has since described himself as loyal to Soviet values until the invasion of Afghanistan in 1979 and has expressed regret at some of his actions as university dean, including his assent in the withdrawal of academic degrees from Jews trying to emigrate to Israel. He resigned from his deanship in 1980 after being criticized for insufficient conformity, but Viktor Grishin helped him keep his teaching position ("Strasti po Moskve," pp. 108–109).

112. Ispolkom decisions dated February 21 and March 27, 1990, ceded the buildings to the party. The gorkom, anticipating a fight, unilaterally made *Moskovskaya pravda* an organ of the party only effective April 15, the day before the inauguration of the new soviet. *Vechernyaya Moskva*'s masthead showed it a joint soviet-party organ until August 1991, but practical control rested from the spring of 1990 onward with the editorial staff.

113. Quotation from "Kak vybirali predsedatelya Mossoveta," p. 9. Luzhkov was appointed on an acting basis by the outgoing ispolkom April 14, the day after Saikin became a deputy premier of the RSFSR.

114. *Vedomosti Mossoveta*, no. 4 (1991), pp. 31–32.

115. O. I. Kachalin in "Kak vybirali predsedatelya Mossoveta," p. 5.

116. *Moskovskaya pravda*, January 3, 1991, p. 1.

117. The organization chart did evolve some. From 1960 to 1966 there was no USSR interior ministry, and from 1966 to 1989 no RSFSR ministry. Bogdanov's predecessor as Moscow chief, V. G. Borisenkov (appointed in April 1984 under Grishin), was evidently the first career policeman to hold the position, Bogdanov being the second.

118. Interview in *Izvestiya*, April 24, 1991, p. 8.

119. Popov in *Kuranty*, September 21, 1991, p. 4.

120. A number of Moscow leaders, including Yeltsin and Yurii Prokof'ev (who never received any credit for his support), had lobbied for permission to rebuild the church before the 1990 election. The CPSU Politburo approved the project in principle at the end of 1989.

121. I was in the crowd at the ceremony.

122. *Moskovskaya pravda*, November 11, 1990, p. 1, and December 23, 1990, p. 3.

123. Ibid., June 22, 1989, p. 1.

124. Yeltsin liquidated nine councils and commissions. The fairly well-tasked committees of factory managers, rectors, and school principals were kept but no longer under party auspices. He also reduced the gorkom secretaries from seven to six, merged two branch departments, and appended new consultative councils to the gorkom for town planning and economics.

125. Shantsev's angry speech is in *Moskovskaya pravda*, December 2, 1990,

pp. 2–3. The record shows Shantsev elected a secretary only, but the position was clearly second ranking and was unofficially referred to as such.

126. Ibid., July 26, 1990, p. 1.

127. Author's interview with Yurii Prokof'ev, June 1991.

128. *Moskovskaya pravda,* November 30, 1990, p. 2. The standard plaint until recently had been that the party organs were unable to extricate themselves from old-style cadres and economic work. Late in 1989 the gorkom bureau was ordering firms to help the railways unload boxcars at the congested Moscow freight yards (ibid., October 27, 1989, p. 2).

129. Five of the municipal members were, like Bryachikhin, ex-raikom secretaries. One was acting head of a Moscow Soviet department, two were deputy heads, and two of the remaining three were lower-ranking still. L. A. Belov, a military researcher and a member of the Mossovet presidium, was the eleventh member. He was a man of some influence but did not hold administrative office at city hall. Also a member of the gorkom was A. T. Vas'kov, secretary of the CPSU committee in the apparatus of the ispolkom.

130. Preobrazhenskii had in fact been elected on the Democratic Russia slate but joined the Moskva faction within the soviet. He got eighty-two votes in April 1990 and Bryachikhin forty-four. Two minor candidates got fourteen votes between them. Bryachikhin was the only Moscow politician elected to the politburo of the RSFSR party in September 1990. He was not reelected to the bureau of the gorkom that winter.

131. *Moskovskaya pravda,* December 4, 1990, p. 2, and December 6, 1990, p. 2; emphasis added.

132. Author's interview with Prokof'ev. Results of the poll were published in various issues of *Moskovskii komsomolets.*

133. One of the three Communists running, Bryachikhin, visited Popov before June 12, declared that the CPSU was waging "a dishonest campaign," and told Popov "that he was basically in agreement with [Popov's] program and was prepared to work for its implementation." Popov, "Strasti po Moskve," p. 107. Popov appointed Bryachikhin to a senior administrative position weeks after the election.

134. *Moskovskaya pravda,* July 18, 1991, p. 2.

135. "'Kapital,' tom poslednii?" *Ogonek,* no. 46 (November 1991), pp. 4–5.

136. *Moskovskaya pravda,* February 21, 1991, p. 2, and June 5, 1991, p. 2. Communists in the Mossovet declined from 280 in April 1990 to 203 in May 1991, and the CPSU fraction from 94 to 82.

137. *Kuranty,* July 30, 1991, p. 1.

138. Popov in *Izvestiya,* February 2, 1993, p. 7, and Michael R. Beschloss and Strobe Talbott, *At the Highest Levels: The Inside Story of the End of the Cold War* (Boston: Little, Brown, 1993), pp. 395–401.

139. The emergency committee may have hoped that the mere sight of the soldiers would quell resistance, as trucks carrying tank shells did not arrive in Moscow until the evening of August 19. The Tamanskaya Division, based at Golitsyno (due west of Moscow), encamped in Tushino, and the Kantemirovskaya Division, from Naro-Fominsk (southwest of Moscow), did so with the Tula paratroops at Khodynka Field.

The Dzerzhinskaya Division operated from four or five points in the area. The Vitebskaya Division, based in northwest Russia, got relatively few troops through to Moscow. Other KGB forces based in Balashikha (east of Moscow) also seem to have taken part.

140. The order was published in *Moskovskaya pravda*, August 20, 1991, p. 2. The best sources for hour-by-hour developments are the chronicle *Khronika putcha: Chas za chasom*, put out shortly afterward by the Russian Information Agency, and the bulletins of the Postfactum news agency, which were made available to me by Sergei A. Grigoriev. S. M. Grigor'ev, *Istina momenta* (Moscow: Respublika, 1992), is also a valuable record.

141. Yeltsin, *Zapiski prezidenta*, p. 116. Information on deployments from ibid.; General Vladimir Dudnik, interviewed in *Nezavisimaya gazeta*, September 3, 1991, p. 6; and *Obshchaya gazeta*, August 21, 1991, p. 4. A later chronicle stated that the two army divisions committed 352 tanks, 288 other armored vehicles, 430 trucks, and 3,809 men to the Moscow operation (*Nezavisimaya gazeta*, August 19, 1992, p. 2). The greatest threat was probably the paratroop division airlifted from Moldova into the Kubinka air force base. It pushed off toward Moscow early on August 21 but was blocked by troops loyal to Yeltsin. According to Dudnik, the 10,000-man force could have "smashed Moscow to smithereens on its own." Yevgeniya Al'bats, *Mina zamedlennogo deistviya (Politicheskii portret KGB SSSR)* (Moscow: Russlit, 1992), p. 246.

142. Al'bats, *Mina zamedlennogo deistviya*, pp. 242, 258; Aleksandr Korsak, "Nam byl otdan prikaz arestovat' Popova," *Literaturnaya gazeta*, no. 36 (September 11, 1991), p. 3.

143. The list is in *Argumenty i fakty*, no. 38 (September 1991), p. 8. A member of Yeltsin's cabinet, Gennadii Burbulis, also claimed that culprits tried to intimidate the Moscow government and population by interfering with bread deliveries and subway operations. Postfactum bulletin, midnight, August 20.

144. Yulii Lebedev in *Nezavisimaya gazeta*, August 24, 1991, p. 2, and Yeltsin, *Zapiski prezidenta*, p. 126.

145. *Kuranty*, August 27, 1991, p. 5.

146. Popov's remarks on Nikol'skii and Belov are in *Vedomosti Mossoveta*, no. 4 (1991), p. 56. Nikol'skii was variously a raikom first secretary, deputy chairman of the Moscow ispolkom, and secretary of the gorkom in charge of administrative organs and retail trade and services from December 1981 until January 1984, when he was appointed party second secretary in the republic of Georgia. He returned to Moscow government in 1990 and was made a deputy chairman of the ispolkom in January 1991.

147. Ibid., p. 59; Al'bats, *Mina zamedlennogo deistviya*, p. 266; Korsak, "Nam byl otdan prikaz"; *Kuranty*, August 31, 1991, p. 5. For a harsh criticism of Popov's conduct, see V. A. Rebrikov, a Russian deputy, in Grigor'ev, *Istina momenta*, p. 169.

148. *Rossiiskaya gazeta*, August 29, 1991, p. 3; *Moskovskiye novosti*, no. 35 (September 1, 1991), p. 7; *Kuranty*, September 25, 1991, p. 2; Grigor'ev, *Istina momenta*, pp. 169, 171. Komissarov's version of his conversation with Popov is in

Nezavisimaya gazeta, September 19, 1991, p. 6. He says the two parted "like brothers."

149. *Kuranty,* September 3, 1991, p. 4.

150. Billington, *Russia Transformed,* p. 102.

151. Speech reprinted in *Moskovskaya pravda,* September 5, 1991, p. 2.

152. *Khronika putcha,* pp. 50–51.

153. The first troop movements were slow, but Luzhkov announced that food shortages and other inconveniences were likely to result from a continued presence of heavy equipment on city streets and that this "is increasing tension and may incite disorders" (ibid., p. 73). Several hours later the withdrawal was accelerated.

154. *Moskovskaya pravda,* September 5, 1991, p. 2.

155. Its issue of August 20 printed GKChP decrees and several letters supporting martial law, including one from a Mossovet deputy, M. M. Yashin. But on August 21 (p. 1) it criticized the banning of other papers. The editors argued that it would be wrong to close their own newspaper in support, since Muscovites were suffering from "information hunger" and needed news from any and all sources.

156. *Moskovskaya pravda,* August 21, 1991, p. 1 (reprinted in issue of August 23, p. 2).

157. *Vedomosti Mossoveta,* no. 4 (1991), p. 59.

158. *Kuranty,* August 24, 1991, p. 2, and *Nezavisimaya gazeta,* August 24, 1991, p. 2.

159. These scenes are described in *Argumenty i fakty,* no. 34 (August 1991), p. 2; *Nezavisimaya gazeta,* August 24, 1991, p. 1 (with a photograph of Prokof'ev amidst the crowd); *Pravda,* September 2, 1991, p. 3; and *Moskovskii komsomolets,* September 28, 1991, p. 1 (interview with Prokof'ev). Popov told me in an interview in October 1994 that he ordered members of his personal guard detail to protect Prokof'ev, and that Prokof'ev later thanked him for possibly saving his life.

160. *Nezavisimaya gazeta,* September 3, 1991, p. 2.

161. *Izvestiya,* September 18, 1991, p. 3.

162. The issue of August 23, the last for five days, criticized the putsch and the Moscow party organs and declared the editors' intent to reregister. The paper reappeared August 28 with the announcement of its change of affiliation. Several correspondents (p. 2) expressed regret that "we all lacked the civil courage to declare a political strike and not publish [on August 19–21] as a sign of solidarity with our colleagues in banned newspapers."

163. Details from *Moskovskaya pravda,* September 13, 1991, p. 2, and September 21, 1991, p. 1; *Moskovskii komsomolets,* September 28, 1991, p. 1; and *Vestnik merii Moskvy,* no. 8 (December 1991), pp. 17–18.

164. *Izvestiya,* August 21, 1992, p. 3.

8. Toward a Post-Socialist Metropolis

1. Adam Przeworski, *Democracy and the Market: Political and Economic Reforms in Eastern Europe and Latin America* (Cambridge: Cambridge University Press, 1991), p. 179.

2. *Izvestiya,* September 18, 1991, p. 3, and *Nezavisimaya gazeta,* December 10, 1993, p. 5.

3. These disagreements are most fully laid out in Gavriil Popov, "Strasti po Moskve: Nestoyavshiisya mer," unpub. ms.

4. Early contradictions are subjected to quantitative analysis in Terry D. Clark, "A House Divided: A Roll-call Analysis of the First Session of the Moscow City Soviet," *Slavic Review,* vol. 51 (Winter 1992), pp. 674–690. Democratic Russia's troubles at the national level are dissected in Yitzhak Brudny, "The Dynamics of 'Democratic Russia,' 1990–1993," *Post-Soviet Affairs,* vol. 9 (April–June 1993), pp. 141–170.

5. Gavriil Popov, "Perspektivy i realii," *Ogonek,* no. 51 (December 1990), p. 5, and *Moskovskaya pravda,* January 16, 1991, p. 2.

6. *Moskovskaya pravda,* July 1, 1990, p. 3.

7. Ibid., May 18, 1991, p. 1.

8. Ibid., November 14, 1991, p. 1.

9. See the interview with Braginskii in *Izvestiya,* October 5, 1993, p. 3.

10. See Luzhkov in *Moskovskaya pravda,* October 8, 1993, p. 3; *Izvestiya,* October 9, 1993, p. 2; Veronika Kutsyllo, *Zapiski iz Belogo doma, 21 sentyabrya–4 oktyabrya* (Moscow: Kommersant, 1993), pp. 53, 109, 117; Vera Tolz, "The Moscow Crisis and the Future of Democracy in Russia," *RFE/RL Research Report,* vol. 2 (October 22, 1993), p. 8. Apparently, none of the arrested deputies had taken part in the armed violence; all were released without charge several days later.

11. For the main decrees concerning Moscow, see *Rossiiskiye vesti,* October 5, 1993, p. 2; *Izvestiya,* October 6, 1993, p. 3, and October 8, 1993, p. 1; *Moskovskaya pravda,* October 29, 1993, pp. 1, 2, 8. Moscow oblast was included because its Small Soviet in late September ordered the chief of administration, Anatolii Tyazhlov, to recognize Rutskoi as president. The full soviet countermanded the resolution, but the damage had been done. The word "duma" had been a trendy appellation for several years. One of the mayor's advisory committees was named the Moscow City Duma in the summer of 1991, and the Small Soviet referred to itself as the Moscow Duma. The biweekly published by the Moscow Soviet in 1992–1993 was called *Duma.*

12. *Rossiiskiye vesti,* October 14, 1993, p. 2, and October 19, 1993, p. 1.

13. On democracy by design, see Michael Urban, "December 1993 as a Replication of Late-Soviet Electoral Practices," *Post-Soviet Affairs,* vol. 10 (April–June 1994), pp. 127–158.

14. In the 1993 national election, half of the seats in the lower house, the State Duma, were filled on the basis of proportional representation, the system most favorable to development of parties. Such an arrangement was rejected as too complicated for the Moscow City Duma.

15. The analysis of the 1990 election in Chapter 7 used the category "semiofficial or unofficial organization," as there were still few genuinely independent associations. The small number of trade union officials, who were classified as core public administrators in 1990, are considered leaders of voluntary associations in 1993.

16. I was present in Moscow the final week of the campaign and was impressed by the quietness of the streets, which in 1990 and to a lesser extent in June 1991 had

been alive with political activity. Some candidates did remind voters of their pre-Gorbachev dissident activity or contributions to the democratic cause. But such information was displayed much less prominently than in 1990.

17. Russia's Choice won 34.7 percent of the Moscow votes in the party-list voting for the State Duma; this was higher than in any other regional unit of Russia and double the party's average cull. Yeltsin's draft constitution was approved by 66.3 percent of Muscovites, 8 points above the national average. The Communists polled 11.0 percent, 1 percent below average, but the near-fascist Liberal-Democrats, at 12.8 percent, were 10 percent below their all-Russian mean.

18. Combining the Russia's Choice vote with that for the three moderate reform slates leaves an even wider range of variance to explain—from 14.4 percent in district 9, beside the Northern TETs, to 63.8 percent in Zelenograd. Local factors again seem to have played an essential role.

19. The survey overpredicted the Russia's Choice vote (by 5.6 percent), hit the moderate vote dead on, and underpredicted the KPRF (by 5.2 percent) and the LDPR (by 2 percent). It does, nonetheless, reliably bring out some relationships among variables.

20. There was also a gender effect on partisan preference, as there was all over Russia in 1993. In the Moscow preelection sample, women were more likely than men to intend to vote for Russia's Choice (by 41.7 percent to 38.5 percent) but men were more likely to favor the LDPR (by 12.3 percent to 7.9 percent) and the Communists (by 10.2 to 2.5 percent). A centrist feminist party, Women of Russia, was favored by 8.7 percent of Moscow women but only 1.1 percent of men.

21. References are to Popov's four-part article in *Izvestiya*, August 21, 24, 25, and 26, 1992; emphasis added.

22. Ye. V. Okhotskii, "Pravyashchaya politicheskaya elita Movksy," in Rossiiskaya akademiya upravleniya, *Moskva i Moskvichi* (Moscow: Luch, 1993), p. 31.

23. Ivanov, formerly of the Moscow ispolkom, was in the Central Committee apparatus from 1986 to 1991, ending as a section head in the department for liaison with the soviets. After that he served as an adviser to Luzhkov and in the fall of 1993 as an organizer of the municipal election. There are family ties among some prominent administrators and pillars of the city leadership under Grishin and Promyslov. It has been reported that Nikol'skii is related by marriage both to A. I. Kostenko, who for many years was deputy chairman of the city ispolkom, and to K. E. Buravlev, his fellow first deputy premier in the present government. Yurii Shchekochikhin, "Strakh," *Literaturnaya gazeta*, no. 24 (June 10, 1992), p. 11.

24. Many former holders of high positions in Moscow have stayed out of politics and administration and found good spots in private commerce. Yurii Prokof'ev, the last leader of the Moscow branch of the CPSU, works today in an auto-leasing firm. Vitalii Prilukov, the head of the Moscow KGB in August 1991, is an executive in a private security company.

25. The letter is in *Moskovskaya pravda*, January 16, 1991, p. 2.

26. Eighty-one percent of those voting approved institution of a mayor in the referendum of March 1991. Asked to forecast the effect, 42 percent of a polling

sample agreed with the statement that they could "expect more decisive measures from a mayor at introducing order in the city," and 41 percent said that he would move more briskly "from words to action" in economic reform. Ibid., June 7, 1991, p. 2.

27. Except for the detailed decree on the Moscow Capital Collegium, these directives are collected in Otdel informatsii Upravleniya delami Merii Moskvy, *Meriya Moskvy i drugiye organy ispolnitel'noi vlasti goroda (Sbornik dokumentov i spravochno-informatsionnykh materialov)*, September 1991, pp. 44–51. The item on the collegium was obtained from the mayor's office.

28. This body, referred to as the Committee on Administration of the City of Moscow in Popov's January memorandum, was at first called the City Duma, the title Moscow's elected council had held until 1917 and was to reacquire in 1993. It was changed to Capital Collegium on August 19, 1991.

29. The Small Soviet was first constituted in November 1991 with 233 members but got nothing done. In January its membership was reduced to the statutory limit contained in the Russian law on local government enacted December 5, 1991.

30. For example, the mayor had the right "to appoint the leaders of the city's executive organs, and also to remove them from their positions, including on resolution of the Moscow Soviet." It was not at all clear if he would have to process an appointment if the soviet chose to make a personnel decision, or if the soviet would have an equal and parallel right of appointment. The temporary statute, adopted April 29, 1991, is in *Vedomosti Mossoveta*, no. 3 (1991), pp. 5–9. An edict issued April 19 by the Presidium of the Supreme Soviet of the RSFSR was equally vague. It is in *Vedomosti S"ezda narodnykh deputatov RSFSR i Verkhovnogo Soveta RSFSR*, no. 17 (April 25, 1991), pp. 471–473.

31. The Moscow Capital Collegium functioned as an information clearer, mostly in the law enforcement area, not the strategic planner of "long-term issues" Popov looked for. The City Assembly, which might have been a mayoral conduit to public opinion, did not meet regularly after the autumn of 1991.

32. There was an obvious difference of opinion on the premier's job between Popov and Luzhkov. Popov said in an interview the day of his resignation (*Moskovskii komsomolets*, June 6, 1992, p. 1) that the mayor should not be head of the city government but should "stand aside from the government, control it, guide it, and be a kind of court of appeal." Luzhkov shunned this advice.

33. The six complexes in the 1991 edicts were reduced in January 1992 to five, for economic reforms, territorial administration, social defense, city services, and long-range urban development.

34. There was some reduction of administrative undergrowth in the late 1980s, but the trend was reversed following the 1990 elections. To use the same categories as in Table B-4 (in Appendix B), eight of the agencies reporting to the premier after Popov's reform were for overhead functions, seven were for physical services, five for transportation, nine for social services, ten for consumer and cultural services, one for town planning, three for local industry, eleven for construction and building materials, and five for state administration, while two agencies were for environ-

mental protection. The Mayor's Department and the Business Office contained, among others, subdepartments for information services, personnel, and legal affairs and the Committee on Long-Range Planning, a trimmed version of Gorplan, the City Economic Planning Commission of Soviet times.

35. Stephen Holmes, "Superpresidentialism and Its Problems," *East European Constitutional Review,* vols. 2–3 (Fall 1993/Winter 1994), pp. 123–126.

36. The presidential document is in *Moskovskaya pravda,* October 29, 1993, p. 8.

37. I follow Holmes, "Superpresidentialism," pp. 123–124.

38. Interview in *Moskovskaya pravda,* November 18, 1993, p. 4.

39. Holmes, "Superpresidentialism," p. 124. See more generally Juan J. Linz, "The Perils of Presidentialism," *Journal of Democracy,* vol. 1 (Winter 1990), pp. 51–69.

40. The others to hold both offices were A. G. Bortsov (in Sverdlovskii raion), G. I. Kutyakov (Frunzenskii raion), S. A. Potapov (Volgogradskii raion), and V. N. Sen'kov (Leninskii raion). Popov claimed that two-thirds of the raion soviets "were under the sway of the raikoms" and "sabotaged every decision" his government took (*Moskovskii komsomolets,* June 11, 1992, p. 1), but his estimate seems quite excessive.

41. The secretary of the ispolkom, Yurii Vinogradov, was candid about the political purpose of the committees: "The development of the self-government councils . . . ought to exclude the kind of situation where Muscovites have literally had to block the way of equipment that is annihilating architectural landmarks or greenery or prevent builders from putting up industrial 'vulcans' harmful to the atmosphere and soil. Urbanites will acquire a real capacity and rights for influencing the vital processes taking place in their raions." He also described inherited mass associations such as house committees and street patrols as being in an advanced state of decomposition. *Moskovskaya pravda,* August 1, 1989, p. 3.

42. See the Krylatskoye charter in *Vestnik ispolkoma Mossoveta,* no. 10 (May 1991), pp. 3–7.

43. The Dzerzhinskii raion soviet's actions are described in *Moskovskaya pravda,* November 29, 1991, p. 1. More than a year after the reorganization, several raion soviets were still funding boards they referred to as ispolkoms and were passing motions on housing and trade as if nothing had changed. "The urge of . . . defunct institutions to hold on at any price," wrote one journalist, "is frustrating prospects for stabilization in the city and disorienting residents of the capital" (ibid., November 5, 1992, p. 4). Pykhtin of Cheremushkinskii raion was toppled by his soviet in March 1993.

44. *Meriya Moskvy i drugiye organy,* p. 69.

45. The streets and sections evoked in the Central Administrative Okrug were Khamovniki, Presnya, Tverskaya, Meshchanskaya, Krasnoye selo, Basmannaya, Taganka, Zamoskvorech'e, Kitaigorod, and Yakimanka. A few of those used in outer okrugs were Ramenki, Izmailovo, Tsaritsyno, Lefortovo, and Pokrovskoye-Streshnevo.

46. V. V. Il'ichev of Kutuzovskii district in *Moskovskaya pravda,* April 8, 1993, p. 5.

47. For the first survey, V. M. Sokolov, "Moskvichi: Otsenka vlasti i zhizni, nastroyeniya i ozhidaniya," in Rossiiskaya akademiya upravleniya, *Moskva i Moskvichi*, p. 5; and for the second, unpublished data from the Institute for the Sociology of Parliamentarism, courtesy of Nugzar Betaneli, director of the institute.

48. The decree is in *Moskovskaya pravda*, December 16, 1993, p. 1. A short list of candidates for chief of municipality is first constructed by the prefect. If the mayor and the local assembly cannot agree on a candidate, the mayor is entitled to act on his own by making a one-year appointment.

49. The legitimacy of the self-government committees was being questioned in the press. Gaik Zulumyan failed miserably to win election to the city duma, getting 3.2 percent of the votes as the PRES candidate in district 21. The decree of December 1993 states that lesser "organs of territorial social self-government" may be established within the municipal districts, with their consent.

50. Source: author's interview with a former aide to Zaikov in June 1991.

51. *Leninskoye znamya*, March 3, 1990, p. 2.

52. Ibid., October 18, 1990, p. 3.

53. I was allowed to see a copy of Popov's letter, dated September 7 and addressed to A. I. Luk'yanov, chairman of the USSR Supreme Soviet, by a legal adviser to the commission.

54. The draft is summarized in *Izvestiya*, October 20, 1990, p. 2.

55. *Vedomosti S"ezda narodnykh deputatov RSFSR i Verkhovnogo Soveta RSFSR*, no. 17 (April 25, 1991), p. 471. The motion was also backed by another RSFSR deputy from the oblast—Stanislav P. Shustov, who had signed the Reutov petition in March 1990.

56. The roll call and texts of the motions are in *Podmoskov'e*, June 15, 1991, p. 3. Popov wrote later that Yeltsin was unwilling to force the oblast to participate in the referendum because he feared this might antagonize the regional elite and cost him votes in the presidential campaign. Popov, "Strasti po Moskve," p. 195.

57. *Podmoskov'e*, June 15, 1991, p. 3.

58. The total oblast land allocated from 1953 to 1990 was 490 square kilometers (49,000 hectares), or 13 square kilometers a year. Allotments were 35 square kilometers in 1991 and 135 in 1992, although the pace slowed in 1993. Some gardening land for Moscow residents will eventually be set aside in neighboring oblasts as well.

59. *Moskovskaya pravda*, July 2, 1992, p. 1, and March 15, 1994, p. 7.

60. Ibid., March 27, 1993, p. 2.

61. *Izvestiya*, April 17, 1991, p. 4; *Vedomosti S"ezda narodnykh deputatov RSFSR i Verkhovnogo Soveta RSFSR*, no. 17 (April 25, 1991), p. 473.

62. The March 1992 decree and the fight between Petrov and Luzhkov are summarized by Andrei Mal'gin in *Novoye Russkoye slovo*, May 18, 1992, p. 5. Luzhkov's statement is in *Kuranty*, August 27, 1991, p. 5. I learned of the fate of the medical facilities through interviews. The Fourth Chief Directorate had already changed name several times before the Russian government restructured it again. One of the Central Committee kindergartens in Yeltsin's decree (No. 838, at 1 ulitsa Davydkovskaya, next to the Stalin dacha) had been explicitly requisitioned by Luzhkov in October 1991. In September 1993 the former Central Committee infir-

mary on ulitsa Granovskogo, now under the Governmental Medical Center, opened
a commercial surgical clinic.

63. *Moskovskaya pravda,* April 9, 1992, p. 2, and March 3, 1994, p. 3. Russian
subsidies reach the city through numerous channels, mostly indirect. The most important items to be negotiated, as in the Soviet past, are the rates the city can impose
on taxpaying organizations. In the end about 50 percent of the budget in 1992 and
1993 came from taxes on enterprise profits, about 20 percent from a value added tax
(a descendant of the Soviet-era turnover tax), and about 20 percent from income tax.
As a report by foreign experts notes, fiscal relations between different levels of
government in Russia remain "unclearly defined," with "multiple bargaining processes" obscuring the result and a widespread perception of unfairness among the local
governments. European Bank for Reconstruction and Development, *Quarterly Economic Review,* vol. 3 (April 1993), p. 103.

64. See on this point *Nezavisimaya gazeta,* April 3, 1992, p. 6.

65. Popov, "Strasti po Moskve," p. 336.

66. Statistics in *Moskva v tsifrakh, 1989* (Moscow: Finansy i statistika, 1989),
p. 44, and *Raiony g. Moskvy v 1990 godu* (Moscow: Mosgorstat, 1991), pp. 21–23.
City statistics give specific profiles for only 48.3 percent of the cooperatives active in
January 1990. In January 1989 the biggest areas of specialization were consumer
services (30.1 percent) and handicrafts (17.9 percent). The cooperatives are well
described in general in Anthony Jones and William Moskoff, *Ko-ops: The Rebirth of
Entrepreneurship in the Soviet Union* (Bloomington: Indiana University Press, 1991).

67. *Kommersant,* no. 25 (June 15–22, 1992), p. 21.

68. Compare to an early poll showing levels of approval of 64 percent for
privatization of the housing stock, 56 percent for small and medium-sized industrial
enterprises, and 43 percent for retail trade. *Moskovskaya pravda,* November 14,
1990, p. 2.

69. The USSR Council of Ministers had endorsed selective sale of apartments in
a resolution of December 1988, and the Moscow government issued an implementing
order in June 1989. Only 1,480 Moscow apartments were transferred and 5,000 more
requests received by December of 1990, when the new ispolkom adopted another
ineffective directive. Unlike the Popov plan, the 1988 scheme charged for the entire
space transferred to the tenant. *Vestnik ispolkoma Mossoveta,* no. 2 (January 1991),
pp. 7–8.

70. The decree is in *Vestnik merii Moskvy,* no. 3 (October 1991), pp. 9–12. The
price for above-quota space was set at 204 rubles per square meter (about one week's
pay for an industrial worker at the time); it has gone up ever since with inflation.
President Yeltsin's edict on privatization in Moscow, dated January 12, 1992, made
a few changes to the original decision, mainly allowing communal flats to be privatized as long as all the tenants agreed. That document is in *Privatizatsiya 1992 god,
Moskva* (Moscow: Garant, 1992), pp. 2–3.

71. The Moscow ispolkom's decision about Mospromstroi (*Vestnik ispolkoma
Mossoveta,* no. 8 [April 1991], pp. 20–21) was typical. The new joint stock company
had the same name as the municipal agency it replaced and was proclaimed its "legal

heir." Mosstroikomitet, the city's coordinating organ for construction, was to own "all shares belonging to the state." Issuance of shares to other investors was made possible but not mandatory.

72. *Kommersant*, no. 26 (June 22–29, 1992), p. 12; *Moscow Times*, June 26, 1992, p. 16. Perestroika was formed in April 1988, the first joint venture in the construction area. Stroyev, then forty-one years old, had been named head of Glavmosinzhstroi, still a government agency, by First Secretary Yeltsin in 1987.

73. *Vestnik merii Moskvy*, no. 7 (December 1991), pp. 3–5.

74. Quotation from *Izvestiya*, April 13, 1993, p. 5.

75. David Remnick, *Lenin's Tomb: The Last Days of the Soviet Empire* (New York: Random House, 1993), pp. 521–522.

76. An excellent short analysis is in Olivier Blanchard et al., *Post-Communist Reform: Pain and Progress* (Cambridge, Mass.: MIT Press, 1993), chap. 3.

77. See John Lloyd in the *Financial Times*, July 25, 1994, p. 8.

78. Source: Russian Election Project. Thirty-five percent of the respondents declined to answer the question on individual income and 16.4 percent did not respond to the question on family income.

79. Quotations from *Moskovskaya pravda*, March 11, 1993, p. 4, and April 2, 1992, p. 1.

80. See *Nezavisimaya gazeta*, July 11, 1992, p. 6; *Izvestiya*, April 13, 1993, p. 5; *Moskovskaya pravda*, December 3, 1992, p. 4; *Gradskiye vesti*, December 15, 1993, p. 3, and January 26, 1994, p. 2.

81. The Osennaya ulitsa house contains twenty apartments and various service and communications facilities. Yeltsin's five-room suite is the largest, with 101 square meters of net dwelling space (170 square meters gross). A picture of the building appears in *Argumenty i fakty*, no. 47 (November 1994), p. 2.

82. *Kuranty*, September 27, 1991, p. 3; *Moskovskaya pravda*, March 3, 1994, p. 3.

83. Dacha purchases by army generals, USSR government officials, and others began in the late 1980s. In October 1990 Prime Minister Nikolai Ryzhkov withdrew his offer to buy a dacha at Nikolina Gora, but a number of his deputies went ahead. Press exposés often mingled description of this practice and other abuses, such as use of military conscripts and state-owned materials to build dachas. See, for example, *Kuranty*, June 7, 1991, p. 1; September 18, 1991, p. 5; April 9, 1993, p. 7.

84. The municipal queue alone expanded from 426,000 in 1980 to 550,000 in 1988, 737,000 in 1990, and 749,000 on January 1, 1992. Mosgorkomstat, *Statisticheskii press-byulleten'*, no. 7 (1992), p. 10.

85. The triggering norm was reset at six square meters per capita in 1989 for all persons resident in Moscow for ten years or more and living in a communal flat (though it remained at five square meters for ten-year residents occupying detached apartments) and for all war invalids in communal accommodation. The seven-square-meter trigger was strictly for employees with fifteen years' continuous service or at least ten years of work in "difficult, harmful, or dangerous conditions," and it allowed the family to enter only the employer's housing queue, not the municipality's.

86. Planners calculate that 50 to 55 percent of the housing built by the Moscow construction industry in the 1990s will be higher than ten stories, 25 percent will be five to ten stories, and 20 to 25 percent will be one to five stories (mostly five). By one estimate, the builders will be able to put up only 1,500 one- or two-family cottages in 1995.

87. Production of net dwelling space was 1,954,000 square meters in 1992 and 1,950,000 square meters in 1993. See *Izvestiya*, April 13, 1993, p. 5, and *Moskovskaya pravda*, February 8, 1994, p. 1.

88. Mosgorkomstat, *Statisticheskii press-byulleten'*, no. 9 (1992), p. 41, reports per capita supply of 11.3 square meters of net dwelling space in 1992. Compare with Table D-2 in Appendix D.

89. See *Vechernyaya Moskva*, January 13, 1994, p. 8, and *Moskovskaya pravda*, February 8, 1994, p. 1. The last statistics I have seen for control of the existing fund are for January 1992, before the acceleration of privatization and before factories stepped up their transfer of apartments to the city. The municipality was landlord at that time to 72.5 percent of the population, enterprises and agencies were to 17.9 percent, and cooperatives were to 9.2 percent, while 0.4 percent of the population lived in private housing. Mosgorkomstat, *Statisticheskii press-byulleten'*, no. 9 (1992), p. 41.

90. *Moskovskaya pravda*, May 7, 1992, p. 1.

91. Leningrad began to review its 1966 general plan in the mid-1970s, and a new plan became effective in 1986. Blair A. Ruble, *Leningrad: Shaping a Soviet City* (Berkeley: University of California Press, 1990), pp. 103–112.

92. G. Makarevich, "Zaglyadyvaya zavtra," *Stroitel'stvo i arkhitektura Moskvy*, no. 2 (February 1982), p. 3.

93. V. Promyslov, "General'nyi plan razvitiya stolitsy," ibid., no. 3 (March 1985), pp. 3–6, and A. Bekker, "Osnovnyye printsipy gradostroitel'noi politiki," ibid., pp. 9–10.

94. *Moskovskaya pravda*, January 25, 1986, p. 2, and July 20, 1986, p. 2.

95. Author's interview with Vavakin in July 1992.

96. There is a summary of the Politburo resolution in *Pravda*, September 26, 1986, p. 1. Some points are discussed by Yeltsin in *Moskovskaya pravda*, October 5, 1986, p. 2.

97. *Moskovskaya pravda*, July 1, 1987, p. 3; February 6, 1988, p. 4; June 7, 1988, p. 3.

98. The fullest summary is in ibid., April 13, 1989, pp. 3–6.

99. Ibid., July 16, 1989, p. 2; Valerii Rabinovich, "Pora skazat' pravdu o genplane Moskvy," *Arkhitektura i stroitel'stvo Moskvy*, no. 6 (June 1989), pp. 2–4.

100. *Moskovskaya pravda*, September 15, 1990, p. 2.

101. I was unable to obtain a population figure for January 1994, but a government spokesman said that month that Moscow's population by the end of the year should be down to 8,676,000. *Argumenty i fakty*, nos. 2–3 (January 1994), p. 3.

102. *Moskovskaya pravda*, April 14, 1993, p. 1. According to *Argumenty i fakty*, no. 25 (June 1993), p. 4, cash incomes in Moscow rose 13.6 times between January

1992 and April 1993, while prices for basic food products rose 17.8 times. The national averages were 24.3 times for incomes and 16.5 times for consumer prices.

103. The decree of November 1991 establishing Moskomarkhitektura specifically exempted the Institute of the Master Plan and several other key subunits from privatization. Moskomarkhitektura and Moskomzem report to the same first deputy premier, at present V. I. Resin, the construction executive whom Gorbachev wanted to make Moscow party leader in 1989.

104. The USSR Constitutional Oversight Committee found in October 1990 that the propiska regulations violated human rights and advocated ending the system in stages. In October 1991 it ruled propiska unconstitutional and ordered it abolished as of January 1, 1992. The Russian Constitutional Court declared the internal passports unsustainable in 1992. One of its main concerns, the item recording ethnic origin, has been taken into account, as the new cards make no mention of nationality.

105. Data from the Institute for the Sociology of Parliamentarism.

106. Vasilii Shakhnovskii in *Moskovskaya pravda*, February 18, 1993, p. 3.

107. Under the plan, non-Muscovites who come to Moscow and buy housing are to pay 500 minimum-monthly-wage units in fees if they are Russian citizens, 1,000 if they are from the Commonwealth of Independent States, and 2,500 if they are from other countries.

108. The new lines are to include a second circular line and two lines extending into the oblast at Mytishchi and Lyubertsy.

109. Reference here is to the article "Will There Be a New 'Greater Moscow?'" by V. Bekker, V. Kuravin, and A. Trifonov, in *Vechernyaya Moskva*, February 16, 1994, p. 3.

110. The original regulations are in *Vestnik merii Moskvy*, no. 9 (May 1992), pp. 5–16. The revised rates for 1994 (*Gradskiye vesti*, January 26, 1994, p. 2) are divided into a "land tax" and a "rental fee," and range in inflated rubles from 2.8 million to 81 million per hectare, a much sharper differentiation than in 1992.

111. V. I. Danilov-Danil'yan, Russia's ecology minister, in *Moskovskaya pravda*, May 26, 1992, p. 1.

112. Ibid., December 17, 1991, p. 1.

113. Ibid., April 2, 1993, p. 2.

114. Luzhkov in ibid., April 15, 1993, p. 3.

115. Richard F. Babcock, *The Zoning Game: Municipal Practices and Policies* (Madison: University of Wisconsin Press, 1966).

116. The physical condition of the cloisters is often appalling. Most of the Simonov Monastery was leveled in the 1930s. Much of Rozhdestvenskii is still taken up by a student dormitory.

117. The general contractor for the project is Mospromstroi, the quasi-privatized city agency for factory construction, and the main designer is Mikhail M. Posokhim, the son of the late chief architect of Moscow. Controversy rages over several aspects of the venture. Some critics fear that the crash pace of construction and the reliance on mechanized techniques will make the final product an ugly and unworthy successor to the original. Others fret that the waterlogged soil of the embankment area, which

bedeviled the attempt to put up the Palace of Soviets, will pose problems for the cathedral. Still others are concerned about cost. Budget estimates range from several hundred million dollars (in ruble equivalents) to one billion dollars. Luzhkov and his ministers assert that no government appropriations will be required, but few Muscovites seem to believe them. Even if city hall makes no direct grants, the assignment of implementation to municipal builders provides ample opportunity for indirect subsidies.

118. *Kuranty,* December 17, 1991, p. 5.

119. A telephone survey of 1,000 Muscovites on October 21, 1993, found 64 percent in favor of interring Lenin in St. Petersburg. Only 6 percent wanted all Lenin monuments in Moscow to be taken down (25 percent preferred to leave them all in place and 62 percent to retain those with "artistic or historic value"). Twenty-four percent supported replacement of the ruby stars on the Kremlin towers with the double-headed eagle, with 42 percent opposed. Data supplied by the Institute for the Sociology of Parliamentarism.

120. There was especially negative reaction to the renaming of ulitsa Pushkinskaya (called since 1937 after Russia's national poet) to the historically correct Bol'shaya Dmitrovka.

121. Luzhkov in *Moskovskaya pravda,* May 7, 1992, p. 1.

122. Ibid., February 11, 1993, p. 5; emphasis added.

123. Kirill Borisov in *Solidarnost',* no. 18 (June 1992), p. 13.

124. Robert D. Putnam, *Making Democracy Work: Civic Traditions in Modern Italy* (Princeton: Princeton University Press, 1993), pp. 184–185; Samuel P. Huntington, *The Third Wave: Democratization in the Late Twentieth Century* (Norman: University of Oklahoma Press, 1991), pp. 266–267.

125. Quotations in these several paragraphs from Putnam, *Making Democracy Work,* pp. 183–184.

126. Ibid., p. 84. Putnam's data also establish that noneconomic factors must be examined to predict democratic success within economic development categories in Italy. Huntington's argument is in *Third Wave,* pp. 59–72 and 271–273. He summarizes his position on p. 59: "An overall correlation exists between the development of economic development and democracy, yet no level or pattern of economic development is in itself either necessary or sufficient to bring about democratization."

127. Sokolov, "Moskvichi," pp. 5–6.

128. This has been borne out by a number of opinion surveys. One investigation, in July 1992, discovered that 27 percent of Muscovites agreed with curbs on political rights if that would help bring about social order and prosperity, whereas 49 percent were opposed; in May 1993 29 percent were in favor and 54 percent were not. Unpublished data from the Institute for the Sociology of Parliamentarism.

129. See the disturbing general description in Stephen Handelman, *Comrade Criminal: The Theft of the Second Russian Revolution* (London: Michael Joseph, 1994).

130. Shchekochikhin, "Strakh." The amounts offered in bribes can be miniscule, but one Western journalist (Celestine Bohlen in the *New York Times,* February 27,

1993, pp. 1, 12) reported that the housing official who cleared the privatization formalities for a communal apartment in central Moscow requested $20,000. He backed off when he learned that the wife of Vice-President Rutskoi was participating in the deal. Converted to rubles at the official rate, the bribe would have represented about fifty years' salary for the functionary.

131. *Moskovskaya pravda*, July 1, 1992, p. 2; Shchekochikhin, "Strakh"; Handelman, *Comrade Criminal*, pp. 136–141; *Argumenty i fakty*, no. 14 (April 1992), p. 1. Bystrov's KGB past is not on the record, but I have heard on reliable authority that he worked in the Twelfth Directorate, the department responsible for electronic eavesdropping, before being brought into Moscow government by Yeltsin.

132. Among other assets, Most has a security service with 1,000 guards and agents, one of them a former deputy chairman of the KGB, Fedor Bobkov. Its politics are generally pro-reform and pro-Western. On Luzhkov's relations with the Most group, see esp. *Rossiiskaya gazeta*, November 19, 1994, pp. 1, 3, and the interview with Gusinskii in *Argumenty i fakty*, no. 48 (November 1994), pp. 1, 3.

133. Data provided by the Institute for the Sociology of Parliamentarism. Sixty-two percent of Muscovites polled in June 1992 expressed the view that bribe taking had become more common in Moscow in the preceding year, compared to only 3 percent who thought it less common (*Izvestiya*, June 22, 1992, p. 5).

134. Readership statistics taken from Mark Rhodes, "The Newspaper in Russia Today," *RFE/RL Research Report*, vol. 2 (November 12, 1993), p. 41. The survey cited shows 50 percent of Muscovites reading some newspaper daily, as compared to 36 percent for European Russians. Rhodes does not include *Segodnya* because it was founded after the survey was done. A later poll (in *Vechernyaya Moskva*, February 23, 1994, p. 1) showed that newspaper at 3 percent and *Nezavisimaya gazeta* below 3 percent.

135. Some of the better coverage of Moscow government is, in fact, in the two English-language dailies, the *Moscow Times* and *Moscow Tribune*, established in 1992 for the growing foreign community. Most Muscovites, of course, do not and cannot read these papers.

136. Sokolov, "Moskvichi," pp. 12–13.

137. The two journals were renamed and retargeted in January 1991. The Mossovet also founded an illustrated weekly magazine in late 1990 called *Stolitsa* (Capital). *Stolitsa* does little serious analysis of political questions, less still on Moscow politics.

138. Only 11 percent of viewers in June 1993 watched the weekly interview series with city administrators ("Face the City") and only 5 percent tuned in to the analogous program with elected officials ("Voice of the Deputy"). *Kuranty*, June 30, 1993, p. 4.

139. Putnam, *Making Democracy Work*, p. 182.

140. *Moskovskaya pravda*, October 28, 1993, p. 5, about leaders of the neighborhood self-government committees.

141. The organization was the Moscow League of Scientific and Production Enterprises from 1990 until August 1992. Its formation was encouraged by the

Moscow CPSU apparatus, and its first chairman, Igor G. Artyukh, was a member of the bureau of the gorkom in 1990–1991. Artyukh is general director of the Tori NPO, a military-industrial firm producing radar and microwave equipment. When I interviewed Yurii Prokof'ev in June 1991, he pointed to Artyukh's membership on the gorkom bureau as proof of the organization's importance and acceptance by the party. The head of the Russian league, Arkadii I. Vol'skii, is a Muscovite who began his career as party secretary in ZIL in the 1960s.

142. Unpublished data from the Institute for the Sociology of Parliamentarism.

143. Sokolov, "Moskvichi," pp. 5–6.

144. M. Steven Fish, "Russia's Fourth Transition," *Journal of Democracy,* vol. 5 (July 1994), p. 34.

145. Because most of Yeltsin's colleagues in the Moscow apparatus denounced him upon his dismissal in 1987, few of them won his favor afterward. Yeltsin has given many more opportunities to officials from Sverdlovsk, where he worked in the party organs until 1985. V. V. Ilyushin, a Sverdlovsk apparatchik who was one of his assistants in the Central Committee and the Moscow gorkom, has headed his personal cabinet since 1990. A. A. Nikitin, one of Luzhkov's deputy premiers, was appointed first deputy head of the Business Office of the Presidential Chancery in February 1994. Mikhail Poltoranin and Sergei Stankevich were the most prominent Muscovites around Yeltsin prior to the 1993 constitutional crisis. Poltoranin was for two years Yeltsin's press minister and now has an advisory role; Stankevich, who quit the Mossovet in 1992 to work full-time as a senior presidential counsellor, resigned in the summer of 1993 and is now a member of the State Duma. Yurii Skokov, the former manager of a Moscow defense plant, Kvant, and a USSR people's deputy from a Moscow constituency, was the very influential secretary of the Russian Security Council, a coordinating body for military and foreign policy. Yeltsin dismissed him in May 1993 after a disagreement over political strategy, but a comeback is possible.

146. Shod Muladzhanov in *Moskovskaya pravda,* December 17, 1991, p. 1.

147. Holmes, "Superpresidentialism," p. 124.

Acknowledgments

Having crafted this book over a dozen years, I find it hard to do justice to the numerous organizations and individuals that have inspired and assisted me along the way. Some of them no doubt are as relieved as I that the job is done.

I am indebted to the University of Toronto, my former academic home, and to the Social Sciences and Humanities Research Council of Canada for sabbatical time and travel support during the opening phases of the project. A fellowship from the Woodrow Wilson International Center for Scholars afforded me an uninterrupted year to conduct library research and begin writing historical text. I had expected to go to press much sooner and with a much slighter product, only to have my plans derailed by two residents of Moscow named Gorbachev and Yeltsin. The winds of change in Russia handed me the opportunity and the obligation to do more, about both the past and the present, and in the process to multiply my debts. Harvard University since 1989 has furnished me with leave time, research expenses, and a wonderfully rich intellectual environment. I owe much also to the Carnegie Corporation for its generous support of my field research.

B. Michael Frolic planted in my head the idea of looking into Moscow governance and got me started with the loan of his file of Moscow-related documents. Blair Ruble, who launched a study of Leningrad around the same time, gave me steady encouragement and the benefit of his insights into Russian cities. Mary Dau of the Danish foreign service and Geoffrey Pearson, then Canadian ambassador to the Soviet Union, helped me immeasurably with access to Moscow in the early 1980s, when much normal academic exchange was in abeyance. Kathleen Berton Murrell shared her peerless trove of knowledge of the metropolis's streets and buildings and introduced me to sections of Moscow province where Westerners rarely tread. T. H. Rigby and Peter Solomon commented incisively on draft essays on Moscow personnel and institutions and sold me on the merit of compiling systematic records on them. Jerry Hough gave me countless leads on administrative structures and leaders' biographies as well as several invaluable contacts with information gatekeepers. Jeffrey Hahn taught me a lot about reform trends in Russian local government and about his work on the city of Yaroslavl.

I am obliged to a number of Western and Japanese scholars for pointers on Russian history and advice on archives. Especially responsive to my at times naive queries were Joseph Bradley, William Chase, David Hoffmann, Nobuo Shimotomai, S. Frederick Starr, Kenneth Straus, and Robert Thurston. Nathaniel Davis kindly prepared for me a memorandum on Orthodox churches in Moscow drawing on his data base on Russia and Ukraine. I made William Craft Brumfield's acquaintance only late in the project, but I owe much to his pioneering architectural scholarship, and I appreciate the chance to reproduce several of his photographs.

A great many colleagues, aware of my Moscow interest, have sent information and bibliographic nuggets my way. I valued, in particular, the tips passed on by James Bater, Seweryn Bialer, George Breslauer, Yitzhak Brudny, Donald Carlisle, Caron Cooper, Theodore Friedgut, Marshall Goldman, Thane Gustafson, Werner Hahn, Edward Keenan, Amy Knight, Mark Kramer, Aleksandr Nekrich, Jonathan Sanders, Steven Solnick, and Nina Tumarkin. Sergei Grigoriev threw unique light on how the Communist Party elite lived in Moscow and environs. Andrei Berezkin, Ellen Hamilton, Blair Ruble, and Vladimir Treml graciously let me utilize unpublished statistical data in their possession. Gary King of the Harvard Government Department helped me with the quantitative analysis of the election returns in Chapter 7. Graham Allison of the Kennedy School of Government involved me in a joint project with the Moscow city government in 1991 that extended my range of contacts.

For energetic research assistance at various stages, I wish to thank Josephine Andrews, George Malick, Jr., James Reisch, Serafima Roll, and above all Gennady Ozornoy. Konstantin Miroshnik located ex-Muscovite architects and municipal administrators in Israel and aided me in interviewing them in 1982. Information that I came upon later to some degree superseded the conversations, but they nonetheless deepened my understanding of Soviet urban management. In Moscow, I profited from the labors of the long-suffering staffs of the Central State Archive of Social Movements of Moscow (the Moscow Party Archive until 1991), the Central State Historical Archive of the City of Moscow, the State Public Historical Library, and the Lenin Library (now the Russian State Library) and from hosting arrangements at the Institute of State and Law, Moscow State University, and the Institute of Legislation. At the Russian Research Center, Michele Wong Albanese, Judith

Mehrmann, and Christine Porto provided efficient and cheery staff support as I moved the volume to completion.

Of the scores of Muscovites who lent a hand, I wish particularly to acknowledge five: Dmitrii Dankin and Vladimir Chernous', who facilitated my work in Communist Party archives at a time when it took courage to do so; Mikhail Shatrov, who told me so much about Moscow cultural life and arranged several indispensable interviews; the late Georgii Barabashev, who helped with interviews and background material on the structure and restructuring of urban government; and Nugzar Betaneli of the Institute for the Sociology of Parliamentarism, who wove several questions of mine into his regular Moscow surveys in 1993 and made other polling results available.

At the Archive of Social Movements, Aleksei Novikov, Leonid Openkin, Anatolii Ponomarev, and Raisa Yurchuk patiently dug out reams of information on my behalf; Openkin and Ponomarev also submitted to hours of questioning about the evolution of the Moscow party apparatus. Andrei Shirokov of city hall's Department for Work of the Soviets made printouts from the department's data bank without which I could not have plumbed the 1990 election. Director Lidiya Solov'eva of the Museum of the History of the City of Moscow permitted me to browse through the museum's photograph archive and to reproduce photos in this book. Sergei Tumanov ably supervised the survey work during the 1993 election campaign. Among the many specialists and officials I interviewed and swapped notes with, Yevgeniya Al'bats, Iosif Diskin, Margarita Astaf'eva-Dlugach, Valerii Fadeyev, Vladimir Gimpel'son, Vyacheslav Glazychev, Leonid Kogan, Yelena Kotova, Sergei Koval'chuk, Vladimir Leksin, Gavriil Popov, Lyudmilla Revenko, Natal'ya Rykova, Yurii Samokhin, Leonid Vavakin, Nikolai Yegorychev, and Oksana Yunina were unusually illuminating sources. Gavriil Popov also allowed me to read and cite his unpublished memoir.

The two anonymous reviewers for Harvard University Press were remarkably thorough and constructive. Many others, already mentioned, also read parts of the manuscript at my request and wrote up critiques.

I express my appreciation to Victor H. Winston for permission to use material from my article on the Moscow Soviet election of 1990 published in *Soviet Economy*, vol. 6 (October–December 1990). I am also glad to note the contributions of Elizabeth Hurwit, the best editor I have ever encountered, of Robert Forget, who sure-handedly drew the maps, and of Aida D. Donald, editor-in-chief of Harvard University Press.

And I thank Patricia Jean Colton for gracefully accepting the Moscow project as part of her life all this time. She has speeded me up when I have moved too slowly and slowed me down when I have raced too fast. She has continued to remind me that there are things in life other than books. Most important, when I was in Moscow investigating one thing or another, or glued to keyboard and computer screen in my study, she alone nurtured the two young women to whom this study is dedicated.

Index